CW01584481

ELSEVIER'S DICTIONARY OF FINANCIAL TERMS

ELSEVIER'S DICTIONARY OF FINANCIAL TERMS

in English, German, Spanish, French, Italian
and Dutch

by

FRANCIS J. THOMSON

Faculty of Applied Economics
State University Centre of Antwerp

ELSEVIER SCIENTIFIC PUBLISHING COMPANY
AMSTERDAM – OXFORD – NEW YORK – TOKYO

ELSEVIER SCIENCE PUBLISHERS B.V.
Sara Burgerhartstraat 25
P.O. Box 211, 1000 AE Amsterdam, The Netherlands

Distributors for the United States and Canada:

ELSEVIER SCIENCE PUBLISHING COMPANY INC.
655 Avenue of the Americas
New York, N.Y. 10010, U.S.A.

First edition 1979
Second impression 1991

ISBN 0-444-41775-3

Library of Congress Cataloging in Publication Data
Main entry under title:
Elsevier's dictionary of financial terms in English,
German, Spanish, French, Italian and Dutch.
Includes indexes.
1. Finance–Dictionaries–Polyglot. 2. Dictionaries,
Polyglot. I. Thomson, Francis J.
HG151.E47 332'.03 79-11810
ISBN 0-444-41775-3

© Elsevier Science Publishers B.V., 1979

All rights reserved. No part of this publication may be reproduced, stored in a retrieval system or transmitted in any form or by any means, electronic, mechanical, photocopying, recording or otherwise, without the prior written permission of the publisher, Elsevier Science Publishers B.V./Physical Sciences and Engineering Division, P.O. Box 330, 1000 AH Amsterdam, The Netherlands.

Special regulations for readers in the U.S.A. – This publication has been registered with the Copyright Clearance Center, Inc. (CCC), Salem, Massachusetts. Information can be obtained from the CCC about conditions under which photocopies of parts of this publication may be made in the U.S.A. All other copyright questions, including photocopying outside of the U.S.A., should be referred to the publisher.

No responsibility is assumed by the Publisher for any injury and/or damage to persons or property as a matter of products liability, negligence or otherwise, or from any use or operation of any methods, products, instructions or ideas contained in the material herein.

Electronic data processing: Büro für Satztechnik W. Meyer KG, Hanau, W. Germany.

Printed in The Netherlands

PREFACE

Originally this dictionary was intended to be a revision of S. Horn's "Glossary of Financial Terms" published by Elsevier in 1965 but it soon became apparent that the inclusion of two more languages, Italian and Dutch, as well as of many new terms, meant the compilation of a new work rather than the revision of the old.

The choice of terms for inclusion in a technical dictionary is subjective for two main reasons: firstly, it is impossible to delineate with exactitude what properly belongs to the world of finance with its many aspects such as banking, accountancy, taxation, monetary policy, insurance, law (with regard to companies, debt, bankruptcy) etc.; secondly, considerations of space determine the extent of the selection.

The business world is in a state of perpetual flux with almost daily changes in monetary policies, banking practices, tax systems, etc., so that neoterism is endemic in economics. It is the work of the much maligned journalist which better reflects this living economic language than that of learned academies or official publications with their adherence to outdated normative "rules". All professions have their jargon and since this dictionary is intended for the use not only of translators, interpreters and students but also of business men, economists, bankers and correspondents, it reflects and records what actually is used, not what "should" be used, and attempts to give the equivalents in the other languages.

It is with regard to this "equivalence" that this dictionary most differs from others. As any translator knows to his cost, the referential meaning and grammatical valence of synonyms never coincide and thus it is pointless to list synonyms as separate entries and in each case give only one "equivalent" in the other language since the semantic fields of the two will also not coincide. The principle adopted here is thus that of the thesaurus - to list under one heading the synonyms of the various languages and leave the choice of the equivalent - which obviously depends on the context - to the user; see, for example, the entries "amortisation" and "appraisal". In addition cross references are given to related terms which may well be appropriate in a particular context, e.g. under the entry "avails" will be found references to "gain, income, incomings, proceeds, return".

One word of warning is appropiate here: owing to differences in national laws and customs the same thing may mean different things in different places, e.g. the person and function of an auditor vary from country to country, as do the services offered by the national giro. In other cases a term may in fact have no precise equivalents, e.g. merchant bank, while in others economists seem to apply the Humpty Dumpty Principle:

" 'When I use a word', Humpty Dumpty said in a rather scornful tone, 'it means just what I choose it to mean, - neither more nor less' " (Lewis Carroll, Through the Looking Glass).

Thus all dictionaries are guides to, not guarantors of, correct equivalents.

Special attention has been paid to words which have various meanings. In the case of English words it is thus most important to consult the English index BEFORE the body of the dictionary since in many cases only one meaning of a word features as the head of an entry, whereas it can be found in other meanings in other entries, e.g. the entry "grant" refers to its meaning of "subsidy", but it is also found in a different sense under "donation".

In other cases a word may feature several times in the dictionary but never as a headword, so that recourse must always be had to the English index before consulting the main body of the dictionary.

Finally, the order is strictly alphabetical irrespective of whether the entry is one word, a hyphenated word or more than one word, e.g. "taxation" comes before "tax avoidance". The principal spelling variations encountered are noted but no attempt has been made to include all the many vagaries which may occur, especially in Dutch. In the case of German, vowels with an umlaut are treated the same as those without.

A bibliography of economics dictionaries published between 1952 and 1974 was published by the compiler in Linguistica Antverpiensia, volume 8, 1974, p. 74–143, which should be of use to those searching for glossaries in any of the many specialized fields of economics and finance.

Francis J. Thomson

ACKNOWLEDGEMENT

The compiler must gratefully acknowledge the cooperation of Misses G. Goeyvaerts and S. Margretts and Mr. F. Van Prooye, who spent many hours dilligently reading financial reports in a search for new terms and equivalents, Mr. M. Van Doren and his staff of the library of the Institute of Translators and Interpreters, Antwerp, who assisted him in meeting his bibliographic requirements, and his patient wife, who frequently had to bear the brunt of his irascible impatience due to the slow progress of the work.

ABBREVIATIONS

The abbreviations listed below signify that the terms after which they appear are used in the following countries:

AL	Latin America	*N*	Netherlands
B	Belgium	*O*	Austria
C	Canada	*Schw*	Switzerland
F	France	*UK*	United Kingdom
L	Luxemburg	*US*	United States of America

The following are used to indicate the languages:

d	Deutsch	*i*	Italiano
e	Español	*n*	Nederlands
f	Français		

Other abbreviations used are:

adj.	adjective	*m*	masculine
adv.	adverb	*n*	neuter
cf.	see also	*pl*	plural
col.	colloquial	*pp.*	past participle
f	feminine	*q.v.*	see there
intr.	intransitive verb	*tr.*	transitive verb
		v	verb

BASIC TABLE

A

1 **abolish** *v* **restrictions; lift** *v* **restrictions; remove** *v* **restrictions; withdraw** *v* **restrictions**
d Beschränkungen abschaffen; Beschränkungen aufheben
e abolir restricciones; levantar restricciones; suprimir restricciones
f abolir des restrictions; lever des restrictions; supprimer des restrictions
i abolire restrizioni; levare restrizioni; sopprimere restrizioni
n beperkingen afschaffen; beperkingen opheffen

2 **abolition of restrictions; lifting of restrictions; removal of restrictions; withdrawal of restrictions**
d Abschaffung *f* von Beschränkungen; Aufhebung *f* von Beschränkungen
e abolición *f* de restricciones; levantamiento *m* de restricciones; supresión *f* de restricciones
f abolition *f* de restrictions; levée *f* de restrictions; suppression *f* de restrictions
i abolizione *f* di restrizioni; levata *f* di restrizioni; soppresione *f* di restrizioni
n afschaffing *f* van beperkingen; opheffing *f* van beperkingen

3 **absorb** *v* **a loss**
d einen Verlust auffangen
e absorber una pérdida
f absorber une perte
i assorbire una perdita
n een verlies opvangen

4 **absorption costing; complete cost accounting; full cost accounting**
d Vollkostenkalkulation *f*; Vollkostenrechnung *f*
e sistema *m* de coste integral
f système *m* de calcul du prix de revient complet; système *m* de calcul du prix de revient intégral
i sistema *m* di calcolo del costo complessivo
n integrale kostenberekening *f*; integrale kostencalculatie *f*

5 **abstract of account; account statement; extract of account; statement of account**
d Kontoauszug *m*; Rechnungsauszug *m*
e extracto *m* de cuenta
f bordereau *m* de compte; extrait *m* de compte; relevé *m* de compte
i estratto *m* (di) conto
n afschrift *n* van een rekening(-courant); rekening(-courant)afschrift *n*; rekening(-courant)uittreksel *n*; uittreksel *n* uit (van) een rekening(-courant)

6 **abundance of money; excessive money circulation; excess money supply; excess of money; glut of money**
d Geldflüssigkeit *f*; Geldfülle *f*; Geldschwemme *f*; Geldüberfluss *m*; Geldüberhang *m*; Geldüberschuss *m*; Überangebot *n* an Geld
e abundancia *f* de dinero; excedente *m* monetario; plétora *f* de dinero; plétora *f* monetaria; superabundancia *f* de dinero; superávit *m* de la circulación monetaria; superávit *m* monetario
f abondance *f* d'argent; excédent *m* de la circulation monétaire; excédent *m* des moyens de paiement; excédent *m* monétaire; pléthore *f* de capitaux; surabondance *f* d'argent
i abbondanza *f* di denaro; eccedenza *f* monetaria; eccessiva circolazione *f* monetaria; pletora *f* di capitali; pletora *f* monetaria; sovrabbondanza *f* di denaro
n geldovervloed *m*; te grote geldcirculatie *f*

7 **accelerated depreciation; declining balance depreciation; reducing depreciation**
d degressive Abschreibung *f*; fallende Abschreibung *f*
e amortización *f* decreciente; depreciación *f* decreciente
f amortissement *m* décroissant; amortissement *m* dégressif
i ammortamento *m* per quote decrescenti
n afnemende afschrijving *f*; degressieve afschrijving *f*

8 **accept** *v* **a bill of exchange**
d einen Wechsel akzeptieren; einen Wechsel annehmen
e aceptar une letra de cambio
f accepter une lettre de change
i accettare una cambiale
n een wissel aannemen; een wissel accepteren

9 **acceptable as collateral; eligible as collateral**
d belehnbar *(O; Schw)*; beleihbar; lombardfähig; lombardierbar
e pignorable; susceptible de pignoración
f susceptible d'être gagé
i suscettibile di essere preso in pegno
n beleenbaar

10 acceptance
d Akzept *n*
e aceptación *f*
f acceptation *f*
i accettazione *f*
n accept *n*; acceptatie *f*

11 acceptance credit; bill credit; paper credit
cf. **documentary credit**
d Akzeptkredit *m*; Wechselkredit *m*; Wechselrembours *m*
e crédito *m* cambiario; crédito *m* de aceptación
f crédit *m* d'acceptation; crédit *m* par acceptation
i credito *m* cambiario; credito *m* di accettazione; fido *m* cambiario
n acceptkrediet *n*; wisselkrediet *n*

12 acceptance house; accepting house
cf. **discount bank**
d Akzeptbank *f*; Akzepthaus *n*; Wechselbank *f*
e banco *m* de aceptaciones; casa *f* de aceptaciones
f banque *f* d'acceptations; maison *f* d'acceptations
i banca *f* d'accettazione; casa *f* d'accettazione
n accepthuis *n*; wisselbank *f*

13 accepting commission; drawee's commission
d Akzeptprovision *f*
e comisión *f* de aceptación
f commission *f* d'acceptation; prime *f* d'acceptation
i commissione *f* d'accettazione; provvigione *f* d'accettazione
n acceptprovisie *f*

14 acceptor
cf. **drawee**
d Akzeptant *m*
e aceptante *m*
f accepteur *m*
i accettante *m*
n acceptant *m*

15 accommodation bill; fictitious bill; kite; wind bill *(UK)*
d fingierter Wechsel *m*; Gefälligkeitsakzept *n*; Gefälligkeitswechsel *m*; Kellerwechsel *m*; Reitwechsel *m*; Scheinwechsel *m*
e letra *f* de acomodación; letra *f* de favor; letra *f* ficticia; letra *f* proforma; pagaré *m* de acomodación
f billet *m* de complaisance; effet *m* de complaisance; papier *m* de complaisance; papier *m* en l'air; traite *f* de cavalerie; traite *f* en l'air
i cambiale *f* di comodo; cambiale *f* di favore; cambiale *f* fittizia; cambiale *f* proforma; cambiale *f* simulata; carta *f* di cavalleria
n accommodatiewissel *m*; beleefdheidsaccept *n*; schoorsteenwissel *m*

16 account *(in bank)*
d Konto *n*
e cuenta *f*
f compte *m*
i conto *m*
n conto *n*; rekening *f*

17 account; bill; invoice
d Faktur *f*; Faktura *f*; Nota *f*; Rechnung *f*
e cuenta *f*; factura *f*; nota *f*
f compte *m*; facture *f*; mémoire *m*; note *f*
i conto *m*; fattura *f*; nota *f*
n factuur *f*; nota *f*; rekening *f*

18 account *(UK)*; **settlement period** *(US)*
d Abrechnungszeitraum *m*; Liquidationstermin *m*
e término *m* de liquidación
f terme *m* de liquidation
i termine *m* di liquidazione
n liquidatietermijn *m*; rescontretermijn *m*

19 on account
d à Konto; auf Abschlag; auf Rechnung
e a cuenta
f à compte; à valoir
i in acconto; in conto
n op rekening

20 accountancy; accounting; bookkeeping
d Buchführung *f*; Buchhaltung *f*
e contabilidad *f*; teneduría *f* de libros
f comptabilité *f*; tenue *f* de livres
i computisteria *f*; contabilità *f*; ragioneria *f*; tenuta *f* dei libri; tenuta *f* della contabilità
n accountancy *f*; boekhouden *n*; boekhouding *f*; comptabiliteit *f*

21 accountant
cf. **bookkeeper**
d Rechnungsprüfer *m*; Wirtschaftsprüfer *m*
e contable *m*; contador *m*; perito *m* contador
f comptable *m*; conseil *m* fiscal; expert *m* comptable

i contabile *m*; ragioniere *m*
n accountant *m*

22 **account classification; accounting plan; accounting system; chart of accounts** *(US)*; **codification of accounts**
d Kontenaufgliederung *f*; Kontengliederung *f*; Kontenplan *m*; Kontenrahmen *m*
e clasificación *f* de cuentas; plan *m* contable; plan *m* de cuentas; sistema *m* de cuentas
f plan *m* comptable; plan *m* de comptabilité
i piano *m* contabile; piano *m* dei conti; sistema *m* contabile
n rekeningstelsel *n*; rekeningsysteem *n*

23 **account current** *(rare)*; **current account; drawing account** *(US)*; **open account; running account** *(rare)*
cf. **check account, giro account**
d Kontokorrent *n*; Kontokorrentkonto *n*; laufende Rechnung *f*; laufendes Konto *n*; offene Rechnung *f*; offenes Konto *n*; offenstehendes Konto *n*
e cuenta *f* abierta; cuenta *f* corriente
f compte *m* à vue; compte *m* courant; compte *m* ouvert
i conto *m* aperto; conto *m* a vista; conto *m* corrente
n conto *n* corrente; lopende rekening *f*; open rekening *f*; openstaande rekening *f*; rekening-courant *f*; zichtrekening *f*

24 **account day; pay day; settlement day; settling day**
d Abrechnungstag *m*; Abrechnungstermin *m*; Liquidationstag *m*; Stichtag *m*
e día *m* de liquidación; día *m* de saldo
f jour *m* de liquidation; jour *m* de règlement; liquidation *f*; règlement *m*
i giorno *m* dei conti; giorno *m* di liquidazione
n betaaldag *m*; liquidatiedag *m*; rescontredag *m*; verrekeningsdag *m*

25 **account heading; account title** *(US)*
d Kontobezeichnung *f*
e denominación *f* de cuenta; designación *f* de cuenta; título *m* de cuenta
f intitulé *m* de compte
i denominazione *f* del conto
n boekingshoofd *n*; rekeningshoofd *n*

26 **account holder; holder of an account**
d Inhaber *m* eines Kontos; Konteninhaber *m*; Kontoinhaber *m*
e cuentacorrentista *m**; titular *m* de una cuenta
f ayant compte *m*; détenteur *m* d'un compte; titulaire *m* d'un compte
i correntista *m**; intestatario *m* di un conto; titolare *m* di un conto
n houder *m* van een rekening; rekeninghouder *m*
* Of a current account.

27 **accounting balance**
d Kontobestand *m*; Rechnungssaldo *m*; Restbetrag *m*; Saldo *m*
e saldo *m* contable; sobrante *m*
f solde *m* comptable
i saldo *m* contabile
n saldo *n*

28 **accounting books; books of account; ledgers**
d Geschäftsbücher *npl*; Handelsbücher *npl*; kaufmännische Bücher *npl*
e libros *mpl* comerciales; libros *mpl* de comercio; libros *mpl* de contabilidad
f livres *mpl* comptables; livres *mpl* d'affaires; livres *mpl* de commerce; livres *mpl* de comptabilité; livres *mpl* de compte; livres *mpl* des marchands
i libri *mpl* commerciali; libri *mpl* contabili; libri *mpl* di commercio
n handelsboeken *npl*; koopmansboeken *npl*

29 **accounting dollar; agreement dollar; clearing dollar; offset dollar**
d Verrechnungsdollar *m*
e dólar *m* de compensación; dólar *m* de convenio; dólar *m* de cuenta
f dollar *m* de compensation; dollar *m* de compte
i dollaro *m* di compensazione
n clearingdollar *m*; verrekeningsdollar *m*

30 **accounting surplus**
d Rechnungsüberschuss *m*
e superávit *m* contable
f excédent *m* comptable
i eccedenza *f* contabile
n boekingsoverschot *n*

31 **accounting unit; unit of account**
d Rechnungseinheit *f*
e unidad *f* de cuenta
f unité *f* de compte
i unità *f* di conto
n rekeneenheid *f*

32 accounting value; book value; carrying value
cf. **balance sheet value, inventory value**
d Buchwert *m*
e valor *m* contable
f valeur *f* comptable
i valore *m* contabile
n boekwaarde *f*

33 accounting voucher; bookkeeping voucher
d Buchführungsbeleg *m*; Buchungsbeleg *m*
e comprobante *m* de asiento; comprobante *m* de contabilidad; justificante *m* de contabilidad
f pièce *f* comptable; pièce *f* de comptabilité
i pezza *f* giustificativa contabile
n boekingsbescheid *n*; boekingsstuk *n*

34 for account of
cf. **chargeable to**
d auf Rechnung von; für Rechnung von; zugunsten
e a favor de; por cuenta de
f à l'acquit de; pour (le) compte de
i per conto di
n voor rekening van

35 for account of a third party; for third party account
d auf (für) dritte Rechnung; auf (für) fremde Rechnung; auf (für) Rechnung Dritter; auf (für) Rechnung eines Dritten
e por cuenta ajena; por cuenta de tercero(s)
f pour (le) compte d'autrui; pour (le) compte de tiers; pour (le) compte d'un tiers
i per conto d'altri; per conto (di) terzi
n voor rekening van derden; voor rekening van een derde

36 account payable *(US)*; debt payable; passive debt
cf. **(current) liabilities, debts**
d Kreditoren *mpl**; passive Schuld *f*; Passivschuld *f*
e acreedores *mpl**; cuenta *f* acreedora; cuenta *f* a pagar; deuda *f* a pagar; deuda *f* pasiva
f compte *m* à payer; dette *f* passive
i conto *m* da pagare; debito *m* passivo
n crediteuren *mpl**; passieve schuld *f*; rekening *f* te voldoen; te betalen rekening *f*; uitschuld *f*
* Plural only.

37 account receivable *(US)*; active debt; debt due; debt receivable; outstanding claim; outstanding debt; receivables *(US)**
cf. **arrearages**
d aktive Forderung *f*; aktive Schuld *f*; Aktivforderung *f*; Aktivschuld *f*; Aussenstände *mpl**; ausstehende Forderung *f*; ausstehende Rechnung *f*; ausstehende Schuld *f*; Debitoren *mpl**; eintreibbare Forderung *f*; einziehbare-Forderung
e cuenta *f* a cobrar; cuenta *f* deudora; deuda *f* a cobrar; deuda *f* activa; deuda *f* exigible; deuda *f* pendiente de cobro
f compte *m* à recevoir; créance *f* à recouvrer; créance *f* exigible; dette *f* active; dette *f* exigible
i conto *m* da esigere; conto *m* da incassare; conto *m* da riscuotere; credito *m* attivo; credito *m* da ricuperare; credito *m* esigibile; credito *m* in essere; credito *m* pendente; debito *m* attivo; debito *m* esigibile
n actieve schuld *f*; debiteuren *mpl**; inschuld *f*; invordering *f*; opeisbare schuld *f*; uitstaande vordering *f*
* Plural only.

38 accrual
cf. **accruals, accumulation**
d Akkumulation *f*; Anfall *m*; Anwachsen *n*; Auflaufen *n*
e acumulación *f*
f accroissement *m*; accumulation *f*
i accumulazione *f*; maturazione *f*
n accumulatie *f*; ophoping *f*

39 accruals *(US)*; accrued charges; accrued expenses; expenses due and unpaid
d antizipative Passiva *npl*; transitorische Passiva *npl (Schw)*
e gastos *mpl* a pagar
f charges *fpl* à payer; frais *mpl* à payer
i costi *mpl* da pagare; spese *fpl* da pagare
n te betalen kosten *mpl*

40 accrue *v*; **accumulate** *v (intr.)*
cf. **accumulate** *v* **(tr.)**
d akkumulieren; anfallen; anwachsen; auflaufen
e acumularse; redituarse
f accroître; courir; s'accumuler; s'acquérir
i accumularsi; maturare
n accumuleren; oplopen; zich op(een)hopen

41 accrued interest
cf. **interest due**
d angefallene Zinsen *mpl*; aufgelaufene Zinsen *mpl*; Stückzinsen *mpl*
e intereses *mpl* acumulados

f intérêts *mpl* accrus; intérêts *mpl* accumulés; intérêts *mpl* courus; intérêts *mpl* cumulés
i interessi *mpl* accumulati; interessi *mpl* maturati
n geaccumuleerde int(e)rest *m*; geaccumuleerde rente *f*; gekweekte int(e)rest *m*; opgelopen rente *f*

42 **accruing interest**
d anfallende Zinsen *mpl*; auflaufende Zinsen *mpl*; entstehende Zinsen *mpl*; fällig werdende Zinsen *mpl*
e intereses *mpl* de próximo vencimiento
f intérêts *mpl* à échoir
i interessi *mpl* da maturare; interessi *mpl* da scadere; interessi *mpl* maturanti
n nog te vervallen rente *f*; te vervallen rente *f*

43 **accumulate** *v (tr.)*; **amass** *v*
cf. **accrue** *v*, **hoard** *v*
d akkumulieren; anhäufen; ansammeln; aufhäufen
e acumular; amontonar
f accumuler; amasser
i accumulare; ammassare; ammucchiare
n accumuleren; opeenhopen; ophopen; vergaren

44 **accumulation**
d Akkumulation *f*; Anhäufung *f*; Ansammlung *f*; Aufhäufung *f*
e acumulación *f*
f accumulation *f*; amassement *m*
i accumulazione *f*; ammassamento *m*; ammucchiamento *m*
n accumulatie *f*; opeenhoping *f*; ophoping *f*; vergaring *f*

45 **acid-test ratio; cash ratio** *(bank)*; **current ratio** *(US)*; **reserve ratio** *(bank)*; **working capital ratio**
d Flüssigkeitsgrad *m*; Flüssigkeitskoeffizient *m*; Flüssigkeitsverhältnis *n*; Liquiditätsgrad *m*; Liquiditätskennzahl *f*; Liquiditätskennziffer *f*; Liquiditätskoeffizient *m*; Liquiditätssatz *m*; Liquiditätsverhältnis *n*; Liquiditätsverhältnisziffer *f*
e coeficiente *m* de liquidez; cuota *f* de liquidez; grado *m* de liquidez; índice *m* de liquidez; relación *f* de liquidez
f coefficient *m* de liquidité; degré *m* de liquidité; quotient *m* de liquidité; rapport *m* de liquidité; ratio *m* de liquidité; taux *m* de liquidité
i coefficiente *m* di liquidità; indice *m* di liquidità; quoziente *m* di liquidità; rapporto *m* di liquidità
n liquiditeitscoëfficiënt *m*; liquiditeitsgraad *m*; liquiditeitsratio *f*; liquiditeitsverhouding *f*; liquiditeitsverhoudingscijfer *n*

46 **acknowledg(e)ment of debt; acknowledg(e)ment of indebtedness**
cf. **certificate of indebtedness, hand bill**
d Schuldanerkenntnis *f/n*
e reconocimiento *m* de deuda
f reconnaissance *f* de dette
i ricognizione *f* di debito; riconoscimento *m* di debito
n schuldbekentenis *f*

47 **acknowledg(e)ment of receipt; confirmation of receipt; receipt**
d Eingangsanzeige *f*; Eingangsbekenntnis *n*; Eingangsbestätigung *f*; Empfangsanzeige *f*; Empfangsbescheinigung *f*; Empfangsbestätigung *f*; Empfangsschein *m*; Quittung *f*
e acuse *m* de recibo; aviso *m* de entrada; comprobante *m*; confirmación *f* de recibo; recibo *m*
f accusé *m* de réception; acquit *m*; avis *m* d'encaissement; avis *m* de réception; quittance *f*; récépissé *m*; reçu *m*
i avviso *m* d'incasso; avviso *m* di ricevimento; avviso *m* di ricevuta; cenno *m* di ricevuta; conferma *f* di ricevuta; quietanza *f*; ricevuta *f*
n kwijtbrief *m*; kwijting *f*; kwijtschrift *n*; kwitantie *f*; ontvangstbericht *n*; ontvangstbevestiging *f*; ontvangstbewijs *n*; recipis *n*; reçu *n*

48 **acquire** *v*
cf. **buy** *v*
d anschaffen; erwerben
e adquirir
f acquérir
i acquistare
n aanschaffen; verkrijgen; verwerven

49 **acquisition**
d Anschaffung *f*; Erwerb *m*; Erwerbung *f*
e adquisición *f*
f acquisition *f*
i acquisizione *f*; acquisto *m*
n aanschaffing *f*; verkrijging *f*; verwerving *f*

50 **acquisition value; cost value; initial value; purchase value; value at cost**
cf. **cost price**
d Anschaffungswert *m*; Einkaufswert *m*; Einstandswert *m*; Erwerbswert *m*; Kauf-

wert *m*; Kostenwert *m*
e valor *m* de adquisición; valor *m* de compra; valor *m* de coste
f valeur *f* à l'achat; valeur *f* d'achat; valeur *f* d'acquisition; valeur *f* initiale
i valore *m* d'acquisto; valore *m* di costo
n aankoopwaarde *f*; aanschaffingswaarde *f*; inkoopwaarde *f*

51 **acquittance; discharge; receipt** *(US)*
d Quittung *f*
e descargo *m*
f quittance *f*
i quietanza *f*
n kwitantie *f*

52 **act** *v* **as surety; go** *v* **surety; secure** *v*; **stand** *v* **security; stand** *v* **surety**
d bürgen; Bürgschaft leisten; Bürgschaft übernehmen; Gewähr übernehmen; Sicherheit leisten; sich verbürgen
e caucionar; dar fianza; dar garantía; prestar fianza; prestar garantía; salir fiador; salir garante; ser fiador; ser garante
f cautionner; donner caution; donner garantie; se porter caution; se porter garant; se rendre caution; se rendre garant
i assumere garanzia; farsi garante; prestare garanzia; rendersi garante
n borg staan; zich borg stellen

53 **active balance of trade; active trade balance; favorable balance of trade** *(US)*; **favorable trade balance** *(US)*; **favourable balance of trade** *(UK)*; **favourable trade balance** *(UK)*
d aktive Aussenhandelsbilanz *f*; aktive Handelsbilanz *f*; günstige Aussenhandelsbilanz *f*; günstige Handelsbilanz *f*
e balanza *f* comercial activa; balanza *f* comercial exedentaria; balanza *f* comercial favorable; balanza *f* comercial propicia
f balance *f* commerciale active; balance *f* commerciale excédentaire; balance *f* commerciale favorable
i bilancia *f* commerciale attiva; bilancia *f* commerciale favorevole
n actieve handelsbalans *f*; gunstige handelsbalans *f*

54 **actual cost; real cost**
d Istkosten *pl*; tatsächliche Kosten *pl*
e coste *m* efectivo; coste *m* real; costo *m* efectivo; costo *m* real
f coût *m* effectif; coût *m* réel
i costo *m* effettivo; costo *m* reale
n effectieve kosten *mpl*; werkelijke kosten *mpl*

55 **actual expenses; out-of-pocket expenses**
cf. **charges**
d Istausgaben *fpl*
e gastos *mpl* efectivos; gastos *mpl* efectuados
f dépenses *fpl* effectives; dépenses *fpl* effectuées
i spese *fpl* effettive; spese *fpl* effettuate
n effectieve uitgaven *fpl*; werkelijke uitgaven *fpl*

56 **actual value; effective value; real value; true value**
d Effektivwert *m*; Istwert *m*; Realwert *m*
e valor *m* efectivo; valor *m* real
f valeur *f* effective; valeur *f* réelle
i valore *m* effettivo; valore *m* reale
n effectieve waarde *f*; reële waarde *f*; werkelijke waarde *f*

57 **actual yield; effective yield; real yield; true yield**
d Effektivverzinsung *f*; Realzins *m*
e rendimiento *m* efectivo; rendimiento *m* real; rentabilidad *f* bursátil
f rendement *m* boursier; rendement *m* effectif; rendement *m* réel
i rendimento *m* borsistico; rendimento *m* effettivo; rendimento *m* reale; rendita *f* borsistica; rendita *f* effettiva; rendita *f* reale
n effectief rendement *n*; reëel rendement *n*; werkelijk rendement *n*

58 **actuary**
d Versicherungsmathematiker *m*; Versicherungsstatistiker *m*
e actuario *m*
f actuaire *m*
i attuario *m*
n actuaris *m*; verzekeringswiskundige *m*; wiskundig adviseur *m*

59 **adaptation inflation; adapted inflation; inflation adaptation**
d Anpassungsinflation *f*
e adaptación *f* inflacionista
f inflation *f* d'adaptation
i inflazione *f* d'adattamento
n aanpassingsinflatie *f*; inflatoir aanpassingsproces *n*

60 **additional charge; extra charge; supplement; surcharge**
cf. **additional charges, increase in price**
d Aufpreis *m*; Aufschlag *m*;

Extragebühr *f*; Mehrpreis *m*; Nachgebühr *f*; Zusatzgebühr *f*; Zuschlag *m*; Zuschlaggebühr *f*
e cargo *m* adicional; recargo *m*; sobreprecio *m*; sobretasa *f*
f droit *m* supplémentaire; supplément *m*; surtaxe *f*; taxe *f* supplémentaire
i soprapprezzo *m*; sopraprezzo *m*; soprattassa *f*; sovrapprezzo *m*; sovraprezzo *m*; sovrattassa *f*; supplemento *m*
n bijslag *m*; extraheffing *f*; opslag *m*; surtaxe *f*; toeslag *m*

61 **additional charges; additional costs; additional expenses; extra charges; extra costs; extra expenses; extras; further charges; further costs; further expenses; incidental charges; incidental costs; incidental expenses; incidentals; special charges; special costs; special expenses; supplementary charges; supplementary costs; supplementary expenses**
cf. **miscellaneous charges**
d Extraausgaben *fpl*; Extrakosten *pl*; Extraspesen *fpl*; Mehrausgaben *fpl*; Mehrkosten *pl*; Nebenausgaben *fpl*; Nebenkosten *pl*; Nebenspesen *fpl*; Sonderausgaben *fpl*; Sonderkosten *pl*; Sonderspesen *fpl*; Zusatzkosten *pl*; zusätzliche Ausgaben *fpl*; zusätzliche Kosten *pl*; zusätzliche Spesen *fpl*; zusätzliche Unkosten *pl*
e costes *mpl* adicionales; costes *mpl* suplementarios; costes *mpl* supletorios; gastos *mpl* accesorios; gastos *mpl* adicionales; gastos *mpl* extraordinarios; gastos *mpl* incidentales; gastos *mpl* suplementarios
f dépenses *fpl* accessoires; dépenses *fpl* spéciales; dépenses *fpl* supplémentaires; faux frais *mpl*; frais *mpl* accessoires; frais *mpl* spéciaux; frais *mpl* supplémentaires
i costi *mpl* addizionali; extra *mpl*; maggiori spese *fpl*; spese *fpl* accessorie; spese *fpl* addizionali; spese *fpl* extra; spese *fpl* straordinarie; spese *fpl* supplementari
n bijkomende kosten *mpl*; bijkomende onkosten *mpl*; bijkomende uitgaven *fpl*; extrakosten *mpl*; extrauitgaven *fpl*; meerkosten *mpl*

62 **additional cover; additional margin; further cover; remargining** *(US)*
d Deckungszuschuss *m*; Nachschuss *m*; zusätzliche Deckung *f*
e cobertura *f* adicional; cobertura *f* suplementaria; margen *m/f* adicional; suplemento *m* de copertura
f couverture *f* additionnelle; couverture *f* complémentaire; couverture *f* supplémentaire; marge *f* supplémentaire; supplément *m* de couverture
i copertura *f* supplementare; margine *m* supplementare; supplemento *m* di copertura
n aanvullende dekking *f*; aanvullende marge *f*; bijkomende dekking *f*

63 **additional credit; further credit; supplemental credit; supplementary credit**
d Ergänzungskredit *m*; Nachtragskredit *m*; Zusatzkredit *m*; zusätzlicher Kredit *m*
e crédito *m* adicional; crédito *m* complementario; crédito *m* suplementario; suplemento *m* de crédito
f crédit *m* additionnel; crédit *m* complémentaire; crédit *m* d'appoint; crédit *m* de complément; crédit *m* supplémentaire; supplément *m* de crédit
i credito *m* adizionale; credito *m* complementare; credito *m* supplementare; supplemento *m* di credito
n aanvullingskrediet *n*; bijkomend krediet *n*; bijkrediet *n*

64 **additional income; casual income; extra income**
d Nebeneinkommen *n*; Nebeneinkünfte *fpl*; Nebeneinnahmen *fpl*; Nebenverdienst *m*; zusätzliche Einkünfte *fpl*; zusätzliche Einnahmen *fpl*
e ingresos *mpl* accesorios; ingresos *mpl* adicionales; ingresos *mpl* suplementarios
f revenus *mpl* accessoires; revenus *mpl* supplémentaires
i redditi *mpl* accessori; redditi *mpl* supplementari
n bijkomende inkomsten *fpl*; supplementaire inkomsten *fpl*

65 **additional security; collateral security; secondary security**
cf. **collateral**
d Nebensicherheit *f*; zusätzliche Sicherheit *f*
e garantía *f* adicional; garantía *f* subsidiaria; garantía *f* suplementaria; seguridad *f* adicional; seguridad *f* subsidiaria; seguridad *f* suplementaria
f garantie *f* accessoire; garantie *f* additionnelle; garantie *f* complémentaire; garantie *f* supplémentaire; sécurité *f* additionnelle; sécurité *f* subsidiaire; sécurité *f* supplémentaire

i garanzia *f* accessoria; garanzia *f* collaterale; garanzia *f* supplementare
n aanvullende zekerheid *f*; additionele zekerheid *f*; bijkomende zekerheid *f*

66 **additional tax; extra tax; supertax; supplementary tax; surtax**
d Extrasteuer *f*; Steueraufschlag *m*; Steuerzuschlag *m*; zusätzliche Steuer *f*; Zusatzsteuer *f*; Zuschlag(s)steuer *f*
e impuesto *m* adicional; impuesto *m* complementario; recargo *m* impositivo; recargo *m* tributario; sobreimposición *f*; sobreimpuesto *m*; sobretasa *f*; suplemento *m* de impuesto
f centimes *mpl* additionnels; impôt *m* additionnel; impôt *m* complémentaire; supplément *m* d'impôt; surtaxe *f*; taxe *f* additionnelle; taxe *f* supplémentaire
i imposta *f* addizionale; imposta *f* complementare; imposta *f* supplementare; soprattassa *f*; sovr(a)imposta *f*; sovrattassa *f*; supplemento *m* d'imposta
n aanvullende belasting *f*; extrabelasting *f*; opcenten *mpl (N)*; opcentiemen *mpl (B)*; surtaxe *f*

67 **addition to the reserve(s); allocation to the reserve(s); appropriation to the reserve(s)**
d Zuführung *f* an die Reserven; Zuführung *f* zu den Reserven; Zuweisung *f* an die Reserven; Zuweisung *f* zu den Reserven
e adición *f* a la reserva; asignación *f* a la reserva
f affectation *f* à la réserve; dotation *f* à la réserve
i assegnazione *f* alle riserve; attribuzione *f* alle riserve; destinazione *f* alle riserve
n toevoeging *f* aan de reserve

68 **add** *v* **to the reserve; carry** *v* **to reserve; carry** *v* **to the reserve fund; place** *v* **to reserve; put** *v* **to the reserve; transfer** *v* **to reserve; transfer** *v* **to the reserve fund**
d an die Reserve abgeben; dem Reservefonds zuführen; dem Reservefonds zuweisen; den Rücklagen zuführen; den Rücklagen zuweisen; der Reserve überweisen; der Reserve zuführen; der Reserve zuweisen; zum Reservefonds schlagen
e afectar a la reserva; afectar al fondo de reserva; asignar a la reserva; asignar al fondo de reserva; destinar a la reserva; destinar al fondo de reserva; llevar al fondo de reserva; pasar a la reserva; pasar al fondo de reserva
f affecter à la réserve; affecter au fonds de réserve; attribuer à la réserve; incorporer aux réserves; passer à la réserve; passer au fonds de réserve; porter à la réserve; porter au fonds de réserve; verser à la réserve; verser au fonds de réserve
i accantonare nella reserva; assegnare al fondo di riserva; assegnare alla riserva; destinare al fondo di riserva; destinare alla riserva; passare al fondo di riserva; passare alla riserva; versare al fondo di riserva; versare alla riserva
n bij de reserve voegen; bij het reservefonds voegen; in de reserve storten; op de reserve plaatsen

69 **adjudication in bankruptcy; adjudication of bankruptcy; declaration of bankruptcy**
d Konkursdeklaration *f*; Konkurserklärung *f*
e declaración *f* (judicial) de quiebra
f déclaration *f* de faillite; déclaration *f* en faillite; jugement *m* déclaratif de faillite
i dichiarazione *f* di fallimento
n faillietverklaring *f*

70 **adjust** *v (statistics)*
d bereinigen
e ajustar
f ajuster
i adeguare; aggiustare
n aanpassen

71 **adjusting entry; adjustment entry; correcting entry; rectifying entry**
cf. **balancing entry**
d Berichtigungsbuchung *f*; Berichtigungseintrag *m*; Berichtigungsposten *m*; Wertberichtigungsbuchung *f*
e asiento *m* de ajuste; asiento *m* de corrección; asiento *m* de rectificación; asiento *m* rectificado; entrada *f* de rectificación; partida *f* de rectificación
f article *m* de régularisation; écriture *f* d'ajustement; écriture *f* de redressement; écriture *f* rectificative
i partita *f* di regolarizzazione; scrittura *f* rettificativa
n correctiepost *m*

72 **adjustment** *(statistics)*
d Bereinigung *f*
e ajuste *m*
f ajustement *m*
i adeguamento *m*; aggiustamento *m*
n aanpassing *f*

73 **adjustment accounts**
d Rechnungsabgrenzungsposten *mpl*

e cuentas *fpl* de regularización
f comptes *mpl* de régularisation
i ratei *mpl*; risconti *mpl*
n transitorische posten *mpl*

74 adjustment in real terms
d reale Anpassung *f*
e ajuste *m* en términos reales
f ajustement *m* en termes réels
i aggiustamento *m* in termini reali
n reële aanpassing *f*

75 adjustment in the exchange rate; exchange adjustment
d Wechselkursänderung *f*; Wechselkursberichtigung *f*; Wechselkurskorrektur *f*
e ajuste *m* del tipo de cambio
f ajustement *m* de change; rajustement *m* monétaire
i aggiustamento *m* della parità monetaria; rettifica *f* di cambio
n aanpassing *f* van de wisselkoers; wisselkoerswijziging *f*

76 adjustment of prices; price adjustment
d Angleichung *f* der Preise; Preisangleichung *f*; Preisanpassung *f*
e ajuste *m* de los precios; reajuste *m* de los precios
f adaptation *f* des prix; ajustement *m* des prix; alignement *m* des prix
i adeguamento *m* dei prezzi; allineamento *m* dei prezzi
n aanpassing *f* van de prijzen; prijsaanpassing *f*

77 adjustment of quotas; redetermination of quotas
d Neufestsetzung *f* von Kontingenten; Neufestsetzung *f* von Quoten
e ajuste *m* de cuotas; nueva fijación *f* de cuotas; revisión *f* de cuotas
f ajustement *m* des quotes-parts; nouvelle fixation *f* des quotes-parts; révision *f* des quotes-parts
i adeguamento *m* delle quote; nuova fissazione *f* delle quote
n herziening *f* van de contingenten; herziening *f* van de quota's; nieuwe vaststelling *f* van de contingenten; nieuwe vaststelling *f* van de quota's

78 administered price; fixed price; set price
cf. **flat price**
d fester Preis *m*; festgesetzter Preis *m*; Festpreis *m*; gebundener Preis *m*; vorgeschriebener Preis *m*
e precio *m* fijado; precio *m* fijo; precio *m* impuesto
f prix *m* fait; prix *m* fixe; prix *m* imposé
i calmiere *m*; prezzo *m* fissato; prezzo *m* fisso; prezzo *m* imposto
n opgelegde prijs *m*; vaste prijs *m*; vastgestelde prijs *m*; voorgeschreven prijs *m*

79 administrative costs; administrative expenses
cf. **business expenses, operating costs**
d Bewirtschaftungskosten *pl*; Verwaltungskosten *pl*
e gastos *mpl* de administración
f dépenses *fpl* administratives; frais *mpl* d'administration; frais *mpl* de gestion
i spese *fpl* amministrative; spese *fpl* di amministrazione; spese *fpl* di gestione
n administratiekosten *mpl*; beheerskosten *mpl*

80 administrative fee; service charge
cf. **handling charge**
d Bearbeitungsgebühr *f*; Verwaltungsgebühr *f*
e derechos *mpl* administrativos; derechos *mpl* de administración; derechos *mpl* de servicio; tasa *f* administrativa
f commission *f* de service; taxe *f* administrative; taxe *f* d'administration
i diritto *m* amministrativo; provvigione *f* di servizio; tassa *f* amministrativa
n administratieve provisie *f*; beheerloon *n*

81 admission to the stock exchange; introduction to the stock exchange; stock exchange listing
d Börseneinführung *f*; Börsenzulassung *f*; Kotierung *f*; Zulassung *f* zur (amtlichen) Börsennotierung; Zulassung *f* zur Kotierung
e admisión *f* a cotización oficial en la bolsa; admisión *f* a la bolsa; admisión *f* a la cotización
f admission *f* à la cote (officielle) de la bourse; admission *f* en bourse
i ammissione *f* alla quotazione (ufficiale) della borsa; ammissione *f* in borsa
n introductie *f* ter beurze; toelating *f* tot de beurs; toelating *f* tot de oficiële notering op de beurs

82 ad valorem duty
d Wertzoll *m*
e arancel *m* (aduanero) ad valorem; arancel *m* sobre el valor; derecho *m* (de aduana) ad valorem
f droit *m* ad valorem; droit *m* de douane ad valorem; droit *m* sur la valeur
i dazio *m* (doganale) ad valorem; dazio *m*

sul valore; diritto *m* (doganale) ad valorem
n ad valorem recht *n*; waarderecht *n*

83 advance; imprest*; sum advanced
cf. **advance payment**
d Vorschuss *m*; Vorschusszahlung *f*
e adelanto *m*; anticipo *m*
f avance *f* (de fonds)
i anticipazione *f*; anticipo *m*
n verschot *n*; voorschot *n*
* Usually only refers to money advanced from government funds.

84 as an advance; by way of an advance
d vorschussweise
e a título de adelanto; a título de anticipo
f à titre d'avance
i a titolo d'anticipazione; a titolo d'anticipo
n bij wijze van voorschot

85 advance *v (money)*
d bevorschussen; vorschiessen; vorstrecken
e anticipar
f avancer
i anticipare
n verschieten; voorschieten

86 advance against collateral (security); advance against security; advance on collateral (security); advance on security; advance upon collateral (security); secured advance
cf. **advance on securities**
d garantierter Vorschuss *m*; gedeckter Vorschuss *m*; gesicherter Vorschuss *m*; Vorschuss *m* gegen Pfand; Vorschuss *m* gegen Sicherheit
e adelanto *m* con garantía; adelanto *m* contra garantía; adelanto *m* garantizado; adelanto *m* pignoraticio; adelanto *m* sobre prenda; anticipo *m* con garantía; anticipo *m* contra garantía; anticipo *m* garantizado; anticipo *m* pignoraticio; anticipo *m* sobre prenda
f avance *f* contre garantie; avance *f* contre (sur) nantissement; avance *f* gagée; avance *f* garantie
i anticipazione *f* garantita; anticipazione *f* pignoratizia; anticipazione *f* su pegno; anticipo *m* garantito; anticipo *m* pignoratizio; anticipo *m* su pegno
n gedekt voorschot *n*; gegarandeerd voorschot *n*; pandvoorschot *n*; voorschot *n* op onderpand; voorschot *n* tegen onderpand

87 advance by overdraft; advance on current account; credit on current account
cf. **borrowing facilities**
d Kontokorrentkredit *m*; Kredit *m* in laufender Rechnung; Überziehungskredit *m*; Überzugskredit *m*; Vorschuss *m* auf laufender Rechnung
e adelanto *m* de descubierto en cuenta; adelanto *m* en cuenta corriente; crédito *m* en cuenta corriente
f avance *f* de (en; sur) compte courant; crédit *m* en compte courant
i anticipazione *f* in conto corrente; credito *m* in conto corrente; credito *m* per scoperto di conto corrente
n rekening-courantkrediet *n*; voorschot *n* in rekening-courant

88 advance commitment; credit commitment
cf. **stand-by**
d Kreditzusage *f*
e promesa *f* de crédito
f promesse *f* de crédit
i promessa *f* di credito
n krediettoezegging *f*

89 advance deduction; deduction in advance; previous deduction; prior deduction
d Abzug *m* im voraus; Vorabzug *m*; Vorausabzug *m*; Vorwegabzug *m*
e deducción *f* previa
f précompte *m*; prélèvement *m*
i previa deduzione *f*
n voorheffing *f*

90 advance on securities
cf. **credit on securities, loan on securities**
d Lombardvorschuss *m*
e adelanto *m* sobre títulos; adelanto *m* sobre valores
f avance *f* sur titres
i anticipazione *f* su titoli
n voorschot *n* tegen effecten; voorschot *n* tegen onderpandeffecten

91 advance *v* **on securities; lend** *v* **on securities**
cf. **collateralize** *v* **securities**
d Effekten belehnen *(Schw)*; Effekten beleihen; Effekten lombardieren
e prestar sobre valores
f avancer sur titres; faire des avances sur titres; lombarder des titres; prêter sur titres
i prestare su titoli
n effecten belenen

92 **advance payment; anticipated payment; early payment; forward payment; payment in advance; prepayment**
cf. **advance**
d Antizipandozahlung *f*; Pränumerandozahlung *f*; Vorausbezahlung *f*; Vorauszahlung *f*; Vorleistung *f*; vorzeitige Zahlung *f*; Zahlung *f* im voraus
e pago *m* adelantado; pago *m* anticipado; pago *m* con anticipación; pago *m* por adelantado; pago *m* por anticipado
f acquittement *m* préalable; paiement *m* à l'avance; paiement *m* anticipatif; paiement *m* anticipé; paiement *m* d'avance; paiement *m* par anticipation; versement *m* à l'avance; versement *m* anticipatif; versement *m* anticipé; versement *m* d'avance; versement *m* par anticipation
i pagamento *m* anticipato; versamento *m* anticipato
n vervroegde betaling *f*; voorafbetaling *f*; vooruitbetaling *f*; voortijdige betaling *f*

93 **adverse balance; balance deficit; debit balance; loss balance; short balance**
cf. **deficiency, overdraft**
d Debetsaldo *m*; Debitorensaldo *m*; Minussaldo *m*; Passivsaldo *m*; Schuldsaldo *m*; Sollsaldo *m*; Verlustsaldo *m*
e saldo *m* deficitario; saldo *m* deudor; saldo *m* negativo; saldo *m* pasivo
f solde *m* débiteur; solde *m* déficitaire; solde *m* en perte; solde *m* négatif
i eccedenza *f* passiva; saldo *m* a debito; saldo *m* debitore; saldo *m* deficitario; saldo *m* passivo
n debetsaldo *n*; nadelig saldo *n*; negatief saldo *n*; passief saldo *n*; schuldsaldo *n*; verliessaldo *n*

94 **adverse balance of trade; adverse trade balance; passive balance of trade; passive trade balance; unfavorable balance of trade *(US)*; unfavorable trade balance *(US)*; unfavourable balance of trade *(UK)*; unfavourable trade balance *(UK)***
d defizitäre Aussenhandelsbilanz *f*; defizitäre Handelsbilanz *f*; passive Aussenhandelsbilanz *f*; passive Handelsbilanz *f*; ungünstige Aussenhandelsbilanz *f*; ungünstige Handelsbilanz *f*
e balanza *f* comercial deficitaria; balanza *f* comercial desfavorable; balanza *f* comercial pasiva
f balance *f* commerciale défavorable; balance *f* déficitaire
i bilancia *f* commerciale deficitaria; bilancia *f* commerciale passiva; bilancia *f* commerciale sfavorevole
n deficitaire handelsbalans *f*; ongunstige handelsbalans *f*; passieve handelsbalans *f*

95 **adverse budget; budget deficit**
d Budgetdefizit *n*; Defizithaushalt *m*; Etatsdefizit *n*; Haushaltsdefizit *n*
e déficit *m* del presupuesto; déficit *m* presupuestario; presupuesto *m* deficitario
f budget *m* déficitaire; déficit *m* budgétaire; impasse *f* budgétaire
i bilancio *m* deficitario; deficit *m* del bilancio; disavanzo *m* del bilancio
n begrotingsdeficit *n*; begrotingstekort *n*; budgettair deficit *n*; budgettair tekort *n*; deficitaire begroting *f*; tekort *n* op de begroting

96 **adverse cash balance *(UK)*; cash deficit; cash short; shortage in the cash**
d Kassenabgang *m*; Kassenausfall *m*; Kassendefizit *n*; Kassenfehlbetrag *m*; Kassenmanko *n*
e deficiencia *f* de caja; déficit *m* de caja; falta *f* de caja
f déficit *m* de caisse; manquant *m* de caisse; tare *f* de caisse
i ammanco *m* di cassa; deficit *m* di cassa; disavanzo *m* di cassa
n kasdeficit *n*; kastekort *n*

97 **advice of payment; notice of payment**
cf. **credit advice**
d Einzahlungsanzeige *f*; Zahlungsanzeige *f*
e aviso *m* de pago
f avis *m* de paiement; avis *m* de versement
i avviso *m* di pagamento; avviso *m* di versamento
n betalingsadvies *n*; kennisgeving *f* van storting; stortingsadvies *n*

98 **affiliate; affiliated company; controlled company; subcompany *(US)*; subsidiary; subsidiary company**
d abhängige Gesellschaft *f*; beherrschte Gesellschaft *f*; Konzerngesellschaft *f*; Organgesellschaft *f*; Tochtergesellschaft *f*; Zweiggesellschaft *f*
e compañía *f* filial; compañía *f* subsidiaria; filial *m/f*; sociedad *f* afiliada; sociedad *f* controlada; sociedad *f* dependiente; sociedad *f* dominada; sociedad *f* filial; subsidiaria *f*
f filiale *f*; société *f* affiliée; société *f* contrôlée; société *f* dominée; société *f* filiale

i filiale *f*; società *f* affiliata; società *f* consociata; società *f* controllata; società *f* dominata; società *f* filiale
n dochtermaatschappij *f*; geaffilieerde maatschappij *f*

99 **afflux of capital; inflow of capital; influx of capital; capital inflow; capital influx; entry of capital**
d Kapitalzufluss *m*; Kapitalzufuhr *f*; Kapitalzustrom *m*
e affluencia *f* de capitales; entrada *f* de capital(es)
f afflux *m* de capitaux; entrée *f* de capitaux
i afflusso *m* di capitali; entrata *f* di capitali
n binnenstromen *n* van kapitaal; kapitaaltoevloed *m*; toevloeiing *f* van kapitalen

100 **afford** *v* **a profit; bring** *v* **in a profit; leave** *v* **a profit; pay** *v*; **return** *v* **a profit; yield** *v* **a profit**
cf. **record** *v* **a profit**
d einen Gewinn abwerfen; einen Gewinn bringen; einen Gewinn einbringen; einen Gewinn ergeben; sich rentieren
e arrojar un beneficio; dar un beneficio; producir (un beneficio); redituar (un beneficio); rendir (un beneficio); rentar
f donner un bénéfice; produire (un bénéfice); rapporter (un bénéfice); rendre (un bénéfice)
i dare un utile; fruttare (un utile); produrre (un utile); rendere (un utile)
n een winst afwerpen; een winst geven; een winst laten; een winst opbrengen; een winst opleveren; renderen

101 **afford** *v* **collateral; furnish** *v* **collateral; give** *v* **collateral security; offer** *v* **collateral**
d besichern; eine Sicherheit bestellen; eine Sicherheit bieten; eine Sicherheit geben; eine Sicherheit gewähren; eine Sicherheit leisten; eine Sicherheit stellen
e constituir una garantía; dar una garantía; ofrecer una garantía; prestar una garantía
f accorder une garantie; constituer une garantie; donner une garantie; fournir une garantie; offrir une garantie
i costituire une garanzia; dare une garanzia; offrire une garanzia; prestare une garanzia
n een zekerheid bieden; een zekerheid geven; een zekerheid stellen

102 **after hours market**
cf. **curb**
d Abendbörse *f*; Nachbörse *f*
e bolsa *f* extraoficial; bolsa *f* nocturna
f après-bourse *f*
i dopoborsa *m*
n avondbeurs *f*; nabeurs *f*

103 **agency**
d Agentur *f*; Vertretung *f*
e agencia *f*
f agence *f*
i agenzia *f*
n agentschap *n*; agentuur *f*

104 **agent**
cf. **broker**
d Agent *m*; Vertreter *m*
e agente *m*
f agent *m*
i agente *m*
n agent *m*; vertegenwoordiger *m*

105 **aggregate; grand total; sum total**
d Endsumme *f*; Gesamtsumme *f*; Gesamtzahl *f*; Totalsumme *f*
e suma *f* final; suma *f* total; total *m* general
f somme *f* finale; somme *f* totale; total *m* général
i somma *f* complessiva; somma *f* finale; somma *f* totale; totale *m* complessivo; totale *m* generale
n eindtotaal *n*; totaal *n* generaal; totale som *f*

106 **aggregate** *v*; **amount** *v* **to a total of; total** *v*
d im ganzen ausmachen; im ganzen betragen; im ganzen ergeben; insgesamt ausmachen; insgesamt betragen; insgesamt ergeben; sich belaufen auf; sich beziffern auf
e ascender a; cifrarse en; elevarse a; importar en total; totalizar
f se chiffrer à; s'élever à; se monter à; totaliser
i ammontare a; ascendere a; totalizzare
n een totaal uitmaken van; in totaal bedragen; in totaal belopen; tot een totaal oplopen van

107 **aggregate amount; global amount; overall amount; total amount**
cf. **lump sum**
d Gesamtbetrag *m*; Globalbetrag *m*; Totalbetrag *m*
e importe *m* global; importe *m* total
f montant *m* global; montant *m* total

i ammontare *m* complessivo; ammontare *m* globale; ammontare *m* totale; importo *m* complessivo; importo *m* globale; importo *m* totale
n gezamenlijk bedrag *n*; globaal bedrag *n*; totaal bedrag *n*

108 aggregate value; total value
d Gesamtwert *m*
e valor *m* global; valor *m* total
f valeur *f* globale; valeur *f* totale
i valore *m* complessivo; valore *m* globale; valore *m* totale
n gezamenlijke waarde *f*; globale waarde *f*; totale waarde *f*

109 agio; exchange premium; premium on exchange; turn on exchange
d Agio *n*; Aufgeld *n*
e agio *m*; prima *f* de cambio
f agio *m*; prime *f* au (de) change
i aggio *m*; premio *m* di cambio
n agio *n*; opgeld *n*

110 agio; premium
d Agio *n*; Aufgeld *n*; Aufzins *m*; Prämie *f*
e agio *m*; prima *f*; premio *m*
f agio *m*; prime *f*
i aggio *m*; premio *m*
n agio *n*; premie *f*; prime *f (B)*

111 agiotage ***(rare)*****; gambling on the stock exchange; stock exchange speculation; stockjobbing**
d Agiotage *f*; Börsenspekulation *f*; Börsenspiel *n*
e agiotaje *m*; especulación *f* en bolsa; juego *m* en bolsa
f agiotage *m*; jeu *m* de bourse; spéculation *f* en bourse
i aggiotaggio *m*; gioco *m* in borsa; speculazione *f* in borsa
n agiotage *f*; beursspeculatie *f*; beursspel *n*

112 agree *v* **accounts; reconcile** *v* **accounts; square** *v* **accounts**
cf. **balance** *v* **an account**
d Konten abgleichen; Konten abstimmen; Konten bereinigen; Konten kollationieren; Konten in Übereinstimmung bringen
e conciliar las cuentas; concordar las cuentas; reconciliar las cuentas
f apurer les comptes; faire accorder les comptes; faire cadrer les comptes; rapprocher les comptes
i appurare i conti; concordare i conti; far quadrare i conti
n rekeningen afstemmen; rekeningen in overeenstemming brengen; rekeningen sluitend maken

113 agree *v* **a price; agree** *v* **on a price**
d einen Preis abmachen; einen Preis ausmachen; einen Preis vereinbaren; sich über einen Preis einigen
e acordar un precio; concertar en precio; concertar por precio; convenir un precio
f convenir d'un prix; se mettre d'accord sur un prix; s'entendre sur un prix; tomber d'accord sur un prix
i convenire su un prezzo; pattuire un prezzo
n een prijs overeenkomen

114 agreed price; all-in price; contract(ing) price; lump-sum price
d abgemachter Preis *m*; Pauschalpreis *m*; vereinbarter Preis *m*; Vertragspreis *m*
e precio *m* concertado; precio *m* contractual; precio *m* convenido; precio *m* global
f prix *m* à forfait; prix *m* convenu; prix *m* forfaitaire; prix *m* global
i prezzo *m* contrattuale; prezzo *m* convenuto; prezzo *m* forfettario; prezzo *m* globale; prezzo *m* pattuito
n contractprijs *m*; forfaitaire prijs *m*; globale prijs *m*; overeengekomen prijs *m*

115 agreement on prices; price agreement; price cartel; price-fixing agreement
d Preisabkommen *n*; Preisabmachung *f*; Preisabrede *f*; Preisabsprache *f*; Preiskartell *n*; Preiskonvention *f*; Preisvereinbarung *f*
e acuerdo *m* sobre los precios; cártel *m* de precios; convenio *m* sobre los precios
f accord *m* de prix; accord *m* sur les prix; cartel *m* de prix; convention *f* sur les prix; entente *f* sur les prix
i accordo *m* sui prezzi; cartello *m* di prezzi; convenzione *f* sui prezzi
n prijsafspraak *f*; prijskartel *n*; prijsovereenkomst *f*

116 alienability; assignability; transferability
d Abtretbarkeit *f*; Transferfähigkeit *f*; Transferierbarkeit *f*; Übertragbarkeit *f*; Veräusserlichkeit *f*; Zedierbarkeit *f*; Zessionsfähigkeit *f*
e alienabilidad *f*; cesibilidad *f*; enajenabilidad *f*; transferibilidad *f*; transmisibilidad *f*
f aliénabilité *f*; cessibilité *f*; transférabilité *f*; transmissibilité *f*
i alienabilità *f*; cedibilità *f*; trasferibilità *f*;

trasmissibilità *f*
n cedeerbaarheid *f*; overdraagbaarheid *f*; transferabiliteit *f*; vervreemdbaarheid *f*

117 alienable; assignable; transferable
d abtretbar; transferabel; transferfähig; transferierbar; übertragbar; veräusserlich; zedierbar; zessionsfähig
e alienable; cesible; enajenable; transferible; transmisible
f aliénable; cessible; transférable; transmissible
i alienabile; cedibile; trasferibile; trasmissibile
n cedeerbaar; overdraagbaar; transferabel; vervreemdbaar

118 alienate *v*; **assign** *v*; **cede** *v*; **convey** *v*; **transfer** *v*
d abtreten; übereignen; überlassen; übertragen; umschreiben; veräussern; zedieren
e alienar; ceder; enajenar; entregar; transferir; transmitir; traspasar
f aliéner; céder; transférer; transmettre
i alienare; cedere; devolvere; tra(n)sferire; trasmettere
n afstaan; cederen; overdragen; overmaken; vervreemden

119 alienation; assignation; assignment; cession; conveyance; transfer
d Abtretung *f*; Übereignung *f*; Überlassung *f*; Übertragung *f*; Umschreibung *f*; Veräusserung *f*; Zession *f*
e alienación *f*; cesión *f*; enajenación *f*; entrega *f*; transferencia *f*; transmisión *f*; traspaso *m*
f aliénation *f*; cession *f*; mutation *f*; transfert *m*; transmission *f*
i alienazione *f*; cessione *f*; devoluzione *f*; trapasso *m*; trasferimento *m*; trasmissione *f*
n afstand *m*; cessie *f*; overdracht *f*; overmaking *f*; vervreemding *f*

120 alienee; assign; assignee; cessionary; transferee
d Abtretungsempfänger *m*; Übernehmer *m*; Zessionar *m*; Zessionär *m*
e cesionario *m*
f aliénataire *m*; cessionaire *m*
i alienatario *m*; cessionario *m*
n cessionaris *m*; overnemer *m*; verkrijger *m*

121 alienor; assignor; cedent; transferor; transfer(r)er *(US)*
d Abtreter *m*; Abtretender *m*; Übertragender *m*; Veräusserer *m*; Zedent *m*
e cedente *m*; cesionista *m*; enajenador *m*
f aliénateur *m*; cédant *m*
i alienante *m*; cedente *m*
n cedent *m*; overdrager *m*; vervreemder *m*

122 allocate *v*; **allot** *v*; **apportion** *v*; **assign** *v*
cf. **appropriate** *v*
d aufteilen; auswerfen; dotieren; kontingentieren*; repartieren; verteilen; zuteilen; zuweisen; zuwenden
e afectar; asignar; contingentar*; designar; distribuir; dotar; proporcionar; prorratear; repartir
f affecter; allouer; assigner; attribuer; contingenter*; distribuer; doter; répartir; ventiler
i accantonare; assegnare; attribuire; contingentare*; destinare; imputare; ripartire; stanziare
n contingenteren*; doteren; omslaan; toedelen; toerekenen; toevoegen; toewijzen; verdelen

* By a quota system.

123 allocation; allotment; apportionment
cf. **analysis, appropriation**
d Aufteilung *f*; Dotierung *f*; Repartierung *f*; Verteilung *f*; Zuführung *f*; Zuordnung *f*; Zuteilung *f*; Zuweisung *f*; Zuwendung *f*
e afectación *f*; asignación *f*; distribución *f*; dotación *f*; imputación *f*; prorrateo *m*; repartición *f*; reparto *m*
f affectation *f*; allocation *f*; attribution *f*; dotation *f*; imputation *f*; répartition *f*; ventilation *f*
i accantonamento *m*; assegnazione *f*; attribuzione *f*; destinazione *f*; imputazione *f*; ripartizione *f*; stanziamento *m*
n allocatie *f*; dotering *f*; omslag *m*; toerekening *f*; toevoeging *f*; toewijzing *f*; ventilatie *f*; verdeling *f*

124 allonge; extension slip; rider
d Allonge *f*; Verlängerungsstück *n*; Wechselallonge *f*; Wechselanhang *m*
e coleta *f* de una letra; suplemento *m* a una letra
f allonge *f*
i allunga *f*; allungamento *m*; coda *f*
n allonge *f*; verlengstuk *n*

125 allotment of shares; apportionment of shares; assignment of shares;

distribution of shares
d Aktienrepartierung *f*; Aktienzuteilung *f*
e asignación *f* de acciones; repartición *f* de acciones; reparto *m* de acciones
f assignation *f* d'actions; répartition *f* d'actions
i assegnazione *f* di azioni; ripartizione *f* di azioni
n toewijzing *f* van aandelen

126 **allow** *v* **a credit; authorise** *v* **a credit** *(UK)*; **authorize** *v* **acredit** *(US)*; **extend** *v* **a credit; grant** *v* **a credit**
d einen Kredit bewilligen; einen Kredit einräumen; einen Kredit genehmigen; einen Kredit gewähren
e acordar un crédito; autorizar un crédito; conceder un crédito; otorgar un crédito
f accorder un crédit; allouer un crédit; autoriser un crédit; consentir un crédit; octroyer un crédit
i accordare un credito; autorizzare un credito; concedere un credito
n een krediet toekennen; een krediet toestaan; een krediet verlenen; een krediet verstrekken

127 **allowance; discount; rebate**
cf. **cut in the price**
d Abschlag *m*; Abzug *m*; Diskont *m*; Ermässigung *f*; Nachlass *m*; Rabatt *m*; Skonto *m/n*; Skontoabzug *m*
e bonificación *f*; descuento *m*; rebaja *f*
f boni *m*; bonification *f*; escompte *m*; rabais *m*; rabat *m*; remise *f*; ristourne *f*
i abbuono *m*; bonifico *m*; ribasso *m*; sconto *m*
n afslag *m*; disconto *n*; korting *f*; rabat *n*

128 **allowance; expense allowance**
d Aufwandsentschädigung *f*
e compensación *f* (de los gastos de representación); indemnización *f* (de los gastos de representación)
f indemnité *f* (des frais de répresentation)
i indennità *f* (di trasferta); indennità *f* (per spese)
n kostenvergoeding *f*; onkosten-vergoeding *f*

129 **allowance; provision; reserve**
d Reserve *f*; Rücklage *f*; Rückstellung *f*
e previsión *f*; provisión *f*; reserva *f*
f prévision *f*; provision *f*; réserve *f*
i accantonamento *m*; riserva *f*
n reserve *f*; voorziening *f*

130 **allowance account; provision account; reserve account; valuation account**
d Reservekonto *n*; Rücklagenkonto *n*; Rückstellungskonto *n*
e cuenta *f* de previsión; cuenta *f* de provisión; cuenta *f* de reserva
f compte *m* de prévision; compte *m* de provision; compte *m* de réserve
i conto *m* di riserva
n reserverekening *f*

131 **after allowance for charges; after allowance for expenses; after allowing for charges; after allowing for expenses; after deducting charges; after deducting expenses; charges deducted; clear of charges; clear of expenses; expenses deducted; quit of charges; quit of expenses**
d abzüglich der Kosten; abzüglich der Spesen; abzüglich der Unkosten; nach Abrechnung der Kosten; nach Abrechnung der Spesen; nach Abrechnung der Unkosten; nach Abzug der Kosten; nach Abzug der Spesen; nach Abzug der Unkosten
e deducción hecha de los gastos; deducidos los gastos; descontados los gastos; previa deducción de los gastos
f après déduction des frais; après défalcation des frais; déduction faite des frais; défalcation faite des frais; frais déduits; frais défalqués
i deduzione fatta delle spese; detrazione fatta delle spese; detratte le spese; dopo dedotte le spese; dopo defalcate le spese; previa detrazione delle spese; spese dedotte
n na aftrek van de kosten; na aftrek van de onkosten

132 **allowance for depreciation; depreciation allowance; depreciation charge; depreciation fund; depreciation reserve; provision for depreciation**
cf. **annual allowance for depreciation**
d Abschreibungsfonds *m*; Abschreibungs-reserve *f*; Abschreibungsrücklage *f*; Abschreibungsrückstellung *f*; Entwertungsrücklage *f*; Rückstellung *f* für Abschreibungen; Rückstellung *f* für Wertberichtigung; Rückstellung *f* für Wertverminderung; Wertminderungs-reserve *f*; Wertverminderungsreserve *f*
e fondo *m* de amortización; fondo *m* de depreciación; previsión *f* por depreciación; provisión *f* para amortizaciones; provisión *f* para depreciación; reserva *f* de depreciación; reserva *f* para amortizaciones; reserva *f* para depreciación

f fonds *m* d'amortissement; fonds *m* de dépréciation; prévision *f* pour dépréciation; provision *f* pour amortissement; provision *f* pour dépréciation; réserve *f* d'amortissement
i fondo *m* di ammortamento; fondo *m* di svalutazione
n afschrijvingsfonds *n*; afschrijvingsreserve *f*; depreciatiereserve *f*; voorziening *f* voor waardevermindering

133 **allowance for errors; cashier's allowance**
d Ausfallgeld *n*; Fehlgeld *n*; Mankogeld *n*
e indemnización *f* de caja; pase *m* de caja
f indemnité *f* de caisse; tare *f* de caisse
i indennità *f* di cassa
n vertelgeld *n*

134 **allowance in kind; benefit in kind; remuneration in kind**
cf. **income in kind**
d Deputat *n*; Naturalbezug *m*; Naturalvergütung *f*; Sachbezug *m*; Sachzuwendung *f*
e remuneración *f* en especie
f avantage *m* en nature; rémunération *f* en nature
i retribuzione *f* in natura; remunerazione *f* in natura; rimunerazione *f* in natura
n vergoeding *f* in natura; voordeel *n* in natura

135 **amalgamation; fusion; merger**
d Fusion *f*; Fusionierung *f*; Integration *f*; Konzentration *f*; Verschmelzung *f*; Zusammenlegung *f*; Zusammenschliessung *f*; Zusammenschluss *m*
e concentración *f*; fusión *f*; integración *f*
f concentration *f*; fusion *f*; fusionnement *m*; intégration *f*
i concentrazione *f*; fusione *f*; integrazione *f*
n concentratie *f*; fusie *f*; integratie *f*; samensmelting *f*

136 **amercement; fine; forfeit (money); mulct; (pecuniary) penalty**
d Busse *f*; Bussgeld *n*; Geldbusse *f*; Geldstrafe *f*; Pönale *n (O)*; Reugeld *n*; Reukauf *m*; Zwangsgeld *n**
e multa *f*; penalidad *f*; pena *f* pecuniaria; sanción (pecuniaria)
f amende *f*; contravention *f**; dédit *m*; peine *f* pécuniaire; pénalité *f*
i ammenda *f*; contravvenzione *f**; multa *f*; penale *f*; penalità *f*; pena *f* pecuniaria
n boete *f*; geldboete *f*; rouwgeld *n*; rouwkoop *m*

* Usually administrative.

137 **amortisable mortgage; amortizable mortgage; sinking fund mortgage loan**
d Amortisationshypothek *f*
e hipoteca *f* amortizable
f hypothèque *f* amortissable
i ipoteca *f* ammortizzabile
n amortiseerbare hypot(h)eek *f*; in termijnen aflosbare hypot(h)ecaire lening *f*

138 **amortisation** *(of assets)*; **amortisement; amortization; amortizement; charge-off; depreciation; write-down; write-off** *(usually complete)*
d Abschreibung *f*; Amortisation *f*; Amortisierung *f*
e amortización *f*; depreciación *f*
f amortissement *m*; dépréciation *f*
i ammortamento *m*; ammortizzamento *m*; ammortizzazione *f*; deprezzamento *m*
n afschrijving *f*; amortisatie *f*; amortizatie *f*

139 **amortisation** *(of debts etc.)*; **amortization; discharge; extinction; liquidation; payment; redemption; repayment; retirement; settlement**
d Abbezahlung *f*; Abdeckung *f*; Abführung *f*; Ablösung *f*; Abtragung *f*; Abzahlung *f*; Amortisation *f*; Amortisierung *f*; Ausgleich *m*; Ausgleichung *f*; Auslöschung *f*; Begleichung *f*; Bezahlung *f*; Einlösung *f*; Entrichtung *f*; Erlöschen *n*; Liquidation *f*; Liquidierung *f*; Löschung *f*; Rückzahlung *f*; Tilgung *f*; Zahlung *f*; Zurückzahlung *f*
e amortización *f*; arreglo *m*; cancelación *f*; descargo *m*; extinción *f*; liquidación *f*; pago *m*; redención *f*; reembolso *m*; rescate *m*; saldo *m*; satisfacción *f*
f acquittement *m*; amortissement *m*; extinction *f*; liquidation *f*; paiement *m*; payement *m*; règlement *m*; remboursement *m*
i ammortamento *m*; ammortizzamento *m*; ammortizzazione *f*; estinzione *f*; liquidazione *f*; pagamento *m*; redenzione *f*; regolamento *m*; rimborso *m*; riscatto *m*; saldo *m*
n aanzuivering *f*; afdoening *f*; aflossing *f*; afrekening *f*; amortisatie *f*; amortizatie *f*; betaling *f*; delging *f*; liquidatie *f*; rescontre *m/f*; terugbetaling *f*; vereffening *f*; verrekening *f*; voldoening *f*; wederbetaling *f*

140 amortisation fund; amortization fund *(US)*; redemption fund *(US)*; sinking fund

d Ablösungsfonds *m*; Amortisationsfonds *m*; Einlösungsfonds *m*; Rückkaufsfonds *m*; Schuldentilgungsfonds *m*; Tilgungsfonds *m*
e fondo *m* de amortización; fondo *m* de rescate
f fonds *m* d'amortissement; fonds *m* de rachat
i fondo *m* d'ammortamento; fondo *m* di riscatto
n aflossingsfonds *n*; amortisatiefonds *n*; delgingsfonds *n*; sinking fund *n*

141 amortisation loan; amortising loan; amortization loan; amortizing loan; redemption loan; sinking fund loan

d Abgeltungsdarleh(e)n *n*; Ablösungsanleihe *f*; Amortisationsanleihe *f*; Amortisationsdarleh(e)n *n*; Tilgungsanleihe *f*; Tilgungsdarleh(e)n *n*
e empréstito *m* amortizable; empréstito *m* de amortización; empréstito *m* redimible; préstamo *m* amortizable; préstamo *m* de amortización; préstamo *m* redimible
f emprunt *m* amortissable; emprunt *m* d'amortissement; prêt *m* amortissable; prêt *m* d'amortissement
i mutuo *m* ammortizzabile; mutuo *m* d'ammortamento; mutuo *m* redimibile; prestito *m* ammortizzabile; prestito *m* d'ammortamento; prestito *m* redimibile
n aflosbare lening *f*; amortisatielening *f*

142 amortisation of a loan; amortization of a loan; redemption of a loan

d Amortisation *f* einer Anleihe; Anleiheablösung *f*; Anleihetilgung *f*
e amortización *f* de un empréstito; redención *f* de un empréstito
f amortissement *m* d'un emprunt
i ammortamento *m* d'un prestito; redenzione *f* d'un prestito
n aflossing *f* van een lening; amortisatie *f* van een lening; leningsaflossing *f*

143 amortisation on replacement value *(UK)*; amortization on replacement value *(US)*; depreciation on replacement value

d Abschreibung *f* auf den Wiederbeschaffungswert
e amortización *f* económica; depreciación *f* económica
f amortissement *m* économique
i ammortamento *m* economico
n afschrijving *f* op basis van de vervangingswaarde

144 amortisation rate *(UK)* *(of assets)*; amortization rate *(US)*; depreciation rate

d Abschreibungsquote *f*; Abschreibungssatz *m*; Amortisationsquote *f*; Amortisationsrate *f*; Amortisationssatz *m*
e coeficiente *m* de amortización; cuota *f* de amortización; tasa *f* de amortización; tasa *f* de depreciación
f coefficient *m* d'amortissement; quota *m* d'amortissement; quote-part *f* d'amortissement; taux *m* d'amortissement; taux *m* de dépréciation
i coefficiente *m* d'ammortamento; quota *f* d'ammortamento; tasso *m* d'ammortamento; tasso *m* di deprezzamento
n afschrijvingspercentage *n*; afschrijvingsvoet *m*; amortisatiepercentage *n*; amortisatievoet *m*

145 amortisation rate *(UK)* *(of debts)*; amortization rate *(US)*; redemption rate
cf. **redemption price**

d Amortisationsquote *f*; Amortisationsrate *f*; Amortisationssatz *m*; Tilgungsquote *f*; Tilgungsrate *f*; Tilgungssatz *m*
e cuota *f* de amortización; tasa *f* de amortización; tipo *m* de amortización
f quota *m* d'amortissement; quote-part *f* d'amortissement; taux *m* d'amortissement
i quota *m* d'ammortamento; tasso *m* d'ammortamento
n amortisatiepercentage *n*; amortisatievoet *m*; delgingsvoet *m*

146 amortisation table *(UK)*; amortization schedule *(US)*; redemption plan; redemption scheme; redemption table; sinking fund table; terms of redemption

d Amortisationsplan *m*; Amortisationstabelle *f*; Einlösungsplan *m*; Tilgungsplan *m*; Tilgungstabelle *f*
e plan *m* de amortización; tabla *f* de amortización
f plan *m* d'amortissement; tableau *m* d'amortissement
i piano *m* d'ammortamento; tavola *f* d'ammortamento
n aflossingsplan *n*; amortisatieplan *n*; amortisatietabel *f*; amortisatietafel *f*; delgingsplan *n*

147 amortise *v* *(of assets)*; amortize *v*; charge *v* off; write *v* down; write *v* off

(usually completely)
cf. **depreciate** *v*
d abschreiben; amortisieren
e amortizar
f amortir
i ammortare; ammortizzare
n afschrijven; amortiseren; amortizeren

148 **amortise** *v (of debts etc.)*; **amortize** *v*; **clear** *v*; **discharge** *v*; **extinguish** *v*; **liquidate** *v*; **pay** *v* **off; redeem** *v*; **repay** *v*; **retire** *v*; **settle** *v*; **sink** *v*; **wipe** *v* **off**
d abbezahlen; abdecken; abführen; ablösen; abzahlen; amortisieren; ausgleichen; auslöschen; begleichen; bezahlen; einlösen; entrichten; liquidieren; löschen; rückzahlen; saldieren; tilgen; zurückzahlen
e amortizar; arreglar; cancelar; enjugar; extinguir; liquidar; pagar; redimir; reembolsar; rescatar; saldar; satisfacer
f acquitter; amortir; éteindre; liquider; payer; régler; rembourser; s'acquitter de; solder
i ammortare; ammortizzare; estinguere; liquidare; pagare; redimere; regolare; rimborsare; riscattare; saldare
n aanzuiveren; afbetalen; afdoen; aflossen; afrekenen; amortiseren; amortizeren; betalen; delgen; liquideren; rescontreren; salderen; terugbetalen; vereffenen; verrekenen; voldoen

149 **amount; sum**
d Betrag *m*; Summe *f*
e importe *m*; monto *m*; suma *f*
f montant *m*; somme *f*
i ammontare *m*; importo *m*; somma *f*
n bedrag *n*; som *f*

150 **amount brought forward (to next account); balance carried forward (to next account); carry-forward; carry-over**
d Saldovortrag *m* auf neue Rechnung; Übertrag *m* auf neue Rechnung; Vortrag *m* auf neue Rechnung
e saldo *m* a cuenta nueva; saldo *m* en cuenta nueva; transporte *m* del saldo a nueva cuenta
f balance *f* à nouveau; report *m* à nouveau
i riporto *m* a nuovo; saldo *m* a nuovo
n overboeking *f* naar nieuwe rekening; overdracht *f* naar nieuwe rekening *(B)*; saldo *n* naar nieuwe rekening; transport *n* naar nieuwe rekening

151 **amount due; amount owing; sum due; sum owing**
cf. **amount outstanding, balance due**
d geschuldeter Betrag *m*; geschuldete Summe *f*; Schuldbetrag *m*; Schuldsumme *f*; schuldiger Betrag *m*; schuldige Summe *f*
e importe *m* adeudado; importe *m* debido; suma *f* adeudada; suma *f* debida
f montant *m* dû; somme *f* due
i importo *m* dovuto; somma *f* dovuta
n verschuldigd bedrag *n*; verschuldigde *n*; verschuldigde som *f*

152 **amount outstanding; outstanding amount**
cf. **amount due, arrearages, balance**
d Aussenstand *m*; ausstehender Betrag *m*; offenstehender Betrag *m*; Rückstand *m*; rückständiger Betrag *m*
e atraso *m*; importe *m* pendiente; remanente *m*
f arriéré *m*; somme *f* à recevoir; somme *f* à recouvrer
i arretrato *m*; importo *m* pendente
n achterstand *m*; uitstaand bedrag *n*

153 **amount subscribed**
d Zeichnungsbetrag *m*
e importe *m* su(b)scrito
f montant *m* de la souscription; montant *m* souscrit
i importo *m* sottoscritto
n inschrijvingsbedrag *n*

154 **amount unpaid**
d nicht eingezahlter Betrag *m*; unbezahlter Betrag *m*
e importe *m* impago; importe *m* no pagado
f montant *m* impayé; non-versé *m*
i importo *m* non pagato; importo *m* non versato
n onbetaald bedrag *n*

155 **analysis; breakdown**
cf. **allocation**
d Aufgliederung *f*; Aufschlüsselung *f*
e clasificación *f*; descomposición *f*
f classification *f*; décomposition *f*; dépouillement *m*
i classificazione *f*; scomposizione *f*
n classificatie *f*; uitsplitsing *f*

156 **anatocism** *(rare)*; **capitalisation of interest** *(UK)*; **capitalization of interest** *(US)*
cf. **compound interest**
d Anatozismus *m*; Kapitalisierung *f* der (fälligen) Zinsen; Zinsenverzinsung *f*
e anatocismo *m*; capitalización *f* de intereses (devengados)
f anatocisme *m*; capitalisation *f* d'intérêts

(dus)
i anatocismo *m*; capitalizzazione *f* d'interessi (dovuti)
n anatocisme *n*; kapitalisatie *f* van (verschuldigde) rente

157 **annual allowance for depreciation; annual depreciation allowance; annual depreciation charge; annual provision for depreciation**
d jährliche Abschreibungsrate *f*
e anualidad *f* de amortización
f annuité *f* d'amortissement
i annualità *f* d'ammortamento
n jaarlijkse afschrijving *f*

158 **annual average**
d Jahresdurchschnitt *m*
e media *f* anual; promedio *m* anual
f moyenne *f* annuelle
i media *f* annua
n jaargemiddelde *n*

159 **annual budget**
d Jahreshaushaltsplan *m*; jährlicher Haushaltsplan *m*
e presupuesto *m* anual
f budget *m* annuel
i bilancio *m* annuale
n jaarlijkse begroting *f*

160 **annual report; annual return; annual statement**
d Jahresausweis *m*; Jahresbericht *m*; Jahresübersicht *f*
e informe *m* anual; memoria *f* anual
f compte rendu *m* annuel; rapport *m* annuel
i rapporto *m* annuale; rapporto *m* annuo; relazione *f* annua; relazione *f* annuale
n jaarbericht *n*; jaarverslag *n*

161 **annuity**
d Annuität *f*; Jahresrente *f*; Jahrgeld *n*
e anualidad *f*; renta *f* anual
f annuité *f*; rente *f* annuelle
i annualità *f*; rendita *f* annuale
n annuïteit *f*; jaargeld *n*; jaarlijkse rente *f*

162 **annuity bond; annuity certificate; perpetual bond**
cf. **bond, fixed interest bearing security**
d Rentenbrief *m*; Rentenpapier *n*; Rentenschein *m*; Rentenschuldverschreibung *f*; Rententitel *m*
e título *m* de renta; valor *m* de renta
f lettre *f* de rente; obligation *f* d'annuité; obligation *f* de rente; titre *m* de rente; valeur *f* de rente
i cartella *f* di rendita; titolo *m* di rendita; valore *m* di rendita
n eeuwigdurende obligatie *f*; rentebewijs *n*; rentebrief *m*; rentetitel *m* *(B)*

163 **annuity for life; life annuity; perpetual annuity**
d Dauerrente *f*; lebenslängliche Rente *f*; Lebensrente *f*; Leibrente *f*; Rente *f* auf Lebenszeit
e annualidad *f* vitalicia; renta *f* perpetua; renta *f* vitalicia
f annuité *f* à vie; annuité *f* viagère; rente *f* perpétuelle; rente *f* viagère; viager *m*
i rendita *f* perpetua; rendita *f* vitalizia; vitalizio *m*
n lijfrente *f*

164 **antedate** *v*; **backdate** *v*; **foredate** *v*; **predate** *v*
d antedatieren; früher datieren; nachdatieren*; postdatieren*; rückdatieren; vorausdatieren; vordatieren*; zurückdatieren
e antedatar; antefechar
f antidater
i antidatare; retrodatare
n antedateren; antidateren

* Also means to postdate.

165 **anticipated interest; anticipatory interest; interest paid in advance**
d Antizipandozinsen *mpl*; Vorauszinsen *mpl*
e intereses *mpl* anticipados
f intérêts *mpl* anticipés
i interessi *mpl* anticipati
n vervroegde int(e)rest *m*

166 **anticipated profit**
cf. **apparent profit**
d erhoffter Gewinn *m*; erwarteter Gewinn *m*
e beneficio *m* esperado; beneficio *m* previsto
f bénéfice *m* espéré; profit *m* espéré
i profitto *m* sperato; utile *m* presunto; utile *m* sperato
n verhoopte winst *f*; verwachte winst *f*

167 **anticipated redemption** *(of a bond)*
d vorzeitiger Rückkauf *m*; vorzeitige Rückzahlung *f*
e rescate *m* anticipado
f rachat *m* anticipé
i riscatto *m* anticipato
n vervroegde inkoop *m*

168 anti-cyclical
d antizyklisch
e anticíclico
f anti-conjoncturel; anti-cyclique
i anticiclico; anticongiunturale; controciclico
n anticyclisch

169 antidumping duty
d Antidumpingzoll *m*
e arancel *m* antidumping; arancel *m* contra el dumping
f droit *m* antidumping; taxe *f* antidumping
i dazio *m* antidumping
n antidumpingrecht *n*

170 anti-inflationary; counterinflationary
d antiinflationär; antiinflationistisch; Antiinflations-; gegeninflatorisch; inflationsfeindlich
e antiinflacionista
f anti-inflationniste; contre-inflationniste
i antiinflazionistico
n anti-inflatoir; anti-inflationistisch

171 apparent profit; assumed profit; fictitious profit; imaginary profit
cf. **anticipated profit**
d imaginärer Gewinn *m*; Scheingewinn *m*
e beneficio *m* ficticio; beneficio *m* imaginario
f bénéfice *m* apparent; bénéfice *m* fictif; bénéfice *m* imaginaire
i utile *m* fittizio; utile *m* immaginario
n denkbeeldige winst *f*; fictieve winst *f*; imaginaire winst *f*; schijnwinst *f*

172 applicant for a loan; applicant for credit; credit applicant; loan applicant
d Anleihesuchender *m*; Darleh(e)nsantragsteller *m*; Darleh(e)nsbewerber *m*; Kreditantragsteller *m*; Kreditbewerber *m*
e solicitante *m* de (un) crédito; solicitante *m* de un empréstito; solicitante *m* de un préstamo
f domandeur *m* de (d'un) crédit; domandeur *m* d'un emprunt; domandeur *m* d'un prêt
i domandante *m* di (un) credito; domandante *m* di un mutuo; domandante *m* di un prestito
n aanvrager *m* van (een) krediet; aanvrager *m* van een lening; kredietaanvrager *m*; leningaanvrager *m*

173 application for a loan; application for credit; credit application; loan application
d Anleihegesuch *n*; Darleh(e)nsantrag *m*; Darleh(e)nsgesuch *n*; Kreditantrag *m*; Kreditgesuch *n*
e solicitud *f* de crédito; solicitud *f* de empréstito; solicitud *f* de préstamo
f demande *f* de crédit; demande *f* d'emprunt; demande *f* de prêt
i domanda *f* di credito; domanda *f* di mutuo; domanda *f* di prestito
n kredietaanvraag *f*; kredietaanvrage *f*; leningaanvraag *f*; leningaanvrage *f*

174 application right; right; stock right *(US)*; subscription right
d Bezugsberechtigung *f*; Bezugsrecht *n*; Subskriptionsrecht *n*; Zeichnungsberechtigung *f*
e derecho *m* de su(b)scripción
f droit *m* de souscription
i diritto *m* di sottoscrizione
n claimrecht *n*; inschrijvingsrecht *n*; recht *n* van inschrijving

175 apply *v* for a loan; ask *v* for a loan
d sich um ein Darleh(e)n bewerben; sich um eine Anleihe bewerben; sich um einen Kredit bewerben
e solicitar un crédito; solicitar un empréstito; solicitar un préstamo
f demander un crédit; demander un emprunt; demander un prêt
i domandare un credito; domandare un mutuo; domandare un prestito
n een krediet aanvragen; een lening aanvragen

176 appraisal; appraisement; assessment; calculation; estimate; estimation; evaluation; valuation
cf. **estimate**
d Abschätzung *f*; Bewertung *f*; Einschätzung *f*; Schätzung *f*; Taxierung *f*; Überschlag *m*; Veranschlagung *f*; Wertansatz *m*; Wertansetzung *f*; Wertberechnung *f*; Wertbestimmung *f*; Wertermittlung *f*; Wertfeststellung *f*; Wertschätzung *f*
e aprecio *m*; avalúo *m*; cálculo *m*; estimación *f*; evaluación *f*; tasación *f*; valoración *f*; valorización *f*; valuación *f*
f appréciation *f*; estimation *f*; évaluation *f*; taxation *f*
i estimazione *f*; perizia *f*; stima *f*; tassazione *f (rare)*; valutazione *f*
n raming *f*; schatting *f*; taxatie *f*; taxering *f*; waardebepaling *f*; waarderaming *f*; waardering *f*; waardeschatting *f*

177 **appraise** *v*; **assess** *v*; **calculate** *v*; **estimate** *v*; **evaluate** *v*; **rate** *v*; **valuate** *v*; **value** *v*
d abschätzen; anschlagen; bewerten; einschätzen; schätzen; taxieren; überschlagen; veranschlagen; werten
e apreciar; avalorar; avaluar; calcular; estimar; evaluar; tasar; valorar; valuar
f apprécier; estimer; évaluer; priser; taxer
i apprezzare; calcolare; estimare; stimare; tassare *(rare)*; valutare
n ramen; schatten; taxeren; waarderen

178 **appreciate** *v (tr.)*; **increase** *v* **the value; raise** *v* **the value; revalorize** *v*; **revaluate** *v*; **revalue** *v*; **upvalue** *v*
cf. **reappraise** *v*
d aufwerten; den Wert erhöhen; den Wert steigern; revalorisieren
e aumentar el valor; elevar el valor; revalorizar; revalorar; revaluar
f augmenter la valeur; élever la valeur; hausser la valeur; réévaluer; revaloriser
i aumentare il valore; rialzare il valore; rivalorizzare; rivalutare
n de waarde vermeerderen; opwaarderen; revaloriseren; revalorizeren; revalueren

179 **appreciate** *v (intr.)*; **go** *v* **up in value; increase** *v* **in value; rise** *v* **in value**
d an Wert gewinnen; an Wert zunehmen; im Wert steigen
e aumentar de valor; subir de (en) valor
f augmenter de (en) valeur; gagner en valeur; monter en valeur
i aumentare di valore
n in waarde stijgen; in waarde vermeerderen

180 **appreciation; increased value; increase in value; increment; rise in value**
cf. **excess value, revalorization**
d Mehrwert *m*; Werterhöhung *f*; Wertsteigerung *f*; Wertzunahme *f*; Wertzuwachs *m*
e aumento *m* de valor; aumento *m* en el valor; incremento *m* de valor; plusvalía *f*
f accroissement *m* de valeur; accroissement *m* en valeur; appréciation *f*; augmentation *f* de valeur; hausse *f* de valeur; plus-value *f*
i aumento *m* di valore; incremento *m* di valore; plusvalenza *f*; plusvalore *m*
n appreciatie *f*; meerwaarde *f*; waardestijging *f*; waardevermeerdering *f*

181 **appropriate** *v*; **earmark** *v*; **obligate** *v*
cf. **allocate** *v*
d anweisen; bereitstellen; zweckbestimmen; zweckgebunden *(pp.)*
e afectar; proveer
f affecter; allouer
i accantonare; stanziare
n aanwijzen; beschikbaar stellen; bestemmen; uittrekken

182 **appropriation**
cf. **allocation**
d Anweisung *f*; Bereitstellung *f*; Zuweisung *f*; Zuwendung *f*; Zweckbestimmung *f*
e afectación *f*; asignación *f*; provisión *f*
f affectation *f*; allocation *f*
i accantonamento *m*; stanziamento *m*
n beschikbaarstelling *f*; besteding *f*; uittrekking *f*

183 **appropriation of profits; distribution of profits; profit distribution**
d Gewinnausschüttung *f*; Gewinnverteilung *f*; Gewinnverwendung *f*
e afectación *f* de beneficios; afectación *f* de ganancias; distribución *f* de beneficios; distribución *f* de ganancias; distribución *f* de utilidades; reparto *m* de beneficios; reparto *m* de ganancias; reparto *m* de utilidades
f affectation *f* de bénéfices; distribution *f* de bénéfices; répartition *f* de bénéfices
i destinazione *f* di utili; distribuzione *f* di utili; divisione *f* di utili; ripartizione *f* di profitti
n winstbestemming *f*; winstuitdeling *f*; winstuitkering *f*; winstverdeling *f*

184 **approximate estimate; approximation; rough estimate**
d annähernde Schätzung *f*; grobe Schätzung *f*; roher Kostenüberschlag *m*; roher Überschlag *m*; rohe Schätzung *f*; ungefährer Kostenüberschlag *m*; ungefährer Überschlag *m*; ungefähre Schätzung *f*
e estimación *f* aproximada; estimación *f* aproximativa; presupuesto *m* aproximado; presupuesto *m* aproximativo
f approximation *f* grossière; devis *m* approximatif; devis *m* estimatif; estimation *f* approximative; estimation *f* globale; évaluation *f* approximative; évaluation *f* en gros
i preventivo *m* estimativo; stima *f* approssimativa; stima *f* globale; valutazione *f* approssimativa
n globale schatting *f*; ruw bestek *n*; ruwe schatting *f*

185 **arbitrage in bullion**
d Goldarbitrage *f*
e arbitraje *m* en oro
f arbitrage *m* sur les matières d'or et d'argent
i arbitraggio *m* sull'oro
n goudarbitrage *f*

186 **arbitrage in (of) exchange; arbitration in (of) exchange; exchange arbitrage; exchange arbitration**
d Devisenarbitrage *f*; Kursarbitrage *f*; Valutenarbitrage *f*; Wechselarbitrage *f*
e arbitraje *m* de cambio; arbitraje *m* de divisas; arbitraje *m* sobre los cambios
f arbitrage *m* de change(s); arbitrage *m* de devises; arbitrage *m* sur les changes; arbitrage *m* sur les devises
i arbitraggio *m* di cambio; arbitraggio *m* di divise; arbitraggio *m* sui cambi
n deviezenarbitrage *f*; koersarbitrage *f*; valuta-arbitrage *f*; wisselarbitrage *f*

187 **arbitrage margins**
d Arbitragespannen *fpl*
e margenes *mpl/fpl* sobre las operaciones de arbitraje
f écarts *mpl* sur les opérations d'arbitrage
i margini *mpl* d'arbitraggio
n marges *fpl* van de arbitrageverrichtingen

188 **arrearages; arrears**
cf. **account receivable, amount outstanding**
d Rückstände *mpl*; rückständige Schulden *fpl*
e atrasos *mpl*; deudas *fpl* atrasadas
f arrérages *mpl*; arriérés *mpl*; dettes *fpl* arriérées
i arretrati *mpl*; debiti *mpl* arretrati
n achterstallige *n*; achterstallige schulden *fpl*; achterstand *m*

189 **in arrears**
cf. **in default**
d im Rückstand; rückständig
e atrasado; en atraso; en retardo; en retraso
f arriéré; en arrière; en retard
i arretrato; in arretrato; in ritardo
n achterop; achterstallig; ten achter(en)

190 **arrears of interest; outstanding interest**
cf. **interest due**
d ausstehende Zinsen *mpl*; rückständige Zinsen *mpl*; Zinsaussenstände *mpl*; Zinsrückstände *mpl*
e intereses *mpl* atrasados
f arrérages *mpl* (d'intérêt); intérêts *mpl* arriérés; intérêts *mpl* en retard
i interessi *mpl* arretrati; interessi *mpl* decorsi
n achterstallige int(e)rest *m*; achterstallige rente *f*

191 **arrest** *(rare)*; **attachment; distraint; distress; seizure; sequestration**
cf. **garnishment**
d Arrest *m*; Beschlag *m*; Beschlagnahme *f*; Pfändung *f*; Sequester *n*; Sequestration *f*; Sequestrierung *f*; Zwangsverwaltung *f*
e embargo *m*; encautación *f*; incautación *f*; secuestración *f*; secuestro *m*
f arrêt *m*; contrainte *f*; mainmise *f*; mise *f* en (sous) séquestre; saisie *f*; séquestration *f*; séquestre *m*
i pignoramento *m*; sequestrazione *f*; sequestro *m*
n arrest *n*; beslag *n*; beslaglegging *f*; sekwester *n*; sekwestratie *f*; sequester *n*; sequestratie *f*

192 **asked and bid; offers and bids**
d Brief *m* und Geld *n*
e oferta *f* y domanda *f*
f l'offre *f* et la demande
i lettera *f* e denaro *m*
n bieden *n* en laten *n*

193 **asked price; asked quotation; asked rate; selling rate**
cf. **offering price, selling price**
d Briefkurs *m*; Verkaufskurs *m*
e cotización *f* de oferta; cotización *f* de venta; cotización *f* ofrecida; tipo *m* de venta; tipo *m* vendedor
f cours *m* à la vente; cours *m* de vente; cours *m* offert; cours *m* vendeur(s); taux *m* de vente
i corso *m* di offerta; corso *m* di vendita; corso *m* lettera; tasso *m* di vendita
n laatkoers *m*; verkoopkoers *m*

194 **assess** *v*; **impose** *v* **a tax (on); levy** *v* **a tax (on); put** *v* **a tax (on); raise** *v* **a tax (on); tax** *v*
cf. **collect** *v* **a tax**
d besteuern; einer Steuer unterwerfen; eine Steuer auferlegen (auf); eine Steuer ausschreiben (auf); eine Steuer erheben (auf); mit einer Steuer belasten; mit einer Steuer belegen
e gravar con un impuesto; imponer una contribución (sobre); imponer un impuesto (sobre)
f frapper d'un impôt; grever d'un impôt;

imposer; lever un impôt (sur); mettre un impôt (sur); taxer
i gravare di una tassa; imporre una tassa (su); mettere una tassa (su); mettere un'imposta (su); tassare
n belasten; een belasting heffen (op); een belasting leggen (op)

195 assess *v*; **rate** *v*
d anschlagen; einschätzen; taxieren; veranlagen
e estimar; evaluar; tasar
f asseoir; coter; estimer; évaluer; taxer
i accertare; estimare; tassare; valutare
n aanslaan; taxeren

196 assessable; liable to tax; rat(e)able *(UK) (mainly property)*; **taxable**
cf. **customable**
d abgabenpflichtig; besteuerbar; einer Steuer unterworfen; steuerbar; steuerpflichtig; veranlagungspflichtig
e contribuyente; gravable; imponible; sujeto a contribución; sujeto a impuesto; sujeto a tributación
f assujetti à l'impôt; imposable; passible d'impôt; soumis à l'impôt; taxable
i imponibile; soggetto a imposta; tassabile
n aan belasting onderhevig; aan belasting onderworpen; belastbaar; belastingsplichtig

197 assessable profit; taxable income *(US)*; **taxable profit**
d steuerpflichtiger Gewinn *m*
e beneficio *m* fiscal; beneficio *m* imponible; ganancia *f* fiscal *(AL)*
f bénéfice *m* fiscal; bénéfice *m* imposable
i reddito *m* imponibile; utile *m* fiscale
n belastbare winst *f*; fiscale winst *f*

198 assessable value; assessed value; rat(e)able value; taxable value; tax value; value for tax purposes
d Einheitswert *m*; steuerbarer Wert *m*; steuerlicher Wert *m*; Steuerwert *m*; Versteuerungswert *m*
e valor *m* fiscal; valor *m* gravable; valor *m* imponible
f valeur *f* fiscale; valeur *f* imposable
i valore *m* fiscale; valore *m* imponibile
n belastbare waarde *f*; fiscale waarde *f*

199 assessed value *(of real property)*; **rat(e)able value**
d Einheitswert *m*; Katastereinheitswert *m*; Katasterwert *m*
e valor *m* catastral
f valeur *f* cadastrale
i valore *m* catastale
n kadastrale waarde *f*

200 assessment *(of tax)*; **rating**
cf. **taxation**
d Anschlag *m*; Einschätzung *f*; Steueranschlag *m*; Steuereinschätzung *f*; Taxierung *f*; Veranlagung *f*
e estimación *f* (impositiva); evaluación *f* (impositiva); tasación *f*
f assiette *f*; cote *f*; cotisation *f*; estimation *f* (fiscale); évaluation *f* (fiscale); taxation *f*
i accertamento *m* (fiscale); accertamento *m* (tributario); estimazione *f* (fiscale); estimazione *f* (tributaria); valutazione *f* (fiscale); valutazione *f* (tributaria)
n aanslag *m*; belastingaanslag *m*; taxatie *f*; taxering *f*

201 asset account
d Aktivkonto *n*
e cuenta *f* de activo
f compte *m* d'actif
i conto *m* dell'attivo
n actief-rekening *f*; rekening *f* van bezit

202 assets
cf. **credit, funds, holdings**
d Aktiva *npl*; Aktiven *npl*; Aktivmasse *f*; Aktivum *n*; Aktivvermögen *n*; Guthaben *npl*; Vermögensgegenstände *mpl*; Wirtschaftsgüter *npl*
e activo(s) *m(pl)*; bienes *mpl*; haberes *mpl*; masa *f* activa
f actif *m*; avoirs *mpl*; biens *mpl*; masse *f* active
i attivi *mpl*; attività *f(pl)*; attivo *m*; averi *mpl*; beni *mpl*; massa *f* attiva
n actief *n*; activa *npl*; goederen *npl*; tegoed(en) *n(pl)*

203 assets and liabilities
d Aktiva *npl* und Passiva *npl*; Aktiven *npl* und Passiven *npl*
e activos *mpl* y pasivos *mpl*
f l'actif *m* et le passif *m*
i attivi *mpl* e passivi *mpl*; attività *f* e passività *f*; attivo *m* e passivo *m*
n actief *n* en passief *n*; activa *npl* en passiva *npl*

204 assets held abroad; external assets; foreign assets
cf. **foreign stock**
d Auslandsguthaben *npl*; Auslandsvermögen *n*; Auslandswerte *mpl*; Guthaben *npl* im Ausland; Vermögenswerte *mpl* im Ausland

e activos *mpl* en el extranjero; activos *mpl* sobre el extranjero; bienes *mpl* en el extranjero; haberes *mpl* en el extranjero
f avoirs *mpl* à l'étranger; avoirs *mpl* sur l'étranger; biens *mpl* à l'étranger; valeurs *fpl* à l'étranger
i averi *mpl* all'estero; beni *mpl* all'estero
n activa *npl* in het buitenland; buitenlands tegoed *n*; buitenlands vermogen *n*; tegoed *n* in het buitenland; vermogen *n* in het buitenland

205 assets in kind (brought into a business); investment in kind; non-cash investment
d eingebrachte Sachwerte *mpl*; Sacheinlage *f*
e aportación *f* en especie; aporte *m* en especie
f apport *m* en nature
i apporto *m* in natura; conferimento *m* (di beni) in natura
n inbreng *m* in natura

206 assets side; black *(col.)*; **credit; creditor side; credit side**
d Aktivseite *f*; Gutschriftseite *f*; Haben *n*; Habenseite *f*; Kredit *m*; Kreditseite *f*
e activo *m*; haber *m*; lado *m* acreedor; lado *m* activo; lado *m* del activo; lado *m* del crédito; lado *m* del haber
f actif *m*; avoir *m*; côté *m* actif; côté *m* créditeur; côté *m* de l'avoir; côté *m* du crédit; crédit *m*
i attivo *m*; avere *m*; lato *m* dell'attivo; lato *m* dell'avere; parte *f* dell'attivo; parte *f* dell'avere
n actiefzijde *f*; credit *n*; creditzijde *f*

207 assign *v* **a claim; transfer** *v* **a claim**
d eine Forderung abtreten; eine Forderung übertragen; eine Forderung zedieren
e ceder un crédito; transferir un crédito
f céder une créance; transférer une créance
i cedere un credito; trasferire un credito
n een vordering cederen; een vordering overdragen

208 assignation of claims; assignment of claims; transfer of claims
d Abtretung *f* von Forderungen; Forderungsabtretung *f*; Forderungsübertragung *f*; Übertragung *f* von Forderungen; Zedierung *f* von Forderungen; Zession *f* von Forderungen
e cesión *f* de créditos; transferencia *f* de créditos; traspaso *m* de créditos
f cession *f* de créances; transfert *m* de créances; transport *m* de créances
i cessione *f* di crediti; trasferimento *m* di crediti
n cessie *f* van vorderingen; overdracht *f* van vorderingen

209 assignee in bankruptcy; bankruptcy trustee; curator in bankruptcy; official receiver; receiver (in bankruptcy); trustee in bankruptcy
cf. **liquidator**
d Konkursbeauftragter *m*; Konkurspfleger *m*; Konkursverwalter *m*; Masse(n)verwalter *m*; Sequester *m*; Verwalter *m* der Konkursmasse; Zwangsverwalter *m*
e administrador *m* de la quiebra; comisario *m* de la quiebra; interventor *m* de la quiebra; sindico *m* de la quiebra
f administrateur *m* de la faillite; administrateur *m* de la masse; administrateur-séquestre *m*; curateur *m* *(B)*; séquestre *m*; syndic *m* de la faillite
i amministratore *m* giudiziario del fallimento; curatore *m* del fallimento; curatore *m* fallimentare; sequestratario *m*
n curator *m* (in het faillissement); sekwester *m*; sequester *m*

210 assured income; fixed income; regular income; settled income
d feste Einkünfte *fpl*; festes Einkommen *n*; fixes Einkommen *n*; regelmässiges Einkommen *n*; sicheres Einkommen *n*; ständiges Einkommen *n*
e ingresos *mpl* fijos; ingresos *mpl* regulares; ingresos *mpl* seguros; renta *f* fija
f revenu *m* fixe; revenu *m* régulier
i reddito *m* fisso; reddito *m* regolare
n gewaarborgd inkomen *n*; vast inkomen *n*

211 attach *v*; **distrain** *v* **(on; upon); levy** *v* **a distress (on; upon); seize** *v*; **sequester** *v*; **sequestrate** *v*
d Beschlag legen (auf); beschlagnahmen; in Beschlag nehmen; mit Beschlag belegen; pfänden; sequestrieren; unter Sequester stellen
e embargar; incautarse (de); poner embargo (sobre); secuestrar
f faire arrêt (sur); mettre arrêt (sur); mettre en (sous) séquestre; placer en (sous) séquestre; saisir; séquestrer
i mettere sotto sequestro; mettere un fermo (su); pignorare; porre sotto sequestro; sequestrare
n arresteren; benaderen; beslag leggen (op);

in beslag nemen; sekwestreren; sequestreren

212 **auction; auction sale; sale by auction**
d Auktion *f*; Verkauf *m* durch Versteigerung; Verkauf *m* im Wege der Versteigerung; Verauktionierung *f*; Versteigerung *f*
e licitación *f (AL)*; remate *m (AL)*; subasta *f*; venta *f* por subasta
f encan *m*; enchère(s) *f(pl)*; vente *f* à la criée; vente *f* à l'encan; vente *f* à l'enchère; vente *f* aux enchères
i asta *f*; incanto *m*; vendita *f* all'asta; vendita *f* all'incanto
n auctie *f*; veiling *f*; vendu *m/n*; vendutie *f*; verkoping *f* bij opbod; verkoop *m* bij opbod

213 **auction** *v*; **sell** *v* **at auction** *(US)*; **sell** *v* **by auction** *(UK)*
d auktionieren; im Wege der Versteigerung verkaufen; verauktionieren; versteigern
e licitar *(AL)*; rematar *(AL)*; subastar; vender en subasta
f vendre à la criée; vendre à l'encan; vendre à l'enchère; vendre aux enchères
i vendere all'asta; vendere all'incanto
n bij opbod verkopen; veilen

214 **audit**
d Abschlussprüfung *f*; Bücherrevision *f*; Buchprüfung *f*; Prüfung *f* der Rechnungslegung; Rechnungsprüfung *f*
e auditoría *f*; censura *f* de cuentas; revisión *f* de cuentas; verificación *f* de cuentas
f contrôle *m* des comptes; vérification *f* des comptes
i controllo *m* dei conti; controllo *m* del bilancio; revisione *f* contabile; verifica *f* dei conti; verificazione *f* dei conti
n controle *f* der boekvoering *f*; controle *f* van de administratie *(N)*; controle *f* van de boekhouding; controle *f* van de (jaar-)-rekening; onderzoek *n* van de boekhouding; verificatie *f* van de boekhouding

215 **audit** *v*
d prüfen; revidieren
e revisar; verificar
f apurer; contrôler; vérifier
i controllare; rivedere; verificare
n controleren; nazien; verifiëren

216 **auditor*; comptroller; controller**
d Abschlussprüfer *m*; Bücherrevisor *m*; Buchprüfer *m*; Prüfer *m*; Rechnungsprüfer *m*; Rechnungsrevisor *m*; Revisor *m*; Wirtschaftsprüfer *m*
e censor *m* de cuentas; contador *m* (público); interventor *m* (de cuentas); revisor *m* de cuentas
f commissaire *m* aux comptes; commissaire *m* de société; contrôleur *m* des comptes; réviseur *m* (comptable); vérificateur *m* (comptable); vérificateur *m* (des comptes)
i revisore *m* (contabile); revisore *m* (dei conti); sindaco *m* (revisore); verificatore *m* (dei conti)
n commissaris *m*; controleur *m*; revisor *m*; verificateur *m (B)*

* The laws governing the person and tasks of the auditor vary considerably.

217 **auditor's report; auditors' report; audit report**
d Bericht *m* des Abschlussprüfers; Buchprüfungsbericht *m*; Prüfungsbericht *m*; Rechnungsbericht *m*; Revisionsbericht *m*
e informe *m* de auditoría; informe *m* de censura; informe *m* de la revisión de cuentas; informe *m* del censor de cuentas
f rapport *m* de vérification; rapport *m* du (des) commissaire(s) aux comptes
i relazione *f* dei sindaci; relazione *f* di verifica
n accountantsrapport *n*; accountantsverslag *n*; verslag *n* van de commissarissen *(B)*

218 **austerity**
d Austerity *f*; wirtschaftliche Einschränkung *f*
e austeridad *f*
f austerité *f*
i austerità *f*; austerity *f*
n austeriteit *f (rare in this sense)*; versobering *f*

219 **autarchy; autarky; self-sufficiency**
d Autarkie *f*; Selbstgenügsamkeit *f*; Selbstversorgung *f*
e autarquía *f*; autosuficiencia *f*
f autarcie *f*; autosuffisance *f*
i autarchia *f*; autosufficienza *f*
n autarkie *f*; zelfgenoegzaamheid *f*; zelfvoorziening *f*

220 **authorisation of credit** *(UK)*; **authorization of credit** *(US)*; **extension of credit; granting of credit; grant of credit**
d Kreditbewilligung *f*; Krediteinräumung *f*; Kreditgenehmigung *f*;

Kreditgewährung *f*
e aprobación *f* de crédito; autorización *f* de crédito; concesión *f* de crédito; otorgamiento *m* de crédito
f allocation *f* de crédit; autorisation *f* de crédit; concession *f* de crédit; octroi *m* de crédit
i autorizzazione *f* di credito; concessione *f* di credito
n kredietverlening *f*; kredietverstrekking *f*; toekenning *f* van krediet

221 **authorisation of payment** *(UK)*; **authorization of payment** *(US)*
cf. **cash order**
d Zahlungsanweisung *f*; Zahlungsauftrag *m*
e orden *f* de pago
f ordre *m* de paiement
i ordine *m* di pagamento
n betalingsopdracht *f*

222 **authorised capital** *(UK)*; **authorized capital stock** *(US)*; **nominal capital; registered capital**
cf. **capitalisation**
d autorisiertes Aktienkapital *n*; autorisiertes Kapital *n*; genehmigtes Gesellschaftskapital *n*; genehmigtes Kapital *n*; Grundkapital *n* (AG); Nennkapital *n*; Stammkapital *n* (GmbH)
e capital *m* autorizado; capital *m* nominal; capital *m* social
f capital *m* autorisé; capital *m* nominal; capital *m* social
i capitale *m* autorizzato; capitale *m* nominale; capitale *m* sociale
n geautoriseerd kapitaal *n*; gewettigd kapitaal *n*; maatschappelijk kapitaal *n*; nominaal kapitaal *n*; statutair kapitaal *n*

223 **authorise** *v* **payment of an account** *(UK)*; **authorize** *v* **payment of an account** *(US)*; **pass** *v* **an account for payment**
d eine Rechnung (zur Zahlung) anweisen
e dar orden de pagar una factura
f ordonnancer une facture
i dare ordine di pagare una fattura
n opdracht geven tot uitbetaling van een rekening; order geven tot uitbetaling van een rekening

224 **auxiliary account; sub-account** *(US)*; **subsidiary account**
d Hilfskonto *n*; Nebenkonto *n*; Unterkonto *n*
e cuenta *f* auxiliar; cuenta *f* subsidiaria; subcuenta *f*
f compte *m* auxiliaire; sous-compte *m*
i conto *m* ausiliario; conto *m* sussidiario; sottoconto *m*
n hulprekening *f*; subrekening *f*

225 **auxiliary book; book of original entry; subsidiary book; subsidiary journal; subsidiary ledger**
cf. **daybook**
d Hilfsbuch *n*; Hilfsjournal *n*; Nebenbuch *n*
e diario *m* auxiliar; libro *m* auxiliar; mayor *m* auxiliar
f journal *m* auxiliaire; livre *m* auxiliaire
i giornale *m* ausiliario; libro *m* ausiliario; libro *m* sussidiario; partitario *m*; sussidiario *m*
n bijboek *n*; hulpboek *n*; hulpjournaal *n*; sub-grootboek *n*

226 **availability of capital**
d Verfügbarkeit *f* von Kapital; Verfügbarkeit *f* von Kapitalien
e disponibilidad *f* de capital
f disponibilité *f* des capitaux
i disponibilità *f* di capitali
n beschikbaarheid *f* van kapitaal

227 **available funds; cash liquidity; funds in hand; liquid assets; liquid funds** *(US)*; **liquid resources; quick assets; ready assets**
cf. **cash assets, cash holdings, liquidity**
d flüssige Aktiven *npl*; flüssige Mittel *npl*; greifbare Mittel *npl*; Kassenliquidität *f*; liquide Mittel *npl*; verfügbare Mittel *npl*
e activo *m* disponible; activo *m* líquido; disponibilidades *fpl*; disponible *m*; fondos *mpl* disponibles; liquidez *f* de caja; tesorería *f*; valores *mpl* disponibles
f actif *m* disponible; actif *m* libre; actif *m* liquide; avoirs *mpl* liquides; disponibilités *fpl*; disponible *m*; fonds *mpl* disponibles; fonds *mpl* libres; liquidité *f* de caisse; liquidités *fpl*; trésorerie *f*; valeurs *fpl* disponibles
i attivi *mpl* liquidi; attività *fpl* liquide; attivo *m* disponibile; attivo *m* liquido; disponibilità *f(pl)*; fondi *mpl* disponibili; liquidità *f(pl)* (di cassa); mezzi *mpl* disponibili; mezzi *mpl* liquidi; tesoreria *f*; valori *mpl* disponibili
n beschikbare middelen *npl*; kasliquiditeit *f*; liquide activa *npl*; liquide middelen *npl*; liquiditeiten *fpl*

228 **availment of credits; use of credits**
d Inanspruchnahme *f* von Krediten; Verwendung *f* von Krediten

e utilización *f* de créditos
f utilisation *f* de crédits
i utilizzo *m* di crediti
n gebruik *n* van kredieten

229 avails *(US)*; **earnings; gains; proceeds; profits**
cf. **gain, income, incomings, proceeds, return**
d Erlös *m*; Ertrag *m*; Erträge *mpl*; Erträgnis(se) *n(pl)*; Gewinne *mpl*; Verdienst *m*
e beneficios *mpl*; ganancias *fpl*; producto(s) *m(pl)*; utilidades *fpl*
f bénéfices *mpl*; gains *mpl*; produit(s) *m(pl)*; profits *mpl*
i benefici *mpl (rare)*; guadagni *mpl*; profitti *mpl*; proventi *mpl*; ricavato *m*; ricavo *m*; utili *mpl*
n baten *fpl*; produkt *n*; provenu *n*; verdienste(n) *f(pl)*; winsten *fpl*

230 aval *(rare)*; **backing for a bill; bill surety**
d Aval *m/n*; Wechselbürgschaft *f*; Wechselgarantie *f*
e aval *m*; fianza *f* cambiaria; garantía *f* cambiaria
f aval *m*
i avallo *m* (cambiario)
n aval *n*; wisselborgtocht *m*; wisselgarantie *f*

231 average *(noun)*
d Durchschnitt *m*
e media *f*; promedio *m*
f moyenne *f*
i media *f*
n gemiddelde *n*

232 average *(adj.)*
d durchschnittlich; Durchschnitts-
e medio
f moyen
i medio
n gemiddeld; midden-

233 average income per head; per-capita average income
d durchschnittliches Pro-Kopf-Einkommen *n*
e renta *f* media por barba; renta *f* media por cabeza; renta *f* media pro-capite
f revenu *m* moyen par tête
i reddito *m* medio pro-capite
n gemiddeld inkomen *n* per hoofd; gemiddeld inkomen *n* per kop

234 average rate *(of shares)*; **mean rate; middle rate**
d Durchschnittskurs *m*; Mittelkurs *m*
e cambio *m* medio; precio *m* medio; tipo *m* medio
f cours *m* moyen
i cambio *m* medio; corso *m* medio
n doorsneekoers *m*; gemiddelde koers *m*; middenkoers *m*

B

235 **back** *v* **a bill; guarantee** *v* **a bill; guarantee** *v* **payment of a bill**
cf. **endorse** *v* **a bill**
d einem Wechsel Bürgschaft leisten; einen Wechsel avalieren; einen Wechsel garantieren; einen Wechsel mit Bürgschaft versehen
e avalar una letra (de cambio); firmar una letra por aval; prestar el aval de (para) una letra (de cambio)
f avaliser un effet; donner aval à (pour) un effet; signer un effet pour aval
i avallare una cambiale; dare il avallo su una cambiale; firmare una cambiale per avallo
n aval geven voor een wissel; een wissel avaleren; een wissel voor aval tekenen

236 **backer** *(of a bill)*; **guarantor; surety**
cf. **bondsman**
d Aval *m/n*; Avalant *m*; Avalist *m*; Wechselbürge *m*
e avalante *m*; avalista *m*; fiador *m*
f avaliseur *m*; avaliste *m*; donneur *m* d'aval
i avallante
n avalgever *m*; avalist *m*

237 **back payment; payment of arrears**
d Nachzahlung *f*; Rückstandsbezahlung *f*
e pago *m* de los atrasos
f paiement *m* des arriérés; règlement *m* des arriérés
i pagamento *m* degli arretrati
n betaling *f* van het achterstallige; nabetaling *f*

238 **back to back guarantee; counterguarantee; countersecurity; countersurety; surety for a surety**
d Gegenbürgschaft *f*; Rückbürgschaft *f*
e contrafianza *f*; fianza *f* de fianza; garantía *f* de fianza
f arrière-caution *f*; arrière-garantie *f*; contre-caution *f*
i controgaranzia *f*; fideiussore *m* del fideiussore
n achterborg *m*; achterborgtocht *m*

239 **backwardation**
d Deport *m*; Kursabschlag *m*
e deport *m*; deporte *m*; deporto *m*
f déport *m*
i deporto *m*
n deport *n*

240 **backwardation rate**
d Deportkurs *m*
e tasa *f* del deport(e)
f cours *m* de déport; taux *m* du déport
i corso *m* del deporto
n deportkoers *m*

241 **bad check*; bouncer** *(UK) (col.)*; **check without cover; check without funds; dud check; N.S.F. check** *(not sufficient funds)*; **rubber check** *(US) (col.)*; **stumer** *(UK) (col.)*; **uncovered check; worthless check**
d Scheck *m* ohne Deckung; ungedeckter Scheck *m*
e cheque *m* al descubierto; cheque *m* en descubierto; cheque *m* sin provisión
f chèque *m* sans contrepartie; chèque *m* sans provision
i assegno *m* a vuoto; assegno *m* scoperto; assegno *m* senza copertura; assegno *m* senza provvista
n cheque *m* zonder dekking; ongedekte cheque *m*

* Check (US); cheque (UK).

242 **bad debt; irrecoverable debt**
d schlechte Forderung *f*; uneinbringliche Forderung *f*
e crédito *m* incobrable; deuda *f* incobrable; no valor *m*
f créance *f* irrécouvrable; mauvaise créance *f*; non-valeur *f*
i credito *m* inesigibile; credito *m* irricuperabile; debito *m* non risc(u)otibile
n non-valeur *m/f*; oninbare schuld *f*; oninbare vordering *f*

243 **bad debt reserve; provision for doubtful debts; reserve for doubtful debts**
cf. **contingency reserve**
d Dubiosenreserve *f*; Dubiosenrückstellung *f*; Reserve *f* für Dubiosen; Reserve *f* für zweifelhafte Forderungen; Rückstellung *f* für Dubiosen; Rückstellung *f* für zweifelhafte Forderungen
e provisión *f* para cuentas dudosas; reserva *f* para créditos dudosos; reserva *f* para deudas dudosas
f provision *f* pour créances douteuses; réserve *f* pour créances douteuses
i riserva *f* per crediti dubbi
n reserve *f* voor dubieuze vorderingen; voorzieningen *fpl* voor dubieuze debiteuren

244 **bad investment; misdirected investment; misinvestment**
d Fehlanlage *f*; Fehlinvestierung *f*; Fehl-

investition *f*; schlechte Kapitalanlage *f*
e inversión *f* desacertada; inversión *f* equivocada; inversión *f* errónea; inversión *f* mal colocada; inversión *f* mal orientada; mala inversión *f*
f investissement *m* erroné; investissement *m* mal orienté; investissement *m* mal placé; mauvais investissement *m*; mauvais placement *m*
i investimento *m* errato; investimento *m* mal orientato; investimento *m* sbagliato
n onjuiste belegging *f*; onjuiste investering *f*; slechte belegging *f*; slechte investering *f*

245 **bad payer**
cf. **defaulter**
d schlechter Zahler *m*
e mal pagador *m*
f mauvais payeur *m*
i cattivo pagatore *m*
n slechte betaler *m*; wanbetaler *m*

246 **balance; remainder; remaining amount; rest**
cf. **amount outstanding**
d Rest *m*; Restbetrag *m*; restlicher Betrag *m*; Restsumme *f*; Saldo *m*; Saldorest *m*; verbleibender Betrag *m*
e importe *m* restante; remanente *m*; resto *m*; saldo *m*; sobrante *m*; suma *f* restante
f décompte *m*; montant *m* restant; reliquat *m*; restant *m*; reste *m*; solde *m*; somme *f* restante
i importo *m* restante; importo *m* rimanente; pareggio *m*; residuo *m*; resto *m*; rimanenza *f*; saldo *m*; somma *f* restante; somma *f* rimanente
n balans *f*; residu *n*; rest *f*; restant *n*; resterend bedrag *n*; resterende *n*; saldo *n*

247 **balance; compensation balance**
d Ausgleichsbetrag *m*; Ausgleichssumme *f*; Soulte *f*
e suma *f* compensada; suma *f* de compensación
f soulte *f*
i conguaglio *m*; tassa *f* di conguaglio
n som *f* ter gelijkmaking; soulte *f*; uitkering *f* tot gelijkmaking

248 **balance** *v (intr.)*
d sich ausgleichen
e saldarse
f se balancer; se solder
i bilanciarsi; pareggiarsi; saldarsi
n elkaar opheffen; sluiten; tegen elkaar opwegen

249 **balance** *v* **an account; liquidate** *v* **an account; make** *v* **up an account; settle** *v* **an account; square** *v* **an account**
cf. **agree** *v* **accounts, close** *v* **an account**
d eine Rechnung abgleichen; eine Rechnung abrechnen; eine Rechnung ausgleichen; eine Rechnung begleichen; eine Rechnung berichtigen; eine Rechnung glattstellen; eine Rechnung saldieren; eine Rechnung skontrieren; ein Konto abgleichen; ein Konto abrechnen; ein Konto ausgleichen; ein Konto begleichen; ein Konto berichtigen; ein Konto glattstellen; ein Konto saldieren; ein Konto skontrieren
e ajustar una cuenta; arreglar una cuenta; balancear una cuenta *(AL)*; hacer el balance de una cuenta; liquidar una cuenta; saldar una cuenta
f balancer un compte; liquider un compte; régler un compte; solder un compte
i bilanciare un conto; liquidare un conto; pareggiare un conto; regolare un conto; saldare un conto
n een rekening liquideren; een rekening salderen; een rekening vereffenen

250 **balance book; balance sheet book**
d Bilanzbuch *n*; Bilanzenbuch *n*
e libro *m* de balance; libro *m* de inventario
f livre *m* des balances de vérification; livre *m* d'inventaire
i libro *m* bilanci; libro *m* dei bilanci di verifica; libro *m* inventario
n balansboek *n*; inventarisboek *n (B)*

251 **balanced budget; budgetary equilibrium**
d ausgeglichener Haushalt *m*; ausgeglichenes Budget *n*; Haushaltsausgleich *m*; Haushaltsgleichgewicht *n*
e equilibrio *m* del presupuesto; equilibrio *m* presupuestario; presupuesto *m* equilibrado
f budget *m* équilibré; équilibre *m* budgétaire; équilibre *m* du budget
i bilancio *m* in equilibrio; bilancio *m* in pareggio; equilibrio *m* del bilancio; pareggio *m* del bilancio
n begrotingsevenwicht *n*; sluitende begroting *f*

252 **balance due; balance owing**
cf. **amount due, amount outstanding**
d fälliger Saldo *m*; geschuldeter Restbetrag *m*; Restschuld *f*; verbleibender

Schuldbetrag *m*
e resto *m* adeudado; saldo *m* debido
f redû *m*; restant *m* dû; solde *m* restant dû
i resto *m* dovuto; saldo *m* dovuto
n nog verschuldigd bedrag *n*; nog verschuldigde *n*; verschuldigd saldo *n*

253 **balance in (on) hand; balance of cash in (on) hand; cash balance**
d Kassenbilanz *f*; Kassensaldo *m*
e balance *m* de caja; saldo *m* de (en) caja
f balance *f* de caisse; solde *m* de (en) caisse
i bilancio *m* di cassa; saldo *m* di (in) cassa
n kasbalans *f*; kassaldo *n*; saldo *n* in kassa

254 **balance of an account; liquidation of an account; settlement of an account**
cf. **close of an account, reconciliation of accounts**
d Abgleichung *f* einer Rechnung (eines Kontos); Abrechnung *f* einer Rechnung (eines Kontos); Ausgleich *m* einer Rechnung (eines Kontos); Begleichung *f* einer Rechnung (eines Kontos); Berichtigung *f* einer Rechnung (eines Kontos); Glattstellung *f* einer Rechnung (eines Kontos); Saldierung *f* einer Rechnung (eines Kontos); Skontrierung *f* einer Rechnung (eines Kontos)
e ajuste *m* de una cuenta; arreglo *m* de una cuenta; balance *m* de una cuenta; liquidación *f* de una cuenta; saldo *m* de una cuenta
f liquidation *f* d'un compte; règlement *m* d'un compte; solde *m* d'un compte
i liquidazione *f* di un conto; pareggiamento *m* di un conto; regolamento *m* di un conto; saldo *m* di un conto
n afrekening *f*; liquidatie *f* van een rekening; saldering *f* van een rekening; vereffening *f* van een rekening

255 **balance of an account; rest**
cf. **position of an account**
d Kontensaldo *m*; Kontobestand *m*; Rechnungssaldo *m*
e saldo *m* contable; saldo *m* de una cuenta
f solde *m* d'un compte
i saldo *m* di un conto
n rekeningssaldo *n*; saldo *n* van een rekening

256 **balance of capital movements; capital balance**
cf. **general balance of transfers and capital movements**
d Kapitalbilanz *f*; Saldo *m* der Kapitalbewegungen
e balance *m* de capitales; balance *m* de los movimientos de capital *(AL)*; balanza *f* de capitales; balanza *f* de los movimientos de capital
f balance *f* des capitaux; balance *f* des mouvements de capitaux
i bilancia *f* dei capitali; bilancia *f* dei movimenti di capitali; bilancio *m* dei capitali
n kapitaalbalans *f*; saldo *n* van de kapitaalbewegingen

257 **balance of current transfers**
d Saldo *m* der laufenden Übertragungen
e saldo *m* de las transferencias corrientes
f solde *m* des transferts courants
i saldo *m* dei trasferimenti correnti
n saldo *n* van de lopende overdrachten

258 **balance of external payments**
d äussere Zahlungsbilanz *f*
e balanza *f* de pagos externos
f balance *f* des comptes extérieurs
i bilancia *f* dei conti esteri
n buitenlandse betalingsbalans *f*

259 **balance of goods and services; balance of transactions in goods and services**
d Saldo *m* des Waren- und Dienstleistungsverkehrs; Waren- und Dienstleistungsbilanz *f*
e balance *m* de pagos de bienes y servicios *(AL)*; balanza *f* de bienes y servicios
f balance *f* des biens et services; solde *m* des opérations de biens et services; solde *m* des transactions sur biens et services
i bilancia *f* dei beni e servizi; saldo *m* delle transazioni su beni e servizi
n goederen- en dienstenbalans *f*; saldo *n* van het goederen- en dienstenverkeer

260 **balance of payments**
d Zahlungsbilanz *f*
e balance *m* de pagos *(AL)*; balanza *f* de pagos
f balance *f* des paiements
i bilancia *f* dei pagamenti
n betalingsbalans *f*

261 **balance of payments deficit; external deficit**
d Zahlungsbilanzdefizit *n*
e déficit *m* de la balanza de pagos; déficit *m* exterior
f déficit *m* de la balance des paiements; déficit *m* extérieur
i disavanzo *m* con l'estero; disavanzo *m*

della bilancia dei pagamenti
n betalingsbalansdeficit *n*; betalingsbalans-tekort *n*

262 **balance of payments on current account**
cf. **balance on current account**
d Ertragsbilanz *f (O; Schw)*; Leistungs-bilanz *f*
e balanza *f* de pagos de las transacciones corrientes
f balance *f* des paiements courants
i bilancia *f* dei pagamenti correnti; bilancia *f* delle partite correnti
n betalingsbalans *f* op lopende rekening

263 **balance of payments surplus**
d Zahlungsbilanzüberschuss *m*
e excedente *m* de la balanza de pagos; saldo *m* activo de la balanza de pagos; superávit *m* de la balanza de pagos
f excédent *m* de la balance des paiements; solde *m* excédentaire de la balance des paiements
i avanzo *m* della bilancia dei pagamenti; saldo *m* attivo della bilancia dei pagamenti
n betalingsbalansoverschot *n*

264 **balance of trade; trade balance**
d Handelsbilanz *f*; Warenbilanz *f**
e balance *m* comercial *(AL)*; balance *m* de comercio *(AL)*; balanza *f* comercial; balanza *f* de comercio
f balance *f* commerciale; balance *f* du commerce
i bilancia *f* commerciale
n goederenbalans *f**; handelsbalans *f*
* Sensu stricto of trade in goods.

265 **balance of trade deficit; deficit in the trade account; deficit in the trade balance; foreign trade deficit; trade deficit**
d Aussenhandelsdefizit *n*; Handelsbilanz-defizit *n*
e déficit *m* del comercio exterior
f déficit *m* du commerce extérieur
i deficit *m* del commercio estero; disavanzo *m* della bilancia commerciale
n deficit *n* op de (buitenlandse) handelsbalans; tekort *n* op de (buitenlandse) handelsbalans

266 **balance of trade surplus; foreign trade surplus; surplus in the trade account; surplus in the trade balance; trade surplus**
d Aussenbeitrag *m*; Aussenhandelsüber-schuss *m*; Handelsbilanzüberschuss *m*; Handelsüberschuss *m*
e excedente *m* de la balanza comercial; saldo *m* activo de la balanza comercial; superávit *m* de la balanza comercial
f excédent *m* de la balance commerciale; solde *m* excédentaire de la balance commerciale
i avanzo *m* della bilancia commerciale; saldo *m* attivo della bilancia commerciale
n overschot *n* op de handelsbalans

267 **balance of transfers**
cf. **general balance of transfers and capital movements**
d Übertragungsbilanz *f*
e balanza *f* de las transferencias
f balance *f* des transferts
i bilancia *f* dei trasferimenti
n balans *f* van de overdrachten

268 **balance on current account**
cf. **balance of payments on current account**
d Saldo *m* der Leistungsbilanz
e saldo *m* de las transacciones corrientes
f solde *m* des opérations courantes
i saldo *m* delle partite correnti
n saldo *n* der lopende transacties

269 **balance on offset account; clearing balance**
d Verrechnungsguthaben *n*; Verrechnungs-saldo *m*; Verrechnungsspitze *f*
e activo *m* de compensación; saldo *m* de compensación
f solde *m* après compensation; solde *m* de compensation
i saldo *m* di compensazione
n verrekeningssaldo *n*

270 **balance sheet**
d Bilanz *f*
e balance *m*
f bilan *m*
i bilancio *m*
n balans *f*; balansblad *n*

271 **balance sheet account**
d Bilanzkonto *n*
e cuenta *f* de balance
f compte *m* de bilan
i conto *m* di bilancio
n balansrekening *f*

272 **balance sheet date**
d Bilanzstichtag *m*
e día *m* de la formación del balance; fecha *f* de cierre del balance
f date *f* d'arrêté du bilan

i data *f* di chiusura del bilancio; giorno *m* di chiusura del bilancio
n balansdatum *m*

273 **balance sheet lay-out; balance sheet structure**
d Bilanzgliederung *f*
e articulación *f* del balance; estructura *f* del balance
f articulation *f* du bilan; présentation *f* du bilan; structure *f* du bilan
i struttura *f* del bilancio
n groepering *f* van de balansposten

274 **balance sheet showing a loss; deficiency statement** *(US)*
d Passivbilanz *f*; Unterbilanz *f*; Verlustbilanz *f*
e balance *m* deficitario; balance *m* pasivo
f bilan *m* déficitaire; bilan *m* passif
i bilancio *m* deficitario; bilancio *m* passivo
n deficitaire balans *f*; nadelige balans *f*; passieve balans *f*

275 **balance sheet showing a profit; earnings statement** *(US)*
d Aktivbilanz *f*; Gewinnbilanz *f*
e balance *m* activo
f bilan *m* actif; bilan *m* bénéficiaire; bilan *m* excédentaire
i bilancio *m* attivo
n actieve balans *f*; voordelige balans *f*

276 **balance sheet total**
d Bilanzsumme *f*; Bilanztotal *n*; Bilanzvolumen *n*
e suma *f* (total) del balance; total *m* del balance
f total *m* du bilan
i totale *m* del bilancio
n balanstelling *f*; balanstotaal *n*

277 **balance sheet value**
cf. **accounting value**
d Bilanzwert *m*
e valor *m* de (en) balance
f montant *m* au bilan; valeur *f* de bilan
i valore *m* di bilancio
n balanswaarde *f*

278 **balance** *v* **the books; close** *v* **the books**
d die Bücher abschliessen; die Bücher saldieren
e balancear los libros *(AL)*; cerrar los libros
f arrêter les livres; balancer les livres; clôturer les livres; régler les livres
i chiudere i libri
n de boeken afsluiten

279 **balance** *v* **the books; draw** *v* **a balance; draw** *v* **up a balance sheet; make** *v* **up a balance sheet; strike** *v* **a balance**
d bilanzieren; eine Bilanz abschliessen; eine Bilanz aufmachen; eine Bilanz aufstellen; eine Bilanz ziehen; einen Saldo ziehen
e cerrar un balance; establecer un balance; establecer un saldo; hacer un balance
f arrêter un solde; dresser un bilan; établir un bilan; établir un solde; faire un bilan; faire une balance; tirer une balance
i chiudere un bilancio; compilare un bilancio; determinare un bilancio; fare un bilancio; redigere un bilancio
n balanceren; een balans afsluiten; een balans opmaken; een balans opstellen; een saldo opmaken; een saldo trekken

280 **balance** *v* **the budget**
d das Budget ausgleichen; das Budget ins Gleichgewicht bringen; den Haushaltsplan ausgleichen; den Haushaltsplan ins Gleichgewicht bringen
e equilibrar el presupuesto; nivelar el presupuesto
f équilibrer le budget; rétablir l'équilibre budgétaire
i equilibrare il bilancio; pareggiare il bilancio
n de begroting in evenwicht brengen; de begroting sluitend maken; het budget in evenwicht brengen; het budget sluitend maken

281 **balancing entry; contra(-entry); counter-entry; cross-entry; offset(-entry); offsetting entry; per contra entry; reversing entry; set-off**
cf. **adjusting entry**
d Ausgleichsposten *m*; Gegenbuchung *f*; Gegeneintrag *m*; Gegenposten *m*; Rückbuchung *f*; Stornierungsbuchung *f*; Stornierungseintrag *m*; Storno *m*; Stornobuchung *f*; Umbuchung *f*
e asiento *m* compensatorio; asiento *m* de compensación; asiento *m* de rescuentro; asiento *m* en contra; contraasiento *m*; contraentrada *f*; contrapartida *f*; entrada *f* de rescuentro; entrada *f* en contra; extorno *m*; partida *f* compensatoria; partida *f* de compensación; partida *f* de rescuentro; rescuentro *m*
f article *m* de compensation; article *m* de contrepassement; article *m* inverse; contre-écriture *f*; contrepartie *f*; contrepassation *f*; contrepassement *m*; écriture *f* de contrepassement; écriture *f* inverse; entrée *f* compensatrice

i contropartita *f*; partita *f* di compensazione; registrazione *f* in contropartita; registrazione *f* inversa; registrazione *f* per storno; scrittura *f* di storno; scrittura *f* inversa; scrittura *f* per storno; storno *m*; voce *f* de conguaglio
n contrapost *m*; storno *m*; stornopost *m*; tegenboeking *f*; tegenpost *m*

282 **bank**
cf. **bank corporation, banking**
d Bank *f*
e banca *f**; banco *m*
f banque *f*
i banca *f*
n bank *f*

* Rare in this sense.

283 **bankable paper; discountable paper; eligible paper**
cf. **money market paper, negotiable document**
d bankfähiges Papier *n*; diskontfähiges Papier *n*; diskontierbares Papier *n*
e papel *m* bancable; papel *m* descontable
f papier *m* bancable; papier *m* escomptable
i carta *f* bancabile; carta *f* scontabile
n bankabel papier *n*; discontabel papier *n*; disconteerbaar papier *n*

284 **bank acceptance*; bank bill; bank draft; banker's acceptance; banker's bill; banker's draft**
d Bankakzept *n*; Bankanweisung *f*; Banktratte *f*; Bankwechsel *m*
e aceptación *f* bancaria; aceptación *f* de banco; giro *m* bancario; letra *f* bancaria; letra *f* de banco; libranza *f* bancaria
f acceptation *f* bancaire; acceptation *f* de banque; assignation *f* de banque; effet *m* de banque; lettre *f* de banque; mandat *m* de banque; papier *m* de banque; traite *f* bancaire
i accettazione *f* bancaria; assegno *m* bancario; cambiale *f* bancaria; carta *f* bancaria; effetto *m* bancario; tratta *f* bancaria; vaglia *m* bancario
n bankaccept *n*; bankaanwijzing *f*; bankassignatie *f*; bankmandaat *n*; banktraite *f*; bankwissel *m*

* The distinction between "bank", i.e. by a bank only, and "banker's", i.e. a bank or other institution, is rarely made. The distinction between "bill" for foreign transactions and "draft" for domestic ones is not consistently made.

285 **bank account**
d Bankkonto *n*
e cuenta *f* bancaria; cuenta *f* en un banco
f compte *m* de banque; compte *m* en banque
i conto *m* bancario; conto *m* in banca
n bankrekening *f*

286 **bank balance; bankroll** *(US)*
cf. **bank deposit**
d Bankguthaben *n*; Banksaldo *m*
e disponibilidad *f* bancaria; saldo *m* en banco
f avoir *m* en banque; disponibilités *fpl* en banque; solde *m* en banque
i avere *m* in banca; disponibilità *f* in banca; saldo *m* in banca
n banksaldo *n*; banktegoed *n*

287 **bank bill** *(US)*; **bank note; bill** *(US)*; **note**
d Banknote *f*
e billete *m* (de banco)
f billet *m* (de banque)
i banconota *f*; biglietto *m* (di banca)
n bankbiljet *n*; banknoot *f*

288 **bank bond**
d Bankschuldverschreibung *f*
e obligación *f* bancaria
f obligation *f* bancaire
i obbligazione *f* bancaria
n bankobligatie *f*

289 **bankbook; passbook** *(US)*
cf. **deposit book**
d Bankbuch *n*; Kontobuch *n*; Kontogegenbuch *n*
e libreta *f* bancaria; libreta *f* de banco; libreta *f* de cuenta
f carnet *m* bancaire; carnet *m* de banque; carnet *m* de compte; livret *m* bancaire; livret *m* de banque; livret *m* de compte
i libretto *m* bancario; libretto *m* di conto
n bankboekje *n*; rekeningboekje *n*

290 **bank certificate; bank confirmation** *(US)*
d Bankbestätigung *f*; Banksaldenbestätigung *f*
e confirmación *f* de saldo bancario
f confirmation *f* de solde bancaire
i conferma *f* di saldo bancario
n banksaldobevestiging *f*

291 **bank charges**
d Bankspesen *pl*
e gastos *mpl* bancarios; gastos *mpl* de banco
f frais *mpl* bancaires; frais *mpl* de

banque
i spese *fpl* bancarie; spese *fpl* di banca
n bankkosten *mpl*; bankonkosten *mpl*

292 **bank clearing; inter-bank clearing**
d Bankenabrechnung *f*; Bankenclearing *n*
e compensación *f* bancaria; compensación *f* interbancaria
f compensation *f* bancaire; compensation *f* entre banques; compensation *f* interbancaire
i compensazione *f* bancaria; compensazione *f* tra banche
n bankclearing *f*; interbancaire clearing *f*

293 **bank commission**
d Bankprovision *f*
e comisión *f* bancaria
f commission *f* bancaire
i commissione *f* bancaria; provvigione *f* bancaria
n bankcommissie *f*; bankprovisie *f*

294 **bank corporation** *(US)*; **banking establishment; banking firm; banking house; banking institution; firm of bankers**
cf. **bank, private bank**
d Bankanstalt *f*; Bankfirma *f*; Bankgeschäft *n*; Bankhaus *n*; Bankinstitut *n*
e establecimiento *m* bancario; institución *f* bancaria; instituto *m* bancario
f établissement *m* bancaire; établissement *m* de banque; institut *m* de banque; maison *f* de banque
i ditta *f* bancaria; istituto *m* bancario
n bankiersfirma *f*; bankiershuis *n*; bankinstelling *f*

295 **bank credit; bank lending**
cf. **banker's advance**
d Bankkredit *m*
e crédito *m* bancario
f crédit *m* bancaire; crédit *m* de banque
i credito *m* bancario
n bankkrediet *n*

296 **bank debts** *(owed to banks)*
d Bankforderungen *fpl*; Bankschulden *fpl*
e adeudos *mpl* bancarios; deudas *fpl* bancarias
f créances *fpl* bancaires; dettes *fpl* bancaires
i crediti *mpl* bancari; debiti *mpl* verso banche
n bankschulden *fpl*; bankvorderingen *fpl*

297 **bank deposit**
cf. **bank balance**
d Bankdepositen *pl*; Bankdepot *n*; Bankeinlage *f*
e depósito *m* bancario; depósito *m* en banco
f dépôt *m* bancaire; dépôt *m* en banque
i deposito *m* bancario; deposito *m* in banca
n bankdeposito *n*

298 **banker's advance; bank loan**
cf. **bank credit**
d Bankdarleh(e)n *n*; Bankvorschuss *m*
e anticipo *m* bancario; préstamo *m* bancario
f avance *f* bancaire; prêt *m* bancaire; prêt *m* de banque
i anticipazione *f* bancaria; fido *m* bancario; mutuo *m* bancario; prestito *m* bancario
n banklening *f*; bankvoorschot *n*

299 **banker's order**
d Bankauftrag *m*
e orden *f* bancaria; orden *f* de banco
f ordre *m* bancaire; ordre *m* de banque
i ordine *m* di banca
n bankopdracht *f*

300 **Bank for International Settlements; BIS**
d Bank *f* für Internationalen Zahlungsausgleich; BIZ
e Banco *m* de Pagos Internacionales; BPI
f Banque *f* des règlements internationaux; BRI
i Banca *f* dei Regolamenti Internazionali; BRI
n Bank *f* voor Internationale Betalingen; BIB

301 **banking**
d Bankbetrieb *m*; Bankgeschäft *n*; Bankwesen *n*
e actividad *f* bancaria; banca *f*; sistema *m* bancario
f activité *f* bancaire; banque *f*; système *m* bancaire
i attività *f* bancaria; banche *fpl*; sistema *m* bancario
n bankbedrijf *n*; bankwezen *n*

302 **banking company**
cf. **incorporated bank**
d Bankgesellschaft *f*
e compañía *f* bancaria; sociedad *f* bancaria
f société *f* bancaire; société *f* de banque
i società *f* bancaria; società *f* di banca
n bankmaatschappij *f (B)*; bankvereniging *f*

303 **banking consortium; banking syndicate**
d Bankenkonsortium *n*; Bankensyndikat *n*
e consorcio *m* de bancos; sindicato *m* de bancos
f consortium *m* de banques; syndicat *m* de banques
i consorzio *m* bancario; sindacato *m* bancario
n bankconsortium *n*; banksyndicaat *n*

304 **banking operations; banking transactions**
d Bankgeschäfte *npl*; Bankoperationen *fpl*; Banktransaktionen *fpl*
e negocios *mpl* bancarios; operaciones *fpl* bancarias; transacciones *fpl* bancarias
f affaires *fpl* bancaires; opérations *fpl* bancaires; opérations *fpl* de banque; transactions *fpl* bancaires; transactions *fpl* de banque
i affari *mpl* bancari; operazioni *fpl* bancarie; operazioni *fpl* di banca; transazioni *fpl* bancarie; transazioni *fpl* di banca
n bankoperaties *fpl*; banktransacties *fpl*; bankverrichtingen *fpl*; bankzaken *fpl*

305 **banking secrecy** *(in general)*; **bank secrecy** *(in general)*; **bank secret** *(particular instance)*
d Bankgeheimnis *n*
e secreto *m* bancario
f secret *m* bancaire
i segreto *m* bancario
n bankgeheim *n*

306 **bank interest**
d Bankzinsen *mpl*
e intereses *mpl* bancarios
f intérêts *mpl* bancaires
i interessi *mpl* bancari
n bankrente *f*

307 **bank money; deposit money; transferable money**
d Bankgeld *n*; Buchgeld *n*; Depositengeld *n*; Depositogeld *n*; Gelddepositen *pl*; Giralgeld *n*; Kreditgeld *n*; Kundengeld *n*
e depósitos *mpl* monetarios; dinero *m* bancario; dinero *m* consignado; dinero *m* de banco; dinero *m* depositado; dinero *m* en cuentas; dinero *m* giral; dinero *m* transferible; moneda *f* bancaria; moneda *f* giral
f monnaie *f* bancaire; monnaie *f* de banque; monnaie *f* de crédit; monnaie *f* scripturale
i denaro *m* depositato; denaro *m* in deposito; moneta *f* bancaria; moneta *f* di conto; moneta *f* di giro; moneta *f* scritturale
n bankgeld *n*; boekgeld *n*; giraalgeld *n*

308 **bank notes in circulation; circulation of bank notes; currency; note circulation; note issue; notes in circulation; notes in issue**
cf. **fiduciary circulation**
d Banknotenumlauf *m*; Banknotenzirkulation *f*; im Umlauf befindliche Noten *fpl*; Notenumlauf *m*
e billetes *mpl* en circulación; circulación *f* de billetes (de banco)
f billets *mpl* en circulation; circulation *f* de billets (de banque)
i biglietti *mpl* in circolazione; circolazione *f* di biglietti (di banca)
n bankbiljettencirculatie *f*; bankbiljetten *npl* in omloop

309 **bank of circulation; bank of issue**
cf. **central bank**
d Ausgabebank *f*; Notenbank *f*; Währungsbank *f*
e banco *m* de emisión; banco *m* emisor
f banque *f* d'émission
i banca *f* di emissione
n circulatiebank *f*; emissiebank *f (B)*

310 **bank of commerce; commercial bank; merchant bank** *(UK)**; **trade bank**
cf. **foreign trade bank**
d Commerzbank *f*; Geschäftsbank *f*; Handelsbank *f*
e banco *m* comercial; banco *m* de comercio
f banque *f* commerciale; banque *f* de commerce
i banca *f* commerciale; banca *f* di commercio
n handelsbank *f*

* Roughly an acceptance house cum investment bank.

311 **bank rate*; bank rate of discount*; minimum lending rate** *(UK)*; **prime lending rate**; prime rate**
cf. **discount rate**
d Bankdiskont *m*; Bankdiskontsatz *m*; Bankrate *f*; Banksatz *m*
e tasa *f* bancaria; tasa *f* de banco; tasa *f* (oficial) de descuento bancario; tipo *m* bancario; tipo *m* de banco; tipo *m* (oficial) de descuento bancario
f escompte *m* bancaire; escompte *m* de banque; escompte *m* officiel; taux *m* de banque; taux *m* d'escompte bancaire;

taux *m* (officiel) d'escompte; taux *m* de l'escompte
i saggio *m* di sconto bancario; sconto *m* bancario; sconto *m* ufficiale; tasso *m* di sconto bancario; tasso *m* ufficiale di banca; tasso *m* (ufficiale) di sconto
n bankdisconto *n*; officieel disconto *n*
* Term abandoned in 1972 in favour of minimum lending rate.
** Used incorrectly in this sense.

312 **bank return**
d Bankausweis *m*
e balance *m* del banco; balance *m* de situación del banco; situación *f* bancaria
f situation *f* de la banque
i situazione *f* della banca
n bankstaat *m*

313 **bankrupt** *(noun)*
d Bank(e)rotteur *m*; Fallit *m (rare)*; Gemeinschuldner *m*; Konkursschuldner *m*; Kridar *m (O)*; Kridatar *m (O)*
e concursado *m*; fallido *m*; quebrado *m*
f banqueroutier *m*; failli *m*
i bancarottiere *m*; fallito *m*
n bankroetier *m*; failliet *m*; gefailleerde *m*

314 **bankrupt** *(adj.)*
d bank(e)rott; fallit; in Konkurs
e en bancarotta; en quiebra; fallido; quebrado
f en banqueroute; en faillite; failli
i fallito; in bancarotta; in fallimento
n bankroet; failliet; in staat van faillissement

315 **bankruptcy; failure**
cf. **insolvency**
d Bank(e)rott *m*; Konkurs *m*
e bancarotta *f*; quiebra *f*
f banqueroute *f*; déconfiture *f*; faillite *f*
i bancarotta *f*; fallimento *m*
n bankbreuk *f*; bankroet *n*; failliet *n (B)*; faillissement *n*

316 **bankruptcy petition; petition in bankruptcy**
d Antrag *m* auf Konkurseröffnung; Konkursanmeldung *f*; Konkursantrag *m*; Konkurseröffnungsantrag *m*
e petición *f* de (apertura de la) quiebra; solicitud *f* de (apertura de la) quiebra
f demande *f* en déclaration de faillite; requête *f* des créanciers
i domanda *f* di dichiarazione di fallimento; richiesta *f* di fallimento
n faillissementsaanvrage *f*; verzoek *n* tot faillietverklaring

317 **bankrupt estate; bankrupt's assets; bankrupt's estate**
d Debitmasse *f (rare)*; Konkursmasse *f*; Masse *f*
e activo *m* de la quiebra; masa *f* de la quiebra
f actif *m* de la faillite; masse *f* de la faillite
i attivo *m* del fallimento; massa *f* fallimentare
n failliete boedel *m*; failliete massa *f*

318 **bank transfer; credit transfer; giro; transfer**
d Banküberweisung *f*; Giro *n*; Überweisung *f*
e giro *m* (bancario); transferencia *f* bancaria
f transfert *m* bancaire; virement *m* (bancaire)
i bancogiro *m*; bonifico *m* (bancario); giro *m*; trasferimento *m* bancario
n bankgiro *m*; bankoverboeking *f*; bankoverschrijving *f*; giro *m*; overboeking *f*; overschrijving *f*

319 **ban on imports; embargo on imports; import ban; import embargo; import prohibition**
d Einfuhrsperre *f*; Einfuhrstopp *m*; Einfuhrverbot *n*
e bloqueo *m* de las importaciones; embargo *m* sobre las importaciones; interdicción *f* de importación; prohibición *f* de importación
f blocage *m* des importations; embargo *m* sur les importations; interdiction *f* d'entrée; interdiction *f* d'importation; prohibition *f* d'entrée; prohibition *f* d'importation
i blocco *m* delle importazioni; divieto *m* di entrata; divieto *m* d'importazione; embargo *m* sulle importazioni
n importverbod *n*; invoerstop *m*; invoerverbod *n*

320 **bargain; deal; dealing*; operation; transaction**
d Geschäft *n*; Handel *m*; Transaktion *f*; Verrichtung *f*
e negociación *f*; negocio *m*; operación *f*; transacción *f*; trato *m*
f affaire *f*; marché *m*; opération *f*; transaction *f*
i affare *m*; negozio *m*; operazione *f*; transazione *f*

n affaire *f*; operatie *f*; transactie *f*; verrichting *f*; zaak *f*

* Rare in singular.

321 bargain; good buy
d Gelegenheitskauf *m*
e compra *f* de ocasión; ganga *f*
f achat *m* d'occasion; bonne affaire *f*; occasion *f*
i acquisto *m* d'occasione; buon affare *m*; buona occasione *f*
n gelegenheidskoopje *n*; koopje *n*

322 bargain price; cut-rate price; give-away price; knock-out price; underprice *(rare)*
cf. **exceptional price**
d Schleuderpreis *m*; Spottpreis *m*
e precio *m* baratísimo; precio *m* irrisorio; vil precio *m*
f prix *m* dérisoire; prix *m* d'occasion; prix *m* sacrifié; vil prix *m*
i prezzo *m* d'occasione; prezzo *m* irrisorio; vil prezzo *m*
n spotprijs *m*; weggeefprijs *m*

323 bar gold; ingot gold
cf. **bullion**
d Barrengold *n*; Gold *n* in Barren; Stangengold *n*
e oro *m* en barras; oro *m* en lingotes
f or *m* en barres; or *m* en lingots
i oro *m* in barre; oro *m* in lingotti; oro *m* in verghe
n goud *n* in baren; goud *n* in staven; staafgoud *n*

324 barred debt; debt barred by limitation; prescribed debt; statute-barred debt
d verjährte Schuld *f*
e deuda *f* prescri(p)ta
f dette *f* caduque; dette *f* prescrite
i debito *m* caduto in prescrizione; debito *m* prescritto
n verjaarde schuld *f*

325 barter
d Tausch *m*; Tauschhandel *m*
e cambio *m*; comercio *m* de trueque; trueco *m*; trueque *m*
f commerce *m* d'échange; échange *m*; troc *m*
i baratto *m*; cambio *m*; scambio *m*
n ruil *m*; ruilhandel *m*

326 barter *v*
d tauschen; Tauschhandel treiben
e baratar *(rare)*; cambiar; hacer negocios de trueque
f échanger; faire le commerce d'échange; faire le troc; troquer
i barattare; cambiare; scambiare
n ruilen; ruilhandel drijven

327 barter transaction; compensation transaction; exchange transaction; offsetting transaction; offset transaction
d Kompensationsgeschäft *n*; Tauschgeschäft *n*
e operación *f* de compensación; operación *f* de trueque; transacción *f* de cambio; transacción *f* de compensación; transacción *f* de trueque
f opération *f* d'échange; opération *f* de compensation; transaction *f* compensatoire; transaction *f* d'échange; transaction *f* de compensation; troc *m*
i operazione *f* di baratto; operazione *f* di compensazione; operazione *f* di scambio; transazione *f* di baratto; transazione *f* di compensazione
n compensatietransactie *f*; ruiltransactie *f*

328 base rate; basic rate; prime rate *(US)*
d Basissatz *m*; Basiszins *m*; Primarate *f*; "prime rate" *f*
e tipo *m* base
f taux *m* de base
i saggio *m* di base; tasso *m* di base
n basisrente *f*; basisvoet *m*

329 basic commodity; primary commodity; primary product; raw material
d Grundstoff *m*; Rohstoff *m*
e materia *f* básica; materia *f* de base; materia *f* prima; producto *m* base; producto *m* basico; producto *m* de base
f matière *f* de base; matière *f* première; produit *m* de base; produit *m* primaire
i materia *f* prima; prodotto *m* (di) base
n grondstof *f*; ruwstof *f* *(rare)*

330 basic price
cf. **normal price**
d Grundpreis *m*
e precio *m* base
f prix *m* de base
i prezzo *m* base
n grondprijs *m*; grondslagprijs *m*

331 basis of assessment; basis of taxation; tax assessment basis
d Bemessungsgrundlage *f*; Besteuerungsgrundlage *f*; Steuerbasis *f*; Steuerbemessungsgrundlage *f*; Steuerberechnungsgrundlage *f*; Steuerfuss *m*; Steuergrundlage *f*
e base *f* de cálculo de la tributación; base *f* de imposición; base *f* del impuesto;

base *f* de tributación; base *f* imponible; base *f* impositiva
f assiette *f* (de l'impôt); base *f* de calcul de l'imposition; base *f* de l'imposition; base *f* de l'impôt; base *f* imposable
i base *f* di calcolo dell'imposta; base *f* imponibile; imponibile *m*
n belastbare grondslag *f*; grondslag *m* der belasting(en) *(B)*; maatstaf *m* voor belastingheffing

332 bear
cf. **go** *v* **a bear**
d Baissier *m*; Baissespekulant *m*; Fixer *m*
e bajista *m*; especulador *m* a la baja
f baissier *m*; bear *m*; spéculateur *m* à la baisse
i ribassista *m*; speculatore *m* al ribasso
n baissier *m*; baissespeculant *m*; contramineur *m*; speculant *m* à la baisse

333 bear *v* **a loss; incur** *v* **a loss; make** *v* **a loss; meet** *v* **with a loss; suffer** *v* **a loss; sustain** *v* **a loss; undergo** *v* **a loss**
d einen Verlust erfahren; einen Verlust erleiden; einen Verlust machen; einen Verlust tragen
e experimentar una pérdida; padecer una pérdida; soportar una pérdida; sufrir una pérdida
f éprouver une perte; essuyer une perte; faire une perte; subir une perte; supporter une perte
i sopportare una perdita; sostenere una perdita; subire una perdita
n een verlies dragen; een verlies lijden; een verlies maken; een verlies ondergaan

334 bear *v* **an interest of X percent; bear** *v* **(a) X percent interest; bear** *v* **interest at a rate of X percent; carry** *v* **an interest of X percent; carry** *v* **(a) X percent interest; carry** *v* **interest at a rate of X percent; draw** *v* **an interest of X percent; draw** *v* **(a) X percent interest; draw** *v* **interest at a rate of X percent; earn** *v* **an interest of X percent; earn** *v* **(a) X percent interest; earn** *v* **interest at a rate of X percent; pay** *v* **an interest of X percent; pay** *v* **(a) X percent interest; pay** *v* **interest at a rate of X percent; return** *v* **an interest of X percent; return** *v* **(a) X percent interest; return** *v* **interest at a rate of X percent; yield** *v* **an interest of X percent**
cf. **interest bearing**
d mit X vom Hundert verzinslich sein; X Prozent Zinsen abwerfen; X Prozent Zinsen bringen; X Prozent Zinsen einbringen; X Prozent Zinsen geben; X Prozent Zinsen tragen; sich mit (zu) X Prozent verzinsen
e arrojar un interés de X por ciento; dar un interés de X por ciento; devengar interés de X por ciento; producir un interés de X por ciento; rendir un interés de X por ciento
f porter intérêt à X pour cent; porter un intérêt de X pour cent; produire intérêt à X pour cent; produire un intérêt de X pour cent; rapporter X pour cent d'intérêt
i dare il X per cento d'interesse; dare un interesse del X per cento; fruttare il X per cento d'interesse; produrre un interesse del X per cento; rendere un interesse del X per cento
n een rente van X procent afwerpen; een rente van X procent dragen; een rente van X procent geven; een rente van X procent opbrengen

335 bear covering *(UK)*; **short covering** *(US)*
d Deckungskauf *m*
e compra *f* de cobertura
f rachat *m* de découvert
i acquisto *m* di copertura; acquisto *m* di rimpiazzo; riacquisto *m* di scoperto
n contraminedekking *f*; dekkingsinkoop *m*

336 bearer; holder
d Besitzer *m*; Inhaber *m*
e portador *m*; poseedor *m*; tenedor *m*; titular *m*
f détenteur *m*; porteur *m*; possesseur *m*; titulaire *m*
i detentore *m*; portatore *m*; possessore *m*; titolare *m*
n bezitter *m*; houder *m*

337 bearer; presenter
d Präsentant *m*; Überbringer *m*; Vorleger *m*; Vorzeiger *m*
e portador *m*; presentador *m*; presentante *m*
f porteur *m*; présentateur *m*
i latore *m*; portatore *m*; presentatore *m*
n aanbieder *m*; brenger *m*; toonder *m*

338 bearer bond
cf. **coupon bond**
d auf den Inhaber lautende Obligation *f*; auf den Inhaber lautende Schuldverschreibung *f*; Inhaberobligation *f*; Inhaberschuldverschreibung *f*
e bono *m* al portador; obligación *f* al portador
f bon *m* au porteur; obligation *f* au porteur

i obbligazione *f* al portatore
n obligatie *f* aan toonder

339 bearer check *(US)*; **open cheque** *(UK)*; **uncrossed check** *(US)*; **uncrossed cheque** *(UK)*
d Barscheck *m*; Inhaberscheck *m*; offener Scheck *m*
e cheque *m* abierto; cheque *m* al portador; cheque *m* no cruzado
f chèque *m* au porteur; chèque *m* non barré; chèque *m* ordinaire; chèque *m* ouvert
i assegno *m* al portatore; assegno *m* non sbarrato; assegno *m* ordinario
n cheque *m* aan toonder; open cheque *m*; toondercheque *m*

340 bearer instrument
d Inhaberpapier *n*
e título *m* al portador
f titre *m* au porteur
i titolo *m* al portatore
n papier *n* aan toonder; toonderpapier *n*

341 bearer of securities; holder of securities; security bearer; security holder
cf. **shareholder**
d Wertpapierbesitzer *m*; Wertpapierinhaber *m*
e portador *m* de valores; poseedor *m* de valores; tenedor *m* de valores
f détenteur *m* de valeurs; porteur *m* de valeurs; possesseur *m* de valeurs
i detentore *m* di valori; portatore *m* di valori; possessore *m* di valori
n effectenbezitter *m*; effectenhouder *m*

342 bearer securities
d Inhabereffekten *pl*; Inhaberpapiere *npl*; Inhaberwertpapiere *npl*
e efectos *mpl* al portador; títulos *mpl* al portador; valores *mpl* al portador
f effets *mpl* au porteur; papiers *mpl* au porteur; titres *mpl* au porteur; valeurs *fpl* au porteur
i effetti *mpl* al portatore; titoli *mpl* al portatore; valori *mpl* al portatore
n effecten *npl* aan toonder; toonderpapieren *npl*; waardepapieren *npl* aan toonder

343 bearer share
d Inhaberaktie *f*
e acción *f* al portador
f action *f* au porteur
i azione *f* al portatore
n aandeel *n* aan toonder; toonderaandeel *n*

344 bearish tone; bearish trend; downtrend; downward trend
d Baisseneigung *f*; Baissestimmung *f*; Baisseströmung *f*; Baissetendenz *f*; fallende Tendenz *f*; Neigung *f* zum Fallen; rückläufige Tendenz *f*
e tendencia *f* a la baja; tendencia *f* bajista; tendencia *f* descendente
f ambiance *f* de baisse; tendance *f* à la baisse
i tendenza *f* al ribasso
n baisseneiging *f*; baissestemming *f*; baissetendens *f*; neergaande tendens *f*; neiging *f* tot dalen; tendens *f* tot dalen

345 bear market
d Baissemarkt *m*; Markt *m* à la Baisse; Markt *m* in Baissestimmung
e mercado *m* bajista; mercado *m* de baja
f marché *m* à la baisse; marché *m* en baisse
i mercato *m* al ribasso
n baissemarkt *f*

346 bear sale *(UK)*; **short sale** *(US)*
d Blankoabgabe *f*; Blankoverkauf *m*; Fixgeschäft *n*; Leerabgabe *f*; Leerverkauf *m*
e venta *f* al descubierto; venta *f* en descubierto
f vente *f* à découvert
i vendita *f* allo scoperto
n baisseverkoop *m*; blancoverkoop *m*

347 become *v* **due; fall** *v* **due; mature** *v*
cf. **due August 15, expire** *v*
d ablaufen; fällig werden; verfallen
e llegar al vencimiento; vencer
f arriver à échéance; échoir; venir à échéance
i giungere a scadenza; maturare; scadere; venire a scadenza
n aflopen; vervallen

348 Belgo-Luxemb(o)urg Economic Union; B.L.U.E.
d Belgisch-luxemburgische Wirtschaftsunion *f*
e Unión *f* Económica Belga-Luxemburguesa
f Union *f* économique belgo-luxembourgeoise
i Unione *f* Economica Belga-Lussemburghese
n Belgisch-Luxemburgse Economische Unie *f*

349 beneficial interest; usufructary right
d Niessbrauch(s)recht *n*; Nutzniessungs-

recht *n*
e derecho *m* de usufructo
f droit *m* d'usufruit
i diritto *m* d'usufrutto
n recht *n* van vruchtgebruik

350 beneficiary; payee
d Begünstigter *m*; Zahlungsberechtigter *m*; Zahlungsempfänger *m*
e beneficiario *m*
f bénéficiaire *m*
i beneficiario *m*
n begunstigde *m*; ontvanger *m*

351 biannual instal(l)ment; half-yearly instal(l)ment; semi-annual instal(l)ment; six-monthly instal(l)ment
d Halbjahresrate *f*; halbjährliche Rate *f*
e cuota *f* semestral; plazo *m* semestral
f acompte *m* semestriel; terme *m* semestriel
i rata *f* semestrale; semestralità *f*
n halfjaarlijkse termijn *m*

352 bid *(general)*; **offer; tender**
d Anerbieten *n*; Angebot *n*; Offerte *f*
e oferta *f*; ofrecimiento *m*
f offre *f*
i offerta *f*
n aanbieding *f*; aanbod *n*; offerte *f*

353 bid *(auction)*
d Gebot *n*
e postura *f*
f enchère *f*; mise *f*
i offerta *f*
n bod *n*

354 bid price; bid quotation; buying rate; demand rate; purchase rate
cf. **buying price**
d Ankaufsatz *m*; Ankaufskurs *m*; Geldkurs *m*; Geldsatz *m*; Kaufkurs *m*
e cambio *m* de compra; cotización *f* de compra; cotización *f* demandada; tipo *m* comprador; tipo *m* de compra
f cours *m* acheteur(s); cours *m* à l'achat; cours *m* argent; cours *m* d'achat; cours *m* de la demande; cours *m* demandé; taux *m* d'achat
i cambio *m* d'acquisto; cambio *m* denaro; corso *m* all'acquisto; corso *m* d'acquisto; corso *m* denaro; corso *m* di domanda; prezzo *m* d'acquisto; prezzo *m* denaro; prezzo *m* di domanda; tasso *m* d'acquisto
n aankoopkoers *m*; biedkoers *m*; inkoopkoers *m*

355 big business
cf. **high finance**
d Grosskapital *n*
e gran capital *m*
f grand capital *m*; gros capital *m*
i grosso capitale *m*
n grootkapitaal *n*

356 bill; bill of exchange; commercial bill; commercial paper; draft; note; trade bill; trade paper
d gezogener Wechsel *m*; Handelspapier *n*; Handelswechsel *m*; Kundenwechsel *m*; Tratte *f*; Warenwechsel *m*; Wechsel *m*
e efecto *m* comercial; efecto *m* de comercio; giro *m*; letra *f* comercial; letra *f* de cambio; libranza *f*; papel *m* comercial; papel *m* de comercio
f change *m* commercial; effet *m* commercial; effet *m* de commerce; lettre *f* de change; papier *m* commercial; papier *m* de commerce; traite *f*
i cambiale *f*; carta *f* commerciale; effetto *m* commerciale; lettera *f* di cambio; tratta *f*; vaglia *m* cambiario
n cambio *n*; commerciële wissel *m*; handelspapier *n*; handelswissel *m*; mandaat *n*; traite *f*; wissel *m*; wisselbrief *m*

357 bill *v*; **invoice** *v*
d fakturieren
e facturar
f facturer
i fatturare
n factureren

358 bill at usance; usance bill; usance draft
d Usowechsel *m*
e letra *f* de vencimiento usual
f effet *m* à usance; lettre *f* de change à usance
i cambiale *f* pagabile secondo l'uso
n usowissel *m*

359 bill book; bill diary; bill journal; bills payable book
d Akzeptbuch *n*; Verfallbuch *n*; Wechselbuch *n*; Wechseljournal *n*
e diario *m* de vencimientos (de letras); libro *m* de efectos (a pagar); registro *m* de efectos (a pagar); registro *m* de vencimientos
f carnet *m* d'échéances; échéancier *m*; journal *m* d'effects (à payer); livre *m* d'effects (à payer)
i libro *m* effetti passivi; libro *m* scadenze; registro *m* degli effetti passivi; scadenzario *m*

n uitgaand wisselboek *n*; vervalboek *n*; vervaldagagenda *f*; vervaldagenboek *n*; wisselboek *n*

360 bill book; bill diary; bill journal; bills receivable book
d Wechselbuch *n*; Wechseldebitorenbuch *n*; Wechseljournal *n*
e diario *m* de letras a cobrar; libro *m* de efectos (a cobrar); registro *m* de efectos (a cobrar)
f journal *m* d'effets (à recevoir); livre *m* d'effets (à recevoir)
i libro *m* effetti attivi; registro *m* degli effetti attivi
n ingaand wisselboek *n*; wisselboek *n*

361 bill broker; cambist; discount broker; exchange broker; note broker
cf. **cambist**
d Cambist *m* *(Schw)*; Diskontmakler *m*; Wechselhändler *m*; Wechselmakler *m*
e agente *m* de descuentos; agente *m* de letras; cambista *m*; corredor *m* de descuentos; corredor *m* de letras
f agent *m* de change; cambiste *m*; courtier *m* de change; courtier *m* d'escompte
i agente *m* di sconto; cambista *m*; negoziatore *m* di cambiali; sensale *m* di cambiali
n cambist *m*; discontomakelaar *m*; wisselmakelaar *m*

362 bill debtor; obligor *(rare)*
d Wechselschuldner *m*; Wechselverpflichteter *m*
e deudor *m* cambiario; obligado *m* por letra de cambio
f débiteur *m* d'une lettre de change; obligé *m*
i debitore *m* cambiario; obbligato *m* cambiario
n wisselschuldenaar *m*

363 bill en pension; bill in pawn; bill on deposit; collateral bill; pawned bill of exchange; pledged bill of exchange
cf. **"bill" for synonyms**
d Depotwechsel *m*; Kostwechsel *m*; Pensionswechsel *m*; sicherungsübereigneter Wechsel *m*; verpfändeter Wechsel *m*
e efecto *m* dado en garantía; efecto *m* dado en prenda; efecto *m* en depósito; efecto *m* pignorado
f effet *m* déposé en garantie; effet *m* déposé en nantissement; effet *m* en nantissement; effet *m* en nourrice; effet *m* en pension; effet *m* nanti
i effetto *m* dato in garanzia; effetto *m* dato in pegno; effetto *m* depositato in garanzia; effetto *m* di smobilizzo; effetto *m* pignorato; effetto *m* tenuto in deposito
n in waarborg gegeven wissel *m*; pensionwissel *m*; verpande wissel *m*; wissel *m* en pension; wissel *m* in pension

364 bill for collection
cf. **bill receivable**
d Inkassowechsel *m*
e efecto *m* al cobro; letra *f* a cobrar; letra *f* al cobro
f effet *m* à l'encaissement; lettre *f* à encaisser; traite *f* d'encaissement
i cambiale *f* all'incasso; effetto *m* all'incasso
n incassowissel *m*

365 bill in distress; bill in suspense; bill returned unpaid; dishonored bill *(US)*; dishonoured bill *(UK)*; overdue bill; past bill; past-due bill; return; returned bill; unpaid bill
cf. **"bill" for synonyms**
d nicht bezahlter Wechsel *m*; nicht eingelöster Wechsel *m*; nicht honorierter Wechsel *m*; notleidender Wechsel *m*; Retour *f*; retournierter Wechsel *m*; Retourwechsel *m*; überfälliger Wechsel *m*; uneingelöster Wechsel *m*; zurücktrassierter Wechsel *m*
e efecto *m* devuelto; efecto *m* impagado; efecto *m* no honrado; efecto *m* no pagado; efecto *m* sobrevencido
f effet *m* en souffrance; effet *m* impayé; effet *m* non honoré; effet *m* renvoyé (impayé); effet *m* retourné (impayé)
i effetto *m* di ritorno; effetto *m* in sofferenza; effetto *m* insoluto; effetto *m* non onorato; effetto *m* non pagato; effetto *m* restituito
n geretourneerde wissel *m*; niet betaalde wissel *m*; niet gehonoreerde wissel *m*; noodlijdende wissel *m*; onbetaalde wissel *m*; onbetaald teruggezonden wissel *m*; retour *m*; retourwissel *m*

366 billing; invoicing
d Fakturierung *f*; Rechnungsstellung *f*
e facturación *f*
f facturation *f*
i fatturazione *f*
n facturering *f*

367 billion *(UK) (1,000,000,000,000)**; **trillion** *(US)*
d Billion *f*

e billón *m*
f billion *m*; trillion *m***
i bilione *m*; trilione *m***
n biljoen *n (N)*
* American usage is becoming increasingly frequent in UK.
** Incorrectly so used.

368 billion *(US) (1,000,000,000)****; milliard** *(rare)*; **thousand million** *(UK)*
d Milliarde *f*
e mil milliones
f billion *m***; milliard *m*
i bilione *m***; miliardo *m*
n biljoen *n (B)*; miljard *n*
* American usage is becoming increasingly frequent in UK.
** Incorrectly so used.

369 bill jobbing; jobbing in bills
d Wechselarbitrage *f*
e arbitraje *m* de letras
f arbitrage *m* sur les lettres de change
i arbitraggio *m* sui cambiali
n wisselarbitrage *f*

370 bill market; discount market
d Diskontmarkt *m*; Wechselmarkt *m*
e mercado *m* de descuento; mercado *m* de letras
f marché *m* de l'escompte; marché *m* des lettres de change
i mercato *m* dello sconto; mercato *m* di cambiali
n discontomarkt *f*; wisselmarkt *f*

371 bill not to order; non-negotiable bill; not-to-order bill; unendorsable bill; unnegotiable bill; untransferable bill
cf. **"bill" for synonyms**
d auf den Namen lautender Wechsel *m*; nicht auf Order lautender Wechsel *m*; nicht begebbarer Wechsel *m*; nicht börsenfähiger Wechsel *m*; nicht handelsfähiger Wechsel *m*; nicht indossierbarer Wechsel *m*; nicht übertragbarer Wechsel *m*; Rektawechsel *m*; unbegebbarer Wechsel *m*; unübertragbarer Wechsel *m*
e letra *f* innegociable; letra *f* intransferible; letra *f* intransmissible; letra *f* no a la orden; letra *f* no comerciable; letra *f* no endosable; letra *f* nominativa; letra *f* no negociable; letra *f* no transferible; letra *f* no transmisible
f effet *m* innégociable; effet *m* intransférable; effet *m* intransmissible; effet *m* nominatif; effet *m* non à ordre; effet *m* non commerçable; effet *m* non endossable; effet *m* non négociable; effet *m* non transférable; effet *m* non transmissible
i effetto *m* intrasferibile; effetto *m* intrasmissibile; effetto *m* non all'ordine; effetto *m* non commerciabile; effetto *m* non negoziabile; effetto *m* non trasferibile; effetto *m* non trasmissibile
n niet endosseerbare wissel *m*; niet verhandelbare wissel *m*; onoverdraagbare wissel *m*; onverhandelbare wissel *m*; rectawissel *m*; wissel *m* op naam

372 bill payable; note payable
d fälliger Wechsel *m*; Schuldwechsel *m*
e documento *m* a pagar; efecto *m* a pagar; letra *f* a pagar
f effet *m* à payer; lettre *f* à payer
i cambiale *f* da pagare; cambiale *f* passiva; effetto *m* da pagare; effetto *m* passivo
n te betalen wissel *m*

373 bill receivable; note receivable *(US)*
cf. **bill for collection**
d Besitzwechsel *m*; einzulösender Wechsel *m*; Wechselforderung *f*
e efecto *m* a cobrar; efecto *m* al cobro; letra *f* a cobrar; letra *f* al cobro
f effet *m* à recevoir
i cambiale *f* attiva; cambiale *f* all'incasso; cambiale *f* da incassare; effetto *m* attivo; effetto *m* all'incasso; effetto *m* da incassare
n te innen wissel *m*

374 bill to order; endorsable bill; negotiable bill; order bill; transferable bill
cf. **"bill" for synonyms**
d auf Order lautender Wechsel *m*; begebbarer Wechsel *m*; börsenfähiger Wechsel *m*; girierbarer Wechsel *m*; handelsfähiger Wechsel *m*; indossabler Wechsel *m*; indossierbarer Wechsel *m*; Orderwechsel *m*; übertragbarer Wechsel *m*
e letra *f* a la orden; letra *f* comerciable; letra *f* endosable; letra *f* negociable; letra *f* transferible; letra *f* transmisible
f effet *m* à ordre; effet *m* commerçable; effet *m* endossable; effet *m* négociable; effet *m* transférable; effet *m* transmissible
i effetto *m* all'ordine; effetto *m* commerciabile; effetto *m* girabile; effetto *m* negoziabile; effetto *m* trasferibile; effetto *m* trasmissibile
n endossabele wissel *m*; endosseerbare wissel *m*; orderwissel *m*; overdraagbare

wissel *m*; verhandelbare wissel *m*; wissel *m* aan order

375 bimetal(l)ism; double standard
d Bimetallismus *m*; Doppelwährung *f*
e bimetalismo *m*; doble patrón *m*; tipo *m* doble
f bimétallisme *m*; double étalon *m*
i bimetallismo *m*; doppio tallone *m*; doppio tipo *m*
n bimetallisme *n*; dubbele standaard *m*

376 black interest; credit interest; interest in black; interest receivable
cf. **interest due**
d Aktivzinsen *mpl*; Habenzinsen *mpl*; Kreditzinsen *mpl*
e intereses *mpl* a cobrar; intereses *mpl* acreedores; intereses *mpl* activos; intereses *mpl* a recibir
f intérêts *mpl* actifs; intérêts *mpl* à recevoir; intérêts *mpl* créditeurs; intérêts *mpl* noirs
i interessi *mpl* attivi; interessi *mpl* creditori; interessi *mpl* da ricevere; interessi *mpl* neri
n creditrente *f*; te ontvangen rente *f*; zwarte rente *f*

377 black market
d schwarzer Markt *m*; Schwarzmarkt *m*
e mercado *m* negro
f marché *m* noir
i mercato *m* nero
n zwarte markt *f*

378 blank check ***(US)*****; blank cheque** ***(UK)***
d Blankoscheck *m*
e cheque *m* en blanco
f chèque *m* en blanc; chèque *m* tiré en blanc
i assegno *m* in bianco
n blancocheque *m*

379 blank credit; open credit; signature loan ***(US)***
cf. **cash credit, fiduciary loan**
d Blankokredit *m*; Kontokorrentkredit *m*; offener Kredit *m*; Überziehungskredit *m*; ungedeckter Kredit *m*; ungesicherter Kredit *m*
e crédito *m* abierto; crédito *m* al descubierto; crédito *m* en blanco; crédito *m* en descubierto; crédito *m* no cubierto
f crédit *m* à découvert; crédit *m* de notoriété; crédit *m* en blanc; crédit *m* libre; crédit *m* non couvert; crédit *m* sur notoriété
i credito *m* allo scoperto; credito *m* in bianco; credito *m* libero; credito *m* non coperto; credito *m* scoperto
n blancokrediet *n*; ongedekt krediet *n*; open krediet *n*

380 block *v (funds etc.)*; **freeze** *v*
cf. **immobilize** *v*
d blockieren; einfrieren; sperren; stoppen
e bloquear; congelar
f bloquer; congeler; geler
i bloccare; congelare
n bevriezen; blokkeren

381 blocked assets
d Sperrguthaben *n*
e haberes *mpl* bloqueados
f avoir *m* bloqué
i avere *m* bloccato
n geblokkeerd tegoed *n*

382 blocked sterling
d Sperrpfunde *npl*
e libras *fpl* bloqueadas
f livres *fpl* bloquées
i sterline *fpl* bloccate
n geblokkeerde ponden *npl*

383 blocking; freezing
d Blockierung *f*; Einfrierung *f*; Sperre *f*; Sperrung *f*
e bloqueo *m*; congelación *f*
f blocage *m*; congélation *f*; gel *m*
i blocco *m*; congelamento *m*
n bevriezing *f*; blokkade *f*; blokkering *f*

384 blocking period *(of securities)*; **period of non-negotiability**
d Sperre *f*; Sperrfrist *f*
e plazo *m* de bloqueo; plazo *m* de suspensión
f délai *m* de blocage; période *f* de suspension
i periodo *m* di blocco; periodo *m* di sospensione
n blokkadetermijn *m*

385 block issue
d Serienausgabe *f*
e emisión *f* en serie
f émission *f* par série
i emissione *f* in serie
n emissie *f* per reeks; in serie uitgegeven emissie *f*

386 block of shares; lot of shares; parcel of shares
d Aktienpaket *n*; Aktienposten *m*
e lote *m* de acciones; paquete *m* de acciones

f bloc *m* d'actions; lot *m* d'actions; paquet *m* d'actions
i lotto *m* azionario; lotto *m* di azioni; pacchetto *m* azionario; pacchetto *m* di azioni
n aandelenpakket *n*; pakket *n* aandelen; post *m* aandelen

387 **blue chips*; blue chip stock(s); gilt-edged securities; gilt-edged stock(s); gilts**
d erstklassige (Wert-)Papiere *npl*; goldgeränderte (Wert-)Papiere *npl*; mündelsichere (Wert-)Papiere *npl*; prima (Wert-)-Papiere *npl*; Spitzenpapiere *npl*; Spitzenwerte *mpl*
e títulos *mpl* de primera categoría; títulos *mpl* de primera clase; títulos *mpl* de primer orden; títulos *mpl* de toda confianza; títulos *mpl* seguros; valores *mpl* de primera categoría; valores *mpl* de primera clase; valores *mpl* de primer orden; valores *mpl* de tota confianza; valores *mpl* seguros
f titres *mpl* de bon père de famille; titres *mpl* de père de famille; titres *mpl* de premier ordre; titres *mpl* de tout premier ordre; titres *mpl* de tout repos; titres *mpl* vedettes; valeurs *fpl* de bon père de famille; valeurs *fpl* de père de famille; valeurs *fpl* de premier ordre; valeurs *fpl* de tout premier ordre; valeurs *fpl* de tout repos; valeurs *fpl* vedettes
i titoli *mpl* di prim'ordine; titoli *mpl* di tutto riposo; titoli *mpl* sicuri(ssimi); valori *mpl* di prim'ordine; valori *mpl* di tutto riposo; valori *mpl* sicuri(ssimi)
n blue chips *mpl*; eersteklas-waardepapieren *npl*; eersterangswaarden *fpl*; goudgerande waarden *fpl*; prima fondsen *npl*; prima waarden *fpl*

* Blue chips are in public companies, gilts usually in government stock.

388 **board of creditors; committee of creditors; committee of inspection** *(UK)*
d Gläubigerausschuss *m*
e junta *f* de acreedores
f commission *f* des créanciers; délégation *f* des créanciers; direction *f* des créanciers; syndicat *m* des créanciers
i comitato *m* dei creditori
n commissie *f* van de schuldeisers

389 **bond*; corporate bond** *(US) (company)*; **debenture** *(company)*; **debenture bond; loan stock; obligation** *(rare)*; **stock** *(UK)***
cf. **annuity bond, certificate of indebtedness**
d Anleihepapier *n*; Anleiheschein *m*; Anleihestück *n*; Anleihetitel *m*; Kassenbon *m****; Kassenobligation *f****; Obligation *f*; Partialobligation *f*; Pfandbrief *m*; Schuldverschreibung *f*; Teilschuldverschreibung *f*
e bono *m* de caja***; bono *m* (de empréstito); obligación *f*; título *m* de empréstito
f bon *m*; bon *m* de caisse***; obligation *f*; titre *m* (d'emprunt); titre *m* (d'obligation)
i buono *m*; buono *m* di cassa***; obbligazione *f*; titolo *m* (obbligazionario)
n kasbon *m****; obligatie *f*; schuldbekentenis *f*; schuldbrief *m*

* In UK usually of state or public authority.
** See note on meaning of this term under "securities".
*** Short or medium term only.

390 **bond creditor; bondholder; debenture holder; loan stockholder; obligee** *(US)*
d Anleihegläubiger *m*; Obligationär *m*; Obligationengläubiger *m*; Obligationeninhaber *m*; Obligationsgläubiger *m*; Obligationsinhaber *m*; Schuldverschreibungsinhaber *m*
e acreedor *m* de obligaciones; debenturista *m (AL)*; obligacionista *m*; tenedor *m* de obligaciones; titular *m* de obligaciones
f créancier *m* obligataire; détenteur *m* d'obligations; obligataire *m*; obligationnaire *m (col.)*; porteur *m* d'obligations; possesseur *m* d'obligations; titulaire *m* d'obligations
i creditore *m* obbligazionista; detentore *m* di obbligazioni; obbligazionista *m*; portatore *m* di obbligazioni; possessore *m* di obbligazioni; titolare *m* di obbligazioni
n obligatiebezitter *m*; obligatiecrediteur *m*; obligatiehouder *m*

391 **bonded debt**
cf. **consolidated debt**
d Anleiheschuld *f*; Obligationenschuld *f*; Obligationsschuld *f*; verbriefte Forderung *f*; verbriefte Schuld *f*
e deuda *f* en obligaciones
f dette *f* d'obligations; dette *f* obligataire
i debito *m* obbligazionario
n obligatieschuld *f*

392 **bond issue; debenture issue**
d Ausgabe *f* von Obligationen; Ausgabe *f* von Pfandbriefen; Ausgabe *f* von Schuldverschreibungen; Emission *f* von

Obligationen; Emission *f* von Pfandbriefen; Emission *f* von Schuldverschreibungen; Obligationenausgabe *f*; Pfandbriefausgabe *f*
e emisión *f* de bonos; emisión *f* de obligaciones
f émission *f* de bons; émission *f* d'obligations
i emissione *f* di buoni; emissione *f* d'obbligazioni; emissione *f* obbligazionaria
n emissie *f* van obligaties; emissie *f* van schuldbrieven; obligatie-emissie *f*; obligatie-uitgifte *f*; uitgifte *f* van obligaties; uitgifte *f* van schuldbrieven

393 **bond market; market in fixed-interest securities**
d Markt *m* für festverzinsliche Werte; Pfandbriefmarkt *m*; Rentenmarkt *m*
e mercado *m* de rentas; mercado *m* de valores de renta fija
f marché *m* des obligations; marché *m* des rentes; marché *m* des valeurs à revenu fixe; marché *m* obligataire
i mercato *m* dei titoli a reddito fisso; mercato *m* dei titoli di rendita; mercato *m* obbligazionario
n markt *f* voor vast renderende waarden; obligatiemarkt *f*

394 **bond of indemnity; declaration of suretyship; deed of surety(ship); guarantee bond; indemnity bond; indemnity letter; letter of guarantee; letter of indemnity; security bond; warrant letter** *(US)*; **warranty deed** *(US)*
d Ausfallbürgschaft *f*; Bürgschaftsbrief *m*; Bürgschaftserklärung *f*; Bürgschaftsschein *m*; Bürgschaftsurkunde *f*; Garantie *f* auf Schadloshaltung; Garantiebrief *m*; Garantieerklärung *f*; Garantieschein *m*; Garantieschreiben *n*; Garantieverpflichtungsschein *m*; Revers *m*; Schadlosbürgschaft *f*
e carta *f* de garantía; carta *f* de indemnidad; carta *f* de indemnización; declaración *f* de garantía; fianza *f* de caución; fianza *f* de indemnidad; fianza *f* de indemnización; garantía *f* de indemnización; obligación *f* de garantía
f acte *m* de caution; acte *m* de cautionnement; cautionnement *m*; déclaration *f* de cautionnement; déclaration *f* de garantie; garantie *f* d'indemnité; lettre *f* de garantie; lettre *f* d'indemnité; obligation *f* de garantie; obligation *f* d'indemnité
i atto *m* di fideiussione; atto *m* di garanzia; dichiarazione *f* di garanzia; fideiussione *f* di indennità; garanzia *f* di indennizzo; lettera *f* di garanzia; lettera *f* di indennità; obbligazione *f* di garanzia; obbligazione *f* di indennizzo
n akte *f* van borgtocht; borgstelling *f*; borgtocht *m*; garantiebewijs *n*; garantiebrief *m*; garantie *f* van schadeloosstelling

395 **bondsman; guarantee; guarantor; surety; warrantor**
cf. **backer**
d Bürge *m*; Garant *m*; Gewährsmann *m*
e afianzador *m*; caucionero *m*; fiador *m*; garante *m*
f caution *f*; donneur *m* de caution; garant *m*; garantisseur *m*; porte-fort *m* *(Schw.)*; répondant *m*
i fideiussore *m*; garante *m*; mallevadore *m*
n borg *m*; garant *m*

396 **bond yield**
d Ertrag *m* aus Obligationen; Erträgnis *n* aus Obligationen
e rendimiento *m* de obligaciones
f rendement *m* d'obligations
i reddito *m* d'obbligazioni; reddito *m* obbligazionario
n opbrengst *f* van obligaties; rendement *n* van obligaties

397 **bonus; bounty** *(governmental)*; **gratuity; premium**
cf. **extra pay**
d Bonifikation *f*; Bonus *m*; Gratifikation *f*; Prämie *f*; Zuwendung *f*
e bonificación *f*; gratificación *f*; prima *f*
f boni *m*; bonus *m*; gratification *f*; prime *f*
i gratifica *f*; gratificazione *f*; premio *m*
n bonus *m*; gratificatie *f*; premie *f*

398 **bonus; extra dividend; special dividend; surplus dividend**
d ausserordentliche Dividende *f*; Bonus *m*; Dividendenbonus *m*; Extradividende *f*; Sonderdividende *f*; Superdividende *f*; Überdividende *f* *(rare)*; Zusatzdividende *f*
e dividendo *m* complementario; dividendo *m* extraordinario; dividendo *m* suplementario; sobredividendo *m*
f boni *m*; dividende *m* extraordinaire; dividende *m* supplémentaire; superdividende *m*
i dividendo *m* extra; dividendo *m* straordinario; dividendo *m*

supplementare; extradividendo *m*
n aanvullend dividend *n*; bonus *m*; bonus-uitkering *f*; extradividend *n*; extra-uitkering *f*; superdividend *n*; surplus-dividend *n*

399 bonus issue; capitalisation issue ***(UK)*****; capitalization issue** ***(US)*****; scrip issue**
d Ausgabe *f* von Gratisaktien; Emission *f* von Gratisaktien
e emisión *f* de acciones gratuitas
f émission *f* d'actions gratuites
i emissione *f* d'azioni gratuite
n emissie *f* van gratis aandelen; uitgifte *f* van gratis aandelen

400 bonus share; scrip; stock dividend ***(US)***
d Genussaktie *f*; Genussschein *m*; Gratis-aktie *f*; Stockdividende *f*
e acción *f* de disfrute; acción *f* de goce; acción *f* gratuita; dividendo *m* en acciones
f action *f* bénéficiaire; action *f* de jouissance; action *f* gratuite; dividende *m* en actions
i azione *f* di godimento; azione *f* gratuita; dividendo *m* in azioni
n bonusaandeel *n*; gratisaandeel *n*; stock-dividend *n*

401 book *v*; **enter** *v* **(in the books); post** *v* ***(US)*****; record** *v*
d buchen; eintragen; verbuchen
e anotar; asentar; contabilizar; dar entrada; registrar; sentar
f comptabiliser; enregistrer; inscrire; passer écriture de; passer en compte
i allibrare; contabilizzare; inscrivere; iscrivere; registrare
n boeken; inboeken; inschrijven; registreren

402 book *v* **as a liability; enter** *v* **as a liability**
cf. **be** *v* **booked as a liability**
d auf das Passivkonto übertragen; auf der Passivseite aufführen; passivieren
e inscribir en el pasivo; pasar al pasivo; sentar en el lado del pasivo
f inscrire au passif; porter au passif
i i(n)scrivere al passivo; portare al passivo
n op het passief schrijven *(B)*; passiveren

403 book *v* **as an asset; enter** *v* **as an asset**
cf. **be** *v* **booked as an asset**
d aktivieren; auf das Aktivkonto übertragen; auf der Aktivseite aufführen; ins Aktiv buchen
e inscribir en el activo; pasar al activo; sentar en el lado del activo
f inscrire à l'actif; passer à l'actif
i i(n)scrivere all'attivo; portare all'attivo
n activeren; op het actief schrijven *(B)*

404 book claim
d Buchforderung *f*; buchmässige Forderung *f*
e crédito *m* contabilizado; crédito *m* contable
f créance *f* comptable
i credito *m* contabile
n boekvordering *f*

405 book creditor
d Buchgläubiger *m*
e acreedor *m* quirografario
f créancier *m* chirographaire; créancier *m* inscrit
i creditore *m* chirografario
n gewone schuldeiser *m*

406 book debt
cf. **unsecured debt**
d Buchschuld *f*
e deuda *f* contabilizada; deuda . contable
f dette *f* comptable
i debito *m* contabile
n boekschuld *f*

407 be *v* **booked as a liability**
cf. **book** *v* **as a liability**
d passivierungspflichtig
e a inscribir en el pasivo
f à inscrire au passif
i da i(n)scrivere al passivo
n te passiveren

408 be *v* **booked as an asset**
cf. **book** *v* **as an asset**
d aktivierungspflichtig
e a inscribir en el activo
f à inscrire à l'actif
i da i(n)scrivere all'attivo
n te activeren

409 book entry; entry; posting ***(US)***
d Bucheintrag *m*; Bucheintragung *f*; Buchung *f*; Buchungsposten *m*; Eintrag *m*; Eintragung *f*; Posten *m*; Verbuchung *f*
e asiento *m* (contable); entrada *f*; partida *f*
f article *m*; écriture *f*; enregistrement *m*; entrée *f*; inscription *f*; passation *f* (d'écriture); poste *m*
i allibramento *m*; entrata *f*; partita *f*; registrazione *f* (contabile); scrittura *f* (contabile); voce *f*

n boeking *f*; boekingspost *m*; geboekte post *m*; post *m*

410 bookkeeper
cf. **accountant**
d Buchführer *m*; Buchhalter *m*; Rechnungsführer *m*
e tenedor *m* de libros
f comptable *m*; teneur *m* de livres
i contabile *m*; ragioniere *m*
n administrateur *m*; boekhouder *n*

411 book loss
d buchmässiger Verlust *m*; Buchverlust *m*
e pérdida *f* contable
f perte *f* comptable
i perdita *f* contabile
n boekverlies *n*

412 book profit
d Buchgewinn *m*; buchmässiger Gewinn *m*; buchmässiger Mehrwert *m*
e beneficio *m* contable; plusvalía *f* contable; utilidad *f* contable
f bénéfice *m* comptable; plus-value *f* comptable
i plusvalore *m* contabile; utile *m* contabile
n boekhoudkundige meerwaarde *f*; boekwinst *f*

413 boom
d Boom *m*; Hausse *f*; Hochkonjunktur *f*
e alta coyuntura *f*; auge *m*
f boom *m*; hausse *f*; haute conjoncture *f*
i alta congiuntura *f*; boom *m*; supercongiuntura *f*
n boom *m*; hausse *f*; hoge conjunctuur *f*; hoogconjunctuur *f*

414 boomflation
d Boomflation *f*
e boomflación *f*
f boomflation *f*
i boomflazione *f*
n boomflatie *f*

415 borrow *v*
d borgen; entleihen; entnehmen; leihen
e emprestar *(rare)*; pedir prestado; recibir prestado; tomar a (en) préstamo; tomar prestado
f emprunter
i mutuare; prendere a prestito; prendere in prestito
n lenen; ontlenen *(B)*

416 borrow *v* **capital; procure** *v* **capital; raise** *v* **capital**
cf. **mobilize**
d Kapital aufbringen; Kapital aufnehmen; Kapital beschaffen
e procurarse capital; proporcionarse capital; recoger capital; reunir capital; tomar capital en préstamo; tomar prestado capital
f emprunter du capital; rassembler des capitaux; réunir des capitaux; se procurer des capitaux
i mutuare capitale; prendere capitale in prestito; procacciarsi capitale; procurarsi capitale; raccogliere capitali
n kapitaal bijeenbrengen; kapitaal lenen; kapitaal opnemen

417 borrowed capital; borrowed funds; outside capital; outside funds
cf. **loanable capital**
d Fremdkapital *n*; Fremdmittel *npl*; Kreditkapital *n*; Leihkapital *n*; Schuldkapital *n*
e capital *m* ajeno; capital *m* prestado; capital *m* tomado en préstamo; fondos *mpl* ajenos; fondos *mpl* prestados; fondos *mpl* tomados en préstamo
f capitaux *mpl* d'emprunt; capitaux *mpl* empruntés; fonds *mpl* empruntés; fonds *mpl* étrangers *(Schw)*
i capitale *m* altrui; capitale *m* di credito; capitale *m* mutuato; capitale *m* prestato; fondi *mpl* attinti al credito
n geleend kapitaal *n*; vreemd kapitaal *n*; vreemd vermogen *n*

418 borrower
d Anleihenehmer *m*; Borger *m*; Darleh(e)nsnehmer *m*; Entleiher *m*; Geldaufnehmer *m*; Geldleiher *m*; Geldnehmer *m*; Kreditnehmer *m*
e beneficiario *m* de(l) crédito; mutuario *m*; mutuatario *m*; prestatario *m*; tomador *m* de(l) crédito
f bénéficiaire *m* du crédit; emprunteur *m*; usager *m* du crédit
i beneficiario *m* del credito; mutuatario *m*; prenditore *m* del credito
n geldnemer *m*; geldopnemer *m*; kredietnemer *m*; lener *m*; ontlener *m* *(B)*

419 borrowing
d Entleihung *f*; Kreditaufnahme *f*
e préstamo
f emprunt *m*
i prestito *m*
n lening *f*; opnemen *n* van krediet

420 borrowing abroad
d Auslandsverschuldung *f*

e endeudamiento *m* exterior
f endettement *m* extérieur
i indebitamento *m* esterno
n aangaan *n* van schulden in het buitenland

421 borrowing facilities; credit facilities; overdraft facilities
cf. **advance by overdraft**
d Krediterleichterungen *fpl*; Kreditfazilitäten *fpl*
e facilidades *fpl* de crédito
f facilités *fpl* de crédit
i agevolazioni *fpl* creditizie; facilitazioni *fpl* di credito
n kredietfaciliteiten *fpl*

422 borrowing limit; debt ceiling; debt limit
cf. **credit ceiling**
d Verschuldungsgrenze *f*
e límite *m* de endeudamiento
f limite *f* d'endettement; plafond *m* d'endettement
i limite *m* d'indebitamento
n schuldlimiet *f*; schuldplafon(d) *n*

423 borrowing rate; loan rate
d Ausleihungssatz *m*; Darleh(e)nssatz *m*; Darleh(e)nszinssatz *m*
e tipo *m* de intereses de préstamo; tipo *m* de préstamos
f taux *m* d'emprunt; taux *m* des avances; taux *m* d'intérêt de prêt
i tasso *m* d'interesse sul prestito
n leningrentevoet *m*; voorschotrentevoet *m*

424 borrowing requirement
d Darleh(e)nsbedarf *m*
e demanda *f* de préstamos; necesidad *f* de préstamos
f besoin *m* d'emprunts
i fabbisogno *m* di prestiti; necessità *f* di prestiti
n leenbehoefte *f*; leningsbehoefte *f*

425 bought note; broker's contract note; broker's note; contract bought note; contract note
cf. **broker's contract note**
d Schlussnote *f*; Schlussschein *m*
e minuta *f* de compra; nota *f* de compra; nota *f* de contrato; talón *m* de compra
f avis *m* d'opéré; bordereau *m* d'achat; bordereau *m* de contrat; note *f* d'achat
i fissato-bollato *m*; stabilito *m* d'acquisto
n afsluitnota *f*; borderel *n (B)*; koopbriefje *n*; sluitbriefje *n*

426 bounty on exportation; export bonus; export bounty
cf. **export subsidy**
d Ausfuhrprämie *f*; Exportprämie *f*
e prima *f* a la exportación; prima *f* de exportación
f prime *f* à l'exportation; prime *f* d'exportation
i premio *m* all'esportazione; premio *m* d'esportazione
n exportpremie *f*; uitvoerpremie *f*

427 branch
d Aussenstelle *f (rare)*; Filiale *f*; Nebenstelle *f*; Niederlassung *f*; Zweiggeschäft *n*; Zweigniederlage *f*; Zweigniederlassung *f*; Zweigstelle *f*
e filial *m/f*; sucursal *f*
f branche *f*; comptoir *m**; succursale *f*
i filiale *f*; succursale *f*
n bijkantoor *n*; filiaal *n*; succursaal *f (B)*; succursale *f*

* Bank only.

428 break *(in trend)*; **reversal; turn**
d Umbruch *m*; Umschwung *m*
e cambio *m* (repentino)
f renversement *m*; retournement *m*; revirement *m*
i cambiamento *m* (repentino); mutuamento *m* (repentino); rivolgimento *m*
n om(me)keer *m*; wending *f*

429 breakdown; detailed account; detailed analysis *(US)*; **detailed statement; itemized account; itemized statement**
d Abrechnung *f*; detaillierte Aufstellung *f*; Einzelaufstellung *f*; Spezifikation *f*; Spezifizierung *f*
e detalle *m*; especificación *f*; estado *m* detallado
f compte *m* specifié; décompte *m*; détail *m*; état *m* détaillé; spécification *f*
i dettaglio *m*; situazione *f* analitica; specifica *f*; specificazione *f*
n afrekening *f*; specificatie *f*; specificatiestaat *m*

430 break-even point
d Gewinnpunkt *m*; Gewinnschwelle *f*; Gleichgewichtspunkt *m*; Nutzschwelle *f (Schw)*; Rentabilitätsgrenze *f*
e punto *m* de equilibrio; punto *m* muerto; umbral *m* de beneficios; umbral *m* de rentabilidad
f point *m* d'équilibre; point *m* mort; seuil *m* de rentabilité
i punto *m* morto; soglia *f* di redditività
n break-even point *n*; dood punt *n*

431 **break in prices; collapse of prices; slump in prices**
cf. **crumbling of prices**
d Kurseinbruch *m*; Kurssturz *m*; Kurszusammenbruch *m*; Preiseinbruch *m*; Preissturz *m*; Preiszusammenbruch *m*
e baja *f* repentina de las cotizaciones; baja *f* de los precios; caída *f* brusca de las cotizaciones; caída *f* de los precios; hundimiento *m* de las cotizaciones; hundimiento *m* de los precios
f affaissement *m* des cours; affaissement *m* des prix; chute *f* des cours; chute *f* des prix; dégringolade *f* des cours; dégringolade *f* des prix; effondrement *m* des cours; effondrement *m* des prix
i crollo *m* dei corsi; crollo *m* dei prezzi; tracollo *m* dei corsi; tracollo *m* dei prezzi
n ineenstorting *f* van de koersen; ineenstorting *f* van de prijzen; inzinking *f* van de koersen; inzinking *f* van de prijzen; kelderen *n* van de koersen; kelderen *n* van de prijzen; omlaagtuimelen *n* van de koersen; omlaagtuimelen *n* van de prijzen

432 **break-up value; liquidating value; liquidation value; net assets value; realisation value *(UK)*; realization value *(US)***
d Liquidationswert *m*; Realisationswert *m*; Substanzwert *m*
e valor *m* de liquidación; valor *m* de realización
f valeur *f* de liquidation; valeur *f* de réalisation; valeur *f* liquidative
i valore *m* di liquidazione; valore *m* di realizzo
n liquidatiewaarde *f*; realisatiewaarde *f*

433 **bridging finance; interim financing; intermediate financing; temporary financing**
d Überbrückungsfinanzierung *f*; Zwischenfinanzierung *f*
e financiación *f* de transición; financiación *f* interina; financiación *f* provisional; financiación *f* temporal; financiación *f* transitorio; financiamiento *m* de transición; financiamiento *m* interino; financiamiento *m* provisional; financiamiento *m* temporal; financiamiento *m* transitorio
f financement *m* de soudure; financement *m* de transition; financement *m* provisoire; financement *m* intérimaire; financement *m* intermédiaire; financement *m* transitoire
i finanziamento *m* di transizione; finanziamento *m* interinale; finanziamento *m* provvisorio; finanziamento *m* temporaneo; finanziamento *m* transitorio
n overbruggingsfinanciering *f*; tussenfinanciering *f*

434 **bridging loan; interim credit; interim loan; intermediate loan; stopgap loan; temporary credit; temporary loan; transitional credit**
cf. **prefinancing**
d Überbrückungskredit *m*; Zwischenkredit *m*
e crédito *m* de transición; crédito *m* interino; crédito *m* provisional; crédito *m* temporal; crédito *m* transitorio
f crédit *m* de soudure; crédit *m* de transition; crédit *m* intérimaire; crédit *m* intermédiaire; crédit *m* provisoire; crédit *m* temporaire; crédit *m* transitoire
i credito *m* di transizione; credito *m* interinale; credito *m* provvisorio; credito *m* temporaneo; credito *m* transitorio
n overbruggingskrediet *n*; tussentijds krediet *n*

435 **bring *v* forward; carry *v* forward; carry *v* over**
cf. **amount brought forward (to next account)**
d übertragen; vortragen
e trasladar; transportar
f reporter
i riportare
n overbrengen; transporteren

436 **bring *v* in capital; contribute *v* capital; inject *v* capital; put *v* in capital; put *v* up capital**
cf. **furnish *v* capital**
d Kapital beisteuern; Kapital einbringen; Kapital einlegen; Kapital einschiessen; Kapital einschleusen; Kapital einspritzen
e aportar capital; contribuir capital; inyectar capital
f apporter du capital; contribuer du capital; faire apport du capital; injecter du capital; verser du capital
i apportare capitale; conferire capitale; contribuire capitale; immettere capitale; iniettare capitale
n kapitaal inbrengen; kapitaal inleggen; kapitaal insteken; kapitaal storten

437 **broker**
cf. **agent, commission agent, securities broker**

d Makler *m*
e corredor *m*
f courtier *m*
i mediatore *m*; sensale *m*
n makelaar *m*

438 brokerage *(fee)*
cf. **commission**
d Courtage *f*; Maklergebühr *f*; Maklerprovision *f*
e correduría *f*; corretaje *m*
f agio *m*; courtage *m*; frais *mpl* de courtage
i mediazione *f*; senseria *f*
n courtage *f*; makelaarsloon *n*

439 brokerage firm; brokerage house; broker's firm; broker's office; firm of stockbrokers
d Börsenkommissionsgeschäft *n**; Maklerbüro *n*; Maklerfirma *f*
e agencia *f* de corredor; agencia *f* de corretaje; oficina *f* de corredor
f agence *f* de courtage; agence *f* de courtier; bureau *m* de courtier; maison *f* de courtage
i agenzia *f* di mediazione; ufficio *m* di mediazione
n effectenkantoor *n**; makelaarsfirma *f*; makelaarskantoor *n*

* Of stockbroker only.

440 broker's contract note; broker's note; contract note; contract sold note; sold note
cf. **bought note**
d Schlussnote *f*; Schlussschein *m*
e minuta *f* de venta; nota *f* de contrato; nota *f* de venta; talón *m* de venta
f avis *m* d'opéré; bordereau *m* de contrat; bordereau *m* de vente; note *f* de vente
i fissato-bollato *m*; stabilito *m* di vendita
n afsluitnota *f*; borderel *n (B)*; sluitbriefje *n*; verkoopsbriefje *n*

441 budget *(noun)*
d Budget *n*; Etat *m*; Haushaltsplan *m*; Voranschlag *m (Schw)*
e presupuesto *m*
f budget *m*
i bilancio *m*; bilancio *m* di previsione; bilancio *m* preventivo; budget *m*
n begroting *f*; budget *n*

442 budget *(adj.)*; **budgetary**
d Budget-; budgetmässig; etatmässig; Etats-; Haushalts-; haushaltsmässig
e del presupuesto; presupuestario
f budgétaire
i budgetario; del bilancio
n begrotings-; budget-; budgettair

443 budget *v*; **budget** *v* **for; enter** *v* **in the budget; include** *v* **in the budget**
d etatisieren; im Haushaltsplan vorsehen
e incluir en el presupuesto; presupuestar
f budgéter; budgétiser; inscrire au budget
i inserire nel bilancio; stanziare nel bilancio
n budgetteren; op de begroting brengen

444 budget appropriations; budgetary appropriations
d bewilligte Etatsansätze *mpl*; bewilligte Haushaltsmittel *npl*; budgetmässige Bewilligungen *fpl*; budgetmässige Zuwendungen *fpl*; Haushaltszuweisungen *fpl*; Zuwendungen *fpl* aus dem Budget; Zuwendungen *fpl* aus dem Haushaltsplan
e asignaciones *fpl* presupuestarias; fondos *mpl* presupuestados; partidas *fpl* presupuestarias
f affectations *fpl* budgétaires; crédits *mpl* budgétaires
i stanziamenti *mpl* di bilancio
n begrotingsgelden *npl*; begrotingskredieten *npl*; budgetkredieten *npl*

445 budgetary depreciation; revenue shortfall*
d Mindereinnahmen *fpl* der öffentlichen Haushalte
e déficit *mpl* de la recaudación presupuestaria
f moins-values *fpl* budgétaires
i minori entrate *fpl* di bilancio
n budgettaire kapitaalverliezen *npl*

* See also revenue shortfall as separate entry.

446 budgetary expenditure
d Haushaltsausgaben *fpl*
e gastos *mpl* presupuestarios
f dépenses *fpl* budgétaires
i spese *fpl* di bilancio
n begrotingsuitgaven *fpl*

447 budgetary receipts; revenues
d etatmässige Eingänge *mpl*; Haushaltseinnahmen *fpl*
e ingresos *mpl* presupuestarios; recaudaciones *fpl* presupuestarias
f recettes *fpl* budgétaires
i entrate *fpl* di bilancio
n begrotingsinkomsten *fpl*; begrotingsontvangsten *fpl*

448 budgetary year; budget year
cf. **financial year, fiscal year**
d Budgetjahr *n*; Etat(s)jahr *n*; Haushalt(s)-jahr *n*
e año *m* presupuestario; ejercicio *m* presupuestario
f année *f* budgétaire; exercice *m* budgétaire
i anno *m* finanziario; esercizio *m* finanziario
n begrotingsjaar *n*

449 budget estimates
d Haushaltsvoranschläge *mpl*
e previsiones *fpl* presupuestarias
f prévisions *fpl* budgétaires
i previsioni *fpl* di bilancio
n budgettaire ramingen *fpl*

450 budget management
d Haushaltsführung *f*
e gestión *f* presupuestaria
f gestion *f* budgétaire
i gestione *f* di bilancio
n begrotingsbeheer *n*

451 budget projections
d Haushaltsprognosen *fpl*; Haushalts-vorausschätzungen *fpl*
e prognósticos *mpl* presupuestarios
f projections *fpl* budgétaires
i proiezioni *fpl* di bilancio
n begrotingsprognosen *fpl*

452 budget surplus
d Budgetüberschuss *m*; Etatsüber-schuss *m*; Haushaltsüberschuss *m*
e excedente *m* del presupuesto; excedente *m* presupuestario
f excédent *m* budgétaire
i eccedenza *f* di bilancio
n begrotingsoverschot *n*

453 building society
cf. **land bank**
d Bausparkasse *f*
e caja *f* de ahorros para la construcción
f caisse *f* d'épargne à la construction; caisse *f* d'épargne-construction
i cassa *f* di credito edilizio; cassa *f* di risparmio immobiliare
n bouwspaarfonds *n*; bouwspaarkas *f*

454 build *v* **up a reserve; create** *v* **a reserve; form** *v* **a reserve**
d eine Reserve aufbauen; eine Reserve bilden; eine Reserve schaffen
e constituir una reserva; crear una reserva; formar una reserva
f constituer une réserve; créer une réserve; former une réserve
i costituire una riserva; creare una riserva; formare una riserva
n een reserve aanleggen; een reserve creëren; een reserve vormen

455 bull *(noun)*
d Haussespekulant *m*; Haussier *m*
e alcista *m*; especulador *m* al alza
f haussier *m*; spéculateur *m* à la hausse
i rialzista *m*; speculatore *m* al rialzo
n haussespeculant *m*; haussier *m*; speculant *m* à la hausse

456 bull *v*; **buy** *v* **for a rise; go** *v* **a bull; speculate** *v* **for a rise**
d à la Hausse spekulieren; auf Hausse spekulieren
e especular al alza
f spéculer à la hausse
i speculare al rialzo
n à la hausse speculeren

457 bullion; gold and silver bullion
cf. **bar gold**
d Gold *n* und Silber *n* in Barren; ungemünztes Gold *n* und Silber *n*
e oro *m* y plata *f* en barras; oro *m* y plata *f* en lingotes
f matières *fpl* d'or et d'argent
i oro *m* ed argento *m* in barre; oro *m* ed argento *m* in lingotti; oro *m* ed argento *m* in verghe
n goud *n* en zilver *n* in baren; goud *n* en zilver *n* in staven; ongemunt goud *n* en zilver *n*

458 bullish market; bull market
d Haussebörse *f*; Haussemarkt *m*
e mercado *m* alcista
f marché *m* à la hausse; marché *m* orienté à la hausse
i mercato *m* al rialzo; mercato *m* orientato al rialzo
n haussemarkt *f*

459 bullish tone; bullish trend; rising trend; uptrend; upward(s) trend
d aufsteigende Tendenz *f*; Hausse-neigung *f*; Haussestimmung *f*; Hausse-tendenz *f*; steigende Tendenz *f*; Tendenz *f* zum Steigen
e tendencia *f* al alza; tendencia *f* alcista; tendencia *f* ascendente
f orientation *f* vers la hausse; tendance *f* à la hausse; tendance *f* ascendante; tendance *f* ascensionnelle
i tendenza *f* al rialzo

n haussestemming *f*; neiging *f* tot stijgen; opgaande tendens *f*; tendens *f* tot stijgen

460 burden; charge; encumbrance; incumbrance
d Belastung *f*; Last *f*
e carga *f*; gravamen *m*
f charge *f*
i carico *m*; gravame *m*; onere *m*
n bezwaring *f*; last *m*

461 burden centre *(UK)*; **cost center** *(US)*; **cost centre** *(UK)*
d Kostenstelle *f*
e centro *m* de costes; sección *f* de costes
f centre *m* de coûts; section *f* de coûts
i centro *m* di costi
n kostenplaats *f*

462 burden of debts; indebtedness
cf. **debts**
d Schuldenlast *f*; Verschuldung *f*
e carga *f* de deudas; endeudamiento *m*
f charge *f* des dettes; endettement *m*; poids *m* des dettes
i carico *m* dei debiti; indebitamento *m*
n schuldenlast *m*

463 burden of taxation; tax burden
d Steuerbelastung *f*; Steuerdruck *m*; Steuerlast *f*; steuerliche Belastung *f*
e carga *f* de los impuestos; carga *f* de los tributos; carga *f* fiscal; presión *f* fiscal
f charge *f* fiscale; poids *m* de la fiscalité; poids *m* des impôts
i aggravio *m* fiscale; carico *m* fiscale; onere *m* fiscale; pressione *f* fiscale
n belastingdruk *m*; fiscale last *m*

464 burden variance *(US)*; **overhead variance**
d Gemeinkostenabweichung *f*
e desviación *f* sobre gastos indirectos
f écart *m* sur frais indirects
i differenza *f* sui costi indiretti
n verschil *n* algemene kosten

465 burden *v* **with a mortgage; encumber** *v* **with a mortgage**
cf. **mortgage** *v*
d hypothekarisch belasten; mit einer Hypothek belasten; mit einer Hypothek beschweren
e gravar con una hipoteca
f grever d'une hypothèque
i gravare di un'ipoteco
n met een hypot(h)eek belasten; met een hypot(h)eek bezwaren

466 burden *v* **with debts; charge** *v* **with debts; encumber** *v* **with debts; load** *v* **with debts**
d mit Schulden beladen; mit Schulden belasten; mit Schulden beschweren
e cargar de deudas; entrampar; gravar con deudas
f charger de dettes; grever de dettes; obérer (de dettes)
i caricare di debiti; gravare di debiti
n met schulden beladen; met schulden belasten; met schulden bezwaren

467 business; business enterprise; enterprise
d Betrieb *m*; Unternehmen *n*; Unternehmung *f (Schw)*
e empresa *f*
f entreprise *f*; fonds *m*
i azienda *f*; impresa *f*
n bedrijf *n*; onderneming *f*

468 business capital; circulating capital; floating assets; floating capital; floating funds; net current assets; operating capital; trading assets; trading capital; trading funds; working assets; working capital; working funds
cf. **current assets**
d Betriebsfonds *m*; Betriebskapital *n*; Betriebsmittel *npl*; Betriebsvermögen *n*; bewegliches Kapital *n*; Geschäftskapital *n*; Geschäftsvermögen *n*; Umlauf(s)kapital *n*; Umlauf(s)mittel *npl*; Umlauf(s)vermögen *n*
e activo *m* circulante; capital *m* activo; capital *m* circulante; capital *m* de comercio; capital *m* de explotación; capital *m* de operación; capital *m* de rotación; capital *m* de trabajo *(AL)*; capital *m* en giro; capital *m* flotante; capital *m* operativo; caudales *mpl* en circulación; fondo(s) *m(pl)* de explotación; fondo(s) *m(pl)* de operación
f actif *m* circulant; capital *m* circulant; capital *m* de roulement; capital *m* d'exploitation; capital *m* engagé; capital *m* flottant; capital *m* mobile; capital *m* mobilier; capital *m* roulant; fonds *m* de commerce; fonds *m* de roulement; fonds *m* d'exploitation
i attivo *m* circolante; capitale *m* circolante; capitale *m* d'esercizio; capitale *m* di rotazione; fondi *mpl* d'esercizio; fondi *mpl* di gestione; fondo *m* d'esercizio; fondo *m* di rotazione
n bedrijfskapitaal *n*; vlottend bedrijfskapitaal *n*; vlottend kapitaal *n*; werkkapitaal *n*

469 **business climate**
d Geschäftslage *f*
e clima *m* de los negocios
f climat *m* des affaires
i clima *m* degli affari
n bedrijfsklimaat *n*

470 **business credit; commercial credit; trade credit**
d Geschäftskredit *m*; Handelskredit *m*; Warenkredit *m*; Wirtschaftskredit *m*
e crédito *m* a la economía; crédito *m* comercial
f crédit *m* à l'économie; crédit *m* commercial
i credito *m* al commercio; credito *m* all'economia; credito *m* commerciale
n handelskrediet *n*

471 **business cycle; economic cycle; trade cycle**
d Konjunkturzyklus *m*; wirtschaftlicher Zyklus *m*; Wirtschaftskreislauf *m*
e ciclo *m* coyuntural; ciclo *m* económico
f cycle *m* conjoncturel; cycle *m* d'affaires; cycle *m* économique
i ciclo *m* congiunturale; ciclo *m* economico
n conjunctuurcyclus *m*

472 **business expenses**
cf. **general charges, operating costs**
d Geschäftsunkosten *pl*
e gastos *mpl* comerciales
f frais *mpl* commerciaux
i spese *fpl* d'esercizio
n zakelijke onkosten *mpl*

473 **business loan; commercial loan; trade loan** *(US)*
d Geschäftskredit *m*; Handelskredit *m*; Warenkredit *m*
e empréstito *m* comercial; préstamo *m* comercial
f emprunt *m* commercial; prêt *m* commercial
i prestito *m* commerciale
n commerciële lening *f*; handelslening *f*

474 **business loss; commercial loss; operating deficit; operating loss; trading deficit; trading loss**
d Betriebsabgang *m*; Betriebsverlust *m*; Geschäftsverlust *m*; Handelsdefizit *n*
e déficit *m* comercial; déficit *m* de explotación; pérdida *f* comercial; pérdida *f* de explotación; pérdida *f* de operación
f déficit *m* commercial; déficit *m* d'exercice; déficit *m* d'exploitation; perte *f* commerciale; perte *f* de gestion; perte *f* d'exploitation; perte *f* en affaires
i deficit *m* commerciale; deficit *m* d'esercizio; perdita *f* commerciale; perdita *f* d'esercizio; perdita *f* di gestione
n bedrijfstekort *n*; bedrijfsverlies *n*; exploitatieverlies *n*; handelsdeficit *n*; handelstekort *n*

475 **business profit; commercial profit; operating profit; trading profit**
cf. **operating surplus**
d Betriebsgewinn *m*; Geschäftsgewinn *m*; Handelsgewinn *m*
e beneficio *m* comercial; beneficio *m* de empresa; beneficio *m* de explotación; utilidades *fpl* de explotación; utilidades *fpl* de operación
f bénéfice *m* commercial; bénéfice *m* d'entreprise; bénéfice *m* d'exploitation
i profitto *m* commerciale; profitto *m* d'esercizio; utile *m* d'esercizio
n bedrijfswinst *f*; exploitatiewinst *f*; handelswinst *f*

476 **business tax** *(US)*; **trade tax**
d Gewerbesteuer *f*
e impuesto *m* sobre las patentes; patente *f*
f impôt *m* des patentes; patente *f*
i patente *f*
n bedrijfsbelasting *f*

477 **business trend; economic trend; economy; state of the economy; trend of business**
cf. **business cycle**
d Konjunktur *f*; Konjunkturablauf *m*; konjunkturelle Entwicklung *f*; Konjunkturentwicklung *f*; Konjunkturverlauf *m*
e coyuntura *f*; evolución *f* coyuntural; evolución *f* de la coyuntura
f conjoncture *f*; évolution *f* conjoncturelle; évolution *f* de la conjoncture
i congiuntura *f*; evoluzione *f* congiunturale; evoluzione *f* della congiuntura
n conjuncturele ontwikkeling *f*; conjunctuur *f*; conjunctuurontwikkeling *f*; conjunctuurverloop *n*

478 **business year; commercial year; trading year; working year**
cf. **company financial year, financial year**
d Betriebsjahr *n*; Geschäftsjahr *n*
e año *m* comercial; ejercicio *m* (comercial)
f année *f* commerciale; exercice *m*

(commercial)
i anno *m* commerciale; esercizio *m* (commerciale)
n bedrijfsjaar *n*; dienstjaar *n*; verslagjaar *n*

479 **buy** *v*; **purchase** *v*
cf. **acquire** *v*
d abkaufen; abnehmen; ankaufen; einkaufen; erstehen; kaufen
e comprar
f acheter
i comp(e)rare
n aankopen; afkopen; afnemen; inkopen; kopen

480 **buy** *v* **back; repurchase** *v*
d rückkaufen; wiederkaufen; zurückkaufen
e readquirir; volver a comprar
f racheter
i riacquistare; ricomp(e)rare
n terugkopen; wederaankopen; wederkopen

481 **buy** *v* **by instal(l)ments; buy** *v* **on hire purchase; buy** *v* **on the instal(l)ment plan** *(US)*; **buy** *v* **on the instal(l)ment system** *(US)*; **buy** *v* **on the never-never** *(col.)*
d auf Abzahlung kaufen; auf Raten kaufen; auf Ratenzahlung kaufen; auf Stottern kaufen *(col.)*; auf Teilzahlung kaufen
e comprar a pagos parciales; comprar a plazos
f acheter à tempérament
i comp(e)rare a rate; comp(e)rare ratealmente
n in huurkoop nemen; op afbetaling kopen

482 **buyer; purchaser; vendee**
d Abnehmer *m*; Ankäufer *m*; Einkäufer *m*; Erwerber *m*; Käufer *m*
e adquirente *m*; comprador *m*
f acheteur *m*; acquéreur *m*; preneur *m*
i acquirente *m*; compratore *m*
n afkoper *m*; afnemer *m*; inkoper *m*; koper *m*; verkrijger *m*; verwerver *m*

483 **buyer's market; buyers' market**
d Käufermarkt *m*
e mercado *m* de compradores
f marché *m* acheteur; marché *m* d'acheteurs; marché *m* des acheteurs
i mercato *m* d'acquirenti; mercato *m* di compratori
n kopersmarkt *f*

484 **buyer's option; call; call option; option to buy; option to purchase**
cf. **call premium, purchase option**
d Bezugsoption *f*; Kaufoption *f*
e opción *f* de compra
f option *f* d'achat
i opzione *f* d'acquisto
n koopoptie *f*

485 **buyer's option to double; call of more; option to repeat*; repeat option***
d Kauf *m* mit dem Recht des Nachforderns; Kauf *m* mit einmal noch; Nachgeschäft *n* in Käufers Wahl; Noch *n* in Käufers Wahl; Nochgeschäft *n* auf Nehmen; Nochgeschäft *n* in Käufers Wahl; Nochgeschäft *n* nach oben; Nochprämiengeschäft *n* in Käufers Wahl
e transacción *f* facultativa a opción del comprador
f doublé *m* à la hausse; doublure *f* à la hausse; faculté *f* à la hausse; faculté *f* de lever double
i facoltà *f* al rialzo; facoltà *f* di ritirare il doppio; transazione *f* facoltativa d'acquisto
n nochaffaire *f* in kopers keuze; premieaffaire *f* met noch in kopers keuze; premieaffaire *f* met noch te leveren

* Can mean seller's option to double, q.v. under option to repeat.

486 **buy** *v* **for future delivery; buy** *v* **for (the) settlement; buy** *v* **forward; purchase** *v* **for future delivery; purchase** *v* **for (the) settlement; purchase** *v* **forward**
d auf Lieferung kaufen; auf Termin kaufen; auf Zeit kaufen; auf Ziel kaufen
e comprar a plazo; comprar a término
f acheter à terme
i comp(e)rare a termine
n op termijn kopen

487 **buying power; purchasing power**
d Kaufkraft *f*
e poder *m* adquisitivo; poder *m* de compra
f pouvoir *m* d'achat
i potere *m* d'acquisto
n koopkracht *f*

488 **buying price; purchase price; purchasing price**
cf. **bid price, cost of acquisition**
d Anschaffungskosten *pl*; Anschaffungspreis *m*; Einkaufskosten *pl*; Einkaufspreis *m*; Erwerbskosten *pl*; Erwerbspreis *m*; Kaufpreis *m*
e coste *m* de adquisición; coste *m* de compra; gastos *mpl* de adquisición; precio *m* de adquisición; precio *m* de compra
f frais *mpl* d'achat; prix *m* d'achat; prix

m d'acquisition
i costi *mpl* d'acquisto; prezzo *m* d'acquisto
n aankoopprijs *m*; aanschaffingskosten *mpl*; aanschaffingsprijs *m*; inkoopprijs *m*; koopprijs *m*

489 buy *v* **up**
d aufkaufen
e acaparar; acopiar
f accaparer; rafler
i accaparrare; incettare
n opkopen

C

490 **calculate** *v*; **compute** *v*; **reckon** *v*; **work** *v* **out**
d ausrechnen; berechnen; errechnen; kalkulieren; rechnen
e calcular; computar
f calculer; computer; supputer
i calcolare; computare
n berekenen; calculeren; rekenen; uitrekenen

491 **calculating error; error in calculation; miscalculation; miscount; mistake in calculation**
d Fehler *m* in der Berechnung; Fehlkalkulation *f*; Fehlrechnung *f*; Kalkulationsfehler *m*; Rechenfehler *m*; Rechnungsfehler *m*
e cálculo *m* erróneo; error *m* de cálculo
f calcul *m* erroné; erreur *f* de calcul; faute *f* de calcul; mécompte *m*
i calcolo *m* errato; calcolo *m* sbagliato; errore *m* di calcolo
n fout *f* in de berekening; misrekening *f*; rekenfout *f*

492 **calculation; computation**
d Ausrechnung *f*; Berechnung *f*; Errechnung *f*; Kalkulation *f*; Rechnung *f*
e cálculo *m*; cómputo *m*
f calcul *m*; calculation *f*; computation *f*; supputation *f*
i calcolazione *f*; calcolo *m*; computazione *f*; computo *m*
n berekening *f*; calculatie *f*; rekening *f*; uitrekening *f*

493 **calendar year; civil year** *(rare)*
d Kalenderjahr *n*
e año *m* civil
f année *f* civile
i anno *m* civile
n kalenderjaar *n*

494 **call; call for funds**
d Aufforderung *f* zur Einzahlung; Aufforderung *f* zur Nachzahlung; Einzahlungsaufforderung *f*; Nachzahlungsaufforderung *f*
e llamamiento *m* de fondos; requerimiento *m* de liberación
f appel *m* de fonds; appel *m* de versement
i richiesta *f* di fondi; richiesta *f* di versamento
n opvraging *f* van bijstorting; opvraging *f* van storting

495 **at call; on call; on demand; on request**
cf. **on presentation**
d auf Abruf; auf Antrag; auf Aufforderung; auf Verlangen
e a (la) demanda
f sur demande
i a richiesta; su domanda
n op aanvraag; op verzoek

496 **callable; withdrawable**
cf. **redeemable, refundable**
d abhebbar; abrufbar; aufkündbar; einforderbar; kündbar
e exigible; retirable
f exigible; retirable
i che si può prelevare; esigibile
n opeisbaar; opvorderbaar

497 **callable bond; callable debenture; optional bond** *(US)*; **redeemable bond; redeemable debenture**
d auslösbare Obligation *f*; auslösbare Schuldverschreibung *f*; einlösbare Obligation *f*; einlösbare Schuldverschreibung *f*; einziehbare Obligation *f*; einziehbare Schuldverschreibung *f*; kündbare Obligation *f*; kündbare Schuldverschreibung *f*; rückzahlbare Obligation *f*; rückzahlbare Schuldverschreibung *f*; tilgbare Obligation *f*; tilgbare Schuldverschreibung *f*; zurückzahlbare Obligation *f*; zurückzahlbare Schuldverschreibung *f*
e obligación *f* amortizable; obligación *f* redimible; obligación *f* reembolsable; obligación *f* rescatable
f obligation *f* amortissable; obligation *f* rachetable; obligation *f* remboursable
i obbligazione *f* ammortizzabile; obbligazione *f* redimibile; obbligazione *f* rimborsabile; obbligazione *f* riscattabile
n afkoopbare obligatie *f*; aflosbare obligatie *f*; amortiseerbare obligatie *f*

498 **callable by lot; redeemable by lot**
d auslosbar; verlosbar
e redimible por sorteo; reembolsable por sorteo; sorteable
f amortissable par tirage (au sort); remboursable par tirage (au sort); tirable au sort
i redimibile per estrazione a sorte; rimborsabile per estrazione a sorte; sorteggiabile
n aflosbaar door loting; uitlootbaar

499 **callable capital**
d einforderbares Kapital *n*

e capital *m* exigible
f capital *m* exigible
i capitale *m* esigibile
n opvraagbaar kapitaal *n*

500 called in capital; called up capital
cf. **paid in capital**
d eingefordertes Kapital *n*; zur Einzahlung aufgerufenes Kapital *n*
e capital *m* exigido; capital *m* llamado (a integración) *(AL)*
f capital *m* appelé
i capitale *m* richiamato
n opgevraagd kapitaal

501 call for additional cover; margin call
d Aufforderung *f* zur Nachschusszahlung; Nachschussaufforderung *f*
e requerimiento *m* de cobertura adicional; requerimiento *m* de margen adicional
f appel *m* de marge; demande *f* de couverture supplémentaire
i richiesta *f* di copertura supplementare; richiesta *f* di margine supplementare
n opvraging *f* van aanvullende dekking

502 call *v* **in** *(bonds)*; **redeem** *v*; **retire** *v*
d ablösen; amortisieren; aufrufen; aus dem Verkehr ziehen; auslösen; einlösen; kündigen; rückkaufen; tilgen; zurückkaufen
e amortizar; redimir; reembolsar; rescatar; retirar
f amortir; racheter; rembourser; retirer; retraire
i ammortare; ammortizzare; redimere; rimborsare; riscattare; ritirare
n aan de circulatie onttrekken; aflossen; amortiseren; amortizeren; delgen; inkopen; lossen

503 call *v* **in (from circulation); demonetize** *v*; **recall** *v* **(from circulation); retire** *v* **(from circulation); withdraw** *v* **(from circulation)**
d aus dem Umlauf zurückziehen; ausser Kurs setzen; ausser Umlauf setzen; demonetisieren; einziehen; entwerten
e desmonetizar; retirar (de la circulación)
f démonétiser; retirer (de la circulation)
i demonetizzare; ritirare (dalla circolazione)
n aan de circulatie onttrekken; buiten omloop stellen; demonetiseren; ontmunten*

* Coins only.

504 call loan; day-to-day loan; demand loan; overnight loan; sight loan
d jederzeit kündbares Darleh(e)n *n*; Sichtdarleh(e)n *n*; Tagesgelddarleh(e)n *n*; täglich kündbares Darleh(e)n *n*
e préstamo *m* a la vista; préstamo *m* de día a día; préstamo *m* diario; préstamo *m* revocable de día en día
f prêt *m* au jour le jour; prêt *m* à vue
i prestito *m* a vista; prestito *m* giornaliero; prestito *m* giorno per giorno
n daggeldlening *f*; zichtlening *f*

505 call money; day-to-day money; money at call; money on call; overnight money
cf. **call loan**
d Callgeld *n*; Geld *n* auf Abruf; Tagesgeld *n*; tägliches Geld *n*; täglich fälliges Geld *n*
e dinero *m* a la vista; dinero *m* de día a día; dinero *m* de vencimiento diario; dinero *m* diario
f argent *m* au jour le jour; argent *m* à vue; call money *m*
i denaro *m* alla giornata; denaro *m* a vista; denaro *m* giornaliero
n callgeld *n*; call-money *n*; daggeld *n*

506 call on the market
d Beanspruchung *f* des Marktes
e llamamiento *m* al mercado; recurso *m* al mercado
f appel *m* au marché
i appello *m* al mercato; ricorso *m* al mercato
n beroep *n* op de markt

507 call premium; premium for the call
cf. **buyer's option**
d Bezugsprämie *f*; Dontprämie *f*; Hausseprämie *f*; Lieferungsprämie *f*; Vorprämie *f*
e prima *f* al alza; prima *f* a recibir; prima *f* de opción de compra
f prime *f* acheteur; prime *f* à la hausse; prime *f* dont; prime *f* pour l'acheteur; prime *f* pour lever; prime *f* simple à la hausse
i premio *m* al rialza; premio *m* a ricevere; premio *m* d'acquisto; premio *m* di cui; premio *m* dont; premio *m* per non ritirare
n dontpremie *f*; haussepremie *f*; premie *f* te leveren

508 calm *(of market)*; **dead; depressed; dull; flat** *(UK)*; **inactive; languid; languishing; lifeless; listless; quiet; sagging; slack; sluggish; stagnant; weak**
d flau; gedrückt; leblos; lustlos; matt; ruhig; schwach; stagnierend; still; stockend;

unbelebt; unlustig
e abatido; apático; débil; deprimido; desanimado; estacionario; estancado; flojo; inactivo; lánguido; muerto; parado; paralizado; poco animado; quieto; tranquilo
f atone; calme; creux; déprimé; faible; inactif; inanimé; languissant; lourd; mort; mou; peu animé; stagnant; terne
i calmo; debole; depresso; fiacco; inattivo; languente; languido; morto; paralizzato; pesante; poco animato; stagnante
n flauw; gedrukt; kalm; kwijnend; loom; lui; lusteloos; mat; slap; stagnerend; stilstaand; traag; zonder animo; zwak

509 **cambist; currency dealer; exchange broker; foreign exchange dealer; money changer; money dealer**
cf. **bill broker**
d Cambist *m (Schw)*; Devisenhändler *m*; Devisenmakler *m*; Geldwechsler *m*; Sortenhändler *m*; Valutenhändler *m*; Valutenmakler *m*; Wechselhändler *m*; Wechselmakler *m*; Wechsler *m*
e agente *m* de cambio(s); agente *m* de divisas; cambista *m*; corredor *m* de divisas; negociante *m* en divisas
f agent *m* de change; cambiste *m*; changeur *m* (de monnaie); courtier *m* de change; courtier *m* en devises
i agente *m* di cambio; cambiamonete *m*; cambiavalute *m*; cambista *m*
n cambist *m (rare)*; deviezenhandelaar *m*; deviezenmakelaar *m*; geldwisselaar *m*; valutahandelaar *m*; valutamakelaar *m*; wisselaar *m*; wisselmakelaar *m*

510 **cancel** *v* **a debt; remit** *v* **a debt; waive** *v* **a debt**
cf. **write** *v* **off a debt**
d eine Schuld erlassen; eine Schuld löschen; eine Schuld nachlassen; eine Schuld niederschlagen; eine Schuld streichen
e cancelar una deuda; castigar una deuda; condonar una deuda; remitir una deuda
f éteindre une dette; faire remise d'une dette; radier une dette; remettre une dette
i cancellare un debito; rimettere un debito
n een schuld kwijtschelden; een schuld schenken *(col.)*

511 **cancel** *v* **a mortgage; extinguish** *v* **a mortgage; pay** *v* **back a mortgage; pay** *v* **off a mortgage; redeem** *v* **a mortgage; repay** *v* **a mortgage; satisfy** *v* **a mortgage; wipe** *v* **off a mortgage**
d eine Hypothek ablösen; eine Hypothek abtragen; eine Hypothek abzahlen; eine Hypothek amortisieren; eine Hypothek einlösen; eine Hypothek löschen; eine Hypothek tilgen; eine Hypothek zurückzahlen
e amortizar una hipoteca; cancelar una hipoteca; desempeñar una hipoteca; deshipotecar; extinguir una hipoteca; redimir una hipoteca; reembolsar una hipoteca; rescatar una hipoteca
f amortir une hypothèque; déshypothéquer; éteindre une hypothèque; purger une hypothèque; racheter une hypothèque; rembourser une hypothèque
i ammortizzare un'ipoteca; cancellare un'ipoteca; disipotecare; estinguere un'ipoteca; redimere un'ipoteca; rimborsare un'ipoteca; riscattare un'ipoteca
n een hypot(h)eek afbetalen; een hypot(h)eek aflossen; een hypot(h)eek amortiseren; een hypot(h)eek delgen; een hypot(h)eek terugbetalen

512 **cancellation** *(of an entry)*; **reversal**
d Stornierung *f*; Stornobuchung *f*
e anulación *f*; rescuentro *m*
f annulation *f*; contrepassation *f*; extourne *f*
i annullamento *m*; storno *m*
n storno *m*; stornoboeking *f*; terugboeking *f*

513 **cancellation of a debt; remission of a debt; waiver of a debt**
d Erlass *m* einer Schuld; Schuldenerlass *m*; Schuldennachlass *m*; Schuldenstreichung *f*; Schulderlass *m*
e cancelación *f* de una deuda; condonación *f* de una deuda; exención *f* de una deuda; remisión *f* de una deuda
f remise *f* d'une dette; remission *f* d'une dette
i remissione *f* di un debito
n kwijtschelding *f* van een schuld

514 **capital**
cf. **funds, principal**
d Kapital *n*
e capital *m*
f capital *m*
i capitale *m*
n kapitaal *n*

515 **capital abroad; capital held abroad; foreign capital*; overseas capital** *(UK)*
d Auslandskapital *n**; Kapital *n* im Ausland

e capital *m* en el extranjero
f capitaux *mpl* à l'étranger
i capitale *m* all'estero
n buitenlands kapitaal *n**; kapitaal *n* in het buitenland

* Can also mean foreign owned capital (q.v. sub foreign capital).

516 **capital account**
d Kapitalkonto *n*
e cuenta *f* de capital
f compte *m* capital; compte *m* capitaux; compte *m* de capital
i conto *m* capitale; conto *m* di capitale
n kapitaalrekening *f*

517 **capital allowance; investment allowance**
d steuerlich zulässige Abschreibungen *fpl*
e amortizaciones *fpl* fiscales
f amortissements *mpl* fiscalement admis
i ammortamento *m* fiscale
n fiscale afschrijving *f*

518 **capital assets; fixed assets; fixed capital; tied-up capital**
cf. **material assets**
d Anlagekapital *n*; Anlagevermögen *n*; feste Aktiven *npl*; feste Kapitalanlagen *fpl*; festes Kapital *n*; festgelegtes Kapital *n*; Kapitalvermögen *n*; Sachanlagen *fpl*; Sachinvestitionen *fpl*
e activo *m* fijo; activo *m* inmovilizado; activo *m* permanente; capital *m* fijo; capital *m* inmovilizado; inmovilizaciones *fpl* corporales; inmovilizaciones *fpl* reales; inmovilizaciones *fpl* tangibles; inversiones *fpl* reales; valores *mpl* inmovilizados
f actif *m* immobilisé; actif *m* permanent; capital *m* fixe; capital *m* immobilisé; capitaux *mpl* fixes; immobilisations *fpl* (corporelles); valeurs *fpl* immobilisées
i attivi *mpl* fissi; attivi *mpl* immobilizzati; attività *fpl* immobilizzate; attivo *m* fisso; capitale *m* fisso; capitale *m* immobile; capitale *m* immobilizzato; immobilizzazioni *fpl*; investimenti *mpl* immobiliari
n materiële duurzame activa *npl*; vaste activa *npl*; vastgelegd kapitaal *n*; vast kapitaal *n*; vastliggend kapitaal *n*

519 **capital budget**
d Investitionsbudget *n*; Investitionshaushalt *m*
e presupuesto *m* de inversiones
f budget *m* d'investissement
i bilancio *m* (preventivo) d'investimenti
n investeringsbegroting *f*

520 **capital charges**
d Kapitallasten *fpl*
e cargas *fpl* de capital
f charges *fpl* de capital
i oneri *mpl* di capitale
n kapitaallasten *mpl*

521 **capital contribution; contribution to capital; injection of capital; investment boost**
cf. **capital invested, capital subscription, payment of capital**
d Einschuss *m*; Investitionsspritze *f*; Kapitaleinbringen *n*; Kapitaleinbringung *f*; Kapitaleinlage *f*; Kapitaleinschuss *m*
e aportación *f* de capital; aporte *m* de capital; inyección *f* de capital
f apport *m* de capital; apport *m* de fonds; capital-apport *m*; injection *f* de capital; mise *f* de fonds
i apporto *m* di capitale; conferimento *m* di capitale; iniezione *f* di capitale
n kapitaalinbreng *m*

522 **capital cost; cost of capital**
d Kapitalkosten *pl*
e costo *m* del capital
f coût *m* du capital
i costo *m* del capitale
n kapitaalkosten *mpl*

523 **capital endowment; capital equipment; capitalisation** *(UK)*; **capitalization** *(US)*
cf. **capital structure**
d Kapitalausrüstung *f*; Kapitalausstattung *f*; Kapitalisierung *f*
e capitalización *f*; dotación *f* de capital
f capitalisation *f*; dotation *f* en capital
i capitalizzazione *f*; dotazione *f* di capitale
n kapitalisatie *f*; kapitaaluitrusting *f*

524 **capital expenditure(s); capital outlay(s); capital spending; investment expenditure(s); investment spending**
d Ausgaben *fpl* in Kapitalrechnung; Kapitalaufwand *m*; Kapitalaufwendungen *fpl*; Kapitalausgaben *fpl*; Kapitalauslagen *fpl*; Investitionsaufwand *m*; Investitionsaufwendungen *fpl*; Investitionsausgaben *fpl*; investive Ausgaben *fpl*; vermögenswirksame Ausgaben *fpl*
e desembolsos *mpl* de capital; egresos *mpl* de capital *(AL)*; gastos *mpl* de capital; gastos *mpl* de inversión
f dépenses *fpl* de capital; dépenses *fpl* d'investissement; dépenses *fpl* en capital; dépenses *fpl* en immobilisation(s)

i spese *fpl* d'immobilizzo; spese *fpl* d'investimento; spese *fpl* in capitale
n investeringsuitgaven *fpl*; kapitaaluitgaven *fpl*

525 **capital export country; capital exporting country**
d Kapitalausfuhrland *n*; Kapital exportierendes Land *n*
e país *m* exportador de capital
f pays *m* exportateur de capitaux
i paese *m* esportatore di capitali
n kapitaalexportland *n*

526 **capital exports; export of capital**
d Kapitalausfuhr *f*; Kapitalexport *m*
e exportación *f* de capital(es)
f exportation *f* de capitaux
i esportazione *f* di capitali
n kapitaalexport *m*; kapitaaluitvoer *m*

527 **capital flight; flight of capital**
d Kapitalflucht *f*
e evasión *f* de capitales; fuga *f* de capitales; huída *f* de capitales
f évasion *f* de capitaux; fuite *f* de capitaux
i evasione *f* di capitali; fuga *f* di capitali
n kapitaalvlucht *f*

528 **capital flow; flow of capital; flux of capital**
cf. **capital movement**
d Kapitalstrom *m*
e flujo *m* de capital(es)
f flux *m* de capitaux; flux *m* financier
i flusso *m* di capitali
n kapitaalstroom *m*

529 **capital formation; formation of capital**
d Kapitalbildung *f*
e formación *f* de capital
f formation *f* de capital
i costituzione *f* di capitale; formazione *f* di capitale
n kapitaalvorming *f*

530 **capital gain**
cf. **capital income**
d Kapitalgewinn *m*
e beneficio *m* de capital; ganancia *f* de capital; utilidad *f* de capital
f bénéfice *m* en capital; gain *m* en capital
i guadagno *m* di capitale; utile *m* di capitale
n kapitaalwinst *f*

531 **capital gain(s)** ***(from transfer)***
d Liquidationsgewinn *m (Schw)*; Veräusserungsgewinn *m*
e plusvalía *f* de cesión
f plus-value *f* de cession
i plusvalenza *f* di cessione
n vervreemdingswinst *f*; winst *f* bij vervreemding

532 **capital gains tax**
cf. **capital yield(s) tax**
d Kapitalgewinnabgabe *f*; Kapitalgewinnsteuer *f*; Kapitalzuwachssteuer *f*; Steuer *f* auf Veräusserungsgewinne
e impuesto *m* sobre el aumento del capital; impuesto *m* sobre el beneficio de capital; impuesto *m* sobre el incremento del capital; impuesto *m* sobre la plusvalía de cesión; impuesto *m* sobre la plusvalía del capital; impuesto *m* sobre las ganancias de capital
f impôt *m* sur le(s) gain(s) en capital; impôt *m* sur les plus-values de cession
i imposta *f* sull'aumento del capitale; imposta *f* sulle plusvalenze
n belasting *f* op de meerwaarde; belasting *f* op de gerealiseerde waardestijging; belasting *f* op kapitaalwinst; kapitaalwinstbelasting *f*; vermogensaanwasbelasting *f*

533 **capital goods; investment goods**
cf. **durable means of production**
d Anlagegüter *npl*; Kapitalgüter *npl*; Investitionsgüter *npl*
e bienes *mpl* de capital; bienes *mpl* de inversión
f biens *mpl* de capital; biens *mpl* d'investissement
i beni *mpl* d'investimento; beni *mpl* strumentali
n investeringsgoederen *npl*; kapitaalgoederen *npl*

534 **capital imports; import of capital**
d Kapitaleinfuhr *f*; Kapitalimport *m*
e importación *f* de capital(es)
f importation *f* de capitaux
i importazione *f* di capitali
n kapitaalimport *m*; kapitaalinvoer *m*

535 **capital income; capital return; capital yield; income from capital; return on capital; revenue from capital; yield of capital**
cf. **capital gain(s), capital interest, income from investments, unearned income**
d Kapitaleinkommen *n*; Kapitaleinkünfte *fpl*; Kapitalertrag *m*; Kapitalerträgnisse *npl*; Kapitalrendite *f*; Kapitalrente *f*; Kapitalverzinsung *f*

e ingresos *mpl* del capital; rédito *m* del capital; remuneración *f* del capital; rendimiento *m* del capital; renta(s) *f(pl)* del capital
f produit *m* du capital; rapport *m* du capital; rémunération *f* du capital; rendement *m* du capital; rente *f* du capital; revenu *m* du capital
i reddito *m* del capitale; remunerazione *f* del capitale; rendimento *m* del capitale; rendita *f* del capitale; rimunerazione *f* del capitale
n inkomen *n* uit kapitaal; inkomsten *fpl* uit kapitaal; kapitaalinkomen *n*; kapitaalinkomsten *fpl*; kapitaal-opbrengst *f*; kapitaalrendement *n*; kapitaalrente *f*

536 **capital increase; increase of capital**
d Kapitalaufstockung *f*; Kapital-ausweitung *f*; Kapitalerhöhung *f*; Kapital-vermehrung *f*
e ampliación *f* de capital; aumento *m* de capital; elevación *f* de capital
f accroissement *m* de capital; augmentation *f* de capital
i aumento *m* di capitale
n kapitaaluitbreiding *f*; kapitaalvergroting *f*; kapitaalverhoging *f*

537 **capital intensification**
d Verstärkung *f* der Kapitalintensität
e aumento *m* de la intensidad de capital
f accroissement *m* de l'intensité de capital
i aumento *m* dell'intensità del capitale
n versterking *f* van de kapitaalintensiteit

538 **capital intensity**
d Kapitalintensität *f*
e intensidad *f* de capital
f intensité *f* de capital
i intensità *f* del capitale
n kapitaalintensiteit *f*

539 **capital-intensive; highly capitalized**
d kapitalintensiv
e con alta proporción de capital
f à fort coefficient de capital; à forte proportion de capital
i fortemente capitalizzato
n kapitaalintensief

540 **capital interest; interest on capital**
cf. **capital income**
d Kapitalinteressen *npl*; Kapital-verzinsung *f*; Kapitalzins(en) *m(pl)*
e interés *m* del capital
f intérêt(s) *m(pl)* du capital
i interesse *m* del capitale
n kapitaalrente *f*

541 **capital invested; invested capital; money sunk** *(UK)*
cf. **capital contribution, investment capital**
d angelegtes Kapital *n*; engagiertes Kapital *n*; investiertes Kapital *n*
e capital *m* colocado; capital *m* investido
f capital *m* engagé; capital *m* investi; capital *m* placé
i capitale *m* impiegato; capitale *m* investito
n belegd kapitaal *n*; geïnvesteerd kapitaal *n*

542 **capital investment; investment of capital**
cf. **employment of capital**
d Kapitalanlage *f*; Kapitalanlegung *f*; Kapitalinvestierung *f*; Kapital-investition *f*
e colocación *f* de capital; inversión *f* de capital
f investissement *m* de capitaux; investissement *m* de fonds; placement *m* de capitaux; placement *m* de fonds
i investimento *m* di capitale
n kapitaalbelegging *f*; kapitaalinvestering *f*

543 **capitalisation** *(UK) (conversion into capital)*; **capitalization** *(US)*
d Kapitalisation *f*; Kapitalisierung *f*
e capitalización *f*
f capitalisation *f*
i capitalizzazione *f*
n kapitalisatie *f*

544 **capitalisation** *(UK)*; **capitalization** *(US)*; **capital stock; corporate capital** *(US)*; **joint stock; share capital; stock*; stock capital**
cf. **authorised capital**
d Aktienkapital *n*; Gesellschaftskapital *n*; Grundkapital *n*; Stammkapital *n*
e capital *m* base; capital *m* básico; capital *m* en acciones; capital *m* social
f capital-actions *m*; capital *m* d'actions; capital *m* social
i capitale *m* azionario; capitale *m* sociale
n aandelenkapitaal *n*; grondkapitaal *n*; maatschappelijk kapitaal *n*; stam-kapitaal *n*; vennootschappelijk kapitaal *n*
* See note sub "stock".

545 **capitalise** *v (UK)*; **capitalize** *v (US)*
d kapitalisieren
e capitalizar

f capitaliser
i capitalizzare
n kapitaliseren

546 **capitalised value** *(UK)*; **capitalized value** *(US)*
d Ertragswert *m*; kapitalisierter Wert *m*
e valor *m* capitalizado; valor *m* de rendimiento
f valeur *f* capitalisée; valeur *f* de rendement
i valore *m* capitalizzato; valore *m* del reddito (potenziale)
n gekapitaliseerde waarde *f*; rentabiliteits-waarde *f*

547 **capitalise** *v* **interest** *(UK)*; **capitalize** *v* **interest** *(US)*
d die Zinsen kapitalisieren; die Zinsen zum Kapital schlagen
e capitalizar los intereses
f capitaliser les intérêts
i capitalizzare gli interessi
n de rente kapitaliseren

548 **capitalise** *v* **profits** *(UK)*; **capitalize** *v* **profits** *(US)*
d Gewinne aktivieren
e capitalizar las ganancias; capitalizar los beneficios
f capitaliser les bénéfices
i capitalizzare gli utili
n de winst kapitaliseren

549 **capital issue**
d Kapitalemission *f*
e emisión *f* de capital
f émission *f* de capitaux
i emissione *f* di capitali
n kapitaaluitgifte *f*

550 **capitalist**
cf. **financier, moneylender**
d Geldmann *m*; Kapitalbesitzer *m*; Kapitalist *m*
e capitalista *m*
f capitaliste *m*
i capitalista *m*
n geldman *m*; kapitaalbezitter *m*; kapitalist *m*

551 **capital levy; capital tax; property tax; tax on capital; wealth tax**
d Besitzsteuer *f*; Kapitalabgabe *f*; Kapital-steuer *f*; Kapitalvermögenssteuer *f*; Vermögensabgabe *f*; Vermögenssteuer *f*
e impuesto *m* a la propiedad; impuesto *m* sobre el capital; impuesto *m* sobre el patrimonio (mueble); impuesto *m* sobre la propiedad
f impôt *m* sur la fortune; impôt *m* sur le capital; impôt *m* sur les capitaux; impôt *m* sur les fortunes; prélèvement *m* sur la fortune; prélèvement *m* sur le capital
i imposta *f* patrimoniale; imposta *f* sul capitale; imposta *f* sulla proprietà; imposta *f* sul patrimonio; prelevamento *m* sul capitale; prelievo *m* sul capitale
n kapitaalbelasting *f (B)*; kapitaalheffing *f*; vermogensbelasting *f*

552 **capital loss; loss of capital**
d Kapitalverlust *m*
e pérdida *f* de capital
f perte *f* de capital; perte *f* en capitaux
i perdita *f* di capitale
n kapitaalverlies *n*

553 **capital loss** *(from transfer)*
d Liquidationsverlust *m (Schw)*; Veräusserungsverlust *m*
e minusvalía *f* de cesión
f moins-value *f* de cession
i minusvalenza *f* di cessione
n vervreemdingsverlies *n*

554 **capital market; finance market; financial market**
cf. **money market**
d Finanzmarkt *m*; Geld- und Kapital-markt *m*; Kapitalmarkt *m*
e mercado *m* de capital(es); mercado *m* financiero
f marché *m* des capitaux; marché *m* financier
i mercato *m* dei capitali; mercato *m* finanziario
n kapitaalmarkt *f*

555 **capital movement; movement of capital**
cf. **capital flow**
d Kapitalbewegung *f*; Kapitalverkehr *m*
e circulación *f* de capital (capitales); movimiento *m* de capital
f circulation *f* de capital (capitaux); mouvement *m* de capital
i circolazione *f* di capitale (capitali); movimento *m* di capitale (capitali)
n kapitaalbeweging *f*; kapitaalverkeer *n*

556 **capital outflow; drain of capital; efflux of capital; emigration of capital; exodus of capital; outflow of capital**
cf. **capital flight**
d Kapitalabfluss *m*; Kapitalabgang *m*; Kapitalabwanderung *f*; Kapital-auswanderung *f*
e drenaje *m* de capitales; emigración *f* de

capitales; éxodo *m* de capitales; salida *f* de capitales
f drainage *m* de capitaux; émigration *f* de capitaux; exode *m* de capitaux; sortie *f* de capitaux
i deflusso *m* di capitali; drenaggio *m* di capitali; efflusso *m* di capitali; emigrazione *f* di capitali; esodo *m* di capitali; uscita *f* di capitali
n afvloeiing *f* van kapitaal; wegvloeiing *f* van kapitaal

557 **capital requirements**
d Kapitalbedarf *m*; Kapitalbedürfnis(se) *n(pl)*
e necesidades *fpl* de capital
f besoins *mpl* en capitaux
i fabbisogno *m* di capitali
n kapitaalbehoefte *f*; vermogensbehoefte *f*

558 **capital resources; financial means; financial resources; funds for financing; means of finance**
cf. **net assets, pecuniary resources**
d Eigenkapital *n*; Eigenmittel *npl*; Eigenvermögen *n*; finanzielle Mittel *npl*; Finanzierungsmittel *npl*; Finanzmittel *npl*; Finanzquellen *fpl*; Kapitalmittel *npl*; Kapitalquellen *fpl*
e medios *mpl* de financiación; medios *mpl* financieros; recursos *mpl* de capital; recursos *mpl* financieros
f fonds *mpl* pour le financement; moyens *mpl* de financement; moyens *mpl* financiers; ressources *fpl* en capital; ressources *fpl* financières
i fondi *mpl* di finanziamento; mezzi *mpl* di finanziamento; mezzi *mpl* finanziari
n financiële middelen *npl*; financieringsmiddelen *npl*

559 **capital shortage; lack of capital; scarcity of capital; shortage of capital; want of capital**
d Kapitalknappheit *f*; Kapitalmangel *m*; Kapitalverknappung *f*
e escasez *f* de capital(es); falta *f* de capital(es); penuria *f* de capital(es); rarefacción *f* de capital(es)
f insuffisance *f* de capitaux; manque *m* de capitaux; pénurie *f* de capitaux; raréfaction *f* de capitaux
i carenza *f* di capitali; deficienza *f* di capitali; mancanza *f* di capitali; penuria *f* di capitali; rarefazione *f* di capitali; scarsità *f* di capitali
n kapitaalgebrek *n*; kapitaalkrapte *f*; kapitaalschaarste *f*

560 **capital stock tax**
d Aktienkapitalsteuer *f*; Gesellschaftskapitalsteuer *f*
e impuesto *m* sobre el capital social
f impôt *m* sur le capital social
i imposta *f* sul capitale azionario; imposta *f* sul capitale sociale
n belasting *f* op het maatschappelijk kapitaal

561 **capital structure; financial structure**
cf. **capital endowment**
d Finanzstruktur *f*; Kapitalstruktur *f*; Kapitalzusammensetzung *f*
e estructura *f* financiera
f structure *f* financière
i struttura *f* finanziaria
n financiële structuur *f*; kapitaalstructuur *f*

562 **capital subscription**
cf. **capital contribution**
d Kapitalzeichnung *f*
e su(b)scripción *f* de capital
f souscription *f* de capital
i sottoscrizione *f* di capitale
n kapitaalinschrijving *f*; kapitaalintekening *f*

563 **capital transfer; transfer of capital**
cf. **foreign transfer, money transfer**
d Kapitaltransfer *m*; Kapitaltransferierung *f*; Kapitalübertragung *f*
e transferencia *f* de capital
f transfert *m* de capitaux; transfert *m* en capital
i trasferimento *m* di capitali
n kapitaaloverdracht *f*; overmaking *f* van kapitaal; transfer *m/n* van kapitaal

564 **capital transfer tax; tax on capital transactions; tax on the movement of capital**
d Kapitalverkehr(s)steuer *f*
e impuesto *m* sobre el movimiento de capital; impuesto *m* sobre la transferencia de capital
f impôt *m* sur les mouvements de capitaux; impôt *m* sur les mutations de capitaux
i imposta *f* sulla circolazione dei capitali
n belasting *f* op het kapitaalverkeer

565 **capital yield(s) tax; tax on distributions**
cf. **capital gains tax**
d Kapitalertragsteuer *f*; Verrechnungssteuer *f (Schw)*
e impuesto *m* sobre el ingreso de capital; impuesto *m* sobre el rendimiento de

capital; impuesto *m* sobre la(s) renta(s) del capital
f impôt *m* sur le revenu des biens mobiliers; impôt *m* sur le revenu des capitaux (mobiliers); impôt *m* sur le revenu des valeurs mobilières; impôt *m* sur le revenu du capital
i imposta *f* sui dividendi e interessi; imposta *f* sui redditi del capitale; imposta *f* sul reddito del capitale
n belasting *f* op de inkomsten uit kapitaal; belasting *f* op het kapitaalinkomen; dividend- en couponbelasting *f*

566 **carry** *v* **a sum to someone's credit; credit** *v* **a sum to someone; credit** *v* **someone with a sum; enter** *v* **a sum to someone's credit; place** *v* **a sum to someone's credit**
cf. **credit** *v* **the account (with)**
d jemandem einen Betrag gutbringen; jemandem einen Betrag gutschreiben; jemandem einen Betrag kreditieren; jemanden für einen Betrag erkennen; jemanden für einen Betrag kreditieren; jemanden mit einem Betrag erkennen; jemanden mit einem Betrag kreditieren
e abonar una suma (en cuenta) a alguien; acreditar a alguien por una suma; llevar una suma al crédito de alguien; pasar una suma al crédito de alguien
f bonifier une somme à quelqu'un; créditer quelqu'un d'une somme; créditer une somme à quelqu'un; passer une somme au crédit de quelqu'un; porter une somme au crédit de quelqu'un
i accreditare a qualcuno una somma; mettere una somma a credito di qualcuno; passare una somma a credito di qualcuno; segnare una somma a credito di qualcuno
n een bedrag in (op) iemands credit boeken; een bedrag in iemands tegoed schrijven; iemand voor een bedrag crediteren; iemand voor een bedrag goedschrijven

567 **carry-over; contango; continuation business**
d Prolongation *f*; Report *m*
e prolongación *f*; reporte *m*; reporto *m* *(AL)*
f prolongation *f (rare)*; report *m*
i riporto *m*
n prolongatie *f*; report *n*

568 **carry** *v* **over a position; contango** *v*; **continue** *v* **a position**
d eine Position prolongieren; eine Position reportieren
e reportar una posición
f reporter une position
i riportare una posizione
n een positie continueren; een positie prolongeren; een positie reporteren

569 **carry-over rate; contango; contango rate; continuation rate**
d Kostgeld *n*; Prolongationsgebühr *f*; Prolongationskurs *m*; Prolongationssatz *m*; Report *m*; Reportgebühr *f*; Reportkurs *m*; Reportprämie *f*; Reportsatz *m*
e gastos *mpl* de prolongación; precio *m* de prolongación; prima *f* de prolongación; reporte *m*; tasa *f* de prolongación; tasa *f* de reporte; tipo *m* de prolongación; tipo *m* de reporte
f cours *m* de prolongation; cours *m* de report; prime *f* de report; prix *m* du report; report *m*; taux *m* du report
i corso *m* di riporto; premio *m* di riporto; prezzo *m* di riporto; riporto *m*; saggio *m* di riporto; tassa *f* di riporto; tasso *m* di riporto
n contango *m*; prolongatiekoers *m*; prolongatiepremie *f*; prolongatierente *f*; prolongatietarief *n*; report *n*; reportkoers *m*

570 **carry** *v* **to account; place** *v* **(in)to account; put** *v* **(in)to account**
cf. **charge** *v* **an account with, charge** *v*
d anrechnen; anschreiben; berechnen; in Ansatz bringen; in Rechnung bringen; in Rechnung stellen
e poner en cuenta; sentar en cuenta
f faire entrer en (ligne de) compte; imputer; mettre en (ligne de) compte; passer en compte; porter en compte
i conteggiare; imputare; mettere in conto
n aanrekenen; berekenen; in rekening brengen

571 **cartel; ring**
cf. **trust**
d Kartell *n*
e cártel *m*
f cartel *m*; entente *f*
i cartello *m*
n kartel *n*

572 **cash; ready money**
cf. **cash holdings, coin, coinage, notes and coin**
d Bargeld *n*; Barschaft *f*; Cash *n*
e contante *m*; dinero *m* contante; efectivo *m* metálico; numerario *m*

f argent *m* comptant; argent *m* en espèces; comptant *m*; espèces *fpl*; numéraire *m*
i contante *m*; denaro *m* contante; denaro *m* in contanti; moneta *f* contante; numerario *m*
n baar geld *n*; cash *n*; chartaal geld *n*; contanten *npl*; contant geld *n*; gereed geld *n*

573 for cash; in cash; cash down; in specie
d bar; gegen bar; gegen Kasse; in bar; in barem Geld; in Bargeld; in klingender Münze; in Metallgeld; per Kasse
e al contado; en efectivo; en metálico; en numerario
f argent comptant; au comptant; comptant; contre caisse; contre argent; en argent; en deniers; en espèces; en numéraire
i a contanti; a pronti (contanti); in contanti; in denaro contante; in moneta metallica; in moneta sonante; per contanti
n contant; in baar; in klinkende munt; tegen contant

574 cashable ***(cheque)*****; collectable; collectible; encashable**
d einkassierbar; einlösbar; einziehbar
e cobrable
f encaissable
i incassabile; riscotibile; riscuotibile
n inbaar; incasseerbaar

575 cash account
d Kassakonto *n*; Kassenkonto *n*
e cuenta *f* de caja
f compte *m* de caisse
i conto *m* (di) cassa
n kasrekening *f*

576 cash *v* **a check** ***(US)*****; cash** *v* **a cheque** ***(UK)*****; collect** *v* **a check (cheque); encash** *v* **a check (cheque)**
d einen Scheck einkassieren; einen Scheck einlösen; einen Scheck einziehen; einen Scheck kassieren
e cobrar un cheque; hacer efectivo un cheque
f encaisser un chèque; toucher un chèque
i incassare un assegno; riscuotere un assegno
n een cheque incasseren; een cheque innen

577 cash assets
cf. **available funds, cash holdings**
d Barkapital *n*; Barvermögen *n*; Barwerte *mpl*
e capital *m* en efectivo; valores *mpl* en efectivo
f capital *m* de numéraire; capital *m* en numéraire; capital-espèces *m*; capital-numéraire *m*; valeurs *fpl* au comptant
i capitale *m* in contanti; valori *mpl* in contanti
n kapitaal *n* in baar geld; kapitaal *n* in contanten

578 cash book
d Kassabuch *n*; Kassenbuch *n*
e diario *m* di caja; libro *m* de caja
f journal *m* de caisse; livre *m* de caisse
i libro *m* cassa; libro *m* di cassa; libro *m* giornale di cassa
n kasboek *n*

579 cash box
d Geldkasse *f*; Geldkassette *f*; Kasse *f*
e caja *f*; cofrecillo *m* para guardar dinero
f caisse *f*; cassette *f*
i cassa *f*; cassetta *f* dei contanti
n kas *f*

580 cash credit
cf. **blank credit**
d Barkredit *m*; Kassenkredit *m*
e crédito *m* de caja
f crédit *m* de caisse; crédit *m* par caisse
i credito *m* in contanti
n kaskrediet *n*

581 cash deal; cash transaction; spot deal; spot transaction
cf. **cash sale**
d Bargeschäft *n*; Bartransaktion *f*; Kassageschäft *n*; Kassatransaktion *f*; Kassengeschäft *n*; Kassentransaktion *f*; Komptantgeschäft *n*; Komptanttransaktion *f*; Kontantgeschäft *n*; Kontanttransaktion *f*; Lokogeschäft *n**
e negocio *m* al contado; negocio *m* en efectivo; operación *f* al contado; operación *f* en efectivo; transacción *f* al contado; transacción *f* en efectivo
f affaire *f* au comptant; opération *f* au comptant; transaction *f* au comptant; transaction *f* en disponible*
i affare *m* a contanti; affare *m* in contanti; affare *m* per contanti; affare *m* sul disponibile*; operazione *f* a contanti; operazione *f* in contanti; operazione *f* per contanti; operazione *f* sul disponibile*; transazione *f* a contanti; transazione *f* in contanti; transazione *f* per contanti; transazione *f* sul disponibile*
n contantaffaire *f*; contantzaak *f*; kastransactie *f*; locoaffaire *f**; locotransactie

*f**; locozaak *f**

* Commodity deal only.

582 **cash disbursements; cash expenditures; cash outgoings; cash outlays**
cf. **cash payment**
d Barausgaben *fpl*; Barausgänge *mpl*; Barauslagen *fpl*; Kassenausgaben *fpl*; Kassenausgänge *mpl*; Kassenauszahlungen *fpl*
e desembolsos *mpl* de caja; desembolsos *mpl* en efectivo; egresos *mpl* de caja *(AL)*; egresos *mpl* en efectivo *(AL)*
f dépenses *fpl* de caisse; sorties *fpl* de caisse
i spese *fpl* di cassa; uscite *fpl* di cassa
n kasuitgaven *fpl*

583 **cash discount; discount for cash**
d Bardiskont *m*; Barzahlungsdiskont *m*; Barzahlungsrabatt *m*; Kassaabzug *m*; Kassadiskont *m*; Kassaskonto *m/n*; Kassenabzug *m*; Kassenskonto *m/n*
e descuento *m* de caja; descuento *m* por pago al contado
f escompte *m* au comptant; escompte *m* de caisse; escompte-intérêt *m*
i sconto *m* cassa; sconto *m* per contanti; sconto *m* per (pagamento) pronto cassa
n korting *f* voor contant

584 **cash dividend**
d Bardividende *f*
e dividendo *m* en efectivo
f dividende *m* en espèces
i dividendo *m* in denaro
n dividend *n* in contanten

585 **cash earnings; cash receipts; cash takings**
d Bareingänge *mpl*; Bareinnahmen *fpl*; Kasseneingänge *mpl*; Kasseneinnahmen *fpl*
e entradas *fpl* en caja; entradas *fpl* en efectivo; ingresos *mpl* en caja; ingresos *mpl* en efectivo
f entrées *fpl* de caisse; recettes *fpl* de caisse; rentrées *fpl* de caisse
i entrate *fpl* di cassa; introiti *mpl* di cassa
n kasontvangsten *fpl*; kasrecettes *fpl*

586 **cash flow**
d Cash-flow *m*; Zu- und Abgang *m* von Barmitteln
e cash flow *m*; movimientos *mpl* de tresorería
f cash flow *m*; flux *m* de trésorerie; mouvement *m* de trésorerie
i cash flow *m*; flusso *m* delle disponibilità
n cash flow *m*; stroom *m* van geldontvangsten en -uitgaven

587 **cash holdings; cash in hand; cash on hand; cash resources; till money**
cf. **available funds, balance in hand, cash, cash assets, cash reserve**
d Barbestand *m*; Barfonds *m*; Barmittel *npl*; Barvorrat *m*; Geldbestand *m*; Geldvorrat *m*; Istbestand *m*; Kassenbestand *m*
e activo *m* en caja; caja *f* disponible; dinero *m* en caja; efectivo *m* en caja; encaje *m*; existencia(s) *f(pl)* en caja; existencia(s) *f(pl)* en efectivo; fondos *mpl* en caja; fondos *mpl* en efectivo; recursos *mpl* en efectivo
f argent *m* en caisse; avoirs *mpl* en caisse; avoirs *mpl* en numéraire; caisse *f*; encaisse *f*; espèces *fpl* en caisse; ressources *fpl* en numéraire
i consistenza *f* di cassa; denaro *m* in cassa; disponibilità *f* in cassa; esistenza *f* di cassa; fondi *mpl* di cassa; giacenza *f* di cassa; giacenza *f* di numerario; giacenza *f* numeraria; incasso *m*; risorse *fpl* di numerario
n contanten *npl* in kas; geld *n* in kas; geldvoorraad *m*; kas *f*; kasgeld *n*; kasmiddelen *npl*; kasvoorraad *m*

588 **cashless payment; non-cash payment; payment by check or by transfer *(US)*; payment by cheque or by transfer *(UK)***
d bargeldlose Zahlung *f*
e pago *m* por cheque o transferencia
f paiement *m* par chèque ou par virement
i pagamento *m* a mezzo (di) assegno o accreditamento
n betaling *f* per cheque of overschrijving

589 **cash on delivery *(UK)*; collect *(US)***
d bei Lieferung zahlbar; gegen Nachnahme; Lieferung gegen (per; unter) Nachnahme; per Nachnahme; unter Nachnahme; Zahlung bei Lieferung
e contra reembolso; entrega contra reembolso; pagadero a la entrega; pago a la entrega; pago contra entrega
f contre remboursement; livraison contre remboursement; paiement à la livraison; paiement contre livraison; payable à la livraison; payable contre livraison
i contrassegno; contro assegno; pagabile alla consegna; pagamento alla consegna; pagamento contrassegno; pagamento contro consegna
n levering tegen betaling bij ontvangst;

levering tegen contante betaling; onder rembours; tegen betaling bij ontvangst; tegen terugbetaling *(B)*; tegen rembours

590 **cash order; cash voucher; disbursement voucher; order for payment; order to pay; pay voucher**
cf. **authorization of payment**
d Auszahlungsanordnung *f*; Auszahlungsanweisung *f*; Auszahlungsauftrag *m*; Kassenbon *m*; Kassenschein *m*; Kassenzettel *m*; Zahlungsanweisung *f*; Zahlungsauftrag *m*; Zahlungsbefehl *m*
e bono *m* de caja; orden *f* de pago; vale *m* de caja
f bon *m* de caisse; mandat *m* de paiement; ordre *m* de paiement; ordre *m* de payer
i buono *m* di cassa; scontrino *m* di cassa
n betalingsaanwijzing *f*; betalingsmandaat *n*; kasbon *m*; opdracht *f* tot betaling

591 **cash payment; payment in cash**
cf. **cash disbursements**
d Barauszahlung *f*; Barzahlung *f*; Kassazahlung *f*
e pago *m* al contado; pago *m* en efectivo; pago *m* en metálico
f paiement *m* au comptant; paiement *m* comptant; paiement *m* en espèces; paiement *m* en numéraire
i pagamento *m* a contanti; pagamento *m* a pronta cassa; pagamento *m* in contanti; pagamento *m* per contanti
n contante betaling *f*

592 **cash position; liquidity position**
d Barliquidität *f*; Kassenlage *f*; Kassenstand *m*; Kassenstatus *m*
e situación *f* de (la) caja; situación *f* de tesorería
f situation *f* de (la) caisse; trésorerie *f*
i situazione *f* della (di)cassa; situazione *f* di tesoreria
n kaspositie *f*

593 **cash price; spot price; spot rate**
d Barpreis *m*; Barzahlungspreis *m*; Kassakurs *m*; Kassapreis *m*
e cotización *f* al contado; precio *m* al contado; precio *m* de pago al contado
f cours *m* au comptant; cours *m* du comptant; prix *m* au comptant; prix *m* comptant; prix *m* pour paiement au comptant
i corso *m* a contanti; prezzo *m* a contanti; prezzo *m* del contante; prezzo *m* per contanti; quotazione *f* del contante; quotazione *f* per contanti
n contante koers *m*; contante prijs *m*; koers *m* à contant; koers *m* voor contant; prijs *m* à contant

594 **cash purchase**
d Barkauf *m*; Kauf *m* gegen Kasse; Kauf *m* ohne Ziel
e compra *f* al contado
f achat *m* au comptant; achat *m* comptant
i acquisto *m* a (per) contanti; acquisto *m* a pronta cassa
n contante inkoop *m*

595 **cash remittance; remittance in cash**
d Anschaffung *f* in bar; Baranschaffung *f*; Barsendung *f*; Barüberweisung *f*; Überweisung *f* in bar
e giro *m* en metálico; remesa *f* en efectivo
f remise *f* en espèces
i rimessa *f* in contante; rimessa *f* in denaro
n overmaking *f* in contanten

596 **cash requirements; liquidity requirements**
d Kassenanforderungen *fpl*; Liquiditätsbedarf *m*; Liquiditätsbedürfnis(se) *n(pl)*
e necesidades *fpl* de liquidez; necesidades *fpl* de tesorería
f besoins *mpl* de (en) caisse; besoins *mpl* en liquidités; besoins *mpl* en trésorerie
i bisogni *mpl* di cassa; bisogni *mpl* di liquidità; bisogni *mpl* di tesoreria; fabbisogno *m* di liquidità; fabbisogno *m* di tesoreria
n kasbehoeften *fpl*; liquiditeitsbehoeften *fpl*; liquiditeitseisen *mpl*

597 **cash reserve**
d bare Reserve *f*; Barreserve *f*; Geldvorrat *m*; Kassenreserve *f*
e reserva *f* en caja; reserva *f* en efectivo
f réserve *f* de caisse; réserve *f* en espèces
i riserva *f* di cassa; riserva *f* in contanti
n contante reserve *f*; kasreserve *f*

598 **cash sale**
cf. **cash transaction**
d Barverkauf *m*; Kassaverkauf *m*
e venta *f* al contado
f vente *f* au comptant
i vendita *f* a contanti; vendita *f* per contanti
n verkoop *m* à contant

599 **cash surplus**
d Kassenüberschuss *m*
e excedente *m* de (en) caja
f excédent *m* de (en) caisse

i eccedenza *f* di cassa
n kasoverschot *n*

600 cash voucher; pay voucher
d Auszahlungsbeleg *m*; Kassenbeleg *m*; Zahlungsbeleg *m*
e comprobante *m* de caja; comprobante *m* de pago; justificante *m* de pago
f pièce *f* (justificative) de caisse
i pezza *f* giustificativa di cassa; pezza *f* di pagamento
n kasbescheid *n*; kasbewijsstuk *n*

601 cash withdrawal; drawing of cash; withdrawal of cash
d Barabhebung *f*; Barentnahme *f*
e retirada *f* en efectivo; retiro *m* en efectivo
f prélèvement *m* d'espèces; prélèvement *m* en espèces; prise *f* d'espèces; retrait *m* d'espèces; retrait *m* en espèces
i prelevamento *m* in contanti; prelievo *m* in contanti; ritiro *m* in contanti
n afhaling *f* in contanten; opneming *f* in contanten; opvraging *f* in contanten

602 caution money; deposit; earnest money; guarantee deposit
cf. **collateral, earnest, margin**
d Angabe *f (rare in this sense)*; Angeld *n*; Draufgabe *f*; Draufgeld *n*; Handgeld *n*; Hinterlage *f*; Kautionsdepot *n*; Sicherheitssumme *f*
e arras *fpl*; caparra *f*; fianza *f*; señal *f*
f arrhes *fpl*; cautionnement *m*; dépôt *m* de caution
i caparra *f*; deposito *m* cauzionale; somma *f* a cauzione
n borgsom *f*; cautiesom *f*; handgeld *n*; waarborgsom *f*

603 cease *v* **payment; discontinue** *v* **payment(s); stop** *v* **payments; suspend** *v* **payments**
d die Zahlungen einstellen; die Zahlungen sistieren *(rare)*
e cesar los pagos; suspender los pagos
f cesser les paiements; suspendre les paiements
i cessare i pagamenti; sospendere i pagamenti
n de betalingen opschorten; de betalingen schorsen; de betalingen staken

604 ceiling on loans on securities; lending limit on securities
d Belehnungsgrenze *f (O; Schw)*; Beleihungsgrenze *f*; Lombardierungsgrenze *f*
e límite *m* de los adelantos sobre títulos
f limite *f* des avances sur titres
i limite *m* delle anticipazioni su titoli
n grens *f* voor leningen tegen onderpandeffecten

605 ceiling price; highest price; maximum price; outside price; top price
cf. **price limit**
d der höchste Preis *m*; Höchstpreis *m*; Maximalpreis *m*
e precio *m* límite; precio *m* máximo; precio *m* tope
f prix *m* de plafond; prix *m* le plus haut; prix *m* limite; prix-limite *m*; prix *m* maximum; prix *m* plafond
i prezzo *m* limite; prezzo *m* massimo
n de hoogste prijs *m*; maximumprijs *m*

606 central bank
cf. **bank of circulation**
d Zentralbank *f*; Zentralnotenbank *f*
e banco *m* central
f banque *f* centrale
i banca *f* centrale
n centrale bank *f*

607 central office(s); head office; headquarters; main office(s); principal office(s)
cf. **registered office(s)**
d Hauptamt *n*; Hauptbüro *n*; Hauptgeschäft *n*; Hauptgeschäftsstelle *f*; Hauptkontor *n*; Hauptniederlassung *f*; Hauptsitz *m*; Hauptstelle *f*; Zentralamt *n*; Zentralbüro *n*; Zentrale *f*; Zentralstelle *f*
e casa *f* central; casa *f* matriz; casa *f* principal; establecimiento *m* central; establecimiento *m* principal; oficina *f* central; oficina *f* principal; sede *f* central; sede *f* principal
f bureau *m* central; bureau *m* principal; établissement *m* central; établissement *m* principal; maison *f* mère; maison *f* principale; siège *m* central; siège *m* principal
i casa *f* madre; casa *f* principale; sede *f* centrale; sede *f* principale; stabilimento *m* centrale; stabilimento *m* principale; ufficio *m* centrale; ufficio *m* principale
n centraal bureau *n*; centraal kantoor *n*; centrale zetel *m*; hoofdbureau *n*; hoofdhuis *n*; hoofdkantoor *n*; hoofdvestiging *f*; hoofdzetel *m*

608 certificate of deposit; deposit receipt; deposit slip; deposit warrant; safe custody receipt; trust receipt
cf. **warehouse receipt**

d Depositalschein *m*; Depositenschein *m*; Depotquittung *f*; Depotschein *m*; Hinterlegungsbescheinigung *f*; Hinterlegungsschein *m*
e boletín *m* de depósito; certificado *m* de depósito; recibo *m* de depósito; resguardo *m* de depósito
f bulletin *m* de dépôt; certificat *m* de dépôt; récépissé *m* de dépôt; reconnaissance *f* de dépôt; reçu *m* de dépôt
i buono *m* di deposito; cedola *f* di deposito; certificato *m* di deposito; distinta *f* di deposito; fede *f* di deposito; ricevuta *f* di deposito
n depositobewijs *n*; depositocertificaat *n*

609 certificate of indebtedness; proof of debt; proof of indebtedness
cf. **acknowledgement of debt, bond, hand bill**
d Schuldschein *m*; Schuldtitel *m*; Schuldurkunde *f*
e certificado *m* de deuda; certificado *m* de endeudamiento; comprobante *m* de deuda; título *m* de deuda
f titre *m* de créance; titre *m* d'obligation
i certificato *m* di debito; prova *f* di debito; titolo *m* di debito
n schuldbewijs *n*; titel *m* van schuldvordering

610 certify *v* a check *(US)*; certify *v* a cheque *(UK)*
d einen Scheck bestätigen
e certificar un cheque; confirmar un cheque
f certifier un chèque; viser un chèque
i confirmare un assegno; vistare un assegno
n een cheque bevestigen; een cheque certificeren; een cheque certifiëren; een cheque waarmerken

611 chamber of commerce (and industry)
d (Industrie- und) Handelskammer *f*; Kammer *f* der gewerblichen Wirtschaft *(O)*
e cámara *f* de comercio (y industria)
f chambre *f* de commerce (et industrie)
i camera *f* di commercio (, industria ed agricoltura)
n kamer *f* van koophandel (en nijverheid)

612 change; loose change; odd change; small change
cf. **copper, divisional coin**
d Kleingeld *n*; Wechselgeld *n*
e cambio *m* (menor); dinero *m* suelto; suelto *m*; vuelta *f*; vuelto *m (AL)*
f appoint *m*; menue monnaie *f*; monnaie *f* d'appoint; petite monnaie *f*
i denaro *m* spiccio; moneta *f* spicciola; soldi *mpl* spiccioli; spicci *mpl*; spiccioli *mpl*
n kleingeld *n*; pasgeld *n*; pasmunt *f*; wisselgeld *n*

613 charge; charging; debit; debiting
d Anrechnung *f*; Belastung *f*; Berechnung *f*; Inrechnungstellung *f*; Lastschrift *f*; Verrechnung *f*
e adeudo *m* (en cuenta); cargo *m*; débito *m*; imputación *f*
f débit *m*; imputation *f*; mise *f* à (la) charge; mise *f* en compte; passation *f* au débit
i addebitamento *m*; addebito *m*; conteggio *m*; imputazione *f*; messa *f* en conto
n aanrekening *f*; belasten *n*; debitering *f*; verrekening *f*

614 charge; dues; duty; fee; rate
cf. **charges, commission, duty**
d Abgabe *f*; Gebühr *f*; Taxe *f*
e derecho *m*; tasa *f*
f droit *m*; redevance *f*; taxe *f*
i diritto *m*; tassa *f*
n recht *n*; retributie *f**; taks *m/f*; taxe *f*
* State.

615 charge *v*; charge *v* to the debit; charge *v* up; debit *v*
cf. **carry *v* to account, charge *v* an account with**
d anrechnen; belasten; debitieren; in Anschlag bringen; in das Debet eintragen; in das Debet stellen; in das Soll eintragen; zu Lasten schreiben; verrechnen
e adeudar (en cuenta); cargar; debitar; imputar; llevar al debe; llevar al débito; pasar al debe; pasar al débito
f charger; débiter; imputer; mettre à (la) charge; passer au débit; porter au débit
i addebitare; imputare; registrare a debito; segnare a debito
n aanrekenen; belasten; debiteren; verrekenen

616 chargeable to; to the debit of
cf. **at the expense of, for account of**
d zu Lasten*
e a cargo de
f à la charge de; au débit de; imputable à (sur); par le débit de
i a carico di; imputabile a

n ten laste van
* Genitive or von.

617 **charge account**
cf. **personal account**
d Anschreibungskonto *n*; Kundenkonto *n*
e cuenta *f* de cliente
f compte *m* client
i conto *m* cliente
n cliëntenrekening *f*

618 **charge *v* an account with; charge *v* to (the debit of) an account; charge *v* up to an account; debit *v* an account with; debit *v* to an account**
cf. **carry *v* to account, charge *v***
d auf das Konto setzen; einem Konto belasten; einem Konto debitieren; ein Konto belasten mit; zu Lasten eines Kontos vortragen
e adeudar la cuenta con; cargar a la cuenta; cargar la cuenta con; debitar la cuenta con
f charger un compte de; débiter à un compte; débiter un compte de; imputer à (sur) un compte; mettre à (sur) un compte; passer au débit d'un compte; passer à (sur) un compte; porter au débit d'un compte
i addebitare un conto per; imputare al conto; mettere sul conto
n een rekening belasten met; een rekening debiteren met

619 **charges**
cf. **expenses**
d Lasten *fpl*
e cargas *fpl*
f charges *fpl*
i oneri *mpl*
n lasten *mpl*

620 **charges for depreciation write-off**
d Aufwendungen *fpl* für Abschreibungen; Abschreibungsaufwendungen *fpl*; Abschreibungen *fpl*
e cargas *fpl* de amortización
f charges *fpl* d'amortissement
i oneri *mpl* di ammortamento
n afschrijvingslasten *mpl*

621 **charges to be deducted; deducting charges; deducting expenses; expenses to be deducted; less charges; less expenses; minus charges; minus expenses**
d abzüglich der Kosten; abzüglich der Spesen; abzüglich der Unkosten; unter Abzug der Kosten; unter Abzug der Spesen; unter Abzug der Unkosten
e descontando los gastos; menos los gastos
f frais à déduire; moins les frais; sous déduction des frais
i defalcando le spese; meno le spese; sotto deduzione delle spese
n min de kosten; min de onkosten; onder aftrek van de kosten; onder aftrek van de onkosten; verminderd met de kosten; verminderd met de onkosten

622 **chattels; goods and chattels; movable property; movables; personal assets; personal estate; personal property; personalty**
d bewegliche Güter *npl*; bewegliche Habe *f*; beweglicher Besitz *m*; bewegliches Eigentum *n*; bewegliches Vermögen *n*; fahrende Habe *f*; Fahrgut *n*; Fahrhabe *f*; Fahrnis *f*; Mobiliar *n*; Mobiliarvermögen *n*; Mobilien *pl*
e bienes *mpl* mobiliarios; bienes *mpl* muebles; muebles *mpl*; propiedad *f* mobiliaria; propiedad *f* mueble; valores *mpl* mobiliarios; valores *mpl* muebles
f biens *mpl* meubles; biens *mpl* mobiliers; effets *mpl* mobiliers; meubles *mpl*; valeurs *fpl* mobilières
i beni *mpl* mobili; beni *mpl* mobiliari; mobili *mpl*; valori *mpl* mobiliari
n mobilair vermogen *n*; mobiliën *pl (B)*; roerend bezit *n*; roerende goederen *npl*

623 **cheap money; easy money *(US)*; soft money**
d billiges Geld *n*
e dinero *m* barato; moneda *f* barata
f argent *m* (à) bon marché
i denaro *m* a buon mercato
n goedkoop geld *n*

624 **check *(US)*; cheque *(UK)***
d Check *m (Schw)*; Scheck *m*
e cheque *m*
f chèque *m*
i assegno *m* (bancario); check *m*; chèque *m*
n check *m*; cheque *m*

625 **check account *(US)*; checking account *(US)*; cheque account *(UK)*; drawing account**
cf. **giro account**
d Scheckkonto *n*; Scheckrechnung *f*
e cuenta *f* de cheques
f compte *m* chèques; compte *m* de chèques

i conto *m* assegni
n chequerekening *f*

626 check-book ***(US)*****; cheque-book** ***(UK)***
d Scheckbuch *n*; Scheckheft *n*
e libreta *f* de cheques; talonario *m* de cheques
f carnet *m* de chèques; chéquier *m*
i carnet *m* d'assegni; libretto *m* (d')assegni
n chequeboek(je) *n*

627 check clearing ***(US)*****; cheque clearing** ***(UK)***
d Scheckabrechnung *f*; Scheck-verrechnung *f*
e compensación *f* de cheques
f compensation *f* de chèques
i compensazione *f* d'assegni
n chequeverrekening *f*

628 check *v* **inflation; control** *v* **inflation; curb** *v* **inflation; restrain** *v* **inflation**
d die Inflation bremsen; die Inflation dämpfen; die Inflation eindämmen; die Inflation kontrollieren; die Inflation steuern
e amortiguar la inflación; controlar la inflación; detener la inflación; refrenar la inflación
f contenir l'inflation; contrôler l'inflation; diriger l'inflation; freiner l'inflation
i contenere l'inflazione; controllare l'inflazione; frenare l'inflazione
n de inflatie afremmen; de inflatie controleren; de inflatie remmen

629 checking of credits; credit control; credit surveillance
d Kreditkontrolle *f*; Kreditüberwachung *f*
e control *m* de los créditos
f contrôle *m* des crédits; surveillance *f* des crédits
i controllo *m* dei crediti
n kredietbewaking *f*; kredietcontrole *f*

630 check not to order ***(US)*****; cheque not to order** ***(UK)*****; not-to-order check** ***(US)*****; not-to-order cheque** ***(UK)***
d Rektascheck *m*
e cheque *m* intransferible; cheque *m* no a la orden
f chèque *m* non à ordre
i assegno *m* non all'ordine; assegno *m* non trasferibile
n rectacheque *m*

631 check to order ***(US)*****; cheque to order** ***(UK)*****; order check** ***(US)*****; order cheque** ***(UK)***
d Orderscheck *m*
e cheque *m* a la orden
f chèque *m* à ordre
i assegno *m* all'ordine
n cheque *m* aan order; ordercheque *m*

632 check transactions ***(US)*****; cheque transactions** ***(UK)***
d Scheckverkehr *m*
e operaciones *fpl* por cheque; transacciones *fpl* por cheque
f opérations *fpl* par cheque(s); transactions *fpl* par cheque(s)
i operazioni *fpl* con assegni; transazioni *fpl* con assegni
n chequeverkeer *n*

633 chief shareholder; leading shareholder; major shareholder; principal shareholder
d Grossaktionär *m*; Hauptaktionär *m*
e accionista *m* principal; gran accionista *m*
f actionnaire *m* principal; gros actionnaire *m*; principal actionnaire *m*
i azionista *m* principale; grande azionista *m*; grosso azionista *m*; principale azionista *m*
n belangrijke aandeelhouder *m*; hoofd-aandeelhouder *m*

634 c.i.f.; cost, insurance, freight
d c.i.f.; Kosten, Versicherung, (und) Fracht
e c.i.f.; costo, seguro, (y) flete
f c.a.f.; coût, assurance, (et) fret; c.i.f.; coût, assurance, (et) fret
i c.i.f.; costo, assicurazione, (e) nolo
n c.i.f.; kost(prijs), verzekering, (en) vracht

635 circulating; in circulation
d im Umlauf (befindlich); zirkulierend
e circulante; en circulación
f circulant; en circulation
i circolante; in circolazione
n circulerend; in circulatie; in omloop

636 circulating medium
d Umlauf(s)mittel *n*
e medio *m* circulante; medio *m* de circulación
f agent *m* de circulation; agent *m* monétaire
i medio *m* circolante; mezzo *m* circolante
n circulerend medium *n*

637 circulation of money; currency circulation; monetary circulation
cf. circulation of notes and coin(s), current money

d Geldkreislauf *m*; Geldumlauf *m*; Geldzirkulation *f*
e circulación *f* de dinero; circulación *f* monetaria
f circulation *f* de l'argent; circulation *f* monétaire
i circolazione *f* di denaro; circolazione *f* monetaria
n geldcirculatie *f*; geld(s)omloop *m*

638 circulation of notes and coin(s); current coin and currency; note and coin circulation; notes and coin(s) in circulation
cf. **circulation of money, fiduciary circulation**
d Bargeldumlauf *m*; im Umlauf befindliche Noten *fpl* und Münzen *fpl*; Zahlungsmittelumlauf *m*
e billetes *mpl* y monedas *fpl* en circulación; circulación *f* de billetes y monedas; circulación *f* de medios de pago
f billets *mpl* et espèces *fpl* en circulation; billets *mpl* et pièces *fpl* en circulation; circulation *f* de billets et espèces; circulation *f* de moyens de paiement
i biglietti *mpl* e monete *fpl* in circolazione; circolazione *f* di biglietti e monete; circolazione *f* di mezzi di pagamento
n biljetten *npl* en munten *fpl* in omloop; circulatie *f* van baar geld; circulatie *f* van betaalmiddelen

639 claim
cf. **debt**
d Forderung *f*; Schuldforderung *f*
e crédito *m*
f créance *f*
i credito *m*
n schuldvordering *f*; vordering *f*

640 claim for refund; claim for restitution
d Rückerstattungsantrag *m*; Rückforderung *f*
e demanda *f* de reembolso; demanda *f* de restitución
f demande *f* de remboursement; demande *f* de restitution
i domanda *f* di restituzione; domanda *f* di rimborso
n eis *m* tot terugbetaling; terugvordering *f*

641 clear *v* a check *(US)*; clear *v* a cheque *(UK)*
d einen Scheck kompensieren; einen Scheck verrechnen
e compensar un cheque
f compenser un chèque
i compensare un assegno
n een cheque verrekenen

642 clearance; clearing
d Clearing *n*; Kompensation *f*; Verrechnung *f*
e clearing *m*; compensación *f*
f clearing *m*; compensation *f*
i clearing *m*; compensazione *f*
n clearing *f*; compensatie *f*; verrekening *f*

643 clearance; clearing; clearing business; clearing transactions
d Abrechnungsgeschäfte *npl*; Abrechnungsverkehr *m*; Clearinggeschäfte *npl*; Clearingverkehr *m*; Giroverkehr *m*; Kompensationsgeschäfte *npl*; Kompensationsverkehr *m*; Verrechnungsgeschäfte *npl*; Verrechnungsverkehr *m*
e compensaciones *fpl*; operaciones *fpl* de clearing; operaciones *fpl* de compensación; operaciones *fpl* de giro; tráfico *m* de compensación; transacciones *fpl* de clearing; transacciones *fpl* de compensación; transacciones *fpl* de giro
f clearing *m*; compensation *f*; opérations *fpl* de clearing; opérations *fpl* de compensation; opérations *fpl* de virement; transactions *fpl* de clearing; transactions *fpl* de compensation; transactions *fpl* de virement
i clearing *m*; operazioni *fpl* di clearing; operazioni *fpl* di compensazione; transazioni *fpl* di clearing; transazioni *fpl* di compensazione
n clearingtransacties *fpl*; clearingverrichtingen *fpl*; compensatietransacties *fpl*; compensatieverrichtingen *fpl*; giroverkeer *n*; verrekeningstransacties *fpl*; verrekeningsverrichtingen *fpl*

644 clearance account; clearing account; offset account
d Clearingkonto *n*; Verrechnungskonto *n*
e cuenta *f* de clearing; cuenta *f* de compensación
f compte *m* de clearing; compte *m* de compensation
i conto *m* di clearing; conto *m* di compensazione
n clearingrekening *f*; compensatierekening *f*

645 clearance through customs; customs clearance
d Freimachung *f*; Klarierung *f*;

Verzollung *f*; Zollabfertigung *f*; Zollerledigung *f*
e aforamiento *m* aduanero; aforo *m* aduanero; despacho *m* aduanero; despacho *m* en la aduana; paso *m* por la aduana
f dédouanement *m*; expédition *f* en douane; passage *m* en douane
i sdaziamento *m*; sdoganamento *m*; spedizione *f* in dogana; svincolo *m* doganale
n dedouaneren *n*; douanevisitatie *f*; inklaring *f**; uitklaring *f***; vrijmaking *f*

* Inwards.
** Outwards.

646 clear gain; clear profit; net; net gain; net profit; pure profit
d Nettogewinn *m*; Reingewinn *m*
e beneficio *m* neto; ganancia(s) *f(pl)* neta(s); utilidad *f* neta
f bénéfice *m* net; gain *m* net
i beneficio *m* netto; guadagno *m* netto; profitto *m* netto; utile *m* netto
n nettowinst *f*; zuivere winst *f*

647 clearing agreement
d Ausgleichsabkommen *n*; Clearingabkommen *n*; Girovertrag *m*; Kompensationsabkommen *n*; Verrechnungsabkommen *n*; Verrechnungsvertrag *m*
e acuerdo *m* de clearing; acuerdo *m* de compensación; ajuste *m* de clearing; ajuste *m* de compensación; arreglo *m* de clearing; arreglo *m* de compensación; convenio *m* de clearing; convenio *m* de compensación
f accord *m* de clearing; accord *m* de compensation; traité *m* de clearing; traité *m* de compensation
i accordo *m* di clearing; accordo *m* di compensazione; trattato *m* di clearing; trattato *m* di compensazione
n clearingovereenkomst *f*; compensatieovereenkomst *f*; verrekeningsovereenkomst *f*

648 clearing bank
d Abrechnungsbank *f*; am Abrechnungsverkehr beteiligte Bank *f*; Clearingbank *f*; Girobank *f*
e banco *m* de clearing; banco *m* de compensación; banco *m* de giro
f banque *f* de clearing; banque *f* de compensation; banque *f* de virement
i banca *f* associata alla stanza di compensazione; banca *f* di clearing; banca *f* di compensazione; banca *f* di giro
n clearingbank *f*; girobank *f*

649 clearing house; clearinghouse; clearing office
d Abrechnungsbüro *n*; Abrechnungshaus *n*; Abrechnungskontor *n*; Abrechnungsstelle *f*; Ausgleichsamt *n*; Ausgleichskasse *f*; Ausgleichsstelle *f*; Clearinghaus *n*; Clearingstelle *f*; Girokasse *f*; Girokontor *n*; Kompensationskasse *f*; Liquidationskasse *f*; Verrechnungskammer *f*; Verrechnungsstelle *f*
e caja *f* de clearing; caja *f* de compensación; caja *f* de giro; cámara *f* de clearing; cámara *f* de compensación; clearinghouse *m*; oficina *f* de compensación; organo *m* de compensación
f bureau *m* de clearing; bureau *m* de compensation; caisse *f* de compensation; chambre *f* de compensation; chambre *f* de liquidation; comptoir *m* de liquidation; comptoir *m* de règlement; comptoir *m* de virement; office *m* de clearing; office *m* de compensation
i camera *f* di compensazione; cassa *f* di compensazione; cassa *f* di liquidazione; stanza *f* di compensazione
n clearinginstituut *n*; clearingkantoor *n*; compensatiekas *f*; liquidatiekas *f*; verrekeningskamer *f*; verrekenkamer *f*; verrekenkantoor *n*

650 clearing rate; settlement price; settlement rate; settling rate
d Abrechnungskurs *m*; Abrechnungspreis *m*; Clearingkurs *m*; Kompensationskurs *m*; Liquidationskurs *m*; Regulierungskurs *m*
e cambio *m* de liquidación; precio *m* de compensación
f cours *m* de clearing; cours *m* de compensation; prix *m* de liquidation
i corso *m* di compensazione; corso *m* di compenso; prezzo *m* di compensazione; prezzo *m* di compenso; prezzo *m* di liquidazione
n clearingkoers *m*; verrekeningskoers *m*

651 clear loss; net loss
d Nettoverlust *m*; Reinverlust *m*
e pérdida *f* neta
f perte *f* nette
i perdita *f* netta
n nettoverlies *n*; zuiver verlies *n*

652 **close** *v* **an account; wind** *v* **up an account**
cf. **balance** *v* **an account**
d eine Rechnung abschliessen; eine Rechnung schliessen; ein Konto abschliessen; ein Konto schliessen
e cerrar una cuenta
f arrêter un compte; clôturer un compte; fermer un compte
i chiudere un conto
n een rekening afsluiten

653 **closed-end investment company** *(US)***; closed-end trust** *(US)***; investment company; investment house; investment trust; portfolio company**
cf. **finance company, investment fund**
d Anlagegesellschaft *f*; Anlagefonds *m* *(Schw)*; Anlagetrust *m*; Investmentgesellschaft *f*; Investmenttrust *m*; Kapitalanlagegesellschaft *f*
e compañía *f* de inversión; compañía *f* de inversiones; compañía *f* inversionista; sociedad *f* de cartera; sociedad *f* de colocación de capitales; sociedad *f* de inversión; sociedad *f* de inversiones; sociedad *f* inversionista
f investment-trust *m*; société *f* d'investissement; société *f* de placement; société *f* de portefeuille
i investment-trust *m*; società *f* d'investimento; società *f* di portafoglio; società *f* finanziaria d'investimenti
n beleggingsmaatschappij *f*; beleggingstrust *m*; investment-trust *m*

654 **close money** *(rare)***; dear money; high money** *(US)***; tight money**
d knappes Geld *n*; teures Geld *n*
e dinero *m* caro; dinero *m* escaso
f argent *m* cher; argent *m* serré
i denaro *m* caro; denaro *m* scarso
n duurgeld *n*; schaarsgeld *n*

655 **close of an account; closing of an account; winding up of an account**
cf. **balance of an account**
d Abschluss *m* einer Rechnung; Abschluss *m* eines Kontos
e cierre *m* de una cuenta
f arrêté *m* d'un compte; clôture *f* d'un compte; fermeture *f* d'un compte
i chiusura *f* di un conto
n afsluiting *f* van een rekening

656 **closing entry**
d Abschlussbuchung *f*; Abschlusseintrag *m*
e asiento *m* de cierre; asiento *m* final
f écriture *f* de clôture
i registrazione *f* di chiusura
n slotboeking *f*

657 **closing price; closing quotation; closing rate**
d Abschlusskurs *m*; letzter Kurs *m*; Schlusskurs *m*; Schlussnotierung *f*; Schlussnotiz *f*
e cambio *m* de cierre; cotización *f* de cierre
f cote *f* de clôture; cours *m* de clôture; dernier cours *m*; prix *m* de clôture
i corso *m* di chiusura; quotazione *f* di chiusura
n slotkoers *m*; slotnotering *f*; slotprijs *m*

658 **co-borrower; joint borrower**
d gemeinsamer Kreditnehmer *m*
e coprestatario *m*
f coemprunteur *m*
i comutuatario
n medekredietnemer *m*

659 **co-debtor; co-obligor; joint debtor; joint obligor**
cf. **joint and several debtor**
d Gemeinschaftsschuldner *m*; Mitschuldner *m*
e codeudor *m*
f codébiteur *m*
i condebitore *m*; coobbligato *m*
n medeschuldenaar *m*

660 **coin; money piece** *(rare)*
d Geldstück *n*; Münze *f*
e moneda *f*; pieza *f*
f monnaie *f*; pièce *f*; pièce *f* d'argent; pièce *f* de monnaie
i moneta *f*; pezzo *m*
n geldstuk(je) *n*; munt *f*; muntstuk *n*

661 **coin** *(US)***; specie**
cf. **cash, coinage**
d Hartgeld *n*; Metallgeld *n*; Münze *f*; Münzgeld *n*
e especie *f*; metálico *m*; moneda *f* metálica; numerario *m*
f monnaie *f* métallique; numéraire *m*
i moneta *f* metallica; numerario *m*
n metaalgeld *n*; metalliek geld *n*; muntgeld *n*; specie *f*

662 **coin** *v***; mint** *v***; monetize** *v***; stamp** *v*
d ausmünzen; ausprägen; münzen; prägen; schlagen
e acuñar; amonedar; monedar; monedear; monetizar
f battre; frapper; monétiser; monnayer

i battere; coniare; monetare
n aanmunten; munten; slaan

663 **coinage; mintage; monetization**
d Ausmünzung *f*; Ausprägung *f*; Münzprägung *f*; Prägung *f*
e acuñación *f*; amonedación *f*; monetización *f*
f frappe *f*; monétisation *f*; monnayage *m*
i coniatura *f*; coniazione *f*; conio *m*; monetazione *f*
n aanmunting *f*; monetisatie *f*; munterij *f*; munting *f*

664 **coinage; monetary system**
d Geldsystem *n*; Münzsystem *n*
e sistema *m* monetario
f système *m* monétaire
i sistema *m* monetario
n geldstelsel *n*; monetair stelsel *n*; muntstelsel *n*

665 **coinage** *(coins)*
cf. **cash, coin**
d Münzen *fpl*
e monedas *fpl*
f espèces *fpl*
i monete *fpl*
n munten *fpl*

666 **coinage gold; coin gold; mint gold; monetary gold; standard gold**
d Gold *n* von gesetzlicher Feinheit; Münzgold *n*; Währungsgold *n*
e oro *m* de título legal; oro *m* monetario
f or *m* à monnayer; or *m* au titre; or *m* monétaire
i oro *m* al titolo legale; oro *m* monetario; oro *m* per monetazione; oro *m* per uso monetario
n monetair goud *n*; muntgoud *n*

667 **coined gold; gold specie; minted gold; monetized gold**
d gemünztes Gold *n*; Münzgold *n*
e oro *m* acuñado; oro *m* amonedado; oro *m* monetizado
f or *m* monétisé; or *m* monnayé
i oro *m* monetato
n gemunt goud *n*; muntgoud *n*

668 **collapse** *(exchange, market etc.)*; **crash; debacle**
d Krach *m*; Zusammenbruch *m*
e crac *m*; desplome *m*; hundimiento *m*
f débâcle *f*; déconfiture *f*; effondrement *m*; krach *m*
i crac *m*; crollo *m*; tracollo *m*
n debâcle *f/n*; ineenstorting *f*; krach *m*

669 **collateral; collateral security**
cf. **additional security, caution money, earnest, margin**
d Sicherheit *f*
e garantía *f*
f garantie *f*; nantissement *m*
i garanzia *f*
n zekerheid *f*

670 **collateral credit; credit against collateral (security); credit against security; credit on collateral (security); credit on security; guaranteed credit; secured credit**
cf. **credit on securities**
d abgesicherter Kredit *m*; garantierter Kredit *m*; gesicherter Kredit *m*; Kredit *m* gegen Sicherheit
e crédito *m* con garantía; crédito *m* contra garantía; crédito *m* garantizado; crédito *m* pignoraticio
f crédit *m* cautionné; crédit *m* contre garantie; crédit *m* contre nantissement; crédit *m* gagé; crédit *m* garanti; crédit *m* sur nantissement
i credito *m* garantito; credito *m* pignoratizio; credito *m* su pegno
n gedekt krediet *n*; gegarandeerd krediet *n*; gewaarborgd krediet *n*; krediet *n* op onderpand; krediet *n* tegen onderpand

671 **collateralize** *v* **securities** *(US)*; **hypothecate** *v* **securities; pawn** *v* **securities; pledge** *v* **securities**
cf. **advance** *v* **on securities**
d Effekten belehnen *(Schw)*; Effekten beleihen; Effekten lombardieren; Effekten verpfänden
e dar valores en garantía; dar valores en prenda; empeñar valores; pignorar valores
f déposer des titres en nantissement; donner des titres en gage (en garantie); engager des titres; gager des titres
i dare titoli in garanzia; dare titoli in pegno; impegnare titoli; pignorare titoli
n effecten als (in) onderpand deponeren; effecten als (in) onderpand geven; effecten als (in) pand deponeren; effecten als (in) pand geven; effecten belenen; effecten verpanden

672 **collateral loan; loan against collateral (security); loan against security; loan on collateral (security); loan on security; secured loan**
cf. **loan on securities**
d abgesichertes Darleh(e)n *n*; Darleh(e)n *n*

gegen Pfand; Darleh(e)n *n* gegen Sicherheit; garantiertes Darleh(e)n *n*; gedecktes Darleh(e)n *n*; gesichertes Darleh(e)n *n*; Pfanddarleh(e)n *n*
e préstamo *m* con (contra) garantía; préstamo *m* cubierto; préstamo *m* garantizado; préstamo *m* pignoraticio; préstamo *m* sobre prenda
f prêt *m* contre garantie; prêt *m* contre (sur) nantissement; prêt *m* couvert; prêt *m* gagé; prêt *m* garanti
i prestito *m* coperto; prestito *m* garantito; prestito *m* pignoratizio; prestito *m* su pegno
n gedekte lening *f*; gegarandeerde lening *f*; lening *f* op onderpand; lening *f* tegen onderpand

673 collation account; collective account; summary account
cf. **control account**
d Kollektivkonto *n*; Sammelkonto *n*
e cuenta *f* colectiva
f compte *m* collectif
i conto *m* collettivo
n verzamelrekening *f*

674 collectability *(of debt)*; **collectibility; receivability; recoverableness**
d Beitreibbarkeit *f*; Eintreibbarkeit *f*; Einziehbarkeit *f*
e cobrabilidad *f*; exigibilidad *f*
f exigibilité *f*
i esigibilità *f*; ricuperabilità *f*
n inbaarheid *f*; invorderbaarheid *f*; opeisbaarheid *f*

675 collectable *(debt)*; **collectible; due; exactable; receivable; recoverable**
d beitreibbar; betreibbar *(Schw)*; einklagbar; eintreibbar; einziehbar
e cobrable; exigible; recaudable
f exigible; recouvrable; récupérable
i esigibile; ricuperabile; riscotibile; riscuotibile
n inbaar; invorderbaar; opeisbaar; opvorderbaar; opvraagbaar

676 collectable *(tax)*; **collectible; leviable**
d beitreibbar; einhebbar *(O)*; eintreibbar; einziehbar; erhebbar
e cobrable; recaudable
f perceptible; percevable; recouvrable
i percepibile; riscotibile; riscuotibile
n inbaar; invorderbaar

677 collect *v* **a debt; recover** *v* **a debt**
d eine Forderung beitreiben; eine Forderung betreiben *(Schw)*; eine Forderung eintreiben; eine Forderung einziehen; eine Schuld beitreiben; eine Schuld betreiben *(Schw)*; eine Schuld eintreiben; eine Schuld einziehen
e cobrar un crédito; cobrar una deuda; recaudar un crédito; recaudar una deuda
f faire rentrer une créance; faire rentrer une dette; mettre une créance en recouvrement; recouvrer une créance; recouvrer une dette; récupérer une créance; récupérer une dette
i ricuperare un credito; ricuperare un debito; riscuotere un credito; riscuotere un debito
n een schuld innen; een schuld invorderen; een vordering innen; een vordering invorderen

678 collect *v* **a tax**
cf. **impose** *v* **a tax on**
d eine Steuer beitreiben; eine Steuer einheben *(O)*; eine Steuer eintreiben; eine Steuer einziehen; eine Steuer erheben
e cobrar un impuesto; percibir un impuesto; recaudar un impuesto
f mettre un impôt en recouvrement; percevoir un impôt; recouvrer un impôt
i percepire una imposta; riscuotere una imposta
n een belasting innen; een belasting invorderen

679 collection; encashment
d Einkassierung *f*; Inkasso *n*
e cobranza *f*; cobro *m*
f encaissement *m*
i incasso *m*
n incassering *f*; incasso *n*; inning *f*

680 collection; recovery
d Beitreibung *f*; Betreibung *f (Schw)*; Eintreibung *f*; Einziehung *f*; Einzug *m*
e recaudación *f*
f recouvrement *m*; récupération *f*
i esazione *f*; ricupero *m*; riscossione *f*
n inning *f*; invordering *f*

681 collection at source; deduction of tax at source; pay as you earn (system); taxation at source; withholding
cf. **tax deducted at source**
d Einbehaltung *f* der Steuern an der Quelle; Quellenabzug *m* der Steuern; Quellenbesteuerung *f*; Steuererhebung *f* an der Quelle
e recaudación *f* de impuestos en la fuente; tributación *f* en el origen; tributación *f* en la fuente

f imposition *f* à la source; retenue *f* d'impôts à la source; stoppage *m* à la source
i imposizione *f* alla fonte; ritenuta *f* d'imposte alla fonte; ritenuta *f* all'origine; ritenuta *f* d'acconto; ritenuta *f* per rivalsa; trattenuta *f* d'imposte alla fonte; trattenuta *f* all'origine; trattenuta *f* d'acconto; trattenuta *f* per rivalsa
n heffing *f* aan de bron; inhouding *f* van belastingen aan de bron; voorheffing *f* *(B)*

682 collection of debts; debt collection; debt recovery; recovery of debts
d Beitreibung *f* von Aussenständen (Forderungen; Schulden); Betreibung *f* *(Schw)* von Aussenständen (Forderungen; Schulden); Eintreibung *f* von Aussenständen (Forderungen; Schulden); Einziehung *f* von Aussenständen (Forderungen; Schulden); Einzug *m* von Aussenständen (Forderungen; Schulden)
e cobranza *f* de créditos (deudas); cobro *m* de créditos (deudas); recaudación *f* de créditos (deudas)
f mise *f* en recouvrement de créances (dettes); recouvrement *m* de créances (dettes); récupération *f* de créances (dettes)
i esazione *f* di crediti (debiti); ricupero *m* di crediti (debiti); riscossione *f* di crediti (debiti)
n inning *f* van schulden (vorderingen); invordering *f* van schulden (vorderingen)

683 collection of taxes; tax collection
cf. **imposition of taxes**
d Steuerbeitreibung *f*; Steuereinhebung *f* *(O)*; Steuereintreibung *f*; Steuereinziehung *f*; Steuererhebung *f*
e cobro *m* de impuestos; percepción *f* de impuestos; recaudación *f* de impuestos
f mise *f* en recouvrement d'impôts; perception *f* d'impôts; recouvrement *m* d'impôts
i esazione *f* d'imposte; percezione *f* d'imposte; riscossione *f* d'imposte
n belastinginning *f*

684 collective benefits; public benefits
d öffentliche Leistungen *fpl*; staatliche Leistungen *fpl*
e prestaciones *fpl* colectivas
f prestations *fpl* collectives
i prestazioni *fpl* collettive
n collectieve voorzieningen *fpl*; openbare voorzieningen *fpl*

685 collective deposit
d Sammeldepot *n*
e depósito *m* colectivo
f dêpôt *m* collectif
i deposito *m* collettivo
n verzameldeposito *n*

686 commercial company; company; trading company
d Compagnie *f* *(rare)*; Gesellschaft *f*; Handelsgesellschaft *f*
e compañía *f* (de comercio); sociedad *f* (comercial); sociedad *f* (mercantil)
f compagnie *f*; société *f* (commerciale)
i compagnia *f*; società *f* (commerciale)
n compagnie *f* *(rare)*; handelscompagnie *f* *(rare)*; handel(s)maatschappij *f*; handelsvennootschap *f*; maatschappij *f*; vennootschap *f*

687 commercial register; trade register
d Handelsregister *n*
e registro *m* mercantil
f registre *m* de commerce
i registro *m* delle imprese; registro *m* di commercio
n handelsregister *n*

688 commercial value; marketable value; market value; sales value
d Handelswert *m*; Marktwert *m*; Verkaufswert *m*; Verkehrswert *m*
e valor *m* comercial; valor *m* de mercado; valor *m* en venta; valor *m* realizable
f valeur *f* commerciale; valeur *f* marchande; valeur *f* négociable; valeur *f* sur le marché; valeur *f* vénale
i valore *m* commerciale; valore *m* di mercato; valore *m* di vendita; valore *m* venale
n marktwaarde *f*; verkoop(s)waarde *f*

689 commission
cf. **brokerage, charge**
d Kommission *f*; Provision *f*; Vermittlungsgebühr *f*
e comisión *f*; derechos *mpl* de comisión
f commission *f*; droit *m* de commission; remise *f*
i commissione *f*; provvigione *f*
n commissie *f*; commissieloon *n*; provisie *f*

690 commission agent
cf. **broker**
d Kommissionär *m*; Kommissionsagent *m*; Kommissionsvertreter *m*
e agente *m* comisionista; agente *m* de comisiones; comisionista *m*
f commissionaire *m*

i commissionario *m*
n commissionair *m*

691 commission rate
d Kommissionssatz *m*; Provisionssatz *m*
e tipo *m* de comisión
f taux *m* de commission
i tasso *m* di provvigione
n commissiekoers *m*

692 commitment
d Bindung *f*; Verpflichtung *f*
e compromiso *m*; obligación *f*
f engagement *m*
i impegno *m*
n engagement *n*; verbintenis *f*; verplichting *f*

693 commitment charge; commitment commission
d Bereitstellungskommission *f*; Bereitstellungsprovision *f*; Krediteröffnungskommission *f*; Krediteröffnungsprovision *f*
e comisión *f* de apertura de crédito
f commission *f* d'ouverture de crédit
i provvigione *f* d'apertura di credito
n kredietopeningskommissie *f*; kredietopeningsprovisie *f*

694 commodities broker
d Kursmakler *m* an der Warenbörse; Warenmakler *m*
e corredor *m* de mercancías; corredor *m* en mercancías
f courtier *m* en marchandises
i mediatore *m* di merci; sensale *m* di merci
n goederenmakelaar *m*; makelaar *m* aan de goederenbeurs

695 commodity exchange; produce exchange
d Handelsbörse *f*; Produktenbörse *f*; Warenbörse *f*
e bolsa *f* de comercio; bolsa *f* de contratación; bolsa *f* de mercancías; lonja *f*
f bourse *f* de commerce; bourse *f* de marchandises
i borsa *f* di commercio; borsa *f* merci
n goederenbeurs *f*; handelsbeurs *f*

696 commodity price index
d Warenpreisindex *m*
e índice *m* de precios de mercancías
f indice *m* des prix des marchandises
i indice *m* dei prezzi delle merci
n goederenprijsindex *m*

697 common capital stock *(US)*; ordinary share capital
cf. **equity capital**
d Stammaktienkapital *n*
e capital *m* en acciones ordinarias
f capital *m* en actions ordinaires
i capitale *m* in azioni ordinarie
n gewoon aandelenkapitaal *n*

698 common denominator
d gemeinsamer Nenner *m*
e denominador *m* común
f dénominateur *m* commun
i comune denominatore *m*; denominatore *m* comune
n gemeenschappelijke noemer *m*

699 common external tariff
d gemeinsamer Aussentarif *m*
e arancel *m* exterior común; tarifa *f* exterior común
f tarif *m* extérieur commun
i tariffa *f* esterna comune
n gemeenschappelijk buitentarief *n*

700 Common Market; Euro-Markt
d Euromarkt *m*; Gemeinsamer Markt *m*
e Euromercado *m*; Mercado *m* Común
f Marché *m* commun; Marché *m* européen
i Euromercato *m*; Mercato *m* Comune
n Euromarkt *f*; Gemeenschappelijke Markt *f*

701 common shares *(US)*; common stock *(US)*; equity; ordinary shares *(UK)*; ordinary stock *(UK)*
d Stammaktien *fpl*
e acciones *fpl* comunes *(AL)*; acciones *fpl* ordinarias
f actions *fpl* ordinaires
i azioni *fpl* comuni; azioni *fpl* ordinarie
n gewone aandelen *npl*

702 Commonwealth preference; imperial preference
d Vorzugstarif *m* für Mitglieder des Commonwealths
e tarifa *f* preferencial para los miembros del Commonwealth
f tarif *m* préférentiel pour les membres du Commonwealth
i tariffa *f* preferenziale per i membri del Commonwealth
n voorkeurtarief *n* voor de leden van het Gemenebest

703 community budget
d Gemeinschaftshaushalt *m*
e presupuesto *m* de la Comunidad

f budget *m* communautaire
i bilancio *m* della Communità
n begroting *f* van de Gemeenschap

704 **commutation bond; conversion bond; debt adjustment debenture *(US)*; redemption bond; refunding bond**
d Ablösungspfandbrief *m*; Ablösungsschuldverschreibung *f*; Konversionsobligation *f*; Konversionsschuldverschreibung *f*; neufundierte Obligation *f*; Umtauschschuldverschreibung *f*
e bono *m* de reintegro; obligación *f* de conversión
f bon *m* de remboursement; obligation *f* de conversion
i buono *m* di rimborso; obbligazione *f* di conversione
n conversieschuldbrief *m*; opnieuw gefundeerde obligatie *f*

705 **company financial year**
cf. **business year, financial year**
d Gesellschaftsjahr *n*
e año *m* financiero
f année *f* sociale; exercice *m* social
i anno *m* sociale; esercizio *m* sociale
n genootschapsjaar *n*

706 **compensate *v*; offset *v*; set *v* off**
d aufrechnen; ausgleichen; in Gegenrechnung bringen; kompensieren; verrechnen
e compensar
f compenser
i compensare
n compenseren; verrekenen

707 **compensate *v* for a loss; cover *v* a loss; make *v* good a loss; make *v* up for a loss; recoup *v* a loss; recover *v* a loss; repair *v* a loss; retrieve *v* a loss**
d einen Verlust ausgleichen; einen Verlust decken; einen Verlust ersetzen; einen Verlust gutmachen; einen Verlust vergüten; einen Verlust wettmachen; einen Verlust wiedereinbringen; einen Verlust wiedergutmachen
e compensar una pérdida; cubrir una pérdida; recuperar una pérdida; reparar una pérdida; resarcirse de una pérdida
f bonifier une perte; combler une perte; compenser une perte; couvrir une perte; réparer une perte; se récupérer d'une perte
i abbonare una perdita; bonificare una perdita; compensare una perdita; coprire una perdita; ricuperare una perdita; riparare una perdita
n een verlies dekken; een verlies goedmaken; een verlies vergoeden; een verlies we(d)er goedmaken

708 **compensation; damages; indemnification; indemnity; reparation***
d Abstandsgeld *n***; Abstandssumme *f***; Entschädigung *f*; Ersatzleistung *f*; Kompensation *f*; Kompensierung *f*; Reparation *f**; Schadenersatz *m*; Schadloshaltung *f*; Vergütung *f*
e compensación *f*; indemnización *f*; reparación *f**; resarcimiento *m*
f compensation *f*; dédommagement *m*; dommages (et) intérêts *mpl*; indemnisation *f*; indemnité *f*; réparation *f*
i compensazione *f*; compenso *m*; indennità *f*; indennizzo *m*; rifusione *f*; riparazione *f**; risarcimento *m*
n afkoopgeld *n***; afkoopsom *f***; compensatie *f*; reparatie *f*; schadeloosstelling *f*; schadevergoeding *f*; vergoeding *f*

* Mostly used in political sense.
** Only for thing bought off or out.

709 **compensation; offset; setoff**
cf. **equalization**
d Aufrechnung *f*; Ausgleich *m*; Ausgleichung *f*; Gegenrechnung *f*; Kompensation *f*; Verrechnung *f (Schw)*
e compensación *f*
f compensation *f*
i compensazione *f*
n compensatie *f*; schuldvergelijking *f*; verrekening *f*

710 **compensation fund *(rare)*; equalization fund**
cf. **stabilization fund**
d Ausgleichsfonds *m*; Ausgleichskasse *f*; Kompensationskasse *f*
e caja *f* de compensación; fondo *m* de compensación; fondo *m* de igualación; fondo *m* de perecuación
f caisse *f* de compensation; caisse *f* de péréquation; fonds *m* de compensation; fonds *m* d'égalisation; fonds *m* de péréquation
i cassa *f* di compensazione; cassa *f* di conguaglio; cassa *f* di perequazione; fondo *m* di compensazione; fondo *m* di equalizzazione; fondo *m* di perequazione
n compensatiekas *f*; egalisatiefonds *n*; perekwatiekas *f (B)*

711 **compensatory duty; countervailing duty; equalizing duty**
d Ausgleichszoll *m*; Kompensationszoll *m*
e arancel *m* compensatorio; arancel *m* de compensación; tasa *f* compensatoria; tasa *f* de compensación
f droit *m* compensateur; droit *m* de compensation
i dazio *m* compensatore; dazio *m* di compensazione
n compensatierecht *n*

712 **compensatory tax; equalization levy; equalization tax**
d Ausgleichsabgabe *f*; Ausgleichssteuer *f*; Ausgleichstaxe *f*
e impuesto *m* compensatorio; impuesto *m* de compensación; tasa *f* compensatoria; tasa *f* de compensación; tasa *f* de perecuación
f taxe *f* compensatoire; taxe *f* de compensation; taxe *f* de péréquation
i imposta *f* di compensazione; imposta *f* di conguaglio; tassa *f* di compensazione; tassa *f* di conguaglio; tassa *f* di perequazione
n compensatietaks *m/f*; egalisatiebelasting *f*

713 **competitive**
d konkurrenzfähig; konkurrierend; wettbewerbsfähig
e competidor; competitivo
f compétitif; concurrentiel
i competitivo; concorrenziale
n concurrerend; mededingend

714 **competitiveness**
d Konkurrenzfähigkeit *f*; Wettbewerbsfähigkeit *f*
e capacidad *f* de competir; competitividad *f*
f capacité *f* compétitive; compétitivité *f*
i capacità *f* concorrenziale; competitività *f*; concorrenzialità *f*
n concurrentiekracht *f*; concurrentievermogen *n*

715 **complete payment; full payment; payment in full**
d Vollbezahlung *f*; vollständige Auszahlung *f*; vollständige Bezahlung *f*; vollständige Zahlung *f*; Vollzahlung *f*
e pago *m* completo; pago *m* entero; pago *m* íntegro; pago *m* total
f paiement *m* entier; paiement *m* intégral; paiement *m* total; parfait paiement *m*
i pagamento *m* completo; pagamento *m* integrale; pagamento *m* intero; pagamento *m* totale
n gehele betaling *f*; volledige betaling *f*

716 **component of demand; demand factor**
d Nachfragefaktor *m*
e componente *m* de la demanda
f composante *f* de la demande
i componente *m/f* della domanda
n vraagelement *n*

717 **composite entry; compound entry; summary posting** *(US)*
d Gesamteintrag *m*; Sammelbuchung *f*
e asiento *m* colectivo; asiento *m* resumen; entrada *f* colectiva; partida *f* colectiva; partida *f* compuesta
f article *m* collectif; article *m* composé; écriture *f* récapitulative
i scrittura *f* riepilogativa
n verzamelboeking *f*

718 **composition** *(with creditors)*; **scheme of arrangement; scheme of composition**
d Abfindung *f*; Akkord *m*; Ausgleich *m* *(O)*; Vergleich *m*; Verständigung *f*
e acomodamiento *m*; arreglo *m* (judicial); compromiso *m*; convenio *m*; transacción *f*
f accommodement *m*; arrangement *m*; concordat *m*; décharge *f*; règlement *m* (judiciaire)
i accomodamento *m*; accordo *m*; concordato *m*; transazione *f*
n akkoord *n*; overeenkomst *f*; vergelijk *n*

719 **composition agreement; deed of arrangement**
d Vergleichsabkommen *n*; Vergleichsvertrag *m*
e contrato *m* de compromiso; contrato *m* de convenio
f concordat *m* préventif à la faillite; contrat *m* d'arrangement
i concordato *m* fallimentare; concordato *m* preventivo
n vergelijkingsakkoord *n*

720 **compound interest**
cf. **anatocism**
d Zinseszins(en) *m(pl)*; zusammengesetzte Zinsen *mpl*
e interés(es) *m(pl)* compuesto(s)
f intérêt(s) *m(pl)* composé(s)
i interesse *m* composto; interesse *m* degli interessi; interessi *mpl* composti
n int(e)rest *m* op int(e)rest; rente *f* op rente; samengestelde int(e)rest *m*

721 compulsory conversion; forced conversion; involuntary conversion
d Zwangskonversion *f*; Zwangskonvertierung *f*
e conversión *f* forzosa
f conversion *f* forcée
i conversione *f* forzata
n gedwongen conversie *f*

722 compulsory exchange; compulsory rate (of exchange); controlled exchange; controlled rate (of exchange); forced exchange; forced rate (of exchange)
d Zwangskurs *m*; Zwangsumrechnungskurs *m*
e cambio *m* forzoso; cambio *m* obligatorio; tipo *m* de cambio forzoso; tipo *m* de cambio obligatorio; tipo *m* forzoso; tipo *m* obligatorio
f cours *m* forcé; taux *m* de change forcé; taux *m* forcé
i cambio *m* forzoso; corso *m* forzoso; tasso *m* (di cambio) forzoso
n gedwongen koers *m*; gedwongen wisselkoers *m*

723 compulsory loan; forced loan
d Zwangsanleihe *f*
e empréstito *m* forzoso
f emprunt *m* forcé
i prestito *m* forzato; prestito *m* forzoso
n gedwongen lening *f*

724 compulsory saving; forced saving
d obligatorisches Sparen *n*; Zwangssparen *n*
e ahorro *m* forzoso; ahorro *m* obligatorio
f épargne *f* forcée; épargne *f* obligatoire
i risparmio *m* coattivo; risparmio *m* forzato; risparmio *m* forzoso
n gedwongen sparen *n*; verplicht sparen *n*

725 concealed inflation; hidden inflation; masked inflation
cf. **creeping inflation**
d unsichtbare Inflation *f*; versteckte Inflation *f*
e inflación *f* latente; inflación *f* oculta
f inflation *f* larvée; inflation *f* latente
i inflazione *f* latente; inflazione *f* larvata; inflazione *f* mascherata
n latente inflatie *f*

726 concealed reserves; hidden reserves; invisible reserves; undisclosed reserves
d stille Reserven *fpl*; unsichtbare Reserven *fpl*; versteckte Reserven *fpl*
e reservas *fpl* encubiertas; reservas *fpl* invisibles; reservas *fpl* latentes; reservas *fpl* no declaradas; reservas *fpl* ocultas; reservas *fpl* tácitas
f réserves *fpl* cachées; réserves *fpl* invisibles; réserves *fpl* latentes; réserves *fpl* non déclarées; réserves *fpl* occultes
i riserve *fpl* invisibili; riserve *fpl* latenti; riserve *fpl* nascoste; riserve *fpl* non dichiarate; riserve *fpl* occulte; riserve *fpl* segrete; riserve *fpl* tacite
n geheime reserves *fpl*; onzichtbare reserves *fpl*; stille reserves *fpl*; verborgen reserves *fpl*

727 concern; group
cf. **consortium, syndicate, trust**
d Gruppe *f*; Konzern *m*
e agrupación *f*; grupo *m*
f groupe *m*; groupement *m*
i complesso *m*; gruppo *m*
n concern *n*; groep *f*

728 concession; franchise *(US)*
d Konzession *f*
e concesión *f*
f concession *f*
i concessione *f*
n concessie *f*

729 conditions of issue of a loan; issuing conditions of a loan
d Ausstattung *f* einer Anleihe; Emissionsbedingungen *fpl* einer Anleihe
e condiciones *fpl* de emisión de un empréstito
f conditions *fpl* d'émission d'un emprunt
i condizioni *fpl* di emissione di un prestito
n emissievoorwaarden *fpl* van een lening

730 conduct of the finances; financial management; handling of the finances; management of the finances
cf. **financial policy**
d Finanzgebaren *n*; Finanzgebarung *f*; finanzielle Gebarung *f*
e gestión *f* financiera
f gestion *f* financière
i gestione *f* finanziaria
n financieel beheer *n*; financieel beleid *n*

731 consideration (in return); quid pro quo
cf. **counterpart**
d Gegenleistung *f*
e contraprestación *f*
f contre-prestation *f*; prestation *f* en retour
i controprestazione *f*
n contraprestatie *f*; tegenprestatie *f*

732 in consideration of the payment of; on payment of
d gegen Zahlung von; mittels Zahlung von
e contra pagam(i)ento de; contra pago de
f moyennant paiement de; moyennant le versement de
i mediante il pagamento di
n tegen betaling van

733 consolidate *v* **a debt; fund** *v* **a debt; unify** *v* **a debt**
d eine Schuld fundieren; eine Schuld konsolidieren; eine Schuld unifizieren
e consolidar una deuda; unificar una deuda
f consolider une dette; fonder une dette; unifier une dette
i consolidare un debito; unificare un debito
n een schuld consolideren; een schuld funderen; een schuld unificeren

734 consolidated bonds *(US)*; **consolidated loan stock; consolidated stock; consols**
d fundierte Staatspapiere *npl*; konsolidierte Staatspapiere *npl*; Konsols *mpl*
e títulos *mpl* de la deuda pública consolidada
f consolidés *mpl*; titres *mpl* de la dette publique consolidée
i consolidati *mpl*; titoli *mpl* del debito pubblico consolidato
n consols *mpl*; geconsolideerde staatspapieren *npl*

735 consolidated debt; funded debt; unified debt
cf. **bonded debt**
d fundierte Schuld *f*; konsolidierte Schuld *f*; unifizierte Schuld *f*
e deuda *f* consolidada; deuda *f* unificada
f dette *f* consolidée; dette *f* unifiée
i debito *m* consolidato; debito *m* unificato
n geconsolideerde schuld *f*; gefundeerde schuld *f*; geünificeerde schuld *f*

736 consolidated statement; group balance sheet
d konsolidierter Jahresabschluss *m*; Konzernabschluss *m*; Konzernbilanz *f*
e balance *m* consolidado (del grupo); estados *mpl* consolidados
f bilan *m* consolidé (du groupe)
i bilancio *m* consolidato (del gruppo)
n concern jaarrekening *f*; geconsolideerde jaarrekening *f*

737 consolidation; funding; unification
cf. **conversion of debts**
d Fundierung *f*; Funding *n*; *Konsolidation f*; Konsolidierung *f*; Umschuldung *f*; Unifizierung *f*
e consolidación *f*; unificación *f*
f consolidation *f*; funding *m*; unification *f*
i consolidamento *m*; consolidazione *f*
n consolidatie *f*; fundering *f*; unificatie *f*

738 consolidation loan; funding loan
cf. **conversion loan**
d Fundierungsanleihe *f*; Konsolidationsanleihe *f*; Konsolidierungsanleihe *f*; Umschuldungsanleihe *f*
e empréstito *m* de consolidación
f emprunt *m* de consolidation; emprunt *m* funding
i prestito *m* di consolidamento; prestito *m* di consolidazione
n consolidatielening *f*

739 consolidation statement
d Konsolidierungsbogen *m*
e estado *m* de consolidación
f état *m* de consolidation
i situazione *f* consolidata
n consolidatiestaat *m*

740 consortium
cf. **concern, pool, syndicate, trust**
d Konsortium *n*
e consorcio *m*
f consortium *m*
i consorzio *m*
n consortium *n*

741 consortium credit; participation loan; syndicated loan; syndicate loan *(US)*
d Konsortialkredit *m*
e crédito *m* consorcial; crédito *m* de consorcio
f crédit *m* consortial; crédit *m* syndical
i credito *m* consorziale
n consortiaal krediet *n*; metakrediet *n*

742 at constant prices
d zu konstanten Preisen
e a precios constantes
f à prix constants
i a prezzi constanti
n in constante prijzen; tegen constante prijzen

743 consumables *(US)*; **consumer goods; consumption goods** *(rare)*
d Konsumgüter *npl*; Verbrauchsgüter *npl*
e bienes *mpl* de consumo
f biens *mpl* de consommation
i beni *mpl* di consumo
n consumptiegoederen *npl*; verbruiksgoederen *npl*

744 consumer
d Konsument *m*; Verbraucher *m*
e consumidor *m*
f consommateur *m*
i consumatore *m*
n consument *m*; verbruiker *m*

745 consumer credit; retail credit *(US)*
cf. **hire purchase credit**
d Konsumentenkredit *m*; Konsumkredit *m*; Konsumtivkredit *m*; Kundenkredit *m*; Verbraucherkredit *m*
e crédito *m* al consumidor; crédito *m* al consumo; crédito *m* de consumo; crédito *m* para el consumidor
f crédit *m* à la consommation; crédit *m* au consommateur
i credito *m* al consumatore; credito *m* al consumo; credito *m* di consumo
n consumentenkrediet *n*; consumptief krediet *n*

746 consumer demand; demand for consumer goods
d Verbrauchsnachfrage *f*
e demanda *f* de consumidores
f demande *f* de biens de consommation
i domanda *f* di beni di consumo
n consumptieve vraag *f*; consumptievraag *f*

747 consumer durables; durable consumer goods
d dauerhafte Konsumgüter *npl*; langlebige Konsumgüter *npl*
e bienes *mpl* durables de consumo; bienes *mpl* duraderos de consumo; durables *mpl* de consumo
f biens *mpl* de consommation durables
i beni *mpl* di consumo durevoli
n duurzame consumptiegoederen *npl*

748 consumer expenditure; consumer spending
d Konsumaufwand *m*; konsumtive Ausgaben *fpl*; Verbraucheraufwand *m*; Verbraucheraufwendung *f*; Verbraucherausgaben *fpl*; Verbrauchsaufwand *m*; Verbrauchsaufwendung *f*; Verbrauchsausgaben *fpl*
e gastos *mpl* de consumo; gastos *mpl* de los consumidores
f dépenses *fpl* de consommation; dépenses *fpl* des consommateurs; dépenses *fpl* en consommation
i spese *fpl* di consumo; spese *fpl* per consumi
n consumentenbesteding *f*; consumptieve besteding *f*

749 consumer price
d Konsumentenpreis *m*; Verbraucherpreis *m*
e precio *m* al consumidor; precio *m* de consumo; precio *m* para el consumidor
f prix *m* à la consommation; prix *m* au consommateur
i prezzo *m* al consumatore; prezzo *m* al consumo
n consumentenprijs *m*; consumptieprijs *m*

750 consumer resistance
d Verbraucherzurückhaltung *f*
e reserva *f* de los consumidores
f réserve *f* des consommateurs
i apatia *f* dei consumatori
n verzet *n* van de consumenten

751 consumption
d Konsum *m*; Verbrauch *m*
e consumo *m*
f consommation *f*
i consumo *m*
n consumptie *f*; verbruik *n*

752 consumption tax; excise; excise duty; excise tax; tax on consumption
d Akzise *f*; Konsumsteuer *f*; Verbrauchsabgabe *f*; Verbrauchssteuer *f*
e contribución *f* de usos y consumos; derecho *m* de consumo; impuesto *m* de consumo(s); impuesto *m* sobre el consumo
f accise *f*; droit *m* de consommation; impôt *m* de consommation; impôt *m* sur la consommation; taxe *f* à la consommation; taxe *f* de consommation; taxe *f* sur la consommation
i accisa *f*; dazio *m* di consumo; imposta *f* di consumo; imposta *f* sui consumi
n accijns *m*; consumptieve belasting *f*; verbruiksbelasting *f*

753 contango transaction
d Kostgeschäft *n*; Pensionsgeschäft *n*; Prolongation *f*; Prolongationsgeschäft *n*; Reportgeschäft *n*
e operación *f* de reporte; operación *f* de reporto *(AL)*; reporte *m*; reporto *m* *(AL)*
f opération *f* de pension; opération *f* de report; report *m*; transaction *f* de report
i operazione *f* a riporto; riporto *m*
n prolongatie *f*; reporttransactie *f*

754 contingencies
d unvorhergesehene Ausgaben *fpl*; unvorhergesehene Belastungen *fpl*
e gastos *mpl* imprevistos
f imprévus *mpl*

i spese *fpl* impreviste
n onvoorziene uitgaven *fpl*

755 contingency fund; contingent fund
cf. **reserve fund**
d ausserordentlicher Reservefonds *m*; Delcrederefonds *m*; Konjunkturfonds *m*; Reservefonds *m* für unvorhergesehene Ausgaben
e fondo *m* coyuntural; fondo *m* de previsión; fondo *m* para contingencias; fondo *m* para eventualidades; fondo *m* para imprevistos
f fonds *m* conjoncturel; fonds *m* de prévision; fonds *m* de prévoyance; fonds *m* de réserve pour dépenses imprévues; fonds *m* prévisionnel
i fondo *m* congiunturale; fondo *m* di previdenza; fondo *m* di riserva per spese impreviste
n conjunctuurfonds *n*; extra-reservefonds *n*; fonds *n* voor onvoorziene uitgaven; voorzieningsfonds *n*

756 contingency reserve; contingent reserve; provision for contingencies; reserve for contingencies
d Delkredererückstellung *f*; Eventualreserve *f*; Rückstellung *f* für unvorhergesehene Ausgaben
e reserva *f* de previsión; reserva *f* para contingencias; reserva *f* para eventualidades; reserva *f* para imprevistos
f réserve *f* de prévoyance; réserve *f* pour dépenses imprévues
i riserva *f* di previdenza; riserva *f* per eventualità; riserva *f* per spese impreviste
n reserve *f* voor onvoorziene uitgaven; voorzieningsreserve *f*

757 contingent claim
d Eventualforderung *f*
e crédito *m* eventual
f créance *f* éventuelle
i credito *m* eventuale
n eventuele schuldvordering *f*

758 contingent liability; contingent obligation
d Eventualverbindlichkeit *f*; Eventualverpflichtung *f*
e obligación *f* eventual; pasivo *m* contingente; pasivo *m* eventual
f obligation *f* éventuelle; passif *m* éventuel
i obbligazione *f* eventuale; passivo *m* contingente; passivo *m* eventuale
n eventuele verplichting *f*

759 contingent tax liability *(US)*; **latent tax liability**
d latente Steuerpflicht *f*
e carga *f* fiscal latente
f charge *f* fiscale latente
i onere *m* fiscale latente
n latente belastingverplichting *f*

760 contra account; offset account *(US)*
d Gegenkonto *n*
e cuenta *f* de contrapartida
f compte *m* de contre-partie
i conto *m* di contropartita
n tegenrekening *f*

761 contract *v* **a debt; incur** *v* **a debt; make** *v* **a debt; run** *v* **up a debt**
cf. **fall** *v* **into debt**
d eine Schuld aufnehmen *(O)*; eine Schuld eingehen; eine Schuld machen
e contraer una deuda; hacer una deuda
f contracter une dette; faire une dette
i contrarre un debito; far un debito
n een schuld aangaan; een schuld maken

762 contract *v* **a loan; raise** *v* **a loan**
cf. **negociate** *v* **a loan**
d eine Anleihe abschliessen; eine Anleihe aufnehmen; eine Anleihe kontrahieren; eine Anleihe machen; eine Anleihe schliessen
e concertar un empréstito; contraer un empréstito; contratar un empréstito; hacer un empréstitio; leventar un empréstito *(AL)*
f contracter un emprunt; faire un emprunt
i contrarre un prestito
n een lening aangaan; een lening afsluiten; een lening doen; een lening opnemen; een lening sluiten

763 contractual liability; liability out of contract
d vertragliche Haftpflicht *f*; vertragliche Haftung *f*; Vertragshaftung *f*
e responsabilidad *f* contractual
f responsabilité *f* contractuelle
i responsabilità *f* contrattuale
n contractuele aansprakelijkheid *f*

764 contractual savings
d Vertragssparen *n*
e ahorros *mpl* contractuales
f épargne *f* contractuelle
i risparmio *m* contrattuale
n contractuele besparingen *fpl*

765 contribution *(of assets etc.)*
cf. **assets in kind, capital contribution**

d Einbringen *n*; Einbringung *f*; Einlage *f*; Einschuss *m*
e aportación *f*; aporte *m*
f apport *m*
i apporto *m*
n inbreng *m*

766 control account
cf. **collation account**
d Kontrollkonto *n*; Sammelkonto *n*
e cuenta *f* colectiva; cuenta *f* de control
f compte *m* collectif
i conto *m* collettivo; conto *m* riassuntivo
n collectieve rekening *f*

767 controlled currency; managed currency
d kontrollierte Währung *f*; manipulierte Währung *f*; regulierte Währung *f*
e moneda *f* controlada; moneda *f* dirigida; moneda *f* manipulada
f monnaie *f* contrôlée; monnaie *f* dirigée; monnaie *f* manipulée
i moneta *f* controllata; moneta *f* manipolata; moneta *f* manovrata; moneta *f* regolata
n gecontroleerde valuta *f*; gemanipuleerde valuta *f*; gereguleerde valuta *f*

768 controlled economy; directed economy; managed economy; planned economy
cf. **dirigisme**
d dirigistische Wirtschaft *f*; gelenkte Wirtschaft *f*; Planwirtschaft *f*
e economía *f* controlada; economía *f* dirigida; economía *f* planificada
f économie *f* dirigée; économie *f* planifiée
i economia *f* dirigista; economia *f* pianificata; economia *f* programmata
n geleide economie *f*; planeconomie *f*; planmatige economie *f*

769 controlling company; parent company; parent firm
cf. **holding company**
d herrschende Gesellschaft *f*; Kontrollgesellschaft *f*; Muttergesellschaft *f*; Obergesellschaft *f*; Stammhaus *n*
e casa *f* matriz; sociedad *f* controladora; sociedad *f* de control; sociedad *f* dominante; sociedad *f* madre; sociedad *f* matriz
f maison *f* mère; société *f* contrôleuse; société *f* de contrôle; société *f* dominante; société *f* mère
i casa *f* madre; società *f* controllante; società *f* di controllo; società *f* dominante; società *f* madre
n moedermaatschappij *f*

770 controlling interest; majority holding; majority interest
d Direktkontrolle *f*; Majoritätsbeteiligung *f*; Mehrheitsbeteiligung *f*; Mehrheitspaket *n*
e control *m* directo; interés *m* mayoritario; participación *f* mayoritaria
f contrôle *m* direct; intérêt(s) *m(pl)* majoritaire(s); participation *f* majoritaire
i controllo *m* diretto; interesse *m* maggioritario; partecipazione *f* di maggioranza; partecipazione *f* maggioritaria
n meerderheidsbelang *n*; meerderheidsdeelname *f*; meerderheidsdeelneming *f*; meerderheidsparticipatie *f*

771 conversion
d Konversion *f*; Konvertierung *f*; Umrechnung *f*; Umtausch *m*; Umwandlung *f*
e cambio *m*; conversión *f*
f conversion *f*; convertissement *m*
i cambio *m*; conversione *f*
n conversie *f*; herleiding *f*; omrekening *f*

772 conversion factor
d Konversionsfaktor *m*; Umrechnungsfaktor *m*
e factor *m* de conversión
f facteur *m* de conversion
i fattore *m* di conversione
n conversiefactor *m*; omrekeningsfactor *m*

773 conversion into cash; conversion into money; liquidation; realisation *(UK)*; **realization** *(US)*
cf. **deblocking**
d Flüssigmachung *f*; Liquidation *f*; Liquidierung *f*; Realisation *f*; Realisierung *f*; Umsetzung *f* in Geld; Umwandlung *f* in Bargeld; Verflüssigung *f*; Versilberung *f*; Verwertung *f*
e conversión *f* en dinero; liquidación *f*; realización *f*
f conversion *f* en argent; conversion *f* en espèces; liquidation *f*; réalisation *f*
i conversione *f* in denaro; liquidazione *f*; realizzazione *f*; realizzo *m*
n liquidatie *f*; realisatie *f*; realisering *f*; tegeldemaking *f*; verzilvering *f*

774 conversion loan
cf. **consolidation loan**
d Konversionsanleihe *f*; Konvertierungsanleihe *f*; Umschuldungsanleihe *f*
e empréstito *m* de conversión
f emprunt *m* de conversion

i prestito *m* di conversione
n conversielening *f*

775 **conversion of a loan; refunding of a loan**
d Konversion *f* einer Anleihe; Konvertierung *f* einer Anleihe; Neufundierung *f* einer Anleihe; Umschuldung *f* einer Anleihe
e conversión *f* de un empréstito
f conversion *f* d'un emprunt
i conversione *f* di un prestito
n conversie *f* van een lening; omzetting *f* van een lening

776 **conversion of debts**
cf. **consolidation**
d Konversion *f* von Schulden; Konvertierung *f* von Schulden; Schuldumwandlung *f*; Umschuldung *f*
e conversión *f* de deudas
f conversion *f* de dettes
i conversione *f* di debiti
n conversie *f* van schulden; omzetting *f* van schulden

777 **conversion option; conversion right**
d Konversionsrecht *n*; Umtauschrecht *n*; Umwandlungsrecht *n*
e derecho *m* de conversión
f droit *m* de conversion
i diritto *m* di conversione
n recht *n* van conversie

778 **conversion rate; rate of conversion**
cf. **exchange**
d Konversionskurs *m*; Konversionssatz *m*; Umrechnungskurs *m*; Umrechnungssatz *m*; Umwandlungskurs *m*; Umwandlungssatz *m*
e cambio *m* de conversión; cotización *f* de conversión; tasa *f* de conversión; tipo *m* de conversión
f cours *m* de conversion; taux *m* de conversion
i corso *m* di conversione; tasso *m* di conversione
n conversiekoers *m*; omrekeningskoers *m*

779 **convert** *v* **a loan; refund** *v* **a loan**
d eine Anleihe konvertieren; eine Anleihe neufundieren; eine Anleihe umschulden
e convertir un empréstito
f convertir un emprunt
i convertire un prestito
n een lening converteren; een lening omzetten

780 **convertibility**
d Konvertibilität *f*; Konvertierbarkeit *f*; Umwandelbarkeit *f*
e convertibilidad *f*
f convertibilité *f*
i convertibilità *f*
n convertibiliteit *f*; inwisselbaarheid *f*

781 **convertibility for residents; internal convertibility**
d Inländerkonvertiblität *f*; Inländerkonvertierbarkeit *f*; innere Konvertibilität *f*; innere Konvertierbarkeit *f*; interne Konvertibilität *f*; interne Konvertierbarkeit *f*
e convertibilidad *f* interna
f convertibilité *f* intérieure; convertibilité *f* interne
i convertibilità *f* interna
n interne convertibiliteit *f*

782 **convertible**
d einlösbar; konvertibel; konvertierbar; umwandelbar
e convertible
f convertible
i convertibile
n converteerbaar; inwisselbaar

783 **convertible bond; convertible debenture**
d Wandelobligation *f*; Wandelschuldverschreibung *f*
e obligación *f* convertible
f obligation *f* convertible
i obbligazione *f* convertibile
n converteerbare obligatie *f*

784 **convertible loan**
d Wandelanleihe *f*
e empréstito *m* convertible
f emprunt *m* convertible; emprunt *m* convertissable
i prestito *m* convertibile
n converteerbare lening *f*

785 **convert** *v* **into cash; convert** *v* **into money; liquidate** *v*; **realise** *v* *(UK)*; **realize** *v* *(US)*; **turn** *v* **into cash; turn** *v* **into money**
cf. **deblock** *v*
d flüssig machen; in Bargeld umwandeln; in Geld umsetzen; liquidieren; liquidisieren; realisieren; verflüssigen; versilbern; verwerten; zu Geld machen
e convertir en dinero (contante); liquidar; monetizar; realizar
f convertir en argent; convertir en espèces; liquider; réaliser
i convertire in denaro (contante); liquidare; monetizzare; realizzare

n liquide maken; realiseren; te gelde maken; verzilveren

786 **cooperative** *(US)*; **co-operative** *(UK)*; **co-operative society**
d Genossenschaft *f*; Kooperativ *n*; Kooperative *f*; Kooperativgenossenschaft *f*; Kooperativgesellschaft *f*
e cooperativa *f*; sociedad *f* cooperativa
f coopérative *f*; société *f* coopérative
i cooperativa *f*; società *f* cooperativa
n coöperatie *f*; coöperatieve vennootschap *f*; samenwerkende vennootschap *f (B)*

787 **co-operative credit bank; credit association; credit co-operative; credit society; credit union** *(US)*; **loan association; loan society; mutual loan society**
d Kreditgenossenschaft *f*; Kreditunion *f*; Kreditverein *m*
e cooperativa *f* de crédito; sociedad *f* de crédito (mutuo); unión *f* de crédito
f association *f* de crédit; coopérative *f* de crédit; société *f* coopérative de crédit; société *f* de crédit (mutuel); union *f* de crédit
i cooperativa *f* di credito; società *f* cooperativa di credito; società *f* mutua di credito; unione *f* di credito
n coöperatieve kredietvereniging *f*; kredietcoöperatie *f*; kredietvereniging *f*

788 **copper; copper coin; copper money**
cf. **change, divisional coin**
d Kupfergeld *n*; Kupfermünze *f*
e calderilla *f*; moneda *f* de cobre
f monnaie *f* de cuivre; pièce *f* de cuivre
i moneta *f* di rame
n koper *n*; koperen munt *f*; kopergeld *n*

789 **corner** *v* **the market**
d den Markt aufkaufen
e acaparar el mercado
f accaparer le marché
i accaparrare il mercato
n de markt opkopen

790 **corporate assets**
d Gesellschaftsvermögen *n*
e activo *m* social; patrimonio *m* social
f actif *m* social; avoir *m* social; patrimoine *m* social
i attivo *m* sociale; patrimonio *m* sociale
n maatschappelijk vermogen *n*; vennootschappelijk vermogen *n*

791 **corporate income**
d Gesellschaftseinkommen *n*; Körperschaftseinkommen *n*
e ingresos *mpl* de la sociedad; renta *f* de la sociedad
f revenu *m* de la société
i reddito *m* della società
n maatschappelijk inkomen *n*; vennootschappelijk inkomen *n*

792 **corporate income tax** *(US)*; **corporate tax; corporation income tax; corporation tax**
d Körperschaftssteuer *f*
e impuesto *m* de sociedades; impuesto *m* sobre los beneficios de sociedades; impuesto *m* sobre sociedades
f impôt *m* des sociétés *(B)*; impôt *m* sur les bénéfices des sociétés; impôt *m* sur les sociétés *(F)*
i imposta *f* sugli utili delle società; imposta *f* sulle società
n belasting *f* op de vennootschappen; vennootschapsbelasting *f*

793 **corporate investor; institutional investor**
d institutioneller Anleger *m*; institutioneller Kapitalanleger *m*; Kapitalsammelstelle *f*
e inversor *m* institucional
f investisseur *m* collectif; investisseur *m* institutionnel
i investitore *m* collettivo; investitore *m* istituzionale
n collectieve belegger *m*; institutionele belegger *m*

794 **correction of the balance of payments**
d Berichtigung *f* der Zahlungsbilanz(en); Besserung *f* der Zahlungsbilanz(en)
e rectificación *f* de la balanza de pagos
f redressement *m* des balances de paiements
i riequilibrio *m* della bilancia dei pagamenti
n herstel *n* van de betalingsbalans(en)

795 **cost**
d Kosten *pl*
e costa *f*; coste *m*; costo *m*
f coût *m*
i costo *m*
n kosten *mpl*

796 **at cost; at cost price**
cf. **at factor cost**
d zum Kostenpreis; zum Selbstkostenpreis
e a coste y costas; a costo y costas; al costo; a precio de coste; a precio de costo

f au prix coûtant; au prix de revient
i a costo; al prezzo di costo
n tegen de kostende prijs; tegen kostprijs

797 cost accounting; costing
cf. **cost price calculation**
d Costing *n*; Einstandsberechnung *f*; Kostenberechnung *f*; Kostenerrechnung *f*; Kostenkalkulation *f*; Kostenkalkulierung *f*; Kostenrechnung *f*
e cálculo *m* de costes; cálculo *m* de costos; cálculo *m* de gastos
f calcul *m* de coûts; calcul *m* de prix coûtants; costing *m*
i calcolo *m* di costi; calcolo *m* di spese; costing *m*
n costing *f*; kostenberekening *f*; kostencalculatie *f*

798 cost accounting *(bookkeeping)*
d Betriebsbuchführung *f*; Kostenberechnung *f*; Kostenbuchführung *f*; Kostenbuchhaltung *f*
e contabilidad *f* analítica de explotación; contabilidad *f* de costes; contabilidad *f* de precios de coste
f comptabilité *f* analytique d'exploitation; comptabilité *f* de prix coûtants; comptabilité *f* du prix de revient
i contabilità *f* analitica d'esercizio; contabilità *f* dei prezzi di costo
n analytische exploitatieboekhouding *f (B)*; bedrijfsboekhouding *f*

799 cost apportionment sheet; cost apportionment statement
d Betriebsabrechnungsbogen *m*
e estado *m* de repartición; hoja *f* de distribución de costes
f état *m* de répartition; feuille *f* de répartition; tableau *m* de répartition
i quadro *m* di ripartizione; stato *m* di ripartizione
n kostenverdeelstaat *m*

800 cost averaging; cost equalisation *(UK)*; **cost equalization** *(US)*; **offsetting of costs**
d Kostenausgleich *m*
e perecuación *f* de gastos
f égalisation *f* des frais; péréquation *f* des frais
i perequazione *f* dei costi
n evenredige verdeling *f* van kosten; gelijkmatige verdeling *f* van kosten

801 cost benefit analysis; cost effectiveness analysis
d Kosten- und Ertragsanalyse *f*; Wirtschaftlichkeitsberechnung *f*
e cálculo *m* de la rentabilidad; estudio *m* de rentabilidad
f prévisions *fpl* de rentabilité
i previsioni *fpl* sulla redditività
n cost benefit analyse *f*; kosten-baten analyse *f*

802 cost control accounts
d Spiegelkonten *npl*
e cuentas *fpl* reflejadas
f comptes *mpl* réfléchis
i conti *mpl* di riferimento
n overboekingsrekeningen *fpl*

803 cost-induced inflation; cost inflation; cost-push inflation
d kostenbedingte Inflation *f*; kosteninduzierte Inflation *f*; Kosteninflation *f*
e inflación *f* de costes; inflación *f* de costos; inflación *f* de gastos
f inflation *f* par les coûts
i inflazione *f* da costi
n kosteninflatie *f*

804 cost of acquisition; historical cost *(US)*
cf. **buying price**
d Anschaffungskosten *pl*; nachkalkulierte Kosten *pl*
e coste *m* de adquisición; coste *m* histórico *(AL)*; gastos *mpl* de adquisición
f coût *m* d'acquisition; prix *m* historique
i costo *m* di acquisto
n aanschaffingskosten *mpl*; historische kosten *mpl*; kosten *mpl* van verkrijging

805 cost of borrowing; cost of credit; credit charges; loan charges
d Kreditgebühren *fpl*; Kreditkosten *pl*; Kreditunkosten *pl*
e coste *m* de crédito; gastos *mpl* de crédito
f coût *m* de crédit; frais *mpl* de crédit
i costi *mpl* di credito; costo *m* di credito
n kredietkosten *mpl*; kosten *mpl* van krediet

806 cost of labor *(US)*; **cost of labour** *(UK)*; **labor costs** *(US)*; **labour costs** *(UK)*
d Arbeitskosten *pl*
e coste *m* de la mano de obra; coste *m* del trabajo; costo *m* de la mano de obra; costo *m* del trabajo
f coût *m* de la main d'œuvre; coût *m* du travail
i costo *m* della manodopera; costo *m* del lavoro
n arbeidskosten *mpl*

807 cost of living
d Lebenshaltungskosten *pl*
e coste *m* de (la) vida; costo *m* de (la) vida
f coût *m* de la vie
i costo *m* della vita
n kosten *mpl* van levensonderhoud; levensduurte *f (B)*

808 cost of living allowance; cost of living bonus
d Teuerungszulage *f*; Teuerungszuschlag *m*
e plus *m* por carestía (de vida); suplemento *m* de carestía (de vida)
f allocation *f* de cherté de vie; allocation *f* de renchérissement; allocation *f* de vie chère; indemnité *f* de cherté de vie; indemnité *f* de renchérissement; indemnité *f* de vie chère
i assegno *m* di carovita; assegno *m* di caroviveri; indennità *f* di carovita; indennità *f* di caroviveri; indennità *f* di contingenza
n duurtebijslag *m*; duurtetoeslag *m*

809 cost of living index
d Index *m* der Lebenshaltungskosten
e índice *m* del coste de vida
f indice *m* du coût de la vie
i indice *m* del costo della vita
n indexcijfer *n* van de kosten van levensonderhoud; index *m* van de levensduurte *(B)*

810 cost of maintenance; maintenance cost; upkeep
d Erhaltungsaufwand *m*; Erhaltungskosten *pl*; Instandhaltungsaufwand *m*; Instandhaltungskosten *pl*; Unterhaltsaufwand *m*; Unterhaltskosten *pl*; Unterhaltungsaufwand *m*; Unterhaltungskosten *pl*
e gastos *mpl* de entretenimiento; gastos *mpl* de mantenimiento; gastos *mpl* de manutención
f dépenses *fpl* d'entretien; frais *mpl* d'entretien
i costo *m* di manutenzione; spese *fpl* di manutenzione
n onderhoudskosten *mpl*

811 cost of manufacture; cost of production; manufacturing cost; production cost(s)
cf. **cost price**
d Erzeugungskosten *pl*; Erzeugungspreis *m*; Fabrikationskosten *pl*; Fabrikationspreis *m*; Fertigungskosten *pl*; Gestehungskosten *pl*; Gestehungspreis *m*; Herstellungskosten *pl*; Herstellungspreis *m*; Produktionskosten *pl*
e coste(s) *m(pl)* de fabricación; coste(s) *m(pl)* de producción; costo(s) *m(pl)* de fabricación; costo(s) *m(pl)* de producción; gastos *mpl* de fabricación; gastos *mpl* de producción; precio *m* de fabricación; precio *m* de producción
f coût(s) *m(pl)* de production; frais *mpl* de fabrication; frais *mpl* de production; prix *m* de production
i costo *m* (costi *mpl*) di fabbricazione; costo *m* (costi *mpl*) di manifattura; costo *m* (costi *mpl*) di produzione; prezzo *m* di produzione
n fabricagekosten *mpl*; fabricageprijs *m*; produktiekosten *mpl*; produktieprijs *m*; voortbrengingskosten *mpl*

812 cost of transfer; transfer charge(s); transfer duty; transfer fee
cf. **registration dues**
d Transfergebühr *f*; Transferkosten *pl*; Transferspesen *fpl*; Übertragungsgebühr *f*; Übertragungsspesen *fpl*; Umschreibungsgebühr *f*; Verkehrssteuer *f*
e derechos *mpl* de transcripción; derechos *mpl* de transferencia; derechos *mpl* de transmisión; gastos *mpl* de transferencia; tasa *f* de transferencia; tasa *f* de transmisión
f droit *m* de mutation; droit *m* de transcription; droit *m* de transfert; droit *m* de transmission; frais *mpl* de transfert; taxe *f* de mutation; taxe *f* de transcription; taxe *f* de transfert; taxe *f* de transmission
i diritto *m* di trascrizione; diritto *m* di trasferimento; diritto *m* di trasmissione; spese *fpl* di trasferimento; tassa *f* di trascrizione; tassa *f* di trasferimento; tassa *f* di trasmissione
n overdrachtskosten *mpl*; overdrachtsrecht *n*; transferkosten *mpl*; transferrecht *n*

813 cost per unit; unit cost
d Einheitskosten *pl*; Kosten *pl* per Einheit; Kosten *pl* pro Einheit; Stückkosten *pl*
e costes *mpl* por unidad; costo *m* por unidad; costo *m* unitario; gastos *mpl* por unidad; gastos *mpl* unificados
f coût *m* par unité; coût *m* unitaire; prix *m* de revient à l'unité; prix *m* de revient unitaire
i costo *m* unitario
n eenheidskosten *mpl*; kosten *mpl* per eenheid

814 **cost price**
cf. **acquisition value, cost of manufacture, direct costs**
d Einkaufspreis *m*; Einstandspreis *m*; Gestehungskosten *pl*; Gestehungspreis *m*; Kostenpreis *m*; Selbstkosten *pl*; Selbstkostenpreis *m*
e precio *m* de coste; precio *m* de costo
f prix *m* coûtant; prix *m* de revient
i prezzo *m* di costo
n kostende prijs *m*; kostprijs *m*

815 **cost price calculation**
cf. **cost accounting**
d Kostenpreisberechnung *f*; Nachkalkulation *f*; Selbstkostenberechnung *f*
e cálculo *m* del precio de coste
f calcul *m* du prix de revient; établissement *m* du prix de revient
i calcolo *m* consuntivo; calcolo *m* del prezzo di costo
n kostprijsberekening *f*; kostprijscalculatie *f*; nacalculatie *f*

816 **cost-price spiral**
d Kosten-Preis-Spirale *f*
e espiral *f* de costos y precios; espiral *f* costos-precios
f spirale *f* coût(s)-prix
i spirale *f* costi-prezzi
n kost-prijsspiraal *f*; spiraal *f* van kosten en prijzen

817 **cost structure**
d Kostenstruktur *f*
e estructura *f* de los costes (costos; gastos)
f structure *f* des coûts
i struttura *f* dei costi
n kostenstructuur *f*

818 **cost unit**
d Kostenträger *m*
e unidad *f* de coste
f support *m* de coût(s); unité *f* à laquelle sont imputés les coûts
i unità *f* di costo
n kostendrager *m*

819 **counter-bill; redraft; return draft**
cf. **bill returned unpaid**
d Gegenwechsel *m*; Retourwechsel *m*; Ricambio *m*; Rikambio *m*; Rikambiowechsel *m*; Rücktratte *f*; Rückwechsel *m*
e contragiro *m*; contralibranza *f*; letra *f* cruzada; letra *f* de resaca; resaca *f*
f rechange *m*; retraite *f*
i ricambio *m*; rivalsa *f* (cambiaria)
n herwissel *m*; retourwissel *m*; retraite *f*

820 **counter-cyclical equalization reserve**
d Konjunkturausgleichsreserve *f*; Konjunkturausgleichsrücklage *f*
e reserva *f* coyuntural; reserva *f* de reajuste coyuntural
f réserve *f* conjoncturelle
i riserva *f* congiunturale
n conjunctuurreserve *f*

821 **counterfoil** *(UK)*; **stub** *(US)*
d Abschnitt *m*; Kontrollabschnitt *m*; Kontrollblatt *n*
e matriz *f*; talón *m* de comprobación; talón *m* de control
f souche *f*; talon *m* (de contrôle)
i madre *f*; matrice *f*; scontrino *m*; tagliando *m* di controllo; talloncino *m* di controllo
n controlestrook *f*; souche *f*; stam *m (B)*; stok *m*; strook *f*

822 **counterpart; counter value; equivalent**
cf. **consideration (in return), exchangeable value**
d Äquivalent *n*; Gegenwert *m*
e contrapartida *f*; contravalor *m*; equivalencia *f*; equivalente *m*
f contrepartie *f*; contrevaleur *f*; équivalent *m*
i contropartita *f*; controvalore *m*; corrispettivo *m*; equivalente *m*
n equivalent *n*; tegenwaarde *f*

823 **counterpart fund**
d Gegenwertfonds *m*
e fondo *m* de contrapartida
f fonds *m* de contrepartie
i fondo *m* di contropartita
n tegenwaardefonds *n*

824 **country in surplus**
d Überschussland *n*
e país *m* excedentario
f pays *m* excédentaire
i paese *m* con un avanzo della bilancia
n overschotland *n*

825 **country of exportation; exporting country**
d Ausfuhrland *n*; Einfuhrland *n**; Exportland *n*; Importland *n**
e país *m* exportador
f pays *m* exportateur
i paese *m* esportatore
n exportland *n*; uitvoerland *n*
* Country receiving (German) exports.

826 **country of importation; importing country**
d Ausfuhrland *n**; Einfuhrland *n*; Export-

land *n**; Importland *n*
e país *m* importador
f pays *m* importateur
i paese *m* importatore
n importland *n*; invoerland *n*
* Country supplying (German) imports.

827 **the country's finances; government finance(s); public finance(s); state finance(s)**
d öffentliche Finanzen *fpl*; öffentliche Finanzwirtschaft *f*; öffentliches Finanzwesen *n*; staatliche Finanzen *fpl*; staatliche Finanzwirtschaft *f*; staatliches Finanzwesen *n*; Staatsfinanzen *fpl*
e economía *f* financiera del estado; finanzas *fpl* del estado; finanzas *fpl* públicas; hacienda *f* pública
f économie *f* financière de l'état; finances *fpl* de l'état; finances *fpl* publiques
i economia *f* finanziaria dello stato; finanze *fpl* dello stato; finanze *fpl* pubbliche
n openbare financiën *pl*; overheidsfinanciën *pl*; 's lands financiën *pl*; staatsfinanciën *pl*

828 **coupon**
cf. **dividend coupon, interest coupon**
d Aktienabschnitt *m*; Aktienanteilschein *m*; Aktienkupon *m*; Anteilschein *m*; Coupon *m*; Kupon *m*
e cupón *m*; talón *m*
f coupon *m*
i cedola *f*; tagliando *m*
n coupon *m*; koepon *m*

829 **with coupon; cum coupon**
cf. **cum dividend**
d einschliesslich Kupon; mit Kupon; samt Kupon
e con cupón
f coupon attaché
i cedola attacata
n inclusief coupon; met coupon

830 **coupon bond**
cf. **bearer bond, fixed interest bearing security**
d Inhaberobligation *f* mit Zinskupon; Inhaberobligation *f* mit Zinsschein; Inhaberschuldverschreibung *f* mit Zinskupon; Inhaberschuldverschreibung *f* mit Zinsschein
e obligación *f* al portador con cupón de intereses
f obligation *f* au porteur avec coupon d'intérêts
i obbligazione *f* al portatore con cedola d'interessi
n obligatie *f* aan toonder met int(e)restcoupon; obligatie *f* aan toonder met rentecoupon

831 **coupon off** ***(US)*****; ex coupon**
cf. **dividend off**
d ausschliesslich Kupon; ex coupon; ohne Kupon
e ex cupón; sin cupón
f coupon détaché; ex coupon; sans coupon
i ex-cedola; senza cedola
n exclusief coupon; ex coupon; zonder coupon

832 **coupon sheet**
d Dividendenbogen *m*; Dividendenscheinbogen *m*; Gewinnanteilscheinbogen *m*; Kuponbogen *m*; Zinsbogen *m*; Zinsscheinbogen *m*
e hoja *f* de cupones
f feuille *f* de coupons
i cartella *f* di cedole; cedolario *m*; foglio *m* (di) cedole
n couponblad *n*; dividendblad *n*

833 **course of business; course of trade; run of business**
d Geschäftsablauf *m*; Geschäftsgang *m*
e curso *m* de los negocios; marcha *f* de los negocios
f cours *m* des affaires; marche *f* des affaires
i andamento *m* degli affari; corso *m* degli affari
n gang *m* van zaken

834 **cover**
d Deckung *f*
e cobertura *f*
f couverture *f*
i copertura *f*
n dekking *f*

835 **without cover; without funds; unbacked; uncovered; unsecured**
d nicht gesichert; ohne Deckung; unbesichert; ungedeckt; ungesichert
e al descubierto; en descubierto; no cubierto; no garantizado; sin cobertura; sin garantía
f à découvert; non couvert; non gagé; non garanti; sans couverture; sans garantie
i a fondo perduto; allo scoperto; non coperto; non garantito; scoperto; senza copertura; senza garanzia
n niet gegarandeerd; ongedekt; zonder dekking

836 cover *v* **a deficit; make** *v* **good a deficit; make** *v* **up a deficit; meet** *v* **a deficit**
d ein Defizit abdecken; ein Defizit ausgleichen; ein Defizit decken; ein Defizit ersetzen; einen Ausfall decken; einen Fehlbetrag abdecken; einen Fehlbetrag ausgleichen; einen Fehlbetrag decken; einen Fehlbetrag ersetzen
e compensar un déficit; compensar un descubierto; cubrir un déficit; cubrir un descubierto; enjugar un déficit; liquidar un déficit; liquidar un descubierto
f combler un découvert; combler un déficit; compenser un découvert; compenser un déficit; couvrir un déficit
i colmare un deficit; colmare un disavanzo; colmare un scoperto; compensare un deficit; compensare un disavanzo; compensare un scoperto; coprire un deficit; coprire un disavanzo
n een deficit dekken; een tekort dekken; in een tekort voorzien

837 coverage requirements; margin requirements; requisite cover
d Deckungsbedarf *m*; Deckungserfordernisse *npl*; Einschussbedarf *m*; erforderliche Deckung *f*
e cobertura *f* requerida; necesidades *fpl* de cobertura
f besoins *mpl* en couverture; couverture *f* requise
i bisogni *mpl* di copertura; copertura *f* richiesta
n dekkingsbehoeften *fpl*; vereiste dekking *f*

838 cover *v* **by mortgage; secure** *v* **by mortgage**
d durch Hypothek absichern; durch Hypothek decken; durch Hypothek sichern; durch Hypothek sicherstellen; hypothekarisch absichern; hypothekarisch decken; hypothekarisch sichern; hypothekarisch sicherstellen
e asegurar hipotecariamente; asegurar por hipoteca; garantizar mediante hipoteca; garantizar por hipoteca
f garantir hypothécairement; garantir par hypothèque
i garantire con ipoteca; garantire mediante ipoteca
n door hypot(h)eek dekken; hypot(h)ecair dekken

839 covering operation; covering transaction; hedging
d Deckungsgeschäft *n*; Hedgegeschäft *n*; Sicherungsgeschäft *n*
e operación *f* de cobertura
f marché *m* de couverture; opération *f* de couverture
i operazione *f* di copertura
n contra-affaire *f*; dekkingsaankoop *m*; dekkingsverkoop *m*; hedging *f*

840 cover ratio
d Deckungskoeffizient *m*
e coeficiente *m* de cobertura
f coefficient *m* de couverture
i coefficiente *m* di copertura
n dekkingscoëfficiënt *m*

841 creation of credit
d Kreditschöpfung *f*
e creación *f* de crédito
f création *f* de crédit
i creazione *f* di credito
n kredietschepping *f*

842 creation of money; money creation
d Geldschöpfung *f*
e creación *f* de dinero; creación *f* de moneda
f création *f* d'argent; création *f* de monnaie; création *f* monétaire
i creazione *f* di disponibilità monetarie; creazione *f* di moneta
n geldschepping *f*

843 credit *(balance in favour)*
cf. **assets**
d Guthaben *n*; Haben *n*; Kredit *m*
e crédito *m*; haber *m*
f accréditif *m*; avoir *m*; crédit *m*
i credito *m*; fido *m*
n credit *n*; krediet *n*; tegoed *n*

844 credit; crediting
cf. **opening of a credit**
d Gutschreibung *f*; Gutschrift *f*; Kreditierung *f*
e abono *m* en cuenta; acreditación *f*; crédito *m*
f crédit *m*
i accreditamento *m*; accredito *m*; credito *m*
n creditboeking *f*; creditering *f*

845 credit; loan
d Darleh(e)n *n*; Darleihen *n (O; Schw)*; Kredit *m*
e crédito *m*; préstamo *m*
f crédit *m*; prêt *m*
i credito *m*; mutuo *m*; prestito *m*
n krediet *n*; lening *f*

846 creditable *(rare)*; **creditworthy; solid; sound**
cf. **solvent**
d kreditfähig; kreditwürdig
e digno de crédito; sólido
f digne de crédit; solide
i degno di credito; degno di fido; meritevole di credito; meritevole di fido; solido
n kredietwaardig; solide; solied

847 credit advice; credit memorandum *(US)*; **credit note**
cf. **advice of payment**
d Gutschriftsanzeige *f*; Gutschriftsaufgabe *f*; Gutschrift(s)beleg *m*; Gutschrift(s)note *f*; Gutschrift(s)zettel *m*; Kreditnota *f*; Kreditnote *f*
e aviso *m* de abono; aviso *m* de crédito; nota *f* de abono; nota *f* de crédito
f avis *m* de crédit; facture *f* d'avoir; note *f* d'avoir; note *f* de crédit
i avviso *m* d'accreditamento; avviso *m* d'accredito; lettera *f* d'accreditamento; lettera *f* d'accredito; nota *f* d'accreditamento; nota *f* d'accredito; nota *f* di credito
n creditadvies *n*; creditnota *f*; creditopgave *f*

848 credit advice; transfer advice; transfer slip
cf. **advice of payment**
d Überweisungsanzeige *f*; Überweisungsträger *m*
e aviso *m* de transferencia; talón *m* de transferencia
f avis *m* de virement
i avviso *m* de bonifico; nota *f* di storno
n bijstrookje *n*; kennisgeving *f* van bijschrijving

849 credit balance; profit balance
d Aktivsaldo *m*; Gewinnsaldo *m*; Guthaben *n*; Guthabensaldo *m*; Habensaldo *m*; Kreditorensaldo *m*; Kreditsaldo *m*
e haber *m*; saldo *m* acreedor; saldo *m* activo; saldo *m* ganancial
f avoir *m*; solde *m* actif; solde *m* bénéficiaire; solde *m* créditeur; solde *m* en bénéfice; solde *m* excédentaire
i avere *m*; saldo *m* a credito; saldo *m* attivo; saldo *m* avere; saldo *m* creditore
n actief saldo *n*; batig saldo *n*; creditsaldo *n*; tegoed *n*; winstsaldo *n*

850 credit bank; credit institution; lending bank; lending institution; loan bank *(UK)*; **loan company** *(US)*; **loaning institution**
d Darleh(e)nsbank *f*; Darleh(e)nskasse *f*; Geldinstitut *n*; Kreditanstalt *f*; Kreditbank *f*; Kreditinstitut *n*
e banco *m* de crédito; banco *m* de préstamos; caja *f* de crédito; caja *f* de préstamos; institución *f* de crédito; instituto *m* de crédito
f banque *f* d'avances; banque *f* de crédit; banque *f* de prêts; caisse *f* de crédit; caisse *f* de prêts; établissement *m* de crédit; établissement *m* de prêts; institut *m* de crédit; institution *f* de crédit; société *f* de crédit
i azienda *f* di credito; banca *f* di credito; banca *f* di prestiti; cassa *f* di prestiti; istituto *m* di credito
n kredietbank *f*; kredietinstelling *f*; leenbank *f*; voorschotbank *f*

851 credit business; credit dealings; credit operations; credit transactions; lending operations
d Kreditgeschäfte *npl*; Kreditoperationen *fpl*; Kredittransaktionen *fpl*
e negocios *mpl* crediticios; operaciones *fpl* crediticias; operaciones *fpl* de crédito; transacciones *fpl* crediticias; transacciones *fpl* de crédito
f opérations *fpl* de crédit; transactions *fpl* de crédit
i operazioni *fpl* di credito; transazioni *fpl* di credito
n kredietoperaties *fpl*; krediettransacties *fpl*; kredietzaken *fpl*

852 credit buying; credit purchase; purchase on account
cf. **forward buying**
d Kauf *m* auf Kredit; Kauf *m* auf Rechnung; Kreditkauf *m*; Rechnungskauf *m*
e compra *f* a crédito; compra *f* a cuenta; compra *f* al fiado
f achat *m* à compte; achat *m* à crédit
i acquisto *m* a credito; acquisto *m* a respiro
n koop *m* op krediet; koop *m* op rekening

853 credit by way of guarantee
d Avalkredit *m*; Bürgschaftskredit *m*; Kautionskredit *m*
e crédito *m* de aval; crédito *m* de caución; crédito *m* de fianza; crédito *m* de garantía
f crédit *m* d'aval; crédit *m* de cautionnement; crédit *m* par aval; crédit *m* par cautionnement

i credito *m* d'avallo; credito *m* di fideiussione; credito *m* di garanzia
n avalkrediet *n*; borgstellingskrediet *n*

854 **credit card**
d Kreditkarte *f*
e tarjeta *f* de crédito
f carte *f* bleue; carte *f* de crédit
i carta *f* di credito
n credit card *f*; kredietkaart *f*

855 **credit ceiling; credit limit** ***(UK)*****; credit line; limit of credit** ***(UK)*****; line of credit; loan ceiling**
cf. **borrowing limit, credit margin**
d Kreditgrenze *f*; Kredithöchstgrenze *f*; Kreditlinie *f*; Kreditplafond *m*
e límite *m* de crédito; línea *f* de crédito; plafón *m* de crédito; tope *m* de crédito
f ligne *f* de crédit; limite *f* de credit; maximum *m* de crédit; plafond *m* de crédit
i castelletto *m*; limite *m* di credito; limite *m* di fido; linea *f* di credito; plafond *m* di credito
n kredietgrens *f*; kredietlijn *f*; krediet-limiet *f*; kredietlinie *f*; krediet-plafon(d) *n*

856 **credit conditions; credit terms**
d Anleihebedingungen *fpl*; Kredit-bedingungen *fpl*
e condiciones *fpl* de crédito
f conditions *fpl* de crédit
i condizioni *fpl* di credito
n kredietvoorwaarden *fpl*

857 **credit entry; credit item**
d Aktivposten *m*; Eintragung *f* auf der Habenseite; Gutschrift *f*; Gutschrift-buchung *f*; Gutschriftposten *m*; Haben-buchung *f*; Habenposten *m*
e asiento *m* activo; asiento *m* de crédito; partida *f* activa; partida *f* de crédito
f article *m* d'avoir; article *m* (porté) au crédit; écriture *f* de crédit; inscription *f* au crédit; poste *m* créditeur; poste *m* (porté) au crédit
i partita *f* di (in) avere; registrazione *f* di accredito; scrittura *f* di accreditamento; voce *f* attiva; voce *f* dell'attivo; voce *f* d'entrata
n creditboeking *f*; creditpost *m*

858 **credit expansion**
d Kreditausdehnung *f*; Kreditausweitung *f*; Kreditexpansion *f*
e expansión *f* crediticia; expansión *f* del crédito
f expansion *f* du crédit
i espansione *f* creditizia; espansione *f* del credito
n kredietexpansie *f*; kredietuitbreiding *f*; kredietverruiming *f*

859 **credit flow; credit flux; flow of credit**
d Kreditstrom *m*
e flujo *m* de crédito
f flux *m* de crédit
i flusso *m* di credito
n kredietstroom *m*

860 **credit guarantee**
d Kreditgarantie *f*
e garantía *f* de crédito
f garantie *f* de crédit
i garanzia *f* di credito
n kredietgarantie *f*

861 **credit inflation**
d Aufblähung *f* des Kredits; Kredit-inflation *f*
e inflación *f* crediticia; inflación *f* del crédito
f gonflement *n* du crédit; inflation *f* du crédit
i inflazione *f* creditizia; inflazione *f* del credito
n kredietinflatie *f*

862 **credit instrument**
d Kreditinstrument *n*; Kreditmittel *n*; Kreditpapier *n*
e instrumento *m* crediticio; instrumento *m* de crédito; título *m* de crédito
f instrument *m* de crédit; titre *m* de crédit
i strumento *m* di credito; titolo *m* di credito
n kredietmiddel *n*; kredietpapier *n*

863 **credit insurance**
d Kreditversicherung *f*
e seguro *m* de crédito(s); seguro *m* sobre el crédito
f assurance-crédit *f*; assurance *f* contre les risques de crédit; assurance *f* de crédit(s)
i assicurazione *f* contro i rischi di credito; assicurazione *f* (di) crediti; assicurazione *f* sul credito
n kredietverzekering *f*

864 **credit margin; swing**
cf. **credit ceiling**
d Kreditmarge *f*; Kreditspielraum *m*; Swing *m*; Swinggrenze *f*; Swing-rahmen *m*
e margen *m/f* de crédito; swing *m*
f marge *f* de crédit; swing *m*

i margine *m* di credito; swing *m*
n kredietmarge *f*; swing *m*

865 **credit on joint account**
d Metakredit *m*
e crédito *m* en cuenta común
f crédit *m* en compte-joint
i credito *m* in conto comune
n krediet *n* in gemeenschappelijke rekening

866 **credit on mortgage; mortgage credit**
cf. **credit on real estate, loan on mortgage**
d Hypothekarkredit *m*; Hypothekenkredit *m*; Pfandbriefkredit *m*
e crédito *m* hipotecario
f crédit *m* hypothécaire; crédit *m* sur hypothèque
i credito *m* ipotecario; credito *m* su ipoteca
n hypot(h)ecair krediet *n*; hypot(h)eekkrediet *n*; krediet *n* op hypot(h)eek

867 **credit on personal estate; credit on personal property**
d Mobiliarkredit *m*
e crédito *m* mobiliario
f crédit *m* mobilier
i credito *m* mobiliare
n krediet *n* op roerende goederen; mobilair krediet *n*

868 **credit on real estate; credit on real property**
cf. **credit on mortgage**
d Grundkredit *m*; Immobiliarkredit *m*; Realkredit *m*
e crédito *m* inmobiliario; crédito *m* real; crédito *m* territorial
f crédit *m* foncier; crédit *m* immobilier; crédit *m* réel
i credito *m* fondiario; credito *m* immobiliare; credito *m* reale
n grondkrediet *n*; krediet *n* op onroerende goederen

869 **credit on securities**
cf. **advance on securities, lending on securities, loan on securities**
d Effektenkredit *m*; Effektenlombardkredit *m*; Kredit *m* gegen Wertpapierlombard; Lombardkredit *m*; Wertpapierkredit *m*
e crédito *m* sobre efectos; crédito *m* sobre títulos; crédito *m* sobre valores
f crédit *m* sur titres
i credito *m* su titoli
n krediet *n* tegen effecten; krediet *n* tegen onderpandeffecten

870 **creditor**
cf. **lender**
d Gläubiger *m*; Kreditor *m*
e acreedor *m*
f créancier *m*; créditeur *m*
i creditore *m*
n crediteur *m*; schuldeiser *m*

871 **creditor country; creditor nation**
d Gläubigerland *n*; Gläubigerstaat *m*
e país *m* acreedor
f pays *m* créditeur
i paese *m* creditore
n crediteurland *n*; crediteurstaat *m*

872 **credit policy**
d Kreditpolitik *f*
e política *f* crediticia; política *f* del crédito
f politique *f* du crédit
i politica *f* creditizia; politica *f* del credito
n kredietbeleid *n*; kredietpolitiek *f*

873 **credit rating; credit standing; credit status; creditworthiness; solidity; soundness**
cf. **solvability**
d Kreditfähigkeit *f*; Kreditwürdigkeit *f*; Solidität *f*
e crédito *m*; solidez *f*
f crédit *m*; solidité *f*
i credito *m*; solidità *f*
n kredietwaardigheid *f*; soliditeit *f*

874 **credit restriction; credit squeeze; restriction of credit; tightening of credit**
cf. **credit stringency**
d Kreditanspannung *f*; Kreditbegrenzung *f*; Kreditbeschränkung *f*; Kreditdrosselung *f*; Krediteinschränkung *f*; Kreditklemme *f*; Kreditrestriktion *f*; Kreditverknappung *f*
e contracción *f* crediticia; contracción *f* del crédito; limitación *f* crediticia; limitación *f* de créditos; rarefacción *f* de créditos; restricción *f* crediticia; restricción *f* de créditos; tirantez *f* del crédito
f limitation *f* des crédits; limitation *f* du crédit; raréfaction *f* des crédits; resserrement *m* du crédit; restriction *f* des crédits; restriction *f* du crédit
i contrazione *f* del credito; limitazione *f* creditizia; limitazione *f* dei crediti; rarefazione *f* dei crediti; restrizione *f* del credito; stretta *f* creditizia
n kredietbeperking *f*; kredietinperking *f*; kredietrestrictie *f*; kredietvernauwing *f*

875 credit sale
cf. **hire purchase sale**
d Kreditverkauf *m*; Verkauf *m* auf Kredit
e venta *f* a crédito
f vente *f* à crédit
i vendita *f* a credito
n verkoop *m* op krediet

876 credit slip; credit voucher
d Bon *m*; Gutschein *m*; Gutschrift *f*
e bono *m*; vale *m*
f bon *m*
i buono *m*
n bon *m*

877 credit slip; deposit receipt; deposit slip *(US)*; deposit ticket *(US)*; paying-in slip *(UK)*; pay-in slip
cf. **deposit form**
d Einzahlungsbeleg *m*; Einzahlungsbescheinigung *f*; Einzahlungsquittung *f*; Einzahlungsschein *m*; Einzahlungszettel *m*
e comprobante *m* de imposición; comprobante *m* de ingreso; justificante *m* de ingreso; resguardo *m* de ingreso; talón *m* de crédito; talón *m* de imposición
f attestation *f* de versement; bordereau *m* de paiement; bordereau *m* de versement; feuille *f* de versement; fiche *f* de versement; reçu *m* de versement
i certificato *m* di versamento; distinta *f* di pagamento; distinta *f* di versamento; ricevuta *f* di versamento
n bewijs *n* van storting; stortingsbewijs *n*; stortingsborderel *n*; stortingsopgave *f*; stortingsreçu *n*

878 credit stringency; tightness of credit
cf. **credit restriction**
d Kreditknappheit *f*; Kreditmangel *m*
e escasez *f* de crédito; penuria *f* de crédito
f manque *m* de crédit; pénurie *f* de crédit
i mancanza *f* creditizia; penuria *f* creditizia
n kredietgebrek *n*; kredietschaarste *f*

879 credit system
d Kreditsystem *n*; Kreditwesen *n*
e crédito *m*; régimen *m* de créditos; sistema *m* crediticio; sistema *m* de créditos
f crédit *m*; régime *m* des crédits; système *m* des crédits
i regime *m* creditizio; sistema *m* creditizio
n kredietstelsel *n*; kredietwezen *n*

880 credit *v* **the account (with)**
cf. **carry** *v* **a sum to some one's credit**
d das Konto erkennen (für, mit); das Konto kreditieren (für, mit); dem Konto gutbringen; dem Konto gutschreiben
e abonar a la cuenta; acreditar en la cuenta; acreditar la cuenta (por)
f créditer le compte (de); porter à l'avoir du compte
i accreditare il conto (di)
n de rekening crediteren (voor, met); op de rekening goedschrijven

881 credit volume
d Kreditvolumen *n*
e volumen *m* de crédito(s)
f volume *m* de crédit
i volume *m* di credito
n kredietvolume *n*

882 creeping inflation
cf. **concealed inflation**
d schleichende Inflation *f*
e inflación *f* reptante
f inflation *f* rampante
i inflazione *f* serpeggiante; inflazione *f* strisciante
n kruipende inflatie *f*

883 crossed check *(US)*; crossed cheque *(UK)*
d gekreuzter Scheck *m*; Verrechnungsscheck *m*
e cheque *m* barrado; cheque *m* cruzado
f chèque *m* à barrement; chèque *m* barré; chèque *m* croisé; chèque *m* de virement
i assegno *m* a sbarramento; assegno *m* incrociato; assegno *m* sbarrato
n gekruiste cheque *m*; verrekeningscheque *m*

884 cross exchange rate; cross rate
d Cross-Rate *f*; intervalutarischer Kurs *m*; Usancekurs *m*
e tipo *m* de cambio cruzado
f taux *m* de change croisé
i cambio *m* incrociato; tasso *m* di cambio incrociato
n cross rate *m*; kruiselingse wisselkoers *m*

885 cross holding
d wechselseitige Beteiligung *f*
e participación *f* recíproca
f participation *f* réciproque
i partecipazione *f* reciproca
n wederzijdse deelneming *f*

886 crumbling of prices; decline in prices; decrease in prices; drop in prices; easing

of prices; fall in prices; sag in prices
cf. **break in prices, cut in the price**
d Abbröckeln *n* der Kurse (Preise); Abbröckelung *f* der Kurse (Preise); Abflauen *n* der Kurse (Preise); Abschwächung *f* der Kurse (Preise); Kursabfall *m*; Kursabschwächung *f*; Kursfall *m*; Kursrückgang *m*; Preisabfall *m*; Preisabnahme *f*; Preisabschwächung *f*; Preisfall *m*; Preisrückgang *m*; Preisrückschlag *m*; Preisverfall *m*
e aflojamiento *m* de las cotizaciones; baja *f* de las cotizaciones (los precios); caída *f* de las cotizaciones (los precios); debilitación *f* de las cotizaciones (los precios); descenso *m* de las cotizaciones (los precios); disminución *f* de las cotizaciones (los precios); retroceso *m* de las cotizaciones (los precios)
f abaissement *m* des cours (prix); affaiblissement *m* des cours (prix); amenuisement *m* des cours (prix); baisse *f* des cours (prix); diminution *f* des cours (prix); effritement *m* des cours (prix); fléchissement *m* des cours (prix); recul *m* des cours (prix); repli *m* des cours (prix)
i caduta *f* dei corsi (prezzi); calo *m* dei corsi (prezzi); cedimento *m* dei (nei) corsi (prezzi); diminuzione *f* dei corsi (prezzi); flessione *f* dei corsi (prezzi); indebolimento *m* dei corsi (prezzi); ribasso *m* dei corsi (prezzi); sgretolamento *m* dei corsi (prezzi); slittamento *m* dei corsi (prezzi)
n koersafbrokkeling *f*; koersachteruitgang *m*; koersdaling *f*; koersval *m*; prijsafbrokkeling *f*; prijsachteruitgang *m*; prijsdaling *f*; teruglopen *n* der koersen; vermindering *f* van de koersen (prijzen)

887 cum dividend; dividend on *(US)*; **with dividend**
cf. **cum coupon**
d cum Dividende; einschliesslich Dividende; mit Dividende
e con dividendo (incluido); incluso dividendo
f avec dividende; dividende inclus
i con dividendo
n cum dividend; inclusief dividend; met dividend

888 cum new; cum rights; rights on *(US)*; **with rights**
d einschliesslich Bezugsrecht; einschliesslich Optionsrecht; mit Bezugsrecht; mit Optionsrecht
e con derechos de opción; con derechos de suscripción
f avec droit; droit attaché
i con diritto d'opzione; diritto attaccato
n cum claim; inclusief claimrecht; met claimrecht

889 cumulative dividend; cumulative prefential dividend
d kumulative Dividende *f*
e dividendo *m* acumulativo
f dividende *m* cumulatif
i dividendo *m* cumulativo
n cumulatief dividend *n*

890 cumulative preference shares; cumulative preferred stock
d kumulative Prioritätsaktien *fpl*; kumulative Vorzugsaktien *fpl*; nachzugsberechtigte Prioritätsaktien *fpl*; nachzugsberechtigte Vorzugsaktien *fpl*; Vorzugsaktien *fpl* mit Nachbezugsrecht
e acciones *fpl* preferentes cumulativas; acciones *fpl* preferidas cumulativas; acciones *fpl* privilegiadas cumulativas
f actions *fpl* de préférence cumulatives; actions *fpl* de priorité cumulatives; actions *fpl* privilégiées cumulatives
i azioni *fpl* preferenziali cumulative; azioni *fpl* privilegiate a dividendo cumulativo; azioni *fpl* privilegiate con accumulo di dividendo; azioni *fpl* privilegiate cumulative
n cumulatief preferente aandelen *npl*; cumulatief prioriteitsaandelen *npl*

891 curb; curb market; free market; outside market; over-the-counter market; unofficial market
cf. **after hours market, dealings before the opening of the stock exchange**
d Freiverkehr *m*; Freiverkehrsmarkt *m*; Kulisse *f*; unnotierter Markt *m*; Winkelbörse *f*
e bolsín *m*; mercado *m* libre; mercado *m* no oficial
f coulisse *f*; hors cote *m*; marché *m* hors cote; marché *m* libre
i coulisse *f*; mercato *m* fuori-borsa; mercato *m* libero
n coulisse *f*; markt *f* in (voor) incourante fondsen; markt *f* in (voor) niet genoteerde fondsen

892 curb stocks *(US)*; **outside securities** *(UK)*; **over-the-counter securities; unlisted securities; unquoted securities**
d an der Börse nicht kotierte Wertpapiere *npl (Schw)*; an der Börse nicht notierte

Effekten *pl*; an der Börse nicht notierte Wertpapiere *npl*; nicht notierte Effekten *pl*; nicht notierte Wertpapiere *npl*; unnotierte Effekten *pl*; unnotierte Wertpapiere *npl*; zur Notierung nicht zugelassene Effekten *pl*; zur Notierung nicht zugelassene Wertpapiere *npl*
e títulos *mpl* no cotizados (en bolsa); valores *mpl* no cotizados (en bolsa)
f titres *mpl* hors cote; titres *mpl* incotés; titres *mpl* non admis à la cote; titres *mpl* non cotés; titres *mpl* non inscrits à la cote; valeurs *fpl* hors cote; valeurs *fpl* incotées; valeurs *fpl* non admises à la cote; valeurs *fpl* non cotées; valeurs *fpl* non inscrites à la cote
i titoli *mpl* non quotati (in bolsa); valori *mpl* non quotati (in bolsa)
n incourante fondsen *npl*; incourante waarden *fpl*; niet genoteerde fondsen *npl*; niet genoteerde waarden *fpl*; ter beurze niet genoteerde fondsen *npl*; ter beurze niet genoteerde waarden *fpl*

893 currency
cf. **current money**
d Devise *f (rare except in pl)**; Valuta *f**; Währung *f*
e divisa *f**; moneda *f*; valuta *f*
f devise *f**; monnaie *f*
i divisa *f**; moneta *f*; valuta *f*
n courant *n*; munt *f*; valuta *f**
* Usually means foreign currency (q.v.).

894 currency; life; period of validity; tenor; term (of validity); validity
cf. **date due, expiration, maturity, usance**
d Dauer *f*; Geltungsdauer *f*; Gültigkeitsdauer *f*; Laufzeit *f*; Verfall(s)zeit *f*
e duración *f* (de validez); período *m* de validez; plazo *m* (de validez); término *m*; validez *f*
f délai *m* de validité; durée *f* (de validité); échéance *f*; période *f* de validité; terme *m* (d'échéance); validité *f*
i durata *f* (di validità); periodo *m* di validità; termine *m* (di validità); validità *f*
n duur *m*; geldigheidsduur *m*; geldigheidstermijn *m*; looptijd *m*; termijn *m*

895 currency; period of circulation
d Umlauf(s)zeit *f*
e plazo *m* de circulación
f délai *m* de circulation; durée *f* de circulation
i durata *f* di circolazione
n omloop(s)tijd *m*

896 currency depreciation; currency erosion; monetary depreciation
cf. **currency devaluation**
d Geldentwertung *f*; Geldwertverschlechterung *f*; Valutaentwertung *f*; Währungsentwertung *f*; Währungsverfall *m*; Währungsverschlechterung *f*; Währungszerfall *m*
e depreciación *f* de la moneda; depreciación *f* monetaria; envilecimiento *m* de la moneda; erosión *f* de la moneda; erosión *f* monetaria
f avilissement *m* de la monnaie; avilissement *m* monétaire; dépréciation *f* de la monnaie; dépréciation *f* monétaire; érosion *f* de la monnaie; érosion *f* monétaire
i deprezzamento *m* della moneta; deprezzamento *m* monetario; erosione *f* della moneta; erosione *f* monetaria; svilimento *m* della moneta; svilimento *m* monetario
n gelddepreciatie *f*; geldontwaarding *f*; muntdepreciatie *f*; muntontwaarding *f*; valutaontwaarding *f*; waardedaling *f* van de munt; waardedaling *f* van het geld

897 currency devaluation; exchange depreciation
cf. **currency depreciation**
d Devaluation *f*; Devalvation *f*; Geldabwertung *f*; Valutaabwertung *f*; Währungsabwertung *f*
e depreciación *f* de cambio; desvalorización *f* de la moneda; desvalorización *f* monetaria; devaluación *f* de la moneda; devaluación *f* monetaria
f dépréciation *f* de change; dépréciation *f* du change; dévalorisation *f* de la monnaie; dévalorisation *f* monétaire; dévaluation *f* de la monnaie; dévaluation *f* monétaire
i devalutazione *f* della moneta; devalutazione *f* monetaria; svalutazione *f* della moneta; svalutazione *f* monetaria
n devaluatie *f* van de munt; devaluatie *f* van het geld; devaluatie *f*; waardevermindering *f* van de munt

898 currency manipulation; manipulation of the currency
d Währungsmanipulation *f*; Währungsmanipulierung *f*
e manipulación *f* de la moneda; manipulación *f* monetaria
f manipulation *f* de la monnaie; manipulation *f* monétaire
i manipolazione *f* della moneta;

manipolazione *f* monetaria
n valutamanipulatie *f*

899 **currency reform; monetary reform**
d Geldneuordnung *f*; Geldreform *f*; Währungsreform *f*; Währungsumstellung *f*
e reforma *f* monetaria
f réforme *f* monétaire
i riforma *f* monetaria
n geldhervorming *f*; munthervorming *f*

900 **currency regulations; exchange control regulations; exchange controls; exchange regulations; foreign exchange controls; foreign exchange regulations**
cf. **exchange control**
d Devisenbestimmungen *fpl*; Devisenbewirtschaftungsvorschriften *fpl*; Devisenkontrollbestimmungen *fpl*; Devisenkontrollen *fpl*; Devisenordnung *f*; Devisenregelungen *fpl*; Devisenvorschriften *fpl*
e controles *mpl* de divisas; disposiciones *fpl* sobre (el control de) cambios; disposiciones *fpl* sobre (el control de) divisas; prescripciones *fpl* sobre (el control de) cambios; régimen *m* de divisas; reglamentación *f* de los cambios
f dispositions *fpl* en matière de change; dispositions *fpl* en matière de devises; prescriptions *fpl* en matière de change; prescriptions *fpl* en matière de devises; régime *m* des changes; régime *m* des devises; réglementation *f* des changes; réglementation *f* du change; réglementation *f* en matière de change
i disposizioni *fpl* valutarie; regime *m* dei cambi; regime *m* delle divise; regolamentazione *f* dei cambi
n deviezenbepalingen *fpl*; deviezenreglementering *f*; deviezenverordeningen *fpl*; deviezenvoorschriften *npl*; wisselreglementering *f*

901 **currency reserve; exchange reserve; foreign exchange reserve**
cf. **monetary reserve**
d Devisenbestand *m*; Devisenpolster *n*; Devisenreserve *f*; Devisenrücklage *f*; Währungsreserve *f*
e reserva *f* de divisas
f réserve *f* de change; réserve *f* de devises; réserve *f* en devises
i riserva *f* (di) divise; riserva *f* di valute; riserva *f* valutaria; scorta *f* di divise
n deviezenreserve *f*; deviezenvoorraad *m*

902 **currency restrictions; exchange restrictions; foreign exchange restrictions**
cf. **rationing of foreign exchange**
d Devisenbeschränkungen *fpl*; Deviseneinschränkungen *fpl*; devisenrechtliche Beschränkungen *fpl*; Devisenrestriktionen *fpl*
e restricciones *fpl* cambiarias; restricciones *fpl* de divisas
f restrictions *f* (en matière) de change; restrictions *f* de devises
i restrizioni *fpl* dei cambi; restrizioni *fpl* di cambio; restrizioni *fpl* sulle divise; restrizioni *fpl* valutarie
n deviezenbeperkingen *fpl*; deviezenrestricties *fpl*

903 **currency stability; monetary stability**
d Geldwertstabilität *f*
e estabilidad *f* de la moneda; estabilidad *f* monetaria
f stabilité *f* de la monnaie; stabilité *f* monétaire
i stabilità *f* della moneta; stabilità *f* monetaria
n monetaire stabiliteit *f*; stabiliteit *f* van de munteenheid

904 **currency unit; monetary unit**
d Geldeinheit *f*; Währungseinheit *f*
e unidad *f* monetaria
f unité *f* monétaire
i unità *f* monetaria
n munteenheid *f*

905 **current assets; realisable assets** ***(UK)*****; realizable assets** ***(US)***
cf. **business capital**
d laufende Aktiven *npl*; realisierbare Aktiven *npl*; verwertbare Aktiven *npl*
e activo(s) *m(pl)* corriente(s); activo(s) *m(pl)* realizable(s) (y disponible(s))
f actif *m* courant; actif *m* réalisable (et disponible)
i attività *fpl* correnti; attivo *m* corrente; attivo *m* realizzabile (e disponibile)
n lopend actief *n*; realiseerbare activa *npl*

906 **current coin**
d gangbare Münze *f*; gängige Münze *f*; Kurantmünze *f*
e moneda *f* circulante; moneda *f* corriente; moneda *f* en circulación; moneda *f* en curso
f monnaie *f* ayant cours; monnaie *f* circulante; monnaie *f* courante; monnaie *f* en circulation; monnaie *f* en cours
i moneta *f* avente corso; moneta *f*

circolante; moneta *f* corrente; moneta *f* in circolazione; moneta *f* in corso
n courante munt *f*; gangbare munt *f*

907 current exchange rate; current rate (of exchange)
d Tageskurs *m*
e cambio *m* corriente; cambio *m* del día
f cours *m* actuel; cours *m* du jour
i cambio *m* del giorno
n dagkoers *m*; huidige koers *m*

908 current expenses; running expenses
d Ausgaben *fpl* in laufender Rechnung; laufende Ausgaben *fpl*; laufende Unkosten *pl*
e gastos *mpl* corrientes
f dépenses *fpl* courantes; frais *mpl* courants
i spese *fpl* correnti
n lopende uitgaven *fpl*

909 current interest; running interest *(rare)*
d laufende Zinsen *mpl*
e interés *m* corriente; intereses *mpl* corrientes
f intérêt(s) *m(pl)* courant(s)
i interesse *m* corrente; interesse *m* in corso; interessi *mpl* correnti; interessi *mpl* in corso
n lopende int(e)rest *m*; lopende rente *f*

910 current liabilities; quick liabilities; short-term debts; short-term liabilities
d kurzfristige Schulden *fpl*; kurzfristige Verbindlichkeiten *fpl*; kurzfristige Verpflichtungen *fpl*; laufende Verbindlichkeiten *fpl*; laufende Verpflichtungen *fpl*
e compromisos *mpl* a corto plazo; débitos *mpl* a corto plazo; obligaciones *fpl* a corto plazo; pasivo *m* a corto plazo; pasivo *m* circulante; pasivo *m* corriente; pasivo *m* exigible
f dettes *fpl* à courte échéance; exigibilités *fpl*; passif *m* à court terme; passif *m* courant; passif *m* exigible
i debiti *mpl* a breve (scadenza); passività *fpl* a breve (termine); passività *fpl* correnti; passività *fpl* esigibili; passivo *m* a breve (termine); passivo *m* circolante; passivo *m* corrente; passivo *m* esigibile
n lopende verplichtingen *fpl*; opvorderbare passiva *npl*; schulden *fpl* op korte termijn

911 current market price; current price; prevailing price; price of the day; ruling price
cf. **market price**
d jeweiliger Preis *m*; Tagespreis *m*
e precio *m* corriente; precio *m* del día
f courant *m* du marché; prix *m* courant (du marché); prix *m* du jour
i prezzo *m* corrente; prezzo *m* del giorno
n dagprijs *m*; huidige prijs *m*; lopende prijs *m*

912 current market value ***(general market)*****; current value; present value**
d Barwert *m*; Gegenwartswert *m*; Tageswert *m*; Verkehrswert *m*; Zeitwert *m*
e valor *m* actual; valor *m* del día
f valeur *f* actuelle; valeur *f* courante; valeur *f* présente
i valore *m* attuale; valore *m* corrente
n actuele waarde *f (B)*; contante waarde *f*; dagwaarde *f*

913 current market value ***(stockmarket)*****; current rate; current value; quotation of the day; rate of the day**
d Tageskurs *m*; Tagesnotierung *f*; Tagesnotiz *f*; Tageswert *m*
e cotización *f* actual; cotización *f* del día
f cote *f* du jour; cours *m* actuel; cours *m* du jour; cours *m* pratiqué
i quotazione *f* del giorno; valore *m* corrente
n dagkoers *m*; dagnotering *f*; dagwaarde *f*

914 current money; money in circulation
cf. **circulation of money, currency**
d gangbares Geld *n*; Geld *n* im Umlauf; im Umlauf befindliches Geld *n*; Kurantgeld *n*; kursierendes Geld *n*
e dinero *m* circulante; dinero *m* corriente; dinero *m* en circulación
f argent *m* circulant; argent *m* courant; argent *m* en circulation
i denaro *m* circolante; denaro *m* corrente; denaro *m* in circolazione
n chartaal geld *n*; courant geld *n*; gangbaar geld *n*; geld *n* in omloop

915 curtail *v* **expenses; cut** *v* **expenses; cut** *v* **down expenses; limit** *v* **expenses; prune** *v* **expenses; reduce** *v* **expenses; restrict** *v* **expenses; retrench** *v* **expenses**
d die Ausgaben begrenzen; die Ausgaben beschneiden; die Ausgaben beschränken; die Ausgaben einschränken; die Ausgaben einsparen; die Ausgaben ermässigen; die Ausgaben herabsetzen; die Ausgaben kürzen; die Ausgaben reduzieren; die Ausgaben senken; die Ausgaben vermindern; die Ausgaben verringern

e cercenar los gastos; cortar los gastos; disminuir los gastos; limitar los gastos; recortar los gastos; reducir los gastos; restringir los gastos
f couper les dépenses; diminuer les dépenses; limiter les dépenses; réduire les dépenses; restreindre les dépenses; rogner les dépenses
i contrarre le spese; decurtare le spese; diminuire le spese; limitare le spese; restringere le spese; ridurre le spese; tagliare le spese
n de uitgaven begrenzen; de uitgaven beperken; de uitgaven besnoeien; de uitgaven bezuinigen; de uitgaven inkrimpen; de uitgaven reduceren; de uitgaven verminderen

916 customable *(rare)*; **dutiable; liable to duty; subject to duty**
cf. **assessable**
d abgabenpflichtig; verzollbar; zollpflichtig
e sujeto a (derechos de) aduana; sujeto al pago de aranceles
f assujetti aux droits de douane; dédouanable; passible des droits de douane; soumis aux droits de douane
i sdaziabile; sdoganabile; soggetto a dazio; soggetto a diritti doganali; soggetto a dogana
n aan douanerechten onderhevig; aan douanerechten onderworpen; tolplichtig

917 customs; customs dues; customs duty; duty
cf. **tariff**
d Zoll *m*; Zollabgabe *f*; Zollgebühr *f*
e aduana *f*; arancel *m*; derecho *m* aduanero; derecho *m* arencelario; derecho *m* de aduana
f douane *f*; droit *m* de douane
i dazio *m* doganale; diritto *m* doganale; dogana *f*
n doeanegelden *npl*; doeanerecht *n*; douanegelden *npl*; douanerecht *n*; tolgelden *npl*; tolrecht *n*

918 customs barrier; tariff wall
d Zollmauer *f*; Zollschranke *f*
e barrera *f* aduanera; muro *m* aduanero; muro *m* arancelario
f barrière *f* douanière; muraille *f* douanière
i barriera *f* doganale; muraglia *f* doganale
n tariefmuur *m*; tolmuur *m*

919 customs declaration; customs entry
d Zollangabe *f*; Zollanmeldung *f*; Zolldeklaration *f*; Zolldeklarierung *f*; Zollerklärung *f*
e declaración *f* aduanera; declaración *f* arancelaria; declaración *f* de aduana
f déclaration *f* de douane; déclaration *f* douanière; déclaration *f* en douane
i dichiarazione *f* di dogana; dichiarazione *f* doganale
n douaneaangifte *f*; douanedeclaratie *f*; douaneverklaring *f*

920 customs-exempt; customs-free; duty-free; exempt from duty; free of duty; non-dutiable
d abgabenfrei; zollfrei
e con (en) franquicia (aduanera); franco de aduana; exento de derechos (de aduana); libre de derechos (de aduana)
f en franchise (de droits); exempt de droits (de douane); franc(o) de (droits de) douane; net de droits (de douane)
i esente da dazio; esente da diritti doganali; esente da dogana; franco di dazio; franco dogana; in franchigia (doganale)
n tolvrij; vrij van (douane-)rechten

921 customs receipts; customs revenue; tariff revenue
d Zolleinnahmen *fpl*
e ingresos *mpl* aduaneros; recaudación *f* aduanera; rentas *fpl* aduaneras
f recettes *fpl* des douanes
i entrate *fpl* doganali; proventi *mpl* doganali
n douaneinkomsten *fpl*; douane-ontvangsten *fpl*

922 customs tariff
d Zolltarif *m*
e arancel *m* aduanero; arancel *m* de aduanas; tarifa *f* aduanera; tarifa *f* arancelaria; tarifa *f* de aduanas
f tarif *m* douanier; tarif *m* des douanes
i tariffa *f* doganale
n douanetarief *n*; toltarief *n*

923 customs union
d Zollunion *f*; Zollverband *m*; Zollverein *m (rare except historically)*
e unión *f* aduanera
f union *f* douanière
i unione *f* doganale
n douane-unie *f*; tolunie *f*

924 cut *v*; **cut** *v* **back; economize** *v*; **retrench** *v*
cf. **curtail** *v* **expenses**
d Abstriche machen; Abstriche vornehmen; Einsparungen machen; Einsparungen vor-

nehmen; sich einschränken
e economizar; hacer economías
f économiser; faire des économies
i economizzare; fare economia
n bezuinigen; economiseren; uitsparen

925 **cut in the dividend; dividend reduction; dividend remission; reduction in the dividend**
d Dividendenherabsetzung *f*; Dividendenkürzung *f*; Dividendenminderung *f*
e reducción *f* del dividendo
f diminution *f* du dividende; réduction *f* du dividende
i riduzione *f* del dividendo
n dividendverlaging *f*

926 **cut in the minimum lending rate *(UK)*; fall in the minimum lending rate *(UK)*; lowering of the minimum lending rate *(UK)*; reduction in the discount rate *(US)*; reduction in the rediscount rate *(US)***
d Diskontermässigung *f*; Diskontherabsetzung *f*; Diskontsenkung *f*; Ermässigung *f* des Diskontsatzes; Herabsetzung *f* des Diskontsatzes; Senkung *f* des Diskontsatzes
e reducción *f* del tipo de descuento
f abaissement *m* du taux d'escompte; réduction *f* de l'escompte; réduction *f* du taux d'escompte
i abbassamento *m* del tasso di sconto; ribasso *m* del tasso di sconto; riduzione *f* del tasso di sconto
n discontoverlaging *f*; verlaging *f* van de discontovoet; verlaging *f* van het disconto

927 **cut in the price; lowering of the price; markdown; price cut; price reduction; reduction in the price**
cf. **allowance, crumbling of prices**
d Preisabbau *m*; Preisabschlag *m*; Preisermässigung *f*; Preisherabsetzung *f*; Preiskürzung *f*; Preisminderung *f*; Preisnachlass *m*; Preisreduktion *f*; Preissenkung *f*
e rebaja *f* del precio; reducción *f* del precio
f abaissement *m* du prix; démarque *f*; rabaissement *m* du prix; réduction *f* du prix
i abbassamento *m* del prezzo; ribasso *m* del prezzo; riduzione *f* del prezzo
n prijsafslag *m*; prijsreductie *f*; prijsverlaging *f*; prijsvermindering *f*

928 **cut *v* one's losses**
d sich mit Verlust zurückziehen
e retirarse con pérdida
f faire la part du feu; se retirer avec perte
i ritirarsi con perdita
n zich met verlies terugtrekken

929 **cyclical budget**
d Konjunkturhaushalt *m*
e presupuesto *m* coyuntural
f budget *m* conjoncturel
i bilancio *m* congiunturale
n conjuncturele begroting *f*

930 **cyclical fluctuation; economic fluctuation; fluctuation in the economic situation; market fluctuation; market swing; swing in the economic situation**
d konjunkturelle Fluktuation *f*; konjunkturelle Schwankung *f*; Konjunkturschwankung *f*; Marktschwankung *f*; zyklische Schwankung *f*
e fluctuación *f* cíclica; fluctuación *f* coyuntural; fluctuación *f* de la coyuntura; fluctuación *f* del mercado; fluctuación *f* económica; oscilación *f* cíclica; oscilación *f* coyuntural; oscilación *f* de la coyuntura; oscilación *f* del mercado; oscilación *f* económica
f fluctuation *f* conjoncturelle; fluctuation *f* cyclique; fluctuation *f* de la conjoncture; fluctuation *f* du marché; fluctuation *f* économique; fluctuation *f* sur le marché
i fluttuazione *f* ciclica; fluttuazione *f* congiunturale; fluttuazione *f* della congiuntura; fluttuazione *f* del mercato; fluttuazione *f* economica; oscillazione *f* ciclica; oscillazione *f* congiunturale; oscillazione *f* della congiuntura; oscillazione *f* del mercato; oscillazione *f* economica
n conjuncturele fluctuatie *f*; conjuncturele schommeling *f*; conjunctuurfluctuatie *f*; conjunctuurschommeling *f*; cyclische fluctuatie *f*; cyclische schommeling *f*; economische fluctuatie *f*; economische schommeling *f*

D

931 date due; date of maturity; due date; maturity date
cf. **expiration date, maturity**
d Fälligkeitsdatum *n*; Fälligkeitstag *m*; Fälligkeitstermin *m*; Verfalldatum *n*; Verfall(s)tag *m*; Verfall(s)termin *m*
e día *m* de vencimiento; fecha *f* de vencimiento; plazo *m* de vencimiento
f date *f* d'échéance; date *f* de l'échéance; jour *m* d'échéance; terme *m* d'échéance
i data *f* di scadenza; giorno *m* di scadenza; termine *m* di scadenza
n vervaldag *m*; vervaldatum *m*

932 daybook; journal
cf. **auxiliary book**
d Journal *n*; Memorial *n*; Tagebuch *n*
e diario *m*; libro *m* diario
f journal *m*; livre-journal *m*; mémorial *m*
i giornale *m*; libro *m* giornale
n dagboek *n (B)*; journaal *n*; memoriaal *n*

933 days of grace; days of respite
cf. **delay**
d Gnadentage *mpl*; Respekttage *mpl*; Respirotage *mpl*; Respittage *mpl*
e días *mpl* de cortesía; días *mpl* de favor; días *mpl* de gracia
f jours *mpl* de grâce; jours *mpl* de répit
i giorni *mpl* di grazia; giorni *mpl* di respiro; giorni *mpl* di rispetto
n respijtdagen *mpl*

934 dead loss; total loss; write-off
d Gesamtschaden *m*; Gesamtverlust *m*; Totalschaden *m*; Totalverlust *m*
e pérdida *f* total
f perte *f* totale
i perdita *f* totale
n geheel verlies *n*; totaal verlies *n*

935 dealer's rebate; trade allowance; trade discount; trade rebate
d Handelsrabatt *m*; Handelsskonto *m/n*; Händlerrabatt *m*; Rabatt *m* an (für) Wiederverkäufer; Warendiskont *m*; Warenrabatt *m*; Warenskonto *m/n*
e descuento *m* comercial; descuento *m* de comerciante; descuento *m* para revendedores; descuento *m* sobre mercancías; rebaja *f* de comercio
f escompte *m* commercial; escompte *m* de revendeur; escompte *m* sur facture; escompte *m* sur marchandises; rabais *m* marchand; remise *f* commerciale; remise *f* de revendeur; remise *f* sur facture; remise *f* sur marchandises
i sconto *m* al rivenditore; sconto *m* commerciale; sconto *m* sulle fatture; sconto *m* su merci
n handelskorting *f*; korting *f* voor handelaars

936 dealing in foreign notes and coins
cf. **exchange transactions**
d Sortengeschäft *n*; Sortenhandel *m*
e comercio *m* en monedas y billetes extranjeros
f commerce *m* en billets et espèces étrangers
i commercio *m* in biglietti e monete esteri
n handel *m* in vreemde biljetten en munten

937 dealings before the opening of the stock exchange
cf. **curb**
d Vorbörse *f*
e antebolsa *f*
f avant-bourse *f*
i affari *mpl* conclusi prima dell'apertura della borsa
n voorbeurs *f*

938 death duty *(UK)*; death tax *(US)*; estate duty *(UK)*; estate tax *(US)*; inheritance tax *(US)*; legacy duty *(UK)*; legacy tax *(US)*; probate duty; succession duty *(UK)*; succession tax *(US)*
d Erbanfallsteuer *f*; Erbschaftssteuer *f*; Nachlasssteuer *f*; Vermächtnissteuer *f*
e derecho *m* de sucesión; impuesto *m* de sucesión; impuesto *m* sobre la herencia; impuesto *m* sucesorio
f droit *m* de succession; impôt *m* successoral; impôt *m* sur la succession; taxe *f* successorale
i diritto *m* di successione; imposta *f* di successione; imposta *f* sull'asse ereditario; imposta *f* sulla successione; tassa *f* di successione
n erfenisrecht *n (B)*; successiebelasting *f*; successierecht *n*

939 debasement of coinage
d Münzverfälschung *f*; Münzverringerung *f*; Münzverschlechterung *f*
e adulteración *f* de la moneda; alteración *f* de la moneda
f adultération *f* de la monnaie; altération *f* de la monnaie
i adulterazione *f* della moneta; alterazione *f* della moneta
n muntschennis *f*; muntvervalsing *f*

940 debenture capital
d Obligationenkapital *n*
e capital-obligaciones *m*
f capital-obligations *m*
i capitale *m* obbligazioni
n obligatiekapitaal *n*

941 debenture loan
d Obligationenanleihe *f*; Obligationsanleihe *f*
e empréstito *m* de obligaciones; empréstito *m* en obligaciones; empréstito-obligaciones *m*; empréstito *m* por obligaciones
f emprunt *m* d'obligations; emprunt *m* obligataire; emprunt-obligations *m*; emprunt *m* par obligations
i prestito *m* obbligazionario; prestito *m* per obbligazioni
n obligatielening *f*

942 debit
d Debet *n*; Soll *n*
e debe *m*; débito *m*
f débit *m*; doit *m*
i addebito *m*; dare *m*; debito *m*
n debet *n*

943 debit; debit side; debtor side; liabilities side; red *(col.)*
d Debet *n*; Debetseite *f*; Passivseite *f*; Soll *n*; Sollseite *f*
e debe *m*; lado *m* del debe; lado *m* del débito; lado *m* del pasivo; lado *m* deudor; lado *m* pasivo; pasivo *m*
f côté *m* débiteur; côté *m* du débit; côté *m* passif; débit *m*; doit *m*; passif *m*
i dare *m*; debito *m*; lato *m* del dare; lato *m* del passivo; parte *f* del dare; parte *f* del passivo; passivo *m*
n debet *n*; debetzijde *f*; passiefzijde *f*

944 be *v* **in debit; be** *v* **in the red**
d im Debet sein; im Debet stehen
e estar en el debe
f être au débit; être débiteur
i essere debitore; essere in disavanzo
n debet staan; debet zijn; in de rode cijfers staan

945 debit advice
cf. **debit note**
d Belastungsanzeige *f*; Belastungsaufgabe *f*; Lastschrift(s)anzeige *f*; Lastschrift(s)aufgabe *f*; Lastschriftzettel *m*
e aviso *m* de débito
f avis *m* de débit
i avviso *m* di debito; lettera *f* di addebitamento
n debetnota *f*

946 debit entry; debit item
d Eintragung *f* auf der Sollseite; Lastschrift *f*; Lastschriftbuchung *f*; Lastschriftposten *m*; Passivposten *m*; Sollbuchung *f*; Sollposten *m*
e asiento *m* de débito; asiento *m* pasivo; entrada *f* al debe; entrada *f* en el debe; partida *f* de cargo; partida *f* de débito; partida *f* del debe; partida *f* deudora; partida *f* pasiva
f article *m* (porté) au débit; écriture *f* de débit; écriture *f* passée au débit; inscription *f* au débit; poste *m* au débit; poste *m* débiteur; poste *m* porté au débit
i partita *f* debitoria; partita *f* del dare; registrazione *f* a debito; registrazione *f* di debito; scrittura *f* d'addebitamento; scrittura *f* di debito; scrittura *f* registrata a debito; voce *f* del dare; voce *f* passiva
n boeking *f* in (op) het debet; debetboeking *f*; debetpost *m*

947 debit interest; interest in red; interest payable; red interest
d Passivzinsen *mpl*; Schuldzinsen *mpl*; Sollzinsen *mpl*
e intereses *mpl* a pagar; intereses *mpl* deudores; intereses *mpl* pasivos
f intérêts *mpl* à payer; intérêts *mpl* débiteurs; intérêts *mpl* passifs; intérêts *mpl* rouges
i interessi *mpl* da pagare; interessi *mpl* debitori; interessi *mpl* passivi; interessi *mpl* rossi
n debetrente *f*; rode rente *f*; te betalen rente *f*

948 debit note
cf. **debit advice**
d Debetnota *f*; Debetnote *f*
e nota *f* de cargo; nota *f* de débito
f facture *f* de débit; note *f* de débit
i nota *f* di addebito
n debetnota *f*

949 deblock *v (funds etc.)*; **release** *v*; **set** *v* **free; unblock** *v*; **unfreeze** *v*
cf. **convert** *v* **into cash, mobilize** *v*
d auftauen; deblockieren; entsperren; freigeben; freisetzen
e desbloquear; descongelar; liberar
f débloquer; dégeler; libérer
i liberare; sbloccare; scongelare; smobilizzare
n deblokkeren; losmaken; ontdooien; vrijmaken

950 **deblocking** *(funds etc.)*; **release; unfreezing**
cf. **conversion into cash, mobilization**
d Auftauen *n*; Deblockierung *f*; Entsperrung *f*; Freigabe *f*; Freisetzung *f*
e desbloqueo *m*; descongelación *f*; liberación *f*
f déblocage *m*; dégel *m*; libération *f*
i liberazione *f*; sblocco *m*; scongelamento *m*; smobilizzo *m*
n deblokkering *f*; ontdooing *f*; vrijgave *f*

951 **debt; indebtedness; liability** *(US)*
cf. **claim, debts**
d Schuld *f*
e adeudo *m*; deuda *f*
f dette *f*
i debito *m*
n schuld *f*

952 **in debt; indebted**
d schuldenbelastet; verschuldet
e adeudado; empeñado; endeudado
f endetté
i carico di debiti; indebitato
n met schulden belast; schuldig

953 **be** *v* **up to one's ears in debt; overextended; overindebted**
d bis über die Ohren in Schulden stecken; überschuldet sein
e estar acribillado de deudas; estar excesivamente endeudado
f être accablé de dettes; être criblé de dettes; être surendetté
i essere eccessivamente indebitato; essere pieno di debiti; essere sovraccarico di debiti
n met schulden overladen zijn; onder schulden bedolven zijn; tot over de oren in de schuld(en) zitten

954 **debt administration; debt management**
d Schuldenverwaltung *f*
e administración *f* de las deudas
f administration *f* des dettes; gestion *f* des dettes
i amministrazione *f* dei debiti
n schuldbeheer *n*

955 **debt collector**
d Inkassobeauftragter *m*
e cobrador *m* de deudas; recaudador *m* de deudas
f agent *m* de recouvrements
i agente *m* per il ricupero di crediti
n schuldincasseerder *m*; schuldinvorderaar *m*

956 **debt financing**
d Finanzierung *f* mittels Abtretung von Forderungen
e financiación *f* mediante la cesión de créditos
f financement *m* au moyen de la cession de créances
i finanziamento *m* mediante la cessione di crediti
n financiering *f* door middel van de cessie van vorderingen

957 **debt on mortgage; mortgage debt**
d Hypothekarschuld *f*; Hypothekenforderung *f*; Hypothekenschuld *f*
e deuda *f* hipotecaria
f créance *f* hypothécaire; dette *f* hypothécaire
i debito *m* ipotecario
n hypot(h)ecaire schuld *f*; hypot(h)eekschuld *f*

958 **debtor**
d Debitor *m*; Schuldner *m*
e deudor *m*
f débiteur *m*
i debitore *m*
n debiteur *m*; schuldenaar *m*

959 **debtor country; debtor nation**
d Schuldnerland *n*; Schuldnerstaat *m*
e país *m* deudor
f pays *m* débiteur
i paese *m* debitore
n debiteurland *n*; debiteurstaat *m*

960 **debtor to sales ratio**
d Debitorenumschlag *m*; Forderungsumschlag *m*
e rotación *f* de créditos
f rotation *f* des créances
i rotazione *f* dei crediti
n debiteurenomslag *m*; omloopsnelheid *f* van de debiteuren

961 **debts; liabilities; obligations**
cf. **account payable, burden of debts, debt**
d Obligos *npl*; Passiva *npl*; Passiven *npl*; Passivmasse *f*; Passivum *n*; Schulden *fpl*; Verbindlichkeiten *fpl*; Verpflichtungen *fpl*
e compromisos *mpl*; débitos *mpl*; deudas *fpl*; empeños *mpl*; masa *f* pasiva; obligaciones *fpl*; pasivo *m*
f dettes *fpl*; engagements *mpl*; masse *f* débitrice; masse *f* passive; obligations *fpl*; passif *m*
i debiti *mpl*; impegni *mpl*; massa *f*

passiva; obbligazioni *fpl*; passivi *mpl*; passività *f*; passivo *m*
n passief *n*; passiva *npl*; schulden *fpl*; uitschulden *fpl*; verplichtingen *fpl*

962 **debt service**
d Schuldendienst *m*
e servicio *m* de la deuda
f service *m* de la dette
i servizio *m* del debito
n schuldendienst *m*

963 **debt to equity ratio; gearing** *(UK)*
d Fremdkapital/Eigenkapital-Verhältnis *n*; Verschuldungs/Eigenkapital-Verhältnis *n*
e relación *f* capital prestado/capital propio
f rapport *m* capitaux empruntés/capitaux propres
i rapporto *m* capitale in prestito/capitale proprio
n verhouding *f* vreemd kapitaal/eigen kapitaal

964 **declaration of a dividend; fixation of a dividend**
cf. **disbursement of dividends**
d Dividendenerklärung *f*; Dividendenfestsetzung *f*
e declaración *f* de un dividendo; fijación *f* de un dividendo
f déclaration *f* d'un dividende; fixation *f* d'un dividende
i dichiarazione *f* di un dividendo; fissazione *f* di un dividendo
n dividendaankondiging *f*; dividenddeclaratie *f*; dividendvaststelling *f*

965 **declare** *v* **a dividend; fix** *v* **a dividend**
cf. **disburse** *v* **a dividend**
d eine Dividende anzeigen; eine Dividende beschliessen; eine Dividende festsetzen
e declarar un dividendo; fijar un dividendo
f déclarer un dividende; fixer un dividende
i dichiare un dividendo; fissare un dividendo
n een dividend aankondigen; een dividend declareren; een dividend vaststellen

966 **declared reserves; disclosed reserves; visible reserves**
d ausgewiesene Reserven *fpl*; ausgewiesene Rücklagen *fpl*; offene Reserven *fpl*; offene Rücklagen *fpl*; sichtbare Reserven *fpl*; sichtbare Rücklagen *fpl*
e reservas *fpl* declaradas; reservas *fpl* visibles
f réserves *fpl* déclarées; réserves *fpl* visibles
i riserve *fpl* dichiarate; riserve *fpl* palesi
n open reserves *fpl*; zichtbare reserves *fpl*

967 **declared value**
d angegebener Wert *m*; deklarierter Wert *m*; Wertangabe *f*
e valor *m* declarado
f valeur *f* déclarée
i valore *m* dichiarato
n aangegeven waarde *f*; gedeclareerde waarde *f*

968 **decline; downswing; downturn; setback; slackening; slide; slowdown; weakening**
cf. **depression, drop**
d Abflauen *n*; Abschwächung *f*; Abschwung *m*; Baisse *f*; Nachlassen *n*; Rückgang *m*; Rücklauf *m*; Rückschlag *m*; Verfall *m*; Zurückgang *m*
e aflojamiento *m*; baja *f*; debilitación *f*; debilitamiento *m*; decremento *m*; descenso *m*; disminución *f*; retroceso *m*
f affaiblissement *m*; baisse *f*; déclin *m*; diminution *f*; fléchissement *m*; ralentissement *m*; recul *m*; relâchement *m*; tassement *m*
i declinazione *f*; diminuzione *f*; indebolimento *m*; rallentamento *m*; regresso *m*; ribasso *m*
n achteruitgang *m*; daling *f*; inzinking *f*; neergang *m*; teruggang *m*; verflauwing *f*; vermindering *f*; verslapping *f*; vertraging *f*; verzwakking *f*

969 **decline in value; decrease in value; depreciation; drop in value; fall in value; loss of value; reduction in value**
cf. **depreciation**
d Minderwert *m*; Wertabnahme *f*; Werteinbusse *f*; Wertherabsetzung *f*; Wertminderung *f*; Wertrückgang *m*; Wertverlust *m*; Wertverminderung *f*; Wertverringerung *f*; Wertverschlechterung *f*
e depreciación *f*; disminución *f* de valor; menor valor *m*; pérdida *f* de valor; rebaja *f* de valor; reducción *f* de valor; retroceso *m* de valor
f amenuisement *m* de valeur; amoindrissement *m* de valeur; baisse *f* de valeur; dépréciation *f*; diminution *f* de valeur; moins-value *f*; perte *f* de valeur; perte *f* en valeur; réduction *f* en valeur
i deprezzamento *m*; diminuzione *f* di valore; minor valore *m*; minusvalenza *f*; perdita *f* di valore; ribasso *m* di valore; ribasso *m* nel valore; riduzione *f* di valore

n depreciatie *f*; minderwaarde *f*; waardedaling *f*; waardevermindering *f*

970 **decline** *v* **in value; decrease** *v* **in value; depreciate** *v*; **diminish** *v* **in value; drop** *v* **in value; fall** *v* **in value; go** *v* **down in value; lose** *v* **(in) value**
d an Wert abnehmen; an Wert einbüssen; an Wert verlieren; eine Wertverminderung erfahren; eine Wertverminderung erleiden; im Wert fallen; im Wert sinken; im Wert zurückgehen; sich im Wert verringern; sich im Wert vermindern
e bajar; depreciarse; descender en valor; desvalorizarse; disminuir de valor; envilecerse; perder (en) valor
f baisser; descendre en valeur; diminuer de valeur; perdre (de) valeur; perdre en valeur; s'avilir; se déprécier; se dévaloriser; subir une dépréciation
i cadere di valore; deprezzarsi; diminuire di valore; perdere (di) valore; ribassare; scendere nel valore; svalutarsi; svilirsi
n (aan) waarde verliezen; depreciëren; in waarde dalen; in waarde verminderen

971 **decontrol of prices; price decontrol**
d Freigabe *f* der Preise; Preisfreigabe *f*
e liberación *f* de los precios
f libération *f* des prix
i liberazione *f* dei prezzi; svincolo *m* dei prezzi
n vrijgeven *n* van de prijzen; vrijmaking *f* van de prijzen

972 **deduct** *v* **at source**
cf. **deduct** *v* **beforehand**
d an der Quelle abziehen
e deducir en la fuente; retener en la fuente
f déduire à la source; retenir à la source
i dedurre alla fonte; detrarre alla fonte; ritenere alla fonte; trattenere alla fonte
n aan de bron afhouden; aan de bron aftrekken; aan de bron inhouden

973 **deduct** *v* **beforehand; deduct** *v* **in advance**
cf. **deduct** *v* **at source**
d im voraus abrechnen; im voraus abziehen; vorweg abrechnen; vorweg abziehen
e deducir con anticipación; deducir por adelantado
f déduire à l'avance; précompter; prélever
i dedurre in anticipo; detrarre in anticipo; prelevare
n vooraf aftrekken

974 **deductible loss**
d abzugfähiger Verlust *m*
e pérdida *f* deducible
f perte *f* déductible
i perdita *f* detraibile
n aftrekbaar verlies *n*

975 **deduction at source**
d Quellenabzug *m*
e deducción *f* en el origen; deducción *f* en la fuente
f déduction *f* à la source; prélèvement *m* à la source; retenue *f* à la source
i deduzione *f* alla fonte; deduzione *f* all'origine; prelevamento *m* alla fonte; prelevamento *m* all'origine; ritenuta *f* alla fonte; ritenuta *f* all'origine; trattenuta *f* alla fonte; trattenuta *f* all'origine
n afhouding *f* aan de bron; aftrek *m* aan de bron; inhouding *f* aan de bron

976 **deed of trust; trust deed**
d Treuhändervertrag *m*; Treuhandvertrag *m*
e contrato *m* fiduciario; escritura *f* fiduciaria
f acte *m* fiduciaire; contrat *m* fiduciaire
i contratto *m* fiduciario; scrittura *f* fiduciaria
n trustakte *f*

977 **defalcate** *v*; **embezzle** *v*; **misappropriate** *v*; **peculate** *v*
d entwenden; sich widerrechtlich aneignen; unterschlagen; veruntreuen
e apropiarse ilegalmente; cometer un desfalco; desfalcar; distraer; hurtar; malversar
f commettre un détournement; dépréder; détourner; distraire; divertir; s'approprier
i appropriarsi indebitamente; defraudare; sottrarre
n verduisteren; verduistering plegen; zich wederrechtelijk toeëigenen

978 **defalcation; embezzlement; misappropriation; peculation**
d Entwendung *f*; Unterschlagung *f*; Unterschleif *m*; Veruntreuung *f*; widerrechtliche Aneignung *f*
e apropiación *f* indebita; desfalco *m*; hurto *m*; malversación *f*; peculado *m*
f concussion *f*; déprédation *f*; détournement *m*; distraction *f*; divertissement *m*; malversation *f*; péculat *m*
i appropriazione *f* indebita; defraudamento *m*; malversazione *f*;

peculato *m*; sottrazione *f*
n verduistering *f*; wederrechtelijke toeëigening *f*

979 in default
cf. **in arrears**
d im Verzug
e en demora; en mora
f en demeure
i in mora
n in gebreke; in mora; in verzuim

980 defaulted bond; defaulted debenture
d notleidende Obligation *f*; notleidende Schuldverschreibung *f*
e bono *m* en mora; obligación *f* en mora
f bon *m* en souffrance; obligation *f* en souffrance
i buono *m* in mora; obbligazione *f* in mora
n noodlijdende obligatie *f*

981 defaulter; defaulting debtor; dilatory debtor; slow debtor; tardy debtor
cf. **bad payer**
d fauler Debitor *m*; fauler Schuldner *m*; säumiger Debitor *m*; säumiger Schuldner *m*
e deudor *m* en retraso; deudor *m* moroso; deudor *m* negligente
f débiteur *m* défaillant; débiteur *m* en retard; débiteur *m* négligent; débiteur *m* retardataire
i debitore *m* inadempiente; debitore *m* in retardo; debitore *m* moroso; debitore *m* negligente
n nalatige debiteur *m*; nalatige schuldenaar *m*

982 default in paying; default in payment; non-payment
cf. **delay in payment**
d Nichtbezahlung *f*; Nichtzahlung *f*
e falta *f* de pago; no pago *m*
f carence *f* de paiement; défaut *m* de paiement; non-paiement *m*
i mancanza *f* di pagamento; mancato pagamento *m*
n niet-betaling *f*; non-betaling *f*; wanbetaling *f*

983 default interest; interest for default; interest on arrears; past-due interest; penal interest
d Verzugszinsen *mpl*
e interés(es) *m(pl)* de demora; interés(es) *m(pl)* moratorio(s)
f intérêt(s) *m(pl)* de retard; intérêt(s) *m(pl)* moratoire(s)
i interesse *m* di mora; interesse *m* moratorio; interessi *mpl* di mora; interessi *mpl* moratori
n moratoire int(e)resten *mpl*; moratoire rente *f*; rente *f* wegens (te) late betaling; rente *f* wegens verzuim

984 defer *v* **a payment; delay** *v* **a payment; postpone** *v* **a payment; respite** *v* **a payment**
d eine Zahlung aufschieben; eine Zahlung hinausschieben; eine Zahlung verschieben; eine Zahlung verzögern
e aplazar un pago; atrasar un pago; demorar un pago; diferir un pago; retrasar un pago
f arriérer un paiement; atermoyer un paiement; différer un paiement; remettre un paiement
i differire un pagamento; dilazionare un pagamento; posticipare un pagamento
n een betaling uitstellen; een betaling verdagen

985 deferred share
d Nachzugsaktie *f*
e acción *f* diferida
f action *f* différée
i azione *f* differita
n uitgesteld aandeel *n*

986 deferred taxation; deferred taxes
d latente Steuerschulden *fpl*
e impuesto *m* diferido
f imposition *f* différée
i imposte *fpl* differite
n latente belastingverplichting *f*

987 on deferred terms; on easy terms; on the instal(l)ment plan ***(US)*****; by instal(l)ments; in instal(l)ments; on the instal(l)ment system** ***(US)***
d auf Abschlag; auf (gegen) Abzahlung; im Abzahlungswege; auf (in) Raten; ratenweise; auf Ratenzahlung; in Ratenzahlungen; in Teilbeträgen; auf Teilzahlung; auf (in) Teilzahlungen; terminweise
e por pagos parciales; a (en; por) plazos; por cuotas
f par abonnement; par acomptes; en plusieurs versements; à tempérament; à (par) termes; en (par) versements échelonnés; en (par) versements fractionnés
i a rate; ratealmente
n bij gedeelten; bij (in) termijnen; op afbetaling

988 deficiency; deficit; short; shortage; shortfall
cf. **adverse balance, loss**
d Abgang *m*; Ausfall *m*; Ausfallbetrag *m*; Defizit *n*; Fehlbestand *m*; Fehlbetrag *m*; Fehlende *n*; Manko *n*; Minderbetrag *m*; Minusbetrag *m*; Unterbilanz *f*
e deficiencia *f*; déficit *m*; descubierto *m*; falta *f*; manco *m*; merma *f*
f découvert *m*; déficit *m*; mali *m*; manquant *m*; manque *m*; moins-value *f*
i ammanco *m*; deficit *m*; disavanzo *m*; mancante *m*; scoperto *m*
n deficit *n*; manco *n*; minder bedrag *n*; ontbrekende *n*; tekort *n*

989 deficit budgeting; deficit financing; deficit spending
d Deficit-spending *n*; Defizitfinanzierung *f*; Defizitwirtschaft *f*
e economía *f* deficitaria; financiación *f* con déficit
f déficit *m* budgétaire systematique; économie *f* déficitaire
i deficit financing *m*; deficit spending *m*; economia *f* deficitaria
n deficitfinanciering *f*; deficit spending *f*

990 deflate *v*
d deflatieren; deflationieren
e desinflar
f amener la déflation
i deflazionare
n deflateren

991 deflation
cf. **disinflation**
d Deflation *f*
e deflación *f*
f déflation *f*
i deflazione *f*
n deflatie *f*

992 deflationary; deflationist
cf. **disinflationary**
d deflationär; deflationistisch; Deflations-; deflatorisch
e deflacionario; deflacionista
f déflationniste
i deflatorio; deflazionistico
n deflatie-; deflationistisch; deflatoir; deflatorisch

993 deflationary spiral
d deflatorische Spirale *f*
e espiral *f* deflacionista
f spirale *f* déflationniste
i spirale *f* deflazionistica
n deflatiespiraal *f*

994 deflationary trend
d deflationistische Tendenz *f*; Deflationstendenz *f*
e tendencia *f* deflacionista
f tendance *f* déflationniste
i tendenza *f* deflazionistica
n deflatoire tendens *f*

995 deflationist *(noun)*
d Deflationist *m*; Deflationsanhänger *m*
e deflacionista *m*
f déflationniste *m*
i deflazionista *m*
n deflationist *m*

996 deflator
d Deflator *m*
e deflator *m*; factor *m* deflacionista
f déflateur *m*; facteur *m* déflationniste
i deflatore *m*; fattore *m* deflazionistico
n deflator *m*

997 degressive tax; regressive tax
d degressive Steuer *f*
e impuesto *m* regresivo
f impôt *m* dégressif
i imposta *f* decrescente
n degressieve belasting *f*

998 delay; period of grace; respite
cf. **days of grace, extension of time for payment**
d Aufschub *m*; Bedenkfrist *f*; Bedenkzeit *f*; Frist *f*; Gnadenfrist *f*; Nachfrist *f*; Respektfrist *f*; Respiro *m/n*; Respit *m*; Schonfrist *f*; Stundung *f*; Stundungsfrist *f*
e plazo *m* (de cortesía); plazo *m* (de gracia); plazo *m* (de respiro); prórroga *f*; respiro *m*; término *m* de cortesía; término *m* de gracia
f atermoiement *m*; délai *m* (de grâce); période *f* de grâce; répit *m*; sursis *m*; terme *m* de grâce
i dilazione *f*; proroga *f*; respiro *m*; termine *m* di grazia; termine *m* di rispetto
n délai *m* (de grâce); respijt *n*; respijttermijn *m*; uitstel *n*

999 delay in payment
d Zahlungsrückstand *m*; Zahlungssäumnis *f/n*; Zahlungsverzögerung *f*; Zahlungsverzug *m*
e demora *f* de pago; demora *f* en el pago; tardanza *f* de pago
f retard *m* dans le paiement; retard *m* de paiement
i mora *f* nel pagamento; morosità *f*;

ritardo *m* di pagamento; ritardo *m* nel pagamento
n vertraging *f* in de betaling

1000 **del credere**
d Delcredere *n*; Delkredere *n*
e delcredere *m*
f ducroire *m*
i del credere *m*
n delcredere *n*

1001 **de luxe articles; deluxe articles** *(US)*; **fancy articles; fancy goods; luxuries; luxury articles; luxury goods**
d Luxusartikel *mpl*; Luxusgegenstände *mpl*; Luxusgüter *npl*; Luxuswaren *fpl*
e artículos *mpl* de lujo; objetos *mpl* de lujo; productos *mpl* de lujo
f articles *mpl* de luxe; objets *mpl* de luxe; produits *mpl* de luxe
i articoli *mpl* di lusso; generi *mpl* di lusso; oggetti *mpl* di lusso; prodotti *mpl* di lusso
n luxeartikelen *npl*; luxegoederen *npl*; weeldeartikelen *npl*

1002 **demand**
d Bedarf *m*; Nachfrage *f*
e demanda *f*
f demande *f*
i domanda *f*; richiesta *f*
n navraag *f*; vraag *f*

1003 **demand bill; demand draft; presentation draft** *(US)*; **sight bill; sight draft**
d Sichttratte *f*; Sichtwechsel *m*; Vistawechsel *m*
e giro *m* a la vista; letra *f* a la vista
f change *m* à vue; effet *m* à vue; lettre *f* de change à vue; traite *f* à vue
i cambiale *f* a vista; tratta *f* a vista
n zichtwissel *m*; zichtwisselbrief *m*

1004 **demand deposit; deposit at call; deposit on call; sight deposit**
cf. **deposit on giro account**
d jederzeit abhebbare Einlage *f*; jederzeit abhebbares Depositum *n*; jederzeit abhebbares Depot *n*; Sichtdepositum *n*; Sichtdepot *n*; Sichteinlage *f*; Soforteinlage *f*
e depósito *m* a demanda; depósito *m* a la vista
f dépôt *m* à vue; dépôt *m* remboursable sur demande
i deposito *m* a richiesta; deposito *m* a vista
n dadelijk opvraagbaar deposito *n*; direct opvraagbaar deposito *n*; zichtdeposito *n*

1005 **demand-induced inflation; demand inflation; demand-pull inflation; excess demand inflation**
d nachfragebedingte Inflation *f*; nachfrageinduzierte Inflation *f*; Nachfrageinflation *f*
e inflación *f* de demanda
f inflation *f* par la demande
i inflazione *f* da domanda
n vraaginflatie *f*

1006 **demand liabilities; demand obligations; liabilities due on presentation; sight liabilities; sight obligations**
d Sichtverbindlichkeiten *fpl*; Sichtverpflichtungen *fpl*
e obligaciones *fpl* a la vista; pasivos *mpl* a la vista
f obligations *fpl* à vue; passif *m* exigible à vue
i obbligazioni *fpl* a vista; passivi *mpl* esigibili a richiesta; passivi *mpl* esigibili a vista
n direct opvorderbare passiva *npl*

1007 **demand note; sight note**
d Sichtpapier *n*
e papel *m* a la vista; título *m* pagadero a la vista
f papier *m* à vue; titre *m* payable à vue
i carta *f* a vista; titolo *m* pagabile a vista
n papier *n* op zicht; zichtpapier *n*

1008 **demonetization; recall; retirement; withdrawal**
d Ausserkurssetzung *f*; Demonetisierung *f*; Einziehung *f*; Entwertung *f*; Zurückziehung *f*
e desmonetización *f*; retiro *m*
f démonétisation *f*; retrait *m*
i demonetizzazione *f*; ritiro *m*
n demonetisatie *f*; ontmunting *f**; onttrekking *f*

* Coins only.

1009 **denationalization**
d Entnationalisierung *f*; Entstaatlichung *f*; Privatisierung *f*; Reprivatisierung *f*
e desnacionalización *f*
f dénationalisation *f*; privatisation *f*; reprivatisation *f*
i privatizzazione *f*; riprivatizzazione *f*; snazionalizzazione *f*
n denationalisatie *f*; denationalisering *f*

1010 **denominated in dollars; expressed in dollars; made out in dollars**
d auf Dollars ausgestellt; auf Dollars lautend; in Dollars ausgedrückt; in

Dollars ausgestellt
e denominado en dólares; extendido en dólares
f exprimé en dollars; libellé en dollars
i espresso in dollari
n in dollars luidend; in dollars uitgedrukt

1011 denomination
d Abschnitt *m*; Stück *n*; Stückelung *f*; Wert *m*
e denominación *f*; título *m*
f coupure *f*
i spezzatura *f*; taglio *m*; valore *m*
n coupure *f*

1012 depletion of the reserves; exhaustion of the reserves
d Erschöpfung *f* der Reserven
e agotamiento *m* de las reservas
f épuisement *m* des réserves
i esaurimento *m* delle riserve
n uitputting *f* van de reserves

1013 deposit *(in bank)*
d Depositum *n*; Depot *n*; Einlage *f*
e depósito *m*
f dépôt *m*
i deposito *m*
n deposito *n*; inlaag *f*; inlage *f*; inleg *m*

1014 deposit; down-payment; payment on account
cf. **instal(l)ment**
d Akontozahlung *f*; Anzahlung *f*
e pago *m* a cuenta; señal *f*
f acompte *m*; paiement *m* à compte
i acconto *m*; pagamento *m* in acconto; pagamento *m* in conto
n aanbetaling *f*; voorschot *n*

1015 deposit *v*; **pay** *v* **in**
d deponieren; einlegen; einzahlen; Einzahlung leisten; hinterlegen
e depositar; enterar *(AL)*; imponer; ingresar
f déposer; verser
i depositare; versare
n deponeren; inleggen; storten

1016 deposit account
d Depositenkonto *n*; Einlagekonto *n*
e cuenta *f* de depósito(s)
f compte *m* de dépôt(s)
i conto *m* depositi; conto *m* di deposito
n depositorekening *f*

1017 depositary; depository
d Depositar *m*; Depositär *m*; Depositenbewahrer *m*; Depothalter *m*; Verwahrer *m*
e depositario *m*
f dépositaire *m*
i depositario *m*
n bewaarnemer *m*; depositaris *m*

1018 deposit *v* **as security; give** *v* **as pledge; give** *v* **as security; lodge** *v* **as security; pawn** *v*; **pledge** *v* **(as security); put** *v* **in pawn; put** *v* **in pledge**
d als (zum) Pfand einsetzen; als (zum) Pfand geben; als (zum) Pfand setzen; als Sicherheit deponieren; als Sicherheit geben; als Sicherheit hinterlegen; als Unterpfand geben; verpfänden; versetzen
e dar a título de garantía; dar a título en garantía; dar a título en prenda; depositar a título de garantía; empeñar; pignorar
f constituer en gage; déposer en nantissement; donner à titre de garantie; donner en gage; donner en garantie; engager; fournir en nantissement; gager; mettre en gage; mettre en pension; remettre en nantissement
i costituire in pegno; dare in garanzia; dare in pegno; depositare in garanzia; impegnare; pignorare
n als onderpand deponeren; als onderpand geven; als pand deponeren; als pand geven; in onderpand geven; in pand geven; panden; verpanden

1019 deposit at notice; notice deposit
d Depositum *n* auf Kündigung; Depositum *n* mit Kündigungsfrist; Einlage *f* auf Kündigung; Einlage *f* mit Kündigungsfrist; Geld *n* auf Kündigung; Kündigungsgeld *n*
e depósito *m* de previo aviso; depósito *m* reembolsable con preaviso
f dépôt *m* à préavis; dépôt *m* avec préavis; dépôt *m* remboursable avec préavis
i deposito *m* a scadenza; deposito *m* con preavviso; deposito *m* rimborsabile con preavviso
n deposito *n* met opzegging; deposito *n* met opzeggingstermijn

1020 deposit bank
d Depositenbank *f*
e banco *m* de depósito(s)
f banque *f* de dépôt(s)
i banca *f* di deposito; banca *f* di depositi
n depositobank *f*

1021 deposit book
cf. **bankbook, savings book**
d Depositenbuch *n*; Einlagebuch *n*
e libreta *f* de depósitos

f carnet *m* de dépôt; livret *m* de déposant; livret *m* de dépôt(s)
i libretto *m* di deposito
n depositoboekje *n*

1022 **deposit form; deposit slip; inpayment form; pay-in form; paying-in form; paying-in slip; pay-in slip**
cf. **credit slip**
d Einzahlungsformular *n*
e formulario *m* de depósito; formulario *m* de ingreso
f bulletin *m* de versement; formulaire *m* de versement *(B)*; formule *f* de versement
i bollettino *m* di versamento; modulo *m* di versamento
n stortingsbiljet *n*; stortingsbulletijn *n (B)*; stortingsformulier *n*

1023 **deposit liabilities**
d Kontokorrentverbindlichkeiten *fpl*; Kontokorrentverpflichtungen *fpl*
e compromisos *mpl* en cuenta corriente; obligaciones *fpl* en cuenta corriente
f engagements *mpl* en compte courant; obligations *fpl* en compte courant
i debiti *mpl* di conto corrente; obbligazioni *fpl* di conto corrente
n rekening-courantverplichtingen *fpl*

1024 **deposit on giro account; deposit on transfer account; giro deposit**
cf. **demand deposit**
d Giroeinlage *f*
e depósito *m* en cuenta de giro(s)
f dépôt *m* de virement; dépôt *m* sur compte de virement; dépôt *m* sur compte giro
i deposito *m* su conto corrente di corrispondenza; deposito *m* su giroconto
n deposito *n* op girorekening; giro-deposito *n*

1025 **depositor** *(who makes a deposit)*
d Deponent *m*; Einleger *m*; Einzahler *m*; Hinterleger *m*
e depositador *m*; depositante *m*
f déposant *m*
i depositante *m*
n deponent *m*; deposant *m*; inlegger *m*

1026 **depositor** *(who owns a deposit)*
d Depositeninhaber *m*
e depositador *m*; depositante *m*
f déposant *m*
i depositante *m*
n deposito-houder *m*

1027 **depreciable assets**
d abschreibungsfähiges Aktivum *n*; abschreibungsfähiges Vermögen *n*
e activo *m* amortizable; activo *m* depreciable *(AL)*
f actif *m* amortissable
i attività *f(pl)* da ammortizzare; attivo *m* ammortizzabile
n af te schrijven activa *npl*

1028 **depreciate** *v (tr.)*; **devalorize** *v*; **devaluate** *v*; **devalue** *v*
cf. **amortise** *v*
d abwerten; devalvieren; entwerten
e depreciar; desvalorar; desvalorizar; envilecer
f avilir; déprécier; dévaloriser; dévaluer
i deprezzare; svalorizzare; svalutare; svilire
n depreciëren; devalueren; ontwaarden

1029 **depreciation; devaluation**
cf. **decline in value**
d Abwertung *f*; Devaluation *f*; Devalvation *f*; Entwertung *f*
e depreciación *f*; desvalorización *f*; devaluación *f*; envilecimiento *m*
f avilissement *m*; dépréciation *f*; dévalorisation *f*; dévaluation *f*
i deprezzamento *m*; devalutazione *f*; svalutazione *f*; svilimento *m*
n depreciatie *f*; devaluatie *f*; devalvatie *f*; ontwaarding *f*

1030 **depreciation for wear and tear**
d Abschreibung *f* entsprechend technischem Verschleiss; technische Abschreibung *f*
e amortización *f* técnica; depreciación *f* técnica
f amortissement *m* technique; dépréciation *f* technique
i ammortamento *m* tecnico; deprezzamento *m* tecnico
n afschrijving *f* op basis van technische slijtage; technische afschrijving *f*

1031 **depression; recession; slump**
cf. **decline**
d Baisse *f*; Depression *f*; Konjunkturrückgang *m*; Konjunkturrückschlag *m*; Rezession *f*; rückläufige Konjunktur *f*; sinkende Konjunktur *f*; Slump *m*; Tiefkonjunktur *f*; Wirtschaftsrückgang *m*
e baja *f* (coyuntural); baja coyuntura *f*; coyuntura *f* regresiva; depresión *f*; recesión *f*
f baisse *f*; basse conjoncture *f*; dépression *f*; récession *f*
i bassa congiuntura *f*; depressione *f*;

recessione *f*; regressione *f* economica; slump *m*
n baisse *f*; dalende conjunctuur *f*; depressie *f*; laagconjunctuur *f*; lage conjunctuur *f*; recessie *f*; slump *m*

1032 **determination of the equivalence of exchange; determination of the exchange parity**
d Festlegung *f* der Währungsparität; Festsetzung *f* der Währungsparität
e determinación *f* de la paridad de cambio
f détermination *f* de la parité de change
i determinazione *f* della parità di cambio
n bepaling *f* van de pariteit; vaststelling *f* der pariwaarde

1033 **determine** *v* **a price; establish** *v* **a price; fix** *v* **a price; lay** *v* **down a price; prescribe** *v* **a price; price** *v*; **set** *v* **a price**
cf. **make** *v* **a price**
d einen Preis ansetzen; einen Preis bestimmen; einen Preis festlegen; einen Preis feststellen; einen Preis vorschreiben
e determinar un precio; fijar un precio; imponer un precio
f déterminer un prix; établir un prix; fixer un prix; imposer un prix
i determinare un prezzo; fissare un prezzo; imporre un prezzo; stabilire un prezzo
n een prijs bepalen; een prijs opleggen; een prijs vastleggen; een prijs vaststellen; een prijs voorschrijven

1034 **development aid; development assistance**
d Entwicklungshilfe *f*
e ayuda *f* al desarrollo; ayuda *f* para el desarrollo
f aide *f* au développement
i aiuto *m* allo sviluppo
n ontwikkelingshulp *f*

1035 **development bank**
d Entwicklungsbank *f*
e banco *m* de desarrollo; banco *m* de fomento
f banque *f* de développement
i banca *f* di sviluppo
n ontwikkelingsbank *f*

1036 **development loan**
d Entwicklungsanleihe *f*
e empréstito *m* para el desarrollo
f emprunt *m* pour le développement
i prestito *m* per lo sviluppo
n ontwikkelingslening *f*

1037 **difference; differential; margin; range; spread**
d Differenz *f*; Gefälle *n*; Marge *f*; Spanne *f*; Spielraum *m*; Unterschied *m*
e diferencia *f*; margen *m/f*
f décalage *m*; différence *f*; écart *m*; marge *f*
i differenza *f*; margine *m*; scarto *m*
n marge *f*; verschil *n*

1038 **difference in price(s); disparity in price(s); price difference; price differential**
cf. **price margin**
d Preisdifferenz *f*; Preisdisparität *f*; Preisgefälle *n*; Preisunterschied *m*
e diferencia *f* de precio(s); diferencia *f* en los precios; diferencia *f* entre los precios; disparidad *f* de precio(s)
f décalage *m* de prix; différence *f* de prix; différence *f* entre les prix; disparité *f* de(s) prix; écart *m* dans les prix; écart *m* des prix
i differenza *f* dei prezzi; differenza *f* di prezzi; differenza *f* di prezzo; disparità *f* dei prezzi; scarto *m* dei prezzi
n prijsdispariteit *f*; prijsverschil *n*

1039 **difference in the rate of exchange**
d Wechselkursdifferenz *f*
e diferencia *f* de cambio
f différence *f* de change
i differenza *f* di cambio
n koersverschil *n*; wisselkoersverschil *n* *(B)*

1040 **differential duty**
cf. **preferential duty**
d Differenzialzoll *m*
e arancel *m* diferencial; derecho *m* (de aduana) diferencial
f droit *m* (de douane) différentiel
i dazio *m* (doganale) differenziale; diritto *m* (doganale) differenziale
n differentieel douanerecht *n*; differentieel recht *n*

1041 **differential tariff; flexible tariff; graded tariff; graduated rates; graduated tariff; sliding-scale tariff**
d Differentialtarif *m*; gestaffelter Tarif *m*; gleitender Tarif *m*; Staffeltarif *m*; Stufentarif *m*
e tarifa *f* diferencial; tarifa *f* escalonada; tarifa *f* graduada; tarifa *f* gradual; tarifa *f* móvil
f tarif *m* à échelons; tarif *m* à paliers; tarif *m* différentiel; tarif *m* échelonné; tarif *m* mobile

i tariffa *f* differenziale; tariffa *f* graduale; tariffa *f* mobile; tariffa *f* scalare
n differentieel tarief *n*; gestaffeld tarief *n*; glijdend tarief *n*; staffeltarief *n*

1042 dip *v* **into the reserves; draw** *v* **(up)on the reserves; encroach** *v* **(up)on the reserves; fall** *v* **back (up)on the reserves; have** *v* **recourse to the reserves; raid** *v* **the reserves**
d auf die Reserven zurückgreifen; die Reserven angreifen; die Reserven in Anspruch nehmen; von den Reserven zehren
e echar mano de las reservas; hacer recurso a las reservas; recurrir a las reservas; tocar las reservas; utilizar las reservas
f avoir recours aux réserves; entamer les réserves; mettre les réserves à contribution; prendre sur les réserves; recourir aux réserves; utiliser les réserves
i far ricorso alle riserve; intaccare le riserve; mettere mano alle riserve; ricorrere alle riserve; utilizzare le riserve
n de reserves aanbreken; de reserves aanspreken; op de reserves beroep doen; uit de reserves putten

1043 direct costs; prime costs
cf. **cost price**
d direkte Kosten *pl*; Einzelkosten *pl*; Primärkosten *pl*
e costes *mpl* directos; costos *mpl* directos; gastos *mpl* directos
f frais *mpl* directs
i costi *mpl* diretti
n directe kosten *mpl*

1044 direction of (capital) investment; investment control
d Investitionskontrolle *f*; Investitionslenkung *f*; Kapitallenkung *f*; Kapitalsteuerung *f*
e control *m* de las inversiones; control *m* del capital; orientación *f* de las inversiones; orientación *f* del capital; regulación *f* del capital
f contrôle *m* des investissements; direction *f* des capitaux; direction *f* des investissements; orientation *f* des capitaux; orientation *f* des investissements
i controllo *m* degli investimenti; direzione *f* degli investimenti; orientamento *m* dei capitali; orientamento *m* degli investimenti
n investeringscontrole *f*; kapitaalbeheer *n*

1045 direct sectional costing; partial cost accounting
d Teilkostenkalkulation *f*; Teilkostenrechnung *f*
e sistema *m* de coste parcial
f système *m* de prix de revient à coûts partiels
i calcolo *m* dei costi parziali
n differentiële kostenberekening *f*; differentiële kostencalculatie *f*

1046 direct tax
d direkte Steuer *f*
e impuesto *m* directo
f impôt *m* direct
i imposta *f* diretta
n directe belasting *f*

1047 dirigisme; economic planning and control
cf. **controlled economy**
d Dirigismus *m*; dirigistische Wirtschaftsordnung *f*; Wirtschaftsdirigismus *m*
e dirigismo *m*
f dirigisme *m* (économique); planisme *m*
i dirigismo *m*; pianismo *m*
n dirigisme *n*

1048 disagio; discount
d Disagio *n*; Diskont *m*; Diskonto *n*
e disagio *m*; discuento *m*
f escompte *m*
i disaggio *m*; sconto *m*
n disagio *n*; disconto *n*

1049 disallowed deductions *(US)*; non-allowable charges
d nicht abzugfähige Ausgaben *fpl*
e gastos *mpl* no deducibles
f charges *fpl* non déductibles
i spese *fpl* indeducibili
n niet aftrekbare kosten *mpl*; niet aftrekbare uitgaven *fpl*

1050 disburse *v*; **lay** *v* **out; pay** *v* **out**
cf. **expend** *v*
d auslegen; auszahlen; verauslagen
e desembolsar
f débourser
i disborsare *(rare)*; esborsare; sborsare
n uitbetalen; uitkeren

1051 disburse *v* **a dividend *(US)*; distribute** *v* **a dividend; pay** *v* **a dividend**
d eine Dividende ausschütten; eine Dividende auszahlen; eine Dividende verteilen; eine Dividende zahlen
e distribuir un dividendo; pagar un dividendo; repartir un dividendo

f distribuer un dividende; payer un dividende; répartir un dividende; verser un dividende
i distribuire un dividendo; pagare un dividendo; ripartire un dividendo
n een dividend betalen; een dividend uitbetalen; een dividend uitkeren; een dividend verdelen

1052 disbursement of dividends; distribution of dividends; payment of dividends
d Dividendenausschüttung *f*; Dividendenauszahlung *f*; Dividendenverteilung *f*; Dividendenzahlung *f*
e distribución *f* de dividendos; pago *m* de dividendos; reparto *m* de dividendos
f distribution *f* de dividendes; paiement *m* de dividendes; répartition *f* de dividendes; versement *m* de dividendes
i distribuzione *f* di dividendi; pagamento *m* di dividendi; ripartizione *f* di dividendi
n dividendbetaling *f*; dividenddistributie *f*; dividenduitbetaling *f*; dividenduitkering *f*; dividendverdeling *f*

1053 disbursements; expenditure(s); outgoings; outlays
cf. **expenditure, expenses**
d Ausgaben *fpl*; Ausgänge *mpl*; Auslagen *fpl*; Auszahlungen *fpl*
e desembolsos *mpl*; egresos *mpl (AL)*; erogaciones *fpl (AL)*; gastos *mpl*; salidas *fpl*
f débours *mpl*; déboursements *mpl*; déboursés *mpl*; dépenses *fpl*; mises *fpl* hors; sorties *fpl*
i disborsi *mpl*; esborsi *mpl*; sborsi *mpl*; spese *fpl*; uscite *fpl*
n uitbetalingen *fpl*; uitgaven *fpl*; uitkeringen *fpl*; uitschotten *npl*

1054 discharge *v* **a bill of exchange; honor** *v* **a bill of exchange** ***(US)*****; honour** *v* **a bill of exchange** ***(UK)*****; meet** *v* **a bill of exchange; pay** *v* **a bill of exchange; protect** *v* **a bill of exchange**
cf. **bill**
d einen Wechsel begleichen; einen Wechsel bezahlen; einen Wechsel einlösen; einen Wechsel honorieren
e atender un efecto; dar buena acogida a un efecto; honrar un efecto; pagar un efecto
f accueillir un effet; acquitter un effet; faire (bon) accueil à un effet; faire honneur à un effet; honorer un effet; payer un effet
i fare onore a un effetto; onorare un effetto; pagare un effetto
n een wissel betalen; een wissel honoreren

1055 discount; discount commission
d Diskontprovision *f*
e comisión *f* de descuento
f commission *f* d'escompte
i commissione *f* di sconto
n discontoprovisie *f*

1056 be *v* **at a discount; be** *v* **below par**
d Disagio erleiden; unter dem Nennwert stehen; unter Pari stehen
e estar bajo la par; estar por debajo de la par
f être au-dessous du pair; faire perte
i essere sotto la pari
n beneden pari staan; disagio doen; onder pari staan

1057 discount *v*
d diskontieren; eskontieren
e descontar
f escompter
i scontare
n disconteren; verdisconteren

1058 discount bank; discount house
cf. **acceptance house**
d Diskont(o)bank *f*; Diskont(o)haus *n*; Wechselbank *f*
e banco *m* de descuento; institución *f* de descuento
f banque *f* d'escompte; maison *f* d'escompte
i banca *f* di sconto; istituto *m* di sconto
n discontobank *f*; discontohuis *n*; wisselbank *f*

1059 discount credit
d Diskontkredit *m*
e crédito *m* de descuento
f crédit *m* d'escompte
i credito *m* di sconto; fido *m* di sconto
n discontokrediet *n*

1060 discounted domestic bill
d Diskont *m (usually pl)*
e efecto *m* descontado sobre el interior
f effet *m* escompté sur l'intérieur
i effetto *m* scontato sull'interno
n gedisconteerde wissel *m* op het binnenland

1061 discount rate
cf. **bank rate**
d Diskontfuss *m*; Diskontrate *f*; Diskontsatz *m*
e tasa *f* de descuento; tipo *m* de descuento

f tarif *m* d'escompte; taux *m* de l'escompte; taux *m* d'escompte
i saggio *m* di sconto; tasso *m* di sconto
n discontotarief *n*; discontovoet *m*

1062 disequilibrium; imbalance; unbalance
d gestörtes Gleichgewicht *n*; Gleichgewichtsstörung *f*; Unausgeglichenheit *f*; Ungleichgewicht *n*
e desequilibrio *m*; perturbación *f* del equilibrio
f déséqulibre *m*; rupture *f* de l'équilibre
i perturbazione *f* del equilibrio; sbilancio *m*; squilibrio *m*
n evenwichtsverstoring *f*; onevenwichtigheid *f*; verstoord evenwicht *n*

1063 dishoarding
d Enthortung *f*
e desatesoramiento *m*
f déthésaurisation *f*
i detesaurizzazione *f*
n ontpotting *f*

1064 disinflation
cf. **deflation**
d Desinflation *f*
e desinflación *f*
f désinflation *f*
i disinflazione *f*
n desinflatie *f*

1065 disinflationary
cf. **deflationary**
d desinflationär; desinflationistisch; Desinflations-; desinflatorisch
e desinflacionario; desinflacionista
f désinflationniste
i disinflatorio; disinflazionistico
n desinflatie-; desinflationistisch; desinflatoir; desinflatorisch

1066 disinvestment
d Anlageabgang *m*; Anlagerückgang *m*; Desinvestition *f*
e desinversión *f*
f désinvestissement *m*
i disinvestimento *m*
n desinvestering *f*

1067 disparity
d Disparität *f*; Unterschied *m*
e disparidad *f*
f disparité *f*
i disparità *f*
n dispariteit *f*

1068 disposable income
d verfügbares Einkommen *n*
e ingresos *mpl* disponibles
f revenu *m* disponible
i reddito *m* disponibile
n beschikbaar inkomen *n*

1069 dissaving
d Entsparung *f*
e desahorro *m*
f désépargne *f*
i riduzione *f* di fondi risparmiati
n ontsparing *f*

1070 dissolution *(of a company)*; **liquidation; winding up**
d Abwicklung *f*; Auflösung *f*; Liquidierung *f*
e disolución *f*; liquidación *f*
f dissolution *f*; liquidation *f*
i liquidazione *f*; scioglimento *m*
n liquidatie *f*; ontbinding *f*; opheffing *f*; vereffening *f*

1071 dissolve *v*; **liquidate** *v*; **wind** *v* **up**
d abwickeln; auflösen; liquidieren
e disolver; liquidar
f dissoudre; liquider
i liquidare; sciogliere
n liquideren; ontbinden; opheffen; vereffenen

1072 distributable profit
d ausschüttungsfähiger Gewinn *m*
e beneficio *m* distribuible; ganancia *f* distribuible; utilidad *f* distribuible
f bénéfice *m* distribuable
i beneficio *m* da ripartire; utile *m* da ripartire
n voor uitkering beschikbare winst *f*

1073 distribution of property
d Vermögensverteilung *f*
e distribución *f* de los patrimonios
f répartition *f* des patrimoines
i ripartizione *f* dei patrimoni
n vermogensverdeling *f*

1074 distribution of wealth
d Vermögensverteilung *f*
e distribución *f* del capital; repartición *f* del capital
f répartition *f* du capital
i ripartizione *f* del capitale
n vermogensverdeling *f*

1075 distribution sector
d Absatzwirtschaft *f*; Verteilungssektor *m*
e sector *m* de la distribución

f secteur *m* de la distribution
i settore *m* della distribuzione
n distributiesector *m*

1076 dividend
cf. **share in the profits**
d Dividende *f*
e dividendo *m*
f dividende *m*
i dividendo *m*
n dividend *n*; uitkering *f*

1077 dividend *(in bankruptcy)*
d Konkursdividende *f*; Konkursquote *f*
e cuota *f* del activo de la quiebra; dividendo *m*
f dividende *m*
i quota *f* di riparto
n dividend *n (B)*; uitkering *f*

1078 dividend coupon; dividend warrant
d Dividendenabschnitt *m*; Dividendenkupon *m*; Dividendenschein *m*; Gewinnanteilschein *m*
e cédula *f* de dividendo; cupón *m* de dividendo
f coupon *m* de dividende
i cedola *f* di dividendo; tagliando *m* di dividendo; talloncino *m* di dividendo
n dividendbewijs *n*; dividendcoupon *m*; dividendtalon *m*

1079 dividend equalization reserve
d Dividendenausgleichsreserve *f*; Dividendengarantierücklage *f*
e reserva *f* de compensación de dividendos; reserva *f* para la igualación de dividendos
f réserve *f* pour régularisation des dividendes
i fondo *m* conguaglio dividendi; fondo *m* perequazione dividendi; riserva *f* per conguaglio dividendi; riserva *f* per la regolarizzazione dei dividendi
n dividendreserve *f*

1080 dividend off *(US)*; **ex dividend**
cf. **coupon off**
d ausschliesslich Dividende; ex Dividende; exklusive Dividende; ohne Dividende
e ex dividendo; sin dividendo
f ex dividende; sans dividende
i ex-dividendo; senza dividendo
n exclusief dividend; ex dividend; zonder dividend

1081 dividend policy
d Dividendenpolitik *f*
e política *f* de dividendos
f politique *f* de dividende(s)
i politica *f* dei dividendi
n dividendpolitiek *f*

1082 dividend yield
d Aktienrendite *f*
e rentabilidad *f* de las acciones
f rendement *m* des actions
i rendimento *m* azionario
n aandelenrendement *n*

1083 divisional coin; divisional currency; fractional coin; fractional currency; fractional money; minor coin; small coin; small money
cf. **change, copper**
d Scheidegeld *n*; Scheidemünze *f*
e moneda *f* divisionaria; moneda *f* fraccionaria
f monnaie *f* de billon; monnaie *f* divisionnaire
i divisionario *m*; moneta *f* divisionale; moneta *f* divisionaria; moneta *f* sussidiaria
n pasmunt *f*

1084 do *v* **business; transact** *v* **business**
d Geschäfte betreiben; Geschäfte machen; Geschäfte tätigen
e efectuar negocios; hacer negocios
f faire des affaires; traiter des affaires
i fare affari; trattare affari
n zaken doen

1085 documentary credit; reimbursement credit
cf. **acceptance credit**
d Dokumentarkredit *m*; Dokumentenakkreditiv *n*; Dokumentenkredit *m*; Rembourskredit *m*
e crédito *m* documentario
f accréditif *m* documentaire; crédit *m* documentaire; remboursement *m* sur banquier
i credito *m* contro documenti; credito *m* di rimborso; credito *m* documentario
n documentair accreditief *n*; documentair krediet *n*; rembourskrediet *n*

1086 dollar area; dollar bloc
d Dollarblock *m*; Dollargebiet *n*; Dollarraum *m*; Dollarwährungsgebiet *n*; Dollarwährungsraum *m*; Dollarzone *f*
e área *f* del dólar; bloque *m* del dólar; zona *f* del dólar
f bloc *m* dollar; zone *f* dollar
i area *f* del dollaro; blocco *m* del dollaro; zona *f* del dollaro
n dollarblok *n*; dollargebied *n*; dollarzone *f*

1087 **dollar bond**
d Dollarbond *m*; Dollarobligation *f*; Dollarschuldverschreibung *f*
e obligación *f* en dólares
f obligation *f* en dollars
i obbligazione *f* in dollari
n dollarobligatie *f*

1088 **dollar clause**
d Dollarklausel *f*
e cláusula *f* dólar
f clause *f* dollar
i clausola *f* dollaro
n dollarclausule *f*

1089 **dollar deficit; dollar gap**
cf. **dollar shortage**
d Dollardefizit *n*; Dollarlücke *f*
e déficit *m* de dólares; laguna *f* de dólares
f déficit *m* de dollars; lacune *f* de dollars
i deficit *m* in dollari
n dollarlacune *f*; dollartekort *n*

1090 **dollar shortage; dollar stringency**
cf. **dollar deficit**
d Dollarknappheit *f*; Dollarmangel *m*
e carestía *f* de dólares; escasez *f* de dólares; falta *f* de dólares; penuria *f* de dólares
f insuffisance *f* de dollars; manque *m* de dollars; pénurie *f* de dollars
i mancanza *f* di dollari; penuria *f* di dollari; scarsezza *f* di dollari; scarsità *f* di dollari
n dollargebrek *n*; dollarschaarste *f*

1091 **domestic bill (of exchange); inland bill (of exchange)**
cf. **discounted domestic bill**
d inländischer Wechsel *m*; inländische Tratte *f*; Inlandstratte *f*; Inlandwechsel *m*
e efecto *m* sobre el interior; letra *f* sobre el interior
f effet *m* sur l'intérieur; lettre *f* de change sur l'intérieur; traite *f* sur l'intérieur
i cambiale *f* sull'interno; effetto *m* sull'interno; tratta *f* sull'interno
n binnenlandse traite *f*; binnenlandse wissel *m*; papier *n* op het binnenland

1092 **domestic consumption; home consumption; home use; internal consumption**
d Eigenverbrauch *m*; inländischer Verbrauch *m*; Inlandsverbrauch *m*; innerer Verbrauch *m*
e consumo *m* interior; consumo *m* interno; consumo *m* nacional
f consommation *f* intérieure; consommation *f* interne; consommation *f* nationale
i consumo *m* interno; consumo *m* nazionale
n binnenlands verbruik *n*; inlandsverbruik *n*

1093 **domestic credits**
d Inlandskredite *mpl*
e créditos *mpl* interiores; créditos *mpl* internos
f crédits *mpl* intérieurs
i crediti *mpl* interni
n binnenlandse kredieten *npl*

1094 **domestic currency; home currency; local currency; national currency**
d eigene Währung *f*; einheimische Währung *f*; heimische Währung *f*; inländische Währung *f*; Inlandswährung *f*; Landeswährung *f*; Landesvaluta *f*
e divisa *f* nacional *(AL)*; moneda *f* del país; moneda *f* nacional; moneda *f* propia
f devise *f* nationale; monnaie *f* du pays; monnaie *f* nationale; monnaie *f* propre
i moneta *f* del paese; moneta *f* nazionale; moneta *f* propria; valuta *f* del paese; valuta *f* nazionale
n eigen valuta *f*; landsmunt *f*; landsvaluta *f*; nationale munt *f*; nationale valuta *f*

1095 **domestic debt; internal debt**
d Inlandsschuld *f*
e deuda *f* interior; deuda *f* interna
f dette *f* intérieure
i debito *m* interno
n binnenlandse schuld *f*

1096 **domestic demand**
d Inlandsnachfrage *f*
e demanda *f* interior
f demande *f* intérieure
i domanda *f* interna
n binnenlandse vraag *f*

1097 **domestic demand; household demand**
d private Nachfrage *f*
e demanda *f* de las familias
f demande *f* des ménages
i domanda *f* proveniente dalle famiglie
n vraag *f* van de gezinshuishoudingen

1098 **domestic equilibrium**
d binnenwirtschaftliches Gleichgewicht *n*
e equilibrio *m* interior; equilibrio *m* interno

f équilibre *m* interne
i equilibrio *m* interno
n intern evenwicht *n*

1099 **domestic loan; inland loan; internal loan; national loan**
cf. **government loan**
d Inlandsanleihe *f*; innere Anleihe *f*; nationale Anleihe *f*
e empréstito *m* interior; empréstito *m* nacional; préstamo *m* interno
f emprunt *m* intérieur; emprunt *m* national
i prestito *m* interno; prestito *m* nazionale
n binnenlandse lening *f*; nationale lening *f*

1100 **domestic market; home market**
d Binnenmarkt *m*; einheimischer Markt *m*; heimischer Markt *m*; Inland(s)-markt *m*
e mercado *m* interior; mercado *m* nacional
f marché *m* intérieur; marché *m* national
i mercato *m* interno; mercato *m* nazionale
n binnenlandse markt *f*

1101 **domestic trade; home trade; inland trade; internal trade**
d Binnenhandel *m*; inländischer Handel *m*; Inland(s)handel *m*; Innen-handel *m*
e comercio *m* interior
f commerce *m* intérieur
i commercio *m* interno
n binnenhandel *m*; binnenlandse handel *m*

1102 **domicile** *(of bill)*
d Domizil *n*
e domicilio *m*
f domicile *m*
i domicilio *m*
n domicilie *n*

1103 **donation; grant**
d Schenkung *f*; Spende *f*; Zuwendung *f*
e dádiva *f*; donación *f*; donativo *m*
f don *m*; donation *f*; liberalité *f*
i donazione *f*; dono *m*; elargizione *f*
n donatie *f*; gift *f*; schenking *f*

1104 **donator; donor**
d Schenker *m*; Spender *m*; Stifter *m*
e donador *m*; donante *m*
f donateur *m*
i donatore *m*; elargitore *m*
n donateur *m*; gever *m*; schenker *m*

1105 **dormant partner; silent partner** *(US)*; **sleeping partner**
cf. **limited partner**
d stiller Gesellschafter *m*; stiller Teilhaber *m*
e socio *m* oculto
f associé *m* occulte; bailleur *m* de fonds
i socio *m* occulto
n slapende vennoot *m*; stille vennoot *m*

1106 **double entry; double posting**
d Doppelbuchung *f*
e partida *f* doble
f partie *f* double
i partita *f* doppia
n dubbele boeking *f*

1107 **double entry bookkeeping**
d doppelte Buchführung *f*
e contabilidad *f* por partida doble
f comptabilité *f* en partie double
i contabilità *f* in partita doppia
n dubbel-boekhouden *n*

1108 **double option; put and call; spread; straddle**
d Doppelprämie *f*; Stellage *f*; Stellage-geschäft *n*; Stellgeschäft *n*; Terminkauf *m* und -verkauf *m*
e doble opción *f*; operación *f* de doble opción
f double option *f*; doubles primes *fpl*; stellage *m*
i stellage *m*; stellagio *m*; transazione *f* a doppio premio
n dubbele premie *f*; stellage *f*

1109 **double taxation**
d Doppelbesteuerung *f*
e doble imposición *f*; doble tributación *f*; tasación *f* doble; tributación *f* doble
f double imposition *f*; double taxation *f*
i doppia imposizione *f*; doppia tassazione *f*; duplice imposizione *f*; imposizione *f* doppia; tassazione *f* doppia
n dubbele belasting *f*; dubbele belastingheffing *f*

1110 **doubtful accounts** *(US)*; **doubtful debts; doubtful notes and accounts** *(US)*; **doubtful receivables** *(US)*
d Dubiosa *pl (incorrectly: Dubiose)*; dubiose Forderungen *fpl*; Dubiosen *pl*; faule Forderungen *fpl*; notleidende Forderungen *fpl*; zweifelhafte Forderungen *fpl*
e créditos *mpl* dudosos; créditos *mpl* inciertos
f créances *fpl* douteuses; créances *fpl* véreuses
i crediti *mpl* di dubbia esazione; crediti

mpl dubbi; crediti *mpl* incerti
n dubieuze vorderingen *fpl*

1111 **draw** *(of bonds)*; **drawing**
d Auslosung *f*; Verlosung *f*; Ziehung *f*
e sorteo *m*
f tirage *m* (au sort)
i estrazione *f* a sorte; sorteggio *m*
n loting *f*; trekking *f*; uitloting *f*; verloting *f*

1112 **draw** *v (of bonds)*; **draw** *v* **by lot**
d auslosen; verlosen; ziehen
e sortear
f sortir au tirage; tirer au sort
i estrarre a sorte; sorteggiare; tirare a sorte
n trekken; uitloten; verloten

1113 **draw** *v (money from account)*; **withdraw** *v*
d abdisponieren; abheben; abziehen; beheben *(O)*; entnehmen
e retirar; sacar
f décaisser; enlever; prélever; retirer
i prelevare; ritirare
n afhalen; onttrekken; opnemen; opvragen

1114 **draw** *v* **a bill of exchange upon somebody**
d auf jemanden einen Wechsel ausstellen; auf jemanden einen Wechsel ziehen; auf jemanden trassieren; auf jemanden ziehen
e girar una letra de cambio contra alguien; librar una letra de cambio contra alguien
f faire traite sur quelqu'un; tirer une lettre de change sur quelqu'un
i spiccare una tratta su qualcuno; trarre una cambiale su qualcuno
n een wissel op iemand afgeven; een wissel op iemand trekken; op iemand trasseren

1115 **draw** *v* **a check** *(US)*; **draw** *v* **a cheque** *(UK)*; **issue** *v* **a check (cheque); make** *v* **out a check (cheque); write** *v* **out a check (cheque)**
d einen Scheck ausfertigen; einen Scheck ausfüllen; einen Scheck ausgeben; einen Scheck ausschreiben; einen Scheck ausstellen; einen Scheck begeben; einen Scheck ziehen
e extender un cheque; girar un cheque; librar un cheque
f créer un chèque; émettre un chèque; établir un chèque; tirer un chèque
i emettere un assegno; spiccare un assegno; trarre un assegno
n een cheque afgeven; een cheque emitteren; een cheque trekken; een cheque uitgeven; een cheque uitschrijven

1116 **drawback**
d Drawback *m*; Rückzoll *m*; Zollrückerstattung *f*; Zollrückvergütung *f*
e drawback *m*; reembolso *m* de los derechos de aduana; reintegro *m* de los derechos de aduana; restitución *f* de los derechos de aduana
f drawback *m*; remboursement *m* des droits de douane; restitution *f* des droits de douane
i dazio *m* di ritorno; dazio *m* doganale rimborsato; drawback *m*; restituzione *f* di dazio; rimborso *m* di diritti doganali; ristorno *m* di dazio
n drawback *m*; restitutie *f* van douanerechten; terugbetaling *f* van douanerechten

1117 **drawee**
cf. **acceptor**
d Bezogener *m*; Trassat *m*
e girado *m*; librado *m*
f tiré *m*
i trassato *m*; trattario *m*
n betrokkene *m*; trassaat *m*

1118 **drawer; maker** *(US)*
d Aussteller *m*; Trassant *m*; Zieher *m*
e girador *m*; girante *m*; librador *m*
f souscripteur *m*; tireur *m*
i traente *m*
n trassant *m*; trekker *m*

1119 **drawing** *(of money from account)*; **withdrawal**
d Abdisponierung *f*; Abhebung *f*; Abzug *m (rare)*; Behebung *f (O)*; Entnahme *f*
e detracción *f*; retirada *f*; retiro *m*
f décaissement *m*; prélèvement *m*; retrait *m*
i prelevamento *m*; prelievo *m*; ritiro *m*
n afhaling *f*; onttrekking *f*; opname *f*; opneming *f*; opvraging *f*

1120 **drawing on the International Monetary Fund**
d Ziehung *f* auf den Internationalen Währungsfonds
e giro *m* contra el Fondo Monetario Internacional
f tirage *m* sur le Fonds monétaire international
i prelievo *m* sul Fondo Monetario Internazionale
n trekking *f* op het Internationaal Monetair Fonds

1121 **drawing rights (on)**
d Ziehungsrechte *npl* (auf); Ziehungsrechte *npl* (bei)
e derechos *mpl* de giro (sobre)
f droits *mpl* de tirage (sur)
i diritti *mpl* di prelievo (su)
n trekkingsrechten *npl* (op)

1122 **draw** *v* **on a loan; draw** *v* **upon a loan; take** *v* **up a loan**
d ein Darleh(e)n aufnehmen; ein Darleh(e)n in Anspruch nehmen; eine Anleihe aufnehmen; eine Anleihe in Anspruch nehmen
e recurrir a un empréstito; recurrir a un préstamo; utilizar un empréstito; utilizar un préstamo
f avoir recours à un emprunt; avoir recours à un prêt; recourir à un emprunt; recourir à un prêt; utiliser un emprunt; utiliser un prêt
i far ricorso a un prestito; ricorrere a un prestito; utilizzare un prestito
n een lening opnemen; op een lening beroep doen

1123 **draw** *v* **on the International Monetary Fund; draw** *v* **upon the International Monetary Fund**
d auf den Internationalen Währungsfonds ziehen
e girar contra el Fondo Monetario Internacional
f tirer sur le Fonds monétaire international
i prelevare sul Fondo Monetario Internazionale
n op het Internationaal Monetair Fonds trekken

1124 **draw** *v* **up the inventory; inventorize** *v* *(rare)*; **inventory** *v*; **make** *v* **the inventory; take** *v* **stock; take** *v* **the inventory**
d das Inventar aufnehmen; das Inventar aufstellen; das Inventar errichten; das Inventar vornehmen; den Bestand aufnehmen; inventarisieren; Inventur machen
e efectuar el inventario; establecer el inventario; formar el inventario; hacer el inventario; inventariar; levantar el inventario; llevar el inventario; tomar inventario
f dresser l'inventaire; établir l'inventaire; faire l'inventaire; inventorier
i compilare l'inventario; erigere l'inventario; fare l'inventario; fornare l'inventario; inventariare; rilevare l'inventario
n de inventaris maken; de inventaris opmaken; inventariseren

1125 **drop; fall**
cf. **decline**
d Fall *m*
e caída *f*
f chute *f*
i caduta *f*; calo *m*
n daling *f*

1126 **due; matured**
cf. **overdue**
d fällig; verfallen
e vencido
f échu
i scaduto
n vervallen

1127 **due; owing**
d geschuldet; schuldig
e adeudado; debido
f dû
i dovuto
n verschuldigd

1128 **when due; at maturity; on maturity**
d bei Fälligkeit; bei Verfall; zur Verfall(s)-zeit
e al vencimiento; a su vencimiento
f à l'échéance
i alla scadenza
n bij verval; op de vervaldag; per vervaldag

1129 **due August 15; falling due on August 15; to mature on August 15**
cf. **become** *v* **due**
d am 15 August fällig
e que vence el 15 de agosto; vencer el 15 de agosto
f échéable le 15 août; échéant le 15 août; venant à l'échéance le 15 août
i che scade il 15 di agosto; con scadenza il 15 di agosto
n te vervallen op 15 augustus

1130 **dullness** *(of market)*; **flatness** *(UK)*; **inactivity; languor; slackness; sluggishness; stagnancy; stagnation; weakness**
d Da(r)niederliegen *n*; Flauheit *f*; Flaute *f*; Gedrücktheit *f*; Leblosigkeit *f*; Lustlosigkeit *f*; Mattheit *f*; Schwäche *f*; Stagnation *f*; Stagnierung *f*; Stille *f*; Stillstand *m*; Stocken *n*; Stockung *f*; Unbelebtheit *f*; Unlust *f*
e abatimiento *m*; calma *f*; debilidad *f*; desanimación *f*; estagnación *f*;

estancación *f*; estancamiento *m*; flaqueza *f*; flojedad *f*; inactividad *f*; languidez *f*; marasmo *m*; paralización *f*; paro *m*
f calme *m*; faiblesse *f*; inactivité *f*; langueur *f*; lourdeur *f*; marasme *m*; mollesse *f*; stagnation *f*
i calma *f*; debolezza *f*; fiacchezza *f*; inattività *f*; languidezza *f*; languore *m*; marasma *m*; paralisi *f*; ristagno *m*; stasi *f*
n flauwheid *f*; gedruktheid *f*; kwijning *f*; loomheid *f*; lusteloosheid *f*; matheid *f*; slapte *f*; stagnatie *f*; stilstand *m*; zwakte *f*

1131 **dumping**
d Dumping *n*; Schleuderausfuhr *f*; Schleuderverkauf *m* (ins Ausland); Verschleuderung *f* (im Ausland)
e dumping *m*
f dumping *m*
i dumping *m*
n dumping *f*

1132 **dump** *v* **on the market; flood** *v* **the market (with cheap articles); glut** *v* **the market (with cheap articles); inundate** *v* **the market (with cheap articles)**
d billig auf den Markt werfen; den Markt (mit billigen Artikeln) übersättigen; den Markt (mit billigen Artikeln) überschwemmen
e inundar el mercado (con artículos baratos); sobresaturar el mercado (con artículos baratos)
f encombrer le marché (d'articles bon marché); inonder le marché (d'articles bon marché); sursaturer le marché (d'articles bon marché)
i inondare il mercato (d'articoli a buon mercato); soprassaturare il mercato (d'articoli a buon mercato)
n de markt (met goedkope artikelen) overspoelen; de markt (met goedkope artikelen) overstromen; de markt (met goedkope artikelen) oververzadigen; de markt (met goedkope artikelen) overvoeren; op de markt dumpen

1133 **durable goods; durables**
d Dauergüter *npl*; dauerhafte Güter *npl*; langlebige Güter *npl*
e bienes *mpl* durables; bienes *mpl* duraderos; durables *mpl*
f biens *mpl* durables
i beni *mpl* durevoli
n duurzame goederen *npl*

1134 **durable means of production; producer goods; producer's goods; producers' goods; production goods**
d dauerhafte Produktionsmittel *npl*; Produktionsgüter *npl*
e bienes *mpl* de equipo; bienes *mpl* de producción; equipo *m* de producción *(AL)*; medios *mpl* de producción durables
f biens *mpl* de production; biens *mpl* d'équipement; moyens *mpl* de production durables
i beni *mpl* strumentali; mezzi *mpl* di produzione durevoli
n duurzame produktiemiddelen *npl*; produktiegoederen *npl*

1135 **duty; imposition; impost; levy; rate*; tax**
cf. **charge**
d Abgabe *f*; Auflage *f*; Steuer *f*; Taxe *f*; Umlage *f*
e arbitrio *m**; contribución *f*; derecho *m*; imposición *f*; impuesto *m*; tasa *f*; tributo *m*
f contribution *f*; droit *m*; imposition *f*; impôt *m*; prélèvement *m*; taxe *f*
i contributo *m*; contribuzione *f*; diritto *m*; imposizione *f*; imposta *f*; prelevamento *m*; prelievo *m*; tassa *f*; tributo *m*
n belasting *f*; heffing *f*; recht *n*; taks *m/f*; taxe *f*

* Usually only municipal tax.

E

1136 **earned income; wage income**
d Arbeitseinkommen *n*; Einkommen *n* aus Arbeit; erarbeitetes Einkommen *n*; Lohneinkommen *n*; unfundiertes Einkommen *n*
e ingresos *mpl* del trabajo; ingresos *mpl* laborales; ingresos *mpl* salariales; renta *f* del trabajo
f revenu *m* du travail; revenus *mpl* salariaux
i reddito *m* di lavoro (salariato)
n arbeidsinkomen *n*; inkomen *n* uit arbeid; looninkomen *n*; verdiend inkomen *n*

1137 **earned surplus *(US)*; retained income**
d zurückbehaltenes Einkommen *n*
e ingreso(s) *m(pl)* retenido(s)
f revenu(s) *m(pl)* retenu(s)
i redditi *mpl* trattenuti
n ingehouden inkomsten *fpl*

1138 **earnest; guarantee; pawn; pledge; security**
cf. **caution money, collateral, guarantee, margin**
d Bürgschaft *f*; Garantie *f*; Kaution *f*; Pfand *n*; Sicherheit *f*; Sicherstellung *f*; Sicherung *f*; Unterpfand *n*
e caución *f*; fianza *f*; garantía *f*; prenda *f*; seguridad *f*
f caution *f*; gage *m*; garantie *f*; nantissement *m*; sûreté *f*
i cauzione *f*; fideiussione *f*; garanzia *f*; malleveria *f*; pegno *m*; sicurezza *f*
n borg *m*; borgstelling *f*; borgtocht *m*; cautie *f*; garantie *f*; onderpand *n*; pand *n*; waarborg *m*; zekerheid *f*

1139 **earning capacity; earning power**
d Ertragsfähigkeit *f*; Ertragskraft *f*; Erwerbsfähigkeit; Erwerbskraft *f*
e capacidad *f* de ganancia; capacidad *f* de rendimiento
f capacité *f* de gain; capacité *f* de rendement
i capacità *f* di guadagno; capacità *f* di reddito; capacità *f* di rendimento
n rendementsvermogen *n*; winstcapaciteit *f*; winstvermogen *n*

1140 **earnings; pay; wage; wages**
cf. **recompense, salary**
d Arbeitsentgelt *n*; Arbeitslohn *m*; Bezahlung *f*; Lohn *m*; Sold *m**; Verdienst *m*
e estipendio *m*; ingresos *mpl*; paga *f*; salario *m***
f gages *mpl*; gain *m*; paie *f*; paye *f*; salaire *m****; solde *m**
i guadagno *m*; guadagni *mpl*; paga *f*; salario *m***
n loon *n*; verdienste *f*

* Chiefly military.
** Does not mean salary.
*** Can also mean salary.

1141 **earnings; wages and salaries**
d Löhne *mpl* und Gehälter *npl*; Verdienst *m*
e salarios *mpl* y sueldos *mpl*
f salaires *mpl*
i salari *mpl* e stipendi *mpl*
n lonen *npl* en salarissen *npl*

1142 **earnings per share**
d Gewinn *m* pro Aktie
e beneficio *m* por acción; ganancia *f* por acción
f bénéfice *m* par action
i utile *m* per azione
n winst *f* per aandeel

1143 **ease *v* credit restrictions; relax *v* credit restrictions**
d die Kreditbeschränkungen lockern; die Kreditbeschränkungen mildern
e relajar las restricciones crediticias
f alléger les restrictions du crédit; assouplir les restrictions du crédit; relâcher les restrictions du crédit
i allentare gli restrizioni del credito
n de kredietbeperkingen vergemakkelijken; de kredietbeperkingen versoepelen

1144 **easing in money rates**
d Entspannung *f* am Geldmarkt
e distensión *f* en el mercado monetario
f détente *f* au marché monétaire
i distensione *f* al mercato monetario
n ontspanning *f* op de geldmarkt

1145 **easing of credit; relaxation of credit**
d Krediterleichterung *f*; Kreditlockerung *f*
e relajación *f* del crédito
f assouplissement *m* du crédit; détente *f* du crédit
i facilitazione *f* del credito
n kredietvergemakkelijking *f*; kredietversoepeling *f*

1146 **economic**
d Konjunktur-; konjunkturell; ökonomisch; wirtschaftlich; Wirtschafts-
e coyuntural; económico

f conjoncturel; économique
i congiunturale; economico
n conjunctureel; conjunctuur-; economisch

1147 **economic; lucrative; paying; profitable; remunerative**
d einträglich; ergiebig; erspriesslich; ertragbringend; ertragreich; gewinnabwerfend; gewinnbringend; lohnend; lukrativ; nutzbringend; ökonomisch; rentabel; wirtschaftlich
e beneficioso; económico; fructifero; lucrativo; provechoso; remunerador; remunerativo; rentable; ventajoso
f avantageux; économique; lucratif; payant; profitable; rémunérant; rémunérateur
i economico; fruttifero; lucrativo; lucroso; profittevole; redditizio; remunerativo; rimunerativo; vantaggioso
n economisch; lonend; lucratief; profijtelijk; profitabel; rendabel; voordelig; winstgevend

1148 **economic balance sheet**
d Wirtschaftsbilanz *f*
e balance *m* económico; balanza *f* económica
f balance *f* économique
i bilancia *f* economica
n economische balans *f*

1149 **economic barrier**
d wirtschaftliche Schranke *f*
e barrera *f* económica
f barrière *f* économique
i barriera *f* economica
n economische hindernis *f*

1150 **economic phase; phase of the business cycle**
d Konjunkturphase *f*
e fase *f* coyuntural
f phase *f* conjoncturelle
i fase *f* congiunturale
n conjuncturele fase *f*; conjunctuurfase *f*

1151 **economics; economic science; political economy**
d Nationalökonomie *f*; politische Ökonomie *f*; Staatswirtschaftslehre *f*; Volkswirtschaft *f*; Volkswirtschaftslehre *f*; Wirtschaftswissenschaft *f*
e ciencias *fpl* económicas; economía *f* política
f économie *f* politique; sciences *fpl* économiques
i economia *f* politica; scienza *f* economica
n economische wetenschap *f*; staatshuishoudkunde *f*

1152 **effect** *v* **payments; make** *v* **payments**
d Zahlungen leisten; Zahlungen vornehmen
e efectuar pagos; hacer pagos
f effectuer des paiements; effectuer des versements; faire des paiements; faire des versements; opérer des paiements; opérer des versements
i effettuare dei pagamenti; fare dei pagamenti
n betalingen doen; betalingen verrichten

1153 **efficiency pay; efficiency wage; payment by results**
cf. **incentive pay**
d Leistungslohn *m*
e salario *m* según rendimiento
f salaire *m* au rendement; salaire *m* de rendement
i salario *m* a rendimento
n loon *n* naar prestatie; prestatieloon *n*

1154 **elasticity of exchange rates; flexibility of exchange rates**
d Elastizität *f* der Wechselkurse; Flexibilität *f* der Wechselkurse
e elasticidad *f* de los tipos de cambio; flexibilidad *f* de los tipos de cambio
f élasticité *f* des cours de change; flexibilité *f* des cours de change; souplesse *f* des cours de change
i elasticità *f* dei tassi di cambio; flessibilità *f* dei tassi di cambio
n elasticiteit *f* van de wisselkoersen; flexibiliteit *f* van de wisselkoersen

1155 **emergency clause; escape clause**
d Ausweichklausel *f*; Notklausel *f*
e cláusula *f* de escape; cláusula *f* escapatoria
f clause *f* d'urgence; clause *f* échappatoire
i clausola *f* di bisogno; clausola *f* di riserva; clausola *f* di salvaguardia; clausola-scappatoia *f*
n ontsnappingsclausule *f*

1156 **emission of bank notes; issue of bank notes; note issue**
d Banknotenausgabe *f*; Notenausgabe *f*
e emisión *f* de billetes (de banco)
f émission *f* de billets (de banque)
i emissione *f* di banconote; emissione *f* di biglietti (di banca)
n emissie *f* van bankbiljetten; uitgifte *f* van bankbiljetten

1157 **emit** *v* **a loan; float** *v* **a loan; issue** *v* **a loan; launch** *v* **a loan**
cf. **negociate** *v* **a loan, place** *v* **a loan**
d eine Anleihe auflegen; eine Anleihe aus-

geben; eine Anleihe begeben; eine Anleihe emittieren; eine Anleihe lancieren
e emitir un empréstito; lanzar un empréstito
f créer un emprunt; émettre un emprunt; lancer un emprunt
i emettere un prestito; lanciare un prestito
n een lening emitteren; een lening lanceren; een lening uitgeven; een lening uitschrijven

1158 **emoluments**
cf. **fee(s), salary**
d Bezüge *mpl*; Diäten *fpl*; Dienstbezüge *mpl*; Emolumente *npl (rare)*
e emolumentos *mpl*
f émoluments *mpl*
i emolumenti *mpl*
n emolumenten *npl*

1159 **employees' shares; staff shares; worker(s') shares**
d Arbeitnehmeraktien *fpl*; Belegschaftsaktien *fpl*
e acciones *fpl* del personal; acciones *fpl* de trabajo
f actions *fpl* de travail
i azioni *fpl* di lavoro
n arbeidersaandelen *npl*

1160 **employment of capital; employment of funds**
cf. **capital investment**
d Kapitalverwendung *f*
e empleo *m* de capital
f emploi *m* de capitaux
i impiego *m* di capitali
n aanwending *f* van kapitaal

1161 **encouragement of saving(s); promotion of saving(s)**
d Sparbegünstigung *f*; Sparförderung *f*
e fomento *m* del ahorro; promoción *f* del ahorro
f encouragement *m* de l'épargne; incitation *f* à l'épargne
i incentivo *m* al risparmio; incoraggiamento *m* del risparmio
n bevordering *f* van het sparen

1162 **endorse** *v* **a bill; indorse** *v* **a bill**
cf. **back** *v* **a bill**
d einen Wechsel gegenzeichnen; einen Wechsel girieren; einen Wechsel indossieren; einen Wechsel übertragen
e endosar una letra di cambio
f endosser un effet
i girare un effetto; indossare un effetto *(rare)*
n een wissel endosseren; een wissel gireren; een wissel indosseren; een wissel rugtekenen *(B)*

1163 **endorsee; indorsee; transferee**
d Girat *m*; Giratar *m*; Indossat *m*; Indossatar *m*; Wechselübernehmer *m*; Zessionar *m*; Zessionär *m*
e cesionario *m*; endosado *m*; endosatario *m*; girado *m*
f cessionaire *m*; endossataire *m*; endossé *m*
i cessionario *m*; giratario *m*; indossato *m* *(rare)*
n cessionaris *m*; geëndosseerde *m*

1164 **endorsement; indorsement**
d Girierung *f*; Giro *n*; Indossament *n*; Indossement *n*; Indossierung *f*; Indosso *n*; Übertragungsvermerk *m*
e endose *m (AL)*; endoso *m*
f endos *m*; endossement *m*
i girata *f*; indossamento *m (rare)*; indosso *m (rare)*
n endossement *n*; giro *m*; indossement *n*; rugtekening *f (B)*

1165 **endorser; indorser; transfer(r)er** *(rare in this sense)*; **transferor**
d Begebender *m*; Begeber *m*; Girant *m*; Indossant *m*; Indossierer *m*; Übertragender *m*; Zedent *m*
e cedente *m*; endosante *m*; girador *m*; girante *m*; transferidor *m*
f cédant *m*; endosseur *m*
i cedente *m*; girante *m*; indossatore *m* *(rare)*
n cedent *m*; endossant *m*; girant *m*; indossant *m*

1166 **endorser's liability**
d Indossamentverbindlichkeiten *fpl*
e garantía *f* del endoso
f engagement *m* d'endos
i obbligazione *f* cambiaria da girata
n verbintenis *f* uit endossement

1167 **endow** *v*
d ausstatten; dotieren
e dotar
f doter
i dotare
n doteren

1168 **endowment**
d Ausstattung *f*; Dotation *f*; Dotierung *f*
e dotación *f*
f dotation *f*

i dotazione *f*
n dotatie *f*

1169 **entertainment allowance; entertainment expenses; representation expenses**
d Aufwandsspesen *pl*; Repräsentationsaufwendungen *fpl*; Repräsentationskosten *pl*
e gastos *mpl* de representación
f frais *mpl* de représentation
i spese *fpl* di rappresentanza
n representatiekosten *mpl*

1170 **entitled to (a) dividend**
d dividendenberechtigt
e con derecho a (percibir) dividendo
f ayant droit au dividende
i avente diritto al dividendo
n met recht op dividend; recht gevend op dividend

1171 **entrepreneur**
d Unternehmer *m*
e empresario *m*
f entrepreneur *m*
i imprenditore *m*
n ondernemer *m*

1172 **equalization**
cf. **compensation**
d Ausgleich *m*; Ausgleichung *f*; Kompensation *f*
e compensación *f*; igualación *f*; perecuación *f*
f compensation *f*; égalisation *f*; péréquation *f*
i compensazione *f*; conguaglio *m*; equalizzazione *f*; pareggiamento *m*; pareggio *m*; perequazione *f*
n compensatie *f*; egalisatie *f*; perekwatie *f* *(B)*

1173 **equalization claim**
d Ausgleichsforderung *f*
e crédito *m* de igualación
f créance *f* de péréquation
i credito *m* di pareggio
n egalisatievordering *f*

1174 **equalization of burdens**
d Lastenausgleich *m*
e igualación *f* de cargas; nivelación *f* de cargas; perecuación *f* de cargas
f égalisation *f* des charges; péréquation *f* des charges
i perequazione *f* degli oneri; perequazione *f* dei carichi
n evenredige verdeling *f* van lasten; gelijkmatige verdeling *f* van lasten

1175 **equalization of taxes; tax equalization**
d Steuerausgleich *m*
e igualación *f* de impuestos; igualación *f* tributaria; perecuación *f* de impuestos; perecuación *f* tributaria
f péréquation *f* des impôts; péréquation *f* fiscale
i conguaglio *m* delle imposte; perequazione *f* delle imposte; perequazione *f* fiscale; perequazione *f* tributaria
n aanpassing *f* der belastingen; perekwatie *f* der belastingen *(B)*

1176 **equilibrium**
d Ausgleich *m*; Gleichgewicht *n*
e equilibrio *m*
f équilibre *m*
i equilibrio *m*
n evenwicht *n*

1177 **equity** *(value of property in excess of liens)*
d Nettowert *m* eines Eigentums
e valor *m* neto de una propiedad
f valeur *f* nette d'une propriété
i valore *m* netto di una proprietà
n netto waarde *f* van een eigendom

1178 **equity capital; risk-bearing capital; risk capital; venture capital**
cf. **common capital stock**
d risikobereites Kapital *n*; Risikokapital *n*; risikotragendes Kapital *n*
e capital *m* a riesgo; capital *m* de riesgo
f capital *m* acceptant les risques; capital *m* à risques
i capitale *m* di rischio
n risicodragend kapitaal *n*

1179 **equity investment**
cf. **variable yield investment**
d Anlagen *fpl* in Börsenwerten
e inversiones *fpl* de bolsa
f placements *mpl* boursiers
i impieghi *mpl* di borsa
n beleggingen *fpl* ter beurze

1180 **equivalence**
d Äquivalenz *f*; Gegenwertigkeit *f*; Gleichwertigkeit *f*
e equivalencia *f*
f équivalence *f*
i equivalenza *f*
n equivalentie *f*; gelijkwaardigheid *f*

1181 **equivalence coefficient**
d Äquivalenzziffer *f*
e coeficiente *m* de equivalencia

f coefficient *m* d'équivalence
i coefficiente *m* di equivalenza
n equivalentiecijfer *n*

1182 equivalence of exchange; exchange parity; monetary parity
cf. **par of exchange**
d Kursparität *f*; Währungsparität *f*; Wechselparität *f*
e paridad *f* cambiaria; paridad *f* de cambio; paridad *f* monetaria
f parité *f* de change; parité *f* monétaire
i parità *f* cambiaria; parità *f* di cambio; parità *f* monetaria
n wisselpariteit *f*

1183 errors and omissions
d Fehler *mpl* und Auslassungen *fpl*; Irrtümer *mpl* und Auslassungen *fpl*
e errores *mpl* y omisiones *fpl*
f erreurs *fpl* et omissions *fpl*
i errori *mpl* ed omissioni *fpl*
n fouten *fpl* en weglatingen *fpl*; onjuistheden *fpl* en weglatingen *fpl*

1184 errors and omissions excepted; E. and O.E.
d Irrtum vorbehalten
e salvo error u omisión; S.E. u O.; salvo error y omisión; S.E. y O.
f sauf erreur et omission; S.E.O.; sauf erreur ou omission
i salvo errore od omissione; S.E. od O.; salvo errori ed omissioni; S.E. ed O.
n behoudens vergissing en weglating; sauf erreur ou omission; S.E.O.O.

1185 in escrow; in trust
d in treuhänderischer Verwahrung; treuhänderisch; zu treuen Händen
e en administración (fiduciaria); en custodia (fiduciaria); en depósito (fiduciario); en fideicomiso
f en administration fiduciaire; en dépôt de garantie (bloqué); en dépôt fiduciaire; par fidéicommis
i in amministrazione fiduciaria; in consegna (legale); in custodia fiduciaria; in fedecommesso; in fidecommesso; in fidecommisso
n in beheer; in bewaring; in fiduciaire bewaring

1186 establish *v* quotas; fix *v* quotas; quota; subject *v* to quota restrictions
d kontingentieren
e contingentar
f contingenter
i contingentare
n contingenteren

1187 estimate
cf. **appraisal**
d Kostenanschlag *m*; Kostenvoranschlag *m*; Voranschlag *m*
e presupuesto *m* (de los gastos)
f devis *m*
i preventivo *m*
n bestek *n*

1188 estimated assessment
d Schätzung *f* der Besteuerungsgrundlagen
e estimación *f* del monto imponible *(AL)*; evaluación *f* de bases imponibles
f évaluation *f* des bases imposables
i determinazione *f* d'ufficio dell'imponibile
n aanslag *m* op basis van schatting; ambtshalve aanslag *m*

1189 estimated cost(s); predetermined cost(s)
d Plankosten *pl*; Sollkosten *pl*; vorkalkulierte Kosten *pl*
e costo(s) *m(pl)* calculado(s) de antemano; costo(s) *m(pl)* estimado(s); costo(s) *m(pl)* estimativo(s)
f coût *m* estimatif; coût *m* prévisionnel; coût *m* prévu
i costo *m* calcolato preventivamente; costo *m* presunto; costo *m* preventivato; costo *m* previsto
n beraamde kosten *mpl*; geraamde kosten *mpl*; voorcalculatorische kosten *mpl*

1190 estimating; preproduction costing
d Vorkalkulation *f*
e presupuesto *m* de coste
f calcul *m* du coût prévisionnel
i calcolo *m* preventivo
n voorcalculatie *f*

1191 Euro-bond market
d Euro-Emissionsmarkt *m*
e mercado *m* de euroemisiones
f marché *m* des euro-émissions
i mercato *m* delle euro-emissioni
n Euro-emissiemarkt *f*

1192 Euro-currency market
d Euro-Divisenmarkt *m*
e mercado *m* de eurodivisas
f marché *m* des euro-devises
i mercato *m* delle euro-divise
n Euro-deviezenmarkt *f*

1193 Eurodollar
d Eurodollar *m*
e Eurodólar *m*

f eurodollar *m*
i eurodollaro *m*
n eurodollar *m*

1194 **European Economic Community; E.E.C.**
d Europäische Wirtschaftsgemeinschaft *f*; E.W.G.
e Comunidad *f* Económica Europea; C.E.E.
f Communauté *f* économique européenne; C.E.E.
i Comunità *f* Economica Europea; C.E.E.
n Europese Economische Gemeenschap *f*; E.E.G.

1195 **European Investment Bank**
d Europäische Investitionsbank *f*
e Banco *m* Europeo de Inversiones
f Banque *f* européenne d'investissement
i Banca *f* Europea per gli Investimenti
n Europese Investeringsbank *f*

1196 **European Monetary Agreement; EMA**
d Europäisches Währungsabkommen; EWA
e Acuerdo *m* Monetario Europeo; AME
f Accord *m* monétaire européen; AME
i Accordo *m* Monetario Europeo; AME
n Europese Monetaire Overeenkomst *f*; EMO

1197 **European Monetary Cooperation Fund**
d Europäischer Fonds *m* für währungspolitische Zusammenarbeit
e Fondo *m* Europeo de Cooperación Monetaria
f Fonds *m* européen de coopération monétaire
i Fondo *m* Europeo di Cooperazione Monetaria
n Europees Fonds *n* voor Monetaire Samenwerking

1198 **European Payments Union; EPU**
d Europäische Zahlungsunion *f*; EZU
e Unión *f* Europea de Pagos; UEP
f Union *f* européenne des paiements; UEP
i Unione *f* Europea dei Pagamenti; UEP
n Europese Betalingsunie *f*; EBU

1199 **evening up; settlement of balance(s)**
d Spitzenausgleich *m*
e compensación *f* de saldos
f compensation *f* de soldes
i compensazione *f* di saldi
n saldovergelijking *f*

1200 **evolution; tendency; trend**
d Entwicklung *f*; Evolution *f*; Neigung *f*; Tendenz *f*; Trend *m*
e evolución *f*; orientación *f*; tendencia *f*
f évolution *f*; orientation *f*; tendance *f*
i evoluzione *f*; orientamento *m*; tendenza *f*
n evolutie *f*; neiging *f*; ontwikkeling *f*; strekking *f*; tendens *f*; tendentie *f*; trend *m*

1201 **exceed** *v* **a credit; overdraw** *v* **a credit**
d einen Kredit überschreiten; einen Kredit überziehen
e exceder un crédito; rebasar un crédito; sobrepasar un crédito
f dépasser un crédit; excéder un crédit
i eccedere un credito; superare un credito
n een krediet overschrijden

1202 **exceptional non-recurring costs**
d betriebsfremder Aufwand *m (Schw)*; neutraler Aufwand *m*
e costes *mpl* no incorporables
f charges *fpl* non-incorporables
i spese *fpl* non incorporabili
n niet in-te-calculeren kosten *mpl*

1203 **exceptional price; preferential price; special price**
cf. **bargain price**
d Ausnahmepreis *m*; Spezialpreis *m*; Vorzugspreis *m*
e precio *m* de favor; precio *m* especial; precio *m* excepcional; precio *m* preferente
f prix *m* de faveur; prix *m* d'exception; prix *m* exceptionnel; prix *m* préférentiel; prix *m* spécial
i prezzo *m* di favore; prezzo *m* eccezionale; prezzo *m* preferenziale; prezzo *m* speciale
n gunstprijs *m (B)*; speciale prijs *m*; uitzonderingsprijs *m*; voorkeurprijs *m*

1204 **excess**
cf. **surplus**
d Überhang *m (of "a" over "b")*; Überschuss *m*
e excedente *m*; exceso *m*
f excédent *m*; excès *m*
i eccedenza *f*; eccesso *m*
n excedent *n*; overschot *n*

1205 **excess amount; sum in excess**
cf. **surplus**
d Mehrbetrag *m*; überschiessender Betrag *m*; überschiessende Summe *f*
e suma *f* excedente
f somme *f* en excédent
i somma *f* eccedente
n overschietend bedrag *n*

1206 **excess demand; excess of demand**
d Nachfrageüberhang *m*
e exceso *m* de demanda
f excédent *m* de la demande; excès *m* de la demande
i eccedenza *f* della domanda; eccesso *m* di domanda
n overtrokken vraag *f*; te grote vraag *f*

1207 **excess indebtedness; excess of liabilities over assets; overextension; overindebtedness**
d Überschuldung *f*
e endeudamiento *m* excesivo; excedente *m* de pasivo; exceso *m* de deudas
f excédent *m* de passif; surendettement *m*
i indebitamento *m* eccessivo; sovraindebitamento *m*
n overstelpende schuldenlast *m*

1208 **excessive price; excess price; overprice** *(rare)*
cf. **exorbitant price**
d Überpreis *m*
e precio *m* excesivo; sobreprecio *m*
f prix *m* excessif; surprix *m*
i prezzo *m* eccessivo; soprapprezzo *m*; sopraprezzo *m*; sovrapprezzo *m*; sovraprezzo *m*
n overprijs *m*

1209 **excessive purchasing power; excess (of) purchasing power**
d Kaufkraftüberhang *m*; überschüssige Kaufkraft *f*
e exceso *m* de poder adquisitivo; poder *m* adquisitivo excesivo
f excédent *m* de pouvoir d'achat; pouvoir *m* d'achat excédentaire; pouvoir *m* d'achat en excès
i eccedenza *f* di potere d'acquisto; potere *m* d'acquisto eccedente
n vlottende koopkracht *f*; zwevende koopkracht *f*

1210 **excessive supply; excess (of) supply; oversupply**
d Überangebot *n*
e exceso *m* de oferta; oferta *f* excesiva; sobreoferta *f*
f excès *m* d'offre; offre *f* excédentaire; offre *f* excessive; suroffre *f*
i eccesso *m* d'offerta; offerta *f* eccessiva
n te groot aanbod *n*

1211 **excess liquidity**
d Überliquidität *f*
e liquidez *f* excesiva
f liquidité *f* excessive
i èccessiva liquidità *f*
n overmatige liquiditeit *f*

1212 **excess of expenditure; overspending**
d Ausgabenüberhang *m*; Ausgabenüberschuss *m*; Mehrausgabe(n) *f(pl)*
e excedente *m* de gastos; exceso *m* de gastos
f excédent *m* de dépenses; excès *m* de dépenses
i eccedenza *f* di spese; eccesso *m* di spese
n excedent *n* van uitgaven; overbesteding *f*

1213 **excess profit; surplus profit** *(US)*
d Mehrgewinn *m*; Sondergewinn *m*; Übergewinn *m*
e beneficio *m* extraordinario; excedente *m* de beneficios; exceso *m* de beneficios; ganancia *f* excesiva; ganancia *f* extraordinaria; superbeneficio *m*
f bénéfice *m* excédentaire; bénéfice *m* exceptionnel; excédent *m* de bénéfice; superbénéfice *m*; superprofit *m*
i extra-profitto *m*; profitto *m* eccezionale; soprapprofitto *m*; sopraprofitto *m*; sovrapprofitto *m*; sovraprofitto *m*
n buitengewone winst *f*; overwinst *f*; superwinst *f*

1214 **excess profits tax**
d Mehrgewinnsteuer *f*; Sondergewinnsteuer *f*; Übergewinnsteuer *f*
e impuesto *m* sobre el excedente de beneficios; impuesto *m* sobre las utilidades excesivas
f impôt *m* sur les bénéfices excédentaires; impôt *m* sur les bénéfices exceptionnels; impôt *m* sur l'excédent de bénéfice
i imposta *f* sui soprapprofitti; imposta *f* sui sovrapprofitti; tassa *f* sui soprapprofitti; tassa *f* sui sovrapprofitti
n belasting *f* op de buitengewone winsten; belasting *f* op overwinsten; overwinstbelasting *f*

1215 **excess value; overvalue; surplus value**
cf. **appreciation**
d Überwert *m*
e exceso *m* de valor
f survaleur *f*
i valore *m* eccessivo
n overwaarde *f*

1216 **exchange; exchange rate; rate of exchange**
cf. **conversion rate**
d Devisenkurs *m*; Valutakurs *m*; Valutenkurs *m*; Wechselkurs *m*
e cambio *m*; tipo *m* de cambio

f change *m*; cours *m* de change; cours *m* du change; échange *m*; taux *m* de change; taux *m* du change
i cambio *m*; corso *m* dei cambi; corso *m* del cambio; corso *m* delle valute; saggio *m* del cambio; tasso *m* del cambio; tasso *m* di cambio
n valutakoers *m*; wisselkoers *m*

1217 **exchange** *(rare)*; **exchange office**
d Wechselkasse *f*; Wechselstelle *f*; Wechselstube *f*
e agencia *f* de cambio(s); oficina *f* de cambio(s)
f bureau *m* de change
i agenzia *f* di cambio; ufficio *m* cambi; ufficio *m* cambio
n wisselagentschap *n*; wisselkantoor *n*

1218 **exchange; stock exchange**
cf. **securities market**
d Aktienbörse *f*; Börse *f*; Effektenbörse *f*; Fondsbörse *f*; Wertpapierbörse *f*
e bolsa *f*; bolsa *f* de acciones; bolsa *f* de cambio; bolsa *f* de valores (mobiliarios)
f bourse *f*; bourse *f* aux actions; bourse *f* d'effets; bourse *f* de(s) valeurs (mobilières)
i borsa *f*; borsa *f* delle azioni; borsa *f* valori (mobiliari)
n beurs *f*; effectenbeurs *f*; fondsenbeurs *f*

1219 **exchangeable value; exchange value; value in exchange**
cf. **counterpart**
d Gegenwert *m*; Tauschwert *m*
e contravalor *m*; valor *m* de cambio
f contre-valeur *f*; valeur *f* d'échange
i controvalore *m*; valore *m* di scambio
n ruilwaarde *f*; tegenwaarde *f*

1220 **exchange bank**
d Wechselbank *f*
e casa *f* de cambio
f maison *f* de change
i banca *f* di cambio
n wisselbank *f*

1221 **exchange business; foreign exchange**
d Devisengeschäft *n*; Devisenhandel *m*; Wechselgeschäft *n*; Wechselhandel *m*
e cambio *m*; comercio *m* de cambio(s); comercio *m* de divisas
f change *m*; commerce *m* de change; commerce *m* de devises
i cambio *m*; commercio *m* dei cambi; commercio *m* delle divise
n deviezenhandel *m*; valutahandel *m*; wisselhandel *m*

1222 **exchange business; security deals; security transactions; stock deals; stock exchange dealings; stock exchange operations; stock exchange transactions; stock transactions**
cf. **stock exchange turnover**
d Börsegeschäfte *npl (O)*; Börsenabschlüsse *mpl*; Börsengeschäfte *npl*; Börsentransaktionen *fpl*; Effektengeschäfte *npl*; Effektentransaktionen *fpl*; Wertpapiergeschäfte *npl*; Wertpapiertransaktionen *fpl*
e contrataciones *fpl* bursátiles; contrataciones *fpl* en bolsa; contratos *mpl* bursátiles; negociaciones *fpl* bursátiles; negociaciones *fpl* de títulos; negociaciones *fpl* de valores; negocios *mpl* bursátiles; negocios *mpl* en títulos; negocios *mpl* en valores; operaciones *fpl* bursátiles; operaciones *fpl* de bolsa; operaciones *fpl* de títulos; operaciones *fpl* de valores; transacciones *fpl* bursátiles; transacciones *fpl* de (en) bolsa; transacciones *fpl* de (en) títulos; transacciones *fpl* de (en) valores
f négociations *fpl* en bourse; opérations *fpl* boursières; opérations *fpl* de (en) bourse; opérations *fpl* sur effets; opérations *fpl* sur titres; opérations *fpl* sur valeurs; transactions *fpl* boursières; transactions *fpl* de (en) bourse; transactions *fpl* sur effets; transactions *fpl* sur titres; transactions *fpl* sur valeurs
i affari *mpl* di borsa; contratti *mpl* di borsa; negoziazioni *fpl* di borsa; operazioni *fpl* borsistiche; operazioni *fpl* di (in) borsa; operazioni *fpl* in (su) titoli; operazioni *fpl* in (su) valori
n beursoperaties *fpl*; beurstransacties *fpl*; beursverrichtingen *fpl*; beurszaken *fpl*; effectentransacties *fpl*; effectenverrichtingen *fpl*; effectenzaken *fpl*

1223 **exchange commitment; exchange liability; foreign exchange commitment; foreign exchange liability**
d Devisenverpflichtung *f*; Devisenzusage *f*
e compromiso *m* en divisas; obligacion *f* en divisas; promesa *f* de divisas
f engagement *m* de change; promesse *f* de devises
i impegno *m* valutario; promessa *f* di divise
n deviezenverplichting *f*; toezegging *f* van deviezen

1224 **exchange control; foreign exchange control**

cf. **currency regulations**
d Devisenbewirtschaftung *f*; Devisenkontrolle *f*; Devisenüberwachung *f*; Devisenzwangswirtschaft *f*
e control *m* de cambios; control *m* de divisas
f contrôle *m* des changes; contrôle *m* des devises
i controllo *m* degli scambi; controllo *m* dei cambi; controllo *m* delle divise; controllo *m* valutario; disciplina *f* dei cambi
n deviezencontrole *f*; wisselcontrole *f*

1225 exchange fluctuation; fluctuation in exchange; fluctuation in (of) the exchange rate
d Fluktuation *f* der Wechselkurse; Kursschwankung *f*; Schwanken *n* der Wechselkurse; Schwankung *f* der Wechselkurse
e fluctuación *f* de los cambios; fluctuación *f* de los tipos de cambio; oscilación *f* de los cambios; oscilación *f* de los tipos de cambio
f fluctuation *f* des cours (de change); fluctuation *f* des taux de change; oscillation *f* des cours (de change); oscillation *f* des taux de change
i fluttuazione *f* dei cambi; fluttuazione *f* dei corsi; fluttuazione *f* dei tassi di cambio; oscillazione *f* dei cambi; oscillazione *f* dei corsi; oscillazione *f* dei tassi di cambio
n fluctuatie *f* in (van) de wisselkoersen; koersfluctuatie *f*; koersschommeling *f*; schommeling *f* in (van) de wisselkoersen

1226 exchange for forward delivery; forward exchange; forward exchange business; forward exchange dealing
cf. **forward exchange deal**
d Devisenterminhandel *m*; Terminhandel *m* in Devisen
e cambio *m* a plazo; cambio *m* a término
f change *m* à terme
i cambio *m* a termine
n termijnhandel *m* in deviezen

1227 exchange for spot delivery; spot exchange; spot exchange business; spot exchange dealing
cf. **spot exchange deal**
d Devisenkassahandel *m*; Kassahandel *m* in Devisen
e cambio *m* al contado
f change *m* au comptant
i cambio *m* a contanti
n contanthandel *m* in deviezen

1228 exchange list; list of quotations; market report; securities' listing *(US)*; stock exchange bulletin; stock exchange list; stock exchange report; stock list; stock market report
d Börsenbericht *m*; Börsenzettel *m*; Börsenkursblatt *n*; Börsenzettel *m*; Kursbericht *m*; Kursblatt *n*; Kursliste *f*; Kurszettel *m*
e boletín *m* de bolsa; boletín *m* de cotización (de la bolsa); cotización *f*; lista *f* de cotización
f bulletin *m* de(s) cours; bulletin *m* de la bourse; bulletin *m* de la cote (de la bourse); cote *f* de la bourse
i bollettino *m* di borsa; listino *m* di borsa
n beursbericht *n*; koersbericht *n*; koersblad *n*; koerslijst *f*; prijscourant *m* van de effectenhandel

1229 exchange loss; loss in exchange; loss on exchange
d Kurseinbusse *f*; Kursverlust *m*
e pérdida *f* de cambio; pérdida *f* en operaciones de cambio
f perte *f* au change; perte *f* au cours; perte *f* résultant d'opérations de change; perte *f* sur le change
i perdita *f* di cambio; perdita *f* sul cambio
n koersverlies *n*

1230 exchange market; foreign exchange market
d Devisenbörse *f*; Devisenmarkt *m*; Wechselmarkt *m*
e bolsa *f* de cambios; mercado *m* de cambios; mercado *m* de divisas
f marché *m* des changes; marché *m* des devises; marché *m* du change
i mercato *m* degli scambi; mercato *m* dei cambi; mercato *m* delle divise; mercato *m* valutario
n deviezenmarkt *f*; valutamarkt *f*; wisselmarkt *f*

1231 exchange of money; money changing
d Geldumtausch *m*; Geldwechsel *m*
e cambio *m* de dinero; cambio *m* de moneda
f change *m* (des monnaies); échange *m* monétaire
i cambio *m* (di denaro); cambio *m* (monetario)
n wisselen *n* van geld

1232 exchange of shares; stock switch *(US)*
d Aktienaustausch *m*; Aktientausch *m*; Aktienumtausch *m*
e cambio *m* de acciones

f échange *m* d'actions
i scambio *m* d'azioni
n aandelenruil *m*

1233 **exchange profit; profit in exchange; profit on exchange; rate gain** *(US)*
d Devisengewinn *m*; Kursgewinn *m*; Valutagewinn *m*; Valutengewinn *m*
e beneficio *m* sobre el cambio; plusvalía *f* de cambio; plusvalía *f* de cotización
f bénéfice *m* au change; bénéfice *m* de cours; bénéfice *m* sur le change; bénéfice *m* sur le cours; plus-value *f* de change; profit *m* au change
i guadagno *m* di cambio; profitto *m* sui cambi; utile *m* sui cambi
n koerswinst *f*

1234 **exchange rate; exchange value; market quotation; market rate; market value; quoted value; stock exchange rate; stock exchange value**
d Börsenkurs *m*; Börsenwert *m*; Kurswert *m*; Marktkurs *m*
e cotización *f* de bolsa; cotización *f* en bolsa; tipo *m* de mercado; valor *m* bursátil; valor *m* cotizado; valor *m* de bolsa; valor *m* de cambio; valor *m* de cotización; valor *m* en bolsa
f cote *f* en bourse; cours *m* coté; cours *m* de la bourse; cours *m* du marché; valeur *f* de bourse; valeur *f* du cours; valeur *f* en bourse
i corso *m* di borsa; quotazione *f* di borsa; valore *m* del cambio; valore *m* di borsa
n beurskoers *m*; beursnotering *f*; koerswaarde *f*

1235 **exchange rate for notes and coin(s); rate for notes and coin(s); rate of exchange for notes and coin(s)**
d Sortenkurs *m*
e cambio *m* de billetes y monedas; tipo *m* de cambio de billetes y metálico; tipo *m* de cambio de billetes y monedas
f cours *m* de change des billets et espèces; taux *m* de change des billets et espèces
i cambio *m* di biglietti e monete; corso *m* di cambio di biglietti e monete; tasso *m* di cambio di biglietti e monete
n wisselkoers *m* voor biljetten en munten

1236 **exchange rate relations; relations between the exchange rates**
d Kursverhältnisse *npl*; Wechselkursverhältnisse *npl*
e relaciones *fpl* de cambio
f relations *fpl* de change
i rapporti *mpl* di cambio
n koersverhoudingen *fpl*

1237 **exchange rate stabilization**
d Kursstabilisierung *f*
e estabilización *f* del cambio
f stabilisation *f* des cours
i stabilizzazione *f* del corso
n koersstabilisatie *f*

1238 **exchange risk**
d Kursrisiko *n*; Valutarisiko *n*; Währungsrisiko *n*; Wechselkursrisiko *n*
e riesgo *m* de cambio; riesgo *m* en el cambio de divisas
f risque *m* de change
i rischio *m* di cambio
n koersrisico *n*; wisselkoersrisico *n*

1239 **exchange stability**
d Stabilität *f* der Devisenkurse; Stabilität *f* der Wechselkurse; Wechselkursstabilität *f*
e estabilidad *f* cambiaria; estabilidad *f* de los cambios
f stabilité *f* des changes
i stabilità *f* dei cambi
n stabiliteit *f* van de wisselkoersen

1240 **exchange system**
d Devisenordnung *f*
e sistema *m* de cambios
f système *m* des changes
i sistema *m* dei cambi
n wisselstelsel *n*; wisselsysteem *n*

1241 **exchange transactions; foreign exchange dealings; foreign exchange transactions**
cf. **dealing in foreign notes and coins, exchange business**
d Devisengeschäfte *npl*; Devisenoperationen *fpl*; Devisentransaktionen *fpl*; Valutageschäfte *npl*
e negocios *mpl* de cambio; negocios *mpl* en divisas; operaciones *fpl* de cambio; operaciones *fpl* en divisas; transacciones *fpl* de cambio; transacciones *fpl* en divisas
f opérations *fpl* de change; opérations *fpl* en devises; transactions *fpl* de change; transactions *fpl* en devises
i operazioni *fpl* di cambio; operazioni *fpl* in cambi; operazioni *fpl* in valuta; operazioni *fpl* su divise; operazioni *fpl* sui cambi; transazioni *fpl* di cambio; transazioni *fpl* in cambi; transazioni *fpl* in valuta; transazioni *fpl* su divise; transazioni *fpl* sui cambi
n deviezenoperaties *fpl*; deviezen-

transacties *fpl*; valutaoperaties *fpl*; valutatransacties *fpl*

1242 **exchequer; fisc *(rare)*; inland revenue *(UK)*; inland revenue department *(UK)*; internal revenue *(US)*; internal revenue service *(US)*; tax authorities**
cf. **treasury**
d Finanzamt *n*; Finanzverwaltung *f*; Fiskus *m*; Steueramt *n*; Steuerbehörden *fpl*; Steuerverwaltung *f*
e administración *f* fiscal; fisco *m*
f administration *f* fiscale; fisc *m*
i amministrazione *f* finanziaria; fisco *m*
n belastingdienst *m*; belastingwezen *n*; fiscus *m*

1243 **exchequer bond *(UK)*; government bond; government obligation; treasury bond**
cf. **treasury bill**
d Staatsobligation *f*; Staatsschuldschein *m*; Staatsschuldverschreibung *f*
e obligación *f* del estado; obligación *f* del tesoro
f obligation *f* d'état; obligation *f* du trésor; obligation *f* publique
i obbligazione *f* dello stato; obbligazione *f* del tesoro
n schatkistobligatie *f*; staatsobligatie *f*

1244 **exchequer stock *(UK)*; government funds *(UK)*; government securities; government stock(s); public funds *(UK)*; public securities; public stock(s); treasury stock(s)**
d Fonds *mpl*; öffentliche Anleihen *fpl*; öffentliche Fonds *mpl*; öffentliche Titel *mpl*; Staatsanleihen *fpl*; Staatsfonds *mpl*; Staatspapiere *npl*
e efectos *mpl* del estado; efectos *mpl* públicos; fondos *mpl* del estado; fondos *mpl* públicos; rentas *fpl*; títulos *mpl* del estado; títulos *mpl* públicos; valores *mpl* del estado; valores *mpl* públicos
f effets *mpl* d'état; effets *mpl* publics; fonds *mpl* d'état; fonds *mpl* publics; rentes *fpl* d'état; titres *mpl* de rentes d'état; titres *mpl* d'état; titres *mpl* publics
i fondi *mpl* di stato; fondi *mpl* pubblici; redditi *mpl*; titoli *mpl* di stato; titoli *mpl* pubblici
n overheidsfondsen *npl*; overheidspapieren *npl*; schatkistpapieren *npl*; staatsfondsen *npl*; staatspapieren *npl*

1245 **excise; excise duty; excise tax; monopoly tax**
d Monopolabgabe *f*; Monopolgebühr *f*; Monopolsteuer *f*
e derecho *m* de monopolio; tasa *f* de monopolio
f droit *m* de régie; taxe *f* de monopole
i diritto *m* di monopolio; tassa *f* di monopolio
n monopoliebelasting *f*; monopolierecht *n*

1246 **exempt *v* from duty**
d von Zoll befreien; zollfrei machen
e exentar de derechos de aduana; eximir de derechos de aduana
f affranchir des droits de douane
i esentare da dogana
n tolvrij maken; vrijstellen van rechten

1247 **exempt from tax; free of tax; non-taxable; tax-exempt; tax-free**
d abgabenfrei; nicht besteuerbar; steuerbefreit; steuerfrei
e exento (del pago) de impuesto(s); libre (del pago) de impuesto(s); no imponible
f exempt d'impôt(s); franc d'impôt(s); net d'impôt(s); non-imposable
i esente d'imposta (imposte); al neto d'imposta; non imponibile
n belastingvrij; niet belastbaar; vrij van belasting(en)

1248 **exemption from taxation; fiscal immunity; non-taxability; tax exemption**
d Abgabenbefreiung *f*; Abgabenfreiheit *f*; Steuerbefreiung *f*; Steuerfreiheit *f*
e exención *f* de impuesto(s); exención *f* fiscal; exención *f* impositiva; franquicia *f* fiscal; franquicia *f* tributaria; inmunidad *f* fiscal; inmunidad *f* tributaria
f exemption *f* d'impôt(s); exemption *f* fiscale; exonération *f* d'impôt(s); exonération *f* fiscale; franchise *f* d'impôt(s); immunité *f* fiscale
i esenzione *f* da imposte; esenzione *f* fiscale; esenzione *f* tributaria; esonero *m* da imposte; esonero *m* fiscale; esonero *m* tributario; immunità *f* fiscale
n belastingvrijdom *m*; belastingvrijheid *f*; vrijstelling *f* van belasting(en)

1249 **ex new; ex rights; rights off *(US)***
d ausschliesslich Bezugsrecht; ausschliesslich Optionsrecht; ex Bezugsrecht; ex Optionsrecht; exklusive Bezugsrecht; exklusive Optionsrecht; ohne Bezugsrecht; ohne Optionsrecht
e ex derechos; sin derechos de suscripción; sin derechos de opción
f droit détaché; ex droit; ex option
i diritto staccato; ex diritto; ex opzione
n ex claim; exclusief claimrecht

1250 exorbitant price; extortionate price; inordinate price; usurious price
cf. **excessive price**
d übermässiger Preis *m*; übermässig hoher Preis *m*; Wucherpreis *m*
e precio *m* exorbitante; precio *m* usurario
f prix *m* exorbitant; prix *m* immodéré; prix *m* usuraire
i prezzo *m* esorbitante; prezzo *m* usurario
n buitensporige prijs *m*; exorbitante prijs *m*; woekerprijs *m*

1251 expansionary measures
d Konjunkturbelebung *f*
e acciones *fpl* de relanzamiento; reactivación *f* de la coyuntura
f actions *fpl* de relance
i misure *fpl* congiunturali di rilancio
n stimuleringsacties *fpl*

1252 expansion in the money supply; growth in the money supply; increase in the money supply; monetary expansion
d Ausdehnung *f* des Geldvolumens; Geldvermehrung *f*; Vermehrung *f* des Geldvolumens; Wachstum *n* der Geldversorgung; Zunahme *f* der Geldmenge; Zunahme *f* des Geldvolumens
e aumento *m* de la masa monetaria; expansión *f* de la masa monetaria; expansión *f* monetaria
f augmentation *f* de la masse monétaire; expansion *f* de la masse monétaire; expansion *f* monétaire
i aumento *m* della massa monetaria; espansione *f* della massa monetaria; espansione *f* monetaria
n monetaire expansie *f (B)*; stijging *f* van de geldhoeveelheid; uitbreiding *f* van het geldvolume

1253 expansion investment; extensive investment; investment in breadth
d Horizontalinvestierung *f*; Horizontalinvestition *f*; Investition *f* für Produktionsausweitung
e inversión *f* horizontal; inversión *f* para expansión
f investissement *m* d'expansion
i investimento *m* di espansione
n breedte-investering *f*

1254 expansion of world trade
d Ausweitung *f* des Welthandels
e expansión *f* del comercio mundial
f expansion *f* des échanges mondiaux; expansion *f* du commerce mondial
i espansione *f* degli scambi mondiali; espansione *f* del commercio mondiale
n uitbreiding *f* van de wereldhandel

1255 expansion rate *(percentage)*; growth rate; rate of expansion; rate of growth; rate of increase
d Steigerungsrate *f*; Steigerungssatz *m*; Wachstumsrate *f*; Zunahmerate *f*; Zuwachsrate *f*
e cuota *f* de crecimiento; tasa *f* de aumento; tasa *f* de crecimiento; tasa *f* de expansión; tasa *f* de progresión; tipo *m* de aumento
f taux *m* d'augmentation; taux *m* de croissance; taux *m* de progression; taux *m* d'expansion
i quota *f* d'incremento; tasso *m* d'espansione; tasso *m* d'incremento; tasso *m* di sviluppo
n groeipercentage *n*; groeivoet *m*; stijgingspercentage *n*; toenemingspercentage *n*

1256 expansion rate *(speed)*; growth rate; rate of expansion; rate of growth; rate of increase
d Expansionsrhythmus *m*; Tempo *n* des Wachstums
e ritmo *m* de aumento; ritmo *m* de crecimiento; ritmo *m* de expansión
f rythme *m* d'augmentation; rythme *m* de croissance; rythme *m* d'expansion
i ritmo *m* d'aumento; ritmo *m* d'espansione
n expansietempo *n*; groeiritme *n*; groeitempo *n*; stijgingstempo *n*

1257 expend *v*; **spend** *v*
cf. **disburse** *v*
d ausgeben; verausgaben
e gastar
f dépenser
i spendere
n uitgeven

1258 expenditure; outlay; spending
d Aufwand *m*; Verausgabung *f*
e desembolso *m*; gasto *m*
f dépense *f*
i dispendio *m*; spesa *f*
n besteding *f*; uitgave *f*

1259 expense account
d Aufwandskonto *n*; Spesenkonto *n*; Unkostenkonto *n*
e cuenta *f* de gastos
f compte *m* de dépenses; compte *m* de(s) frais
i conto *m* spese
n onkostenrekening *f*

1260 **at the expense of**
cf. **chargeable to**
d auf Kosten*
e a costa de; a expensas de; por cuenta de
f aux frais de
i a spese di
n op kosten van
* Genitive or von.

1261 **expenses**
cf. **charges, disbursements**
d Aufwendungen *fpl*; Ausgaben *fpl*; Spesen *fpl*; Unkosten *pl*
e gastos *mpl*
f dépenses *fpl*; frais *mpl*
i spese *fpl*
n onkosten *mpl*; uitgaven *fpl*

1262 **expiration** *(rare)*; **expiry; term**
cf. **currency, date due, maturity**
d Ablauf *m*; Ablaufzeit *f*; Erlöschen *n*; Termin *m*
e expiración *f*; término *m*
f déchéance *f*; expiration *f*; terme *m*
i scadenza *f*; termine *m*
n afloop *m*; termijn *m*; verstrijking *f*

1263 **expiration date; expiry date**
cf. **date due**
d Ablaufstag *m*; Ablaufstermin *m*
e fecha *f* de expiración; plazo *m* de expiración
f date *f* d'expiration; jour *m* de déchéance; jour *m* d'expiration
i data *f* di scadenza; giorno *m* di scadenza; termine *m* di scadenza
n datum *m* van afloop

1264 **expire** *v*
cf. **become** *v* **due**
d ablaufen; erlöschen; verfallen; verstreichen
e expirar; vencer
f échoir; expirer; venir à expiration
i decorrere; scadere; spirare
n aflopen; verlopen; verstrijken

1265 **export; exportation**
d Ausfuhr *f*; Export *m*
e exportación *f*
f exportation *f*
i esportazione *f*
n export *m*; uitvoer *m*

1266 **export commodities; export goods**
d Ausfuhrartikel *mpl*; Ausfuhrgüter *npl*; Ausfuhrwaren *fpl*; Exportartikel *mpl*; Exportgüter *npl*; Exportwaren *fpl*
e artículos *mpl* de exportación; mercancías *fpl* de exportación
f articles *mpl* d'exportation; marchandises *fpl* d'exportation
i articoli *mpl* d'esportazione; merci *fpl* d'esportazione
n exportartikelen *npl*; exportgoederen *npl*; exportwaren *fpl*; uitvoerartikelen *npl*; uitvoergoederen *npl*; uitvoerwaren *fpl*

1267 **export credit(s) guarantee**
d Ausfuhrkreditgarantie *f*; Exportkreditgarantie *f*; Exportrisikogarantie *f*
e garantía *f* de crédito a la exportación
f garantie *f* de crédit à l'exportation
i garanzia *f* di credito all'esportazione
n exportgarantie *f*; exportkredietgarantie *f*

1268 **export licence** *(UK)*; **export license** *(US)*; **export permit**
d Ausfuhrbewilligung *f*; Ausfuhrerlaubnis *f*; Ausfuhrgenehmigung *f*; Ausfuhrlizenz *f*; Exportbewilligung *f*; Exporterlaubnis *f*; Exportgenehmigung *f*; Exportlizenz *f*
e autorización *f* para exportar; licencia *f* de exportación; permiso *m* de exportación
f autorisation *f* d'exportation; licence *f* d'exportation; permis *m* de sortie; permis *m* d'exportation; permis *m* d'exporter
i autorizzazione *f* d'esportazione; licenza *f* d'esportazione; permesso *m* d'esportazione
n exportbewilliging *f*; exportconsent *n*; exportlicentie *f*; exportvergunning *f*; uitvoerbewilliging *f*; uitvoerconsent *n*; uitvoerlicentie *f*; uitvoervergunning *f*

1269 **export subsidy**
cf. **bounty on exportation**
d Ausfuhrbeihilfe *f*; Ausfuhrsubvention *f*; Exportbeihilfe *f*; Exportsubvention *f*
e subsidio *m* a la exportación; subvención *f* a la exportación
f subvention *f* à l'exportation
i sovvenzione *f* all'esportazione
n exportsubsidie *f*; uitvoersubsidie *f/n*

1270 **expropriate** *v*
d enteignen; expropiieren
e expropiar
f exproprier
i espropriare
n expropriëren; onteigenen

1271 **expropriation**
d Enteignung *f*; Expropriation *f*; Expropiierung *f*

e expropiación *f*
f expropriation *f*
i espropriazione *f*; esproprio *m*
n expropriatie *f*; onteigening *f*

1272 **extend** *v* **a credit; prolong** *v* **a credit; renew** *v* **a credit**
d einen Kredit prolongieren; einen Kredit stillhalten; einen Kredit verlängern
e prolongar un crédito; prorrogar un crédito; renovar un crédito
f atermoyer un crédit; prolonger un crédit; proroger un crédit; renouveler un crédit
i prorogare un credito; rinnovare un credito
n een krediet prolongeren; een krediet verlengen

1273 **extend** *v* **a term; prolong** *v* **a term**
d eine Frist prolongieren; eine Frist verlängern
e prolongar un término; prorrogar un término
f prolonger un terme; proroger un terme
i prorogare un termine
n een termijn prolongeren; een termijn verlengen

1274 **extend** *v* **the time of payment; grant** *v* **a respite for payment; respite** *v* **a payment**
d die Zahlungsfrist verlängern; einen Zahlungsaufschub bewilligen; einen Zahlungsaufschub gewähren; einen Zahlungsaufschub zugestehen; eine Zahlung stunden
e acordar una prórroga para un pago; acordar un plazo para un pago; acordar un respiro para un pago; conceder una prórroga para un pago; conceder un plazo para un pago; conceder un respiro para un pago; prorrogar el plazo de pago; prorrogar un pago
f accorder un délai de paiement; accorder un répit de paiement; accorder un sursis de paiement; admettre un atermoiement; atermoyer un paiement; proroger le terme de paiement; proroger un paiement
i accordare una dilazione di pagamento; accordare una proroga di pagamento; accordare unrespiro di pagamento; prorogare il termine di pagamento; prorogare un pagamento
n de betalingstermijn verlengen; uitstel van betaling verlenen

1275 **extension of credit; prolongation of credit; renewal of credit**
d Kreditprolongation *f*; Kreditverlängerung *f*; Stillhaltung *f* eines Kredits
e prolongación *f* de un crédito; prórroga *f* de un crédito; renovación *f* de un crédito
f prolongation *f* d un crédit; prorogation *f* (de la durée) d'un crédit; renouvellement *m* d'un crédit
i proroga *f* d'un credito; rinnovo *m* d'un credito
n kredietverlenging *f*; prolongatie *f* van een krediet

1276 **extension of time for payment; moratorium; respite for payment; suspension of payment**
cf. **delay, standstill agreement**
d Moratorium *n*; Stundungsfrist *f*; Zahlungsaufschub *m*; Zahlungsfristverlängerung *f*; Zahlungsstundung *f*
e aplazamiento *m* de pago; moratoria *f*; prórroga *f* (del plazo) de pago; respiro *m* de pago; suspensión *f* de pago
f atermoiement *m*; moratoire *m*; moratorium *m*; prorogation *f* du délai de paiement; répit *m* de paiement; sursis *m* de paiement; suspension *f* de paiement
i differimento *m* di pagamento; dilazione *f* di pagamento; moratoria *f*; proroga *f* di pagamento; respiro *m* di pagamento; sospensione *f* di pagamento
n betalingsuitstel *n*; moratorium *n*; opschorting *f* van betaling; surséance *f* van betaling; uitstel *n* van betaling

1277 **external balance; external trade balance; foreign balance; foreign trade balance**
d Aussenhandelssaldo *m*; Leistungsbilanzsaldo *m*
e saldo *m* del comercio exterior; saldo *m* exterior
f solde *m* des échanges extérieurs; solde *m* extérieur
i saldo *m* degli scambi con l'estero; saldo *m* con l'estero
n exportsaldo *n*; uitvoersaldo *n*

1278 **external convertibility; non-resident convertibility**
d Ausländerkonvertibilität *f*; Ausländerkonvertierbarkeit *f*; äussere Konvertibilität *f*; äussere Konvertierbarkeit *f*; externe Konvertibilität *f*; externe Konvertierbarkeit *f*
e convertibilidad *f* externa
f convertibilité *f* extérieure; convertibilité *f* externe
i convertibilità *f* esterna
n externe convertibiliteit *f*

1279 external customs tariff; external tariff
d Aussentarif *m*
e arancel *m* (aduanero) exterior; tarifa *f* (aduanera) exterior
f tarif *m* (douanier) extérieur
i tariffa *f* (doganale) esterna
n buitentarief *n*

1280 external debt; foreign debt
d Auslandsschuld *f*
e deuda *f* exterior; deuda *f* externa
f dette *f* extérieure
i debito *m* estero
n buitenlandse schuld *f*

1281 external financing; financing with borrowed funds; financing with outside funds; outside financing
d Aussenfinanzierung *f*; Finanzierung *f* mit Fremdkapital; Fremdfinanzierung *f*
e financiación *f* con fondos ajenos; financiación *f* con fondos externos; financiación *f* externa; financiamiento *m* con fondos ajenos; financiamiento *m* con fondos externos; financiamiento *m* externo
f financement *m* extérieur; financement *m* par des fonds empruntés; financement *m* par des fonds extérieurs
i finanziamento *m* con capitali altrui; finanziamento *m* esterno
n externe financiering *f*; financiering *f* met vreemd vermogen

1282 external loan; foreign loan
d Auslandsanleihe *f*; äussere Anleihe *f*; auswärtige Anleihe *f*
e empréstito *m* en el extranjero; empréstito *m* exterior; empréstito *m* externo
f emprunt *m* extérieur
i prestito *m* all'estero; prestito *m* estero
n buitenlandse lening *f*; lening *f* in het buitenland

1283 external trade; foreign trade; oversea(s) trade
d Aussenhandel *m*; Aussenwirtschaft *f*; auswärtiger Handel *m*; Handel *m* mit dem Ausland; Überseehandel *m*; überseeischer Handel *m*
e comercio *m* de ultramar; comercio *m* exterior
f commerce *m* d'outre-mer; commerce *m* extérieur; échanges *mpl* extérieurs
i commercio *m* con l'estero; commercio *m* d'oltremare; commercio *m* estero; scambi *mpl* con l'estero
n buitenlandse handel *m*; handel *m* op het buitenland; overzeese handel *m*

1284 extra allowance; fringe benefit; special allowance
cf. **extra pay**
d Extravergütung *f*; Nebenvergütung *f*; Sondervergütung *f*; zusätzliche Vergütung *f*
e remuneración *f* accesoria; remuneración *f* adicional; remuneración *f* especial; remuneración *f* suplementaria
f rémunération *f* accessoire; rémunération *f* spéciale; rémunération *f* supplémentaire
i remunerazione *f* accessoria; remunerazione *f* addizionale; remunerazione *f* speciale; remunerazione *f* supplementare; rimunerazione *f* accessoria; rimunerazione *f* addizionale; rimunerazione *f* speciale; rimunerazione *f* supplementare
n bijkomende vergoeding *f*; extra-vergoeding *f*; speciale vergoeding *f*

1285 extra benefit; fringe benefit
d Ergänzungsleistung *f*; Mehrleistung *f*; Nebenleistung *f*; Zusatzleistung *f*; zusätzliche Leistung *f*
e prestación *f* adicional; prestación *f* suplementaria
f avantage *m* accessoire; avantage *m* complémentaire; avantage *m* extra-légal; prestation *f* complémentaire; prestation *f* supplémentaire
i prestazione *f* addizionale; prestazione *f* supplementare
n bijkomende prestatie *f*; bijkomend voordeel *n*; extra-legaal voordeel *n (B)*

1286 extra-budgetary
d ausseretatmässig
e extrapresupuestario
f extra-budgétaire; hors budget
i estrabudgetario; extrabudgetario; fuori bilancio
n buiten de begroting (om); extrabudgettair

1287 extraordinary receipts; non-recurrent receipts; non-recurring receipts
d ausserordentliche Einnahmen *fpl*; einmalige Einnahmen *fpl*; nicht wiederkehrende Einnahmen *fpl*; Sondereinnahmen *fpl*
e ingresos *mpl* extraordinarios; ingresos *mpl* no recurrentes
f recettes *fpl* extraordinaires; recettes *fpl* non périodiques; recettes *fpl* non récurrentes

i entrate *fpl* non ricorrenti; entrate *fpl* straordinarie
n buitengewone inkomsten *fpl*; niet terugkerende inkomsten *fpl*

1288 extra pay
cf. **bonus, extra allowance**
d Draufgabe *f*; Draufgeld *n*; Gehaltszulage *f*; Überlohn *m*; Zulage *f*
e sobrepaga *f*; sobresueldo *m*
f surpaie *f*; surpaye *f*; sursalaire *m*
i soprappaga *f*
n extrabetaling *f*; loontoeslag *m*; overloon *n*

F

1289 **face value; nominal value**
cf. **denomination, parity value**
d Nennwert *m*; Nominalnennwert *m*; Nominalwert *m*
e valor *m* nominal
f valeur *f* nominale
i valore *m* nominale
n nominale waarde *f*

1290 **face value of a share; nominal value of a share**
d Nennwert *m* einer Aktie
e nominal *m* de una acción; valor *m* nominal de una acción
f nominal *m* d'une action; valeur *f* nominale d'une action
i valore *m* nominale di una azione
n nominale waarde *f* van een aandeel

1291 **at factor cost**
cf. **at cost**
d zu Faktorkosten
e al costo de los factores
f aux coûts des facteurs
i al costo dei fattori
n tegen factorkosten

1292 **factor income**
d Faktoreinkommen *n*
e ingresos *mpl* de los factores
f revenu *m* des facteurs
i reddito *m* da fattori
n factoorinkomen *n*; factorinkomen *n*

1293 **factoring**
d Factoring *n*; Faktorengeschäft *n*; Faktorgeschäft *n*; Forderungsabkauf *m*
e factoring *m*; factorización *f*
f factoring *m*
i factoring *m*; fattorizzazione *f*
n factoorsbedrijf *n*; factoring *f*

1294 **fall** *v* **into debt; get** *v* **into debt; run** *v* **into debt**
d in Schulden geraten; in Schulden stecken; sich verschulden
e adeudar; endeudarse
f s'endetter
i indebitarsi
n in de schuld(en) zitten; zich in de schuld(en) steken

1295 **fee(s)**
cf. **emoluments, recompense**
d Gebühren *fpl*; Honorar *n*
e honorarios *mpl*
f droits *mpl*; honoraires *mpl*
i onorario *m*
n ereloon *n*; honorarium *n*

1296 **fiat money; fiduciary money; token money**
cf. **folding money**
d Zeichengeld *n*
e moneda *f* fiduciaria
f monnaie *f* conventionnelle; monnaie *f* fictive; monnaie *f* fiduciaire; monnaie *f* obsidionale *(rare)*
i moneta *f* fiduciaria; moneta *f* fittizia
n fiduciair geld *n*; tekengeld *n*

1297 **fictional assets; fictitious assets**
d fictive Aktiva *npl*; Scheinaktiva *npl*
e activo *m* ficticio
f actif *m* fictif
i attivo *m* fittizio
n fictieve activa *npl*

1298 **fiduciary; trustee**
d Treuhänder *m*
e fideicomisario *m*; fiduciario *m*
f fiduciaire *m*; fiduciant *m (Schw)*
i fiduciario *m*; trustee *m*
n trustee *m*

1299 **fiduciary circulation**
cf. **bank notes in circulation, circulation of notes and coin(s)**
d fiduziärer Notenumlauf *m*; fiduziärer Umlauf *m*; fiduziarischer Notenumlauf *m*; fiduziarischer Umlauf *m*; Papiergeldumlauf *m*
e circulación *f* fiduciaria
f circulation *f* fiduciaire
i circolazione *f* fiduciaria
n fiduciaire circulatie *f*

1300 **fiduciary issue**
d fiduziäre Notenausgabe *f*; fiduziarische Notenausgabe *f*; ungedeckte Notenausgabe *f*
e emisión *f* fiduciaria
f émission *f* fiduciaire
i emissione *f* fiduciaria
n fiduciaire emissie *f*; fiduciaire uitgifte *f*

1301 **fiduciary loan; loan without security; uncovered loan; unsecured loan**
cf. **blank credit**
d Darleh(e)n *n* ohne Deckung; fiduziarisches Darleh(e)n *n*; nicht gesichertes Darleh(e)n *n*; ungedecktes Darleh(e)n *n*; ungesichertes Darleh(e)n *n*
e préstamo *m* fiduciario; préstamo *m* no cubierto; préstamo *m* no garantizado;

préstamo *m* sin garantía
f prêt *m* à découvert; prêt *m* fiduciaire; prêt *m* non couvert; prêt *m* non gagé; prêt *m* non garanti; prêt *m* sans garantie
i prestito *m* allo scoperto; prestito *m* fiduciario; prestito *m* libero; prestito *m* non coperto; prestito *m* non garantito
n fiduciaire lening *f*; lening *f* zonder dekking; ongedekte lening *f*

1302 final balance sheet; list of closing balances
d Schlussbilanz *f*
e balance *m* de cierre; balance *m* final
f bilan *m* de clôture; bilan *m* définitif
i bilancio *m* di chiusura; bilancio *m* finale
n slotbalans *f*; sluitingsbalans *f*

1303 final dividend
d Abschlussdividende *f*; Restdividende *f*; Schlussdividende *f*
e complemento *m* de dividendo; dividendo *m* de liquidación; dividendo *m* final
f complément *m* de dividende; dividende *m* final; solde *m* de dividende
i dividendo *m* finale; saldo *m* (di) dividendo
n slotdividend *n*

1304 finance; finances; financial economy; financial system
d Finanzen *fpl*; Finanzwesen *n*; Finanzwirtschaft *f*; Geldwesen *n*; Geldwirtschaft *f*
e economía *f* financiera; finanzas *fpl*; sistema *m* financiero
f économie *f* financière; finance(s) *f(pl)*; système *m* financier
i economia *f* finanziaria; finanza *f*; finanze *fpl*; sistema *m* finanziario
n financiën *pl*; financies *pl*; financiewezen *n*; geldwezen *n*

1305 finance; financial circles; financial community; financial world; world of finance
d Finanz *f*; Finanzkreise *mpl*; Finanzwelt *f*
e círculos *mpl* financieros; mundo *m* de las finanzas; mundo *m* financiero
f finance *f*; milieux *mpl* financiers; monde *m* de la finance; monde *m* financier
i circoli *mpl* finanziari; finanza *f*; mondo *m* della finanza; mondo *m* finanziario
n financiële kringen *mpl*; financiële wereld *f*; geldwereld *f*

1306 finance *v*
d finanzieren
e financiar
f financer
i finanziare
n financieren

1307 finance bill; financial bill; financial paper
d Finanzierungswechsel *m*; Finanzwechsel *m*
e efecto *m* financiero; papel *m* financiero
f effet *m* de finance; effet *m* de financement; papier *m* financier
i carta *f* finanziaria; effetto *m* finanziario
n financiële wissel *m*; financieringswissel *m*

1308 finance company; finance house
cf. **closed-end investment company**
d Finanzgesellschaft *f*; Finanzierungsgesellschaft *f*
e compañía *f* de financiación; compañía *f* financiera; sociedad *f* de financiación; sociedad *f* financiera
f compagnie *f* de financement; société *f* de finance; société *f* de financement; société *f* financière
i compagnia *f* finanziatrice; società *f* di finanziamento; società *f* finanziaria
n financieringsmaatschappij *f*

1309 financial adviser; financial advisor; financial consultant
d Finanzbeirat *m*; Finanzberater *m*; Finanzkonsulent *m*
e consejero *m* financiero; consultor *m* financiero
f conseil *m* financier; conseiller *m* financier; consultant *m* financier
i consigliere *m* finanziario; consulente *m* finanziario
n financiële adviseur *m*; financiële consulent *m*

1310 financial aid; financial assistance
d Finanzbeihilfe *f*; finanzielle Beihilfe *f*; finanzielle Hilfe *f*
e asistencia *f* financiera; ayuda *f* financiera
f aide *f* financière; assistance *f* financière
i aiuto *m* finanziario; assistenza *f* finanziaria
n financiële bijstand *m*; financiële hulp *f*; financiële steun *m*

1311 financial broker; money broker
d Finanzmakler *m*; Geldhändler *m*; Geldmakler *m*; Geldvermittler *m*

e agente *m* financiero; corredor *m* de dinero; corredor *m* financiero
f agent *m* de change; courtier *m* de change
i mediatore *m* di capitali
n geldhandelaar *m*; geldmakelaar *m*

1312 **financial budget; financial program** *(US)*; **financial programme** *(UK)*; **financial scheme**
d Finanzanschlag *m*; Finanzhaushalt *m*; Finanzierungsplan *m*; Finanzplan *m*; Finanzprogramm *n*
e plan *m* de financiación; plan *m* financiero; presupuesto *m* financiero; programa *m* de financiación; programa *m* financiero
f budget *m* financier; plan *m* de financement; plan *m* financier; programme *m* de financement; programme *m* financier
i bilancio *m* finanziario; piano *m* di finanziamento; piano *m* finanziario; programma *m* di finanziamento; programma *m* finanziario
n financieel budget *n*; financieringsbegroting *f*

1313 **financial burden; financial charges; financial expenses; financial outlays; financing charges** *(US)*; **financing costs** *(US)*
d Finanzaufwendungen *fpl*; finanzielle Belastung *f*
e cargas *fpl* financieras; gastos *mpl* financieros
f charges *fpl* financières; frais *mpl* financiers
i oneri *mpl* finanziari; spese *fpl* finanziarie
n financiële lasten *mpl (B)*; financieringskosten *mpl*

1314 **financial difficulties; financial embarrassment; financial straits; financial trouble; money squeeze; pecuniary difficulties**
d finanzielle Schwierigkeiten *fpl*; Geldklemme *f*; Geldnot *f*; Geldschwierigkeiten *fpl*; Geldverlegenheit *f*
e apuro(s) *m(pl)* económico(s); apuro(s) *m(pl)* financiero(s); dificultades *fpl* económicas; dificultades *fpl* financieras; dificultades *fpl* monetarias; dificultades *fpl* pecuniarias
f difficultés *fpl* d'argent; difficultés *fpl* de trésorerie; difficultés *fpl* financières; difficultés *fpl* pécuniaires; embarras *m(pl)* d'argent; embarras *m(pl)* financier(s); embarras *m(pl)* pécuniaire(s); gêne *f* pécuniare
i difficoltà *fpl* finanziarie; imbarazzi *mpl* finanziari; imbarazzo *m* finanziario; stretta *f* finanziaria; stretta *f* monetaria
n financiële moeilijkheden *fpl*; geldelijke moeilijkheden *fpl*; geldnood *m*; geldverlegenheid *f*

1315 **financial house; financial institution**
d Finanzinstitut *n*; Geldinstitut *n*
e establecimiento *m* financiero; instituto *m* financiero
f établissement *m* financier; institut *m* financier
i istituto *m* finanziario
n financiële instelling *f*

1316 **financial needs; financial requirements**
d Finanzierungsbedarf *m*; Finanzierungsbedürfnisse *npl*
e necesidades *fpl* financieras
f besoins *mpl* de financement; besoins *mpl* financiers
i fabbisogni *mpl* di finanziamento; fabbisogni *mpl* finanziari
n financieringsbehoeften *fpl*

1317 **financial policy**
cf. **conduct of the finances**
d Finanzpolitik *f*
e política *f* financiera
f politique *f* financière
i politica *f* finanziaria
n financiële politiek *f*

1318 **financial reconstruction; financial rehabilitation; financial reorganization; reconstruction of the finances; rehabilitation of the finances; reorganization of the finances**
d finanzielle Gesundung *f*; finanzielle Sanierung *f*; Sanierung *f* der Finanzen
e reorganización *f* financiera; saneamiento *m* financiero
f assainissement *m* des finances; redressement *m* financier; réorganisation *f* financière
i riorganizzazione *f* finanziaria; risanamento *m* finanziario
n financiële reorganisatie *f*; rehabilitatie *f* van de financiën; reorganisatie *f* van de financiën; sanering *f* van de financiën

1319 **financial statement**
d Finanzausweis *m*; Finanzbericht *m*; Finanzstatus *m*; Finanzübersicht *f*
e estado *m* financiero; informe *m* financiero; relación *f* sobre las finanzas

f état *m* des finances; état *m* financier; situation *f* de trésorerie
i prospetto *m* finanziario; situazione *f* finanziaria; stato *m* finanziario
n financieel bericht *n*; financieel overzicht *n*; financiële staat *m*

1320 **financial year**
cf. **budgetary year, business year, company financial year, fiscal year**
d Finanzjahr *n*; Rechnungsjahr *n*; Wirtschaftsjahr *n*
e año *m* económico; año *m* financiero; ejercicio *m* (financiero)
f année *f* comptable; année *f* financière; exercice *m* (comptable); exercice *m* (financier)
i anno *m* contabile; anno *m* d'esercizio; anno *m* economico; anno *m* finanziario; esercizio *m* (finanziario)
n boekjaar *n*; financieel jaar *n*

1321 **financier**
cf. **capitalist, moneylender**
d Finanzier *m*; Finanzmann *m*
e financiero *m*
f financier *m*; homme *m* de finance
i finanziere *m*; finanziatore *m*
n financier *m*

1322 **financing**
d Finanzierung *f*
e financiación *f*; financiamiento *m*
f financement *m*
i finanziamento *m*
n financiering *f*

1323 **fine bill *(UK)*; fine trade bill *(UK)*; first-class bill; first-class paper; prime bill *(US)*; prime trade bill *(US)***
cf. **"bill" for synonyms, first of exchange**
d erstklassiger Wechsel *m*; erstklassiges Handelspapier *n*; Primadiskont *m*; Primahandelspapier *n*; Primapapier *n*; prima Wechsel *m**; Privatdiskont *m*
e efecto *m* de primera clase; efecto *m* de primer orden
f effet *m* de première banque; effet *m* de (tout) premier ordre; papier *m* de haut commerce
i carta *f* di prim'ordine; effetto *m* di prim'ordine
n eersteklaswissel *m*; prima handelspapier *n*

* Rare in this sense.

1324 **fine gold**
d Feingold *n*
e oro *m* de ley; oro *m* fino
f or *m* fin
i oro *m* fino
n fijn goud *n*

1325 **fineness**
cf. **gold content**
d Feingehalt *m*; Feinheit *f*
e ley *f*; título *m* (legal)
f titre *m*
i finezza *f*; fino *m*; lega *f*; titolo *m* (legale)
n gehalte *n* (aan edel metaal)

1326 **firmness of prices; price stability; steadiness of prices**
d Preisbehauptung *f*; Preisbeständigkeit *f*; Preisfestigkeit *f*; Preisstabilität *f*
e estabilidad *f* de los precios; firmeza *f* de los precios
f fermeté *f* des prix; solidité *f* des prix; stabilité *f* des prix
i fermezza *f* dei prezzi; stabilità *f* dei prezzi
n bestendigheid *f* van de prijzen; prijsstabiliteit *f*; vastheid *f* van de prijzen

1327 **first of exchange**
d Erstausfertigung *f*; Prima *m/f* Primawechsel *m*; Wechselprima *m/f*
e primera *f* (de cambio)
f première *f* de change
i prima *f* di cambio
n prima *f*; primawissel *m*

1328 **first right; preference; preferential right; priority; priority right; right of preference; right of priority**
cf. **application right**
d Priorität *f*; Prioritätsrecht *n*; Vorrecht *n*; Vorzugsrecht *n*
e derecho *m* de preferencia; derecho *m* de prioridad; derecho *m* preferente; preferencia *f*
f droit *m* de préférence; droit *m* de priorité; droit *m* préférentiel; préférence *f*
i diritto *m* di poziorità; diritto *m* di preferenza; diritto *m* di priorità
n prioriteitsrecht *n*; recht *n* van voorkeur; voorkeurrecht *n*

1329 **fiscal**
d Fiskal-; fiskalisch
e fiscal
f fiscal
i fiscale
n fiscaal

1330 **fiscal deficit; shortfall in (of) tax revenue; tax deficit**

d Steuerausfall *m*; Steuerdefizit *n*
e déficit *m* de impuestos; déficit *m* de (en) la recaudación fiscal; déficit *m* fiscal
f déficit *m* des recouvrements fiscaux; déficit *m* fiscal; moins-perçu *m* d'impôts
i ammanco *m* fiscale; deficit *m* fiscale
n belastingtekort *n*; tekort *n* van de belastingopbrengst

1331 **fiscal domicile**
d steuerlicher Wohnsitz
e domicilio *m* fiscal
f domicile *m* fiscal
i domicilio *m* fiscale
n fiscaal domicilie *n*; fiscale zetel *m*

1332 **fiscal instrument**
d fiskalpolitisches Instrument *n*; steuerpolitisches Instrument *n*
e instrumento *m* fiscal
f instrument *m* fiscal
i strumento *m* fiscale
n fiscaal instrument *n*

1333 **fiscal regulator**
d Steuerregulator *m*
e regulador *m* fiscal
f régulateur *m* fiscal
i regolatore *m* fiscale
n fiscale regelaar *m*; fiscale regulator *m*

1334 **fiscal system; taxation system; tax system**
d Fiskalität *f*; Fiskalwesen *n*; Steuersystem *n*; Steuerwesen *n*
e régimen *m* fiscal; régimen *m* tributario; sistema *m* de contribuciones; sistema *m* fiscal; sistema *m* tributario
f fiscalité *f*; régime *m* fiscal; système *m* de taxation; système *m* d'impôts; système *m* fiscal
i fiscalità *f*; regime *m* fiscale; sistema *m* fiscale; sistema *m* tributario
n belastingstelsel *n*; belastingsystem *n*; fiscaliteit *f*

1335 **fiscal year; tax year**
cf. **budgetary year, financial year**
d Fiskaljahr *n*; Steuerjahr *n*
e año *m* fiscal; ejercicio *m* fiscal
f année *f* fiscale; exercice *m* fiscal
i anno *m* fiscale; anno *m* tributario; esercizio *m* fiscale; esercizio *m* tributario
n belastingjaar *n*; fiscaal jaar *n*

1336 **fixed costs; fixed expenses**
d Ausgabekonstanten *fpl*; feste Ausgaben *fpl*; feste Kosten *pl*; feste Unkosten *pl*; Festkosten *pl*; festliegende Kosten *pl*; fixe Kosten *pl*
e costes *mpl* constantes; costes *mpl* fijos; gastos *mpl* constantes; gastos *mpl* fijos
f charges *fpl* fixes; dépenses *fpl* fixes; frais *mpl* fixes
i spese *fpl* constanti; spese *fpl* fisse
n constante kosten *mpl*; vaste kosten *mpl*

1337 **fixed deposit; fixed-period deposit; money lent for fixed period; time deposit**
d befristete Einlage *f*; Einlage *f* mit fester Laufzeit *f*; feste Einlage *f*; festes Geld *n*; Festgeld *n*; gebundene Einlage *f*; Termindepositum *n*; Termineinlage *f*; Termingeld *n*; Zeitdepositum *n*; Zeiteinlage *f*; Zeitgeld *n*
e depósito *m* a plazo (fijo); depósito *m* a término; depósito *m* a (de) vencimiento fijo; dinero *m* a plazo (fijo); dinero *m* a término
f argent *m* à echéance (fixe); argent *m* à terme (fixe); dépôt *m* à échéance (fixe); dépôt *m* à temps *(C)*; dépôt *m* à terme (fixe)
i denaro *m* a termine (fisso); deposito *m* a scadenza fissa; deposito *m* a termine (fisso); deposito *m* vincolato
n deposito *n* met (op) (vaste) termijn; termijndeposito *n*; termijngeld *n*

1338 **fixed interest** *(adj.)*; **fixed interest bearing; fixed yield** *(adj.)*
d festverzinslich
e a interés fijo; de interés fijo; de renta fija
f à intérêt fixe; à revenu fixe; rapportant un intérêt fixe
i a interesse fisso; a reddito fisso; a tasso fisso
n met vaste rente; vast renderend; vast rentend

1339 **fixed interest bearing security; fixed interest security; fixed yield security**
cf. **annuity bond, bond**
d Agiopapier *n**; festverzinslicher Titel *m*; festverzinsliches Wertpapier *n*
e título *m* a (de) interés fijo; título *m* de renta fija; valor *m* a (de) interés fijo; valor *m* de renta fija
f titre *m* à revenu(s) fixe(s); valeur *f* à revenu(s) fixe(s)
i titolo *m* a reddito fisso; valore *m* a reddito fisso
n vast renderend waardepapier *n*; vast rentend waardepapier *n*; waardepapier *n* met (een) vaste rente

* Redeemable at a premium.

1340 fixed investment
d Anlageinvestition *f*; feste Anlage *f*; feste Investition *f*
e inversión *f* fija; inversión *f* inmovilizada
f investissement *m* fixe; investissement *m* immobilisé
i investimento *m* fisso; investimento *m* immobilizzato
n vaste investering *f*

1341 fixed rate of exchange
d festgesetzter Wechselkurs *m*
e tipo *m* de cambio fijo
f cours *m* de change fixe; taux *m* de change fixe
i corso *m* di cambio fisso; tasso *m* di cambio fisso
n vaste wisselkoers *m*

1342 fixing a ceiling; setting a ceiling
d Festsetzung *f* einer Höchstgrenze; Festsetzung *f* eines Plafonds
e fijación *f* de un máximo
f plafonnement *m*
i fissazione *f* di un massimale
n vastlegging *f* van een plafon(d); vaststelling *f* van een plafon(d)

1343 fixing of parity rates
d Festsetzung *f* der Paritätsverhältnisse
e fijación *f* de las razones de paridad
f fixation *f* des rapports de parité
i fissazione *f* dei rapporti di parità
n vaststelling *f* van de pariteitsverhoudingen

1344 flat price; uniform price
cf. **normal price, unit price**
d Einheitspreis *m*
e precio *m* único
f prix *m* unique; uniprix *m*
i prezzo *m* unico
n eenheidsprijs *m*

1345 flat rate
d Einheitssatz *m*
e tasa *f* uniforme
f taux *m* uniforme
i tasso *m* unitario
n eenheidsvoet *m*

1346 flexibility margin between exchange rates; fluctuation margin in exchange rates; margin of fluctuation for exchange rates
d Bandbreite *f* der Wechselkurse; Bandbreite *f* der Wechselkursschwankungen
e banda *f* de fluctuación de los tipos de cambio; margen *m/f* de fluctuación de los tipos de cambio
f marge *f* de fluctuation des cours; marge *f* de fluctuation des taux de change
i margine *m* di fluttuazione dei corsi; margine *m* di fluttuazione dei tassi di cambio
n fluctuatiemarge *f* tussen de wisselkoersen; marge *f* voor de fluctuatie van de wisselkoersen

1347 flexible rate of exchange; floating rate of exchange; fluctuating rate of exchange; free rate of exchange; variable rate of exchange
d flexibler Wechselkurs *m*; floatender Wechselkurs *m*; fluktuierender Wechselkurs *m*; freier Wechselkurs *m*; schwankender Wechselkurs *m*; variabler Wechselkurs *m*; veränderlicher Wechselkurs *m*
e tipo *m* de cambio flexible; tipo *m* de cambio flotante; tipo *m* de cambio fluctuante; tipo *m* de cambio libre; tipo *m* de cambio oscilante; tipo *m* de cambio variable
f cours *m* de change flexible; cours *m* de change flottant; cours *m* de change fluctuant; cours *m* de change libre; cours *m* de change oscillant; cours *m* de change variable; taux *m* de change flexible; taux *m* de change flottant; taux *m* de change fluctuant; taux *m* de change libre; taux *m* de change oscillant; taux *m* de change variable
i corso *m* dei cambi flessibile; corso *m* dei cambi flottante; corso *m* dei cambi fluttuante; corso *m* dei cambi libero; corso *m* dei cambi oscillante; corso *m* dei cambi variabile; tasso *m* di cambio flessibile; tasso *m* di cambio flottante; tasso *m* di cambio fluttuante; tasso *m* di cambio libero; tasso *m* di cambio oscillante; tasso *m* di cambio variabile
n flexibele wisselkoers *m*; fluctuerende wisselkoers *m*; schommelende wisselkoers *m*; variabele wisselkoers *m*; vlottende wisselkoers *m*; vrije wisselkoers *m*; wisselende valutakoers *m*; zwevende wisselkoers *m*

1348 flexible scale; sliding scale
d bewegliche Skala *f*; gleitende Skala *f*
e escala *f* móvil
f échelle *f* mobile
i scala *f* mobile
n glijdende schaal *f*

1349 flight capital
d Fluchtgelder *npl*; Fluchtkapital *n*

e capital *m* de evasión; capital *m* evadido
f capitaux *mpl* d'évasion; capitaux *mpl* fugitifs
i capitale *m* d'evasione; capitale *m* fuggitivo
n vluchtkapitaal *n*

1350 floating currency; fluctuating currency; unstable currency
cf. **soft currency**
d floatende Währung *f*; labile Währung *f*; schwankende Währung *f*; unbeständige Währung *f*; veränderliche Währung *f*
e moneda *f* flotante; moneda *f* inestable; moneda *f* variable
f monnaie *f* flottante; monnaie *f* instable; monnaie *f* variable
i moneta *f* flottante; moneta *f* fluttuante; moneta *f* instabile; moneta *f* variabile
n onstabiele valuta *f*; vlottende valuta *f*; zwevende valuta *f*

1351 floating debt; unfunded debt
d schwebende Schuld *f*; unfundierte Schuld *f*
e deuda *f* flotante; deuda *f* no consolidada
f dette *f* flottante; dette *f* non consolidée
i debito *m* fluttuante; debito *m* non consolidato
n ongefundeerde schuld *f*; vlottende schuld *f*

1352 flotation *(issue, loan etc.)*; **issuance; issue; launch**
cf. **placement**
d Auflegung *f*; Ausgabe *f*; Begebung *f*; Emission *f*; Lancierung *f*
e emisión *f*; lanzamiento *m*
f émission *f*; lancement *m*
i emissione *f*; lanciamento *m*; lancio *m*
n emissie *f*; lancering *f*; uitgifte *f*; uitschrijving *f*

1353 flotation cost; issue costs; issue expenses; issuing costs; issuing expenses
d Ausgabekosten *pl (Schw)*; Begebungskosten *pl*; Emissionskosten *pl*
e costo *m* de emisión; gastos *mpl* de emisión
f coût *m* de l'émission; frais *mpl* d'émission
i costo *m* di emissione; costi *mpl* di emissione; spese *fpl* di emissione
n emissiekosten *mpl*; uitgiftekosten *mpl*

1354 fob; free on board
d fob; franko (an) Bord; frei (an) Bord
e fob; franco (a) bordo
f fob; franco (à) bord
i fob; franco (a) bordo
n fob; vrij aan boord

1355 folding money *(US)*; **paper currency; paper money; soft money** *(US)*
cf. **fiduciary money**
d Papiergeld *n*; Papierwährung *f*
e papel moneda *m*
f monnaie *f* (de) papier*; monnaie-papier *f**; papier-monnaie *m***
i carta *f* moneta; cartamoneta *f*; moneta *f* cartacea
n papieren geld *n*; papiergeld *n*

* Convertible.
** Inconvertible.

1356 forced circulation; forced currency
d Zwangskurs *m*; Zwangsumlauf *m*
e circulación *f* forzada; curso *m* forzoso
f circulation *f* forcée; cours *m* forcé
i circolazione *f* forzosa; corso *m* forzoso
n gedwongen circulatie *f*; gedwongen koers *m*

1357 foreign bill (of exchange)
d ausländische Tratte *f*; ausländischer Wechsel *m*; Auslandstratte *f*; Auslandswechsel *m*
e efecto *m* sobre el extranjero; letra *f* sobre el extranjero
f effet *m* sur l'extérieur; lettre *f* de change (à l'extérieur); traite *f* sur l'extérieur
i cambiale *f* sull'estero; effetto *m* sull'estero; tratta *f* sull'estero
n buitenlandse traite *f*; buitenlandse wissel *m*; papier *n* op het buitenland

1358 foreign business; foreign dealings; foreign operations; foreign transactions
d Auslandsgeschäfte *npl*; Auslandsoperationen *fpl*; Auslandstransaktionen *fpl*; Geschäfte *npl* mit dem Ausland; Operationen *fpl* mit dem Ausland; Transaktionen *fpl* mit dem Ausland
e negocios *mpl* con el extranjero; operaciones *fpl* con el extranjero; transacciones *fpl* con el extranjero
f affaires *fpl* avec l'étranger; opérations *fpl* avec l'étranger; transactions *fpl* avec l'étranger
i affari *mpl* con l'estero; operazioni *fpl* con l'estero; transazioni *fpl* con l'estero
n operaties *fpl* met het buitenland; transacties *fpl* met het buitenland; zaken *fpl* met het buitenland

1359 foreign capital*; foreign owned capital
d ausländisches Kapital *n*; Auslandskapital *n**

e capital *m* extranjero
f capitaux *mpl* étrangers
i capitale *m* estero
n buitenlands kapitaal *n**

* Can also mean capital (held) abroad (q.v.).

1360 foreign creditor
d Auslandsgläubiger *m*
e acreedor *m* extranjero
f créancier *m* étranger
i creditore *m* estero
n buitenlandse crediteur *m*; buitenlandse schuldeiser *m*

1361 foreign currency; foreign exchange; foreign money
cf. **foreign notes and coins**
d ausländisches Geld *n*; ausländische Währung *f*; Devisen *fpl*; fremdes Geld *n*; fremde Währung *f*; Fremdwährung *f*; Valuta *f*
e divisas *fpl*; moneda *f* extranjera; valuta *f* (extranjera)
f devises *fpl*; monnaie *f* étrangère
i divise *fpl*; moneta *f* estera; valuta *f* estera
n buitenlandse munt *f*; buitenlandse valuta *f*; buitenlands geld *n*; deviezen *npl*; valuta *f*; vreemde munt *f*; vreemde valuta *f*; vreemd geld *n*

1362 foreign exchange balances; foreign exchange holdings
d Auslandsguthaben *npl*; Devisenbestand *m*; Devisenguthaben *n*; Valutaguthaben *n*; Valutenguthaben *n*
e existencias *fpl* de divisas
f avoirs *mpl* en devises
i avere *m* in divise; disponibilità *fpl* in divise; disponibilità *fpl* in valuta
n deviezentegoed *n*; deviezenvoorraad *m*

1363 foreign exchange position
d Devisenposition *f*
e posición *f* de divisas
f position *f* devises
i posizione *f* divise
n deviezenpositie *f*

1364 foreign exchange value of the currency
d Devisenwert *m* der Währung
e valor *m* de la moneda en divisa extranjera
f valeur *f* de change de la monnaie
i valore *m* di cambio della moneta
n buitenlandse waarde *f* van de valuta

1365 foreign interest *(of foreigners)**
d ausländische Beteiligung *f*; Auslandsbeteiligung *f**
e participación *f* extranjera
f participation *f* étrangère
i partecipazione *f* estera
n buitenlandse deelneming *f**; buitenlandse participatie *f**

* Can also mean interest abroad (q.v.).

1366 foreign interest*; interest abroad; interest overseas
d Auslandsbeteiligung *f**; Beteiligung *f* im Ausland
e participación *f* en el extranjero
f participation *f* à l'étranger
i partecipazione *f* all'estero
n buitenlandse deelneming *f**; buitenlandse participatie *f**; deelneming *f* in het buitenland; participatie *f* in het buitenland

* Can also mean foreign interest (of foreigners) (q.v.).

1367 foreign investment*; foreign owned investment
d ausländische Anlage *f*; ausländische Investierung *f*; ausländische Investition *f*; Auslandsanlage *f**; Auslandsinvestierung *f**; Auslandsinvestition *f**
e colocación *f* extranjera; inversión *f* extranjera
f investissement *m* étranger; placement *m* étranger
i investimento *m* estero
n buitenlandse belegging *f**; buitenlandse investering *f**; vreemde belegging *f*; vreemde investering *f*

* Can also mean investment abroad (q.v.).

1368 foreign investment*; investment abroad; overseas investment *(UK)*
d Anlage *f* im Ausland; Auslandsanlage *f**; Auslandsinvestierung *f**; Auslandsinvestition *f**; Investierung *f* im Ausland; Investition *f* im Ausland
e colocación *f* en el extranjero; inversión *f* en el extranjero
f investissement *m* à l'étranger; placement *m* à l'étranger
i investimento *m* all'estero
n belegging *f* in het buitenland; buitenlandse belegging *f**; buitenlandse investering *f**; investering *f* in het buitenland

* Can also mean foreign owned investment (q.v.).

1369 foreign notes and coins
cf. **foreign currency**
d ausländische Noten *fpl* und Münzen *fpl*; Sorten *fpl*
e billetes *mpl* y monedas *fpl* extranjeros
f billets *mpl* et espèces *fpl* étrangers
i biglietti *mpl* e monete *fpl* esteri
n buitenlandse biljetten *npl* en munten *fpl*; vreemde biljetten *npl* en munten *fpl*

1370 foreign stock
cf. **assets held abroad**
d Auslandswerte *mpl*
e valores *mpl* extranjeros
f valeurs *fpl* étrangères
i valori *mpl* esteri
n buitenlandse waarden *fpl*

1371 foreign trade bank
cf. **acceptance house, bank of commerce**
d Aussenhandelsbank *f*; Bank *f* für Aussenhandel
e banco *m* (de comercio) exterior
f banque *f* de (pour le) commerce extérieur
i banca *f* di (per il) commercio estero
n bank *f* voor buitenlandse handel; buitenlandse handelsbank *f*

1372 foreign transfer; transfer abroad
d Transfer *m* ins Ausland; Übertragung *f* ins Ausland
e transferencia *f* al exterior
f transfert *m* à l'étranger
i trasferimento *m* all'estero
n overmaking *f* naar het buitenland; transfer *m/n* naar het buitenland

1373 formation of assets
d Vermögensbildung *f*
e formación *f* del patrimonio
f formation *f* de patrimoine
i formazione *f* dei patrimoni
n bezitvorming *f*

1374 formation of savings
d Ersparnisbildung *f*
e formación *f* de ahorros
f formation *f* de l'épargne
i formazione *f* di risparmio
n vorming *f* van spaarmiddelen

1375 form of payment; method of payment; mode of payment
cf. **terms of payment**
d Zahlungsmodalität *f*; Zahlungsmodus *m*; Zahlungsweise *f*
e forma *f* de pago; modalidad *f* de pago; modo *m* de pago
f modalité *f* de paiement; modalité *f* de règlement; mode *m* de paiement; mode *m* de règlement
i modalità *f* di pagamento; modalità *f* di regolamento; modo *m* di pagamento; modo *m* di regolamento
n betalingswijze *f*

1376 forward buying; forward purchase; future purchase *(US)*; purchase for forward delivery; purchase on term; term purchase
cf. **credit buying**
d Kauf *m* auf Lieferung; Lieferungskauf *m*; Terminkauf *m*; Zeitkauf *m*; Zielkauf *m*
e compra *f* a plazo; compra *f* a término; compra *f* para entrega futura
f achat *m* à livrer; achat *m* à terme; achat *m* sur livraison
i acquisto *m* a termine; acquisto *m* per consegna futura
n koop *m* op levering; koop *m* op termijn

1377 forward cover
d Deckung *f* auf Termin
e cobertura *f* a término
f couverture *f* à terme
i copertura *f* a termine
n dekking *f* op termijn

1378 forward currencies; forward exchanges
d Devisen *fpl* auf Termin; Termindevisen *fpl*
e cambios *mpl* a plazo; cambios *mpl* a término; divisas *fpl* a plazo; divisas *fpl* a término
f changes *mpl* à terme; devises *fpl* à terme
i cambi *mpl* a termine; divise *fpl* a termine
n termijndeviezen *npl*; valuta's *fpl* op termijn

1379 forward deal; forward transaction; future; time bargain
cf. **option**
d Distanzgeschäft *n*; Fixgeschäft *n*; Lieferungsgeschäft *n*; Sichtgeschäft *n*; Termingeschäft *n*; Zeitgeschäft *n*
e negocio *m* a la vista; negocio *m* a plazo; negocio *m* a término; operación *f* a la vista; operación *f* a plazo; operación *f* a término; transacción *f* a la vista; transacción *f* a plazo; transacción *f* a término
f affaire *f* à terme; marché *m* à livrer; marché *m* à terme; opération *f* à terme;

opération *f* à vue; transaction *f* à terme; transaction *f* à vue
i affare *m* a termine; affare *m* a vista; contratto *m* a termine; operazione *f* a termine; operazione *f* a vista; transazione *f* a termine; transazione *f* a vista
n termijnaffaire *f*; termijntransactie *f*; termijnzaak *f*; tijdaffaire *f*; tijdtransactie *f*

1380 **forward delivery; future delivery**
d Terminlieferung *f*
e entrega *f* a plazo; entrega *f* a término
f livraison *f* à terme
i consegna *f* a termine
n termijnlevering *f*

1381 **forward exchange deal; forward exchange operation; forward exchange transaction**
cf. **exchange for forward delivery**
d Devisentermingeschäft *n*; Devisentermintransaktion *f*; Termingeschäft *n* in Devisen
e negocio *m* a plazo en moneda extranjera; negocio *m* a término en moneda extranjera; negocio *m* de cambio a plazo; negocio *m* de divisas a término; operación *f* a plazo en moneda extranjera; operación *f* a término con divisas; operación *f* de cambio a plazo; operación *f* de divisas a término; transacción *f* a término en moneda extranjera; transacción *f* de cambio a plazo; transacción *f* de divisas a término
f opération *f* à terme sur les changes; opération *f* à terme sur les devises; opération *f* de change à terme; transaction *f* à terme sur les changes; transaction *f* à terme sur les devises; transaction *f* de change à terme
i operazione *f* a termine su divise; operazione *f* di cambio a termine; transazione *f* a termine su divise; transazione *f* di cambio a termine
n termijnaffaire *f* in deviezen; termijnaffaire *f* in valuta; termijntransactie *f* in deviezen; termijntransactie *f* in valuta; termijnzaak *f* in deviezen; termijnzaak *f* in valuta; valutatermijnaffaire *f*; valutatermijntransactie *f*; valutatermijnzaak *f*

1382 **forward exchange market; forward foreign exchange market**
d Devisenterminmarkt *m*
e mercado *m* de cambios a plazo; mercado *m* de cambios a término; mercado *m* de divisas a plazo; mercado *m* de divisas a término
f marché *m* à terme des changes; marché *m* des changes à terme; marché *m* des devises à terme
i mercato *m* a termine delle divise; mercato *m* dei cambi a termine; mercato *m* delle divise a termine
n termijndeviezenmarkt *f*; valutatermijnmarkt *f*

1383 **forward exchange rate; forward rate; future rate; rate of exchange for forward delivery**
d Devisenterminkurs *m*; Devisenterminsatz *m*; Termindevisenkurs *m*
e cambio *m* a término; tipo *m* de cambio a plazo; tipo *m* de cambio a término
f cours *m* à terme; cours *m* de change à terme; taux *m* à terme; taux *m* de change à terme
i corso *m* a termine; corso *m* di cambio a termine; saggio *m* di cambio a termine; tasso *m* di cambio a termine
n termijndeviezenkoers *m*

1384 **forward price; forward rate; future price; future rate; price for forward delivery**
d Terminkurs *m*; Terminpreis *m*
e cambio *m* a plazo; cambio *m* a término; precio *m* a plazo; precio *m* a término
f cours *m* à terme; prix *m* à terme
i corso *m* a termine; prezzo *m* a termine
n termijnkoers *m*; termijnprijs *m*

1385 **foundation**
d Stiftung *f*
e fundación *f*
f fondation *f*
i fondazione *f*
n stichting *f*

1386 **founders' shares; founders' stocks; management shares; promoters' shares**
d Gründeraktien *fpl*
e acciones *fpl* de fundador; partes *fpl* de fundador
f actions *fpl* d'apport; parts *fpl* de fondateur(s)
i azioni *fpl* di fondazione; azioni *fpl* per i fondatori
n aandelen *npl* voor inbreng in natura *(B)*; oprichtersaandelen *npl*; oprichtersbewijzen *npl*

1387 **fraction of shares; share fraction**
d Aktienspitze *f*; Spitze *f*
e fracción *f* de acciones
f fraction *f* d'actions; rompu *m*

i frazione *f* d'azioni; spezzatura *f* d'azioni
n aandelenfractie *f*

1388 franc area; franc bloc
d Franc-Zone *f*; Frankenblock *m*; Frankengebiet *n*; Frankenraum *m*; Frankenwährungsraum *m*; Frankenzone *f*
e área *f* del franco; bloque *m* del franco; zona *f* del franco
f bloc *m* franc; zone *f* franc
i area *f* del franco; blocco *m* del franco; zona *f* del franco
n frankblok *n*; frankgebied *n*; frankzone *f*

1389 frank *v*
d frankieren; freimachen
e franquear
f affranchir
i affrancare
n frankeren

1390 free competition; freedom of competition
d freie Konkurrenz *f*; freier Wettbewerb *m*; Konkurrenzfreiheit *f*; Wettbewerbsfreiheit *f*
e libertad *f* de competencia; libre competencia *f*
f liberté *f* de concurrence; libre concurrence *f*
i libera concorrenza *f*; libertà *f* di concorrenza
n vrije concurrentie *f*; vrije mededinging *f*; vrijheid *f* van concurrentie; vrijheid *f* van mededinging

1391 freedom of enterprise; free enterprise
cf. **free economy**
d freies Unternehmertum *n*; Unternehmungsfreiheit *f*
e libertad *f* de empresa; libre empresa *f*
f liberté *f* d'entreprise; libre entreprise *f*
i libera impresa *f*; libera iniziativa *f*
n vrijheid *f* van onderneming

1392 freedom of trade; free trade
d freier Handel *m*; Freihandel *m*; Handelsfreiheit *f*
e comercio *m* libre; libertad *f* de comercio; libre cambio *m*; librecambio *m*
f commerce *m* libre; échange *m* libre; liberté *f* des échanges (commerciaux); liberté *f* du commerce; libre-commerce *m*; libre-échange *m*
i liberismo *m*; libero scambio *m*; libertà *f* di commercio
n handelsvrijheid *f*; vrijhandel *m*; vrijheid *f* van het handelsverkeer

1393 free economy; free market economy
d freie Marktwirtschaft *f*; freie Wirtschaft *f*; ungebundene Wirtschaft *f*
e economía *f* de mercado libre; economía *f* libre (de mercados)
f économie *f* de marché libre; économie *f* libérale; économie *f* libre (des marchés)
i economia *f* di mercato libera; economia *f* libera (dei mercati); economia *f* liberale
n vrije economie *f*; vrije-markteconomie *f*

1394 free list
d Zollfreiliste *f*
e lista *f* de mercancías exentas de aranceles
f liste *f* de marchandises exemptes de droits
i elenco *m* di merci non soggette a dazio
n lijst *f* van tolvrije goederen

1395 free market; open market
d freier Markt *m*; offener Markt *m*
e mercado *m* abierto; mercado *m* libre
f marché *m* libre; marché *m* ouvert
i mercato *m* aperto; mercato *m* libero
n open markt *f*; vrije markt *f*

1396 free market rate; free rate; open market rate
d Freiverkehrskurs *m*
e tipo *m* del mercado libre; tipo *m* en el mercado libre
f cours *m* du marché libre; cours *m* libre; taux *m* du marché libre
i corso *m* sul mercato libero; tasso *m* sul mercato libero
n vrije-marktkoers *m*

1397 free reserve(s)
d freie Rücklage *f*; freiwillige Rücklage *f*
e reserva *f* facultativa; reserva *f* libre *(AL)*; reserva *f* voluntaria
f réserve *f* facultative; réserve *f* libre
i riserva *f* facoltativa; riserva *f* libera
n facultatieve reserve *f (B)*; vrije reserve *f*

1398 free trade area*; free trade zone
d Freihandelszone *f*
e zona *f* de comercio libre
f zone *f* de libre-échange
i zona *f* di libero scambio
n vrijhandelszone *f*

* Free trade zone is used of free ports etc., free trade area is between states.

1399 free trader
d Freihändler *m*
e librecambista *m*
f libre-échangiste *m*

i liberista *m*; liberoscambista *m*
n vrijhandelaar *m*

1400 **freeze of prices; price freeze; price stop**
d Einfrierung *f* der Preise; Preisstop *m*
e bloqueo *m* de los precios; congelación *f* de los precios
f blocage *m* des prix; congélation *f* des prix
i blocco *m* dei prezzi; congelamento *m* dei prezzi
n bevriezing *f* van de prijzen; prijsstop *m*

1401 **frozen credits**
d eingefrorene Kredite *mpl*
e créditos *mpl* congelados
f crédits *mpl* congelés; crédits *mpl* gelés
i crediti *mpl* congelati
n bevroren kredieten *npl*

1402 **full gold standard; gold specie standard**
d Goldumlaufswährung *f*; reine Goldwährung *f*
e moneda *f* oro; patrón *m* de numerario oro
f étalon *m* de numéraire-or; monnaie-or *f*
i gold specie standard *m*; moneta *f* aurea; moneta *f* oro; valuta *f* aurea; valuta *f* oro
n goudspeciestandaard *m*

1403 **fully paid shares; fully paid stocks; paid-up shares; paid-up stocks**
d liberierte Aktien *fpl*; Vollaktien *fpl*; voll eingezahlte Aktien *fpl*
e acciones *fpl* completamente (totalmente) desembolsadas; acciones *fpl* completamente (totalmente) liberadas; acciones *fpl* completamente (totalmente) integradas *(AL)*
f actions *fpl* entièrement (intégralement) libérées
i azioni *fpl* interamente liberate
n volgefourneerde aandelen *npl*; volgestorte aandelen *npl*

1404 **fund**
cf. **funds**
d Fonds *m*
e fondo *m*
f fonds *m*
i fondo *m*
n fonds *n*

1405 **fund raising; procurement of capital; raising of capital; raising of funds**
cf. **mobilization**
d Kapitalansammlung *f*; Kapitalaufbringung *f*; Kapitalbeschaffung *f*
e mobilización *f* de capital; mobilización *f* de fondos; obtención *f* de capital; obtención *f* de fondos
f collecte *f* de capitaux; collecte *f* de fonds; mobilisation *f* de capitaux; mobilisation *f* de fonds
i mobilitazione *f* di capitali; mobilitazione *f* di fondi; raccolta *f* di capitali; raccolta *f* di fondi
n aantrekken *n* van kapitaal; aantrekken *n* van middelen; mobilisering *f* van kapitaal; mobilisering *f* van middelen

1406 **funds; means; resources**
cf. **assets, capital**
d Fonds *mpl*; Mittel *npl*; Vermögen *n*
e fondos *mpl*; medios *mpl*; recursos *mpl*
f fonds *mpl*; moyens *mpl*; ressources *fpl*
i fondi *mpl*; mezzi *mpl*; risorse *fpl*
n fondsen *npl*; middelen *npl*

1407 **furnish** *v* **capital; provide** *v* **capital; supply** *v* **capital**
cf. **bring** *v* **in capital**
d Kapital beistellen *(O)*; Kapital bereitstellen; Kapital beschaffen; Kapital verschaffen; Kapital zur Verfügung stellen
e hacer provisión de capital; poner capital a la disposición; proporcionar capital; procurar capital; proveer capital
f fournir des capitaux; mettre des capitaux à la disposition; pouvoir des capitaux; procurer des capitaux
i fornire capitale; mettere capitale a disposizione; procacciare capitale; procurare capitale; provvedere capitale
n kapitaal beschikbaar stellen; kapitaal bezorgen; kapitaal ter beschikking stellen; kapitaal verschaffen; van kapitaal voorzien

1408 **furnishing of capital; provision of capital**
d Kapitalbeistellung *f (O)*; Kapitalbereitstellung *f*; Kapitalbeschaffung *f*; Kapitalleistung *f*
e prestación *f* de capitales; provisión *f* de capital
f fourniture *f* de capitaux; prestation *f* de capitaux; provision *f* de capitaux
i approvvigionamento *m* di capitali; provvista *f* di capitali
n beschikbaarstelling *f* van kapitaal; kapitaalvoorziening *f*; verschaffing *f* van kapitaal

G

1409 **gain; profit**
cf. **avails**
d Gewinn *m*; Nutzen *m*; Profit *m*
e beneficio *m*; ganancia *f*; lucro *m*; provecho *m*; utilidad *f*
f bénéfice *m*; gain *m*; lucre *m**; profit *m*
i beneficio *m*; guadagno *m*; lucro *m**; profitto *m*; utile *m*; utilità *f*
n profijt *n (rare)*; voordeel *n*; winst *f*
* Frequently pejorative in popular use.

1410 **gain sharing; participation in profits; profit sharing**
cf. **share in the profits**
d Ertragsbeteiligung *f*; Gewinnbeteiligung *f*
e participación *f* en las ganancias; participación *f* en las utilidades; participación *f* en los beneficios
f participation *f* aux bénéfices
i compartecipazione *f* agli utili; partecipazione *f* agli utili
n deelneming *f* aan de winst; winstdeling *f*

1411 **galloping inflation; runaway inflation; snowballing inflation**
d galoppierende Inflation *f*; unaufhaltsame Inflation *f*; zügellose Inflation *f*
e inflación *f* desenfrenada; inflación *f* galopante; inflación *f* irrefrenable
f inflation *f* galopante; inflation *f* incontrôlable
i inflazione *f* galoppante; inflazione *f* sfrenata
n galopperende inflatie *f*; hollende inflatie *f*

1412 **gap between the interest rates; interest differential; interest margin; interest rate differential; interest spread** *(US)*
d Zinsgefälle *n*; Zinsspanne *f*
e diferencia *f* entre los tipos de interés; margen *m/f* de intereses; margen *m/f* entre los tipos de interés
f différence *f* de niveau des intérêts; différence *f* entre les taux d'intérêt; écart *m* entre les taux d'intérêt; marge *f* d'intérêts; marge *f* entre les taux d'intérêt
i differenza *f* dei tasse d'interesse; margine *m* d'interesse; margine *m* fra le tasse d'interesse; scarto *m* fra le tasse d'interesse
n rentemarge *f*; renteverschil *n*; verschil *n* in de rentestand

1413 **garnishee**
d Drittschuldner *m*
e deudor *m* tercero; tercer deudor *m*
f tiers débiteur *m*; tiers-saisi *m*
i terzo debitore *m*; terzo *m* pignorato; terzo *m* sequestrato
n derde beslagene *m*

1414 **garnishment**
cf. **arrest**
d Beschlag *m* beim Drittschuldner; Beschlag *m* in der dritten Hand; Beschlagnahme *f* beim Drittschuldner; Pfändung *f* beim Drittschuldner; Vorpfändung *f* beim Drittschuldner
e embargo *m* contra un deudor tercero; embargo *m* de los bienes de un tercer deudor
f opposition *f*; saisie-arrêt *f*; tiers-saisie *f*
i opposizione *f*; pignoramento *m* presso terzi; sequestro *m* presso terzi
n beslag *n* onder derden; derdenarrest *n*; derdenbeslag *n*

1415 **General Agreement on Tariffs and Trade; GATT**
d Allgemeines Zoll- und Handelsabkommen *n*; AZH *n*; GATT *n*
e Acuerdo *m* general sobre aranceles y comercio; GATT *m*
f Accord *m* général sur les tarifs douaniers et le commerce; GATT *m*
i Accordo *m* generale sulle tariffe (doganali) e sul commercio; GATT *m*
n Algemene Overeenkomst *f* inzake Tarieven en Handel; GATT *m*

1416 **general balance of transfers and capital movements**
d Gesamtsaldo *m* der Übertragungen und der Kapitalbewegungen
e saldo *m* global de las transferencias y de los movimientos de capitales
f solde *m* général des transferts et des mouvements de capitaux
i saldo *m* generale dei trasferimenti e dei movimenti di capitale
n globaal saldo *n* bij de overdrachten en in het kapitaalverkeer

1417 **general charges; general expenses; indirect charges; indirect costs; indirect expenses; oncost; overhead charges; overhead costs; overhead expenses; overheads**
cf. **business expenses**
d allgemeine Kosten *pl*; allgemeine Unkosten *pl*; Allgemeinunkosten *pl*; Gemeinkosten *pl*; Generalunkosten *pl*;

Handlungskosten *pl*; Handlungsunkosten *pl*; indirekte Kosten *pl*; Sekundärkosten *pl*
e costes *mpl* indirectos; costos *mpl* indirectos; gastos *mpl* generales; gastos *mpl* indirectos
f charges *fpl* indirectes; dépenses *fpl* générales; frais *mpl* généraux; frais *mpl* indirects
i costi *mpl* generali; costi *mpl* indiretti; spese *fpl* generali; spese *fpl* indirette
n algemene kosten *mpl*; algemene onkosten *mpl*; indirecte kosten *mpl*

1418 general ledger; ledger
d Hauptbuch *n*
e libro *m* mayor; mayor *m* (general)
f grand livre *m* (général); grand-livre *m* (général)
i libro *m* maestro; libro *m* mastro; mastro *m*
n grootboek *n*; legger *m*

1419 general partner
d Komplementär *m*; persönlich haftender Gesellschafter *m*; unbeschränkt haftender Gesellschafter *m*; Vollhafter *m*
e socio *m* general; socio *m* personalmente responsable
f associé *m* commandité; commandité *m*
i accomandatario *m*; socio *m* accomandatario
n beherend vennoot *m*; persoonlijk aansprakelijk vennoot *m*

1420 general partnership
d Kollektivgesellschaft *f*; offene Handelsgesellschaft *f*; oHG
e sociedad *f* colectiva *(AL)*; sociedad *f* regular colectiva; SRC
f société *f* en nom collectif; SNC
i società *f* in nome collettivo; Snc
n vennootschap *f* onder firma; VOF

1421 get *v* **one's money back; recover** *v* **one's money**
d sein Geld wiederbekommen; sein Geld wiedererhalten; sein Geld wiedererlangen; sein Geld zurückbekommen; sein Geld zurückerhalten; sein Geld zurückerlangen; zu seinem Gelde kommen
e recobrar su dinero; recuperar su dinero
f recouvrer son argent; récupérer son argent; rentrer dans ses fonds
i ricuperare il suo denaro; riscuotere il suo denaro
n zijn geld herkrijgen; zijn geld terugkrijgen; zijn geld we(d)erkrijgen

1422 gift tax; tax on donations
d Schenkungssteuer *f*
e impuesta *f* sobre las donaciones
f droit *m* sur les donations
i imposta *f* sulle donazioni
n schenkingsrecht *n*

1423 giro; national giro; postal giro service
d Postscheckdienst *m*
e servicio *m* de giro postal
f service *m* des chèques postaux
i servizio *m* dei conti correnti postali
n girodienst *m*; postcheque- en girodienst *m*

1424 giro account; transfer account
cf. **check account, current account, national giro account**
d Girokonto *n*
e cuenta *f* de giro(s)
f compte *m* de virement; compte *m* giro
i conto *m* corrente di corrispondenza; giroconto *m*
n girorekening *f*

1425 giro cheque ***(UK)*; postal check** ***(US)*; post office cheque** ***(UK)***
cf. **money order**
d Postscheck *m*
e cheque *m* postal
f chèque *m* postal
i assegno *m* postale
n postcheck *m*; postcheque *m*

1426 give *v* **X days' notice; give** *v* **notice X days in advance**
d mit einer Frist von X Tagen kündigen; mit X-tägiger Frist kündigen; X Tage vorher kündigen; X-tägig kündigen
e avisar con X días de anticipación; dar aviso con X días de anticipación
f donner un préavis de X jours; prévenir X jours à l'avance; prévenir X jours d'avance
i dare X giorni di preavviso; dare un preavviso di X giorni
n X dagen vooraf opzeggen; met X dagen opzeggen

1427 go *v* **a bear; sell** *v* **for a fall; sell** *v* **short; speculate** *v* **for a fall**
d à la Baisse spekulieren; auf das Fallen spekulieren; blanko verkaufen; fixen; leer verkaufen
e especular a la baja; vender al descubierto
f spéculer à la baisse; vendre à découvert
i speculare al ribasso; speculare sul ribasso; vendere allo scoperto
n à la baisse speculeren; contramineren; in

blanco verkopen; in de contramine zijn; in de wind zijn

1428 **go** *v* **into liquidation; liquidate** *v*
d in Liquidation gehen; in Liquidation geraten; in Liquidation treten; liquidieren
e entrar en liquidación; liquidarse
f entrer en liquidation; liquider
i andare in liquidazione; entrare in liquidazione; liquidare
n in liquidatie gaan; liquideren

1429 **gold and foreign exchange holdings; gold and foreign exchange reserves**
d Gold- und Devisenbestände *mpl*; Gold- und Devisenreserven *fpl*; Gold- und Devisenvorrat *m*
e reservas *fpl* de (en) oro y divisas
f réserves *fpl* d'(en) or de (en) devises
i riserve *fpl* auree e valutarie; scorta *f* d'oro e di divise
n goud- en deviezenreserves *fpl*; goud- en deviezenvoorraad *m*

1430 **gold assets; gold coin and bullion; gold holdings; gold stocks**
cf. **gold reserve**
d Goldbestand *m*; Goldvorrat *m*
e existencias *fpl* de oro
f avoirs *mpl* en or; encaisse-or *f*; existence *f* en or; fonds *m* d'or; stock *m* d'or
i giacenza *f* d'oro; scorte *fpl* auree; scorte *fpl* d'oro
n goudvermogen *n*; goudvoorraad *m*

1431 **gold bullion standard; gold nucleus standard**
d Goldbarrenwährung *f*; Goldkernwährung *f*
e moneda *f* de núcleo aureo (en lingotes); moneda *f* de núcleo oro; patrón *m* lingote oro
f étalon *m* de lingots-or; étalon *m* or de lingot; étalon-or *m* de lingot
i gold bullion standard *m*; moneta *f* di nucleo aureo
n goudkernstandaard *m*

1432 **gold clause**
d Goldklausel *f*; Goldwertklausel *f*
e cláusula *f* oro
f clause *f* or; clause-or *f*
i clausola *f* oro
n goudclausule *f*

1433 **gold coin; gold piece**
d Goldmünze *f*; Goldstück *n*
e moneda *f* de oro; pieza *f* de oro
f monnaie *f* d'or; pièce *f* d'or; pièce *f* en or
i moneta *f* d'oro; pezzo *m* d'oro
n gouden munt *f*; goudmunt *f*; goudstuk *n*

1434 **gold content**
cf. **fineness**
d Goldgehalt *m*
e contenido *m* (de) oro
f teneur *m* en or
i contenuto *m* in oro; tenore *m* d'oro
n goudgehalte *n*

1435 **gold cover**
d Golddeckung *f*
e cobertura *f* (en) oro
f couverture *f* en or; couverture *f* or; couverture-or *f*
i copertura *f* aurea; copertura *f* oro
n gouddekking *f*

1436 **gold exchange standard; indirect foreign exchange standard**
d Gold-Devisenstandard *m*; Golddevisenstandard *m*; Gold-Devisenwährung *f*; Golddevisenwährung *f*; Goldkurswährung *f*
e moneda *f* de cobertura en oro y divisas; patrón *m* de cambio oro; patrón *m* de (en) divisas-oro; patrón *m* oro-divisas
f étalon *m* de change-or; étalon *m* or de change; étalon-or *m* de change; monnaie *f* à couverture or et devises
i cambio *m* in divise auree; gold exchange standard *m*; sistema *m* monetario a (di) cambio aureo
n goudwisselstandaard *m*

1437 **gold guarantee**
d Goldgarantie *f*
e garantía *f* oro; garantía-oro *f*
f garantie-or *f*
i garanzia *f* aurea; garanzia *f* oro
n goudgarantie *f*

1438 **gold loan**
d Goldanleihe *f*
e empréstito *m* con garantía oro
f emprunt-or *m*
i prestito *m* con garanzia oro; prestito *m* oro
n goudlening *f*

1439 **gold parity**
d Goldparität *f*
e paridad *f* oro
f parité *f* or; parité-or *f*
i parità *f* aurea; parità *f* oro
n goudpariteit *f*

1440 gold reserve
cf. **gold assets**
d Goldreserve *f*
e reserva *f* de oro; reserva *f* en oro
f réserve *f* d'or; réserve-or *f*
i riserva *f* aurea; riserva *f* d'oro; riserva *f* in oro
n goudreserve *f*

1441 gold standard
d Goldstandard *m*; Goldwährung *f*
e patrón *m* oro; sistema *m* monetario oro; talón *m* oro; tipo *m* oro
f étalon *m* d'or; étalon *m* or; étalon-or *m*
i base *f* aurea; gold standard *m*; tallone *m* aureo; tallone *m* d'oro; tipo *m* d'oro
n gouden standaard *m*

1442 gold value; value in gold
d Goldwert *m*; Valuta *f* in Gold
e valor *m* en oro; valor *m* oro
f valeur *f* en or; valeur *f* or; valeur-or *f*
i valore *m* in oro; valore *m* oro
n goudwaarde *f*

1443 goods and services
d Güter *npl* und Dienstleistungen *fpl*; Waren *fpl* und Dienstleistungen *fpl*
e bienes *mpl* y servicios *mpl*
f biens *mpl* et services *mpl*
i beni *mpl* e servizi *mpl*
n goederen *npl* en diensten *mpl*

1444 goodwill
d Firmenwert *m*; Goodwill *m/n*
e buena voluntad *f (AL)*; fondo *m* de comercio
f fonds *m* de commerce; goodwill *m*
i avviamento *m*; valore *m* di avviamento
n goodwill *m*

1445 government aid; state aid
cf. **government grant**
d staatliche Unterstützung *f*; Staatshilfe *f*; Staatsunterstützung *f*
e ayuda *f* del estado; ayuda *f* gubernamental
f aide *f* de l'état; aide *f* gouvernementale; appui *m* de l'état
i aiuto *m* dello stato; appoggio *m* statale
n overheidshulp *f*; overheidssteun *m*; staatshulp *f*; staatssteun *m*

1446 government budget; national budget; state budget
d öffentlicher Haushalt *m*; Staatsbudget *n*; Staatshaushalt *m*; Staatshaushaltsplan *m*
e presupuesto *m* del estado; presupuesto *m* nacional; presupuesto *m* público
f budget *m* de l'état; budget *m* national; budget *m* public
i bilancio *m* dello stato; bilancio *m* nazionale; bilancio *m* pubblico
n nationale begroting *f*; openbare begroting *f*; overheidsbegroting *f*; staatsbegroting *f*

1447 government credit guarantee; government loan guarantee; state credit guarantee; state loan guarantee
d öffentliche Garantie *f* für ein Darleh(e)n; Staatsgarantie *f* für ein Darleh(e)n
e garantía *f* gubernamental de un crédito
f garantie *f* de bonne fin d'un crédit
i garanzia *f* di buon fine di un credito
n overheidsgarantie *f* voor een lening

1448 government enterprise; government owned enterprise; government run enterprise; public enterprise; publicly owned enterprise; state controlled enterprise; state enterprise; state owned enterprise; state run enterprise
d öffentlicher Betrieb *m*; öffentliches Unternehmen *n*; öffentliche Unternehmung *f*; Regiebetrieb *m*; Regierungsbetrieb *m*; staatlicher Betrieb *m*; staatliches Unternehmen *n*; staatliche Unternehmung *f*; Staatsbetrieb *m*; Staatsunternehmen *n*; Wirtschaftsbetrieb *m* der öffentlichen Hand
e empresa *f* del estado; empresa *f* estatal; empresa *f* nacional; empresa *f* pública
f entreprise *f* d'état; entreprise *f* de l'état; entreprise *f* nationale; entreprise *f* publique
i azienda *f* di stato; azienda *f* pubblica; azienda *f* nazionale; azienda *f* statale; impresa *f* di stato; impresa *f* pubblica; impresa *f* nazionale; impresa *f* statale
n openbaar bedrijf *n*; overheidsbedrijf *n*; staatsbedrijf *n*; staatsonderneming *f*

1449 government grant; government subsidy; grant-in-aid*; state grant; state subsidy
cf. **government aid**
d öffentlicher Zuschuss *m*; öffentliche Subvention *f*; Regierungsbeihilfe *f*; Regierungszuschuss *m*; staatliche Beihilfe *f*; staatlicher Zuschuss *m*; staatliche Subvention *f*; Staatsbeihilfe *f*; Staatssubvention *f*; Staatszuschuss *m*
e subsidio *m* del estado; subvención *f* del estado; subvención *f* del gobierno; subvención *f* estatal; subvención *f* gubernamental

f subside *m* de l'état; subvention *f* budgétaire; subvention *f* de l'état; subvention *f* du gouvernement; subvention *f* gouvernementale
i contributo *m* erariale; contributo *m* governativo; contributo *m* statale; sovvenzione *f* dello stato; sovvenzione *f* statale; sussidio *m* statale
n overheidssubsidie *f/n*; overheidstoelage *f*; rijkssubsidie *f/n*; rijkstoelage *f*; staatssubsidie *f/n*; staatstoelage *f*

* Usually only of central government to local authority.

1450 **government guarantee; state guarantee**
d öffentliche Bürgschaft *f*; öffentliche Garantie *f*; staatliche Bürgschaft *f*; staatliche Garantie *f*; Staatsbürgschaft *f*; Staatsgarantie *f*
e garantía *f* del estado; garantía *f* estatal; garantía *f* gubernamental
f garantie *f* de l'état
i garanzia *f* dello stato; garanzia *f* statale
n overheidsgarantie *f*; staatsgarantie *f*; staatswaarborg *m*

1451 **government income; government revenue; public revenue; state revenue**
d öffentliche Einnahmen *fpl*; staatliche Einnahmen *fpl*; Staatseinkommen *n*; Staatseinkünfte *fpl*; Staatseinnahmen *fpl*
e ingresos *mpl* del Estado; ingresos *mpl* públicos; recaudaciones *fpl* públicas; rentas *fpl* del Estado; rentas *fpl* públicas
f recettes *fpl* de l'Etat; recettes *fpl* publiques; revenu(s) *m(pl)* de l'Etat; revenus *mpl* publics
i entrate *fpl* erariali; entrate *fpl* pubbliche; redditi *mpl* pubblici; redditi *mpl* statali
n overheidsontvangsten *fpl*; staatsinkomsten *fpl*

1452 **government interference*; government intervention; state interference*; state intervention**
d staatliche Einmischung *f*; staatliche Intervention *f*; Staatseingriff(e) *m(pl)*; Staatseinmischung *f*; Staatsintervention *f*
e ingerencia *f* del estado*; ingerencia *f* del gobierno*; intervención *f* del estado
f ingérence *f* de l'état*; intervention *f* de l'état
i ingerenza *f* dello stato*; intervento *m* dello stato
n overheidsbemoeiing *f**; overheidsinmenging *f*; overheidsinterventie *f*; staatsinmenging *f*; staatsinterventie *f*; staatstussenkomst *f*

* Usually pejorative.

1453 **government loan; public loan; state loan**
cf. **domestic loan**
d öffentliche Anleihe *f*; staatliche Anleihe *f*; Staatsanleihe *f*
e empréstito *m* del estado; empréstito *m* del gobierno; empréstito *m* estatal; empréstito *m* gubernamental; empréstito *m* público
f emprunt *m* d'état; emprunt *m* du gouvernement; emprunt *m* gouvernemental; emprunt *m* public
i prestito *m* dello stato; prestito *m* di stato; prestito *m* governativo; prestito *m* pubblico
n openbare lening *f*; overheidslening *f*; staatslening *f*

1454 **government monopoly; regie; state monopoly**
d Regie *f*; Regiebetrieb *m*; Staatsmonopol *n*
e monopolio *m* del estado
f monopole *m* d'état; régie *f*
i monopolio *m* di stato; regia *f*
n regie *f*; regiebedrijf *n*; staatsmonopolie *n*

1455 **government stock equalization account**
d Rentenfonds *m*
e fondo *m* de rentas
f fonds *m* des rentes
i fondo *m* dei titoli di stato
n rentefonds *n*

1456 **graded tax; graduated tax; progressive tax**
d gestaffelte Steuer *f*; progressive Steuer *f*; Progressivsteuer *f*; Staffelsteuer *f*
e impuesto *m* graduado; impuesto *m* progresivo
f impôt *m* progressif
i imposta *f* progressiva
n progressieve belasting *f*

1457 **graduated interest**
d gestaffelte(r) Zins(en) *m(pl)*; Staffelzins(en) *m(pl)*
e interés(es) *m(pl)* escalonado(s)
f intérêt(s) *m(pl)* échelonné(s)
i interesse *m* rateizzato; interesse *m* scaglionato; interessi *mpl* rateizzati; interessi *mpl* scaglionati

n gestaffelde int(e)rest *m*; gestaffelde rente *f*

1458 grant; subsidy; subvention
d Beihilfe *f*; Subsidien *npl*; Subvention *f*; Zuschuss *m*
e subsidio *m*; subvención *f*
f subside *m*; subvention *f*
i contributo *m*; sovvenzione *f*; sussidio *m*
n subsidie *f/n*; subventie *f*; toelage *f*

1459 gross *(noun)*; gross profit
d Bruttogewinn *m*; Rohgewinn *m*
e beneficio *m* bruto; ganancia(s) *f(pl)* bruta(s); utilidad *f* bruta
f bénéfice *m* brut
i beneficio *m* lordo; profitto *m* lordo; utile *m* lordo
n brutowinst *f*

1460 gross amount
d Bruttobetrag *m*; Rohbetrag *m*
e importe *m* bruto; monto *m* bruto
f montant *m* brut
i ammontare *m* lordo; importo *m* lordo
n brutobedrag *n*

1461 gross domestic product; GDP
d Bruttoinlandsprodukt *n*; BIP
e producto *m* interior bruto; PIB
f produit *m* intérieur brut; PIB
i prodotto *m* interno lordo
n bruto binnenlands produkt *n*

1462 gross domestic saving
d Brutto-Inlandsersparnisse *fpl*
e ahorro *m* interior bruto
f épargne *f* intérieure brute
i risparmio *m* interno lordo
n binnenlandse brutobesparingen *fpl*

1463 gross income; gross revenue
d Bruttoeinkommen *n*; Bruttoeinkünfte *fpl*; Roheinkommen *n*
e ingresos *mpl* brutos; renta *f* bruta
f revenu *m* brut
i reddito *m* lordo
n bruto-inkomen *n*; bruto-inkomsten *fpl*; brutorevenu *n*

1464 gross loss; negative gross margin *(US)*
d Bruttoverlust *m*; Rohverlust *m*
e pérdida *f* bruta
f perte *f* brute
i perdita *f* lorda
n brutoverlies *n*

1465 gross margin; gross profit margin
cf. **margin of income**
d Bruttoverdienstspanne *f*
e margen *m/f* de beneficio bruto; margen *m/f* de ganancia bruta
f marge *f* de bénéfice brut
i margine *m* di utile lordo
n bruto winstmarge *f*

1466 gross national product; GNP
d Bruttonationalprodukt *n*; Bruttosozialprodukt *n*; BSP
e producto *m* nacional bruto; PNB
f produit *m* national brut; PNB
i prodotto *m* nazionale lordo; PNL
n bruto nationaal produkt *n*; BNP

1467 gross sales; gross turnover
d Bruttoumsatz *m*
e cifra *f* bruta de negocios; ventas *fpl* brutas
f chiffre *m* d'affaires brut; ventes *fpl* brutes
i giro *m* d'affari lordo; ricavi *mpl* lordi
n bruto-omzet *m*

1468 gross value
d Bruttowert *m*; Rohwert *m*
e valor *m* bruto
f valeur *f* brute
i valore *m* lordo
n brutowaarde *f*

1469 growth potential
d Wachstumspotential *n*; Wachstumsvermögen *n*
e potencial *m* de crecimiento
f potentiel *m* de croissance
i potenziale *m* di crescita
n groeikracht *f*; groeivermogen *n*

1470 growth sector
d Wachstumsbereich *m/n*; Wachstumsbranche *f*; Wachstumssektor *m*
e sector *m* de crecimiento
f secteur *m* de croissance
i settore *m* in espansione; settore *m* in sviluppo
n groeisector *m*

1471 guarantee; guaranty *(US)*; warrant; warranty
cf. **earnest**
d Garantie *f*; Gewähr *f*; Gewährleistung *f*
e garantía *f*
f garantie *f*
i garanzia *f*
n garantie *f*; waarborg *m*

1472 guarantee fund; guaranty fund *(US)*
d Garantiefonds *m*; Sicherheitsfonds *m*;

Sicherstellungsfonds *m*; Sicherungsfonds *m*
e fondo *m* de garantía
f fonds *m* de garantie
i fondo *m* di garanzia
n garantiefonds *n*; waarborgfonds *n*

1473 guarantee of a loan; loan guarantee
d Anleihegarantie *f*
e garantía *f* de un empréstito
f garantie *f* d'un emprunt
i garanzia *f* di un prestito
n leengarantie *f*; leenwaarborg *m*

1474 guarantee of meeting a bill
d Garantie *f* der Honorierung
e garantía *f* de buen fin
f garantie *f* de bonne fin
i garanzia *f* di buon fine
n waarborg *m* van honorering

H

1475 **half-yearly coupon; semi-annual coupon**
d Halbjahreskupon *m*
e cupón *m* semestral
f coupon *m* semestriel
i cedola *f* semestrale
n halfjaarlijkse coupon *m*

1476 **halting standard; limping standard**
d hinkende Währung *f*
e patrón *m* claudicante; patrón *m* cojo; talón *m* claudicante; talón *m* cojo
f étalon *m* boiteux; étalon *m* imparfait
i bimetallismo *m* claudicante; bimetallismo *m* zoppo; tallone *m* claudicante; tallone *m* zoppo
n hinkende standaard *m*

1477 **hand bill** *(rare)*; **I.O.U.; note; note to hand; promissory note**
cf. **acknowledgement of debt, certificate of indebtedness, single bill**
d eigener Wechsel *m*; eigenes Akzept *n*; Eigenwechsel *m*; Handschein *m*; Handschuldschein *m*; Promesse *f*; Schuldschein *m*; Schuldverschreibung *f*; Schuldversprechen *n*
e cambio *m* seco; letra *f* a la propia orden; letra *f* al propio cargo; pagaré *m*; promesa *f* de deuda; vale *m*
f billet *m* à ordre; billet *m* de créance simple; billet *m* promissoire *(C)*; billet *m* simple; bon *m*; cédule *f* *(rare)*; promesse *f*
i cambiale *f* pagherò; cambiale *f* propria; pagherò *m* (cambiario); promessa *f* (di debito); vaglia *m* cambiario
n orderbiljet *n* *(B)*; orderbriefje *n*; promesse *f*; schuldbekentenis *f*; schuldbrief *m*

1478 **handling charge; handling fee; processing fee**
cf. **administrative fee**
d Bearbeitungsgebühr *f*; Manipulationsgebühr *f*
e derechos *mpl* de tramitación; gastos *mpl* de manipulación
f droit *m* de constitution de dossier; droit *m* d'établissement de dossier; frais *mpl* de constitution de dossier; frais *mpl* de dossier; frais *mpl* d'établissement de dossier; frais *mpl* de manipulation
i diritti *mpl* amministrativi; diritti *mpl* fissi; diritto *m* di manipolazione
n behandelingskosten *mpl*; dossierkosten *mpl*; dossierrecht *n*

1479 **hard currency; strong currency**
cf. **sound currency, stable currency**
d feste Währung *f*; Hartdevise *f*; harte Währung *f*; Hartwährung *f*; hochwertige Devise *f*; hochwertige Währung *f*; starke Währung *f*
e divisa *f* fuerte; moneda *f* dura; moneda *f* fuerte
f devise *f* dure; devise *f* forte; monnaie *f* forte; monnaie *f* solide
i divisa *f* forte; divisa *f* pregiata; moneta *f* forte; valuta *f* dura; valuta *f* forte; valuta *f* pregiata
n harde valuta *f*; sterke valuta *f*

1480 **hard currency country**
d Hartwährungsland *n*; Land *n* mit harter Währung *f*
e país *m* de moneda fuerte
f pays *m* à monnaie forte
i paese *m* a valuta forte
n land *n* met harde valuta

1481 **have** *v* **a bill of exchange protested; protest** *v* **a bill of exchange**
cf. **"bill" for synonyms**
d einen Wechsel protestieren; einen Wechsel protestieren lassen; einen Wechsel zum Protest geben; einen Wechsel zu Protest gehen lassen
e hacer protestar un efecto; mandar un efecto al protesto; protestar un efecto
f faire le protêt d'un effet; faire protester un effet; lever protêt d'un effet; protester un effet
i far protestare une cambiale; protestare una cambiale
n een wissel laten protesteren; een wissel protesteren

1482 **hidden distribution**
d verdeckte Gewinnausschüttung *f*
e distribución *f* oculta
f distribution *f* occulte
i distribuzione *f* occulta
n verkapte winstuitkering *f*

1483 **high cost of living**
d Lebensteuerung *f*; Lebensverteuerung *f*
e carestía *f* de la vida
f cherté *f* de la vie
i carovita *m*; caroviveri *m*
n levensduurte *f*

1484 **higher bid; overbid**
d höheres Gebot *n*; Mehrgebot *n*; Überbietung *f*; Übergebot *n*
e sobrepostura *f*
f surenchère *f*

i maggiore offerta *f*
n hoger bod *n*; opbod *n*

1485 **highest bidder**
d Meistbietender *m*
e mayor postor *m*; mejor postor *m*
f dernier enchérisseur *m*; le plus offrant *m*
i maggior offerente *m*; miglior offerente *m*
n meestbiedende *m*

1486 **high finance**
cf. **big business**
d Finanzaristokratie *f*; Grossfinanz *f*; Hochfinanz *f*
e alta(s) finanza(s) *f(pl)*; alto mundo *m* financiero; bancocracia *f*
f bancocratie *f*; haute banque *f*; haute finance *f*
i alta finanza *f*; bancocrazia *f*
n haute-finance *f*

1487 **hire purchase**
cf. **instal(l)ment buying**
d Kaufmiete *f*; Mietkauf *m*
e locación venta *f*
f location-vente *f*
i locazione-vendita *f*
n huurkoop *m*

1488 **hire purchase credit** *(UK)*; **instal(l)ment credit** *(US)*
cf. **consumer credit**
d Abzahlungskredit *m*; Ratenzahlungskredit *m*; Teilzahlungskredit *m*
e crédito *m* de pago a plazos; crédito *m* para (financiar) compras a plazos
f crédit *m* finançant des ventes à tempérament
i credito *m* per la compravendita rateale
n afbetalingskrediet *n*

1489 **hire purchase deal; hire purchase transaction; instal(l)ment deal; instal(l)ment transaction**
d Abzahlungsgeschäft *n*; Abzahlungstransaktion *f*; Teilzahlungsgeschäft *n*; Teilzahlungstransaktion *f*
e negocio *m* a plazos; operación *f* a plazos; transacción *f* a plazos
f affaire *f* à tempérament; marché *m* à tempérament; opération *f* à tempérament; transaction *f* à tempérament
i affare *m* a rate; affare *m* rateale; operazione *f* a rate; operazione *f* rateale; transazione *f* a rate; transazione *f* rateale
n afbetalingstransactie *f*; afbetalingszaak *f*

1490 **hire purchase finance** *(UK)*; **hire purchase financing** *(UK)*; **instal(l)ment financing**
d Abzahlungsfinanzierung *f*; Finanzierung *f* von Abzahlungsgeschäften; Ratenzahlungsfinanzierung *f*; Teilzahlungsfinanzierung *f*
e financiación *f* de compras a plazos; financiación *f* de pagos a plazos; financiación *f* de ventas a plazos
f financement *m* des achats à tempérament; financement *m* des opérations à tempérament; financement *m* des ventes à tempérament
i finanziamento *m* degli acquisti rateali; finanziamento *m* della compravendita rateale
n huurkoopfinanciering *f*

1491 **hire purchase sale** *(UK)*; **instal(l)ment sale**
cf. **credit sale**
d Abzahlungsverkauf *m*; Teilzahlungsverkauf *m*
e venta *f* a plazos
f vente *f* à tempérament
i vendita *f* a rate
n verkoop *m* op afbetaling

1492 **hoard** *v*
cf. **accumulate** *v*
d hamstern*; horten; thesaurieren**
e acaparar*; atesorar**
f accaparer*; thésauriser
i accaparrare*; tesaurizzare**
n hamsteren*; oppotten**

* Usually goods.
** Usually money.

1493 **hoarding**
d Hamsterei *f**; Hortung *f*; Thesaurierung *f***
e acaparamiento *m**; atesoramiento *m***
f accaparement *m**; thésaurisation *f***
i accaparramento *m**; bagarinaggio *m**; tesaurizzazione *f***
n hamsteren *n**; oppotting *f***

* Usually goods.
** Usually money.

1494 **holding company**
cf. **controlling company**
d Beteiligungsgesellschaft *f*; Dachgesellschaft *f*; Holding *f*; Holdinggesellschaft *f*
e compañía *f* holding; holding *m/f*;

sociedad *f* holding
f holding *m/f*; société *f* de participation; société *f* holding
i holding *f*; società *f* holding
n holding (company) *f*; holdingmaatschappij *f*; houdstermaatschappij *f*; participatiemaatschappij *f* *(B)*

1495 **holding (in); interest (in); stake (in)**
d Beteiligung *f* (an); Interesse *n* (an); Teilnahme *f* (an)
e interés *m* (en); participación *f* (en)
f intérêt(s) *m(pl)* (dans); participation *f* (à)
i interesse *m* (in); interessi *mpl* (in); partecipazione *f* (a)
n belang *n* (in); deelname *f* (in); deelneming *f* (in); participatie *f* (in) *(B)*

1496 **holdings**
cf. **assets, inventory**
d Bestände *mpl*; Guthaben *npl*
e existencias *fpl*
f avoirs *mpl*
i averi *mpl*
n tegoeden *npl*

1497 **home consumption; own consumption**
d Eigenverbrauch *m*; Selbstverbrauch *m*
e autoconsumo *m*; consumo *m* propio
f auto(-)consommation *f*; consommation *f* propre
i autoconsumo *m*; consumo *m* proprio
n autoconsumptie *f*; eigen verbruik *n*

1498 **hot money**
d Fluchtgeld *n*; heisses Geld *n*; hot money *n*; vagabundierendes Kapital *n*
e capital(es) *m(pl)* errante(s); hot money *m*
f capitaux *mpl* errants; capitaux *mpl* fébriles; capitaux *mpl* vagabonds; hot money *m*
i capitali *mpl* vaganti; hot money *m*
n hot money *m*; vagebonderend kapitaal *n*

1499 **household consumption; private consumer expenditure**
d privater Verbrauch *m*; Privatverbrauch *m*
e consumo *m* familiar; consumo *m* privado
f consommation *f* des ménages; consommation *f* privée
i consumo *m* delle famiglie; consumo *m* privato
n gezinsbesteding *f*; gezinsverbruik *n*; privaat verbruik *n*; privé-verbruik *n*

1500 **hyperinflation**
d Hyperinflation *f*; Superinflation *f*
e hiperinflación *f*
f hyperinflation *f*
i iperinflazione *f*
n hyperinflatie *f*

1501 **hypothecation of securities *(US)*; pawning of securities; pledging of securities**
cf. **lending on securities**
d Belehnung *f* von Effekten *(Schw)*; Beleihung *f* von Effekten; Lombardierung *f*; Verpfändung *f* von Effekten
e empeño *m* de efectos; empeño *m* de títulos; empeño *m* de valores; pignoración *f* de efectos; pignoración *f* de títulos; pignoración *f* de valores
f engagement *m* de titres; engagement *m* de valeurs; mise *f* en gage de titres; mise *f* en gage de valeurs; nantissement *m* de titres; nantissement *m* de valeurs
i dare *m* in pegno di titoli; impegnare *m* di titoli
n belening *f* van effecten; inpandgeving *f* van effecten; verpanding *f* van effecten

I

1502 **idle capital; unproductive capital**
d brachliegendes Kapital *n*; totes Kapital *n*; unproduktives Kapital *n*
e capital *m* improductivo; capital *m* inactivo; capital *m* muerto; capital *m* ocioso
f capital *m* dormant; capital *m* improductif; capital *m* mort; capital *m* oisif
i capitale *m* improduttivo; capitale *m* inattivo; capitale *m* morto
n dood kapitaal *n*; onproductief kapitaal *n*; renteloos kapitaal *n*

1503 **illiquid; non-liquid; not liquid**
d illiquid; nicht flüssig; nicht liquid
e ilíquido; no líquido
f illiquide; non liquide
i illiquido; non liquido
n illiquide; niet liquide

1504 **illiquidity; non-liquidity**
d Illiquidität *f*; Mangel *m* an flüssigen Mitteln
e falta *f* de liquidez; iliquidez *f*; no liquidez *f*
f manque *m* de liquidité; non-liquidité *f*
i illiquidità *f*; mancanza *f* di liquidità
n gebrek *n* aan liquide middelen; illiquititeit *f*

1505 **immaterial assets; intangible assets; intangibles**
d Immaterialgüter *npl*; immateriale Aktiva *npl*; immateriale Aktiven *npl*; immateriale Anlagen *fpl*; immateriale Vermögenswerte *mpl*; immateriale Werte *mpl*; immateriale Wirtschaftsgüter *npl*; nicht greifbare Aktiva *npl*; nicht greifbare Aktiven *npl*; nicht greifbare Vermögenswerte *mpl*; nicht greifbare Werte *mpl*; nicht greifbare Wirtschaftsgüter *npl*; unkörperliche Wirtschaftsgüter *npl*
e activos *mpl* inmateriales; activos *mpl* intangibles; bienes *mpl* incorporales; bienes *mpl* inmateriales; bienes *mpl* intangibles; inmovilizaciones *fpl* incorporales; inmovilizaciones *fpl* inmateriales; inmovilizaciones *fpl* intangibles; valores *mpl* inmateriales; valores *mpl* intangibles
f biens *mpl* incorporels; biens *mpl* immatériels; immobilisations *fpl* immatérielles; immobilisations *fpl* incorporelles; valeurs *fpl* immatérielles; valeurs *fpl* incorporelles; valeurs *fpl* intangibles
i attivi *mpl* immateriali; attivi *mpl* intangibili; attività *f* immateriale; beni *mpl* immateriali; immobilizzazioni *fpl* immateriali; valori *mpl* immateriali; valori *mpl* intangibili
n immateriële activa *npl*; immateriële goederen *npl*; onaantastbare activa *npl*; onlichamelijke goederen *npl*

1506 **immobilization** *(of capital etc.)*
cf. **sterilization**
d Bindung *f*; Festlegung *f*; Immobilisierung *f*
e inmovilización *f*
f immobilisation *f*
i immobilizzazione *f*; immobilizzo *m*
n immobilisatie *f*; vastlegging *f*

1507 **immobilize** *v (capital etc.)*; **lock** *v* **up; tie** *v* **up**
cf. **block** *v*, **sterilize** *v*
d binden; fest anlegen; festlegen; immobilisieren
e inmovilizar
f immobiliser
i immobilizzare
n immobiliseren; vastleggen

1508 **immovable property; immovables; real assets; real estate; real property; realty**
cf. **landed property**
d Immobiliareigentum *n*; Immobiliargüter *npl*; Immobiliarvermögen *n*; Immobilien *pl*; liegende Güter *npl*; liegende Habe *f*; Liegenschaften *fpl*; Realitäten *fpl*; unbewegliche Güter *npl*; unbewegliche Habe *f*; unbewegliches Eigentum *n*; unbewegliches Vermögen *n*
e bienes *mpl* inmobiliarios; bienes *mpl* inmuebles; bienes *mpl* raíces; inmuebles *mpl*; patrimonio *m* inmueble; propiedad *f* inmobiliaria; propiedad *f* inmueble; valores *mpl* inmobiliarios; valores *mpl* inmuebles
f avoirs *mpl* immobiliers; biens *mpl* en immeubles; biens *mpl* immeubles; biens *mpl* immobiliers; effets *mpl* immobiliers; immeubles *mpl*; patrimoine *m* immobilier; propriété *f* immobilière; valeurs *fpl* immobilières
i beni *mpl* immobili; beni *mpl* immobiliari; beni *mpl* stabili; immobili *mpl*; patrimonio *m* immobiliare; proprietà *f* immobile; proprietà *f* immobiliare; valori *mpl* immobiliari
n immobiliën *pl*; liggende goederen *npl*;

onroerende goederen *npl*; vaste goederen *npl*

1509 **import; importation**
d Einfuhr *f*; Import *m*
e importación *f*
f importation *f*
i importazione *f*
n import *m*; invoer *m*

1510 **import commodities; import goods**
d Einfuhrartikel *mpl*; Einfuhrgüter *npl*; Einfuhrwaren *fpl*; Importartikel *mpl*; Importgüter *npl*; Importwaren *fpl*
e artículos *mpl* de importación; mercancías *fpl* de importación
f articles *mpl* d'importation; marchandises *fpl* d'importation
i articoli *mpl* d'importazione; merci *fpl* d'importazione
n importartikelen *npl*; importgoederen *npl*; importwaren *fpl*; invoerartikelen *npl*; invoergoederen *npl*; invoerwaren *fpl*

1511 **imported inflation**
d importierte Inflation *f*
e inflación *f* importada
f inflation *f* importée
i inflazione *f* importata
n geïmporteerde inflatie *f*

1512 **import licence *(UK)*; import license *(US)*; import permit**
d Einfuhrbewilligung *f*; Einfuhrerlaubnis *f*; Einfuhrgenehmigung *f*; Einfuhrlizenz *f*; Importbewilligung *f*; Importerlaubnis *f*; Importgenehmigung *f*; Importlizenz *f*
e autorización *f* para importar; licencia *f* de importación; permiso *m* de importación
f autorisation *f* d'importation; licence *f* d'importation; permis *m* d'entrée; permis *m* d'importation; permis *m* d'importer
i autorizzazione *f* d'importazione; licenza *f* d'importazione; permesso *m* d'importazione
n importbewilliging *f*; importconsent *n*; importlicentie *f*; importvergunning *f*; invoerbewilliging *f*; invoerconsent *n*; invoerlicentie *f*; invoervergunning *f*

1513 **import restriction; restriction on imports**
d Einfuhrbeschränkung *f*; Importbeschränkung *f*
e restricción *f* a la importación; restricción *f* de las importaciones
f restriction *f* à l'importation; restriction *f* des importations
i restrizione *f* all'importazione; restrizione *f* delle importazioni
n invoerbeperking *f*

1514 **impose *v* a surcharge; surcharge *v***
d mit einem Zuschlag belegen
e gravar con una sobretasa; recargar
f frapper d'une surtaxe; grever d'une surtaxe; surtaxer
i gravare di una sovrattasa; soprattassare; sovrattassare
n een toeslag heffen (op); een toeslag leggen (op)

1515 **imposition of prices; price fixing; price maintenance**
cf. **pegging of prices, price determination**
d Preisbindung *f*; Preisfestsetzung *f*
e fijación *f* de precios; imposición *f* de precios
f fixation *f* des prix; imposition *f* des prix
i fissazione *f* dei prezzi; imposizione *f* dei prezzi
n prijsbinding *f*; prijszetting *f*; prijzenbinding *f*

1516 **imposition of taxes; levy of taxes; raising of taxes**
cf. **collection of taxes, taxation**
d Steuerauferlegung *f*; Steuerausschreibung *f*; Steuererhebung *f*
e imposición *f* de contribuciones
f imposition *f* de taxes; levée *f* de contributions
i esazione *f* d'imposte; imposizione *f* di tasse
n belastingheffing *f*

1517 **imprest fund**
d fester Kassenbestand *m*
e fondo *m* fijo de caja
f fonds *m* fixe de caisse
i fondo *m* cassa in dotazione; fondo *m* fisso di cassa
n vaste kasvoorraad *m*

1518 **imputed interest**
d kalkulatorische Zinsen *mpl*
e intereses *mpl* calculados
f intérêt *m* fictif
i interessi *mpl* fittizi
n fictieve int(e)rest *m*; schijnint(e)rest *m*

1519 **incentive**
d Anreiz *m*
e incentivo *m*
f incitation *f*
i incentivo *m*
n stimulans *m*

1520 **incentive pay; incentive wage**
cf. **efficiency pay**
d Prämienlohn *m*
e salario *m* a prima; salario *m* con primas
f salaire *m* à la prime; salaire *m* au devis-prime
i salario *m* a premio
n premieloon *n*

1521 **incidence of a tax**
d Anfall *m* einer Steuer; Inzidenz *f* einer Steuer
e incidencia *f* de un impuesto
f incidence *f* d'un impôt
i incidenza *f* di un'imposta
n doorberekening *f* van een belasting; terugslag *m* van een belasting

1522 **income; revenue**
cf. **avails, incomings, proceeds, return**
d Einkommen *n*; Einkünfte *fpl*; Rente *f*
e ingresos *mpl*; rédito *m*; renta *f*
f rente *f*; revenu(s) *m(pl)*
i redditi *mpl*; reddito *m*
n inkom *m (B)*; inkomen *n*; inkomsten *fpl*; rente *f*; revenu(en) *n(pl)*

1523 **income account; income statement *(US)*; profit and loss account; profit and loss statement**
d Erfolgskonto *n*; Erfolgsrechnung *f*; Ertragskonto *n*; Ertragsrechnung *f*; Gewinn- und Verlustkonto *n*; Gewinn- und Verlustrechnung *f*
e cuenta *f* de ganancías y pérdidas; cuenta *f* de pérdidas y ganancías; cuenta *f* de resultados
f compte *m* de pertes et profits; compte *m* de profits et pertes; compte *m* de(s) résultats
i conto *m* dei ricavi; conto *m* economico; conto *m* perdite e profitti; conto *m* profitti e perdite; conto *m* spese e rendite
n resultatenrekening *f*; verlies-en-winst-rekening *f*; winst-en-verliesrekening *f*

1524 **income account; revenue account**
d Einnahmekonto *n*; Einnahmen-rechnung *f*
e cuenta *f* de entradas; cuenta *f* de ingresos
f compte *m* de recettes; compte *m* de revenus; compte *m* recettes; compte *m* revenus
i conto *m* (delle) entrate
n inkomstenrekening *f*

1525 **income and expenses; incomings and outgoings; receipts and expenditure(s); receipts and expenses; receipts and payments**
d Eingänge *mpl* und Ausgänge *mpl*; Einnahmen *fpl* und Ausgaben *fpl*
e entradas *fpl* y salidas *fpl*; ingresos *mpl* y egresos *mpl (AL)*; ingresos *mpl* y gastos *mpl*
f entrées *fpl* et sorties *fpl*; recettes *fpl* et dépenses *fpl*; recettes *fpl* et paiements *mpl*; rentrées *fpl* et sorties *fpl*
i entrate *fpl* ed uscite *fpl*; introiti *mpl* e pagamenti *mpl*
n ontvangsten *fpl* en uitbetalingen *fpl*; ontvangsten *fpl* en uitgaven *fpl*

1526 **income bond; participating bond**
d Gewinnobligation *f*; Gewinn-schuldverschreibung *f*
e bono *m* de ingresos; obligación *f* de participación
f bon *m* de revenus; obligation *f* participant aux bénéfices
i buono *m* delle entrate; obbligazione *f* partecipante agli utili
n inkomstenobligatie *f*; inkomstobligatie *f*; winstdelende obligatie *f*

1527 **income bracket; income class; income group**
d Einkommensgruppe *f*; Einkommens-klasse *f*; Einkommensschicht *f*; Einkommensstufe *f*
e categoría *f* de ingresos; categoría *f* de rentas; clase *f* de ingresos; clase *f* de rentas; grado *m* de ingresos; grado *m* de rentas; grupo *m* de ingresos; grupo *m* de rentas
f catégorie *f* de revenus; classe *f* de revenus; échelon *m* de revenus; groupe *m* de revenus; tranche *f* de revenus
i categoria *f* di redditi; classe *f* di redditi; scaglione *m* di redditi
n inkomensgroep *f*; inkomensklasse *f*; inkomensschijf *f*

1528 **income from investments; income on investments; investment income**
cf. **capital income, unearned income**
d Einkommen *n* aus Kapitalanlagen; Einkommen *n* aus Vermögensanlagen; Erträge *mpl* aus Beteiligungen; Erträgnisse *npl* aus Kapitalanlagen; Erträgnisse *npl* aus Vermögensanlagen
e ingresos *mpl* (derivados) de inversiones
f revenus *mpl* de placements; revenus *mpl* d'investissements; revenus *mpl* mobiliers

i redditi *mpl* d'investimenti; redditi *mpl* mobiliari
n beleggingsinkomen *n*; inkomen *n* uit beleggingen; inkomen *n* uit investeringen; investeringsinkomen *n*

1529 **income in kind**
cf. **allowance in kind**
d Naturaleinkommen *n*
e ingresos *mpl* en especie
f revenu *m* en nature
i reddito *m* in natura
n inkomen *n* in natura; inkomsten *fpl* in natura

1530 **income tax**
d Einkommenssteuer *f*
e impuesto *m* a los réditos *(AL)*; impuesto *m* sobre la renta
f impôt *m* sur le revenu
i imposta *f* sul reddito
n inkomstenbelasting *f*

1531 **income tax return**
d Einkommenssteuererklärung *f*
e declaración *f* de ingresos
f déclaration *f* de revenus
i denuncia *f* dei redditi; denunzia *f* dei redditi; dichiarazione *f* dei redditi
n aangifte *f* inkomstenbelasting

1532 **incomings; receipts; takings**
cf. **avails, income, proceeds, return**
d Eingänge *mpl*; Einnahmen *fpl*; Zugänge *mpl*
e entradas *fpl*; ingresos *mpl*; recibos *mpl*
f entrées *fpl*; recettes *fpl*; rentrées *fpl*
i entrate *fpl*; incassi *mpl*; introiti *mpl*
n inkomsten *fpl*; ontvangsten *fpl*; recettes *fpl*

1533 **inconvertibility; non-convertibility; unconvertibility**
d Inkonvertibilität *f*; Nichteinlösbarkeit *f*; Nichtkonvertierbarkeit *f*; Nichtumwandelbarkeit *f*
e inconvertibilidad *f*; no convertibilidad *f*
f inconvertibilité *f*; non-convertibilité *f*
i inconvertibilità *f*
n inconvertibiliteit *f*; niet-converteerbaarheid *f*; niet-inwisselbaarheid *f*

1534 **inconvertible; non-convertible; unconvertible**
d inkonvertibel; inkonvertierbar; nicht einlösbar; nicht konvertierbar; nicht umwandelbar
e inconvertible; no convertible
f inconvertible; non convertible
i inconvertibile; non convertibile
n niet-converteerbaar; niet-inwisselbaar

1535 **inconvertible paper money; irredeemable money**
d nicht einlösbares Papiergeld *n*
e papel moneda *m* no convertible
f papier-monnaie *m* (inconvertible)
i cartamoneta *f* inconvertibile
n niet inwisselbaar papiergeld *n*

1536 **incorporated bank** *(US)*; **joint stock bank** *(UK)*
cf. **banking company**
d Aktienbank *f*; Bankgesellschaft *f* auf Aktien
e banco *m* por acciones; sociedad *f* bancaria por acciones
f banque *f* par actions; société *f* bancaire par actions
i banca *f* per azioni; società *f* bancaria per azioni
n bankmaatschappij *f* op aandelen *(B)*; bank *f* op aandelen

1537 **incorporated company** *(US)**; **Inc.** *(US)**; **joint stock company***; **limited liability company***; **Co. Ltd.***; **public limited company***; **stock company***; **stock corporation*** *(US)*
cf. **limited liability company**
d Aktiengesellschaft *f*; A.G.; Kapitalgesellschaft *f*
e sociedad *f* anónima; S.A.; sociedad *f* de capitales; sociedad *f* por acciones
f société *f* anonyme; S.A.; société *f* de capital; société *f* de capitaux; société *f* par actions
i società *f* anonima; società *f* di capitali; società *f* per azioni; S.p.A.
n kapitaalvennootschap *f*; naamloze vennootschap *f*; N.V.; vennootschap *f* op aandelen

* Local legislation varies greatly.

1538 **increase in liquidity**
d Liquidisierung *f*; Verflüssigung *f*
e aumento *m* de la liquidez
f augmentation *f* de la liquidité
i aumento *m* della liquidità
n verhoging *f* van de liquiditeit

1539 **increase in price(s); markup; price increase; price rise; rise in price(s)**
cf. **additional charge, rally**
d Preisanhebung *f*; Preisanstieg *m*; Preisaufschlag *m*; Preisaufstieg *m*; Preisauftrieb *m*; Preiserhöhung *f*; Preis-

steigerung *f*; Preissteigung *f*; Teuerung *f*; Verteuerung *f*
e alza *f* de precio(s); aumento *m* de precio(s); elevación *f* del precio; encarecimiento *m*; incremento *m* de los precios; subida *f* de precio(s)
f augmentation *f* de(s) prix; élévation *f* de(s) prix; enchérissement *m*; hausse *f* de(s) prix; majoration *f* de(s) prix; relèvement *m* de(s) prix; renchérissement *m*
i ascesa *f* dei prezzi; aumento *m* del prezzo; aumento *m* dei prezzi; lievitazione *f* dei prezzi; maggiorazione *f* del prezzo; maggiorazione *f* dei prezzi; rialzo *m* del prezzo; rialzo *m* dei prezzi; rincaro *m*
n prijsstijging *f*; prijsverhoging *f*; prijzenstijging *f*

1540 increase in salary; raise ***(US)*****; rise; salary increase**
d Besoldigungserhöhung *f*; Gehaltsaufbesserung *f*; Gehaltserhöhung *f*; Gehaltssteigerung *f*
e aumento *m* de sueldo
f amélioration *f* de salaire; amélioration *f* de traitement; augmentation *f* de salaire; augmentation *f* de traitement; relèvement *m* de salaire; relèvement *m* de traitement
i aumento *m* di stipendio; miglioramento *m* di stipendio
n salarisverhoging *f*

1541 increase in the discount rate ***(US)*****; increase in the minimum lending rate** ***(UK)*****; increase in the rediscount rate** ***(US)*****; raising of the minimum lending rate** ***(UK)*****; rise in the minimum lending rate** ***(UK)***
d Diskonterhöhung *f*; Diskontheraufsetzung *f*; Erhöhung *f* des Diskontsatzes; Heraufsetzung *f* des Diskontsatzes
e aumento *m* del tipo de descuento; elevación *f* del tipo de descuento; incremento *m* del tipo de descuento
f augmentation *f* du taux de (l')escompte; élévation *f* du taux de (l')escompte; majoration *f* du taux de (l')escompte; relèvement *m* du taux de (l')escompte
i aumento *m* del tasso di sconto; rialzo *m* del tasso di sconto
n discontoverhoging *f*; verhoging *f* van de discontovoet; verhoging *f* van het disconto

1542 increase in wages; raise ***(US)*****; rise; wage increase**
d Lohnaufbesserung *f*; Lohnerhöhung *f*; Lohnsteigerung *f*
e aumento *m* de paga; aumento *m* de salario
f amélioration *f* de gages; amélioration *f* de salaire; augmentation *f* de gages; augmentation *f* de salaire; relèvement *m* de gages; relèvement *m* de salaire
i aumento *m* di paga; aumento *m* di salario; aumento *m* salariale; miglioramento *m* di salario
n loonsverhoging *f*

1543 increase of X per cent; rise of X per cent
d Erhöhung *f* um X Prozent; X prozentige Erhöhung *f*
e aumento *m* del X por ciento; incremento *m* del X por ciento
f augmentation *f* de X pour cent; majoration *f* de X pour cent
i aumento *m* del X per cento; rialzo *m* del X per cento
n X percent verhoging *f*; verhoging *f* met X percent; verhoging *f* van X percent

1544 increase *v* **the capital (stock); raise** *v* **the capital stock**
d das Kapital aufstocken; das Kapital erhöhen; das Kapital vermehren
e ampliar el capital; aumentar el capital; elevar el capital
f accroître le capital; augmenter le capital
i aumentare il capitale
n het kapitaal uitbreiden; het kapitaal vergroten; het kapitaal verhogen

1545 increasing charge depreciation ***(US)*****; progressive depreciation**
d progressive Abschreibung *f*; steigende Abschreibung *f*
e amortización *f* creciente; amortización *f* progresiva; depreciación *f* creciente; depreciación *f* progresiva
f amortissement *m* croissant; amortissement *m* progressif
i ammortamento *m* per quote crescenti; ammortamento *m* progressivo
n progressieve afschrijving *f*; toenemende afschrijving *f*

1546 index
cf. **index figure**
d Index *m*
e índice *m*
f index *m (B)*; indice *m*
i indice *m*
n index *m*

1547 **index** *v*; **index-link** *v*; **link** *v* **to an index; tie** *v* **to an index**
d an einen Index binden; an einen Index koppeln; indexkoppeln
e variar con un índice económico
f indexer
i ancorare a un indice; indicizzare
n aan een index binden; aan een index koppelen; indexeren

1548 **indexation**
d Indexbindung *f*; indexmässige Bindung *f*
e ajustamiento *m* por un índice
f indexation *f*
i ancoramento *m* a un indice; indicizzazione *f*
n indexering *f*

1549 **indexed bond; index-linked bond**
d indexgebundene Obligation *f*; indexgebundene Schuldverschreibung *f*; indexgekoppelte Obligation *f*; indexgekoppelte Schuldverschreibung *f*; Indexobligation *f*; Indexschuldverschreibung *f*; Obligation *f* mit Indexschutz; Obligation *f* mit Wertsicherungsklauseln
e obligación *f* ajustable por un índice; obligación *f* índice; obligación *f* variable por un índice
f obligation *f* indexée
i obbligazione *f* con adeguamento; obbligazione *f* parametrata; obbligazione *f* vincolata ad un indice
n geïndexeerde obligatie *f*; indexobligatie *f*

1550 **index figure; index number**
d Indexzahl *f*; Indexziffer *f*; Messzahl *f*; Messziffer *f*
e cifra *f* índice; índice *m*; número *m* índice
f chiffre *m* indice; indice *m*; nombre *m* indice
i indice *m*; numero *m* indice
n indexcijfer *n*

1551 **indicator**
d Indikator *m*
e indicador *m*
f indicatateur *m*
i indicatore *m*
n indicator *m*

1552 **indirect tax**
d indirekte Steuer *f*
e impuesto *m* indirecto
f impôt *m* indirect
i imposta *f* indiretta
n indirecte belasting *f*

1553 **inflate** *v*
d aufblähen; inflatieren; inflationieren
e inflar
f gonfler; inflater
i gonfiare; inflazionare
n inflateren; inflationeren; opdrijven; opvoeren

1554 **inflation**
cf. **overheating**
d Geldentwertung *f*; Inflation *f*
e inflación *f*
f inflation *f*
i inflazione *f*
n geldontwaarding *f*; inflatie *f*

1555 **inflationary**
d inflationär; inflationistisch; Inflations-; inflatorisch
e inflacionista
f inflationniste
i inflazionistico
n inflatie-; inflationistisch; inflatoir; inflatoor

1556 **inflationary factor**
d Inflationsfaktor *m*
e factor *m* inflacionista
f facteur *m* inflationniste
i fattore *m* inflazionistico
n inflatoire factor *m*

1557 **inflationary gap**
d Inflationslücke *f*; inflatorische Lücke *f*; Nachfrageüberhang *m*
e déficit *m* inflacionista; hueco *m* inflacionista
f déficit *m* inflationniste; écart *m* inflationniste
i disavanzo *m* inflazionistico; gap *m* inflazionistico
n bestedingsoverschot *n*; inflatoir deficit *n*

1558 **inflationary pressure**
d inflationäre Spannung *f*; Inflationsdruck *m*; Inflationsschub *m*; inflatorische Kraft *f*
e presión *f* inflacionista
f force *f* inflationniste; poussée *f* inflationniste; pression *f* inflationniste
i pressione *f* inflazionistica; spinta *f* inflazionistica
n inflatoire druk *m*; inflatoire kracht *f*

1559 **inflationary spiral**
d Inflationsschraube *f*; Inflationsspirale *f*
e espiral *f* inflacionista
f spirale *f* inflationniste

i spirale *f* inflazionistica
n inflatiespiraal *f*

1560 inflationism
d Inflationismus *m*
e inflacionismo *m*
f inflationnisme *m*
i inflazionismo *m*
n inflationisme *n*

1561 inflationist
d Inflationist *m*; Inflationsanhänger *m*
e inflacionista *m*
f inflationniste *m*
i inflazionista *m*
n inflationist *m*

1562 inflation-proof; inflation-proofed
d inflationsgeschützt
e protegido contra la inflación
f protégé contre l'inflation
i protetto contro l'inflazione
n inflatiebestand; inflatiebestendig

1563 inflation rate; pace of inflation; rate of inflation
d Inflationsrate *f*; Inflationstempo *n*
e ritmo *m* de la inflación; tasa *f* de inflación
f rythme *m* de l'inflation; taux *m* d'inflation
i ritmo *m* dell'inflazione; tasso *m* d'inflazione
n inflatiepercentage *n*; inflatietempo *n*; inflatievoet *m*

1564 initial capital; opening capital; original capital
d Anfangskapital *n*; Einlagekapital *n*; Grundkapital *n*; Gründungskapital *n*
e capital *m* de establecimiento; capital *m* de fundación; capital *m* fundacional; capital *m* inicial
f capital *m* d'apport; capital *m* d'établissement; capital *m* initial; capital *m* originaire
i capitale *m* d'apporto; capitale *m* di conferimento; capitale *m* di fondazione; capitale *m* iniziale
n aanvangskapitaal *n*; beginkapitaal *n*; grondkapitaal *n*; oprichtingskapitaal *n*

1565 inland revenue; tax receipts; tax revenue
d Steueraufkommen *n*; Steuereingänge *mpl*; Steuereinkommen *n*; Steuereinkünfte *fpl*; Steuereinnahmen *fpl*; Steuerertrag *m*; Steuererträgnisse *npl*
e ingresos *mpl* fiscales; producto *m* de los impuestos; rendimiento *m* impositivo; rentas *fpl* fiscales; rentas *fpl* tributarias
f recettes *fpl* fiscales; rendement *m* des impôts; rentrées *fpl* fiscales; revenu *m* fiscal
i entrate *fpl* del fisco; entrate *fpl* fiscali; gettito *m* delle imposte; gettito *m* fiscale; introiti *m* fiscali; reddito *m* fiscale; ricavo *m* delle imposte
n belastinginkomsten *fpl*; belastingontvangsten *fpl*; belastingopbrengst *f*

1566 inland revenue inspection *(UK)*; tax field audit *(US)*
d Betriebsprüfung *f*; Steuerrevision *f*
e inspección *f* fiscal
f contrôle *m* fiscal
i verifica *f* fiscale
n belastingonderzoek *n*; fiscale controle *f*

1567 inpayment; payment
d Einzahlung *f*
e entero *m (AL)*; imposición *f*; ingreso *m*; pago *m*
f versement *m*
i versamento *m*
n storting *f*

1568 inscribed securities *(UK)*; registered securities; registered shares; registered stock *(US)*
d auf (den) Namen lautende Wertpapiere *npl*; Namensaktien *fpl*; Namenspapiere *npl*; Rektapapiere *npl*
e acciones *fpl* nominativas; acciones *fpl* registradas; títulos *mpl* nominativos; títulos *mpl* registrados; títulos-valores *mpl* nominativos
f actions *fpl* nominatives; titres *mpl* nominatifs; valeurs *fpl* nominatives
i azioni *fpl* nominative; titoli *mpl* nominativi; valori *mpl* nominativi
n aandelen *npl* op naam; effecten *npl* op naam; op naam gestelde waarden *fpl*; waarden *fpl* op naam; waardepapieren *npl* op naam

1569 insolvency
cf. **bankruptcy**
d Insolvenz *f*; Zahlungsunfähigkeit *f*
e insolvencia *f*
f insolvabilité *f*
i insolvenza *f*; insolvibilità *f*
n insolventie *f*; onvermogen *n*

1570 insolvent
d insolvent; zahlungsunfähig
e insolvente
f insolvable

i insolvente; insolvibile
n insolvabel; insolvent

1571 instal(l)ment
cf. **deposit, part payment**
d Abschlagszahlung *f*; Abzahlungsrate *f*; Rate *f*; Ratenzahlung *f*
e cuota *f*; pago *m* a plazos; plazo *m*
f acompte *m (rare)*; paiement *m* à tempérament; paiement *m* par termes; terme *m*
i pagamento *m* rateale; rata *f*
n afbetaling *f*; aflossing *f*; termijnbetaling *f*

1572 instal(l)ment *(of loan)*; **portion; tranche**
d Anleiheabschnitt *m*; Rate *f*; Teilabschnitt *m*; Tranche *f*
e cuota *f*
f tranche *f*
i rata *f*; tranche *f*
n gedeelte *n*; tranche *f*

1573 instal(l)ment buying; instal(l)ment purchase
cf. **hire purchase**
d Abzahlungskauf *m*; Kauf *m* auf Raten; Ratenkauf *m*; Teilzahlungskauf *m*
e compra *f* a plazos
f achat *m* à tempérament
i acquisto *m* a rate; acquisto *m* rateale
n aankoop *m* op afbetaling

1574 instal(l)ment debt
d Amortisationsschuld *f*
e deuda *f* amortizable
f dette *f* amortissable
i debito *m* ammortizzabile
n aflosbare schuld *f*

1575 institution of bankruptcy proceedings
d Eröffnung *f* des Konkurses; Konkurseröffnung *f*
e apertura *f* de la quiebra
f ouverture *f* de la faillite
i apertura *f* del fallimento
n opening *f* van het faillissement

1576 insurance*
d Versicherung *f*
e seguro *m*
f assurance *f*
i assicurazione *f*
n verzekering *f*

* Assurance only applies to life assurance (q.v.).

1577 insurance policy
d Versicherungspolice *f*; Versicherungspolizze *f (O)*; Versicherungsschein *m*
e póliza *f* de seguro
f police *f* d'assurance
i polizza *f* di assicurazione
n verzekeringspolis *f*

1578 insurance premium
d Versicherungsprämie *f*
e prima *f* de seguro
f prime *f* d'assurance
i premio *m* d'assicurazione
n verzekeringspremie *f*

1579 integrated national accounts
d volkswirtschaftliche Gesamtrechnung *f*
e cuentas *fpl* económicas integradas
f comptes *mpl* économiques intégrés
i conti *mpl* economici integrati
n geïntegreerde economische rekeningen *fpl*

1580 intensive investment; investment in depth; rationalization investment
d Rationalisierungsinvestition *f*; Vertikalinvestierung *f*; Vertikalinvestition *f*
e inversión *f* para racionalización; inversión *f* vertical
f investissement *m* de productivité; investissement *m* de rationalization
i investimento *m* di razionalizzazione
n diepte-investering *f*

1581 Inter-American Development Bank
d Interamerikanische Entwicklungsbank *f*
e Banco *m* Interamericano de Desarrollo
f Banque *f* interaméricaine de développement
i Banca *f* Interamericana di Sviluppo
n Interamerikaanse Ontwikkelingsbank *f*

1582 inter-bank deposits
d Bank-bei-Bank-Einlagen *fpl*; Interbankeinlagen *fpl*; wechselseitige Bankguthaben *npl*
e depósitos *mpl* interbancarios
f dépôts *mpl* interbancaires
i depositi *mpl* interbancari
n interbancaire deposito's *npl*; interbankdeposito's *npl*

1583 inter-bank loan
d Bank-an-Bank-Kredit *m*; gegenseitige Bankforderung *f*; Interbankkredit *m*
e crédito *m* interbancario
f crédit *m* interbancaire
i credito *m* tra banche
n interbancair krediet *n*

1584 interconvertibility
d Interkonvertibilität *f*; Interkonvertierbarkeit *f*
e interconvertibilidad *f*
f interconvertibilité *f*
i interconvertibilità *f*
n interconvertibiliteit *f*

1585 interest
d Interessen *npl*; Zins(en) *m(pl)*
e interés *m*; intereses *mpl*; rédito *m*
f intérêt(s) *m(pl)*; loyer *m* (de l'argent)
i interesse *m*; interessi *mpl*
n int(e)rest *m*; rente *f*

1586 interest bearing; interest-bearing
cf. **bear** *v* **(a) X percent interest**
d verzinsbar; verzinslich; zinsbar; zinsbringend; zinsentragend; zinstragend
e a interés; pagando interés (intereses); productivo de interés (intereses)
f à intérêt(s); portant intérêt(s); porteur d'intérêt(s); productif d'intérêt(s)
i fruttante interesse (interessi); fruttifero; produttivo di interesse (interessi)
n rentedragend; rentegevend

1587 interest charges
d Zinsbelastung *f*; Zinsenlasten *fpl*
e cargas *fpl* de intereses
f charges *fpl* d'intérêt
i oneri *mpl* d'interesse
n rentelasten *mpl*

1588 interest coupon; interest warrant
d Zinsabschnitt *m*; Zinscoupon *m*; Zinskupon *m*; Zinsschein *m*
e cupón *m* de intereses; talón *m* de intereses
f coupon *m* d'intérêt(s)
i cedola *f* d'interessi
n int(e)restcoupon *m*; rentecoupon *m*

1589 interest due
cf. **accrued interest, arrears of interest, black interest**
d fällige Zinsen *mpl*; fällig gewordene Zinsen *mpl*
e intereses *mpl* débitos; intereses *mpl* devengados; intereses *mpl* vencidos
f intérêts *mpl* dus; intérêts *mpl* échus
i interessi *mpl* maturati; interessi *mpl* scaduti
n verschenen int(e)rest *m*; verschenen rente *f*; verschuldigde int(e)rest *m*; verschuldigde rente *f*; vervallen int(e)rest *m*; vervallen rente *f*

1590 interest-free; non-interest-bearing
d unverzinsbar; unverzinslich; zinsenfrei *(O)*; zinsfrei; zinslos
e exento de interés (intereses); improductivo de interés (intereses); sin interés (intereses)
f exempt d'intérêt(s); improductif d'intérêt(s); ne portant pas d'intérêt; non productif d'intérêt(s); sans intérêt(s)
i esente da interesse (interessi); infruttifero; non fruttifero (di interessi); non produttivo di interesse (interessi); senza interesse (interessi)
n niet rentedragend; niet rentegevend; renteloos

1591 interest in limited partnership; share in limited partnership
d Kommanditanteil *m*; Kommanditeinlage *f*
e participación *f* en comandita
f commandite *f*
i quota *f* dell'accomandante
n aandeel *n* van de commanditair

1592 interest payment; interestservice; payment of interest
d Verzinsung *f*; Zinsendienst *m*; Zinsenzahlung *f*; Zinszahlung *f*
e pago *m* de intereses; servicio *m* de intereses
f paiement *m* d'intérêts; service *m* d'intérêts; versement *m* d'intérêts
i corresponsione *f* d'interessi; pagamento *m* d'interessi; servizio *m* d'interessi
n int(e)restbetaling *f*; rentebetaling *f*; rentedienst *m*

1593 interest rate; rate of interest
d Verzinsung *f*; Zinsfuss *m*; Zinsrate *f*; Zinssatz *m*
e tasa *f* de interés; tipo *m* de interés
f taux *m* d'intérêt
i percentuale *f* d'interesse; saggio *m* d'interesse; tasso *m* d'interesse
n int(e)restvoet *m*; rentekoers *m*; rentestand *m*; rentestandaard *m*; rentetarief *n*; rentevoet *m*

1594 interest rate rebate; interest rate subsidy; interest rebate; interest subsidy
d Zinsenvergütung *f (O)*; Zinsenzuschuss *m (O)*; Zinssubvention *f*; Zinsvergütung *f*; Zinszuschuss *m*
e abono *m* de intereses; bonificación *f* de intereses; subvención *f* de intereses
f bonification *f* d'intérêts; subvention *f* d'intérêts
i abbuono *m* d'interessi; bonifico *m*

d'interessi; sovvenzione *f* d'interessi
n int(e)restsubsidie *f/n*; int(e)rest-vergoeding *f*; rentesubsidie *f/n*; rente-vergoeding *f*

1595 **interest yield**
d Verzinsung *f*; Zinsenertrag *m*; Zins-ertrag *m*
e producto *m* de los intereses; rédito *m* de los intereses
f produit *m* d'intérêts; rapport *m* d'intérêts
i reddito *m* di interessi
n renteopbrengst *f*

1596 **interim balance sheet; interim (financial) statement; provisional balance sheet**
d Zwischenabschluss *m*; Zwischenbilanz *f*
e balance *m* interino; balance *m* intermediario; balance *m* provisional; balance *m* provisorio
f bilan *m* intérimaire; bilan *m* intermédiaire; bilan *m* provisoire
i bilancio *m* interinale; bilancio *m* intermedio; bilancio *m* provvisorio
n tussenbalans *f*; tussentijdse balans *f*; voorlopige balans *f*

1597 **interim certificate; interim share; promise of shares; provisional certificate; provisional share; scrip; scrip certificate**
cf. **share certificate**
d Aktienpromesse *f*; Interimsaktie *f*; Interimsschein *m*; provisorischer Anteil-schein *m*; Scrip *m*; Zwischenschein *m*
e acción *f* provisional; certificado *m* provisional; promesa *f* de acciones; resguardo *m* provisional; título *m* provisional
f action *f* provisoire; certificat *m* provisoire; promesse *f* d'actions; scrip(t) *m*; titre *m* provisoire
i azione *f* provvisoria; certificato *m* provvisorio; promessa *f* d'azioni; titolo *m* provvisorio
n interimaandeel *n*; scrip *m*; recipis *n*; voorlopig aandeel *n*; voorlopig certificaat *n*

1598 **interim dividend**
d Abschlagsdividende *f*; Interims-dividende *f*; Zwischendividende *f*
e dividendo *m* a cuenta; dividendo *m* interino; dividendo *m* provisional
f acompte *m* sur le dividende; dividende *m* intérimaire; dividende *m* provisoire
i acconto *m* dividendo; acconto *m* sul dividendo; dividendo *m* d'acconto; dividendo *m* provvisorio
n interimdividend *n*

1599 **interim interest; mesne interest** *(rare)*
d Interkalarzinsen *mpl*; Zwischenzinsen *mpl*
e intereses *mpl* interinos
f intérêts *mpl* intercalaires; intérêts *mpl* intérimaires; intérimaires *mpl*
i interessi *mpl* intercalari; interessi *mpl* interinali
n tussenrente *f*

1600 **internal audit**
d betriebseigene Revision *f*; Innen-revision *f*; innerbetriebliche Revision *f*; interne Revision *f*
e auditoría *f* interna; censura *f* interna; revisión *f* interna
f révision *f* interne
i revisione *f* interna
n interne accountantscontrole *f*

1601 **internal financing; self-finance; self-financing**
d Eigenfinanzierung *f*; Innen-finanzierung *f*; Selbstfinanzierung *f*
e autofinanciación *f*; autofinanciamiento *m*; financiación *f* interna; financiación *f* por fondos propios; financiamiento *m* interno; financiamiento *m* por fondos propios
f autofinancement *m*; financement *m* interne; financement *m* par des fonds propres
i autofinanziamento *m*; finanziamento *m* interno; finanziamento *m* con mezzi propri
n autofinanciering *f (B)*; financiering *f* met eigen middelen; interne financiering *f*; zelffinanciering *f*

1602 **International Bank for Reconstruction and Development; IB; IBRD; WorldBank**
d Internationale Bank *f* für Wiederaufbau und Wirtschaftsförderung; IBRD; Welt-bank *f*
e Banco *m* Internacional de Reconstrucción y Desarrollo; BIRD; Banco *m* Internacional de Reconstrucción y Fomento; BIRF; Banco *m* Mundial
f Banque *f* internationale pour la reconstruction et le développement; BIRD; Banque *f* mondiale
i Banca *f* Internazionale per la Ricostruzione e lo Sviluppo; BIRS; Banca *f* Mondiale

n Internationale Bank *f* voor Herstel en Ontwikkeling; IBRD; Internationale Bank *f* voor Wederopbouw en Ontwikkeling; Wereldbank *f*

1603 International Chamber of Commerce; ICS
d Internationale Handelskammer *f*; IHK
e Cámara *f* de Comercio Internacional; CCI
f Chambre *f* de commerce internationale; CCI
i Camera *f* di Commercio Internazionale; CCI
n Internationale Kamer *f* van Koophandel; IKK

1604 International Development Association
d Internationale Entwicklungsorganisation *f*; IDA
e Asociación *f* Internacional de Desarrollo; AID
f Association *f* internationale de développement; AID; Association *f* internationale pour le développement
i Associazione *f* Internazionale per lo Sviluppo; IDA
n Internationale Ontwikkelingsorganisatie *f*; IDA

1605 International Finance Corporation; IFC
d Internationale Finanz-Corporation *f*; IFC; Internationale Finanzgesellschaft *f*; Internationale Finanzkorporation *f*
e Corporación *f* Financiera Internacional; CFI; Sociedad *f* Financiera Internacional; SFI
f Société *f* financière internationale; SFI
i Società *f* Finanziaria Internazionale; SFI
n Internationale Financieringsmaatschappij *f*; IFM

1606 International Labor Organization *(US)*; ILO; International Labour Organization *(UK)*
d Internationale Arbeitsorganisation *f*; IAO
e Organización *f* Internacional del Trabajo; OIT
f Organisation *f* internationale du travail; OIT
i Organizzazione *f* Internazionale del Lavoro; OIL
n Internationale Arbeidsorganisatie *f*; IAO

1607 International Monetary Fund; IMF
d Internationaler Währungsfonds *m*; IWF
e Fondo *m* Monetario Internacional; FMI
f Fonds *m* monétaire international; FMI
i Fondo *m* Monetario Internazionale; FMI
n Internationaal Monetair Fonds *n*; IMF

1608 interventionism
d Interventionismus *m*
e intervencionismo *m*
f interventionnisme *m*
i interventismo *m*
n interventionisme *n*

1609 intervention point; support point
d Interventionspunkt *m*; Stützungspunkt *m*
e punto *m* de apoyo; punto *m* de intervención; punto *m* de sostén
f point *m* d'appui; point *m* d'intervention; point *m* de soutien
i punto *m* d'appoggio; punto *m* d'intervento; punto *m* di sostegno
n interventiepunt *n*; steunpunt *n*

1610 intervention rate; pegged rate; support rate
d Interventionskurs *m*; Stützkurs *m*; Stützungskurs *m*
e cambio *m* de apoyo; cambio *m* de intervención; cambio *m* de sostén
f cours *m* d'appui; cours *m* de soutien; cours *m* d'intervention
i corso *m* d'appoggio; corso *m* d'intervento; corso *m* di sostegno
n interventiekoers *m*; steunkoers *m*

1611 intra-community payment
d innergemeinschaftliche Zahlung *f*
e pago *m* intracomunitario
f paiement *m* intracommunautaire
i pagamento *m* intracomunitario
n betaling *f* binnen de Gemeenschap

1612 intrinsic value
d eigentlicher Wert *m*; innerer Wert *m*
e valor *m* intrínseco
f valeur *f* intrinsèque
i valore *m* intrinseco
n intrinsieke waarde *f*

1613 introductory price; publicity price
d Einführungspreis *m*; Reklamepreis *m*; Werbepreis *m*
e precio *m* de propaganda; precio *m* de reclamo
f prix *m* de lancement; prix *m* de réclame; prix-réclame *m*
i prezzo *m* di lancio; prezzo *m* di propaganda; prezzo réclame *m*
n lanceerprijs *m*; reclameprijs *m*

1614 inventory *(list)*
d Inventar *n*
e inventario *m*
f inventaire *m*

i inventario *m*
n boedelbeschrijving *f*; boedellijst *f*; inventaris *m*; inventarislijst *f*

1615 inventory ***(US)*; stock; supply**
d Bestand *m*; Inventar *n*; Stock *m*; Vorrat *m*
e existencia *f*; inventario *m*; provisión *f*; stock *m*
f existence *f*; inventaire *m*; provision *f*; stock *m*
i esistenza *f*; giacenza *f*; inventario *m*; provvista *f*; scorta *f*; stock *m*
n inventaris *m*; stock *m*; voorraad *m*

1616 inventory; inventory taking; stocktaking
d Bestand(s)aufnahme *f*; Inventaraufnahme *f*; Inventaraufstellung *f*; Inventarerrichtung *f*; Inventarisation *f*; Inventarisierung *f*; Inventur *f*; Inventuraufnahme *f*
e facción *f* del inventario *(AL)*; formación *f* del inventario; inventario *m*; levantamiento *m* del inventario
f confection *f* de l'inventaire; établissement *m* de l'inventaire; inventaire *m*
i formazione *f* dell'inventario; inventariazione *f*; inventario *m*; redazione *f* dell'inventario
n inventarisatie *f*; opmaken *n* van de inventaris

1617 inventory value
cf. **accounting value**
d Inventarwert *m*
e valor *m* de inventario
f valeur *f* d'inventaire
i valore *m* di inventario
n inventariswaarde *f*

1618 invest *v (money etc.)*; **place** *v*
d anlegen; investieren; placieren; plazieren
e colocar; invertir
f investir; placer
i collocare; impiegare; investire
n beleggen; investeren; plaatsen; uitzetten

1619 investment; placement
d Anlage *f*; Investierung *f*; Investition *f*; Investment *n*; Kapitalanlage *f*; Placierung *f*; Plazierung *f*
e colocación *f*; inversión *f*
f investissement *m*; placement *m*
i collocamento *m*; impiego *m*; investimento *m*
n belegging *f*; investering *f*; plaatsing *f*; uitzetting *f*

1620 investment appropriations; investment credits
d Investitionsmittel *npl*
e créditos *mpl* de inversión
f crédits *mpl* d'investissement
i stanziamenti *mpl* destinati agli investimenti
n investeringskredieten *npl*

1621 investment bank
d Anlagebank *f (Schw)*; Investitionsbank *f*
e banco *m* de inversiones
f banque *f* d'affaires; banque *f* d'investissements
i banca *f* d'investimenti
n investeringsbank *f*

1622 investment capital
cf. **capital invested**
d Anlagekapital *n*; Anlagevermögen *n*; Investitionskapital *n*
e capital *m* de colocación; capital *m* de inversión
f capitaux *mpl* de placement; fonds *mpl* d'investissement
i capitale *m* d'investimento
n beleggingskapitaal *n*; investeringskapitaal *n*

1623 investment expansion
d Ausweitung *f* der Investitionen
e expansión *f* de las inversiones
f expansion *f* des investissements
i espansione *f* degli investimenti
n uitbreiding *f* van de investeringen

1624 investment fund; mutual fund; open-end investment company* ***(US)*; open-end trust*** ***(US)*; unit trust*** ***(UK)***
cf. **closed-end investment company**
d Anlagefonds *m*; gemeinsamer Anlagefonds *m*; gemeinsamer Investmentfonds *m*; Investitionsfonds *m*; Investmentfonds *m*
e fondo *m* de inversión; fondo *m* de inversiones; fondo *m* mutual de inversiones
f fonds *m* commun de placement; fonds *m* commun d'investissement; fonds *m* de placement; fonds *m* d'investissement
i fondo *m* comune d'investimento; fondo *m* d'investimento
n beleggingsfonds *n*; gemeenschappelijk beleggingsfonds *n*

* No exact equivalent exists elsewhere.

1625 investment incentive
d Investitionsanreiz *m*; Investitionsimpuls *m*

e estímulo *m* a la inversión; incentivo *m* a la inversión
f incitation *f* à l'investissement
i incentivo *m* al investimento; sollecitazione *f* ad investire
n investeringsprikkel *m*; investeringsstimulans *m*

1626 investment in securities; investment in stock; portfolio investment
d Anlage *f* in Portefeuilleeffekten; Wertpapieranlage *f*
e colocación *f* en títulos (de cartera); colocación *f* en valores (de cartera); inversión *f* en títulos (de cartera); inversión *f* en valores (de cartera)
f investissement *m* en titres (de portefeuille); investissement *m* en valeurs (de portefeuille); placement *m* en titres (de portefeuille); placement *m* en valeurs (de portefeuille)
i investimento *m* in titoli (di portafoglio); investimento *m* in valori (di portafoglio)
n belegging *f* in effecten; belegging *f* in waardepapieren; investering *f* in effecten; investering *f* in waardepapieren

1627 investment needs; investment requirements
d Anlagebedarf *m*; Investitionsbedarf *m*
e necesidades *fpl* de inversión
f besoins *mpl* d'investissement
i fabbisogni *mpl* d'investimento; necessità *fpl* d'investimento
n investeringsbehoeften *fpl*

1628 investment portfolio; portfolio of securities; security holdings; shareholdings; stockholdings
d Aktienbesitz *m*; Aktienbestand *m*; Aktienportefeuille *n*; Anlageportefeuille *n*; Effektenbesitz *m*; Effektenbestand *m*; Effektenportefeuille *n*; Wertpapierbesitz *m*; Wertpapierbestand *m*; Wertpapierportefeuille *n*; Wertschriftenbesitz *m*; Wertschriftenbestand *m*; Wertschriftenportefeuille *n*
e cartera *f* de acciones; cartera *f* de títulos; cartera *f* de valores; efectivo *m* en cartera
f existence *f* (en) titres; portefeuille *m* (d')actions; portefeuille *m* (de) titres; portefeuille *m* (de) valeurs
i giacenza *f* in titoli; portafoglio *m* (di) azioni; portafoglio *m* (di) titoli; portafoglio *m* (di) valori
n aandelenbezit *n*; aandelenportefeuille *m*; effectenbezit *n*; effectenportefeuille *m*; effectenvoorraad *m*

1629 investment rate; investment ratio; rate of investment
d Investitionsquote *f*; Investitionsrate *f*
e tasa *f* de inversión; tasa *f* de las inversiones
f taux *m* des investissements; taux *m* d'investissement
i tasso *m* degli investimenti; tasso *m* d'investimento
n investeringsquote *f*

1630 investment securities; portfolio securities
d Anlageeffekten *pl*; Anlagepapiere *npl*; Anlagetitel *mpl*; Anlagewerte *mpl*; Anlagewertpapiere *npl*; Portefeuilleeffekten *pl*
e títulos *mpl* de cartera; títulos *mpl* de inversión; valores *mpl* de cartera; valores *mpl* de colocación; valores *mpl* de inversión
f titres *mpl* de placement; titres *mpl* de portefeuille; titres *mpl* d'investissement; valeurs *fpl* de placement; valeurs *fpl* de portefeuille; valeurs *fpl* d'investissement
i titoli *mpl* d'investimento; titoli *mpl* in portafoglio; valori *mpl* d'investimento; valori *mpl* in portafoglio
n beleggingspapieren *npl*; beleggingswaarden *fpl*

1631 investor
cf. **moneylender**
d Anleger *m*; Geldanleger *m*; Investor *m*; Kapitalanleger *m*; Kapitaleinleger *m*; Kapitalgeber *m*
e aportador *m* de capital; inversionista *m*; inversor *m*
f apporteur *m* de capital; bailleur *m* de capitaux; investisseur *m*
i apportatore *m* di capitale; investitore *m*
n belegger *m*; investeerder *m*

1632 invisible exports; invisibles
d unsichtbare Ausfuhr(en) *f(pl)*; unsichtbare Exporte *mpl*
e exportaciones *fpl* invisibles
f exportations *fpl* invisibles
i esportazioni *fpl* invisibili
n onzichtbare export *m*; onzichtbare uitvoer *m*

1633 invisible imports
d unsichtbare Einfuhr(en) *f(pl)*; unsichtbare Importe *mpl*
e importaciones *fpl* invisibles
f importations *fpl* invisibles

i importazioni *fpl* invisibili
n onzichtbare import *m*; onzichtbare invoer *m*

1634 **invite** *v* **subscriptions for a loan; offer** *v* **a loan for subscription**
d eine Anleihe zur Zeichnung auflegen; zur Zeichnung einer Anleihe auffordern
e abrir la suscripción de un empréstito; invitar a la suscripción de un empréstito; ofrecer un empréstito a (la) su(b)scripción; ofrecer un empréstito en su(b)scripción; sacar un empréstito a (la) su(b)scripción
f inviter à la souscription d'un emprunt; mettre un emprunt en souscription; offrir un emprunt à la souscription; offrir un emprunt en souscription; ouvrir la souscription d'un emprunt; ouvrir un emprunt à la souscription
i aprire la sottoscrizione di un prestito; invitare a la sottoscrizione di un prestito; mettere un prestito in sottoscrizione; offrire un prestito in sottoscrizione
n de inschrijving op een lening openstellen; een lening ter inschrijving aanbieden; tot het inschrijven op een lening uitnodigen

1635 **invite** *v* **tenders**
d ausschreiben
e llamar a licitación
f mettre en adjudication
i bandire una gara di appalto; indire una gara per l'appalto
n aanbesteden; in aanbesteding geven

1636 **irredeemable bond; irredeemable debenture; unredeemable bond**
d nicht einziehbare Obligation *f*; nicht einziehbare Schuldverschreibung *f*; nicht rückzahlbare Obligation *f*; nicht rückzahlbare Schuldverschreibung *f*; nicht tilgbare Obligation *f*; nicht tilgbare Schuldverschreibung *f*; nicht zurückzahlbare Obligation *f*; nicht zurückzahlbare Schuldverschreibung *f*; unkündbare Obligation *f*; unkündbare Schuldverschreibung *f*; untilgbare Obligation *f*; untilgbare Schuldverschreibung *f*
e obligación *f* irredimible; obligación *f* irrescatable; obligación *f* no amortizable; obligación *f* no reembolsable; obligación *f* no rescatable
f obligation *f* irrachetable; obligation *f* irremboursable; obligation *f* non amortissable; obligation *f* non remboursable
i obbligazione *f* irredimibile; obbligazione *f* non ammortizzabile; obbligazione *f* non rimborsabile; obbligazione *f* non riscattabile
n niet aflosbare obligatie *f*; niet amortiseerbare obligatie *f*; onafkoopbare obligatie *f*; onaflosbare obligatie *f*

1637 **issue** *v* **bonds; put** *v* **out bonds**
d Obligationen ausgeben; Schuldverschreibungen ausgeben
e emitir obligaciones
f émettre des obligations
i emettere obbligazioni
n obligaties emitteren; obligaties uitgeven

1638 **issued capital; issued capital stock** ***(US)*****; issued stock** ***(US)*****; outstanding capital stock** ***(US)*****; outstanding share capital** ***(UK)*****; outstanding shares** ***(UK)***
d ausgegebenes Aktienkapital *n*; ausgegebenes Kapital *n*; begebenes Kapital *n*; Emissionskapital *n*; emittiertes Kapital *n*
e capital *m* en acciones emitido; capital *m* emitido
f capital-actions *m* émis; capital *m* émis
i capitale *m* azionario emesso; capitale *m* emesso
n geëmitteerd aandelenkapitaal *n*; geëmitteerd kapitaal *n*; uitgegeven aandelenkapitaal *n*; uitgegeven kapitaal *n*

1639 **issue of securities**
d Effektenausgabe *f*; Effektenemission *f*
e emisión *f* de títulos-valores
f émission *f* de valeurs
i emissione *f* di valori
n effectenemissie *f*; effectenuitgifte *f*

1640 **issue of shares; share issue; stock issue** ***(US)***
cf. **rights issue**
d Aktienausgabe *f*; Aktienemission *f*; Ausgabe *f* von Aktien; Emission *f* von Aktien
e emisión *f* de acciones
f émission *f* d'actions
i emissione *f* azionaria; emissione *f* d'azioni
n emissie *f* van aandelen; uitgifte *f* van aandelen

1641 **issue premium; issuing premium; premium on an issue; share premium**
d Aktienagio *n*; Aktienaufgeld *n*; Aktienaufpreis *m*; Ausgabeprämie *f*; Emissionsagio *n*; Emissionsaufgeld *n*; Emissionsprämie *f*

e agio *m* sobre la emisión; prima *f* de emisión
f prime *f* à l'émission; prime *f* d'émission
i premio *m* d'emissione; sovrapprezzo *m* d'emissione
n emissieagio *n*; emissiepremie *f*; uitgiftepremie *f*

1642 issue price; issuing price; rate of issue
cf. **subscription price**
d Ausgabekurs *m*; Ausgabepreis *m*; Begebungskurs *m*; Begebungspreis *m*; Emissionskurs *m*; Emissionspreis *m*
e cotización *f* de emisión; precio *m* de emisión; tipo *m* de emisión
f cours *m* d'émission; prix *m* d'émission; taux *m* d'émission
i corso *m* d'emissione; prezzo *m* d'emissione; tasso *m* d'emissione
n emissiekoers *m*; emissieprijs *m*; koers *m* van uitgifte; uitgiftekoers *m*; uitgifteprijs *m*

1643 issue prospectus; subscription prospectus; underwriting prospectus
d Begebungsprospekt *m*; Emissionsprospekt *m*; Subskriptionsprospekt *m*; Zeichnungsprospekt *m*
e prospecto *m* de emisión; prospecto *m* de suscripción
f prospectus *m* d'émission; prospectus *m* de souscription
i programma *m* d'emissione; programma *m* di sottoscrizione
n emissieprospectus *m/n*; inschrijvingsprospectus *m/n*

1644 issuer
d Emittent *m*
e emisor *m*
f émetteur *m*
i emittente *m*
n emittent *m*

1645 issuing bank; issuing house; underwriting house
d Effektenbank *f*; Emissionsbank *f*; Emissionshaus *n*
e banco *m* de emisión de valores; banco *m* de valores; casa *f* de emisiones
f banque *f* émettrice; banque *f* de placement; banque *f* de valeurs; maison *f* d'émission
i banca *f* d'emissione di valori; banca *f* emittente
n effectenbank *f*; emissiebank *f (N)*; emissiehuis *n*

1646 items of value; objects of value; valuables
d Kostbarkeiten *fpl*; Wertgegenstände *mpl*; Wertobjekte *npl*; Wertsachen *fpl*
e objetos *mpl* de valor; prendas *fpl* de valor; valores *mpl*
f objets *mpl* de prix; objets *mpl* de valeur; valeurs *fpl*
i oggetti *mpl* di valore; preziosi *mpl*; valori *mpl*
n kostbaarheden *fpl*; voorwerpen *npl* van waarde

J

1647 jobber; market speculator ***(US)*****; stock exchange gambler; stock exchange operator; stock exchange speculator**
d Agioteur *m*; Börsenschieber *m*; Börsenspekulant *m*; Börsenspieler *m*; Börsianer *m*
e agiotador *m*; agiotista *m*; bolsista *m*; especulador *m* en bolsa; jugador *m* de bolsa; operador *m* *(AL)*
f agioteur *m*; boursicoteur *m*; boursicotier *m*; boursier *m*; joueur *m* à la bourse; joueur *m* de bourse; opérateur *m*; spéculateur *m* en bourse
i aggiotatore *m*; borsista *m*; giocatore *m* di borsa; giocatore *m* in borsa; operatore *m* di borsa; speculatore *m* di borsa
n agioteur *m*; beursman *m*; beursspeculant *m*; gokker *m* aan de beurs; speler *m* aan de beurs

1648 jobber; stockjobber
d Aktienzwischenhändler *m*; Börsenjobber *m*; Jobber *m*; Zwischenmakler *m*
e intermediario *m* de corredores de bolsa
f courtier *m* intermédiaire de bourse; jobber *m*
i intermediario *m* fra agenti di borsa; jobber *m*
n hoekman *m*; jobber *m*; tussenmakelaar *m*

1649 joint account
cf. **joint venture account**
d gemeinsames Konto *n*; gemeinschaftliches Konto *n*; Gemeinschaftskonto *n*; Oderkonto *n**; Undkonto *n***
e cuenta *f* colectiva; cuenta *f* común; cuenta *f* conjunta; cuenta *f* en común; cuenta *f* mancomunada
f compte *m* collectif; compte *m* commun; compte *m* conjoint; compte *m* joint; compte-joint *m*
i conto *m* collettivo; conto *m* comune; conto *m* congiunto; conto *m* in comune
n gemeenschappelijke rekening *f*; gemene rekening *f*; gezamenlijke rekening *f*

* Any signatory can sign alone.
** All signatories must sign.

1650 joint and several debt
d Gesamtschuld *f*; Solidarschuld *f*
e deuda *f* in sólidum; deuda *f* solidaria
f dette *f* solidaire
i debito *m* in solido; debito *m* solidale
n hoofdelijke schuld *f*; solidaire schuld *f*

1651 joint and several debtor
cf. **co-debtor**
d Gesamtschuldner *m*; Solidarschuldner *m*
e deudor *m* in sólidum; deudor *m* solidario
f débiteur *m* solidaire
i debitore *m* in solido; debitore *m* solidale
n hoofdelijke schuldenaar *m*; solidaire schuldenaar *m*

1652 joint and several liability
d gesamtschuldnerische Haftpflicht *f*; gesamtschuldnerische Haftung *f*; Gesamtschuldnerschaft *f*; Solidarhaftung *f*; solidarische Haftpflicht *f*; solidarische Haftung *f*
e responsabilidad *f* solidaria; solidaridad *f* pasiva
f responsabilité *f* solidaire; solidarité *f* passive
i responsabilità *f* solidale; solidarità *f* passiva
n hoofdelijke aansprakelijkheid *f*; solidaire aansprakelijkheid *f*

1653 joint transaction; joint venture; transaction on joint account
d Metageschäft *n*; Partizipationsgeschäft *n*
e negocio *m* a medias; negocio *m* en participación; transacción *f* a medias; transacción *f* en participación
f opération *f* en compte à demi; opération *f* en participation; transaction *f* en compte à demi; transaction *f* en participation
i affare *m* a metà; affare *m* in partecipazione; operazione *f* a metà; operazione *f* in partecipazione
n meta-affaire *f*; meta-transactie *f*; transactie *f* voor gemeenschappelijke rekening

1654 joint venture account; participation account ***(US)*****; syndicate account**
cf. **joint account**
d Beteiligungskonto *n*; Konsortialkonto *n*; Konto *n* a meta; Metakonto *n*; Partizipationskonto *n*
e cuenta *f* a mitad; cuenta *f* de participación; cuenta *f* en participación
f compte *m* à demi; compte *m* de participation; compte *m* en participation
i conto *m* a compartecipazione; conto *m* a più firme; conto *m* di partecipazione; conto *m* in partecipazione
n conto *n* a meta; halve rekening *f*; metaconto *n*; metarekening *f*; participatierekening *f* *(B)*

1655 **journal entry**
d Buchungsposten *m* im Journal
e asiento *m* de diario
f article *m* de journal
i articolo *m* di giornale
n dagboekpost *m*; journaalpost *m*

K

1656 keep *v* **the accounts; keep** *v* **the books**
d die Bücher führen; die Buchführung machen; die Buchhaltung führen; Konten führen; Rechnung führen
e llevar la contabilidad; llevar las cuentas; llevar los libros; tener los libros
f tenir la comptabilité; tenir les comptes; tenir les écritures; tenir les livres
i tenere i conti; tenere i libri; tenere la contabilità
n boekhouden; de boeken houden

1657 keynesian
d keynesisch
e keynesiano
f keynésien
i keynesiano
n keynesiaans

1658 in kind
d in natura; in Naturalien; in Waren; Natural-; Sach-
e en especie
f en nature
i in natura
n in natura

1659 kite flying
d Wechselreiterei *f*
e libranza *f* de letras de colusión
f cavalerie *f*; tirage *m* en l'air
i giro *m* di cambiali a vuoto
n wisselruiterij *f*

L

1660 land bank *(US)*; **mortgage bank**
cf. **building society**
d Grundkreditanstalt *f*; Hypothekenbank *f*; Realkreditinstitut *n*
e banco *m* de crédito inmobiliario; banco *m* de crédito territorial; banco *m* hipotecario; instituto *m* de crédito inmobiliario
f banque *f* de crédit foncier; banque *f* de crédit hypothécaire; banque *f* hypothécaire; établissement *m* de crédit foncier; établissement *m* de crédit immobilier; institut *m* de crédit foncier; institut *m* de crédit immobilier
i banca *f* di credito fondiario; banca *f* di credito immobiliare; banca *f* ipotecaria; istituto *m* di credito fondiario; istituto *m* di credito immobiliare
n grondkredietbank *f*; hypot(h)eekbank *f*

1661 landed estate; landed property
cf. **immovable property**
d Grundbesitz *m*; Grundeigentum *n*; Grundstücksbesitz *m*; Grundstückseigentum *n*; Grundstücksvermögen *n*; Grund *m* und Boden *m*; Grundvermögen *n*
e arraigo *m*; bienes *mpl* raíces; propiedad *f* fundiaria *(AL)*; propiedad *f* territorial
f bien-fonds *m(pl)*; fonds *m* de terre; propriété *f* foncière
i beni *mpl* fondiari; proprietà *f* fondiaria; proprietà *f* terriera
n grondbezit *n*; grondeigendom *n*; liggende gronden *mpl*

1662 land tax; property tax
cf. **property tax (as separate entry)**
d Grundsteuer *f*; Grundstückssteuer *f*; Grundvermögensabgabe *f*; Grundvermögenssteuer *f*; Grundwertabgabe *f*
e contribución *f* territorial; impuesto *m* predial; impuesto *m* sobre la propiedad territorial; impuesto *m* territorial
f contribution *f* foncière; impôt *m* foncier; taxe *f* sur la valeur foncière
i imposta *f* fondiaria; imposta *f* prediale; imposta *f* sui terreni; prediale *f*
n grondbelasting *f*

1663 languish *v*; **stagnate** *v*; **stand** *v* **still**
d da(r)niederliegen; stagnieren; stillstehen; stocken
e estancarse; languidecer; paralizarse
f languir; stagner
i languire; ristagnare; stagnare
n kwijnen; stagneren; stilstaan; stokken *(rare)*

1664 lapsed coupon; statute-barred coupon
d verjährter Kupon *m*
e cupón *m* prescri(p)to
f coupon *m* périmé; coupon *m* prescrit
i cedola *f* prescritta
n verjaarde coupon *m*

1665 launch *v* **on the market; throw** *v* **on the market; unload** *v* **on the market**
cf. **market** *v*
d auf den Markt lancieren; auf den Markt werfen
e arrojar al mercado; echar al mercado; lanzar al mercado
f jeter sur le marché; lancer sur le marché
i gettare sul mercato; lanciare sul mercato
n op de markt gooien; op de markt lanceren

1666 lease; lease agreement *(US)*; **lease contract**
d Miete *f*; Mietkontrakt *m*; Mietvertrag *m*; Pacht *f*; Pachtbrief *m*; Pachtkontrakt *m*; Pachtvertrag *m*
e arrendamiento *m*; arriendo *m*; contrato *m* de alquiler; contrato *m* de arrendamiento; contrato *m* de locación; escritura *f* de arrendamiento
f bail *m* (à loyer); contrat *m* de bail; contrat *m* de location; ferme *f (rare)*
i affittanza *f*; affitto *m*; contratto *m* d'affitto; contratto *m* di locazione; fitto *m*
n huur *f*; huurcedel *f/n*; huurceel *f/n*; huurcontract *n*; huurovereenkomst *f*; pacht *f*; pachtbrief *m*; pachtcedel *f/n*; pachtceel *f/n*; pachtcontract *n*; pachtovereenkomst *f*

1667 leaseholder; lessee
d Mieter *m*; Pächter *m*; Pachtnehmer *m*
e arrendador *m (col.)*; arrendatario *m*; arrendante *m (AL)*; conductor *m (rare)*; locatario *m*
f fermier *m (rare)*; locataire *m*; preneur *m* (à bail); preneur *m* (à ferme)
i affittuario *m*; conduttore *m*; locatario *m*
n huurder *m*; pachter *m*

1668 leasing
d Anlagenpachtung *f*; Anlageverpachtung *f*; Ausrüstungsvermietung *f*; Leasing *n*
e arrendamiento *m* financiero; leasing *m*
f crédit-bail *m*; leasing *m*
i affitto *m* di impianti industriali; credito-

affitto *m*; credito-locazione *m*; leasing *m*
n leasing *f*

1669 legal currency *(US)*; legal tender
d gesetzliches Zahlungsmittel *n*; gesetzliche Währung *f*
e moneda *f* de curso legal; moneda *f* legal
f monnaie *f* de cours légal; monnaie *f* légale; monnaie *f* libératoire
i moneta *f* di corso legale; moneta *f* legale
n wettig betaalmiddel *n*

1670 legal reserves; minimum reserve requirements; minimum reserves; obligatory reserves; reserve requirements
d gesetzliche Reserven *fpl*; Mindestreserven *fpl*; Pflichtreserven *fpl*; Reservesoll *n*
e reservas *fpl* legales; reservas *fpl* mínimas (legales); reservas *fpl* obligatorias
f réserves *fpl* légales; réserves *fpl* obligatoires
i riserva *f* dovuta per legge; riserva *f* ordinaria; riserve *fpl* legali; riserve *fpl* obbligatorie
n minimumreserves *fpl*; verplichte reserves *fpl*; wettelijke reserves *fpl*; wettelijk voorgeschreven reserves *fpl*

1671 lend *v*; loan *v*
d ausleihen; borgen; leihen; verborgen; verleihen
e dar a préstamo; dar en préstamo; dar prestado; emprestar *(col.)*; prestar
f donner en prêt; prêter
i dare a prestito; dare in prestito; imprestare; prestare
n borgen *(rare)*; lenen; uitlenen

1672 lender
cf. **creditor, moneylender**
d Anleihegeber *m*; Ausleiher *m*; Borger *m*; Darleh(e)nsgeber *m*; Darleiher *m (O; Schw)*; Kreditgeber *m*; Verleiher *m*
e dador *m* de crédito; mutuante *m*; prestador *m*; prestamista *m*
f donneur *m* de crédit; prêteur *m*
i datore *m* di credito; mutuante *m*; prestatore *m*
n kredietgever *m*; lener *m*; uitlener *m*

1673 lending
d Ausleihungen *fpl*
e prestamos *mpl*
f emprunts *mpl*; prêts *mpl*
i prestiti *mpl*
n leningen *fpl*

1674 lending on securities
cf. **credit on securities, hypothecation of securities, loan on securities**
d Belehnung *f* von Effekten *(Schw)*; Beleihung *f* von Effekten; Lombard *m/n*; Lombardierung *f*
e préstamo *m* sobre efectos; préstamo *m* sobre títulos; préstamo *m* sobre valores
f prêt *m* sur titres; prêt *m* sur valeurs
i prestito *m* su titoli
n belening *f* van effecten

1675 lend *v* money at (on) interest; put *v* out money at (on) interest
d Geld auf (gegen) Zinsen ausleihen; Geld auf (gegen) Zinsen leihen; Geld auf (gegen) Zinsen verleihen
e prestar dinero a interés
f prêter de l'argent à (contre) intérêt(s)
i prestare denaro a interesse (interessi)
n geld op (tegen) int(e)rest lenen; geld op (tegen) int(e)rest uitlenen; geld op rente lenen; geld op rente uitlenen

1676 lessor
d Vermieter *m*; Verpächter *m*
e arrendador *m*; arrendante *m (AL)*; locador *m (AL)*
f affermeur *m (rare)*; bailleur *m*
i locatore *m*
n verhuurder *m*; verpachter *m*

1677 less tax(es); after tax; after taxes; tax deducted; taxes deducted; taxes paid; tax paid
d nach Abzug der Steuer(n); nach Bezahlung der Steuer(n); nach Steuerabzug; unter Abzug der Steuer(n)
e deducidos los impuestos; después de deducir el impuesto (los impuestos); después de impuestos; después de la deducción del impuesto (de los impuestos); pagados los impuestos
f après déduction de l'impôt (des impôts); après paiement de l'impôt (des impôts); après taxe(s); déduction faite d'impôt(s); impôts déduits; sous déduction d'impôt(s)
i al lordo delle imposte; dedotte le imposte; dedotte le tasse; deduzione fatta della tassa (delle imposte); defalcate le imposte; defalcate le tasse; detratte le imposte; detratte le tasse; dopo deduzione della tassa (delle imposte)
n na aftrek van de belasting(en); na belasting; na belastingen; na belastingaftrek

1678 letter of credit
d Akkreditiv *n*; Kreditbrief *m*

e carta *f* de crédito; carta-orden *f* de crédito; letra *f* de crédito
f accréditif *m*; lettre *f* accréditive; lettre *f* de créance; lettre *f* de crédit
i credenziale *f*; lettera *f* credenziale; lettera *f* d'accreditamento; lettera *f* di credito
n accreditief *n*; kredietbrief *m*

1679 **level of investments**
d Investitionshöhe *f*
e nivel *m* de inversiones
f niveau *m* des investissements
i livello *m* dell'investimento
n niveau *n* van de investeringen

1680 **level of prices; price level**
d Kursniveau *n*; Kursstand *m*; Preisniveau *n*; Preisstand *m*
e nivel *m* de (las) cotizaciones; nivel *m* de (los) precios
f niveau *m* des cours; niveau *m* des prix
i livello *m* dei corsi; livello *m* dei prezzi
n koersniveau *n*; koerspeil *n*; prijsniveau *n*; prijspeil *n*; stand *m* der prijzen

1681 **liability**
d Haftbarkeit *f*; Haftpflicht *f*; Haftung *f*
e responsabilidad *f*
f responsabilité *f*
i responsabilità *f*
n aansprakelijkheid *f*

1682 **liability account**
d Passivkonto *n*
e cuenta *f* de pasivo
f compte *m* de passif
i conto *m* del passivo
n passief-rekening *f*

1683 **liability to tax; tax liability**
cf. **tax liability**
d Steuerpflicht *f*; Steuerverpflichtung *f*
e obligación *f* de pagar impuestos
f assujettissement *m* à l'impôt; devoir *m* de l'impôt; devoir *m* fiscal
i obbligo *m* di pagare le tasse; soggettamento *m* all'imposta; soggettività *f* all'imposta
n belastingverplichting *f*

1684 **liberalization of commerce**
d Befreiung *f* des Handelsverkehrs; Liberalisierung *f* des Handels
e liberalización *f* del comercio
f libéralisation *f* des échanges commerciaux; libéralisation *f* du commerce; libération *f* des échanges commerciaux
i liberalizzazione *f* degli scambi commerciali; liberalizzazione *f* del commercio
n liberalisatie *f* van de handel; liberalisering *f* van de handel; vrijmaking *f* van het handelsverkeer

1685 **liberalize** *v*
d liberalisieren
e liberalizar
f libéraliser
i liberalizzare
n liberaliseren

1686 **licence fee; royalty**
d Ertragsanteil *m*; Gewinnanteil *m*; Lizenz *f*; Lizenzabgabe *f*; Lizenzgebühr *f*; Tantieme *f*
e canon *m* de licencia; derecho *m* de licencia; licencia *f*; royalty *m/f*; tasa *f* de licencia
f droit *m* de licence; licence *f*; redevance *f*; royalty *f*
i canone *m* di licenza; diritto *m* di licenza; royalty *f*
n aandeel *n* in de opbrengst; licentierecht *n*; royalty *f*

1687 **lien (on)**
d Pfandrecht *n* (an); Retentionsrecht *n* (an) *(Schw)*; Rückbehaltungsrecht *n* (an) *(O)*; Zurückbehaltungsrecht *n* (an)
e derecho *m* de embargo (sobre); derecho *m* de prenda (sobre); derecho *m* de retención (sobre); derecho *m* prendario (sobre)
f droit *m* de gage (sur); droit *m* de nantissement (sur); droit *m* de retention (sur)
i diritto *m* cauzionale (su); diritto *m* di pegno (su); diritto *m* di ritenzione (su)
n pandrecht *n* (op); recht *n* van retentie (op); recht *n* van terughouding (op); retentierecht *n* (op)

1688 **life assurance** *(UK)*; **life insurance** *(US)*
d Lebensversicherung *f*
e siguro *m* de vida; siguro *m* sobre la vida *(AL)*
f assurance *f* vie; assurance-vie *f*; assurance *f* sur la vie
i assicurazione *f* (sulla) vita
n levensverzekering *f*

1689 **limited liability**
d beschränkte Haftpflicht *f*; beschränkte Haftung *f*
e responsabilidad *f* limitada

f responsabilité *f* limitée
i responsabilità *f* limitata
n beperkte aansprakelijkheid *f*

1690 **limited liability company*; private limited company*; Co. Ltd.**
cf. **incorporated company**
d Gesellschaft *f* mit beschränkter Haftung; G.m.b.H.
e sociedad *f* de responsabilidad limitada; S.L.; S.R.L.
f société *f* à responsabilité limitée; S.A.R.L.; société *f* de personnes à responsabilité limitée; S.P.R.L. *(B)*
i società *f* a responsabilità limitata; S.R.L.
n besloten vennootschap *f*; B.V. *(N)*; personenvennootschap *f* met beperkte aansprakelijkheid; P.V.B.A. *(B)*; vennootschap *f* met beperkte aansprakelijheid *(N)*
* Local legislation varies greatly.

1691 **limited partner; special partner**
cf. **dormant partner**
d beschränkt haftender Gesellschafter *m*; Kommanditär *m (Schw)*; Kommanditist *m*
e comanditario *m*; socio *m* comanditario
f associé *m* commanditaire; commanditaire *m*
i accomandante *m*; socio *m* accomandante
n commanditair *m*; commanditair vennoot *m*; commanditaris *m*

1692 **limited partnership**
cf. **partnership limited by shares**
d Kommandite *f*; Kommanditgesellschaft *f*
e comandita *f*; sociedad *f* comanditaria; sociedad *f* en comandita (simple)
f commandite *f*; société *f* en commandite (simple)
i accomandita *f*; società *f* in accomandita (semplice)
n commandite *f*; commanditaire vennootschap *f*

1693 **liquid**
d flüssig; liquid
e líquido
f liquide
i liquido
n liquide

1694 **liquidator**
cf. **assignee in bankruptcy**
d Abwickler *m*; Liquidator *m*
e liquidador *m*
f liquidateur *m*
i liquidatore *m*
n liquidateur *m*; liquidator *m*; vereffenaar *m*

1695 **liquidity**
cf. **available funds**
d Flüssigkeit *f*; Liquidität *f*
e liquidez *f*
f liquidité *f*
i liquidità *f*
n liquiditeit *f*

1696 **liquidity reserves; liquid reserves**
cf. **cash reserve**
d liquide Reserven *fpl*; Liquiditätsreserven *fpl*
e reservas *fpl* de liquidez; reservas *fpl* líquidas
f réserves *fpl* de liquidité; réserves *fpl* liquides
i riserve *fpl* di liquidità; riserve *fpl* liquide
n liquide reserves *fpl*; liquiditeitsreserves *fpl*

1697 **liquidity squeeze**
d Eindämmung *f* der Liquidität
e contracción *f* de la liquidez
f resserrement *m* des liquidités
i contrazione *f* delle liquidità
n indamming *f* van de liquiditeit

1698 **list** *v (US) (shares)**; **mark** *v*; **quote** *v*
d kotieren*; notieren; quotieren
e cotizar
f coter
i quotare
n noteren
* Usually in sense of to admit to quotation.

1699 **listed securities; quoted securities; securities admitted to the stock exchange; stock exchange securities**
d an der Börse zugelassene Effekten *pl*; an der Börse zugelassene Wertpapiere *npl*; Börseneffekten *pl*; börsenfähige Effekten *pl*; börsenfähige Wertpapiere *npl*; börsengängige Effekten *pl*; börsengängige Wertpapiere *npl*; börsenmässige Effekten *pl*; börsenmässige Wertpapiere *npl*; börsennotierte Effekten *pl*; börsennotierte Wertpapiere *npl*; Börsenpapiere *npl*; Börsenwerte *mpl*; Börsenwertpapiere *npl*; kotierte Wertpapiere *npl (Schw)*; notierte Effekten *pl*; notierte Wertpapiere *npl*
e papeles *mpl* bursátiles; títulos *mpl* admitidos en bolsa; títulos *mpl* cotizados

(en bolsa); títulos *mpl* de bolsa; títulos *mpl* inscritos en la bolsa; valores *mpl* admitidos en bolsa; valores *mpl* bursátiles; valores *mpl* cotizados (en bolsa); valores *mpl* de bolsa; valores *mpl* inscritos en la bolsa

f titres *mpl* admis à la cote; titres *mpl* cotés (en bourse); titres *mpl* de bourse; titres *mpl* inscrits à la bourse; valeurs *fpl* admises à la cote; valeurs *fpl* boursières; valeurs *fpl* cotées (en bourse); valeurs *fpl* de bourse; valeurs *fpl* inscrites à la bourse

i titoli *mpl* ammessi alla quotazione; titoli *mpl* di borsa; titoli *mpl* di listino; titoli *mpl* quotati (in bolsa); valori *mpl* ammessi alla quotazione; valori *mpl* di borsa; valori *mpl* quotati (in bolsa)

n aan de beurs genoteerde fondsen *npl*; aan de beurs genoteerde waarden *fpl*; beursfondsen *npl*; beurswaarden *fpl*; genoteerde fondsen *npl*; genoteerde waarden *fpl*; genoteerde waardepapieren *npl*; ter beurze genoteerde fondsen *npl*; ter beurze genoteerde waarden *fpl*; ter beurze genoteerde waardepapieren *npl*

1700 list of opening balances; opening balance sheet

d Eröffnungsbilanz *f*

e balance *m* de apertura

f bilan *m* d'entrée; bilan *m* d'ouverture

i bilancio *m* di apertura

n openingsbalans *f*

1701 list of shareholders; list of stockholders *(US)*; register of members; register of shareholders; register of stockholders *(US)*; share ledger; share register; stock book; stockholders' ledger *(US)*; stock record *(US)*; stock register

d Aktienbuch *n*; Aktienliste *f*; Aktienregister *n*; Aktionär(s)register *n*; Aktionär(s)verzeichnis *n*; Gesellschafterliste *f*; Gesellschafterregister *n*; Hauptbuch *n* der Aktionäre; Liste *f* der Aktionäre; Mitgliederverzeichnis *n*; Verzeichnis *n* der Aktionäre

e libro *m* de acciones; libro *m* de (los) accionistas; libro *m* mayor de los accionistas; lista *f* de los accionistas; registro *m* de acciones; registro *m* de (los) accionistas; registro *m* de (los) socios

f grand(-)livre *m* des actionnaires; grand(-)livre *m* des titres; liste *f* des actionnaires; livre *m* des actionnaires; livre *m* des actions; livre *m* des titres; registre *m* des actionnaires; registre *m* des actions; registre *m* des sociétaires; registre *m* des titres

i elenco *m* degli azionisti; libro *m* degli azionisti; libro *m* dei soci; libro *m* mastro delle azioni; registro *m* degli azionisti; registro *m* delle azioni

n aandeelhoudersboek *n*; aandeelhoudersregister *n*; aandelenregister *n*; grootboek *n* van de aandeelhouders; lijst *f* van aandeelhouders; lijst *f* van vennoten

1702 live *v* **beyond one's means**

d mit seinen Mitteln nicht auskommen; über seine Verhältnisse leben

e gastar más de lo que se gana; no llegar con su dinero; vivir dentro de sus recursos

f dépenser plus que son revenu; vivre au-delà (au-dessus) de ses moyens

i spendere più di quello che si guadagna; vivere al di sopra dei propri mezzi

n boven zijn middelen leven

1703 live *v* **within one's means; make** *v* **(both) ends meet**

d mit seinen Mitteln auskommen; seinen Verhältnissen entsprechend leben

e pasar con lo que se gana; vivir uno de sus ingresos

f joindre les deux bouts; ne pas dépasser son revenu

i sbarcare il lunario; vivere alla meglio

n de eindjes aan elkaar knopen; rondkomen

1704 living standard; standard of living

d Lebenshaltung *f*; Lebensstandard *m*

e nivel *m* de vida; standard *m* de vida

f niveau *m* de vie; standard *m* de vie

i standard *m* di vita; tenore *m* di vita

n levenspeil *n*; levensstandaard *m*

1705 loan *(government, company)*
cf. **credit**

d Anleihe *f*; Anleihen *n (Schw)*

e empréstito *m*

f emprunt *m*

i prestito *m*

n lening *f*

* For general or personal loan see under credit.

1706 as a loan; by way of a loan

d leihweise

e a título de préstamo

f à titre de prêt

i a titolo di prestito

n bij wijze van lening

1707 loanable capital; loan capital
cf. **borrowed capital**
d Anleihekapital *n*; Leihkapital *n*
e capital *m* de empréstito; capital *m* de préstamo
f capital *m* d'emprunt
i capitale *m* di prestito
n leenkapitaal *n*; leningkapitaal *n*

1708 loan by the central banks
d Notenbankkredit *m*; Notenbank-vorschuss *m*
e anticipo *m* de los bancos centrales; préstamo *m* de los bancos centrales
f avance *f* des banques centrales
i anticipazione *f* delle banche centrali
n krediet *n* van de centrale banken

1709 loan certificate
d Darleh(e)nsschein *m*; Darleh(e)ns-urkunde *f*
e certificado *m* de préstamo; título *m* de préstamo
f certificat *m* de prêt; titre *m* de prêt
i certificato *m* di prestito; titolo *m* di prestito
n bewijs *n* van voorschot; schuldbewijs *n*

1710 loan fund
d Darleh(e)nsfonds *m*
e fondo *m* de crédito; fondo *m* de préstamos
f fonds *m* de crédit; fonds *m* de prêts
i fondo *m* di credito; fondo *m* di prestiti
n kredietfonds *n*; leningsfonds *n*

1711 loan on mortgage; mortgage loan
cf. **credit on mortgage**
d Hypothekardarleh(e)n *n*; Hypotheken-anleihe *f*; Hypothekendarleh(e)n *n*
e préstamo *m* hipotecario
f emprunt *m* hypothécaire; prêt *m* hypothécaire; prêt *m* sur hypothèque
i mutuo *m* ipotecario; prestito *m* ipotecario
n hypot(h)ecaire lening *f*; lening *f* op hypot(h)eek

1712 loan on securities; lombard loan
cf. **advance on securities, credit on securities, lending on securities**
d Faustpfanddarleh(e)n *n*; Lombard-anleihe *f*; Lombarddarleh(e)n *n*
e préstamo *m* sobre efectos; préstamo *m* sobre títulos; préstamo *m* sobre valores
f emprunt *m* sur titres; emprunt *m* sur valeurs; prêt *m* sur titres; prêt *m* sur valeurs
i mutuo *m* su titoli; mutuo *m* su valori; prestito *m* su titoli; prestito *m* su valori
n lening *f* tegen effecten; lening *f* tegen onderpandeffecten

1713 local authority bond *(UK)*; local bond *(UK)*; municipal; municipal bond
d Kommunalanleihen *fpl*; Kommunal-obligation *f*; Kommunalschuldschein *m*; Kommunalschuldverschreibung *f*
e obligación *f* comunal; obligación *f* municipal
f obligation *f* communale; obligation *f* municipale
i obbligazione *f* comunale; obbligazione *f* municipale
n gemeenteobligatie *f*

1714 lombard rate; rate for advances on securities; rate for loans on securities
cf. **rate for advances on collateral**
d Lombardsatz *m*; Lombardzinsfuss *m*
e tasa *f* de préstamos sobre efectos; tasa *f* de préstamos sobre títulos; tasa *f* de préstamos sobre valores; tipo *m* de préstamos sobre efectos; tipo *m* de préstamos sobre títulos; tipo *m* de préstamos sobre valores
f taux *m* des avances sur titres; taux *m* des avances sur valeurs
i saggio *m* delle anticipazioni su titoli; saggio *m* delle anticipazioni su valori; tasso *m* sulle anticipazioni su titoli; tasso *m* sulle anticipazioni su valori
n beleningsrente *f* op effecten; belenings-rente *f* op waardepapieren

1715 long; long-dated*; long-term
d lang; langfristig
e a largo plazo; a plazo largo
f à long terme; à longue échéance*
i a lunga scadenza*; a lungo termine
n lang; langlopend; langzicht-*; op lange termijn

* Of bills etc.

1716 loro account; vostro account
d Lorokonto *n*; Vostrokonto *n*
e cuenta *f* suya; su cuenta *f*
f compte *m* loro; compte *m* vostro; votre compte *m*
i conto *m* loro; conto *m* vostro
n conto *n* loro; conto *n* vostro; loro-rekening *f*; vostrorekening *f*

1717 loss
cf. **deficiency**
d Einbusse *f*; Verlust *m*
e pérdida *f*
f perte *f*

i perdita *f*
n verlies *n*

1718 **loss of earnings; loss of income** *(US)*; **loss of profit(s); profit shortfall**
d entgangener Gewinn *m*; Ertragsausfall *m*; Ertragseinbusse *f*; Gewinnausfall *m*; Gewinneinbusse *f*; Gewinnentgang *m*; Verdienstausfall *m*; Verdiensteinbusse *f*; Verdienstentgang *m*
e beneficio *m* perdido; falta *f* de beneficio; falta *f* de ganancia; lucro *m* cesante; pérdida *f* de beneficios; pérdida *f* de ganancias; pérdida *f* de lucro
f gain *m* manqué; manque *m* à gagner; perte *f* de bénéfice(s); perte *f* de gain; perte *f* de profit(s)
i lucro *m* cessante; mancato guadagno *m*; perdita *f* di guadagno; perdita *f* di profitto; perdita *f* di proventi; perdita *f* d'utile; perdita *f* d'utilità
n derving *f* van verdienste(n); winstderving *f*

1719 **lottery bond; premium bond**
d auslosbare Obligation *f*; Prämienlos *n*; Prämienobligation *f*; Prämienschein *m*; Prämienschuldverschreibung *f*
e bono *m* de prima; bono *m* de sorteo; obligación *f* a prima
f bon *m* à lots; obligation *f* à lots; obligation *f* à primes; titre *m* à lots
i buono *m* di premio; obbligazione *f* a premio; obbligazione *f* di premio
n lotenobligatie *f*; premielot *n*; premieobligatie *f*

1720 **lottery loan; premium bond loan; premium loan**
d Auslosungsanleihe *f*; Losanleihe *f*; Lotterieanleihe *f*; Prämienanleihe *f*; Trefferanleihe *f (O)*
e empréstito *m* a prima; empréstito *m* a sorteo; empréstito *m* con prima; empréstito *m* de lotería; empréstito *m* de sorteo; empréstito *m* por bonos de sorteo
f emprunt *m* à lots; emprunt *m* à primes; emprunt *m* par tirage au sort
i prestito *m* a premi; prestito *m* a premio
n lotenlening *f*; premielening *f*

1721 **lower value method; minimum value principle**
d Niederstwertprinzip *n*
e principio *m* del valor mínimo
f principe *m* de la valeur minimale
i principio *m* del minimo valore
n principe *n* van de laagste waarde

1722 **lump sum**
cf. **aggregate amount**
d Pauschalbetrag *m*; Pauschale *n (rarely f)*; Pauschalsumme *f*
e importe *m* a tanto alzado; suma *f* a tanto alzada
f montant *m* forfaitaire; somme *f* à forfait; somme *f* forfaitaire
i importo *m* forfettario; somma *f* forfettaria
n forfaitair bedrag *n*

1723 **luxury tax; tax on luxuries**
d Aufwand(s)steuer *f*; Luxussteuer *f*
e contribución *f* suntuaria; impuesto *m* al lujo; impuesto *m* de lujo; impuesto *m* sobre los artículos de lujo; impuesto *m* sobre el lujo; impuesto *m* suntuario
f impôt *m* de luxe; impôt *m* somptuaire; impôt *m* sur le luxe; impôt *m* sur les articles de luxe; taxe *f* de luxe; taxe *f* somptuaire
i imposta *f* sui consumi di lusso; imposta *f* sul lusso; tassa *f* di lusso; tassa *f* sugli articoli di lusso
n belasting *f* op luxeartikelen; luxebelasting *f*; weeldebelasting *f*

M

1724 **machine accounting; mechanized accounting**
d Maschinenbuchführung *f*; Maschinenbuchhaltung *f*
e contabilidad *f* mecánica; contabilidad *f* mecanizada
f mécanographie *f* comptable
i contabilità *f* meccanografica; meccanografia *f* contabile
n mechanische boekhouding *f*

1725 **macro-economic**
d grosswirtschaftlich; makro-ökonomisch
e macroeconómico
f macro-économique
i macro-economico
n macro-economisch

1726 **made out to order; payable to order; to order**
d Order-
e a la orden
f à ordre
i all'ordine
n order-

1727 **make *v* a cash settlement; pay *v* cash; pay *v* cash down; pay *v* spot cash; settle *v* in cash**
d bar auf den Tisch bezahlen; bar bezahlen; bar zahlen; in bar begleichen; in bar bezahlen; in bar zahlen; in barem Geld zahlen; in Geld bezahlen
e arreglar al contado; arreglar en efectivo; pagar al contado; pagar en dinero; pagar en efectivo
f payer argent sur table; payer au comptant compté; payer comptant; payer en argent (comptant); payer en espèces; payer en numéraire; régler au comptant
i pagare a contanti; pagare a pronti contanti; pagare in contanti; pagare in denaro; pagare in numerario; regolare a contanti; regolare in contanti
n cash betalen; contant betalen; contant vereffenen; in baar geld betalen; in contanten betalen; prompt contant betalen

1728 **make *v* a price; name *v* a price; quote *v* a price; state *v* a price**
cf. **determine *v* a price**
d einen Preis angeben; einen Preis ansetzen; einen Preis benennen; einen Preis festsetzen; einen Preis quotieren
e cotizar un precio; indicar un precio; señalar un precio
f coter un prix; donner un prix; faire un prix; indiquer un prix
i fare un prezzo; indicare un prezzo; quotare un prezzo
n een prijs noemen; een prijs opgeven; een prijs zeggen

1729 **make *v* a profit; realise *v* a profit; realize *v* a profit *(US)*; turn *v* a profit**
d einen Gewinn erzielen; einen Gewinn machen; einen Gewinn realisieren
e obtener un beneficio; obtener una ganancia; realizar un beneficio; realizar una ganancia; sacar un beneficio; sacar una ganancia
f faire un bénéfice; faire un profit; réaliser un bénéfice; réaliser un profit; retirer un bénéfice; retirer un profit
i fare un guadagno; realizzare un profitto; realizzare un utile; ricavare un profitto; ricavare un utile
n een winst maken; een winst realiseren; een winst verwezenlijken

1730 **manipulation on the stock exchange; market rigging; rigging**
d Börsenmanipulation *f*; Börsenmanöver *n*; Börsenschiebung *f*; Kursmanipulation *f*; Kurstreiberei *f*
e manipulación *f* bursátil; manipulación *f* de los cambios; maniobra *f* bursátil
f manipulation *f* des cours; manipulation *f* sur les cours; manœuvre *f* de bourse; tripotage *m* de bourse
i manipolazione *f* dei corsi; manovra *f* di borsa
n beursmaneuver *f/n*; beursmanœuvre *f/n*; koersmanipulatie *f*

1731 **margin** *(between option deal and forward deal)*
d Ekart *m*
e diferencia *f* de prima
f écart *m* (de prime)
i scarto *m* (di prima)
n ecart *m*

1732 **margin** *(collateral deposited with broker)*
cf. **caution money, collateral, earnest**
d Bareinschuss *m*; Deckung *f*; Deckungsbetrag *m*; Einschuss *m*; Hinterlegungssumme *f*; Marge *f*; Sicherheitssumme *f*
e cobertura *f*; margen *m/f*
f couverture *f*; marge *f*
i copertura *f*; margine *m*
n dekking *f*; marge *f*

1733 **marginal cost**
d Grenzkosten *pl*
e coste *m* marginal; costo *m* marginal
f coût *m* marginal
i costo *m* marginale
n marginale kosten *mpl*

1734 **margin of income** *(US)*; **margin of profit; markup; profit margin; trade profit margin; trading margin**
cf. **gross margin**
d Gewinnspanne *f*; Handelsspanne *f*; Verdienstspanne *f*
e margen *m/f* comercial; margen *m/f* de beneficio; margen *m/f* de ganancia; margen *m/f* de utilidad
f marge *f* bénéficiaire; marge *f* commerciale; marge *f* de bénéfice; taux *m* de marque
i coefficiente *m* di maggiorazione; margine *m* commerciale; margine *m* di guadagno; margine *m* di profitto; margine *m* di utile
n handelsmarge *f*; winstmarge *f*

1735 **market** *(place)*
d Markt *m*
e mercado *m*
f marché *m*
i mercato *m*
n markt *f*

1736 **market** *(region)*; **marketing area; outlet; sales area**
d Absatzbereich *m*; Absatzfeld *n*; Absatzgebiet *n*; Absatzmarkt *m*; Absatzquelle *f*
e área *f* de mercado; área *f* de salida; área *f* de venta; campo *m* de venta; mercado *m* (de salida); zona *f* de mercado; zona *f* de venta
f débouché *m*; marché *m* (de vente); zone *f* de vente
i campo *m* di smercio; mercato *m* (di sbocco); mercato *m* (di vendita); sbocco *m*; zona *f* di vendita
n afzetgebied *n*; afzetmarkt *f*; debouché *n*

1737 **market** *v*; **put** *v* **on the market**
cf. **launch** *v* **on the market, sell** *v*
d auf den Markt bringen
e introducir en el mercado; llevar al mercado
f introduire sur le marché; mettre sur le marché
i immettere nel (sul) mercato; introdurre sul mercato
n aan (op) de markt brengen

1738 **marketable; merchantable; salable** *(US)*; **saleable** *(UK)*; **vendable; vendible**
d absatzfähig; absetzbar; gangbar; handelsfähig; marktfähig; marktgängig; umsetzbar; veräusserlich; verkäuflich; verkaufsfähig
e comerciable; negociable; vendible
f commerçable; marchand; négociable; vendable
i commerciabile; esitabile; negoziabile; smerciabile; vendibile
n verhandelbaar; verkoopbaar

1739 **marketable securities; negotiable securities; transferable securities**
d begebbare Effekten *pl*; begebbare Wertpapiere *npl*; börsenfähige Effekten *pl*; börsenfähige Wertpapiere *npl*; handelsfähige Effekten *pl*; handelsfähige Wertpapiere *npl*; marktfähige Effekten *pl*; marktfähige Wertpapiere *npl*; übertragbare Effekten *pl*; übertragbare Wertpapiere *npl*; verkehrsfähige Effekten *pl*; verkehrsfähige Wertpapiere *npl*
e títulos *mpl* comerciables; títulos *mpl* mobiliarios; títulos *mpl* negociables; títulos *mpl* transferibles; valores *mpl* comerciables; valores *mpl* mobiliarios; valores *mpl* negociables; valores *mpl* transferibles
f titres *mpl* commerçables; titres *mpl* mobiliers; titres *mpl* négociables; titres *mpl* transférables; valeurs *fpl* commerçables; valeurs *fpl* mobilières; valeurs *fpl* négociables; valeurs *fpl* transférables
i titoli *mpl* commerciabili; titoli *mpl* mobiliari; titoli *mpl* negoziabili; titoli *mpl* trasferibili; valori *mpl* commerciabili; valori *mpl* mobiliari; valori *mpl* negoziabili; valori *mpl* trasferibili
n geldswaardige papieren *npl*; overdraagbare waardepapieren *npl*; roerende effecten *npl*; roerende waarden *fpl*; verhandelbare effecten *npl*; verhandelbare waardepapieren *npl*

1740 **market analysis; market investigation; market research; market study; market survey**
d Absatzanalyse *f*; Absatzforschung *f*; Absatzstudie *f*; Marktanalyse *f*; Marktbeobachtung *f*; Markterkundung *f*; Marktforschung *f*; Marktstudie *f*; Marktuntersuchung *f*
e análisis *m/f* del mercado; estudio *m* del mercado; examen *m* del mercado;

investigación *f* del mercado; mercadología *f (AL)*; prospección *f* del mercado
f analyse *f* du marché; enquête *f* sur le marché; étude *f* du marché; prospection *f* du marché
i analisi *f* del mercato; indagine *f* del mercato; ricerca *f* del mercato; studio *m* del mercato
n marktanalyse *f*; marktonderzoek *n*; marktprospectie *f (B)*; marktstudie *f*

1741 **market economy**
d Marktwirtschaft *f*
e economía *f* de mercado
f économie *f* du marché
i economia *f* di mercato
n markteconomie *f*

1742 **marketing**
d Absatzkunde *f*; Kommerzialisierung *f*; Marketing *n*; Markttechnik *f*; Vermarktung *f*
e comercialización *f*; marketing *m*; mercadotecnia *f (AL)*
f commercialisation *f*; marketing *m*; technique *f* du marché
i commercializzazione *f*; marketing *m*; mercatistica *f*
n marketing *f*; markttechniek *f*

1743 **market position; market situation; state of the market**
d Lage *f* des Marktes; Marktlage *f*; Markt-situation *f*; Stand *m* des Marktes
e estado *m* del mercado; situación *f* del mercado
f état *m* du marché; position *f* de place; situation *f* du marché
i situazione *f* del mercato
n marktpositie *f*; marktsituatie *f*; stand *m* van de markt

1744 **market price**
cf. **current market price**
d Marktpreis *m*
e precio *m* de(l) mercado
f prix *m* de (du) marché; prix *m* sur la place
i prezzo *m* del (di) mercado
n marktprijs *m*

1745 **market sharing**
d Aufteilung *f* des Marktes; Aufteilung *f* der Märkte; Marktaufteilung *f*
e repartición *f* del mercado; repartición *f* de mercados
f partage *m* du marché; partage *m* des marchés; répartition *f* du marché; répartition *f* des marchés
i ripartizione *f* del mercato; ripartizione *f* dei mercati; spartizione *f* del mercato; spartizione *f* dei mercati
n onderlinge verdeling *f* van de markt; onderlinge verdeling *f* der markten

1746 **marking (of share prices); quotation (of share prices)**
d Kotierung *f*; Kursnotierung *f*; Notierung *f*; Quotierung *f*
e cotización *f*
f cotation *f* (des cours); cote *f* (des cours)
i quotazione *f* (dei corsi)
n koersnotering *f*; notering *f*

1747 **material assets; tangible assets**
cf. **capital assets**
d greifbare Aktiva *npl*; greifbare Aktiven *npl*; greifbare Vermögenswerte *mpl*; greifbare Werte *mpl*; greifbare Wirtschaftsgüter *npl*; körperliche Wirtschaftsgüter *npl*; materielle Aktiva *npl*; materielle Aktiven *npl*; materielle Vermögenswerte *mpl*; materielle Werte *mpl*; materielle Wirtschaftsgüter *npl*
e activos *mpl* materiales; activos *mpl* tangibles; bienes *mpl* corporales; bienes *mpl* materiales; bienes *mpl* tangibles
f biens *mpl* corporels; biens *mpl* matériels; valeurs *fpl* corporelles; valeurs *fpl* matérielles; valeurs *fpl* tangibles
i attivi *mpl* materiali; attivi *mpl* tangibili; attività *f* materiale; beni *mpl* materiali
n lichamelijke goederen *npl*; materiële goederen *npl*; reële activa *npl*; stoffelijke activa *npl*

1748 **maturity**
cf. **currency, date due, expiration**
d Fälligkeit *f*; Verfall *m*; Verfall(s)zeit *f*
e vencimiento *m*
f échéance *f*
i maturazione *f**; scadenza *f*
n verval *n*; vervaltijd *m*
* Interest.

1749 **maturity of X years**
d X-jährige Laufzeit *f*
e plazo *m* de vencimiento de X años; vencimiento *m* de X años
f X années d'échéance; échéance *f* de X années
i scadenza *f* di X anni
n X-jarige looptijd *m*

1750 **maturity premium; premium on redemption; redemption premium**
d Einlösungsprämie *f*; Rückkaufsprämie *f*;

Rückprämie *f*; Rückzahlungsagio *n*; Rückzahlungsprämie *f*
e prima *f* de reembolso; prima *f* de rescate
f prime *f* de remboursement
i premio *m* di rimborso
n aflossingspremie *f*; terugbetalingspremie *f*

1751 means of payment; means of settlement
d Zahlungsmittel *npl*
e medios *mpl* de pago
f moyens *mpl* de paiement
i mezzi *mpl* di pagamento
n betaalmiddelen *npl*

1752 medium-dated*; medium-term
d mittelfristig
e a medio plazo; a plazo medio
f à moyenne échéance*; à moyen terme
i a media scadenza*; a medio termine
n half lang *(B)*; middellang; op middellange termijn
* Of bills etc.

1753 medium-term credit
d mittelfristiger Kredit *m*
e crédito *m* a medio plazo
f crédit *m* à moyen terme
i credito *m* a medio termine; mediocredito *m*
n middellang krediet *n*

1754 memo book *(US)*; waste book
d Kladde *f*; Strazze *f*
e borrador *m*; libro *m* borrador
f brouillard *m*; main *f* courante
i brogliaccio *m*
n kladboek *n*

1755 method of gross presentation; principle of gross presentation
d Bruttoprinzip *n*
e principio *m* de no compensación
f méthode *f* de non-compensation
i metodo *m* dei compensi di partite; principio *m* dei compensi di partite
n bruto-methode *f*

1756 method of net presentation; principle of net presentation
d Nettoprinzip *n*
e principio *m* de la compensación de saldos
f méthode *f* de la compensation des soldes
i metodo *m* del compenso di partite; principio *m* del compenso di partite
n netto-methode *f*

1757 micro-economic
d kleinwirtschaftlich; mikro-ökonomisch
e microeconómico
f micro-économique
i micro-economico
n micro-economisch

1758 migratory balance
d Einwanderungssaldo *m*; Wanderungsbilanz *f*
e balance *m* migratorio; balanza *f* migratoria *(AL)*
f solde *m* migratoire
i saldo *m* migratore
n migratiesaldo *n*

1759 minimum reserve ratio
d Mindestreservesatz *m*
e coeficiente *m* de reserva obligatoria; tipo *m* de reserva mínima
f coefficient *m* de réserve obligatoire
i coefficiente *m* di riserva obbligatoria
n coëfficiënt *m* van de verplichte reserves

1760 minority holding; minority interest
d Minderheitsbeteiligung *f*; Minderheitspaket *n*; Minoritätsbeteiligung *f*
e interés *m* minoritario; participación *f* minoritaria
f intérêt(s) *m(pl)* minoritaire(s); participation *f* minoritaire
i interesse *m* minoritario; partecipazione *f* di minoranza; partecipazione *f* minoritaria
n minderheidsbelang *n*; minderheidsdeelname *f*; minderheidsdeelneming *f*; minderheidsparticipatie *f*

1761 mint
d Münzamt *n*; Münzanstalt *f*; Münze *f*; Münzstätte *f*
e casa *f* (de la) moneda; ceca *f*; Moneda *f*; monedería *f*
f hôtel *m* de la monnaie; hôtel *m* des monnaies; Monnaie *f*
i zecca *f*
n Munt *f*; munterij *f*; muntfabriek *f*; munthuis *n*

1762 mint par (of exchange)
cf. **par of exchange**
d Münzpari *n*; Münzparität *f*
e paridad *f* intrínseca
f pair *m* (du change) intrinsèque; pair *m* (du change) métallique
i parità *f* intrinseca
n muntpari *n*; muntpariteit *f*

1763 misallocation of funds
d Fehlleitung *f* von Mitteln; unsachgemässe Verteilung *f* von Mitteln
e repartición *f* ineficiente de fondos
f allocation *f* inappropriée de moyens
i ripartizione *f* inadeguata di fondi
n onjuiste allocatie *f* van middelen; onjuiste toewijzing *f* van middelen

1764 miscellaneous charges; miscellaneous costs; miscellaneous expenses; petty charges; petty expenses; sundries; sundry charges; sundry costs; sundry expenses
cf. **additional charges**
d Diversa *npl*; Diverse *pl*; diverse Ausgaben *fpl*; diverse Unkosten *pl*; kleine Ausgaben *fpl*; kleine Auslagen *fpl*; kleine Kosten *pl*; kleine Spesen *fpl*; kleine Unkosten *pl*; sonstige Ausgaben *fpl*; sonstige Auslagen *fpl*; sonstige Spesen *fpl*; sonstige Unkosten *pl*; Verschiedene *pl*; verschiedene Ausgaben *fpl*; verschiedene Unkosten *pl*
e diversos *mpl*; gastos *mpl* chicos; gastos *mpl* diversos; gastos *mpl* menores; gastos *mpl* menudos; otros gastos *mpl*; varios *mpl*
f dépenses *fpl* diverses; divers *mpl*; frais *mpl* divers; menues dépenses *fpl*; menus frais *mpl*; petites dépenses *fpl*; petits frais *mpl*
i diversi *mpl*; piccole spese *fpl*; spese *fpl* diverse; spese *fpl* minute; spese *fpl* varie; varie *fpl*
n diversen *pl*; diverse kosten *mpl*; diverse onkosten *mpl*; diverse uitgaven *fpl*; kleine kosten *mpl*; kleine onkosten *mpl*; kleine uitgaven *fpl*

1765 miscellaneous income; miscellaneous revenues; other income
d neutrale Erträge *mpl*; sonstige Einkünfte *fpl*; sonstige Erträge *mpl*
e ingresos *mpl* varios; otros ingresos *mpl*
f revenu *m* de sources diverses; revenu *m* non incorporé; revenus *mpl* divers
i ricavi *mpl* diversi
n andere inkomsten *fpl*; bijzondere baten *fpl*

1766 mobilization *(funds etc.)*
cf. **conversion into cash, deblocking, fund raising**
d Flüssigmachung *f*; Mobilisation *f*; Mobilisierung *f*
e movilización *f*
f mobilisation *f*
i mobilitazione *f*; mobilizzazione *f*
n mobilisering *f*

1767 mobilize *v (funds etc.)*
cf. **borrow** *v* **capital, convert** *v* **into cash, deblock** *v*
d flüssig machen; mobilisieren
e movilizar
f mobiliser
i mobilitare; mobilizzare
n mobiliseren; vlottend maken

1768 monetarist
d Monetarist *m*
e monetarista *m*
f monétariste *m*
i monetarista *m*
n monetarist *m*

1769 monetary policy
d Geldpolitik *f*; Währungspolitik *f*
e política *f* monetaria
f politique *f* de la monnaie; politique *f* monétaire
i politica *f* monetaria; politica *f* valutaria
n geldbeleid *n*; geldpolitiek *f*; monetair beleid *n*; monetaire politiek *f*; munt-politiek *f*

1770 monetary reserve; money reserve
cf. **currency reserve**
d Geldreserve *f*
e reserva *f* monetaria
f réserve *f* monétaire
i riserva *f* monetaria; scorta *f* monetaria
n geldreserve *f*

1771 monetary support
d Währungsbeistand *m*
e ayuda *f* monetaria
f soutien *m* monétaire
i sostegno *m* monetario
n monetaire hulp *f*

1772 monetization *(establishing as money)*
d Monetisierung *f*
e monetización *f*
f monétisation *f*
i monetazione *f*
n monetisatie *f*

1773 monetize *v (establish as money)*
d monetisieren; zum gesetzlichen Zahlungsmittel machen
e monetizar
f monétiser
i monetare
n als wettig betaalmiddel in circulatie brengen; monetiseren

1774 **money demand**
d Geldbedarf *m*; Geldnachfrage *f*
e demanda *f* de dinero
f demande *f* monétaire
i domanda *f* monetaria
n geldvraag *f*; monetaire vraag *f*; vraag *f* naar geld

1775 **money economy**
d Geldwirtschaft *f*
e economía *f* monetaria
f économie *f* monétaire
i economia *f* monetaria
n geldhuishouding *f*; monetaire economie *f*

1776 **money equivalents; secondary liquidity**
cf. **supply of near money**
d Liquiditäten *fpl* zweiten Grades; Quasigeldbestände *mpl*; Sekundarliquiditäten *fpl*; zentralbankfähige Titel *mpl*
e liquideces *fpl* cuasimonetarias; liquideces *fpl* secundarias
f disponibilités *fpl* quasi-monétaires; liquidités *fpl* quasi-monétaires; liquidités *fpl* secondaires
i liquidità *fpl* quasi-monetarie; liquidità *fpl* secondarie
n quasimonetaire liquiditeiten *fpl*; secondaire liquiditeiten *fpl*; secundaire liquiditeiten *fpl*

1777 **moneylender**
cf. **capitalist, financier, investor, lender**
d Geldausleiher *m*; Geldgeber *m*; Geldleiher *m*; Geldverleiher *m*; Kapitalgeber *m*
e prestador *m* de dinero; prestamista *m*
f bailleur *m* de fonds; prêteur *m* d'argent
i fornitore *m* di fondi; prestatore *m* di denaro; prestatore *m* di fondi
n geldgever *m*; geldschieter *m*; geldverstrekker *m*

1778 **money market**
cf. **capital market**
d Geldmarkt *m*
e mercado *m* de dinero; mercado *m* monetario
f marché *m* de l'argent; marché *m* monétaire
i mercato *m* del denaro; mercato *m* monetario
n geldmarkt *f*

1779 **money market paper**
cf. **bankable paper**
d Geldmarktpapier *n*; Geldmarkttitel *m*
e papel *m* monetario
f papier *m* monétaire
i carta *f* monetaria
n geldmarktpapier *n*

1780 **money of exchange**
d Umrechnungsmünze *f*; Wechselgeld *n*
e moneda *f* de cambio; moneda *f* de intercambio
f monnaie *f* d'échange; monnaie *f* de change; monnaie *f* de conversion
i moneta *f* di cambio; moneta *f* di scambio
n omrekeningsmunt *f*

1781 **money order *(US)*; postal money order; postal order; post office order *(UK)***
cf. **giro cheque**
d Geldanweisung *f*; Postanweisung *f*; Zahlkarte *f*
e giro *m* postal; mandato *m* postal
f mandat-carte *m*; mandat *m* de poste; mandat *m* de virement postal; mandat *m* postal; mandat-poste *m*
i cartolina *f* vaglia; mandato *m* postale; vaglia *m* di giro postale; vaglia *m* postale
n girokaart *f*; postgirobiljet *n*; postwissel *m*

1782 **money rate**
d Geldsatz *m*
e tipo *m* de interés del dinero; tipo *m* monetario
f taux *m* de l'argent; taux *m* monétaire
i tasso *m* del denaro; tasso *m* monetario
n geldkoers *m*

1783 **money supply; volume of money**
d Geldmenge *f*; Geldversorgung *f*; Geldvolumen *n*; Geldvorrat *m*
e disponibilidad(es) *f(pl)* monetaria(s); masa *f* monetaria; volumen *m* de dinero; volumen *m* dinerario; volumen *m* monetario
f disponibilités *fpl* monétaires; masse *f* monétaire; stock *m* monétaire; volume *m* monétaire
i disponibilità *fpl* monetarie; massa *f* monetaria; scorta *f* monetaria; volume *m* monetario
n geldhoeveelheid *f*; geldvolume *n*; geldvoorraad *m*; liquiditeitenmassa *f*; liquiditeitsvolume *n*

1784 **money transfer; remittance; transfer of funds; transfer of money**
cf. **capital transfer**
d Anweisung *f*; Einsendung *f*; Geldsendung *f*; Geldüberweisung *f*; Transferierung *f*; Übersendung *f*
e envío *m* de dinero; envío *m* de fondos;

giro *m* de dinero; giro *m* de fondos; remesa *f*; transferencia *f* de dinero; transferencia *f* de fondos; transferencia *f* monetaria
f envoi *m* d'argent; envoi *m* de fonds; remise *f*; transfert *m* d'argent; transfert *m* de fonds; versement *m* de fonds; virement *m* de fonds
i giro *m* (di) fondi; invio *m* di fondi; rimessa *f*; trasferimento *m* di denaro; trasferimento *m* di fondi; versamento *m* di fondi
n geldoverdracht *f*; geldovermaking *f*; geldzending *f*; overboeking *f* van geld; overmaking *f* van geld; overschrijving *f* van geld; remise *f*; transfer *m/n* van geld

1785 monometal(l)ism; single standard
d einfache Währung *f*; Einzelwährung *f*; Monometallismus *m*
e monometalismo *m*; patrón *m* único; tipo *m* único
f étalon *m* unique; monométallisme *m*
i monometallismo *m*; tallone *m* unico; tipo *m* unico
n enkele standaard *m*; monometallisme *n*

1786 monopoly
d Alleinhandel *m*; Monopol *n*
e monopolio *m*
f monopole *m*
i monopolio *m*
n alleenhandel *m*; monopolie *n*

1787 monthly allowance; monthly remittance; monthly salary
d Monatsgehalt *n*; Monatsgeld *n*
e mensualidad *f*; mesada *f*; sueldo *m* mensual
f mensualité *f*; salaire *m* mensuel; traitement *m* mensuel
i mensile *m*; mensilità *f*; mensualità *f*; mesata *f*; stipendio *m* mensile; stipendio *m* mensuale *(rare)*
n maandgeld *n*; maandsalaris *n*; maandwedde *f*

1788 monthly instal(l)ment
d monatliche Rate *f*; monatliche Teilzahlung *f*; Monatsrate *f*
e mensualidad *f*; plazo *m* mensual
f acompte *m* mensuel; mensualité *f*; versement *m* mensuel
i mensilità *f*; mensualità *f*; mesata *f*; rata *f* mensile; rata *f* mensuale *(rare)*
n maandelijkse afbetaling *f*; maandelijkse aflossing *f*

1789 moratory
d moratorisch; Moratoriums-; Stundungs-
e moratorio
f moratoire
i moratorio
n moratoir; moratoor

1790 mortgage
d Hypothek *f*
e hipoteca *f*
f hypothèque *f*
i ipoteca *f*
n hypot(h)eek *f*; onderzetting *f**
* Legal only.

1791 mortgage *v*
cf. **burden** *v* **with a mortgage, raise** *v* **a mortgage (on)**
d hypothekarisch belasten; hypothekieren *(rare)*; verpfänden
e hipotecar
f hypothéquer
i ipotecare
n hypot(h)ekeren; verhypot(h)ekeren; verpanden

1792 mortgage bond ***(US)*****; mortgage certificate; mortgage debenture** ***(UK)***
d hypothekarischer Pfandbrief *m*; hypothekarische Schuldverschreibung *f*; Hypothekarschuldverschreibung *f*; Hypothekenobligation *f*; Hypothekenpfandbrief *m*; Hypothekenschein *m*; Hypothekenschuldverschreibung *f*; Hypothekentitel *m*
e cédula *f* hipotecaria; obligación *f* hipotecaria; título *m* hipotecario
f cédule *f* hypothécaire; lettre *f* (de gage) hypothécaire; obligation *f* foncière; obligation *f* hypothécaire; titre *m* hypothécaire
i cartella *f* fondiaria; cartella *f* ipotecaria; obbligazione *f* ipotecaria; titolo *m* ipotecario
n hypot(h)ecaire obligatie *f*; hypot(h)eekbrief *m*; hypot(h)eekpandbrief *m*; pandbrief *m*

1793 mortgage charge
d hypothekarische Belastung *f*; Hypothekenbelastung *f*; Hypothekenlast *f*
e carga *f* hipotecaria; gravamen *m* hipotecario
f charge *f* hypothécaire
i onere *m* ipotecario; vincolo *m* ipotecario
n hypot(h)eeklast *m*

1794 **mortgage interest**
d Hypothekenzinsen *mpl*
e intereses *mpl* hipotecarios
f intérêts *mpl* hypothécaires
i interessi *mpl* ipotecari
n hypot(h)eekrente *f*

1795 **mortmain**
d tote Hand *f*
e manos *fpl* muertas
f mainmorte *f*
i manomorta *f*; mano *f* morta
n dode hand *f*

1796 **multiple vote share; multi-voting share; share with plural voting rights**
d Mehrstimmaktie *f*; Mehrstimmenaktie *f*; Mehrstimmrechtsaktie *f*
e acción *f* de voto múltiple; acción *f* de voto plural
f action *f* à vote plural
i azione *f* a voto multiplo; azione *f* a voto plurimo
n aandeel *n* met meervoudig stemrecht

N

1797 **national accounting; national accounts**
d volkswirtschaftliche Gesamtrechnung *f*
e contabilidad *f* nacional
f comptabilité *f* nationale
i contabilità *f* nazionale
n nationale boekhouding *f*; nationale rekeningen *fpl*

1798 **national debt; public debt**
d Landesschuld *f*; Nationalschuld *f*; öffentliche Schuld *f*; öffentliche Verschuldung *f*; Staatsschuld *f*; Staatsverschuldung *f*
e deuda *f* del Estado; deuda *f* nacional; deuda *f* pública; endeudamiento *m* del Estado
f dette *f* de l'État; dette *f* nationale; dette *f* publique; endettement *m* de l'État
i debito *m* dello Stato; debito *m* nazionale; debito *m* pubblico; indebitamento *m* dello Stato
n nationale schuld *f*; openbare schuld *f*; publieke schuld *f*; rijksschuld *f*; staatsschuld *f*

1799 **national dividend** *(now rare)*; **national income**
d Nationaleinkommen *n*; nationales Einkommen *n*; Volkseinkommen *n*
e renta *f* nacional
f revenu *m* national
i reddito *m* nazionale
n nationaal inkomen *n*; volksinkomen *n*

1800 **national giro account** *(UK)*; **postal check account** *(US)*; **post office cheque account** *(UK)*
d Postscheckkonto *n*
e cuenta *f* corriente postal; cuenta *f* de cheques postales
f compte *m* chèque postal; compte *m* de chèques postaux
i conto *m* cheques postali; conto *m* corrente postale
n postchequerekening *f (B)*; postgirorekening *f (N)*; postrekening *f*

1801 **nationalization; socialization**
d Nationalisierung *f*; Sozialisierung *f*; Vergesellschaftung *f*; Verstaatlichung *f*
e estatificación *f*; nacionalización *f*; socialización *f*
f étatisation *f*; nationalisation *f*; socialisation *f*
i nazionalizzazione *f*; socializzazione *f*; statalizzazione *f*; statizzazione *f*
n nationalisatie *f*; nationalisering *f*; socialisatie *f*; socialisering *f*; verstaatsing *f*

1802 **nationalize** *v*; **socialize** *v*
d nationalisieren; sozialisieren; vergesellschaften; verstaatlichen
e estatificar; nacionalizar; socializar
f étatiser; nationaliser; socialiser
i nazionalizzare; socializzare; statalizzare; statizzare
n nationaliseren; socialiseren; verstaatsen

1803 **national product**
d Nationalprodukt *n*; Sozialprodukt *n*
e producto *m* nacional
f produit *m* national
i prodotto *m* nazionale
n nationaal produkt *n*

1804 **national wealth**
d Nationalvermögen *n*; Volksvermögen *n*
e patrimonio *m* nacional; riqueza *f* nacional
f fortune *f* nationale; patrimoine *m* national; richesse *f* nationale
i patrimonio *m* nazionale; ricchezza *f* nazionale
n nationaal vermogen *n*; volksvermogen *n*

1805 **near money; quasi money**
cf. **money-equivalents**
d Quasigeld *n*
e casi dinero *m*; cuasidinero *m*
f quasi monnaie *f*
i quasimoneta *f*
n bijnageld *n*

1806 **negotiable document** *(US)*; **negotiable instrument**
cf. **bankable paper**
d begebbares Papier *n*; Orderpapier *n*; übertragbares Papier *n*
e papel *m* negociable; título *m* a la orden; título *m* negociable; valor *m* a la orden; valor *m* negociable
f papier *m* à ordre; papier *m* négociable; titre *m* à ordre; titre *m* négociable; valeur *f* négociable
i carta *f* all'ordine; carta *f* negoziabile; documento *m* negoziabile; titolo *m* all'ordine; titolo *m* negoziabile; valore *m* negoziabile
n orderpapier *n*; verhandelbaar papier *n*

1807 **negotiate** *v* **a loan**
cf. **contract** *v* **a loan, place** *v* **a loan**
d eine Anleihe vermitteln
e negociar un empréstito

f négocier un emprunt
i negoziare un prestito
n een lening negotiëren

1808 **net amount**
d Nettobetrag *m*
e importe *m* neto; monto *m* neto
f montant *m* net
i ammontare *m* netto; importo *m* netto
n nettobedrag *n*

1809 **net assets** *(of a company)*; **net worth; shareholders' equity**
cf. **capital resources**
d Aktivüberschuss *m (Schw)*; Eigenkapital *n*; Eigenmittel *npl*; Eigenvermögen *n*; Nettovermögen *n*; Nettowert *m*; Reinvermögen *n*
e activo *m* neto; patrimonio *m* neto; valor *m* neto
f actif *m* net; patrimoine *m* net; valeur *f* nette
i attivo *m* netto; patrimonio *m* netto; valore *m* netto
n nettoactief *n*; netto activa *npl (B)*; zuiver vermogen *n*

1810 **net borrowing**
d Nettobetrag *m* aufgenommener Kredite
e importe *m* neto de los créditos utilizados
f montant *m* net des crédits utilisés
i ammontare *m* netto dei crediti utilizzati
n nettobedrag *n* van opgenomen kredieten

1811 **net income; net revenue**
d Nettoeinkommen *n*; Nettoeinkünfte *fpl*; Reineinkommen *n*
e ingresos *mpl* netos; renta *f* neta
f revenu *m* net
i reddito *m* netto
n netto-inkomen *n*; netto-inkomsten *fpl*; zuiver inkomen *n*

1812 **net lending**
d Nettobetrag *m* gewährter Kredite
e importe *m* neto de los créditos concedidos
f montant *m* net des crédits accordés
i ammontare *m* netto dei crediti accordati
n nettobedrag *n* van toegestane kredieten

1813 **net margin; net profit margin**
d Nettoverdienstspanne *f*
e margen *m/f* de beneficio neto; margen *m/f* de ganancia neta
f marge *f* de bénéfice net
i margine *m* di utile netto
n netto winstmarge *f*

1814 **net national product**
d Nettonationalprodukt *n*; Nettosozialprodukt *n*
e producto *m* nacional neto
f produit *m* national net
i prodotto *m* nazionale netto
n netto nationaal produkt *n*

1815 **net profit ratio**
d Umsatzrentabilität *f*
e rendimiento *m* sobre el volumen de ventas
f rendement *m* des ventes
i percentuale *f* di utile sul giro d'affari
n omzetrendement *n*

1816 **net sales; net turnover**
d Nettoumsatz *m*; Reinumsatz *m*
e cifra *f* neta de negocios; ventas *fpl* netas
f chiffre *m* d'affaires net; ventes *fpl* nettes
i giro *m* d'affari netto; ricavi *mpl* netti
n netto-omzet *m*

1817 **net value**
d Nettowert *m*; Reinwert *m*
e valor *m* neto
f valeur *f* nette
i valore *m* netto
n nettowaarde *f*

1818 **new investment**
cf. **reinvestment**
d Neuanlage *f*; neue Kapitalanlage *f*; Neuinvestition *f*
e colocación *f* nueva; inversión *f* nueva
f nouveau placement *m*; nouvel investissement *m*
i impiego *m* nuovo; investimento *m* nuovo
n nieuwe belegging *f*; nieuwe investering *f*

1819 **new issue shares; new shares; new stock**
d Bezugsaktien *fpl*; junge Aktien *fpl*; neue Aktien *fpl*
e acciones *fpl* nuevas
f actions *fpl* nouvelles
i azioni *fpl* nuove; azioni *fpl* optate
n nieuwe aandelen *npl*

1820 **nominal amount**
d Nennbetrag *m*; Nominalbetrag *m*
e importe *m* nominal
f montant *m* nominal
i importo *m* nominale
n nominaal bedrag *n*

1821 **nominal interest rate; nominal rate (of interest)**
d Nominalsatz *m*; Nominalzins *m*;

Nominalzinsfuss *m*
e tipo *m* de interés nominal; tipo *m* nominal
f taux *m* d'intérêt nominal; taux *m* nominal
i tasso *m* d'interesse nominale; tasso *m* nominale
n nominale rentevoet *m*

1822 **nominal rebate**
d fiktiver Rabatt *m*
e rebaja *f* ficticia
f rabais *m* fictif
i sconto *m* fittizio
n fictieve korting *f*

1823 **non-budgetary expenditure**
d haushaltsfremde Ausgaben *fpl*
e gastos *mpl* ajenos al presupuesto; gastos *mpl* fuera del presupuesto
f dépenses *fpl* débudgétisées
i spese *fpl* fuori bilancio
n niet in de begroting opgenomen uitgaven *fpl*

1824 **non-contractual liability**
d ausservertragliche Haftpflicht *f*; ausservertragliche Haftung *f*
e responsabilidad *f* extracontractual
f responsabilité *f* non contractuelle
i responsabilità *f* extracontrattuale
n niet contractuele aansprakelijkheid *f*

1825 **non-current liabilities**
d noch nicht fällige Verbindlichkeiten *fpl*; noch nicht fällige Verpflichtungen *fpl*
e pasivo *m* no exigible; pasivo *m* no vencido
f passif *m* inexigible; passif *m* non exigible
i passivo *m* inesigibile; passivo *m* non scaduto
n nog niet opeisbare schulden *fpl*

1826 **non-distribution** *(US)*; **passing of a dividend**
d Dividendenausfall *m*
e no distribución *f* de dividendo
f non-distribution *f* de dividende
i mancata distribuzione *f* di dividendo; non distribuzione *f* di dividendo
n dividendpassering *f*

1827 **nondurable goods; nondurables**
d kurzlebige Güter *npl*; nicht dauerhafte Güter *npl*
e bienes *mpl* no durables; bienes *mpl* no duraderos
f biens *mpl* non durables
i beni *mpl* non durevoli
n niet duurzame goederen *npl*

1828 **non-inflationary**
d geldwertneutral; nicht inflationistisch
e no inflacionista
f non inflationniste
i non inflazionistico
n niet inflatoir

1829 **non-profit association; non-profit-making association**
d gemeinnütziger Verein *m*; idealer Verein *m*; Idealverein *m*; nichtwirtschaftlicher Verein *m*; Verein *m* ohne Erwerbszweck; Verein *m* ohne Gewinn(erzielungs)absicht; Verein *m* ohne Gewinnzweck
e asociación *f* sin fin lucrativo
f association *f* sans but lucratif
i associazione *f* senza scopo di lucro
n vereniging *f* zonder winstbejag; vereniging *f* zonder winstoogmerk

1830 **non-voting shares** *(US)*; **non-voting stock** *(UK)*
d Aktien *fpl* ohne Stimmrecht; stimmrechtslose Aktien *fpl*
e acciones *fpl* sin derecho a (de) voto
f actions *fpl* sans droit de vote
i azioni *fpl* senza diritto di voto
n aandelen *npl* zonder stemrecht

1831 **no-par shares; no-par stock; no par value shares; no par value stock; shares without par value; stock without par value**
d nennwertlose Aktien *fpl*; Quotenaktien *fpl*
e acciones *fpl* sin valor nominal
f actions *fpl* sans valeur nominale
i azioni *fpl* senza valore nominale
n aandelen *n* zonder nominale waarde

1832 **normal price; regular price; standard price**
cf. **basic price, flat price**
d Grundpreis *m*; Normalpreis *m*; Richtpreis *m*; Standardpreis *m*
e precio *m* normal; precio *m* normativo
f prix *m* normal; prix *m* standard
i prezzo *m* normativo; prezzo *m* standard
n normale prijs *m*; richtprijs *m*; standaardprijs *m*

1833 **nostro account**
d Nostrokonto *n*
e cuenta *f* nuestra; nuestra cuenta *f*
f compte *m* nostro; notre compte *m*

i conto *m* nostro
n conto *n* nostro; nostrorekening *f*

1834 **notes and coin(s)**
cf. **cash**
d Noten *fpl* und Münzen *fpl*; Stückgeld *n*
e billetes *mpl* y monedas *fpl*
f billets *mpl* et espèces *fpl*; billets *mpl* et pièces *fpl*
i biglietti *mpl* e monete *fpl*
n biljetten *npl* en munten *fpl*

1835 **notice** *(action)*
d Kündigung *f*
e preaviso *m*
f préavis *m*
i preavviso *m*
n opzegging *f*

1836 **notice; term of notice**
d Kündigungsfrist *f*; Kündigungstermin *m*
e plazo *m* de preaviso; plazo *m* de previo aviso
f délai *m* de préavis; terme *m* de préavis
i termine *m* di preavviso
n opvragingstermijn *m*; opzeggingstermijn *m*

1837 **at X days' notice; subject to X days' notice; upon X days' notice**
d mit X-tägiger Kündigung(sfrist)
e con X días de preaviso; sujeto a aviso con X días de antelación; sujeto a X días de preaviso
f à X jours de préavis; avec préavis de X jours; moyennant un préavis de X jours
i con preavviso di X giorni; soggetto a un preavviso di X giorni
n met X dagen opvraging; met X dagen opzegging; met een opvragingstermijn van X dagen; met een opzeggingstermijn van X dagen

1838 **without (previous) (prior) notice**
d ohne Kündigung
e sin preaviso; sin previo aviso
f sans avis préalable; sans préavis
i senza preavviso; senza previo avviso
n zonder opzegging

1839 **notice of assessment; tax assessment notice**
d Steuerbescheid *m*; Steuereinschränkung *f (Schw)*
e acta *f* de liquidación (de impuestos); aviso *m* impositivo; hoja *f* de impuestos
f avertissement *m* d'imposition; avis *m* d'imposition; feuille *f* de contribution(s); feuille *f* d'impôt(s); taxation *f (Schw)*
i avviso *m* di accertamento; cartella *f* esattoriale; cartella *f* delle imposte
n aanslagbiljet *n*; belastingbiljet *n*

1840 **notice of withdrawal of deposits**
d Einlagenkündigung *f*; Kündigung *f* von Einlagen
e aviso *m* de retirada de depósitos; preaviso *m* de retirada de depósitos
f avis *m* de retrait de dépôts; congé *m* de retrait de dépôts *(L)*; préavis *m* de retrait de dépôts
i avviso *m* di ritiro di depositi; preavviso *m* di ritiro di depositi
n opzegging *f* van deposito's

O

1841 offer *v* **for sale; put** *v* **on sale; put** *v* **up for sale**
d feilbieten; zum Kauf anbieten; zum Verkauf anbieten; zum Verkauf bringen
e ofrecer a la venta; ofrecer en venta; poner a la venta; poner en venta
f mettre à la vente; mettre en vente; offrir à la vente; offrir en vente
i mettere alla vendita; mettere in vendita; offrire alla vendita; offrire in vendita
n te koop aanbieden; verkrijgbaar stellen

1842 offering (for subscription); tender
d Zeichnungsangebot *n*; Zeichnungsofferte *f*
e oferta *f* de suscripción
f offre *f* de souscription
i offerta *f* di sottoscrizione *f*
n openstelling *f* van inschrijving

1843 offering price; offer price
cf. **asked price**
d angebotener Preis *m*; Angebotspreis *m*
e precio *m* de oferta; precio *m* ofrecido
f prix *m* d'offre; prix *m* offert
i prezzo *m* d'offerta
n aangeboden prijs *m*

1844 offer to pay; tender of payment
d Zahlungsangebot *n*
e oferta *f* de pago
f offre *f* de paiement; offre *f* de règlement
i offerta *f* di pagamento
n aanbod *n* tot betalingsregeling

1845 official market
d amtliche Börse *f*
e bolsa *f* oficial
f bourse *f* à parquet; bourse *f* officielle; corbeille *f**; marché *m* à parquet*; marché *m* de corbeille*; marché *m* du parquet*; parquet *m**
i borsa *f* ufficiale
n corbeille *f (B)**; corbeillemarkt *f (B)**; korf *m (B)**; officiële beurs *f*; parquet *m (B)**; parquetmarkt *f (B)**

* In Brussels Stock Exchange the corbeille is the market with fluctuating daily rates, the parquet with only one daily rate.

1846 open account; outstanding account; unsettled account*
d ausstehende Rechnung *f*; nicht abgerechnete Rechnung *f**; offene Rechnung *f*; offenstehende Rechnung *f*; unbeglichene Rechnung *f*; unsaldierte Rechnung *f*
e cuenta *f* abierta; cuenta *f* no liquidada*; cuenta *f* no saldada
f compte *m* non liquidé*; compte *m* non réglé; compte *m* non saldé; compte *m* ouvert
i conto *m* aperto; conto *m* non liquidato*; conto *m* non saldato
n ongesaldeerde rekening *f**; onvereffende rekening *f*; open rekening *f*; uitstaande rekening *f*

* Cf. "balance *v* an account" for synonyms.

1847 open *v* **a credit in favor of** ***(US)*****; open** *v* **a credit in favour of** ***(UK)***
cf. **carry** *v* **a sum to some one's credit**
d jemanden akkreditieren; zu jemandes Gunsten einen Kredit eröffnen
e abrir un crédito a (en) favor de; acreditar a alguien
f accréditer quelqu'un; ouvrir un crédit en faveur de
i accreditare a qualcuno; aprire un credito a favore di
n iemand accrediteren; ten gunste van iemand een krediet openen

1848 opening of a credit
cf. **credit**
d Akkreditierung *f*; Krediteröffnung *f*
e acreditación *f*; apertura *f* de un crédito
f ouverture *f* d'un crédit
i accreditamento *m*; apertura *f* di un credito
n kredietopening *f*; openen *n* van een krediet

1849 opening price; opening quotation; opening rate
d Eröffnungskurs *m*; Eröffnungsnotierung *f*; Eröffnungsnotiz *f*
e cambio *m* de apertura; cotización *f* de apertura
f cote *f* d'ouverture; cours *m* de début; cours *m* d'ouverture; premier cours *m*
i corso *m* d'apertura; quotazione *f* d'apertura
n beginkoers *m*; openingskoers *m*; openingsnotering *f*

1850 operating costs; operating expenses; running costs; running expenses; working costs; working expenses
cf. **business expenses**
d Betriebsaufwand *m*; Betriebsaufwendungen *fpl*; Betriebsausgaben

fpl; Betriebskosten *pl*; Betriebsunkosten *pl*
e costos *mpl* de explotación; costos *mpl* de operación; gastos *mpl* de explotación; gastos *mpl* de operación
f charges *fpl* d'exploitation; dépenses *fpl* d'exploitation; frais *mpl* d'exploitation
i costi *mpl* aziendali; costo *m* d'esercizio; costo *m* di gestione; spese *fpl* d'esercizio; spese *fpl* di gestione
n bedrijfskosten *mpl*; bedrijfsonkosten *mpl*; exploitatiekosten *mpl*; exploitatieonkosten *mpl*

1851 **operating statistics**
d interne Betriebsstatistik *f*
e estadísticas *fpl* internas; estadísticas *fpl* operativas
f statistiques *fpl* internes
i statistica *f* aziendale; statistica *f* interna d'impresa
n interne bedrijfsstatistiek *f*

1852 **operating surplus**
cf. **business profit**
d Betriebsüberschuss *m*
e excedente *m* de explotación
f excédent *m* d'exploitation
i avanzo *m* d'esercizio; eccedenza *f* d'esercizio
n bedrijfsoverschot *n*; exploitatieoverschot *n*

1853 **opportunity cost**
d alternative Kosten *pl*
e coste *m* alternativo; costo *m* alternativo
f coût *m* alternatif
i costo *m* alternativo
n alternatieve kosten *mpl*

1854 **option; right of option**
d Option *f*; Optionsrecht *n*; Wahlrecht *n*
e derecho *m* de opción; opción *f*
f droit *m* d'option; faculté *f*; option *f*
i diritto *m* d'opzione; opzione *f*
n keuzerecht *n*; optie *f*; optierecht *n*

1855 **option; option bargain; option deal; share option; stock option**
cf. **forward deal**
d Dontgeschäft *n*; Prämiengeschäft *n*
e negocio *m* a prima; operación *f* a prima; transacción *f* a prima
f affaire *f* à prime; marché *m* à prime; opération *f* à prime; transaction *f* à prime
i affare *m* a premio; transazione *f* a premio
n dontaffaire *f*; premieaffaire *f*; premietransactie *f*

1856 **option money**
d Abstandsgeld *n*; Prämie *f*; Prämiengeld *n*
e prima *f*
f prime *f*
i premio *m*
n optiegeld *n*; premie *f*

1857 **option to repeat*; put of more; repeat option*; seller's option to double**
d Nachgeschäft *n* in Verkäufers Wahl; Noch *n* in Verkäufers Wahl; Nochgeschäft *n* auf Geben; Nochgeschäft *n* in Verkäufers Wahl; Nochgeschäft *n* nach unten; Nochprämiengeschäft *n* in Verkäufers Wahl; Verkauf *m* mit dem Recht des Nachlieferns; Verkauf *m* mit einmal noch
e transacción *f* facultativa a opción del vendedor
f doublé *m* à la baisse; doublure *f* à la baisse; faculté *f* à la baisse; faculté *f* de livrer double
i facoltà *f* a ribasso; facoltà *f* di consegnare il doppio; transazione *f* facoltativa di vendita
n nochaffaire *f* in verkopers keuze; premieaffaire *f* met noch in verkopers keuze; premieaffaire *f* met noch te ontvangen

* Can mean buyer's option to double (q.v.).

1858 **option to sell; put; put option; seller's option; selling option**
cf. **premium for the put**
d Verkaufsoption *f*
e opción *f* de venta
f option *f* de vente
i opzione *f* di vendita
n verkoopoptie *f*

1859 **ordinary budget**
d ordentlicher Haushalt *m*; ordentlicher Haushaltsplan *m*
e presupuesto *m* ordinario
f budget *m* ordinaire
i bilancio *m* ordinario
n gewone begroting *f*

1860 **Organization for Economic Co-operation and Development*; OECD**
d Organisation *f* für wirtschaftliche Zusammenarbeit und Entwicklung; OECD
e Organización *f* de Cooperación y Desarrollo Económico; OCDE

f Organisation *f* de coopération et de développement économique; OCDE
i Organizzazione *f* della Cooperazione e dello Sviluppo Economico; OCSE
n Organisatie *f* voor Economische Samenwerking en Ontwikkeling; OECD; OESO
* Formerly the OEEC.

1861 **Organization for European Economic Co-operation*; OEEC**
d Organisation *f* für europäische wirtschaftliche Zusammenarbeit
e Organización *f* Europea de Cooperación Económica; OECE
f Organisation *f* européenne de coopération économique; OECE
i Organizzazione *f* Europea della Cooperazione Economica; OECE
n Organisatie *f* voor Europese Economische Samenwerking; OEES
* Superseded by the OECD.

1862 **overall balance of payments**
d Gesamtzahlungsbilanz *f*
e balance *m* total de pagos; balanza *f* total de pagos
f balance *f* globale des paiements
i bilancia *f* globale dei pagamenti
n totale betalingsbalans *f*

1863 **overassess** *v*; **overestimate** *v*; **overrate** *v* *(rare)*; **overvalue** *v*
d überbewerten; überschätzen; übertaxieren *(rare)*; überwerten
e sobre(e)stimar; sobre(e)valorar; sobre(e)valuar; sobretasar; supervalorar
f surestimer; surévaluer; surtaxer *(rare)*
i sopravvalutare; supervalutare
n overschatten; overtaxeren *(rare)*; overwaarderen

1864 **overassessment; overestimate; overestimation; overvaluation**
d Überbewertung *f*; Überschätzung *f*; Übertaxierung *f (rare)*; Überwertung *f*
e sobre(e)stimación *f*; sobre(e)valoración *f*; sobre(e)valuación *f*; sobretasación *f*; supervaloración *f*
f surestimation *f*; surévaluation *f*; surtaxation *f (rare)*
i sopravvalutazione *f*; supervalutazione *f*
n overschatting *f*; overwaardering *f*

1865 **overcapitalization**
d Überkapitalisation *f*; Überkapitalisierung *f*
e sobrecapitalización *f*
f surcapitalisation *f*
i sovra(c)capitalizzazione *f*
n overkapitalisatie *f*

1866 **overcharge** *v*; **surcharge** *v*
d überfordern; überteuern; zuviel anrechnen; zuviel berechnen; zuviel fordern
e exigir demasiado; pedir demasiado; sobrecargar
f compter en trop; compter trop (cher); demander trop (cher); faire payer trop (cher); surfaire
i chiedere troppo; far pagare troppo (caro)
n overvragen; teveel berekenen; teveel vragen

1867 **overdraft**
cf. **adverse balance**
d Kontenüberziehung *f*; Kontoüberziehung *f*; Kreditüberschreitung *f*; Überdisposition *f*; Überschreitung *f*; Überziehung *f*
e descubierto *m* (en cuenta); giro *m* en descubierto; sobregiro *m*
f découvert *m* (de compte)
i scoperto *m* (di conto)
n overdisponering *f*; overdispositie *f*; overtrekking *f*

1868 **overdraw** *v* **an account**
d ein Konto überdisponieren; ein Konto überschreiten; ein Konto überziehen
e girar en descubierto (sobre una cuenta); rebasar una cuenta; sobregirar una cuenta; sobrepasar una cuenta
f découvrir un compte; dépasser un compte; mettre un compte à découvert; tirer à découvert (sur un compte)
i mandare un conto allo scoperto; scoprire un conto; trarre allo scoperto (su un conto)
n een rekening overtrekken; op een rekening overdisponeren

1869 **overdue; past due; past-due**
cf. **due**
d überfällig
e sobrevencido
f en souffrance
i in sofferenza
n achterstallig

1870 **overestimate of costs**
d Überdeckung *f* der Kosten
e exceso *m* de cobertura de gastos
f excédent *m* de couverture des frais
i eccesso *m* di copertura delle spese
n overdekking *f* van kosten

1871 overheating
cf. **inflation**
d Überhitzung *f*
e recalentamiento *m*
f surchauffe *f*
i surriscaldamento *m*
n oververhitting *f*

1872 oversaving
d Sparüberhang *m*; Sparüberschuss *m*
e ahorro *m* excesivo; exceso *m* de ahorro
f épargne *f* excessive; excès *m* d'épargne
i eccesso *m* di risparmio; risparmio *m* eccessivo
n overbesparing *f*

1873 oversubscribe *v*
d überzeichnen
e sobresuscribir *(AL)*; su(b)scribir con (en) exceso
f surpasser la souscription *f*; sur-souscrire
i sottoscrivere in eccedenza; superare la sottoscrizione
n overtekenen

1874 oversubscription
d Überzeichnung *f*
e sobresuscripción *f (AL)*; su(b)scripción *f* en exceso
f souscription *f* surpassée
i sottoscrizione *f* superata
n overtekening *f*

1875 overtime
d Überstunden *fpl*
e horas *fpl* extraordinarias; horas *fpl* suplementarias
f heures *fpl* supplémentaires
i orario *m* supplementare; ore *fpl* straordinarie
n overuren *npl*

1876 owe *v*
d schulden; schuldig sein
e adeudar; deber; ser deudor de
f devoir; être débiteur de; être redevable de
i dovere; essere debitore di
n schuldig zijn; verschuldigd zijn

1877 for (one's) own account
d auf eigene Rechnung; für eigene Rechnung
e por cuenta propia; por su cuenta
f pour compte propre; pour (son) propre compte
i per conto proprio
n voor eigen rekening

1878 owner; proprietor
d Besitzer *m*; Eigentümer *m*
e amo *m*; dueño *m*; propietario *m*
f propriétaire *m*
i proprietario *m*
n bezitter *m*; eigenaar *m*

P

1879 **paid***
d eingelöst
e recibí
f pour acquit
i per quietanza
n betaald
* Term on invoice etc. showing payment effected.

1880 **paid in capital *(US)*; paid-up capital**
cf. **called in capital**
d eingezahltes Kapital *n*
e capital *m* desembolsado; capital *m* exhibido; capital *m* integrado *(AL)*; capital *m* pagado
f capital *m* libéré; capital *m* versé
i capitale *m* liberato; capitale *m* versato
n gestort kapitaal *n*

1881 **paper standard**
d Papierwährung *f*
e sistema *m* monetario papel
f étalon *m* papier; étalon-papier *m*
i sistema *m* monetario cartaceo
n papieren standaard *m*

1882 **at par; at parity**
d al pari; paritätisch; zum Nennwert; zu Pari
e a la par
f à parité; à la parité; au pair
i alla pari
n à pari; tegen pari

1883 **be *v* above par; be *v* at a premium**
d Agio geniessen; über dem Nennwert stehen; über Pari stehen
e estar por encima de la par; estar sobre la par; tener agio; tener prima
f être au-dessus du pair; être en prime; faire prime
i essere sopra la pari; far premio
n agio doen; boven pari staan

1884 **be *v* at par**
d al pari stehen; auf Pari stehen; pari stehen
e estar a la par
f être au pair; se tenir à parité
i essere alla pari
n à pari staan; op pari staan; pari staan

1885 **parallel market; unofficial exchange market**
d freier Devisenmarkt *m*; Parallelmarkt *m*
e mercado *m* libre de cambios; mercado *m* libre de divisas; mercado *m* paralelo
f marché *m* libre des changes; marché *m* libre des devises; marché *m* parallèle
i mercato *m* libero dei cambi; mercato *m* libero di divise; mercato *m* parallelo
n parallelmarkt *f*; vrije deviezenmarkt *f*

1886 **parity**
d Parität *f*
e paridad *f*
f parité *f*
i parità *f*
n pariteit *f*

1887 **parity price; par price; par rate**
d Parikurs *m*; Paritätskurs *m*; Paritätspreis *m*
e cambio *m* a la par; precio *m* de paridad
f cours *m* au pair; cours *m* du pair; prix *m* à parité; prix *m* du pair
i cambio *m* alla pari; corso *m* alla pari; prezzo *m* alla pari
n parikoers *m*; pariteitsprijs *m*

1888 **parity rate; parity ratio**
d Paritätsverhältnis *n*
e razón *f* de paridad
f rapport *m* de parité
i rapporto *m* di parità
n pariteitsverhouding *f*

1889 **parity value; par value**
cf. **face value**
d Nennwert *m*; Nominalwert *m*; Pari *n*; Parität *f*; Paritätswert *m*; Pariwert *m*
e paridad *f*; valor *m* a la par; valor *m* de paridad; valor *m* nominal
f montant *m* nominal; pair *m*; parité *f*; valeur *f* au pair; valeur *f* nominale
i pari *f*; parità *f*; valore *m* alla pari; valore *m* nominale
n nominale waarde *f*; pari *n*; pariteit *f*; pariwaarde *f*

1890 **par of exchange**
cf. **equivalence of exchange, mint par of exchange**
d Wechselpari *n*
e paridad *f* de cambio
f pair *m* du change
i parità *f* cambiaria
n wisselpari *n*

1891 **participating preference share; participating preferred share**
d Vorzugsaktie *f* mit Gewinnbeteiligung; Vorzugsaktie *f* mit Teilhaberschaft am Gewinn

e acción *f* preferente con participación en el beneficio
f action *f* de préférence ayant part dans les bénéfices; action *f* privilégiée participant aux bénéfices
i azione *f* di preferenza con partecipazione al beneficio; azione *f* privilegiata nella ripartizione dell'utile
n winstdelend preferent aandeel *n*

1892 partnership*
d Personalgesellschaft *f*; Personengesellschaft *f*
e sociedad *f* de personas
f société *f* de personnes
i società *f* di persone
n personenvennootschap *f*

* This is approximate as English law knows no exact equivalent.

1893 partnership limited by shares*
cf. **limited partnership**
d Kommanditaktiengesellschaft *(Schw)*; Kommanditgesellschaft *f* auf Aktien
e sociedad *f* comanditaria por acciones
f société *f* en commandite par actions
i società *f* in accomandita per azioni
n commanditaire vennootschap *f* op aandelen

* This is approximate as English law does not know this type of partnership.

1894 part payment; part-payment; payment in part
cf. **instal(l)ment**
d Teilzahlung *f*
e pago *m* parcial
f paiement *m* partiel; versement *m* partiel
i pagamento *m* parziale
n gedeeltelijke betaling *f*

1895 pawned securities; pledged securities; securities held in pawn; securities held in pledge; securities lodged as collateral; securities pledged as collateral
cf. **advance *v* on securities**
d Lombardeffekten* *pl*; lombardierte Effekten *pl*; verpfändete Effekten *pl*
e valores* *mpl* dados en garantía; valores* *mpl* dados en prenda; valores* *mpl* empeñados; valores* *mpl* pignorados
f titres* *mpl* déposés en nantissement; titres* *mpl* détenus en gage; titres* *mpl* donnés en gage; titres* *mpl* en pension; titres* *mpl* gagés; titres* *mpl* nantis; titres* *mpl* remis en nantissement
i titoli* *mpl* dati in garanzia; titoli* *mpl* dati in pegno; titoli* *mpl* impegnati; titoli* *mpl* pignorati; titoli* *mpl* tenuti in pegno
n als onderpand gedeponeerde effecten* *npl*; als pand gedeponeerde effecten* *npl*; beleende effecten *npl*; verpande effecten *npl*

* See under "securities" for synonyms.

1896 payable at sight; payable on demand
d auf Sicht zahlbar; bei Sicht zahlbar
e pagadero a la presentación; pagadero a la vista
f payable à vue
i pagabile a richiesta; pagabile a vista
n betaalbaar op vertoon; betaalbaar op zicht

1897 payable in cash; terms strictly cash
d in bar zahlbar; in bar zu zahlen
e pagadero al contado; pagadero en efectivo
f payable au comptant; payable comptant
i pagabile in contanti
n contant betaalbaar

1898 payable in foreign currency
d in ausländischer Währung zahlbar; in Devisen zahlbar
e pagable en divisas; pagable en moneda extranjero; pagadero en divisas; pagadero en moneda extranjera
f payable en devises; payable en monnaie étrangère
i pagabile in divisa estera; pagabile in divise
n betaalbaar in buitenlandse valuta; betaalbaar in deviezen

1899 pay *v* a call of X % on a share
d eine Einzahlung von X % auf eine Aktie leisten
e liberar una acción del X %
f libérer une action de (du) X %
i liberare un'azione del X %
n X % op een aandeel fourneren; X % op een aandeel storten

1900 pay *v* back; refund *v*; reimburse *v*; repay *v*; return *v*
d rückerstatten; rückvergüten; rückzahlen; wiederbezahlen; wiedererstatten; zurückbezahlen; zurückerstatten; zurückvergüten; zurückzahlen
e devolver; reembolsar; reintegrar; restituir*
f rembourser; rendre; restituer; ristourner**
i rendere; restituire; rifondere; rimborsare; ripagare *(rare)*
n rembourseren; restitueren; terugbetalen;

vergoeden; wederbetalen

* Repagar means to pay too much.
** Repayer means to pay again.

1901 pay *v* **by check** *(US)*; **pay** *v* **by cheque** *(UK)*
d durch Scheck zahlen; mit einem Scheck bezahlen; per Scheck zahlen
e pagar con cheque; pagar mediante cheque; pagar por medio de un cheque
f payer par chèque
i pagare con assegno; pagare mediante assegno
n per cheque betalen

1902 payee *(of bill)**
d Remittent *m*; Wechselempfänger *m*; Wechselnehmer *m*
e beneficiario *m* de un efecto; tenedor *m* de un efecto por endorso; tomador *m* de un efecto
f bénéficiaire *m* d'un effet; preneur *m* d'un effet
i beneficiario *m* d'un effetto; prenditore *m* d'un effetto
n nemer *m* van een wissel; ontvanger *m* van een wissel; remittent *m*; wisselnemer *m*

* Payee in general sense see "beneficiary".

1903 payer; payor
d Auszahler *m*; Bezahler *m*; Zahler *m*
e pagador *m*
f payant *m*; payeur *m*
i pagatore *m*
n betaler *m*

1904 pay *v* **in advance; prepay** *v*
d im voraus zahlen; pränumerando zahlen; vorausbezahlen; vorauszahlen; vorleisten
e pagar anticipadamente; pagar con anticipación; pagar por adelanto; pagar por anticipado
f acquitter par anticipation; payer à l'avance; payer d'avance; payer par avance; payer préalablement
i pagare anticipatamente; pagare in anticipo
n bij voorbaat betalen; voorafbetalen; vooruitbetalen

1905 pay *v* **in full; pay** *v* **up**
d voll begleichen; voll bezahlen; voll zahlen
e pagar integralmente; pagar íntegramente
f payer intégralement
i pagare integralmente
n geheel betalen

1906 payment agreement; payments agreement
d Zahlungsabkommen *n*
e acuerdo *m* de pagos; convenio *m* de pagos
f accord *m* de paiement
i accordo *m* di pagamento
n betalingsovereenkomst *f*

1907 payment by the job; job wage; task wage
cf. **piecework pay**
d Akkordlohn *m*
e salario *m* a destajo
f salaire *m* à forfait; salaire *m* à la tâche
i cottimo *m*; salario *m* a cottimo
n accoordloon *n*; akkoordloon *n*

1908 payment in full of a share
d Volleinzahlung *f* einer Aktie
e liberación *f* total de una acción
f libération *f* intégrale d'une action
i liberazione *f* integrale di un'azione
n volstorting *f* van een aandeel

1909 payment of capital
cf. **capital contribution**
d Kapitaleinzahlung *f*
e ingreso *m* de capital
f versement *m* de capital
i versamento *m* di capitale
n kapitaalstorting *f*

1910 payment on due date
d Terminzahlung *f*
e pago *m* a término
f paiement *m* à terme
i pagamento *m* a termine
n betaling *f* op termijn

1911 payments; payment transactions
d Zahlungsverkehr *m*
e movimiento *m* de pagos; operaciones *fpl* de pago; pagos *mpl*
f mouvement *m* des paiements; opérations *fpl* de paiement; paiements *mpl*; trafic *m* des paiements
i movimento *m* dei pagamenti; operazioni *fpl* di pagamento; pagamenti *mpl*
n betalingsverkeer *n*

1912 payroll; pay sheet
d Besoldungsliste *f*; Gehalt(s)liste *f*; Lohnliste *f*
e nómina *f* de sueldos
f bordereau *m* de paie (paye); feuille *f* d'appointements; feuille *f* de paie (paye); rôle *m* d'appointements
i foglio *m* paga
n betaalstaat *m*; loonlijst *f*

1913 pay slip
d Auszahlungsschein *m*
e aviso *m* de pago
f avis *m* de paiement
i avviso *m* di pagamento
n betaalstrook *f*

1914 pay *v* **the balance; settle** *v* **the balance**
d den Saldo ausgleichen
e arreglar el saldo
f régler le solde; solder le redû
i regolare il saldo
n het saldo vereffenen

1915 pay *v* **up a share (in full)**
d eine Aktie voll einzahlen
e liberar una acción completamente; liberar una acción totalmente
f libérer une action entièrement; libérer une action intégralement
i liberare un'azione interamente
n een aandeel volfourneren; een aandeel volstorten

1916 pecuniary resources
cf. **capital resources**
d Geldmittel *npl*
e recursos *mpl* pecuniarios
f ressources *fpl* pécuniaires
i risorse *fpl* pecuniarie
n geldmiddelen *npl*

1917 pegging of prices; price maintenance; price support
cf. **imposition of prices**
d Preisstützung *f*; Preisunterstützung *f*
e mantenimiento *m* de los precios; sostén *m* de los precios; sostenimiento *m* de los precios
f maintien *m* des prix; soutien *m* des prix
i mantenimento *m* dei prezzi; sostegno *m* dei prezzi
n prijsondersteuning *f*

1918 pension fund; superannuation fund
d Pensionsfonds *m*; Pensionskasse *f*; Rentenanstalt *f*
e caja *f* de pensiones; fondo *m* de pensiones
f caisse *f* de pensions; caisse *f* de retraite(s); fonds *m* de pensions
i cassa *f* (di) pensioni; cassa *f* previdenza aziendale; fondo *m* pensioni
n pensioenfonds *n*; pensioenkas *f*

1919 pent-up inflation
d zurückgestaute Inflation *f*
e inflación *f* reprimida
f inflation *f* refoulée
i inflazione *f* repressa
n onderdrukte inflatie *f*; teruggedrongen inflatie *f*

1920 per-capita consumption
d Prokopfverbrauch *m*; Pro-Kopf-Verbrauch *m*; Verbrauch *m* je Einwohner; Verbrauch *m* pro Kopf (der Bevölkerung)
e consumo *m* per cápita; consumo *m* por cada habitante
f consommation *f* par habitant; consommation *f* par personne; consommation *f* par tête
i consumo *m* per abitante; consumo *m* pro capite
n consumptie *f* per hoofd (van de bevolking)

1921 per cent *(UK) (noun)****; percent; percentage; per centum**
d Hundertsatz *m*; Prozent *n*; Prozentsatz *m*; Vomhundertsatz *m*
e porcentaje *m*; tanto *m* por ciento
f pour-cent *m*; pourcentage *m*; tant *m* pour cent
i percento *m*; percentuale *f*; tanto *m* per cento
n percent *n*; percentage *n*; procent *n*

* The distinction between percent (= part) and percentage (= rate) is seldom consistently made in any language in common usage.

1922 per cent *(UK) (adv.)*; **percent**
d prozent; Prozent; vom Hundert
e por ciento
f pour cent
i per cento
n percent; procent; ten honderd

1923 percentage of profits; tantième *(rare)*
cf. **share in the profits**
d Tantieme *f*; Tantiemenanteil *m*
e porcentaje *m* de participación en los beneficios
f tantième *m*
i percentuale *f* sugli utili; tantième *m*
n tantième *n*

1924 period for payment; term of payment; time for payment
d Zahlungsfrist *f*; Zahlungstermin *m*
e plazo *m* de pago
f délai *m* de paiement; terme *m* de paiement
i termine *m* di pagamento
n betalingstermijn *m*

1925 **perpetual debenture**
d Dauerschuldverschreibung *f*
e obligación *f* perpetua
f obligation *f* perpétuelle
i obbligazione *f* perpetua
n eeuwigdurende obligatie *f*; niet aflosbare obligatie *f*; obligatie *f* zonder aflossingstermijn

1926 **personal account; private account**
cf. **charge account**
d Personalkonto *n*; Privatkonto *n*
e cuenta *f* personal; cuenta *f* privada
f compte *m* particulier; compte *m* personnel; compte *m* privé
i conto *m* individuale; conto *m* personale; conto *m* privato
n persoonlijke rekening *f*; privé-rekening *f*

1927 **personal credit**
d Personalkredit *m*; Privatkredit *m*
e crédito *m* personale; crédito *m* privado
f crédit *m* personnel; crédit *m* privé
i credito *m* personale; credito *m* privato
n persoonlijk krediet *n*

1928 **personal debt; private debt**
d Personalschuld *f (rare)*; persönliche Schuld *f*; private Schuld *f*; Privatschuld *f*
e deuda *f* personal; deuda *f* privada
f dette *f* civile; dette *f* personnelle; dette *f* privée
i debito *m* personale
n particuliere schuld *f*; privé-schuld *f*

1929 **personal income; private income**
d Privateinkommen *n*; Privateinkünfte *fpl*
e ingresos *mpl* personales; ingresos *mpl* privados; renta *f* personal; renta *f* privada
f revenu *m* personnel; revenus *mpl* particuliers; revenus *mpl* privés
i redditi *mpl* privati; reddito *m* personale
n persoonlijk inkomen *n*; privé-inkomen *n*

1930 **personal income tax**
d Einkommenssteuer *f* für natürliche Personen
e impuesto *m* sobre la renta de las personas físicas
f impôt *m* sur le revenu des personnes physiques
i imposta *f* sul reddito delle persone fisiche
n inkomstenbelasting *f* op natuurlijke personen

1931 **petty cash**
d Barkasse *f*; kleine Kasse *f*
e caja *f* chica *(AL)*; caja *f* pequeña
f petite caisse *f*
i piccola cassa *f*
n kleine kas *f*

1932 **piecework pay; piecework wage**
cf. **payment by the job**
d Stücklohn *m*
e salario *m* por pieza; salario *m* por unidad
f salaire *m* à la pièce; salaire *m* aux pièces
i cottimo *m*; salario *m* a cottimo
n stukloon *n*

1933 **place** *v* **a loan**
cf. **emit** *v* **a loan, negociate** *v* **a loan**
d eine Anleihe placieren; eine Anleihe plazieren; eine Anleihe unterbringen
e colocar un empréstito
f écouler un emprunt; placer un emprunt
i collocare un prestito; piazzare un prestito
n een lening onderbrengen; ee lening plaatsen

1934 **place** *v* **an issue**
d eine Emission placieren; eine Emission plazieren; eine Emission unterbringen
e colocar una emisión
f écouler une émission; placer une émission
i collocare una emissione; piazzare una emissione
n een uitgifte onderbrengen; een uitgifte plaatsen

1935 **placement** *(issue, loan etc.)**; **placing**
cf. **flotation**
d Placement *n*; Placierung *f*; Plazierung *f*; Unterbringung *f*
e colocación *f*
f écoulement *m*; placement *m*
i collocamento *m*; piazzamento *m*
n onderbrengen *n*; plaatsen *n*

* For placement of capital, money etc. see "investment".

1936 **plough** *v* **back; plow** *v* **back** *(US)*; **reinvest** *v*
d neu anlegen; neu investieren; reinvestieren; wiederanlegen; wiederinvestieren
e reinvertir
f réemployer; réinvestir; remployer; replacer
i reimpiegare; reinvestire; rimpiegare

(rare); rinvestire
n herbeleggen; herinvesteren

1937 **pocket** *v* **a profit; rake** *v* **in a profit**
d einen Gewinn einheimsen; einen Gewinn einstecken; einen Gewinn einstreichen
e embolsar una ganancia
f empocher un bénfice
i intascare un guadagno
n een winst opstrijken

1938 **pool**
cf. **consortium**
d Pool *m*
e pool *m*
f pool *m*
i pool *m*
n pool *m*

1939 **pooling**
d Poolung *f*; Zusammenlegung *f*
e puesta *f* en pool
f mise *f* en commun; mise *f* en pool; pooling *m*
i messa *f* in pool
n poolen *n*; pooling *f*

1940 **position of an account; state of an account**
cf. **balance of an account**
d Kontenstand *m*; Kontostand *m*; Rechnungsstand *m*; Stand *m* einer Rechnung
e estado *m* de una cuenta; posición *f* de una cuenta; situación *f* de una cuenta
f état *m* d'un compte; position *f* d'un compte; situation *f* d'un compte
i posizione *f* di un conto; situazione *f* di un conto
n positie *f* van een rekening; stand *m* van een rekening

1941 **postal savings bank** *(US)*; **post office savings bank** *(UK)*
d Postsparkasse *f*
e caja *f* postal de ahorros
f caisse *f* d'épargne postale
i cassa *f* di risparmio postale
n postspaarbank *f*

1942 **postdate** *v*
d nachdatieren*; postdatieren**; später datieren; vordatieren**
e pos(t)fechar
f postdater
i pos(t)datare
n postdateren
* This use of nachdatieren is found but is in fact incorrect, it really means to antedate.
** Also means to antedate.

1943 **pound sterling**
cf. **sterling**
d Pfund *n* Sterling
e libra *f* esterlina
f livre *f* sterling
i lira *f* sterlina
n pond *n* sterling

1944 **preceding endorser; previous endorser**
d Vordermann *m*; Vorgirant *m*; vorhergehender Indossant *m*; Vorindossant *m*; Vormann *m*
e endosante *m* anterior
f endosseur *m* antérieur; endosseur *m* précédent
i girante *m* precedente
n voorgaande endossant *m*; voorman *m*

1945 **preference dividend; preferential dividend; preferred dividend** *(US)*
d Prioritätsdividende *f*; Vorzugsdividende *f*
e dividendo *m* de prioridad; dividendo *m* preferencial; dividendo *m* preferente; dividendo *m* preferido *(AL)*; dividendo *m* privilegiado
f dividende *m* de priorité; dividende *m* prioritaire; dividende *m* privilégié
i dividendo *m* privilegiato
n preferent dividend *n*

1946 **preference share; preference stock** *(US)*; **preferred stock** *(US)*
d Aktie *f* mit Vorzugsrecht; bevorrechtigte Aktie *f*; Priorität(en) *f(pl)*; Prioritätsaktie *f*; Stammpriorität *f*; Stammprioritätsaktie *f*; Vorrechtsaktie *f*; Vorzugsaktie *f*
e acción *f* de preferencia; acción *f* de prioridad; acción *f* preferente; acción *f* preferida *(AL)*; acción *f* privilegiada
f action *f* de préférence; action *f* de priorité; action *f* privilégiée
i azione *f* di priorità; azione *f* preferenziale; azione *f* privilegiata
n preferent aandeel *n*; prioriteitsaandeel *n*

1947 **preference tariff; preferential tariff**
cf. **preferential duty**
d Begünstigungstarif *m*; Präferenztarif *m*; Vergünstigungstarif *m*; Vorzugstarif *m*
e arancel *m* de preferencia; arancel *m* preferencial; arancel *m* preferente; tarifa *f* de favor; tarifa *f* de preferencia; tarifa *f* preferencial; tarifa *f* preferente
f tarif *m* de faveur; tarif *m* préférentiel
i tariffa *f* di favore; tariffa *f* preferenziale

n gunsttarief *n (B)*; preferentieel tarief *n*; voorkeurtarief *n*

1948 preferential creditor; preferred creditor; prior creditor
cf. **secured creditor**
d Absonderungsberechtigter *m*; Absonderungsgläubiger *m*; bevorrechtigter Gläubiger *m*; bevorzugter Gläubiger *m*; Prioritätsgläubiger *m*; privilegierter Gläubiger *m (Schw)*; vorrangiger Gläubiger *m*; Vorrangsgläubiger *m*; Vorzugsgläubiger *m*
e acreedor *m* preferente; acreedor *m* prioritario; acreedor *m* privilegiado
f créditeur *m* à droit de priorité; créditeur *m* prioritaire; créditeur *m* privilégié
i creditore *m* prioritario; creditore *m* privilegiato
n bevoorrechte crediteur *m*; bevoorrechte schuldeiser *m*; preferente crediteur *m*; preferente schuldeiser *m*; prioriteitsschuldeiser *m*

1949 preferential duty
cf. **differential duty, preferential tariff**
d Begünstigungszoll *m*; Präferenzzoll *m*; Vergünstigungszoll *m*; Vorzugszoll *m*
e arancel *m* preferencial; arancel *m* preferente; derecho *m* (de aduana) preferencial; derecho *m* (de aduana) preferente
f droit *m* (de douane) préférentiel
i dazio *m* (doganale) preferenziale
n preferentieel recht *n*

1950 preferential rate of exchange
d Vorzugsumrechnungskurs *m*
e tipo *m* de cambio preferente
f taux *m* de change préférentiel
i tasso *m* di cambio preferenziale
n preferentiële omrekeningskoers *m*

1951 prefinance *v*; **provide** *v* **anticipatory finance**
d vorfinanzieren
e financiar anticipadamente; financiar provisionalmente; prefinanciar
f financer provisoirement; préfinancer
i finanziare in anticipo; finanziare provvisoriamente; prefinanziare
n voorfinancieren; voorlopig financieren; vooruitfinancieren

1952 prefinancing; provision of anticipatory finance
cf. **bridging finance, bridging loan**
d Vorfinanzierung *f*
e financiación *f* anticipada; financiación *f* provisional; financiamiento *m* anticipado; financiamiento *m* provisional; prefinanciación *f*; prefinanciamiento *m*
f financement *m* anticipatif; financement *m* provisoire; préfinancement *m*
i finanziamento *m* anticipato; finanziamento *m* provvisorio; prefinanziamento *m*
n voorfinanciering *f*; voorlopige financiering *f*; vooruitfinanciering *f*

1953 premium for the put; put premium
cf. **option to sell**
d Baisseprämie *f*; Empfangsprämie *f*; Rückprämie *f*
e prima *f* a la baja; prima *f* a la venta; prima *f* de opción a vender
f prime *f* à la baisse; prime *f* pour le vendeur; prime *f* pour livrer; prime *f* renversée; prime *f* simple à la baisse; prime *f* vendeur
i premio *m* a dare; premio *m* al ribasso; premio *m* per non consegnare; premio *m* put
n baissepremie *f*; premie *f* te ontvangen

1954 prescribed dividend
d verfallene Dividende *f*
e dividendo *m* prescrito
f dividende *m* prescrit
i dividendo *m* prescritto
n vervallen dividend *n*

1955 prescription; statute of limitation(s)
d Verjährung *f*
e prescripción *f*
f prescription *f*
i prescrizione *f*
n prescriptie *f*; verjaring *f*

1956 on presentation; at sight
cf. **at call**
d bei Präsentation; auf Sicht; bei Sicht; bei Vorkommen; bei Vorlage; bei Vorzeigung; gegen Vorzeigung
e a (la) presentación; a (la) vista
f à présentation; à vue
i a presentazione; a vista; contro presentazione
n op vertoon; op zicht

1957 presentation of the balance sheet
d Bilanzvorlegung *f*
e presentación *f* del balance
f présentation *f* du bilan
i presentazione *f* del bilancio
n voorlegging *f* van de balans

1958 (up)on presentation of the coupon; (up)on surrender of the coupon
d gegen Abgabe des Kupons*; gegen Einreichung des Kupons*; gegen Übergabe des Kupons*
e contra entrega del cupón*
f contre remise du coupon
i contro rimessa della cedola*
n tegen inlevering van de coupon*

* Cf. "coupon" for synonyms.

1959 pre-tax; before tax; before taxes
d vor Abzug der Steuer(n); vor Steuer(n); vor Steuerabzug
e antes de la deducción del impuesto (de los impuestos); antes de deducir el impuesto (los impuestos); antes del impuesto (de los impuestos)
f avant déduction de l'impôt (des impôts); avant impôt(s); avant paiement de l'impôt (des impôts); avant taxe(s)
i prima della deduzione della tassa; prima della deduzione delle imposte; prima della tassa; prima delle imposte
n voor aftrek van de belasting(en); voor belasting; voor belastingaftrek; voor belastingen

1960 price ***(of a share)*****; quotation; rate**
d Kurs *m*; Kursnotierung *f*; Kursnotiz *f*; Notierung *f*; Notiz *f*; Preis *m*
e cambio *m*; cotización *f*; precio *m*
f cotation *f*; cote *f*; cours *m*; prix *m*
i corso *m*; quotazione *f*; prezzo *m*
n koers *m*; koersnotering *f*; notering *f*; prijs *m*

1961 price administration ***(US)*****; price control; price regulation**
d Preiskontrolle *f*; Preislenkung *f*; Preisregelung *f*; Preisüberwachung *f*
e control *m* de los precios; reglamentación *f* de los precios; regulación *f* de los precios
f contrôle *m* des prix; réglementation *f* des prix; régulation *f* des prix; surveillance *f* des prix
i controllo *m* dei prezzi; regolamentazione *f* dei prezzi; regolamento *m* dei prezzi; vigilanza *f* sui prezzi
n prijsbeheersing *f*; prijscontrole *f*; prijsregeling *f*; prijzencontrole *f*

1962 price determination; price fixing; pricing
cf. **imposition of prices**
d Preisansatz *m*; Preisbestimmung *f*; Preisermittlung *f*; Preisfestlegung *f*; Preisfestsetzung *f*; Preisfeststellung *f*; Preisfixierung *f*
e determinación *f* de los precios; fijación *f* de los precios
f détermination *f* des prix; fixation *f* des prix; taxation *f* des prix
i determinazione *f* dei prezzi; fissazione *f* dei prezzi
n fixeren *n* van prijzen; prijsbepaling *f*; vastleggen *n* van prijzen

1963 price-earnings ratio; price to earnings ratio
d Ertragspreisverhältnis *n*; Kursertrags(kraft)verhältnis *n*; Kursgewinnrelation *f*; Kursgewinnverhältnis *n*; Preisertragsverhältnis *n*
e relación *f* precio-beneficios
f rapport *m* cours-bénéfice
i rapporto *m* cambio-utile
n koers-winst verhouding *f*

1964 price index
d Preisindex *m*
e índice *m* de precios
f indice *m* des prix
i indice *m* dei prezzi
n index *m* der prijzen *(B)*; prijsindex *m*; prijsindexcijfer *n*; prijzenindex *m*

1965 price limit; reserve price
cf. **ceiling price**
d Grenzkurs *m*; Grenzpreis *m*; Kurslimit *n*; Preisgrenze *f*; Preislimit *n*
e límite *m* de precio; precio *m* límite
f cours-limite *m*; limite *f* de cours; limite *f* de prix; prix-limite *m*; prix *m* limite
i corso *m* limite; limite *m* di prezzo; prezzo *m* limite
n grensprijs *m*; koerslimiet *f*; limietkoers *m*; limietprijs *m*; prijsgrens *f*; prijslimiet *f*

1966 price margin; price range; price spread
cf. **difference in price(s)**
d Preisspanne *f*
e margen *m/f* de precios
f décalage *m* de prix; marge *f* de prix
i margine *m* di prezzi
n prijsmarge *f*

1967 price of money
d Geldpreis *m*; Kapitalmarktzins *m*
e precio *m* del dinero
f coût *m* de l'argent; prix *m* de l'argent
i prezzo *m* del denaro
n prijs *m* van het geld

1968 price restraint
d Preisbeschränkung *f*
e restricción *f* de los precios

f restriction *f* des prix
i restrizione *f* dei prezzi
n prijsbeperking *f*

1969 price stabilization
d Festigung *f* der Preise; Preisstabilisierung *f*
e estabilización *f* de los precios
f stabilisation *f* des prix
i stabilizzazione *f* dei prezzi
n prijsstabilisatie *f*

1970 primary incomes
d primäre Einkommen *npl*; Primäreinkommen *npl*
e ingresos *mpl* primarios
f revenus *mpl* primaires
i redditi *mpl* primari
n primaire inkomens *npl*

1971 primary liquidity
d Primärliquidität *f*
e liquidez *f* primaria
f liquidité *f* primaire
i liquidità *f* primaria
n primaire liquiditeit *f*

1972 principal *(capital sum)*
d Kapital *n*
e principal *m*
f principal *m*
i capitale *m*
n hoofdsom *f*

1973 principal *(person)*
d Auftraggeber *m*; Besteller *m*; Kommittent *m*; Mandant *m*
e comitente *m*; mandante *m*; principal *m*
f commettant *m*; donneur *m* d'ordre; mandant *m*
i committente *m*; mandante *m*
n committent *m*; lastgever *m*; opdrachtgever *m*; principaal *m*

1974 private bank
d Privatbank *f*; Privatbankhaus *n*
e banco *m* privado
f banque *f* d'intérêt privé; banque *f* privée
i banca *f* privata
n particuliere bank *f*; privé-bank *f*

1975 private capital
d Privatkapital *n*
e capital *m* privado
f capital *m* privé
i capitale *m* privato
n privé-kapitaal *n*

1976 private enterprise *(system)*
d privates Unternehmertum *n*; Privatinitiative *f*; Privatwirtschaft *f*
e economía *f* privada; iniciativa *f* privada
f économie *f* privée; initiative *f* privée
i economia *f* privata; iniziativa *f* privata
n particulier initiatief *n*; privé-initiatief *n*

1977 private enterprise *(firm)*
d Privatbetrieb *m*; Privatunternehmen *n*; Privatunternehmung *f (Schw)*; privatwirtschaftlicher Betrieb *m*
e empresa *f* privada
f entreprise *f* privée
i azienda *f* privata; impresa *f* privata
n particulier bedrijf *n*; particuliere onderneming *f*; privé-bedrijf *n*; privé-onderneming *f*

1978 private investment
d private Investition *f*; private Kapitalanlage *f*
e inversión *f* privada
f investissement *m* privé
i investimento *m* privato
n particuliere belegging *f*; particuliere investering *f*

1979 private ownership; private property
d Privatbesitz *m*; Privateigentum *n*; privater Besitz *m*; privates Eigentum *n*
e propiedad *f* privada
f propriété *f* privée
i proprietà *f* privata
n particulier bezit *n*; particuliere eigendom *m**; particulier eigendom *n**; privaatbezit *n*; privé-bezit *n*; privé-eigendom *m/n**

* When *m* it signifies ownership, when *n* thing owned.

1980 private savings
d private Ersparnisbildung *f*
e ahorro *m* privado
f épargne *f* privée
i risparmio *m* privato
n particuliere besparingen *fpl*

1981 private sector
d privater Sektor *m*; Privatsektor *m*
e sector *m* privado
f secteur *m* privé
i settore *m* privato
n particuliere sector *m*; private sector *m*; privé-sector *m*

1982 proceeds; returns
cf. **avails, income, incomings, return**
d Erlös *m*; Ertrag *m*; Erträgnis *n*

e producto *m*
f produit *m*
i provento *m*; ricavato *m*; ricavo *m*
n produkt *n*; provenu *n*

1983 **producer cooperative; producers' cooperative**
d Erzeugergenossenschaft *f*; Produktionsgenossenschaft *f*; Produktivgenossenschaft *f*
e cooperativa *f* de producción; sociedad *f* cooperativa de producción
f coopérative *f* de production; société *f* coopérative de production
i cooperativa *f* di produzione; società *f* cooperativa di produzione
n coöperatieve produktievereniging *f*; produktiecoöperatie *f*

1984 **profitability; profitableness**
cf. **earning capacity, viability**
d Einträglichkeit *f*; Ergiebigkeit *f*; Rentabilität *f*; Wirtschaftlichkeit *f*
e economicidad *f*; rentabilidad *f*
f économicité *f*; rentabilité *f*
i economicità *f*; redditività *f*
n rendabiliteit *f*; rentabiliteit *f*

1985 **profit balance brought forward; profit balance carried forward; profit brought forward; profit carried forward**
d Gewinnvortrag *m*
e beneficio *m* traslado
f bénéfice *m* reporté
i utile *m* riportato
n overgebrachte winst *f*

1986 **profit-making association**
d Verein *m* mit Erwerbszweck; Verein *m* mit Gewinn(erzielungs)absicht; Verein *m* mit Gewinnzweck
e asociación *f* con fin lucrativo
f association *f* à but lucratif
i associazione *f* con scopo di lucro
n vereniging *f* met winstbejag; vereniging *f* met winstoogmerk

1987 **profit retention; retention of profits**
d Einbehaltung *f* von Gewinnen; Gewinnrücklage *f*; Gewinnrückstellung *f*; Rücklagenzuweisung *f* aus dem Gewinn
e asignación *f* de beneficios al fondo de reserva
f mise *f* en réserve de bénéfices
i assegnazione *f* di utili a riserva
n winstinhouding *f*

1988 **profit squeeze**
d Druck *m* auf den Gewinn
e presión *f* sobre las utilidades
f pression *f* sur les bénéfices
i pressione *f* sugli utili
n druk *m* op de winst

1989 **profits tax; tax on earnings**
d Ertrag(s)steuer *f*; Gewinnsteuer *f*
e impuesto *m* sobre las utilidades; impuesto *m* sobre los beneficios
f impôt *m* sur les bénéfices
i imposta *f* sugli utili; imposta *f* sui profitti
n belasting *f* op de bedrijfswinst; winstbelasting *f*

1990 **profit taking**
d Gewinnmitnahme *f*; Gewinnrealisation *f*; Gewinnrealisierung *f*; Gewinnsicherung *f*
e realización *f* de beneficios; realización *f* de ganancias; realización *f* de utilidades
f dégagement *m* bénéficiaire *(B)*; prise *f* de bénéfices; réalisation *f* de bénéfices
i presa *f* di profitti; presa *f* di utili; realizzazione *f* di profitti; realizzazione *f* di utili; realizzo *m* di profitti; realizzo *m* di utili
n winstneming *f*

1991 **pro forma invoice; proforma invoice**
d Proforma-Rechnung *f*; Proformarechnung *f*
e cuenta *f* pro-forma; cuenta *f* proforma; factura *f* pro-forma; factura *f* proforma
f facture *f* pro-forma
i fattura *f* pro forma; fattura *f* proforma
n pro forma factuur *f*; pro-forma factuur *f*

1992 **progressive rate of a tax**
d Progression *f* einer Steuer; Staffelung *f* einer Steuer
e progresividad *f* de un impuesto
f progressivité *f* d'un impôt
i progressività *f* di un'imposto
n progressief tarief *n* van een belasting

1993 **prohibitive duty**
d Prohibitivzoll *m*; Sperrzoll *m*
e aduana *f* prohibitiva; arancel *m* prohibitivo; arancel *m* prohibitorio; derecho *m* aduanero prohibitivo; derecho *m* aduanero prohibitorio
f droit *m* prohibitif
i dazio *m* proibitivo; diritto *m* doganale proibitivo
n prohibitief recht *n*

1994 **prolongation** *(of a bill)*
d Prolongation *f*; Prolongierung *f*;

Verlängerung *f*
e prolongación *f*; prórroga *f*
f prolongation *f*; prorogation *f*
i proroga *f*
n prolongatie *f*; verlenging *f*

1995 property tax; real estate tax
cf. **land tax**
d Immobiliarsteuer *f*; Realsteuer *f*; Sachsteuer *f*
e impuesto *m* inmobiliario; impuesto *m* real; impuesto *m* sobre el patrimonio inmueble; impuesto *m* sobre los bienes raíces
f impôt *m* immobilier; impôt *m* réel; impôt *m* sur le patrimoine immobilier; impôt *m* sur les biens immobiliers
i imposta *f* immobiliare; imposta *f* reale; imposta *f* sui beni immobiliari; imposta *f* sul patrimonio immobiliare
n belasting *f* op immobiliën; belasting *f* op onroerende goederen; reële belasting *f*

1996 proprietors' capital; proprietors' equity; shareholders' equity; stockholders' equity *(US)*
d Beteiligungskapital *n*; Eigenkapital *n*; Eigenvermögen *n*
e capital *m* accionista; capital *m* de participación; capitales *mpl* propios; capital *m* propio
f capital *m* propre; capitaux *mpl* propres
i capitale *m* proprio
n eigen kapitaal *n*; eigen vermogen *n*

1997 protectionist
d Protektionist *m*; Schutzzöllner *m*; Schutzzollpolitiker *m*
e proteccionista *m*
f protectionniste *m*
i protezionista *m*
n protectionist *m*

1998 protective duty
d Schutzzoll *m*
e aduana *f* protectora; arancel *m* proteccionista; arancel *m* protector; derecho *m* aduanero protector
f droit *m* protecteur
i dazio *m* protettivo; diritto *m* doganale protettivo
n beschermend recht *n*

1999 provisional payment
d vorläufige Zahlung *f*
e pago *m* provisional
f paiement *m* provisoire; versement *m* provisoire
i pagamento *m* provvisorio
n voorlopige betaling *f*

2000 provisional return
d Voranmeldung *f*; vorläufige Steuererklärung *f*; vorläufige Veranlagung *f (Schw)*
e declaración *f* provisional
f déclaration *f* provisoire
i dichiarazione *f* provvisoria
n voorlopige aangifte *f*

2001 provision for tax; provision for taxation; reserve for taxation; tax reserve
d Steuerreserve *f*; Steuerrücklage *f*; Steuerrückstellung *f*
e provisión *f* para impuestos; reserva *f* para (el pago de los) impuestos
f provision *f* pour taxes et impôts; réserve *f* fiscale; réserve *f* pour les impôts
i accantonamento *m* per imposte e tasse; fondo *m* imposte e tasse; riserva *f* fiscale; riserva *f* per le imposte
n belastingreserve *f*; fiscale reserve *f*; voorzieningen *fpl* voor belastingen

2002 public consumption
d öffentliche Konsumausgaben *fpl*; öffentlicher Verbrauch *m*
e consumo *m* público
f consommation *f* publique
i consumo *m* pubblico
n overheidsverbruik *n*

2003 public expenditure; public spending
d öffentliche Ausgaben *fpl*
e gastos *mpl* públicos
f dépenses *fpl* publiques
i spese *fpl* pubbliche
n overheidsuitgaven *fpl*

2004 public finance body
d öffentlich-rechtliches Finanzinstitut *n*
e organismo *m* financiero público
f organisme *m* public financier
i organismo *m* pubblico finanziario
n financiële overheidsinstelling *f*

2005 public funds; public money; state funds
d öffentliche Fonds *mpl*; öffentliche Gelder *npl*; staatliche Fonds *mpl*; staatliche Gelder *npl*; Staatsfonds *mpl*; Staatsgelder *npl*
e fondos *mpl* del estado; fondos *mpl* públicos
f deniers *mpl* de l'état; deniers *mpl* publics; fonds *mpl* de l'état; fonds *mpl* publics
i denaro *m* pubblico; fondi *mpl* dello

stato; fondi *mpl* pubblici
n overheidsgelden *npl*; staatsgelden *npl*

2006 **public investment**
d Investition *f* der öffentlichen Hand; öffentliche Investition *f*
e inversión *f* del sector público; inversión *f* pública
f investissement *m* du secteur public; investissement *m* public
i investimento *m* del settore pubblico; investimento *m* pubblico
n openbare belegging *f*; openbare investering *f*; overheidsinvestering *f*

2007 **public resources**
d öffentliche Mittel *npl*
e recursos *mpl* públicos
f ressources *fpl* publiques
i pubbliche risorse *fpl*
n overheidsmiddelen *npl*

2008 **public sector**
d öffentlicher Sektor *m*
e sector *m* público
f secteur *m* public
i settore *m* pubblico
n openbare sector *m*; overheidssector *m*

2009 **public service corporation** *(US)*; **public utility; public utility company** *(UK)*
d gemeinnütziger Betrieb *m*; gemeinnütziges Unternehmen *n*; gemeinnützige Unternehmung *f*; gemeinwirtschaftliches Unternehmen *n (rare)*; öffentlicher Versorgungsbetrieb *m*; öffentliches Versorgungsunternehmen *n*
e empresa *f* de servicio(s) público(s); empresa *f* de utilidad pública
f entreprise *f* de service public; entreprise *f* d'utilité publique
i impresa *f* di servizio pubblico; impresa *f* di servizi pubblici; impresa *f* d'utilità pubblica
n bedrijf *n* van openbaar nut; openbaar nutsbedrijf *n*

2010 **public works**
d öffentliche Arbeiten *fpl*; öffentliche Bauten *mpl*
e obras *fpl* públicas
f travaux *mpl* publics
i lavori *mpl* pubblici; opere *fpl* pubbliche
n openbare werken *npl*

2011 **pump priming**
d Massnahmen *fpl* zur Konjunkturbelebung; Massnahmen *fpl* zur Wirtschaftsankurbelung
e médidas *fpl* de relanzamiento; médidas *fpl* para estimular la recuperación económica
f mesures *fpl* de relance; mesures *fpl* pour stimuler la reprise économique
i misure *fpl* di relancio; misure *fpl* per stimolare la ripresa economica
n maatregelen *mpl* ter stimulering van de economie

2012 **purchase**
d Ankauf *m*; Einkauf *m*; Kauf *m*
e compra *f*
f achat *m*
i acquisto *m*
n aankoop *m*; inkoop *m*; koop *m*

2013 **purchase option; right of pre-emption**
cf. **buyer's option**
d Einstandsrecht *n*; Vorkaufsrecht *n*
e derecho *m* de tanteo
f droit *m* de préemption
i diritto *m* di prelazione
n voorkooprecht *n*

2014 **purchase tax** *(UK)*; **sales tax** *(US)*; **turnover tax**
d Umsatzabgabe *f*; Umsatzsteuer *f*; Warenumsatzsteuer *f*
e impuesto *m* al giro comercial; impuesto *m* sobre el movimiento de ventas; impuesto *m* sobre la cifra de negocios; impuesto *m* sobre las ventas
f impôt *m* sur le chiffre d'affaires; taxe *f* de transmission; taxe *f* sur le chiffre d'affaires
i imposta *f* generale sull'entrata; imposta *f* sugli scambi (di merci); imposta *f* sul giro d'affari; imposta *f* sulla cifra d'affari
n omzetbelasting *f*; overdrachtstaks *f (B)*; overdrachtstaxe *f (B)*

Q

2015 qualifying share
d Kautionsaktie *f*; Pflichtaktie *f*
e acción *f* de garantía
f action *f* de garantie
i azione *f* di garanzia
n garantieaandeel *n*

2016 quarter *(of a year)*
d Quartal *n*; Vierteljahr *n*
e trimestre *m*
f trimestre *m*
i trimestre *m*
n kwartaal *n*; trimester *n*

2017 quota
d Anteil *m*; Kontingent *n*; Quote *f*
e contingente *m*; cuota *f*; cupo *m*
f contingent *m*; cote *f*; quota *m*; quote-part *f*
i contingente *m*; quota *f*
n contingent *n*; quota *f*; quote *f*; quotum *n*

2018 quota restrictions
d Kontingentierung *f*
e contingentación *f*
f contingentement *m*
i contingentamento *m*
n contingentering *f*

R

2019 **raise** *v* **a mortgage (on); take** *v* **a mortgage (on)**
cf. **mortgage** *v*
d eine Hypothek aufnehmen (auf)
e tomar una hipoteca (sobre)
f prendre une hypothèque (sur)
i prendere un'ipoteca (su)
n een hypot(h)eek nemen (op)

2020 **rally** *(of prices)*
cf. **recovery**
d Anziehen *n*; Erholung *f*; Reprise *f*
e recuperación *f*
f reprise *f*
i rafforzamento *m*; ricupero *m*; ripresa *f*
n herstel *n*

2021 **rate** *(amount measured per unit of another amount)**
d Fuss *m*; Rate *f*; Satz *m*
e tasa *f*; tipo *m*
f taux *m*
i saggio *m*; tasso *m*
n koers *m*; voet *m*
* For other meanings of rate see charge, duty, price.

2022 **rate for advances on collateral (security); rate for loans on collateral (security); rate for secured advances; rate for secured loans**
cf. **lombard rate**
d Beleihungssatz *m*
e tasa *f* de préstamos con garantía; tasa *f* de préstamos su prenda; tipo *m* de préstamos con garantía; tipo *m* de préstamos su prenda
f taux *m* des avances contre garantie; taux *m* des avances sur nantissement; taux *m* des prêts contre garantie; taux *m* des prêts contre nantissement
i saggio *m* delle anticipazioni garantite; saggio *m* delle anticipazione su pegno; tasso *m* sui prestiti garantiti; tasso *m* sui prestiti su pegno
n beleningsrentevoet *m*

2023 **rate of assessment; rate of tax; rate of taxation; tax rate**
d Besteuerungssatz *m*; Steuerfuss *m (O)*; Steuersatz *m*
e tasa *f* de imposición; tasa *f* de(l) impuesto; tipo *m* de(l) impuesto; tipo *m* imponible; tipo *m* impositivo
f taux *m* de l'impôt; taux *m* d'imposition; taux *m* d'impôt; taux *m* fiscal
i aliquota *f* (dell'imposta); aliquota *f* (d'imposta); saggio *m* d'imposizione; saggio *m* d'imposta; tasso *m* dell'imposta; tasso *m* d'imposizione; tasso *m* d'imposta
n belastingvoet *m*

2024 **rate of exchange for spot delivery; spot exchange rate; spot rate**
d Bardevisenkurs *m*; Devisenkassakurs *m*; Devisenkassasatz *m*
e cambio *m* al contado; tipo *m* de cambio al contado
f cours *m* au comptant; cours *m* de change au comptant; taux *m* au comptant; taux *m* de change au comptant
i corso *m* a contanti; corso *m* di cambio a contanti; saggio *m* a contanti; saggio *m* di cambio a contanti; tasso *m* a contanti; tasso *m* di cambio a contanti
n contante wisselkoers *m* (van deviezen)

2025 **rate of return**
d Ertragsrate *f*
e tipo *m* de rédito; tipo *m* de rendimiento
f taux *m* de rendement
i tasso *m* di rendimento; tasso *m* di rendita
n rendementspercentage *n*

2026 **rate of saving(s); saving(s) rate**
d Sparquote *f*; Sparrate *f*
e tasa *f* de ahorro; tipo *m* de ahorro
f taux *m* de l'épargne
i tasso *m* di risparmio
n spaarquote *f*

2027 **rate of turnover; turnover rate; velocity of circulation**
d Umlauf(s)geschwindigkeit *f*
e velocidad *f* de circulación
f vitesse *f* de circulation
i velocità *f* di circolazione
n omloopsnelheid *f*

2028 **ratepayer*; taxpayer; tax-payer**
d Besteuerter *m*; Steuerpflichtiger *m*; Steuerzahler *m*
e causante *m (AL)*; contribuidor *m*; contributario *m*; contribuyente *m*; tributante *m*
f contribuable *m*
i contribuente *m*
n belastingbetaler *m*; belastingplichtige *m*; belastingschuldige *m*
* Usually only of municipal taxes.

2029 **ratio**
d Proportion *f*; Verhältnis *n*
e razón *f*; relación *f*
f proportion *f*; quotient *m*; raison *f*; rapport *m*; ratio *m*
i proporzione *f*; quoziente *m*; ragione *f*; rapporto *m*
n ratio *f*; verhouding *f*

2030 **rationing of foreign exchange**
cf. **currency restrictions**
d Devisenkontingentierung *f*
e contingentación *f* de divisas
f contingentement *m* des devises
i contingentamento *m* delle divise
n deviezencontingentering *f*

2031 **realignment of par values; realinement of par values**
d Neufestsetzung *f* der Paritäten
e reajuste *m* de las paridades
f réalignement *m* des parités; réaménagement *m* des parités
i riallineamento *m* delle parità; riequilibrio *m* delle parità
n herwaardering *f* van de pariteiten

2032 **real income**
d effektives Einkommen *n*; Realeinkommen *n*; tatsächliches Einkommen *n*; wirkliches Einkommen *n*
e ingreso(s) *m(pl)* efectivo(s); ingreso(s) *m(pl)* real(es); renta *f* efectiva; renta *f* real
f revenu(s) *m(pl)* effectif(s); revenu(s) *m(pl)* réel(s)
i redditi *mpl* effettivi; reddito *m* effettivo; reddito *m* reale
n reëel inkomen *n*; werkelijk inkomen *n*

2033 **realisability** ***(UK)*****; realizability** ***(US)***
d Realisierbarkeit *f*; Verwertbarkeit *f*
e realizabilidad *f*
f réalisabilité *f*
i realizzabilità
n realiseerbaarheid *f*; realizeerbaarheid *f*

2034 **realisable** ***(UK)*****; realizable** ***(US)***
d realisierbar; verwertbar
e realizable
f réalisable
i realizzabile
n realiseerbaar; realizeerbaar

2035 **real security; security on mortgage**
d dingliche Sicherheit *f*; hypothekarische Sicherheit *f*; hypothekarisches Pfand *n*; Hypothekengarantie *f*; Realsicherheit *f*
e garantía *f* hipotecaria; garantía *f* real; prenda *f* hipotecaria
f gage *m* hypothécaire; garantie *f* hypothécaire; garantie *f* réelle; sûreté *f* réelle
i garanzia *f* ipotecaria; garanzia *f* reale
n zakelijke zekerheid *f*; zakelijk onderpand *n*

2036 **reappraisal; revaluation**
cf. **revalorization**
d Neubewertung *f*
e revalorización *f*; reevaluación *f*; revaluación *f*
f réappréciation *f*; réévaluation *f*
i rivalutazione *f*
n herschatting *f*; herwaardering *f*; revaluatie *f*

2037 **reappraise** *v*; **revaluate** *v*; **revalue** *v*
cf. **appreciate** *v* **(tr.)**
d neu bewerten
e reevaluar; revalorizar; revaluar
f réapprécier; réévaluer
i rivalutare
n herschatten; herwaarderen; revalueren

2038 **rebate of tax; refund of tax; tax rebate; tax refund**
d Steuererstattung *f*; Steuerrückerstattung *f*; Steuerrückvergütung *f*; Steuerrückzahlung *f*; Steuervergütung *f*
e devolución *f* de impuestos; reembolso *m* de impuestos; restitución *f* de impuestos
f bonification *f* de taxe; remboursement *m* d'impôts; remboursement *m* fiscal; restitution *f* d'impôts; ristourne *f* d'impôts
i restituzione *f* d'imposte; rimborso *m* d'imposte
n belastingrestitutie *f*; belastingterugbetaling *f*

2039 **rebuild** *v* **the reserve; replenish** *v* **the reserve**
d die Reserve auffüllen; die Reserve wiederaufbauen; die Reserve wiederauffüllen
e reconstituir la reserva; rellenar la reserva
f combler la réserve; réapprovisionner la réserve; reconstituer la réserve
i ricostituire la riserva; rifornire la riserva
n de reserve aanvullen

2040 **receivership** ***(UK)*****; sequestration; trusteeship in bankruptcy** ***(US)***
d Geschäftsaufsicht *f*; Konkursverwaltung *f*; Zwangsverwaltung *f*
e administración *f* de (la masa de) la quiebra; secuestro *m* (judicial); sindicatura *f*

f administration *f* de la faillite; administration *f* de la masse; administration-séquestre *f*; séquestre *m* (judiciaire); syndicat *m* de la faillite
i amministrazione *f* della massa fallimentare; amministrazione *f* fallimentare; curatela *f* del (di) fallimento; curatela *f* fallimentare; sequestro *m* (giudiziario)
n curatorschap *n*

2041 **recompense; remuneration**
d Belohnung *f*; Besoldung *f*; Entgelt *n*; Entlohnung *f*; Remuneration *f*; Vergeltung *f*; Vergütung *f*
e recompensa *f*; remuneración *f*; retribución *f*
f récompense *f*; rémunération *f*; rétribution *f*
i compenso *m*; remunerazione *f*; retribuzione *f*; ricompensa *f*; rimunerazione *f*
n beloning *f*; bezoldiging *f*; remuneratie *f*; vergelding *f*; vergoeding *f*

2042 **recompense** *v*; **remunerate** *v*
d belohnen; besolden; entgelten; entlohnen; entlöhnen *(Schw)*; remunerieren; vergelten; vergüten
e abonar; recompensar; remunerar; retribuir
f récompenser; rémunérer; rétribuer
i remunerare; retribuire; ricompensare; rimunerare
n belonen; bezoldigen; remunereren; vergelden; vergoeden

2043 **reconciliation of accounts; squaring of accounts**
cf. **balance of an account**
d Abgleichung *f* von Konten; Abstimmung *f* von Konten; Bereinigung *f* von Konten; Kollationierung *f* von Konten
e conciliación *f* de cuentas; reconciliación *f* de cuentas
f apurement *m* de comptes; concordance *f* de comptes; rapprochement *m* de comptes
i appuramento *m* di conti
n afstemming *f* van rekeningen

2044 **reconstruct** *v* **the finances; rehabilitate** *v* **the finances; reorganize** *v* **the finances**
d die Finanzen sanieren
e reorganizar las finanzas; sanear las finanzas
f assainir les finances; redresser les finances; réorganiser les finances
i riorganizzare le finanze; risanare le finanze
n de financiën reorganiseren; de financiën saneren

2045 **record** *v* **a fall (a gain) of X points; show** *v* **a fall (a gain) of X points**
d einen Rückgang (einen Gewinn) von X Punkten aufweisen; einen Rückgang (einen Gewinn) von X Punkten verzeichnen
e acusar una baja (una ganancia; un avance) de X enteros (puntos); registrar una baja (una ganancia; un avance) de X enteros (puntos)
f accuser une baisse (un gain) de X points; enregistrer une baisse (un gain) de X points
i accusare una flessione (un guadagno) di X punti; registrare una flessione (un guadagno) di X punti
n een daling (een winst) van X punten noteren; een daling (een winst) van X punten vertonen

2046 **record** *v* **a loss (a profit); show** *v* **a loss (a profit)**
d einen Verlust (einen Gewinn) aufweisen; einen Verlust (einen Gewinn) ausweisen; einen Verlust (einen Gewinn) verzeichnen
e acusar una pérdida (una ganancia); arrojar una pérdida (una ganancia); registrar una pérdida (una ganancia)
f accuser une perte (un bénéfice); enregistrer une perte (un bénéfice); faire ressortir une perte (un bénéfice); se traduire par une perte (un bénéfice)
i accusare una perdita (un utile); presentare una perdita (un utile); registrare una perdita (un utile)
n een verlies (een winst) aanwijzen; een verlies (een winst) laten zien; een verlies (een winst) vertonen

2047 **recourse** *(in law)*
d Regress *m*; Rückgriff *m*
e recurso *m*
f recours *m*
i regresso *m*
n regres *n*; verhaal *n*

2048 **recovery** *(market etc.)*
cf. **rally, rise**
d Belebung *f*; Erholung *f*; Reprise *f*; Wiederaufleben *n*; Wiederaufschwung *m*; Wiederaufstieg *m*; Wiedergesundung *f*
e reactivación *f*; recobro *m*; recuperación *f*; relanzamiento *m*

f récupération *f*; redressement *m*; relance *f*; relèvement *m*; reprise *f*
i rialzo *m*; ricupero *m*; rilancio *m*; ripresa *f*
n herstel *n*; opleving *f*; wederopleving *f*

2049 recurrent receipts; recurring receipts
d wiederkehrende Einnahmen *fpl*
e ingresos *mpl* periódicos; ingresos *mpl* recurrentes
f recettes *fpl* périodiques; recettes *fpl* récurrentes
i entrate *fpl* periodiche; entrate *fpl* ricorrenti
n periodieke inkomsten *fpl*

2050 recycling of capital
d Rückführung *f* von Kapital; Rückschleusung *f* von Kapital
e reciclaje *m* de capital
f recyclage *m* de capitaux
i riciclaggio *m* di capitali; riciclo *m* di capitali
n recycleren *n* van kapitaal; recycling *f* van kapitaal; terugvoering *f* van kapitaal

2051 redeemability
d Ablösbarkeit *f*; Auslösbarkeit *f*; Einlösbarkeit *f*; Kündbarkeit *f*; Rückzahlbarkeit *f*; Tilgbarkeit *f*
e amortizabilidad *f*; redimibilidad *f*; reembolsabilidad *f*; rescatabilidad *f*
f possibilité *f* d'amortir; possibilité *f* de racheter; possibilité *f* de rembourser; remboursabilité *f*
i redimibilità *f*; rimborsabilità *f*; riscattabilità *f*
n afkoopbaarheid *f*; aflosbaarheid *f*

2052 redeemable
cf. **callable, refundable**
d ablösbar; auslösbar; einlösbar; kündbar; rückkaufbar; rückkäuflich; rückzahlbar; tilgbar
e amortizable; redimible; reembolsable; rescatable
f amortissable; rachetable; remboursable
i ammortizzabile; redimibile; rimborsabile; riscattabile
n afkoopbaar; aflosbaar; amortiseerbaar

2053 redemption *(of bonds etc.)*; **retirement**
cf. **amortisation**
d Ablösung *f*; Amortisation *f*; Amortisierung *f*; Aufruf *m*; Einlösung *f*; Kündigung *f*; Rückkauf *m*; Rückzahlung *f*; Tilgung *f*; Wiederkauf *m*
e amortización *f*; redención *f*; reembolso *m*; rescate *m*; retirada *f*; retiro *m*
f amortissement *m*; rachat *m*; remboursement *m*; retrait *m*
i ammortamento *m*; ammortizzamento *m*; ammortizzazione *f*; redenzione *f*; rimborso *m*; riscatto *m*; ritiro *m*
n aflossing *f*; amortisatie *f*; amortizatie *f*; delging *f*; inkoop *m*; lossing *f*

2054 redemption price; redemption rate; retirement rate
cf. **amortisation rate**
d Einlösungskurs *m*; Rückkaufspreis *m*; Rückkaufssatz *m*; Rückzahlungskurs *m*; Rückzahlungspreis *m*; Rückzahlungsrate *f*
e cambio *m* de reembolso; cotización *f* de reembolso; cotización *f* de rescate; precio *m* de redención; precio *m* de reembolso; precio *m* de rescate
f cours *m* de rachat; cours *m* de remboursement; prix *m* de rachat
i corso *m* di rimborso; corso *m* di riscatto; prezzo *m* di rimborso; prezzo *m* di riscatto
n aflossingskoers *m*; aflossingsprijs *m*

2055 redemption value
cf. **surrender value**
d Ablösungswert *m*; Einlösungswert *m*; Rückkaufswert *m*; Rückzahlungswert *m*; Tilgungswert *m*
e valor *m* de redención; valor *m* de reembolso; valor *m* de rescate
f valeur *f* de rachat; valeur *f* de remboursement
i valore *m* di rimborso; valore *m* di riscatto
n aflossingswaarde *f*; inkoopwaarde *f*; terugbetalingswaarde *f*

2056 rediscount; rediscounting
d Neudiskontierung *f*; Rediskont *m*; Rediskontierung *f*; Rückdiskont *m*; Rückdiskontierung *f*
e redescuento *m*
f réescompte *m*
i risconto *m*
n herdiscontering *f*; herdisconto *n*

2057 rediscount *v*
d neudiskontieren; rediskontieren; rückdiskontieren
e redescontar
f réescompter
i riscontare
n herdisconteren

2058 rediscountable
d rediskontfähig; rediskontierbar; rückdiskontierbar; zum Rediskont zugelassen
e redescontable
f réescomptable
i riscontabile
n herdiscontabel; herdisconteerbaar

2059 rediscount rate
cf. **bank rate**
d Rediskontsatz *m*
e tasa *f* de redescuento; tipo *m* de redescuento
f taux *m* de réescompte
i saggio *m* di risconto; tasso *m* di risconto
n herdiscontovoet *m*

2060 redistribution
d Redistribution *f*; Umverteilung *f*; Wiederverteilung *f*
e redistribución *f*
f redistribution *f*
i ridistribuzione *f*
n herdistributie *f*; herverdeling *f*

2061 reduce *v* **capital stock; reduce** *v* **share capital**
d Aktien zusammenlegen; das Aktienkapital zusammenlegen
e agrupar acciones; reducir el capital social
f réduire le capital-actions; regrouper des actions
i aggruppare azioni; raggruppare azioni; ridurre il capitale azionario
n het aandelenkapitaal verkleinen; het aandelenkapitaal verminderen

2062 reduce *v* **the par value**
d die Parität herabsetzen
e rebajar la paridad
f abaisser la parité
i abbassare la parità
n de pariteit verlagen; de pariteit verminderen

2063 reduction of capital
d Kapitalabschnitt *m*; Kapitalherabsetzung *f*; Kapitalverminderung *f*; Kapitalzusammenlegung *f*
e reducción *f* de capital
f réduction *f* de capital
i riduzione *f* di capitale
n kapitaalvermindering *f*

2064 reduction of capital stock; reduction of share capital
d Aktienzusammenlegung *f*; Zusammenlegung *f* des Aktienkapitals
e agrupación *f* de acciones; reducción *f* del capital social
f réduction *f* du capital-actions; regroupement *m* d'actions
i aggruppamento *m* di azioni; raggruppamento *m* di azioni; riduzione *f* del capitale azionario
n verkleining *f* van het aandelenkapitaal; vermindering *f* van het aandelenkapitaal

2065 reduction of flexibility margins; reduction of fluctuation margins
d Einengung *f* der Bandbreiten
e reducción *f* de los márgines de fluctuación
f rétrécissement *m* des marges de fluctuation
i riduzione *f* dei margini di fluttuazione
n vermindering *f* van de fluctuatiemarges

2066 reexport; reexportation
d Reexport *m*; Wiederausfuhr *f*
e reexportación *f*
f réexportation *f*
i riesportazione *f*
n herexport *m*; wederuitvoer *m*

2067 refinance *v*
d refinanzieren
e refinanciar
f refinancer
i rifinanziare
n herfinancieren

2068 refinancing
d Neufinanzierung *f*; Refinanzierung *f*
e refinanciación *f*; refinanciamiento *m*
f refinancement *m*
i rifinanziamento *m*
n herfinanciering *f*

2069 reflate *v*
d eine Reflation bewirken; reflatieren
e provocar una reflación; reflar
f provoquer une reflation; reflater
i provocare una reflazione; riflazionare
n een reflatie bewerken; reflateren; reflationeren

2070 reflation
d Reflation *f*
e reflación *f*
f reflation *f*
i reflazione *f*; riflazione *f*
n reflatie *f*

2071 reflow of capital; reflux of capital
d Rückfluss *m* von Kapital
e reflujo *m* de capitales
f reflux *m* de capitaux

i riflusso *m* di capitali
n terugvloeiing *f* van kapitaal

2072 refund; reimbursement; repayment
d Rückerstattung *f*; Rückvergütung *f*; Rückzahlung *f*; Wiederbezahlung *f*; Wiedererstattung *f*; Zurückbezahlung *f*; Zurückerstattung *f*; Zurückvergütung *f*; Zurückzahlung *f*
e reembolso *m*; reintegro *m*; restitución *f*
f remboursement *m*; restitution *f*; ristourne *f*
i restituzione *f*; rifusione *f*; rimborso *m*
n rembours *n*; remboursement *n*; restitutie *f*; terugbetaling *f*; wederbetaling *f*

2073 refundable; reimbursable; repayable; returnable
cf. **callable, redeemable**
d erstattungsfähig; rückerstattungsfähig; rückzahlbar; zurückzahlbar
e reembolsable; reintegrable; restituible
f remboursable; restituable
i restituibile; rifondibile; rimborsabile
n terugbetaalbaar; wederbetaalbaar

2074 refusal of payment; refusal to pay
d Ablehnung *f* der Zahlung; Zahlungsverweigerung *f*
e denegación *f* de pago; negativa *f* de pago; rehusamiento *m* de pago; rehuso *m* de pago
f refus *m* de paiement
i rifiuto *m* di pagamento
n weigering *f* tot betaling; weigering *f* van betaling

2075 registered office(s)
cf. **central office(s)**
d Gesellschaftssitz *m*; satzungsmässiger Sitz *m*; statutarischer Sitz *m (Schw)*
e domicilio *m* social; sede *f* estatutaria; sede *f* social
f siège *m* social; siège *m* statutaire
i sede *f* sociale; sede *f* statutaria
n maatschappelijke zetel *m*; statutaire zetel *m*

2076 registered shareholder; shareholder of record; stockholder of record *(US)*
d (im Hauptbuch) eingetragener Aktionär *m*
e accionista *m* registrado
f actionnaire *m* enregistré
i azionista *m* iscritto nel libro dei soci
n geregistreerde aandeelhouder *m*

2077 registration dues; registration fee(s); transfer fee *(US)*
cf. **cost of transfer**
d Eintragungsgebühr *f*; Registrierungsgebühr *f*
e derecho *m* de registro; tasa *f* de registro
f droit *m* d'enregistrement; droit *m* d'inscription
i diritto *m* di iscrizione; diritto *m* di registrazione; imposta *f* di registro; tassa *f* di registro
n registratierecht *n*

2078 reinvestment
cf. **new investment**
d Neuanlage *f*; Neuinvestition *f*; Reinvestition *f*; Wiederanlage *f*
e reinversión *f*
f réemploi *m*; réinvestissement *m*; remploi *m*; replacement *m*
i reimpiego *m*; reinvestimento *m*; rimpiego *m (rare)*; rinvestimento *m*
n herbelegging *f*; herinvestering *f*

2079 relend *v*
d weiterleihen; wieder ausleihen; wieder leihen
e prestar de nuevo
f reprêter
i prestare di nuovo; riprestare
n we(d)erlenen; we(d)eruitlenen

2080 remit *v (funds etc.)*; **send** *v*; **transfer** *v*
d anweisen; einsenden; girieren; remittieren; transferieren; übermachen; übersenden; überweisen
e enviar; girar; remesar; transferir
f envoyer; remettre; transférer; verser; virer
i girare; inviare; rimettere; tra(n)sferire; versare
n gireren; overboeken; overdragen; overmaken; overschrijven; remitteren; transfereren

2081 remittance charge(s); remittance fee; transfer charge(s); transfer fee
d Überweisungsgebühr *f*
e tasa *f* de transferencia
f droit *m* de transfert; frais *mpl* de virement
i diritto *m* di rimessa; diritto *m* di trasferimento
n overboekingskosten *mpl*; overschrijvingskosten *mpl*

2082 remittee; transferee
d Anweisungsempfänger *m*; Empfänger *m*; Überweisungsempfänger *m*

e destinatario *m*
f destinataire *m*
i destinatario *m*
n ontvanger *m*

2083 remitter; transferor; transfer(r)er *(rare in this sense)*
d Remittent *m*; Übersender *m*; Überweisender *m*
e remitente *m*; transferidor *m*
f remettant *m*; remetteur *m*
i ordinante *m*
n overdrager *m*; remittent *m*

2084 rendering of services
cf. **services**
d Dienstleistung *f*
e prestación *f* de servicios
f prestation *f* de services
i prestazione *f* di servizi
n dienstbetoon *n*; dienstverlening *f*

2085 renewal coupon; talon
d Erneuerungsschein *m*; Talon *m*; Zinsleiste *f*
e talón *m* de renovación
f talon *m* de recouponnement; talon *m* de renouvellement
i cedola *f* di riaffogliamento
n talon *m*

2086 renewal fund; replacement reserve
d Erneuerungsfonds *m*; Erneuerungsrücklage *f*
e fondo *m* de reemplazo; fondo *m* de reposición; reserva *f* de reemplazo; reserva *f* de reposición
f fonds *m* de renouvellement; réserve *f* de renouvellement
i fondo *m* di rinnovamento; fondo *m* per l'ammodernamento
n vernieuwingsfonds *n*; vernieuwingsreserve *f*; vervangingsfonds *n*; vervangingsreserve *f*

2087 renewal of coupons
d Dividendenscheinerneuerung *f*; Zinsscheinerneuerung *f*
e renovación *f* de la hoja de cupones
f recouponnement *m*
i riaffogliamento *m*
n vernieuwing *f* van het couponblad

2088 rent; rental
d Miete *f*; Mietpreis *m*; Mietzins *m*; Pacht *f*; Zins *m*
e alquiler *m*; arriendo *m*; renta *f (AL)*; precio *m* del alquiler
f location *f*; loyer *m*; prix *m* de location; prix *m* du loyer; prix *m* locatif
i affitto *m*; canone *m* d'affitto; canone *m* di locazione; fitto *m*; locazione *f*; pigione *f*
n huur *f*; huurgeld *n*; huurprijs *m*; pacht *f*; pachtgeld *n*; pachtprijs *m*

2089 repatriate *v (profits etc.)*; **transfer** *v* **home**
d repatriieren; rückführen; zurückführen
e repatriar
f rapatrier
i rimpatriare
n repatriëren; terugvoeren

2090 repatriation *(of profits etc.)*
d Repatriierung *f*; Rückführung *f*; Rückwanderung *f*; Zurückführung *f*
e repatriación *f*
f rapatriement *m*
i rimpatrio *m*
n repatriëring *f*; terugvoering *f*

2091 replacement cost(s); replacement price; replacement value
d Ersatzkosten *pl*; Ersatzwert *m*; Wiederanschaffungskosten *pl*; Wiederanschaffungspreis *m*; Wiederanschaffungswert *m*; Wiederbeschaffungskosten *pl*; Wiederbeschaffungspreis *m*; Wiederbeschaffungswert *m*
e costo *m* de reposición; gastos *m* de reposición; precio *m* de reemplazo; valor *m* de reemplazo; valor *m* de reposición; valor *m* de sustitución
f coût *m* de remplacement; prix *m* de remplacement; valeur *f* de remplacement
i costo *m* di rimpiazzo; costo *m* di sostituzione; spese *fpl* di sostituzione; valore *m* di rimpiazzo; valore *m* di sostituzione
n heraanschaffingswaarde *f (B)*; vervangingskosten *mpl*; vervangingsprijs *m*; vervangingswaarde *f*

2092 repudiate *v* **a debt**
d eine Schuld bestreiten; eine Schuld nicht anerkennen
e repudiar una deuda
f nier une dette; renier une dette; répudier une dette
i rifiutare di riconoscere un debito
n een schuld niet erkennen

2093 repudiation of a debt
d Nichtanerkenntnis *n* einer Schuld; Nichtanerkennung *f* einer Schuld
e no reconocimiento *m* de una deuda; repudiación *f* de una deuda

f reniement *m* d'une dette; répudiation *f* d'une dette
i rifiuto *m* di riconoscere un debito
n niet-erkennen *n* van een schuld

2094 repurchase
d Rückkauf *m*; Wiederkauf *m*
e readquisición *f*; recompra *f*
f rachat *m*
i riacquisto *m*; ricomp(e)ra *f*
n terugkoop *m*; wederaankoop *m*; wederinkoop *m*

2095 repurchase price
d Rückkaufspreis *m*; Rückkaufssatz *m*; Rücknahmepreis *m*; Rücknahmesatz *m*
e precio *m* de recompra
f prix *m* de rachat
i prezzo *m* di riscatto
n koers *m* van terugkoop; koers *m* van wederinkoop

2096 resale price; retail price
d Detailpreis *m*; Einzelhandelspreis *m*; Einzelverkaufspreis *m*; Kleinhandelspreis *m*; Kleinverkaufspreis *m*; Wiederverkaufspreis *m*
e precio *m* al detall(e); precio *m* al por menor; precio *m* de detalle; precio *m* de menudeo; precio *m* de reventa; precio *m* de venta al por menor
f prix *m* au détail; prix *m* de détail; prix *m* de revente; prix *m* de vente au détail
i prezzo *m* al dettaglio; prezzo *m* al minuto; prezzo *m* di rivendita; prezzo *m* di vendita al minuto
n detailhandelsprijs *m*; detailprijs *m*; detailverkoopprijs *m*; kleinhandelsprijs *m*; wederverkoopprijs *m*

2097 resale price maintenance; vertical price-fixing
d Preisbindung *f* der zweiten Hand; Preisbindung *f* zweiter Hand; vertikale Preisbindung *f*
e fijación *f* vertical de los precios; mantenimiento *m* del precio de reventa
f fixation *f* verticale des prix; pratique *f* des prix imposés
i fissazione *f* verticale dei prezzi; sistema *m* dei prezzi imposti
n verticale prijsbinding *f*

2098 reserve; reserves
cf. **allowance, reserve fund, retained earnings**
d Reserve(n) *f(pl)*; Rücklage(n) *f(pl)*
e reserva(s) *f(pl)*
f réserve(s) *f(pl)*
i riserva *f*; riserve *fpl*
n reserve(s) *f(pl)*

2099 under reserve; under the usual reserves
d Eingang vorbehalten; unter den üblichen Vorbehalten; unter üblichem Vorbehalt; unter Vorbehalt; vorbehaltlich des richtigen Einganges
e salvo buen cobro; salvo buen fin
f sauf bonne fin
i salvo buon fine
n onder gewoon voorbehoud; onder voorbehoud van inkomst

2100 reserve currency
d Reservewährung *f*
e moneda *f* de reserva
f monnaie *f* de réserve
i moneta *f* di riserva
n reservevaluta *f*

2101 reserve fund
cf. **contingency fund, reserve, retained earnings**
d Reservefonds *m*; Rücklage *f*; Rücklagefonds *m*
e fondo *m* de reserva
f fonds *m* de réserve
i fondo *m* di riserva
n reservefonds *n*

2102 reserve prescribed by the articles; statutory reserve
d statutarische Reserve *f*; statutarische Rücklage *f*
e reserva *f* estatutaria
f réserve *f* statutaire
i riserva *f* statutaria
n statutaire reserve *f*

2103 residual value
d Restwert *m*
e valor *m* residual; valor *m* restante
f valeur *f* résiduelle
i valore *m* residuo; valore *m* rimanente
n residuwaarde *f*; restwaarde *f*

2104 restriction of liquidity
d Liquiditätsbeschränkung *f*; Liquiditätsbegrenzung *f*; Liquiditätshemmung *f*; Liquiditätsverknappung *f*
e limitación *f* de la liquidez; restricción *f* de la liquidez
f restriction *f* de la liquidité
i limitazione *f* della liquidità; restrizione *f* della liquidità
n liquiditeitsbeperking *f*; liquiditeitsinperking *f*

2105 **retailer**
d Detailhändler *m*; Detaillist *m*; Einzelhändler *m*; Kleinhändler *m*; Wiederverkäufer *m*
e comerciante *m* al detall(e); comerciante *m* al por menor; comerciante *m* minorista; detallista *m*; expendedor *m*; menorista *m (AL)*; minorista *m*; revendedor *m*
f débitant *m*; détaillant *m*; petit commerçant *m*; revendeur *m*
i commerciante *m* al minuto; dettagliante *m*; piccolo commerciante *m*; rivenditore *m*
n detailhandelaar *m*; détaillant *m (B)*; detaillist *m*; kleinhandelaar *m*; wederverkoper *m*

2106 **retail price index**
d Einzelhandels(preis)index *m*; Index *m* der Einzelhandelspreise; Index *m* der Kleinhandelspreise; Kleinhandels(preis)-index *m*
e índice *m* de los precios al por menor
f indice *m* des prix au (de) détail
i indice *m* dei prezzi al minuto
n indexcijfer *n* van de detailhandelsprijzen; indexcijfer *n* van de kleinhandelsprijzen; index *m* van de detailhandelsprijzen; index *m* van de kleinhandelsprijzen; kleinhandelsprijzenindex *m*

2107 **retail trade**
d Detailhandel *m*; Einzelhandel *m*; Kleinhandel *m*
e comercio *m* al detall(e); comercio *m* al por menor; comercio *m* detallista; comercio *m* minorista; menudeo *m*
f commerce *m* au détail; commerce *m* de détail; commerce *m* en détail; détail *m*; petit commerce *m*
i commercio *m* al dettaglio; commercio *m* al minuto; piccolo commercio *m*
n detailhandel *m*; kleinhandel *m*

2108 **retained earnings; retained profits; undistributed profits**
cf. **reserve**
d einbehaltene Gewinne *mpl*; nicht ausgeschüttete Gewinne *mpl*; nicht entnommene Gewinne *mpl*; thesaurierte Gewinne *mpl*; unausgeschütteter Reingewinn *m*; zurückbehaltene Gewinne *mpl*
e beneficios *mpl* acumulados; beneficios *mpl* no distribuidos; beneficios *mpl* retenidos; ganancias *fpl* acumuladas; ganancias *fpl* no distribuidas; ganancias *fpl* retenidas; utilidades *fpl* acumuladas; utilidades *fpl* no distribuidas; utilidades *fpl* retenidas
f bénéfices *mpl* accumulés; bénéfices *mpl* non distribués; bénéfices *mpl* non prélevés; bénéfices *mpl* réservés; bénéfices *mpl* retenus; profits *mpl* accumulés; profits *mpl* non distribués; profits *mpl* non prélevés; profits *mpl* réservés; profits *mpl* retenus
i utili *mpl* accantonati; utili *mpl* non distributi; utili *mpl* non prelevati
n ingehouden winsten *fpl*; niet uitgekeerde winsten *fpl*

2109 **retention money**
d einbehaltene Garantiesumme *f*; Sicherheitssumme *f*
e retención *f* en garantía
f retenue *f* de garantie
i ritenuta *f* a garanzia
n ingehouden waarborgsom *f*

2110 **return; yield**
cf. **avails, income, incomings, proceeds**
d Anfall *m*; Ertrag *m*; Erträgnis *n*; Rendite *f* Verzinsung *f*
e rédito *m*; rendimiento *m*
f rendement *m*
i rendimento *m*; rendita *f*
n opbrengst *f*; rendement *n*

2111 **revalorization; revaluation**
cf. **appreciation, reappraisal**
d Aufwertung *f*; Revalorisierung *f*
e revalorización *f*; revaluación *f*
f réévaluation *f*; revalorisation *f*
i rivalorizzazione *f*; rivalutazione *f*
n opwaardering *f*; revalorisatie *f*; revaluatie *f*

2112 **revenue shortfall; shortfall in receipts**
cf. **budgetary depreciation**
d Mindereinnahme(n) *f(pl)*
e menor(es) ingreso(s) *m(pl)*
f moins-perçu *m*; recette(s) *f(pl)* inférieure(s)
i entrata *f* minore; minori entrate *fpl*
n mindere ontvangst(en) *f(pl)*

2113 **revocable credit**
d widerruflicher Kredit *m*
e crédito *m* revocable
f crédit *m* révocable
i credito *m* revocabile
n herroepelijk krediet *n*

2114 **revolving credit**
d revolvierender Kredit *m*; Revolving-

kredit m; rotierender Kredit *m*; sich automatisch erneuernder Kredit *m*; Umlaufkredit *m*
e crédito *m* renovable automáticamente; crédito *m* rotativo; crédito *m* rotatorio
f crédit *m* automatiquement renouvelable; crédit *m* revolving; crédit *m* rotatif
i credito *m* revolving; credito *m* rinnovabile automaticamente; credito *m* rotativo
n automatisch hernieuwd krediet *n*; renouvellerend krediet *n*; revolver-krediet *n*; revolving krediet *n*

2115 **right; stock allotment warrant** *(US)*; **stock subscription warrant; subscription right certificate; subscription warrant; warrant**
d Aktienbezugsschein *m*; Bezugs-berechtigungsschein *m*; Bezugsschein *m*
e certificado *m* de suscripción; derecho *m* de suscripción
f certificat *m* de souscription; droit *m* de souscription
i certificato *m* di sottoscrizione; diritto *m* di sottoscrizione
n certificaat *n* van inschrijving; recht *n* van inschrijving

2116 **rights issue**
cf. **issue of shares**
d Ausgabe *f* von Bezugsaktien; Emission *f* von Bezugsaktien
e emisión *f* de acciones nuevas
f émission *f* d'actions nouvelles
i emissione *f* d'azioni optate; emissione *f* di nuove azioni
n emissie *f* van nieuwe aandelen; uitgifte *f* van nieuwe aandelen

2117 **rise; upsurge; upswing; upturn**
cf. **recovery**
d Aufschwung *m*; Aufstieg *m*; Auftrieb *m*; Hausse *f*; Steigen *n*
e alza *f*; ascenso *m*; auge *m*
f essor *m*; hausse *f*; relèvement *m*
i ascesa *f*; aumento *m*; rialzo *m*
n hausse *f*; opleving *f*; stijging *f*

2118 **roll-over loan**
d Roll-over Anleihe *f*; Roll-over Kredit *m*
e crédito *m* roll-over
f crédit *m* roll-over; emprunt *m* à charnière
i credito *m* roll-over; prestito *m* a cerniera
n roll-over krediet *n*

2119 **in round figures**
d abgerundet; aufgerundet; in runden Zahlen
e en cifras redondas
f en chiffres ronds
i in cifra tonda
n in ronde getallen

2120 **run** *v* **counter to the general trend**
d der allgemeinen Tendenz zuwiderlaufen
e estar contrario a la tendencia general
f aller à l'encontre de la tendance générale
i essere contrario alla tendenza generale
n tegen de algemene tendens indruisen

2121 **run on the bank**
d Ansturm *m* auf die Bank(schalter); Bank-panik *f*; Run *m* auf die Bank; Sturm *m* auf die Bank
e asedio *m* del banco; corrida *f* sobre el banco; pánico *m* bancario
f assaut *m* de la banque; course *f* aux guichets de la banque; descente *f* (en masse) sur la banque; panique *f* bancaire; ruée *f* sur (les guichets de) la banque
i assalto *m* agli sportelli (della banca); assedio *m* della banca; corsa *f* agli sportelli della banca; panico *m* bancario; run *m* ai depositi bancari
n bestorming *f* van de bank; run *m* op de bank; stormloop *m* op de bank

S

2122 safe; strong box
d Geldschrank *m*; Panzerschrank *m*; Safe *m/n*; Stahlkasse *f*; Tresor *m*
e caja *f* acorazada; caja *f* de caudales; caja *f* fuerte; cofre *m* fuerte
f coffre-fort *m*; safe *m*
i cassaforte *f* (blindata); cassaforte *f* (corazzata); safe *m*
n brandkast *f*; safe *m*

2123 safe deposit box; safety deposit box
d Schliessfach *n*; Sicherheitsfach *n*; Stahlfach *n*; Stahlkassette *f*; Tresorfach *n*
e caja *f* de seguridad; caja *f* fuerte de alquiler; cofrecillo *m* de seguridad
f boîte *f* de coffre-fort; coffre *m*; compartiment *m* de coffre-fort
i cassa *f* di sicurezza; cassetta *f* di sicurezza
n kluisloket *n*; safeloket *n*

2124 safe deposit charge
d Depotgebühr *f*
e derechos *mpl* de custodia
f droit *m* de garde
i diritti *mpl* di custodia
n bewaarloon *n*

2125 safe deposit vault; safety deposit vault; strong room; vault
d Panzergewölbe *n*; Stahlkammer *f*; Tresor *m*; Tresorraum *m*
e cámara *f* acorazada; cámara *f* blindada; cámara *f* de seguridad; depósito *m* de seguridad
f cave *f* des coffres-forts; chambre *f* blindée; chambre *f* forte; salle *f* blindée; salle *f* des coffres
i camera *f* blindata; camera *f* corazzata; camera *f* di sicurezza; deposito *m* di sicurezza
n bewaarkluis *f*; kluis *f*; safe-inrichting *f*

2126 salary
cf. **earnings, emoluments, recompense**
d Besoldung *f*; Gehalt *n*; Salär *n (Schw)*
e sueldo *m**
f appointements *mpl*; salaire *m***; traitement *m*
i stipendio *m****
n salaris *n*; wedde *f*

* Salario means earnings (q.v.).
** Salaire also means earnings (q.v.).
*** Salario means earnings (q.v.).

2127 sale *(act of selling)*
d Verkauf *m*
e venta *f*
f vente *f*
i vendita *f*
n verkoop *m*

2128 sale *(selling off cheaply)*
d Ausverkauf *m*; Resteverkauf *m*
e saldo *m*
f soldes *mpl*
i saldi *mpl*
n solde *f (B)*; uitverkoop *m*

2129 sale at a loss; selling at a loss
d Schleuderverkauf *m*; Verkauf *m* mit Schaden; Verkauf *m* mit Verlust; Verlustverkauf *m*; Verschleuderung *f*
e venta *f* con pérdida
f mévente *f*; vente *f* à perte; vente *f* avec perte
i svendita *f*; vendita *f* a perdita; vendita *f* con perdita
n verkoop *m* met schade; verkoop *m* met verlies

2130 sales *(US)*; **turnover; volume of business**
d Geschäftsumfang *m*; Geschäftsumsatz *m*; Geschäftsvolumen *n*; Umsatz *m*; Verkäufe *mpl*
e cifra *f* de negocios; giro *m* de negocios; ventas *fpl*; volumen *m* de negocios
f chiffre *m* d'affaires; ventes *fpl*; volume *m* d'affaires
i cifra *f* d'affari; fatturato *m*; giro *m* d'affari; vendite *fpl*; volume *m* d'affari
n omzet *m*; verkopen *mpl*; zakencijfer *n (B)*; zakenomvang *m*

2131 sales index
d Umsatzindex *m*
e índice *m* de ventas
f indice *m* des chiffres d'affaires; indice *m* des ventes
i indice *m* delle vendite
n index *m* van het omzetcijfer *(B)*; omzetindexcijfer *n*

2132 sale with right of repurchase
d Kauf *m* mit Rückkaufsrecht
e venta *f* con derecho de retracto; venta *f* con derecho de retroventa
f vente *f* à réméré
i vendita *f* con diritto di riacquisto; vendita *f* con diritto di riscatto
n verkoop *m* met recht van wederinkoop

2133 save *v*
d sparen

e ahorrar
f épargner; mettre de côté
i risparmiare
n sparen

2134 saver
d Sparer *m*
e ahorrador *m*
f épargnant *m*
i risparmiatore *m*
n spaarder *m*

2135 saving by investment in securities
d Effektensparen *n*; Wertpapiersparen *n*
e ahorro *m* en forma de valores; ahorro *m* mediante inversión en valores mobiliarios
f épargne *f* (de placement) en valeurs; épargne *f* mobilière
i risparmio *m* in titoli; risparmio *m* mobiliare
n effectensparen *n*; sparen *n* in effecten

2136 saving on savings accounts
d Kontensparen *n*
e ahorro *m* en cuenta(s) de ahorros
f épargne *f* en compte(s) d'épargne
i risparmio *m* in conto di risparmio
n sparen *n* op spaarrekeningen

2137 savings
cf. **savings capital**
d Einsparungen *fpl*; Ersparnisse *fpl*; Spargelder *npl*
e ahorros *mpl*
f épargne *f*
i risparmio *m*
n besparingen *fpl*; spaargelden *npl*; spaarpenningen *mpl*

2138 savings account
d Sparkonto *n*
e cuenta *f* de ahorros
f compte *m* d'épargne
i conto *m* di risparmio
n spaarrekening *f*

2139 savings bank
d Sparbank *f*; Sparkasse *f*
e banco *m* de ahorros; caja *f* de ahorros
f banque *f* d'épargne; caisse *f* d'épargne
i banca *f* di risparmio; cassa *f* di risparmio
n spaarbank *f*; spaarkas *f*

2140 savings bank book; savings bank deposit book
cf. **savings book**
d Sparkassenbuch *n*
e libreta *f* de caja de ahorros
f carnet *m* de caisse d'épargne; livret *m* de caisse d'épargne
i libretto *m* di cassa di risparmio
n spaarbankboekje *n*

2141 savings bond; savings certificate
d Sparanleihestück *n*; Sparbon *m*; Sparbrief *m*; Sparschein *m*
e bono *m* de ahorro
f bon *m* d'épargne
i buono *m* di risparmio
n rentespaarbrief *m*; spaarbrief *m*

2142 savings book
cf. **deposit book, savings bank book**
d Sparbuch *n*
e libreta *f* de ahorros
f carnet *m* d'épargne; livret *m* d'épargne
i libretto *m* di risparmio
n spaarboekje *n*

2143 savings capital
cf. **savings**
d Sparkapital *n*
e capital *m* de ahorro
f capital *m* d'épargne
i capitale *m* di risparmio
n spaarkapitaal *n*

2144 savings deposit
d Spareinlage *f*; Sparguthaben *n*
e depósito *m* de ahorro(s)
f dépôt *m* d'épargne
i deposito *m* a risparmio; deposito *m* di risparmio
n spaardeposito *n*; spaarinlaag *f*; spaarinlage *f*; spaarinleg *m*; spaartegoed *n*

2145 savings fund
d Sparfonds *m*
e fondo *m* de ahorros
f fonds *m* d'épargne
i fondo *m* di risparmio
n spaarfonds *n*

2146 secondary income
d Sekundäreinkommen *n*; Sekundäreinkünfte *fpl*
e ingresos *mpl* secundarios
f revenus *mpl* secondaires
i entrate *fpl* secondarie; redditi *mpl* secondari
n secondaire inkomens *npl*; secundaire inkomens *npl*

2147 secondary market
d Sekondärmarkt *m*
e mercado *m* secundario

f marché *m* secondaire
i mercato *m* secondario
n secondaire markt *f*; secundaire markt *f*

2148 second of exchange
d Sekunda *m/f*; Sekundawechsel *m*; Wechselsekunda *m/f*; Zweitausfertigung *f*; zweite Wechselausfertigung *f*
e segunda *f* de cambio
f deuxième *f* de change; seconde *f* de change
i seconda *f* di cambio
n secunda *f*; secundawissel *m*

2149 secured bond
d besicherte Obligation *f*; besicherte Schuldverschreibung *f*; gesicherte Obligation *f*; gesicherte Schuldverschreibung *f*; sichergestellte Obligation *f*; sichergestellte Schuldverschreibung *f*
e obligación *f* con garantía; obligación *f* garantizada
f obligation *f* gagée; obligation *f* garantie
i obbligazione *f* garantita
n gegarandeerde obligatie *f*

2150 secured creditor
cf. **preferential creditor**
d gesicherter Gläubiger *m*; sichergestellter Gläubiger *m*
e acreedor *m* garantizado
f créditeur *m* garanti; créditeur *m* nanti
i creditore *m* garantito
n gedekte crediteur *m*; gedekte schuldeiser *m*

2151 securities; stock*; stocks*
d Effekten *pl*; Papiere *npl*; Papierwerte *mpl*; Stücke *npl*; Titel *mpl*; Valoren *pl*; Werte *mpl*; Wertpapiere *npl*; Wertschriften *fpl (Schw)*
e efectos *mpl*; papeles *mpl*; títulos *mpl*; títulos-valores *mpl*; valores *mpl*
f effets *mpl*; papiers-valeurs *mpl*; titres *mpl*; valeurs *fpl*
i carte-valori *fpl*; effetti *mpl*; titoli *mpl*; valori *mpl*
n effecten *npl*; effekten *npl*; fondsen *npl*; papieren *npl*; stukken *npl*; titels *mpl (B)*; waarden *fpl*; waardepapieren *npl*

* Stock(s) in UK usage is mostly synonymous with shares, in US usage with bonds or debentures. Technically the term denotes an individual capital contribution which can be held and transferred in any amount, i.e. by definition always fully paid up. Linguistically it is (usually) used in the singular as a collective noun and in the plural to denote individual certificates.

2152 securities broker *(US)*; stockbroker
cf. **jobber**
d Aktienhändler *m*; Aktienmakler *m*; Börsenhändler *m*; Börsenmakler *m*; Effektenhändler *m*; Effektenmakler *m*; Fondsmakler *m*; Kursmakler *m*; Wechselmakler *m*; Wertpapiermakler *m*
e agente *m* de cambio; agente *m* de valores; corredor *m* de bolsa; corredor *m* de cambios; corredor *m* de valores
f agent *m* de bourse; agent *m* de change; courtier *m* de bourse; courtier *m* de change; courtier *m* en valeurs; marchand *m* de titres
i agente *m* di borsa; agente *m* di cambio; commissionario *m* di borsa; mediatore *m* di borsa; sensale *m* di borsa; sensale *m* di cambio
n beursmakelaar *m*; commissionair *m* in effecten; effectencommissionair *m*; effectenhandelaar *m*; effectenmakelaar *m*; wisselagent *m (B)*

2153 securities market; security market; share market; stock market
cf. **exchange**
d Aktienmarkt *m*; Effektenmarkt *m*; Fondsmarkt *m*; Wertpapiermarkt *m*
e mercado *m* de acciones; mercado *m* de valores (mobiliarios)
f marché *m* des actions; marché *m* des titres; marché *m* des valeurs (mobilières)
i mercato *m* azionario; mercato *m* dei titoli; mercato *m* dei valori (mobiliari); mercato *m* delle azioni; mercato *m* mobiliare
n aandelenmarkt *f*; effectenmarkt *f*; fondsenmarkt *f*

2154 seigneurage; seign(i)orage
d Münzgewinn *m*
e beneficio *m* de monetización
f bénéfice *m* de monnayage
i utile *m* di coniatura
n muntloon *n*

2155 self-balancing accounting
d Nebenbuchhaltung *f (Schw)*; selbständige Teilbuchführung *f*
e contabilidad *f* autónoma
f comptabilité *f* autonome
i contabilità *f* autonoma
n zelfstandige boekhouding *f*

2156 self-liquidating loan
d Kredit *m* der automatisch abgedeckt wird
e crédito *m* autoamortizable *(AL)*; crédito *m* de liquidación automática
f crédit *m* de liquidation automatique
i credito *m* di liquidazione automatica
n krediet *n* dat automatisch gedekt wordt

2157 sell *v*; **vend** *v*
cf. **market** *v*
d absetzen; käuflich überlassen; veräussern; verkaufen
e expender; vender
f écouler; vendre
i smerciare; vendere
n afzetten; van de hand doen; verkopen

2158 sell *v* **at a loss; sell** *v* **with a loss**
d mit Schaden verkaufen; mit Verlust verkaufen; verschleudern
e malvender; vender con pérdida
f mévendre; vendre à perte; vendre avec perte
i svendere; vendere a perdita; vendere con perdita
n met schade verkopen; met verlies verkopen

2159 seller; vender; vendor
d Veräusserer *m*; Verkäufer *m*
e vendedor *m*
f vendeur *m*
i venditore *m*
n verkoper *m*

2160 seller's market
d Verkäufermarkt *m*
e mercado *m* de vendedores
f marché *m* de(s) vendeurs; marché *m* vendeur
i mercato *m* di venditori
n verkopersmarkt *f*

2161 sell *v* **for future delivery; sell** *v* **for (the) settlement; sell** *v* **forward**
d auf Lieferung verkaufen; auf Termin verkaufen; auf Zeit verkaufen; auf Ziel verkaufen
e vender a plazo; vender a término
f vendre à terme
i vendere a termine
n op termijn verkopen

2162 selling price
cf. **asked price, offering price**
d Verkaufspreis *m*
e precio *m* de venta
f prix *m* de vente
i prezzo *m* di vendita; prezzo *m* venale
n laatprijs *m*; verkoopprijs *m*

2163 sell *v* **on credit; sell** *v* **on trust**
d auf Kredit verkaufen
e vender a(l) crédito; vender al fiado
f vendre à crédit
i vendere a credito; vendere a fido
n op krediet verkopen

2164 semi-variable costs
d teilproportionale Kosten *pl*
e costes *mpl* semi-variables
f frais *mpl* semi-variables
i spese *fpl* semi-variabili
n semi-variabele kosten *mpl*

2165 serve *v* **a loan; service** *v* **a loan**
d eine Anleihe bedienen
e hacer el servicio de un empréstito; pagar los intereses de un empréstito
f faire le service d'un emprunt; payer les intérêts d'un emprunt; servir un emprunt *(rare)*
i fare il servizio di un prestito; pagare gli interessi di un prestito
n een lening bedienen

2166 serve *v* **as cover**
d als Deckung dienen
e servir de cubierta
f servir de couverture
i servire da copertura
n als dekking dienen

2167 service of a loan
d Anleihedienst *m*
e servicio *m* de un empréstito
f service *m* d'un emprunt
i servizio *m* di un prestito
n dienst *m* van een lening; leningsdienst *m*

2168 services
cf. **rendering of services**
d Dienste *mpl*; Dienstleistungen *fpl*
e prestaciones *fpl* de servicios; servicios *mpl*
f prestations *fpl* de services; services *mpl*
i prestazioni *fpl* di servizi; servizi *mpl*
n diensten *mpl*; dienstprestaties *fpl*; dienstverleningen *fpl*; dienstverrichtingen *fpl*

2169 share; stock *(US)**
d Aktie *f*
e acción *f*
f action *f*
i azione *f*

n aandeel *n*

* See note under "securities" for meaning of this term.

2170 share certificate; share warrant; stock certificate *(US)*; **stock warrant** *(US)*
cf. **interim certificate**
d Aktienschein *m*; Aktienzertifikat *n*; Anteilschein *m*
e certificato *m* de accion(es); titulo *m* de accion(es)
f certificat *m* d'action(s); titre *m* d'action(s)
i certificato *m* azionario; certificato *m* d'azione (azioni); titolo *m* azionario; titolo *m* d'azione (azioni)
n aandeelbewijs *n*; aandeelcertificaat *n*; aandelenbewijs *n*; aandelencertificaat *n*; certificaat *n* van aandeel; titel *m* van aandeel; titel *m* van aandelen

2171 shareholder *(UK)*; **stockholder** *(US)*; **stock owner** *(US)*
cf. **bearer of securities**
d Aktienbesitzer *m*; Aktieninhaber *m*; Aktionär *m*; Anteilscheinbesitzer *m*; Anteilscheininhaber *m*; Anteilseigner *m*; Effektenbesitzer *m*; Effekteninhaber *m*; Gesellschafter *m**; Wertpapierbesitzer *m*; Wertpapierinhaber *m*
e accionista *m*; socio *m**; tenedor *m* de acciones; tenedor *m* de títulos; tenedor *m* de valores; titular *m* de acciones; titular *m* de valores
f actionnaire *m*; détenteur *m* d'actions; détenteur *m* de titres; détenteur *m* de valeurs; porteur *m* d'actions; porteur *m* de titres; porteur *m* de valeurs; possesseur *m* d'actions; possesseur *m* de titres; possesseur *m* de valeurs; sociétaire *m**; titulaire *m* d'actions; titulaire *m* de valeurs
i azionista *m*; caratista *m*; detentore *m* d'azioni; detentore *m* di titoli; detentore *m* di valori; portatore *m* d'azioni; portatore *m* di titoli; portatore *m* di valori; possessore *m* d'azioni; possessore *m* di titoli; possessore *m* di valori; socio *m**; titolare *m* d'azioni; titolare *m* di valori
n aandeelhouder *m*; aandelenbezitter *m*; actionair *m*; actionaris *m*; effectenbezitter *m*; effectenhouder *m*; vennoot *m**

* Viz. in incorporated company (q.v.) and limited liability company (q.v.).

2172 shareholding *(in one company)*
cf. **investment portfolio**
d Aktienbeteiligung *f*
e participación *f* en acciones
f participation *f* en actions
i partecipazione *f* azionaria
n kapitaaldeelneming *f*

2173 share in the profits
cf. **dividend, gain sharing, percentage of profits**
d Gewinnanteil *m*
e parte *f* de los beneficios
f part *f* des bénéfices
i quota *f* di utile
n winstaandeel *n*

2174 share price; stock price *(US)*; **share quotation**
d Aktienkurs *m*; Aktienpreis *m*
e cotización *f* de las acciones; precio *m* de las acciones
f cours *m* des actions; prix *m* des actions
i corso *m* azionario; corso *m* delle azioni; prezzo *m* delle azioni
n aandelenkoers *m*; prijs *m* van de aandelen

2175 share split(-up); split(-up); stock split(-up)
d Aktiensplit *m/n*; Aktienzerlegung *f*; Split *m/n*; Splitting *n*
e fraccionamiento *m* de acciones; split *m*
f fractionnement *m* d'actions; scission *f* d'actions; split up *m*
i frazionamento *m* azionario; frazionamento *m* di azioni
n aandelensplitsing *f*; splitsing *f*; split-up *f/n*

2176 share without coupon sheet
d Mantel *m*
e acción *f* sin la hoja de cupones
f manteau *m*
i mantello *m*
n mantel *m*

2177 short; short-dated*; short-term
d kurz; kurzfristig
e a breve plazo; a corto plazo
f à courte échéance*; à court terme
i a breve scadenza*; a breve termine
n kort; kortlopend; op korte termijn

* Of bills etc.

2178 be *v* **short of cash**
d knapp bei Kasse sein; nicht bei Kasse sein
e andar escaso de fondos; estar apurado de fondos; estar escaso de fondos
f être (à) court de fonds

i essere a corto di fondi
n krap (bij kas) zitten; niet bij kas zijn

2179 **simple interest**
d einfacher Zins *m*
e interés *m* simple
f intérêt *m* simple
i interesse *m* simplice
n eenvoudige int(e)rest *m*

2180 **single bill; sola; sola bill; sole bill of exchange; sole of exchange**
d Solawechsel *m*
e sola *f* de cambio
f seule *f* de change
i sola *f* di cambio
n sola *f*; sola-wissel *m*

2181 **single entry bookkeeping**
d einfache Buchführung *f*
e contabilidad *f* por partida simple
f comptabilité *f* en partie simple
i contabilità *f* in partita semplice
n enkel-boekhouden *n*

2182 **slumpflation**
d Slumpflation *f*
e slumpflación *f*
f slumpflation *f*
i slumpflazione *f*
n slumpflatie *f*

2183 **snake**
d Schlange *f*; Währungsschlange *f*
e serpiente *f* (monetaria)
f serpent *m* (monétaire)
i serpente *m* (monetario)
n muntslang *f*; slang *f*

2184 **social security**
d soziale Sicherheit *f*; Sozialversicherung *f*
e seguridad *f* social
f sécurité *f* sociale
i previdenza *f* sociale; sicurezza *f* sociale
n maatschappelijke zekerheid *f (B)*; sociale verzekering *f*; sociale zekerheid *f*

2185 **social security benefit**
d soziale Leistung *f*; Sozialleistung *f*
e prestación *f* social
f prestation *f* de la sécurité sociale; prestation *f* sociale
i prestazione *f* sociale
n sociaal voordeel *n*; sociale prestatie *f*

2186 **social security contributions; social security taxes**
d Sozialabgaben *fpl*; Sozialbeiträge *mpl*; soziale Abgaben *fpl*; soziale Lasten *fpl*; Soziallasten *fpl*; Sozialversicherungsbeiträge *mpl*
e cargas *fpl* sociales; contribuciones *fpl* sociales; cuotas *fpl* sociales; gastos *mpl* sociales
f charges *fpl* sociales
i carichi *mpl* sociali; contributi *mpl* sociali; oneri *mpl* sociali
n sociale lasten *mpl*

2187 **soft currency; weak currency**
cf. **floating currency**
d schwache Währung *f*; weiche Währung *f*; Weichwährung *f*
e divisa *f* débil; moneda *f* blanda; moneda *f* débil; moneda *f* floja
f devise *f* faible; devise *f* légère; devise *f* molle; monnaie *f* faible
i divisa *f* debole; moneta *f* debole; valuta *f* debole
n zachte valuta *f*; zwakke valuta *f*

2188 **soft currency country**
d Land *n* mit weicher Währung; Weichwährungsland *n*
e país *m* de moneda débil
f pays *m* à monnaie faible
i paese *m* a valuta debole
n land *n* met zachte valuta

2189 **solvability** *(rare)*; **solvency**
cf. **credit rating**
d Bonität *f*; Leistungsfähigkeit *f*; Solvenz *f*; Zahlungsfähigkeit *f*
e solvencia *f*
f solvabilité *f*
i solvenza *f*; solvibilità *f*
n solvabiliteit *f*; solventie *f*

2190 **solvent**
d leistungsfähig; solvabel *(rare)*; solvent; zahlungsfähig; zahlungskräftig
e solvente
f solvable
i solvibile
n betaalkrachtig; solvabel; solvent

2191 **sound currency**
cf. **hard currency, stable currency**
d gesunde Währung *f*
e moneda *f* sana
f monnaie *f* saine
i moneta *f* sana
n gezonde munt *f*

2192 **source of finance**
d Finanzierungsquelle *f*
e fuente *f* de financiación; fuente *f* de financiamiento

f source *f* de financement
i cespite *m* di finanziamento; fonte *f* di finanziamento
n financieringsbron *f*

2193 **source of income; source of revenue**
d Einkommensquelle *f*; Einnahmequelle *f*
e fuente *f* de entradas; fuente *f* de ingresos
f source *f* de recettes; source *f* de revenus
i cespite *m* d'entrate; cespite *m* di redditi; fonte *f* d'entrate; fonte *f* di redditi
n bron *f* van inkomsten

2194 **special credit**
d Sonderkredit *m*
e crédito *m* especial
f crédit *m* spécial
i credito *m* speciale
n speciaal krediet *n*

2195 **special drawing rights; S.D.R.**
d Sonderziehungsrechte *npl*; S.Z.R.
e derechos *mpl* especiales de giro; D.E.G.
f droits *mpl* de tirage speciaux; D.T.S.
i diritti *mpl* speciali di prelievo; D.S.P.
n speciale trekkingsrechten *npl*; S.T.R.

2196 **speculate** *v*
d spekulieren
e especular
f spéculer
i speculare
n speculeren

2197 **speculation**
d Spekulation *f*
e especulación *f*
f spéculation *f*
i speculazione *f*
n speculatie *f*

2198 **speculative purchase**
d Meinungskauf *m*
e compra *f* especulativa
f achat *m* spéculatif
i acquisto *m* speculativo
n speculatieve aankoop *m*

2199 **speculative securities; speculative stocks**
d Spekulationspapiere *npl*; Spekulationswerte *mpl*; Spielpapiere *npl*
e títulos *mpl* de especulación; títulos *mpl* especulativos; valores *mpl* de especulación; valores *mpl* especulativos
f titres *mpl* de spéculation; titres *mpl* spéculatifs; valeurs *fpl* de spéculation; valeurs *fpl* spéculatives
i titoli *mpl* di speculazione; titoli *mpl* speculativi; valori *mpl* di speculazione; valori *mpl* speculativi
n speculatiepapieren *npl*; speculatieve waarden *fpl*

2200 **speculator**
cf. **jobber**
d Spekulant *m*
e especulador *m*
f spéculateur *m*
i speculatore *m*
n speculant *m*

2201 **split** *v* **the difference**
d sich in den Unterschied teilen; sich in die Differenz teilen
e dividir la diferencia; repartir la diferencia
f partager la différence
i dividere la differenza; ripartire la differenza
n het verschil delen

2202 **spot exchange deal; spot exchange operation; spot exchange transaction**
cf. **exchange for spot delivery**
d Devisenkassageschäft *n*; Devisenkassatransaktion *f*; Kassageschäft *n* in Devisen
e negocio *m* de cambio al contado; negocio *m* de divisas al contado; operación *f* de cambio al contado; operación *f* de divisas al contado; transacción *f* de cambio al contado; transacción *f* de divisas al contado
f opération *f* au comptant sur les changes; opération *f* au comptant sur les devises; opération *f* de change au comptant; transaction *f* au comptant sur les changes; transaction *f* de change au comptant
i operazione *f* di cambio a (in) (per) contanti; transazione *f* di cambio a (in) (per) contanti
n contantaffaire *f* in deviezen; contantaffaire *f* in valuta; contanttransactie *f* in deviezen; contanttransactie *f* in valuta

2203 **spot price** *(commodities)*; **spot rate**
cf. **cash price**
d Lokopreis *m*
e precio *m* en plaza
f cours *m* du disponible; cours *m* sur place
i prezzo *m* del disponibile; prezzo *m* del pronto; prezzo *m* sul posto
n locoprijs *m*

2204 **spread** *v* **out payments over X years; spread** *v* **payments over X years**

d Zahlungen auf (über) X Jahre verteilen
e distribuir los pagos sobre X años; escalonar los pagos sobre X años; repartir los pagos sobre X años
f échelonner les paiements sur X années; fractionner le paiement sur X années; répartir les paiements sur X années
i distribuire i pagamenti su X anni; rateare i pagamenti su X anni; rateizzare i pagamenti su X anni; ripartire i pagamenti su X anni; scaglionare i pagamenti su X anni
n de betalingen over X jaren echelonneren; de betalingen over X jaren spreiden; de betalingen over X jaren verdelen

2205 stabilization fund
cf. **compensation fund**
d Stabilisierungsfonds *m*
e fondo *m* de estabilización
f fonds *m* de stabilisation
i fondo *m* di stabilizzazione
n stabilisatiefonds *n*

2206 stabilization loan
d Aufwertungsanleihe *f*; Stabilisierungsanleihe *f*
e empréstito *m* de estabilización
f emprunt *m* de stabilisation; emprunt *m* de valorisation
i prestito *m* di stabilizzazione
n stabilisatielening *f*

2207 stable currency
cf. **hard currency, sound currency**
d beständige Währung *f*; stabile Währung *f*; wertbeständige Währung *f*; wertstabile Währung *f*
e moneda *f* estable
f devise *f* stable; monnaie *f* stable
i moneta *f* stabile
n stabiele munt *f*; stabiele valuta *f*

2208 stagflation
d Stagflation *f*
e estagflación *f*; stagflación *f*
f stagflation *f*
i stagflazione *f*
n stagflatie *f*

2209 stamp
d Marke *f*; Stempel *m*; Stempelmarke *f*
e póliza *f*; sello *m*; timbre *m*
f timbre *m*; vignette *f*
i bollo *m*; marca *f* da bollo; stampiglia *f*; timbro *m*
n stempel *n (incorrectly in this sense* m*)*; zegel *m (incorrectly in this sense* n*)*

2210 stamp *v (shares)*
d abstempeln
e estampillar
f estampiller
i stampigliare
n afstempelen

2211 stamp duty; stamp tax
d Stempelabgabe *f*; Stempelgebühr *f*; Stempelsteuer *f*
e derecho *m* de sello; derecho *m* de timbre; impuesto *m* de timbre; impuesto *m* de sellos *(AL)*
f droit *m* de timbre; impôt *m* de timbre; impôt *m* du timbre; timbre *m*
i imposta *f* di bollo; tassa *f* di bollo
n zegel *n*; zegelgeld *n*; zegelrecht *n*

2212 stamping of shares
d Abstempelung *f* von Aktien
e estampillado *m* de acciones
f estampillage *m* d'actions
i stampigliatura *f* di azioni
n afstempeling *f* van aandelen

2213 standard value; uniform value
d Einheitswert *m*; Festwert *m*; Standardwert *m*
e valor *m* standard; valor *m* unitario
f valeur *f* standard; valeur *f* unitaire
i valore *m* standard; valore *m* unitario
n eenheidswaarde *f*; standaardwaarde *f*

2214 stand-by; stand-by credit
cf. **advance commitment**
d Abrufkredit *m*; Bereitschaftskredit *m*; Stand-by-Kredit *m*
e crédito *m* contingente; crédito *m* stand-by
f crédit *m* stand-by
i credito *m* stand-by
n afroepkrediet *n*; stand-by-krediet *n*

2215 stand-by agreement
d Stand-by-Kreditabkommen *n*; Stand-by-Kreditvereinbarung *f*
e acuerdo *m* (de) stand-by
f accord *m* (de) stand-by
i accordo *m* (di) stand-by
n stand-by-kredietovereenkomst *f*

2216 standstill agreement
cf. **extension of time for payment**
d Stillhalteabkommen *n*; Stillhalteübereinkommen *n*; Stillhaltevereinbarung *f*
e acuerdo *m* de inmovilización; acuerdo *m* de moratoria; convenio *m* de prórroga
f accord *m* de prorogation; accord *m* de standstill; accord *m* moratoire

i accordo *m* d'immobilizzazione; accordo *m* di moratoria; accordo *m* di proroga
n overeenkomst *f* tot opschorting van betaling; stilhalte-overeenkomst *f (rare)*

2217 **statement; summary** *(US)*
d Aufstellung *f*; Ausweis *m*; Bericht *m*; Status *m (Schw)*; Übersicht *f*
e estado *m*; informe *m*; relación *f*
f bordereau *m*; état *m*; exposé *m*; relevé *m*
i rendiconto *m*; situazione *f*; stato *m*
n bericht *n*; borderel *n*; overzicht *n*; staat *m*

2218 **statement of expenses**
d Ausgabenaufstellung *f*; Spesenaufstellung *f*; Unkostenaufstellung *f*
e estado *m* de gastos; relación *f* de gastos
f état *m* de(s) dépenses; état *m* de(s) frais
i distinta *f* delle spese
n staat *m* van onkosten; staat *m* van uitgaven

2219 **statistical data; statistics**
cf. **statistics (science)**
d statistische Angaben *fpl*; Statistiken *fpl*
e datos *mpl* estadísticos; estadísticas *fpl*
f données *fpl* statistiques; statistiques *fpl*
i dati *mpl* statistici; statistiche *fpl*
n statistieken *fpl*; statistische gegevens *npl*

2220 **statistiques** *(science)*
cf. **statistical data**
d Statistik *f*
e estadística *f*
f statistique *f*
i statistica *f*
n statistiek *f*

2221 **sterilization** *(of funds etc.)*
cf. **immobilization**
d Inaktivierung *f*; Sterilisierung *f*; Stillegung *f*
e esterilización *f*
f stérilisation *f*
i sterilizzazione *f*
n sterilisering *f*

2222 **sterilize** *v (funds etc.)*
cf. **immobilize** *v*
d inaktivieren; sterilisieren; stillegen
e esterilizar
f stériliser
i sterilizzare
n steriliseren

2223 **sterling**
cf. **pound sterling**
d Sterling *m*; Sterlingwährung *f*
e esterlina *f*
f sterling *m*
i sterlina *f*
n sterling *m*

2224 **sterling area; sterling bloc**
d Pfundzone *f*; Sterlingblock *m*; Sterlinggebiet *n*; Sterlingraum *m*; Sterlingwährungsgebiet *n*; Sterlingwährungsraum *m*; Sterlingzone *f*
e área *f* de la (libra) esterlina; bloque *m* de la (libra) esterlina; zona *f* de la (libra) esterlina
f bloc *m* sterling; zone *f* sterling
i area *f* della sterlina; blocco *m* della sterlina; zona *f* della sterlina
n sterlingblok *n*; sterlinggebied *n*; sterlingzone *f*

2225 **stock exchange turnover; volume of business in the stockmarket**
cf. **exchange business**
d Börsenumsatz *m*; Umsatz *m* an der Börse
e movimiento *m* bursátil; volumen *m* de las transacciones en bolsa
f mouvement *m* boursier; volume *m* des transactions en bourse
i movimento *m* borsistico; quantitativo *m* trattato in borsa; volume *m* degli affari di borsa
n beursomzet *m*; omzet *m* ter beurze

2226 **stock watering; watering of capital; watering of share capital; watering of stock**
d Kapitalverwässerung *f*; Verwässerung *f* des Aktienkapitals
e dilución *f* del capital (en acciones)
f dilution *f* du capital(-actions)
i annacquamento *m* del capitale (azionario)
n kapitaalverwatering *f*; verwatering *f* van het aandelenkapitaal

2227 **stop** *v* **a cheque; stop** *v* **payment of a cheque** *(UK)*; **stop** *v* **payment on a check** *(US)*
d die Zahlung eines Schecks sperren; einen Scheck sperren (lassen)
e bloquear un cheque; suspender el pago de un cheque
f arrêter le paiement d'un chèque; bloquer un chèque; suspendre le paiement d'un chèque
i bloccare un assegno; mettere il fermo su

un assegno; sospendere il pagamento di un assegno
n de betaling van een cheque opschorten; de betaling van een cheque schorsen; een cheque blokkeren

2228 **straight line depreciation**
d lineare Abschreibung *f*
e amortización *f* constante; depreciación *f* constante
f amortissement *m* linéaire
i ammortamento *m* fisso
n lineaire afschrijving *f*; vaste afschrijving *f*

2229 **structural surplus**
d struktureller Überschuss *m*
e excedente *m* estructural
f surplus *m* structurel
i eccedenza *f* strutturale
n structureel overschot *n*

2230 **subdivided share; sub-share**
d Aktienabschnitt *m*; Aktienanteil *m*; Teilaktie *f*
e parte *f* de acción; subacción *f*
f coupure *f* d'action
i parte *f* d'azione
n onderaandeel *n*

2231 **subject to the payment of interest**
d zinsbar; zinspflichtig
e sujeto al pago de interés (intereses)
f sujet au paiement d'intérêt(s)
i soggetto al pagamento di interesse (interessi)
n renteplichtig

2232 **subscribed capital**
d gezeichnetes Kapital *n*
e capital *m* su(b)scrito
f capital *m* souscrit
i capitale *m* sottoscritto
n ingeschreven kapitaal *n*; voltekend kapitaal *n*

2233 **subscribe** *v* **(for); take** *v* **up; tender** *v* **for**
d subskribieren *(rare)*; übernehmen; zeichnen (auf)
e su(b)scribir
f souscrire (à)
i sottoscrivere
n inschrijven (op); intekenen (op); overnemen

2234 **subscriber**
d Zeichner *m*
e su(b)scriptor *m*
f souscripteur *m*
i sottoscrittore *m*
n inschrijver *m*; intekenaar *m*

2235 **subscription** *(contribution)*
d Beitrag *m*
e cuota *f*
f cotisation *f*
i quota *f*
n bijdrage *f*

2236 **subscription; take-up**
d Subskription *f (rare)*; Zeichnung *f*
e su(b)scripción *f*
f souscription *f*
i sottoscrizione *f*
n inschrijving *f*; intekening *f*

2237 **subscription period**
d Bezugsfrist *f*; Zeichnungsfrist *f*
e plazo *m* de su(b)scripción
f délai *m* de souscription; terme *m* de souscription
i termine *m* di sottoscrizione
n inschrijvingstermijn *m*; intekentermijn *m*

2238 **subscription price; subscription rate**
cf. **issue price**
d Bezugskurs *m*; Bezugspreis *m*; Zeichnungskurs *m*; Zeichnungspreis *m*
e cotización *f* de su(b)scripción; precio *m* de su(b)scripción
f cours *m* de souscription; prix *m* de souscription
i corso *m* di sottoscrizione; prezzo *m* di sottoscrizione
n inschrijvingskoers *m*; inschrijvingsprijs *m*; intekenprijs *m*

2239 **subsequent endorser**
d Hintermann *m*; nachfolgender Indossant *m*; Nachgirant *m*; Nachindossant *m*; Nachmann *m*
e endosante *m* subsiguiente
f endosseur *m* postérieur; endosseur *m* subséquent
i girante *m* susseguente
n achterman *m*; naman *m*; volgende endossant *m*

2240 **subsidize** *v*; **subvention** *v (US)*; **subventionize** *v (US)*
d durch Subsidien unterstützen; durch Zuschüsse unterstützen; subventionieren
e subsidiar; subvencionar
f subventionner
i sovvenzionare; sussidiare
n subsidiëren

2241 summary statement
d zusammenfassende Übersicht *f*
e estado *m* recapitulativo; estado-resumen *m*
f état *m* récapitulatif
i situazione *f* sintetica
n recapitulatie *f*; verzamelstaat *m*

2242 supply and demand
d Angebot *n* und Nachfrage *f*
e oferta *f* y demanda *f*
f l'offre *f* et la demande *f*
i domanda *f* ed offerta *f*
n vraag *f* en aanbod *n*

2243 supply of near money
cf. **money equivalents**
d quasi-monetäre Mittel *npl*
e disponibilidades *fpl* cuasi monetarias
f disponibilités *fpl* quasi-monétaires
i disponibilità *fpl* quasi monetarie
n quasimonetaire middelen *npl*

2244 surplus
cf. **excess, excess amount**
d Mehrbetrag *m*; Surplus *n*; Überschuss *m*
e excedente *m*; sobrante *m*; superávit *m*; surplus *m*
f boni *m*; excédent *m*; surplus *m*
i avanzo *m*; eccedenza *f*; soprappiú *m*; sovrappiú *m*; surplus *m*
n excedent *n*; overschot *n*; surplus *n*

2245 surplus of receipts; surplus receipts; surplus takings
d Einnahme(n)überhang *m*; Einnahme(n)-überschuss *m*; Mehreinkommen *n*; Mehreinnahme(n) *f(pl)*; überschüssiges Einkommen
e excedente *m* de ingresos
f excédent *m* de recettes
i eccedenza *f* di entrate
n overschot *n* van ontvangsten

2246 surplus revenues
d Mehreinnahmen *fpl*
e plusvalías *fpl* de entradas
f plus-values *fpl* de recettes
i plusvalenze *fpl* di entrate
n extraopbrengsten *fpl*

2247 surrender value *(insurance policy)*
cf. **redemption value**
d Rückkaufwert *m*
e valor *m* de rescate
f valeur *f* de rachat
i valore *m* di riscatto
n afkoopwaarde *f*

2248 suspense account
d Auffangkonto *n*; Durchgangskonto *n*; Durchlaufskonto *n*; Interimskonto *n*; Schwebekonto *n*; Übergangskonto *n*; Verwahrkonto *n*; Zwischenkonto *n*
e cuenta *f* de orden; cuenta *f* de tránsito; cuenta *f* en suspensa *(AL)*; cuenta *f* provisional; cuenta *f* puente; cuenta *f* transitoria
f compte *m* d'attente; compte *m* d'engagement; compte *m* de passage; compte *m* d'ordre; compte *m* intermédiaire; compte *m* provisoire
i conto *m* d'ordine; conto *m* intermedio; conto *m* provvisorio; conto *m* sospeso; conto *m* transitorio
n orderrekening *f (B)*; tussenrekening *f*; wachtrekening *f*

2249 suspense entry; suspense item; transitory item
d Durchgangsposten *m*; durchlaufender Posten *m*; Zwischeneintrag *m*; Zwischeneintragung *f*
e entrada *f* intermédiaria; entrada *f* transitoria; partida *f* transitoria
f article *m* d'ordre; article *m* transitoire; écriture *f* d'ordre; poste *m* d'ordre
i partita *f* in sospeso; scrittura *f* d'ordine; scrittura *f* in sospeso
n transitorische post *m*; tussenpost *m*

2250 suspension of payments*
d Zahlungseinstellung *f*
e cesación *f* de pagos; suspensión *f* de pagos
f cessation *f* des paiements; suspension *f* des paiements
i cessazione *f* dei pagamenti; sospensione *f* dei pagamenti
n staking *f* van betaling

* Not to be confused with "suspension of payment" (q.v. under "extension of time for payment").

2251 swap; swap transaction
d Swap *m*; Swapgeschäft *n*
e operación *f* de reporte; operación *f* de swap; operación *f* vinculada
f opération *f* de report; opération *f* liée; opération *f* swap
i operazione *f* a termine con contropartita; operazione *f* di cambio a riporto; operazione *f* swap
n swap *m*; swapaffaire *f*; swaptransactie *f*

2252 swap credit
d Swapkredit *m*
e crédito *m* swap

f crédit *m* swap
i credito *m* swap
n swapkrediet *n*

2253 **switch; switch(ed) transaction; triangular transaction**
d Dreiecksgeschäft *n*; Switch *m*; Switchgeschäft *n*
e operación *f* switch; operación *f* triangular; switch *m*; transacción *f* switch; transacción *f* triangular
f opération *f* switch; opération *f* triangulaire; switch *m*; transaction *f* switch; transaction *f* triangulaire
i operazione *f* switch; operazione *f* triangolare; switch *m*; transazione *f* switch; transazione *f* triangolare
n driehoekstransactie *f*; switch *m*; switchtransactie *f*

2254 **switch; switching**
d Effektenaustausch *m*; Umtausch *m* von Effekten
e canje *m* de valores
f échange *m* de titres
i scambio *m* di titoli
n omwisseling *f* van effecten

2255 **syndicate**
cf. **concern, consortium, trust**
d Syndikat *n*
e sindicato *m*
f syndicat *m*
i sindacato *m*
n syndicaat *n*

T

2256 **table**
d Tabelle *f*; Tafel *f*
e cuadro *m*; tabla *f*
f table *f*; tableau *m*
i quadro *m*; tabella *f*; tavola *f*
n tabel *f*; tafel *f*

2257 **take-over**
d Aufnahme *f*; Übernahme *f*
e absorción *f*
f absorption *f*; reprise *f*
i assorbimento *m*; rilevamento *m*
n overname *f*; overneming *f*

2258 **tangible security**
d dingliche Sicherheit *f*
e garantía *f* real
f garantie *f* réelle
i garanzia *f* reale
n werkelijke garantie *f*; zakelijke garantie *f*

2259 **tap issue**
d Daueremission *f*
e emisión *f* constante
f émission *f* à guichets ouverts; émission *f* au robinet; émission *f* continue
i emissione *f* a rubinetto; emissione *f* continua
n continu-emissie *f*; continu-uitgifte *f*

2260 **tariff***
d Tarif *m**
e arancel *m**; tarifa *f**
f tarif *m**
i tariffa *f**
n tarief *n**

* It can mean both a schedule of duties and an individual duty, see customs.

2261 **tax abatement; tax allowance; tax deduction; tax reduction; tax release *(US)*; tax relief; tax remission *(US)***
cf. **tax advantage**
d Steuerabzug *m*; Steuererlass *m*; Steuererleichterung *f*; Steuerermässigung *f*; Steuerherabsetzung *f*; Steuermilderung *f*; Steuerminderung *f*; Steuernachlass *m*
e deducción *f* de impuestos; deducción *f* fiscal; desgravación *f* fiscal; rebaja *f* de impuestos; reducción *f* de impuestos; reducción *f* fiscal
f abattement *m* fiscal; allégement *m* fiscal; déduction *f* d'impôts; déduction *f* fiscale; décote *f*; dégrèvement *m* fiscal; détaxe *f*; réduction *f* d'impôts; réduction *f* fiscale; réfaction *f* fiscale; remise *f* d'impôts
i deduzione *f* fiscale; detrazione *f* fiscale; riduzione *f* d'imposta; riduzione *f* fiscale; sgravio *m* fiscale
n belastingaftrek *m*; belastingverlichting *f*; belastingvermindering *f*; ontheffing *f* (van belasting)

2262 **taxable income***
d steuerpflichtiges Einkommen *n*
e ingresos *mpl* imponibles; réditos *mpl* gravados *(AL)*; renta *f* imponible
f revenu *m* globalisé *(B)*; revenu *m* imposable; revenu *m* taxable
i imponibile *m*; reddito *m* imponibile
n belastbaar inkomen *n*; geglobaliseerd inkomen *n (B)*

* In US also used to mean "assessable profit" (q.v.).

2263 **tax advantage; tax benefit; tax concession; tax privilege**
cf. **tax abatement**
d Steuerbegünstigung *f*; Steuervergünstigung *f*; Steuervorteil *m*
e privilegio *m* fiscal; privilegio *m* tributario; ventaja *f* fiscal
f avantage *m* fiscal; faveur *f* fiscale; privilège *m* fiscal
i agevolazione *f* fiscale; agevolazione *f* tributaria; vantaggio *m* fiscale
n belastingconcessie *f*; belastingvoordeel *n*; fiscaal voordeel *n*

2264 **tax adviser; tax advisor; tax consultant; tax expert**
d Berater *m* in Steuersachen; Steuerberater *m*
e asesor *m* fiscal; perito *m* en leyes fiscales
f conseil *m* fiscal; conseiller *m* fiscal; expert *m* fiscal
i consulente *m* fiscale; perito *m* fiscale
n belastingadviseur *m*; belasting(s)-consulent *m*; consulent *m* in belastingzaken

2265 **taxation**
cf. **assessment, imposition of taxes**
d Besteuerung *f*
e tasación *f*; tributación *f*
f taxation *f*
i tassazione *f*
n belasting *f*; belastingheffing *f*

2266 **tax avoidance; tax dodging; tax evasion**
d Steuerflucht *f*; Steuerhinterziehung *f*;

Steuerumgehung *f*
e defraudación *f* de impuestos; evasión *f* de impuestos; evasión *f* fiscal; fraude *m* fiscal; fraude *m* tributario
f évasion *f* d'impôt(s); évasion *f* fiscale; fraude *f* fiscale
i evasione *f* fiscale; frode *f* fiscale; frode *f* tributaria
n belastingfraude *f*; belastingontduiking *f*; belastingontwijking *f*; belastingvlucht *f*

2267 tax bracket
d Steuergruppe *f*; Steuerklasse *f*
e categoría *f* impositiva; categoría *f* tributaria; grupo *m* fiscal
f catégorie *f* d'imposition; cédule *f* d'impôts; classe *f* d'impôt
i categoria *f* contribuente; categoria *f* d'imposizione; categoria *f* fiscale
n belastinggroep *f*; belastingschijf *f*

2268 tax deducted at source; witholding tax *(US)*
cf. **collection at source**
d Quellensteuer *f*
e impuesto *m* deducido en el origen; impuesto *m* en la fuente
f impôt *m* prélevé à la source; impôt *m* retenu à la source; précompte *m* (professionnel) *(B)*
i imposta *f* ritenuta alla fonte; imposta *f* all'origine; imposta *f* trattenuta alla fonte; imposta *f* all'origine
n aan de bron ingehouden belasting *f*

2269 tax haven
d Steueroase *f*
e refugio *m* fiscal
f refuge *m* fiscal
i rifugio *m* fiscale
n fiscale toevlucht *f*

2270 tax incentive
d Steueranreiz *m*
e incentivo *m* fiscal
f incitation *f* fiscale; stimulant *m* fiscal
i incentivo *m* fiscale
n fiscale aanmoediging *f*

2271 tax liability
cf. **liability to tax**
d Steuerschuld *f*; Steuerverbindlichkeit *f*; Steuerverpflichtung *f*
e deuda *f* fiscal; deuda *f* impositiva; deuda *f* tributaria; obligación *f* contributiva; obligación *f* fiscal; obligación *f* tributaria
f dette *f* d'impôt; dette *f* fiscale; obligation *f* contributive; obligation *f* fiscale; redevance *f* fiscale
i debito *m* d'imposta; debito *m* fiscale; obbligazione *f* fiscale; obbligazione *f* tributaria
n belastingschuld *f*

2272 tax loss carry-back
d Verlustrücktrag *m*
e deducción *f* retroactiva de pérdidas
f déduction *f* rétroactive d'un déficit
i deduzione *f* retroattiva di perdite
n carry-back *m/f*; retroactieve verliescompensatie *f*

2273 tax loss carry-forward
d Verlustabzug *m*
e deducción *f* de pérdidas
f déduction *f* du report déficitaire
i deduzione *f* di perdite
n carry-forward *m/f*; verliescompensatie *f*

2274 tax reform
d Steuerreform *f*
e reforma *f* fiscal; reforma *f* tributaria
f réforme *f* de la fiscalité; réforme *f* fiscale
i riforma *f* fiscale; riforma *f* tributaria
n belastinghervorming *f*

2275 tax return
d Steuererklärung *f*
e declaración *f* fiscal; declaración *f* tributaria
f déclaration *f* fiscale
i dichiarazione *f* fiscale
n belastingaangifte *f*

2276 tender *(written offer to supply)*
cf. **bid, offering (for subscription)**
d Submissionsangebot *n*; Submissionsofferte *f*
e oferta *f* (de concurso-subasta)
f soumission *f*
i offerta *f* (d'appalto)
n inschrijving *f*

2277 term loan; time loan
d befristetes Darleh(e)n *n*
e préstamo *m* a plazo fijo
f prêt *m* à échéance fixe; prêt *m* à terme fixe
i prestito *m* a scadenza fissa; prestito *m* a termine fisso
n lening *f* op vaste termijn

2278 terms of payment
cf. **form of payment**
d Zahlungsbedingungen *fpl*; Zahlungsmodalitäten *fpl*
e condiciones *fpl* de pago; modalidades

fpl de pago
f conditions *fpl* de paiement; conditions *fpl* de règlement; modalités *fpl* de paiement; modalités *fpl* de règlement
i condizioni *fpl* di pagamento; condizioni *fpl* di regolamento; modalità *fpl* di pagamento; modalità *fpl* di regolamento
n betalingscondities *fpl*; betalingsvoorwaarden *fpl*; voorwaarden *fpl* van betaling

2279 terms of trade
d Austauschbedingungen *fpl*; Austauschpreisverhältnis *n*; Austauschrelation(en) *f(pl)*; Austauschverhältnis(se) *n(pl)*; Terms *mpl* of trade
e relación *f* real de intercambio; términos *mpl* del intercambio
f termes *mpl* de l'échange
i ragione *f* di scambio
n ruilvoet *m*; terms *mpl* of trade

2280 three-cornered trade; triangular trade
d Dreieckshandel *m*; Dreiecksverkehr *m*
e comercio *m* triangular; intercambio *m* triangular
f commerce *m* triangulaire; échanges *mpl* triangulaires
i commercio *m* triangolare; scambi *mpl* triangolari
n driehoekshandel *m*; driehoeksverkeer *n*

2281 tied loan
d gebundene Anleihe *f*
e empréstito *m* legado a un fin determinado
f emprunt *m* affecté à un but déterminé; emprunt *m* lié à un but déterminé
i prestito *m* legato ad uno scopo determinato
n gebonden lening *f*

2282 tied share
d gebundene Aktie *f*; vinkulierte Aktie *f*
e acción *f* sindicada; acción *f* vinculada
f action *f* à cessibilité restreinte; action *f* liée
i azione *f* a cessione condizionata
n aandeel *n* met blokkeringsclausule

2283 token coin
cf. **fiat money**
d Zeichenmünze *f*
e moneda *f* fiduciaria
f pièce *f* de monnaie fiduciaire
i moneta *f* fiduciaria
n tekenmunt *f*

2284 toll
d Maut *f*; Mautgebühr *f*
e peaje *m*; portazgo *m*
f droit *m* de péage; péage *m*
i diritto *m* di pedaggio; pedaggio *m*
n tol *m*; tolgeld *n*

2285 total asset value
d Aktivsumme *f*
e activo *m* contable
f actif *m* comptable
i attivo *m* contabile
n som *f* der activa

2286 trade acceptance
d Handelsakzept *n*; Kundenakzept *n*; Warenakzept *n*
e aceptación *f* comercial
f acceptation *f* commerciale
i accettazione *f* commerciale
n handelsaccept *n*

2287 trade monopoly
d Handelsmonopol *n*
e monopolio *m* comercial
f monopole *m* commercial
i monopolio *m* commerciale
n handelsmonopolie *n*

2288 trade price; wholesale price
d Engrospreis *m*; Grosshandelspreis *m*; Grossistenpreis *m*
e precio *m* al por mayor; precio *m* de mayorista; precio *m* de venta al por mayor; precio *m* mayorista
f prix *m* de gros; prix *m* grossiste
i prezzo *m* all'ingrosso
n en-gros-prijs *m*; groothandelsprijs *m*; grossiersprijs *m*

2289 trading account
d Betriebskonto *n*; Betriebskostenrechnung *f*
e cuenta *f* de explotación
f compte *m* d'exploitation
i conto *m* di esercizio
n exploitatierekening *f*

2290 trading stamp
d Rabattmarke *f*
e cupón *m* comercial; sello *m* de premio
f timbre *m* de rabais; timbre-prime *m*
i bollo premio *m*; punto-premio *m*
n kortingzegel *m*; rabatzegel *m*

2291 transferable sterling
d transferable Pfunde *npl*
e libras *fpl* (esterlinas) transferibles
f livres *fpl* (sterling) transférables

i lire *fpl* (sterline) trasferibili
n transferabele ponden *npl*

2292 **transfer income**
d Übertragungseinkommen *n*
e ingreso *m* de transferencia
f revenu *m* de transfert
i reddito *m* da trasferimento
n overdrachtsinkomen *n*

2293 **transfer payment**
d Transferzahlung *f*
e transferencia *f*
f transfert *m*
i trasferimento *m*
n transferbetaling *f*

2294 **transit trade**
d Durchfuhrhandel *m*; Durchgangshandel *m*; Transithandel *m*
e comercio *m* de tránsito
f commerce *m* de transit; commerce *m* en transit
i commercio *m* di transito
n doorvoerhandel *m*; transithandel *m*

2295 **transport costs**
d Beförderungskosten *pl*; Speditionskosten *pl*; Transportkosten *pl*
e costes *mpl* de expedición; costes *mpl* de transporte; gastos *mpl* de expedición; gastos *mpl* de transporte
f frais *mpl* de transport; frais *mpl* d'expédition
i spese *fpl* di spedizione; spese *fpl* di trasporto
n expeditiekosten *mpl*; transportkosten *mpl*; vervoerkosten *mpl*

2296 **travel allowance; travel expenses; traveling allowance *(US)*; traveling expenses *(US)*; travelling allowance *(UK)*; travelling expenses *(UK)***
d Reiseentschädigung *f*; Reisekostenentschädigung *f*; Reisekostenvergütung *f*; Reisevergütung *f*
e indemnización *f* de gastos de viaje
f déplacement *m*; indemnité *f* de déplacement; indemnité *f* de route; indemnité *f* de voyage
i indennità *f* di trasferta; indennità *f* di viaggio
n reisvergoeding *f*

2297 **traveler's check *(US)*; traveller's cheque *(UK)***
d Reisescheck *m*; Travellerscheck *m*
e cheque *m* de turista; cheque *m* de viaje; cheque *m* de viajero(s); travellor's cheque *m*
f chèque *m* de voyage; mandat *m* de voyage; traveller's cheque *m*
i assegno *m* per viaggiatori; assegno *m* turistico; traveller's cheque *m*
n reischeque *m*; traveller's cheque *m*

2298 **travel expenses*; traveling expenses *(US)**; travelling expenses *(UK)****
d Reiseauslagen *fpl*; Reisekosten *pl*; Reisespesen *pl*; Reiseunkosten *pl*
e gastos *mpl* de desplazamiento; gastos *mpl* de viaje
f frais *mpl* de course; frais *mpl* de déplacement; frais *mpl* de route; frais *mpl* de tournée; frais *mpl* de voyage
i spese *fpl* di trasferta; spese *fpl* di viaggio
n reiskosten *mpl*
* Can also mean "travel allowance" (q.v.).

2299 **treasury**
cf. **exchequer**
d Ärar *n*; Schatzamt *n*; Staatsärar *n*; Staatskasse *f*; Staatsschatz *m*
e erario *m* (público); tesorería *f*; tesoro *m* público
f trésorerie *f*; trésor *m* publique
i erario *m*; tesoreria *f*; tesoro *m* pubblico
n schatkist *f*; staatskas *f*; thesaurie *f*

2300 **treasury assets**
d Guthaben *npl* des Schatzamts
e haberes *mpl* del tesoro
f avoirs *mpl* du trésor
i disponibilità *f(pl)* del tesoro
n tegoeden *npl* van de schatkist

2301 **treasury bill; treasury bond *(US)*; treasury note *(US)***
cf. **exchequer bond**
d Schatzanweisung *f*; Schatzschein *m*; Schatzwechsel *m*; Kassenschein *m*; Staatskassenschein *m*
e bono *m* del tesoro; bono *m* de tesorería; certificado *m* del tesoro; letra *f* de tesorería; vale *m* del tesoro
f billet *m* du trésor; bon *m* du trésor; certificat *m* du trésor; promesse *f* du trésor
i buono *m* del tesoro; cambiale *f* di stato; certificato *m* del tesoro
n schatkistbiljet *n*; schatkistbon *m*; schatkistcertificaat *n*; schatkistpromesse *f*; schatkistwissel *m*

2302 **treasury currency**
d von der Staatskasse ausgegebenes Geld *n*

e moneda *f* emitida por el tesoro
f monnaie *f* émise par le trésor
i moneta *f* emessa dal tesoro
n door de schatkist in omloop gebracht geld *n*

2303 trial balance
d Probebilanz *f*; Rohbilanz *f*
e balance *m* de comprobación; balance *m* de prueba
f bilan *m* de vérification; bilan *m* d'ordre
i bilancio *m* di verifica; bilancio *m* di verificazione
n proefbalans *f*

2304 trust
cf. **cartel, concern, consortium, syndicate**
d Trust *m*
e trust *m*
f trust *m*
i trust *m*
n trust *m*

2305 trust account
d Anderkonto *n*; Treuhänderkonto *n*
e cuenta *f* fiduciaria
f compte *m* de consignation; compte *m* rubriqué *(B)*
i conto *m* fiduciario
n q.q.* rekening *f (N)*; rubriek-rekening *f (B)*

* Qualitate qua.

2306 trust company; trust corporation
d Treuhandgesellschaft *f*
e compañía *f* de fideicomiso; compañía *f* fiduciaria; sociedad *f* de fideicomiso; sociedad *f* fiduciaria
f société *f* fiduciaire
i società *f* fiduciaria
n administratiekantoor *n*; trustmaatschappij *f*

2307 trust fund
d Treuhandfonds *m*; Treuhandgelder *npl*
e fondo *m* fiduciario
f fonds *m* fiduciaire
i fondo *m* fiduciario
n beheerfonds *n*

2308 trust property
d Treugut *n*; Treuhandgut *n*; Treuhandvermögen *n*
e propiedad *f* fiduciaria
f propriété *f* fiduciaire
i bene *m* fiduciario
n trustvermogen *n*

2309 two-tier foreign exchange market
d gespaltener Devisenmarkt *m*
e doble mercado *m* de cambios
f double marché *m* des changes
i doppio mercato *m* dei cambi; duplice mercato *m* valutario
n dubbele deviezenmarkt *f*; tweeledige wisselmarkt *f*

2310 two-tier price system for gold
d System *n* des gespaltenen Goldpreises
e régimen *m* del doble precio para el oro
f régime *m* du double prix pour l'or
i regime *m* del doppio prezzo dell'oro
n tweevoudig goudprijssysteem *n*

U

2311 **unappropriated profits; undivided profits**
cf. **retained earnings**
d nicht verteilte Gewinne *mpl*; unverteilte Gewinne *mpl*; unverteilter Reingewinn *m*
e beneficios *mpl* no repartidos; ganancias *fpl* no repartidas; utilidades *fpl* no repartidas
f bénéfices *mpl* non répartis
i utili *mpl* indivisi; utili *mpl* non ripartiti
n niet toegewezen winsten *fpl*; onverdeelde winsten *fpl*

2312 **unbalanced entry**
d nicht ausgeglichener Posten *m*; nicht saldierter Posten *m*; unausgeglichener Posten *m*
e asiento *m* no saldado
f poste *m* non soldé
i partita *f* non saldata
n niet gesaldeerde post *m*; onvereffende post *m*

2313 **uncalled capital; unpaid capital**
d (noch) nicht aufgerufenes Kapital *n*; (noch) nicht eingefordertes Kapital *n*; (noch) nicht eingezahltes Kapital *n*
e capital *m* no desembolsado; capital *m* no integrado *(AL)*; capital *m* no llamado *(AL)*
f capital *m* non (encore) appelé; capital *m* non versé
i capitale *m* non richiamato; capitale *m* non versato
n (nog) niet gestort kapitaal *n*; (nog) te storten kapitaal *n*; onopgevraagd kapitaal *n*

2314 **undeclared income**
d Schwarzgeld *n*
e dinero *m* clandestino; dinero *m* negro
f argent *m* noir
i denaro *m* clandestino; denaro *m* non dichiarato
n zwart geld *n*

2315 **undercapitalization**
d Unterkapitalisation *f*; Unterkapitalisierung *f*
e subcapitalización *f*
f souscapitalisation *f*
i sottocapitalizzazione *f*
n onderkapitalisatie *f*

2316 **undercharge** *v*
d zu wenig anrechnen; zu wenig berechnen; zu wenig fordern
e cargar demasiado poco; exigir demasiado poco; pedir demasiado poco
f compter trop peu; demander trop peu; faire payer trop peu
i far pagare meno del dovuto; far pagare meno del giusto
n te weinig aanrekenen; te weinig berekenen; te weinig in rekening brengen

2317 **undercut** *v*; **undersell** *v*
d unterbieten
e ofrecer mejor precio; vender más barato
f offrir à un prix inférieur; vendre à un prix inférieur
i offrire a minor prezzo; vendere a minor prezzo
n onderkruipen; tegen lagere prijs verkopen

2318 **underestimate; undervaluation**
d Unterbewertung *f*; Unterschätzung *f*
e subestimación *f*; subvaloración *f*
f sous-estimation *f*; sous-évaluation *f*
i sottovalutazione *f*
n onderschatting *f*; onderwaardering *f*; te lage schatting *f*

2319 **underestimate** *v*; **understate** *v*; **undervalue** *v*
d unterbewerten; unter dem Wert einschätzen; unter dem Wert schätzen; unterschätzen
e subestimar; subvalorar
f sous-estimer; sous-évaluer
i sottovalutare
n onderschatten; onderwaarderen

2320 **underwrite** *v* **an issue**
d die Unterbringung einer Emission garantieren; die Unterbringung einer Emission übernehmen; eine Emission (zur Unterbringung) garantieren
e garantizar una emisión
f garantir une émission
i garantire una emissione
n een emissie garanderen; een emissie waarborgen

2321 **underwriting contract**
d Übernahmeabkommen *n*; Übernahmevertrag *m*
e contrato *m* de su(b)scripción
f contrat *m* de prise ferme
i contratto *m* di collocazione vincolata
n overnemingscontract *n*

2322 underwriting syndicate
d Emissionskonsortium *n*; Garantiekonsortium *n*; Garantiesyndikat *n*; Placierungskonsortium *n*; Plazierungskonsortium *n*; Übernahmekonsortium *n*
e consorcio *m* de emisión; consorcio *m* de garantía; sindicato *m* de colocación; sindicato *m* de emisión; sindicato *m* de garantía
f consortium *m* d'émission; consortium *m* de placement; syndicat *m* de garantie; syndicat *m* d'émission; syndicat *m* de placement
i consorzio *m* d'emissione; consorzio *m* di collocamento; consorzio *m* di garanzia; sindacato *m* (finanziario) d'emissione
n emissieconsortium *n*; emissiesyndicaat *n*; garantiesyndicaat *n*; overnameconsortium *n*; overnamesyndicaat *n*

2323 unearned income
cf. **capital income, income from investments, personal income**
d arbeitsloses Einkommen *n*
e ingresos *mpl* no laborales
f rente(s) *f(pl)*; revenu *m* non gagné
i reddito *m* non di lavoro; rendita *f*
n arbeidsloos inkomen *n*

2324 uneconomic(al); unprofitable; unremunerative
d ertraglos; gewinnlos; nicht einträglich*; nutzlos; uneinträglich; unergiebig; unrentabel; unwirtschaftlich
e antieconómico; no económico; no lucrativo; no rentable*; poco lucrativo; poco remunerador*
f improfitable; inéconomique; non économique; non lucratif; non rentable*; peu lucratif; peu rémunérateur
i antieconomico; non economico; non lucroso; non redditizio; non rimunerativo*; poco lucrativo; poco rimunerativo*
n niet economisch; niet voordelig; niet winstgevend*; oneconomisch; onrendabel; onvoordelig

* For synonyms see "economic".

2325 uniform costing
d einheitliche Einheitskostenrechnung *f*
e cálculo *m* del precio de coste tipo
f calcul *m* de prix de revient type
i sistema *m* di costi uniformi
n uniform calculatieschema *n* voor kostprijsberekening

2326 uniform price *(shares etc.)*; **uniform quotation**
cf. **flat price**
d Einheitskurs *m*; Konzentrationskurs *m*
e cotización *f* única
f cours *m* unique; cours *m* unitaire
i corso *m* unico; corso *m* unitario
n eenheidskoers *m*

2327 unitholder
d Anteilscheinbesitzer *m* eines gemeinsamen Investmentfonds
e titular *m* de participaciones de un fondo mutual de inversión
f titulaire *m* de parts d'un fonds commun de placement
i azionista *m* di un fondo commune d'investimento
n aandeelhouder *m* van een gemeenschappelijk beleggingsfonds

2328 unit price
cf. **flat price**
d Einheitspreis *m*; Einzelpreis *m*; Preis *m* per Einheit; Preis *m* pro Einheit; Stückpreis *m*
e precio *m* por pieza; precio *m* por unidad; precio *m* unitario
f prix *m* à la pièce; prix *m* unitaire
i prezzo *m* al pezzo; prezzo *m* unitario
n eenheidsprijs *m*; prijs *m* per eenheid; stukprijs *m*

2329 unlimited liability
d unbeschränkte Haftpflicht *f*; unbeschränkte Haftung *f*
e responsabilidad *f* ilimitada
f responsabilité *f* illimitée
i responsabilità *f* illimitata
n onbeperkte aansprakelijkheid *f*

2330 unmatured coupon
d nicht verfallener Anteilschein *m*; nicht verfallener Coupon *m*; nicht verfallener Kupon *m*
e cupón *m* no vencido; talón *m* no vencido
f coupon *m* non échu
i cedola *f* non scaduta
n niet vervallen coupon *m*; niet vervallen koepon *m*

2331 unsecured bond
d unbesicherte Obligation *f*; unbesicherte Schuldverschreibung *f*; ungesicherte Obligation *f*; ungesicherte Schuldverschreibung *f*
e obligación *f* no garantizada; obligación *f* sin garantía
f obligation *f* non gagée; obligation *f* non

garantie
i obbligazione *f* non garantita
n niet gegarandeerde obligatie *f*

2332 unsecured debt
cf. **book debt**
d ungesicherte Forderung *f*
e deuda *f* quirografaria
f créance *f* chirographaire
i debito *m* chirografario
n gewone schuldvordering *f*

2333 usance
d Usance *f*; Usanz *f*; Uso *m*
e uso *m*
f usance *f*
i usanza *f*; uso *m*
n usance *f*; usantie *f*; uso *n*

2334 usufruct
d Fruchtgenuss *m (O)*; Niessbrauch *m*; Niessnutz *m*; Nutzniessung *f*
e usofructo *m*
f usufruit *m*
i usufrutto *m*
n vruchtgebruik *n*

2335 usurious interest
d Wucherzins(en) *m(pl)*
e interés(es) *m(pl)* usurario(s)
f intérêt(s) *m(pl)* usuraire(s); taux *m* usuraire
i interesse *m* usurario; interessi *mpl* usuari
n woekerrente *f*

2336 usurious loan
d Darleh(e)n *n* zu Wucherzinsen; Wucherdarleh(e)n *n*; wucherisches Darleh(e)n *n*
e préstamo *m* usurario
f prêt *m* usuraire
i mutuo *m* usurario; prestito *m* usurario
n lening *f* tegen woekerrente

2337 usury
d Wucher *m*
e logro *m*; usura *f*
f usure *f*
i usura *f*
n woeker *m*

V

2338 valorization
d Valorisation *f*; Valorisierung *f*
e valorización *f*
f valorisation *f*
i valorizzazione *f*
n valorisatie *f*

2339 valorize *v*
d valorisieren
e valorizar
f valoriser
i valorizzare
n valoriseren

2340 value added by industry
d Wertschöpfung *f* der Industrie
e valor *m* añadido por la industria
f valeur *f* ajoutée par l'industrie
i valore *m* aggiunto dall'industria
n door de industrie toegevoegde waarde *f*

2341 value added tax; VAT
d Mehrwertsteuer *f*; MwSt
e impuesto *m* sobre el valor agregado *(AL)*; IVA; impuesto *m* sobre el valor añadido
f taxe *f* à la valeur ajoutée; TVA; taxe *f* sur la valeur ajoutée
i imposta *f* sul valore aggiunto; IVA
n belasting *f* op de toegevoegde waarde; BTW

2342 value (as on) 1 January
cf. **value date**
d Valuta (per) 1 Januar; Wert (per) 1 Januar
e valor del 1º de enero
f valeur (au) 1er janvier
i valuta al 1 gennaio
n (met) valuta 1 januari; valuta (per) 1 januari

2343 value date
cf. **value (as on) 1 January**
d Valuta *f*; Valutierungstag *m*; Wertstellung *f*; Wertstellungstermin *m*; Werttag *m*
e fecha *f* (de) valor
f date *f* de valeur
i valuta *f*
n valuta *f*; valutadatum *m*

2344 valuelessness; worthlessness
d Wertlosigkeit *f*
e carencia *f* de valor; falta *f* de valor; no valor *m*
f manque *m* de valeur; non-valeur *f*
i mancanza *f* di valore
n waardeloosheid *f*

2345 valueless securities; valueless stock; worthless securities; worthless stock
d Nonvaleurs *mpl*; wertlose Papiere *npl*
e no valores *mpl*; títulos *mpl* sin valor
f non-valeurs *fpl*; titres *mpl* sans valeur
i titoli *mpl* senza valore
n non-valeurs *mpl/fpl*; waardeloze effecten *npl*

2346 variable costs
d variable Kosten *pl*
e gastos *mpl* variables
f frais *mpl* variables
i spese *fpl* variabili
n variabele kosten *mpl*

2347 variable depreciation
d schwankende Abschreibung *f*; variable Abschreibung *f*
e amortización *f* variable; depreciación *f* variable
f amortissement *m* variable
i ammortamento *m* variabile
n variabele afschrijving *f*; wisselende afschrijving *f*

2348 variable yield investment
cf. **equity investment**
d Anlage *f* mit schwankendem Ertrag
e inversión *f* de rédito variable
f placement *m* à revenu(s) variable(s)
i investimento *m* a reddito variabile
n belegging *f* met veranderlijk inkomen

2349 viability
cf. **profitability**
d Lebensfähigkeit *f*
e viabilidad *f*
f viabilité *f*
i vitalità *f*
n levensvatbaarheid *f*

2350 viable
d lebensfähig
e viable
f viable
i vitale
n levensvatbaar

2351 visible exports; visibles
d sichtbare Ausfuhr(en) *f(pl)*; sichtbare Exporte *mpl*
e exportaciones *fpl* visibles
f exportations *fpl* visibles

i esportazioni *fpl* visibili
n zichtbare export *m*; zichtbare uitvoer *m*

2352 visible imports
d sichtbare Einfuhr(en) *f(pl)*; sichtbare Importe *mpl*
e importaciones *fpl* visibles
f importations *fpl* visibles
i importazioni *fpl* visibili
n zichtbare import *m*; zichtbare invoer *m*

2353 volume of savings
d Sparvolumen *n*
e volumen *m* de ahorros
f volume *m* de l'épargne
i volume *m* di risparmio
n spaarvolume *n*

2354 volume of trade
d Handelsvolumen *n*
e volumen *m* comercial; volumen *m* de intercambio; volumen *m* del comercio
f volume *m* des échanges (commerciaux); volume *m* du commerce
i volume *m* degli scambi (commerciali); volume *m* del comercio
n handelsvolume *n*

2355 voluntary restraint agreement
d Selbstbeschränkungsabkommen *n*
e acuerdo *m* de autolimitación
f accord *m* d'autolimitation
i accordo *m* di autolimitazione
n afspraak *f* inzake zelfbeperking

2356 voting rights of nominee shareholders
d Depotstimmrecht *n*
e derecho *m* de voto de títulos en depósito
f droit *m* de vote des titres en dépôt
i diritto *m* di voto su titoli in deposito
n depotstemrecht *n*

2357 voting shares *(UK)*; voting stock *(US)*
d stimmberechtigte Aktien *fpl*; Stimmrechtsaktien *fpl*
e acciones *fpl* con derecho a (de) voto
f actions *fpl* à droit de vote
i azioni *fpl* con diritto di voto
n aandelen *npl* met stemrecht

2358 voucher
d Beleg *m*; Belegschein *m*; Belegstück *n*; Beweisstück *n*; Unterlage *f*
e comprobante *m*; justificante *m*
f justificatif *m*; pièce *f* à l'appui; pièce *f* certificative; pièce *f* justificative
i giustificativo *m*; pezza *f* d'appoggio; pezza *f* giustificativa
n bewijsstuk *n*; verantwoordingsstuk *n (B)*

W

2359 **wage bill; wage costs; wages and salaries bill**
d Lohnkosten *pl*; Lohnsumme *f*
e costes *mpl* salariales; costos *mpl* salariales; masa *f* salarial
f coûts *mpl* salariaux; masse *f* salariale
i costi *mpl* salariali; massa *f* salariale
n loonkosten *mpl*; loonsom *f*

2360 **wage control(s)**
d Lohnkontrolle *f*
e control *m* de (los) salarios
f contrôle *m* des salaires
i controllo *m* dei salari
n looncontrole *f*

2361 **wage-induced inflation; wage-led inflation; wage-push inflation**
d durch Lohnsteigerung bedingte Inflation *f*; lohninduzierte Inflation *f*
e inflación *f* provocada por el aumento de los salarios
f inflation *f* provoquée par (la hausse des) les salaires
i inflazione *f* provocata da aumenti salariali
n door loonsverhogingen veroorzaakte inflatie *f*

2362 **wage investment scheme**
d Investivlohnsystem *n*
e sistema *m* de salario inversión
f système *m* de salaire-investissement
i sistema *m* salario investimento
n investeringsloonstelsel *n*

2363 **wage-price spiral**
d Lohn-Preis-Spirale *f*
e espiral *f* de precios y salarios; espiral *f* precios-salarios
f mouvement *m* en spirale des prix et des salaires; spirale *f* des salaires et des prix; spirale *f* prix-salaires
i movimento *m* a spirale dei prezzi e dei salari; spirale *f* dei prezzi e dei salari; spirale *f* prezzi-salari
n lonen- en prijzenspiraal *f*; loon- en prijsspiraal *f*; loon-prijsspiraal *f*

2364 **warehouse receipt; warehouse warrant; warrant**
cf. **certificate of deposit**
d Lagerschein *m*; Warrant *m*
e comprobante *m* de almacén; resguardo *m* de almacén; talón *m* de almacén; warrant *m* (de almacén)
f certificat *m* d'entrepôt; récépissé-warrant *m*; warrant *m*; warrant-cédule *m (B)*
i buono *m* di magazzino; nota *f* di pegno; scontrino *m* di magazzino; warrant *m*
n cedel *f/n*; ceel *f/n*; opslagbewijs *n*; veemceel *f/n*; warrant *m*; warrant-cedel *m (B)*

2365 **watered capital stock; watered share capital; watered stock**
d verwässertes Aktienkapital *n*
e capital *m* en acciones diluido
f capital-actions *m* dilué
i capitale *m* azionario annacquato
n verwaterd aandelenkapitaal *n*

2366 **wear** *(of a coin)*
d Abnützung *f*; Abnutzung *f*
e uso *m*
f frai *m*; usure *f*
i usura *f*
n slijtage *f*; slijting *f*

2367 **wear and tear**
d Abnutzung *f*; Abnützung *f*; Verschleiss *m*
e desgaste *m*; deterioro *m*; uso *m*
f dégradation *f*; détérioration *f*; usure *f*
i deperimento *m*; deterioramento *m*; logoramento *m*; logorio *m*; usura *f*
n slijtage *f*; slijting *f*

2368 **weight** *(statistics)*
d Gewicht *n*
e peso *m*
f poids *m*
i peso *m*
n gewicht *n*

2369 **weight** *v*
d bewerten; gewichten; wiegen
e ponderar
f pondérer
i ponderare
n wegen

2370 **weighted index**
d gewogener Index *m*
e índice *m* ponderado
f indice *m* pondéré
i indice *m* ponderato
n gewogen index *m*; gewogen indexcijfer *n*

2371 **weighting** *(statistics)*
d Gewichtung *f*; Wägung *f*
e ponderación *f*
f pondération *f*

i ponderazione *f*
n weging *f*

2372 weighting coefficient
d Gewichtungskoeffizient *m*; Wägungskoeffizient *m*
e coeficiente *m* de ponderación
f coefficient *m* de pondération
i coefficiente *m* di ponderazione
n wegingscoëfficiënt *m*

2373 welfare state
d Sozialstaat *m*; Wohlfahrtsstaat *m*
e estado *m* providencia; estado *m* social
f état *m* providence; état *m* social
i stato *m* assistenziale; stato *m* sociale
n welvaartsstaat *m*

2374 wholesale price index
d Grosshandels(preis)index *m*; Index *m* der Grosshandelspreise
e índice *m* de los precios al por mayor
f indice *m* des prix de gros
i indice *m* dei prezzi all'ingrosso
n groothandelsprijzenindex *m*; indexcijfer *n* van de groothandelsprijzen; index *m* van de groothandelsprijzen

2375 wholesaler
d Engroshändler *m*; Engrossist *m (O)*; Grosshändler *m*; Grossist *m*
e almacenista *m*; comerciante *m* al por mayor; comerciante *m* mayorista; mayorista *m*
f commerçant *m* de gros; commerçant *m* en gros; grossiste *m*
i commerciante *m* all'ingrosso; grossista *m*
n groothandelaar *m*; grossier *m*

2376 wholesale trade
d Engroshandel *m*; Grosshandel *m*
e comercio *m* al por mayor; comercio *m* mayorista *(AL)*; mayoreo *m (AL)*
f commerce *m* de gros; commerce *m* en gros
i commercio *m* all'ingrosso
n en-gros-handel *m*; groothandel *m*; grossierderij *f*

2377 withdrawal from reserves
d Entnahme *f* aus Rücklagen; Reserveentnahme *f (Schw)*
e detracción *f* de reservas
f prélèvement *m* sur réserves
i prelevamento *m* da riserve; prelievo *m* da riserve
n onttrekking *f* aan reserves

2378 worn *(of a coin)*
d abgegriffen; abgenutzt; abgenützt
e gastado; usado
f fruste; usé
i consumato; logoro
n afgesleten

2379 write *v* **off a debt**
cf. **cancel** *v* **a debt**
d eine Forderung abbuchen; eine Forderung abschreiben; eine Forderung ausbuchen
e amortizar una deuda
f amortir une créance
i ammortare un debito; ammortizzare un debito
n een vordering afboeken; een vordering amortiseren

ENGLISH

GB

abatement, tax ~ 2261
abolish restrictions 1
abolition of restrictions 2
absorb a loss 3
absorption costing 4
abstract of account 5
abundance of money 6
accelerated depreciation 7
accept a bill of exchange 8
acceptable as collateral 9
acceptance 10
acceptance, bank ~ 284
acceptance credit 11
acceptance house 12
acceptance, trade ~ 2286
accepting commission 13
accepting house 12
acceptor 14
accommodation bill 15
account 16, 17, 18
account, allowance ~ 130
accountancy 20
accountant 21
account, asset ~ 201
account, auxiliary ~ 224
account, balance an ~ 249
account, balance of an ~ 254, 255
account, balance sheet ~ 271
account, bank ~ 285
account, capital ~ 516
account, carry to ~ 570
account, cash ~ 575
account, charge ~ 617
account, charge to (the debit of) an ~ 618
account, charge up to an ~ 618
account, check ~ 625
account, checking ~ 625
account classification 22
account, clearance ~ 644
account, clearing ~ 644
account, close an ~ 652
account, close of an ~ 655
account, closing of an ~ 655
account, collation ~ 673
account, collective ~ 673
account, contra ~ 760
account, control ~ 766
account current 23
account day 24
account, debit to an ~ 618
account, deposit ~ 1016
account, detailed ~ 429
account, drawing ~ 23, 625
account, expense ~ 1259
account, for (one's) own ~ 1877
account, giro ~ 1424
account, government stock equalization ~ 1455
account heading 25
account holder 26
account, income ~ 1523, 1524
accounting 20
accounting balance 27
accounting books 28
accounting dollar 29
accounting, machine ~ 1724
accounting, mechanized ~ 1724
accounting, national ~ 1797
accounting plan 22
accounting, self-balancing ~ 2155
accounting surplus 30
accounting system 22
accounting unit 31
accounting value 32
accounting voucher 33
account, itemized ~ 429
account, joint venture ~ 1654
account, liability ~ 1682
account, liquidate an ~ 249
account, liquidation of an ~ 254
account, loro ~ 1716
account, make up an ~ 249
account, national giro ~ 1800
account of a third party, for ~ 35
account of, for ~ 34
account, offset ~ 644, 760
account, on ~ 19
account, open ~ 23, 1846
account, outstanding ~ 1846
account, overdraw an ~ 1868
account, participation ~ 1654
account payable 36
account, personal ~ 1926
account, place (in)to ~ 570
account, position of an ~ 1940
account, postal check ~ 1800
account, post office cheque ~ 1800
account, private ~ 1926
account, profit and loss ~ 1523
account, provision ~ 130
account, purchase on ~ 852
account, put (in)to ~ 570
account receivable 37
account, reserve ~ 130
account, revenue ~ 1524
account, running ~ 23
accounts, agree ~ 112
account, savings ~ 2138
accounts, chart of ~ 22
accounts, codification of ~ 22
accounts, cost control ~ 802
accounts, doubtful ~ 1110
account, settle an ~ 249
account, settlement of an ~ 254
accounts, integrated national ~ 1579
accounts, keep the ~ 1656
accounts, national ~ 1797
account, square an ~ 249
accounts, reconcile ~ 112
accounts, reconciliation of ~ 2043
accounts, square ~ 112
accounts, squaring of ~ 2043
account statement 5
account, state of an ~ 1940
account, subsidiary ~ 224
account, summary ~ 673
account, suspense ~ 2248
account, syndicate ~ 1654
account title 25
account, trading ~ 2289
account, transfer ~ 1424
account, trust ~ 2305
account, unsettled ~ 1846
account, valuation ~ 130
account, vostro ~ 1716
account, winding up of an ~ 655
account, wind up an ~ 652
account with, charge an ~ 618
account (with), credit the ~ 880
account with, debit an ~ 618
accrual 38
accruals 39
accrue 40
accrued charges 39
accrued expenses 39
accrued interest 41
accruing interest 42
accumulate 40, 43
accumulation 44
acid-test ratio 45
acknowledg(e)ment of debt 46
acknowledg(e)ment of indebtedness 46
acknowledg(e)ment of receipt 47
acquire 48
acquisition 49
acquisition value 50
acquittance 51
act as surety 52
active balance of trade 53
active debt 37
active trade balance 53
actual cost 54
actual expenses 55
actual value 56
actual yield 57
actuary 58
adaptation inflation 59
adapted inflation 59
additional charge 60
additional charges 61
additional costs 61
additional cover 62
additional credit 63
additional expenses 61
additional income 64
additional margin 62
additional security 65
additional tax 66
addition to the reserve(s) 67
add to the reserve 68
adjudication in bankruptcy 69
adjudication of bankruptcy 69
adjust 70
adjusting entry 71
adjustment 72
adjustment accounts 73
adjustment entry 71
adjustment in real terms 74
adjustment in the exchange rate 75
adjustment of prices 76
adjustment of quotas 77
administered price 78
administration, debt ~ 954
administration, price ~ 1961
administrative costs 79
administrative expenses 79
administrative fee 80
admission to the stock exchange 81
ad valorem duty 82
advance 83, 85
advance against collateral (security) 86

advance against security 86
advance, as an ~ 84
advance, banker's ~ 298
advance by overdraft 87
advance, by way of an ~ 84
advance commitment 88
advance deduction 89
advance on collateral (security) 86
advance on current account 87
advance on securities 90, 91
advance on security 86
advance payment 92
advance, secured ~ 86
advances on collateral (security), rate for ~ 2022
advances on securities, rate for ~ 1714
advance upon collateral (security) 86
advantage, tax ~ 2263
adverse balance 93
adverse balance of trade 94
adverse budget 95
adverse cash balance 96
adverse trade balance 94
advice, credit ~ 847, 848
advice, debit ~ 945
advice of payment 97
advice, transfer ~ 848
adviser, financial ~ 1309
adviser, tax ~ 2264
advisor, financial ~ 1309
advisor, tax ~ 2264
affiliate 98
affiliated company 98
afflux of capital 99
afford a profit 100
afford collateral 101
after hours market 102
agency 103
agent 104
agent, commission ~ 690
aggregate 105, 106
aggregate amount 107
aggregate value 108
agio 109, 110
agiotage 111
agree accounts 112
agree a price 113
agreed price 114
agreement, clearing ~ 647
agreement, composition ~ 719
agreement dollar 29
Agreement, European Monetary ~ 1196
agreement, lease ~ 1666
agreement on prices 115
Agreement on Tariffs and Trade, General ~ 1415
agreement, payment ~ 1906
agreement, payments ~ 1906
agreement, stand-by ~ 2215
agreement, standstill ~ 2216
agreement, voluntary restraint ~ 2355
agree on a price 113
aid, development ~ 1034
aid, financial ~ 1310
aid, government ~ 1445
aid, state ~ 1445
alienability 116
alienable 117
alienate 118
alienation 119
alienee 120
alienor 121
all-in price 114
allocate 122
allocation 123
allocation to the reserve(s) 67
allonge 124
allot 122
allotment 123
allotment of shares 125
allow a credit 126
allowance 127, 128, 129
allowance account 130
allowance, capital ~ 517
allowance, cashier's ~ 133
allowance, cost of living ~ 808
allowance, depreciation ~ 132
allowance, entertainment ~ 1169
allowance, extra ~ 1284
allowance for charges, after ~ 131
allowance for depreciation 132
allowance for depreciation, annual ~ 157
allowance for errors 133
allowance for expenses, after ~ 131
allowance in kind 134
allowance, investment ~ 517
allowance, monthly ~ 1787
allowance, special ~ 1284
allowance, tax ~ 2261
allowance, trade ~ 935
allowance, travel ~ 2296
allowance, travelling ~ 2296
allowing for charges, after ~ 131
allowing for expenses, after ~ 131
amalgamation 135
amass 43
amercement 136
amortisable mortgage 137
amortisation 138, 139
amortisation fund 140
amortisation loan 141
amortisation of a loan 142
amortisation on replacement value 143
amortisation rate 144, 145
amortisation table 146
amortise 147, 148
amortisement 138
amortising loan 141
amortizable mortgage 137
amortization 138, 139
amortization fund 140
amortization loan 141
amortization of a loan 142
amortization on replacement value 143
amortization rate 144, 145
amortization schedule 146
amortize 147, 148
amortizement 138
amortizing loan 141
amount 149
amount, aggregate ~ 107
amount brought forward (to next account) 150
amount due 151
amount, excess ~ 1205
amount, global ~ 107
amount, gross ~ 1460
amount, net ~ 1808
amount, nominal ~ 1820
amount outstanding 152
amount, overall ~ 107
amount owing 151
amount, remaining ~ 246
amount subscribed 153
amount to a total of 106
amount, total ~ 107
amount unpaid 154
analysis 155
analysis, cost benefit ~ 801
analysis, cost effectiveness ~ 801
analysis, detailed ~ 429
analysis, market ~ 1740
anatocism 156
annual allowance for depreciation 157
annual average 158
annual budget 159
annual depreciation allowance 157
annual depreciation charge 157
annual provision for depreciation 157
annual report 160
annual return 160
annual statement 160
annuity 161
annuity bond 162
annuity certificate 162
annuity for life 163
annuity, perpetual ~ 163
antedate 164
anticipated interest 165
anticipated payment 92
anticipated profit 166
anticipated redemption 167
anticipatory finance, provide ~ 1951
anticipatory finance, provision of ~ 1952
anticipatory interest 165
anti-cyclical 168
antidumping duty 169
anti-inflationary 170
apparent profit 171
applicant for a loan 172
applicant for credit 172
application for a loan 173
application for credit 173
application right 174
apply for a loan 175
apportion 122
apportionment 123
apportionment of shares 125
appraisal 176
appraise 177
appraisement 176
appreciate 178, 179
appreciation 180
appropriate 181
appropriation 182

appropriation of profits 183
appropriations, budget ~ 444
appropriations, budgetary ~ 444
appropriations, investment ~ 1620
appropriation to the reserve(s) 67
approximate estimate 184
approximation 184
arbitrage in bullion 185
arbitrage in (of) exchange 186
arbitrage margins 187
arbitration in (of) exchange 186
area, dollar ~ 1086
area, franc ~ 1388
area, free trade ~ 1398
area, marketing ~ 1736
area, sales ~ 1736
area, sterling ~ 2224
arrangement, deed of ~ 719
arrangement, scheme of ~ 718
arrearages 188
arrears 188
arrears, in ~ 189
arrears, interest on ~ 983
arrears of interest 190
arrears, payment of ~ 237
arrest 191
articles, de luxe ~ 1001
articles, deluxe ~ 1001
articles, fancy ~ 1001
articles, luxury ~ 1001
articles, reserve prescribed by the ~ 2102
asked and bid 192
asked price 193
asked quotation 193
asked rate 193
ask for a loan 175
assess 177, 194, 195
assessable 196
assessable profit 197
assessable value 198
assessed value 198, 199
assessment 176, 200
assessment, basis of ~ 331
assessment, estimated ~ 1188
assessment, notice of ~ 1839
assessment, rate of ~ 2023
asset account 201
asset, be booked as an ~ 408
asset, book as an ~ 403
asset, enter as an ~ 403
assets 202
assets and liabilities 203
assets, bankrupt's ~ 317
assets, blocked ~ 381
assets, capital ~ 518
assets, cash ~ 577
assets, corporate ~ 790
assets, current ~ 905
assets, depreciable ~ 1027
assets, external ~ 204
assets, fictional ~ 1297
assets, fictitious ~ 1297
assets, fixed ~ 518
assets, floating ~ 468
assets, foreign ~ 204
assets, formation of ~ 1373
assets, gold ~ 1430
assets held abroad 204
assets, immaterial ~ 1505
assets in kind (brought into a business) 205
assets, intangible ~ 1505
assets, liquid ~ 227
assets, material ~ 1747
assets, net ~ 1809
assets, net current ~ 468
assets, personal ~ 622
assets, quick ~ 227
assets, ready ~ 227
assets, real ~ 1508
assets, realisable ~ 905
assets, realizable ~ 905
assets side 206
assets, tangible ~ 1747
assets, trading ~ 468
assets, treasury ~ 2300
assets, working ~ 468
assign 118, 120, 122
assignability 116
assignable 117
assign a claim 207
assignation 119
assignation of claims 208
assignee 120
assignee in bankruptcy 209
assignment 119
assignment of claims 208
assignment of shares 125
assignor 121
assistance, development ~ 1034
assistance, financial ~ 1310
association, credit ~ 787
Association, International Development ~ 1604
association, loan ~ 787
association, non-profit ~ 1829
association, non-profit-making ~ 1829
association, profit-making ~ 1986
assumed profit 171
assurance, life ~ 1688
assured income 210
attach 211
attachment 191
auction 212, 213
auction sale 212
audit 214, 215
audit, internal ~ 1600
auditor 216
auditor's report 217, 217
audit report 217
audit, tax field ~ 1566
austerity 218
autarchy 219
autarky 219
authorisation of credit 220
authorisation of payment 221
authorise a credit 126
authorised capital 222
authorise payment of an account 223
authorities, tax ~ 1242
authorization of credit 220
authorization of payment 221
authorize acredit 126
authorized capital stock 222
authorize payment of an account 223
auxiliary account 224
auxiliary book 225
availability of capital 226
available funds 227
availment of credits 228
avails 229
aval 230
average 231, 232
average, annual ~ 158
average income per head 233
average rate 234
averaging, cost ~ 800
avoidance, tax ~ 2266

back a bill 235
backdate 164
backer 236
backing for a bill 230
back payment 237
back to back guarantee 238
backwardation 239
backwardation rate 240
bad check 241
bad debt 242
bad debt reserve 243
bad investment 244
bad payer 245
balance 246, 247, 248
balance, accounting ~ 27
balance, adverse ~ 93
balance an account 249
balance, bank ~ 286
balance book 250
balance brought forward, profit ~ 1985
balance, capital ~ 256
balance carried forward, profit ~ 1985
balance carried forward (to next account) 150
balance, clearing ~ 269
balance, credit ~ 849
balanced budget 251
balance, debit ~ 93
balance deficit 93
balance, draw a ~ 279
balance due 252
balance, external ~ 1277
balance, foreign ~ 1277
balance in (on) hand 253
balance, loss ~ 93
balance, migratory ~ 1758
balance of an account 254, 255
balance of capital movements 256
balance of cash in (on) hand 253
balance of current transfers 257
balance of external payments 258
balance of goods and services 259
balance of payments 260
balance of payments, correction of the ~ 794
balance of payments deficit 261
balance of payments on current account 262
balance of payments, overall ~ 1862

balance of payments surplus 263
balance of trade 264
balance of trade, active ~ 53
balance of trade, adverse ~ 94
balance of trade deficit 265
balance of trade, favourable ~ 53
balance of trade, passive ~ 94
balance of trade surplus 266
balance of trade, unfavorable ~ 94
balance of trade, unfavourable ~ 94
balance of transactions in goods and services 259
balance of transfers 267
balance of transfers and capital movements, general ~ 1416
balance on current account 268
balance on offset account 269
balance owing 252
balance, pay the ~ 1914
balance, profit ~ 849
balance, settle the ~ 1914
balances, foreign exchange ~ 1362
balance sheet 270
balance sheet account 271
balance sheet book 250
balance sheet date 272
balance sheet, draw up a ~ 279
balance sheet, economic ~ 1148
balance sheet, final ~ 1302
balance sheet, group ~ 736
balance sheet, interim ~ 1596
balance sheet lay-out 273
balance sheet, make up a ~ 279
balance sheet, opening ~ 1700
balance sheet, presentation of the ~ 1957
balance sheet, provisional ~ 1596
balance sheet showing a loss 274
balance sheet showing a profit 275
balance sheet structure 273
balance sheet total 276
balance sheet value 277
balance, short ~ 93
balances, list of opening ~ 1700
balance(s), settlement of ~ 1199
balance, strike a ~ 279
balance the books 278, 279
balance the budget 280
balance, trial ~ 2303
balancing entry 281
bank 282
bankable paper 283
bank acceptance 284
bank account 285
bank balance 286
bank bill 284, 287
bank bond 288
bankbook 289
bank, central ~ 606
bank certificate 290
bank charges 291
bank clearing 292
bank, clearing ~ 648
bank commission 293
bank confirmation 290
bank corporation 294
bank credit 295
bank, credit ~ 850
bank debts 296
bank deposit 297
bank, deposit ~ 1020
bank, development ~ 1035
bank, discount ~ 1058
bank draft 284
banker's acceptance 284
banker's advance 298
banker's bill 284
banker's draft 284
banker's order 299
Bank, European Investment ~ 1195
bank, exchange ~ 1220
Bank for International Settlements 300
Bank for Reconstruction and Development, International ~ 1602
bank, incorporated ~ 1536
banking 301
banking company 302
banking consortium 303
banking establishment 294
banking firm 294
banking house 294
banking institution 294
banking operations 304
banking secrecy 305
banking syndicate 303
banking transactions 304
Bank, Inter-American Development ~ 1581
bank interest 306
bank, investment ~ 1621
bank, issuing ~ 1645
bank, joint stock ~ 1536
bank, land ~ 1660
bank lending 295
bank, lending ~ 850
bank loan 298
bank, loan ~ 850
bank, merchant ~ 310
bank money 307
bank, mortgage ~ 1660
bank note 287
bank notes, emission of ~ 1156
bank notes in circulation 308
bank notes, issue of ~ 1156
bank of circulation 309
bank of commerce 310
bank of issue 309
bank, postal savings ~ 1941
bank, post office savings ~ 1941
bank, private ~ 1974
bank rate 311
bank rate of discount 311
bank return 312
bankroll 286
bankrupt 313, 314
bankruptcy 315
bankruptcy, adjudication in ~ 69
bankruptcy, declaration of ~ 69
bankruptcy petition 316
bankruptcy proceedings, institution of ~ 1575
bankruptcy trustee 209
bankruptcy, trusteeship in ~ 2040
bankrupt estate 317
bankrupt's assets 317
bankrupt's estate 317
bank, savings ~ 2139
bank secrecy 305
bank secret 305
bank, trade ~ 310
bank transfer 318
Bank, World~ 1602
ban on imports 319
bargain 320, 321
bargain, option ~ 1855
bargain price 322
bargain, time ~ 1379
bar gold 323
barred debt 324
barrier, customs ~ 918
barrier, economic ~ 1149
barter 325, 326
barter transaction 327
base rate 328
basic commodity 329
basic price 330
basic rate 328
basis of assessment 331
basis of taxation 331
bear 332
bear a loss 333
bear an interest of X percent 334
bear (a) X percent interest 334
bear covering 335
bearer 336, 337
bearer bond 338
bearer check 339
bearer instrument 340
bearer of securities 341
bearer securities 342
bearer share 343
bear, go a ~ 1427
bearing, interest ~ 1586
bear interest at a rate of X percent 334
bearish tone 344
bearish trend 344
bear market 345
bear sale 346
become due 347
Belgo-Luxemb(o)urg Economic Union 348
beneficial interest 349
beneficiary 350
benefit, extra ~ 1285
benefit, fringe ~ 1284, 1285
benefit in kind 134
benefits, collective ~ 684
benefit, social security ~ 2185
benefits, public ~ 684
benefit, tax ~ 2263
biannual instal(l)ment 351
bid 352, 353
bid, asked and ~ 192
bidder, highest ~ 1485
bid, higher ~ 1484
bid price 354
bid quotation 354
bids, offers and ~ 192
big business 355
bill 17, 287, 356, 357
bill, accommodation ~ 15

bill at usance 358
bill, back a ~ 235
bill, backing for a ~ 230
bill, bank ~ 284, 287
bill book 359, 360
bill broker 361
bill, collateral ~ 363
bill, commercial ~ 356
bill credit 11
bill debtor 362
bill, demand ~ 1003
bill diary 359, 360
bill, discounted domestic ~ 1060
bill, dishonored ~ 365
bill, endorsable ~ 374
bill en pension 363
bill, fictitious ~ 15
bill, finance ~ 1307
bill, financial ~ 1307
bill, fine ~ 1323
bill, first-class ~ 1323
bill for collection 364
bill, guarantee a ~ 235
bill, guarantee payment of a ~ 235
bill, hand ~ 1477
bill in distress 365
billing 366
bill in pawn 363
bill in suspense 365
billion 367, 368
bill jobbing 369
bill journal 359, 360
bill market 370
bill, negotiable ~ 374
bill, non-negotiable ~ 371
bill not to order 371
bill of exchange 356
bill of exchange, accept a ~ 8
bill of exchange, discharge a ~ 1054
bill (of exchange), domestic ~ 1091
bill (of exchange), foreign ~ 1357
bill of exchange, honor a ~ 1054
bill of exchange, honour a ~ 1054
bill (of exchange), inland ~ 1091
bill of exchange, meet a ~ 1054
bill of exchange, pawned ~ 363
bill of exchange, pay a ~ 1054
bill of exchange, pledged ~ 363
bill of exchange, protect a ~ 1054
bill of exchange, sole ~ 2180
bill of exchange upon somebody, draw a ~ 1114
bill on deposit 363
bill, overdue ~ 365
bill, past ~ 365
bill, past-due ~ 365
bill payable 372
bill, prime ~ 1323
bill receivable 373
bill, returned ~ 365
bill returned unpaid 365
bill, sight ~ 1003
bill, single ~ 2180
bill, sola ~ 2180
bills payable book 359
bills receivable book 360
bill surety 230
bill to order 374
bill, trade ~ 356
bill, transferable ~ 374
bill, treasury ~ 2301
bill, unendorsable ~ 371
bill, unnegotiable ~ 371
bill, unpaid ~ 365
bill, untransferable ~ 371
bill, wage ~ 2359
bill, wind ~ 15
bimetal(l)ism 375
BIS 300
black 206
black interest 376
black market 377
blank check 378
blank cheque 378
blank credit 379
bloc, dollar ~ 1086
bloc, franc ~ 1388
block 380
blocked assets 381
blocked sterling 382
blocking 383
blocking period 384
block issue 385
block of shares 386
bloc, sterling ~ 2224
B.L.U.E. 348
blue chips 387
blue chip stock(s) 387
board of creditors 388
body, public finance ~ 2004
bond 389
bond, annuity ~ 162
bond, bank ~ 288
bond, bearer ~ 338
bond, callable ~ 497
bond, commutation ~ 704
bond, conversion ~ 704
bond, convertible ~ 783
bond, corporate ~ 389
bond, coupon ~ 830
bond creditor 390
bond, debenture ~ 389
bond, defaulted ~ 980
bond, dollar ~ 1087
bonded debt 391
bond, exchequer ~ 1243
bond, government ~ 1243
bond, guarantee ~ 394
bondholder 390
bond, income ~ 1526
bond, indemnity ~ 394
bond, indexed ~ 1549
bond, index-linked ~ 1549
bond, irredeemable ~ 1636
bond issue 392
bond, local ~ 1713
bond, local authority ~ 1713
bond, lottery ~ 1719
bond market 393
bond, mortgage ~ 1792
bond, municipal ~ 1713
bond of indemnity 394
bond, optional ~ 497
bond, participating ~ 1526
bond, perpetual ~ 162
bond, premium ~ 1719
bond, redeemable ~ 497
bond, redemption ~ 704
bond, refunding ~ 704
bond, savings ~ 2141
bonds, consolidated ~ 734
bond, secured ~ 2149
bond, security ~ 394
bonds, issue ~ 1637
bondsman 395
bonds, put out ~ 1637
bond, treasury ~ 1243, 2301
bond, unredeemable ~ 1636
bond, unsecured ~ 2331
bond yield 396
bonus 397, 398
bonus, cost of living ~ 808
bonus, export ~ 426
bonus issue 399
bonus share 400
book 401
book as a liability 402
book as an asset 403
book, auxiliary ~ 225
book, balance ~ 250
book, balance sheet ~ 250
book, bank~ 289
book, bill ~ 359, 360
book, bills payable ~ 359
book, bills receivable ~ 360
book, cash ~ 578
book, check-~ 626
book claim 404
book creditor 405
book, day~ 932
book debt 406
book, deposit ~ 1021
booked as a liability, be ~ 407
booked as an asset, be ~ 408
book entry 409
bookkeeper 410
bookkeeping 20
bookkeeping, double entry ~ 1107
bookkeeping, single entry ~ 2181
bookkeeping voucher 33
book loss 411
book, memo ~ 1754
book of original entry 225
book, pass~ 289
book profit 412
book, savings ~ 2142
book, savings bank ~ 2140
books, balance the ~ 278, 279
books, close the ~ 278
books, keep the ~ 1656
books of account 28
book, stock ~ 1701
book, subsidiary ~ 225
book value 32
book, waste ~ 1754
boom 413
boomflation 414
boost, investment ~ 521
borrow 415
borrow capital 416
borrowed capital 417
borrowed funds 417
borrower 418
borrower, joint ~ 658

borrowing 419
borrowing abroad 420
borrowing, cost of ~ 805
borrowing facilities 421
borrowing limit 422
borrowing, net ~ 1810
borrowing rate 423
borrowing requirement 424
bought note 425
bought note, contract ~ 425
bouncer 241
bounty 397
bounty on exportation 426
box, cash ~ 579
box, safe deposit ~ 2123
box, strong ~ 2122
bracket, income ~ 1527
bracket, tax ~ 2267
branch 427
break 428
breakdown 155, 429
break-even point 430
break in prices 431
break-up value 432
bridging finance 433
bridging loan 434
bring forward 435
bring in a profit 100
bring in capital 436
broker 437
brokerage 438
brokerage firm 439
brokerage house 439
broker, bill ~ 361
broker, commodities ~ 694
broker, discount ~ 361
broker, exchange ~ 361, 509
broker, financial ~ 1311
broker, money ~ 1311
broker, note ~ 361
broker's contract note 425, 440
broker, securities ~ 2152
broker's firm 439
broker's note 425, 440
broker's office 439
broker, stock~ 2152
brought forward, profit ~ 1985
brought forward (to next account), amount ~ 150
budget 441, 442, 443
budget, adverse ~ 95
budget, annual ~ 159
budget appropriations 444
budgetary 442
budgetary appropriations 444
budgetary depreciation 445
budgetary equilibrium 251
budgetary expenditure 446
budgetary receipts 447
budgetary year 448
budget, balanced ~ 251
budget, balance the ~ 280
budget, capital ~ 519
budget, community ~ 703
budget, cyclical ~ 929
budget deficit 95
budget, enter in the ~ 443
budget estimates 449
budget, financial ~ 1312
budget for 443
budget, government ~ 1446
budget, include in the ~ 443
budgeting, deficit ~ 989
budget management 450
budget, national ~ 1446
budget, ordinary ~ 1859
budget projections 451
budget, state ~ 1446
budget surplus 452
budget year 448
building society 453
build up a reserve 454
bull 455, 456
bulletin, stock exchange ~ 1228
bull, go a ~ 456
bullion 457
bullion, arbitrage in ~ 185
bullion, gold coin and ~ 1430
bullish market 458
bullish tone 459
bullish trend 459
bull market 458
burden 460
burden centre 461
burden, financial ~ 1313
burden of debts 462
burden of taxation 463
burden variance 464
burden with a mortgage 465
burden with debts 466
business 467
business, big ~ 355
business capital 468
business, clearing ~ 643
business climate 469
business, continuation ~ 567
business, course of ~ 833
business credit 470
business, credit ~ 851
business cycle 471
business, do ~ 1084
business enterprise 467
business, exchange ~ 1221, 1222
business expenses 472
business, foreign ~ 1358
business loan 473
business loss 474
business profit 475
business, run of ~ 833
business tax 476
business, transact ~ 1084
business trend 477
business year 478
buy 479
buy back 480
buy by instal(l)ments 481
buyer 482
buyer's market 483, 483
buyer's option 484
buyer's option to double 485
buy for a rise 456
buy for future delivery 486
buy for (the) settlement 486
buy forward 486
buy, good ~ 321
buying, credit ~ 852
buying, forward ~ 1376
buying, instal(l)ment ~ 1573
buying power 487
buying price 488
buying rate 354
buy on hire purchase 481
buy on the instal(l)ment plan 481
buy on the instal(l)ment system 481
buy on the never-never 481
buy up 489

calculate 177, 490
calculating error 491
calculation 176, 492
calculation, cost price ~ 815
calendar year 493
call 484, 494
callable 496
callable bond 497
callable by lot 498
callable capital 499
callable debenture 497
call, at ~ 495
call, deposit at ~ 1004
call, deposit on ~ 1004
called in capital 500
called up capital 500
call for additional cover 501
call for funds 494
call in 502
call in (from circulation) 503
call loan 504
call, margin ~ 501
call money 505
call of more 485
call of X % on a share, pay a ~ 1899
call, on ~ 495
call on the market 506
call option 484
call premium 507
calm 508
cambist 361, 509
cancel a debt 510
cancel a mortgage 511
cancellation 512
cancellation of a debt 513
capital 514
capital abroad 515
capital account 516
capital, afflux of ~ 99
capital allowance 517
capital assets 518
capital balance 256
capital, borrow ~ 416
capital, borrowed ~ 417
capital, bring in ~ 436
capital budget 519
capital, business ~ 468
capital, called in ~ 500
capital, called up ~ 500
capital charges 520
capital, circulating ~ 468
capital, contribute ~ 436
capital contribution 521
capital, corporate ~ 544
capital cost 522
capital, debenture ~ 940

capital, drain of ~ 556
capital, efflux of ~ 556
capital, emigration of ~ 556
capital, employment of ~ 1160
capital endowment 523
capital, entry of ~ 99
capital equipment 523
capital, equity ~ 1178
capital, exodus of ~ 556
capital expenditure(s) 524
capital export country 525
capital exporting country 525
capital exports 526
capital, fixed ~ 518
capital flight 527
capital, flight ~ 1349
capital, floating ~ 468
capital flow 528
capital, foreign ~ 515, 1359
capital, foreign owned ~ 1359
capital formation 529
capital, furnish ~ 1407
capital, furnishing of ~ 1408
capital gain 530
capital gain(s) 531
capital gains tax 532
capital goods 533
capital held abroad 515
capital, idle ~ 1502
capital imports 534
capital income 535
capital increase 536
capital inflow 99
capital influx 99
capital, initial ~ 1564
capital, inject ~ 436
capital, injection of ~ 521
capital intensification 537
capital intensity 538
capital-intensive 539
capital interest 540
capital invested 541
capital investment 542
capitalisation 523, 543, 544
capitalisation issue 399
capitalisation of interest 156
capitalise 545
capitalised value 546
capitalise interest 547
capitalise profits 548
capital issue 549
capital, issued ~ 1638
capitalist 550
capitalization 523, 543, 544
capitalization issue 399
capitalization of interest 156
capitalize 545
capitalized value 546
capitalize interest 547
capitalize profits 548
capital, lack of ~ 559
capital levy 551
capital, loan ~ 1707
capital, loanable ~ 1707
capital loss 552, 553
capital market 554
capital movement 555
capital movements, balance of ~ 256
capital, opening ~ 1564
capital, operating ~ 468
capital, original ~ 1564
capital outflow 556
capital outlay(s) 524
capital, outside ~ 417
capital, overseas ~ 515
capital, paid in ~ 1880
capital, paid-up ~ 1880
capital, private ~ 1975
capital, procure ~ 416
capital, procurement of ~ 1405
capital, proprietors' ~ 1996
capital, provide ~ 1407
capital, provision of ~ 1408
capital, put in ~ 436
capital, put up ~ 436
capital, raise ~ 416
capital, raising of ~ 1405
capital, recycling of ~ 2050
capital, reduction of ~ 2063
capital, reflow of ~ 2071
capital, reflux of ~ 2071
capital requirements 557
capital resources 558
capital return 535
capital, risk ~ 1178
capital, risk-bearing ~ 1178
capital, savings ~ 2143
capital, scarcity of ~ 559
capital, share ~ 544
capital shortage 559
capital spending 524
capital stock 544
capital, stock ~ 544
capital stock, common ~ 697
capital (stock), increase the ~ 1544
capital stock, issued ~ 1638
capital stock, outstanding ~ 1638
capital stock, raise the ~ 1544
capital stock, reduce ~ 2061
capital stock, reduction of ~ 2064
capital stock tax 560
capital stock, watered ~ 2365
capital structure 561
capital, subscribed ~ 2232
capital subscription 562
capital, supply ~ 1407
capital tax 551
capital, tied-up ~ 518
capital, trading ~ 468
capital transfer 563
capital transfer tax 564
capital, uncalled ~ 2313
capital, unpaid ~ 2313
capital, unproductive ~ 1502
capital, venture ~ 1178
capital, want of ~ 559
capital, working ~ 468
capital yield 535
capital yield(s) tax 565
card, credit ~ 854
carried forward, profit ~ 1985
carry an interest of X percent 334
carry a sum to someone's credit 566
carry (a) X percent interest 334
carry-back, tax loss ~ 2272
carry-forward 150, 435
carry-forward, tax loss ~ 2273
carrying value 32
carry interest at a rate of X percent 334
carry-over 150, 435, 567
carry over a position 568
carry-over rate 569
carry to account 570
carry to reserve 68
carry to the reserve fund 68
cartel 571
cartel, price ~ 115
cash 572
cashable 574
cash account 575
cash a check 576
cash a cheque 576
cash assets 577
cash balance 253
cash balance, adverse ~ 96
cash book 578
cash box 579
cash, conversion into ~ 773
cash, convert into ~ 785
cash credit 580
cash deal 581
cash deficit 96
cash disbursements 582
cash discount 583
cash dividend 584
cash down 573
cash, drawing of ~ 601
cash earnings 585
cash expenditures 582
cash flow 586
cash, for ~ 573
cash holdings 587
cashier's allowance 133
cash, in ~ 573
cash in hand 587
cashless payment 588
cash liquidity 227
cash on delivery 589
cash on hand 587
cash order 590
cash outgoings 582
cash outlays 582
cash, pay ~ 1727
cash, payable in ~ 1897
cash payment 591
cash, petty ~ 1931
cash position 592
cash price 593
cash purchase 594
cash ratio 45
cash receipts 585
cash remittance 595
cash requirements 596
cash reserve 597
cash resources 587
cash sale 598
cash settlement, make a ~ 1727
cash short 96
cash surplus 599
cash takings 585
cash, terms strictly ~ 1897

cash transaction 581
cash voucher 590, 600
cash withdrawal 601
casual income 64
caution money 602
cease payment 603
cede 118
cedent 121
ceiling, credit ~ 855
ceiling, debt ~ 422
ceiling, fixing a ~ 1342
ceiling, loan ~ 855
ceiling on loans on securities 604
ceiling price 605
ceiling, setting a ~ 1342
central bank 606
central banks, loan by the ~ 1708
central office(s) 607
centre, burden ~ 461
centre, cost ~ 461
certificate, annuity ~ 162
certificate, bank ~ 290
certificate, interim ~ 1597
certificate, loan ~ 1709
certificate, mortgage ~ 1792
certificate of deposit 608
certificate of indebtedness 609
certificate, provisional ~ 1597
certificate, savings ~ 2141
certificate, scrip ~ 1597
certificate, share ~ 2170
certificate, stock ~ 2170
certificate, subscription right ~ 2115
certify a check 610
certify a cheque 610
cession 119
cessionary 120
chamber of commerce (and industry) 611
Chamber of Commerce, International ~ 1603
change 612
changer, money ~ 509
changing, money ~ 1231
charge 460, 613, 614, 615
chargeable to 616
charge account 617
charge, additional ~ 60
charge an account with 618
charge, commitment ~ 693
charge, depreciation ~ 132
charge, extra ~ 60
charge, handling ~ 1478
charge, mortgage ~ 1793
charge-off 138, 147
charges 619
charges, accrued ~ 39
charges, additional ~ 61
charge, safe deposit ~ 2124
charges, after allowance for ~ 131
charges, after deducting ~ 131
charges, bank ~ 291
charges, capital ~ 520
charges, clear of ~ 131
charges, credit ~ 805
charges deducted 131
charge, service ~ 80
charges, extra ~ 61
charges, financial ~ 1313
charges, financing ~ 1313
charges for depreciation write-off 620
charges, further ~ 61
charges, general ~ 1417
charges, incidental ~ 61
charges, indirect ~ 1417
charges, interest ~ 1587
charges, less ~ 621
charges, loan ~ 805
charges, minus ~ 621
charges, miscellaneous ~ 1764
charges, non-allowable ~ 1049
charges, overhead ~ 1417
charges, petty ~ 1764
charges, quit of ~ 131
charge(s), remittance ~ 2081
charges, special ~ 61
charges, sundry ~ 1764
charges, supplementary ~ 61
charges to be deducted 621
charge(s), transfer ~ 812, 2081
charge to the debit 615
charge to (the debit of) an account 618
charge up 615
charge up to an account 618
charge with debts 466
charging 613
chart of accounts 22
chattels 622
cheap money 623
check 624
check account 625
check, bearer ~ 339
check, blank ~ 378
check-book 626
check, cash a ~ 576
check, certify a ~ 610
check (cheque), collect a ~ 576
check (cheque), encash a ~ 576
check (cheque), issue a ~ 1115
check (cheque), make out a ~ 1115
check (cheque), write out a ~ 1115
check, clear a ~ 641
check clearing 627
check, draw a ~ 1115
check, dud ~ 241
check inflation 628
checking account 625
checking of credits 629
check not to order 630
check, N.S.F. ~ 241
check, pay by ~ 1901
check, postal ~ 1425
check, rubber ~ 241
check to order 631
check transactions 632
check, traveler's ~ 2297
check, uncovered ~ 241
check, uncrossed ~ 339
check without cover 241
check without funds 241
check, worthless ~ 241
cheque 624
cheque account 625
cheque-book 626
cheque, cash a ~ 576
cheque, certify a ~ 610
cheque clearing 627
cheque, draw a ~ 1115
cheque, giro ~ 1425
cheque not to order 630
cheque, pay by ~ 1901
cheque, post office ~ 1425
cheque, stop a ~ 2227
cheque to order 631
cheque transactions 632
cheque, traveller's ~ 2297
chief shareholder 633
c.i.f. 634
circles, financial ~ 1305
circulating 635
circulating capital 468
circulating medium 636
circulation), call in (from ~ 503
circulation, fiduciary ~ 1299
circulation, forced ~ 1356
circulation, in ~ 635
circulation, note ~ 308
circulation of bank notes 308
circulation of money 637
circulation of notes and coin(s) 638
circulation, velocity of ~ 2027
civil year 493
claim 639
claim, assign a ~ 207
claim, book ~ 404
claim, contingent ~ 757
claim, equalization ~ 1173
claim for refund 640
claim for restitution 640
claim, outstanding ~ 37
claims, assignation of ~ 208
claims, assignment of ~ 208
claims, transfer of ~ 208
claim, transfer a ~ 207
classification, account ~ 22
class, income ~ 1527
clause, dollar ~ 1088
clause, emergency ~ 1155
clause, escape ~ 1155
clause, gold ~ 1432
clear 148
clear a check 641
clear a cheque 641
clearance 642, 643
clearance account 644
clearance through customs 645
clear gain 646
clearing 642, 643
clearing account 644
clearing agreement 647
clearing balance 269
clearing, bank ~ 292
clearing bank 648
clearing business 643
clearing, check ~ 627
clearing dollar 29
clearing house 649
clearinghouse 649
clearing, inter-bank ~ 292
clearing office 649
clearing rate 650
clearing transactions 643

clear loss 651
clear of charges 131
clear of expenses 131
clear profit 646
climate, business ~ 469
close an account 652
closed-end investment company 653
closed-end trust 653
close money 654
close of an account 655
close the books 278
closing balances, list of ~ 1302
closing entry 656
closing of an account 655
closing price 657
closing quotation 657
closing rate 657
co-borrower 658
co-debtor 659
codification of accounts 22
coefficient, equivalence ~ 1181
coefficient, weighting ~ 2372
coin 660, 661, 662
coinage 663, 664, 665
coinage, debasement of ~ 939
coinage gold 666
coin, copper ~ 788
coin, current ~ 906
coin, divisional ~ 1083
coined gold 667
coin, fractional ~ 1083
coin gold 666
coin, gold ~ 1433
coin, minor ~ 1083
coin, small ~ 1083
coin(s), notes and ~ 1834
coin, token ~ 2283
collapse 668
collapse of prices 431
collateral 669
collateral, acceptable as ~ 9
collateral, afford ~ 101
collateral bill 363
collateral credit 670
collateral, eligible as ~ 9
collateral, furnish ~ 101
collateralize securities 671
collateral loan 672
collateral, offer ~ 101
collateral security 65, 669
collateral (security), advance against ~ 86
collateral security, give ~ 101
collation account 673
collect 589
collectability 674
collectable 574, 675, 676
collect a check (cheque) 576
collect a debt 677
collect a tax 678
collectibility 674
collectible 574, 675, 676
collection 679, 680
collection at source 681
collection of debts 682
collection of taxes 683
collective account 673
collective benefits 684
collective deposit 685
collector, debt ~ 955
Co. Ltd. 1537, 1690
commerce, liberalization of ~ 1684
commercial bank 310
commercial bill 356
commercial company 686
commercial credit 470
commercial loan 473
commercial loss 474
commercial paper 356
commercial profit 475
commercial register 687
commercial value 688
commercial year 478
commission 689
commission, accepting ~ 13
commission agent 690
commission, bank ~ 293
commission, commitment ~ 693
commission, drawee's ~ 13
commission rate 691
commitment 692
commitment, advance ~ 88
commitment charge 693
commitment commission 693
commitment, credit ~ 88
commitment, exchange ~ 1223
commitment, foreign exchange ~ 1223
committee of creditors 388
committee of inspection 388
commodities broker 694
commodities, export ~ 1266
commodities, import ~ 1510
commodity, basic ~ 329
commodity exchange 695
commodity price index 696
commodity, primary ~ 329
common capital stock 697
common denominator 698
common external tariff 699
Common Market 700
common shares 701
common stock 701
Commonwealth preference 702
community budget 703
community, financial ~ 1305
commutation bond 704
company 686
company, affiliated ~ 98
company, commercial ~ 686
company, controlled ~ 98
company, controlling ~ 769
company, finance ~ 1308
company financial year 705
company, holding ~ 1494
company, incorporated ~ 1537
company, investment ~ 653
company, joint stock ~ 1537
company, limited liability ~ 1537, 1690
company, loan ~ 850
company, parent ~ 769
company, portfolio ~ 653
company, private limited ~ 1690
company, public limited ~ 1537
company, public utility ~ 2009
company, stock ~ 1537
company, subsidiary ~ 98
company, trading ~ 686
company, trust ~ 2306
compensate 706
compensate for a loss 707
compensation 708, 709
compensation balance 247
compensation fund 710
compensation transaction 327
compensatory duty 711
compensatory tax 712
competition, free ~ 1390
competitive 713
competitiveness 714
complete cost accounting 4
complete payment 715
component of demand 716
composite entry 717
composition 718
composition agreement 719
compound entry 717
compound interest 720
comptroller 216
compulsory conversion 721
compulsory exchange 722
compulsory loan 723
compulsory rate (of exchange) 722
compulsory saving 724
computation 492
compute 490
concealed inflation 725
concealed reserves 726
concern 727
concession 728
concession, tax ~ 2263
conditions, credit ~ 856
conditions of issue of a loan 729
conduct of the finances 730
confirmation, bank ~ 290
confirmation of receipt 47
consideration (in return) 731
consideration of the payment of, in ~ 732
consolidate a debt 733
consolidated bonds 734
consolidated debt 735
consolidated loan stock 734
consolidated statement 736
consolidated stock 734
consolidation 737
consolidation loan 738
consolidation statement 739
consols 734
consortium 740
consortium credit 741
constant prices, at ~ 742
consultant, financial ~ 1309
consultant, tax ~ 2264
consumables 743
consumer 744
consumer credit 745
consumer demand 746
consumer durables 747
consumer expenditure 748
consumer goods 743
consumer goods, durable ~ 747
consumer price 749

consumer resistance 750
consumer spending 748
consumption 751
consumption, domestic ~ 1092
consumption goods 743
consumption, home ~ 1092, 1497
consumption, household ~ 1499
consumption, internal ~ 1092
consumption, own ~ 1497
consumption, per-capita ~ 1920
consumption, public ~ 2002
consumption tax 752
contango 567, 568, 569
contango rate 569
contango transaction 753
content, gold ~ 1434
contingencies 754
contingency fund 755
contingency reserve 756
contingent claim 757
contingent fund 755
contingent liability 758
contingent obligation 758
contingent reserve 756
contingent tax liability 759
continuation business 567
continuation rate 569
continue a position 568
contra account 760
contract a debt 761
contract a loan 762
contract bought note 425
contract(ing) price 114
contract, lease ~ 1666
contract note 425, 440
contract note, broker's ~ 425, 440
contract sold note 440
contractual liability 763
contractual savings 764
contract, underwriting ~ 2321
contra(-entry) 281
contribute capital 436
contribution 765
contributions, social security ~ 2186
contribution to capital 521
control account 766
control, credit ~ 629
control, exchange ~ 1224
control, foreign exchange ~ 1224
control inflation 628
control, investment ~ 1044
controlled company 98
controlled currency 767
controlled economy 768
controlled exchange 722
controlled rate (of exchange) 722
controller 216
controlling company 769
controlling interest 770
control, price ~ 1961
controls, exchange ~ 900
controls, foreign exchange ~ 900
control(s), wage ~ 2360
conversion 771
conversion bond 704
conversion, compulsory ~ 721
conversion factor 772
conversion, forced ~ 721
conversion into cash 773
conversion into money 773
conversion, involuntary ~ 721
conversion loan 774
conversion of a loan 775
conversion of debts 776
conversion option 777
conversion rate 778
conversion right 777
convert a loan 779
convertibility 780
convertibility, external ~ 1278
convertibility for residents 781
convertibility, internal ~ 781
convertibility, non-resident ~ 1278
convertible 782
convertible bond 783
convertible debenture 783
convertible loan 784
convert into cash 785
convert into money 785
convey 118
conveyance 119
co-obligor 659
cooperative 786
co-operative 786
co-operative, credit ~ 787
co-operative credit bank 787
cooperative, producer ~ 1983
cooperative, producers' ~ 1983
co-operative society 786
copper 788
copper coin 788
copper money 788
corner the market 789
corporate assets 790
corporate bond 389
corporate capital 544
corporate income 791
corporate income tax 792
corporate investor 793
corporate tax 792
corporation, bank ~ 294
corporation income tax 792
Corporation, International Finance ~ 1605
corporation, public service ~ 2009
corporation, stock ~ 1537
corporation tax 792
corporation, trust ~ 2306
correcting entry 71
correction of the balance of payments 794
cost 795
cost accounting 797, 798
cost accounting, complete ~ 4
cost accounting, full ~ 4
cost accounting, partial ~ 1045
cost, actual ~ 54
cost apportionment sheet 799
cost apportionment statement 799
cost, at ~ 796
cost averaging 800
cost benefit analysis 801
cost center 461
cost centre 461
cost control accounts 802
cost effectiveness analysis 801
cost equalisation 800
cost equalization 800
cost, flotation ~ 1353
cost, historical ~ 804
cost-induced inflation 803
cost inflation 803
costing 797
costing, absorption ~ 4
costing, preproduction ~ 1190
costing, uniform ~ 2325
cost, insurance, freight 634
cost, marginal ~ 1733
cost of acquisition 804
cost of borrowing 805
cost of capital 522
cost of credit 805
cost of labor 806
cost of labour 806
cost of living 807
cost of living allowance 808
cost of living bonus 808
cost of living, high ~ 1483
cost of living index 809
cost of maintenance 810
cost of manufacture 811
cost of production 811
cost of transfer 812
cost, opportunity ~ 1853
cost per unit 813
cost price 814
cost price, at ~ 796
cost price calculation 815
cost-price spiral 816
cost-push inflation 803
cost, real ~ 54
costs, additional ~ 61
costs, administrative ~ 79
costs, direct ~ 1043
cost(s), estimated ~ 1189
costs, exceptional non-recurring ~ 1202
costs, extra ~ 61
costs, financing ~ 1313
costs, fixed ~ 1336
costs, further ~ 61
costs, incidental ~ 61
costs, indirect ~ 1417
costs, issue ~ 1353
costs, miscellaneous ~ 1764
costs, operating ~ 1850
costs, overestimate of ~ 1870
costs, overhead ~ 1417
cost(s), predetermined ~ 1189
costs, prime ~ 1043
cost(s), replacement ~ 2091
costs, running ~ 1850
costs, semi-variable ~ 2164
costs, special ~ 61
costs, sundry ~ 1764
costs, supplementary ~ 61
costs, transport ~ 2295
cost structure 817
costs, variable ~ 2346
costs, wage ~ 2359
costs, working ~ 1850
cost unit 818
cost value 50
counter-bill 819

counter-cyclical equalization reserve 820
counter-entry 281
counterfoil 821
counterguarantee 238
counterinflationary 170
counterpart 822
counterpart fund 823
countersecurity 238
countersurety 238
countervailing duty 711
counter value 822
country, capital export ~ 525
country, capital exporting ~ 525
country, creditor ~ 871
country, debtor ~ 959
country, hard currency ~ 1480
country in surplus 824
country of exportation 825
country of importation 826
country's finances, the ~ 827
country, soft currency ~ 2188
coupon 828
coupon bond 830
coupon, cum ~ 829
coupon, dividend ~ 1078
coupon, ex ~ 831
coupon, half-yearly ~ 1475
coupon, interest ~ 1588
coupon, lapsed ~ 1664
coupon off 831
coupon, renewal ~ 2085
coupon, semi-annual ~ 1475
coupon sheet 832
coupon sheet, share without ~ 2176
coupons, renewal of ~ 2087
coupon, statute-barred ~ 1664
coupon, unmatured ~ 2330
coupon, (up)on presentation of the ~ 1958
coupon, (up)on surrender of the ~ 1958
coupon, with ~ 829
course of business 833
course of trade 833
cover 834
cover, additional ~ 62
cover a deficit 836
coverage requirements 837
cover a loss 707
cover by mortgage 838
cover, forward ~ 1377
cover, further ~ 62
cover, gold ~ 1435
covering, bear ~ 335
covering operation 839
covering, short ~ 335
covering transaction 839
cover ratio 840
cover, requisite ~ 837
cover, serve as ~ 2166
cover, without ~ 835
crash 668
create a reserve 454
creation of credit 841
creation of money 842
credit 206, 843, 844, 845
creditable 846
credit, acceptance ~ 11
credit, additional ~ 63
credit advice 847, 848
credit against collateral (security) 670
credit against security 670
credit, allow a ~ 126
credit applicant 172
credit application 173
credit association 787
credit a sum to someone 566
credit, authorisation of ~ 220
credit, authorise a ~ 126
credit, authorization of ~ 220
credit, authorize a~ 126
credit balance 849
credit, bank ~ 295
credit bank 850
credit bank, co-operative ~ 787
credit, bill ~ 11
credit, blank ~ 379
credit, business ~ 470
credit business 851
credit buying 852
credit by way of guarantee 853
credit card 854
credit, cash ~ 580
credit ceiling 855
credit charges 805
credit, commercial ~ 470
credit commitment 88
credit conditions 856
credit, consortium ~ 741
credit, consumer ~ 745
credit control 629
credit co-operative 787
credit, cost of ~ 805
credit, creation of ~ 841
credit dealings 851
credit, discount ~ 1059
credit, documentary ~ 1085
credit, easing of ~ 1145
credit entry 857
credit, exceed a ~ 1201
credit expansion 858
credit, extend a ~ 126, 1272
credit, extension of ~ 220, 1275
credit facilities 421
credit flow 859
credit flux 859
credit, further ~ 63
credit, grant a ~ 126
credit, granting of ~ 220
credit, grant of ~ 220
credit guarantee 860
credit, guaranteed ~ 670
credit, hire purchase ~ 1488
credit in favor of, open a ~ 1847
credit in favour of, open a ~ 1847
credit inflation 861
crediting 844
credit, instal(l)ment ~ 1488
credit institution 850
credit instrument 862
credit insurance 863
credit interest 376
credit, interim ~ 434
credit item 857
credit, letter of ~ 1678
credit limit 855
credit line 855
credit margin 864
credit, medium-term ~ 1753
credit memorandum 847
credit note 847
credit on collateral (security) 670
credit on current account 87
credit on joint account 865
credit on mortgage 866
credit on personal estate 867
credit on personal property 867
credit on real estate 868
credit on real property 868
credit on securities 869
credit on security 670
credit, open ~ 379
credit, opening of a ~ 1848
credit operations 851
creditor 870
creditor, bond ~ 390
creditor, book ~ 405
creditor country 871
creditor, foreign ~ 1360
creditor nation 871
creditor, preferential ~ 1948
creditor, preferred ~ 1948
creditor, prior ~ 1948
creditors, board of ~ 388
creditors, committee of ~ 388
creditor, secured ~ 2150
creditor side 206
credit, overdraw a ~ 1201
credit, paper ~ 11
credit, personal ~ 1927
credit policy 872
credit, prolong a ~ 1272
credit, prolongation of ~ 1275
credit purchase 852
credit rating 873
credit, reimbursement ~ 1085
credit, relaxation of ~ 1145
credit, renew a ~ 1272
credit, renewal of ~ 1275
credit restriction 874
credit restrictions, ease ~ 1143
credit restrictions, relax ~ 1143
credit, retail ~ 745
credit, revocable ~ 2113
credit, revolving ~ 2114
credit sale 875
credits, checking of ~ 629
credits, domestic ~ 1093
credit, secured ~ 670
credit, sell on ~ 2163
credits, frozen ~ 1401
credit side 206
credits, investment ~ 1620
credit slip 876, 877
credit society 787
credit someone with a sum 566
credit, special ~ 2194
credit squeeze 874
credit standing 873
credit status 873
credit stringency 878
credit, supplemental ~ 63

credit, supplementary ~ 63
credit surveillance 629
credit, swap ~ 2252
credit system 879
credit, temporary ~ 434
credit terms 856
credit the account (with) 880
credit, tightness of ~ 878
credit, trade ~ 470
credit transactions 851
credit transfer 318
credit, transitional ~ 434
credit union 787
credit volume 881
credit voucher 876
creditworthiness 873
creditworthy 846
creeping inflation 882
crossed check 883
crossed cheque 883
cross-entry 281
cross exchange rate 884
cross holding 885
cross rate 884
crumbling of prices 886
cum coupon 829
cum dividend 887
cum new 888
cum rights 888
cumulative dividend 889
cumulative prefential dividend 889
cumulative preference shares 890
cumulative preferred stock 890
curator in bankruptcy 209
curb 891
curb inflation 628
curb market 891
curb stocks 892
currencies, forward ~ 1378
currency 308, 893, 894, 895
currency circulation 637
currency, controlled ~ 767
currency dealer 509
currency depreciation 896
currency devaluation 897
currency, divisional ~ 1083
currency, domestic ~ 1094
currency erosion 896
currency, floating ~ 1350
currency, fluctuating ~ 1350
currency, forced ~ 1356
currency, foreign ~ 1361
currency, fractional ~ 1083
currency, hard ~ 1479
currency, home ~ 1094
currency, legal ~ 1669
currency, local ~ 1094
currency, managed ~ 767
currency manipulation 898
currency, national ~ 1094
currency, paper ~ 1355
currency reform 899
currency regulations 900
currency reserve 901
currency, reserve ~ 2100
currency restrictions 902
currency, soft ~ 2187
currency, sound ~ 2191
currency stability 903
currency, stable ~ 2207
currency, strong ~ 1479
currency, treasury ~ 2302
currency unit 904
currency, unstable ~ 1350
currency, weak ~ 2187
current account 23
current account, advance on ~ 87
current account, balance of payments on ~ 262
current account, credit on ~ 87
current assets 905
current coin 906
current coin and currency 638
current exchange rate 907
current expenses 908
current interest 909
current liabilities 910
current market price 911
current market value 912, 913
current money 914
current price 911
current rate 913
current rate (of exchange) 907
current ratio 45
current transfers, balance of ~ 257
current value 912, 913
curtail expenses 915
customable 916
customs 917
customs barrier 918
customs clearance 645
customs declaration 919
customs dues 917
customs duty 917
customs entry 919
customs-exempt 920
customs-free 920
customs receipts 921
customs revenue 921
customs tariff 922
customs tariff, external ~ 1279
customs union 923
cut 924
cut back 924
cut down expenses 915
cut expenses 915
cut in the dividend 925
cut in the minimum lending rate 926
cut in the price 927
cut one's losses 928
cut-rate price 322
cycle, business ~ 471
cycle, economic ~ 471
cycle, trade ~ 471
cyclical budget 929
cyclical fluctuation 930

damages 708
date, balance sheet ~ 272
date due 931
date, expiration ~ 1263
date, expiry ~ 1263
date of maturity 931
date, value ~ 2343
day, account ~ 24
daybook 932
day, pay ~ 24
day, settlement ~ 24
day, settling ~ 24
days of grace 933
days of respite 933
day-to-day loan 504
day-to-day money 505
dead 508
dead loss 934
deal 320
deal, cash ~ 581
dealer, currency ~ 509
dealer, foreign exchange ~ 509
dealer, money ~ 509
dealer's rebate 935
deal, forward ~ 1379
deal, forward exchange ~ 1381
deal, hire purchase ~ 1489
dealing 320
dealing in foreign notes and coins 936
dealings before the opening of the stock exchange 937
dealings, credit ~ 851
dealings, foreign ~ 1358
dealings, foreign exchange ~ 1241
deal, instal(l)ment ~ 1489
deal, option ~ 1855
deal, spot ~ 581
deal, spot exchange ~ 2202
deals, security ~ 1222
deals, stock ~ 1222
dear money 654
death duty 938
death tax 938
debacle 668
debasement of coinage 939
debenture 389
debenture bond 389
debenture, callable ~ 497
debenture capital 940
debenture, convertible ~ 783
debenture, debt adjustment ~ 704
debenture, defaulted ~ 980
debenture holder 390
debenture, irredeemable ~ 1636
debenture issue 392
debenture loan 941
debenture, mortgage ~ 1792
debenture, perpetual ~ 1925
debenture, redeemable ~ 497
debit 613, 615, 942, 943
debit advice 945
debit an account with 618
debit balance 93
debit, be in ~ 944
debit entry 946
debiting 613
debit interest 947
debit item 946
debit note 948
debit of, to the ~ 616
debit side 943
debit to an account 618
deblock 949
deblocking 950
debt 951

debt, acknowledg(e)ment of ~ 46
debt, active ~ 37
debt adjustment debenture 704
debt administration 954
debt, bad ~ 242
debt barred by limitation 324
debt, be up to one's ears in ~ 953
debt, bonded ~ 391
debt, book ~ 406
debt, cancel a ~ 510
debt, cancellation of a ~ 513
debt ceiling 422
debt, collect a ~ 677
debt collection 682
debt collector 955
debt, consolidate a ~ 733
debt, consolidated ~ 735
debt, contract a ~ 761
debt, domestic ~ 1095
debt due 37
debt, external ~ 1280
debt, fall into ~ 1294
debt financing 956
debt, floating ~ 1351
debt, foreign ~ 1280
debt, fund a ~ 733
debt, funded ~ 735
debt, get into ~ 1294
debt, in ~ 952
debt, incur a ~ 761
debt, instal(l)ment ~ 1574
debt, internal ~ 1095
debt, irrecoverable ~ 242
debt, joint and several ~ 1650
debt limit 422
debt, make a ~ 761
debt management 954
debt, national ~ 1798
debt on mortgage 957
debtor 958
debtor, bill ~ 362
debtor country 959
debtor, defaulting ~ 981
debtor, dilatory ~ 981
debtor, joint ~ 659
debtor, joint and several ~ 1651
debtor nation 959
debtor side 943
debtor, slow ~ 981
debtor, tardy ~ 981
debtor to sales ratio 960
debt, outstanding ~ 37
debt, passive ~ 36
debt payable 36
debt, personal ~ 1928
debt, prescribed ~ 324
debt, private ~ 1928
debt, proof of ~ 609
debt, public ~ 1798
debt receivable 37
debt, recover a ~ 677
debt recovery 682
debt, remission of a ~ 513
debt, remit a ~ 510
debt, repudiate a ~ 2092
debt, repudiation of a ~ 2093
debt, run into ~ 1294
debt, run up a ~ 761
debts 961
debts, bank ~ 296
debts, burden with ~ 466
debts, charge with ~ 466
debts, conversion of ~ 776
debts, doubtful ~ 1110
debts, encumber with ~ 466
debt service 962
debts, load with ~ 466
debts, short-term ~ 910
debt, statute-barred ~ 324
debt to equity ratio 963
debt, unfunded ~ 1351
debt, unified ~ 735
debt, unify a ~ 733
debt, unsecured ~ 2332
debt, waive a ~ 510
debt, waiver of a ~ 513
declaration, customs ~ 919
declaration of a dividend 964
declaration of bankruptcy 69
declaration of suretyship 394
declare a dividend 965
declared reserves 966
declared value 967
decline 968
decline in prices 886
decline in value 969, 970
declining balance depreciation 7
decontrol of prices 971
decrease in prices 886
decrease in value 969, 970
deduct at source 972
deduct beforehand 973
deductible loss 974
deduct in advance 973
deducting charges 621
deducting charges, after ~ 131
deducting expenses 621
deducting expenses, after ~ 131
deduction at source 975
deduction in advance 89
deduction of tax at source 681
deduction, previous ~ 89
deduction, prior ~ 89
deductions, disallowed ~ 1049
deduction, tax ~ 2261
deed of arrangement 719
deed of surety(ship) 394
deed of trust 976
deed, warranty ~ 394
defalcate 977
defalcation 978
defaulted bond 980
defaulted debenture 980
defaulter 981
default, in ~ 979
defaulting debtor 981
default in paying 982
default in payment 982
default interest 983
defer a payment 984
deferred share 985
deferred taxation 986
deferred taxes 986
deferred terms, on ~ 987
deficiency 988
deficiency statement 274
deficit 988
deficit, balance ~ 93
deficit, balance of payments ~ 261
deficit, budget ~ 95
deficit budgeting 989
deficit, cash ~ 96
deficit, cover a ~ 836
deficit, dollar ~ 1089
deficit, external ~ 261
deficit financing 989
deficit, fiscal ~ 1330
deficit in the trade account 265
deficit in the trade balance 265
deficit, make good a ~ 836
deficit, make up a ~ 836
deficit, meet a ~ 836
deficit, operating ~ 474
deficit spending 989
deficit, tax ~ 1330
deficit, trading ~ 474
deflate 990
deflation 991
deflationary 992
deflationary spiral 993
deflationary trend 994
deflationist 992, 995
deflator 996
degressive tax 997
delay 998
delay a payment 984
delay in payment 999
del credere 1000
delivery, forward ~ 1380
delivery, future ~ 1380
de luxe articles 1001
deluxe articles 1001
demand 1002
demand bill 1003
demand, component of ~ 716
demand deposit 1004
demand, domestic ~ 1096, 1097
demand draft 1003
demand factor 716
demand for consumer goods 746
demand, household ~ 1097
demand-induced inflation 1005
demand inflation 1005
demand liabilities 1006
demand loan 504
demand, money ~ 1774
demand note 1007
demand obligations 1006
demand, on ~ 495
demand, payable on ~ 1896
demand-pull inflation 1005
demand rate 354
demand, supply and ~ 2242
demonetization 1008
demonetize 503
denationalization 1009
denominated in dollars 1010
denomination 1011
denominator, common ~ 698
department, inland revenue ~ 1242
depletion of the reserves 1012
deposit 602, 1013, 1014, 1015
deposit account 1016
depositary 1017

deposit as security 1018
deposit at call 1004
deposit at notice 1019
deposit, bank ~ 297
deposit bank 1020
deposit book 1021
deposit book, savings bank ~ 2140
deposit box, safety ~ 2123
deposit, certificate of ~ 608
deposit, collective ~ 685
deposit, demand ~ 1004
deposit, fixed ~ 1337
deposit, fixed-period ~ 1337
deposit form 1022
deposit, guarantee ~ 602
deposit liabilities 1023
deposit money 307
deposit on call 1004
deposit on giro account 1024
deposit on transfer account 1024
depositor 1025, 1026
depository 1017
deposit receipt 608, 877
deposit, savings ~ 2144
deposit, sight ~ 1004
deposits, inter-bank ~ 1582
deposit slip 608, 877, 1022
deposit ticket 877
deposit, time ~ 1337
deposit warrant 608
depreciable assets 1027
depreciate 970, 1028
depreciation 138, 969, 1029
depreciation, accelerated ~ 7
depreciation allowance 132
depreciation allowance, annual ~ 157
depreciation, allowance for ~ 132
depreciation, budgetary ~ 445
depreciation charge 132
depreciation charge, annual ~ 157
depreciation, currency ~ 896
depreciation, declining balance ~ 7
depreciation, exchange ~ 897
depreciation for wear and tear 1030
depreciation fund 132
depreciation, increasing charge ~ 1545
depreciation, monetary ~ 896
depreciation on replacement value 143
depreciation, progressive ~ 1545
depreciation, provision for ~ 132
depreciation rate 144
depreciation, reducing ~ 7
depreciation reserve 132
depreciation, straight line ~ 2228
depreciation, variable ~ 2347
depreciation write-off, charges for ~ 620
depressed 508
depression 1031
detailed account 429
detailed analysis 429
detailed statement 429
determination of the equivalence of exchange 1032
determination of the exchange parity 1032
determination, price ~ 1962
determine a price 1033
devalorize 1028
devaluate 1028
devaluation 1029
devaluation, currency ~ 897
devalue 1028
development aid 1034
development assistance 1034
development bank 1035
development loan 1036
diary, bill ~ 359, 360
difference 1037
difference in price(s) 1038
difference in the rate of exchange 1039
difference, split the ~ 2201
differential 1037
differential duty 1040
differential, interest ~ 1412
differential, price ~ 1038
differential tariff 1041
difficulties, financial ~ 1314
difficulties, pecuniary ~ 1314
dilatory debtor 981
diminish in value 970
dip into the reserves 1042
direct costs 1043
directed economy 768
direction of (capital) investment 1044
direct sectional costing 1045
direct tax 1046
dirigisme 1047
disagio 1048
disallowed deductions 1049
disburse 1050
disburse a dividend 1051
disbursement of dividends 1052
disbursements 1053
disbursements, cash ~ 582
disbursement voucher 590
discharge 51, 139, 148
discharge a bill of exchange 1054
disclosed reserves 966
discontinue payment(s) 603
discount 127, 1048, 1055, 1057
discountable paper 283
discount bank 1058
discount, be at a ~ 1056
discount broker 361
discount commission 1055
discount credit 1059
discounted domestic bill 1060
discount for cash 583
discount house 1058
discount market 370
discount rate 1061
discount rate, increase in the ~ 1541
discount rate, reduction in the ~ 926
discount, trade ~ 935
disequilibrium 1062
dishoarding 1063
dishonored bill 365
dishonoured bill 365
disinflation 1064
disinflationary 1065
disinvestment 1066
disparity 1067
disparity in price(s) 1038
disposable income 1068
dissaving 1069
dissolution 1070
dissolve 1071
distrain (on; upon) 211
distraint 191
distress 191
distributable profit 1072
distribute a dividend 1051
distribution, hidden ~ 1482
distribution, non-~ 1826
distribution of dividends 1052
distribution of profits 183
distribution of property 1073
distribution of shares 125
distribution of wealth 1074
distribution sector 1075
distributions, tax on ~ 565
dividend 1076, 1077
dividend, cash ~ 584
dividend coupon 1078
dividend, cum ~ 887
dividend, cumulative ~ 889
dividend, cut in the ~ 925
dividend, declaration of a ~ 964
dividend, declare a ~ 965
dividend, disburse a ~ 1051
dividend, distribute a ~ 1051
dividend, entitled to (a) ~ 1170
dividend equalization reserve 1079
dividend, extra ~ 398
dividend, final ~ 1303
dividend, fix a ~ 965
dividend, fixation of a ~ 964
dividend, interim ~ 1598
dividend, national ~ 1799
dividend off 1080
dividend on 887
dividend, passing of a ~ 1826
dividend, pay a ~ 1051
dividend policy 1081
dividend, preference ~ 1945
dividend, preferential ~ 1945
dividend, preferred ~ 1945
dividend, prescribed ~ 1954
dividend reduction 925
dividend remission 925
dividends, disbursement of ~ 1052
dividends, distribution of ~ 1052
dividends, payment of ~ 1052
dividend, special ~ 398
dividend, stock ~ 400
dividend, surplus ~ 398
dividend warrant 1078
dividend, with ~ 887
dividend yield 1082
divisional coin 1083
divisional currency 1083
do business 1084
documentary credit 1085
document, negotiable ~ 1806
dodging, tax ~ 2266

dollar, accounting ~ 29
dollar, agreement ~ 29
dollar area 1086
dollar bloc 1086
dollar bond 1087
dollar clause 1088
dollar, clearing ~ 29
dollar deficit 1089
dollar, Euro~ 1193
dollar gap 1089
dollar, offset ~ 29
dollars, denominated in ~ 1010
dollars, expressed in ~ 1010
dollar shortage 1090
dollars, made out in ~ 1010
dollar stringency 1090
domestic bill (of exchange) 1091
domestic consumption 1092
domestic credits 1093
domestic currency 1094
domestic debt 1095
domestic demand 1096, 1097
domestic equilibrium 1098
domestic loan 1099
domestic market 1100
domestic trade 1101
domicile 1102
domicile, fiscal ~ 1331
donation 1103
donator 1104
donor 1104
dormant partner 1105
double entry 1106
double entry bookkeeping 1107
double option 1108
double posting 1106
double standard 375
double taxation 1109
doubtful accounts 1110
doubtful debts 1110
doubtful notes and accounts 1110
doubtful receivables 1110
down-payment 1014
downswing 968
downtrend 344
downturn 968
downward trend 344
draft 356
draft, bank ~ 284
draft, demand ~ 1003
draft, presentation ~ 1003
draft, return ~ 819
draft, sight ~ 1003
draft, usance ~ 358
drain of capital 556
draw 1111, 1112, 1113
draw a balance 279
draw a bill of exchange upon somebody 1114
draw a check 1115
draw a cheque 1115
draw an interest of X percent 334
draw (a) X percent interest 334
drawback 1116
draw by lot 1112
drawee 1117
drawee's commission 13
drawer 1118
drawing 1111, 1119
drawing account 23, 625
drawing of cash 601
drawing on the International Monetary Fund 1120
drawing rights (on) 1121
drawing rights, special ~ 2195
draw interest at a rate of X percent 334
draw on a loan 1122
draw on the International Monetary Fund 1123
draw up a balance sheet 279
draw upon a loan 1122
draw upon the International Monetary Fund 1123
draw (up)on the reserves 1042
draw up the inventory 1124
drop 1125
drop in prices 886
drop in value 969, 970
dud check 241
due 675, 1126, 1127
due, amount ~ 151
due August 15 1129
due, balance ~ 252
due, become ~ 347
due date 931
due date, payment on ~ 1910
due, fall ~ 347
due, interest ~ 1589
due on August 15, falling ~ 1129
due, past ~ 1869
dues 614
dues, customs ~ 917
dues, registration ~ 2077
due, sum ~ 151
due, when ~ 1128
dull 508
dullness 1130
dumping 1131
dump on the market 1132
durable consumer goods 747
durable goods 1133
durable means of production 1134
durables 1133
durables, consumer ~ 747
dutiable 916
duty 614, 917, 1135
duty, ad valorem ~ 82
duty, antidumping ~ 169
duty, compensatory ~ 711
duty, countervailing ~ 711
duty, death ~ 938
duty, differential ~ 1040
duty, equalizing ~ 711
duty, estate ~ 938
duty, excise ~ 752, 1245
duty, exempt from ~ 1246
duty-free 920
duty, legacy ~ 938
duty, liable to ~ 916
duty, preferential ~ 1949
duty, probate ~ 938
duty, prohibitive ~ 1993
duty, protective ~ 1998
duty, stamp ~ 2211
duty, subject to ~ 916
duty, succession ~ 938
duty, transfer ~ 812

E. and O.E. 1184
early payment 92
earmark 181
earn an interest of X percent 334
earn (a) X percent interest 334
earned income 1136
earned surplus 1137
earnest 1138
earnest money 602
earning capacity 1139
earning power 1139
earnings 229, 1140, 1141
earnings, cash ~ 585
earnings, loss of ~ 1718
earnings per share 1142
earnings, retained ~ 2108
earnings statement 275
earnings, tax on ~ 1989
earn interest at a rate of X percent 334
ease credit restrictions 1143
easing in money rates 1144
easing of credit 1145
easing of prices 886
easy money 623
easy terms, on ~ 987
economic 1146, 1147
economic balance sheet 1148
economic barrier 1149
Economic Community, European ~ 1194
economic cycle 471
economic fluctuation 930
economic phase 1150
economic planning and control 1047
economics 1151
economic science 1151
economic trend 477
economize 924
economy 477
economy, controlled ~ 768
economy, directed ~ 768
economy, financial ~ 1304
economy, free ~ 1393
economy, managed ~ 768
economy, market ~ 1741
economy, money ~ 1775
economy, planned ~ 768
economy, political ~ 1151
E.E.C. 1194
effective value 56
effective yield 57
effect payments 1152
efficiency pay 1153
efficiency wage 1153
efflux of capital 556
elasticity of exchange rates 1154
eligible as collateral 9
eligible paper 283
EMA 1196
embargo on imports 319
embarrassment, financial ~ 1314
embezzle 977
embezzlement 978
emergency clause 1155

emigration of capital 556
emission of bank notes 1156
emit a loan 1157
emoluments 1158
employees' shares 1159
employment of capital 1160
employment of funds 1160
encashable 574
encash a check (cheque) 576
encashment 679
encouragement of saving(s) 1161
encroach (up)on the reserves 1042
encumber with a mortgage 465
encumber with debts 466
encumbrance 460
endorsable bill 374
endorse a bill 1162
endorsee 1163
endorsement 1164
endorser 1165
endorser, preceding ~ 1944
endorser, previous ~ 1944
endorser's liability 1166
endorser, subsequent ~ 2239
endow 1167
endowment 1168
endowment, capital ~ 523
enter as a liability 402
enter as an asset 403
enter a sum to someone's credit 566
enter (in the books) 401
enter in the budget 443
enterprise 467
enterprise, free ~ 1391
enterprise, government ~ 1448
enterprise, private ~ 1976, 1977
enterprise, public ~ 1448
enterprise, state ~ 1448
entertainment allowance 1169
entertainment expenses 1169
entitled to (a) dividend 1170
entrepreneur 1171
entry 409
entry, adjusting ~ 71
entry, balancing ~ 281
entry, book ~ 409
entry, composite ~ 717
entry, compound ~ 717
entry, correcting ~ 71
entry, credit ~ 857
entry, customs ~ 919
entry, debit ~ 946
entry, double ~ 1106
entry, journal ~ 1655
entry of capital 99
entry, offsetting ~ 281
entry, per contra ~ 281
entry, rectifying ~ 71
entry, reversing ~ 281
entry, suspense ~ 2249
entry, unbalanced ~ 2312
EPU 1198
equalisation, cost ~ 800
equalization 1172
equalization claim 1173
equalization fund 710
equalization levy 712
equalization of burdens 1174
equalization of taxes 1175
equalization reserve, dividend ~ 1079
equalization tax 712
equalizing duty 711
equilibrium 1176
equilibrium, budgetary ~ 251
equilibrium, domestic ~ 1098
equipment, capital ~ 523
equity 701, 1177
equity capital 1178
equity investment 1179
equity, proprietors' ~ 1996
equity, shareholders' ~ 1809, 1996
equity, stockholders' ~ 1996
equivalence 1180
equivalence coefficient 1181
equivalence of exchange 1182
equivalence of exchange, determination of the ~ 1032
equivalent 822
equivalents, money ~ 1776
erosion, currency ~ 896
error in calculation 491
errors, allowance for ~ 133
errors and omissions 1183
errors and omissions excepted 1184
escape clause 1155
escrow, in ~ 1185
establish a price 1033
establishment, banking ~ 294
establish quotas 1186
estate, bankrupt ~ 317
estate, bankrupt's ~ 317
estate duty 938
estate, landed ~ 1661
estate, personal ~ 622
estate, real ~ 1508
estate tax 938
estimate 176, 177, 1187
estimate, approximate ~ 184
estimated assessment 1188
estimated cost(s) 1189
estimate, rough ~ 184
estimates, budget ~ 449
estimating 1190
estimation 176
Euro-bond market 1191
Euro-currency market 1192
Eurodollar 1193
Euro-Market 700
European Economic Community 1194
European Investment Bank 1195
European Monetary Agreement 1196
European Monetary Cooperation Fund 1197
European Payments Union 1198
evaluate 177
evaluation 176
evasion, tax ~ 2266
evening up 1199
evolution 1200
exactable 675
exceed a credit 1201
exceptional non-recurring costs 1202
exceptional price 1203
excess 1204
excess amount 1205
excess demand 1206
excess demand inflation 1005
excess indebtedness 1207
excessive money circulation 6
excessive price 1208
excessive purchasing power 1209
excessive supply 1210
excess liquidity 1211
excess money supply 6
excess of demand 1206
excess of expenditure 1212
excess of liabilities over assets 1207
excess of money 6
excess (of) purchasing power 1209
excess (of) supply 1210
excess price 1208
excess profit 1213
excess profits tax 1214
excess value 1215
exchange 1216, 1217, 1218
exchangeable value 1219
exchange adjustment 75
exchange arbitrage 186
exchange arbitration 186
exchange bank 1220
exchange broker 361, 509
exchange business 1221, 1222
exchange commitment 1223
exchange, commodity ~ 695
exchange, compulsory ~ 722
exchange control 1224
exchange, controlled ~ 722
exchange control regulations 900
exchange controls 900
exchange depreciation 897
exchange, equivalence of ~ 1182
exchange fluctuation 1225
exchange, forced ~ 722
exchange, foreign ~ 1221, 1361
exchange for forward delivery 1226
exchange for spot delivery 1227
exchange liability 1223
exchange list 1228
exchange loss 1229
exchange market 1230
exchange market, forward ~ 1382
exchange market, unofficial ~ 1885
exchange, money of ~ 1780
exchange office 1217
exchange of money 1231
exchange of shares 1232
exchange parity 1182
exchange parity, determination of the ~ 1032
exchange, par of ~ 1890
exchange premium 109
exchange, produce ~ 695
exchange profit 1233
exchange rate 1216, 1234
exchange rate, adjustment in the ~ 75
exchange rate, cross ~ 884
exchange rate, current ~ 907
exchange rate for notes and coin(s) 1235
exchange rate relations 1236
exchange rates, elasticity of ~ 1154

exchange rates, flexibility of ~ 1154
exchange rates, margin of fluctuation for ~ 1346
exchange rate, spot ~ 2024
exchange rate stabilization 1237
exchange regulations 900
exchange reserve 901
exchange restrictions 902
exchange risk 1238
exchange, second of ~ 2148
exchanges, forward ~ 1378
exchange stability 1239
exchange system 1240
exchange transaction 327
exchange transactions 1241
exchange value 1219, 1234
exchequer 1242
exchequer bond 1243
exchequer stock 1244
excise 752, 1245
excise duty 752, 1245
excise tax 752, 1245
ex coupon 831
ex dividend 1080
exempt from duty 920, 1246
exempt from tax 1247
exemption from taxation 1248
exhaustion of the reserves 1012
ex new 1249
exodus of capital 556
exorbitant price 1250
expansionary measures 1251
expansion, credit ~ 858
expansion in the money supply 1252
expansion investment 1253
expansion, investment ~ 1623
expansion of world trade 1254
expansion rate 1255, 1256
expend 1257
expenditure 1258
expenditure, budgetary ~ 446
expenditure, consumer ~ 748
expenditure, excess of ~ 1212
expenditure, non-budgetary ~ 1823
expenditure, private consumer ~ 1499
expenditure, public ~ 2003
expenditure(s) 1053
expenditure(s), capital ~ 524
expenditures, cash ~ 582
expenditure(s), investment ~ 524
expenditure(s), receipts and ~ 1525
expense account 1259
expense allowance 128
expense of, at the ~ 1260
expenses 1261
expenses, accrued ~ 39
expenses, actual ~ 55
expenses, additional ~ 61
expenses, administrative ~ 79
expenses, after allowance for ~ 131
expenses, after deducting ~ 131
expenses, business ~ 472
expenses, clear of ~ 131
expenses, current ~ 908
expenses, curtail ~ 915
expenses, cut ~ 915
expenses, cut down ~ 915
expenses deducted 131
expenses due and unpaid 39
expenses, entertainment ~ 1169
expenses, extra ~ 61
expenses, financial ~ 1313
expenses, fixed ~ 1336
expenses, further ~ 61
expenses, general ~ 1417
expenses, incidental ~ 61
expenses, income and ~ 1525
expenses, indirect ~ 1417
expenses, issue ~ 1353
expenses, less ~ 621
expenses, limit ~ 915
expenses, minus ~ 621
expenses, miscellaneous ~ 1764
expenses, operating ~ 1850
expenses, out-of-pocket ~ 55
expenses, overhead ~ 1417
expenses, petty ~ 1764
expenses, prune ~ 915
expenses, quit of ~ 131
expenses, receipts and ~ 1525
expenses, reduce ~ 915
expenses, representation ~ 1169
expenses, restrict ~ 915
expenses, retrench ~ 915
expenses, running ~ 908, 1850
expenses, special ~ 61
expenses, statement of ~ 2218
expenses, sundry ~ 1764
expenses, supplementary ~ 61
expenses to be deducted 621
expenses, travel ~ 2296, 2298
expenses, traveling ~ 2298
expenses, travelling ~ 2296, 2298
expenses, working ~ 1850
expert, tax ~ 2264
expiration 1262
expiration date 1263
expire 1264
expiry 1262
expiry date 1263
export 1265
exportation 1265
export bonus 426
export bounty 426
export commodities 1266
export credit(s) guarantee 1267
export goods 1266
exporting country 825
export licence 1268
export license 1268
export of capital 526
export permit 1268
exports, invisible ~ 1632
export subsidy 1269
exports, visible ~ 2351
expressed in dollars 1010
expropriate 1270
expropriation 1271
ex rights 1249
extend a credit 126, 1272
extend a term 1273
extend the time of payment 1274
extension of credit 220, 1275
extension of time for payment 1276
extension slip 124
extensive investment 1253
external assets 204
external balance 1277
external convertibility 1278
external customs tariff 1279
external debt 1280
external deficit 261
external financing 1281
external loan 1282
external payments, balance of ~ 258
external tariff 1279
external tariff, common ~ 699
external trade 1283
external trade balance 1277
extinction 139
extinguish 148
extinguish a mortgage 511
extortionate price 1250
extra allowance 1284
extra benefit 1285
extra-budgetary 1286
extra charge 60
extra charges 61
extra costs 61
extract of account 5
extra dividend 398
extra expenses 61
extra income 64
extraordinary receipts 1287
extra pay 1288
extras 61
extra tax 66

face value 1289
face value of a share 1290
facilities, borrowing ~ 421
facilities, credit ~ 421
facilities, overdraft ~ 421
factor, conversion ~ 772
factor cost, at ~ 1291
factor, demand ~ 716
factor income 1292
factor, inflationary ~ 1556
factoring 1293
failure 315
fall 1125
fall back (up)on the reserves 1042
fall due 347
falling due on August 15 1129
fall in prices 886
fall in the minimum lending rate 926
fall into debt 1294
fall in value 969, 970
fall, sell for a ~ 1427
fall, speculate for a ~ 1427
fancy articles 1001
fancy goods 1001
favorable balance of trade 53
favorable trade balance 53
favor of, open a credit in ~ 1847
favourable balance of trade 53
favourable trade balance 53
favour of, open a credit in ~ 1847
fee 614
fee, administrative ~ 80
fee, handling ~ 1478
fee, licence ~ 1686

fee, processing ~ 1478
fee, remittance ~ 2081
fee(s) 1295
fee(s), registration ~ 2077
fee, transfer ~ 812, 2077, 2081
fiat money 1296
fictional assets 1297
fictitious assets 1297
fictitious bill 15
fictitious profit 171
fiduciary 1298
fiduciary circulation 1299
fiduciary issue 1300
fiduciary loan 1301
fiduciary money 1296
figures, in round ~ 2119
final balance sheet 1302
final dividend 1303
finance 1304, 1305, 1306
finance bill 1307
finance, bridging ~ 433
finance company 1308
finance, high ~ 1486
finance, hire purchase ~ 1490
finance house 1308
finance market 554
finance, means of ~ 558
finances 1304
finances, conduct of the ~ 730
finance, self-~ 1601
finance(s), government ~ 827
finances, handling of the ~ 730
finances, management of the ~ 730
finance, source of ~ 2192
finance(s), public ~ 827
finances, reconstruct the ~ 2044
finances, rehabilitate the ~ 2044
finances, reorganize the ~ 2044
finance(s), state ~ 827
finances, the country's ~ 827
financial adviser 1309
financial advisor 1309
financial aid 1310
financial assistance 1310
financial bill 1307
financial broker 1311
financial budget 1312
financial burden 1313
financial charges 1313
financial circles 1305
financial community 1305
financial consultant 1309
financial difficulties 1314
financial economy 1304
financial embarrassment 1314
financial expenses 1313
financial house 1315
financial institution 1315
financial management 730
financial market 554
financial means 558
financial needs 1316
financial outlays 1313
financial paper 1307
financial policy 1317
financial program 1312
financial programme 1312
financial reconstruction 1318
financial rehabilitation 1318
financial reorganization 1318
financial requirements 1316
financial resources 558
financial scheme 1312
financial statement 1319
financial straits 1314
financial structure 561
financial system 1304
financial trouble 1314
financial world 1305
financial year 1320
financier 1321
financing 1322
financing charges 1313
financing costs 1313
financing, debt ~ 956
financing, deficit ~ 989
financing, funds for ~ 558
financing, hire purchase ~ 1490
financing, instal(l)ment ~ 1490
financing, interim ~ 433
financing, intermediate ~ 433
financing, internal ~ 1601
financing, temporary ~ 433
financing with borrowed funds 1281
financing with outside funds 1281
fine 136
fine bill 1323
fine gold 1324
fineness 1325
fine trade bill 1323
firm, banking ~ 294
firm, brokerage ~ 439
firm, broker's ~ 439
firmness of prices 1326
firm of bankers 294
firm of stockbrokers 439
firm, parent ~ 769
first-class bill 1323
first-class paper 1323
first of exchange 1327
first right 1328
fisc 1242
fiscal 1329
fiscal deficit 1330
fiscal domicile 1331
fiscal immunity 1248
fiscal instrument 1332
fiscal regulator 1333
fiscal system 1334
fiscal year 1335
fix a dividend 965
fix a price 1033
fixation of a dividend 964
fixed assets 518
fixed capital 518
fixed costs 1336
fixed deposit 1337
fixed expenses 1336
fixed income 210
fixed interest 1338
fixed interest bearing 1338
fixed interest bearing security 1339
fixed-interest securities, market in ~ 393
fixed interest security 1339
fixed investment 1340
fixed-period deposit 1337
fixed price 78
fixed rate of exchange 1341
fixed yield 1338
fixed yield security 1339
fixing a ceiling 1342
fixing of parity rates 1343
fixing, price ~ 1515, 1962
fix quotas 1186
flat 508
flatness 1130
flat price 1344
flat rate 1345
flexibility margin between exchange rates 1346
flexibility margins, reduction of ~ 2065
flexibility of exchange rates 1154
flexible rate of exchange 1347
flexible scale 1348
flexible tariff 1041
flight capital 1349
flight of capital 527
float a loan 1157
floating assets 468
floating capital 468
floating currency 1350
floating debt 1351
floating funds 468
floating rate of exchange 1347
flood the market (with cheap articles) 1132
flotation 1352
flotation cost 1353
flow, cash ~ 586
flow of capital 528
flow of credit 859
fluctuating currency 1350
fluctuating rate of exchange 1347
fluctuation, cyclical ~ 930
fluctuation, economic ~ 930
fluctuation in exchange 1225
fluctuation in (of) the exchange rate 1225
fluctuation in the economic situation 930
fluctuation margin in exchange rates 1346
fluctuation margins, reduction of ~ 2065
fluctuation, market ~ 930
flux, credit ~ 859
flux of capital 528
flying, kite ~ 1659
fob 1354
folding money 1355
forced circulation 1356
forced conversion 721
forced currency 1356
forced exchange 722
forced loan 723
forced rate (of exchange) 722
forced saving 724
foredate 164
foreign assets 204
foreign balance 1277
foreign bill (of exchange) 1357
foreign business 1358

foreign capital 515, 1359
foreign creditor 1360
foreign currency 1361
foreign dealings 1358
foreign debt 1280
foreign exchange 1221, 1361
foreign exchange balances 1362
foreign exchange commitment 1223
foreign exchange control 1224
foreign exchange controls 900
foreign exchange dealer 509
foreign exchange dealings 1241
foreign exchange holdings 1362
foreign exchange liability 1223
foreign exchange market 1230
foreign exchange market, two-tier ~ 2309
foreign exchange position 1363
foreign exchange, rationing of ~ 2030
foreign exchange regulations 900
foreign exchange reserve 901
foreign exchange restrictions 902
foreign exchange transactions 1241
foreign exchange value of the currency 1364
foreign interest 1365, 1366
foreign investment 1367, 1368
foreign loan 1282
foreign money 1361
foreign notes and coins 1369
foreign notes and coins, dealing in ~ 936
foreign operations 1358
foreign owned capital 1359
foreign owned investment 1367
foreign stock 1370
foreign trade 1283
foreign trade balance 1277
foreign trade bank 1371
foreign trade deficit 265
foreign trade surplus 266
foreign transactions 1358
foreign transfer 1372
forfeit (money) 136
form a reserve 454
formation of assets 1373
formation of capital 529
formation of savings 1374
form, deposit ~ 1022
form, inpayment ~ 1022
form of payment 1375
form, pay-in ~ 1022
form, paying-in ~ 1022
forward buying 1376
forward cover 1377
forward currencies 1378
forward deal 1379
forward delivery 1380
forward exchange 1226
forward exchange business 1226
forward exchange deal 1381
forward exchange dealing 1226
forward exchange market 1382
forward exchange operation 1381
forward exchange rate 1383
forward exchanges 1378
forward exchange transaction 1381
forward foreign exchange market 1382
forward payment 92
forward price 1384
forward purchase 1376
forward rate 1383, 1384
forward, sell ~ 2161
forward transaction 1379
foundation 1385
founders' shares 1386
founders' stocks 1386
fractional coin 1083
fractional currency 1083
fractional money 1083
fraction of shares 1387
franc area 1388
franc bloc 1388
franchise 728
frank 1389
free competition 1390
freedom of competition 1390
freedom of enterprise 1391
freedom of trade 1392
free economy 1393
free enterprise 1391
free, interest-~ 1590
free list 1394
free market 891, 1395
free market economy 1393
free market rate 1396
free of duty 920
free of tax 1247
free on board 1354
free rate 1396
free rate of exchange 1347
free reserve(s) 1397
free trade 1392
free trade area 1398
free trader 1399
free trade zone 1398
freeze 380
freeze of prices 1400
freezing 383
fringe benefit 1284, 1285
frozen credits 1401
full cost accounting 4
full gold standard 1402
full of a share, payment in ~ 1908
full, pay in ~ 1905
full payment 715
fully paid shares 1403
fully paid stocks 1403
fund 1404
fund a debt 733
fund, amortisation ~ 140
fund, amortization ~ 140
fund, compensation ~ 710
fund, contingency ~ 755
fund, contingent ~ 755
fund, counterpart ~ 823
fund, depreciation ~ 132
funded debt 735
fund, equalization ~ 710
Fund, European Monetary Cooperation ~ 1197
fund, guarantee ~ 1472
fund, guaranty ~ 1472
fund, imprest ~ 1517
funding 737
funding loan 738
Fund, International Monetary ~ 1607
fund, investment ~ 1624
fund, loan ~ 1710
fund, mutual ~ 1624
fund, pension ~ 1918
fund raising 1405
fund, redemption ~ 140
fund, renewal ~ 2086
fund, reserve ~ 2101
funds 1406
funds, available ~ 227
fund, savings ~ 2145
funds, borrowed ~ 417
funds, employment of ~ 1160
funds, floating ~ 468
funds for financing 558
funds, government ~ 1244
funds in hand 227
fund, sinking ~ 140
funds, liquid ~ 227
funds, misallocation of ~ 1763
funds, outside ~ 417
funds, public ~ 1244, 2005
funds, state ~ 2005
fund, stabilization ~ 2205
funds, trading ~ 468
funds, transfer of ~ 1784
fund, superannuation ~ 1918
funds, without ~ 835
funds, working ~ 468
fund, trust ~ 2307
furnish capital 1407
furnish collateral 101
furnishing of capital 1408
further charges 61
further costs 61
further cover 62
further credit 63
further expenses 61
fusion 135
future 1379
future delivery 1380
future delivery, buy for ~ 486
future delivery, sell for ~ 2161
future price 1384
future purchase 1376
future rate 1383, 1384

gain 1409
gain, capital ~ 530
gain, clear ~ 646
gain, net ~ 646
gain, rate ~ 1233
gains 229
gain sharing 1410
galloping inflation 1411
gambler, stock exchange ~ 1647
gambling on the stock exchange 111
gap between the interest rates 1412
gap, dollar ~ 1089
gap, inflationary ~ 1557
garnishee 1413
garnishment 1414
GATT 1415
GDP 1461

gearing 963
General Agreement on Tariffs and Trade 1415
general balance of transfers and capital movements 1416
general charges 1417
general expenses 1417
general ledger 1418
general partner 1419
general partnership 1420
get into debt 1294
get one's money back 1421
gift tax 1422
gilt-edged securities 387
gilt-edged stock(s) 387
gilts 387
giro 318, 1423
giro account 1424
giro account, deposit on ~ 1024
giro cheque 1425
giro deposit 1024
give as pledge 1018
give as security 1018
give-away price 322
give collateral security 101
give notice X days in advance 1426
give X days' notice 1426
global amount 107
glut of money 6
glut the market (with cheap articles) 1132
GNP 1466
go a bear 1427
go a bull 456
go down in value 970
go into liquidation 1428
gold and foreign exchange holdings 1429
gold and foreign exchange reserves 1429
gold and silver bullion 457
gold assets 1430
gold, bar ~ 323
gold bullion standard 1431
gold clause 1432
gold, coin ~ 666
gold coin 1433
gold, coinage ~ 666
gold coin and bullion 1430
gold, coined ~ 667
gold content 1434
gold cover 1435
gold exchange standard 1436
gold, fine ~ 1324
gold guarantee 1437
gold holdings 1430
gold, ingot ~ 323
gold loan 1438
gold, mint ~ 666
gold, minted ~ 667
gold, monetary ~ 666
gold, monetized ~ 667
gold nucleus standard 1431
gold parity 1439
gold piece 1433
gold reserve 1440
gold specie 667
gold specie standard 1402
gold, standard ~ 666
gold standard 1441
gold standard, full ~ 1402
gold stocks 1430
gold, two-tier price system for ~ 2310
gold value 1442
good buy 321
goods and chattels 622
goods and services 1443
goods and services, balance of ~ 259
goods, capital ~ 533
goods, consumer ~ 743
goods, consumption ~ 743
goods, durable ~ 1133
goods, export ~ 1266
goods, fancy ~ 1001
goods, import ~ 1510
goods, investment ~ 533
goods, luxury ~ 1001
goods, nondurable ~ 1827
goods, producer ~ 1134
goods, production ~ 1134
goodwill 1444
go surety 52
go up in value 179
government aid 1445
government bond 1243
government budget 1446
government credit guarantee 1447
government enterprise 1448
government finance(s) 827
government funds 1244
government grant 1449
government guarantee 1450
government income 1451
government interference 1452
government intervention 1452
government loan 1453
government loan guarantee 1447
government monopoly 1454
government obligation 1243
government owned enterprise 1448
government revenue 1451
government run enterprise 1448
government securities 1244
government stock equalization account 1455
government stock(s) 1244
government subsidy 1449
grace, days of ~ 933
grace, period of ~ 998
graded tariff 1041
graded tax 1456
graduated interest 1457
graduated rates 1041
graduated tariff 1041
graduated tax 1456
grand total 105
grant 1103, 1458
grant a credit 126
grant a respite for payment 1274
grant, government ~ 1449
grant-in-aid 1449
granting of credit 220
grant of credit 220
grant, state ~ 1449
gratuity 397
gross 1459
gross amount 1460
gross domestic product 1461
gross domestic saving 1462
gross income 1463
gross loss 1464
gross margin 1465
gross national product 1466
gross presentation, method of ~ 1755
gross presentation, principle of ~ 1755
gross profit 1459
gross profit margin 1465
gross revenue 1463
gross sales 1467
gross turnover 1467
gross value 1468
group 727
group balance sheet 736
group, income ~ 1527
growth in the money supply 1252
growth potential 1469
growth rate 1255, 1256
growth sector 1470
guarantee 395, 1138, 1471
guarantee a bill 235
guarantee, back to back ~ 238
guarantee bond 394
guarantee, credit ~ 860
guarantee, credit by way of ~ 853
guaranteed credit 670
guarantee deposit 602
guarantee fund 1472
guarantee, gold ~ 1437
guarantee, government ~ 1450
guarantee, government credit ~ 1447
guarantee, government loan ~ 1447
guarantee of a loan 1473
guarantee of meeting a bill 1474
guarantee payment of a bill 235
guarantee, state ~ 1450
guarantee, state credit ~ 1447
guarantee, state loan ~ 1447
guarantor 236, 395
guaranty 1471
guaranty fund 1472

half-yearly coupon 1475
half-yearly instal(l)ment 351
halting standard 1476
hand bill 1477
handling charge 1478
handling fee 1478
handling of the finances 730
hard currency 1479
hard currency country 1480
have a bill of exchange protested 1481
haven, tax ~ 2269
have recourse to the reserves 1042
head office 607
headquarters 607
hedging 839
hidden distribution 1482
hidden inflation 725

hidden reserves 726
high cost of living 1483
higher bid 1484
highest bidder 1485
highest price 605
high finance 1486
highly capitalized 539
high money 654
hire purchase 1487
hire purchase, buy on ~ 481
hire purchase credit 1488
hire purchase deal 1489
hire purchase finance 1490
hire purchase financing 1490
hire purchase sale 1491
hire purchase transaction 1489
historical cost 804
hoard 1492
hoarding 1493
holder 336
holder, bond~ 390
holder, debenture ~ 390
holder of an account 26
holder of securities 341
holding company 1494
holding, cross ~ 885
holding (in) 1495
holding, majority ~ 770
holding, minority ~ 1760
holdings 1496
holdings, cash ~ 587
holdings, foreign exchange ~ 1362
holdings, gold ~ 1430
holdings, gold and foreign exchange ~ 1429
holdings, security ~ 1628
home consumption 1092, 1497
home currency 1094
home market 1100
home trade 1101
home use 1092
honor a bill of exchange 1054
honour a bill of exchange 1054
hot money 1498
house, banking ~ 294
house, brokerage ~ 439
house, clearing ~ 649
house, discount ~ 1058
house, finance ~ 1308
house, financial ~ 1315
household consumption 1499
household demand 1097
house, investment ~ 653
house, issuing ~ 1645
house, underwriting ~ 1645
hyperinflation 1500
hypothecate securities 671
hypothecation of securities 1501

IB 1602
IBRD 1602
ICS 1603
idle capital 1502
IFC 1605
illiquid 1503
illiquidity 1504
ILO 1606
imaginary profit 171
imbalance 1062
IMF 1607
immaterial assets 1505
immobilization 1506
immobilize 1507
immovable property 1508
immovables 1508
immunity, fiscal ~ 1248
imperial preference 702
import 1509
importation 1509
import ban 319
import commodities 1510
imported inflation 1511
import embargo 319
import goods 1510
importing country 826
import licence 1512
import license 1512
import of capital 534
import permit 1512
import prohibition 319
import restriction 1513
imports, invisible ~ 1633
imports, visible ~ 2352
impose a surcharge 1514
impose a tax (on) 194
imposition 1135
imposition of prices 1515
imposition of taxes 1516
impost 1135
imprest 83
imprest fund 1517
imputed interest 1518
inactive 508
inactivity 1130
Inc. 1537
incentive 1519
incentive, investment ~ 1625
incentive pay 1520
incentive, tax ~ 2270
incentive wage 1520
incidence of a tax 1521
incidental charges 61
incidental costs 61
incidental expenses 61
incidentals 61
include in the budget 443
income 1522
income account 1523, 1524
income, additional ~ 64
income and expenses 1525
income, assured ~ 210
income bond 1526
income bracket 1527
income, casual ~ 64
income class 1527
income, disposable ~ 1068
income, earned ~ 1136
income, extra ~ 64
income, factor ~ 1292
income, fixed ~ 210
income from capital 535
income from investments 1528
income, government ~ 1451
income, gross ~ 1463
income group 1527
income in kind 1529
income, loss of ~ 1718
income, margin of ~ 1734
income, miscellaneous ~ 1765
income, national ~ 1799
income, net ~ 1811
income on investments 1528
income, other ~ 1765
income, per-capita average ~ 233
income per head, average ~ 233
income, personal ~ 1929
income, private ~ 1929
income, regular ~ 210
income, retained ~ 1137
income, secondary ~ 2146
income, settled ~ 210
income, source of ~ 2193
incomes, primary ~ 1970
income statement 1523
income tax 1530
income, taxable ~ 197
income tax, corporate ~ 792
income tax, corporation ~ 792
income tax, personal ~ 1930
income tax return 1531
income, transfer ~ 2292
income, undeclared ~ 2314
income, unearned ~ 2323
income, wage ~ 1136
incomings 1532
incomings and outgoings 1525
inconvertibility 1533
inconvertible 1534
inconvertible paper money 1535
incorporated bank 1536
incorporated company 1537
increased value 180
increase in liquidity 1538
increase in price(s) 1539
increase in salary 1540
increase in the discount rate 1541
increase in the minimum lending rate 1541
increase in the money supply 1252
increase in the rediscount rate 1541
increase in value 179, 180
increase in wages 1542
increase of capital 536
increase of X per cent 1543
increase the capital (stock) 1544
increase the value 178
increasing charge depreciation 1545
increment 180
incumbrance 460
incur a debt 761
incur a loss 333
indebted 952
indebtedness 462, 951
indebtedness, acknowledg(e)ment of ~ 46
indebtedness, certificate of ~ 609
indebtedness, excess ~ 1207
indebtedness, proof of ~ 609
indemnification 708
indemnity 708
indemnity bond 394
indemnity, bond of ~ 394
indemnity letter 394
index 1546, 1547

indexation 1548
index, commodity price ~ 696
index, cost of living ~ 809
indexed bond 1549
index figure 1550
index-link 1547
index-linked bond 1549
index number 1550
index, price ~ 1964
index, retail price ~ 2106
index, sales ~ 2131
index, weighted ~ 2370
index, wholesale price ~ 2374
indicator 1551
indirect charges 1417
indirect costs 1417
indirect expenses 1417
indirect foreign exchange standard 1436
indirect tax 1552
indorse a bill 1162
indorsee 1163
indorsement 1164
indorser 1165
inflate 1553
inflation 1554
inflation, adaptation ~ 59
inflation adaptation 59
inflation, adapted ~ 59
inflationary 1555
inflationary factor 1556
inflationary gap 1557
inflationary pressure 1558
inflationary spiral 1559
inflation, check ~ 628
inflation, concealed ~ 725
inflation, control ~ 628
inflation, cost ~ 803
inflation, cost-induced ~ 803
inflation, cost-push ~ 803
inflation, credit ~ 861
inflation, creeping ~ 882
inflation, curb ~ 628
inflation, demand ~ 1005
inflation, demand-induced ~ 1005
inflation, demand-pull ~ 1005
inflation, excess demand ~ 1005
inflation, galloping ~ 1411
inflation, hidden ~ 725
inflation, imported ~ 1511
inflationism 1560
inflationist 1561
inflation, masked ~ 725
inflation, pent-up ~ 1919
inflation-proof 1562
inflation-proofed 1562
inflation rate 1563
inflation, restrain ~ 628
inflation, runaway ~ 1411
inflation, snowballing ~ 1411
inflation, wage-induced ~ 2361
inflation, wage-led ~ 2361
inflation, wage-push ~ 2361
inflow of capital 99
influx of capital 99
ingot gold 323
inheritance tax 938
initial capital 1564
initial value 50
inject capital 436
injection of capital 521
inland bill (of exchange) 1091
inland loan 1099
inland revenue 1242, 1565
inland revenue department 1242
inland revenue inspection 1566
inland trade 1101
inordinate price 1250
inpayment 1567
inpayment form 1022
inscribed securities 1568
insolvency 1569
insolvent 1570
inspection, committee of ~ 388
inspection, inland revenue ~ 1566
instal(l)ment 1571, 1572
instal(l)ment, biannual ~ 351
instal(l)ment buying 1573
instal(l)ment credit 1488
instal(l)ment deal 1489
instal(l)ment debt 1574
instal(l)ment financing 1490
instal(l)ment, half-yearly ~ 351
instal(l)ment, monthly ~ 1788
instal(l)ment plan, buy on the ~ 481
instal(l)ment plan, on the ~ 987
instal(l)ment purchase 1573
instal(l)ment sale 1491
instal(l)ments, buy by ~ 481
instal(l)ments, by ~ 987
instal(l)ment, semi-annual ~ 351
instal(l)ments, in ~ 987
instal(l)ment, six-monthly ~ 351
instal(l)ment system, buy on the ~ 481
instal(l)ment system, on the ~ 987
instal(l)ment transaction 1489
institutional investor 793
institution, banking ~ 294
institution, credit ~ 850
institution, financial ~ 1315
institution, lending ~ 850
institution, loaning ~ 850
institution of bankruptcy proceedings 1575
instrument, bearer ~ 340
instrument, credit ~ 862
instrument, fiscal ~ 1332
instrument, negotiable ~ 1806
insurance 1576
insurance, credit ~ 863
insurance, life ~ 1688
insurance policy 1577
insurance premium 1578
intangible assets 1505
intangibles 1505
integrated national accounts 1579
intensification, capital ~ 537
intensity, capital ~ 538
intensive investment 1580
Inter-American Development Bank 1581
inter-bank clearing 292
inter-bank deposits 1582
inter-bank loan 1583
interconvertibility 1584
interest 1585
interest abroad 1366
interest, accrued ~ 41
interest, accruing ~ 42
interest, anticipated ~ 165
interest, anticipatory ~ 165
interest, arrears of ~ 190
interest at a rate of X percent, bear ~ 334
interest, bank ~ 306
interest bearing 1586, 1586
interest, beneficial ~ 349
interest, capitalisation of ~ 156
interest, capitalise ~ 547
interest, capitalize ~ 547
interest charges 1587
interest, compound ~ 720
interest, controlling ~ 770
interest coupon 1588
interest, credit ~ 376
interest, current ~ 909
interest, debit ~ 947
interest differential 1412
interest due 1589
interest, fixed ~ 1338
interest for default 983
interest, foreign ~ 1366
interest-free 1590
interest, graduated ~ 1457
interest, imputed ~ 1518
interest (in) 1495
interest in black 376
interest in limited partnership 1591
interest in red 947
interest, interim ~ 1599
interest, majority ~ 770
interest margin 1412
interest, mesne ~ 1599
interest, minority ~ 1760
interest, mortgage ~ 1794
interest of X percent, bear an ~ 334
interest on arrears 983
interest on capital 540
interest, outstanding ~ 190
interest overseas 1366
interest paid in advance 165
interest, past-due ~ 983
interest payable 947
interest payment 1592
interest, penal ~ 983
interest, put out money at (on) ~ 1675
interest rate 1593
interest rate differential 1412
interest rate, nominal ~ 1821
interest rate rebate 1594
interest rate subsidy 1594
interest rebate 1594
interest receivable 376
interest, running ~ 909
interestservice 1592
interest, simple ~ 2179
interest spread 1412
interest subsidy 1594
interest, usurious ~ 2335
interest warrant 1588
interest yield 1595
interference, government ~ 1452

interference, state ~ 1452
interim balance sheet 1596
interim certificate 1597
interim credit 434
interim dividend 1598
interim (financial) statement 1596
interim financing 433
interim interest 1599
interim loan 434
interim share 1597
intermediate financing 433
intermediate loan 434
internal audit 1600
internal consumption 1092
internal convertibility 781
internal debt 1095
internal financing 1601
internal loan 1099
internal revenue 1242
internal revenue service 1242
internal trade 1101
International Bank for Reconstruction and Development 1602
International Chamber of Commerce 1603
International Development Association 1604
International Finance Corporation 1605
International Labor Organization 1606
International Labour Organization 1606
International Monetary Fund 1607
International Monetary Fund, draw on the ~ 1123
International Monetary Fund, draw upon the ~ 1123
intervention, government ~ 1452
interventionism 1608
intervention point 1609
intervention rate 1610
intervention, state ~ 1452
intra-community payment 1611
intrinsic value 1612
introduction to the stock exchange 81
introductory price 1613
inundate the market (with cheap articles) 1132
inventorize 1124
inventory 1124, 1614, 1615, 1616
inventory, draw up the ~ 1124
inventory, make the ~ 1124
inventory, take the ~ 1124
inventory taking 1616
inventory value 1617
invest 1618
invested capital 541
investigation, market ~ 1740
investment 1619
investment abroad 1368
investment allowance 517
investment appropriations 1620
investment, bad ~ 244
investment bank 1621
investment boost 521
investment capital 1622
investment company 653
investment company, closed-end ~ 653
investment company, open-end ~ 1624
investment control 1044
investment credits 1620
investment, direction of (capital) ~ 1044
investment, equity ~ 1179
investment, expansion ~ 1253
investment expansion 1623
investment expenditure(s) 524
investment, extensive ~ 1253
investment, fixed ~ 1340
investment, foreign ~ 1367, 1368
investment, foreign owned ~ 1367
investment fund 1624
investment goods 533
investment house 653
investment in breadth 1253
investment incentive 1625
investment income 1528
investment in depth 1580
investment in kind 205
investment in securities 1626
investment in securities, saving by ~ 2135
investment in stock 1626
investment, intensive ~ 1580
investment, misdirected ~ 244
investment needs 1627
investment, new ~ 1818
investment, non-cash ~ 205
investment of capital 542
investment, overseas ~ 1368
investment, portfolio ~ 1626
investment portfolio 1628
investment, private ~ 1978
investment, public ~ 2006
investment rate 1629
investment ratio 1629
investment, rationalization ~ 1580
investment requirements 1627
investment scheme, wage ~ 2362
investment securities 1630
investments, level of ~ 1679
investment spending 524
investment trust 653
investment, variable yield ~ 2348
investor 1631
investor, corporate ~ 793
investor, institutional ~ 793
invisible exports 1632
invisible imports 1633
invisible reserves 726
invisibles 1632
invite subscriptions for a loan 1634
invite tenders 1635
invoice 17, 357
invoice, pro forma ~ 1991
invoicing 366
involuntary conversion 721
I.O.U. 1477
irrecoverable debt 242
irredeemable bond 1636
irredeemable debenture 1636
irredeemable money 1535
issuance 1352
issue 1352
issue a check (cheque) 1115
issue a loan 1157
issue, block ~ 385
issue, bond ~ 392
issue bonds 1637
issue, bonus ~ 399
issue, capital ~ 549
issue, capitalisation ~ 399
issue, capitalization ~ 399
issue costs 1353
issued capital 1638
issued capital stock 1638
issue, debenture ~ 392
issued stock 1638
issue expenses 1353
issue, fiduciary ~ 1300
issue, note ~ 308
issue of bank notes 1156
issue of securities 1639
issue of shares 1640
issue, place an ~ 1934
issue premium 1641
issue price 1642
issue prospectus 1643
issuer 1644
issue, rate of ~ 1642
issue, rights ~ 2116
issue, scrip ~ 399
issue, tap ~ 2259
issuing bank 1645
issuing conditions of a loan 729
issuing costs 1353
issuing expenses 1353
issuing house 1645
issuing premium 1641
issuing price 1642
item, credit ~ 857
item, debit ~ 946
itemized account 429
itemized statement 429
items of value 1646
item, suspense ~ 2249
item, transitory ~ 2249

jobber 1647, 1648
jobbing in bills 369
job wage 1907
joint account 1649
joint account, credit on ~ 865
joint and several debt 1650
joint and several debtor 1651
joint and several liability 1652
joint borrower 658
joint debtor 659
joint obligor 659
joint stock 544
joint stock bank 1536
joint stock company 1537
joint transaction 1653
joint venture 1653
joint venture account 1654
journal 932
journal, bill ~ 359, 360
journal entry 1655
journal, subsidiary ~ 225

keep the accounts 1656
keep the books 1656
keynesian 1657
kind, allowance in ~ 134
kind, benefit in ~ 134
kind (brought into a business), assets in ~ 205
kind, in ~ 1658
kind, income in ~ 1529
kind, investment in ~ 205
kind, remuneration in ~ 134
kite 15
kite flying 1659
knock-out price 322

labor costs 806
labour costs 806
lack of capital 559
land bank 1660
landed estate 1661
landed property 1661
land tax 1662
languid 508
languish 1663
languishing 508
languor 1130
lapsed coupon 1664
latent tax liability 759
launch 1352
launch a loan 1157
launch on the market 1665
lay down a price 1033
lay out 1050
lay-out, balance sheet ~ 273
leading shareholder 633
lease 1666
lease agreement 1666
lease contract 1666
leaseholder 1667
leasing 1668
leave a profit 100
ledger 1418
ledgers 28
ledger, share ~ 1701
ledger, stockholders' ~ 1701
ledger, subsidiary ~ 225
legacy duty 938
legacy tax 938
legal currency 1669
legal reserves 1670
legal tender 1669
lend 1671
lender 1672
lending 1673
lending, bank ~ 295
lending bank 850
lending institution 850
lending limit on securities 604
lending, net ~ 1812
lending on securities 1674
lending operations 851
lend money at (on) interest 1675
lend on securities 91
less charges 621
lessee 1667
less expenses 621
lessor 1676
less tax(es) 1677
letter, indemnity ~ 394
letter of credit 1678
letter of guarantee 394
letter of indemnity 394
letter, warrant ~ 394
level of investments 1679
level of prices 1680
leviable 676
levy 1135
levy a distress (on; upon) 211
levy a tax (on) 194
levy, capital ~ 551
levy, equalization ~ 712
levy of taxes 1516
liabilities 961
liabilities, assets and ~ 203
liabilities, current ~ 910
liabilities, demand ~ 1006
liabilities, deposit ~ 1023
liabilities due on presentation 1006
liabilities, non-current ~ 1825
liabilities, quick ~ 910
liabilities, short-term ~ 910
liabilities side 943
liabilities, sight ~ 1006
liability 951, 1681
liability account 1682
liability, be booked as a ~ 407
liability, book as a ~ 402
liability, contingent ~ 758
liability, endorser's ~ 1166
liability, enter as a ~ 402
liability, exchange ~ 1223
liability, foreign exchange ~ 1223
liability, joint and several ~ 1652
liability, limited ~ 1689
liability, non-contractual ~ 1824
liability out of contract 763
liability to tax 1683
liability, unlimited ~ 2329
liable to duty 916
liable to tax 196
liberalization of commerce 1684
liberalize 1685
licence, export ~ 1268
licence fee 1686
licence, import ~ 1512
license, export ~ 1268
license, import ~ 1512
lien (on) 1687
life 894
life annuity 163
life assurance 1688
life insurance 1688
lifeless 508
lifting of restrictions 2
lift restrictions 1
limitation(s), statute of ~ 1955
limit, borrowing ~ 422
limit, debt ~ 422
limited liability 1689
limited liability company 1537, 1690
limited partner 1691
limited partnership 1692
limited partnership, interest in ~ 1591
limited partnership, share in ~ 1591
limit expenses 915
limit of credit 855
limit on securities, lending ~ 604
limit, price ~ 1965
limping standard 1476
line, credit ~ 855
line of credit 855
link to an index 1547
liquid 1693
liquid assets 227
liquidate 148, 785, 1071, 1428
liquidate an account 249
liquidating value 432
liquidation 139, 773, 1070
liquidation, go into ~ 1428
liquidation of an account 254
liquidation value 432
liquidator 1694
liquid funds 227
liquidity 1695
liquidity, cash ~ 227
liquidity, excess ~ 1211
liquidity, increase in ~ 1538
liquidity position 592
liquidity, primary ~ 1971
liquidity requirements 596
liquidity reserves 1696
liquidity, restriction of ~ 2104
liquidity, secondary ~ 1776
liquidity squeeze 1697
liquid reserves 1696
liquid resources 227
list 1698
listed securities 1699
list, exchange ~ 1228
list, free ~ 1394
listing, securities' ~ 1228
listless 508
list of closing balances 1302
list of opening balances 1700
list of quotations 1228
list of shareholders 1701
list of stockholders 1701
list, stock ~ 1228
live beyond one's means 1702
live within one's means 1703
living standard 1704
load with debts 466
loan 845, 1671, 1705
loanable capital 1707
loan against collateral (security) 672
loan against security 672
loan, amortisation ~ 141
loan, amortisation of a ~ 142
loan, amortising ~ 141
loan, amortization ~ 141
loan, amortization of a ~ 142
loan, amortizing ~ 141
loan applicant 172
loan application 173
loan, apply for a ~ 175
loan, as a ~ 1706
loan, ask for a ~ 175
loan association 787
loan, bank ~ 298
loan bank 850
loan, bridging ~ 434
loan, business ~ 473
loan by the central banks 1708

loan, by way of a ~ 1706
loan, call ~ 504
loan capital 1707
loan ceiling 855
loan certificate 1709
loan charges 805
loan, collateral ~ 672
loan, commercial ~ 473
loan company 850
loan, compulsory ~ 723
loan, consolidation ~ 738
loan, contract a ~ 762
loan, conversion ~ 774
loan, conversion of a ~ 775
loan, convert a ~ 779
loan, convertible ~ 784
loan, day-to-day ~ 504
loan, debenture ~ 941
loan, demand ~ 504
loan, development ~ 1036
loan, domestic ~ 1099
loan, draw on a ~ 1122
loan, draw upon a ~ 1122
loan, emit a ~ 1157
loan, external ~ 1282
loan, fiduciary ~ 1301
loan, float a ~ 1157
loan, forced ~ 723
loan, foreign ~ 1282
loan for subscription, offer a ~ 1634
loan fund 1710
loan, funding ~ 738
loan, gold ~ 1438
loan, government ~ 1453
loan guarantee 1473
loaning institution 850
loan, inland ~ 1099
loan, interim ~ 434
loan, intermediate ~ 434
loan, internal ~ 1099
loan, issue a ~ 1157
loan, launch a ~ 1157
loan, lombard ~ 1712
loan, lottery ~ 1720
loan, national ~ 1099
loan, negotiate a ~ 1807
loan on collateral (security) 672
loan on mortgage 1711
loan on securities 1712
loan on security 672
loan, overnight ~ 504
loan, participation ~ 741
loan, place a ~ 1933
loan, premium ~ 1720
loan, premium bond ~ 1720
loan, public ~ 1453
loan, raise a ~ 762
loan rate 423
loan, redemption ~ 141
loan, redemption of a ~ 142
loan, refund a ~ 779
loan, refunding of a ~ 775
loan, roll-over ~ 2118
loan, secured ~ 672
loan, self-liquidating ~ 2156
loan, serve a ~ 2165
loan, service a ~ 2165
loan, sight ~ 504
loan, signature ~ 379
loan, sinking fund ~ 141
loan, sinking fund mortgage ~ 137
loan society 787
loans on collateral (security), rate for ~ 2022
loans on securities, rate for ~ 1714
loan, stabilization ~ 2206
loan, state ~ 1453
loan stock 389
loan stock, consolidated ~ 734
loan stockholder 390
loan, stopgap ~ 434
loan, syndicate ~ 741
loan, syndicated ~ 741
loan, take up a ~ 1122
loan, temporary ~ 434
loan, term ~ 2277
loan, tied ~ 2281
loan, time ~ 2277
loan, trade ~ 473
loan, uncovered ~ 1301
loan, unsecured ~ 1301
loan, usurious ~ 2336
loan without security 1301
local authority bond 1713
local bond 1713
local currency 1094
lock up 1507
lodge as security 1018
lombard loan 1712
lombard rate 1714
long 1715
long-dated 1715
long-term 1715
loose change 612
loro account 1716
lose (in) value 970
loss 1717
loss, absorb a ~ 3
loss (a profit), record a ~ 2046
loss (a profit), show a ~ 2046
loss balance 93
loss, balance sheet showing a ~ 274
loss, bear a ~ 333
loss, business ~ 474
loss, clear ~ 651
loss, commercial ~ 474
loss, compensate for a ~ 707
loss, cover a ~ 707
loss, dead ~ 934
loss, deductible ~ 974
losses, cut one's ~ 928
loss, gross ~ 1464
loss, incur a ~ 333
loss in exchange 1229
loss, make a ~ 333
loss, make good a ~ 707
loss, make up for a ~ 707
loss, meet with a ~ 333
loss, net ~ 651
loss of capital 552
loss of earnings 1718
loss of income 1718
loss of profit(s) 1718
loss of value 969
loss on exchange 1229
loss, operating ~ 474
loss, recoup a ~ 707
loss, recover a ~ 707
loss, repair a ~ 707
loss, retrieve a ~ 707
loss, sale at a ~ 2129
loss, sell at a ~ 2158
loss, selling at a ~ 2129
loss, sell with a ~ 2158
loss, suffer a ~ 333
loss, sustain a ~ 333
loss, total ~ 934
loss, trading ~ 474
loss, undergo a ~ 333
lot, callable by ~ 498
lot of shares 386
lot, redeemable by ~ 498
lottery bond 1719
lottery loan 1720
lowering of the minimum lending rate 926
lowering of the price 927
lower value method 1721
Ltd., Co. ~ 1537, 1690
lucrative 1147
lump sum 1722
lump-sum price 114
luxuries 1001
luxury articles 1001
luxury goods 1001
luxury tax 1723

machine accounting 1724
macro-economic 1725
made out in dollars 1010
made out to order 1726
main office(s) 607
maintenance cost 810
maintenance, price ~ 1515, 1917
majority holding 770
majority interest 770
major shareholder 633
make a cash settlement 1727
make a debt 761
make a loss 333
make a price 1728
make a profit 1729
make (both) ends meet 1703
make good a deficit 836
make good a loss 707
make out a check (cheque) 1115
make payments 1152
maker 1118
make the inventory 1124
make up a balance sheet 279
make up a deficit 836
make up an account 249
make up for a loss 707
managed currency 767
managed economy 768
management, budget ~ 450
management, debt ~ 954
management of the finances 730
management shares 1386
manipulation of the currency 898
manipulation on the stock exchange 1730
manufacturing cost 811
margin 1037, 1731, 1732

margin, additional ~ 62
marginal cost 1733
margin between exchange rates, flexibility ~ 1346
margin call 501
margin, credit ~ 864
margin, gross ~ 1465
margin, gross profit ~ 1465
margin, interest ~ 1412
margin, negative gross ~ 1464
margin, net ~ 1813
margin of fluctuation for exchange rates 1346
margin of income 1734
margin of profit 1734
margin, price ~ 1966
margin requirements 837
margins, arbitrage ~ 187
margin, trade profit ~ 1734
margin, trading ~ 1734
mark 1698
markdown 927
market 1735, 1736, 1737
marketable 1738
marketable securities 1739
marketable value 688
market, after hours ~ 102
market analysis 1740
market, bear ~ 345
market, bill ~ 370
market, black ~ 377
market, bond ~ 393
market, bull ~ 458
market, bullish ~ 458
market, buyer's ~ 483, 483
market, capital ~ 554
Market, Common ~ 700
market, corner the ~ 789
market, discount ~ 370
market, domestic ~ 1100
market, dump on the ~ 1132
market economy 1741
market economy, free ~ 1393
Market, Euro-~ 700
market, Euro-bond ~ 1191
market, Euro-currency ~ 1192
market, exchange ~ 1230
market, finance ~ 554
market, financial ~ 554
market fluctuation 930
market, foreign exchange ~ 1230
market, forward foreign exchange ~ 1382
market, free ~ 891, 1395
market, home ~ 1100
market in fixed-interest securities 393
marketing 1742
marketing area 1736
market investigation 1740
market, launch on the ~ 1665
market, money ~ 1778
market, official ~ 1845
market, open ~ 1395
market, outside ~ 891
market, over-the-counter ~ 891
market, parallel ~ 1885
market position 1743
market price 1744
market quotation 1234
market rate 1234
market report 1228
market research 1740
market rigging 1730
market, secondary ~ 2147
market, securities ~ 2153
market, security ~ 2153
market, share ~ 2153
market sharing 1745
market situation 1743
market speculator 1647
market, stock ~ 2153
market study 1740
market survey 1740
market swing 930
market, throw on the ~ 1665
market, unload on the ~ 1665
market, unofficial ~ 891
market value 688, 1234
market value, current ~ 912, 913
market (with cheap articles), flood the ~ 1132
market (with cheap articles), glut the ~ 1132
market (with cheap articles), inundate the ~ 1132
marking (of share prices) 1746
markup 1539, 1734
masked inflation 725
material assets 1747
mature 347
matured 1126
mature on August 15, to ~ 1129
maturity 1748
maturity, at ~ 1128
maturity date 931
maturity of X years 1749
maturity, on ~ 1128
maturity premium 1750
maximum price 605
mean rate 234
means 1406
means, financial ~ 558
means, live beyond one's ~ 1702
means, live within one's ~ 1703
means of finance 558
means of payment 1751
means of production, durable ~ 1134
means of settlement 1751
mechanized accounting 1724
medium, circulating ~ 636
medium-dated 1752
medium-term 1752
medium-term credit 1753
meet a bill of exchange 1054
meet a deficit 836
meeting a bill, guarantee of ~ 1474
meet with a loss 333
members, register of ~ 1701
memo book 1754
memorandum, credit ~ 847
merchantable 1738
merchant bank 310
merger 135
mesne interest 1599
method, lower value ~ 1721
method of gross presentation 1755
method of net presentation 1756
method of payment 1375
micro-economic 1757
middle rate 234
migratory balance 1758
milliard 368
minimum lending rate 311
minimum lending rate, cut in the ~ 926
minimum lending rate, fall in the ~ 926
minimum lending rate, increase in the ~ 1541
minimum lending rate, lowering of the ~ 926
minimum lending rate, raising of the ~ 1541
minimum lending rate, rise in the ~ 1541
minimum reserve ratio 1759
minimum reserve requirements 1670
minimum reserves 1670
minimum value principle 1721
minor coin 1083
minority holding 1760
minority interest 1760
mint 662, 1761
mintage 663
minted gold 667
mint gold 666
mint par (of exchange) 1762
minus charges 621
minus expenses 621
misallocation of funds 1763
misappropriate 977
misappropriation 978
miscalculation 491
miscellaneous charges 1764
miscellaneous costs 1764
miscellaneous expenses 1764
miscellaneous income 1765
miscellaneous revenues 1765
miscount 491
misdirected investment 244
misinvestment 244
mistake in calculation 491
mobilization 1766
mobilize 1767
mode of payment 1375
monetarist 1768
monetary circulation 637
monetary depreciation 896
monetary expansion 1252
monetary gold 666
monetary parity 1182
monetary policy 1769
monetary reform 899
monetary reserve 1770
monetary stability 903
monetary support 1771
monetary system 664
monetary unit 904
monetization 663, 1772
monetize 662, 1773
monetized gold 667
money at call 505

money at (on) interest, lend ~ 1675
money back, get one's ~ 1421
money broker 1311
money, call ~ 505
money, caution ~ 602
money changer 509
money changing 1231
money, cheap ~ 623
money circulation, excessive ~ 6
money, close ~ 654
money, conversion into ~ 773
money, convert into ~ 785
money, copper ~ 788
money creation 842
money, current ~ 914
money, day-to-day ~ 505
money dealer 509
money, dear ~ 654
money demand 1774
money, earnest ~ 602
money, easy ~ 623
money economy 1775
money equivalents 1776
money, fiat ~ 1296
money, fiduciary ~ 1296
money, folding ~ 1355
money, foreign ~ 1361
money, fractional ~ 1083
money, high ~ 654
money, hot ~ 1498
money in circulation 914
money, irredeemable ~ 1535
moneylender 1777
money lent for fixed period 1337
money market 1778
money market paper 1779
money, near ~ 1805
money of exchange 1780
money on call 505
money, option ~ 1856
money order 1781
money, overnight ~ 505
money, paper ~ 1355
money piece 660
money, price of ~ 1967
money, public ~ 2005
money, quasi ~ 1805
money rate 1782
money rates, easing in ~ 1144
money, ready ~ 572
money, recover one's ~ 1421
money reserve 1770
money, small ~ 1083
money, soft ~ 623, 1355
money squeeze 1314
money sunk 541
money supply 1783
money supply, excess ~ 6
money supply, expansion in the ~ 1252
money, tight ~ 654
money, till ~ 587
money, token ~ 1296
money transfer 1784
money, volume of ~ 1783
monometal(l)ism 1785
monopoly 1786
monopoly, government ~ 1454
monopoly, state ~ 1454
monopoly tax 1245
monopoly, trade ~ 2287
monthly allowance 1787
monthly instal(l)ment 1788
monthly remittance 1787
monthly salary 1787
moratorium 1276
moratory 1789
mortgage 1790, 1791
mortgage, amortisable ~ 137
mortgage, amortizable ~ 137
mortgage bank 1660
mortgage bond 1792
mortgage, burden with a ~ 465
mortgage, cancel a ~ 511
mortgage certificate 1792
mortgage charge 1793
mortgage, cover by ~ 838
mortgage credit 866
mortgage debenture 1792
mortgage debt 957
mortgage, encumber with a ~ 465
mortgage, extinguish a ~ 511
mortgage interest 1794
mortgage loan 1711
mortgage (on), raise a ~ 2019
mortgage (on), take a ~ 2019
mortgage, pay back a ~ 511
mortgage, pay off a ~ 511
mortgage, redeem a ~ 511
mortgage, repay a ~ 511
mortgage, satisfy a ~ 511
mortgage, secure by ~ 838
mortgage, wipe off a ~ 511
mortmain 1795
movable property 622
movables 622
movement of capital 555
movement of capital, tax on the ~ 564
mulct 136
multiple vote share 1796
multi-voting share 1796
municipal 1713
municipal bond 1713
mutual fund 1624
mutual loan society 787

name a price 1728
national accounting 1797
national accounts 1797
national budget 1446
national currency 1094
national debt 1798
national dividend 1799
national giro 1423
national giro account 1800
national income 1799
nationalization 1801
nationalize 1802
national loan 1099
national product 1803
national product, net ~ 1814
national wealth 1804
nation, creditor ~ 871
nation, debtor ~ 959
near money 1805
near money, supply of ~ 2243
needs, financial ~ 1316
needs, investment ~ 1627
negative gross margin 1464
negotiable bill 374
negotiable document 1806
negotiable instrument 1806
negotiable securities 1739
negotiate a loan 1807
net 646
net amount 1808
net assets 1809
net assets value 432
net borrowing 1810
net current assets 468
net gain 646
net income 1811
net lending 1812
net loss 651
net margin 1813
net national product 1814
net presentation, principle of ~ 1756
net profit 646
net profit margin 1813
net profit ratio 1815
net revenue 1811
net sales 1816
net turnover 1816
net value 1817
net worth 1809
never-never, buy on the ~ 481
new, cum ~ 888
new, ex ~ 1249
new investment 1818
new issue shares 1819
new shares 1819
new stock 1819
nominal amount 1820
nominal capital 222
nominal interest rate 1821
nominal rate (of interest) 1821
nominal rebate 1822
nominal value 1289
nominal value of a share 1290
nominee shareholders, voting rights of ~ 2356
non-allowable charges 1049
non-budgetary expenditure 1823
non-cash investment 205
non-cash payment 588
non-contractual liability 1824
non-convertibility 1533
non-convertible 1534
non-current liabilities 1825
non-distribution 1826
nondurable goods 1827
nondurables 1827
non-dutiable 920
non-inflationary 1828
non-interest-bearing 1590
non-liquid 1503
non-liquidity 1504
non-negotiable bill 371
non-payment 982
non-profit association 1829
non-profit-making association 1829
non-recurrent receipts 1287

non-recurring receipts 1287
non-resident convertibility 1278
non-taxability 1248
non-taxable 1247
non-voting shares 1830
non-voting stock 1830
no-par shares 1831
no-par stock 1831
no par value shares 1831
no par value stock 1831
normal price 1832
nostro account 1833
note 287, 356, 1477
note and coin circulation 638
note, bank ~ 287
note, bought ~ 425
note broker 361
note, broker's ~ 425, 440
note circulation 308
note, contract ~ 425, 440
note, credit ~ 847
note, demand ~ 1007
note issue 308, 1156
note payable 372
note receivable 373
notes and accounts, doubtful ~ 1110
notes and coin(s) 1834
notes and coins, foreign ~ 1369
notes and coin(s) in circulation 638
note, sight ~ 1007
notes in circulation 308
notes in issue 308
note, sold ~ 440
note to hand 1477
note, treasury ~ 2301
notice 1835, 1836
notice, at X days' ~ 1837
notice deposit 1019
notice, give X days' ~ 1426
notice of assessment 1839
notice of payment 97
notice of withdrawal of deposits 1840
notice, tax assessment ~ 1839
notice, upon X days' ~ 1837
notice, without (previous) (prior) ~ 1838
notice X days in advance, give ~ 1426
not liquid 1503
not-to-order bill 371
not-to-order check 630
not-to-order cheque 630
N.S.F. check 241

objects of value 1646
obligate 181
obligation 389
obligation, contingent ~ 758
obligation, government ~ 1243
obligations 961
obligations, demand ~ 1006
obligations, sight ~ 1006
obligatory reserves 1670
obligee 390
obligor 362
obligor, joint ~ 659
odd change 612
OECD 1860
OEEC 1861
offer 352
offer a loan for subscription 1634
offer collateral 101
offer for sale 1841
offering (for subscription) 1842
offering price 1843
offer price 1843
offers and bids 192
offer to pay 1844
office, clearing ~ 649
office, head ~ 607
office(s), central ~ 607
office(s), main ~ 607
office(s), principal ~ 607
office(s), registered ~ 2075
official market 1845
official receiver 209
offset 706, 709
offset account 644, 760
offset account, balance on ~ 269
offset dollar 29
offset(-entry) 281
offsetting entry 281
offsetting of costs 800
offsetting transaction 327
offset transaction 327
omissions, errors and ~ 1183
oncost 1417
open account 23, 1846
open a credit in favor of 1847
open a credit in favour of 1847
open cheque 339
open credit 379
open-end investment company 1624
open-end trust 1624
opening balance sheet 1700
opening capital 1564
opening of a credit 1848
opening price 1849
opening quotation 1849
opening rate 1849
open market 1395
open market rate 1396
operating capital 468
operating costs 1850
operating deficit 474
operating expenses 1850
operating loss 474
operating profit 475
operating statistics 1851
operating surplus 1852
operation 320
operation, covering ~ 839
operation, forward exchange ~ 1381
operations, banking ~ 304
operations, credit ~ 851
operations, foreign ~ 1358
operations, lending ~ 851
operation, spot exchange ~ 2202
operator, stock exchange ~ 1647
opportunity cost 1853
option 1854, 1855
optional bond 497
option bargain 1855
option, buyer's ~ 484
option, call ~ 484
option, conversion ~ 777
option deal 1855
option, double ~ 1108
option money 1856
option, purchase ~ 2013
option, put ~ 1858
option, repeat ~ 485
option, seller's ~ 1858
option, share ~ 1855
option, stock ~ 1855
option to buy 484
option to double, buyer's ~ 485
option to double, seller's ~ 1857
option to purchase 484
option to repeat 485, 1857
option to sell 1858
order, banker's ~ 299
order bill 374
order, cash ~ 590
order check 631
order cheque 631
order for payment 590
order, money ~ 1781
order, postal ~ 1781
order, post office ~ 1781
order, to ~ 1726
order to pay 590
ordinary budget 1859
ordinary share capital 697
ordinary shares 701
ordinary stock 701
Organization for Economic Co-operation and Development 1860
Organization for European Economic Co-operation 1861
Organization, International Labor ~ 1606
original capital 1564
other income 1765
outflow of capital 556
outgoings 1053
outgoings, cash ~ 582
outgoings, incomings and ~ 1525
outlay 1258
outlays 1053
outlay(s), capital ~ 524
outlays, cash ~ 582
outlays, financial ~ 1313
outlet 1736
out-of-pocket expenses 55
outside capital 417
outside financing 1281
outside funds 417
outside market 891
outside price 605
outside securities 892
outstanding account 1846
outstanding amount 152
outstanding capital stock 1638
outstanding claim 37
outstanding debt 37
outstanding interest 190
outstanding share capital 1638
outstanding shares 1638
overall amount 107
overall balance of payments 1862
overassess 1863
overassessment 1864

overbid 1484
overcapitalization 1865
overcharge 1866
overdraft 1867
overdraft, advance by ~ 87
overdraft facilities 421
overdraw a credit 1201
overdraw an account 1868
overdue 1869
overdue bill 365
overestimate 1863, 1864
overestimate of costs 1870
overestimation 1864
overextended 953
overextension 1207
overhead charges 1417
overhead costs 1417
overhead expenses 1417
overheads 1417
overhead variance 464
overheating 1871
overindebted 953
overindebtedness 1207
overnight loan 504
overnight money 505
overprice 1208
overrate 1863
oversaving 1872
overseas capital 515
overseas, interest ~ 1366
overseas investment 1368
oversea(s) trade 1283
overspending 1212
oversubscribe 1873
oversubscription 1874
oversupply 1210
over-the-counter market 891
over-the-counter securities 892
overtime 1875
overvaluation 1864
overvalue 1215, 1863
owe 1876
owing 1127
owing, amount ~ 151
owing, balance ~ 252
owing, sum ~ 151
own account, for (one's) ~ 1877
own consumption 1497
owner 1878
ownership, private ~ 1979
owner, stock ~ 2171

pace of inflation 1563
paid 1879
paid in capital 1880
paid-up capital 1880
paid-up shares 1403
paid-up stocks 1403
paper, bankable ~ 283
paper, commercial ~ 356
paper credit 11
paper currency 1355
paper, discountable ~ 283
paper, eligible ~ 283
paper, financial ~ 1307
paper, first-class ~ 1323
paper money 1355
paper money, inconvertible ~ 1535
paper, money market ~ 1779
paper standard 1881
paper, trade ~ 356
parallel market 1885
par, at ~ 1882
par, be above ~ 1883
par, be at ~ 1884
par, be below ~ 1056
parcel of shares 386
parent company 769
parent firm 769
parity 1886
parity, at ~ 1882
parity, exchange ~ 1182
parity, gold ~ 1439
parity, monetary ~ 1182
parity price 1887
parity rate 1888
parity rates, fixing of ~ 1343
parity ratio 1888
parity value 1889
par of exchange 1890
par (of exchange), mint ~ 1762
par price 1887
par rate 1887
partial cost accounting 1045
participating bond 1526
participating preference share 1891
participating preferred share 1891
participation account 1654
participation in profits 1410
participation loan 741
partner, dormant ~ 1105
partner, general ~ 1419
partner, limited ~ 1691
partnership 1892
partnership, general ~ 1420
partnership, limited ~ 1692
partnership limited by shares 1893
partner, silent ~ 1105
partner, sleeping ~ 1105
partner, special ~ 1691
part payment 1894, 1894
par value 1889
par value, reduce the ~ 2062
par values, realignment of ~ 2031
pass an account for payment 223
passbook 289
passing of a dividend 1826
passive balance of trade 94
passive debt 36
passive trade balance 94
past bill 365
past due 1869, 1869
past-due bill 365
past-due interest 983
pawn 1018, 1138
pawned bill of exchange 363
pawned securities 1895
pawning of securities 1501
pawn, put in ~ 1018
pawn securities 671
pay 100, 1140
pay a bill of exchange 1054
payable at sight 1896
payable in cash 1897
payable in foreign currency 1898
payable on demand 1896
payable to order 1726
pay a call of X % on a share 1899
pay a dividend 1051
pay an interest of X percent 334
pay as you earn (system) 681
pay (a) X percent interest 334
pay back 1900
pay back a mortgage 511
pay by check 1901
pay by cheque 1901
pay cash 1727
pay cash down 1727
pay day 24
payee 350, 1902
pay, efficiency ~ 1153
payer 1903
payer, bad ~ 245
pay, extra ~ 1288
pay in 1015
pay in advance 1904
pay, incentive ~ 1520
pay-in form 1022
pay in full 1905
paying 1147
paying, default in ~ 982
paying-in form 1022
paying-in slip 877, 1022
pay-in slip 877, 1022
pay interest at a rate of X percent 334
payment 139, 1567
payment, advance ~ 92
payment, advice of ~ 97
payment agreement 1906
payment, anticipated ~ 92
payment, authorisation of ~ 221
payment, authorization of ~ 221
payment, back ~ 237
payment by check or by transfer 588
payment by cheque or by transfer 588
payment by results 1153
payment by the job 1907
payment, cashless ~ 588
payment, cease ~ 603
payment, complete ~ 715
payment, defer a ~ 984
payment, delay a ~ 984
payment, delay in ~ 999
payment, early ~ 92
payment, extension of time for ~ 1276
payment, form of ~ 1375
payment, forward ~ 92
payment in advance 92
payment in cash 591
payment in full 715
payment in full of a share 1908
payment in part 1894
payment, intra-community ~ 1611
payment, means of ~ 1751
payment, method of ~ 1375
payment, mode of ~ 1375
payment, non-cash ~ 588
payment, notice of ~ 97
payment of a cheque, stop ~ 2227
payment of arrears 237

payment of capital 1909
payment of dividends 1052
payment of interest 1592
payment of interest, subject to the ~ 2231
payment of, on ~ 732
payment on account 1014
payment on due date 1910
payment, part ~ 1894
payment, period for ~ 1924
payment, postpone a ~ 984
payment, provisional ~ 1999
payment, refusal of ~ 2074
payment, respite a ~ 984, 1274
payment, respite for ~ 1276
payments 1911
payments agreement 1906
payment(s), discontinue ~ 603
payments, effect ~ 1152
payments, make ~ 1152
payments over X years, spread ~ 2204
payments, receipts and ~ 1525
payments, stop ~ 603
payments, suspend ~ 603
payment, suspension of ~ 1276
payment, tender of ~ 1844
payment, term of ~ 1924
payment, terms of ~ 2278
payment, time for ~ 1924
payment transactions 1911
payment, transfer ~ 2293
pay off 148
pay off a mortgage 511
pay, offer to ~ 1844
payor 1903
pay out 1050
pay, piecework ~ 1932
pay, refusal to ~ 2074
payroll 1912
pay sheet 1912
pay slip 1913
pay spot cash 1727
pay the balance 1914
pay up 1905
pay up a share (in full) 1915
pay voucher 590, 600
peculate 977
peculation 978
pecuniary difficulties 1314
(pecuniary) penalty 136
pecuniary resources 1916
pegged rate 1610
pegging of prices 1917
penal interest 983
penalty, (pecuniary) ~ 136
pension fund 1918
pent-up inflation 1919
per-capita average income 233
per-capita consumption 1920
per cent 1921
percent 1921
per cent 1922
percent 1922
percentage 1921
percentage of profits 1923
per cent, increase of X ~ 1543
percent interest, bear (a) X ~ 334
per cent, rise of X ~ 1543
per centum 1921
per contra entry 281
period, blocking ~ 384
period for payment 1924
period of circulation 895
period of grace 998
period of non-negotiability 384
period of validity 894
period, subscription ~ 2237
permit, export ~ 1268
permit, import ~ 1512
perpetual annuity 163
perpetual bond 162
perpetual debenture 1925
personal account 1926
personal assets 622
personal credit 1927
personal debt 1928
personal estate 622
personal estate, credit on ~ 867
personal income 1929
personal income tax 1930
personal property 622
personal property, credit on ~ 867
personalty 622
petition in bankruptcy 316
petty cash 1931
petty charges 1764
petty expenses 1764
phase of the business cycle 1150
piece, gold ~ 1433
piece, money ~ 660
piecework pay 1932
piecework wage 1932
place 1618
place a loan 1933
place an issue 1934
place a sum to someone's credit 566
place (in)to account 570
placement 1619, 1935
place to reserve 68
placing 1935
planned economy 768
planning and control, economic ~ 1047
plan, redemption ~ 146
pledge 1138
pledge (as security) 1018
pledged bill of exchange 363
pledged securities 1895
pledge, give as ~ 1018
pledge, put in ~ 1018
pledge securities 671
pledging of securities 1501
plough back 1936
plow back 1936
pocket a profit 1937
point, break-even ~ 430
point, intervention ~ 1609
points, record a fall (a gain) of X ~ 2045
points, show a fall (a gain) of X ~ 2045
point, support ~ 1609
policy, credit ~ 872
policy, dividend ~ 1081
policy, financial ~ 1317
policy, insurance ~ 1577
policy, monetary ~ 1769
political economy 1151
pool 1938
pooling 1939
portfolio company 653
portfolio investment 1626
portfolio, investment ~ 1628
portfolio of securities 1628
portfolio securities 1630
portion 1572
position, cash ~ 592
position, foreign exchange ~ 1363
position, liquidity ~ 592
position, market ~ 1743
position of an account 1940
post 401
postal check 1425
postal check account 1800
postal giro service 1423
postal money order 1781
postal order 1781
postal savings bank 1941
postdate 1942
posting 409
posting, double ~ 1106
posting, summary ~ 717
post office cheque 1425
post office cheque account 1800
post office order 1781
post office savings bank 1941
postpone a payment 984
potential, growth ~ 1469
pound sterling 1943
power, buying ~ 487
power, purchasing ~ 487
preceding endorser 1944
predate 164
predetermined cost(s) 1189
pre-emption, right of ~ 2013
prefential dividend, cumulative ~ 889
preference 1328
preference, Commonwealth ~ 702
preference dividend 1945
preference, imperial ~ 702
preference share 1946
preference share, participating ~ 1891
preference shares, cumulative ~ 890
preference stock 1946
preference tariff 1947
preferential creditor 1948
preferential dividend 1945
preferential duty 1949
preferential price 1203
preferential rate of exchange 1950
preferential right 1328
preferential tariff 1947
preferred creditor 1948
preferred dividend 1945
preferred share, participating ~ 1891
preferred stock 1946
preferred stock, cumulative ~ 890
prefinance 1951
prefinancing 1952
premium 110, 397

premium, be at a ~ 1883
premium bond 1719
premium bond loan 1720
premium for the call 507
premium for the put 1953
premium, insurance ~ 1578
premium loan 1720
premium, maturity ~ 1750
premium on an issue 1641
premium on exchange 109
premium on redemption 1750
premium, share ~ 1641
prepay 1904
prepayment 92
preproduction costing 1190
prescribe a price 1033
prescribed debt 324
prescribed dividend 1954
prescription 1955
presentation draft 1003
presentation, liabilities due on ~ 1006
presentation of the balance sheet 1957
presentation of the coupon, (up)on ~ 1958
presentation, on ~ 1956
presenter 337
present value 912
pressure, inflationary ~ 1558
pre-tax 1959
prevailing price 911
previous deduction 89
previous endorser 1944
price 1033, 1960
price adjustment 76
price, administered ~ 78
price administration 1961
price, agree a ~ 113
price, agreed ~ 114
price agreement 115
price, agree on a ~ 113
price, all-in ~ 114
price, asked ~ 193
price, at cost ~ 796
price, bargain ~ 322
price, basic ~ 330
price, bid ~ 354
price, buying ~ 488
price cartel 115
price, cash ~ 593
price, ceiling ~ 605
price, closing ~ 657
price, consumer ~ 749
price, contract(ing) ~ 114
price control 1961
price, cost ~ 814
price, current ~ 911
price, current market ~ 911
price cut 927
price, cut-rate ~ 322
price decontrol 971
price determination 1962
price, determine a ~ 1033
price difference 1038
price differential 1038
price-earnings ratio 1963
price, establish a ~ 1033
price, exceptional ~ 1203
price, excess ~ 1208
price, excessive ~ 1208
price, exorbitant ~ 1250
price, extortionate ~ 1250
price, fix a ~ 1033
price, fixed ~ 78
price fixing 1515, 1962
price-fixing agreement 115
price-fixing, vertical ~ 2097
price, flat ~ 1344
price for forward delivery 1384
price, forward ~ 1384
price freeze 1400
price, future ~ 1384
price, give-away ~ 322
price, highest ~ 605
price increase 1539
price index 1964
price, inordinate ~ 1250
price, introductory ~ 1613
price, issue ~ 1642
price, issuing ~ 1642
price, knock-out ~ 322
price, lay down a ~ 1033
price level 1680
price limit 1965
price, lowering of the ~ 927
price, lump-sum ~ 114
price maintenance 1515, 1917
price maintenance, resale ~ 2097
price, make a ~ 1728
price margin 1966
price, market ~ 1744
price, maximum ~ 605
price, name a ~ 1728
price, normal ~ 1832
price, offer ~ 1843
price, offering ~ 1843
price of money 1967
price of the day 911
price, opening ~ 1849
price, outside ~ 605
price, par ~ 1887
price, parity ~ 1887
price, preferential ~ 1203
price, prescribe a ~ 1033
price, prevailing ~ 911
price, publicity ~ 1613
price, purchase ~ 488
price, purchasing ~ 488
price, quote a ~ 1728
price range 1966
price, redemption ~ 2054
price reduction 927
price, regular ~ 1832
price regulation 1961
price, replacement ~ 2091
price, repurchase ~ 2095
price, resale ~ 2096
price, reserve ~ 1965
price restraint 1968
price, retail ~ 2096
price rise 1539
price, ruling ~ 911
prices, at constant ~ 742
prices, break in ~ 431
prices, collapse of ~ 431
prices, crumbling of ~ 886
prices, decline in ~ 886
prices, decrease in ~ 886
price(s), disparity in ~ 1038
prices, drop in ~ 886
prices, easing of ~ 886
price, selling ~ 2162
price, set ~ 78
price, set a ~ 1033
price, settlement ~ 650
prices, fall in ~ 886
prices, firmness of ~ 1326
price, share ~ 2174
prices, imposition of ~ 1515
price, special ~ 1203
prices, pegging of ~ 1917
price, spot ~ 593, 2203
price spread 1966
prices, sag in ~ 886
prices, slump in ~ 431
prices, steadiness of ~ 1326
price stability 1326
price stabilization 1969
price, standard ~ 1832
price, state a ~ 1728
price, stock ~ 2174
price stop 1400
price, subscription ~ 2238
price support 1917
price system for gold, two-tier ~ 2310
price to earnings ratio 1963
price, top ~ 605
price, trade ~ 2288
price, uniform ~ 1344, 2326
price, unit ~ 2328
price, usurious ~ 1250
price, wholesale ~ 2288
pricing 1962
primary commodity 329
primary incomes 1970
primary liquidity 1971
primary product 329
prime bill 1323
prime costs 1043
prime lending rate 311
prime rate 311, 328
prime trade bill 1323
priming, pump ~ 2011
principal 1972, 1973
principal office(s) 607
principal shareholder 633
principle, minimum value ~ 1721
principle of gross presentation 1755
principle of net presentation 1756
prior creditor 1948
prior deduction 89
priority 1328
priority right 1328
private account 1926
private bank 1974
private capital 1975
private consumer expenditure 1499
private debt 1928
private enterprise 1976, 1977
private income 1929
private investment 1978
private limited company 1690

private ownership 1979
private property 1979
private savings 1980
private sector 1981
privilege, tax ~ 2263
probate duty 938
proceeds 229, 1982
processing fee 1478
procure capital 416
procurement of capital 1405
produce exchange 695
producer cooperative 1983
producer goods 1134
producers' cooperative 1983
producer's goods 1134, 1134
product, gross domestic ~ 1461
production cost(s) 811
production goods 1134
product, national ~ 1803
product, primary ~ 329
profit 1409
profitability 1984
profitable 1147
profitableness 1984
profit, afford a ~ 100
profit and loss account 1523
profit and loss statement 1523
profit, anticipated ~ 166
profit, apparent ~ 171
profit, assessable ~ 197
profit, assumed ~ 171
profit balance 849
profit balance brought forward 1985
profit balance carried forward 1985
profit, balance sheet showing a ~ 275
profit, book ~ 412
profit, bring in a ~ 100
profit brought forward 1985
profit, business ~ 475
profit carried forward 1985
profit, clear ~ 646
profit, commercial ~ 475
profit, distributable ~ 1072
profit distribution 183
profit, excess ~ 1213
profit, fictitious ~ 171
profit, gross ~ 1459
profit, imaginary ~ 171
profit in exchange 1233
profit, leave a ~ 100
profit, make a ~ 1729
profit-making association 1986
profit margin 1734
profit margin, net ~ 1813
profit, net ~ 646
profit on exchange 1233
profit, operating ~ 475
profit, pocket a ~ 1937
profit, pure ~ 646
profit, rake in a ~ 1937
profit ratio, net ~ 1815
profit, realise a ~ 1729
profit, realize a ~ 1729
profit retention 1987
profit, return a ~ 100
profits 229
profits, appropriation of ~ 183
profits, capitalise ~ 548
profits, capitalize ~ 548
profit sharing 1410
profit shortfall 1718
profit(s), loss of ~ 1718
profits, percentage of ~ 1923
profit squeeze 1988
profits, retained ~ 2108
profits, share in the ~ 2173
profits tax 1989
profits, unappropriated ~ 2311
profits, undistributed ~ 2108
profits, undivided ~ 2311
profit, surplus ~ 1213
profit taking 1990
profit, taxable ~ 197
profit, trading ~ 475
profit, turn a ~ 1729
profit, yield a ~ 100
pro forma invoice 1991
proforma invoice 1991
program, financial ~ 1312
progressive depreciation 1545
progressive rate of a tax 1992
progressive tax 1456
prohibition, import ~ 319
prohibitive duty 1993
projections, budget ~ 451
prolong a credit 1272
prolong a term 1273
prolongation 1994
prolongation of credit 1275
promise of shares 1597
promissory note 1477
promoters' shares 1386
promotion of saving(s) 1161
proof, inflation-~ 1562
proof of debt 609
proof of indebtedness 609
property, distribution of ~ 1073
property, immovable ~ 1508
property, landed ~ 1661
property, movable ~ 622
property, personal ~ 622
property, private ~ 1979
property, real ~ 1508
property tax 551, 1662, 1995
property, trust ~ 2308
proprietor 1878
proprietors' capital 1996
proprietors' equity 1996
prospectus, issue ~ 1643
prospectus, subscription ~ 1643
prospectus, underwriting ~ 1643
protect a bill of exchange 1054
protectionist 1997
protective duty 1998
protest a bill of exchange 1481
provide anticipatory finance 1951
provide capital 1407
provision 129
provision account 130
provisional balance sheet 1596
provisional certificate 1597
provisional payment 1999
provisional return 2000
provisional share 1597
provision for contingencies 756
provision for depreciation 132
provision for depreciation, annual ~ 157
provision for doubtful debts 243
provision for tax 2001
provision for taxation 2001
provision of anticipatory finance 1952
provision of capital 1408
prune expenses 915
public benefits 684
public consumption 2002
public debt 1798
public enterprise 1448
public expenditure 2003
public finance body 2004
public finance(s) 827
public funds 1244, 2005
public investment 2006
publicity price 1613
public limited company 1537
public loan 1453
publicly owned enterprise 1448
public money 2005
public resources 2007
public revenue 1451
public sector 2008
public securities 1244
public service corporation 2009
public spending 2003
public stock(s) 1244
public utility 2009
public utility company 2009
public works 2010
pump priming 2011
purchase 479, 2012
purchase, cash ~ 594
purchase, credit ~ 852
purchase for forward delivery 1376
purchase for future delivery 486
purchase for (the) settlement 486
purchase forward 486
purchase, forward ~ 1376
purchase, future ~ 1376
purchase, hire ~ 1487
purchase, instal(l)ment ~ 1573
purchase on account 852
purchase on term 1376
purchase option 2013
purchase price 488
purchaser 482
purchase rate 354
purchase, speculative ~ 2198
purchase tax 2014
purchase, term ~ 1376
purchase value 50
purchasing power 487
purchasing power, excessive ~ 1209
purchasing price 488
pure profit 646
put 1858
put and call 1108
put a tax (on) 194
put in capital 436
put in pawn 1018
put in pledge 1018
put (in)to account 570
put of more 1857

put on sale 1841
put on the market 1737
put option 1858
put out bonds 1637
put out money at (on) interest 1675
put premium 1953
put to the reserve 68
put up capital 436
put up for sale 1841

qualifying share 2015
quarter 2016
quasi money 1805
quick assets 227
quick liabilities 910
quid pro quo 731
quiet 508
quit of charges 131
quit of expenses 131
quota 1186, 2017
quota restrictions 2018
quota restrictions, subject to ~ 1186
quotation 1960
quotation, asked ~ 193
quotation, bid ~ 354
quotation, closing ~ 657
quotation, market ~ 1234
quotation (of share prices) 1746
quotation of the day 913
quotation, opening ~ 1849
quotation, share ~ 2174
quotation, uniform ~ 2326
quote 1698
quote a price 1728
quoted securities 1699
quoted value 1234

raid the reserves 1042
raise 1540, 1542
raise a loan 762
raise a mortgage (on) 2019
raise a tax (on) 194
raise capital 416
raise the capital stock 1544
raise the value 178
raising of capital 1405
raising of funds 1405
raising of taxes 1516
raising of the minimum lending rate 1541
rake in a profit 1937
rally 2020
range 1037
range, price ~ 1966
rate 177, 195, 614, 1135, 1960, 2021
rat(e)able 196
rat(e)able value 198, 199
rate, amortisation ~ 144, 145
rate, amortization ~ 144, 145
rate, asked ~ 193
rate, average ~ 234
rate, backwardation ~ 240
rate, bank ~ 311
rate, base ~ 328
rate, basic ~ 328
rate, borrowing ~ 423
rate, buying ~ 354
rate, carry-over ~ 569
rate, clearing ~ 650
rate, closing ~ 657
rate, commission ~ 691
rate, contango ~ 569
rate, continuation ~ 569
rate, cross ~ 884
rate, current ~ 913
rate, demand ~ 354
rate, depreciation ~ 144
rate differential, interest ~ 1412
rate, discount ~ 1061
rate, exchange ~ 1234
rate, flat ~ 1345
rate for advances on collateral (security) 2022
rate for advances on securities 1714
rate for loans on collateral (security) 2022
rate for loans on securities 1714
rate for notes and coin(s) 1235
rate for secured advances 2022
rate for secured loans 2022
rate, forward ~ 1383, 1384
rate, forward exchange ~ 1383
rate, free ~ 1396
rate, free market ~ 1396
rate, future ~ 1383, 1384
rate gain 1233
rate, intervention ~ 1610
rate, loan ~ 423
rate, lombard ~ 1714
rate, market ~ 1234
rate, mean ~ 234
rate, middle ~ 234
rate, minimum lending ~ 311
rate, money ~ 1782
rate of assessment 2023
rate of a tax, progressive ~ 1992
rate of conversion 778
rate of discount, bank ~ 311
rate of exchange 1216
rate (of exchange), compulsory ~ 722
rate (of exchange), controlled ~ 722
rate (of exchange), current ~ 907
rate of exchange, difference in the ~ 1039
rate of exchange, fixed ~ 1341
rate of exchange, flexible ~ 1347
rate of exchange, floating ~ 1347
rate of exchange, fluctuating ~ 1347
rate (of exchange), forced ~ 722
rate of exchange for forward delivery 1383
rate of exchange for notes and coin(s) 1235
rate of exchange for spot delivery 2024
rate of exchange, free ~ 1347
rate of exchange, preferential ~ 1950
rate of exchange, variable ~ 1347
rate of expansion 1255, 1256
rate of growth 1255, 1256
rate of increase 1255, 1256
rate of inflation 1563
rate of interest 1593
rate (of interest), nominal ~ 1821
rate of investment 1629
rate of issue 1642
rate of return 2025
rate of saving(s) 2026
rate of tax 2023
rate of taxation 2023
rate of the day 913
rate of turnover 2027
rate, opening ~ 1849
rate, open market ~ 1396
rate, par ~ 1887
rate, parity ~ 1888
ratepayer 2028
rate, pegged ~ 1610
rate, prime ~ 328
rate, prime lending ~ 311
rate, purchase ~ 354
rate, redemption ~ 145, 2054
rate, rediscount ~ 2059
rate, retirement ~ 2054
rate, selling ~ 193
rate, settlement ~ 650
rate, settling ~ 650
rates, graduated ~ 1041
rate, spot ~ 593, 2024, 2203
rate, stock exchange ~ 1234
rate, subscription ~ 2238
rate, support ~ 1610
rating 200
rating, credit ~ 873
ratio 2029
ratio, cash ~ 45
ratio, cover ~ 840
ratio, debtor to sales ~ 960
ratio, debt to equity ~ 963
ratio, investment ~ 1629
ratio, minimum reserve ~ 1759
rationalization investment 1580
rationing of foreign exchange 2030
ratio, parity ~ 1888
ratio, price-earnings ~ 1963
raw material 329
ready assets 227
ready money 572
real assets 1508
real cost 54
real estate 1508
real estate, credit on ~ 868
real estate tax 1995
realignment of par values 2031
real income 2032
realinement of par values 2031
realisability 2033
realisable 2034
realisable assets 905
realisation 773
realisation value 432
realise 785
realise a profit 1729
realizability 2033
realizable 2034
realizable assets 905
realization 773
realization value 432
realize 785
realize a profit 1729
real property 1508
real property, credit on ~ 868

real security 2035
realty 1508
real value 56
real yield 57
reappraisal 2036
reappraise 2037
rebate 127
rebate, dealer's ~ 935
rebate, interest ~ 1594
rebate, interest rate ~ 1594
rebate, nominal ~ 1822
rebate of tax 2038
rebate, trade ~ 935
rebuild the reserve 2039
recall 1008
recall (from circulation) 503
receipt 47, 51
receipt, deposit ~ 608, 877
receipts 1532
receipt, safe custody ~ 608
receipts and expenditure(s) 1525
receipts and expenses 1525
receipts and payments 1525
receipts, budgetary ~ 447
receipts, cash ~ 585
receipts, customs ~ 921
receipts, extraordinary ~ 1287
receipts, non-recurrent ~ 1287
receipts, non-recurring ~ 1287
receipts, recurrent ~ 2049
receipts, recurring ~ 2049
receipts, surplus ~ 2245
receipts, tax ~ 1565
receipt, trust ~ 608
receipt, warehouse ~ 2364
receivability 674
receivable 675
receivables 37
receivables, doubtful ~ 1110
receiver (in bankruptcy) 209
receivership 2040
recession 1031
reckon 490
recompense 2041, 2042
reconcile accounts 112
reconciliation of accounts 2043
reconstruction of the finances 1318
reconstruct the finances 2044
record 401
record a fall (a gain) of X points 2045
record a loss (a profit) 2046
record, stock ~ 1701
recoup a loss 707
recourse 2047
recoverable 675
recoverableness 674
recover a debt 677
recover a loss 707
recover one's money 1421
recovery 680, 2048
recovery of debts 682
rectifying entry 71
recurrent receipts 2049
recurring receipts 2049
recycling of capital 2050
red 943
red, be in the ~ 944
redeem 148, 502
redeemability 2051
redeemable 2052
redeemable bond 497
redeemable by lot 498
redeemable debenture 497
redeem a mortgage 511
redemption 139, 2053
redemption, anticipated ~ 167
redemption bond 704
redemption fund 140
redemption loan 141
redemption of a loan 142
redemption plan 146
redemption premium 1750
redemption price 2054
redemption rate 145, 2054
redemption scheme 146
redemption table 146
redemption value 2055
redetermination of quotas 77
red interest 947
rediscount 2056, 2057
rediscountable 2058
rediscounting 2056
rediscount rate 2059
rediscount rate, increase in the ~ 1541
rediscount rate, reduction in the ~ 926
redistribution 2060
redraft 819
reduce capital stock 2061
reduce expenses 915
reduce share capital 2061
reduce the par value 2062
reducing depreciation 7
reduction in the discount rate 926
reduction in the dividend 925
reduction in the price 927
reduction in the rediscount rate 926
reduction in value 969
reduction of capital 2063
reduction of capital stock 2064
reduction of flexibility margins 2065
reduction of fluctuation margins 2065
reduction of share capital 2064
reduction, tax ~ 2261
reexport 2066
reexportation 2066
refinance 2067
refinancing 2068
reflate 2069
reflation 2070
reflow of capital 2071
reflux of capital 2071
reform, currency ~ 899
reform, monetary ~ 899
reform, tax ~ 2274
refund 1900, 2072
refundable 2073
refund a loan 779
refund, claim for ~ 640
refunding bond 704
refunding of a loan 775
refund of tax 2038
refusal of payment 2074
refusal to pay 2074
regie 1454
register, commercial ~ 687
registered capital 222
registered office(s) 2075
registered securities 1568
registered shareholder 2076
registered shares 1568
registered stock 1568
register of members 1701
register of shareholders 1701
register of stockholders 1701
register, share ~ 1701
register, stock ~ 1701
register, trade ~ 687
registration dues 2077
registration fee(s) 2077
regressive tax 997
regular income 210
regular price 1832
regulation, price ~ 1961
regulations, currency ~ 900
regulations, exchange ~ 900
regulations, exchange control ~ 900
regulations, foreign exchange ~ 900
regulator, fiscal ~ 1333
rehabilitate the finances 2044
rehabilitation of the finances 1318
reimbursable 2073
reimburse 1900
reimbursement 2072
reimbursement credit 1085
reinvest 1936
reinvestment 2078
relations between the exchange rates 1236
relaxation of credit 1145
relax credit restrictions 1143
release 949, 950
release, tax ~ 2261
relend 2079
relief, tax ~ 2261
remainder 246
remaining amount 246
remargining 62
remission, dividend ~ 925
remission of a debt 513
remission, tax ~ 2261
remit 2080
remit a debt 510
remittance 1784
remittance charge(s) 2081
remittance fee 2081
remittance in cash 595
remittance, monthly ~ 1787
remittee 2082
remitter 2083
removal of restrictions 2
remove restrictions 1
remunerate 2042
remuneration 2041
remuneration in kind 134
remunerative 1147
rendering of services 2084
renew a credit 1272
renewal coupon 2085
renewal fund 2086
renewal of coupons 2087

renewal of credit 1275
rent 2088
rental 2088
reorganization of the finances 1318
reorganize the finances 2044
repair a loss 707
reparation 708
repatriate 2089
repatriation 2090
repay 148, 1900
repayable 2073
repay a mortgage 511
repayment 139, 2072
repeat option 485, 1857
replacement cost(s) 2091
replacement price 2091
replacement reserve 2086
replacement value 2091
replacement value, amortisation on ~ 143
replacement value, amortization on ~ 143
replacement value, depreciation on ~ 143
replenish the reserve 2039
report, annual ~ 160
report, audit ~ 217
report, auditor's ~ 217, 217
report, stock market ~ 1228
representation expenses 1169
repudiate a debt 2092
repudiation of a debt 2093
repurchase 480, 2094
repurchase price 2095
request, on ~ 495
requirement, borrowing ~ 424
requirements, capital ~ 557
requirements, cash ~ 596
requirements, coverage ~ 837
requirements, financial ~ 1316
requirements, investment ~ 1627
requirements, liquidity ~ 596
requirements, margin ~ 837
requirements, minimum reserve ~ 1670
requirements, reserve ~ 1670
requisite cover 837
resale price 2096
resale price maintenance 2097
research, market ~ 1740
reserve 129, 2098
reserve account 130
reserve, build up a ~ 454
reserve, carry to ~ 68
reserve, cash ~ 597
reserve, contingency ~ 756
reserve, contingent ~ 756
reserve, counter-cyclical equalization ~ 820
reserve, create a ~ 454
reserve, currency ~ 901
reserve currency 2100
reserve, depreciation ~ 132
reserve, exchange ~ 901
reserve for contingencies 756
reserve for doubtful debts 243
reserve, foreign exchange ~ 901
reserve, form a ~ 454
reserve for taxation 2001
reserve fund 2101
reserve fund, carry to the ~ 68
reserve, gold ~ 1440
reserve, monetary ~ 1770
reserve, money ~ 1770
reserve prescribed by the articles 2102
reserve price 1965
reserve ratio 45
reserve, rebuild the ~ 2039
reserve, replacement ~ 2086
reserve, replenish the ~ 2039
reserve requirements 1670
reserves 2098
reserves, concealed ~ 726
reserves, declared ~ 966
reserves, depletion of the ~ 1012
reserves, dip into the ~ 1042
reserves, disclosed ~ 966
reserves, draw (up)on the ~ 1042
reserves, encroach (up)on the ~ 1042
reserves, exhaustion of the ~ 1012
reserves, fall back (up)on the ~ 1042
reserve(s), free ~ 1397
reserves, gold and foreign exchange ~ 1429
reserves, have recourse to the ~ 1042
reserves, hidden ~ 726
reserves, invisible ~ 726
reserves, legal ~ 1670
reserves, minimum ~ 1670
reserves, obligatory ~ 1670
reserves, raid the ~ 1042
reserve, statutory ~ 2102
reserves, undisclosed ~ 726
reserves, visible ~ 966
reserves, withdrawal from ~ 2377
reserve, under ~ 2099
residual value 2103
resistance, consumer ~ 750
resources 1406
resources, capital ~ 558
resources, cash ~ 587
resources, financial ~ 558
resources, liquid ~ 227
resources, pecuniary ~ 1916
resources, public ~ 2007
respite 998
respite a payment 984, 1274
respite, days of ~ 933
respite for payment 1276
rest 246, 255
restitution, claim for ~ 640
restrain inflation 628
restraint, price ~ 1968
restrict expenses 915
restriction of credit 874
restriction of liquidity 2104
restriction on imports 1513
restrictions, abolish ~ 1
restrictions, abolition of ~ 2
restrictions, currency ~ 902
restrictions, exchange ~ 902
restrictions, foreign exchange ~ 902
restrictions, lift ~ 1
restrictions, lifting of ~ 2
restrictions, quota ~ 2018
restrictions, removal of ~ 2
restrictions, remove ~ 1
restrictions, withdraw ~ 1
restrictions, withdrawal of ~ 2
retail credit 745
retailer 2105
retail price 2096
retail price index 2106
retail trade 2107
retained earnings 2108
retained income 1137
retained profits 2108
retention money 2109
retention of profits 1987
retire 148, 502
retire (from circulation) 503
retirement 139, 1008, 2053
retirement rate 2054
retrench 924
retrench expenses 915
retrieve a loss 707
return 365, 1900, 2110
returnable 2073
return an interest of X percent 334
return, annual ~ 160
return a profit 100
return (a) X percent interest 334
return, bank ~ 312
return draft 819
returned bill 365
return, income tax ~ 1531
return interest at a rate of X percent 334
return on capital 535
return, provisional ~ 2000
return, rate of ~ 2025
returns 1982
return, tax ~ 2275
revalorization 2111
revalorize 178
revaluate 178, 2037
revaluation 2036, 2111
revalue 178, 2037
revenue 1522
revenue account 1524
revenue, customs ~ 921
revenue from capital 535
revenue, government ~ 1451
revenue, gross ~ 1463
revenue, inland ~ 1242, 1565
revenue, internal ~ 1242
revenue, net ~ 1811
revenue, public ~ 1451
revenues 447
revenue shortfall 445, 2112
revenues, miscellaneous ~ 1765
revenue, source of ~ 2193
revenue, state ~ 1451
revenue, tariff ~ 921
revenue, tax ~ 1565
reversal 428, 512
reversing entry 281
revocable credit 2113
revolving credit 2114
rider 124

rigging 1730
right 174, 2115
right, application ~ 174
right, conversion ~ 777
right, first ~ 1328
right of option 1854
right of pre-emption 2013
right of preference 1328
right of priority 1328
right of repurchase, sale with ~ 2132
right, preferential ~ 1328
rights, cum ~ 888
rights, ex ~ 1249
rights issue 2116
rights off 1249
rights on 888
rights (on), drawing ~ 1121
right, stock ~ 174
right, subscription ~ 174
rights, with ~ 888
right, usufructary ~ 349
ring 571
rise 1540, 1542, 2117
rise, buy for a ~ 456
rise in price(s) 1539
rise in the minimum lending rate 1541
rise in value 179, 180
rise of X per cent 1543
rise, speculate for a ~ 456
rising trend 459
risk-bearing capital 1178
risk capital 1178
risk, exchange ~ 1238
roll-over loan 2118
rough estimate 184
round figures, in ~ 2119
royalty 1686
rubber check 241
ruling price 911
runaway inflation 1411
run counter to the general trend 2120
run into debt 1294
running account 23
running costs 1850
running expenses 908, 1850
running interest 909
run of business 833
run on the bank 2121
run up a debt 761

safe 2122
safe custody receipt 608
safe deposit box 2123
safe deposit charge 2124
safe deposit vault 2125
safety deposit box 2123
safety deposit vault 2125
sagging 508
sag in prices 886
salable 1738
salaries, wages and ~ 1141
salary 2126
salary increase 1540
salary, monthly ~ 1787
sale 2127, 2128
saleable 1738
sale at a loss 2129
sale, bear ~ 346
sale by auction 212
sale, cash ~ 598
sale, credit ~ 875
sale, hire purchase ~ 1491
sale, instal(l)ment ~ 1491
sale, offer for ~ 1841
sale, put on ~ 1841
sale, put up for ~ 1841
sales 2130
sales area 1736
sales, gross ~ 1467
sale, short ~ 346
sales index 2131
sales, net ~ 1816
sales tax 2014
sales value 688
sale with right of repurchase 2132
satisfy a mortgage 511
save 2133
saver 2134
saving by investment in securities 2135
saving, compulsory ~ 724
saving, forced ~ 724
saving, gross domestic ~ 1462
saving on savings accounts 2136
savings 2137
savings account 2138
savings accounts, saving on ~ 2136
savings bank 2139
savings bank book 2140
savings bank deposit book 2140
savings bond 2141
savings book 2142
savings capital 2143
savings certificate 2141
savings, contractual ~ 764
savings deposit 2144
saving(s), encouragement of ~ 1161
savings fund 2145
savings, private ~ 1980
saving(s), promotion of ~ 1161
saving(s) rate 2026
scale, flexible ~ 1348
scale, sliding ~ 1348
scarcity of capital 559
schedule, amortization ~ 146
scheme, financial ~ 1312
scheme of arrangement 718
scheme of composition 718
scheme, redemption ~ 146
scrip 400, 1597
scrip certificate 1597
scrip issue 399
S.D.R. 2195
secondary income 2146
secondary liquidity 1776
secondary market 2147
secondary security 65
second of exchange 2148
secrecy, bank ~ 305
secrecy, banking ~ 305
secret, bank ~ 305
sectional costing, direct ~ 1045
sector, distribution ~ 1075
sector, growth ~ 1470
sector, private ~ 1981
sector, public ~ 2008
secure 52
secure by mortgage 838
secured advance 86
secured advances, rate for ~ 2022
secured bond 2149
secured credit 670
secured creditor 2150
secured loan 672
secured loans, rate for ~ 2022
securities 2151
securities admitted to the stock exchange 1699
securities, advance on ~ 90, 91
securities, bearer ~ 342
securities broker 2152
securities, collateralize ~ 671
securities, credit on ~ 869
securities, gilt-edged ~ 387
securities, government ~ 1244
securities held in pawn 1895
securities held in pledge 1895
securities, hypothecate ~ 671
securities, hypothecation of ~ 1501
securities, inscribed ~ 1568
securities, investment ~ 1630
securities, investment in ~ 1626
securities, lending on ~ 1674
securities, lend on ~ 91
securities, listed ~ 1699
securities' listing 1228
securities, loan on ~ 1712
securities lodged as collateral 1895
securities market 2153
securities, marketable ~ 1739
securities, negotiable ~ 1739
securities, outside ~ 892
securities, over-the-counter ~ 892
securities, pawn ~ 671
securities, pawned ~ 1895
securities, pawning of ~ 1501
securities, pledge ~ 671
securities, pledged ~ 1895
securities pledged as collateral 1895
securities, pledging of ~ 1501
securities, portfolio ~ 1630
securities, public ~ 1244
securities, quoted ~ 1699
securities, registered ~ 1568
securities, speculative ~ 2199
securities, stock exchange ~ 1699
securities, transferable ~ 1739
securities, unlisted ~ 892
securities, unquoted ~ 892
security 1138
security, additional ~ 65
security, advance against ~ 86
security bearer 341
security bond 394
security, collateral ~ 65, 669
security, credit against ~ 670
security deals 1222
security, deposit as ~ 1018
security, fixed interest ~ 1339
security, fixed interest bearing ~ 1339

security, fixed yield ~ 1339
security, give as ~ 1018
security holder 341
security holdings 1628
security, lodge as ~ 1018
security market 2153
security on mortgage 2035
security, real ~ 2035
security, secondary ~ 65
security, social ~ 2184
security, stand ~ 52
security, tangible ~ 2258
security transactions 1222
seigneurage 2154
seign(i)orage 2154
seize 211
seizure 191
self-balancing accounting 2155
self-finance 1601
self-financing 1601
self-liquidating loan 2156
self-sufficiency 219
sell 2157
sell at a loss 2158
sell at auction 213
sell by auction 213
seller 2159
seller's market 2160
seller's option 1858
seller's option to double 1857
sell for a fall 1427
sell for future delivery 2161
sell for (the) settlement 2161
sell forward 2161
selling at a loss 2129
selling option 1858
selling price 2162
selling rate 193
sell on credit 2163
sell on trust 2163
sell, option to ~ 1858
sell short 1427
sell with a loss 2158
semi-annual coupon 1475
semi-annual instal(l)ment 351
semi-variable costs 2164
send 2080
sequester 211
sequestrate 211
sequestration 191, 2040
serve a loan 2165
serve as cover 2166
service a loan 2165
service charge 80
service, debt ~ 962
service, interest~ 1592
service, internal revenue ~ 1242
service of a loan 2167
service, postal giro ~ 1423
services 2168
services, goods and ~ 1443
services, rendering of ~ 2084
set a price 1033
setback 968
set free 949
set-off 281, 706
setoff 709
set price 78
setting a ceiling 1342
settle 148
settle an account 249
settled income 210
settle in cash 1727
settlement 139
settlement, buy for (the) ~ 486
settlement day 24
settlement, means of ~ 1751
settlement of an account 254
settlement of balance(s) 1199
settlement period 18
settlement price 650
settlement rate 650
settlement, sell for (the) ~ 2161
settle the balance 1914
settling day 24
settling rate 650
share 2169
share, bearer ~ 343
share, bonus ~ 400
share capital 544
share capital, ordinary ~ 697
share capital, outstanding ~ 1638
share capital, reduce ~ 2061
share capital, reduction of ~ 2064
share capital, watered ~ 2365
share certificate 2170
share, deferred ~ 985
share, earnings per ~ 1142
share fraction 1387
shareholder 2171
shareholder, chief ~ 633
shareholder, leading ~ 633
shareholder, major ~ 633
shareholder of record 2076
shareholder, principal ~ 633
shareholder, registered ~ 2076
shareholders' equity 1809, 1996
shareholders, list of ~ 1701
shareholders, register of ~ 1701
shareholding 2172
shareholdings 1628
share (in full), pay up a ~ 1915
share in limited partnership 1591
share, interim ~ 1597
share in the profits 2173
share issue 1640
share ledger 1701
share market 2153
share, multiple vote ~ 1796
share, multi-voting ~ 1796
share option 1855
share, preference ~ 1946
share premium 1641
share price 2174
share, provisional ~ 1597
share, qualifying ~ 2015
share quotation 2174
share register 1701
shares, allotment of ~ 125
shares, apportionment of ~ 125
shares, assignment of ~ 125
shares, block of ~ 386
shares, common ~ 701
shares, distribution of ~ 125
shares, employees' ~ 1159
shares, exchange of ~ 1232
shares, founders' ~ 1386
shares, fully paid ~ 1403
shares, lot of ~ 386
shares, management ~ 1386
shares, new ~ 1819
shares, new issue ~ 1819
shares, non-voting ~ 1830
shares, no-par ~ 1831
shares, ordinary ~ 701
shares, outstanding ~ 1638
shares, paid-up ~ 1403
shares, parcel of ~ 386
share split(-up) 2175
shares, promoters' ~ 1386
shares, registered ~ 1568
shares, staff ~ 1159
shares, stamping of ~ 2212
share, subdivided ~ 2230
shares, voting ~ 2357
shares without par value 1831
shares, worker(s') ~ 1159
share, tied ~ 2282
share warrant 2170
share without coupon sheet 2176
share with plural voting rights 1796
sharing, gain ~ 1410
sharing, market ~ 1745
sharing, profit ~ 1410
sheet, cost apportionment ~ 799
sheet, coupon ~ 832
sheet, pay ~ 1912
short 988, 2177
shortage 983
shortage, dollar ~ 1090
shortage in the cash 96
shortage of capital 559
short balance 93
short, cash ~ 96
short covering 335
short-dated 2177
shortfall 983
shortfall in (of) tax revenue 1330
shortfall in receipts 2112
shortfall, profit ~ 1718
shortfall, revenue ~ 445, 2112
short of cash, be ~ 2178
short sale 346
short, sell ~ 1427
short-term 2177
short-term debts 910
short-term liabilities 910
show a fall (a gain) of X points 2045
show a loss (a profit) 2046
side, assets ~ 206
side, credit ~ 206
side, creditor ~ 206
side, debit ~ 943
side, debtor ~ 943
side, liabilities ~ 943
sight, at ~ 1956
sight bill 1003
sight deposit 1004
sight draft 1003
sight liabilities 1006
sight loan 504
sight note 1007
sight obligations 1006
sight, payable at ~ 1896

signature loan 379
silent partner 1105
simple interest 2179
single bill 2180
single entry bookkeeping 2181
single standard 1785
sink 148
sinking fund 140
sinking fund loan 141
sinking fund mortgage loan 137
sinking fund table 146
situation, market ~ 1743
six-monthly instal(l)ment 351
slack 508
slackening 968
slackness 1130
sleeping partner 1105
slide 968
sliding scale 1348
sliding-scale tariff 1041
slip, credit ~ 876, 877
slip, deposit ~ 608, 877, 1022
slip, extension ~ 124
slip, pay ~ 1913
slip, pay-in ~ 877, 1022
slip, paying-in ~ 877, 1022
slip, transfer ~ 848
slow debtor 981
slowdown 968
sluggish 508
sluggishness 1130
slump 1031
slumpflation 2182
slump in prices 431
small change 612
small coin 1083
small money 1083
snake 2183
snowballing inflation 1411
socialization 1801
socialize 1802
social security 2184
social security benefit 2185
social security contributions 2186
social security taxes 2186
society, building ~ 453
society, co-operative ~ 786
society, credit ~ 787
society, loan ~ 787
society, mutual loan ~ 787
soft currency 2187
soft currency country 2188
soft money 623, 1355
sola 2180
sola bill 2180
sold note 440
sold note, contract ~ 440
sole bill of exchange 2180
sole of exchange 2180
solid 846
solidity 873
solvability 2189
solvency 2189
solvent 2190
sound 846
sound currency 2191
soundness 873
source, collection at ~ 681
source, deduct at ~ 972
source, deduction at ~ 975
source, deduction of tax at ~ 681
source of finance 2192
source of income 2193
source of revenue 2193
source, taxation at ~ 681
source, tax deducted at ~ 2268
special allowance 1284
special charges 61
special costs 61
special credit 2194
special dividend 398
special drawing rights 2195
special expenses 61
special partner 1691
special price 1203
specie 661
specie, gold ~ 667
specie, in ~ 573
specie standard, gold ~ 1402
speculate 2196
speculate for a fall 1427
speculate for a rise 456
speculation 2197
speculation, stock exchange ~ 111
speculative purchase 2198
speculative securities 2199
speculative stocks 2199
speculator 2200
speculator, market ~ 1647
speculator, stock exchange ~ 1647
spend 1257
spending 1258
spending, capital ~ 524
spending, consumer ~ 748
spending, deficit ~ 989
spending, investment ~ 524
spending, public ~ 2003
spiral, cost-price ~ 816
spiral, deflationary ~ 993
spiral, inflationary ~ 1559
spiral, wage-price ~ 2363
split the difference 2201
split(-up) 2175
spot deal 581
spot delivery, rate of exchange for ~ 2024
spot exchange 1227
spot exchange business 1227
spot exchange deal 2202
spot exchange dealing 1227
spot exchange operation 2202
spot exchange rate 2024
spot exchange transaction 2202
spot price 593, 2203
spot rate 593, 2024, 2203
spot transaction 581
spread 1037, 1108
spread, interest ~ 1412
spread out payments over X years 2204
spread payments over X years 2204
spread, price ~ 1966
square accounts 112
square an account 249
squaring of accounts 2043
squeeze, credit ~ 874
squeeze, liquidity ~ 1697
squeeze, money ~ 1314
squeeze, profit ~ 1988
stability, currency ~ 903
stability, exchange ~ 1239
stability, monetary ~ 903
stability, price ~ 1326
stabilization, exchange rate ~ 1237
stabilization fund 2205
stabilization loan 2206
stabilization, price ~ 1969
stable currency 2207
staff shares 1159
stagflation 2208
stagnancy 1130
stagnant 508
stagnate 1663
stagnation 1130
stake (in) 1495
stamp 662, 2209, 2210
stamp duty 2211
stamping of shares 2212
stamp tax 2211
stamp, trading ~ 2290
standard, double ~ 375
standard gold 666
standard, gold ~ 1441
standard, gold bullion ~ 1431
standard, gold exchange ~ 1436
standard, gold nucleus ~ 1431
standard, halting ~ 1476
standard, indirect foreign exchange ~ 1436
standard, limping ~ 1476
standard of living 1704
standard, paper ~ 1881
standard price 1832
standard, single ~ 1785
standard value 2213
stand-by 2214
stand-by agreement 2215
stand-by credit 2214
standing, credit ~ 873
stand security 52
stand still 1663
standstill agreement 2216
stand surety 52
state aid 1445
state a price 1728
state budget 1446
state controlled enterprise 1448
state credit guarantee 1447
state enterprise 1448
state finance(s) 827
state funds 2005
state grant 1449
state guarantee 1450
state interference 1452
state intervention 1452
state loan 1453
state loan guarantee 1447
statement 2217
statement, account ~ 5
statement, annual ~ 160
statement, consolidated ~ 736
statement, consolidation ~ 739
statement, cost apportionment ~ 799

statement, deficiency ~ 274
statement, detailed ~ 429
statement, earnings ~ 275
statement, financial ~ 1319
statement, income ~ 1523
statement, interim (financial) ~ 1596
statement, itemized ~ 429
statement of account 5
statement of expenses 2218
statement, profit and loss ~ 1523
statement, summary ~ 2241
state monopoly 1454
state of an account 1940
state of the economy 477
state of the market 1743
state owned enterprise 1448
state revenue 1451
state run enterprise 1448
state subsidy 1449
state, welfare ~ 2373
statistical data 2219
statistics 2219
statistics, operating ~ 1851
statistiques 2220
status, credit ~ 873
statute-barred coupon 1664
statute-barred debt 324
statute of limitation(s) 1955
statutory reserve 2102
steadiness of prices 1326
sterilization 2221
sterilize 2222
sterling 2223
sterling area 2224
sterling bloc 2224
sterling, blocked ~ 382
sterling, pound ~ 1943
sterling, transferable ~ 2291
stock 389, 544, 1615, 2151, 2169
stock allotment warrant 2115
stock book 1701
stockbroker 2152
stock, capital ~ 544
stock capital 544
stock certificate 2170
stock, common ~ 701
stock company 1537
stock, consolidated ~ 734
stock corporation 1537
stock deals 1222
stock dividend 400
stock exchange 1218
stock exchange bulletin 1228
stock exchange dealings 1222
stock exchange gambler 1647
stock exchange list 1228
stock exchange listing 81
stock exchange, manipulation on the ~ 1730
stock exchange operations 1222
stock exchange operator 1647
stock exchange rate 1234
stock exchange report 1228
stock exchange securities 1699
stock exchange speculation 111
stock exchange speculator 1647
stock exchange transactions 1222
stock exchange turnover 2225
stock exchange value 1234
stock, exchequer ~ 1244
stock, foreign ~ 1370
stockholder 2171
stockholder, loan ~ 390
stockholder of record 2076
stockholders' equity 1996
stockholders' ledger 1701
stockholders, list of ~ 1701
stockholders, register of ~ 1701
stockholdings 1628
stock, investment in ~ 1626
stock issue 1640
stock, issued ~ 1638
stockjobber 1648
stockjobbing 111
stock, joint ~ 544
stock list 1228
stock, loan ~ 389
stock market 2153
stock market report 1228
stock, new ~ 1819
stock, non-voting ~ 1830
stock, no-par ~ 1831
stock option 1855
stock, ordinary ~ 701
stock owner 2171
stock, preference ~ 1946
stock, preferred ~ 1946
stock price 2174
stock record 1701
stock register 1701
stock, registered ~ 1568
stock right 174
stocks 2151
stocks, curb ~ 892
stocks, founders' ~ 1386
stocks, fully paid ~ 1403
stock(s), gilt-edged ~ 387
stocks, gold ~ 1430
stock(s), government ~ 1244
stocks, paid-up ~ 1403
stock split(-up) 2175
stock(s), public ~ 1244
stocks, speculative ~ 2199
stock(s), treasury ~ 1244
stock subscription warrant 2115
stock switch 1232
stock, take ~ 1124
stocktaking 1616
stock transactions 1222
stock, voting ~ 2357
stock warrant 2170
stock, watered ~ 2365
stock watering 2226
stock without par value 1831
stop a cheque 2227
stopgap loan 434
stop payment of a cheque 2227
stop payment on a check 2227
stop payments 603
stop, price ~ 1400
straddle 1108
straight line depreciation 2228
straits, financial ~ 1314
strike a balance 279
stringency, credit ~ 878
stringency, dollar ~ 1090
strong box 2122
strong currency 1479
strong room 2125
structural surplus 2229
structure, balance sheet ~ 273
structure, capital ~ 561
structure, cost ~ 817
structure, financial ~ 561
stub 821
study, market ~ 1740
stumer 241
sub-account 224
subcompany 98
subdivided share 2230
subject to duty 916
subject to quota restrictions 1186
subject to the payment of interest 2231
subject to X days' notice 1837
subscribed, amount ~ 153
subscribed capital 2232
subscribe (for) 2233
subscriber 2234
subscription 2235, 2236
subscription capital ~ 562
subscription period 2237
subscription price 2238
subscription prospectus 1643
subscription rate 2238
subscription right 174
subscription right certificate 2115
subscriptions for a loan, invite ~ 1634
subscription warrant 2115
subsequent endorser 2239
sub-share 2230
subsidiary 98
subsidiary account 224
subsidiary book 225
subsidiary company 98
subsidiary journal 225
subsidiary ledger 225
subsidize 2240
subsidy 1458
subsidy, export ~ 1269
subsidy, government ~ 1449
subsidy, interest ~ 1594
subsidy, interest rate ~ 1594
subsidy, state ~ 1449
subvention 1458, 2240
subventionize 2240
succession duty 938
succession tax 938
suffer a loss 333
sum 149
sum advanced 83
sum, credit someone with a ~ 566
sum due 151
sum in excess 1205
sum, lump ~ 1722
summary 2217
summary account 673
summary posting 717
summary statement 2241
sum owing 151
sum to someone, credit a ~ 566

sum to someone's credit, carry a ~ 566
sum to someone's credit, enter a ~ 566
sum to someone's credit, place a ~ 566
sum total 105
sundries 1764
sundry charges 1764
sundry costs 1764
sundry expenses 1764
superannuation fund 1918
supertax 66
supplement 60
supplemental credit 63
supplementary charges 61
supplementary costs 61
supplementary credit 63
supplementary expenses 61
supplementary tax 66
supply 1615
supply and demand 2242
supply capital 1407
supply, excessive ~ 1210
supply, money ~ 1783
supply of near money 2243
support, monetary ~ 1771
support point 1609
support, price ~ 1917
support rate 1610
surcharge 60, 1514, 1866
surety 236, 395
surety, act as ~ 52
surety, bill ~ 230
surety for a surety 238
surety, go ~ 52
suretyship, declaration of ~ 394
surety(ship), deed of ~ 394
surety, stand ~ 52
surplus 2244
surplus, accounting ~ 30
surplus, balance of payments ~ 263
surplus, budget ~ 452
surplus, cash ~ 599
surplus, country in ~ 824
surplus dividend 398
surplus, earned ~ 1137
surplus in the trade account 266
surplus in the trade balance 266
surplus of receipts 2245
surplus, operating ~ 1852
surplus profit 1213
surplus receipts 2245
surplus revenues 2246
surplus, structural ~ 2229
surplus takings 2245
surplus value 1215
surrender of the coupon, (up)on ~ 1958
surrender value 2247
surtax 66
surveillance, credit ~ 629
survey, market ~ 1740
suspend payments 603
suspense account 2248
suspense entry 2249
suspense item 2249
suspension of payment 1276
suspension of payments 2250
sustain a loss 333
swap 2251
swap credit 2252
swap transaction 2251
swing 864
swing in the economic situation 930
swing, market ~ 930
switch 2253, 2254
switch(ed) transaction 2253
switching 2254
switch, stock ~ 1232
syndicate 2255
syndicate account 1654
syndicated loan 741
syndicate loan 741
syndicate, underwriting ~ 2322
system, credit ~ 879
system, exchange ~ 1240
system, fiscal ~ 1334
system, monetary ~ 664
system, tax ~ 1334
system, taxation ~ 1334

table 2256
table, amortisation ~ 146
table, redemption ~ 146
table, sinking fund ~ 146
take a mortgage (on) 2019
take-over 2257
take stock 1124
take the inventory 1124
take up 2233, 2236
take up a loan 1122
taking, profit ~ 1990
takings 1532
takings, cash ~ 585
takings, surplus ~ 2245
talon 2085
tangible assets 1747
tangible security 2258
tantième 1923
tap issue 2259
tardy debtor 981
tariff 2260
tariff, customs ~ 922
tariff, differential ~ 1041
tariff, external ~ 1279
tariff, flexible ~ 1041
tariff, graded ~ 1041
tariff, graduated ~ 1041
tariff, preference ~ 1947
tariff, preferential ~ 1947
tariff revenue 921
tariff, sliding-scale ~ 1041
tariff wall 918
task wage 1907
tax 194, 1135
tax abatement 2261
taxable 196
taxable income 197, 2262
taxable profit 197
taxable value 198
tax, additional ~ 66
tax advantage 2263
tax adviser 2264
tax advisor 2264
tax, after ~ 1677
tax allowance 2261
tax assessment basis 331
tax assessment notice 1839
taxation 2265
taxation at source 681
taxation, basis of ~ 331
taxation, deferred ~ 986
taxation, double ~ 1109
taxation system 1334
tax authorities 1242
tax avoidance 2266
tax, before ~ 1959
tax benefit 2263
tax bracket 2267
tax burden 463
tax, business ~ 476
tax, capital ~ 551
tax, capital gains ~ 532
tax, capital stock ~ 560
tax, capital transfer ~ 564
tax, capital yield(s) ~ 565
tax, collect a ~ 678
tax collection 683
tax, compensatory ~ 712
tax concession 2263
tax consultant 2264
tax, consumption ~ 752
tax, corporate ~ 792
tax, corporation ~ 792
tax, death ~ 938
tax deducted 1677
tax deducted at source 2268
tax deduction 2261
tax deficit 1330
tax, degressive ~ 997
tax, direct ~ 1046
tax dodging 2266
tax, equalization ~ 712
tax equalization 1175
taxes, after ~ 1677
taxes, before ~ 1959
taxes deducted 1677
taxes, deferred ~ 986
taxes, imposition of ~ 1516
taxes, levy of ~ 1516
taxes paid 1677
taxes, raising of ~ 1516
taxes, social security ~ 2186
tax, estate ~ 938
tax evasion 2266
tax, excess profits ~ 1214
tax, excise ~ 752, 1245
tax-exempt 1247
tax exemption 1248
tax expert 2264
tax, extra ~ 66
tax field audit 1566
tax-free 1247
tax, gift ~ 1422
tax, graded ~ 1456
tax, graduated ~ 1456
tax haven 2269
tax incentive 2270
tax, income ~ 1530
tax, indirect ~ 1552
tax, inheritance ~ 938
tax, land ~ 1662
tax, legacy ~ 938

tax liability 1683, 2271
tax liability, contingent ~ 759
tax liability, latent ~ 759
tax loss carry-back 2272
tax loss carry-forward 2273
tax, monopoly ~ 1245
tax on capital 551
tax on capital transactions 564
tax on consumption 752
tax on distributions 565
tax on donations 1422
tax on earnings 1989
tax (on), impose a ~ 194
tax (on), levy a ~ 194
tax on luxuries 1723
tax (on), put a ~ 194
tax (on), raise a ~ 194
tax on the movement of capital 564
tax paid 1677
taxpayer 2028
tax-payer 2028
tax privilege 2263
tax, profits ~ 1989
tax, progressive ~ 1456
tax, property ~ 551, 1662, 1995
tax, provision for ~ 2001
tax, purchase ~ 2014
tax rate 2023
tax, real estate ~ 1995
tax rebate 2038
tax receipts 1565
tax reduction 2261
tax reform 2274
tax refund 2038
tax, regressive ~ 997
tax release 2261
tax relief 2261
tax remission 2261
tax reserve 2001
tax return 2275
tax revenue 1565
tax revenue, shortfall in (of) ~ 1330
tax, sales ~ 2014
tax, stamp ~ 2211
tax, succession ~ 938
tax system 1334
tax, trade ~ 476
tax, turnover ~ 2014
tax value 198
tax, value added ~ 2341
tax, wealth ~ 551
tax, witholding ~ 2268
tax year 1335
temporary credit 434
temporary financing 433
temporary loan 434
tendency 1200
tender 352, 1842, 2276
tender for 2233
tender, legal ~ 1669
tender of payment 1844
tenders, invite ~ 1635
tenor 894
term 1262
term, extend a ~ 1273
term loan 2277
term of notice 1836
term of payment 1924
term (of validity) 894
term, prolong a ~ 1273
term purchase 1376
terms, credit ~ 856
terms of payment 2278
terms of redemption 146
terms of trade 2279
terms, on deferred ~ 987
terms, on easy ~ 987
terms strictly cash 1897
third party account, for ~ 35
thousand million 368
three-cornered trade 2280
throw on the market 1665
ticket, deposit ~ 877
tied loan 2281
tied share 2282
tied-up capital 518
tie to an index 1547
tie up 1507
tightening of credit 874
tight money 654
tightness of credit 878
till money 587
time bargain 1379
time deposit 1337
time for payment 1924
time loan 2277
time of payment, extend the ~ 1274
token coin 2283
token money 1296
toll 2284
tone, bearish ~ 344
tone, bullish ~ 459
top price 605
total 106
total amount 107
total asset value 2285
total, balance sheet ~ 276
total, grand ~ 105
total loss 934
total, sum ~ 105
total value 108
trade acceptance 2286
trade allowance 935
trade balance 264
trade balance, active ~ 53
trade balance, adverse ~ 94
trade balance, external ~ 1277
trade balance, favourable ~ 53
trade balance, foreign ~ 1277
trade balance, passive ~ 94
trade balance, unfavorable ~ 94
trade balance, unfavourable ~ 94
trade bank 310
trade bank, foreign ~ 1371
trade bill 356
trade bill, fine ~ 1323
trade bill, prime ~ 1323
trade, course of ~ 833
trade credit 470
trade cycle 471
trade deficit 265
trade discount 935
trade, domestic ~ 1101
trade, external ~ 1283
trade, foreign ~ 1283
trade, free ~ 1392
trade, home ~ 1101
trade, inland ~ 1101
trade, internal ~ 1101
trade loan 473
trade monopoly 2287
trade, oversea(s) ~ 1283
trade paper 356
trade price 2288
trade profit margin 1734
trade rebate 935
trade register 687
trade, retail ~ 2107
trade surplus 266
trade tax 476
trade, terms of ~ 2279
trade, three-cornered ~ 2280
trade, transit ~ 2294
trade, triangular ~ 2280
trade, volume of ~ 2354
trade, wholesale ~ 2376
trading account 2289
trading assets 468
trading capital 468
trading company 686
trading deficit 474
trading funds 468
trading loss 474
trading margin 1734
trading profit 475
trading stamp 2290
trading year 478
tranche 1572
transact business 1084
transaction 320
transaction, barter ~ 327
transaction, cash ~ 581
transaction, compensation ~ 327
transaction, contango ~ 753
transaction, covering ~ 839
transaction, exchange ~ 327
transaction, forward ~ 1379
transaction, forward exchange ~ 1381
transaction, hire purchase ~ 1489
transaction, instal(l)ment ~ 1489
transaction, joint ~ 1653
transaction, offset ~ 327
transaction, offsetting ~ 327
transaction on joint account 1653
transactions, banking ~ 304
transactions, check ~ 632
transactions, cheque ~ 632
transactions, clearing ~ 643
transactions, credit ~ 851
transactions, exchange ~ 1241
transactions, foreign ~ 1358
transactions, foreign exchange ~ 1241
transactions in goods and services, balance of ~ 259
transactions, payment ~ 1911
transaction, spot ~ 581
transaction, spot exchange ~ 2202
transactions, stock ~ 1222
transaction, swap ~ 2251
transaction, switch(ed) ~ 2253
transaction, triangular ~ 2253
transfer 118, 119, 318, 2080

transferability 116
transferable 117
transferable bill 374
transferable money 307
transferable securities 1739
transferable sterling 2291
transfer abroad 1372
transfer account 1424
transfer account, deposit on ~ 1024
transfer a claim 207
transfer advice 848
transfer, bank ~ 318
transfer charge(s) 812, 2081
transfer, cost of ~ 812
transfer, credit ~ 318
transfer duty 812
transferee 120, 1163, 2082
transfer fee 812, 2077, 2081
transfer, foreign ~ 1372
transfer home 2089
transfer income 2292
transfer of capital 563
transfer of claims 208
transfer of funds 1784
transfer of money 1784
transferor 121, 1165, 2083
transfer payment 2293
transfer(r)er 121, 1165, 2083
transfers, balance of ~ 267
transfer slip 848
transfer to reserve 68
transfer to the reserve fund 68
transitional credit 434
transitory item 2249
transit trade 2294
transport costs 2295
travel allowance 2296
traveler's check 2297
travel expenses 2296, 2298
traveling allowance 2296
traveling expenses 2296, 2298
traveller's cheque 2297
travelling allowance 2296
travelling expenses 2296, 2298
treasury 2299
treasury assets 2300
treasury bill 2301
treasury bond 1243, 2301
treasury currency 2302
treasury note 2301
treasury stock(s) 1244
trend 1200
trend, bearish ~ 344
trend, bullish ~ 459
trend, business ~ 477
trend, deflationary ~ 994
trend, downward ~ 344
trend, economic ~ 477
trend of business 477
trend, rising ~ 459
trend, upward(s) ~ 459
trial balance 2303
triangular trade 2280
triangular transaction 2253
trillion 367
trouble, financial ~ 1314
true value 56
true yield 57
trust 2304
trust account 2305
trust, closed-end ~ 653
trust company 2306
trust corporation 2306
trust deed 976
trustee 1298
trustee in bankruptcy 209
trusteeship in bankruptcy 2040
trust fund 2307
trust, in ~ 1185
trust, investment ~ 653
trust, open-end ~ 1624
trust property 2308
trust receipt 608
trust, sell on ~ 2163
trust, unit ~ 1624
turn 428
turn a profit 1729
turn into cash 785
turn into money 785
turn on exchange 109
turnover 2130
turnover, gross ~ 1467
turnover, net ~ 1816
turnover rate 2027
turnover, stock exchange ~ 2225
turnover tax 2014
two-tier foreign exchange market 2309
two-tier price system for gold 2310

unappropriated profits 2311
unbacked 835
unbalance 1062
unbalanced entry 2312
unblock 949
uncalled capital 2313
unconvertibility 1533
unconvertible 1534
uncovered 835
uncovered check 241
uncovered loan 1301
uncrossed check 339
uncrossed cheque 339
undeclared income 2314
undercapitalization 2315
undercharge 2316
undercut 2317
underestimate 2318, 2319
undergo a loss 333
underprice 322
undersell 2317
understate 2319
undervaluation 2318
undervalue 2319
underwrite an issue 2320
underwriting contract 2321
underwriting house 1645
underwriting prospectus 1643
underwriting syndicate 2322
undisclosed reserves 726
undistributed profits 2108
undivided profits 2311
unearned income 2323
uneconomic(al) 2324
unendorsable bill 371
unfavorable balance of trade 94
unfavorable trade balance 94
unfavourable balance of trade 94
unfavourable trade balance 94
unfreeze 949
unfreezing 950
unfunded debt 1351
unification 737
unified debt 735
uniform costing 2325
uniform price 1344, 2326
uniform quotation 2326
uniform value 2213
unify a debt 733
union, credit ~ 787
union, customs ~ 923
Union, European Payments ~ 1198
unit, accounting ~ 31
unit cost 813
unit, currency ~ 904
unitholder 2327
unit, monetary ~ 904
unit of account 31
unit price 2328
unit trust 1624
unlimited liability 2329
unlisted securities 892
unload on the market 1665
unmatured coupon 2330
unnegotiable bill 371
unofficial exchange market 1885
unofficial market 891
unpaid, amount ~ 154
unpaid bill 365
unpaid capital 2313
unproductive capital 1502
unprofitable 2324
unquoted securities 892
unredeemable bond 1636
unremunerative 2324
unsecured 835
unsecured bond 2331
unsecured debt 2332
unsecured loan 1301
unsettled account 1846
unstable currency 1350
untransferable bill 371
upkeep 810
upsurge 2117
upswing 2117
uptrend 459
upturn 2117
upvalue 178
upward(s) trend 459
usance 2333
usance bill 358
usance draft 358
use, home ~ 1092
use of credits 228
usual reserves, under the ~ 2099
usufruct 2334
usufructary right 349
usurious interest 2335
usurious loan 2336
usurious price 1250
usury 2337
utility, public ~ 2009

validity 894

valorization 2338
valorize 2339
valuables 1646
valuate 177
valuation 176
valuation account 130
value 177
value, accounting ~ 32
value, acquisition ~ 50
value, actual ~ 56
value added by industry 2340
value added tax 2341
value, aggregate ~ 108
value (as on) 1 January 2342
value, assessable ~ 198
value, assessed ~ 198, 199
value at cost 50
value, balance sheet ~ 277
value, book ~ 32
value, break-up ~ 432
value, capitalised ~ 546
value, capitalized ~ 546
value, carrying ~ 32
value, commercial ~ 688
value, cost ~ 50
value, current ~ 912, 913
value date 2343
value, declared ~ 967
value, decline in ~ 969, 970
value, decrease in ~ 969, 970
value, diminish in ~ 970
value, drop in ~ 969, 970
value, effective ~ 56
value, excess ~ 1215
value, exchange ~ 1234
value, exchangeable ~ 1219
value, face ~ 1289
value, fall in ~ 969, 970
value for tax purposes 198
value, go down in ~ 970
value, go up in ~ 179
value, gross ~ 1468
value, increased ~ 180
value, increase in ~ 179, 180
value, increase the ~ 178
value in exchange 1219
value in gold 1442
value, initial ~ 50
value, intrinsic ~ 1612
value, inventory ~ 1617
value, items of ~ 1646
valuelessness 2344
valueless securities 2345
valueless stock 2345
value, liquidating ~ 432
value, lose (in) ~ 970
value, loss of ~ 969
value, market ~ 688, 1234
value, marketable ~ 688
value, net ~ 1817
value, net assets ~ 432
value, nominal ~ 1289
value, objects of ~ 1646
value of the currency, foreign exchange ~ 1364
value, par ~ 1889
value, parity ~ 1889
value, present ~ 912
value, purchase ~ 50
value, quoted ~ 1234
value, raise the ~ 178
value, rat(e)able ~ 198, 199
value, real ~ 56
value, realisation ~ 432
value, redemption ~ 2055
value, reduction in ~ 969
value, replacement ~ 2091
value, residual ~ 2103
value, rise in ~ 179, 180
value, sales ~ 688
value, standard ~ 2213
value, stock exchange ~ 1234
value, surplus ~ 1215
value, surrender ~ 2247
value, tax ~ 198
value, taxable ~ 198
value, total ~ 108
value, total asset ~ 2285
value, true ~ 56
value, uniform ~ 2213
variable costs 2346
variable depreciation 2347
variable rate of exchange 1347
variable yield investment 2348
variance, burden ~ 464
variance, overhead ~ 464
VAT 2341
vault 2125
vault, safe deposit ~ 2125
vault, safety deposit ~ 2125
velocity of circulation 2027
vend 2157
vendable 1738
vendee 482
vender 2159
vendible 1738
vendor 2159
venture capital 1178
venture, joint ~ 1653
vertical price-fixing 2097
viability 2349
viable 2350
visible exports 2351
visible imports 2352
visible reserves 966
visibles 2351
volume, credit ~ 881
volume of business 2130
volume of business in the stockmarket 2225
volume of money 1783
volume of savings 2353
volume of trade 2354
voluntary restraint agreement 2355
vostro account 1716
voting rights of nominee shareholders 2356
voting rights, share with plural ~ 1796
voting shares 2357
voting stock 2357
voucher 2358
voucher, accounting ~ 33
voucher, bookkeeping ~ 33
voucher, cash ~ 590, 600
voucher, credit ~ 876
voucher, disbursement ~ 590
voucher, pay ~ 590, 600

wage 1140
wage bill 2359
wage control(s) 2360
wage costs 2359
wage, efficiency ~ 1153
wage, incentive ~ 1520
wage income 1136
wage increase 1542
wage-induced inflation 2361
wage investment scheme 2362
wage-led inflation 2361
wage, piecework ~ 1932
wage-price spiral 2363
wage-push inflation 2361
wages 1140
wages and salaries 1141
wages and salaries bill 2359
wage, task ~ 1907
waive a debt 510
waiver of a debt 513
wall, tariff ~ 918
want of capital 559
warehouse receipt 2364
warehouse warrant 2364
warrant 1471, 2115, 2364
warrant, deposit ~ 608
warrant, dividend ~ 1078
warrant, interest ~ 1588
warrant letter 394
warrantor 395
warrant, share ~ 2170
warrant, stock ~ 2170
warrant, stock allotment ~ 2115
warrant, stock subscription ~ 2115
warrant, subscription ~ 2115
warrant, warehouse ~ 2364
warranty 1471
warranty deed 394
waste book 1754
watered capital stock 2365
watered share capital 2365
watered stock 2365
watering of capital 2226
watering of share capital 2226
watering of stock 2226
weak 508
weak currency 2187
weakening 968
weakness 1130
wealth, distribution of ~ 1074
wealth, national ~ 1804
wealth tax 551
wear 2366
wear and tear 2367
wear and tear, depreciation for ~ 1030
weight 2368, 2369
weighted index 2370
weighting 2371
weighting coefficient 2372
welfare state 2373
wholesale price 2288
wholesale price index 2374
wholesaler 2375
wholesale trade 2376

wind bill 15
winding up 1070
winding up of an account 655
wind up 1071
wind up an account 652
wipe off 148
wipe off a mortgage 511
withdraw 1113
withdrawable 496
withdrawal 1008, 1119
withdrawal from reserves 2377
withdrawal of cash 601
withdrawal of deposits, notice of ~ 1840
withdrawal of restrictions 2
withdraw (from circulation) 503
withdraw restrictions 1
withholding 681
witholding tax 2268
worker(s') shares 1159
working assets 468
working capital 468
working capital ratio 45
working costs 1850
working expenses 1850
working funds 468
working year 478
work out 490
works, public ~ 2010
WorldBank 1602
world of finance 1305
world trade, expansion of ~ 1254
worn 2378
worthless check 241
worthlessness 2344
worthless securities 2345
worthless stock 2345
worth, net ~ 1809
write-down 138, 147
write-off 138, 147, 934
write off a debt 2379
write out a check (cheque) 1115

year, budget ~ 448
year, budgetary ~ 448
year, business ~ 478
year, calendar ~ 493
year, civil ~ 493
year, commercial ~ 478
year, company financial ~ 705
year, financial ~ 1320
year, fiscal ~ 1335
year, tax ~ 1335
year, trading ~ 478
year, working ~ 478
yield 2110
yield, actual ~ 57
yield an interest of X percent 334
yield a profit 100
yield, bond ~ 396
yield, dividend ~ 1082
yield, effective ~ 57
yield, fixed ~ 1338
yield, interest ~ 1595
yield of capital 535
yield, real ~ 57
yield, true ~ 57

zone, free trade ~ 1398

DEUTSCH

abbau, Preis~ 927
abbezahlen 148
Abbezahlung 139
Abbröckeln der Kurse (Preise) 886
Abbröckelung der Kurse (Preise) 886
abbuchen, eine Forderung ~ 2379
abdecken 148
abdecken, ein Defizit ~ 836
abdecken, einen Fehlbetrag ~ 836
Abdeckung 139
abdisponieren 1113
Abdisponierung 1119
Abendbörse 102
abfall, Kurs~ 886
abfall, Preis~ 886
abfertigung, Zoll~ 645
Abfindung 718
Abflauen 968
Abflauen der Kurse (Preise) 886
abfluss, Kapital~ 556
abführen 148
Abführung 139
Abgabe 614, 1135
abgabe, Ausgleichs~ 712
abgabe, Blanko~ 346
Abgabe des Kupons, gegen ~ 1958
abgabe, Grundvermögens~ 1662
abgabe, Grundwert~ 1662
abgabe, Kapital~ 551
abgabe, Kapitalgewinn~ 532
abgabe, Leer~ 346
abgabe, Lizenz~ 1686
abgabe, Monopol~ 1245
Abgabenbefreiung 1248
abgabenfrei 920, 1247
Abgabenfreiheit 1248
abgabenpflichtig 196, 916
abgaben, Sozial~ 2186
Abgaben, soziale ~ 2186
abgabe, Stempel~ 2211
abgabe, Umsatz~ 2014
abgabe, Verbrauchs~ 752
abgabe, Vermögens~ 551
abgabe, Zoll~ 917
Abgang 988
abgang, Anlage~ 1066
abgang, Betriebs~ 474
abgang, Kapital~ 556
abgang, Kassen~ 96
Abgang von Barmitteln, Zu- und ~ 586
abgeben, an die Reserve ~ 68
abgegriffen 2378
Abgeltungsdarleh(e)n 141
abgemachter Preis 114
abgenutzt 2378
abgenützt 2378
abgerundet 2119
abgesicherter Kredit 670
abgesichertes Darleh(e)n 672
abgleichen, eine Rechnung ~ 249
abgleichen, ein Konto ~ 249
abgleichen, Konten ~ 112
Abgleichung einer Rechnung (eines Kontos) 254
Abgleichung von Konten 2043
abhängige Gesellschaft 98
abhebbar 496
abheben 1113
Abhebung 1119
abhebung, Bar~ 601
abkaufen 479
abkauf, Forderungs~ 1293
abkommen, Ausgleichs~ 647
abkommen, Clearing~ 647
abkommen, Europäisches Währungs~ 1196
abkommen, Kompensations~ 647
abkommen, Preis~ 115
abkommen, Selbstbeschränkungs~ 2355
abkommen, Stand-by-Kredit~ 2215
abkommen, Stillhalte~ 2216
abkommen, Übernahme~ 2321
abkommen, Vergleichs~ 719
abkommen, Verrechnungs~ 647
abkommen, Zahlungs~ 1906
Ablauf 1262
ablaufen 347, 1264
ablauf, Geschäfts~ 833
ablauf, Konjunktur~ 477
Ablaufstag 1263
Ablaufstermin 1263
Ablaufzeit 1262
Ablehnung der Zahlung 2074
ablösbar 2052
Ablösbarkeit 2051
ablösen 148, 502
ablösen, eine Hypothek ~ 511
Ablösung 139, 2053
ablösung, Anleihe~ 142
Ablösungsanleihe 141
Ablösungsfonds 140
Ablösungspfandbrief 704
Ablösungsschuldverschreibung 704
Ablösungswert 2055
abmachen, einen Preis ~ 113
abmachung, Preis~ 115
abnahme, Preis~ 886
abnahme, Wert~ 969
abnehmen 479
abnehmen, an Wert ~ 970
Abnehmer 482
Abnutzung 2366, 2367
Abnützung 2366, 2367
abrechnen, eine Rechnung ~ 249
abrechnen, ein Konto ~ 249
abrechnen, im voraus ~ 973
abrechnen, vorweg ~ 973
Abrechnung 429
abrechnung, Banken~ 292
Abrechnung der Kosten, nach ~ 131
Abrechnung der Spesen, nach ~ 131
Abrechnung der Unkosten, nach ~ 131
Abrechnung einer Rechnung (eines Kontos) 254
Abrechnungsbank 648
Abrechnungsbüro 649
abrechnung, Scheck~ 627
Abrechnungsgeschäfte 643
Abrechnungshaus 649
Abrechnungskontor 649
Abrechnungskurs 650
Abrechnungspreis 650
Abrechnungsstelle 649
Abrechnungstag 24
Abrechnungstermin 24
Abrechnungsverkehr 643
Abrechnungsverkehr beteiligte Bank, am ~ 648
Abrechnungszeitraum 18
abrede, Preis~ 115
Abruf, auf ~ 495
abrufbar 496
Abrufkredit 2214
Absatzanalyse 1740
Absatzbereich 1736
absatzfähig 1738
Absatzfeld 1736
Absatzforschung 1740
Absatzgebiet 1736
Absatzkunde 1742
Absatzmarkt 1736
Absatzquelle 1736
Absatzstudie 1740
Absatzwirtschaft 1075
Abschaffung von Beschränkungen 2
abschätzen 177
Abschätzung 176
Abschlag 127
Abschlag, auf ~ 19, 987
abschlag, Preis~ 927
Abschlagsdividende 1598
Abschlagszahlung 1571
abschliessen, die Bücher ~ 278
abschliessen, eine Anleihe ~ 762
abschliessen, eine Bilanz ~ 279
abschliessen, eine Rechnung ~ 652
abschliessen, ein Konto ~ 652
Abschlussbuchung 656
Abschlussdividende 1303
abschlüsse, Börsen~ 1222
Abschluss einer Rechnung 655
Abschluss eines Kontos 655
Abschlusseintrag 656
abschluss, Konzern~ 736
Abschlusskurs 657
Abschlussprüfer 216
Abschlussprüfung 214
abschluss, Zwischen~ 1596
Abschnitt 821, 1011
abschnitt, Aktien~ 828, 2230
abschnitt, Anleihe~ 1572
abschnitt, Dividenden~ 1078
abschnitt, Kapital~ 2063
abschnitt, Kontroll~ 821
abschnitt, Teil~ 1572
abschnitt, Zins~ 1588
abschreiben 147
abschreiben, eine Forderung ~ 2379
Abschreibung 138
Abschreibung auf den Wiederbeschaffungswert 143
Abschreibung, degressive ~ 7
Abschreibungen 620
Abschreibungen, steuerlich zulässige ~ 517
Abschreibung entsprechend technischem Verschleiss 1030
Abschreibung, fallende ~ 7
Abschreibung, lineare ~ 2228
Abschreibung, progressive ~ 1545

Abschreibungsaufwendungen 620
Abschreibung, schwankende ~ 2347
abschreibungsfähiges Aktivum 1027
abschreibungsfähiges Vermögen 1027
Abschreibungsfonds 132
Abschreibungsquote 144
Abschreibungsrate, jährliche ~ 157
Abschreibungsreserve 132
Abschreibungsrücklage 132
Abschreibungsrückstellung 132
Abschreibungssatz 144
Abschreibung, steigende ~ 1545
Abschreibung, technische ~ 1030
Abschreibung, variable ~ 2347
Abschwächung 968
Abschwächung der Kurse (Preise) 886
abschwächung, Kurs~ 886
abschwächung, Preis~ 886
Abschwung 968
absetzbar 1738
absetzen 2157
absichern, durch Hypothek ~ 838
absichern, hypothekarisch ~ 838
Absonderungsberechtigter 1948
Absonderungsgläubiger 1948
absprache, Preis~ 115
Abstandsgeld 708, 1856
Abstandssumme 708
abstempeln 2210
Abstempelung von Aktien 2212
abstimmen, Konten ~ 112
Abstimmung von Konten 2043
Abstriche machen 924
Abstriche vornehmen 924
abtragen, eine Hypothek ~ 511
Abtragung 139
abtretbar 117
Abtretbarkeit 116
abtreten 118
Abtretender 121
abtreten, eine Forderung ~ 207
Abtreter 121
Abtretung 119
Abtretungsempfänger 120
Abtretung von Forderungen 208
abwanderung, Kapital~ 556
abweichung, Gemeinkosten~ 464
abwerfen, einen Gewinn ~ 100
abwerfen, X Prozent Zinsen ~ 334
abwerten 1028
Abwertung 1029
abwertung, Geld~ 897
abwertung, Valuta~ 897
abwertung, Währungs~ 897
abwickeln 1071
Abwickler 1694
Abwicklung 1070
abzahlen 148
abzahlen, eine Hypothek ~ 511
Abzahlung 139
Abzahlung, auf (gegen) ~ 987
Abzahlung kaufen, auf ~ 481
Abzahlungsfinanzierung 1490
Abzahlungsgeschäft 1489
Abzahlungskauf 1573
Abzahlungskredit 1488
Abzahlungsrate 1571
Abzahlungstransaktion 1489
Abzahlungsverkauf 1491
Abzahlungswege, im ~ 987
abziehen 1113
abziehen, an der Quelle ~ 972
abziehen, im voraus ~ 973
Abzug 127, 1119
Abzug der Kosten, nach ~ 131
Abzug der Kosten, unter ~ 621
Abzug der Spesen, nach ~ 131
Abzug der Spesen, unter ~ 621
Abzug der Steuer(n), nach ~ 1677
Abzug der Steuer(n), unter ~ 1677
Abzug der Steuer(n), vor ~ 1959
Abzug der Unkosten, nach ~ 131
Abzug der Unkosten, unter ~ 621
abzugfähiger Verlust 974
Abzug im voraus 89
abzug, Kassa~ 583
abzug, Kassen~ 583
abzüglich der Kosten 131, 621
abzüglich der Spesen 131, 621
abzüglich der Unkosten 131, 621
abzug, Quellen~ 975
abzug, Skonto~ 127
abzug, Steuer~ 2261
abzug, Verlust~ 2273
abzug, Vor~ 89
abzug, Voraus~ 89
abzug, Vorweg~ 89
A.G. 1537
Agent 104
agent, Kommissions~ 690
Agentur 103
Agio 109, 110
agio, Aktien~ 1641
agio, Emissions~ 1641
Agio geniessen 1883
Agiopapier 1339
agio, Rückzahlungs~ 1750
Agiotage 111
Agioteur 1647
Akkord 718
Akkordlohn 1907
akkreditieren, jemanden ~ 1847
Akkreditierung 1848
Akkreditiv 1678
akkreditiv, Dokumenten~ 1085
Akkumulation 38, 44
akkumulieren 40, 43
Akontozahlung 1014
Aktie 2169
Aktie, bevorrechtigte ~ 1946
Aktie, gebundene ~ 2282
aktie, Genuss~ 400
aktie, Gratis~ 400
aktie, Inhaber~ 343
aktie, Interims~ 1597
aktie, Mehrstimm~ 1796
aktie, Mehrstimmen~ 1796
aktie, Mehrstimmrechts~ 1796
Aktie mit Vorzugsrecht 1946
Aktienabschnitt 828, 2230
aktie, Nachzugs~ 985
Aktienagio 1641
Aktienanteil 2230
Aktienanteilschein 828
aktien, Arbeitnehmer~ 1159
Aktienaufgeld 1641
Aktienaufpreis 1641
Aktienausgabe 1640
Aktienaustausch 1232
Aktienbank 1536
aktien, Belegschafts~ 1159
Aktienbesitz 1628
Aktienbesitzer 2171
Aktienbestand 1628
Aktienbeteiligung 2172
aktien, Bezugs~ 1819
Aktienbezugsschein 2115
Aktienbörse 1218
Aktienbuch 1701
Aktienemission 1640
Aktiengesellschaft 1537
aktiengesellschaft, Kommandit~ 1893
aktien, Gründer~ 1386
Aktienhändler 2152
Aktieninhaber 2171
Aktien, junge ~ 1819
Aktienkapital 544
Aktienkapital, ausgegebenes ~ 1638
Aktienkapital, autorisiertes ~ 222
aktienkapital, Stamm~ 697
Aktienkapitalsteuer 560
Aktienkapital, verwässertes ~ 2365
Aktienkapital zusammenlegen, das ~ 2061
Aktienkupon 828
Aktienkurs 2174
Aktien, liberierte ~ 1403
Aktienliste 1701
Aktienmakler 2152
Aktienmarkt 2153
aktien, Namens~ 1568
Aktien, nennwertlose ~ 1831
Aktien, neue ~ 1819
Aktien ohne Stimmrecht 1830
Aktienpaket 386
Aktienportefeuille 1628
Aktienposten 386
Aktienpreis 2174
Aktienpromesse 1597
aktien, Quoten~ 1831
Aktienregister 1701
Aktienrendite 1082
Aktienrepartierung 125
Aktienschein 2170
Aktienspitze 1387
Aktiensplit 2175
aktien, Stamm~ 701
Aktien, stimmberechtigte ~ 2357
aktien, Stimmrechts~ 2357
Aktien, stimmrechtslose ~ 1830
Aktientausch 1232
Aktienumtausch 1232
aktien, Voll~ 1403
Aktien, voll eingezahlte ~ 1403
Aktienzerlegung 2175
Aktienzertifikat 2170
Aktien zusammenlegen 2061
Aktienzusammenlegung 2064
Aktienzuteilung 125
Aktienzwischenhändler 1648
aktie, Pflicht~ 2015

aktie, Prioritäts~ 1946
aktie, Stammprioritäts~ 1946
aktie, Teil~ 2230
Aktie, vinkulierte ~ 2282
Aktie voll einzahlen, eine ~ 1915
aktie, Vorrechts~ 1946
aktie, Vorzugs~ 1946
Aktionär 2171
aktionär, Gross~ 633
aktionär, Haupt~ 633
Aktionär, (im Hauptbuch) eingetragener ~ 2076
Aktionär(s)register 1701
Aktionär(s)verzeichnis 1701
Aktiva 202
Aktiva, fictive ~ 1297
Aktiva, greifbare ~ 1747
Aktiva, immateriale ~ 1505
Aktiva, materielle ~ 1747
Aktiva, nicht greifbare ~ 1505
aktiva, Schein~ 1297
Aktiva und Passiva 203
Aktivbilanz 275
Aktiv buchen, ins ~ 403
aktive Aussenhandelsbilanz 53
aktive Forderung 37
aktive Handelsbilanz 53
Aktiven 202
Aktiven, feste ~ 518
Aktiven, flüssige ~ 227
Aktiven, greifbare ~ 1747
Aktiven, immateriale ~ 1505
Aktiven, laufende ~ 905
Aktiven, materielle ~ 1747
Aktiven, nicht greifbare ~ 1505
Aktiven, realisierbare ~ 905
Aktiven und Passiven 203
Aktiven, verwertbare ~ 905
aktive Schuld 37
Aktivforderung 37
aktivieren 403
aktivieren, Gewinne ~ 548
aktivierungspflichtig 408
Aktivkonto 201
Aktivkonto übertragen, auf das ~ 403
Aktivmasse 202
Aktivposten 857
Aktivsaldo 849
Aktivschuld 37
Aktivseite 206
Aktivseite aufführen, auf der ~ 403
Aktivsumme 2285
Aktivüberschuss 1809
Aktivum 202
Aktivum, abschreibungsfähiges ~ 1027
Aktivvermögen 202
Aktivzinsen 376
Akzept 10
Akzeptant 14
akzept, Bank~ 284
Akzeptbank 12
Akzeptbuch 359
Akzept, eigenes ~ 1477
akzept, Gefälligkeits~ 15
akzept, Handels~ 2286
Akzepthaus 12
akzeptieren, einen Wechsel ~ 8
Akzeptkredit 11
akzept, Kunden~ 2286
Akzeptprovision 13
akzept, Waren~ 2286
Akzise 752
Alleinhandel 1786
allgemeine Kosten 1417
allgemeinen Tendenz zuwiderlaufen, der ~ 2120
Allgemeines Zoll- und Handelsabkommen 1415
allgemeine Unkosten 1417
Allgemeinunkosten 1417
Allonge 124
allonge, Wechsel~ 124
alternative Kosten 1853
Amortisation 138, 139, 2053
Amortisation einer Anleihe 142
Amortisationsanleihe 141
Amortisationsdarleh(e)n 141
Amortisationsfonds 140
Amortisationshypothek 137
Amortisationsplan 146
Amortisationsquote 144, 145
Amortisationsrate 144, 145
Amortisationssatz 144, 145
Amortisationsschuld 1574
Amortisationstabelle 146
amortisieren 147, 148, 502
amortisieren, eine Hypothek ~ 511
Amortisierung 138, 139, 2053
amt, Ausgleichs~ 649
amt, Finanz~ 1242
amt, Haupt~ 607
amtliche Börse 1845
amt, Münz~ 1761
amt, Schatz~ 2299
amt, Steuer~ 1242
amt, Zentral~ 607
analyse, Absatz~ 1740
analyse, Kosten- und Ertrags~ 801
analyse, Markt~ 1740
Anatozismus 156
anbieten, zum Kauf ~ 1841
anbieten, zum Verkauf ~ 1841
Anderkonto 2305
änderung, Wechselkurs~ 75
aneignen, sich widerrechtlich ~ 977
Aneignung, widerrechtliche ~ 978
Anerbieten 352
anerkenntnis, Schuld~ 46
Anfall 38, 2110
Anfall einer Steuer 1521
anfallen 40
anfallende Zinsen 42
Anfangskapital 1564
anforderungen, Kassen~ 596
Angabe 602
angabe, Wert~ 967
angabe, Zoll~ 919
angeben, einen Preis ~ 1728
Angebot 352
angebotener Preis 1843
Angebotspreis 1843
angebot, Submissions~ 2276
Angebot und Nachfrage 2242
angebot, Zahlungs~ 1844
angebot, Zeichnungs~ 1842
angefallene Zinsen 41
angegebener Wert 967
Angeld 602
angelegtes Kapital 541
Angleichung der Preise 76
angleichung, Preis~ 76
angreifen, die Reserven ~ 1042
anhang, Wechsel~ 124
anhäufen 43
Anhäufung 44
anhebung, Preis~ 1539
Ankauf 2012
ankaufen 479
Ankäufer 482
Ankaufsatz 354
Ankaufskurs 354
Anlage 1619
Anlageabgang 1066
Anlage, ausländische ~ 1367
anlage, Auslands~ 1367, 1368
Anlagebank 1621
Anlagebedarf 1627
Anlageeffekten 1630
anlage, Fehl~ 244
Anlage, feste ~ 1340
Anlagefonds 653, 1624
Anlagegesellschaft 653
Anlagegüter 533
Anlage im Ausland 1368
Anlage in Portefeuilleeffekten 1626
Anlageinvestition 1340
anlage, Kapital~ 542, 1619
Anlagekapital 518, 1622
Anlage mit schwankendem Ertrag 2348
anlage, Neu~ 1818
Anlagen, immateriale ~ 1505
Anlagen in Börsenwerten 1179
Anlagenpachtung 1668
anlagen, Sach~ 518
Anlagepapiere 1630
Anlageportefeuille 1628
Anlagerückgang 1066
Anlagetitel 1630
Anlagetrust 653
Anlagevermögen 518, 1622
Anlageverpachtung 1668
Anlagewerte 1630
anlage, Wertpapier~ 1626
Anlagewertpapiere 1630
anlegen 1618
anlegen, fest ~ 1507
Anleger 1631
anleger, Geld~ 1631
Anleger, institutioneller ~ 793
anleger, Kapital~ 1631
anlegung, Kapital~ 542
Anleihe 1705
Anleiheablösung 142
anleihe, Ablösungs~ 141
Anleihe abschliessen, eine ~ 762
Anleiheabschnitt 1572
anleihe, Amortisations~ 141
Anleihe auflegen, eine ~ 1157
Anleihe aufnehmen, eine ~ 762, 1122
anleihe, Aufwertungs~ 2206

Anleihe ausgeben, eine ~ 1157
anleihe, Auslands~ 1282
anleihe, Auslosungs~ 1720
Anleihe, äussere ~ 1282
Anleihe, auswärtige ~ 1282
Anleihe bedienen, eine ~ 2165
Anleihebedingungen 856
Anleihe begeben, eine ~ 1157
Anleihe bewerben, sich um eine ~ 175
Anleihedienst 2167
Anleihe emittieren, eine ~ 1157
anleihe, Entwicklungs~ 1036
anleihe, Fundierungs~ 738
Anleihegarantie 1473
Anleihegeber 1672
Anleihe, gebundene ~ 2281
Anleihegesuch 173
Anleihegläubiger 390
anleihe, Gold~ 1438
anleihe, Hypotheken~ 1711
Anleihe in Anspruch nehmen, eine ~ 1122
anleihe, Inlands~ 1099
Anleihe, innere ~ 1099
Anleihekapital 1707
anleihe, Konsolidations~ 738
anleihe, Konsolidierungs~ 738
Anleihe kontrahieren, eine ~ 762
anleihe, Konversions~ 774
Anleihe konvertieren, eine ~ 779
anleihe, Konvertierungs~ 774
Anleihe lancieren, eine ~ 1157
anleihe, Lombard~ 1712
anleihe, Los~ 1720
anleihe, Lotterie~ 1720
Anleihe machen, eine ~ 762
Anleihen 1705
Anleihe, nationale ~ 1099
Anleihenehmer 418
Anleihe neufundieren, eine ~ 779
anleihen, Kommunal~ 1713
anleihen, Staats~ 1244
anleihe, Obligationen~ 941
anleihe, Obligations~ 941
Anleihe, öffentliche ~ 1453
Anleihepapier 389
Anleihe placieren, eine ~ 1933
Anleihe plazieren, eine ~ 1933
anleihe, Prämien~ 1720
Anleihe, Roll-over ~ 2118
Anleiheschein 389
Anleihe schliessen, eine ~ 762
Anleiheschuld 391
Anleihe, staatliche ~ 1453
anleihe, Staats~ 1453
anleihe, Stabilisierungs~ 2206
Anleihestück 389
anleihestück, Spar~ 2141
Anleihesuchender 172
Anleihetilgung 142
anleihe, Tilgungs~ 141
Anleihetitel 389
anleihe, Treffer~ 1720
Anleihe umschulden, eine ~ 779
anleihe, Umschuldungs~ 738, 774
Anleihe unterbringen, eine ~ 1933
Anleihe vermitteln, eine ~ 1807
anleihe, Wandel~ 784
Anleihe zur Zeichnung auflegen, eine ~ 1634
anleihe, Zwangs~ 723
anmeldung, Konkurs~ 316
anmeldung, Zoll~ 919
annähernde Schätzung 184
annehmen, einen Wechsel ~ 8
Annuität 161
anordnung, Auszahlungs~ 590
anpassung, Preis~ 76
Anpassung, reale ~ 74
Anpassungsinflation 59
anrechnen 570, 615
anrechnen, zuviel ~ 1866
anrechnen, zu wenig ~ 2316
Anrechnung 613
Anreiz 1519
anreiz, Investitions~ 1625
anreiz, Steuer~ 2270
ansammeln 43
Ansammlung 44
ansammlung, Kapital~ 1405
Ansatz bringen, in ~ 570
ansatz, Preis~ 1962
ansatz, Wert~ 176
anschaffen 48
Anschaffung 49
Anschaffung in bar 595
Anschaffungskosten 488, 804
Anschaffungspreis 488
Anschaffungswert 50
Anschlag 200
Anschlag bringen, in ~ 615
anschlagen 177, 195
anschlag, Finanz~ 1312
anschlag, Kosten~ 1187
anschreiben 570
Anschreibungskonto 617
ansetzen, einen Preis ~ 1033, 1728
ansetzung, Wert~ 176
anspannung, Kredit~ 874
Anspruch nehmen, die Reserven in ~ 1042
Anspruch nehmen, ein Darleh(e)n in ~ 1122
Anspruch nehmen, eine Anleihe in ~ 1122
anstalt, Bank~ 294
anstalt, Grundkredit~ 1660
anstalt, Kredit~ 850
anstalt, Münz~ 1761
anstalt, Renten~ 1918
anstieg, Preis~ 1539
Ansturm auf die Bank(schalter) 2121
antedatieren 164
Anteil 2017
anteil, Aktien~ 2230
anteil, Ertrags~ 1686
anteil, Gewinn~ 1686, 2173
anteil, Kommandit~ 1591
Anteilschein 828, 2170
anteilschein, Aktien~ 828
Anteilscheinbesitzer 2171
Anteilscheinbesitzer eines gemeinsamen Investmentfonds 2327
Anteilscheininhaber 2171
Anteilschein, nicht verfallener ~ 2330
Anteilschein, provisorischer ~ 1597
Anteilseigner 2171
anteil, Tantiemen~ 1923
Antidumpingzoll 169
antiinflationär 170
antiinflationistisch 170
Antiinflations- 170
Antizipandozahlung 92
Antizipandozinsen 165
antizipative Passiva 39
antizyklisch 168
Antrag, auf ~ 495
Antrag auf Konkurseröffnung 316
antrag, Darleh(e)ns~ 173
antrag, Konkurs~ 316
antrag, Kredit~ 173
antrag, Rückerstattungs~ 640
antragsteller, Darleh(e)ns~ 172
antragsteller, Kredit~ 172
anwachsen 40
Anwachsen 38
anweisen 181, 2080
anweisen, eine Rechnung (zur Zahlung) ~ 223
Anweisung 182, 1784
anweisung, Auszahlungs~ 590
anweisung, Bank~ 284
anweisung, Geld~ 1781
anweisung, Post~ 1781
anweisung, Schatz~ 2301
Anweisungsempfänger 2082
anweisung, Zahlungs~ 221, 590
Anzahlung 1014
anzeige, Belastungs~ 945
anzeige, Eingangs~ 47
anzeige, Einzahlungs~ 97
anzeige, Empfangs~ 47
anzeige, Gutschrifts~ 847
anzeige, Lastschrift(s)~ 945
anzeigen, eine Dividende ~ 965
anzeige, Überweisungs~ 848
anzeige, Zahlungs~ 97
Anziehen 2020
Äquivalent 822
Äquivalenz 1180
Äquivalenzziffer 1181
Ärar 2299
Arbeiten, öffentliche ~ 2010
Arbeitnehmeraktien 1159
Arbeitseinkommen 1136
Arbeitsentgelt 1140
Arbeitskosten 806
Arbeitslohn 1140
arbeitsloses Einkommen 2323
arbitrage, Devisen~ 186
arbitrage, Gold~ 185
arbitrage, Kurs~ 186
Arbitragespannen 187
arbitrage, Valuten~ 186
arbitrage, Wechsel~ 186, 369
Arrest 191
artikel, Ausfuhr~ 1266
artikel, Einfuhr~ 1510
artikel, Export~ 1266
artikel, Import~ 1510
artikel, Luxus~ 1001

aufbauen, eine Reserve ~ 454
aufbesserung, Gehalts~ 1540
aufbesserung, Lohn~ 1542
aufblähen 1553
Aufblähung des Kredits 861
aufbringen, Kapital ~ 416
aufbringung, Kapital~ 1405
auferlegen (auf), eine Steuer ~ 194
auferlegung, Steuer~ 1516
Auffangkonto 2248
auffordern, zur Zeichnung einer Anleihe ~ 1634
Aufforderung, auf ~ 495
Aufforderung zur Einzahlung 494
Aufforderung zur Nachschusszahlung 501
Aufforderung zur Nachzahlung 494
aufführen, auf der Aktivseite ~ 403
aufführen, auf der Passivseite ~ 402
auffüllen, die Reserve ~ 2039
aufgabe, Belastungs~ 945
aufgabe, Gutschrifts~ 847
aufgabe, Lastschrift(s)~ 945
aufgelaufene Zinsen 41
Aufgeld 109, 110
aufgeld, Aktien~ 1641
aufgeld, Emissions~ 1641
aufgerundet 2119
Aufgliederung 155
aufgliederung, Konten~ 22
aufhäufen 43
Aufhäufung 44
Aufhebung von Beschränkungen 2
aufkaufen 489
aufkaufen, den Markt ~ 789
aufkommen, Steuer~ 1565
aufkündbar 496
Auflage 1135
auflaufen 40
Auflaufen 38
auflaufende Zinsen 42
auflegen, eine Anleihe ~ 1157
auflegen, eine Anleihe zur Zeichnung ~ 1634
Auflegung 1352
auflösen 1071
Auflösung 1070
aufmachen, eine Bilanz ~ 279
Aufnahme 2257
aufnahme, Bestand(s)~ 1616
aufnahme, Inventar~ 1616
aufnahme, Inventur~ 1616
aufnehmen (auf), eine Hypothek ~ 2019
aufnehmen, das Inventar ~ 1124
aufnehmen, den Bestand ~ 1124
aufnehmen, ein Darleh(e)n ~ 1122
aufnehmen, eine Anleihe ~ 762, 1122
aufnehmen, eine Schuld ~ 761
aufnehmen, Kapital ~ 416
Aufpreis 60
aufpreis, Aktien~ 1641
aufrechnen 706
Aufrechnung 709
Aufruf 2053
aufrufen 502
aufschieben, eine Zahlung ~ 984
Aufschlag 60
aufschlag, Preis~ 1539
aufschlag, Steuer~ 66
Aufschlüsselung 155
Aufschub 998
aufschub, Zahlungs~ 1276
Aufschwung 2117
aufsicht, Geschäfts~ 2040
aufsteigende Tendenz 459
aufstellen, das Inventar ~ 1124
aufstellen, eine Bilanz ~ 279
Aufstellung 2217
aufstellung, Ausgaben~ 2218
Aufstellung, detaillierte ~ 429
aufstellung, Einzel~ 429
aufstellung, Inventar~ 1616
aufstellung, Spesen~ 2218
aufstellung, Unkosten~ 2218
Aufstieg 2117
aufstieg, Preis~ 1539
aufstocken, das Kapital ~ 1544
auftauen 949
Auftauen 950
aufteilen 122
Aufteilung 123
Aufteilung der Märkte 1745
Aufteilung des Marktes 1745
auftrag, Auszahlungs~ 590
auftrag, Bank~ 299
Auftraggeber 1973
auftrag, Zahlungs~ 221, 590
Auftrieb 2117
auftrieb, Preis~ 1539
Aufwand 1258
aufwand, Betriebs~ 1850
Aufwand, betriebsfremder ~ 1202
aufwand, Erhaltungs~ 810
aufwand, Instandhaltungs~ 810
aufwand, Investitions~ 524
aufwand, Kapital~ 524
aufwand, Konsum~ 748
Aufwand, neutraler ~ 1202
Aufwandsentschädigung 128
Aufwandskonto 1259
Aufwandsspesen 1169
Aufwand(s)steuer 1723
aufwand, Unterhalts~ 810
aufwand, Unterhaltungs~ 810
aufwand, Verbraucher~ 748
aufwand, Verbrauchs~ 748
aufweisen, einen Rückgang (einen Gewinn) von X Punkten ~ 2045
aufweisen, einen Verlust (einen Gewinn) ~ 2046
Aufwendungen 1261
aufwendungen, Betriebs~ 1850
aufwendungen, Finanz~ 1313
Aufwendungen für Abschreibungen 620
aufwendungen, Investitions~ 524
aufwendungen, Kapital~ 524
aufwendungen, Repräsentations~ 1169
aufwendung, Verbraucher~ 748
aufwendung, Verbrauchs~ 748
aufwerten 178
Aufwertung 2111
Aufwertungsanleihe 2206
Aufzins 110
Auktion 212
auktionieren 213
ausbuchen, eine Forderung ~ 2379
Ausdehnung des Geldvolumens 1252
ausdehnung, Kredit~ 858
Ausfall 988
Ausfallbetrag 988
Ausfallbürgschaft 394
Ausfall decken, einen ~ 836
ausfall, Dividenden~ 1826
ausfall, Ertrags~ 1718
Ausfallgeld 133
ausfall, Gewinn~ 1718
ausfall, Kassen~ 96
ausfall, Steuer~ 1330
ausfall, Verdienst~ 1718
ausfertigen, einen Scheck ~ 1115
ausfertigung, Zweit~ 2148
Ausfuhr 1265
Ausfuhrartikel 1266
Ausfuhrbeihilfe 1269
Ausfuhrbewilligung 1268
Ausfuhr(en), sichtbare ~ 2351
Ausfuhr(en), unsichtbare ~ 1632
Ausfuhrerlaubnis 1268
Ausfuhrgenehmigung 1268
Ausfuhrgüter 1266
ausfuhr, Kapital~ 526
Ausfuhrkreditgarantie 1267
Ausfuhrland 825, 826
Ausfuhrlizenz 1268
Ausfuhrprämie 426
ausfuhr, Schleuder~ 1131
Ausfuhrsubvention 1269
Ausfuhrwaren 1266
ausfüllen, einen Scheck ~ 1115
Ausgabe 1352
Ausgabebank 309
ausgabe, Banknoten~ 1156
ausgabe, Effekten~ 1639
Ausgabekonstanten 1336
Ausgabekosten 1353
Ausgabekurs 1642
Ausgaben 1053, 1261
Ausgabenaufstellung 2218
ausgaben, Bar~ 582
Ausgaben begrenzen, die ~ 915
Ausgaben beschneiden, die ~ 915
Ausgaben beschränken, die ~ 915
ausgaben, Betriebs~ 1850
Ausgaben, diverse ~ 1764
Ausgaben, Einnahmen und ~ 1525
Ausgaben einschränken, die ~ 915
Ausgaben einsparen, die ~ 915
Ausgaben ermässigen, die ~ 915
Ausgaben, feste ~ 1336
ausgaben, Haushalts~ 446
Ausgaben, haushaltsfremde ~ 1823
Ausgaben herabsetzen, die ~ 915
Ausgaben in Kapitalrechnung 524
Ausgaben in laufender Rechnung 908
ausgaben, Investitions~ 524
Ausgaben, investive ~ 524
ausgaben, Ist~ 55
ausgaben, Kapital~ 524
ausgaben, Kassen~ 582

Ausgaben, kleine ~ 1764
Ausgaben, konsumtive ~ 748
Ausgaben kürzen, die ~ 915
Ausgaben, laufende ~ 908
ausgabe(n), Mehr~ 1212
Ausgaben, nicht abzugfähige ~ 1049
Ausgaben, öffentliche ~ 2003
ausgabe, Noten~ 1156
Ausgaben reduzieren, die ~ 915
Ausgaben senken, die ~ 915
Ausgaben, sonstige ~ 1764
Ausgabenüberhang 1212
Ausgabenüberschuss 1212
Ausgaben, unvorhergesehene ~ 754
ausgaben, Verbraucher~ 748
ausgaben, Verbrauchs~ 748
Ausgaben vermindern, die ~ 915
Ausgaben, vermögenswirksame ~ 524
Ausgaben verringern, die ~ 915
Ausgaben, verschiedene ~ 1764
Ausgaben, zusätzliche ~ 61
Ausgabeprämie 1641
Ausgabepreis 1642
ausgabe, Serien~ 385
Ausgabe von Aktien 1640
Ausgabe von Bezugsaktien 2116
Ausgabe von Gratisaktien 399
Ausgabe von Obligationen 392
Ausgabe von Pfandbriefen 392
Ausgabe von Schuldverschreibungen 392
Ausgänge 1053
ausgänge, Bar~ 582
Ausgänge, Eingänge und ~ 1525
ausgänge, Kassen~ 582
ausgeben 1257
ausgeben, eine Anleihe ~ 1157
ausgeben, einen Scheck ~ 1115
ausgeben, Obligationen ~ 1637
ausgeben, Schuldverschreibungen ~ 1637
ausgedrückt, in Dollars ~ 1010
ausgegebenes Aktienkapital 1638
ausgegebenes Kapital 1638
ausgeglichener Haushalt 251
ausgeglichenes Budget 251
ausgestellt, auf Dollars ~ 1010
ausgestellt, in Dollars ~ 1010
ausgewiesene Reserven 966
ausgewiesene Rücklagen 966
Ausgleich 139, 709, 718, 1172, 1176
Ausgleich einer Rechnung (eines Kontos) 254
ausgleichen 148, 706
ausgleichen, das Budget ~ 280
ausgleichen, den Haushaltsplan ~ 280
ausgleichen, den Saldo ~ 1914
ausgleichen, ein Defizit ~ 836
ausgleichen, einen Fehlbetrag ~ 836
ausgleichen, einen Verlust ~ 707
ausgleichen, eine Rechnung ~ 249
ausgleichen, ein Konto ~ 249
ausgleichen, sich ~ 248
ausgleich, Haushalts~ 251
ausgleich, Kosten~ 800
ausgleich, Lasten~ 1174
Ausgleichsabgabe 712
Ausgleichsabkommen 647
Ausgleichsamt 649
Ausgleichsbetrag 247
Ausgleichsfonds 710
Ausgleichsforderung 1173
Ausgleichskasse 649, 710
ausgleich, Spitzen~ 1199
Ausgleichsposten 281
ausgleichsreserve, Dividenden~ 1079
Ausgleichsstelle 649
Ausgleichssteuer 712
Ausgleichssumme 247
Ausgleichstaxe 712
ausgleich, Steuer~ 1175
Ausgleichszoll 711
Ausgleichung 139, 709, 1172
auskommen, mit seinen Mitteln ~ 1703
auskommen, mit seinen Mitteln nicht ~ 1702
Auslagen 1053
auslagen, Bar~ 582
auslagen, Kapital~ 524
Auslagen, kleine ~ 1764
auslagen, Reise~ 2298
Auslagen, sonstige ~ 1764
Ausländerkonvertibilität 1278
Ausländerkonvertierbarkeit 1278
ausländische Anlage 1367
ausländische Beteiligung 1365
ausländische Investierung 1367
ausländische Investition 1367
ausländische Noten und Münzen 1369
ausländischer Währung zahlbar, in ~ 1898
ausländischer Wechsel 1357
ausländisches Geld 1361
ausländisches Kapital 1359
ausländische Tratte 1357
ausländische Währung 1361
Auslandsanlage 1367, 1368
Auslandsanleihe 1282
Auslandsbeteiligung 1365, 1366
Auslandsgeschäfte 1358
Auslandsgläubiger 1360
Auslandsguthaben 204, 1362
Auslandsinvestierung 1367, 1368
Auslandsinvestition 1367, 1368
Auslandskapital 515, 1359
Auslandsoperationen 1358
Auslandsschuld 1280
Auslandstransaktionen 1358
Auslandstratte 1357
Auslandsvermögen 204
Auslandsverschuldung 420
Auslandswechsel 1357
Auslandswerte 204, 1370
Auslassungen, Fehler und ~ 1183
auslegen 1050
ausleihen 1671
ausleihen, Geld auf (gegen) Zinsen ~ 1675
Ausleiher 1672
ausleiher, Geld~ 1777
Ausleihungen 1673
Ausleihungssatz 423
auslosbar 498
auslösbar 2052
auslosbare Obligation 1719
auslösbare Obligation 497
auslösbare Schuldverschreibung 497
Auslösbarkeit 2051
auslöschen 148
Auslöschung 139
auslosen 1112
auslösen 502
Auslosung 1111
Auslosungsanleihe 1720
ausmachen, einen Preis ~ 113
ausmachen, im ganzen ~ 106
ausmachen, insgesamt ~ 106
ausmünzen 662
Ausmünzung 663
Ausnahmepreis 1203
ausprägen 662
Ausprägung 663
ausrechnen 490
Ausrechnung 492
ausrüstung, Kapital~ 523
Ausrüstungsvermietung 1668
ausschliesslich Dividende 1080
ausschliesslich Kupon 831
ausschreiben 1635
ausschreiben (auf), eine Steuer ~ 194
ausschreiben, einen Scheck ~ 1115
ausschreibung, Steuer~ 1516
ausschuss, Gläubiger~ 388
ausschütten, eine Dividende ~ 1051
ausschüttung, Dividenden~ 1052
ausschüttung, Gewinn~ 183
ausschüttungsfähiger Gewinn 1072
Aussenbeitrag 266
Aussenfinanzierung 1281
Aussenhandel 1283
Aussenhandelsbank 1371
Aussenhandelsbilanz, aktive ~ 53
Aussenhandelsbilanz, defizitäre ~ 94
Aussenhandelsbilanz, günstige ~ 53
Aussenhandelsbilanz, passive ~ 94
Aussenhandelsbilanz, ungünstige ~ 94
Aussenhandelsdefizit 265
Aussenhandelssaldo 1277
Aussenhandelsüberschuss 266
Aussenstand 152
Aussenstände 37
aussenstände, Zins~ 190
Aussenstelle 427
Aussentarif 1279
Aussentarif, gemeinsamer ~ 699
Aussenwirtschaft 1283
äussere Anleihe 1282
äussere Konvertibilität 1278
äussere Konvertierbarkeit 1278
ausseretatmässig 1286
äussere Zahlungsbilanz 258
Ausserkurssetzung 1008
ausserordentliche Dividende 398
ausserordentliche Einnahmen 1287
ausserordentlicher Reservefonds 755
ausservertragliche Haftpflicht 1824

ausservertragliche Haftung 1824
ausstatten 1167
Ausstattung 1168
Ausstattung einer Anleihe 729
ausstattung, Kapital~ 523
ausstehende Forderung 37
ausstehender Betrag 152
ausstehende Rechnung 37, 1846
ausstehende Schuld 37
ausstehende Zinsen 190
ausstellen, auf jemanden einen Wechsel ~ 1114
ausstellen, einen Scheck ~ 1115
Aussteller 1118
austausch, Aktien~ 1232
Austauschbedingungen 2279
austausch, Effekten~ 2254
Austauschpreisverhältnis 2279
Austauschrelation(en) 2279
Austauschverhältnis(se) 2279
Austerity 218
Ausverkauf 2128
auswanderung, Kapital~ 556
auswärtige Anleihe 1282
auswärtiger Handel 1283
Ausweichklausel 1155
Ausweis 2217
ausweis, Bank~ 312
ausweisen, einen Verlust (einen Gewinn) ~ 2046
ausweis, Finanz~ 1319
ausweis, Jahres~ 160
Ausweitung der Investitionen 1623
Ausweitung des Welthandels 1254
ausweitung, Kredit~ 858
auswerfen 122
auszahlen 1050
auszahlen, eine Dividende ~ 1051
Auszahler 1903
auszahlung, Bar~ 591
auszahlung, Dividenden~ 1052
Auszahlungen 1053
auszahlungen, Kassen~ 582
Auszahlungsanordnung 590
Auszahlungsanweisung 590
Auszahlungsauftrag 590
Auszahlungsbeleg 600
Auszahlungsschein 1913
Auszahlung, vollständige ~ 715
auszug, Konto~ 5
auszug, Rechnungs~ 5
Autarkie 219
autorisiertes Aktienkapital 222
autorisiertes Kapital 222
Aval 230, 236
Avalant 236
avalieren, einen Wechsel ~ 235
Avalist 236
Avalkredit 853
AZH 1415

Baisse 968, 1031
Baissemarkt 345
Baisseneigung 344
Baisseprämie 1953
Baissespekulant 332
Baisse spekulieren, à la ~ 1427
Baissestimmung 344
Baisseströmung 344
Baissetendenz 344
Baissier 332
Bandbreite der Wechselkurse 1346
Bandbreite der Wechselkursschwankungen 1346
Bank 282
bank, Abrechnungs~ 648
bank, Aktien~ 1536
bank, Akzept~ 12
Bankakzept 284
Bank, am Abrechnungsverkehr beteiligte ~ 648
Bank-an-Bank-Kredit 1583
bank, Anlage~ 1621
Bankanstalt 294
Bankanweisung 284
Bankauftrag 299
bank, Ausgabe~ 309
Bankausweis 312
Bank-bei-Bank-Einlagen 1582
Bankbestätigung 290
Bankbetrieb 301
Bankbuch 289
bank, Clearing~ 648
bank, Commerz~ 310
Bankdarleh(e)n 298
bank, Darleh(e)ns~ 850
bank, Depositen~ 1020
Bankdepositen 297
Bankdepot 297
Bankdiskont 311
bank, Diskont(o)~ 1058
Bankdiskontsatz 311
bank, Effekten~ 1645
Bankeinlage 297
bank, Emissions~ 1645
Bankenabrechnung 292
Bankenclearing 292
Bankenkonsortium 303
Bankensyndikat 303
bank, Entwicklungs~ 1035
bank(e)rott 314
Bank(e)rott 315
Bank(e)rotteur 313
bank, Europäische Investitions~ 1195
bankfähiges Papier 283
Bankfirma 294
Bankforderungen 296
Bankforderung, gegenseitige ~ 1583
Bank für Aussenhandel 1371
Bank für Internationalen Zahlungsausgleich 300
Bank für Wiederaufbau und Wirtschaftsförderung, Internationale ~ 1602
Bankgeheimnis 305
Bankgeld 307
Bankgeschäft 294, 301
Bankgeschäfte 304
bank, Geschäfts~ 310
Bankgesellschaft 302
Bankgesellschaft auf Aktien 1536
bank, Giro~ 648
Bankguthaben 286
Bankguthaben, wechselseitige ~ 1582
bank, Handels~ 310
Bankhaus 294
bankhaus, Privat~ 1974
bank, Hypotheken~ 1660
Bankinstitut 294
bank, Interamerikanische Entwicklungs~ 1581
bank, Investitions~ 1621
Bankkonto 285
bank, Kredit~ 850
Bankkredit 295
Banknote 287
bank, Noten~ 309
Banknotenausgabe 1156
Banknotenumlauf 308
Banknotenzirkulation 308
Bankoperationen 304
Bankpanik 2121
bank, Privat~ 1974
Bankprovision 293
Bankrate 311
Banksaldenbestätigung 290
Banksaldo 286
Banksatz 311
Bankschulden 296
Bankschuldverschreibung 288
bank, Spar~ 2139
Bankspesen 291
Banktransaktionen 304
Banktratte 284
Banküberweisung 318
Bankvorschuss 298
bank, Währungs~ 309
bank, Wechsel~ 12, 1058, 1220
Bankwechsel 284
bank, Welt~ 1602
Bankwesen 301
bank, Zentral~ 606
Bankzinsen 306
bar 573
Barabhebung 601
Baranschaffung 595
bar auf den Tisch bezahlen 1727
Barausgaben 582
Barausgänge 582
Barauslagen 582
Barauszahlung 591
bar begleichen, in ~ 1727
Barbestand 587
bar bezahlen 1727
bar bezahlen, in ~ 1727
Bardevisenkurs 2024
Bardiskont 583
Bardividende 584
Bareingänge 585
Bareinnahmen 585
Bareinschuss 1732
barem Geld, in ~ 573
barem Geld zahlen, in ~ 1727
Barentnahme 601
bare Reserve 597
Barfonds 587
bar, gegen ~ 573
Bargeld 572
Bargeld, in ~ 573
bargeldlose Zahlung 588
Bargeldumlauf 638
Bargeld umwandeln, in ~ 785

Bargeschäft 581
bar, in ~ 573
Barkapital 577
Barkasse 1931
Barkauf 594
Barkredit 580
Barliquidität 592
Barmittel 587
Barpreis 593
Barrengold 323
Barreserve 597
Barschaft 572
Barscheck 339
Barsendung 595
Bartransaktion 581
Barüberweisung 595
Barverkauf 598
Barvermögen 577
Barvorrat 587
Barwert 912
Barwerte 577
bar zahlbar, in ~ 1897
bar zahlen 1727
bar zahlen, in ~ 1727
Barzahlung 591
Barzahlungsdiskont 583
Barzahlungspreis 593
Barzahlungsrabatt 583
bar zu zahlen, in ~ 1897
Basissatz 328
basis, Steuer~ 331
Basiszins 328
Bausparkasse 453
Bauten, öffentliche ~ 2010
Beanspruchung des Marktes 506
Bearbeitungsgebühr 80, 1478
beauftragter, Inkasso~ 955
beauftragter, Konkurs~ 209
Bedarf 1002
bedarf, Anlage~ 1627
bedarf, Darleh(e)ns~ 424
bedarf, Deckungs~ 837
bedarf, Einschuss~ 837
bedarf, Finanzierungs~ 1316
bedarf, Geld~ 1774
bedarf, Investitions~ 1627
bedarf, Kapital~ 557
bedarf, Liquiditäts~ 596
Bedenkfrist 998
Bedenkzeit 998
bedienen, eine Anleihe ~ 2165
bedingungen, Anleihe~ 856
bedingungen, Austausch~ 2279
bedingungen einer Anleihe, Emissions~ 729
bedingungen, Kredit~ 856
bedingungen, Zahlungs~ 2278
bedürfnisse, Finanzierungs~ 1316
bedürfnis(se), Kapital~ 557
bedürfnis(se), Liquiditäts~ 596
befehl, Zahlungs~ 590
Beförderungskosten 2295
befreien, von Zoll ~ 1246
befreit, steuer~ 1247
befreiung, Abgaben~ 1248
Befreiung des Handelsverkehrs 1684
befreiung, Steuer~ 1248
befristete Einlage 1337
befristetes Darleh(e)n 2277
begebbare Effekten 1739
begebbarer Wechsel 374
begebbares Papier 1806
begebbare Wertpapiere 1739
Begebender 1165
begeben, eine Anleihe ~ 1157
begeben, einen Scheck ~ 1115
begebenes Kapital 1638
Begeber 1165
Begebung 1352
Begebungskosten 1353
Begebungskurs 1642
Begebungspreis 1642
Begebungsprospekt 1643
begleichen 148
begleichen, einen Wechsel ~ 1054
begleichen, eine Rechnung ~ 249
begleichen, ein Konto ~ 249
begleichen, in bar ~ 1727
begleichen, voll ~ 1905
Begleichung 139
Begleichung einer Rechnung (eines Kontos) 254
begrenzen, die Ausgaben ~ 915
begrenzung, Kredit~ 874
begrenzung, Liquiditäts~ 2104
Begünstigter 350
begünstigung, Spar~ 1161
Begünstigungstarif 1947
begünstigung, Steuer~ 2263
Begünstigungszoll 1949
behauptung, Preis~ 1326
beheben 1113
Behebung 1119
beherrschte Gesellschaft 98
behörden, Steuer~ 1242
Beihilfe 1458
beihilfe, Ausfuhr~ 1269
beihilfe, Export~ 1269
beihilfe, Finanz~ 1310
Beihilfe, finanzielle ~ 1310
beihilfe, Regierungs~ 1449
Beihilfe, staatliche ~ 1449
beihilfe, Staats~ 1449
beirat, Finanz~ 1309
beistand, Währungs~ 1771
beistellen, Kapital ~ 1407
beistellung, Kapital~ 1408
beisteuern, Kapital ~ 436
Beitrag 2235
beiträge, Sozial~ 2186
beiträge, Sozialversicherungs~ 2186
beitreibbar 675, 676
Beitreibbarkeit 674
beitreiben, eine Forderung ~ 677
beitreiben, eine Schuld ~ 677
beitreiben, eine Steuer ~ 678
Beitreibung 680
beitreibung, Steuer~ 683
Beitreibung von Aussenständen (Forderungen; Schulden) 682
bekenntnis, Eingangs~ 47
beladen, mit Schulden ~ 466
belasten 615
belasten, einem Konto ~ 618
belasten, hypothekarisch ~ 465, 1791
belasten, mit einer Hypothek ~ 465
belasten, mit einer Steuer ~ 194
belasten mit, ein Konto ~ 618
belasten, mit Schulden ~ 466
Belastung 460, 613
Belastungen, unvorhergesehene ~ 754
Belastung, finanzielle ~ 1313
Belastung, hypothekarische ~ 1793
belastung, Hypotheken~ 1793
Belastungsanzeige 945
Belastungsaufgabe 945
belastung, Steuer~ 463
belastung, Zins~ 1587
belaufen auf, sich ~ 106
Belebung 2048
Beleg 2358
beleg, Auszahlungs~ 600
beleg, Buchführungs~ 33
beleg, Buchungs~ 33
beleg, Einzahlungs~ 877
belegen, mit einem Zuschlag ~ 1514
belegen, mit einer Steuer ~ 194
beleg, Gutschrift(s)~ 847
beleg, Kassen~ 600
Belegschaftsaktien 1159
Belegschein 2358
Belegstück 2358
beleg, Zahlungs~ 600
belehnbar 9
belehnen, Effekten ~ 91, 671
Belehnungsgrenze 604
Belehnung von Effekten 1501, 1674
beleihbar 9
beleihen, Effekten ~ 91, 671
Beleihungsgrenze 604
Beleihungssatz 2022
Beleihung von Effekten 1501, 1674
Belgisch-luxemburgische Wirtschaftsunion 348
belohnen 2042
Belohnung 2041
Bemessungsgrundlage 331
benennen, einen Preis ~ 1728
beobachtung, Markt~ 1740
berater, Finanz~ 1309
Berater in Steuersachen 2264
berechnen 490, 570
berechnen, zuviel ~ 1866
berechnen, zu wenig ~ 2316
Berechnung 492, 613
berechnung, Einstands~ 797
berechnung, Kosten~ 797, 798
berechnung, Kostenpreis~ 815
berechnung, Selbstkosten~ 815
berechnungsgrundlage, Steuer~ 331
berechnung, Wert~ 176
berechnung, Wirtschaftlichkeits~ 801
berechtigt, dividenden~ 1170
berechtigter, Absonderungs~ 1948
berechtigter, Zahlungs~ 350
berechtigung, Bezugs~ 174
berechtigung, Zeichnungs~ 174
bereich, Absatz~ 1736
bereich, Wachstums~ 1470
bereinigen 70
bereinigen, Konten ~ 112

Bereinigung 72
Bereinigung von Konten 2043
Bereitschaftskredit 2214
bereitstellen 181
bereitstellen, Kapital ~ 1407
Bereitstellung 182
bereitstellung, Kapital~ 1408
Bereitstellungskommission 693
Bereitstellungsprovision 693
Bericht 2217
bericht, Börsen~ 1228
bericht, Buchprüfungs~ 217
Bericht des Abschlussprüfers 217
bericht, Finanz~ 1319
berichtigen, eine Rechnung ~ 249
berichtigen, ein Konto ~ 249
Berichtigung der Zahlungsbilanz(en) 794
Berichtigung einer Rechnung (eines Kontos) 254
Berichtigungsbuchung 71
Berichtigungseintrag 71
Berichtigungsposten 71
berichtigung, Wechselkurs~ 75
bericht, Jahres~ 160
bericht, Kurs~ 1228
bericht, Prüfungs~ 217
bericht, Rechnungs~ 217
bericht, Revisions~ 217
beschaffen, Kapital ~ 416, 1407
beschaffung, Kapital~ 1405, 1408
bescheid, Steuer~ 1839
bescheinigung, Einzahlungs~ 877
bescheinigung, Empfangs~ 47
bescheinigung, Hinterlegungs~ 608
Beschlag 191
Beschlag beim Drittschuldner 1414
Beschlag belegen, mit ~ 211
Beschlag in der dritten Hand 1414
Beschlag legen (auf) 211
Beschlagnahme 191
Beschlagnahme beim Drittschuldner 1414
beschlagnahmen 211
Beschlag nehmen, in ~ 211
beschliessen, eine Dividende ~ 965
beschneiden, die Ausgaben ~ 915
beschränken, die Ausgaben ~ 915
beschränkte Haftpflicht 1689
beschränkte Haftung 1689
beschränkt haftender Gesellschafter 1691
beschränkung, Einfuhr~ 1513
Beschränkungen abschaffen 1
Beschränkungen, Abschaffung von ~ 2
Beschränkungen aufheben 1
Beschränkungen, Aufhebung von ~ 2
beschränkungen, Devisen~ 902
Beschränkungen, devisenrechtliche ~ 902
beschränkung, Import~ 1513
beschränkung, Kredit~ 874
beschränkung, Liquiditäts~ 2104
beschränkung, Preis~ 1968
beschweren, mit einer Hypothek ~ 465
beschweren, mit Schulden ~ 466
besichern 101
besicherte Obligation 2149
besicherte Schuldverschreibung 2149
besitz, Aktien~ 1628
Besitz, beweglicher ~ 622
besitz, Effekten~ 1628
Besitzer 336, 1878
besitzer, Aktien~ 2171
besitzer, Anteilschein~ 2171
besitzer, Effekten~ 2171
besitzer eines gemeinsamen Investmentfonds, Anteilschein~ 2327
besitzer, Wertpapier~ 341, 2171
besitz, Grund~ 1661
besitz, Grundstücks~ 1661
besitz, Privat~ 1979
Besitz, privater ~ 1979
Besitzsteuer 551
Besitzwechsel 373
besitz, Wertpapier~ 1628
besitz, Wertschriften~ 1628
besolden 2042
Besoldigungserhöhung 1540
Besoldung 2041, 2126
Besoldungsliste 1912
Besserung der Zahlungsbilanz(en) 794
Bestand 1615
bestand, Aktien~ 1628
Bestand aufnehmen, den ~ 1124
bestand, Bar~ 587
bestand, Devisen~ 901, 1362
Bestände 1496
bestand, Effekten~ 1628
bestände, Gold- und Devisen~ 1429
bestände, Quasigeld~ 1776
bestand, Fehl~ 988
bestand, Geld~ 587
bestand, Gold~ 1430
beständige Währung 2207
beständigkeit, Preis~ 1326
bestand, Ist~ 587
bestand, Kassen~ 587
bestand, Konto~ 27, 255
Bestand(s)aufnahme 1616
bestand, Wertpapier~ 1628
bestand, Wertschriften~ 1628
bestätigen, einen Scheck ~ 610
bestätigung, Bank~ 290
bestätigung, Banksalden~ 290
bestätigung, Eingangs~ 47
bestätigung, Empfangs~ 47
bestellen, eine Sicherheit ~ 101
Besteller 1973
besteuerbar 196
besteuerbar, nicht ~ 1247
besteuern 194
Besteuerter 2028
Besteuerung 2265
besteuerung, Doppel~ 1109
besteuerung, Quellen~ 681
Besteuerungsgrundlage 331
Besteuerungssatz 2023
bestimmen, einen Preis ~ 1033
bestimmungen, Devisen~ 900
bestimmungen, Devisenkontroll~ 900
bestimmung, Preis~ 1962
bestimmung, Wert~ 176
bestreiten, eine Schuld ~ 2092
beteiligung, Aktien~ 2172
Beteiligung (an) 1495
Beteiligung, ausländische ~ 1365
beteiligung, Auslands~ 1365, 1366
beteiligung, Ertrags~ 1410
beteiligung, Gewinn~ 1410
Beteiligung im Ausland 1366
beteiligung, Majoritäts~ 770
beteiligung, Mehrheits~ 770
beteiligung, Minderheits~ 1760
beteiligung, Minoritäts~ 1760
Beteiligungsgesellschaft 1494
Beteiligungskapital 1996
Beteiligungskonto 1654
Beteiligung, wechselseitige ~ 885
Betrag 149
betrag aufgenommener Kredite, Netto~ 1810
betrag, Ausfall~ 988
betrag, Ausgleichs~ 247
Betrag, ausstehender ~ 152
betrag, Brutto~ 1460
betrag, Deckungs~ 1732
betragen, im ganzen ~ 106
betragen, insgesamt ~ 106
Betrag erkennen, jemanden für einen ~ 566
Betrag erkennen, jemanden mit einem ~ 566
betrag, Fehl~ 988
betrag, Gesamt~ 107
Betrag, geschuldeter ~ 151
betrag gewährter Kredite, Netto~ 1812
betrag, Global~ 107
Betrag gutbringen, jemandem einen ~ 566
Betrag gutschreiben, jemandem einen ~ 566
Betrag kreditieren, jemandem einen ~ 566
Betrag kreditieren, jemanden für einen ~ 566
Betrag kreditieren, jemanden mit einem ~ 566
betrag, Mehr~ 1205, 2244
betrag, Minder~ 988
betrag, Minus~ 988
betrag, Nenn~ 1820
betrag, Netto~ 1808
Betrag, nicht eingezahlter ~ 154
betrag, Nominal~ 1820
Betrag, offenstehender ~ 152
betrag, Pauschal~ 1722
betrag, Rest~ 27, 246
Betrag, restlicher ~ 246
betrag, Roh~ 1460
Betrag, rückständiger ~ 152
betrag, Schuld~ 151
Betrag, schuldiger ~ 151
betrag, Total~ 107
Betrag, überschiessender ~ 1205
Betrag, unbezahlter ~ 154

Betrag, verbleibender ~ 246
betrag, Zeichnungs~ 153
betreibbar 675
betreiben, eine Forderung ~ 677
betreiben, eine Schuld ~ 677
Betreibung 680
Betreibung von Aussenständen (Forderungen; Schulden) 682
Betrieb 467
betrieb, Bank~ 301
betrieb der öffentlichen Hand, Wirtschafts~ 1448
Betrieb, gemeinnütziger ~ 2009
Betrieb, öffentlicher ~ 1448
betrieb, Privat~ 1977
Betrieb, privatwirtschaftlicher ~ 1977
betrieb, Regie~ 1448, 1454
betrieb, Regierungs~ 1448
Betriebsabgang 474
Betriebsabrechnungsbogen 799
Betriebsaufwand 1850
Betriebsaufwendungen 1850
Betriebsausgaben 1850
Betriebsbuchführung 798
betriebseigene Revision 1600
Betriebsfonds 468
betriebsfremder Aufwand 1202
Betriebsgewinn 475
Betriebsjahr 478
Betriebskapital 468
Betriebskonto 2289
Betriebskosten 1850
Betriebskostenrechnung 2289
Betriebsmittel 468
Betriebsprüfung 1566
Betrieb, staatlicher ~ 1448
betrieb, Staats~ 1448
Betriebsüberschuss 1852
Betriebsunkosten 1850
Betriebsverlust 474
Betriebsvermögen 468
bevorrechtigte Aktie 1946
bevorrechtigter Gläubiger 1948
bevorschussen 85
bevorzugter Gläubiger 1948
bewegliche Güter 622
bewegliche Habe 622
beweglicher Besitz 622
bewegliches Eigentum 622
bewegliche Skala 1348
bewegliches Kapital 468
bewegliches Vermögen 622
bewegung, Kapital~ 555
Beweisstück 2358
bewerben, sich um ein Darleh(e)n ~ 175
bewerben, sich um eine Anleihe ~ 175
bewerben, sich um einen Kredit ~ 175
bewerber, Darleh(e)ns~ 172
bewerber, Kredit~ 172
bewerten 177, 2369
bewerten, neu ~ 2037
Bewertung 176
bewilligen, einen Kredit ~ 126
bewilligen, einen Zahlungsaufschub ~ 1274
bewilligte Etatsansätze 444
bewilligte Haushaltsmittel 444
bewilligung, Ausfuhr~ 1268
bewilligung, Einfuhr~ 1512
Bewilligungen, budgetmässige ~ 444
bewilligung, Export~ 1268
bewilligung, Import~ 1512
bewilligung, Kredit~ 220
bewirtschaftung, Devisen~ 1224
Bewirtschaftungskosten 79
bezahlen 148
bezahlen, bar auf den Tisch ~ 1727
bezahlen, einen Wechsel ~ 1054
bezahlen, in Geld ~ 1727
bezahlen, mit einem Scheck ~ 1901
bezahlen, voll ~ 1905
Bezahler 1903
Bezahlung 139, 1140
Bezahlung der Steuer(n), nach ~ 1677
bezahlung, Nicht~ 982
bezahlung, Rückstands~ 237
bezahlung, Voll~ 715
Bezahlung, vollständige ~ 715
bezeichnung, Konto~ 25
beziffern auf, sich ~ 106
Bezogener 1117
Bezüge 1158
bezug, Natural~ 134
bezug, Sach~ 134
Bezugsaktien 1819
Bezugsberechtigung 174
Bezugsberechtigungsschein 2115
Bezugsfrist 2237
Bezugskurs 2238
Bezugsoption 484
Bezugsprämie 507
Bezugspreis 2238
Bezugsrecht 174
Bezugsrecht, ausschliesslich ~ 1249
Bezugsrecht, mit ~ 888
Bezugsrecht, ohne ~ 1249
Bezugsschein 2115
bietender, Meist~ 1485
bieten, eine Sicherheit ~ 101
Bilanz 270
Bilanz abschliessen, eine ~ 279
bilanz, Aktiv~ 275
Bilanz aufmachen, eine ~ 279
Bilanz aufstellen, eine ~ 279
Bilanzbuch 250
Bilanzenbuch 250
bilanz, Eröffnungs~ 1700
bilanz, Ertrags~ 262
bilanz, Gewinn~ 275
Bilanzgliederung 273
bilanz, Handels~ 264
bilanzieren 279
bilanz, Kapital~ 256
bilanz, Kassen~ 253
Bilanzkonto 271
bilanz, Konzern~ 736
bilanz, Leistungs~ 262
bilanz, Passiv~ 274
bilanz, Probe~ 2303
bilanz, Roh~ 2303
bilanz, Schluss~ 1302
Bilanzstichtag 272
Bilanzsumme 276
Bilanztotal 276
bilanz, Übertragungs~ 267
bilanz, Unter~ 274, 988
bilanz, Verlust~ 274
Bilanzvolumen 276
Bilanzvorlegung 1957
bilanz, Wanderungs~ 1758
bilanz, Waren~ 264
Bilanzwert 277
bilanz, Wirtschafts~ 1148
bilanz, Zahlungs~ 260
Bilanz ziehen, eine ~ 279
bilanz, Zwischen~ 1596
bilden, eine Reserve ~ 454
bildung, Ersparnis~ 1374
bildung, Kapital~ 529
bildung, Vermögens~ 1373
billig auf den Markt werfen 1132
billiges Geld 623
Billion 367
Bimetallismus 375
binden 1507
binden, an einen Index ~ 1547
Bindung 692, 1506
bindung, Index~ 1548
Bindung, indexmässige ~ 1548
bindung, Preis~ 1515
Binnenhandel 1101
Binnenmarkt 1100
binnenwirtschaftliches Gleichgewicht 1098
BIP 1461
BIZ 300
Blankoabgabe 346
Blankokredit 379
Blankoscheck 378
Blankoverkauf 346
blanko verkaufen 1427
blatt, Börsenkurs~ 1228
blatt, Kontroll~ 821
blatt, Kurs~ 1228
block, Dollar~ 1086
block, Franken~ 1388
blockieren 380
Blockierung 383
block, Sterling~ 2224
bogen, Betriebsabrechnungs~ 799
bogen, Dividenden~ 832
bogen, Dividendenschein~ 832
bogen, Gewinnanteilschein~ 832
bogen, Konsolidierungs~ 739
bogen, Kupon~ 832
bogen, Zins~ 832
bogen, Zinsschein~ 832
Bon 876
bond, Dollar~ 1087
Bonifikation 397
Bonität 2189
bon, Kassen~ 389, 590
bon, Spar~ 2141
Bonus 397, 398
bonus, Dividenden~ 398
Boom 413
Boomflation 414
borgen 415, 1671

Borger 418, 1672
Börse 1218
börse, Abend~ 102
Börse, amtliche ~ 1845
börse, Devisen~ 1230
Börsegeschäfte 1222
börse, Handels~ 695
börse, Hausse~ 458
Börsenabschlüsse 1222
börse, Nach~ 102
Börsenbericht 1228
Börseneffekten 1699
Börseneinführung 81
börsenfähige Effekten 1699, 1739
börsenfähiger Wechsel 374
börsenfähige Wertpapiere 1699, 1739
börsengängige Effekten 1699
börsengängige Wertpapiere 1699
Börsengeschäfte 1222
Börsenhändler 2152
Börse nicht kotierte Wertpapiere, an der ~ 892
Börse nicht notierte Effekten, an der ~ 892
Börse nicht notierte Wertpapiere, an der ~ 892
Börsenjobber 1648
Börsenkommissionsgeschäft 439
Börsenkurs 1234
Börsenkursblatt 1228
Börsenmakler 2152
Börsenmanipulation 1730
Börsenmanöver 1730
börsenmässige Effekten 1699
börsenmässige Wertpapiere 1699
börsennotierte Effekten 1699
börsennotierte Wertpapiere 1699
Börsenpapiere 1699
Börsenschieber 1647
Börsenschiebung 1730
Börsenspekulant 1647
Börsenspekulation 111
Börsenspiel 111
Börsenspieler 1647
Börsentransaktionen 1222
Börsenumsatz 2225
Börsenwert 1234
Börsenwerte 1699
Börsenwertpapiere 1699
Börsenzettel 1228, 1228
Börsenzulassung 81
börse, Produkten~ 695
börse, Waren~ 695
börse, Winkel~ 891
Börsianer 1647
brachliegendes Kapital 1502
branche, Wachstums~ 1470
bremsen, die Inflation ~ 628
brief, Bürgschafts~ 394
brief, Garantie~ 394
brief, Kredit~ 1678
Briefkurs 193
brief, Pacht~ 1666
brief, Pfand~ 389
brief, Renten~ 162
brief, Spar~ 2141
Brief und Geld 192
bringen, einen Gewinn ~ 100
bringen, in Anschlag ~ 615
bringen, X Prozent Zinsen ~ 334
bringen, zum Verkauf ~ 1841
Bruttobetrag 1460
Bruttoeinkommen 1463
Bruttoeinkünfte 1463
Bruttogewinn 1459
Brutto-Inlandsersparnisse 1462
Bruttoinlandsprodukt 1461
Bruttonationalprodukt 1466
Bruttoprinzip 1755
Bruttosozialprodukt 1466
Bruttoumsatz 1467
Bruttoverdienstspanne 1465
Bruttoverlust 1464
Bruttowert 1468
BSP 1466
buch, Aktien~ 1701
buch, Akzept~ 359
buch, Bank~ 289
buch, Bilanz~ 250
buch, Bilanzen~ 250
buch, Depositen~ 1021
buch, Einlage~ 1021
Bucheintrag 409
Bucheintragung 409
buchen 401
buchen, ins Aktiv ~ 403
Bücher abschliessen, die ~ 278
Bücher führen, die ~ 1656
bücher, Geschäfts~ 28
bücher, Handels~ 28
Bücher, kaufmännische ~ 28
Bücherrevision 214
Bücherrevisor 216
Bücher saldieren, die ~ 278
Buchforderung 404
Buchführer 410
Buchführung 20
buchführung, Betriebs~ 798
Buchführung, doppelte ~ 1107
Buchführung, einfache ~ 2181
buchführung, Kosten~ 798
Buchführung machen, die ~ 1656
buchführung, Maschinen~ 1724
Buchführungsbeleg 33
Buchgeld 307
Buchgewinn 412
Buchgläubiger 405
Buchhalter 410
Buchhaltung 20
Buchhaltung führen, die ~ 1656
buchhaltung, Kosten~ 798
buchhaltung, Maschinen~ 1724
buchhaltung, Neben~ 2155
buch, Haupt~ 1418
buch, Hilfs~ 225
buch, Kassa~ 578
buch, Kassen~ 578
buch, Konto~ 289
buchmässige Forderung 404
buchmässiger Gewinn 412
buchmässiger Mehrwert 412
buchmässiger Verlust 411
buch, Neben~ 225
Buchprüfer 216
Buchprüfung 214
Buchprüfungsbericht 217
buch, Scheck~ 626
Buchschuld 406
buch, Spar~ 2142
buch, Sparkassen~ 2140
buch, Tage~ 932
Buchung 409
buchung, Abschluss~ 656
buchung, Berichtigungs~ 71
buchung, Doppel~ 1106
buchung, Gegen~ 281
buchung, Gutschrift~ 857
buchung, Haben~ 857
buchung, Lastschrift~ 946
buchung, Rück~ 281
buchung, Sammel~ 717
Buchungsbeleg 33
buchung, Soll~ 946
Buchungsposten 409
Buchungsposten im Journal 1655
buchung, Stornierungs~ 281
buchung, Storno~ 281, 512
buchung, Wertberichtigungs~ 71
buch, Verfall~ 359
Buchverlust 411
buch, Wechsel~ 359, 360
buch, Wechseldebitoren~ 360
Buchwert 32
Budget 441, 442
Budget, ausgeglichenes ~ 251
Budget ausgleichen, das ~ 280
Budgetdefizit 95
Budget ins Gleichgewicht bringen, das ~ 280
budget, Investitions~ 519
Budgetjahr 448
budgetmässig 442
budgetmässige Bewilligungen 444
budgetmässige Zuwendungen 444
budget, Staats~ 1446
Budgetüberschuss 452
Bürge 395
bürgen 52
Bürgschaft 1138
bürgschaft, Ausfall~ 394
Bürgschaft leisten 52
Bürgschaft leisten, einem Wechsel ~ 235
Bürgschaft, öffentliche ~ 1450
Bürgschaftsbrief 394
bürgschaft, Schadlos~ 394
Bürgschaftserklärung 394
Bürgschaftskredit 853
Bürgschaftsschein 394
Bürgschaft, staatliche ~ 1450
bürgschaft, Staats~ 1450
Bürgschaftsurkunde 394
Bürgschaft übernehmen 52
Bürgschaft versehen, einen Wechsel mit ~ 235
bürgschaft, Wechsel~ 230
büro, Abrechnungs~ 649
büro, Haupt~ 607
büro, Makler~ 439
büro, Zentral~ 607
Busse 136
Bussgeld 136

Callgeld 505

Cambist 361, 509
Cash 572
Cash-flow 586
Check 624
c.i.f. 634
Clearing 642
Clearingabkommen 647
Clearingbank 648
clearing, Banken~ 292
Clearinggeschäfte 643
Clearinghaus 649
Clearingkonto 644
Clearingkurs 650
Clearingstelle 649
Clearingverkehr 643
Commerzbank 310
Compagnie 686
Corporation, Internationale Finanz- ~ 1605
Costing 797
Coupon 828
Coupon, nicht verfallener ~ 2330
coupon, Zins~ 1588
Courtage 438
Cross-Rate 884
cum Dividende 887

Dachgesellschaft 1494
dämpfen, die Inflation ~ 628
Darleh(e)n 845
darleh(e)n, Abgeltungs~ 141
Darleh(e)n, abgesichertes ~ 672
darleh(e)n, Amortisations~ 141
Darleh(e)n aufnehmen, ein ~ 1122
darleh(e)n, Bank~ 298
Darleh(e)n, befristetes ~ 2277
Darleh(e)n bewerben, sich um ein ~ 175
darleh(e)n, Faustpfand~ 1712
Darleh(e)n, fiduziarisches ~ 1301
Darleh(e)n, garantiertes ~ 672
Darleh(e)n, gedecktes ~ 672
Darleh(e)n gegen Pfand 672
Darleh(e)n gegen Sicherheit 672
Darleh(e)n, gesichertes ~ 672
darleh(e)n, Hypothekar~ 1711
darleh(e)n, Hypotheken~ 1711
Darleh(e)n in Anspruch nehmen, ein ~ 1122
Darleh(e)n, jederzeit kündbares ~ 504
darleh(e)n, Lombard~ 1712
Darleh(e)n, nicht gesichertes ~ 1301
Darleh(e)n ohne Deckung 1301
darleh(e)n, Pfand~ 672
Darleh(e)nsantrag 173
Darleh(e)nsantragsteller 172
Darleh(e)nsbank 850
Darleh(e)nsbedarf 424
Darleh(e)nsbewerber 172
Darleh(e)nsfonds 1710
Darleh(e)nsgeber 1672
Darleh(e)nsgesuch 173
darleh(e)n, Sicht~ 504
Darleh(e)nskasse 850
Darleh(e)nsnehmer 418
Darleh(e)nssatz 423
Darleh(e)nsschein 1709
Darleh(e)nsurkunde 1709
Darleh(e)nszinssatz 423
darleh(e)n, Tagesgeld~ 504
Darleh(e)n, täglich kündbares ~ 504
darleh(e)n, Tilgungs~ 141
Darleh(e)n, ungedecktes ~ 1301
Darleh(e)n, ungesichertes ~ 1301
darleh(e)n, Wucher~ 2336
Darleh(e)n, wucherisches ~ 2336
Darleh(e)n zu Wucherzinsen 2336
Darleihen 845
Darleiher 1672
da(r)niederliegen 1663
Da(r)niederliegen 1130
datum, Fälligkeits~ 931
datum, Verfall~ 931
Dauer 894
Daueremission 2259
Dauergüter 1133
dauerhafte Güter 1133
dauerhafte Konsumgüter 747
dauerhafte Produktionsmittel 1134
Dauerrente 163
Dauerschuldverschreibung 1925
Debet 942, 943
Debet eintragen, in das ~ 615
Debetnota 948
Debetnote 948
Debetsaldo 93
Debet sein, im ~ 944
Debetseite 943
Debet stehen, im ~ 944
Debet stellen, in das ~ 615
debitieren 615
debitieren, einem Konto ~ 618
Debitmasse 317
Debitor 958
Debitoren 37
Debitorensaldo 93
Debitorenumschlag 960
Debitor, fauler ~ 981
Debitor, säumiger ~ 981
deblockieren 949
Deblockierung 950
decken, durch Hypothek ~ 838
decken, ein Defizit ~ 836
decken, einen Ausfall ~ 836
decken, einen Fehlbetrag ~ 836
decken, einen Verlust ~ 707
decken, hypothekarisch ~ 838
Deckung 834, 1732
Deckung auf Termin 1377
Deckung dienen, als ~ 2166
Deckung, erforderliche ~ 837
deckung, Gold~ 1435
Deckung, ohne ~ 835
Deckungsbedarf 837
Deckungsbetrag 1732
Deckungserfordernisse 837
Deckungsgeschäft 839
Deckungskauf 335
Deckungskoeffizient 840
Deckungszuschuss 62
Deckung, zusätzliche ~ 62
Deficit-spending 989
Defizit 988
Defizit abdecken, ein ~ 836
defizitäre Aussenhandelsbilanz 94
defizitäre Handelsbilanz 94
Defizit ausgleichen, ein ~ 836
defizit, Aussenhandels~ 265
defizit, Budget~ 95
Defizit decken, ein ~ 836
defizit, Dollar~ 1089
Defizit ersetzen, ein ~ 836
defizit, Etats~ 95
Defizitfinanzierung 989
defizit, Handels~ 474
defizit, Handelsbilanz~ 265
Defizithaushalt 95
defizit, Haushalts~ 95
defizit, Kassen~ 96
defizit, Steuer~ 1330
Defizitwirtschaft 989
defizit, Zahlungsbilanz~ 261
deflatieren 990
Deflation 991
deflationär 992
deflationieren 990
Deflationist 995
deflationistisch 992
deflationistische Tendenz 994
Deflations- 992
Deflationsanhänger 995
Deflationstendenz 994
Deflator 996
deflatorisch 992
deflatorische Spirale 993
degressive Abschreibung 7
degressive Steuer 997
deklaration, Konkurs~ 69
deklaration, Zoll~ 919
deklarierter Wert 967
deklarierung, Zoll~ 919
Delcredere 1000
Delcrederefonds 755
Delkredere 1000
Delkredererückstellung 756
demonetisieren 503
Demonetisierung 1008
Deponent 1025
deponieren 1015
Deport 239
Deportkurs 240
Depositalschein 608
Depositar 1017
Depositär 1017
depositen, Bank~ 297
Depositenbank 1020
Depositenbewahrer 1017
Depositenbuch 1021
depositen, Geld~ 307
Depositengeld 307
Depositeninhaber 1026
Depositenkonto 1016
Depositenschein 608
Depositogeld 307
Depositum 1013
Depositum auf Kündigung 1019
Depositum, jederzeit abhebbares ~ 1004
Depositum mit Kündigungsfrist 1019
depositum, Sicht~ 1004
depositum, Termin~ 1337
depositum, Zeit~ 1337
Depot 1013

depot, Bank~ 297
Depotgebühr 2124
Depothalter 1017
Depot, jederzeit abhebbares ~ 1004
depot, Kautions~ 602
Depotquittung 608
depot, Sammel~ 685
Depotschein 608
depot, Sicht~ 1004
Depotstimmrecht 2356
Depotwechsel 363
Depression 1031
Deputat 134
Desinflation 1064
desinflationär 1065
desinflationistisch 1065
Desinflations- 1065
desinflatorisch 1065
Desinvestition 1066
Detailhandel 2107
Detailhändler 2105
detaillierte Aufstellung 429
Detaillist 2105
Detailpreis 2096
Devaluation 897, 1029
Devalvation 897, 1029
devalvieren 1028
Devise 893
devise, Hart~ 1479
Devise, hochwertige ~ 1479
Devisen 1361
Devisenarbitrage 186
Devisen auf Termin 1378
Devisenbeschränkungen 902
Devisenbestand 901, 1362
Devisenbestimmungen 900
Devisenbewirtschaftung 1224
Devisenbewirtschaftungsvorschriften 900
Devisenbörse 1230
Deviseneinschränkungen 902
Devisengeschäft 1221
Devisengeschäfte 1241
Devisengewinn 1233
Devisenguthaben 1362
Devisenhandel 1221
Devisenhändler 509
Devisenkassageschäft 2202
Devisenkassahandel 1227
Devisenkassakurs 2024
Devisenkassasatz 2024
Devisenkassatransaktion 2202
Devisenkontingentierung 2030
Devisenkontrollbestimmungen 900
Devisenkontrolle 1224
Devisenkontrollen 900
Devisenkurs 1216
devisenkurs, Termin~ 1383
Devisenmakler 509
Devisenmarkt 1230
Devisenmarkt, freier ~ 1885
Devisenmarkt, gespaltener ~ 2309
Devisenoperationen 1241
Devisenordnung 900, 1240
Devisenpolster 901
Devisenposition 1363
devisenrechtliche Beschränkungen 902
Devisenregelungen 900
Devisenreserve 901
Devisenrestriktionen 902
Devisenrücklage 901
devisen, Termin~ 1378
Devisentermingeschäft 1381
Devisenterminhandel 1226
Devisenterminkurs 1383
Devisenterminmarkt 1382
Devisenterminsatz 1383
Devisentermintransaktion 1381
Devisentransaktionen 1241
Devisenüberwachung 1224
Devisenverpflichtung 1223
Devisenvorschriften 900
Devisenwert der Währung 1364
Devisen zahlbar, in ~ 1898
Devisenzusage 1223
Devisenzwangswirtschaft 1224
Diäten 1158
dienen, als Deckung ~ 2166
dienst, Anleihe~ 2167
Dienstbezüge 1158
Dienste 2168
Dienstleistung 2084
Dienstleistungen 2168
Dienstleistungen, Güter und ~ 1443
Dienstleistungen, Waren und ~ 1443
dienst, Postscheck~ 1423
dienst, Schulden~ 962
dienst, Zinsen~ 1592
Differentialtarif 1041
Differentialzoll 1040
Differenz 1037
differenz, Preis~ 1038
Differenz teilen, sich in die ~ 2201
differenz, Wechselkurs~ 1039
dingliche Sicherheit 2035, 2258
direkte Kosten 1043
direkte Steuer 1046
Direktkontrolle 770
Dirigismus 1047
dirigistische Wirtschaft 768
dirigistische Wirtschaftsordnung 1047
Disagio 1048
Disagio erleiden 1056
Diskont 127, 1048, 1060
diskont, Bank~ 311
diskont, Bar~ 583
diskont, Barzahlungs~ 583
Diskonterhöhung 1541
Diskontermässigung 926
diskontfähiges Papier 283
Diskontfuss 1061
Diskontherabsetzung 926
Diskontheraufsetzung 1541
diskontierbares Papier 283
diskontieren 1057
diskont, Kassa~ 583
Diskontkredit 1059
Diskontmakler 361
Diskontmarkt 370
Diskonto 1048
Diskont(o)bank 1058
Diskont(o)haus 1058
diskont, Prima~ 1323
diskont, Privat~ 1323
Diskontprovision 1055
Diskontrate 1061
Diskontsatz 1061
diskontsatz, Bank~ 311
Diskontsenkung 926
diskont, Waren~ 935
Disparität 1067
disparität, Preis~ 1038
Distanzgeschäft 1379
Diversa 1764
Diverse 1764
diverse Ausgaben 1764
diverse Unkosten 1764
Dividende 1076
dividende, Abschlags~ 1598
dividende, Abschluss~ 1303
Dividende anzeigen, eine ~ 965
Dividende ausschütten, eine ~ 1051
Dividende, ausserordentliche ~ 398
Dividende auszahlen, eine ~ 1051
dividende, Bar~ 584
Dividende beschliessen, eine ~ 965
dividende, Extra~ 398
Dividende festsetzen, eine ~ 965
dividende, Interims~ 1598
dividende, Konkurs~ 1077
Dividende, kumulative ~ 889
Dividende, mit ~ 887
Dividendenabschnitt 1078
Dividendenausfall 1826
Dividendenausgleichsreserve 1079
Dividendenausschüttung 1052
Dividendenauszahlung 1052
dividendenberechtigt 1170
Dividendenbogen 832
Dividendenbonus 398
Dividendenerklärung 964
Dividendenfestsetzung 964
Dividendengarantierücklage 1079
Dividendenherabsetzung 925
Dividendenkupon 1078
Dividendenkürzung 925
Dividendenminderung 925
Dividendenpolitik 1081
Dividendenschein 1078
Dividendenscheinbogen 832
Dividendenscheinerneuerung 2087
Dividendenverteilung 1052
Dividendenzahlung 1052
Dividende, ohne ~ 1080
dividende, Prioritäts~ 1945
dividende, Rest~ 1303
dividende, Schluss~ 1303
dividende, Sonder~ 398
dividende, Stock~ 400
dividende, Super~ 398
Dividende, verfallene ~ 1954
Dividende verteilen, eine ~ 1051
dividende, Vorzugs~ 1945
Dividende zahlen, eine ~ 1051
dividende, Zusatz~ 398
Dokumentarkredit 1085
Dokumentenakkreditiv 1085
Dokumentenkredit 1085
Dollarblock 1086
Dollarbond 1087
Dollardefizit 1089
dollar, Euro~ 1193

Dollargebiet 1086
Dollarklausel 1088
Dollarknappheit 1090
Dollarlücke 1089
Dollarmangel 1090
Dollarobligation 1087
Dollarraum 1086
Dollars ausgedrückt, in ~ 1010
Dollars ausgestellt, auf ~ 1010
Dollars ausgestellt, in ~ 1010
Dollarschuldverschreibung 1087
Dollars lautend, auf ~ 1010
dollar, Verrechnungs~ 29
Dollarwährungsgebiet 1086
Dollarwährungsraum 1086
Dollarzone 1086
Domizil 1102
Dontgeschäft 1855
Dontprämie 507
Doppelbesteuerung 1109
Doppelbuchung 1106
Doppelprämie 1108
doppelte Buchführung 1107
Doppelwährung 375
Dotation 1168
dotieren 122, 1167
Dotierung 123, 1168
Draufgabe 602, 1288
Draufgeld 602, 1288
Drawback 1116
Dreiecksgeschäft 2253
Dreieckshandel 2280
Dreiecksverkehr 2280
dritte Rechnung, auf (für) ~ 35
Drittschuldner 1413
drosselung, Kredit~ 874
Druck auf den Gewinn 1988
druck, Inflations~ 1558
druck, Steuer~ 463
Dubiosa 1110
dubiose Forderungen 1110
Dubiosen 1110
Dubiosenreserve 243
Dubiosenrückstellung 243
Dumping 1131
Durchfuhrhandel 2294
Durchgangshandel 2294
Durchgangskonto 2248
Durchgangsposten 2249
durchlaufender Posten 2249
Durchlaufskonto 2248
Durchschnitt 231
durchschnitt, Jahres~ 158
durchschnittlich 232
durchschnittliches Pro-Kopf-Einkommen 233
Durchschnitts- 232
Durchschnittskurs 234

Effekten 2151
Effekten, an der Börse nicht notierte ~ 892
Effekten, an der Börse zugelassene ~ 1699
effekten, Anlage~ 1630
Effektenausgabe 1639
Effektenaustausch 2254
Effektenbank 1645
Effekten, begebbare ~ 1739
Effekten belehnen 91, 671
Effekten beleihen 91, 671
Effektenbesitz 1628
Effektenbesitzer 2171
Effektenbestand 1628
Effektenbörse 1218
effekten, Börsen~ 1699
Effekten, börsenfähige ~ 1699, 1739
Effekten, börsengängige ~ 1699
Effekten, börsenmässige ~ 1699
Effekten, börsennotierte ~ 1699
Effektenemission 1639
Effektengeschäfte 1222
Effekten, handelsfähige ~ 1739
Effektenhändler 2152
effekten, Inhaber~ 342
Effekteninhaber 2171
Effektenkredit 869
effekten, Lombard~ 1895
Effekten lombardieren 91, 671
Effekten, lombardierte ~ 1895
Effektenlombardkredit 869
Effektenmakler 2152
Effektenmarkt 2153
Effekten, marktfähige ~ 1739
Effekten, nicht notierte ~ 892
Effekten, notierte ~ 1699
effekten, Portefeuille~ 1630
Effektenportefeuille 1628
Effektensparen 2135
Effektentransaktionen 1222
Effekten, übertragbare ~ 1739
Effekten, unnotierte ~ 892
Effekten, verkehrsfähige ~ 1739
Effekten verpfänden 671
Effekten, verpfändete ~ 1895
Effekten, zur Notierung nicht zugelassene ~ 892
effektives Einkommen 2032
Effektivverzinsung 57
Effektivwert 56
eigene Rechnung, auf ~ 1877
eigene Rechnung, für ~ 1877
eigener Wechsel 1477
eigenes Akzept 1477
eigene Währung 1094
Eigenfinanzierung 1601
Eigenkapital 558, 1809, 1996
Eigenmittel 558, 1809
eigentlicher Wert 1612
Eigentum, bewegliches ~ 622
Eigentümer 1878
eigentum, Grund~ 1661
eigentum, Grundstücks~ 1661
eigentum, Immobiliar~ 1508
eigentum, Privat~ 1979
Eigentum, privates ~ 1979
Eigentum, unbewegliches ~ 1508
Eigenverbrauch 1092, 1497
Eigenvermögen 558, 1809, 1996
Eigenwechsel 1477
einbehaltene Garantiesumme 2109
einbehaltene Gewinne 2108
Einbehaltung der Steuern an der Quelle 681
Einbehaltung von Gewinnen 1987
Einbringen 765
einbringen, einen Gewinn ~ 100
einbringen, Kapital ~ 436, 521
einbringen, X Prozent Zinsen ~ 334
Einbringung 765
einbringung, Kapital~ 521
einbruch, Kurs~ 431
einbruch, Preis~ 431
Einbusse 1717
einbusse, Ertrags~ 1718
einbusse, Gewinn~ 1718
einbusse, Kurs~ 1229
einbüssen, an Wert ~ 970
einbusse, Verdienst~ 1718
einbusse, Wert~ 969
eindämmen, die Inflation ~ 628
Eindämmung der Liquidität 1697
Einengung der Bandbreiten 2065
einfache Buchführung 2181
einfacher Zins 2179
einfache Währung 1785
einforderbar 496
einforderbares Kapital 499
einfrieren 380
Einfrierung 383
Einfrierung der Preise 1400
Einfuhr 1509
Einfuhrartikel 1510
Einfuhrbeschränkung 1513
Einfuhrbewilligung 1512
Einfuhr(en), sichtbare ~ 2352
Einfuhrerlaubnis 1512
Einfuhrgenehmigung 1512
Einfuhrgüter 1510
einfuhr, Kapital~ 534
Einfuhrland 825, 826
Einfuhrlizenz 1512
Einfuhrsperre 319
Einfuhrstopp 319
einführung, Börsen~ 81
Einführungspreis 1613
Einfuhrverbot 319
Einfuhrwaren 1510
Eingänge 1532
eingänge, Bar~ 585
Eingänge, etatmässige ~ 447
eingänge, Kassen~ 585
eingänge, Steuer~ 1565
Eingänge und Ausgänge 1525
Eingangsanzeige 47
Eingangsbekenntnis 47
Eingangsbestätigung 47
Eingang vorbehalten 2099
eingebrachte Sachwerte 205
eingefordertes Kapital 500
eingefrorene Kredite 1401
eingehen, eine Schuld ~ 761
eingelöst 1879
eingetragener Aktionär, (im Hauptbuch) ~ 2076
eingezahltes Kapital 1880
eingriff(e), Staats~ 1452
einhebbar 676
einheben, eine Steuer ~ 678
einhebung, Steuer~ 683
einheimischer Markt 1100
einheimische Währung 1094
einheimsen, einen Gewinn ~ 1937
einheit, Geld~ 904

einheitliche Einheitskostenrechnung 2325
einheit, Rechnungs~ 31
Einheitskosten 813
Einheitskostenrechnung, einheitliche ~ 2325
Einheitskurs 2326
Einheitspreis 1344, 2328
Einheitssatz 1345
Einheitswert 198, 199, 2213
einheit, Währungs~ 904
einigen, sich über einen Preis ~ 113
einkassierbar 574
einkassieren, einen Scheck ~ 576
Einkassierung 679
Einkauf 2012
einkaufen 479
Einkäufer 482
Einkaufskosten 488
Einkaufspreis 488, 814
Einkaufswert 50
einklagbar 675
Einkommen 1522
einkommen, Arbeits~ 1136
Einkommen, arbeitsloses ~ 2323
Einkommen aus Arbeit 1136
Einkommen aus Kapitalanlagen 1528
Einkommen aus Vermögensanlagen 1528
einkommen, Brutto~ 1463
Einkommen, effektives ~ 2032
Einkommen, erarbeitetes ~ 1136
einkommen, Faktor~ 1292
Einkommen, festes ~ 210
Einkommen, fixes ~ 210
einkommen, Gesellschafts~ 791
einkommen, Kapital~ 535
einkommen, Körperschafts~ 791
einkommen, Lohn~ 1136
einkommen, Mehr~ 2245
einkommen, National~ 1799
Einkommen, nationales ~ 1799
einkommen, Natural~ 1529
einkommen, Neben~ 64
einkommen, Netto~ 1811
einkommen, Primär~ 1970
Einkommen, primäre ~ 1970
einkommen, Privat~ 1929
einkommen, Real~ 2032
Einkommen, regelmässiges ~ 210
einkommen, Rein~ 1811
einkommen, Roh~ 1463
einkommen, Sekundär~ 2146
Einkommensgruppe 1527
Einkommen, sicheres ~ 210
Einkommensklasse 1527
Einkommensquelle 2193
Einkommensschicht 1527
Einkommenssteuer 1530
Einkommenssteuererklärung 1531
Einkommenssteuer für natürliche Personen 1930
Einkommensstufe 1527
einkommen, Staats~ 1451
Einkommen, ständiges ~ 210
einkommen, Steuer~ 1565
Einkommen, steuerpflichtiges ~ 2262
Einkommen, tatsächliches ~ 2032
Einkommen, überschüssiges ~ 2245
einkommen, Übertragungs~ 2292
Einkommen, unfundiertes ~ 1136
Einkommen, verfügbares ~ 1068
einkommen, Volks~ 1799
Einkommen, wirkliches ~ 2032
Einkommen, zurückbehaltenes ~ 1137
Einkünfte 1522
einkünfte, Brutto~ 1463
Einkünfte, feste ~ 210
einkünfte, Kapital~ 535
einkünfte, Neben~ 64
einkünfte, Netto~ 1811
einkünfte, Privat~ 1929
einkünfte, Sekundär~ 2146
Einkünfte, sonstige ~ 1765
einkünfte, Staats~ 1451
einkünfte, Steuer~ 1565
Einkünfte, zusätzliche ~ 64
Einlage 765, 1013
Einlage auf Kündigung 1019
einlage, Bank~ 297
Einlage, befristete ~ 1337
Einlagebuch 1021
Einlage, feste ~ 1337
Einlage, gebundene ~ 1337
einlage, Giro~ 1024
Einlage, jederzeit abhebbare ~ 1004
einlage, Kapital~ 521
Einlagekapital 1564
einlage, Kommandit~ 1591
Einlagekonto 1016
Einlage mit fester Laufzeit 1337
Einlage mit Kündigungsfrist 1019
Einlagen, Bank-bei-Bank-~ 1582
einlagen, Interbank~ 1582
Einlagenkündigung 1840
einlage, Sach~ 205
einlage, Sicht~ 1004
einlage, Sofort~ 1004
einlage, Spar~ 2144
einlage, Termin~ 1337
einlage, Zeit~ 1337
einlegen 1015
einlegen, Kapital ~ 436
Einleger 1025
einleger, Kapital~ 1631
einlösbar 574, 782, 2052
einlösbare Obligation 497
einlösbare Schuldverschreibung 497
Einlösbarkeit 2051
einlösen 148, 502
einlösen, eine Hypothek ~ 511
einlösen, einen Scheck ~ 576
einlösen, einen Wechsel ~ 1054
Einlösung 139, 2053
Einlösungsfonds 140
Einlösungskurs 2054
Einlösungsplan 146
Einlösungsprämie 1750
Einlösungswert 2055
einmalige Einnahmen 1287
Einmischung, staatliche ~ 1452
einmischung, Staats~ 1452
Einnahmekonto 1524
Einnahmen 1532
Einnahmen, ausserordentliche ~ 1287
einnahmen, Bar~ 585
Einnahmen, einmalige ~ 1287
einnahmen, Haushalts~ 447
einnahmen, Kassen~ 585
einnahme(n), Mehr~ 2245, 2246
einnahmen, Neben~ 64
Einnahmen, nicht wiederkehrende ~ 1287
Einnahmen, öffentliche ~ 1451
Einnahmenrechnung 1524
einnahmen, Sonder~ 1287
Einnahmen, staatliche ~ 1451
einnahmen, Staats~ 1451
einnahmen, Steuer~ 1565
Einnahme(n)überhang 2245
Einnahme(n)überschuss 2245
Einnahmen und Ausgaben 1525
Einnahmen, wiederkehrende ~ 2049
einnahmen, Zoll~ 921
Einnahmen, zusätzliche ~ 64
Einnahmequelle 2193
einräumen, einen Kredit ~ 126
einräumung, Kredit~ 220
Einreichung des Kupons, gegen ~ 1958
einschätzen 177, 195
einschätzen, unter dem Wert ~ 2319
Einschätzung 176, 200
einschiessen, Kapital ~ 436
einschleusen, Kapital ~ 436
einschliesslich Bezugsrecht 888
einschliesslich Dividende 887
einschliesslich Kupon 829
einschliesslich Optionsrecht 888
einschränken, die Ausgaben ~ 915
einschränken, sich ~ 924
einschränkungen, Devisen~ 902
einschränkung, Kredit~ 874
einschränkung, Steuer~ 1839
Einschränkung, wirtschaftliche ~ 218
Einschuss 521, 765, 1732
einschuss, Bar~ 1732
Einschussbedarf 837
einschuss, Kapital~ 521
einsenden 2080
Einsendung 1784
einsparen, die Ausgaben ~ 915
Einsparungen 2137
Einsparungen machen 924
Einsparungen vornehmen 924
einspritzen, Kapital ~ 436
Einstandsberechnung 797
Einstandspreis 814
Einstandsrecht 2013
Einstandswert 50
einstecken, einen Gewinn ~ 1937
einstellen, die Zahlungen ~ 603
einstellung, Zahlungs~ 2250
einstreichen, einen Gewinn ~ 1937
Eintrag 409
eintrag, Abschluss~ 656
eintrag, Berichtigungs~ 71
eintrag, Buch~ 409

eintragen 401
eintragen, in das Debet ~ 615
eintragen, in das Soll ~ 615
eintrag, Gegen~ 281
eintrag, Gesamt~ 717
einträglich 1147
Einträglichkeit 1984
eintrag, Stornierungs~ 281
Eintragung 409
Eintragung auf der Habenseite 857
Eintragung auf der Sollseite 946
eintragung, Buch~ 409
Eintragungsgebühr 2077
eintragung, Zwischen~ 2249
eintrag, Zwischen~ 2249
eintreibbar 675, 676
eintreibbare Forderung 37
Eintreibbarkeit 674
eintreiben, eine Forderung ~ 677
eintreiben, eine Schuld ~ 677
eintreiben, eine Steuer ~ 678
Eintreibung 680
eintreibung, Steuer~ 683
Eintreibung von Aussenständen (Forderungen; Schulden) 682
Einwanderungssaldo 1758
einzahlen 1015
einzahlen, eine Aktie voll ~ 1915
Einzahler 1025
Einzahlung 1567
Einzahlung aufgerufenes Kapital, zur ~ 500
einzahlung einer Aktie, Voll~ 1908
einzahlung, Kapital~ 1909
Einzahlung leisten 1015
Einzahlungsanzeige 97
Einzahlungsaufforderung 494
Einzahlungsbeleg 877
Einzahlungsbescheinigung 877
Einzahlungsformular 1022
Einzahlungsquittung 877
Einzahlungsschein 877
Einzahlungszettel 877
Einzahlung von X % auf eine Aktie leisten, eine ~ 1899
Einzelaufstellung 429
Einzelhandel 2107
Einzelhandelspreis 2096
Einzelhandels(preis)index 2106
Einzelhändler 2105
Einzelkosten 1043
Einzelpreis 2328
Einzelverkaufspreis 2096
Einzelwährung 1785
einziehbar 574, 675, 676
einziehbareForderung 37
einziehbare Obligation 497
einziehbare Schuldverschreibung 497
Einziehbarkeit 674
einziehen 503
einziehen, eine Forderung ~ 677
einziehen, einen Scheck ~ 576
einziehen, eine Schuld ~ 677
einziehen, eine Steuer ~ 678
Einziehung 680, 1008
einziehung, Steuer~ 683
Einziehung von Aussenständen (Forderungen; Schulden) 682
Einzug 680
Einzug von Aussenständen (Forderungen; Schulden) 682
einzulösender Wechsel 373
Ekart 1731
Elastizität der Wechselkurse 1154
Emission 1352
emission, Dauer~ 2259
emission, Effekten~ 1639
emission, Kapital~ 549
Emission placieren, eine ~ 1934
Emission plazieren, eine ~ 1934
Emissionsagio 1641
Emissionsaufgeld 1641
Emissionsbank 1645
Emissionsbedingungen einer Anleihe 729
Emissionshaus 1645
Emissionskapital 1638
Emissionskonsortium 2322
Emissionskosten 1353
Emissionskurs 1642
Emissionsprämie 1641
Emissionspreis 1642
Emissionsprospekt 1643
Emission unterbringen, eine ~ 1934
Emission von Aktien 1640
Emission von Bezugsaktien 2116
Emission von Gratisaktien 399
Emission von Obligationen 392
Emission von Pfandbriefen 392
Emission von Schuldverschreibungen 392
Emission (zur Unterbringung) garantieren, eine ~ 2320
Emittent 1644
emittieren, eine Anleihe ~ 1157
emittiertes Kapital 1638
Emolumente 1158
Empfänger 2082
empfänger, Abtretungs~ 120
empfänger, Anweisungs~ 2082
empfänger, Überweisungs~ 2082
empfänger, Wechsel~ 1902
empfänger, Zahlungs~ 350
Empfangsanzeige 47
Empfangsbescheinigung 47
Empfangsbestätigung 47
Empfangsprämie 1953
Empfangsschein 47
Endsumme 105
engagiertes Kapital 541
Engroshandel 2376
Engroshändler 2375
Engrospreis 2288
Engrossist 2375
enteignen 1270
Enteignung 1271
entgangener Gewinn 1718
entgang, Gewinn~ 1718
entgang, Verdienst~ 1718
Entgelt 2041
entgelt, Arbeits~ 1140
entgelten 2042
Enthortung 1063
entleihen 415
Entleiher 418
Entleihung 419
entlohnen 2042
entlöhnen 2042
Entlohnung 2041
Entnahme 1119
Entnahme aus Rücklagen 2377
entnahme, Bar~ 601
Entnationalisierung 1009
entnehmen 415, 1113
entrichten 148
Entrichtung 139
Entschädigung 708
entschädigung, Aufwands~ 128
entschädigung, Reise~ 2296
entschädigung, Reisekosten~ 2296
Entspannung am Geldmarkt 1144
Entsparung 1069
entsperren 949
Entsperrung 950
Entstaatlichung 1009
entstehende Zinsen 42
entwenden 977
Entwendung 978
entwerten 503, 1028
Entwertung 1008, 1029
entwertung, Geld~ 896, 1554
Entwertungsrücklage 132
entwertung, Valuta~ 896
entwertung, Währungs~ 896
Entwicklung 1200
Entwicklung, konjunkturelle ~ 477
Entwicklungsanleihe 1036
Entwicklungsbank 1035
Entwicklungshilfe 1034
erarbeitetes Einkommen 1136
Erbanfallsteuer 938
Erbschaftssteuer 938
erfahren, einen Verlust ~ 333
Erfolgskonto 1523
Erfolgsrechnung 1523
erforderliche Deckung 837
erfordernisse, Deckungs~ 837
Ergänzungskredit 63
Ergänzungsleistung 1285
ergeben, einen Gewinn ~ 100
ergeben, im ganzen ~ 106
ergeben, insgesamt ~ 106
ergiebig 1147
Ergiebigkeit 1984
Erhaltungsaufwand 810
Erhaltungskosten 810
erhebbar 676
erheben (auf), eine Steuer ~ 194
erheben, eine Steuer ~ 678
erhebung, Steuer~ 683, 1516
erhoffter Gewinn 166
erhöhen, das Kapital ~ 1544
erhöhen, den Wert ~ 178
erhöhung, Besoldigungs~ 1540
Erhöhung des Diskontsatzes 1541
erhöhung, Diskont~ 1541
erhöhung, Gehalts~ 1540
erhöhung, Lohn~ 1542
erhöhung, Preis~ 1539
Erhöhung um X Prozent 1543
erhöhung, Wert~ 180
Erholung 2020, 2048

erkennen (für, mit), das Konto ~ 880
erkennen, jemanden für einen Betrag ~ 566
erkennen, jemanden mit einem Betrag ~ 566
erklärung, Bürgschafts~ 394
erklärung, Dividenden~ 964
erklärung, Einkommenssteuer~ 1531
erklärung, Garantie~ 394
erklärung, Konkurs~ 69
erklärung, Steuer~ 2275
erklärung, Zoll~ 919
erkundung, Markt~ 1740
Erlass einer Schuld 513
erlassen, eine Schuld ~ 510
erlass, Schulden~ 513
erlass, Steuer~ 2261
erlaubnis, Ausfuhr~ 1268
erlaubnis, Einfuhr~ 1512
erlaubnis, Export~ 1268
erlaubnis, Import~ 1512
erledigung, Zoll~ 645
erleichterungen, Kredit~ 421
erleichterung, Kredit~ 1145
erleichterung, Steuer~ 2261
erleiden, einen Verlust ~ 333
Erlös 229, 1982
erlöschen 1264
Erlöschen 139, 1262
ermässigen, die Ausgaben ~ 915
Ermässigung 127
Ermässigung des Diskontsatzes 926
ermässigung, Diskont~ 926
ermässigung, Preis~ 927
ermässigung, Steuer~ 2261
ermittlung, Preis~ 1962
ermittlung, Wert~ 176
erneuernder Kredit, sich automatisch ~ 2114
erneuerung, Dividendenschein~ 2087
Erneuerungsfonds 2086
Erneuerungsrücklage 2086
Erneuerungsschein 2085
erneuerung, Zinsschein~ 2087
Eröffnung des Konkurses 1575
eröffnung, Kredit~ 1848
Eröffnungsbilanz 1700
Eröffnungskurs 1849
Eröffnungsnotierung 1849
Eröffnungsnotiz 1849
errechnen 490
Errechnung 492
errechnung, Kosten~ 797
errichten, das Inventar ~ 1124
errichtung, Inventar~ 1616
Ersatzkosten 2091
Ersatzleistung 708
Ersatzwert 2091
Erschöpfung der Reserven 1012
ersetzen, ein Defizit ~ 836
ersetzen, einen Fehlbetrag ~ 836
ersetzen, einen Verlust ~ 707
Ersparnisbildung 1374
Ersparnisbildung, private ~ 1980
Ersparnisse 2137
ersparnisse, Brutto-Inlands~ 1462
erspriesslich 1147
erstattungsfähig 2073
erstattung, Steuer~ 2038
Erstausfertigung 1327
erstehen 479
erstklassiger Wechsel 1323
erstklassiges Handelspapier 1323
erstklassige (Wert-)Papiere 387
Ertrag 229, 1982, 2110
Ertrag aus Obligationen 396
ertragbringend 1147
Erträge 229
Erträge aus Beteiligungen 1528
Erträge, neutrale ~ 1765
Erträge, sonstige ~ 1765
ertrag, Kapital~ 535
ertraglos 2324
Erträgnis 1982, 2110
Erträgnis aus Obligationen 396
Erträgnis(se) 229
Erträgnisse aus Kapitalanlagen 1528
Erträgnisse aus Vermögensanlagen 1528
erträgnisse, Kapital~ 535
erträgnisse, Steuer~ 1565
ertragreich 1147
Ertragsanteil 1686
Ertragsausfall 1718
Ertragsbeteiligung 1410
Ertragsbilanz 262
Ertragseinbusse 1718
Ertragsfähigkeit 1139
Ertragskonto 1523
Ertragskraft 1139
Ertragspreisverhältnis 1963
Ertragsrate 2025
Ertragsrechnung 1523
Ertrag(s)steuer 1989
ertrag, Steuer~ 1565
Ertragswert 546
ertrag, Zins~ 1595
ertrag, Zinsen~ 1595
erwarteter Gewinn 166
Erwerb 49
erwerben 48
Erwerber 482
Erwerbsfähigkeit 1139
Erwerbskosten 488
Erwerbskraft 1139
Erwerbspreis 488
Erwerbswert 50
Erwerbszweck, Verein mit ~ 1986
Erwerbszweck, Verein ohne ~ 1829
Erwerbung 49
Erzeugergenossenschaft 1983
Erzeugungskosten 811
Erzeugungspreis 811
erzielen, einen Gewinn ~ 1729
eskontieren 1057
Etat 441
etatisieren 443
etatmässig 442
etatmässige Eingänge 447
Etats- 442
Etatsansätze, bewilligte ~ 444
Etatsdefizit 95
Etat(s)jahr 448
Etatsüberschuss 452
Euro-Divisenmarkt 1192
Eurodollar 1193
Euro-Emissionsmarkt 1191
Euromarkt 700
Europäische Investitionsbank 1195
Europäischer Fonds für währungspolitische Zusammenarbeit 1197
Europäisches Währungsabkommen 1196
Europäische Wirtschaftsgemeinschaft 1194
Europäische Zahlungsunion 1198
Eventualforderung 757
Eventualreserve 756
Eventualverbindlichkeit 758
Eventualverpflichtung 758
Evolution 1200
EWA 1196
E.W.G. 1194
ex Bezugsrecht 1249
ex coupon 831
ex Dividende 1080
exklusive Bezugsrecht 1249
exklusive Dividende 1080
exklusive Optionsrecht 1249
ex Optionsrecht 1249
expansion, Kredit~ 858
Expansionsrhythmus 1256
Export 1265
Exportartikel 1266
Exportbeihilfe 1269
Exportbewilligung 1268
Exporterlaubnis 1268
Exporte, sichtbare ~ 2351
Exporte, unsichtbare ~ 1632
Exportgenehmigung 1268
Exportgüter 1266
export, Kapital~ 526
Exportkreditgarantie 1267
Exportland 825, 826
Exportlizenz 1268
Exportprämie 426
Exportrisikogarantie 1267
Exportsubvention 1269
Exportwaren 1266
expropiieren 1270
Expropiierung 1271
Expropriation 1271
externe Konvertibilität 1278
externe Konvertierbarkeit 1278
Extraausgaben 61
Extradividende 398
Extragebühr 60
Extrakosten 61
Extraspesen 61
Extrasteuer 66
Extravergütung 1284
EZU 1198

Fabrikationskosten 811
Fabrikationspreis 811
Factoring 1293
fahrende Habe 622
Fahrgut 622
Fahrhabe 622
Fahrnis 622
Faktoreinkommen 1292

Faktorengeschäft 1293
Faktorgeschäft 1293
faktor, Inflations~ 1556
faktor, Konversions~ 772
Faktorkosten, zu ~ 1291
faktor, Nachfrage~ 716
faktor, Umrechnungs~ 772
Faktur 17
Faktura 17
fakturieren 357
Fakturierung 366
Fall 1125
fallende Abschreibung 7
fallende Tendenz 344
Fallen spekulieren, auf das ~ 1427
fällig 1126
fällig, am 15 August ~ 1129
fälliger Saldo 252
fälliger Wechsel 372
fällige Zinsen 1589
fällig gewordene Zinsen 1589
Fälligkeit 1748
Fälligkeit, bei ~ 1128
Fälligkeitsdatum 931
Fälligkeitstag 931
Fälligkeitstermin 931
fällig werden 347
fällig werdende Zinsen 42
fallit 314
Fallit 313
fall, Kurs~ 886
fall, Preis~ 886
faule Forderungen 1110
fauler Debitor 981
fauler Schuldner 981
Faustpfanddarleh(e)n 1712
fazilitäten, Kredit~ 421
Fehlanlage 244
Fehlbestand 988
Fehlbetrag 988
Fehlbetrag abdecken, einen ~ 836
Fehlbetrag ausgleichen, einen ~ 836
Fehlbetrag decken, einen ~ 836
Fehlbetrag ersetzen, einen ~ 836
fehlbetrag, Kassen~ 96
Fehlende 988
Fehler in der Berechnung 491
fehler, Kalkulations~ 491
fehler, Rechen~ 491
fehler, Rechnungs~ 491
Fehler und Auslassungen 1183
Fehlgeld 133
Fehlinvestierung 244
Fehlinvestition 244
Fehlkalkulation 491
Fehlleitung von Mitteln 1763
Fehlrechnung 491
feilbieten 1841
Feingehalt 1325
Feingold 1324
Feinheit 1325
feld, Absatz~ 1736
Fertigungskosten 811
fest anlegen 1507
feste Aktiven 518
feste Anlage 1340
feste Ausgaben 1336
feste Einkünfte 210
feste Einlage 1337
feste Investition 1340
feste Kapitalanlagen 518
feste Kosten 1336
fester Kassenbestand 1517
fester Preis 78
festes Einkommen 210
festes Geld 1337
festes Kapital 518
feste Unkosten 1336
feste Währung 1479
Festgeld 1337
festgelegtes Kapital 518
festgesetzter Preis 78
festgesetzter Wechselkurs 1341
festigkeit, Preis~ 1326
Festigung der Preise 1969
Festkosten 1336
festlegen 1507
festlegen, einen Preis ~ 1033
Festlegung 1506
Festlegung der Währungsparität 1032
festlegung, Preis~ 1962
festliegende Kosten 1336
Festpreis 78
festsetzen, eine Dividende ~ 965
festsetzen, einen Preis ~ 1728
Festsetzung der Paritätsverhältnisse 1343
Festsetzung der Währungsparität 1032
festsetzung, Dividenden~ 964
Festsetzung einer Höchstgrenze 1342
Festsetzung eines Plafonds 1342
festsetzung, Preis~ 1515, 1962
feststellen, einen Preis ~ 1033
feststellung, Preis~ 1962
feststellung, Wert~ 176
festverzinslich 1338
festverzinslicher Titel 1339
festverzinsliches Wertpapier 1339
Festwert 2213
fictive Aktiva 1297
fiduziäre Notenausgabe 1300
fiduziärer Notenumlauf 1299
fiduziärer Umlauf 1299
fiduziarische Notenausgabe 1300
fiduziarischer Notenumlauf 1299
fiduziarischer Umlauf 1299
fiduziarisches Darleh(e)n 1301
fiktiver Rabatt 1822
Filiale 427
Finanz 1305
Finanzamt 1242
Finanzanschlag 1312
Finanzaristokratie 1486
Finanzaufwendungen 1313
Finanzausweis 1319
Finanzbeihilfe 1310
Finanzbeirat 1309
Finanzberater 1309
Finanzbericht 1319
Finanzen 1304
Finanzen, öffentliche ~ 827
Finanzen sanieren, die ~ 2044
Finanzen, staatliche ~ 827
finanzen, Staats~ 827
Finanzgebaren 730
Finanzgebarung 730
Finanzgesellschaft 1308
finanz, Gross~ 1486
Finanzhaushalt 1312
finanz, Hoch~ 1486
finanzielle Beihilfe 1310
finanzielle Belastung 1313
finanzielle Gebarung 730
finanzielle Gesundung 1318
finanzielle Hilfe 1310
finanzielle Mittel 558
finanzielle Sanierung 1318
finanzielle Schwierigkeiten 1314
Finanzier 1321
finanzieren 1306
Finanzierung 1322
finanzierung, Abzahlungs~ 1490
finanzierung, Aussen~ 1281
finanzierung, Defizit~ 989
finanzierung, Eigen~ 1601
finanzierung, Fremd~ 1281
finanzierung, Innen~ 1601
Finanzierung mit Fremdkapital 1281
Finanzierung mittels Abtretung von Forderungen 956
finanzierung, Ratenzahlungs~ 1490
Finanzierungsbedarf 1316
Finanzierungsbedürfnisse 1316
finanzierung, Selbst~ 1601
Finanzierungsgesellschaft 1308
Finanzierungsmittel 558
Finanzierungsplan 1312
Finanzierungsquelle 2192
Finanzierungswechsel 1307
finanzierung, Teilzahlungs~ 1490
finanzierung, Überbrückungs~ 433
Finanzierung von Abzahlungsgeschäften 1490
finanzierung, Zwischen~ 433
Finanzinstitut 1315
Finanzinstitut, öffentlich-rechtliches ~ 2004
Finanzjahr 1320
Finanzkonsulent 1309
Finanzkreise 1305
Finanzmakler 1311
Finanzmann 1321
Finanzmarkt 554
Finanzmittel 558
Finanzplan 1312
Finanzpolitik 1317
Finanzprogramm 1312
Finanzquellen 558
Finanzstatus 1319
Finanzstruktur 561
Finanzübersicht 1319
Finanzverwaltung 1242
Finanzwechsel 1307
Finanzwelt 1305
Finanzwesen 1304
Finanzwesen, öffentliches ~ 827
Finanzwesen, staatliches ~ 827
Finanzwirtschaft 1304
Finanzwirtschaft, öffentliche ~ 827
Finanzwirtschaft, staatliche ~ 827
fingierter Wechsel 15

firma, Bank~ 294
firma, Makler~ 439
Firmenwert 1444
Fiskal- 1329
fiskalisch 1329
Fiskalität 1334
Fiskaljahr 1335
fiskalpolitisches Instrument 1332
Fiskalwesen 1334
Fiskus 1242
fixe Kosten 1336
fixen 1427
Fixer 332
fixes Einkommen 210
Fixgeschäft 346, 1379
fixierung, Preis~ 1962
flau 508
Flauheit 1130
Flaute 1130
Flexibilität der Wechselkurse 1154
flexibler Wechselkurs 1347
floatender Wechselkurs 1347
floatende Währung 1350
Fluchtgeld 1498
Fluchtgelder 1349
flucht, Kapital~ 527
Fluchtkapital 1349
flucht, Steuer~ 2266
Fluktuation der Wechselkurse 1225
Fluktuation, konjunkturelle ~ 930
fluktuierender Wechselkurs 1347
flüssig 1693
flüssige Aktiven 227
flüssige Mittel 227
Flüssigkeit 1695
flüssigkeit, Geld~ 6
Flüssigkeitsgrad 45
Flüssigkeitskoeffizient 45
Flüssigkeitsverhältnis 45
flüssig machen 785, 1767
Flüssigmachung 773, 1766
fob 1354
Fonds 1244, 1404, 1406
fonds, Ablösungs~ 140
fonds, Abschreibungs~ 132
fonds, Amortisations~ 140
fonds, Anlage~ 653, 1624
fonds, Ausgleichs~ 710
fonds, Bar~ 587
fonds, Betriebs~ 468
Fondsbörse 1218
fonds, Darleh(e)ns~ 1710
fonds, Delcredere~ 755
fonds, Einlösungs~ 140
fonds, Erneuerungs~ 2086
Fonds für währungspolitische Zusammenarbeit, Europäischer ~ 1197
fonds, Garantie~ 1472
fonds, Gegenwert~ 823
fonds, Internationaler Währungs~ 1607
fonds, Investitions~ 1624
fonds, Investment~ 1624
fonds, Konjunktur~ 755
Fondsmakler 2152
Fondsmarkt 2153
Fonds, öffentliche ~ 2005
fonds, Pensions~ 1918
fonds, Renten~ 1455
fonds, Reserve~ 2101
fonds, Rückkaufs~ 140
fonds, Rücklage~ 2101
fonds, Schuldentilgungs~ 140
fonds, Sicherheits~ 1472
fonds, Sicherstellungs~ 1472
fonds, Sicherungs~ 1472
fonds, Spar~ 2145
Fonds, staatliche ~ 2005
fonds, Staats~ 1244, 2005
fonds, Stabilisierungs~ 2205
fonds, Tilgungs~ 140
fonds, Treuhand~ 2307
fordern, zuviel ~ 1866
fordern, zu wenig ~ 2316
Forderung 639
Forderung abbuchen, eine ~ 2379
Forderung abschreiben, eine ~ 2379
Forderung abtreten, eine ~ 207
Forderung, aktive ~ 37
Forderung ausbuchen, eine ~ 2379
forderung, Ausgleichs~ 1173
Forderung, ausstehende ~ 37
Forderung beitreiben, eine ~ 677
Forderung betreiben, eine ~ 677
forderung, Buch~ 404
Forderung, buchmässige ~ 404
Forderung, eintreibbare ~ 37
Forderung eintreiben, eine ~ 677
Forderung, einziehbare~ 37
Forderung einziehen, eine ~ 677
Forderungen, Abtretung von ~ 208
forderungen, Bank~ 296
Forderungen, dubiose ~ 1110
Forderungen, faule ~ 1110
Forderungen, notleidende ~ 1110
Forderungen, Übertragung von ~ 208
Forderungen, Zedierung von ~ 208
Forderungen, Zession von ~ 208
Forderungen, zweifelhafte ~ 1110
forderung, Eventual~ 757
forderung, Hypotheken~ 957
Forderungsabkauf 1293
Forderungsabtretung 208
Forderung, schlechte ~ 242
förderung, Spar~ 1161
Forderungsübertragung 208
Forderungsumschlag 960
Forderung übertragen, eine ~ 207
Forderung, uneinbringliche ~ 242
Forderung, ungesicherte ~ 2332
Forderung, verbriefte ~ 391
forderung, Wechsel~ 373
Forderung zedieren, eine ~ 207
formular, Einzahlungs~ 1022
forschung, Absatz~ 1740
forschung, Markt~ 1740
Franc-Zone 1388
Frankenblock 1388
Frankengebiet 1388
Frankenraum 1388
Frankenwährungsraum 1388
Frankenzone 1388
frankieren 1389
franko (an) Bord 1354
frei, abgaben~ 1247
frei (an) Bord 1354
freie Konkurrenz 1390
freie Marktwirtschaft 1393
freier Devisenmarkt 1885
freier Handel 1392
freier Markt 1395
freie Rücklage 1397
freier Wechselkurs 1347
freier Wettbewerb 1390
freies Unternehmertum 1391
freie Wirtschaft 1393
Freigabe 950
Freigabe der Preise 971
freigeben 949
Freihandel 1392
Freihandelszone 1398
Freihändler 1399
freiheit, Abgaben~ 1248
freiheit, Steuer~ 1248
freimachen 1389
Freimachung 645
freisetzen 949
Freisetzung 950
frei, steuer~ 1247
Freiverkehr 891
Freiverkehrskurs 1396
Freiverkehrsmarkt 891
freiwillige Rücklage 1397
fremde Rechnung, auf (für) ~ 35
fremdes Geld 1361
fremde Währung 1361
Fremdfinanzierung 1281
Fremdkapital 417
Fremdkapital/Eigenkapital-Verhältnis 963
Fremdmittel 417
Fremdwährung 1361
Frist 998
frist, Bedenk~ 998
frist, Bezugs~ 2237
frist, Gnaden~ 998
Frist kündigen, mit X-tägiger ~ 1426
frist, Kündigungs~ 1836
frist, Nach~ 998
Frist prolongieren, eine ~ 1273
frist, Respekt~ 998
frist, Schon~ 998
frist, Sperr~ 384
frist, Stundungs~ 998, 1276
Frist verlängern, eine ~ 1273
Frist von X Tagen kündigen, mit einer ~ 1426
frist, Zahlungs~ 1924
frist, Zeichnungs~ 2237
Fruchtgenuss 2334
früher datieren 164
führen, die Bücher ~ 1656
führen, die Buchhaltung ~ 1656
führen, Konten ~ 1656
führen, Rechnung ~ 1656
führung, Haushalts~ 450
fülle, Geld~ 6
fundieren, eine Schuld ~ 733
fundierte Schuld 735
fundierte Staatspapiere 734
Fundierung 737

Fundierungsanleihe 738
Funding 737
Fusion 135
Fusionierung 135
Fuss 2021
fuss, Diskont~ 1061
fuss, Steuer~ 2023
fuss, Zins~ 1593

gabe, Drauf~ 602, 1288
galoppierende Inflation 1411
gangbar 1738
gangbare Münze 906
gangbares Geld 914
gang, Geschäfts~ 833
gängige Münze 906
ganzen ausmachen, im ~ 106
ganzen betragen, im ~ 106
ganzen ergeben, im ~ 106
Garant 395
Garantie 1138, 1471
garantie, Anleihe~ 1473
Garantie auf Schadloshaltung 394
garantie, Ausfuhrkredit~ 1267
Garantiebrief 394
Garantie der Honorierung 1474
Garantieerklärung 394
garantie, Exportkredit~ 1267
garantie, Exportrisiko~ 1267
Garantiefonds 1472
Garantie für ein Darleh(e)n, öffentliche ~ 1447
garantie für ein Darleh(e)n, Staats~ 1447
garantie, Gold~ 1437
Garantiekonsortium 2322
garantie, Kredit~ 860
Garantie, öffentliche ~ 1450
garantieren, die Unterbringung einer Emission ~ 2320
garantieren, eine Emission (zur Unterbringung) ~ 2320
garantieren, einen Wechsel ~ 235
garantierter Kredit 670
garantierter Vorschuss 86
garantiertes Darleh(e)n 672
garantierücklage, Dividenden~ 1079
Garantieschein 394
Garantieschreiben 394
Garantie, staatliche ~ 1450
garantie, Staats~ 1450
Garantiesumme, einbehaltene ~ 2109
Garantiesyndikat 2322
Garantieverpflichtungsschein 394
garantie, Wechsel~ 230
GATT 1415
gebaren, Finanz~ 730
gebarung, Finanz~ 730
Gebarung, finanzielle ~ 730
geben, eine Sicherheit ~ 101
geben, X Prozent Zinsen ~ 334
geber, Anleihe~ 1672
geber, Darleh(e)ns~ 1672
geber, Geld~ 1777
geber, Kapital~ 1631, 1777
geber, Kredit~ 1672
gebiet, Absatz~ 1736
gebiet, Dollar~ 1086
gebiet, Franken~ 1388
gebiet, Sterling~ 2224
Gebot 353
Gebot, höheres ~ 1484
gebot, Mehr~ 1484
Gebühr 614
gebühr, Bearbeitungs~ 80, 1478
gebühr, Depot~ 2124
gebühr, Eintragungs~ 2077
Gebühren 1295
gebühren, Kredit~ 805
gebühr, Lizenz~ 1686
gebühr, Makler~ 438
gebühr, Manipulations~ 1478
gebühr, Maut~ 2284
gebühr, Monopol~ 1245
gebühr, Prolongations~ 569
gebühr, Registrierungs~ 2077
gebühr, Report~ 569
gebühr, Stempel~ 2211
gebühr, Transfer~ 812
gebühr, Übertragungs~ 812
gebühr, Überweisungs~ 2081
gebühr, Umschreibungs~ 812
gebühr, Vermittlungs~ 689
gebühr, Verwaltungs~ 80
gebühr, Zoll~ 917
gebundene Aktie 2282
gebundene Anleihe 2281
gebundene Einlage 1337
gebundener Preis 78
gedeckter Vorschuss 86
gedecktes Darleh(e)n 672
gedrückt 508
Gedrücktheit 1130
Gefälle 1037
gefälle, Preis~ 1038
gefälle, Zins~ 1412
Gefälligkeitsakzept 15
Gefälligkeitswechsel 15
gegenbuch, Konto~ 289
Gegenbuchung 281
Gegenbürgschaft 238
Gegeneintrag 281
gegeninflatorisch 170
Gegenkonto 760
Gegenleistung 731
Gegenposten 281
Gegenrechnung 709
Gegenrechnung bringen, in ~ 706
gegenseitige Bankforderung 1583
gegenstände, Luxus~ 1001
gegenstände, Wert~ 1646
Gegenwartswert 912
Gegenwechsel 819
Gegenwert 822, 1219
Gegenwertfonds 823
Gegenwertigkeit 1180
gegenzeichnen, einen Wechsel ~ 1162
Gehalt 2126
Gehälter, Löhne und ~ 1141
gehalt, Gold~ 1434
gehalt, Monats~ 1787
Gehaltsaufbesserung 1540
Gehaltserhöhung 1540
Gehalt(s)liste 1912
Gehaltssteigerung 1540
Gehaltszulage 1288
geheimnis, Bank~ 305
gekreuzter Scheck 883
geld, Abstands~ 708, 1856
Geldabwertung 897
Geldanleger 1631
Geldanweisung 1781
Geld auf Abruf 505
Geld auf (gegen) Zinsen ausleihen 1675
Geld auf (gegen) Zinsen leihen 1675
Geld auf (gegen) Zinsen verleihen 1675
Geld auf Kündigung 1019
Geldaufnehmer 418
geld, Ausfall~ 133
Geld, ausländisches ~ 1361
Geldausleiher 1777
geld, Bank~ 307
geld, Bar~ 572
Geldbedarf 1774
Geldbestand 587
Geld bezahlen, in ~ 1727
Geld, billiges ~ 623
Geld, Brief und ~ 192
geld, Buch~ 307
geld, Buss~ 136
Geldbusse 136
geld, Call~ 505
geld, Depositen~ 307
Gelddepositen 307
geld, Deposito~ 307
geld, Drauf~ 602, 1288
Geldeinheit 904
Gelde kommen, zu seinem ~ 1421
Geldentwertung 896, 1554
gelder, Flucht~ 1349
Gelder, öffentliche ~ 2005
gelder, Spar~ 2137
Gelder, staatliche ~ 2005
gelder, Staats~ 2005
gelder, Treuhand~ 2307
geld, Fehl~ 133
geld, Fest~ 1337
Geld, festes ~ 1337
geld, Flucht~ 1498
Geldflüssigkeit 6
Geld, fremdes ~ 1361
Geldfülle 6
Geld, gangbares ~ 914
Geldgeber 1777
geld, Giral~ 307
geld, Hand~ 602
Geldhändler 1311
geld, Hart~ 661
Geld, heisses ~ 1498
Geld im Umlauf 914
Geld, im Umlauf befindliches ~ 914
Geldinstitut 850, 1315
geld, Jahr~ 161
Geldkasse 579
Geldkassette 579
geld, Klein~ 612
Geldklemme 1314
Geld, knappes ~ 654
geld, Kost~ 569
geld, Kredit~ 307

Geldkreislauf 637
geld, Kunden~ 307
geld, Kündigungs~ 1019
geld, Kupfer~ 788
geld, Kurant~ 914
Geldkurs 354
Geld, kursierendes ~ 914
Geldleiher 418, 1777
Geld machen, zu ~ 785
Geldmakler 1311
geld, Manko~ 133
Geldmann 550
Geldmarkt 1778
Geldmarktpapier 1779
Geldmarkttitel 1779
Geldmenge 1783
geld, Metall~ 661
Geldmittel 1916
geld, Monats~ 1787
geld, Münz~ 661
Geldnachfrage 1774
Geldnehmer 418
Geldneuordnung 899
Geldnot 1314
geld, Papier~ 1355
Geldpolitik 1769
geld, Prämien~ 1856
Geldpreis 1967
geld, Quasi~ 1805
Geldreform 899
Geldreserve 1770
geld, Reu~ 136
Geldsatz 354, 1782
geld, Scheide~ 1083
Geldschöpfung 842
Geldschrank 2122
geld, Schwarz~ 2314
Geldschwemme 6
Geldschwierigkeiten 1314
Geldsendung 1784
Geldstrafe 136
geld, Stück~ 1834
Geldstück 660
Geldsystem 664
geld, Tages~ 505
Geld, tägliches ~ 505
Geld, täglich fälliges ~ 505
geld, Termin~ 1337
Geld, teures ~ 654
Geldüberfluss 6
Geldüberhang 6
Geldüberschuss 6
Geldüberweisung 1784
Geldumlauf 637
Geld umsetzen, in ~ 785
Geldumtausch 1231
Geld- und Kapitalmarkt 554
Geldverlegenheit 1314
Geldverleiher 1777
Geldvermehrung 1252
Geldvermittler 1311
Geldversorgung 1783
Geldvolumen 1783
Geld, von der Staatskasse ausgegebenes ~ 2302
Geldvorrat 587, 597, 1783
geld, Wechsel~ 612, 1780
Geldwechsel 1231
Geldwechsler 509
geldwertneutral 1828
Geldwertstabilität 903
Geldwertverschlechterung 896
Geldwesen 1304
Geld wiederbekommen, sein ~ 1421
Geld wiedererhalten, sein ~ 1421
Geld wiedererlangen, sein ~ 1421
Geldwirtschaft 1304, 1775
geld, Zeichen~ 1296
geld, Zeit~ 1337
Geldzirkulation 637
Geld zurückbekommen, sein ~ 1421
Geld zurückerhalten, sein ~ 1421
Geld zurückerlangen, sein ~ 1421
geld, Zwangs~ 136
Gelegenheitskauf 321
gelenkte Wirtschaft 768
Geltungsdauer 894
Gemeinkosten 1417
Gemeinkostenabweichung 464
gemeinnütziger Betrieb 2009
gemeinnütziger Verein 1829
gemeinnütziges Unternehmen 2009
gemeinnützige Unternehmung 2009
gemeinsamer Anlagefonds 1624
gemeinsamer Aussentarif 699
gemeinsamer Investmentfonds 1624
gemeinsamer Kreditnehmer 658
Gemeinsamer Markt 700
gemeinsamer Nenner 698
gemeinsames Konto 1649
gemeinschaftliches Konto 1649
Gemeinschaftshaushalt 703
Gemeinschaftskonto 1649
Gemeinschaftsschuldner 659
Gemeinschuldner 313
gemeinwirtschaftliches Unternehmen 2009
gemünztes Gold 667
genehmigen, einen Kredit ~ 126
genehmigtes Gesellschaftskapital 222
genehmigtes Kapital 222
genehmigung, Ausfuhr~ 1268
genehmigung, Einfuhr~ 1512
genehmigung, Export~ 1268
genehmigung, Import~ 1512
genehmigung, Kredit~ 220
Generalunkosten 1417
Genossenschaft 786
genossenschaft, Erzeuger~ 1983
genossenschaft, Kooperativ~ 786
genossenschaft, Kredit~ 787
genossenschaft, Produktions~ 1983
genossenschaft, Produktiv~ 1983
Genussaktie 400
Genussschein 400
gesamt ausmachen, ins~ 106
Gesamtbetrag 107
gesamt betragen, ins~ 106
Gesamteintrag 717
gesamt ergeben, ins~ 106
Gesamtrechnung, volkswirtschaftliche ~ 1579, 1797
Gesamtsaldo der Übertragungen und der Kapitalbewegungen 1416
Gesamtschaden 934
Gesamtschuld 1650
Gesamtschuldner 1651
gesamtschuldnerische Haftpflicht 1652
gesamtschuldnerische Haftung 1652
Gesamtschuldnerschaft 1652
Gesamtsumme 105
Gesamtverlust 934
Gesamtwert 108
Gesamtzahl 105
Gesamtzahlungsbilanz 1862
Geschäft 320
geschäft, Abzahlungs~ 1489
geschäft auf Geben, Noch~ 1857
geschäft auf Nehmen, Noch~ 485
geschäft, Bank~ 294, 301
geschäft, Bar~ 581
geschäft, Börsenkommissions~ 439
geschäft, Deckungs~ 839
geschäft, Devisen~ 1221
geschäft, Devisenkassa~ 2202
geschäft, Devisentermin~ 1381
geschäft, Distanz~ 1379
geschäft, Dont~ 1855
geschäft, Dreiecks~ 2253
geschäfte, Abrechnungs~ 643
geschäfte, Auslands~ 1358
geschäfte, Bank~ 304
Geschäfte betreiben 1084
geschäfte, Börse~ 1222
geschäfte, Börsen~ 1222
geschäfte, Clearing~ 643
geschäfte, Devisen~ 1241
geschäfte, Effekten~ 1222
geschäfte, Kompensations~ 643
geschäfte, Kredit~ 851
Geschäfte machen 1084
Geschäfte mit dem Ausland 1358
Geschäfte tätigen 1084
geschäfte, Valuta~ 1241
geschäfte, Verrechnungs~ 643
geschäfte, Wertpapier~ 1222
geschäft, Faktor~ 1293
geschäft, Faktoren~ 1293
geschäft, Fix~ 346, 1379
geschäft, Haupt~ 607
geschäft, Hedge~ 839
geschäft in Käufers Wahl, Nach~ 485
geschäft in Käufers Wahl, Noch~ 485
geschäft in Verkäufers Wahl, Nach~ 1857
geschäft in Verkäufers Wahl, Noch~ 1857
geschäft, Kassa~ 581
geschäft, Kassen~ 581
geschäft, Kompensations~ 327
geschäft, Komptant~ 581
geschäft, Kontant~ 581
geschäft, Kost~ 753
geschäft, Lieferungs~ 1379
geschäft, Loko~ 581
geschäft, Meta~ 1653
geschäft nach oben, Noch~ 485
geschäft nach unten, Noch~ 1857
geschäft, Partizipations~ 1653
geschäft, Pensions~ 753
geschäft, Prämien~ 1855

geschäft, Prolongations~ 753
geschäft, Report~ 753
Geschäftsablauf 833
Geschäftsaufsicht 2040
Geschäftsbank 310
Geschäftsbücher 28
Geschäftsgang 833
Geschäftsgewinn 475
geschäft, Sicherungs~ 839
geschäft, Sicht~ 1379
Geschäftsjahr 478
Geschäftskapital 468
Geschäftskredit 470, 473
Geschäftslage 469
geschäft, Sorten~ 936
geschäftsstelle, Haupt~ 607
geschäft, Stell~ 1108
geschäft, Stellage~ 1108
Geschäftsumfang 2130
Geschäftsumsatz 2130
Geschäftsunkosten 472
Geschäftsverlust 474
Geschäftsvermögen 468
Geschäftsvolumen 2130
geschäft, Swap~ 2251
geschäft, Switch~ 2253
geschäft, Tausch~ 327
geschäft, Teilzahlungs~ 1489
geschäft, Termin~ 1379
geschäft, Wechsel~ 1221
geschäft, Zeit~ 1379
geschuldet 1127
geschuldeter Betrag 151
geschuldeter Restbetrag 252
geschuldete Summe 151
geschwindigkeit, Umlauf(s)~ 2027
Gesellschaft 686
Gesellschaft, abhängige ~ 98
gesellschaft, Aktien~ 1537
gesellschaft, Anlage~ 653
gesellschaft auf Aktien, Kommandit~ 1893
gesellschaft, Bank~ 302
Gesellschaft, beherrschte ~ 98
gesellschaft, Beteiligungs~ 1494
gesellschaft, Dach~ 1494
Gesellschafter 2171
Gesellschafter, beschränkt haftender ~ 1691
Gesellschafterliste 1701
Gesellschafter, persönlich haftender ~ 1419
Gesellschafterregister 1701
Gesellschafter, stiller ~ 1105
Gesellschafter, unbeschränkt haftender ~ 1419
gesellschaft, Finanz~ 1308
gesellschaft, Finanzierungs~ 1308
gesellschaft, Handels~ 686
Gesellschaft, herrschende ~ 769
gesellschaft, Internationale Finanz~ 1605
gesellschaft, Investment~ 653
gesellschaft, Kapital~ 1537
gesellschaft, Kapitalanlage~ 653
gesellschaft, Kollektiv~ 1420
gesellschaft, Kommandit~ 1692
gesellschaft, Kontroll~ 769
gesellschaft, Konzern~ 98
gesellschaft, Kooperativ~ 786
Gesellschaft mit beschränkter Haftung 1690
gesellschaft, Mutter~ 769
gesellschaft, Ober~ 769
gesellschaft, Organ~ 98
gesellschaft, Personal~ 1892
gesellschaft, Personen~ 1892
Gesellschaftseinkommen 791
Gesellschaftsjahr 705
Gesellschaftskapital 544
Gesellschaftskapital, genehmigtes ~ 222
Gesellschaftskapitalsteuer 560
Gesellschaftssitz 2075
Gesellschaftsvermögen 790
gesellschaft, Tochter~ 98
gesellschaft, Treuhand~ 2306
gesellschaft, Zweig~ 98
gesetzliche Reserven 1670
gesetzliches Zahlungsmittel 1669
gesetzliche Währung 1669
gesicherte Obligation 2149
gesicherter Gläubiger 2150
gesicherter Kredit 670
gesicherter Vorschuss 86
gesicherte Schuldverschreibung 2149
gesichertes Darleh(e)n 672
gesichert, nicht ~ 835
gespaltener Devisenmarkt 2309
gestaffelter Tarif 1041
gestaffelte(r) Zins(en) 1457
gestaffelte Steuer 1456
Gestehungskosten 811, 814
Gestehungspreis 811, 814
gestörtes Gleichgewicht 1062
gesuch, Anleihe~ 173
gesuch, Darleh(e)ns~ 173
gesuch, Kredit~ 173
gesunde Währung 2191
Gesundung, finanzielle ~ 1318
Gewähr 1471
gewähren, einen Kredit ~ 126
gewähren, einen Zahlungsaufschub ~ 1274
gewähren, eine Sicherheit ~ 101
Gewährleistung 1471
Gewährsmann 395
Gewähr übernehmen 52
gewährung, Kredit~ 220
Gewerbesteuer 476
Gewicht 2368
gewichten 2369
Gewichtung 2371
Gewichtungskoeffizient 2372
Gewinn 1409
gewinnabwerfend 1147
Gewinn abwerfen, einen ~ 100
Gewinnanteil 1686, 2173
Gewinnanteilschein 1078
Gewinnanteilscheinbogen 832
Gewinnausfall 1718
Gewinnausschüttung 183
Gewinn, ausschüttungsfähiger ~ 1072
Gewinnausschüttung, verdeckte ~ 1482
Gewinnbeteiligung 1410
gewinn, Betriebs~ 475
Gewinnbilanz 275
gewinnbringend 1147
Gewinn bringen, einen ~ 100
gewinn, Brutto~ 1459
gewinn, Buch~ 412
Gewinn, buchmässiger ~ 412
gewinn, Devisen~ 1233
Gewinne 229
Gewinne aktivieren 548
Gewinne, einbehaltene ~ 2108
Gewinn einbringen, einen ~ 100
Gewinneinbusse 1718
Gewinn einheimsen, einen ~ 1937
Gewinn einstecken, einen ~ 1937
Gewinn einstreichen, einen ~ 1937
gewinnen, an Wert ~ 179
Gewinne, nicht ausgeschüttete ~ 2108
Gewinne, nicht entnommene ~ 2108
Gewinne, nicht verteilte ~ 2311
Gewinnentgang 1718
Gewinn, entgangener ~ 1718
Gewinn ergeben, einen ~ 100
Gewinn, erhoffter ~ 166
Gewinn, erwarteter ~ 166
Gewinn erzielen, einen ~ 1729
Gewinn(erzielungs)absicht, Verein mit ~ 1986
Gewinn(erzielungs)absicht, Verein ohne ~ 1829
Gewinne, thesaurierte ~ 2108
Gewinne, unverteilte ~ 2311
Gewinne, zurückbehaltene ~ 2108
gewinn, Geschäfts~ 475
gewinn, Handels~ 475
Gewinn, imaginärer ~ 171
gewinn, Kapital~ 530
gewinn, Kurs~ 1233
gewinn, Liquidations~ 531
gewinnlos 2324
Gewinn machen, einen ~ 1729
gewinn, Mehr~ 1213
Gewinnmitnahme 1990
gewinn, Münz~ 2154
gewinn, Netto~ 646
Gewinnobligation 1526
Gewinn pro Aktie 1142
Gewinnpunkt 430
Gewinnrealisation 1990
Gewinn realisieren, einen ~ 1729
Gewinnrealisierung 1990
gewinn, Rein~ 646
gewinn, Roh~ 1459
Gewinnrücklage 1987
Gewinnrückstellung 1987
Gewinnsaldo 849
gewinn, Schein~ 171
Gewinnschuldverschreibung 1526
Gewinnschwelle 430
Gewinnsicherung 1990
gewinn, Sonder~ 1213
Gewinnspanne 1734
Gewinnsteuer 1989
Gewinn, steuerpflichtiger ~ 197
Gewinn- und Verlustkonto 1523
Gewinn- und Verlustrechnung 1523

gewinn, Valuta~ 1233
gewinn, Valuten~ 1233
gewinn, Veräusserungs~ 531
Gewinnverteilung 183
Gewinnverwendung 183
Gewinnvortrag 1985
Gewinnzweck, Verein mit ~ 1986
Gewinnzweck, Verein ohne ~ 1829
gewogener Index 2370
gezeichnetes Kapital 2232
gezogener Wechsel 356
Giralgeld 307
Girant 1165
girant, Nach~ 2239
girant, Vor~ 1944
Girat 1163
Giratar 1163
girierbarer Wechsel 374
girieren 2080
girieren, einen Wechsel ~ 1162
Girierung 1164
Giro 318, 1164
Girobank 648
Giroeinlage 1024
Girokasse 649
Girokonto 1424
Girokontor 649
Giroverkehr 643
Girovertrag 647
glattstellen, eine Rechnung ~ 249
glattstellen, ein Konto ~ 249
Glattstellung einer Rechnung (eines Kontos) 254
Gläubiger 870
gläubiger, Absonderungs~ 1948
gläubiger, Anleihe~ 390
gläubiger, Auslands~ 1360
Gläubigerausschuss 388
Gläubiger, bevorrechtigter ~ 1948
Gläubiger, bevorzugter ~ 1948
gläubiger, Buch~ 405
Gläubiger, gesicherter ~ 2150
Gläubigerland 871
gläubiger, Obligationen~ 390
gläubiger, Obligations~ 390
gläubiger, Prioritäts~ 1948
Gläubiger, privilegierter ~ 1948
Gläubiger, sichergestellter ~ 2150
Gläubigerstaat 871
Gläubiger, vorrangiger ~ 1948
gläubiger, Vorrangs~ 1948
gläubiger, Vorzugs~ 1948
Gleichgewicht 1176
Gleichgewicht, binnenwirtschaftliches ~ 1098
Gleichgewicht bringen, das Budget ins ~ 280
Gleichgewicht bringen, den Haushaltsplan ins ~ 280
Gleichgewicht, gestörtes ~ 1062
gleichgewicht, Haushalts~ 251
Gleichgewichtspunkt 430
Gleichgewichtsstörung 1062
Gleichwertigkeit 1180
gleitender Tarif 1041
gleitende Skala 1348
gliederung, Bilanz~ 273
gliederung, Konten~ 22
Globalbetrag 107
G.m.b.H. 1690
Gnadenfrist 998
Gnadentage 933
Goldanleihe 1438
Goldarbitrage 185
gold, Barren~ 323
Goldbarrenwährung 1431
Goldbestand 1430
Golddeckung 1435
Gold-Devisenstandard 1436
Golddevisenstandard 1436
Gold-Devisenwährung 1436
Golddevisenwährung 1436
gold, Fein~ 1324
Goldgarantie 1437
Goldgehalt 1434
Gold, gemünztes ~ 667
goldgeränderte (Wert-)Papiere 387
Gold in Barren 323
Goldkernwährung 1431
Goldklausel 1432
Goldkurswährung 1436
gold, Münz~ 666, 667
Goldmünze 1433
Goldparität 1439
Goldpreises, System des gespaltenen ~ 2310
Goldreserve 1440
Goldstandard 1441
gold, Stangen~ 323
Goldstück 1433
Goldumlaufswährung 1402
Gold- und Devisenbestände 1429
Gold- und Devisenreserven 1429
Gold- und Devisenvorrat 1429
Gold und Silber in Barren 457
Gold und Silber, ungemünztes ~ 457
Gold von gesetzlicher Feinheit 666
Goldvorrat 1430
Goldwährung 1441
Goldwährung, reine ~ 1402
gold, Währungs~ 666
Goldwert 1442
Goldwertklausel 1432
Goodwill 1444
grad, Flüssigkeits~ 45
grad, Liquiditäts~ 45
Gratifikation 397
Gratisaktie 400
greifbare Aktiva 1747
greifbare Aktiven 1747
greifbare Mittel 227
greifbare Vermögenswerte 1747
greifbare Werte 1747
greifbare Wirtschaftsgüter 1747
grenze, Beleihungs~ 604
grenze, Kredit~ 855
grenze, Lombardierungs~ 604
grenze, Preis~ 1965
grenze, Rentabilitäts~ 430
grenze, Swing~ 864
grenze, Verschuldungs~ 422
Grenzkosten 1733
Grenzkurs 1965
Grenzpreis 1965
grobe Schätzung 184
Grossaktionär 633
Grossfinanz 1486
Grosshandel 2376
Grosshandelspreis 2288
Grosshandels(preis)index 2374
Grosshändler 2375
Grossist 2375
Grossistenpreis 2288
Grosskapital 355
grosswirtschaftlich 1725
Grundbesitz 1661
Grundeigentum 1661
Gründeraktien 1386
Grundkapital 544, 1564
Grundkapital (AG) 222
Grundkredit 868
Grundkreditanstalt 1660
grundlage, Bemessungs~ 331
grundlage, Besteuerungs~ 331
grundlage, Steuer~ 331
Grundpreis 330, 1832
Grundsteuer 1662
Grundstoff 329
Grundstücksbesitz 1661
Grundstückseigentum 1661
Grundstückssteuer 1662
Grundstücksvermögen 1661
Grund und Boden 1661
Gründungskapital 1564
Grundvermögen 1661
Grundvermögensabgabe 1662
Grundvermögenssteuer 1662
Grundwertabgabe 1662
Gruppe 727
gruppe, Einkommens~ 1527
gruppe, Steuer~ 2267
Gültigkeitsdauer 894
Gunsten einen Kredit eröffnen, zu jemandes ~ 1847
günstige Aussenhandelsbilanz 53
günstige Handelsbilanz 53
gutbringen, dem Konto ~ 880
gutbringen, jemandem einen Betrag ~ 566
güter, Anlage~ 533
güter, Ausfuhr~ 1266
Güter, bewegliche ~ 622
güter, Dauer~ 1133
Güter, dauerhafte ~ 1133
güter, Einfuhr~ 1510
güter, Export~ 1266
güter, Immaterial~ 1505
güter, Immobiliar~ 1508
güter, Import~ 1510
güter, Investitions~ 533
güter, Kapital~ 533
güter, Konsum~ 743
Güter, kurzlebige ~ 1827
Güter, langlebige ~ 1133
Güter, liegende ~ 1508
güter, Luxus~ 1001
Güter, nicht dauerhafte ~ 1827
güter, Produktions~ 1134
Güter, unbewegliche ~ 1508
Güter und Dienstleistungen 1443
güter, Verbrauchs~ 743
gut, Fahr~ 622
Guthaben 202, 843, 849, 1496

guthaben, Auslands~ 204, 1362
guthaben, Bank~ 286
Guthaben des Schatzamts 2300
guthaben, Devisen~ 1362
Guthaben im Ausland 204
Guthabensaldo 849
guthaben, Spar~ 2144
guthaben, Sperr~ 381
guthaben, Valuta~ 1362
guthaben, Verrechnungs~ 269
gutmachen, einen Verlust ~ 707
Gutschein 876
gutschreiben, dem Konto ~ 880
gutschreiben, jemandem einen Betrag ~ 566
Gutschreibung 844
Gutschrift 844, 857, 876
Gutschriftbuchung 857
Gutschriftposten 857
Gutschriftsanzeige 847
Gutschriftsaufgabe 847
Gutschrift(s)beleg 847
Gutschriftseite 206
Gutschrift(s)note 847
Gutschrift(s)zettel 847

Habe, bewegliche ~ 622
habe, Fahr~ 622
Habe, fahrende ~ 622
Habe, liegende ~ 1508
Haben 206, 843
Habenbuchung 857
Habenposten 857
Habensaldo 849
Habenseite 206
Habenzinsen 376
Habe, unbewegliche ~ 1508
Haftbarkeit 1681
Haftpflicht 1681
Haftpflicht, ausservertragliche ~ 1824
Haftpflicht, beschränkte ~ 1689
Haftpflicht, gesamtschuldnerische ~ 1652
Haftpflicht, solidarische ~ 1652
Haftpflicht, unbeschränkte ~ 2329
Haftpflicht, vertragliche ~ 763
Haftung 1681
Haftung, ausservertragliche ~ 1824
Haftung, beschränkte ~ 1689
Haftung, gesamtschuldnerische ~ 1652
haftung, Solidar~ 1652
Haftung, solidarische ~ 1652
Haftung, unbeschränkte ~ 2329
Haftung, vertragliche ~ 763
haftung, Vertrags~ 763
Halbjahreskupon 1475
Halbjahresrate 351
halbjährliche Rate 351
haltung, Lebens~ 1704
Hamsterei 1493
hamstern 1492
Handel 320
handel, Aussen~ 1283
Handel, auswärtiger ~ 1283
handel, Binnen~ 1101
handel, Detail~ 2107
handel, Devisen~ 1221
handel, Dreiecks~ 2280
handel, Durchfuhr~ 2294
handel, Durchgangs~ 2294
handel, Einzel~ 2107
handel, Engros~ 2376
handel, Gross~ 2376
Handel, inländischer ~ 1101
handel, Inland(s)~ 1101
handel, Innen~ 1101
handel, Klein~ 2107
Handel mit dem Ausland 1283
Handelsakzept 2286
Handelsbank 310
handelsbank, Aussen~ 1371
Handelsbilanz 264
Handelsbilanz, aktive ~ 53
Handelsbilanzdefizit 265
Handelsbilanz, defizitäre ~ 94
Handelsbilanz, günstige ~ 53
Handelsbilanz, passive ~ 94
Handelsbilanzüberschuss 266
Handelsbilanz, ungünstige ~ 94
Handelsbörse 695
Handelsbücher 28
Handelsdefizit 474
handelsfähig 1738
handelsfähige Effekten 1739
handelsfähiger Wechsel 374
handelsfähige Wertpapiere 1739
Handelsfreiheit 1392
Handelsgesellschaft 686
Handelsgesellschaft, offene ~ 1420
Handelsgewinn 475
Handelskammer, (Industrie- und) ~ 611
Handelskammer, Internationale ~ 1603
Handelskredit 470, 473
Handelsmonopol 2287
handel, Sorten~ 936
Handelspapier 356
Handelspapier, erstklassiges ~ 1323
handelspapier, Prima~ 1323
Handelsrabatt 935
Handelsregister 687
Handelsskonto 935
Handelsspanne 1734
Handelsüberschuss 266
Handelsvolumen 2354
Handelswechsel 356
Handelswert 688
handel, Transit~ 2294
handel, Übersee~ 1283
handel, Wechsel~ 1221
Handgeld 602
händler, Aktien~ 2152
händler, Börsen~ 2152
händler, Detail~ 2105
händler, Effekten~ 2152
händler, Einzel~ 2105
händler, Engros~ 2375
händler, Geld~ 1311
händler, Gross~ 2375
händler, Klein~ 2105
Händlerrabatt 935
händler, Wechsel~ 361
Handlungskosten 1417
Handlungsunkosten 1417
Handschein 1477
Handschuldschein 1477
Hartdevise 1479
harte Währung 1479
Hartgeld 661
Hartwährung 1479
Hartwährungsland 1480
Hauptaktionär 633
Hauptamt 607
Hauptbuch 1418
Hauptbuch der Aktionäre 1701
Hauptbüro 607
Hauptgeschäft 607
Hauptgeschäftsstelle 607
Hauptkontor 607
Hauptniederlassung 607
Hauptsitz 607
Hauptstelle 607
haus, Abrechnungs~ 649
haus, Bank~ 294
haus, Clearing~ 649
haus, Diskont(o)~ 1058
haus, Emissions~ 1645
Haushalt, ausgeglichener ~ 251
haushalt, Defizit~ 95
haushalt, Finanz~ 1312
haushalt, Gemeinschafts~ 703
haushalt, Investitions~ 519
haushalt, Konjunktur~ 929
Haushalt, öffentlicher ~ 1446
Haushalt, ordentlicher ~ 1859
Haushalts- 442
Haushaltsausgaben 446
Haushaltsausgleich 251
Haushaltsdefizit 95
Haushaltseinnahmen 447
haushaltsfremde Ausgaben 1823
Haushaltsführung 450
Haushaltsgleichgewicht 251
Haushalt(s)jahr 448
haushaltsmässig 442
Haushaltsmittel, bewilligte ~ 444
Haushaltsplan 441
Haushaltsplan ausgleichen, den ~ 280
Haushaltsplan ins Gleichgewicht bringen, den ~ 280
Haushaltsplan, jährlicher ~ 159
Haushaltsplan, ordentlicher ~ 1859
haushaltsplan, Staats~ 1446
Haushaltsplan vorsehen, im ~ 443
Haushaltsprognosen 451
haushalt, Staats~ 1446
Haushaltsüberschuss 452
Haushaltsvoranschläge 449
Haushaltsvorausschätzungen 451
Haushaltszuweisungen 444
Hausse 413, 2117
Haussebörse 458
Haussemarkt 458
Hausseneigung 459
Hausseprämie 507
Haussespekulant 455
Hausse spekulieren, à la ~ 456
Hausse spekulieren, auf ~ 456
Haussestimmung 459
Haussetendenz 459

Haussier 455
haus, Stamm~ 769
Hedgegeschäft 839
heft, Scheck~ 626
heimischer Markt 1100
heimische Währung 1094
heisses Geld 1498
hemmung, Liquiditäts~ 2104
herabsetzen, die Ausgaben ~ 915
herabsetzen, die Parität ~ 2062
Herabsetzung des Diskontsatzes 926
herabsetzung, Diskont~ 926
herabsetzung, Dividenden~ 925
herabsetzung, Kapital~ 2063
herabsetzung, Preis~ 927
herabsetzung, Steuer~ 2261
herabsetzung, Wert~ 969
Heraufsetzung des Diskontsatzes 1541
heraufsetzung, Diskont~ 1541
herrschende Gesellschaft 769
Herstellungskosten 811
Herstellungspreis 811
hilfe, Entwicklungs~ 1034
Hilfe, finanzielle ~ 1310
hilfe, Staats~ 1445
Hilfsbuch 225
Hilfsjournal 225
Hilfskonto 224
hinausschieben, eine Zahlung ~ 984
hinkende Währung 1476
Hinterlage 602
hinterlegen 1015
Hinterleger 1025
Hinterlegungsbescheinigung 608
Hinterlegungsschein 608
Hinterlegungssumme 1732
Hintermann 2239
hinterziehung, Steuer~ 2266
Hochfinanz 1486
Hochkonjunktur 413
höchste Preis, der ~ 605
höchstgrenze, Kredit~ 855
Höchstpreis 605
hochwertige Devise 1479
hochwertige Währung 1479
höhe, Investitions~ 1679
höheres Gebot 1484
Holding 1494
Holdinggesellschaft 1494
Honorar 1295
honorieren, einen Wechsel ~ 1054
Honorierung, Garantie der ~ 1474
Horizontalinvestierung 1253
Horizontalinvestition 1253
horten 1492
Hortung 1493
hot money 1498
Hundertsatz 1921
Hundert verzinslich sein, mit X vom ~ 334
Hyperinflation 1500
Hypothek 1790
Hypothek ablösen, eine ~ 511
Hypothek absichern, durch ~ 838
Hypothek abtragen, eine ~ 511
Hypothek abzahlen, eine ~ 511
hypothek, Amortisations~ 137
Hypothek amortisieren, eine ~ 511
Hypothekardarleh(e)n 1711
hypothekarisch absichern 838
hypothekarisch belasten 465, 1791
hypothekarisch decken 838
hypothekarische Belastung 1793
hypothekarischer Pfandbrief 1792
hypothekarische Schuldverschreibung 1792
hypothekarische Sicherheit 2035
hypothekarisches Pfand 2035
hypothekarisch sichern 838
hypothekarisch sicherstellen 838
Hypothekarkredit 866
Hypothekarschuld 957
Hypothekarschuldverschreibung 1792
Hypothek aufnehmen (auf), eine ~ 2019
Hypothek belasten, mit einer ~ 465
Hypothek beschweren, mit einer ~ 465
Hypothek decken, durch ~ 838
Hypothek einlösen, eine ~ 511
Hypothekenanleihe 1711
Hypothekenbank 1660
Hypothekenbelastung 1793
Hypothekendarleh(e)n 1711
Hypothekenforderung 957
Hypothekengarantie 2035
Hypothekenkredit 866
Hypothekenlast 1793
Hypothekenobligation 1792
Hypothekenpfandbrief 1792
Hypothekenschein 1792
Hypothekenschuld 957
Hypothekenschuldverschreibung 1792
Hypothekentitel 1792
Hypothekenzinsen 1794
hypothekieren 1791
Hypothek löschen, eine ~ 511
Hypothek sichern, durch ~ 838
Hypothek sicherstellen, durch ~ 838
Hypothek tilgen, eine ~ 511
Hypothek zurückzahlen, eine ~ 511

IAO 1606
IBRD 1602
IDA 1604
idealer Verein 1829
Idealverein 1829
IFC 1605
IHK 1603
illiquid 1503
Illiquidität 1504
imaginärer Gewinn 171
immateriale Aktiva 1505
immateriale Aktiven 1505
immateriale Anlagen 1505
immateriale Vermögenswerte 1505
immateriale Werte 1505
immateriale Wirtschaftsgüter 1505
Immaterialgüter 1505
Immobiliareigentum 1508
Immobiliargüter 1508
Immobiliarkredit 868
Immobiliarsteuer 1995
Immobiliarvermögen 1508
Immobilien 1508
immobilisieren 1507
Immobilisierung 1506
Import 1509
Importartikel 1510
Importbeschränkung 1513
Importbewilligung 1512
Importerlaubnis 1512
Importe, sichtbare ~ 2352
Importe, unsichtbare ~ 1633
Importgenehmigung 1512
Importgüter 1510
importierte Inflation 1511
import, Kapital~ 534
Importland 825, 826
Importlizenz 1512
Importwaren 1510
impuls, Investitions~ 1625
inaktivieren 2222
Inaktivierung 2221
Inanspruchnahme von Krediten 228
Index 1546
Index binden, an einen ~ 1547
Indexbindung 1548
Index der Einzelhandelspreise 2106
Index der Grosshandelspreise 2374
Index der Kleinhandelspreise 2106
Index der Lebenshaltungskosten 809
indexgebundene Obligation 1549
indexgebundene Schuldverschreibung 1549
indexgekoppelte Obligation 1549
indexgekoppelte Schuldverschreibung 1549
Index, gewogener ~ 2370
index, Grosshandels(preis)~ 2374
indexkoppeln 1547
Index koppeln, an einen ~ 1547
indexmässige Bindung 1548
Indexobligation 1549
index, Preis~ 1964
Indexschuldverschreibung 1549
index, Umsatz~ 2131
index, Warenpreis~ 696
Indexzahl 1550
Indexziffer 1550
Indikator 1551
indirekte Kosten 1417
indirekte Steuer 1552
indossabler Wechsel 374
Indossament 1164
Indossamentverbindlichkeiten 1166
Indossant 1165
indossant, Nach~ 2239
Indossant, nachfolgender ~ 2239
indossant, Vor~ 1944
Indossant, vorhergehender ~ 1944
Indossat 1163
Indossatar 1163
Indossement 1164
indossierbarer Wechsel 374
indossieren, einen Wechsel ~ 1162
Indossierer 1165
Indossierung 1164
Indosso 1164
(Industrie- und) Handelskammer 611
inflatieren 1553

Inflation 1554
inflation, Anpassungs~ 59
inflationär 1555
inflationäre Spannung 1558
Inflation bremsen, die ~ 628
Inflation dämpfen, die ~ 628
Inflation, durch Lohnsteigerung bedingte ~ 2361
Inflation eindämmen, die ~ 628
Inflation, galoppierende ~ 1411
inflationieren 1553
Inflation, importierte ~ 1511
Inflationismus 1560
Inflationist 1561
inflationistisch 1555
Inflation kontrollieren, die ~ 628
inflation, Kosten~ 803
Inflation, kostenbedingte ~ 803
Inflation, kosteninduzierte ~ 803
inflation, Kredit~ 861
Inflation, lohninduzierte ~ 2361
inflation, Nachfrage~ 1005
Inflation, nachfragebedingte ~ 1005
Inflation, nachfrageinduzierte ~ 1005
Inflations- 1555
Inflationsanhänger 1561
Inflation, schleichende ~ 882
Inflationsdruck 1558
Inflationsfaktor 1556
inflationsfeindlich 170
inflationsgeschützt 1562
Inflationslücke 1557
Inflationsrate 1563
Inflationsschraube 1559
Inflationsschub 1558
Inflationsspirale 1559
Inflationstempo 1563
Inflation steuern, die ~ 628
Inflation, unaufhaltsame ~ 1411
Inflation, unsichtbare ~ 725
Inflation, versteckte ~ 725
Inflation, zügellose ~ 1411
Inflation, zurückgestaute ~ 1919
inflatorisch 1555
inflatorische Kraft 1558
inflatorische Lücke 1557
Inhaber 336
Inhaberaktie 343
inhaber, Aktien~ 2171
inhaber, Anteilschein~ 2171
inhaber, Effekten~ 2171
Inhabereffekten 342
Inhaber eines Kontos 26
Inhaber lautende Obligation, auf den ~ 338
Inhaber lautende Schuldverschreibung, auf den ~ 338
Inhaberobligation 338
inhaber, Obligationen~ 390
Inhaberobligation mit Zinskupon 830
Inhaberobligation mit Zinsschein 830
inhaber, Obligations~ 390
Inhaberpapier 340
Inhaberpapiere 342
Inhaberscheck 339
Inhaberschuldverschreibung 338
Inhaberschuldverschreibung mit Zinskupon 830
Inhaberschuldverschreibung mit Zinsschein 830
inhaber, Schuldverschreibungs~ 390
inhaber, Wertpapier~ 341, 2171
Inhaberwertpapiere 342
initiative, Privat~ 1976
Inkasso 679
Inkassobeauftragter 955
Inkassowechsel 364
inkonvertibel 1534
Inkonvertibilität 1533
inkonvertierbar 1534
Inländerkonvertiblität 781
Inländerkonvertierbarkeit 781
inländischer Handel 1101
inländischer Verbrauch 1092
inländischer Wechsel 1091
inländische Tratte 1091
inländische Währung 1094
Inlandsanleihe 1099
Inland(s)handel 1101
Inlandskredite 1093
Inland(s)markt 1100
Inlandsnachfrage 1096
Inlandsschuld 1095
Inlandstratte 1091
Inlandsverbrauch 1092
Inlandswährung 1094
Inlandwechsel 1091
Innenfinanzierung 1601
Innenhandel 1101
Innenrevision 1600
innerbetriebliche Revision 1600
innere Anleihe 1099
innere Konvertibilität 781
innere Konvertierbarkeit 781
innerer Verbrauch 1092
innerer Wert 1612
innergemeinschaftliche Zahlung 1611
Inrechnungstellung 613
insolvent 1570
Insolvenz 1569
Instandhaltungsaufwand 810
Instandhaltungskosten 810
institut, Bank~ 294
institut, Finanz~ 1315
institut, Geld~ 850, 1315
institutioneller Anleger 793
institutioneller Kapitalanleger 793
institut, Kredit~ 850
institut, Realkredit~ 1660
Instrument, fiskalpolitisches ~ 1332
instrument, Kredit~ 862
Instrument, steuerpolitisches ~ 1332
Integration 135
intensität, Kapital~ 538
Interamerikanische Entwicklungsbank 1581
Interbankeinlagen 1582
Interbankkredit 1583
Interesse (an) 1495
Interessen 1585
interessen, Kapital~ 540
Interimsaktie 1597
Interimsdividende 1598
Interimskonto 2248
Interimsschein 1597
Interkalarzinsen 1599
Interkonvertibilität 1584
Interkonvertierbarkeit 1584
Internationale Arbeitsorganisation 1606
Internationale Bank für Wiederaufbau und Wirtschaftsförderung 1602
Internationale Entwicklungsorganisation 1604
Internationale Finanz-Corporation 1605
Internationale Finanzgesellschaft 1605
Internationale Finanzkorporation 1605
Internationale Handelskammer 1603
Internationalen Währungsfonds ziehen, auf den ~ 1123
Internationaler Währungsfonds 1607
interne Betriebsstatistik 1851
interne Konvertibilität 781
interne Konvertierbarkeit 781
interne Revision 1600
intervalutarischer Kurs 884
Interventionismus 1608
Interventionskurs 1610
Interventionspunkt 1609
Intervention, staatliche ~ 1452
intervention, Staats~ 1452
Inventar 1614, 1615
Inventaraufnahme 1616
Inventar aufnehmen, das ~ 1124
Inventar aufstellen, das ~ 1124
Inventaraufstellung 1616
Inventar errichten, das ~ 1124
Inventarerrichtung 1616
Inventarisation 1616
inventarisieren 1124
Inventarisierung 1616
Inventar vornehmen, das ~ 1124
Inventarwert 1617
Inventur 1616
Inventuraufnahme 1616
Inventur machen 1124
investieren 1618
investiertes Kapital 541
Investierung 1619
Investierung, ausländische ~ 1367
investierung, Auslands~ 1367, 1368
investierung, Fehl~ 244
investierung, Horizontal~ 1253
Investierung im Ausland 1368
investierung, Kapital~ 542
investierung, Vertikal~ 1580
Investition 1619
investition, Anlage~ 1340
Investition, ausländische ~ 1367
investition, Auslands~ 1367, 1368
Investition der öffentlichen Hand 2006
investitionen, Sach~ 518
investition, Fehl~ 244
Investition, feste ~ 1340

Investition für Produktionsausweitung 1253
investition, Horizontal~ 1253
Investition im Ausland 1368
investition, Kapital~ 542
investition, Neu~ 1818
Investition, öffentliche ~ 2006
Investition, private ~ 1978
investition, Rationalisierungs~ 1580
Investitionsanreiz 1625
Investitionsaufwand 524
Investitionsaufwendungen 524
Investitionsausgaben 524
Investitionsbank 1621
Investitionsbedarf 1627
Investitionsbudget 519
Investitionsfonds 1624
Investitionsgüter 533
Investitionshaushalt 519
Investitionshöhe 1679
Investitionsimpuls 1625
Investitionskapital 1622
Investitionskontrolle 1044
Investitionslenkung 1044
Investitionsmittel 1620
Investitionsquote 1629
Investitionsrate 1629
Investitionsspritze 521
investive Ausgaben 524
Investivlohnsystem 2362
Investment 1619
Investmentfonds 1624
Investmentgesellschaft 653
Investmenttrust 653
Investor 1631
Inzidenz einer Steuer 1521
Irrtümer und Auslassungen 1183
Irrtum vorbehalten 1184
Istausgaben 55
Istbestand 587
Istkosten 54
Istwert 56
IWF 1607

jahr, Betriebs~ 478
jahr, Budget~ 448
Jahresabschluss, konsolidierter ~ 736
Jahresausweis 160
Jahresbericht 160
Jahresdurchschnitt 158
Jahreshaushaltsplan 159
Jahresrente 161
Jahresübersicht 160
jahr, Etat(s)~ 448
jahr, Finanz~ 1320
jahr, Fiskal~ 1335
Jahrgeld 161
jahr, Geschäfts~ 478
jahr, Gesellschafts~ 705
jahr, Haushalt(s)~ 448
jährige Laufzeit, X-~ 1749
jahr, Kalender~ 493
jährliche Abschreibungsrate 157
jährlicher Haushaltsplan 159
jahr, Rechnungs~ 1320
jahr, Steuer~ 1335
jahr, Wirtschafts~ 1320

jederzeit abhebbare Einlage 1004
jederzeit abhebbares Depositum 1004
jederzeit abhebbares Depot 1004
jederzeit kündbares Darleh(e)n 504
jeweiliger Preis 911
Jobber 1648
Journal 932
journal, Hilfs~ 225
journal, Wechsel~ 359, 360
junge Aktien 1819

Kalenderjahr 493
Kalkulation 492
kalkulation, Fehl~ 491
kalkulation, Kosten~ 797
Kalkulationsfehler 491
kalkulation, Vor~ 1190
kalkulatorische Zinsen 1518
kalkulieren 490
kalkulierung, Kosten~ 797
Kammer der gewerblichen Wirtschaft 611
kammer, Verrechnungs~ 649
Kapital 514, 1972
Kapitalabfluss 556
Kapitalabgabe 551
Kapitalabgang 556
Kapitalabschnitt 2063
Kapitalabwanderung 556
kapital (AG), Grund~ 222
kapital, Aktien~ 544
kapital, Anfangs~ 1564
Kapital, angelegtes ~ 541
kapital, Anlage~ 518, 1622
Kapitalanlage 542, 1619
Kapitalanlagegesellschaft 653
Kapitalanlage, neue ~ 1818
Kapitalanlagen, feste ~ 518
Kapitalanlage, private ~ 1978
Kapitalanlage, schlechte ~ 244
Kapitalanleger 1631
Kapitalanleger, institutioneller ~ 793
Kapitalanlegung 542
kapital, Anleihe~ 1707
Kapitalansammlung 1405
Kapital aufbringen 416
Kapitalaufbringung 1405
Kapital aufnehmen 416
Kapital aufstocken, das ~ 1544
Kapitalaufstockung 536
Kapitalaufwand 524
Kapitalaufwendungen 524
Kapitalausfuhr 526
Kapitalausfuhrland 525
Kapitalausgaben 524
Kapitalauslagen 524
Kapital, ausländisches ~ 1359
kapital, Auslands~ 515, 1359
Kapitalausrüstung 523
Kapitalausstattung 523
Kapitalauswanderung 556
Kapitalausweitung 536
Kapital, autorisiertes ~ 222
kapital, Bar~ 577
Kapitalbedarf 557
Kapitalbedürfnis(se) 557

Kapital, begebenes ~ 1638
Kapital beistellen 1407
Kapitalbeistellung 1408
Kapital beisteuern 436
Kapital bereitstellen 1407
Kapitalbereitstellung 1408
Kapital beschaffen 416, 1407
Kapitalbeschaffung 1405, 1408
Kapitalbesitzer 550
kapital, Beteiligungs~ 1996
kapital, Betriebs~ 468
Kapital, bewegliches ~ 468
Kapitalbewegung 555
Kapitalbewegungen, Saldo der ~ 256
Kapitalbilanz 256
Kapitalbildung 529
Kapital, brachliegendes ~ 1502
kapital, Eigen~ 558, 1809, 1996
Kapital einbringen 436
Kapitaleinbringen 521
Kapitaleinbringung 521
Kapital, einforderbares ~ 499
Kapitaleinfuhr 534
Kapital, eingefordertes ~ 500
Kapital, eingezahltes ~ 1880
Kapitaleinkommen 535
Kapitaleinkünfte 535
kapital, Einlage~ 1564
Kapitaleinlage 521
Kapital einlegen 436
Kapitaleinleger 1631
Kapital einschiessen 436
Kapital einschleusen 436
Kapitaleinschuss 521
Kapital einspritzen 436
Kapitaleinzahlung 1909
Kapitalemission 549
kapital, Emissions~ 1638
Kapital, emittiertes ~ 1638
Kapital, engagiertes ~ 541
Kapital erhöhen, das ~ 1544
Kapitalerhöhung 536
Kapitalertrag 535
Kapitalerträgnisse 535
Kapitalertragsteuer 565
Kapitalexport 526
Kapital exportierendes Land 525
Kapital, festes ~ 518
Kapital, festgelegtes ~ 518
kapital, Flucht~ 1349
Kapitalflucht 527
kapital, Fremd~ 417
Kapitalgeber 1631, 1777
Kapital, genehmigtes ~ 222
kapital, Geschäfts~ 468
Kapitalgesellschaft 1537
kapital, Gesellschafts~ 544
Kapitalgewinn 530
Kapitalgewinnabgabe 532
Kapitalgewinnsteuer 532
Kapital, gezeichnetes ~ 2232
kapital (GmbH), Stamm~ 222
kapital, Gross~ 355
kapital, Grund~ 544, 1564
kapital, Gründungs~ 1564
Kapitalgüter 533
Kapitalherabsetzung 2063

Kapital im Ausland 515
Kapitalimport 534
Kapitalintensität 538
kapitalintensiv 539
Kapitalinteressen 540
Kapital, investiertes ~ 541
Kapitalinvestierung 542
Kapitalinvestition 542
kapital, Investitions~ 1622
Kapitalisation 543
kapitalisieren 545
kapitalisieren, die Zinsen ~ 547
kapitalisierter Wert 546
Kapitalisierung 523, 543
Kapitalisierung der (fälligen) Zinsen 156
Kapitalist 550
Kapitalknappheit 559
Kapitalkonto 516
Kapitalkosten 522
kapital, Kredit~ 417
Kapitallasten 520
kapital, Leih~ 417, 1707
Kapitalleistung 1408
Kapitallenkung 1044
Kapitalmangel 559
Kapitalmarkt 554
Kapitalmarktzins 1967
Kapitalmittel 558
kapital, Nenn~ 222
Kapital, (noch) nicht aufgerufenes ~ 2313
Kapital, (noch) nicht eingefordertes ~ 2313
Kapital, (noch) nicht eingezahltes ~ 2313
kapital, Obligationen~ 940
kapital, Privat~ 1975
Kapitalquellen 558
Kapitalrendite 535
Kapitalrente 535
kapital, Risiko~ 1178
Kapital, risikobereites ~ 1178
Kapitalsammelstelle 793
kapital, Schuld~ 417
kapital, Spar~ 2143
kapital, Stamm~ 544
Kapitalsteuer 551
Kapitalsteuerung 1044
Kapitalstrom 528
Kapitalstruktur 561
Kapital, totes ~ 1502
Kapitaltransfer 563
Kapitaltransferierung 563
Kapitalübertragung 563
kapital, Umlauf(s)~ 468
Kapital, unproduktives ~ 1502
Kapital, vagabundierendes ~ 1498
Kapitalverkehr 555
Kapitalverkehr(s)steuer 564
Kapitalverknappung 559
Kapitalverlust 552
Kapital vermehren, das ~ 1544
Kapitalvermehrung 536
Kapitalverminderung 2063
Kapitalvermögen 518
Kapitalvermögenssteuer 551
Kapital verschaffen 1407
Kapitalverwässerung 2226
Kapitalverwendung 1160
Kapitalverzinsung 535, 540
Kapitalzeichnung 562
Kapitalzins(en) 540
Kapitalzufluss 99
Kapitalzufuhr 99
Kapital, zur Einzahlung aufgerufenes ~ 500
Kapital zur Verfügung stellen 1407
Kapitalzusammenlegung 2063
Kapitalzusammensetzung 561
Kapitalzustrom 99
Kapitalzuwachssteuer 532
karte, Kredit~ 854
Kartell 571
kartell, Preis~ 115
karte, Zahl~ 1781
Kassaabzug 583
Kassabuch 578
Kassadiskont 583
Kassageschäft 581
Kassageschäft in Devisen 2202
Kassahandel in Devisen 1227
Kassakonto 575
Kassakurs 593
Kassapreis 593
Kassaskonto 583
Kassatransaktion 581
Kassaverkauf 598
Kassazahlung 591
Kasse 579
kasse, Ausgleichs~ 649, 710
kasse, Bar~ 1931
kasse, Bauspar~ 453
kasse, Darleh(e)ns~ 850
Kasse, gegen ~ 573
kasse, Geld~ 579
kasse, Giro~ 649
Kasse, kleine ~ 1931
kasse, Kompensations~ 649, 710
kasse, Liquidations~ 649
Kassenabgang 96
Kassenabzug 583
Kassenanforderungen 596
Kassenausfall 96
Kassenausgaben 582
Kassenausgänge 582
Kassenauszahlungen 582
Kassenbeleg 600
Kassenbestand 587
Kassenbestand, fester ~ 1517
Kassenbilanz 253
Kassenbon 389, 590
Kassenbuch 578
Kassendefizit 96
Kasseneingänge 585
Kasseneinnahmen 585
Kassenfehlbetrag 96
Kassengeschäft 581
Kassenkonto 575
Kassenkredit 580
Kassenlage 592
Kassenliquidität 227
Kassenmanko 96
Kassenobligation 389
Kassenreserve 597
Kassensaldo 253
Kassenschein 590, 2301
Kassenskonto 583
Kassenstand 592
Kassenstatus 592
Kassentransaktion 581
Kassenüberschuss 599
Kassenzettel 590
kasse, Pensions~ 1918
Kasse, per ~ 573
kasse, Postspar~ 1941
Kasse sein, nicht bei ~ 2178
kasse, Spar~ 2139
kasse, Staats~ 2299
kasse, Stahl~ 2122
kassette, Geld~ 579
kasse, Wechsel~ 1217
kassieren, einen Scheck ~ 576
Katastereinheitswert 199
Katasterwert 199
Kauf 2012
kauf, Abzahlungs~ 1573
Kauf anbieten, zum ~ 1841
Kauf auf Kredit 852
Kauf auf Lieferung 1376
Kauf auf Raten 1573
Kauf auf Rechnung 852
kauf, Bar~ 594
kauf, Deckungs~ 335
kaufen 479
kaufen, auf Abzahlung ~ 481
kaufen, auf Lieferung ~ 486
kaufen, auf Raten ~ 481
kaufen, auf Ratenzahlung ~ 481
kaufen, auf Stottern ~ 481
kaufen, auf Teilzahlung ~ 481
kaufen, auf Termin ~ 486
kaufen, auf Zeit ~ 486
kaufen, auf Ziel ~ 486
Käufer 482
Käufermarkt 483
Kauf gegen Kasse 594
kauf, Gelegenheits~ 321
Kaufkraft 487
Kaufkraftüberhang 1209
Kaufkraft, überschüssige ~ 1209
kauf, Kredit~ 852
Kaufkurs 354
käuflich überlassen 2157
kauf, Lieferungs~ 1376
kaufmännische Bücher 28
kauf, Meinungs~ 2198
kauf, Miet~ 1487
Kaufmiete 1487
Kauf mit dem Recht des Nachforderns 485
Kauf mit einmal noch 485
Kauf mit Rückkaufsrecht 2132
Kauf ohne Ziel 594
Kaufoption 484
Kaufpreis 488
kauf, Rechnungs~ 852
kauf, Reu~ 136
kauf, Teilzahlungs~ 1573
kauf, Termin~ 1376
Kaufwert 50
kauf, Zeit~ 1376
kauf, Ziel~ 1376
Kaution 1138

Kautionsaktie 2015
Kautionsdepot 602
Kautionskredit 853
Kellerwechsel 15
kennzahl, Liquiditäts~ 45
kennziffer, Liquiditäts~ 45
keynesisch 1657
Kladde 1754
Klarierung 645
klasse, Einkommens~ 1527
klasse, Steuer~ 2267
klausel, Ausweich~ 1155
klausel, Dollar~ 1088
klausel, Gold~ 1432
klausel, Goldwert~ 1432
klausel, Not~ 1155
kleine Ausgaben 1764
kleine Auslagen 1764
kleine Kasse 1931
kleine Kosten 1764
kleine Spesen 1764
kleine Unkosten 1764
Kleingeld 612
Kleinhandel 2107
Kleinhandelspreis 2096
Kleinhandels(preis)index 2106
Kleinhändler 2105
Kleinverkaufspreis 2096
kleinwirtschaftlich 1757
klemme, Geld~ 1314
klemme, Kredit~ 874
klingender Münze, in ~ 573
knapp bei Kasse sein 2178
knappes Geld 654
knappheit, Dollar~ 1090
knappheit, Kapital~ 559
knappheit, Kredit~ 878
koeffizient, Deckungs~ 840
koeffizient, Flüssigkeits~ 45
koeffizient, Gewichtungs~ 2372
koeffizient, Liquiditäts~ 45
koeffizient, Wägungs~ 2372
kollationieren, Konten ~ 112
Kollationierung von Konten 2043
Kollektivgesellschaft 1420
Kollektivkonto 673
Kommanditaktiengesellschaft 1893
Kommanditanteil 1591
Kommanditär 1691
Kommandite 1692
Kommanditeinlage 1591
Kommanditgesellschaft 1692
Kommanditgesellschaft auf Aktien 1893
Kommanditist 1691
Kommerzialisierung 1742
Kommission 689
Kommissionär 690
kommission, Bereitstellungs~ 693
kommission, Krediteröffnungs~ 693
Kommissionsagent 690
Kommissionssatz 691
Kommissionsvertreter 690
Kommittent 1973
Kommunalanleihen 1713
Kommunalobligation 1713
Kommunalschuldschein 1713
Kommunalschuldverschreibung 1713
Kompensation 642, 708, 709, 1172
Kompensationsabkommen 647
Kompensationsgeschäft 327
Kompensationsgeschäfte 643
Kompensationskasse 649, 710
Kompensationskurs 650
Kompensationsverkehr 643
Kompensationszoll 711
kompensieren 706
kompensieren, einen Scheck ~ 641
Kompensierung 708
Komplementär 1419
Komptantgeschäft 581
Komptanttransaktion 581
Konjunktur 477, 1146
Konjunkturablauf 477
Konjunkturausgleichsreserve 820
Konjunkturausgleichsrücklage 820
Konjunkturbelebung 1251
konjunkturell 1146
konjunkturelle Entwicklung 477
konjunkturelle Fluktuation 930
konjunkturelle Schwankung 930
Konjunkturentwicklung 477
Konjunkturfonds 755
Konjunkturhaushalt 929
konjunktur, Hoch~ 413
Konjunkturphase 1150
Konjunkturrückgang 1031
Konjunktur, rückläufige ~ 1031
Konjunkturrückschlag 1031
Konjunkturschwankung 930
Konjunktur, sinkende ~ 1031
konjunktur, Tief~ 1031
Konjunkturverlauf 477
Konjunkturzyklus 471
konkurrenzfähig 713
Konkurrenzfähigkeit 714
Konkurrenzfreiheit 1390
konkurrierend 713
Konkurs 315
Konkursanmeldung 316
Konkursantrag 316
Konkursbeauftragter 209
Konkursdeklaration 69
Konkursdividende 1077
Konkurserklärung 69
Konkurseröffnung 1575
Konkurseröffnungsantrag 316
Konkurs, in ~ 314
Konkursmasse 317
Konkurspfleger 209
Konkursquote 1077
Konkursschuldner 313
Konkursverwalter 209
Konkursverwaltung 2040
Konsolidation 737
Konsolidationsanleihe 738
konsolidieren, eine Schuld ~ 733
konsolidierter Jahresabschluss 736
konsolidierte Schuld 735
konsolidierte Staatspapiere 734
Konsolidierung 737
Konsolidierungsanleihe 738
Konsolidierungsbogen 739
Konsols 734
Konsortialkonto 1654
Konsortialkredit 741
Konsortium 740
konsortium, Banken~ 303
konsortium, Emissions~ 2322
konsortium, Garantie~ 2322
konsortium, Placierungs~ 2322
konsortium, Plazierungs~ 2322
konsortium, Übernahme~ 2322
konstanten, Ausgabe~ 1336
konstanten Preisen, zu ~ 742
konsulent, Finanz~ 1309
Konsum 751
Konsumaufwand 748
Konsumausgaben, öffentliche ~ 2002
Konsument 744
Konsumentenkredit 745
Konsumentenpreis 749
Konsumgüter 743
Konsumgüter, dauerhafte ~ 747
Konsumgüter, langlebige ~ 747
Konsumkredit 745
Konsumsteuer 752
konsumtive Ausgaben 748
Konsumtivkredit 745
Kontantgeschäft 581
Kontanttransaktion 581
Konten abgleichen 112
Konten abstimmen 112
Kontenaufgliederung 22
Konten bereinigen 112
Konten führen 1656
Kontengliederung 22
Konteninhaber 26
Konten in Übereinstimmung bringen 112
Konten kollationieren 112
Kontenplan 22
Kontenrahmen 22
Kontensaldo 255
Kontensparen 2136
konten, Spiegel~ 802
Kontenstand 1940
Kontenüberziehung 1867
Kontingent 2017
kontingentieren 122, 1186
Kontingentierung 2018
kontingentierung, Devisen~ 2030
Konto 16
Konto, à ~ 19
Konto abgleichen, ein ~ 249
Konto abrechnen, ein ~ 249
Konto abschliessen, ein ~ 652
konto, Aktiv~ 201
Konto a meta 1654
konto, Ander~ 2305
konto, Anschreibungs~ 617
konto, Auffang~ 2248
konto, Aufwands~ 1259
Konto ausgleichen, ein ~ 249
Kontoauszug 5
konto, Bank~ 285
Konto begleichen, ein ~ 249
Konto belasten, einem ~ 618
Konto belasten mit, ein ~ 618
Konto berichtigen, ein ~ 249
Kontobestand 27, 255
konto, Beteiligungs~ 1654
konto, Betriebs~ 2289

Kontobezeichnung 25
konto, Bilanz~ 271
Kontobuch 289
konto, Clearing~ 644
Konto debitieren, einem ~ 618
konto, Depositen~ 1016
konto, Durchgangs~ 2248
konto, Durchlaufs~ 2248
konto, Einlage~ 1016
konto, Einnahme~ 1524
konto, Erfolgs~ 1523
Konto erkennen (für, mit), das ~ 880
konto, Ertrags~ 1523
konto, Gegen~ 760
Kontogegenbuch 289
Konto, gemeinsames ~ 1649
Konto, gemeinschaftliches ~ 1649
konto, Gemeinschafts~ 1649
konto, Gewinn- und Verlust~ 1523
konto, Giro~ 1424
Konto glattstellen, ein ~ 249
Konto gutbringen, dem ~ 880
Konto gutschreiben, dem ~ 880
konto, Hilfs~ 224
Kontoinhaber 26
konto, Interims~ 2248
konto, Kapital~ 516
konto, Kassa~ 575
konto, Kassen~ 575
konto, Kollektiv~ 673
konto, Konsortial~ 1654
konto, Kontokorrent~ 23
konto, Kontroll~ 766
Kontokorrent 23
Kontokorrentkonto 23
Kontokorrentkredit 87, 379
Kontokorrentverbindlichkeiten 1023
Kontokorrentverpflichtungen 1023
Konto kreditieren (für, mit), das ~ 880
konto, Kunden~ 617
Konto, laufendes ~ 23
konto, Loro~ 1716
konto, Meta~ 1654
konto, Neben~ 224
konto, Nostro~ 1833
Konto, offenes ~ 23
Konto, offenstehendes ~ 23
konto, Partizipations~ 1654
konto, Passiv~ 1682
konto, Personal~ 1926
konto, Postscheck~ 1800
konto, Privat~ 1926
kontor, Abrechnungs~ 649
konto, Reserve~ 130
kontor, Giro~ 649
kontor, Haupt~ 607
konto, Rücklagen~ 130
konto, Rückstellungs~ 130
Konto saldieren, ein ~ 249
konto, Sammel~ 673, 766
konto, Scheck~ 625
Konto schliessen, ein ~ 652
konto, Schwebe~ 2248
Konto setzen, auf das ~ 618
Konto skontrieren, ein ~ 249
konto, Spar~ 2138
konto, Spesen~ 1259
Kontostand 1940
konto, Treuhänder~ 2305
Konto überdisponieren, ein ~ 1868
konto, Übergangs~ 2248
Konto überschreiten, ein ~ 1868
Konto überziehen, ein ~ 1868
Kontoüberziehung 1867
konto, Unkosten~ 1259
konto, Unter~ 224
konto, Verrechnungs~ 644
konto, Verwahr~ 2248
konto, Vostro~ 1716
konto, Zwischen~ 2248
kontrahieren, eine Anleihe ~ 762
kontrakt, Miet~ 1666
kontrakt, Pacht~ 1666
Kontrollabschnitt 821
Kontrollblatt 821
kontrolle, Devisen~ 1224
kontrolle, Direkt~ 770
kontrolle, Investitions~ 1044
kontrolle, Kredit~ 629
kontrolle, Lohn~ 2360
kontrollen, Devisen~ 900
kontrolle, Preis~ 1961
Kontrollgesellschaft 769
kontrollieren, die Inflation ~ 628
kontrollierte Währung 767
Kontrollkonto 766
konvention, Preis~ 115
Konversion 771
Konversion einer Anleihe 775
Konversionsanleihe 774
Konversionsfaktor 772
Konversionskurs 778
Konversionsobligation 704
Konversionsrecht 777
Konversionssatz 778
Konversionsschuldverschreibung 704
Konversion von Schulden 776
konversion, Zwangs~ 721
konvertibel 782
Konvertibilität 780
konvertibilität, Ausländer~ 1278
Konvertibilität, äussere ~ 1278
Konvertibilität, externe ~ 1278
Konvertibilität, innere ~ 781
Konvertibilität, interne ~ 781
konvertiblität, Inländer~ 781
konvertierbar 782
Konvertierbarkeit 780
konvertierbarkeit, Ausländer~ 1278
Konvertierbarkeit, äussere ~ 1278
Konvertierbarkeit, externe ~ 1278
konvertierbarkeit, Inländer~ 781
Konvertierbarkeit, innere ~ 781
Konvertierbarkeit, interne ~ 781
konvertieren, eine Anleihe ~ 779
Konvertierung 771
Konvertierung einer Anleihe 775
Konvertierungsanleihe 774
Konvertierung von Schulden 776
konvertierung, Zwangs~ 721
Konzentration 135
Konzentrationskurs 2326
Konzern 727
Konzernabschluss 736
Konzernbilanz 736
Konzerngesellschaft 98
Konzession 728
Kooperativ 786
Kooperative 786
Kooperativgenossenschaft 786
Kooperativgesellschaft 786
körperliche Wirtschaftsgüter 1747
Körperschaftseinkommen 791
Körperschaftssteuer 792
korrektur, Wechselkurs~ 75
Kostbarkeiten 1646
Kosten 795
Kosten, abzüglich der ~ 131, 621
Kosten, allgemeine ~ 1417
Kosten, alternative ~ 1853
kosten, Anschaffungs~ 488, 804
Kostenanschlag 1187
kosten, Arbeits~ 806
Kosten, auf ~ 1260
kosten, Ausgabe~ 1353
Kostenausgleich 800
kostenbedingte Inflation 803
kosten, Beförderungs~ 2295
kosten, Begebungs~ 1353
Kostenberechnung 797, 798
kosten, Betriebs~ 1850
kosten, Bewirtschaftungs~ 79
Kostenbuchführung 798
Kostenbuchhaltung 798
Kosten, direkte ~ 1043
kosten, Einkaufs~ 488
kosten, Einzel~ 1043
kosten, Emissions~ 1353
kosten, Erhaltungs~ 810
Kostenerrechnung 797
kosten, Ersatz~ 2091
kosten, Erwerbs~ 488
kosten, Erzeugungs~ 811
kosten, Fabrikations~ 811
kosten, Fertigungs~ 811
kosten, Fest~ 1336
Kosten, feste ~ 1336
Kosten, festliegende ~ 1336
Kosten, fixe ~ 1336
kosten, Gemein~ 1417
kosten, Gestehungs~ 811, 814
kosten, Grenz~ 1733
kosten, Handlungs~ 1417
kosten, Herstellungs~ 811
Kosten, indirekte ~ 1417
kosteninduzierte Inflation 803
Kosteninflation 803
kosten, Instandhaltungs~ 810
kosten, Ist~ 54
Kostenkalkulation 797
kostenkalkulation, Teil~ 1045
kostenkalkulation, Voll~ 4
Kostenkalkulierung 797
kosten, Kapital~ 522
Kosten, kleine ~ 1764
kosten, Kredit~ 805
kosten, Lebenshaltungs~ 807
kosten, Lohn~ 2359
Kosten, nach Abrechnung der ~ 131
Kosten, nach Abzug der ~ 131
Kosten, nachkalkulierte ~ 804
Kosten per Einheit 813

kosten, Plan~ 1189
Kostenpreis 814
Kostenpreisberechnung 815
kostenpreis, Selbst~ 814
Kosten-Preis-Spirale 816
Kostenpreis, zum ~ 796
kosten, Primär~ 1043
kosten, Produktions~ 811
Kosten pro Einheit 813
Kostenrechnung 797
kostenrechnung, Voll~ 4
kosten, Reise~ 2298
kosten, Repräsentations~ 1169
kosten, Sekundär~ 1417
kosten, Selbst~ 814
kosten, Soll~ 1189
kosten, Speditions~ 2295
Kostenstelle 461
Kostenstruktur 817
kosten, Stück~ 813
Kosten, tatsächliche ~ 54
Kosten, teilproportionale ~ 2164
Kostenträger 818
kosten, Transfer~ 812
kosten, Transport~ 2295
Kostenüberschlag, roher ~ 184
Kostenüberschlag, ungefährer ~ 184
Kosten- und Ertragsanalyse 801
Kosten, unter Abzug der ~ 621
kosten, Unterhalts~ 810
kosten, Unterhaltungs~ 810
Kosten, variable ~ 2346
Kosten, Versicherung, (und) Fracht 634
kosten, Verwaltungs~ 79
Kostenvoranschlag 1187
Kosten, vorkalkulierte ~ 1189
Kostenwert 50
kosten, Wiederanschaffungs~ 2091
kosten, Wiederbeschaffungs~ 2091
Kosten, zusätzliche ~ 61
Kostgeld 569
Kostgeschäft 753
Kostwechsel 363
kotieren 1698
kotierte Wertpapiere 1699
Kotierung 81, 1746
Krach 668
Kraft, inflatorische ~ 1558
Kredit 206, 843, 845
Kredit, abgesicherter ~ 670
kredit, Abruf~ 2214
kredit, Abzahlungs~ 1488
kredit, Akzept~ 11
Kreditanspannung 874
Kreditanstalt 850
Kreditantrag 173
Kreditantragsteller 172
Kreditaufnahme 419
Kreditausdehnung 858
Kreditausweitung 858
kredit, Aval~ 853
kredit, Bank~ 295
Kreditbank 850
Kredit, Bank-an-Bank-~ 1583
kredit, Bar~ 580
Kreditbedingungen 856
Kreditbegrenzung 874
kredit, Bereitschafts~ 2214
Kreditbeschränkung 874
Kreditbeschränkungen lockern, die ~ 1143
Kreditbeschränkungen mildern, die ~ 1143
Kredit bewerben, sich um einen ~ 175
Kreditbewerber 172
Kredit bewilligen, einen ~ 126
Kreditbewilligung 220
kredit, Blanko~ 379
Kreditbrief 1678
kredit, Bürgschafts~ 853
Kredit der automatisch abgedeckt wird 2156
kredit, Diskont~ 1059
kredit, Dokumentar~ 1085
kredit, Dokumenten~ 1085
Kreditdrosselung 874
Kredite, eingefrorene ~ 1401
kredit, Effekten~ 869
kredit, Effektenlombard~ 869
kredite, Inlands~ 1093
Kredit einräumen, einen ~ 126
Krediteinräumung 220
Krediteinschränkung 874
kredit, Ergänzungs~ 63
Krediterleichterung 1145
Krediterleichterungen 421
Kredit eröffnen, zu jemandes Gunsten einen ~ 1847
Krediteröffnung 1848
Krediteröffnungskommission 693
Krediteröffnungsprovision 693
Kreditexpansion 858
kreditfähig 846
Kreditfähigkeit 873
Kreditfazilitäten 421
Kreditgarantie 860
Kredit, garantierter ~ 670
Kreditgeber 1672
Kreditgebühren 805
Kredit gegen Sicherheit 670
Kredit gegen Wertpapierlombard 869
Kreditgeld 307
Kredit genehmigen, einen ~ 126
Kreditgenehmigung 220
Kreditgenossenschaft 787
Kreditgeschäfte 851
kredit, Geschäfts~ 470, 473
Kredit, gesicherter ~ 670
Kreditgesuch 173
Kredit gewähren, einen ~ 126
Kreditgewährung 220
Kreditgrenze 855
kredit, Grund~ 868
kredit, Handels~ 470, 473
Kredithöchstgrenze 855
kredit, Hypothekar~ 866
kredit, Hypotheken~ 866
kreditieren (für, mit), das Konto ~ 880
kreditieren, jemandem einen Betrag ~ 566
kreditieren, jemanden für einen Betrag ~ 566
kreditieren, jemanden mit einem Betrag ~ 566
Kreditierung 844
kredit, Immobiliar~ 868
Kreditinflation 861
Kredit in laufender Rechnung 87
Kreditinstitut 850
Kreditinstrument 862
kredit, Interbank~ 1583
Kreditkapital 417
Kreditkarte 854
kredit, Kassen~ 580
Kreditkauf 852
kredit, Kautions~ 853
Kreditklemme 874
Kreditknappheit 878
kredit, Konsortial~ 741
kredit, Konsum~ 745
kredit, Konsumenten~ 745
kredit, Konsumtiv~ 745
kredit, Kontokorrent~ 87, 379
Kreditkontrolle 629
Kreditkosten 805
kredit, Kunden~ 745
Kreditlinie 855
Kreditlockerung 1145
kredit, Lombard~ 869
Kreditmangel 878
Kreditmarge 864
kredit, Meta~ 865
Kreditmittel 862
Kredit, mittelfristiger ~ 1753
kredit, Mobiliar~ 867
kredit, Nachtrags~ 63
Kreditnehmer 418
Kreditnehmer, gemeinsamer ~ 658
Kreditnota 847
Kreditnote 847
kredit, Notenbank~ 1708
Kredit, offener ~ 379
Kreditoperationen 851
Kreditor 870
Kreditoren 36
Kreditorensaldo 849
Kreditpapier 862
kredit, Personal~ 1927
kredit, Pfandbrief~ 866
Kreditplafond 855
Kreditpolitik 872
kredit, Privat~ 1927
Kreditprolongation 1275
Kredit prolongieren, einen ~ 1272
kredit, Ratenzahlungs~ 1488
kredit, Real~ 868
kredit, Rembours~ 1085
Kreditrestriktion 874
Kredit, revolvierender ~ 2114
kredit, Revolving~ 2114
Kredit, Roll-over ~ 2118
Kredit, rotierender ~ 2114
Kreditsaldo 849
Kreditschöpfung 841
Kreditseite 206
Kredit, sich automatisch erneuernder ~ 2114
kredit, Sonder~ 2194
Kreditspielraum 864
Kredit, Stand-by-~ 2214

Kredit stillhalten, einen ~ 1272
Kreditstrom 859
kredit, Swap~ 2252
Kreditsystem 879
kredit, Teilzahlungs~ 1488
Kredittransaktionen 851
kredit, Überbrückungs~ 434
Kredit überschreiten, einen ~ 1201
Kreditüberschreitung 1367
Kreditüberwachung 629
Kredit überziehen, einen ~ 1201
kredit, Überziehungs~ 87, 379
kredit, Überzugs~ 87
kredit, Umlauf~ 2114
Kredit, ungedeckter ~ 379
Kredit, ungesicherter ~ 379
Kreditunion 787
Kreditunkosten 805
kredit, Verbraucher~ 745
Kreditverein 787
Kreditverkauf 875
Kredit verkaufen, auf ~ 2163
Kreditverknappung 874
Kredit verlängern, einen ~ 1272
Kreditverlängerung 1275
Kreditversicherung 863
Kreditvolumen 881
kredit, Waren~ 470, 473
kredit, Wechsel~ 11
kredit, Wertpapier~ 869
Kreditwesen 879
Kredit, widerruflicher ~ 2113
kredit, Wirtschafts~ 470
kreditwürdig 846
Kreditwürdigkeit 873
Kreditzinsen 376
Kreditzusage 88
Kredit, zusätzlicher ~ 63
kredit, Zwischen~ 434
kreise, Finanz~ 1305
kreislauf, Geld~ 637
kreislauf, Wirtschafts~ 471
Kridar 313
Kridatar 313
Kulisse 891
kumulative Dividende 889
kumulative Prioritätsaktien 890
kumulative Vorzugsaktien 890
kündbar 496, 2052
kündbare Obligation 497
kündbare Schuldverschreibung 497
Kündbarkeit 2051
Kundenakzept 2286
Kundengeld 307
Kundenkonto 617
Kundenkredit 745
Kundenwechsel 356
kündigen 502
kündigen, mit einer Frist von X Tagen ~ 1426
kündigen, mit X-tägiger Frist ~ 1426
kündigen, X-tägig ~ 1426
Kündigung 1835, 2053
kündigung, Einlagen~ 1840
Kündigung, ohne ~ 1838
Kündigungsfrist 1836
Kündigung(sfrist), mit X-tägiger ~ 1837
Kündigungsgeld 1019
Kündigungstermin 1836
Kündigung von Einlagen 1840
Kupfergeld 788
Kupfermünze 788
Kupon 828
kupon, Aktien~ 828
Kupon, ausschliesslich ~ 831
Kuponbogen 832
kupon, Dividenden~ 1078
kupon, Halbjahres~ 1475
Kupon, mit ~ 829
Kupon, nicht verfallener ~ 2330
Kupon, ohne ~ 831
Kupon, samt ~ 829
Kupons, gegen Abgabe des ~ 1958
Kupons, gegen Einreichung des ~ 1958
Kupons, gegen Übergabe des ~ 1958
Kupon, verjährter ~ 1664
kupon, Zins~ 1588
Kurantgeld 914
Kurantmünze 906
Kurs 1960
Kursabfall 886
kurs, Abrechnungs~ 650
Kursabschlag 239
kurs, Abschluss~ 657
Kursabschwächung 886
kurs, Aktien~ 2174
kurs, Ankaufs~ 354
Kursarbitrage 186
kurs, Ausgabe~ 1642
kurs, Bardevisen~ 2024
kurs, Begebungs~ 1642
Kursbericht 1228
kurs, Bezugs~ 2238
Kursblatt 1228
kurs, Börsen~ 1234
kurs, Brief~ 193
kurs, Clearing~ 650
kurs, Deport~ 240
kurs, Devisen~ 1216
kurs, Devisenkassa~ 2024
kurs, Durchschnitts~ 234
Kurseinbruch 431
Kurseinbusse 1229
kurs, Einheits~ 2326
kurs, Einlösungs~ 2054
kurs, Emissions~ 1642
kurs, Eröffnungs~ 1849
Kursertrags(kraft)verhältnis 1963
Kursfall 886
kurs, Freiverkehrs~ 1396
kurs, Geld~ 354
Kursgewinn 1233
Kursgewinnrelation 1963
Kursgewinnverhältnis 1963
kurs, Grenz~ 1965
kursierendes Geld 914
Kurs, intervalutarischer ~ 884
kurs, Interventions~ 1610
kurs, Kassa~ 593
kurs, Kauf~ 354
kurs, Kompensations~ 650
kurs, Konversions~ 778
kurs, Konzentrations~ 2326
Kurs, letzter ~ 657
Kurslimit 1965
kurs, Liquidations~ 650
Kursliste 1228
Kursmakler 2152
Kursmakler an der Warenbörse 694
Kursmanipulation 1730
kurs, Markt~ 1234
kurs, Mittel~ 234
Kursniveau 1680
Kursnotierung 1746, 1960
Kursnotiz 1960
kurs, Pari~ 1887
Kursparität 1182
kurs, Paritäts~ 1887
kurs, Prolongations~ 569
kurs, Regulierungs~ 650
kurs, Report~ 569
Kursrisiko 1238
Kursrückgang 886
kurs, Rückzahlungs~ 2054
kurs, Schluss~ 657
Kursschwankung 1225
Kurs setzen, ausser ~ 503
kurs, Sorten~ 1235
Kursstabilisierung 1237
Kursstand 1680
Kurssturz 431
kurs, Stütz~ 1610
kurs, Stützungs~ 1610
kurs, Tages~ 907
kurs, Termin~ 1384
Kurstreiberei 1730
kurs, Umrechnungs~ 778
kurs, Umwandlungs~ 778
kurs, Usance~ 884
kurs, Valuta~ 1216
kurs, Valuten~ 1216
Kursverhältnisse 1236
kurs, Verkaufs~ 193
Kursverlust 1229
kurs, Vorzugsumrechnungs~ 1950
kurs, Wechsel~ 1216
Kurswert 1234
kurs, Zeichnungs~ 2238
Kurszettel 1228
Kurszusammenbruch 431
kurs, Zwangs~ 722, 1356
kurz 2177
kürzen, die Ausgaben ~ 915
kurzfristig 2177
kurzfristige Schulden 910
kurzfristige Verbindlichkeiten 910
kurzfristige Verpflichtungen 910
kurzlebige Güter 1827
kürzung, Dividenden~ 925
kürzung, Preis~ 927

labile Währung 1350
Lage des Marktes 1743
lage, Geschäfts~ 469
lage, Kassen~ 592
Lagerschein 2364
lancieren, auf den Markt ~ 1665
lancieren, eine Anleihe ~ 1157
Lancierung 1352

land, Ausfuhr~ 825, 826
land, Einfuhr~ 825, 826
Landesschuld 1798
Landesvaluta 1094
Landeswährung 1094
land, Export~ 825, 826
land, Gläubiger~ 871
land, Hartwährungs~ 1480
land, Import~ 825, 826
land, Kapitalausfuhr~ 525
Land, Kapital exportierendes ~ 525
Land mit harter Währung 1480
Land mit weicher Währung 2188
land, Schuldner~ 959
land, Überschuss~ 824
lang 1715
langfristig 1715
langlebige Güter 1133
langlebige Konsumgüter 747
Last 460
Lasten 619
Lastenausgleich 1174
Lasten eines Kontos vortragen, zu ~ 618
lasten, Kapital~ 520
Lasten schreiben, zu ~ 615
lasten, Sozial~ 2186
Lasten, soziale ~ 2186
lasten, Zinsen~ 1587
Lasten, zu ~ 616
last, Hypotheken~ 1793
Lastschrift 613, 946
Lastschriftbuchung 946
Lastschriftposten 946
Lastschrift(s)anzeige 945
Lastschrift(s)aufgabe 945
Lastschriftzettel 945
last, Schulden~ 462
last, Steuer~ 463
latente Steuerpflicht 759
latente Steuerschulden 986
laufende Aktiven 905
laufende Ausgaben 908
laufenden Übertragungen, Saldo der ~ 257
laufende Rechnung 23
laufender Rechnung, Kredit in ~ 87
laufendes Konto 23
laufende Unkosten 908
laufende Verbindlichkeiten 910
laufende Verpflichtungen 910
laufende Zinsen 909
Laufzeit 894
Laufzeit, X-jährige ~ 1749
lautend, auf Dollars ~ 1010
Leasing 1668
leben, seinen Verhältnissen entsprechend ~ 1703
lebensfähig 2350
Lebensfähigkeit 2349
Lebenshaltung 1704
Lebenshaltungskosten 807
lebenslängliche Rente 163
Lebensrente 163
Lebensstandard 1704
Lebensteuerung 1483
Lebensversicherung 1688
Lebensverteuerung 1483
leben, über seine Verhältnisse ~ 1702
leblos 508
Leblosigkeit 1130
Leerabgabe 346
Leerverkauf 346
leer verkaufen 1427
Leibrente 163
leihen 415, 1671
leihen, Geld auf (gegen) Zinsen ~ 1675
leiher, Geld~ 1777
Leihkapital 417, 1707
leihweise 1706
leisten, eine Sicherheit ~ 101
leistung, Dienst~ 2084
Leistungen, öffentliche ~ 684
Leistungen, staatliche ~ 684
leistung, Ergänzungs~ 1285
leistung, Kapital~ 1408
leistung, Mehr~ 1285
leistung, Neben~ 1285
Leistungsbilanz 262
Leistungsbilanzsaldo 1277
leistungsfähig 2190
Leistungsfähigkeit 2189
Leistungslohn 1153
leistung, Sozial~ 2185
Leistung, soziale ~ 2185
leistung, Zusatz~ 1285
lenkung, Investitions~ 1044
lenkung, Kapital~ 1044
lenkung, Preis~ 1961
letzter Kurs 657
liberalisieren 1685
Liberalisierung des Handels 1684
liberierte Aktien 1403
Lieferung gegen (per; unter) Nachnahme 589
Lieferung kaufen, auf ~ 486
Lieferungsgeschäft 1379
Lieferungskauf 1376
Lieferungsprämie 507
lieferung, Termin~ 1380
Lieferung verkaufen, auf ~ 2161
Lieferung zahlbar, bei ~ 589
liegende Güter 1508
liegende Habe 1508
Liegenschaften 1508
limit, Kurs~ 1965
limit, Preis~ 1965
lineare Abschreibung 2228
linie, Kredit~ 855
liquid 1693
Liquidation 139, 773
Liquidation gehen, in ~ 1428
Liquidation geraten, in ~ 1428
Liquidationsgewinn 531
Liquidationskasse 649
Liquidationskurs 650
Liquidationstag 24
Liquidationstermin 18
Liquidationsverlust 553
Liquidationswert 432
Liquidation treten, in ~ 1428
Liquidator 1694
liquide Mittel 227
liquide Reserven 1696
liquidieren 148, 785, 1071, 1428
Liquidierung 139, 773, 1070
liquidisieren 785
Liquidisierung 1538
Liquidität 1695
liquidität, Bar~ 592
liquiditäten, Sekundar~ 1776
Liquiditäten zweiten Grades 1776
liquidität, Kassen~ 227
liquidität, Primär~ 1971
Liquiditätsbedarf 596
Liquiditätsbedürfnis(se) 596
Liquiditätsbegrenzung 2104
Liquiditätsbeschränkung 2104
Liquiditätsgrad 45
Liquiditätshemmung 2104
Liquiditätskennzahl 45
Liquiditätskennziffer 45
Liquiditätskoeffizient 45
Liquiditätsreserven 1696
Liquiditätssatz 45
Liquiditätsverhältnis 45
Liquiditätsverhältnisziffer 45
Liquiditätsverknappung 2104
liste, Aktien~ 1701
liste, Besoldungs~ 1912
Liste der Aktionäre 1701
liste, Gehalt(s)~ 1912
liste, Gesellschafter~ 1701
liste, Kurs~ 1228
liste, Lohn~ 1912
liste, Zollfrei~ 1394
Lizenz 1686
Lizenzabgabe 1686
lizenz, Ausfuhr~ 1268
lizenz, Einfuhr~ 1512
lizenz, Export~ 1268
Lizenzgebühr 1686
lizenz, Import~ 1512
lockern, die Kreditbeschränkungen ~ 1143
lockerung, Kredit~ 1145
Lohn 1140
lohn, Akkord~ 1907
lohn, Arbeits~ 1140
Lohnaufbesserung 1542
Lohneinkommen 1136
lohnend 1147
Lohnerhöhung 1542
Löhne und Gehälter 1141
lohninduzierte Inflation 2361
Lohnkontrolle 2360
Lohnkosten 2359
lohn, Leistungs~ 1153
Lohnliste 1912
lohn, Prämien~ 1520
Lohn-Preis-Spirale 2363
Lohnsteigerung 1542
Lohnsteigerung bedingte Inflation, durch ~ 2361
lohn, Stück~ 1932
Lohnsumme 2359
Lokogeschäft 581
Lokopreis 2203
Lombard 1674
Lombardanleihe 1712
Lombarddarleh(e)n 1712
Lombardeffekten 1895

lombardfähig 9
lombardierbar 9
lombardieren, Effekten ~ 91, 671
lombardierte Effekten 1895
Lombardierung 1501, 1674
Lombardierungsgrenze 604
Lombardkredit 869
Lombardsatz 1714
Lombardvorschuss 90
Lombardzinsfuss 1714
Lorokonto 1716
Losanleihe 1720
löschen 148
löschen, eine Hypothek ~ 511
löschen, eine Schuld ~ 510
Löschung 139
los, Prämien~ 1719
Lotterieanleihe 1720
lücke, Dollar~ 1089
lücke, Inflations~ 1557
Lücke, inflatorische ~ 1557
lukrativ 1147
lustlos 508
Lustlosigkeit 1130
Luxusartikel 1001
Luxusgegenstände 1001
Luxusgüter 1001
Luxussteuer 1723
Luxuswaren 1001

machen, eine Anleihe ~ 762
machen, einen Verlust ~ 333
machen, eine Schuld ~ 761
Majoritätsbeteiligung 770
Makler 437
makler, Aktien~ 2152
makler, Börsen~ 2152
Maklerbüro 439
makler, Devisen~ 509
makler, Diskont~ 361
makler, Effekten~ 2152
makler, Finanz~ 1311
Maklerfirma 439
makler, Fonds~ 2152
Maklergebühr 438
makler, Geld~ 1311
makler, Kurs~ 2152
Maklerprovision 438
makler, Valuten~ 509
makler, Waren~ 694
makler, Wechsel~ 361, 509, 2152
makler, Wertpapier~ 2152
makler, Zwischen~ 1648
makro-ökonomisch 1725
Mandant 1973
Mangel an flüssigen Mitteln 1504
mangel, Dollar~ 1090
mangel, Kapital~ 559
mangel, Kredit~ 878
manipulation, Börsen~ 1730
manipulation, Kurs~ 1730
Manipulationsgebühr 1478
manipulation, Währungs~ 898
manipulierte Währung 767
manipulierung, Währungs~ 898
Manko 988
Mankogeld 133
manko, Kassen~ 96
manöver, Börsen~ 1730
Mantel 2176
Marge 1037, 1732
marge, Kredit~ 864
Marke 2209
marke, Rabatt~ 2290
Marketing 1742
Markt 1735
markt, Absatz~ 1736
markt, Aktien~ 2153
Markt à la Baisse 345
Marktanalyse 1740
Markt aufkaufen, den ~ 789
Marktaufteilung 1745
Marktbeobachtung 1740
markt, Binnen~ 1100
Markt bringen, auf den ~ 1737
markt, Devisen~ 1230
markt, Diskont~ 370
markt, Effekten~ 2153
Markt, einheimischer ~ 1100
Markterkundung 1740
markt, Euro~ 700
markt, Euro-Divisen~ 1192
markt, Euro-Emissions~ 1191
marktfähig 1738
marktfähige Effekten 1739
marktfähige Wertpapiere 1739
markt, Finanz~ 554
markt, Fonds~ 2153
Marktforschung 1740
Markt, freier ~ 1395
markt, Freiverkehrs~ 891
Markt für festverzinsliche Werte 393
marktgängig 1738
markt, Geld~ 1778
markt, Geld- und Kapital~ 554
Markt, Gemeinsamer ~ 700
markt, Hausse~ 458
Markt, heimischer ~ 1100
Markt in Baissestimmung 345
markt, Inland(s)~ 1100
markt, Kapital~ 554
markt, Käufer~ 483
Marktkurs 1234
Marktlage 1743
Markt lancieren, auf den ~ 1665
Markt (mit billigen Artikeln) übersättigen, den ~ 1132
Markt (mit billigen Artikeln) überschwemmen, den ~ 1132
Markt, offener ~ 1395
markt, Parallel~ 1885
markt, Pfandbrief~ 393
Marktpreis 1744
markt, Renten~ 393
Marktschwankung 930
Markt, schwarzer ~ 377
markt, Sekondär~ 2147
Marktsituation 1743
Marktstudie 1740
Markttechnik 1742
Markt, unnotierter ~ 891
Marktuntersuchung 1740
markt, Verkäufer~ 2160
markt, Wechsel~ 370, 1230
Markt werfen, auf den ~ 1665
Markt werfen, billig auf den ~ 1132
Marktwert 688
markt, Wertpapier~ 2153
Marktwirtschaft 1741
Marktwirtschaft, freie ~ 1393
Maschinenbuchführung 1724
Maschinenbuchhaltung 1724
Masse 317
masse, Debit~ 317
masse, Konkurs~ 317
Masse(n)verwalter 209
masse, Passiv~ 961
Massnahmen zur Konjunkturbelebung 2011
Massnahmen zur Wirtschaftsankurbelung 2011
materielle Aktiva 1747
materielle Aktiven 1747
materielle Vermögenswerte 1747
materielle Werte 1747
materielle Wirtschaftsgüter 1747
mathematiker, Versicherungs~ 58
matt 508
Mattheit 1130
mauer, Zoll~ 918
Maut 2284
Mautgebühr 2284
Maximalpreis 605
Mehrausgaben 61, 1212
Mehrbetrag 1205, 2244
Mehreinkommen 2245
Mehreinnahme(n) 2245, 2246
Mehrgebot 1484
Mehrgewinn 1213
Mehrgewinnsteuer 1214
Mehrheitsbeteiligung 770
Mehrheitspaket 770
Mehrkosten 61
Mehrleistung 1285
Mehrpreis 60
Mehrstimmaktie 1796
Mehrstimmenaktie 1796
Mehrstimmrechtsaktie 1796
Mehrwert 180
Mehrwert, buchmässiger ~ 412
Mehrwertsteuer 2341
Meinungskauf 2198
Meistbietender 1485
Memorial 932
menge, Geld~ 1783
Messzahl 1550
Messziffer 1550
Metageschäft 1653
Metakonto 1654
Metakredit 865
Metallgeld 661
Metallgeld, in ~ 573
Miete 1666, 2088
miete, Kauf~ 1487
Mieter 1667
Mietkauf 1487
Mietkontrakt 1666
Mietpreis 2088
Mietvertrag 1666
Mietzins 2088
mikro-ökonomisch 1757
mildern, die Kreditbeschränkungen ~ 1143
milderung, Steuer~ 2261

Milliarde 368
Minderbetrag 988
Mindereinnahme(n) 2112
Mindereinnahmen der öffentlichen Haushalte 445
Minderheitsbeteiligung 1760
Minderheitspaket 1760
minderung, Dividenden~ 925
minderung, Preis~ 927
minderung, Steuer~ 2261
minderung, Wert~ 969
Minderwert 969
Mindestreserven 1670
Mindestreservesatz 1759
Minoritätsbeteiligung 1760
Minusbetrag 988
Minussaldo 93
Mitgliederverzeichnis 1701
mitnahme, Gewinn~ 1990
Mitschuldner 659
Mittel 1406
mittel, Bar~ 587
mittel, Betriebs~ 468
mittel, Eigen~ 558, 1809
mittel, Finanz~ 558
Mittel, finanzielle ~ 558
mittel, Finanzierungs~ 558
Mittel, flüssige ~ 227
mittel, Fremd~ 417
mittelfristig 1752
mittelfristiger Kredit 1753
mittel, Geld~ 1916
Mittel, greifbare ~ 227
mittel, Investitions~ 1620
mittel, Kapital~ 558
mittel, Kredit~ 862
Mittelkurs 234
Mittel, liquide ~ 227
Mitteln auskommen, mit seinen ~ 1703
Mitteln nicht auskommen, mit seinen ~ 1702
Mittel, öffentliche ~ 2007
Mittel, quasi-monetäre ~ 2243
mittel, Umlauf(s)~ 468, 636
Mittel, verfügbare ~ 227
mittel, Zahlungs~ 1751
Mobiliar 622
Mobiliarkredit 867
Mobiliarvermögen 622
Mobilien 622
Mobilisation 1766
mobilisieren 1767
Mobilisierung 1766
modalitäten, Zahlungs~ 2278
modalität, Zahlungs~ 1375
modus, Zahlungs~ 1375
monatliche Rate 1788
monatliche Teilzahlung 1788
Monatsgehalt 1787
Monatsgeld 1787
Monatsrate 1788
Monetarist 1768
monetisieren 1773
Monetisierung 1772
Monometallismus 1785
Monopol 1786
Monopolabgabe 1245
Monopolgebühr 1245
monopol, Handels~ 2287
monopol, Staats~ 1454
Monopolsteuer 1245
moratorisch 1789
Moratorium 1276
Moratoriums- 1789
mündelsichere (Wert-)Papiere 387
Münzamt 1761
Münzanstalt 1761
Münze 660, 661, 1761
Münze, gangbare ~ 906
Münze, gängige ~ 906
münze, Gold~ 1433
münze, Kupfer~ 788
münze, Kurant~ 906
münzen 662
Münzen 665
Münzen, Noten und ~ 1834
münze, Scheide~ 1083
münze, Umrechnungs~ 1780
münze, Zeichen~ 2283
Münzgeld 661
Münzgewinn 2154
Münzgold 666, 667
Münzpari 1762
Münzparität 1762
Münzprägung 663
Münzstätte 1761
Münzsystem 664
Münzverfälschung 939
Münzverringerung 939
Münzverschlechterung 939
Muttergesellschaft 769
MwSt 2341

Nachbörse 102
nachdatieren 164, 1942
nachfolgender Indossant 2239
Nachfrage 1002
Nachfrage, Angebot und ~ 2242
nachfragebedingte Inflation 1005
Nachfragefaktor 716
nachfrage, Geld~ 1774
nachfrageinduzierte Inflation 1005
Nachfrageinflation 1005
nachfrage, Inlands~ 1096
Nachfrage, private ~ 1097
Nachfrageüberhang 1206, 1557
nachfrage, Verbrauchs~ 746
Nachfrist 998
Nachgebühr 60
Nachgeschäft in Käufers Wahl 485
Nachgeschäft in Verkäufers Wahl 1857
Nachgirant 2239
Nachindossant 2239
Nachkalkulation 815
nachkalkulierte Kosten 804
Nachlass 127
Nachlassen 968
nachlassen, eine Schuld ~ 510
nachlass, Preis~ 927
nachlass, Schulden~ 513
nachlass, Steuer~ 2261
Nachlasssteuer 938
Nachmann 2239
Nachnahme, gegen ~ 589
Nachnahme, per ~ 589
Nachnahme, unter ~ 589
Nachschuss 62
Nachschussaufforderung 501
Nachtragskredit 63
Nachzahlung 237
Nachzahlungsaufforderung 494
Nachzugsaktie 985
nachzugsberechtigte Prioritätsaktien 890
nachzugsberechtigte Vorzugsaktien 890
Namen lautender Wechsel, auf den ~ 371
Namen lautende Wertpapiere, auf (den) ~ 1568
Namensaktien 1568
Namenspapiere 1568
nationale Anleihe 1099
Nationaleinkommen 1799
nationales Einkommen 1799
nationalisieren 1802
Nationalisierung 1801
Nationalökonomie 1151
Nationalprodukt 1803
nationalprodukt, Netto~ 1814
Nationalschuld 1798
Nationalvermögen 1804
natura, in ~ 1658
Natural- 1658
Naturalbezug 134
Naturaleinkommen 1529
Naturalien, in ~ 1658
Naturalvergütung 134
Nebenausgaben 61
Nebenbuch 225
Nebenbuchhaltung 2155
Nebeneinkommen 64
Nebeneinkünfte 64
Nebeneinnahmen 64
Nebenkonto 224
Nebenkosten 61
Nebenleistung 1285
Nebensicherheit 65
Nebenspesen 61
Nebenstelle 427
Nebenverdienst 64
Nebenvergütung 1284
nehmer, Wechsel~ 1902
Neigung 1200
neigung, Baisse~ 344
neigung, Hausse~ 459
Neigung zum Fallen 344
Nennbetrag 1820
Nenner, gemeinsamer ~ 698
Nennkapital 222
Nennwert 1289, 1889
Nennwert einer Aktie 1290
nennwertlose Aktien 1831
Nennwert stehen, über dem ~ 1883
Nennwert stehen, unter dem ~ 1056
Nennwert, zum ~ 1882
Nettobetrag 1808
Nettobetrag aufgenommener Kredite 1810
Nettobetrag gewährter Kredite 1812
Nettoeinkommen 1811
Nettoeinkünfte 1811

Nettogewinn 646
Nettonationalprodukt 1814
Nettoprinzip 1756
Nettosozialprodukt 1814
Nettoumsatz 1816
Nettoverdienstspanne 1813
Nettoverlust 651
Nettovermögen 1809
Nettowert 1809, 1817
Nettowert eines Eigentums 1177
Neuanlage 1818, 2078
neu anlegen 1936
neu bewerten 2037
Neubewertung 2036
neudiskontieren 2057
Neudiskontierung 2056
neue Aktien 1819
neue Kapitalanlage 1818
neue Rechnung, Saldovortrag auf ~ 150
Neufestsetzung der Paritäten 2031
Neufestsetzung von Kontingenten 77
Neufestsetzung von Quoten 77
Neufinanzierung 2068
neufundieren, eine Anleihe ~ 779
neufundierte Obligation 704
Neufundierung einer Anleihe 775
neu investieren 1936
Neuinvestition 1818, 2078
neuordnung, Geld~ 899
neutrale Erträge 1765
neutraler Aufwand 1202
nicht abgerechnete Rechnung 1846
nicht abzugfähige Ausgaben 1049
Nichtanerkenntnis einer Schuld 2093
Nichtanerkennung einer Schuld 2093
nicht aufgerufenes Kapital, (noch) ~ 2313
nicht auf Order lautender Wechsel 371
nicht ausgeglichener Posten 2312
nicht ausgeschüttete Gewinne 2108
nicht begebbarer Wechsel 371
nicht besteuerbar 1247
nicht bezahlter Wechsel 365
Nichtbezahlung 982
nicht börsenfähiger Wechsel 371
nicht dauerhafte Güter 1827
nicht eingefordertes Kapital, (noch) ~ 2313
nicht eingelöster Wechsel 365
nicht eingezahlter Betrag 154
nicht eingezahltes Kapital, (noch) ~ 2313
nicht einlösbar 1534
nicht einlösbares Papiergeld 1535
Nichteinlösbarkeit 1533
nicht einträglich 2324
nicht einziehbare Obligation 1636
nicht einziehbare Schuldverschreibung 1636
nicht entnommene Gewinne 2108
nicht flüssig 1503
nicht gesichertes Darleh(e)n 1301
nicht greifbare Aktiva 1505
nicht greifbare Aktiven 1505
nicht greifbare Vermögenswerte 1505
nicht greifbare Werte 1505
nicht greifbare Wirtschaftsgüter 1505
nicht handelsfähiger Wechsel 371
nicht honorierter Wechsel 365
nicht indossierbarer Wechsel 371
nicht inflationistisch 1828
nicht konvertierbar 1534
Nichtkonvertierbarkeit 1533
nicht liquid 1503
nicht notierte Effekten 892
nicht notierte Wertpapiere 892
nicht rückzahlbare Obligation 1636
nicht rückzahlbare Schuldverschreibung 1636
nicht saldierter Posten 2312
nicht tilgbare Obligation 1636
nicht tilgbare Schuldverschreibung 1636
nicht übertragbarer Wechsel 371
nicht umwandelbar 1534
Nichtumwandelbarkeit 1533
nicht verfallener Anteilschein 2330
nicht verfallener Coupon 2330
nicht verfallener Kupon 2330
nicht verteilte Gewinne 2311
nicht wiederkehrende Einnahmen 1287
nichtwirtschaftlicher Verein 1829
Nichtzahlung 982
nicht zurückzahlbare Obligation 1636
nicht zurückzahlbare Schuldverschreibung 1636
Niederlassung 427
niederlassung, Haupt~ 607
niederschlagen, eine Schuld ~ 510
Niederstwertprinzip 1721
Niessbrauch 2334
Niessbrauch(s)recht 349
Niessnutz 2334
niveau, Kurs~ 1680
niveau, Preis~ 1680
Nochgeschäft auf Geben 1857
Nochgeschäft auf Nehmen 485
Nochgeschäft in Käufers Wahl 485
Nochgeschäft in Verkäufers Wahl 1857
Nochgeschäft nach oben 485
Nochgeschäft nach unten 1857
Noch in Käufers Wahl 485
Noch in Verkäufers Wahl 1857
noch nicht fällige Verbindlichkeiten 1825
noch nicht fällige Verpflichtungen 1825
Nochprämiengeschäft in Käufers Wahl 485
Nochprämiengeschäft in Verkäufers Wahl 1857
Nominalbetrag 1820
Nominalnennwert 1289
Nominalsatz 1821
Nominalwert 1289, 1889
Nominalzins 1821
Nominalzinsfuss 1821
Nonvaleurs 2345
Normalpreis 1832
Nostrokonto 1833
Nota 17
nota, Debet~ 948
nota, Kredit~ 847
note, Bank~ 287
note, Debet~ 948
note, Gutschrift(s)~ 847
note, Kredit~ 847
Notenausgabe 1156
Notenausgabe, fiduziäre ~ 1300
Notenausgabe, fiduziarische ~ 1300
Notenausgabe, ungedeckte ~ 1300
Notenbank 309
Notenbankkredit 1708
Notenbankvorschuss 1708
notenbank, Zentral~ 606
Noten, im Umlauf befindliche ~ 308
Notenumlauf 308
Notenumlauf, fiduziärer ~ 1299
Notenumlauf, fiduziarischer ~ 1299
Noten und Münzen 1834
Noten und Münzen, ausländische ~ 1369
Noten und Münzen, im Umlauf befindliche ~ 638
note, Schluss~ 425, 440
not, Geld~ 1314
notieren 1698
notierte Effekten 1699
notierte Wertpapiere 1699
Notierung 1746, 1960
notierung, Eröffnungs~ 1849
notierung, Kurs~ 1960
Notierung nicht zugelassene Effekten, zur ~ 892
Notierung nicht zugelassene Wertpapiere, zur ~ 892
notierung, Schluss~ 657
Notiz 1960
notiz, Eröffnungs~ 1849
notiz, Kurs~ 1960
notiz, Schluss~ 657
Notklausel 1155
notleidende Forderungen 1110
notleidende Obligation 980
notleidender Wechsel 365
notleidende Schuldverschreibung 980
nutzbringend 1147
Nutzen 1409
nutzlos 2324
Nutzniessung 2334
Nutzniessungsrecht 349
Nutzschwelle 430

oase, Steuer~ 2269
Obergesellschaft 769
objekte, Wert~ 1646
Obligation 389
Obligationär 390
Obligation, auslosbare ~ 1719
Obligation, auslösbare ~ 497
Obligation, besicherte ~ 2149
obligation, Dollar~ 1087
Obligation, einlösbare ~ 497
Obligation, einziehbare ~ 497

Obligationenanleihe 941
Obligationenausgabe 392
Obligationen ausgeben 1637
Obligationengläubiger 390
Obligationeninhaber 390
Obligationenkapital 940
Obligationenschuld 391
Obligation, gesicherte ~ 2149
obligation, Gewinn~ 1526
obligation, Hypotheken~ 1792
obligation, Index~ 1549
Obligation, indexgebundene ~ 1549
Obligation, indexgekoppelte ~ 1549
obligation, Inhaber~ 338
obligation, Kassen~ 389
obligation, Kommunal~ 1713
obligation, Konversions~ 704
Obligation, kündbare ~ 497
Obligation mit Indexschutz 1549
Obligation mit Wertsicherungsklauseln 1549
obligation mit Zinskupon, Inhaber~ 830
obligation mit Zinsschein, Inhaber~ 830
Obligation, neufundierte ~ 704
Obligation, nicht einziehbare ~ 1636
Obligation, nicht rückzahlbare ~ 1636
Obligation, nicht tilgbare ~ 1636
Obligation, nicht zurückzahlbare ~ 1636
Obligation, notleidende ~ 980
obligation, Partial~ 389
obligation, Prämien~ 1719
Obligation, rückzahlbare ~ 497
Obligationsanleihe 941
Obligationsgläubiger 390
Obligation, sichergestellte ~ 2149
Obligationsinhaber 390
Obligationsschuld 391
obligation, Staats~ 1243
Obligation, tilgbare ~ 497
Obligation, unbesicherte ~ 2331
Obligation, ungesicherte ~ 2331
Obligation, unkündbare ~ 1636
Obligation, untilgbare ~ 1636
obligation, Wandel~ 783
Obligation, zurückzahlbare ~ 497
obligatorisches Sparen 724
Obligos 961
Oderkonto 1649
OECD 1860
offene Handelsgesellschaft 1420
offene Rechnung 23, 1846
offene Reserven 966
offener Kredit 379
offener Markt 1395
offener Scheck 339
offene Rücklagen 966
offenes Konto 23
offenstehender Betrag 152
offenstehende Rechnung 1846
offenstehendes Konto 23
öffentliche Anleihe 1453
öffentliche Anleihen 1244
öffentliche Arbeiten 2010
öffentliche Ausgaben 2003
öffentliche Bauten 2010
öffentliche Bürgschaft 1450
öffentliche Einnahmen 1451
öffentliche Finanzen 827
öffentliche Finanzwirtschaft 827
öffentliche Fonds 1244, 2005
öffentliche Garantie 1450
öffentliche Garantie für ein Darleh(e)n 1447
öffentliche Gelder 2005
öffentliche Investition 2006
öffentliche Konsumausgaben 2002
öffentliche Leistungen 684
öffentliche Mittel 2007
öffentlicher Betrieb 1448
öffentlicher Haushalt 1446
öffentlicher Sektor 2008
öffentlicher Verbrauch 2002
öffentlicher Versorgungsbetrieb 2009
öffentlicher Zuschuss 1449
öffentliche Schuld 1798
öffentliches Finanzwesen 827
öffentliche Subvention 1449
öffentliches Unternehmen 1448
öffentliches Versorgungsunternehmen 2009
öffentliche Titel 1244
öffentliche Unternehmung 1448
öffentliche Verschuldung 1798
öffentlich-rechtliches Finanzinstitut 2004
Offerte 352
offerte, Submissions~ 2276
offerte, Zeichnungs~ 1842
oHG 1420
ökonomie, National~ 1151
Ökonomie, politische ~ 1151
ökonomisch 1146, 1147
operationen, Auslands~ 1358
operationen, Bank~ 304
operationen, Devisen~ 1241
operationen, Kredit~ 851
Operationen mit dem Ausland 1358
Option 1854
option, Bezugs~ 484
option, Kauf~ 484
Optionsrecht 1854
Optionsrecht, ausschliesslich ~ 1249
Optionsrecht, mit ~ 888
Optionsrecht, ohne ~ 1249
option, Verkaufs~ 1858
ordentlicher Haushalt 1859
ordentlicher Haushaltsplan 1859
Order- 1726
Order lautender Wechsel, auf ~ 374
Orderpapier 1806
Orderscheck 631
Orderwechsel 374
ordnung, Devisen~ 900, 1240
Organgesellschaft 98
Organisation für europäische wirtschaftliche Zusammenarbeit 1861
Organisation für wirtschaftliche Zusammenarbeit und Entwicklung 1860
organisation, Internationale Arbeits~ 1606
organisation, Internationale Entwicklungs~ 1604
Pacht 1666, 2088
Pachtbrief 1666
Pächter 1667
Pachtkontrakt 1666
Pachtnehmer 1667
pachtung, Anlagen~ 1668
Pachtvertrag 1666
paket, Aktien~ 386
paket, Mehrheits~ 770
paket, Minderheits~ 1760
panik, Bank~ 2121
Panzergewölbe 2125
Panzerschrank 2122
papier, Agio~ 1339
papier, Anleihe~ 389
Papier, bankfähiges ~ 283
Papier, begebbares ~ 1806
Papier, diskontfähiges ~ 283
Papier, diskontierbares ~ 283
Papiere 2151
papiere, Anlage~ 1630
papiere, Börsen~ 1699
Papiere, erstklassige (Wert-)~ 387
Papiere, goldgeränderte (Wert-)~ 387
papiere, Inhaber~ 342
Papiere, mündelsichere (Wert-)~ 387
papiere, Namens~ 1568
Papiere, prima (Wert-)~ 387
papiere, Rekta~ 1568
papiere, Spekulations~ 2199
papiere, Spiel~ 2199
papiere, Spitzen~ 387
papiere, Staats~ 1244
Papiere, wertlose ~ 2345
Papiergeld 1355
papier, Geldmarkt~ 1779
Papiergeld, nicht einlösbares ~ 1535
Papiergeldumlauf 1299
papier, Handels~ 356
papier, Inhaber~ 340
papier, Kredit~ 862
papier, Order~ 1806
papier, Prima~ 1323
papier, Renten~ 162
papier, Sicht~ 1007
Papier, übertragbares ~ 1806
Papierwährung 1355, 1881
Papierwerte 2151
Parallelmarkt 1885
Pari 1889
pari, al ~ 1882
Parikurs 1887
pari, Münz~ 1762
pari stehen 1884
pari stehen, al ~ 1884
Pari stehen, auf ~ 1884
Pari stehen, über ~ 1883
Pari stehen, unter ~ 1056
Parität 1886, 1889
parität, Gold~ 1439
Parität herabsetzen, die ~ 2062
paritätisch 1882
parität, Kurs~ 1182

parität, Münz~ 1762
Paritätskurs 1887
Paritätspreis 1887
Paritätsverhältnis 1888
Paritätswert 1889
parität, Währungs~ 1182
parität, Wechsel~ 1182
pari, Wechsel~ 1890
Pariwert 1889
Pari, zu ~ 1882
Partialobligation 389
Partizipationsgeschäft 1653
Partizipationskonto 1654
Passiva 961
Passiva, Aktiva und ~ 203
Passiva, antizipative ~ 39
Passiva, transitorische ~ 39
Passivbilanz 274
passive Aussenhandelsbilanz 94
passive Handelsbilanz 94
Passiven 961
Passiven, Aktiven und ~ 203
passive Schuld 36
passivieren 402
passivierungspflichtig 407
Passivkonto 1682
Passivkonto übertragen, auf das ~ 402
Passivmasse 961
Passivposten 946
Passivsaldo 93
Passivschuld 36
Passivseite 943
Passivseite aufführen, auf der ~ 402
Passivum 961
Passivzinsen 947
Pauschalbetrag 1722
Pauschale 1722
Pauschalpreis 114
Pauschalsumme 1722
Pensionsfonds 1918
Pensionsgeschäft 753
Pensionskasse 1918
Pensionswechsel 363
Personalgesellschaft 1892
Personalkonto 1926
Personalkredit 1927
Personalschuld 1928
Personengesellschaft 1892
persönliche Schuld 1928
persönlich haftender Gesellschafter 1419
Pfand 1138
Pfandbrief 389
pfandbrief, Ablösungs~ 704
Pfandbriefausgabe 392
Pfandbrief, hypothekarischer ~ 1792
pfandbrief, Hypotheken~ 1792
Pfandbriefkredit 866
Pfandbriefmarkt 393
Pfanddarleh(e)n 672
Pfand einsetzen, als (zum) ~ 1018
pfänden 211
Pfand geben, als (zum) ~ 1018
Pfand, hypothekarisches ~ 2035
Pfandrecht (an) 1687
Pfand setzen, als (zum) ~ 1018
Pfändung 191
Pfändung beim Drittschuldner 1414
Pfand, Vorschuss gegen ~ 86
pfleger, Konkurs~ 209
Pflichtaktie 2015
Pflichtreserven 1670
pflicht, Steuer~ 1683
pfunde, Sperr~ 382
Pfunde, transferable ~ 2291
Pfund Sterling 1943
Pfundzone 2224
phase, Konjunktur~ 1150
Placement 1935
placieren 1618
placieren, eine Anleihe ~ 1933
placieren, eine Emission ~ 1934
Placierung 1619, 1935
Placierungskonsortium 2322
plafond, Kredit~ 855
plan, Amortisations~ 146
plan, Einlösungs~ 146
plan, Finanz~ 1312
plan, Finanzierungs~ 1312
plan, Konten~ 22
Plankosten 1189
plan, Tilgungs~ 146
Planwirtschaft 768
plazieren 1618
plazieren, eine Anleihe ~ 1933
plazieren, eine Emission ~ 1934
Plazierung 1619, 1935
Plazierungskonsortium 2322
police, Versicherungs~ 1577
politik, Dividenden~ 1081
politik, Finanz~ 1317
politik, Geld~ 1769
politik, Kredit~ 872
politik, Währungs~ 1769
politische Ökonomie 1151
polizze, Versicherungs~ 1577
polster, Devisen~ 901
Pönale 136
Pool 1938
Poolung 1939
portefeuille, Aktien~ 1628
portefeuille, Anlage~ 1628
portefeuille, Effekten~ 1628
Portefeuilleeffekten 1630
portefeuille, Wertpapier~ 1628
portefeuille, Wertschriften~ 1628
position, Devisen~ 1363
Position prolongieren, eine ~ 568
Position reportieren, eine ~ 568
Postanweisung 1781
postdatieren 164, 1942
Posten 409
posten, Aktien~ 386
posten, Aktiv~ 857
posten, Ausgleichs~ 281
posten, Berichtigungs~ 71
posten, Buchungs~ 409
posten, Durchgangs~ 2249
Posten, durchlaufender ~ 2249
posten, Gegen~ 281
posten, Gutschrift~ 857
posten, Haben~ 857
posten im Journal, Buchungs~ 1655
posten, Lastschrift~ 946
Posten, nicht ausgeglichener ~ 2312
Posten, nicht saldierter ~ 2312
posten, Passiv~ 946
posten, Rechnungsabgrenzungs~ 73
posten, Soll~ 946
Posten, unausgeglichener ~ 2312
Postscheck 1425
Postscheckdienst 1423
Postscheckkonto 1800
Postsparkasse 1941
potential, Wachstums~ 1469
Präferenztarif 1947
Präferenzzoll 1949
prägen 662
Prägung 663
Prämie 110, 397, 1856
prämie, Ausfuhr~ 426
prämie, Ausgabe~ 1641
prämie, Baisse~ 1953
prämie, Bezugs~ 507
prämie, Dont~ 507
prämie, Doppel~ 1108
prämie, Einlösungs~ 1750
prämie, Emissions~ 1641
prämie, Empfangs~ 1953
prämie, Export~ 426
prämie, Hausse~ 507
prämie, Lieferungs~ 507
Prämienanleihe 1720
Prämiengeld 1856
Prämiengeschäft 1855
prämiengeschäft in Käufers Wahl, Noch~ 485
prämiengeschäft in Verkäufers Wahl, Noch~ 1857
Prämienlohn 1520
Prämienlos 1719
Prämienobligation 1719
Prämienschein 1719
Prämienschuldverschreibung 1719
prämie, Report~ 569
prämie, Rück~ 1750, 1953
prämie, Rückkaufs~ 1750
prämie, Rückzahlungs~ 1750
prämie, Versicherungs~ 1578
pränumerando zahlen 1904
Pränumerandozahlung 92
Präsentant 337
Präsentation, bei ~ 1956
Preis 1960
Preisabbau 927
Preisabfall 886
Preis, abgemachter ~ 114
Preisabkommen 115
Preis abmachen, einen ~ 113
Preisabmachung 115
Preisabnahme 886
preis, Abrechnungs~ 650
Preisabrede 115
Preisabschlag 927
Preisabschwächung 886
Preisabsprache 115
preis, Aktien~ 2174
Preis angeben, einen ~ 1728
Preis, angebotener ~ 1843
preis, Angebots~ 1843
Preisangleichung 76
Preisanhebung 1539

Preisanpassung 76
Preisansatz 1962
preis, Anschaffungs~ 488
Preis ansetzen, einen ~ 1033, 1728
Preisanstieg 1539
Preisaufschlag 1539
Preisaufstieg 1539
Preisauftrieb 1539
preis, Ausgabe~ 1642
Preis ausmachen, einen ~ 113
preis, Ausnahme~ 1203
preis, Bar~ 593
preis, Barzahlungs~ 593
preis, Begebungs~ 1642
Preisbehauptung 1326
Preis benennen, einen ~ 1728
Preisbeschränkung 1968
Preisbeständigkeit 1326
Preis bestimmen, einen ~ 1033
Preisbestimmung 1962
preis, Bezugs~ 2238
Preisbindung 1515
Preisbindung der zweiten Hand 2097
Preisbindung, vertikale ~ 2097
Preisbindung zweiter Hand 2097
Preis, der höchste ~ 605
preis, Detail~ 2096
Preisdifferenz 1038
Preisdisparität 1038
Preiseinbruch 431
preis, Einführungs~ 1613
preis, Einheits~ 1344, 2328
Preis einigen, sich über einen ~ 113
preis, Einkaufs~ 488, 814
preis, Einstands~ 814
preis, Einzel~ 2328
preis, Einzelhandels~ 2096
preis, Einzelverkaufs~ 2096
preis, Emissions~ 1642
preis, Engros~ 2288
Preisen, zu konstanten ~ 742
Preiserhöhung 1539
Preisermässigung 927
Preisermittlung 1962
Preisertragsverhältnis 1963
preis, Erwerbs~ 488
preis, Erzeugungs~ 811
preis, Fabrikations~ 811
Preisfall 886
Preis, fester ~ 78
Preis, festgesetzter ~ 78
Preisfestigkeit 1326
Preis festlegen, einen ~ 1033
Preisfestlegung 1962
Preis festsetzen, einen ~ 1728
Preisfestsetzung 1515, 1962
Preis feststellen, einen ~ 1033
Preisfeststellung 1962
Preisfixierung 1962
Preisfreigabe 971
Preis, gebundener ~ 78
Preisgefälle 1038
preis, Geld~ 1967
preis, Gestehungs~ 811, 814
preis, Grenz~ 1965
Preisgrenze 1965
preis, Grosshandels~ 2288
preis, Grossisten~ 2288
preis, Grund~ 330, 1832
Preisherabsetzung 927
preis, Herstellungs~ 811
preis, Höchst~ 605
Preisindex 1964
Preis, jeweiliger ~ 911
Preiskartell 115
preis, Kassa~ 593
preis, Kauf~ 488
preis, Kleinhandels~ 2096
preis, Kleinverkaufs~ 2096
preis, Konsumenten~ 749
Preiskontrolle 1961
Preiskonvention 115
preis, Kosten~ 814
Preiskürzung 927
Preislenkung 1961
Preislimit 1965
preis, Loko~ 2203
preis, Markt~ 1744
preis, Maximal~ 605
preis, Miet~ 2088
Preisminderung 927
Preisnachlass 927
Preisniveau 1680
preis, Normal~ 1832
preis, Paritäts~ 1887
preis, Pauschal~ 114
Preis per Einheit 2328
Preis pro Einheit 2328
Preis quotieren, einen ~ 1728
Preisreduktion 927
Preisregelung 1961
preis, Reklame~ 1613
preis, Richt~ 1832
Preisrückgang 886
preis, Rückkaufs~ 2054, 2095
preis, Rücknahme~ 2095
Preisrückschlag 886
preis, Rückzahlungs~ 2054
preis, Schleuder~ 322
Preissenkung 927
Preisspanne 1966
preis, Spezial~ 1203
preis, Spott~ 322
Preisstabilisierung 1969
Preisstabilität 1326
Preisstand 1680
preis, Standard~ 1832
Preissteigerung 1539
Preissteigung 1539
Preisstop 1400
preis, Stück~ 2328
Preissturz 431
Preisstützung 1917
preis, Tages~ 911
preis, Termin~ 1384
Preis, übermässiger ~ 1250
Preisüberwachung 1961
Preisunterschied 1038
Preisunterstützung 1917
preis, Verbraucher~ 749
Preis vereinbaren, einen ~ 113
Preis, vereinbarter ~ 114
Preisvereinbarung 115
Preisverfall 886
preis, Verkaufs~ 2162
preis, Vertrags~ 114
Preis, vorgeschriebener ~ 78
Preis vorschreiben, einen ~ 1033
preis, Vorzugs~ 1203
preis, Werbe~ 1613
preis, Wiederanschaffungs~ 2091
preis, Wiederbeschaffungs~ 2091
preis, Wiederverkaufs~ 2096
preis, Wucher~ 1250
preis, Zeichnungs~ 2238
preis, zum Kosten~ 796
preis, zum Selbstkosten~ 796
Preiszusammenbruch 431
Prima 1327
Primadiskont 1323
Primahandelspapier 1323
Primapapier 1323
Primarate 328
primäre Einkommen 1970
Primäreinkommen 1970
Primärkosten 1043
Primärliquidität 1971
prima Wechsel 1323
prima, Wechsel~ 1327
Primawechsel 1327
prima (Wert-)Papiere 387
"prime rate" 328
prinzip, Brutto~ 1755
prinzip, Netto~ 1756
prinzip, Niederstwert~ 1721
Priorität 1328
Priorität(en) 1946
Prioritätsaktie 1946
Prioritätsaktien, kumulative ~ 890
Prioritätsaktien, nachzugsberechtigte ~ 890
Prioritätsdividende 1945
Prioritätsgläubiger 1948
Prioritätsrecht 1328
priorität, Stamm~ 1946
Privatbank 1974
Privatbankhaus 1974
Privatbesitz 1979
Privatbetrieb 1977
Privatdiskont 1323
private Ersparnisbildung 1980
Privateigentum 1979
Privateinkommen 1929
Privateinkünfte 1929
private Investition 1978
private Kapitalanlage 1978
private Nachfrage 1097
privater Besitz 1979
privater Sektor 1981
privater Verbrauch 1499
private Schuld 1928
privates Eigentum 1979
privates Unternehmertum 1976
Privatinitiative 1976
Privatisierung 1009
Privatkapital 1975
Privatkonto 1926
Privatkredit 1927
Privatschuld 1928
Privatsektor 1981
Privatunternehmen 1977
Privatunternehmung 1977
Privatverbrauch 1499

Privatwirtschaft 1976
privatwirtschaftlicher Betrieb 1977
privilegierter Gläubiger 1948
Probebilanz 2303
produkt, Bruttoinlands~ 1461
produkt, Bruttonational~ 1466
produkt, Bruttosozial~ 1466
Produktenbörse 695
Produktionsgenossenschaft 1983
Produktionsgüter 1134
Produktionskosten 811
Produktionsmittel, dauerhafte ~ 1134
Produktivgenossenschaft 1983
produkt, National~ 1803
produkt, Sozial~ 1803
Profit 1409
Proforma-Rechnung 1991
Proformarechnung 1991
prognosen, Haushalts~ 451
programm, Finanz~ 1312
Progression einer Steuer 1992
progressive Abschreibung 1545
progressive Steuer 1456
Progressivsteuer 1456
Prohibitivzoll 1993
Pro-Kopf-Einkommen, durchschnittliches ~ 233
Prokopfverbrauch 1920
Pro-Kopf-Verbrauch 1920
Prolongation 567, 753, 1994
prolongation, Kredit~ 1275
Prolongationsgebühr 569
Prolongationsgeschäft 753
Prolongationskurs 569
Prolongationssatz 569
prolongieren, eine Frist ~ 1273
prolongieren, einen Kredit ~ 1272
prolongieren, eine Position ~ 568
Prolongierung 1994
Promesse 1477
promesse, Aktien~ 1597
Proportion 2029
prospekt, Begebungs~ 1643
prospekt, Emissions~ 1643
prospekt, Subskriptions~ 1643
prospekt, Zeichnungs~ 1643
Protektionist 1997
Protest geben, einen Wechsel zum ~ 1481
protestieren, einen Wechsel ~ 1481
Provision 689
provision, Akzept~ 13
provision, Bank~ 293
provision, Bereitstellungs~ 693
provision, Diskont~ 1055
provision, Krediteröffnungs~ 693
provision, Makler~ 438
Provisionssatz 691
provisorischer Anteilschein 1597
prozent 1922
Prozent 1921, 1922
prozentige Erhöhung, X ~ 1543
Prozentsatz 1921
Prozent verzinsen, sich mit (zu) X ~ 334
Prozent Zinsen abwerfen, X ~ 334
Prozent Zinsen bringen, X ~ 334
Prozent Zinsen einbringen, X ~ 334
Prozent Zinsen geben, X ~ 334
Prozent Zinsen tragen, X ~ 334
prüfen 215
Prüfer 216
prüfer, Abschluss~ 216
prüfer, Buch~ 216
prüfer, Rechnungs~ 21, 216
prüfer, Wirtschafts~ 21, 216
prüfung, Abschluss~ 214
prüfung, Betriebs~ 1566
prüfung, Buch~ 214
Prüfung der Rechnungslegung 214
prüfung, Rechnungs~ 214
Prüfungsbericht 217
Punkten aufweisen, einen Rückgang (einen Gewinn) von X ~ 2045
Punkten verzeichnen, einen Rückgang (einen Gewinn) von X ~ 2045
punkt, Gewinn~ 430
punkt, Gleichgewichts~ 430
punkt, Interventions~ 1609
punkt, Stützungs~ 1609

Quartal 2016
Quasigeld 1805
Quasigeldbestände 1776
quasi-monetäre Mittel 2243
quelle, Absatz~ 1736
Quelle abziehen, an der ~ 972
quelle, Einkommens~ 2193
quelle, Einnahme~ 2193
quelle, Finanzierungs~ 2192
Quellenabzug 975
Quellenabzug der Steuern 681
Quellenbesteuerung 681
quellen, Finanz~ 558
quellen, Kapital~ 558
Quellensteuer 2268
Quittung 47, 51
quittung, Depot~ 608
quittung, Einzahlungs~ 877
Quote 2017
quote, Abschreibungs~ 144
quote, Amortisations~ 144, 145
quote, Investitions~ 1629
quote, Konkurs~ 1077
Quotenaktien 1831
quote, Spar~ 2026
quote, Tilgungs~ 145
quotieren 1698
quotieren, einen Preis ~ 1728
Quotierung 1746

Rabatt 127
Rabatt an (für) Wiederverkäufer 935
rabatt, Barzahlungs~ 583
Rabatt, fiktiver ~ 1822
rabatt, Handels~ 935
rabatt, Händler~ 935
Rabattmarke 2290
rabatt, Waren~ 935
rahmen, Konten~ 22
rahmen, Swing~ 864
Rate 1571, 1572, 2021
rate, Abzahlungs~ 1571
rate, Amortisations~ 144, 145
rate, Bank~ 311
rate, Diskont~ 1061
rate, Ertrags~ 2025
rate, Halbjahres~ 351
Rate, halbjährliche ~ 351
rate, Inflations~ 1563
rate, Investitions~ 1629
Rate, monatliche ~ 1788
rate, Monats~ 1788
Raten, auf (in) ~ 987
Ratenkauf 1573
Raten kaufen, auf ~ 481
ratenweise 987
Ratenzahlung 1571
Ratenzahlung, auf ~ 987
Ratenzahlungen, in ~ 987
Ratenzahlung kaufen, auf ~ 481
Ratenzahlungsfinanzierung 1490
Ratenzahlungskredit 1488
rate, Prima~ 328
rate, Rückzahlungs~ 2054
rate, Spar~ 2026
rate, Steigerungs~ 1255
rate, Tilgungs~ 145
rate, Wachstums~ 1255
rate, Zins~ 1593
rate, Zunahme~ 1255
rate, Zuwachs~ 1255
Rationalisierungsinvestition 1580
raum, Dollar~ 1086
raum, Franken~ 1388
raum, Sterling~ 2224
reale Anpassung 74
Realeinkommen 2032
Realisation 773
realisation, Gewinn~ 1990
Realisationswert 432
realisierbar 2034
realisierbare Aktiven 905
Realisierbarkeit 2033
realisieren 785
realisieren, einen Gewinn ~ 1729
Realisierung 773
realisierung, Gewinn~ 1990
Realitäten 1508
Realkredit 868
Realkreditinstitut 1660
Realsicherheit 2035
Realsteuer 1995
Realwert 56
Realzins 57
Rechenfehler 491
rechnen 490
Rechnung 17, 492
Rechnung abgleichen, eine ~ 249
Rechnung abrechnen, eine ~ 249
Rechnung abschliessen, eine ~ 652
Rechnung, auf ~ 19
Rechnung, auf eigene ~ 1877
Rechnung ausgleichen, eine ~ 249
Rechnung, ausstehende ~ 37, 1846
Rechnung begleichen, eine ~ 249
Rechnung berichtigen, eine ~ 249
rechnung, Betriebskosten~ 2289
Rechnung bringen, in ~ 570
Rechnung Dritter, auf (für) ~ 35
Rechnung eines Dritten, auf (für) ~ 35

rechnung, Einnahmen~ 1524
rechnung, Erfolgs~ 1523
rechnung, Ertrags~ 1523
rechnung, Fehl~ 491
Rechnung führen 1656
Rechnung, für eigene ~ 1877
rechnung, Gewinn- und Verlust~ 1523
Rechnung glattstellen, eine ~ 249
rechnung, Kosten~ 797
Rechnung, laufende ~ 23
Rechnung, nicht abgerechnete ~ 1846
Rechnung, offene ~ 23, 1846
Rechnung, offenstehende ~ 1846
rechnung, Proforma~ 1991
Rechnungsabgrenzungsposten 73
Rechnung saldieren, eine ~ 249
Rechnungsauszug 5
Rechnungsbericht 217
rechnung, Scheck~ 625
Rechnung schliessen, eine ~ 652
Rechnungseinheit 31
Rechnungsfehler 491
Rechnungsführer 410
Rechnungsjahr 1320
Rechnungskauf 852
Rechnung skontrieren, eine ~ 249
Rechnungsprüfer 21, 216
Rechnungsprüfung 214
Rechnungsrevisor 216
Rechnungssaldo 27, 255
Rechnungsstand 1940
Rechnungsstellung 366
Rechnung stellen, in ~ 570
Rechnungsüberschuss 30
Rechnung, unbeglichene ~ 1846
Rechnung, unsaldierte ~ 1846
Rechnung von, auf ~ 34
Rechnung von, für ~ 34
Rechnung (zur Zahlung) anweisen, eine ~ 223
recht (an), Pfand~ 1687
recht (an), Retentions~ 1687
recht (an), Rückbehaltungs~ 1687
recht (an), Zurückbehaltungs~ 1687
recht, Bezugs~ 174
rechte (auf), Ziehungs~ 1121
rechte (bei), Ziehungs~ 1121
recht, Einstands~ 2013
recht, Konversions~ 777
recht, Niessbrauch(s)~ 349
recht, Nutzniessungs~ 349
recht, Options~ 1854
recht, Prioritäts~ 1328
recht, Subskriptions~ 174
recht, Umtausch~ 777
recht, Umwandlungs~ 777
recht, Vorkaufs~ 2013
recht, Vorzugs~ 1328
recht, Wahl~ 1854
Rediskont 2056
rediskontfähig 2058
rediskontierbar 2058
rediskontieren 2057
Rediskontierung 2056
Rediskontsatz 2059
Rediskont zugelassen, zum ~ 2058
Redistribution 2060
reduktion, Preis~ 927
reduzieren, die Ausgaben ~ 915
Reexport 2066
refinanzieren 2067
Refinanzierung 2068
reflatieren 2069
Reflation 2070
Reflation bewirken, eine ~ 2069
reform, Geld~ 899
reform, Steuer~ 2274
reform, Währungs~ 899
regelmässiges Einkommen 210
regelungen, Devisen~ 900
regelung, Preis~ 1961
Regie 1454
Regiebetrieb 1448, 1454
Regierungsbeihilfe 1449
Regierungsbetrieb 1448
Regierungszuschuss 1449
register, Aktien~ 1701
register, Aktionär(s)~ 1701
register, Gesellschafter~ 1701
register, Handels~ 687
Registrierungsgebühr 2077
Regress 2047
regulator, Steuer~ 1333
regulierte Währung 767
Regulierungskurs 650
reine Goldwährung 1402
Reineinkommen 1811
Reingewinn 646
Reingewinn, unausgeschütteter ~ 2108
Reingewinn, unverteilter ~ 2311
Reinumsatz 1816
Reinverlust 651
Reinvermögen 1809
reinvestieren 1936
Reinvestition 2078
Reinwert 1817
Reiseauslagen 2298
Reiseentschädigung 2296
Reisekosten 2298
Reisekostenentschädigung 2296
Reisekostenvergütung 2296
Reisescheck 2297
Reisespesen 2298
Reiseunkosten 2298
Reisevergütung 2296
reiterei, Wechsel~ 1659
Reitwechsel 15
Reklamepreis 1613
Rektapapiere 1568
Rektascheck 630
Rektawechsel 371
relation(en), Austausch~ 2279
relation, Kursgewinn~ 1963
Rembourskredit 1085
rembours, Wechsel~ 11
Remittent 1902, 2083
remittieren 2080
Remuneration 2041
remunerieren 2042
Rendite 2110
rendite, Aktien~ 1082
rendite, Kapital~ 535
rentabel 1147
Rentabilität 1984
Rentabilitätsgrenze 430
rentabilität, Umsatz~ 1815
Rente 1522
Rente auf Lebenszeit 163
rente, Dauer~ 163
rente, Jahres~ 161
rente, Kapital~ 535
rente, Lebens~ 163
Rente, lebenslängliche ~ 163
rente, Leib~ 163
Rentenanstalt 1918
Rentenbrief 162
Rentenfonds 1455
Rentenmarkt 393
Rentenpapier 162
Rentenschein 162
Rentenschuldverschreibung 162
Rententitel 162
rentieren, sich ~ 100
Reparation 708
repartieren 122
Repartierung 123
repartierung, Aktien~ 125
repatriieren 2089
Repatriierung 2090
Report 567, 569
Reportgebühr 569
Reportgeschäft 753
reportieren, eine Position ~ 568
Reportkurs 569
Reportprämie 569
Reportsatz 569
Repräsentationsaufwendungen 1169
Repräsentationskosten 1169
Reprise 2020, 2048
Reprivatisierung 1009
Reserve 129
Reserve abgeben, an die ~ 68
reserve, Abschreibungs~ 132
Reserve aufbauen, eine ~ 454
Reserve auffüllen, die ~ 2039
Reserve, bare ~ 597
Reserve bilden, eine ~ 454
reserve, Devisen~ 901
Reserveentnahme 2377
reserve, Eventual~ 756
Reservefonds 2101
Reservefonds, ausserordentlicher ~ 755
Reservefonds für unvorhergesehene Ausgaben 755
Reservefonds schlagen, zum ~ 68
Reservefonds zuführen, dem ~ 68
Reservefonds zuweisen, dem ~ 68
Reserve für Dubiosen 243
Reserve für zweifelhafte Forderungen 243
reserve, Geld~ 1770
reserve, Gold~ 1440
reserve, Kassen~ 597
reserve, Konjunkturausgleichs~ 820
Reservekonto 130
Reserve(n) 2098
Reserven angreifen, die ~ 1042
Reserven, ausgewiesene ~ 966
Reserven, gesetzliche ~ 1670
reserven, Gold- und Devisen~ 1429

Reserven in Anspruch nehmen, die ~ 1042
Reserven, liquide ~ 1696
reserven, Liquiditäts~ 1696
reserven, Mindest~ 1670
Reserven, offene ~ 966
reserven, Pflicht~ 1670
Reserven, sichtbare ~ 966
Reserven, stille ~ 726
Reserven, unsichtbare ~ 726
Reserven, versteckte ~ 726
Reserven zehren, von den ~ 1042
Reserven zurückgreifen, auf die ~ 1042
Reserve schaffen, eine ~ 454
Reservesoll 1670
Reserve, statutarische ~ 2102
reserve, Steuer~ 2001
Reserve überweisen, der ~ 68
Reservewährung 2100
reserve, Währungs~ 901
reserve, Wertminderungs~ 132
reserve, Wertverminderungs~ 132
Reserve wiederaufbauen, die ~ 2039
Reserve wiederauffüllen, die ~ 2039
Reserve zuführen, der ~ 68
Reserve zuweisen, der ~ 68
Respektfrist 998
Respekttage 933
Respiro 998
Respirotage 933
Respit 998
Respittage 933
Rest 246
Restbetrag 27, 246
Restbetrag, geschuldeter ~ 252
Restdividende 1303
Resteverkauf 2128
restlicher Betrag 246
restriktionen, Devisen~ 902
restriktion, Kredit~ 874
Restschuld 252
Restsumme 246
Restwert 2103
Retentionsrecht (an) 1687
Retour 365
retournierter Wechsel 365
Retourwechsel 365, 819
Reugeld 136
Reukauf 136
revalorisieren 178
Revalorisierung 2111
Revers 394
revidieren 215
Revision, betriebseigene ~ 1600
revision, Bücher~ 214
revision, Innen~ 1600
Revision, innerbetriebliche ~ 1600
Revision, interne ~ 1600
Revisionsbericht 217
revision, Steuer~ 1566
Revisor 216
revisor, Bücher~ 216
revisor, Rechnungs~ 216
revolvierender Kredit 2114
Revolvingkredit 2114
Rezession 1031
rhythmus, Expansions~ 1256
Ricambio 819
Richtpreis 1832
Rikambio 819
Rikambiowechsel 819
risikobereites Kapital 1178
Risikokapital 1178
risiko, Kurs~ 1238
risikotragendes Kapital 1178
risiko, Valuta~ 1238
risiko, Währungs~ 1238
risiko, Wechselkurs~ 1238
Rohbetrag 1460
Rohbilanz 2303
Roheinkommen 1463
roher Kostenüberschlag 184
roher Überschlag 184
rohe Schätzung 184
Rohgewinn 1459
Rohstoff 329
Rohverlust 1464
Rohwert 1468
Roll-over Anleihe 2118
Roll-over Kredit 2118
rotierender Kredit 2114
Rückbehaltungsrecht (an) 1687
Rückbuchung 281
Rückbürgschaft 238
rückdatieren 164
Rückdiskont 2056
rückdiskontierbar 2058
rückdiskontieren 2057
Rückdiskontierung 2056
rückerstatten 1900
Rückerstattung 2072
Rückerstattungsantrag 640
rückerstattungsfähig 2073
rückerstattung, Steuer~ 2038
rückerstattung, Zoll~ 1116
Rückfluss von Kapital 2071
Rückforderung 640
rückführen 2089
Rückführung 2090
Rückführung von Kapital 2050
Rückgang 968
rückgang, Anlage~ 1066
Rückgang (einen Gewinn) von X Punkten aufweisen, einen ~ 2045
Rückgang (einen Gewinn) von X Punkten verzeichnen, einen ~ 2045
rückgang, Konjunktur~ 1031
rückgang, Kurs~ 886
rückgang, Preis~ 886
rückgang, Wert~ 969
rückgang, Wirtschafts~ 1031
Rückgriff 2047
Rückkauf 2053, 2094
rückkaufbar 2052
rückkaufen 480, 502
rückkäuflich 2052
Rückkaufsfonds 140
Rückkaufsprämie 1750
Rückkaufspreis 2054, 2095
Rückkaufssatz 2054, 2095
Rückkaufswert 2055
Rückkauf, vorzeitiger ~ 167
Rückkaufwert 2247
Rücklage 129, 2101
rücklage, Abschreibungs~ 132
rücklage, Devisen~ 901
rücklage, Entwertungs~ 132
rücklage, Erneuerungs~ 2086
Rücklagefonds 2101
Rücklage, freie ~ 1397
Rücklage, freiwillige ~ 1397
rücklage, Gewinn~ 1987
rücklage, Konjunkturausgleichs~ 820
Rücklage(n) 2098
Rücklagen, ausgewiesene ~ 966
Rücklagenkonto 130
Rücklagen, offene ~ 966
Rücklagen, sichtbare ~ 966
Rücklagen zuführen, den ~ 68
Rücklagen zuweisen, den ~ 68
Rücklagenzuweisung aus dem Gewinn 1987
Rücklage, statutarische ~ 2102
rücklage, Steuer~ 2001
Rücklauf 968
rückläufige Konjunktur 1031
rückläufige Tendenz 344
Rücknahmepreis 2095
Rücknahmesatz 2095
Rückprämie 1750, 1953
Rückschlag 968
rückschlag, Konjunktur~ 1031
rückschlag, Preis~ 886
Rückschleusung von Kapital 2050
Rückstand 152
Rückstände 188
rückstände, Zins~ 190
rückständig 189
rückständiger Betrag 152
rückständige Schulden 188
rückständige Zinsen 190
Rückstand, im ~ 189
Rückstandsbezahlung 237
rückstand, Zahlungs~ 999
Rückstellung 129
rückstellung, Abschreibungs~ 132
rückstellung, Delkredere~ 756
Rückstellung für Abschreibungen 132
Rückstellung für Dubiosen 243
Rückstellung für unvorhergesehene Ausgaben 756
Rückstellung für Wertberichtigung 132
Rückstellung für Wertverminderung 132
Rückstellung für zweifelhafte Forderungen 243
rückstellung, Gewinn~ 1987
Rückstellungskonto 130
rückstellung, Steuer~ 2001
rücktrag, Verlust~ 2272
Rücktratte 819
rückvergüten 1900
Rückvergütung 2072
rückvergütung, Steuer~ 2038
rückvergütung, Zoll~ 1116
Rückwanderung 2090
Rückwechsel 819
rückzahlbar 2052, 2073
rückzahlbare Obligation 497

rückzahlbare Schuldverschreibung 497
Rückzahlbarkeit 2051
rückzahlen 148, 1900
Rückzahlung 139, 2053, 2072
Rückzahlungsagio 1750
Rückzahlungskurs 2054
Rückzahlungsprämie 1750
Rückzahlungspreis 2054
Rückzahlungsrate 2054
rückzahlung, Steuer~ 2038
Rückzahlungswert 2055
Rückzahlung, vorzeitige ~ 167
Rückzoll 1116
ruhig 508
Run auf die Bank 2121
runden Zahlen, in ~ 2119

Sach- 1658
Sachanlagen 518
Sachbezug 134
Sacheinlage 205
sachen, Wert~ 1646
Sachinvestitionen 518
Sachsteuer 1995
Sachwerte, eingebrachte ~ 205
Sachzuwendung 134
Safe 2122
Salär 2126
saldieren 148
saldieren, die Bücher ~ 278
saldieren, eine Rechnung ~ 249
saldieren, ein Konto ~ 249
Saldierung einer Rechnung (eines Kontos) 254
Saldo 27, 246
saldo, Aktiv~ 849
Saldo ausgleichen, den ~ 1914
saldo, Aussenhandels~ 1277
saldo, Bank~ 286
saldo, Debet~ 93
saldo, Debitoren~ 93
Saldo der Kapitalbewegungen 256
Saldo der laufenden Übertragungen 257
Saldo der Leistungsbilanz 268
saldo der Übertragungen und der Kapitalbewegungen, Gesamt~ 1416
Saldo des Waren- und Dienstleistungsverkehrs 259
saldo, Einwanderungs~ 1758
Saldo, fälliger ~ 252
saldo, Gewinn~ 849
saldo, Guthaben~ 849
saldo, Haben~ 849
saldo, Kassen~ 253
saldo, Konten~ 255
saldo, Kredit~ 849
saldo, Kreditoren~ 849
saldo, Leistungsbilanz~ 1277
saldo, Minus~ 93
saldo, Passiv~ 93
saldo, Rechnungs~ 27, 255
Saldorest 246
saldo, Schuld~ 93
saldo, Soll~ 93
saldo, Verlust~ 93
saldo, Verrechnungs~ 269
Saldovortrag auf neue Rechnung 150
Saldo ziehen, einen ~ 279
Sammelbuchung 717
Sammeldepot 685
Sammelkonto 673, 766
sanieren, die Finanzen ~ 2044
Sanierung der Finanzen 1318
Sanierung, finanzielle ~ 1318
Satz 2021
satz, Abschreibungs~ 144
satz, Amortisations~ 144, 145
satz, Ankauf~ 354
satz, Ausleihungs~ 423
satz, Bank~ 311
satz, Basis~ 328
satz, Beleihungs~ 2022
satz, Besteuerungs~ 2023
satz, Darleh(e)ns~ 423
satz, Devisenkassa~ 2024
satz, Diskont~ 1061
satz, Einheits~ 1345
satz, Geld~ 354, 1782
satz, Kommissions~ 691
satz, Konversions~ 778
satz, Liquiditäts~ 45
satz, Lombard~ 1714
satz, Mindestreserve~ 1759
satz, Nominal~ 1821
satz, Prolongations~ 569
satz, Provisions~ 691
satz, Rediskont~ 2059
satz, Report~ 569
satz, Rückkaufs~ 2054, 2095
satz, Rücknahme~ 2095
satz, Steigerungs~ 1255
satz, Steuer~ 2023
satz, Tilgungs~ 145
satz, Umrechnungs~ 778
satz, Umwandlungs~ 778
satzungsmässiger Sitz 2075
satz, Zins~ 1593
säumiger Debitor 981
säumiger Schuldner 981
säumnis, Zahlungs~ 999
Schadenersatz 708
schaden, Gesamt~ 934
schaden, Total~ 934
Schaden verkaufen, mit ~ 2158
Schadlosbürgschaft 394
Schadloshaltung 708
schaffen, eine Reserve ~ 454
Schatzamt 2299
Schatzanweisung 2301
schätzen 177
schätzen, unter dem Wert ~ 2319
Schatzschein 2301
Schätzung 176
Schätzung, annähernde ~ 184
Schätzung der Besteuerungsgrundlagen 1188
Schätzung, grobe ~ 184
Schätzung, rohe ~ 184
Schätzung, ungefähre ~ 184
schätzung, Wert~ 176
Schatzwechsel 2301
Scheck 624
Scheckabrechnung 627
Scheck ausfertigen, einen ~ 1115
Scheck ausfüllen, einen ~ 1115
Scheck ausgeben, einen ~ 1115
Scheck ausschreiben, einen ~ 1115
Scheck ausstellen, einen ~ 1115
scheck, Bar~ 339
Scheck begeben, einen ~ 1115
Scheck bestätigen, einen ~ 610
Scheck bezahlen, mit einem ~ 1901
scheck, Blanko~ 378
Scheckbuch 626
Scheck einkassieren, einen ~ 576
Scheck einlösen, einen ~ 576
Scheck einziehen, einen ~ 576
Scheckheft 626
scheck, Inhaber~ 339
Scheck kassieren, einen ~ 576
Scheck kompensieren, einen ~ 641
Scheckkonto 625
Scheck, offener ~ 339
Scheck ohne Deckung 241
scheck, Order~ 631
scheck, Post~ 1425
Scheckrechnung 625
scheck, Reise~ 2297
scheck, Rekta~ 630
Scheck sperren (lassen), einen ~ 2227
scheck, Traveller~ 2297
Scheck, ungedeckter ~ 241
Scheckverkehr 632
Scheck verrechnen, einen ~ 641
Scheckverrechnung 627
Scheck zahlen, durch ~ 1901
Scheck zahlen, per ~ 1901
Scheck ziehen, einen ~ 1115
Scheidegeld 1083
Scheidemünze 1083
schein, Aktien~ 2170
schein, Aktienbezugs~ 2115
Scheinaktiva 1297
schein, Anleihe~ 389
schein, Anteil~ 2170
schein, Auszahlungs~ 1913
schein, Beleg~ 2358
schein, Bezugs~ 2115
schein, Bezugsberechtigungs~ 2115
schein, Bürgschafts~ 394
schein, Darleh(e)ns~ 1709
schein, Deposital~ 608
schein, Depositen~ 608
schein, Depot~ 608
schein, Dividenden~ 1078
schein, Einzahlungs~ 877
schein, Empfangs~ 47
schein, Erneuerungs~ 2085
schein, Garantie~ 394
schein, Genuss~ 400
Scheingewinn 171
schein, Gewinnanteil~ 1078
schein, Hand~ 1477
schein, Hinterlegungs~ 608
schein, Hypotheken~ 1792
schein, Interims~ 1597
schein, Kassen~ 590
schein, Lager~ 2364
schein, Prämien~ 1719
schein, Renten~ 162

schein, Schatz~ 2301
schein, Schluss~ 425, 440
schein, Schuld~ 609, 1477
schein, Spar~ 2141
schein, Versicherungs~ 1577
Scheinwechsel 15
schein, Zins~ 1588
Schenker 1104
Schenkung 1103
Schenkungssteuer 1422
schicht, Einkommens~ 1527
schieber, Börsen~ 1647
schiebung, Börsen~ 1730
schlagen 662
schlagen, die Zinsen zum Kapital ~ 547
schlagen, zum Reservefonds ~ 68
Schlange 2183
schlechte Forderung 242
schlechte Kapitalanlage 244
schlechter Zahler 245
schleichende Inflation 882
Schleuderausfuhr 1131
Schleuderpreis 322
Schleuderverkauf 2129
Schleuderverkauf (ins Ausland) 1131
schliessen, eine Anleihe ~ 762
schliessen, eine Rechnung ~ 652
schliessen, ein Konto ~ 652
Schliessfach 2123
Schlussbilanz 1302
Schlussdividende 1303
Schlusskurs 657
Schlussnote 425, 440
Schlussnotierung 657
Schlussnotiz 657
Schlussschein 425, 440
Schonfrist 998
schöpfung, Geld~ 842
schöpfung, Kredit~ 841
Schranke, wirtschaftliche ~ 1149
schranke, Zoll~ 918
schraube, Inflations~ 1559
schreiben, Garantie~ 394
schreiben, zu Lasten ~ 615
schub, Inflations~ 1558
Schuld 951
Schuld, aktive ~ 37
schuld, Amortisations~ 1574
Schuldanerkenntnis 46
schuld, Anleihe~ 391
Schuld aufnehmen, eine ~ 761
schuld, Auslands~ 1280
Schuld, ausstehende ~ 37
Schuld beitreiben, eine ~ 677
Schuld bestreiten, eine ~ 2092
Schuldbetrag 151
Schuldbetrag, verbleibender ~ 252
Schuld betreiben, eine ~ 677
schuld, Buch~ 406
Schuld eingehen, eine ~ 761
Schuld eintreiben, eine ~ 677
Schuld einziehen, eine ~ 677
schulden 1876
Schulden 961
schulden, Bank~ 296
Schulden beladen, mit ~ 466
Schulden belasten, mit ~ 466
schuldenbelastet 952
Schulden beschweren, mit ~ 466
Schuldendienst 962
Schuldenerlass 513
Schulden geraten, in ~ 1294
Schulden, kurzfristige ~ 910
Schuldenlast 462
Schuldennachlass 513
Schulden, rückständige ~ 188
Schulden stecken, bis über die Ohren in ~ 953
Schulden stecken, in ~ 1294
Schuldenstreichung 513
Schuldentilgungsfonds 140
Schuldenverwaltung 954
Schulderlass 513
Schuld erlassen, eine ~ 510
Schuldforderung 639
Schuld fundieren, eine ~ 733
Schuld, fundierte ~ 735
schuld, Gesamt~ 1650
schuld, Hypothekar~ 957
schuld, Hypotheken~ 957
schuldig 1127
schuldiger Betrag 151
schuldige Summe 151
schuldig sein 1876
schuld, Inlands~ 1095
Schuldkapital 417
Schuld konsolidieren, eine ~ 733
Schuld, konsolidierte ~ 735
schuld, Landes~ 1798
Schuld löschen, eine ~ 510
Schuld machen, eine ~ 761
Schuld nachlassen, eine ~ 510
schuld, National~ 1798
Schuldner 958
Schuldner, fauler ~ 981
schuldner, Gemeinschafts~ 659
schuldner, Gesamt~ 1651
Schuldnerland 959
Schuldner, säumiger ~ 981
schuldner, Solidar~ 1651
Schuldnerstaat 959
schuldner, Wechsel~ 362
Schuld nicht anerkennen, eine ~ 2092
Schuld niederschlagen, eine ~ 510
schuld, Obligationen~ 391
schuld, Obligations~ 391
Schuld, öffentliche ~ 1798
Schuld, passive ~ 36
schuld, Personal~ 1928
Schuld, persönliche ~ 1928
schuld, Privat~ 1928
Schuld, private ~ 1928
schuld, Rest~ 252
Schuldsaldo 93
Schuldschein 609, 1477
schuldschein, Hand~ 1477
schuldschein, Kommunal~ 1713
schuldschein, Staats~ 1243
Schuld, schwebende ~ 1351
schuld, Solidar~ 1650
schuld, Staats~ 1798
schuld, Steuer~ 2271
Schuld streichen, eine ~ 510
Schuldsumme 151
Schuldtitel 609
Schuldumwandlung 776
Schuld, unfundierte ~ 1351
Schuld unifizieren, eine ~ 733
Schuld, unifizierte ~ 735
Schuldurkunde 609
Schuld, verbriefte ~ 391
Schuld, verjährte ~ 324
Schuldverschreibung 389, 1477
schuldverschreibung, Ablösungs~ 704
Schuldverschreibung, auslösbare ~ 497
schuldverschreibung, Bank~ 288
Schuldverschreibung, besicherte ~ 2149
schuldverschreibung, Dauer~ 1925
schuldverschreibung, Dollar~ 1087
Schuldverschreibung, einlösbare ~ 497
Schuldverschreibung, einziehbare ~ 497
Schuldverschreibungen ausgeben 1637
Schuldverschreibung, gesicherte ~ 2149
schuldverschreibung, Gewinn~ 1526
schuldverschreibung, Hypothekar~ 1792
Schuldverschreibung, hypothekarische ~ 1792
schuldverschreibung, Hypotheken~ 1792
schuldverschreibung, Index~ 1549
Schuldverschreibung, indexgebundene ~ 1549
Schuldverschreibung, index-gekoppelte ~ 1549
schuldverschreibung, Inhaber~ 338
schuldverschreibung, Kommunal~ 1713
schuldverschreibung, Konversions~ 704
Schuldverschreibung, kündbare ~ 497
schuldverschreibung mit Zinskupon, Inhaber~ 830
schuldverschreibung mit Zinsschein, Inhaber~ 830
Schuldverschreibung, nicht einziehbare ~ 1636
Schuldverschreibung, nicht rückzahlbare ~ 1636
Schuldverschreibung, nicht tilgbare ~ 1636
Schuldverschreibung, nicht zurück-zahlbare ~ 1636
Schuldverschreibung, notleidende ~ 980
schuldverschreibung, Prämien~ 1719
schuldverschreibung, Renten~ 162
Schuldverschreibung, rück-zahlbare ~ 497
Schuldverschreibung, sicher-gestellte ~ 2149
Schuldverschreibungsinhaber 390
schuldverschreibung, Staats~ 1243

schuldverschreibung, Teil~ 389
Schuldverschreibung, tilgbare ~ 497
schuldverschreibung, Umtausch~ 704
Schuldverschreibung, unbesicherte ~ 2331
Schuldverschreibung, ungesicherte ~ 2331
Schuldverschreibung, unkündbare ~ 1636
Schuldverschreibung, untilgbare ~ 1636
schuldverschreibung, Wandel~ 783
Schuldversprechen 1477
Schuldwechsel 372
Schuldzinsen 947
Schutzzoll 1998
Schutzzöllner 1997
Schutzzollpolitiker 1997
schwach 508
Schwäche 1130
schwache Währung 2187
schwankende Abschreibung 2347
schwankender Wechselkurs 1347
Schwanken der Wechselkurse 1225
schwankende Währung 1350
Schwankung der Wechselkurse 1225
schwankung, Konjunktur~ 930
Schwankung, konjunkturelle ~ 930
schwankung, Markt~ 930
Schwankung, zyklische ~ 930
schwarzer Markt 377
Schwarzgeld 2314
Schwarzmarkt 377
Schwebekonto 2248
schwebende Schuld 1351
schwelle, Gewinn~ 430
schwelle, Nutz~ 430
schwemme, Geld~ 6
Schwierigkeiten, finanzielle ~ 1314
schwierigkeiten, Geld~ 1314
Scrip 1597
seite, Aktiv~ 206
seite, Debet~ 943
seite, Gutschrift~ 206
seite, Haben~ 206
seite, Kredit~ 206
seite, Passiv~ 943
seite, Soll~ 943
Sekondärmarkt 2147
Sektor, öffentlicher ~ 2008
sektor, Privat~ 1981
Sektor, privater ~ 1981
sektor, Verteilungs~ 1075
sektor, Wachstums~ 1470
Sekunda 2148
Sekundäreinkommen 2146
Sekundäreinkünfte 2146
Sekundärkosten 1417
Sekundarliquiditäten 1776
Sekundawechsel 2148
selbständige Teilbuchführung 2155
Selbstbeschränkungsabkommen 2355
Selbstfinanzierung 1601
Selbstgenügsamkeit 219
Selbstkosten 814
Selbstkostenberechnung 815
Selbstkostenpreis 814
Selbstkostenpreis, zum ~ 796
Selbstverbrauch 1497
Selbstversorgung 219
sendung, Bar~ 595
sendung, Geld~ 1784
senken, die Ausgaben ~ 915
Senkung des Diskontsatzes 926
senkung, Diskont~ 926
senkung, Preis~ 927
Sequester 191, 209
Sequester stellen, unter ~ 211
Sequestration 191
sequestrieren 211
Sequestrierung 191
Serienausgabe 385
setzen, auf das Konto ~ 618
sicheres Einkommen 210
sichergestellte Obligation 2149
sichergestellter Gläubiger 2150
sichergestellte Schuldverschreibung 2149
Sicherheit 669, 1138
Sicherheit bestellen, eine ~ 101
Sicherheit bieten, eine ~ 101
Sicherheit deponieren, als ~ 1018
Sicherheit, dingliche ~ 2035, 2258
Sicherheit geben, als ~ 1018
Sicherheit geben, eine ~ 101
Sicherheit gewähren, eine ~ 101
Sicherheit hinterlegen, als ~ 1018
Sicherheit, hypothekarische ~ 2035
Sicherheit leisten 52
Sicherheit leisten, eine ~ 101
sicherheit, Neben~ 65
sicherheit, Real~ 2035
Sicherheitsfach 2123
Sicherheitsfonds 1472
Sicherheit, soziale ~ 2184
Sicherheitssumme 602, 1732, 2109
Sicherheit stellen, eine ~ 101
Sicherheit, Vorschuss gegen ~ 86
Sicherheit, zusätzliche ~ 65
sichern, durch Hypothek ~ 838
sichern, hypothekarisch ~ 838
sicherstellen, durch Hypothek ~ 838
sicherstellen, hypothekarisch ~ 838
Sicherstellung 1138
Sicherstellungsfonds 1472
Sicherung 1138
sicherung, Gewinn~ 1990
Sicherungsfonds 1472
Sicherungsgeschäft 839
sicherungsübereigneter Wechsel 363
Sicht, auf ~ 1956
sichtbare Ausfuhr(en) 2351
sichtbare Einfuhr(en) 2352
sichtbare Exporte 2351
sichtbare Importe 2352
sichtbare Reserven 966
sichtbare Rücklagen 966
Sicht, bei ~ 1956
Sichtdarleh(e)n 504
Sichtdepositum 1004
Sichtdepot 1004
Sichteinlage 1004
Sichtgeschäft 1379
Sichtpapier 1007
Sichttratte 1003
Sichtverbindlichkeiten 1006
Sichtverpflichtungen 1006
Sichtwechsel 1003
Sicht zahlbar, auf ~ 1896
Sicht zahlbar, bei ~ 1896
sinkende Konjunktur 1031
sistieren, die Zahlungen ~ 603
sitz, Gesellschafts~ 2075
sitz, Haupt~ 607
Sitz, satzungsmässiger ~ 2075
Sitz, statutarischer ~ 2075
Skala, bewegliche ~ 1348
Skala, gleitende ~ 1348
Skonto 127
Skontoabzug 127
skonto, Handels~ 935
skonto, Kassa~ 583
skonto, Kassen~ 583
skonto, Waren~ 935
skontrieren, eine Rechnung ~ 249
skontrieren, ein Konto ~ 249
Skontrierung einer Rechnung (eines Kontos) 254
Slump 1031
Slumpflation 2182
Soforteinlage 1004
Solawechsel 2180
Sold 1140
Solidarhaftung 1652
solidarische Haftpflicht 1652
solidarische Haftung 1652
Solidarschuld 1650
Solidarschuldner 1651
Solidität 873
Soll 942, 943
Sollbuchung 946
Soll eintragen, in das ~ 615
Sollkosten 1189
Sollposten 946
Sollsaldo 93
Sollseite 943
Sollzinsen 947
solvabel 2190
solvent 2190
Solvenz 2189
Sonderausgaben 61
Sonderdividende 398
Sondereinnahmen 1287
Sondergewinn 1213
Sondergewinnsteuer 1214
Sonderkosten 61
Sonderkredit 2194
Sonderspesen 61
Sondervergütung 1284
Sonderziehungsrechte 2195
sonstige Ausgaben 1764
sonstige Auslagen 1764
sonstige Einkünfte 1765
sonstige Erträge 1765
sonstige Spesen 1764
sonstige Unkosten 1764
Sorten 1369
Sortengeschäft 936
Sortenhandel 936
Sortenhändler 509
Sortenkurs 1235
Soulte 247
Sozialabgaben 2186

Sozialbeiträge 2186
soziale Abgaben 2186
soziale Lasten 2186
soziale Leistung 2185
soziale Sicherheit 2184
sozialisieren 1802
Sozialisierung 1801
Soziallasten 2186
Sozialleistung 2185
Sozialprodukt 1803
sozialprodukt, Netto~ 1814
Sozialstaat 2373
Sozialversicherung 2184
Sozialversicherungsbeiträge 2186
Spanne 1037
spanne, Bruttoverdienst~ 1465
spanne, Gewinn~ 1734
spanne, Handels~ 1734
spannen, Arbitrage~ 187
spanne, Preis~ 1966
spanne, Verdienst~ 1734
spanne, Zins~ 1412
Spannung, inflationäre ~ 1558
Sparanleihestück 2141
Sparbank 2139
Sparbegünstigung 1161
Sparbon 2141
Sparbrief 2141
Sparbuch 2142
Spareinlage 2144
sparen 2133
sparen, Effekten~ 2135
sparen, Konten~ 2136
Sparen, obligatorisches ~ 724
sparen, Vertrags~ 764
sparen, Wertpapier~ 2135
sparen, Zwangs~ 724
Sparer 2134
Sparfonds 2145
Sparförderung 1161
Spargelder 2137
Sparguthaben 2144
Sparkapital 2143
Sparkasse 2139
Sparkassenbuch 2140
Sparkonto 2138
Sparquote 2026
Sparrate 2026
Sparschein 2141
Sparüberhang 1872
Sparüberschuss 1872
Sparvolumen 2353
später datieren 1942
Speditionskosten 2295
Spekulant 2200
spekulant, Baisse~ 332
spekulant, Börsen~ 1647
spekulant, Hausse~ 455
Spekulation 2197
spekulation, Börsen~ 111
Spekulationspapiere 2199
Spekulationswerte 2199
spekulieren 2196
spekulieren, à la Baisse ~ 1427
spekulieren, à la Hausse ~ 456
spekulieren, auf das Fallen ~ 1427
spekulieren, auf Hausse ~ 456
Spende 1103
Spender 1104
Sperre 383, 384
sperre, Einfuhr~ 319
sperren 380
sperren, die Zahlung eines Schecks ~ 2227
sperren (lassen), einen Scheck ~ 2227
Sperrfrist 384
Sperrguthaben 381
Sperrpfunde 382
Sperrung 383
Sperrzoll 1993
Spesen 1261
Spesen, abzüglich der ~ 131, 621
Spesenaufstellung 2218
spesen, Aufwands~ 1169
spesen, Bank~ 291
Spesen, kleine ~ 1764
Spesenkonto 1259
Spesen, nach Abrechnung der ~ 131
Spesen, nach Abzug der ~ 131
spesen, Reise~ 2298
Spesen, sonstige ~ 1764
spesen, Transfer~ 812
spesen, Übertragungs~ 812
Spesen, unter Abzug der ~ 621
Spesen, zusätzliche ~ 61
Spezialpreis 1203
Spezifikation 429
Spezifizierung 429
Spiegelkonten 802
spiel, Börsen~ 111
spieler, Börsen~ 1647
Spielpapiere 2199
Spielraum 1037
spielraum, Kredit~ 864
Spirale, deflatorische ~ 993
spirale, Inflations~ 1559
Spirale, Kosten-Preis-~ 816
Spirale, Lohn-Preis-~ 2363
Spitze 1387
Spitzenausgleich 1199
Spitzenpapiere 387
Spitzenwerte 387
spitze, Verrechnungs~ 269
Split 2175
Splitting 2175
Spottpreis 322
spritze, Investitions~ 521
staat, Gläubiger~ 871
staatliche Anleihe 1453
staatliche Beihilfe 1449
staatliche Bürgschaft 1450
staatliche Einmischung 1452
staatliche Einnahmen 1451
staatliche Finanzen 827
staatliche Finanzwirtschaft 827
staatliche Fonds 2005
staatliche Garantie 1450
staatliche Gelder 2005
staatliche Intervention 1452
staatliche Leistungen 684
staatlicher Betrieb 1448
staatlicher Zuschuss 1449
staatliches Finanzwesen 827
staatliche Subvention 1449
staatliches Unternehmen 1448
staatliche Unternehmung 1448
staatliche Unterstützung 1445
Staatsanleihe 1453
Staatsanleihen 1244
Staatsärar 2299
Staatsbeihilfe 1449
Staatsbetrieb 1448
Staatsbudget 1446
Staatsbürgschaft 1450
staat, Schuldner~ 959
Staatseingriff(e) 1452
Staatseinkommen 1451
Staatseinkünfte 1451
Staatseinmischung 1452
Staatseinnahmen 1451
Staatsfinanzen 827
Staatsfonds 1244, 2005
Staatsgarantie 1450
Staatsgarantie für ein Darleh(e)n 1447
Staatsgelder 2005
Staatshaushalt 1446
Staatshaushaltsplan 1446
Staatshilfe 1445
Staatsintervention 1452
Staatskasse 2299
Staatskasse ausgegebenes Geld, von der ~ 2302
Staatskassenschein 2301
Staatsmonopol 1454
Staatsobligation 1243
staat, Sozial~ 2373
Staatspapiere 1244
Staatspapiere, fundierte ~ 734
Staatspapiere, konsolidierte ~ 734
Staatsschatz 2299
Staatsschuld 1798
Staatsschuldschein 1243
Staatsschuldverschreibung 1243
Staatssubvention 1449
Staatsunternehmen 1448
Staatsunterstützung 1445
Staatsverschuldung 1798
Staatswirtschaftslehre 1151
Staatszuschuss 1449
staat, Wohlfahrts~ 2373
stabile Währung 2207
stabilisierung, Kurs~ 1237
stabilisierung, Preis~ 1969
Stabilisierungsanleihe 2206
Stabilisierungsfonds 2205
Stabilität der Devisenkurse 1239
Stabilität der Wechselkurse 1239
stabilität, Geldwert~ 903
stabilität, Preis~ 1326
Staffelsteuer 1456
Staffeltarif 1041
Staffelung einer Steuer 1992
Staffelzins(en) 1457
Stagflation 2208
Stagnation 1130
stagnieren 1663
stagnierend 508
Stagnierung 1130
Stahlfach 2123
Stahlkammer 2125
Stahlkasse 2122

Stahlkassette 2123
Stammaktien 701
Stammaktienkapital 697
Stammhaus 769
Stammkapital 544
Stammkapital (GmbH) 222
Stammpriorität 1946
Stammprioritätsaktie 1946
standard, Gold~ 1441
standard, Gold-Devisen~ 1436
standard, Lebens~ 1704
Standardpreis 1832
Standardwert 2213
Stand-by-Kredit 2214
Stand-by-Kreditabkommen 2215
Stand-by-Kreditvereinbarung 2215
Stand des Marktes 1743
Stand einer Rechnung 1940
ständiges Einkommen 210
stand, Kassen~ 592
stand, Konten~ 1940
stand, Konto~ 1940
stand, Kurs~ 1680
stand, Preis~ 1680
stand, Rechnungs~ 1940
Stangengold 323
starke Währung 1479
Statistik 2220
Statistiken 2219
statistiker, Versicherungs~ 58
statistik, interne Betriebs~ 1851
statistische Angaben 2219
Status 2217
status, Finanz~ 1319
status, Kassen~ 592
statutarische Reserve 2102
statutarischer Sitz 2075
statutarische Rücklage 2102
Steigen 2117
steigende Abschreibung 1545
steigende Tendenz 459
steigen, im Wert ~ 179
steigern, den Wert ~ 178
steigerung, Gehalts~ 1540
steigerung, Lohn~ 1542
steigerung, Preis~ 1539
Steigerungsrate 1255
Steigerungssatz 1255
steigerung, Wert~ 180
steigung, Preis~ 1539
Stellage 1108
Stellagegeschäft 1108
stelle, Abrechnungs~ 649
stelle, Ausgleichs~ 649
stelle, Clearing~ 649
stelle, Haupt~ 607
stelle, Kosten~ 461
stellen, eine Sicherheit ~ 101
stellen, in das Debet ~ 615
stelle, Verrechnungs~ 649
stelle, Wechsel~ 1217
stelle, Zentral~ 607
Stellgeschäft 1108
Stempel 2209
Stempelabgabe 2211
Stempelgebühr 2211
Stempelmarke 2209
Stempelsteuer 2211
sterilisieren 2222
Sterilisierung 2221
Sterling 2223
Sterlingblock 2224
Sterlinggebiet 2224
Sterlingraum 2224
Sterlingwährung 2223
Sterlingwährungsgebiet 2224
Sterlingwährungsraum 2224
Sterlingzone 2224
Steuer 1135
Steuerabzug 2261
Steuerabzug, nach ~ 1677
Steuerabzug, vor ~ 1959
steuer, Aktienkapital~ 560
Steueramt 1242
Steueranreiz 2270
Steueranschlag 200
Steuer auferlegen (auf), eine ~ 194
Steuerauferlegung 1516
Steueraufkommen 1565
Steueraufschlag 66
Steuer auf Veräusserungsgewinne 532
steuer, Aufwand(s)~ 1723
Steuerausfall 1330
Steuerausgleich 1175
steuer, Ausgleichs~ 712
Steuer ausschreiben (auf), eine ~ 194
Steuerausschreibung 1516
steuerbar 196
steuerbarer Wert 198
Steuerbasis 331
steuerbefreit 1247
Steuerbefreiung 1248
Steuerbegünstigung 2263
Steuerbehörden 1242
Steuer beitreiben, eine ~ 678
Steuerbeitreibung 683
Steuer belasten, mit einer ~ 194
Steuerbelastung 463
Steuer belegen, mit einer ~ 194
Steuerbemessungsgrundlage 331
Steuerberater 2264
Steuerberechnungsgrundlage 331
Steuerbescheid 1839
steuer, Besitz~ 551
Steuerdefizit 1330
Steuer, degressive ~ 997
Steuer, direkte ~ 1046
Steuerdruck 463
Steuereingänge 1565
Steuer einheben, eine ~ 678
Steuereinhebung 683
Steuereinkommen 1565
steuer, Einkommens~ 1530
Steuereinkünfte 1565
Steuereinnahmen 1565
Steuereinschätzung 200
Steuereinschränkung 1839
Steuer eintreiben, eine ~ 678
Steuereintreibung 683
Steuer einziehen, eine ~ 678
Steuereinziehung 683
steuer, Erbanfall~ 938
steuer, Erbschafts~ 938
Steuer erheben (auf), eine ~ 194
Steuer erheben, eine ~ 678
Steuererhebung 683, 1516
Steuererhebung an der Quelle 681
Steuererklärung 2275
Steuererklärung, vorläufige ~ 2000
Steuererlass 2261
Steuererleichterung 2261
Steuerermässigung 2261
Steuererstattung 2038
Steuerertrag 1565
Steuererträgnisse 1565
steuer, Ertrag(s)~ 1989
steuer, Extra~ 66
Steuerflucht 2266
steuerfrei 1247
Steuerfreiheit 1248
Steuerfuss 331, 2023
steuer, Gesellschaftskapital~ 560
Steuer, gestaffelte ~ 1456
steuer, Gewerbe~ 476
steuer, Gewinn~ 1989
steuer, Grund~ 1662
Steuergrundlage 331
steuer, Grundstücks~ 1662
steuer, Grundvermögens~ 1662
Steuergruppe 2267
Steuerherabsetzung 2261
Steuerhinterziehung 2266
steuer, Immobiliar~ 1995
Steuer, indirekte ~ 1552
Steuerjahr 1335
steuer, Kapital~ 551
steuer, Kapitalertrag~ 565
steuer, Kapitalgewinn~ 532
steuer, Kapitalverkehr(s)~ 564
steuer, Kapitalvermögens~ 551
steuer, Kapitalzuwachs~ 532
Steuerklasse 2267
steuer, Konsum~ 752
steuer, Körperschafts~ 792
Steuerlast 463
steuerliche Belastung 463
steuerlicher Wert 198
steuerlicher Wohnsitz 1331
steuerlich zulässige Abschreibungen 517
steuer, Luxus~ 1723
steuer, Mehrgewinn~ 1214
steuer, Mehrwert~ 2341
Steuermilderung 2261
Steuerminderung 2261
steuer, Monopol~ 1245
steuer, Nachlass~ 938
Steuernachlass 2261
steuern, die Inflation ~ 628
Steuer(n), vor ~ 1959
Steueroase 2269
Steuerpflicht 1683
steuerpflichtig 196
Steuerpflichtiger 2028
steuerpflichtiger Gewinn 197
steuerpflichtiges Einkommen 2262
Steuerpflicht, latente ~ 759
steuerpolitisches Instrument 1332
Steuer, progressive ~ 1456
steuer, Quellen~ 2268
steuer, Real~ 1995
Steuerreform 2274

Steuerregulator 1333
Steuerreserve 2001
Steuerrevision 1566
Steuerrückerstattung 2038
Steuerrücklage 2001
Steuerrückstellung 2001
Steuerrückvergütung 2038
Steuerrückzahlung 2038
steuer, Sach~ 1995
Steuersatz 2023
steuer, Schenkungs~ 1422
Steuerschuld 2271
Steuerschulden, latente ~ 986
steuer, Sondergewinn~ 1214
steuer, Staffel~ 1456
steuer, Stempel~ 2211
Steuersystem 1334
steuer, Übergewinn~ 1214
Steuerumgehung 2266
steuer, Umsatz~ 2014
steuerung, Kapital~ 1044
Steuer unterwerfen, einer ~ 194
Steuer unterworfen, einer ~ 196
Steuerverbindlichkeit 2271
steuer, Verbrauchs~ 752
Steuervergünstigung 2263
Steuervergütung 2038
steuer, Verkehrs~ 812
steuer, Vermächtnis~ 938
steuer, Vermögens~ 551
Steuerverpflichtung 1683, 2271
steuer, Verrechnungs~ 565
Steuerverwaltung 1242
Steuervorteil 2263
steuer, Warenumsatz~ 2014
Steuerwert 198
Steuerwesen 1334
Steuerzahler 2028
Steuer, zusätzliche ~ 66
Steuerzuschlag 66
steuer, Zuschlag(s)~ 66
Stichtag 24
Stifter 1104
Stiftung 1385
still 508
Stille 1130
stillegen 2222
Stillegung 2221
stille Reserven 726
stiller Gesellschafter 1105
stiller Teilhaber 1105
Stillhalteabkommen 2216
stillhalten, einen Kredit ~ 1272
Stillhalteübereinkommen 2216
Stillhaltevereinbarung 2216
Stillhaltung eines Kredits 1275
Stillstand 1130
stillstehen 1663
stimmberechtigte Aktien 2357
stimmrecht, Depot~ 2356
Stimmrechtsaktien 2357
stimmrechtslose Aktien 1830
stimmung, Baisse~ 344
stimmung, Hausse~ 459
Stock 1615
Stockdividende 400
stocken 1663
Stocken 1130
stockend 508
Stockung 1130
stopp, Einfuhr~ 319
stoppen 380
stop, Preis~ 1400
Stornierung 512
Stornierungsbuchung 281
Stornierungseintrag 281
Storno 281
Stornobuchung 281, 512
störung, Gleichgewichts~ 1062
Stottern kaufen, auf ~ 481
strafe, Geld~ 136
Strazze 1754
streichen, eine Schuld ~ 510
streichung, Schulden~ 513
strom, Kapital~ 528
strom, Kredit~ 859
strömung, Baisse~ 344
struktureller Überschuss 2229
struktur, Finanz~ 561
struktur, Kapital~ 561
struktur, Kosten~ 817
stube, Wechsel~ 1217
Stück 1011
stück, Anleihe~ 389
Stücke 2151
Stückelung 1011
stück, Geld~ 660
Stückgeld 1834
stück, Gold~ 1433
Stückkosten 813
Stücklohn 1932
Stückpreis 2328
Stückzinsen 41
studie, Absatz~ 1740
studie, Markt~ 1740
stufe, Einkommens~ 1527
Stufentarif 1041
stunden, eine Zahlung ~ 1274
Stundung 998
Stundungs- 1789
Stundungsfrist 998, 1276
stundung, Zahlungs~ 1276
Sturm auf die Bank 2121
sturz, Kurs~ 431
sturz, Preis~ 431
Stützkurs 1610
stützung, Preis~ 1917
Stützungskurs 1610
Stützungspunkt 1609
Submissionsangebot 2276
Submissionsofferte 2276
Subsidien 1458
Subsidien unterstützen, durch ~ 2240
subskribieren 2233
Subskription 2236
Subskriptionsprospekt 1643
Subskriptionsrecht 174
Substanzwert 432
Subvention 1458
subvention, Ausfuhr~ 1269
subvention, Export~ 1269
subventionieren 2240
Subvention, öffentliche ~ 1449
Subvention, staatliche ~ 1449
subvention, Staats~ 1449
subvention, Zins~ 1594
suchender, Anleihe~ 172
Summe 149
summe, Abstands~ 708
summe, Aktiv~ 2285
summe, Ausgleichs~ 247
summe, Bilanz~ 276
summe, End~ 105
summe, Gesamt~ 105
Summe, geschuldete ~ 151
summe, Hinterlegungs~ 1732
summe, Lohn~ 2359
summe, Pauschal~ 1722
summe, Rest~ 246
summe, Schuld~ 151
Summe, schuldige ~ 151
summe, Sicherheits~ 602, 1732, 2109
summe, Total~ 105
Summe, überschiessende ~ 1205
Superdividende 398
Superinflation 1500
Surplus 2244
Swap 2251
Swapgeschäft 2251
Swapkredit 2252
Swing 864
Swinggrenze 864
Swingrahmen 864
Switch 2253
Switchgeschäft 2253
Syndikat 2255
syndikat, Banken~ 303
syndikat, Garantie~ 2322
System des gespaltenen Goldpreises 2310
system, Geld~ 664
system, Investivlohn~ 2362
system, Kredit~ 879
system, Münz~ 664
system, Steuer~ 1334
S.Z.R. 2195

Tabelle 2256
tabelle, Amortisations~ 146
tabelle, Tilgungs~ 146
Tafel 2256
tag, Ablaufs~ 1263
tag, Abrechnungs~ 24
tag, Bilanzstich~ 272
Tagebuch 932
tage, Gnaden~ 933
tage, Respekt~ 933
tage, Respiro~ 933
tage, Respit~ 933
Tagesgeld 505
Tagesgelddarleh(e)n 504
Tageskurs 907, 913
Tagesnotierung 913
Tagesnotiz 913
Tagespreis 911
Tageswert 912, 913
tag, Fälligkeits~ 931
tägliches Geld 505
täglich fälliges Geld 505
täglich kündbares Darleh(e)n 504
tag, Liquidations~ 24
tag, Stich~ 24
tag, Valutierungs~ 2343

tag, Verfall(s)~ 931
tag, Wert~ 2343
Talon 2085
Tantieme 1686, 1923
Tantiemenanteil 1923
Tarif 2260
tarif, Aussen~ 1279
tarif, Begünstigungs~ 1947
tarif, Differential~ 1041
tarif für Mitglieder des Commonwealths, Vorzugs~ 702
Tarif, gestaffelter ~ 1041
Tarif, gleitender ~ 1041
tarif, Präferenz~ 1947
tarif, Staffel~ 1041
tarif, Stufen~ 1041
tarif, Vergünstigungs~ 1947
tarif, Vorzugs~ 1947
tarif, Zoll~ 922
tatsächliche Kosten 54
tatsächliches Einkommen 2032
Tausch 325
tausch, Aktien~ 1232
tauschen 326
Tauschgeschäft 327
Tauschhandel 325
Tauschhandel treiben 326
Tauschwert 1219
Taxe 614, 1135
taxe, Ausgleichs~ 712
taxieren 177, 195
Taxierung 176, 200
technische Abschreibung 1030
Teilabschnitt 1572
Teilaktie 2230
Teilbeträgen, in ~ 987
Teilbuchführung, selbständige ~ 2155
teilen, sich in den Unterschied ~ 2201
teilen, sich in die Differenz ~ 2201
Teilhaber, stiller ~ 1105
Teilkostenkalkulation 1045
Teilkostenrechnung 1045
Teilnahme (an) 1495
teilproportionale Kosten 2164
Teilschuldverschreibung 389
Teilzahlung 1894
Teilzahlung, auf ~ 987
Teilzahlungen, auf (in) ~ 987
Teilzahlung kaufen, auf ~ 481
Teilzahlung, monatliche ~ 1788
Teilzahlungsfinanzierung 1490
Teilzahlungsgeschäft 1489
Teilzahlungskauf 1573
Teilzahlungskredit 1488
Teilzahlungstransaktion 1489
Teilzahlungsverkauf 1491
Tempo des Wachstums 1256
tempo, Inflations~ 1563
Tendenz 1200
Tendenz, aufsteigende ~ 459
tendenz, Baisse~ 344
Tendenz, deflationistische ~ 994
tendenz, Deflations~ 994
Tendenz, fallende ~ 344
tendenz, Hausse~ 459
Tendenz, rückläufige ~ 344
Tendenz, steigende ~ 459
Tendenz zum Steigen 459
Tendenz zuwiderlaufen, der allgemeinen ~ 2120
Termin 1262
termin, Ablaufs~ 1263
termin, Abrechnungs~ 24
Termindepositum 1337
Termindevisen 1378
Termindevisenkurs 1383
Termineinlage 1337
termin, Fälligkeits~ 931
Termingeld 1337
Termingeschäft 1379
Termingeschäft in Devisen 1381
Terminhandel in Devisen 1226
Terminkauf 1376
Termin kaufen, auf ~ 486
Terminkauf und -verkauf 1108
termin, Kündigungs~ 1836
Terminkurs 1384
terminkurs, Devisen~ 1383
Terminlieferung 1380
termin, Liquidations~ 18
terminmarkt, Devisen~ 1382
Terminpreis 1384
terminsatz, Devisen~ 1383
termintransaktion, Devisen~ 1381
termin, Verfall(s)~ 931
Termin verkaufen, auf ~ 2161
terminweise 987
termin, Wertstellungs~ 2343
Terminzahlung 1910
termin, Zahlungs~ 1924
Terms of trade 2279
Teuerung 1539
teuerung, Lebens~ 1483
Teuerungszulage 808
Teuerungszuschlag 808
teures Geld 654
thesaurieren 1492
thesaurierte Gewinne 2108
Thesaurierung 1493
Tiefkonjunktur 1031
tilgbar 2052
tilgbare Obligation 497
tilgbare Schuldverschreibung 497
Tilgbarkeit 2051
tilgen 148, 502
tilgen, eine Hypothek ~ 511
Tilgung 139, 2053
tilgung, Anleihe~ 142
Tilgungsanleihe 141
Tilgungsdarleh(e)n 141
Tilgungsfonds 140
Tilgungsplan 146
Tilgungsquote 145
Tilgungsrate 145
Tilgungssatz 145
Tilgungstabelle 146
Tilgungswert 2055
Titel 2151
titel, Anlage~ 1630
titel, Anleihe~ 389
Titel, festverzinslicher ~ 1339
titel, Geldmarkt~ 1779
titel, Hypotheken~ 1792
titel, Renten~ 162
titel, Schuld~ 609
Titel, zentralbankfähige ~ 1776
Tochtergesellschaft 98
Totalbetrag 107
total, Bilanz~ 276
Totalschaden 934
Totalsumme 105
Totalverlust 934
tote Hand 1795
totes Kapital 1502
tragen, einen Verlust ~ 333
tragen, X Prozent Zinsen ~ 334
träger, Kosten~ 818
träger, Überweisungs~ 848
Tranche 1572
Transaktion 320
transaktion, Abzahlungs~ 1489
transaktion, Bar~ 581
transaktion, Devisenkassa~ 2202
transaktionen, Auslands~ 1358
transaktionen, Bank~ 304
transaktionen, Börsen~ 1222
transaktionen, Devisen~ 1241
transaktionen, Effekten~ 1222
transaktionen, Kredit~ 851
Transaktionen mit dem Ausland 1358
transaktionen, Wertpapier~ 1222
transaktion, Kassa~ 581
transaktion, Kassen~ 581
transaktion, Komptant~ 581
transaktion, Kontant~ 581
transaktion, Teilzahlungs~ 1489
transferabel 117
transferable Pfunde 2291
transferfähig 117
Transferfähigkeit 116
Transfergebühr 812
transferierbar 117
Transferierbarkeit 116
transferieren 2080
Transferierung 1784
transferierung, Kapital~ 563
Transfer ins Ausland 1372
transfer, Kapital~ 563
Transferkosten 812
Transferspesen 812
Transferzahlung 2293
Transithandel 2294
transitorische Passiva 39
Transportkosten 2295
Trassant 1118
Trassat 1117
trassieren, auf jemanden ~ 1114
Tratte 356
Tratte, ausländische ~ 1357
tratte, Auslands~ 1357
tratte, Bank~ 284
Tratte, inländische ~ 1091
tratte, Inlands~ 1091
tratte, Rück~ 819
tratte, Sicht~ 1003
Travellerscheck 2297
Trefferanleihe 1720
treiberei, Kurs~ 1730
Trend 1200
Tresor 2122, 2125
Tresorfach 2123

Tresorraum 2125
treuen Händen, zu ~ 1185
Treugut 2308
Treuhänder 1298
treuhänderisch 1185
treuhänderischer Verwahrung, in ~ 1185
Treuhänderkonto 2305
Treuhändervertrag 976
Treuhandfonds 2307
Treuhandgelder 2307
Treuhandgesellschaft 2306
Treuhandgut 2308
Treuhandvermögen 2308
Treuhandvertrag 976
Trust 2304
trust, Anlage~ 653
trust, Investment~ 653

Überangebot 1210
Überangebot an Geld 6
überbewerten 1863
Überbewertung 1864
Überbietung 1484
Überbringer 337
Überbrückungsfinanzierung 433
Überbrückungskredit 434
Überdeckung der Kosten 1870
überdisponieren, ein Konto ~ 1868
Überdisposition 1867
Überdividende 398
übereignen 118
Übereignung 119
übereinkommen, Stillhalte~ 2216
Übereinstimmung bringen, Konten in ~ 112
überfällig 1869
überfälliger Wechsel 365
überfluss, Geld~ 6
überfordern 1866
Übergabe des Kupons, gegen ~ 1958
Übergangskonto 2248
Übergebot 1484
Übergewinn 1213
Übergewinnsteuer 1214
Überhang 1204
überhang, Ausgaben~ 1212
überhang, Einnahme(n)~ 2245
überhang, Geld~ 6
überhang, Kaufkraft~ 1209
überhang, Nachfrage~ 1206, 1557
überhang, Spar~ 1872
Überhitzung 1871
Überkapitalisation 1865
Überkapitalisierung 1865
überlassen 118
Überlassung 119
Überliquidität 1211
Überlohn 1288
übermachen 2080
übermässiger Preis 1250
übermässig hoher Preis 1250
Übernahme 2257
Übernahmeabkommen 2321
Übernahmekonsortium 2322
Übernahmevertrag 2321
übernehmen 2233
übernehmen, die Unterbringung einer Emission ~ 2320
Übernehmer 120
Überpreis 1208
übersättigen, den Markt (mit billigen Artikeln) ~ 1132
überschätzen 1863
Überschätzung 1864
überschiessender Betrag 1205
überschiessende Summe 1205
Überschlag 176
überschlagen 177
Überschlag, roher ~ 184
Überschlag, ungefährer ~ 184
überschreiten, einen Kredit ~ 1201
überschreiten, ein Konto ~ 1868
Überschreitung 1867
überschuldet sein 953
Überschuldung 1207
Überschuss 1204, 2244
überschuss, Aktiv~ 1809
überschuss, Ausgaben~ 1212
überschuss, Aussenhandels~ 266
überschuss, Betriebs~ 1852
überschuss, Budget~ 452
überschuss, Einnahme(n)~ 2245
überschuss, Etats~ 452
überschuss, Geld~ 6
überschuss, Handels~ 266
überschuss, Handelsbilanz~ 266
überschuss, Haushalts~ 452
überschüssige Kaufkraft 1209
überschüssiges Einkommen 2245
überschuss, Kassen~ 599
Überschussland 824
überschuss, Rechnungs~ 30
überschuss, Spar~ 1872
Überschuss, struktureller ~ 2229
überschuss, Zahlungsbilanz~ 263
überschwemmen, den Markt (mit billigen Artikeln) ~ 1132
Überseehandel 1283
überseeischer Handel 1283
übersenden 2080
Übersender 2083
Übersendung 1784
Übersicht 2217
übersicht, Finanz~ 1319
übersicht, Jahres~ 160
Übersicht, zusammenfassende ~ 2241
Überstunden 1875
übertaxieren 1863
Übertaxierung 1864
überteuern 1866
Übertrag auf neue Rechnung 150
übertragbar 117
übertragbare Effekten 1739
übertragbarer Wechsel 374
übertragbares Papier 1806
übertragbare Wertpapiere 1739
Übertragbarkeit 116
übertragen 118, 435
übertragen, auf das Aktivkonto ~ 403
übertragen, auf das Passivkonto ~ 402
Übertragender 121, 1165
übertragen, eine Forderung ~ 207
übertragen, einen Wechsel ~ 1162
Übertragung 119
Übertragung ins Ausland 1372
übertragung, Kapital~ 563
Übertragungsbilanz 267
Übertragungseinkommen 2292
Übertragungsgebühr 812
Übertragungsspesen 812
Übertragungsvermerk 1164
Übertragung von Forderungen 208
überwachung, Devisen~ 1224
überwachung, Kredit~ 629
überwachung, Preis~ 1961
überweisen 2080
Überweisender 2083
überweisen, der Reserve ~ 68
Überweisung 318
überweisung, Bank~ 318
überweisung, Bar~ 595
überweisung, Geld~ 1784
Überweisung in bar 595
Überweisungsanzeige 848
Überweisungsempfänger 2082
Überweisungsgebühr 2081
Überweisungsträger 848
Überwert 1215
überwerten 1863
Überwertung 1864
überzeichnen 1873
Überzeichnung 1874
überziehen, einen Kredit ~ 1201
überziehen, ein Konto ~ 1868
Überziehung 1867
Überziehungskredit 87, 379
Überzugskredit 87
üblichem Vorbehalt, unter ~ 2099
üblichen Vorbehalten, unter den ~ 2099
Umbruch 428
Umbuchung 281
umfang, Geschäfts~ 2130
umgehung, Steuer~ 2266
Umlage 1135
umlauf, Banknoten~ 308
umlauf, Bargeld~ 638
Umlauf befindliche Noten, im ~ 308
Umlauf befindliche Noten und Münzen, im ~ 638
Umlauf befindliches Geld, im ~ 914
Umlauf (befindlich), im ~ 635
Umlauf, fiduziärer ~ 1299
Umlauf, fiduziarischer ~ 1299
umlauf, Geld~ 637
Umlaufkredit 2114
umlauf, Noten~ 308
umlauf, Papiergeld~ 1299
Umlauf setzen, ausser ~ 503
Umlauf(s)geschwindigkeit 2027
Umlauf(s)kapital 468
Umlauf(s)mittel 468, 636
Umlauf(s)vermögen 468
Umlauf(s)zeit 895
umlauf, Zahlungsmittel~ 638
Umlauf zurückziehen, aus dem ~ 503
umlauf, Zwangs~ 1356
Umrechnung 771

Umrechnungsfaktor 772
Umrechnungskurs 778
umrechnungskurs, Zwangs~ 722
Umrechnungsmünze 1780
Umrechnungssatz 778
Umsatz 2130
Umsatzabgabe 2014
Umsatz an der Börse 2225
umsatz, Brutto~ 1467
umsatz, Geschäfts~ 2130
Umsatzindex 2131
umsatz, Netto~ 1816
umsatz, Rein~ 1816
Umsatzrentabilität 1815
Umsatzsteuer 2014
umschlag, Debitoren~ 960
umschlag, Forderungs~ 960
umschreiben 118
Umschreibung 119
Umschreibungsgebühr 812
umschulden, eine Anleihe ~ 779
Umschuldung 737, 776
Umschuldung einer Anleihe 775
Umschuldungsanleihe 738, 774
Umschwung 428
umsetzbar 1738
umsetzen, in Geld ~ 785
Umsetzung in Geld 773
umstellung, Währungs~ 899
Umtausch 771
umtausch, Aktien~ 1232
umtausch, Geld~ 1231
Umtauschrecht 777
Umtauschschuldverschreibung 704
Umtausch von Effekten 2254
Umverteilung 2060
umwandelbar 782
Umwandelbarkeit 780
umwandeln, in Bargeld ~ 785
Umwandlung 771
Umwandlung in Bargeld 773
umwandlung, Schuld~ 776
Umwandlungskurs 778
Umwandlungsrecht 777
Umwandlungssatz 778
unaufhaltsame Inflation 1411
unausgeglichener Posten 2312
Unausgeglichenheit 1062
unausgeschütteter Reingewinn 2108
unbegebbarer Wechsel 371
unbeglichene Rechnung 1846
unbelebt 508
Unbelebtheit 1130
unbeschränkte Haftpflicht 2329
unbeschränkte Haftung 2329
unbeschränkt haftender Gesellschafter 1419
unbesichert 835
unbesicherte Obligation 2331
unbesicherte Schuldverschreibung 2331
unbeständige Währung 1350
unbewegliche Güter 1508
unbewegliche Habe 1508
unbewegliches Eigentum 1508
unbewegliches Vermögen 1508
unbezahlter Betrag 154
Undkonto 1649
uneinbringliche Forderung 242
uneingelöster Wechsel 365
uneinträglich 2324
unergiebig 2324
unfundierte Schuld 1351
unfundiertes Einkommen 1136
ungebundene Wirtschaft 1393
ungedeckt 835
ungedeckte Notenausgabe 1300
ungedeckter Kredit 379
ungedeckter Scheck 241
ungedecktes Darleh(e)n 1301
ungefährer Kostenüberschlag 184
ungefährer Überschlag 184
ungefähre Schätzung 184
ungemünztes Gold und Silber 457
ungesichert 835
ungesicherte Forderung 2332
ungesicherte Obligation 2331
ungesicherter Kredit 379
ungesicherte Schuldverschreibung 2331
ungesichertes Darleh(e)n 1301
Ungleichgewicht 1062
ungünstige Aussenhandelsbilanz 94
ungünstige Handelsbilanz 94
unifizieren, eine Schuld ~ 733
unifizierte Schuld 735
Unifizierung 737
union, Europäische Zahlungs~ 1198
union, Kredit~ 787
union, Zoll~ 923
unkörperliche Wirtschaftsgüter 1505
Unkosten 1261
Unkosten, abzüglich der ~ 131, 621
unkosten, Allgemein~ 1417
Unkosten, allgemeine ~ 1417
Unkostenaufstellung 2218
unkosten, Betriebs~ 1850
Unkosten, diverse ~ 1764
Unkosten, feste ~ 1336
unkosten, General~ 1417
unkosten, Geschäfts~ 472
unkosten, Handlungs~ 1417
Unkosten, kleine ~ 1764
Unkostenkonto 1259
unkosten, Kredit~ 805
Unkosten, laufende ~ 908
Unkosten, nach Abrechnung der ~ 131
Unkosten, nach Abzug der ~ 131
unkosten, Reise~ 2298
Unkosten, sonstige ~ 1764
Unkosten, unter Abzug der ~ 621
Unkosten, verschiedene ~ 1764
Unkosten, zusätzliche ~ 61
unkündbare Obligation 1636
unkündbare Schuldverschreibung 1636
Unlust 1130
unlustig 508
unnotierte Effekten 892
unnotierter Markt 891
unnotierte Wertpapiere 892
unproduktives Kapital 1502
unrentabel 2324
unsachgemässe Verteilung von Mitteln 1763
unsaldierte Rechnung 1846
unsichtbare Ausfuhr(en) 1632
unsichtbare Einfuhr(en) 1633
unsichtbare Exporte 1632
unsichtbare Importe 1633
unsichtbare Inflation 725
unsichtbare Reserven 726
unterbewerten 2319
Unterbewertung 2318
unterbieten 2317
Unterbilanz 274, 988
unterbringen, eine Anleihe ~ 1933
unterbringen, eine Emission ~ 1934
Unterbringung 1935
Unterbringung einer Emission garantieren, die ~ 2320
Unterbringung einer Emission übernehmen, die ~ 2320
Unterhaltsaufwand 810
Unterhaltskosten 810
Unterhaltungsaufwand 810
Unterhaltungskosten 810
Unterkapitalisation 2315
Unterkapitalisierung 2315
Unterkonto 224
Unterlage 2358
Unternehmen 467
Unternehmen, gemeinnütziges ~ 2009
Unternehmen, gemeinwirtschaftliches ~ 2009
Unternehmen, öffentliches ~ 1448
unternehmen, Privat~ 1977
Unternehmen, staatliches ~ 1448
unternehmen, Staats~ 1448
Unternehmer 1171
Unternehmertum, privates ~ 1976
Unternehmung 467
Unternehmung, gemeinnützige ~ 2009
Unternehmung, öffentliche ~ 1448
unternehmung, Privat~ 1977
Unternehmungsfreiheit 1391
Unternehmung, staatliche ~ 1448
Unterpfand 1138
Unterpfand geben, als ~ 1018
unterschätzen 2319
Unterschätzung 2318
Unterschied 1037, 1067
unterschied, Preis~ 1038
Unterschied teilen, sich in den ~ 2201
unterschlagen 977
Unterschlagung 978
Unterschleif 978
unterstützen, durch Subsidien ~ 2240
unterstützen, durch Zuschüsse ~ 2240
unterstützung, Preis~ 1917
Unterstützung, staatliche ~ 1445
unterstützung, Staats~ 1445
untersuchung, Markt~ 1740
unterwerfen, einer Steuer ~ 194
untilgbare Obligation 1636
untilgbare Schuldverschreibung 1636
unübertragbarer Wechsel 371
unverteilte Gewinne 2311

unverteilter Reingewinn 2311
unverzinsbar 1590
unverzinslich 1590
unvorhergesehene Ausgaben 754
unvorhergesehene Belastungen 754
unwirtschaftlich 2324
urkunde, Bürgschafts~ 394
urkunde, Darleh(e)ns~ 1709
urkunde, Schuld~ 609
Usance 2333
Usancekurs 884
Usanz 2333
Uso 2333
Usowechsel 358

vagabundierendes Kapital 1498
Valoren 2151
Valorisation 2338
valorisieren 2339
Valorisierung 2338
Valuta 893, 1361, 2343
Valutaabwertung 897
Valutaentwertung 896
Valutageschäfte 1241
Valutagewinn 1233
Valutaguthaben 1362
Valuta in Gold 1442
Valutakurs 1216
valuta, Landes~ 1094
Valuta (per) 1 Januar 2342
Valutarisiko 1238
Valutenarbitrage 186
Valutengewinn 1233
Valutenguthaben 1362
Valutenhändler 509
Valutenkurs 1216
Valutenmakler 509
Valutierungstag 2343
variable Abschreibung 2347
variable Kosten 2346
variabler Wechselkurs 1347
veränderlicher Wechselkurs 1347
veränderliche Währung 1350
veranlagen 195
Veranlagung 200
veranlagungspflichtig 196
Veranlagung, vorläufige ~ 2000
veranschlagen 177
Veranschlagung 176
verauktionieren 213
Verauktionierung 212
verausgaben 1257
Verausgabung 1258
verauslagen 1050
Veräusserer 121, 2159
veräusserlich 117, 1738
Veräusserlichkeit 116
veräussern 118, 2157
Veräusserung 119
Veräusserungsgewinn 531
Veräusserungsverlust 553
verband, Zoll~ 923
Verbindlichkeiten 961
verbindlichkeiten, Indossament~ 1166
verbindlichkeiten, Kontokorrent~ 1023
Verbindlichkeiten, kurzfristige ~ 910
Verbindlichkeiten, laufende ~ 910
Verbindlichkeiten, noch nicht fällige ~ 1825
verbindlichkeiten, Sicht~ 1006
verbindlichkeit, Eventual~ 758
verbindlichkeit, Steuer~ 2271
verbleibender Betrag 246
verbleibender Schuldbetrag 252
verborgen 1671
verbot, Einfuhr~ 319
Verbrauch 751
verbrauch, Eigen~ 1092, 1497
Verbraucher 744
Verbraucheraufwand 748
Verbraucheraufwendung 748
Verbraucherausgaben 748
Verbraucherkredit 745
Verbraucherpreis 749
Verbraucherzurückhaltung 750
Verbrauch, inländischer ~ 1092
verbrauch, Inlands~ 1092
Verbrauch, innerer ~ 1092
Verbrauch je Einwohner 1920
Verbrauch, öffentlicher ~ 2002
Verbrauch, privater ~ 1499
verbrauch, Prokopf~ 1920
Verbrauch pro Kopf (der Bevölkerung) 1920
Verbrauchsabgabe 752
Verbrauchsaufwand 748
Verbrauchsaufwendung 748
Verbrauchsausgaben 748
verbrauch, Selbst~ 1497
Verbrauchsgüter 743
Verbrauchsnachfrage 746
Verbrauchssteuer 752
verbriefte Forderung 391
verbriefte Schuld 391
verbuchen 401
Verbuchung 409
verbürgen, sich ~ 52
verdeckte Gewinnausschüttung 1482
Verdienst 229, 1140, 1141
Verdienstausfall 1718
Verdiensteinbusse 1718
Verdienstentgang 1718
verdienst, Neben~ 64
Verdienstspanne 1734
verdienstspanne, Netto~ 1813
vereinbaren, einen Preis ~ 113
vereinbarter Preis 114
vereinbarung, Preis~ 115
vereinbarung, Stand-by-Kredit~ 2215
vereinbarung, Stillhalte~ 2216
Verein, gemeinnütziger ~ 1829
verein, Ideal~ 1829
Verein, idealer ~ 1829
verein, Kredit~ 787
Verein mit Erwerbszweck 1986
Verein mit Gewinn(erzielungs)-absicht 1986
Verein mit Gewinnzweck 1986
Verein, nichtwirtschaftlicher ~ 1829
Verein ohne Erwerbszweck 1829
Verein ohne Gewinn(erzielungs)absicht 1829
Verein ohne Gewinnzweck 1829
verein, Zoll~ 923
Verfall 968, 1748
Verfall, bei ~ 1128
Verfallbuch 359
Verfalldatum 931
verfallen 347, 1126, 1264
verfallene Dividende 1954
verfall, Preis~ 886
Verfall(s)tag 931
Verfall(s)termin 931
Verfall(s)zeit 894, 1748
Verfall(s)zeit, zur ~ 1128
verfall, Währungs~ 896
verfälschung, Münz~ 939
verflüssigen 785
Verflüssigung 773, 1538
verfügbare Mittel 227
verfügbares Einkommen 1068
Verfügbarkeit von Kapital 226
Verfügbarkeit von Kapitalien 226
Verfügung stellen, Kapital zur ~ 1407
vergelten 2042
Vergeltung 2041
vergesellschaften 1802
Vergesellschaftung 1801
Vergleich 718
Vergleichsabkommen 719
Vergleichsvertrag 719
Vergünstigungstarif 1947
vergünstigung, Steuer~ 2263
Vergünstigungszoll 1949
vergüten 2042
vergüten, einen Verlust ~ 707
Vergütung 708, 2041
vergütung, Extra~ 1284
vergütung, Natural~ 134
vergütung, Neben~ 1284
vergütung, Reise~ 2296
vergütung, Reisekosten~ 2296
vergütung, Sonder~ 1284
vergütung, Steuer~ 2038
vergütung, Zins~ 1594
vergütung, Zinsen~ 1594
Vergütung, zusätzliche ~ 1284
Verhältnis 2029
verhältnis, Austauschpreis~ 2279
verhältnis, Ertragspreis~ 1963
verhältnis, Flüssigkeits~ 45
Verhältnis, Fremdkapital/Eigenkapital-~ 963
verhältnis, Kursertrags(kraft)~ 1963
verhältnis, Kursgewinn~ 1963
verhältnis, Liquiditäts~ 45
verhältnis, Paritäts~ 1888
verhältnis, Preisertrags~ 1963
verhältnis(se), Austausch~ 2279
verhältnisse, Kurs~ 1236
Verhältnisse leben, über seine ~ 1702
Verhältnissen entsprechend leben, seinen ~ 1703
verhältnisse, Wechselkurs~ 1236
Verhältnis, Verschuldungs/Eigenkapital-~ 963

verhältnisziffer, Liquiditäts~ 45
verjährter Kupon 1664
verjährte Schuld 324
Verjährung 1955
Verkauf 2127
verkauf, Abzahlungs~ 1491
Verkauf anbieten, zum ~ 1841
Verkauf auf Kredit 875
verkauf, Bar~ 598
verkauf, Blanko~ 346
Verkauf bringen, zum ~ 1841
Verkauf durch Versteigerung 212
Verkäufe 2130
verkaufen 2157
verkaufen, auf Kredit ~ 2163
verkaufen, auf Lieferung ~ 2161
verkaufen, auf Termin ~ 2161
verkaufen, auf Zeit ~ 2161
verkaufen, auf Ziel ~ 2161
verkaufen, blanko ~ 1427
verkaufen, leer ~ 1427
verkaufen, mit Schaden ~ 2158
verkaufen, mit Verlust ~ 2158
Verkäufer 2159
Verkäufermarkt 2160
Verkauf im Wege der Versteigerung 212
verkauf (ins Ausland), Schleuder~ 1131
verkauf, Kassa~ 598
verkauf, Kredit~ 875
verkauf, Leer~ 346
verkäuflich 1738
Verkauf mit dem Recht des Nachlieferns 1857
Verkauf mit einmal noch 1857
Verkauf mit Schaden 2129
Verkauf mit Verlust 2129
verkauf, Schleuder~ 2129
verkaufsfähig 1738
Verkaufskurs 193
Verkaufsoption 1858
Verkaufspreis 2162
Verkaufswert 688
verkauf, Teilzahlungs~ 1491
verkehr, Abrechnungs~ 643
verkehr, Clearing~ 643
verkehr, Dreiecks~ 2280
verkehr, Frei~ 891
verkehr, Giro~ 643
verkehr, Kapital~ 555
verkehr, Kompensations~ 643
verkehr, Scheck~ 632
verkehrsfähige Effekten 1739
verkehrsfähige Wertpapiere 1739
Verkehrssteuer 812
Verkehrswert 688, 912
verkehr, Verrechnungs~ 643
verkehr, Zahlungs~ 1911
Verkehr ziehen, aus dem ~ 502
verknappung, Kapital~ 559
verknappung, Kredit~ 874
verknappung, Liquiditäts~ 2104
Verlangen, auf ~ 495
verlängern, die Zahlungsfrist ~ 1274
verlängern, eine Frist ~ 1273
verlängern, einen Kredit ~ 1272
Verlängerung 1994
verlängerung, Kredit~ 1275
Verlängerungsstück 124
verlängerung, Zahlungsfrist~ 1276
verlauf, Konjunktur~ 477
verlegenheit, Geld~ 1314
verleihen 1671
verleihen, Geld auf (gegen) Zinsen ~ 1675
Verleiher 1672
verleiher, Geld~ 1777
verlieren, an Wert ~ 970
verlosbar 498
verlosen 1112
Verlosung 1111
Verlust 1717
Verlustabzug 2273
Verlust, abzugfähiger ~ 974
Verlust auffangen, einen ~ 3
Verlust ausgleichen, einen ~ 707
verlust, Betriebs~ 474
Verlustbilanz 274
verlust, Brutto~ 1464
verlust, Buch~ 411
Verlust, buchmässiger ~ 411
Verlust decken, einen ~ 707
Verlust (einen Gewinn) aufweisen, einen ~ 2046
Verlust (einen Gewinn) ausweisen, einen ~ 2046
Verlust (einen Gewinn) verzeichnen, einen ~ 2046
Verlust erfahren, einen ~ 333
Verlust erleiden, einen ~ 333
Verlust ersetzen, einen ~ 707
verlust, Gesamt~ 934
verlust, Geschäfts~ 474
Verlust gutmachen, einen ~ 707
verlust, Kapital~ 552
verlust, Kurs~ 1229
verlust, Liquidations~ 553
Verlust machen, einen ~ 333
verlust, Netto~ 651
verlust, Rein~ 651
verlust, Roh~ 1464
Verlustrücktrag 2272
Verlustsaldo 93
verlust, Total~ 934
Verlust tragen, einen ~ 333
verlust, Veräusserungs~ 553
Verlust vergüten, einen ~ 707
Verlustverkauf 2129
Verlust verkaufen, mit ~ 2158
verlust, Wert~ 969
Verlust wettmachen, einen ~ 707
Verlust wiedereinbringen, einen ~ 707
Verlust wiedergutmachen, einen ~ 707
Verlust zurückziehen, sich mit ~ 928
Vermächtnissteuer 938
Vermarktung 1742
vermehren, das Kapital ~ 1544
Vermehrung des Geldvolumens 1252
vermerk, Übertragungs~ 1164
Vermieter 1676
vermietung, Ausrüstungs~ 1668
vermindern, die Ausgaben ~ 915
verminderung, Kapital~ 2063
verminderung, Wert~ 969
vermitteln, eine Anleihe ~ 1807
vermittler, Geld~ 1311
Vermittlungsgebühr 689
Vermögen 1406
Vermögen, abschreibungsfähiges ~ 1027
vermögen, Aktiv~ 202
vermögen, Anlage~ 518, 1622
vermögen, Auslands~ 204
vermögen, Bar~ 577
Vermögen, bewegliches ~ 622
vermögen, Eigen~ 558, 1809, 1996
vermögen, Geschäfts~ 468
vermögen, Gesellschafts~ 790
vermögen, Grund~ 1661
vermögen, Grundstücks~ 1661
vermögen, Immobiliar~ 1508
vermögen, Kapital~ 518
vermögen, Mobiliar~ 622
vermögen, National~ 1804
vermögen, Netto~ 1809
vermögen, Rein~ 1809
Vermögensabgabe 551
Vermögensbildung 1373
Vermögensgegenstände 202
Vermögenssteuer 551
Vermögensverteilung 1073, 1074
Vermögenswerte, greifbare ~ 1747
Vermögenswerte im Ausland 204
Vermögenswerte, immateriale ~ 1505
Vermögenswerte, materielle ~ 1747
Vermögenswerte, nicht greifbare ~ 1505
vermögenswirksame Ausgaben 524
vermögen, Treuhand~ 2308
vermögen, Umlauf(s)~ 468
Vermögen, unbewegliches ~ 1508
vermögen, Volks~ 1804
vermögen, Wachstums~ 1469
Verpächter 1676
verpachtung, Anlage~ 1668
verpfänden 1018, 1791
verpfänden, Effekten ~ 671
verpfändete Effekten 1895
verpfändeter Wechsel 363
Verpfändung von Effekten 1501
verpflichteter, Wechsel~ 362
Verpflichtung 692
verpflichtung, Devisen~ 1223
Verpflichtungen 961
verpflichtungen, Kontokorrent~ 1023
Verpflichtungen, kurzfristige ~ 910
Verpflichtungen, laufende ~ 910
Verpflichtungen, noch nicht fällige ~ 1825
verpflichtungen, Sicht~ 1006
verpflichtung, Eventual~ 758
verpflichtungsschein, Garantie~ 394
verpflichtung, Steuer~ 1683, 2271
verrechnen 615, 706
verrechnen, einen Scheck ~ 641
Verrechnung 613, 642, 709
Verrechnungsabkommen 647
verrechnung, Scheck~ 627

Verrechnungsdollar 29
Verrechnungsgeschäfte 643
Verrechnungsguthaben 269
Verrechnungskammer 649
Verrechnungskonto 644
Verrechnungssaldo 269
Verrechnungsscheck 883
Verrechnungsspitze 269
Verrechnungsstelle 649
Verrechnungssteuer 565
Verrechnungsverkehr 643
Verrechnungsvertrag 647
Verrichtung 320
verringern, die Ausgaben ~ 915
verringerung, Münz~ 939
verringerung, Wert~ 969
verschaffen, Kapital ~ 1407
verschieben, eine Zahlung ~ 984
Verschiedene 1764
verschiedene Ausgaben 1764
verschiedene Unkosten 1764
verschlechterung, Münz~ 939
verschlechterung, Währungs~ 896
verschlechterung, Wert~ 969
Verschleiss 2367
verschleudern 2158
Verschleuderung 2129
Verschleuderung (im Ausland) 1131
Verschmelzung 135
verschreibung, Schuld~ 1477
verschulden, sich ~ 1294
verschuldet 952
Verschuldung 462
verschuldung, Auslands~ 420
Verschuldung, öffentliche ~ 1798
Verschuldungs/Eigenkapital-Verhältnis 963
Verschuldungsgrenze 422
verschuldung, Staats~ 1798
versetzen 1018
Versicherung 1576
versicherung, Kredit~ 863
versicherung, Lebens~ 1688
Versicherungsmathematiker 58
versicherung, Sozial~ 2184
Versicherungspolice 1577
Versicherungspolizze 1577
Versicherungsprämie 1578
Versicherungsschein 1577
Versicherungsstatistiker 58
versilbern 785
Versilberung 773
versorgung, Geld~ 1783
Versorgungsbetrieb, öffentlicher ~ 2009
Versorgungsunternehmen, öffentliches ~ 2009
versprechen, Schuld~ 1477
verstaatlichen 1802
Verstaatlichung 1801
Verständigung 718
Verstärkung der Kapitalintensität 537
versteckte Inflation 725
versteckte Reserven 726
versteigern 213
Versteigerung 212
Versteigerung verkaufen, im Wege der ~ 213
Versteuerungswert 198
verstreichen 1264
verteilen 122
verteilen, eine Dividende ~ 1051
verteilen, Zahlungen auf (über) X Jahre ~ 2204
Verteilung 123
verteilung, Dividenden~ 1052
verteilung, Gewinn~ 183
Verteilungssektor 1075
verteilung, Vermögens~ 1073, 1074
Verteilung von Mitteln, unsachgemässe ~ 1763
Verteuerung 1539
verteuerung, Lebens~ 1483
vertikale Preisbindung 2097
Vertikalinvestierung 1580
Vertikalinvestition 1580
vertrag, Giro~ 647
vertragliche Haftpflicht 763
vertragliche Haftung 763
vertrag, Miet~ 1666
vertrag, Pacht~ 1666
Vertragshaftung 763
Vertragspreis 114
Vertragssparen 764
vertrag, Treuhand~ 976
vertrag, Treuhänder~ 976
vertrag, Übernahme~ 2321
vertrag, Vergleichs~ 719
vertrag, Verrechnungs~ 647
Vertreter 104
vertreter, Kommissions~ 690
Vertretung 103
veruntreuen 977
Veruntreuung 978
Verwahrer 1017
Verwahrkonto 2248
Verwahrung, in treuhänderischer ~ 1185
Verwalter der Konkursmasse 209
verwalter, Konkurs~ 209
verwalter, Masse(n)~ 209
verwalter, Zwangs~ 209
verwaltung, Finanz~ 1242
verwaltung, Konkurs~ 2040
verwaltung, Schulden~ 954
Verwaltungsgebühr 80
Verwaltungskosten 79
verwaltung, Steuer~ 1242
verwaltung, Zwangs~ 2040
verwässertes Aktienkapital 2365
Verwässerung des Aktienkapitals 2226
verweigerung, Zahlungs~ 2074
verwendung, Gewinn~ 183
verwendung, Kapital~ 1160
Verwendung von Krediten 228
verwertbar 2034
verwertbare Aktiven 905
Verwertbarkeit 2033
verwerten 785
Verwertung 773
verzeichnen, einen Rückgang (einen Gewinn) von X Punkten ~ 2045
verzeichnen, einen Verlust (einen Gewinn) ~ 2046
verzeichnis, Aktionär(s)~ 1701
Verzeichnis der Aktionäre 1701
verzeichnis, Mitglieder~ 1701
verzinsbar 1586
verzinsen, sich mit (zu) X Prozent ~ 334
verzinslich 1586
verzinslich sein, mit X vom Hundert ~ 334
Verzinsung 1592, 1593, 1595, 2110
verzinsung, Effektiv~ 57
verzinsung, Kapital~ 535, 540
verzinsung, Zinsen~ 156
verzögern, eine Zahlung ~ 984
verzögerung, Zahlungs~ 999
verzollbar 916
Verzollung 645
Verzug, im ~ 979
Verzugszinsen 983
verzug, Zahlungs~ 999
Vierteljahr 2016
vinkulierte Aktie 2282
Vistawechsel 1003
Volkseinkommen 1799
Volksvermögen 1804
Volkswirtschaft 1151
volkswirtschaftliche Gesamtrechnung 1579, 1797
Volkswirtschaftslehre 1151
Vollaktien 1403
voll begleichen 1905
voll bezahlen 1905
Vollbezahlung 715
voll eingezahlte Aktien 1403
Volleinzahlung einer Aktie 1908
Vollhafter 1419
Vollkostenkalkulation 4
Vollkostenrechnung 4
vollständige Auszahlung 715
vollständige Bezahlung 715
vollständige Zahlung 715
voll zahlen 1905
Vollzahlung 715
volumen, Bilanz~ 276
volumen, Geld~ 1783
volumen, Geschäfts~ 2130
volumen, Handels~ 2354
volumen, Kredit~ 881
volumen, Spar~ 2353
vom Hundert 1922
Vomhundertsatz 1921
Vorabzug 89
Voranmeldung 2000
Voranschlag 441, 1187
voranschläge, Haushalts~ 449
voranschlag, Kosten~ 1187
voraus abrechnen, im ~ 973
voraus abziehen, im ~ 973
Vorausabzug 89
vorausbezahlen 1904
Vorausbezahlung 92
vorausdatieren 164
vorausschätzungen, Haushalts~ 451
vorauszahlen 1904
voraus zahlen, im ~ 1904
Vorauszahlung 92

Vorauszinsen 165
vorbehaltlich des richtigen Einganges 2099
Vorbehalt, unter ~ 2099
Vorbörse 937
vordatieren 164, 1942
Vordermann 1944
vorfinanzieren 1951
Vorfinanzierung 1952
vorgeschriebener Preis 78
Vorgirant 1944
vorhergehender Indossant 1944
vorher kündigen, X Tage ~ 1426
Vorindossant 1944
Vorkalkulation 1190
vorkalkulierte Kosten 1189
Vorkaufsrecht 2013
Vorkommen, bei ~ 1956
Vorlage, bei ~ 1956
vorläufige Steuererklärung 2000
vorläufige Veranlagung 2000
vorläufige Zahlung 1999
Vorleger 337
vorlegung, Bilanz~ 1957
vorleisten 1904
Vorleistung 92
Vormann 1944
vornehmen, das Inventar ~ 1124
Vorpfändung beim Drittschuldner 1414
Vorprämie 507
vorrangiger Gläubiger 1948
Vorrangsgläubiger 1948
Vorrat 1615
vorrat, Bar~ 587
vorrat, Geld~ 587, 597, 1783
vorrat, Gold~ 1430
vorrat, Gold- und Devisen~ 1429
Vorrecht 1328
Vorrechtsaktie 1946
vorschiessen 85
vorschreiben, einen Preis ~ 1033
vorschriften, Devisen~ 900
vorschriften, Devisenbewirtschaftungs~ 900
Vorschuss 83
Vorschuss auf laufender Rechnung 87
vorschuss, Bank~ 298
Vorschuss, garantierter ~ 86
Vorschuss, gedeckter ~ 86
Vorschuss gegen Pfand 86
Vorschuss gegen Sicherheit 86
Vorschuss, gesicherter ~ 86
vorschuss, Lombard~ 90
vorschuss, Notenbank~ 1708
vorschussweise 84
Vorschusszahlung 83
vorstrecken 85
vorteil, Steuer~ 2263
Vortrag auf neue Rechnung 150
vortragen 435
vortragen, zu Lasten eines Kontos ~ 618
vortrag, Gewinn~ 1985
vorweg abrechnen 973
vorweg abziehen 973
Vorwegabzug 89
Vorzeiger 337
Vorzeigung, bei ~ 1956
Vorzeigung, gegen ~ 1956
vorzeitiger Rückkauf 167
vorzeitige Rückzahlung 167
vorzeitige Zahlung 92
Vorzugsaktie 1946
Vorzugsaktie mit Gewinnbeteiligung 1891
Vorzugsaktie mit Teilhaberschaft am Gewinn 1891
Vorzugsaktien, kumulative ~ 890
Vorzugsaktien mit Nachbezugsrecht 890
Vorzugsaktien, nachzugsberechtigte ~ 890
Vorzugsdividende 1945
Vorzugsgläubiger 1948
Vorzugspreis 1203
Vorzugsrecht 1328
Vorzugstarif 1947
Vorzugstarif für Mitglieder des Commonwealths 702
Vorzugsumrechnungskurs 1950
Vorzugszoll 1949
Vostrokonto 1716

Wachstum der Geldversorgung 1252
Wachstumsbereich 1470
Wachstumsbranche 1470
Wachstumspotential 1469
Wachstumsrate 1255
Wachstumssektor 1470
Wachstumsvermögen 1469
Wägung 2371
Wägungskoeffizient 2372
Wahlrecht 1854
Währung 893
Währung, ausländische ~ 1361
Währung, beständige ~ 2207
währung, Doppel~ 375
Währung, eigene ~ 1094
Währung, einfache ~ 1785
Währung, einheimische ~ 1094
währung, Einzel~ 1785
Währung, feste ~ 1479
Währung, floatende ~ 1350
währung, Fremd~ 1361
Währung, fremde ~ 1361
Währung, gesetzliche ~ 1669
Währung, gesunde ~ 2191
währung, Gold~ 1441
währung, Goldbarren~ 1431
währung, Gold-Devisen~ 1436
währung, Golddevisen~ 1436
währung, Goldkern~ 1431
währung, Goldkurs~ 1436
währung, Goldumlaufs~ 1402
Währung, harte ~ 1479
Währung, heimische ~ 1094
Währung, hinkende ~ 1476
Währung, hochwertige ~ 1479
Währung, inländische ~ 1094
währung, Inlands~ 1094
Währung, kontrollierte ~ 767
Währung, labile ~ 1350
währung, Landes~ 1094
Währung, manipulierte ~ 767
währung, Papier~ 1355, 1881
Währung, regulierte ~ 767
währung, Reserve~ 2100
Währungsabwertung 897
Währungsbank 309
Währungsbeistand 1771
Währung, schwache ~ 2187
Währung, schwankende ~ 1350
Währungseinheit 904
Währungsentwertung 896
Währungsgold 666
Währungsmanipulation 898
Währungsmanipulierung 898
Währungsparität 1182
Währungspolitik 1769
währungsraum, Franken~ 1388
Währungsreform 899
Währungsreserve 901
Währungsrisiko 1238
Währungsschlange 2183
Währung, stabile ~ 2207
Währung, starke ~ 1479
währung, Sterling~ 2223
Währungsumstellung 899
Währungsverfall 896
Währungsverschlechterung 896
Währungszerfall 896
Währung, unbeständige ~ 1350
Währung, veränderliche ~ 1350
Währung, weiche ~ 2187
Währung, wertbeständige ~ 2207
Währung, wertstabile ~ 2207
Wandelanleihe 784
Wandelobligation 783
Wandelschuldverschreibung 783
Wanderungsbilanz 1758
Warenakzept 2286
waren, Ausfuhr~ 1266
Warenbilanz 264
Warenbörse 695
Warendiskont 935
waren, Einfuhr~ 1510
waren, Export~ 1266
waren, Import~ 1510
Waren, in ~ 1658
Warenkredit 470, 473
waren, Luxus~ 1001
Warenmakler 694
Warenpreisindex 696
Warenrabatt 935
Warenskonto 935
Warenumsatzsteuer 2014
Waren und Dienstleistungen 1443
Waren- und Dienstleistungsbilanz 259
Waren- und Dienstleistungsverkehrs, Saldo des ~ 259
Warenwechsel 356
Warrant 2364
Wechsel 356
Wechsel akzeptieren, einen ~ 8
Wechselallonge 124
Wechselanhang 124
Wechsel annehmen, einen ~ 8
Wechselarbitrage 186, 369
Wechsel, auf den Namen lautender ~ 371
Wechsel, auf Order lautender ~ 374

Wechselausfertigung, zweite ~ 2148
Wechsel, ausländischer ~ 1357
wechsel, Auslands~ 1357
Wechsel ausstellen, auf jemanden einen ~ 1114
Wechsel avalieren, einen ~ 235
wechsel, Bank~ 284
Wechselbank 12, 1058, 1220
Wechsel, begebbarer ~ 374
Wechsel begleichen, einen ~ 1054
wechsel, Besitz~ 373
Wechsel bezahlen, einen ~ 1054
Wechsel, börsenfähiger ~ 374
Wechselbuch 359, 360
Wechselbürge 236
Wechselbürgschaft 230
Wechsel Bürgschaft leisten, einem ~ 235
Wechseldebitorenbuch 360
wechsel, Depot~ 363
wechsel, Eigen~ 1477
Wechsel, eigener ~ 1477
Wechsel einlösen, einen ~ 1054
Wechsel, einzulösender ~ 373
Wechselempfänger 1902
Wechsel, erstklassiger ~ 1323
Wechsel, fälliger ~ 372
wechsel, Finanz~ 1307
wechsel, Finanzierungs~ 1307
Wechsel, fingierter ~ 15
Wechselforderung 373
Wechselgarantie 230
Wechsel garantieren, einen ~ 235
wechsel, Gefälligkeits~ 15
wechsel, Gegen~ 819
Wechsel gegenzeichnen, einen ~ 1162
wechsel, Geld~ 1231
Wechselgeld 612, 1780
Wechselgeschäft 1221
Wechsel, gezogener ~ 356
Wechsel, girierbarer ~ 374
Wechsel girieren, einen ~ 1162
Wechselhandel 1221
wechsel, Handels~ 356
Wechsel, handelsfähiger ~ 374
Wechselhändler 361, 509
Wechsel honorieren, einen ~ 1054
Wechsel, indossabler ~ 374
Wechsel, indossierbarer ~ 374
Wechsel indossieren, einen ~ 1162
wechsel, Inkasso~ 364
wechsel, Inland~ 1091
Wechsel, inländischer ~ 1091
Wechseljournal 359, 360
Wechselkasse 1217
wechsel, Keller~ 15
wechsel, Kost~ 363
Wechselkredit 11
wechsel, Kunden~ 356
Wechselkurs 1216
Wechselkursänderung 75
Wechselkursberichtigung 75
Wechselkursdifferenz 1039
Wechselkurs, festgesetzter ~ 1341
Wechselkurs, flexibler ~ 1347
Wechselkurs, floatender ~ 1347
Wechselkurs, fluktuierender ~ 1347
Wechselkurs, freier ~ 1347
Wechselkurskorrektur 75
Wechselkursrisiko 1238
Wechselkurs, schwankender ~ 1347
Wechselkursstabilität 1239
Wechselkurs, variabler ~ 1347
Wechselkurs, veränderlicher ~ 1347
Wechselkursverhältnisse 1236
Wechselmakler 361, 509, 2152
Wechselmarkt 370, 1230
Wechsel mit Bürgschaft versehen, einen ~ 235
Wechselnehmer 1902
Wechsel, nicht auf Order lautender ~ 371
Wechsel, nicht begebbarer ~ 371
Wechsel, nicht bezahlter ~ 365
Wechsel, nicht börsenfähiger ~ 371
Wechsel, nicht eingelöster ~ 365
Wechsel, nicht handelsfähiger ~ 371
Wechsel, nicht honorierter ~ 365
Wechsel, nicht indossierbarer ~ 371
Wechsel, nicht übertragbarer ~ 371
Wechsel, notleidender ~ 365
wechsel, Order~ 374
Wechselpari 1890
Wechselparität 1182
wechsel, Pensions~ 363
wechsel, Prima~ 1327
Wechsel, prima ~ 1323
Wechselprima 1327
Wechsel protestieren, einen ~ 1481
Wechsel protestieren lassen, einen ~ 1481
wechsel, Reit~ 15
Wechselreiterei 1659
wechsel, Rekta~ 371
Wechselrembours 11
wechsel, Retour~ 819
Wechsel, retournierter ~ 365
wechsel, Rikambio~ 819
wechsel, Rück~ 819
wechsel, Schatz~ 2301
wechsel, Schein~ 15
wechsel, Schuld~ 372
Wechselschuldner 362
wechselseitige Bankguthaben 1582
wechselseitige Beteiligung 885
wechsel, Sekunda~ 2148
Wechselsekunda 2148
Wechsel, sicherungsübereigneter ~ 363
wechsel, Sicht~ 1003
wechsel, Sola~ 2180
Wechselstelle 1217
Wechselstube 1217
Wechsel, überfälliger ~ 365
Wechselübernehmer 1163
Wechsel, übertragbarer ~ 374
Wechsel übertragen, einen ~ 1162
Wechsel, unbegebbarer ~ 371
Wechsel, uneingelöster ~ 365
Wechsel, unübertragbarer ~ 371
wechsel, Uso~ 358
Wechsel, verpfändeter ~ 363
Wechselverpflichteter 362
wechsel, Vista~ 1003
wechsel, Waren~ 356
Wechsel ziehen, auf jemanden einen ~ 1114
Wechsel zum Protest geben, einen ~ 1481
Wechsel zu Protest gehen lassen, einen ~ 1481
Wechsel, zurücktrassierter ~ 365
Wechsler 509
wechsler, Geld~ 509
weiche Währung 2187
Weichwährung 2187
Weichwährungsland 2188
weise, Zahlungs~ 1375
weiterleihen 2079
Weltbank 1602
welt, Finanz~ 1305
wenig anrechnen, zu ~ 2316
wenig berechnen, zu ~ 2316
wenig fordern, zu ~ 2316
Werbepreis 1613
werfen, auf den Markt ~ 1665
Wert 1011
wert, Ablösungs~ 2055
Wertabnahme 969
Wert abnehmen, an ~ 970
Wertangabe 967
Wert, angegebener ~ 967
Wertansatz 176
wert, Anschaffungs~ 50
Wertansetzung 176
wert, Bar~ 912
Wertberechnung 176
Wertberichtigungsbuchung 71
wertbeständige Währung 2207
Wertbestimmung 176
wert, Bilanz~ 277
wert, Börsen~ 1234
wert, Brutto~ 1468
wert, Buch~ 32
Wert, deklarierter ~ 967
wert der Währung, Devisen~ 1364
Werte 2151
werte, Anlage~ 1630
werte, Auslands~ 204, 1370
werte, Bar~ 577
werte, Börsen~ 1699
wert, Effektiv~ 56
Werte, greifbare ~ 1747
Wert, eigentlicher ~ 1612
Werte, immateriale ~ 1505
Werteinbusse 969
Wert einbüssen, an ~ 970
wert eines Eigentums, Netto~ 1177
wert, Einheits~ 198, 2213
wert, Einkaufs~ 50
wert, Einlösungs~ 2055
Wert einschätzen, unter dem ~ 2319
wert, Einstands~ 50
Werte, materielle ~ 1747
werten 177
Werte, nicht greifbare ~ 1505
Wert erhöhen, den ~ 178
Werterhöhung 180
Wertermittlung 176
wert, Ersatz~ 2091
wert, Ertrags~ 546
wert, Erwerbs~ 50
werte, Spekulations~ 2199

werte, Spitzen~ 387
Wert fallen, im ~ 970
wert, Fest~ 2213
Wertfeststellung 176
wert, Firmen~ 1444
Wertgegenstände 1646
wert, Gegenwarts~ 912
wert, Gesamt~ 108
Wert gewinnen, an ~ 179
wert, Gold~ 1442
wert, Handels~ 688
Wertherabsetzung 969
Wert, innerer ~ 1612
wert, Inventar~ 1617
wert, Ist~ 56
Wert, kapitalisierter ~ 546
wert, Kauf~ 50
wert, Kosten~ 50
wert, Kurs~ 1234
wert, Liquidations~ 432
wertlose Papiere 2345
Wertlosigkeit 2344
wert, Markt~ 688
wert, Minder~ 969
Wertminderung 969
Wertminderungsreserve 132
wert, Nenn~ 1289, 1889
wert, Netto~ 1809, 1817
wert, Nominal~ 1289, 1889
Wertobjekte 1646
Wertpapieranlage 1626
Wertpapierbesitz 1628
Wertpapierbesitzer 341, 2171
Wertpapierbestand 1628
Wertpapierbörse 1218
Wertpapiere 2151
Wertpapiere, an der Börse nicht kotierte ~ 892
Wertpapiere, an der Börse nicht notierte ~ 892
Wertpapiere, an der Börse zugelassene ~ 1699
wertpapiere, Anlage~ 1630
Wertpapiere, auf (den) Namen lautende ~ 1568
Wertpapiere, begebbare ~ 1739
wertpapiere, Börsen~ 1699
Wertpapiere, börsenfähige ~ 1699, 1739
Wertpapiere, börsengängige ~ 1699
Wertpapiere, börsenmässige ~ 1699
Wertpapiere, börsennotierte ~ 1699
(Wert-)Papiere, erstklassige ~ 387
(Wert-)Papiere, goldgeränderte ~ 387
Wertpapiere, handelsfähige ~ 1739
wertpapiere, Inhaber~ 342
Wertpapiere, kotierte ~ 1699
Wertpapiere, marktfähige ~ 1739
(Wert-)Papiere, mündelsichere ~ 387
Wertpapiere, nicht notierte ~ 892
Wertpapiere, notierte ~ 1699
(Wert-)Papiere, prima ~ 387
Wertpapiere, übertragbare ~ 1739
Wertpapiere, unnotierte ~ 892
Wertpapiere, verkehrsfähige ~ 1739
Wertpapiere, zur Notierung nicht zugelassene ~ 892
Wertpapier, festverzinsliches ~ 1339
Wertpapiergeschäfte 1222
Wertpapierinhaber 341, 2171
Wertpapierkredit 869
Wertpapiermakler 2152
Wertpapiermarkt 2153
Wertpapierportefeuille 1628
Wertpapiersparen 2135
Wertpapiertransaktionen 1222
wert, Pari~ 1889
wert, Paritäts~ 1889
Wert (per) 1 Januar 2342
wert, Real~ 56
wert, Realisations~ 432
wert, Rein~ 1817
wert, Rest~ 2103
wert, Roh~ 1468
Wertrückgang 969
wert, Rückkauf~ 2247
wert, Rückkaufs~ 2055
wert, Rückzahlungs~ 2055
Wertsachen 1646
Wert schätzen, unter dem ~ 2319
Wertschätzung 176
Wertschöpfung der Industrie 2340
Wertschriften 2151
Wertschriftenbesitz 1628
Wertschriftenbestand 1628
Wertschriftenportefeuille 1628
Wert sinken, im ~ 970
wertstabile Währung 2207
wert, Standard~ 2213
Wert steigen, im ~ 179
Wert steigern, den ~ 178
Wertsteigerung 180
Wertstellung 2343
Wertstellungstermin 2343
wert, Steuer~ 198
Wert, steuerbarer ~ 198
Wert, steuerlicher ~ 198
wert, Substanz~ 432
Werttag 2343
wert, Tages~ 912
wert, Tausch~ 1219
wert, Tilgungs~ 2055
wert, Verkaufs~ 688
wert, Verkehrs~ 688, 912
Wert verlieren, an ~ 970
Wertverlust 969
Wert vermindern, sich im ~ 970
Wertverminderung 969
Wertverminderung erfahren, eine ~ 970
Wertverminderung erleiden, eine ~ 970
Wertverminderungsreserve 132
Wert verringern, sich im ~ 970
Wertverringerung 969
Wertverschlechterung 969
wertverschlechterung, Geld~ 896
wert, Versteuerungs~ 198
wert, Wiederanschaffungs~ 2091
wert, Wiederbeschaffungs~ 2091
wert, Zeit~ 912
Wertzoll 82
Wertzunahme 180
Wert zunehmen, an ~ 179
Wert zurückgehen, im ~ 970
Wertzuwachs 180
wettbewerbsfähig 713
Wettbewerbsfähigkeit 714
Wettbewerbsfreiheit 1390
wettmachen, einen Verlust ~ 707
widerrechtlich aneignen, sich ~ 977
widerrechtliche Aneignung 978
widerruflicher Kredit 2113
Wiederanlage 2078
wiederanlegen 1936
Wiederanschaffungskosten 2091
Wiederanschaffungspreis 2091
Wiederanschaffungswert 2091
wiederaufbauen, die Reserve ~ 2039
wiederauffüllen, die Reserve ~ 2039
Wiederaufleben 2048
Wiederaufschwung 2048
Wiederaufstieg 2048
Wiederausfuhr 2066
wieder ausleihen 2079
wiederbekommen, sein Geld ~ 1421
Wiederbeschaffungskosten 2091
Wiederbeschaffungspreis 2091
Wiederbeschaffungswert 2091
Wiederbeschaffungswert, Abschreibung auf den ~ 143
wiederbezahlen 1900
Wiederbezahlung 2072
wiedereinbringen, einen Verlust ~ 707
wiedererhalten, sein Geld ~ 1421
wiedererlangen, sein Geld ~ 1421
wiedererstatten 1900
Wiedererstattung 2072
Wiedergesundung 2048
wiedergutmachen, einen Verlust ~ 707
wiederinvestieren 1936
Wiederkauf 2053, 2094
wiederkaufen 480
wiederkehrende Einnahmen 2049
wieder leihen 2079
Wiederverkäufer 2105
Wiederverkaufspreis 2096
Wiederverteilung 2060
wiegen 2369
Winkelbörse 891
wirkliches Einkommen 2032
wirtschaft, Absatz~ 1075
wirtschaft, Aussen~ 1283
wirtschaft, Defizit~ 989
Wirtschaft, dirigistische ~ 768
wirtschaft, Finanz~ 1304
Wirtschaft, freie ~ 1393
wirtschaft, Geld~ 1304, 1775
Wirtschaft, gelenkte ~ 768
wirtschaftlich 1146, 1147
wirtschaftliche Einschränkung 218
wirtschaftlicher Zyklus 471
wirtschaftliche Schranke 1149
Wirtschaftlichkeit 1984
Wirtschaftlichkeitsberechnung 801
wirtschaft, Markt~ 1741
wirtschaft, Plan~ 768
wirtschaft, Privat~ 1976
Wirtschafts- 1146

Wirtschaftsbetrieb der öffentlichen Hand 1448
Wirtschaftsbilanz 1148
Wirtschaftsdirigismus 1047
Wirtschaftsgemeinschaft, Europäische ~ 1194
Wirtschaftsgüter 202
Wirtschaftsgüter, greifbare ~ 1747
Wirtschaftsgüter, immateriale ~ 1505
Wirtschaftsgüter, körperliche ~ 1747
Wirtschaftsgüter, materielle ~ 1747
Wirtschaftsgüter, nicht greifbare ~ 1505
Wirtschaftsgüter, unkörperliche ~ 1505
Wirtschaftsjahr 1320
Wirtschaftskredit 470
Wirtschaftskreislauf 471
wirtschaftslehre, Staats~ 1151
wirtschaftslehre, Volks~ 1151
Wirtschaftsordnung, dirigistische ~ 1047
Wirtschaftsprüfer 21, 216
Wirtschaftsrückgang 1031
Wirtschaftswissenschaft 1151
Wirtschaft, ungebundene ~ 1393
wirtschaft, Volks~ 1151
Wohlfahrtsstaat 2373
Wohnsitz, steuerlicher ~ 1331
Wucher 2337
Wucherdarleh(e)n 2336
wucherisches Darleh(e)n 2336
Wucherpreis 1250
Wucherzins(en) 2335

zahlbar, auf Sicht ~ 1896
zahlbar, bei Sicht ~ 1896
zahlbar, in ausländischer Währung ~ 1898
zahlbar, in bar ~ 1897
zahlbar, in Devisen ~ 1898
zahlen, bar ~ 1727
zahlen, durch Scheck ~ 1901
zahlen, eine Dividende ~ 1051
zahlen, im voraus ~ 1904
zahlen, in bar zu ~ 1897
Zahlen, in runden ~ 2119
zahlen, per Scheck ~ 1901
zahlen, pränumerando ~ 1904
zahlen, voll ~ 1905
Zahler 1903
Zahler, schlechter ~ 245
zahler, Steuer~ 2028
zahl, Index~ 1550
Zahlkarte 1781
zahl, Mess~ 1550
Zahlung 139
zahlung, Abschlags~ 1571
zahlung, Akonto~ 1014
zahlung, Antizipando~ 92
Zahlung aufschieben, eine ~ 984
zahlung, Bar~ 591
Zahlung, bargeldlose ~ 588
Zahlung bei Lieferung 589
zahlung, Dividenden~ 1052
Zahlung eines Schecks sperren, die ~ 2227
Zahlungen auf (über) X Jahre verteilen 2204
Zahlungen einstellen, die ~ 603
Zahlungen leisten 1152
Zahlungen sistieren, die ~ 603
Zahlungen vornehmen 1152
Zahlung hinausschieben, eine ~ 984
Zahlung im voraus 92
Zahlung, innergemeinschaftliche ~ 1611
zahlung, Kassa~ 591
zahlung, Nicht~ 982
zahlung, Pränumerando~ 92
Zahlungsabkommen 1906
Zahlungsangebot 1844
Zahlungsanweisung 221, 590
Zahlungsanzeige 97
Zahlungsaufschub 1276
Zahlungsaufschub bewilligen, einen ~ 1274
Zahlungsaufschub gewähren, einen ~ 1274
Zahlungsaufschub zugestehen, einen ~ 1274
Zahlungsauftrag 221, 590
Zahlungsbedingungen 2278
Zahlungsbefehl 590
Zahlungsbeleg 600
Zahlungsberechtigter 350
Zahlungsbilanz 260
Zahlungsbilanz, äussere ~ 258
Zahlungsbilanzdefizit 261
zahlungsbilanz, Gesamt~ 1862
Zahlungsbilanzüberschuss 263
Zahlungseinstellung 2250
Zahlungsempfänger 350
zahlungsfähig 2190
Zahlungsfähigkeit 2189
Zahlungsfrist 1924
Zahlungsfrist verlängern, die ~ 1274
Zahlungsfristverlängerung 1276
zahlungskräftig 2190
Zahlungsmittel 1751
Zahlungsmittel, gesetzliches ~ 1669
Zahlungsmittel machen, zum gesetzlichen ~ 1773
Zahlungsmittelumlauf 638
Zahlungsmodalität 1375
Zahlungsmodalitäten 2278
Zahlungsmodus 1375
Zahlungsrückstand 999
Zahlungssäumnis 999
Zahlungsstundung 1276
Zahlungstermin 1924
Zahlung stunden, eine ~ 1274
zahlungsunfähig 1570
Zahlungsunfähigkeit 1569
Zahlungsverkehr 1911
Zahlungsverweigerung 2074
Zahlungsverzögerung 999
Zahlungsverzug 999
Zahlungsweise 1375
zahlung, Teil~ 1894
zahlung, Termin~ 1910
zahlung, Transfer~ 2293
Zahlung verschieben, eine ~ 984
Zahlung verzögern, eine ~ 984
zahlung, Voll~ 715
Zahlung, vollständige ~ 715
Zahlung von, gegen ~ 732
Zahlung von, mittels ~ 732
Zahlung, vorläufige ~ 1999
zahlung, Vorschuss~ 83
Zahlung, vorzeitige ~ 92
zahlung, Zins~ 1592
zahlung, Zinsen~ 1592
Zedent 121, 1165
zedierbar 117
Zedierbarkeit 116
zedieren 118
zedieren, eine Forderung ~ 207
Zedierung von Forderungen 208
zehren, von den Reserven ~ 1042
Zeichengeld 1296
Zeichenmünze 2283
zeichnen (auf) 2233
Zeichner 2234
Zeichnung 2236
Zeichnung einer Anleihe auffordern, zur ~ 1634
zeichnung, Kapital~ 562
Zeichnungsangebot 1842
Zeichnungsberechtigung 174
Zeichnungsbetrag 153
Zeichnungsfrist 2237
Zeichnungskurs 2238
Zeichnungsofferte 1842
Zeichnungspreis 2238
Zeichnungsprospekt 1643
zeit, Ablauf~ 1262
zeit, Bedenk~ 998
Zeitdepositum 1337
Zeiteinlage 1337
Zeitgeld 1337
Zeitgeschäft 1379
Zeitkauf 1376
Zeit kaufen, auf ~ 486
zeit, Lauf~ 894
zeit, Umlauf(s)~ 895
zeit, Verfall(s)~ 894, 1748
Zeit verkaufen, auf ~ 2161
Zeitwert 912
Zentralamt 607
Zentralbank 606
zentralbankfähige Titel 1776
Zentralbüro 607
Zentrale 607
Zentralnotenbank 606
Zentralstelle 607
zerfall, Währungs~ 896
zerlegung, Aktien~ 2175
zertifikat, Aktien~ 2170
Zession 119
Zessionar 120, 1163
Zessionär 120, 1163
zessionsfähig 117
Zessionsfähigkeit 116
Zession von Forderungen 208
zettel, Börsen~ 1228, 1228
zettel, Einzahlungs~ 877
zettel, Gutschrift(s)~ 847
zettel, Kassen~ 590
zettel, Kurs~ 1228
zettel, Lastschrift~ 945
ziehen 1112

ziehen, auf den Internationalen Währungsfonds ~ 1123
ziehen, auf jemanden ~ 1114
ziehen, auf jemanden einen Wechsel ~ 1114
ziehen, eine Bilanz ~ 279
ziehen, einen Saldo ~ 279
ziehen, einen Scheck ~ 1115
Zieher 1118
Ziehung 1111
Ziehung auf den Internationalen Währungsfonds 1120
Ziehungsrechte (auf) 1121
Ziehungsrechte (bei) 1121
ziehungsrechte, Sonder~ 2195
Zielkauf 1376
Ziel kaufen, auf ~ 486
Ziel verkaufen, auf ~ 2161
ziffer, Äquivalenz~ 1181
ziffer, Index~ 1550
ziffer, Mess~ 1550
Zins 2088
Zinsabschnitt 1588
Zinsaussenstände 190
zinsbar 1586, 2231
zins, Basis~ 328
Zinsbelastung 1587
Zinsbogen 832
zinsbringend 1586
Zinscoupon 1588
Zins, einfacher ~ 2179
Zins(en) 1585
zinsen, Aktiv~ 376
Zinsen, anfallende ~ 42
Zinsen, angefallene ~ 41
zinsen, Antizipando~ 165
Zinsen, aufgelaufene ~ 41
Zinsen, auflaufende ~ 42
Zinsen ausleihen, Geld auf (gegen) ~ 1675
Zinsen, ausstehende ~ 190
zinsen, Bank~ 306
Zinsendienst 1592
Zinsen, entstehende ~ 42
Zinsenertrag 1595
Zinsen, fällige ~ 1589
Zinsen, fällig gewordene ~ 1589
Zinsen, fällig werdende ~ 42
zinsenfrei 1590
Zins(en), gestaffelte(r) ~ 1457
zinsen, Haben~ 376
zinsen, Hypotheken~ 1794
zinsen, Interkalar~ 1599
Zinsen, kalkulatorische ~ 1518
zins(en), Kapital~ 540
Zinsen kapitalisieren, die ~ 547
zinsen, Kredit~ 376
Zinsenlasten 1587
Zinsen, laufende ~ 909
Zinsen leihen, Geld auf (gegen) ~ 1675
zinsen, Passiv~ 947
Zinsen, rückständige ~ 190
zinsen, Schuld~ 947
zinsen, Soll~ 947
zins(en), Staffel~ 1457
zinsen, Stück~ 41
zinsentragend 1586
Zinsenvergütung 1594
Zinsen verleihen, Geld auf (gegen) ~ 1675
Zinsenverzinsung 156
zinsen, Verzugs~ 983
zins(en), Wucher~ 2335
Zinsenzahlung 1592
zins(en), Zinses~ 720
Zinsen zum Kapital schlagen, die ~ 547
Zinsen, zusammengesetzte ~ 720
Zinsenzuschuss 1594
Zinsertrag 1595
Zinseszins(en) 720
zinsfrei 1590
Zinsfuss 1593
zinsfuss, Lombard~ 1714
zinsfuss, Nominal~ 1821
Zinsgefälle 1412
zins, Kapitalmarkt~ 1967
Zinskupon 1588
Zinsleiste 2085
zinslos 1590
zins, Miet~ 2088
zins, Nominal~ 1821
zinspflichtig 2231
Zinsrate 1593
zins, Real~ 57
Zinsrückstände 190
Zinssatz 1593
zinssatz, Darleh(e)ns~ 423
Zinsschein 1588
Zinsscheinbogen 832
Zinsscheinerneuerung 2087
Zinsspanne 1412
Zinssubvention 1594
zinstragend 1586
Zinsvergütung 1594
Zinszahlung 1592
Zinszuschuss 1594
zirkulation, Banknoten~ 308
zirkulation, Geld~ 637
zirkulierend 635
Zoll 917
Zollabfertigung 645
Zollabgabe 917
Zollangabe 919
Zollanmeldung 919
zoll, Antidumping~ 169
zoll, Ausgleichs~ 711
Zoll befreien, von ~ 1246
zoll, Begünstigungs~ 1949
Zolldeklaration 919
Zolldeklarierung 919
zoll, Differential~ 1040
Zolleinnahmen 921
Zollerklärung 919
Zollerledigung 645
zollfrei 920
Zollfreiliste 1394
zollfrei machen 1246
Zollgebühr 917
zoll, Kompensations~ 711
Zollmauer 918
zöllner, Schutz~ 1997
zollpflichtig 916
zoll, Präferenz~ 1949
zoll, Prohibitiv~ 1993
Zollrückerstattung 1116
Zollrückvergütung 1116
Zollschranke 918
zoll, Schutz~ 1998
zoll, Sperr~ 1993
Zolltarif 922
Zoll- und Handelsabkommen, Allgemeines ~ 1415
Zollunion 923
Zollverband 923
Zollverein 923
zoll, Vergünstigungs~ 1949
zoll, Vorzugs~ 1949
zoll, Wert~ 82
zone, Dollar~ 1086
Zone, Franc-~ 1388
zone, Franken~ 1388
zone, Freihandels~ 1398
zone, Pfund~ 2224
zone, Sterling~ 2224
zufluss, Kapital~ 99
zuführen, dem Reservefonds ~ 68
zufuhr, Kapital~ 99
Zuführung 123
Zuführung an die Reserven 67
Zuführung zu den Reserven 67
Zugänge 1532
zugelassene Effekten, an der Börse ~ 1699
zugelassene Wertpapiere, an der Börse ~ 1699
zügellose Inflation 1411
zugestehen, einen Zahlungsaufschub ~ 1274
zugunsten 34
Zulage 1288
zulage, Gehalts~ 1288
zulage, Teuerungs~ 808
zulassung, Börsen~ 81
Zulassung zur (amtlichen) Börsennotierung 81
Zulassung zur Kotierung 81
Zunahme der Geldmenge 1252
Zunahme des Geldvolumens 1252
Zunahmerate 1255
zunahme, Wert~ 180
zunehmen, an Wert ~ 179
Zuordnung 123
zurückbehaltene Gewinne 2108
zurückbehaltenes Einkommen 1137
Zurückbehaltungsrecht (an) 1687
zurückbekommen, sein Geld ~ 1421
zurückbezahlen 1900
Zurückbezahlung 2072
zurückdatieren 164
zurückerhalten, sein Geld ~ 1421
zurückerlangen, sein Geld ~ 1421
zurückerstatten 1900
Zurückerstattung 2072
zurückführen 2089
Zurückführung 2090
Zurückgang 968
zurückgestaute Inflation 1919
zurückgreifen, auf die Reserven ~ 1042
zurückhaltung, Verbraucher~ 750
zurückkaufen 480, 502
zurücktrassierter Wechsel 365

zurückvergüten 1900
Zurückvergütung 2072
zurückzahlbar 2073
zurückzahlbare Obligation 497
zurückzahlbare Schuldverschreibung 497
zurückzahlen 148, 1900
zurückzahlen, eine Hypothek ~ 511
Zurückzahlung 139, 2072
zurückziehen, aus dem Umlauf ~ 503
zurückziehen, sich mit Verlust ~ 928
Zurückziehung 1008
zusage, Devisen~ 1223
zusage, Kredit~ 88
Zusammenbruch 668
zusammenbruch, Kurs~ 431
zusammenbruch, Preis~ 431
zusammenfassende Übersicht 2241
zusammengesetzte Zinsen 720
zusammenlegen, Aktien ~ 2061
zusammenlegen, das Aktienkapital ~ 2061
Zusammenlegung 135, 1939
Zusammenlegung des Aktienkapitals 2064
zusammenlegung, Kapital~ 2063
Zusammenschliessung 135
Zusammenschluss 135
zusammensetzung, Kapital~ 561
Zusatzdividende 398
Zusatzgebühr 60
Zusatzkosten 61
Zusatzkredit 63
Zusatzleistung 1285
zusätzliche Ausgaben 61
zusätzliche Deckung 62
zusätzliche Einkünfte 64
zusätzliche Einnahmen 64
zusätzliche Kosten 61
zusätzliche Leistung 1285
zusätzlicher Kredit 63
zusätzliche Sicherheit 65
zusätzliche Spesen 61
zusätzliche Steuer 66
zusätzliche Unkosten 61
zusätzliche Vergütung 1284
Zusatzsteuer 66
Zuschlag 60
Zuschlag belegen, mit einem ~ 1514
Zuschlaggebühr 60
Zuschlag(s)steuer 66
zuschlag, Steuer~ 66
zuschlag, Teuerungs~ 808
Zuschuss 1458
zuschuss, Deckungs~ 62
Zuschüsse unterstützen, durch ~ 2240
Zuschuss, öffentlicher ~ 1449
zuschuss, Regierungs~ 1449
Zuschuss, staatlicher ~ 1449
zuschuss, Staats~ 1449
zuschuss, Zins~ 1594
zuschuss, Zinsen~ 1594
zustrom, Kapital~ 99
zuteilen 122
Zuteilung 123
zuteilung, Aktien~ 125
Zu- und Abgang von Barmitteln 586
zuviel anrechnen 1866
zuviel berechnen 1866
zuviel fordern 1866
Zuwachsrate 1255
zuwachs, Wert~ 180
zuweisen 122
zuweisen, dem Reservefonds ~ 68
Zuweisung 123, 182
Zuweisung an die Reserven 67
zuweisung aus dem Gewinn, Rücklagen~ 1987
zuweisungen, Haushalts~ 444
Zuweisung zu den Reserven 67
zuwenden 122
Zuwendung 123, 182, 397, 1103
Zuwendungen aus dem Budget 444
Zuwendungen aus dem Haushaltsplan 444
Zuwendungen, budgetmässige ~ 444
zuwendung, Sach~ 134
zuwiderlaufen, der allgemeinen Tendenz ~ 2120
Zwangsanleihe 723
Zwangsgeld 136
Zwangskonversion 721
Zwangskonvertierung 721
Zwangskurs 722, 1356
Zwangssparen 724
Zwangsumlauf 1356
Zwangsumrechnungskurs 722
Zwangsverwalter 209
Zwangsverwaltung 191, 2040
zwangswirtschaft, Devisen~ 1224
zweckbestimmen 181
Zweckbestimmung 182
zweckgebunden 181
zweifelhafte Forderungen 1110
Zweiggeschäft 427
Zweiggesellschaft 98
Zweigniederlage 427
Zweigniederlassung 427
Zweigstelle 427
Zweitausfertigung 2148
zweite Wechselausfertigung 2148
Zwischenabschluss 1596
Zwischenbilanz 1596
Zwischendividende 1598
Zwischeneintrag 2249
Zwischeneintragung 2249
Zwischenfinanzierung 433
zwischenhändler, Aktien~ 1648
Zwischenkonto 2248
Zwischenkredit 434
Zwischenmakler 1648
Zwischenschein 1597
Zwischenzinsen 1599
zyklische Schwankung 930
zyklus, Konjunktur~ 471
Zyklus, wirtschaftlicher ~ 471

ESPAÑOL

abatido 508
abatimiento 1130
abolición de restricciones 2
abolir restricciones 1
abonar 2042
abonar a la cuenta 880
abonar una suma (en cuenta) a alguien 566
abono de intereses 1594
abono en cuenta 844
abrir la suscripción de un empréstito 1634
abrir un crédito a (en) favor de 1847
absorber una pérdida 3
absorción 2257
abundancia de dinero 6
acaparamiento 1493
acaparar 489, 1492
acaparar el mercado 789
acción 2169
acción al portador 343
acción de disfrute 400
acción de garantía 2015
acción de goce 400
acción de preferencia 1946
acción de prioridad 1946
acción de voto múltiple 1796
acción de voto plural 1796
acción diferida 985
acciones completamente (totalmente) desembolsadas 1403
acciones completamente (totalmente) integradas 1403
acciones completamente (totalmente) liberadas 1403
acciones comunes 701
acciones con derecho a (de) voto 2357
acciones de fundador 1386
acciones del personal 1159
acciones de relanzamiento 1251
acciones de trabajo 1159
acciones nominativas 1568
acciones nuevas 1819
acciones ordinarias 701
acciones preferentes cumulativas 890
acciones preferidas cumulativas 890
acciones privilegiadas cumulativas 890
acciones registradas 1568
acciones sin derecho a (de) voto 1830
acciones sin valor nominal 1831
acción gratuita 400
accionista 2171
accionista, gran ~ 633
accionista principal 633
accionista registrado 2076
acción preferente 1946
acción preferente con participación en el beneficio 1891
acción preferida 1946
acción privilegiada 1946
acción provisional 1597
acción sindicada 2282
acción sin la hoja de cupones 2176
acción vinculada 2282
aceptación 10
aceptación bancaria 284
aceptación comercial 2286
aceptación, comisión de ~ 13
aceptación, crédito de ~ 11
aceptación de banco 284
aceptante 14
aceptar une letra de cambio 8
acogida a un efecto, dar buena ~ 1054
acomodamiento 718
acopiar 489
acordar una prórroga para un pago 1274
acordar un crédito 126
acordar un plazo para un pago 1274
acordar un precio 113
acordar un respiro para un pago 1274
acreditación 844, 1848
acreditar a alguien 1847
acreditar a alguien por una suma 566
acreditar en la cuenta 880
acreditar la cuenta (por) 880
acreedor 870
acreedor de obligaciones 390
acreedores 36
acreedor extranjero 1360
acreedor garantizado 2150
acreedor preferente 1948
acreedor prioritario 1948
acreedor privilegiado 1948
acreedor quirografario 405
acta de liquidación (de impuestos) 1839
actividad bancaria 301
activo 206
activo, a inscribir en el ~ 408
activo amortizable 1027
activo circulante 468
activo contable 2285
activo de compensación 269
activo de la quiebra 317
activo depreciable 1027
activo disponible 227
activo en caja 587
activo ficticio 1297
activo fijo 518
activo inmovilizado 518
activo líquido 227
activo neto 1809
activo permanente 518
activo(s) 202
activo(s) corriente(s) 905
activos en el extranjero 204
activos inmateriales 1505
activos intangibles 1505
activos materiales 1747
activo social 790
activo(s) realizable(s) (y disponible(s)) 905
activos sobre el extranjero 204
activos tangibles 1747
activos y pasivos 203
actuario 58
acuerdo de autolimitación 2355
acuerdo de clearing 647
acuerdo de compensación 647
acuerdo de inmovilización 2216
acuerdo de moratoria 2216
acuerdo de pagos 1906
acuerdo (de) stand-by 2215
Acuerdo general sobre aranceles y comercio 1415
Acuerdo Monetario Europeo 1196
acuerdo sobre los precios 115
acumulación 38, 44
acumular 43
acumularse 40
acuñación 663
acuñar 662
acusar una baja (una ganancia; un avance) de X enteros (puntos) 2045
acusar una pérdida (una ganancia) 2046
acuse de recibo 47
adaptación inflacionista 59
adelanto 83
adelanto, a título de ~ 84
adelanto con garantía 86
adelanto contra garantía 86
adelanto de descubierto en cuenta 87
adelanto en cuenta corriente 87
adelanto garantizado 86
adelanto pignoraticio 86
adelanto sobre prenda 86
adelanto sobre títulos 90
adelanto sobre valores 90
adeudada, suma ~ 151
adeudado 952, 1127
adeudado, importe ~ 151
adeudar 1294, 1876
adeudar (en cuenta) 615
adeudar la cuenta con 618
adeudo 951
adeudo (en cuenta) 613
adeudos bancarios 296
adición a la reserva 67
administración de (la masa de) la quiebra 2040
administración de las deudas 954
administración (fiduciaria), en ~ 1185
administración fiscal 1242
administrador de la quiebra 209
admisión a cotización oficial en la bolsa 81
admisión a la bolsa 81
admisión a la cotización 81
adquirente 482
adquirir 48
adquisición 49
aduana 917
aduana prohibitiva 1993
aduana protectora 1998
adulteración de la moneda 939
afectación 123, 182
afectación de beneficios 183
afectación de ganancias 183
afectar 122, 181
afectar a la reserva 68
afectar al fondo de reserva 68
affluencia de capitales 99

afianzador 395
aflojamiento 968
aflojamiento de las cotizaciones 886
aforamiento aduanero 645
aforo aduanero 645
agencia 103
agencia de cambio(s) 1217
agencia de corredor 439
agencia de corretaje 439
agente 104
agente comisionista 690
agente de cambio 2152
agente de cambio(s) 509
agente de comisiones 690
agente de descuentos 361
agente de divisas 509
agente de letras 361
agente de valores 2152
agente financiero 1311
agio 109, 110
agio sobre la emisión 1641
agiotador 1647
agiotaje 111
agio, tener ~ 1883
agiotista 1647
agotamiento de las reservas 1012
agrupación 727
agrupación de acciones 2064
agrupar acciones 2061
ahorrador 2134
ahorrar 2133
ahorro en cuenta(s) de ahorros 2136
ahorro en forma de valores 2135
ahorro excesivo 1872
ahorro forzoso 724
ahorro interior bruto 1462
ahorro mediante inversión en valores mobiliarios 2135
ahorro obligatorio 724
ahorro privado 1980
ahorros 2137
ahorros contractuales 764
AID 1604
ajustamiento por un índice 1548
ajustar 70
ajustar una cuenta 249
ajuste 72
ajuste de clearing 647
ajuste de compensación 647
ajuste de cuotas 77
ajuste de los precios 76
ajuste del tipo de cambio 75
ajuste de una cuenta 254
ajuste en términos reales 74
alcista 455
alienabilidad 116
alienable 117
alienación 119
alienar 118
almacenista 2375
alquiler 2088
alta coyuntura 413
alta proporción de capital, con ~ 539
alta(s) finanza(s) 1486
alteración de la moneda 939
alto mundo financiero 1486
alza 2117
alza de precio(s) 1539
AME 1196
amo 1878
amonedación 663
amonedar 662
amontonar 43
amortiguar la inflación 628
amortizabilidad 2051
amortizable 2052
amortización 138, 139, 2053
amortización constante 2228
amortización creciente 1545
amortización decreciente 7
amortización de un empréstito 142
amortización económica 143
amortizaciones fiscales 517
amortización progresiva 1545
amortización técnica 1030
amortización variable 2347
amortizar 147, 148, 502
amortizar una deuda 2379
amortizar una hipoteca 511
ampliación de capital 536
ampliar el capital 1544
análisis del mercado 1740
anatocismo 156
annualidad vitalicia 163
anotar 401
antebolsa 937
antedatar 164
antefechar 164
anticíclico 168
anticipar 85
anticipo 83
anticipo, a título de ~ 84
anticipo bancario 298
anticipo con garantía 86
anticipo contra garantía 86
anticipo de los bancos centrales 1708
anticipo garantizado 86
anticipo pignoraticio 86
anticipo sobre prenda 86
antieconómico 2324
antiinflacionista 170
anualidad 161
anualidad de amortización 157
anulación 512
año civil 493
año comercial 478
año económico 1320
año financiero 705, 1320
año fiscal 1335
año presupuestario 448
apático 508
apertura de la quiebra 1575
apertura de un crédito 1848
aplazamiento de pago 1276
aplazar un pago 984
aportación 765
aportación de capital 521
aportación en especie 205
aportador de capital 1631
aportar capital 436
aporte 765
aporte de capital 521
aporte en especie 205
apreciar 177
aprecio 176
aprobación de crédito 220
apropiación indebita 978
apropiarse ilegalmente 977
apurado de fondos, estar ~ 2178
apuro(s) económico(s) 1314
apuro(s) financiero(s) 1314
arancel 917, 2260
arancel aduanero 922
arancel (aduanero) ad valorem 82
arancel (aduanero) exterior 1279
arancel antidumping 169
arancel compensatorio 711
arancel contra el dumping 169
arancel de aduanas 922
arancel de compensación 711
arancel de preferencia 1947
arancel diferencial 1040
arancel exterior común 699
arancel preferencial 1947, 1949
arancel preferente 1947, 1949
arancel prohibitivo 1993
arancel prohibitorio 1993
arancel proteccionista 1998
arancel protector 1998
arancel sobre el valor 82
arbitraje de cambio 186
arbitraje de divisas 186
arbitraje de letras 369
arbitraje en oro 185
arbitraje sobre los cambios 186
arbitrio 1135
área de la (libra) esterlina 2224
área del dólar 1086
área del franco 1388
área de mercado 1736
área de salida 1736
área de venta 1736
arraigo 1661
arras 602
arreglar 148
arreglar al contado 1727
arreglar el saldo 1914
arreglar en efectivo 1727
arreglar una cuenta 249
arreglo 139
arreglo de clearing 647
arreglo de compensación 647
arreglo de una cuenta 254
arreglo (judicial) 718
arrendador 1667, 1676
arrendamiento 1666
arrendamiento financiero 1668
arrendante 1667, 1676
arrendatario 1667
arriendo 1666, 2088
arrojar al mercado 1665
arrojar una pérdida (una ganancia) 2046
arrojar un beneficio 100
arrojar un interés de X por ciento 334
articulación del balance 273
artículos de exportación 1266
artículos de importación 1510
artículos de lujo 1001
ascender a 106
ascenso 2117

asedio del banco 2121
asegurar hipotecariamente 838
asegurar por hipoteca 838
asentar 401
asesor fiscal 2264
asiento activo 857
asiento colectivo 717
asiento compensatorio 281
asiento (contable) 409
asiento de ajuste 71
asiento de cierre 656
asiento de compensación 281
asiento de corrección 71
asiento de crédito 857
asiento de débito 946
asiento de diario 1655
asiento de rectificación 71
asiento de rescuentro 281
asiento en contra 281
asiento final 656
asiento no saldado 2312
asiento pasivo 946
asiento rectificado 71
asiento resumen 717
asignación 123, 182
asignación a la reserva 67
asignación de acciones 125
asignación de beneficios al fondo de reserva 1987
asignaciones presupuestarias 444
asignar 122
asignar a la reserva 68
asignar al fondo de reserva 68
asistencia financiera 1310
asociación con fin lucrativo 1986
Asociación Internacional de Desarrollo 1604
asociación sin fin lucrativo 1829
atender un efecto 1054
atesoramiento 1493
atesorar 1492
atrasado 189
atrasar un pago 984
atraso 152
atraso, en ~ 189
atrasos 188
auditoria 214
auditoria interna 1600
auge 413, 2117
aumentar de valor 179
aumentar el capital 1544
aumentar el valor 178
aumento de capital 536
aumento de la intensidad de capital 537
aumento de la liquidez 1538
aumento de la masa monetaria 1252
aumento del tipo de descuento 1541
aumento del X por ciento 1543
aumento de paga 1542
aumento de precio(s) 1539
aumento de salario 1542
aumento de sueldo 1540
aumento de valor 180
aumento en el valor 180
austeridad 218
autarquía 219
autoconsumo 1497
autofinanciación 1601
autofinanciamiento 1601
autorización de crédito 220
autorización para exportar 1268
autorización para importar 1512
autorizar un crédito 126
autosuficiencia 219
aval 230
avalante 236
avalar una letra (de cambio) 235
avalista 236
avalorar 177
avaluar 177
avalúo 176
avisar con X días de anticipación 1426
aviso con X días de anticipación, dar ~ 1426
aviso de abono 847
aviso de crédito 847
aviso de débito 945
aviso de entrada 47
aviso de pago 97, 1913
aviso de retirada de depósitos 1840
aviso de transferencia 848
aviso impositivo 1839
ayuda al desarrollo 1034
ayuda del estado 1445
ayuda financiera 1310
ayuda gubernamental 1445
ayuda monetaria 1771
ayuda para el desarrollo 1034

baja 968
baja coyuntura 1031
baja (coyuntural) 1031
baja de las cotizaciones (los precios) 886
baja de los precios 431
bajar 970
baja repentina de las cotizaciones 431
bajista 332
balance 270
balance activo 275
balancear los libros 278
balancear una cuenta 249
balance comercial 264
balance consolidado (del grupo) 736
balance de apertura 1700
balance de caja 253
balance de capitales 256
balance de cierre 1302
balance de comercio 264
balance de comprobación 2303
balance deficitario 274
balance del banco 312
balance de los movimientos de capital 256
balance de pagos 260
balance de pagos de bienes y servicios 259
balance de prueba 2303
balance de situación del banco 312
balance de una cuenta 254
balance económico 1148
balance final 1302
balance interino 1596
balance intermediario 1596
balance migratorio 1758
balance pasivo 274
balance provisional 1596
balance provisorio 1596
balance total de pagos 1862
balanza comercial 264
balanza comercial activa 53
balanza comercial deficitaria 94
balanza comercial desfavorable 94
balanza comercial exedentaria 53
balanza comercial favorable 53
balanza comercial pasiva 94
balanza comercial propicia 53
balanza de bienes y servicios 259
balanza de capitales 256
balanza de comercio 264
balanza de las transferencias 267
balanza de los movimientos de capital 256
balanza de pagos 260
balanza de pagos de las transacciones corrientes 262
balanza de pagos externos 258
balanza económica 1148
balanza migratoria 1758
balanza total de pagos 1862
banca 282, 301
bancarotta 315
bancarotta, en ~ 314
banco 282
banco central 606
banco comercial 310
bancocracia 1486
banco de aceptaciones 12
banco de ahorros 2139
banco de clearing 648
banco de comercio 310
banco (de comercio) exterior 1371
banco de compensación 648
banco de crédito 850
banco de crédito inmobiliario 1660
banco de crédito territorial 1660
banco de depósito(s) 1020
banco de desarrollo 1035
banco de descuento 1058
banco de emisión 309
banco de emisión de valores 1645
banco de fomento 1035
banco de giro 648
banco de inversiones 1621
Banco de Pagos Internacionales 300
banco de préstamos 850
banco de valores 1645
banco emisor 309
Banco Europeo de Inversiones 1195
banco hipotecario 1660
Banco Interamericano de Desarrollo 1581
Banco Internacional de Reconstrucción y Desarrollo 1602
Banco Internacional de Reconstrucción y Fomento 1602
Banco Mundial 1602
banco por acciones 1536
banco privado 1974
banda de fluctuación de los tipos de cambio 1346

baratar 326
barrera aduanera 918
barrera económica 1149
base de cálculo de la tributación 331
base de imposición 331
base del impuesto 331
base de tributación 331
base imponible 331
base impositiva 331
beneficiario 350
beneficiario de(l) crédito 418
beneficiario de un efecto 1902
beneficio 1409
beneficio, arrojar un ~ 100
beneficio bruto 1459
beneficio comercial 475
beneficio contable 412
beneficio, dar un ~ 100
beneficio de capital 530
beneficio de empresa 475
beneficio de explotación 475
beneficio de monetización 2154
beneficio distribuible 1072
beneficio esperado 166
beneficio extraordinario 1213
beneficio ficticio 171
beneficio fiscal 197
beneficio imaginario 171
beneficio imponible 197
beneficio neto 646
beneficio perdido 1718
beneficio por acción 1142
beneficio previsto 166
beneficios 229
beneficios acumulados 2108
beneficios no distribuidos 2108
beneficios no repartidos 2311
beneficioso 1147
beneficio sobre el cambio 1233
beneficios retenidos 2108
beneficio traslado 1985
bienes 202
bienes corporales 1747
bienes de capital 533
bienes de consumo 743
bienes de equipo 1134
bienes de inversión 533
bienes de producción 1134
bienes durables 1133
bienes durables de consumo 747
bienes duraderos 1133
bienes duraderos de consumo 747
bienes en el extranjero 204
bienes incorporales 1505
bienes inmateriales 1505
bienes inmobiliarios 1508
bienes inmuebles 1508
bienes intangibles 1505
bienes materiales 1747
bienes mobiliarios 622
bienes muebles 622
bienes no durables 1827
bienes no duraderos 1827
bienes raíces 1508, 1661
bienes tangibles 1747
bienes y servicios 1443
bienes y servicios, balanza de ~ 259
billete (de banco) 287
billetes en circulación 308
billetes y monedas 1834
billetes y monedas en circulación 638
billetes y monedas extranjeros 1369
billón 367
bimetalismo 375
BIRD 1602
BIRF 1602
bloquear 380
bloquear un cheque 2227
bloque de la (libra) esterlina 2224
bloque del dólar 1086
bloque del franco 1388
bloqueo 383
bloqueo de las importaciones 319
bloqueo de los precios 1400
boletín de bolsa 1228
boletín de cotización (de la bolsa) 1228
boletín de depósito 608
bolsa 1218
bolsa de acciones 1218
bolsa de cambio 1218
bolsa de cambios 1230
bolsa de comercio 695
bolsa de contratación 695
bolsa de mercancías 695
bolsa de valores (mobiliarios) 1218
bolsa extraoficial 102
bolsa nocturna 102
bolsa oficial 1845
bolsín 891
bolsista 1647
bonificación 127, 397
bonificación de intereses 1594
bono 876
bono al portador 338
bono de ahorro 2141
bono de caja 389, 590
bono (de empréstito) 389
bono de ingresos 1526
bono del tesoro 2301
bono de prima 1719
bono de reintegro 704
bono de sorteo 1719
bono de tesorería 2301
bono en mora 980
boomflación 414
borrador 1754
BPI 300
breve plazo, a ~ 2177
buena voluntad 1444
buen cobro, salvo ~ 2099
buen fin, garantía de ~ 1474
buen fin, salvo ~ 2099

caída 1125
caída brusca de las cotizaciones 431
caída de las cotizaciones (los precios) 886
caída de los precios 431
caja 579
caja acorazada 2122
caja chica 1931
caja de ahorros 2139
caja de ahorros para la construcción 453
caja de caudales 2122
caja de clearing 649
caja de compensación 649, 710
caja de crédito 850
caja de giro 649
caja de pensiones 1918
caja de préstamos 850
caja de seguridad 2123
caja disponible 587
caja fuerte 2122
caja fuerte de alquiler 2123
caja pequeña 1931
caja postal de ahorros 1941
calcular 177, 490
cálculo 176, 492
cálculo de costes 797
cálculo de costos 797
cálculo de gastos 797
cálculo de la rentabilidad 801
cálculo del precio de coste 815
cálculo del precio de coste tipo 2325
cálculo erróneo 491
calderilla 788
calma 1130
cámara acorazada 2125
cámara blindada 2125
cámara de clearing 649
Cámara de Comercio Internacional 1603
cámara de comercio (y industria) 611
cámara de compensación 649
cámara de seguridad 2125
cambiar 326
cambio 325, 771, 1216, 1221, 1960
cambio a la par 1887
cambio al contado 1227, 2024
cambio a plazo 1226, 1384
cambio a término 1226, 1383, 1384
cambio corriente 907
cambio de acciones 1232
cambio de apertura 1849
cambio de apoyo 1610
cambio de billetes y monedas 1235
cambio de cierre 657
cambio de compra 354
cambio de conversión 778
cambio de dinero 1231
cambio de intervención 1610
cambio del día 907
cambio de liquidación 650
cambio de moneda 1231
cambio de reembolso 2054
cambio de sostén 1610
cambio forzoso 722
cambio, libre ~ 1392
cambio medio 234
cambio (menor) 612
cambio obligatorio 722
cambio (repentino) 428
cambios a plazo 1378
cambios a término 1378
cambio seco 1477
cambista 361, 509
campo de venta 1736
cancelación 139
cancelación de una deuda 513
cancelar 148

cancelar una deuda 510
cancelar una hipoteca 511
canje de valores 2254
canon de licencia 1686
capacidad de competir 714
capacidad de ganancia 1139
capacidad de rendimiento 1139
caparra 602
capital 514
capital accionista 1996
capital activo 468
capital ajeno 417
capital a riesgo 1178
capital autorizado 222
capital base 544
capital básico 544
capital circulante 468
capital colocado 541
capital, con alta proporción de ~ 539
capital de ahorro 2143
capital de colocación 1622
capital de comercio 468
capital de empréstito 1707
capital de establecimiento 1564
capital de evasión 1349
capital de explotación 468
capital de fundación 1564
capital de inversión 1622
capital de operación 468
capital de participación 1996
capital de préstamo 1707
capital de riesgo 1178
capital de rotación 468
capital desembolsado 1880
capital de trabajo 468
capital emitido 1638
capital en acciones 544
capital en acciones diluido 2365
capital en acciones emitido 1638
capital en acciones ordinarias 697
capital en efectivo 577
capital en el extranjero 515
capital en giro 468
capital(es) errante(s) 1498
capitales propios 1996
capital evadido 1349
capital exhibido 1880
capital exigible 499
capital exigido 500
capital extranjero 1359
capital fijo 518
capital flotante 468
capital fundacional 1564
capital, gran ~ 355
capital improductivo 1502
capital inactivo 1502
capital inicial 1564
capital inmovilizado 518
capital integrado 1880
capital investido 541
capitalista 550
capitalización 523, 543
capitalización de intereses (devengados) 156
capitalizar 545
capitalizar las ganancias 548
capitalizar los beneficios 548
capitalizar los intereses 547
capital llamado (a integración) 500
capital muerto 1502
capital no desembolsado 2313
capital no integrado 2313
capital no llamado 2313
capital nominal 222
capital-obligaciones 940
capital ocioso 1502
capital operativo 468
capital pagado 1880
capital prestado 417
capital privado 1975
capital propio 1996
capital social 222, 544
capital su(b)scrito 2232
capital tomado en préstamo 417
carencia de valor 2344
carestía de dólares 1090
carestía de la vida 1483
carga 460
carga de deudas 462
carga de los impuestos 463
carga de los tributos 463
carga fiscal 463
carga fiscal latente 759
carga hipotecaria 1793
cargar 615
cargar a la cuenta 618
cargar de deudas 466
cargar demasiado poco 2316
cargar la cuenta con 618
cargas 619
cargas de amortización 620
cargas de capital 520
cargas de intereses 1587
cargas financieras 1313
cargas sociales 2186
cargo 613
cargo adicional 60
cargo de, a ~ 616
carta de crédito 1678
carta de garantía 394
carta de indemnidad 394
carta de indemnización 394
carta-orden de crédito 1678
cártel 571
cártel de precios 115
cartera de acciones 1628
cartera de títulos 1628
cartera de valores 1628
casa central 607
casa de aceptaciones 12
casa de cambio 1220
casa de emisiones 1645
casa (de la) moneda 1761
casa matriz 607, 769
casa principal 607
cash flow 586
casi dinero 1805
castigar una deuda 510
categoría de ingresos 1527
categoría de rentas 1527
categoría impositiva 2267
categoría tributaria 2267
caución 1138
caucionar 52
caucionero 395
caudales en circulación 468
causante 2028
CCI 1603
ceca 1761
cedente 121, 1165
ceder 118
ceder un crédito 207
cédula de dividendo 1078
cédula hipotecaria 1792
C.E.E. 1194
censor de cuentas 216
censura de cuentas 214
censura interna 1600
centro de costes 461
cercenar los gastos 915
cerrar los libros 278
cerrar una cuenta 652
cerrar un balance 279
certificado de depósito 608
certificado de deuda 609
certificado de endeudamiento 609
certificado del tesoro 2301
certificado de préstamo 1709
certificado de suscripción 2115
certificado provisional 1597
certificar un cheque 610
certificato de accion(es) 2170
cesación de pagos 2250
cesar los pagos 603
cesibilidad 116
cesible 117
cesión 119
cesionario 120, 1163
cesión de créditos 208
cesionista 121
CFI 1605
ciclo coyuntural 471
ciclo económico 471
ciencias económicas 1151
cierre de una cuenta 655
c.i.f. 634
cifra bruta de negocios 1467
cifra de negocios 2130
cifra índice 1550
cifra neta de negocios 1816
cifrarse en 106
cifras redondas, en ~ 2119
circulación de billetes (de banco) 308
circulación de billetes y monedas 638
circulación de capital (capitales) 555
circulación de dinero 637
circulación de medios de pago 638
circulación, en ~ 635
circulación fiduciaria 1299
circulación forzada 1356
circulación monetaria 637
circulación monetaria, superávit de la ~ 6
circulante 635
círculos financieros 1305
clase de ingresos 1527
clase de rentas 1527
clasificación 155
clasificación de cuentas 22
cláusula de escape 1155
cláusula dólar 1088
cláusula escapatoria 1155

cláusula oro 1432
clearing 642
clearinghouse 649
clima de los negocios 469
cobertura 834, 1732
cobertura adicional 62
cobertura a término 1377
cobertura (en) oro 1435
cobertura requerida 837
cobertura, sin ~ 835
cobertura suplementaria 62
cobrabilidad 674
cobrable 574, 675, 676
cobrador de deudas 955
cobranza 679
cobranza de créditos (deudas) 682
cobrar una deuda 677
cobrar un crédito 677
cobrar un cheque 576
cobrar un impuesto 678
cobro 679
cobro de créditos (deudas) 682
cobro de impuestos 683
cobro, salvo buen ~ 2099
codeudor 659
coeficiente de amortización 144
coeficiente de cobertura 840
coeficiente de equivalencia 1181
coeficiente de liquidez 45
coeficiente de ponderación 2372
coeficiente de reserva obligatoria 1759
cofrecillo de seguridad 2123
cofrecillo para guardar dinero 579
cofre fuerte 2122
coleta de una letra 124
colocación 1619, 1935
colocación de capital 542
colocación en el extranjero 1368
colocación en títulos (de cartera) 1626
colocación en valores (de cartera) 1626
colocación extranjera 1367
colocación nueva 1818
colocar 1618
colocar una emisión 1934
colocar un empréstito 1933
comandita 1692
comanditario 1691
comerciable 1738
comercialización 1742
comerciante al detall(e) 2105
comerciante al por mayor 2375
comerciante al por menor 2105
comerciante mayorista 2375
comerciante minorista 2105
comercio al detall(e) 2107
comercio al por mayor 2376
comercio al por menor 2107
comercio de cambio(s) 1221
comercio de divisas 1221
comercio detallista 2107
comercio de tránsito 2294
comercio de trueque 325
comercio de ultramar 1283
comercio en monedas y billetes extranjeros 936
comercio exterior 1283
comercio interior 1101
comercio libre 1392
comercio mayorista 2376
comercio minorista 2107
comercio triangular 2280
cometer un desfalco 977
comisario de la quiebra 209
comisión 689
comisión bancaria 293
comisión de aceptación 13
comisión de apertura de crédito 693
comisión de descuento 1055
comisionista 690
comitente 1973
compañía bancaria 302
compañía (de comercio) 686
compañía de fideicomiso 2306
compañía de financiación 1308
compañía de inversión 653
compañía de inversiones 653
compañía fiduciaria 2306
compañía filial 98
compañía financiera 1308
compañía holding 1494
compañía inversionista 653
compañía subsidiaria 98
compensación 642, 708, 709, 1172
compensación bancaria 292
compensación de cheques 627
compensación (de los gastos de representación) 128
compensación de saldos 1199
compensaciones 643
compensación interbancaria 292
compensar 706
compensar una pérdida 707
compensar un cheque 641
compensar un déficit 836
compensar un descubierto 836
competencia, libre ~ 1390
competidor 713
competitividad 714
competitivo 713
complemento de dividendo 1303
componente de la demanda 716
compra 2012
compra a crédito 852
compra a cuenta 852
compra al contado 594
compra al fiado 852
compra a plazo 1376
compra a plazos 1573
compra a término 1376
compra de cobertura 335
compra de ocasión 321
comprador 482
compra especulativa 2198
compra para entrega futura 1376
comprar 479
comprar a pagos parciales 481
comprar a plazo 486
comprar a plazos 481
comprar a término 486
comprobante 47, 2358
comprobante de almacén 2364
comprobante de asiento 33
comprobante de caja 600
comprobante de contabilidad 33
comprobante de deuda 609
comprobante de imposición 877
comprobante de ingreso 877
comprobante de pago 600
compromiso 692, 718
compromiso en divisas 1223
compromisos 961
compromisos a corto plazo 910
compromisos en cuenta corriente 1023
computar 490
cómputo 492
Comunidad Económica Europea 1194
conceder una prórroga para un pago 1274
conceder un crédito 126
conceder un plazo para un pago 1274
conceder un respiro para un pago 1274
concentración 135
concertar en precio 113
concertar por precio 113
concertar un empréstito 762
concesión 728
concesión de crédito 220
conciliación de cuentas 2043
conciliar las cuentas 112
concordar las cuentas 112
concursado 313
condiciones de crédito 856
condiciones de emisión de un empréstito 729
condiciones de pago 2278
condonación de una deuda 513
condonar una deuda 510
conductor 1667
confirmación de recibo 47
confirmación de saldo bancario 290
confirmar un cheque 610
congelación 383
congelación de los precios 1400
congelar 380
consejero financiero 1309
consolidación 737
consolidar una deuda 733
consorcio 740
consorcio de bancos 303
consorcio de emisión 2322
consorcio de garantía 2322
constituir una garantía 101
constituir una reserva 454
consultor financiero 1309
consumidor 744
consumo 751
consumo familiar 1499
consumo interior 1092
consumo interno 1092
consumo nacional 1092
consumo per cápita 1920
consumo por cada habitante 1920
consumo privado 1499
consumo propio 1497
consumo público 2002
contabilidad 20
contabilidad analítica de explotación 798

contabilidad autónoma 2155
contabilidad de costes 798
contabilidad de precios de coste 798
contabilidad mecánica 1724
contabilidad mecanizada 1724
contabilidad nacional 1797
contabilidad por partida doble 1107
contabilidad por partida simple 2181
contabilizar 401
contable 21
contado, al ~ 573
contador 21
contador (público) 216
contante 572
contenido (de) oro 1434
contingentación 2018
contingentación de divisas 2030
contingentar 122, 1186
contingente 2017
contraasiento 281
contracción crediticia 874
contracción de la liquidez 1697
contracción del crédito 874
contraentrada 281
contraer una deuda 761
contraer un empréstito 762
contrafianza 238
contragiro 819
contralibranza 819
contrapartida 281, 822
contraprestación 731
contrario a la tendencia general, estar ~ 2120
contrataciones bursátiles 1222
contrataciones en bolsa 1222
contratar un empréstito 762
contrato de alquiler 1666
contrato de arrendamiento 1666
contrato de compromiso 719
contrato de convenio 719
contrato de locación 1666
contrato de su(b)scripción 2321
contrato fiduciario 976
contratos bursátiles 1222
contravalor 822, 1219
contribución 1135
contribución de usos y consumos 752
contribuciones sociales 2186
contribución suntuaria 1723
contribución territorial 1662
contribuidor 2028
contribuir capital 436
contributario 2028
contribuyente 196, 2028
controlar la inflación 628
control de cambios 1224
control de divisas 1224
control de las inversiones 1044
control del capital 1044
control de los créditos 629
control de los precios 1961
control de (los) salarios 2360
control directo 770
controles de divisas 900
convenio 718
convenio de clearing 647
convenio de compensación 647
convenio de pagos 1906
convenio de prórroga 2216
convenio sobre los precios 115
convenir un precio 113
conversión 771
conversión de deudas 776
conversión de un empréstito 775
conversión en dinero 773
conversión forzosa 721
convertibilidad 780
convertibilidad externa 1278
convertibilidad interna 781
convertible 782
convertir en dinero (contante) 785
convertir un empréstito 779
cooperativa 786
cooperativa de crédito 787
cooperativa de producción 1983
coprestatario 658
Corporación Financiera Internacional 1605
corredor 437
corredor de bolsa 2152
corredor de cambios 2152
corredor de descuentos 361
corredor de dinero 1311
corredor de divisas 509
corredor de letras 361
corredor de mercancías 694
corredor de valores 2152
corredor en mercancías 694
corredor financiero 1311
correduría 438
corretaje 438
corrida sobre el banco 2121
cortar los gastos 915
corto plazo, a ~ 2177
costa 795
costa de, a ~ 1260
coste 795
coste alternativo 1853
coste de adquisición 488, 804
coste de compra 488
coste de crédito 805
coste de la mano de obra 806
coste de (la) vida 807
coste del trabajo 806
coste efectivo 54
coste histórico 804
coste integral, sistema de ~ 4
coste marginal 1733
coste real 54
costes adicionales 61
costes constantes 1336
costes de expedición 2295
coste(s) de fabricación 811
coste(s) de producción 811
costes de transporte 2295
costes directos 1043
costes fijos 1336
costes indirectos 1417
costes no incorporables 1202
costes por unidad 813
costes salariales 2359
costes semi-variables 2164
costes suplementarios 61
costes supletorios 61
coste y costas, a ~ 796
costo 795
costo, al ~ 796
costo alternativo 1853
costo de emisión 1353
costo de la mano de obra 806
costo de (la) vida 807
costo del capital 522
costo de los factores, al ~ 1291
costo del trabajo 806
costo de reposición 2091
costo efectivo 54
costo marginal 1733
costo por unidad 813
costo real 54
costo(s) calculado(s) de antemano 1189
costos de explotación 1850
costo(s) de fabricación 811
costos de operación 1850
costo(s) de producción 811
costos directos 1043
costo, seguro, (y) flete 634
costo(s) estimado(s) 1189
costo(s) estimativo(s) 1189
costos indirectos 1417
costos salariales 2359
costo unitario 813
costo y costas, a ~ 796
cotización 1228, 1746, 1960
cotización actual 913
cotización al contado 593
cotización de apertura 1849
cotización de bolsa 1234
cotización de cierre 657
cotización de compra 354
cotización de conversión 778
cotización de emisión 1642
cotización de las acciones 2174
cotización del día 913
cotización demandada 354
cotización de oferta 193
cotización de reembolso 2054
cotización de rescate 2054
cotización de su(b)scripción 2238
cotización de venta 193
cotización en bolsa 1234
cotización ofrecida 193
cotización única 2326
cotizar 1698
cotizar un precio 1728
coyuntura 477
coyuntura, alta ~ 413
coyuntura, baja ~ 1031
coyuntural 1146
coyuntura regresiva 1031
crac 668
creación de crédito 841
creación de dinero 842
creación de moneda 842
crear una reserva 454
crédito 639, 843, 844, 845, 873, 879
crédito abierto 379
crédito, acordar un ~ 126
crédito adicional 63
crédito a la economía 470
crédito al consumidor 745
crédito al consumo 745
crédito al descubierto 379

crédito a medio plazo 1753
crédito, aprobación de ~ 220
crédito autoamortizable 2156
crédito, autorización de ~ 220
crédito, autorizar un ~ 126
crédito bancario 295
crédito cambiario 11
crédito, ceder un ~ 207
crédito comercial 470
crédito complementario 63
crédito, conceder un ~ 126
crédito, concesión de ~ 220
crédito con garantía 670
crédito consorcial 741
crédito contabilizado 404
crédito contable 404
crédito contingente 2214
crédito contra garantía 670
crédito de aceptación 11
crédito de aval 853
crédito de caja 580
crédito de caución 853
crédito de consorcio 741
crédito de consumo 745
crédito de descuento 1059
crédito de fianza 853
crédito de garantía 853
crédito de igualación 1173
crédito de liquidación automática 2156
crédito de pago a plazos 1488
crédito de transición 434
crédito documentario 1085
crédito en blanco 379
crédito en cuenta común 865
crédito en cuenta corriente 87
crédito en descubierto 379
crédito especial 2194
crédito eventual 757
crédito garantizado 670
crédito hipotecario 866
crédito incobrable 242
crédito inmobiliario 868
crédito interbancario 1583
crédito interino 434
crédito mobiliario 867
crédito no cubierto 379
crédito, otorgamiento de ~ 220
crédito, otorgar un ~ 126
crédito para el consumidor 745
crédito para (financiar) compras a plazos 1488
crédito personale 1927
crédito pignoraticio 670
crédito privado 1927
crédito provisional 434
crédito real 868
crédito renovable automáticamente 2114
crédito revocable 2113
crédito roll-over 2118
crédito rotativo 2114
crédito rotatorio 2114
créditos, cesión de ~ 208
créditos congelados 1401
créditos de inversión 1620
créditos dudosos 1110
créditos inciertos 1110
créditos interiores 1093
créditos internos 1093
crédito sobre efectos 869
crédito sobre títulos 869
crédito sobre valores 869
crédito, solicitar un ~ 175
crédito stand-by 2214
créditos, transferencia de ~ 208
créditos, traspaso de ~ 208
crédito suplementario 63
crédito swap 2252
crédito temporal 434
crédito territorial 868
crédito, transferir un ~ 207
crédito transitorio 434
cuadro 2256
cuasidinero 1805
cubierta, servir de ~ 2166
cubierto, no ~ 835
cubrir una pérdida 707
cubrir un déficit 836
cubrir un descubierto 836
cuenta 16, 17
cuenta, a ~ 19
cuenta abierta 23, 1846
cuenta a cobrar 37
cuenta acreedora 36
cuenta ajena, por ~ 35
cuenta a mitad 1654
cuenta a pagar 36
cuenta auxiliar 224
cuenta bancaria 285
cuenta colectiva 673, 766, 1649
cuenta común 1649
cuenta conjunta 1649
cuentacorrentista 26
cuenta corriente 23
cuenta corriente, adelanto en ~ 87
cuenta corriente, crédito en ~ 87
cuenta corriente postal 1800
cuenta de activo 201
cuenta de ahorros 2138
cuenta de balance 271
cuenta de caja 575
cuenta de capital 516
cuenta de clearing 644
cuenta de cliente 617
cuenta de compensación 644
cuenta de contrapartida 760
cuenta de control 766
cuenta de cheques 625
cuenta de cheques postales 1800
cuenta de depósito(s) 1016
cuenta de entradas 1524
cuenta de explotación 2289
cuenta de ganancías y pérdidas 1523
cuenta de gastos 1259
cuenta de giro(s) 1424
cuenta de ingresos 1524
cuenta, denominación de ~ 25
cuenta de orden 2248
cuenta de participación 1654
cuenta de pasivo 1682
cuenta de pérdidas y ganancías 1523
cuenta de, por ~ 34, 1260
cuenta de previsión 130
cuenta de provisión 130
cuenta de reserva 130
cuenta de resultados 1523
cuenta de tercero(s), por ~ 35
cuenta de tránsito 2248
cuenta deudora 37
cuenta en común 1649
cuenta en participación 1654
cuenta en suspensa 2248
cuenta en un banco 285
cuenta fiduciaria 2305
cuenta mancomunada 1649
cuenta no liquidada 1846
cuenta no saldada 1846
cuenta nuestra 1833
cuenta nueva, saldo a ~ 150
cuenta personal 1926
cuenta, por su ~ 1877
cuenta privada 1926
cuenta pro-forma 1991
cuenta proforma 1991
cuenta propia, por ~ 1877
cuenta provisional 2248
cuenta puente 2248
cuentas, clasificación de ~ 22
cuentas de regularización 73
cuentas económicas integradas 1579
cuentas, plan de ~ 22
cuentas reflejadas 802
cuentas, sistema de ~ 22
cuenta subsidiaria 2[illegible]
cuenta suya 1716
cuenta, titular de una ~ 26
cuenta, título de ~ 25
cuenta transitoria 2248
cuota 1571, 1572, 2017, 2235
cuota de amortización 144, 145
cuota de crecimiento 1255
cuota del activo de la quiebra 1077
cuota de liquidez 45
cuota semestral 351
cuotas, por ~ 987
cuotas sociales 2186
cupo 2017
cupón 828
cupón comercial 2290
cupón, con ~ 829
cupón, contra entrega del ~ 1958
cupón de dividendo 1078
cupón de intereses 1588
cupón no vencido 2330
cupón prescri(p)to 1664
cupón semestral 1475
cupón, sin ~ 831
curso de los negocios 833
curso forzoso 1356
custodia (fiduciaria), en ~ 1185

cheque 624
cheque abierto 339
cheque a la orden 631
cheque al descubierto 241
cheque al portador 339
cheque barrado 883
cheque cruzado 883
cheque de turista 2297
cheque de viaje 2297
cheque de viajero(s) 2297
cheque en blanco 378
cheque en descubierto 241

cheque intransferible 630
cheque no a la orden 630
cheque no cruzado 339
cheque, pagar con ~ 1901
cheque postal 1425
cheque sin provisión 241

dádiva 1103
dador de crédito 1672
dar a préstamo 1671
dar a título de garantía 1018
dar a título en garantía 1018
dar a título en prenda 1018
dar aviso con X días de anticipación 1426
dar buena acogida a un efecto 1054
dar en préstamo 1671
dar entrada 401
dar fianza 52
dar garantía 52
dar orden de pagar una factura 223
dar prestado 1671
dar una garantía 101
dar un beneficio 100
dar un interés de X por ciento 334
dar valores en garantía 671
dar valores en prenda 671
datos estadísticos 2219
debe 942, 943
debe, estar en el ~ 944
debenturista 390
deber 1876
debida, suma ~ 151
debido 1127
debido, importe ~ 151
débil 508
debilidad 1130
debilitación 968
debilitación de las cotizaciones (los precios) 886
debilitamiento 968
debitar 615
debitar la cuenta con 618
débito 613, 942
débitos 961
débitos a corto plazo 910
declaración aduanera 919
declaración arancelaria 919
declaración de aduana 919
declaración de garantía 394
declaración de ingresos 1531
declaración de un dividendo 964
declaración fiscal 2275
declaración (judicial) de quiebra 69
declaración provisional 2000
declaración tributaria 2275
declarar un dividendo 965
decremento 968
deducción de impuestos 2261
deducción del impuesto (de los impuestos), antes de la ~ 1959
deducción del impuesto (de los impuestos), después de la ~ 1677
deducción de los gastos, previa ~ 131
deducción de pérdidas 2273
deducción en el origen 975
deducción en la fuente 975
deducción fiscal 2261
deducción hecha de los gastos 131
deducción previa 89
deducción retroactiva de pérdidas 2272
deducible, pérdida ~ 974
deducidos los gastos 131
deducidos los impuestos 1677
deducir con anticipación 973
deducir el impuesto (los impuestos), antes de ~ 1959
deducir el impuesto (los impuestos), después de ~ 1677
deducir en la fuente 972
deducir por adelantado 973
deficiencia 988
deficiencia de caja 96
déficit 988
déficit comercial 474
déficit de caja 96
déficit de dólares 1089
déficit de (en) la recaudación fiscal 1330
déficit de explotación 474
déficit de impuestos 1330
déficit de la balanza de pagos 261
déficit de la recaudación presupuestaria 445
déficit del comercio exterior 265
déficit del presupuesto 95
déficit exterior 261
déficit fiscal 1330
déficit inflacionista 1557
déficit presupuestario 95
deflación 991
deflacionario 992
deflacionista 992, 995
deflator 996
defraudación de impuestos 2266
D.E.G. 2195
delcredere 1000
demanda 1002
demanda, a (la) ~ 495
demanda de consumidores 746
demanda de dinero 1774
demanda de las familias 1097
demanda de préstamos 424
demanda de reembolso 640
demanda de restitución 640
demanda interior 1096
demanda, oferta y ~ 2242
demora de pago 999
demora, en ~ 979
demora en el pago 999
demorar un pago 984
denegación de pago 2074
denominación 1011
denominación de cuenta 25
denominado en dólares 1010
denominador común 698
deport 239
deporte 239
deporto 239
depositador 1025, 1026
depositante 1025, 1026
depositar 1015
depositar a título de garantía 1018
depositario 1017
depósito 1013
depósito a demanda 1004
depósito a (de) vencimiento fijo 1337
depósito a la vista 1004
depósito a plazo (fijo) 1337
depósito a término 1337
depósito bancario 297
depósito colectivo 685
depósito de ahorro(s) 2144
depósito de previo aviso 1019
depósito de seguridad 2125
depósito en banco 297
depósito en cuenta de giro(s) 1024
depósito (fiduciario), en ~ 1185
depósito reembolsable con preaviso 1019
depósitos interbancarios 1582
depósitos monetarios 307
depreciación 138, 969, 1029
depreciación constante 2228
depreciación creciente 1545
depreciación de cambio 897
depreciación decreciente 7
depreciación de la moneda 896
depreciación económica 143
depreciación monetaria 896
depreciación progresiva 1545
depreciación técnica 1030
depreciación variable 2347
depreciar 1028
depreciarse 970
depresión 1031
deprimido 508
derecho 614, 1135
derecho aduanero 917
derecho aduanero prohibitivo 1993
derecho aduanero prohibitorio 1993
derecho aduanero protector 1998
derecho a (percibir) dividendo, con ~ 1170
derecho arencelario 917
derecho de aduana 917
derecho (de aduana) ad valorem 82
derecho (de aduana) diferencial 1040
derecho (de aduana) preferencial 1949
derecho (de aduana) preferente 1949
derecho de consumo 752
derecho de conversión 777
derecho de embargo (sobre) 1687
derecho de licencia 1686
derecho de monopolio 1245
derecho de opción 1854
derecho de preferencia 1328
derecho de prenda (sobre) 1687
derecho de prioridad 1328
derecho de registro 2077
derecho de retención (sobre) 1687
derecho de sello 2211
derecho de su(b)scripción 174
derecho de sucesión 938
derecho de suscripción 2115
derecho de tanteo 2013
derecho de timbre 2211
derecho de usufructo 349
derecho de voto de títulos en depósito 2356
derecho preferente 1328

derecho prendario (sobre) 1687
derechos administrativos 80
derechos de administración 80
derechos de comisión 689
derechos de custodia 2124
derechos de giro (sobre) 1121
derechos de opción, con ~ 888
derechos de opción, sin ~ 1249
derechos de servicio 80
derechos de suscripción, con ~ 888
derechos de suscripción, sin ~ 1249
derechos de tramitación 1478
derechos de transcripción 812
derechos de transferencia 812
derechos de transmisión 812
derechos especiales de giro 2195
desahorro 1069
desanimación 1130
desanimado 508
desatesoramiento 1063
desbloquear 949
desbloqueo 950
descargo 51, 139
descender en valor 970
descenso 968
descenso de las cotizaciones (los precios) 886
descomposición 155
descongelación 950
descongelar 949
descontados los gastos 131
descontando los gastos 621
descontar 1057
descubierto 988
descubierto, al ~ 835
descubierto, en ~ 835
descubierto (en cuenta) 1867
descuento 127
descuento comercial 935
descuento de caja 583
descuento de comerciante 935
descuento para revendedores 935
descuento por pago al contado 583
descuento sobre mercancías 935
desembolsar 1050
desembolso 1258
desembolsos 1053
desembolsos de caja 582
desembolsos de capital 524
desembolsos en efectivo 582
desempeñar una hipoteca 511
desequilibrio 1062
desfalcar 977
desfalco 978
desfalco, cometer un ~ 977
desgaste 2367
desgravación fiscal 2261
deshipotecar 511
designación de cuenta 25
designar 122
desinflación 1064
desinflacionario 1065
desinflacionista 1065
desinflar 990
desinversión 1066
desmonetización 1008
desmonetizar 503
desnacionalización 1009
despacho aduanero 645
despacho en la aduana 645
desplome 668
destinar a la reserva 68
destinar al fondo de reserva 68
destinatario 2082
desvalorar 1028
desvalorización 1029
desvalorización de la moneda 897
desvalorización monetaria 897
desvalorizar 1028
desvalorizarse 970
desviación sobre gastos indirectos 464
detalle 429
detallista 2105
detener la inflación 628
deterioro 2367
determinación de la paridad de cambio 1032
determinación de los precios 1962
determinar un precio 1033
detracción 1119
detracción de reservas 2377
deuda 951
deuda a cobrar 37
deuda activa 37
deuda amortizable 1574
deuda a pagar 36
deuda consolidada 735
deuda contabilizada 406
deuda contable 406
deuda del Estado 1798
deuda en obligaciones 391
deuda exigible 37
deuda exterior 1280
deuda externa 1280
deuda fiscal 2271
deuda flotante 1351
deuda hipotecaria 957
deuda impositiva 2271
deuda incobrable 242
deuda in sólidum 1650
deuda interior 1095
deuda interna 1095
deuda nacional 1798
deuda no consolidada 1351
deuda pasiva 36
deuda pendiente de cobro 37
deuda personal 1928
deuda prescri(p)ta 324
deuda privada 1928
deuda pública 1798
deuda quirografaria 2332
deudas 961
deudas atrasadas 188
deudas bancarias 296
deudas, estar acribillado de ~ 953
deuda solidaria 1650
deuda tributaria 2271
deuda unificada 735
deudor 958
deudor cambiario 362
deudor de, ser ~ 1876
deudor en retraso 981
deudor in sólidum 1651
deudor moroso 981
deudor negligente 981
deudor solidario 1651
deudor tercero 1413
devaluación 1029
devaluación de la moneda 897
devaluación monetaria 897
devengar interés de X por ciento 334
devolución de impuestos 2038
devolver 1900
día de la formación del balance 272
día de liquidación 24
día de saldo 24
día de vencimiento 931
diario 932
diario auxiliar 225
diario de letras a cobrar 360
diario de vencimientos (de letras) 359
diario di caja 578
días de cortesía 933
días de favor 933
días de gracia 933
diferencia 1037
diferencia de cambio 1039
diferencia de precio(s) 1038
diferencia de prima 1731
diferencia en los precios 1038
diferencia entre los precios 1038
diferencia entre los tipos de interés 1412
diferir un pago 984
dificultades económicas 1314
dificultades financieras 1314
dificultades monetarias 1314
dificultades pecuniarias 1314
digno de crédito 846
dilución del capital (en acciones) 2226
dinero a interés, prestar ~ 1675
dinero a la vista 505
dinero a plazo (fijo) 1337
dinero a término 1337
dinero bancario 307
dinero barato 623
dinero caro 654
dinero, casi ~ 1805
dinero circulante 914
dinero clandestino 2314
dinero consignado 307
dinero contante 572
dinero corriente 914
dinero de banco 307
dinero de día a día 505
dinero depositado 307
dinero de vencimiento diario 505
dinero diario 505
dinero en caja 587
dinero en circulación 914
dinero en cuentas 307
dinero escaso 654
dinero giral 307
dinero negro 2314
dinero suelto 612
dinero transferible 307
dirigismo 1047
disagio 1048
discuento 1048
disminución 968

disminución de las cotizaciones (los precios) 886
disminución de valor 969
disminuir de valor 970
disminuir los gastos 915
disolución 1070
disolver 1071
disparidad 1067
disparidad de precio(s) 1038
disponibilidad bancaria 286
disponibilidad de capital 226
disponibilidades 227
disponibilidades cuasi monetarias 2243
disponibilidad(es) monetaria(s) 1783
disponible 227
disposiciones sobre (el control de) cambios 900
disposiciones sobre (el control de) divisas 900
distensión en el mercado monetario 1144
distraer 977
distribución 123
distribución de beneficios 183
distribución de dividendo, no ~ 1826
distribución de dividendos 1052
distribución de ganancias 183
distribución del capital 1074
distribución de los patrimonios 1073
distribución de utilidades 183
distribución oculta 1482
distribuir 122
distribuir los pagos sobre X años 2204
distribuir un dividendo 1051
diversos 1764
dividendo 1076, 1077
dividendo a cuenta 1598
dividendo acumulativo 889
dividendo complementario 398
dividendo, con derecho a (percibir) ~ 1170
dividendo de liquidación 1303
dividendo de prioridad 1945
dividendo en acciones 400
dividendo en efectivo 584
dividendo extraordinario 398
dividendo final 1303
dividendo (incluido), con ~ 887
dividendo interino 1598
dividendo preferencial 1945
dividendo preferente 1945
dividendo preferido 1945
dividendo prescrito 1954
dividendo privilegiado 1945
dividendo provisional 1598
dividendo, sin ~ 1080
dividendo suplementario 398
dividir la diferencia 2201
divisa 893
divisa débil 2187
divisa fuerte 1479
divisa nacional 1094
divisas 1361
divisas a plazo 1378
divisas a término 1378
doble imposición 1109
doble mercado de cambios 2309
doble opción 1108
doble patrón 375
doble tributación 1109
documento a pagar 372
dólar de compensación 29
dólar de convenio 29
dólar de cuenta 29
dólar, Euro~ 1193
domanda, oferta y ~ 192
domicilio 1102
domicilio fiscal 1331
domicilio social 2075
donación 1103
donador 1104
donante 1104
donativo 1103
dotación 123, 1168
dotación de capital 523
dotar 122, 1167
drawback 1116
drenaje de capitales 556
dueño 1878
dumping 1131
durables 1133
durables de consumo 747
duración (de validez) 894

economía controlada 768
economía deficitaria 989
economía de mercado 1741
economía de mercado libre 1393
economía dirigida 768
economía financiera 1304
economía financiera del estado 827
economía libre (de mercados) 1393
economía monetaria 1775
economía planificada 768
economía política 1151
economía privada 1976
economías, hacer ~ 924
economicidad 1984
económico 1146, 1147
economizar 924
echar al mercado 1665
echar mano de las reservas 1042
efectivo, en ~ 573
efectivo en caja 587
efectivo en cartera 1628
efectivo metálico 572
efecto a cobrar 373
efecto al cobro 364, 373
efecto a pagar 372
efecto comercial 356
efecto dado en garantía 363
efecto dado en prenda 363
efecto de comercio 356
efecto de primera clase 1323
efecto de primer orden 1323
efecto descontado sobre el interior 1060
efecto devuelto 365
efecto en depósito 363
efecto financiero 1307
efecto impagado 365
efecto no honrado 365
efecto no pagado 365
efecto pignorado 363
efectos 2151
efectos al portador 342
efectos del estado 1244
efecto sobre el extranjero 1357
efecto sobre el interior 1091
efecto sobrevencido 365
efectos públicos 1244
efectuar el inventario 1124
efectuar negocios 1084
efectuar pagos 1152
egresos 1053
egresos de caja 582
egresos de capital 524
egresos en efectivo 582
egresos, ingresos y ~ 1525
ejercicio (comercial) 478
ejercicio (financiero) 1320
ejercicio fiscal 1335
ejercicio presupuestario 448
elasticidad de los tipos de cambio 1154
elevación de capital 536
elevación del precio 1539
elevación del tipo de descuento 1541
elevar el capital 1544
elevar el valor 178
elevarse a 106
embargar 211
embargo 191
embargo contra un deudor tercero 1414
embargo de los bienes de un tercer deudor 1414
embargo sobre las importaciones 319
embolsar una ganancia 1937
emigración de capitales 556
emisión 1352
emisión constante 2259
emisión de acciones 1640
emisión de acciones gratuitas 399
emisión de acciones nuevas 2116
emisión de billetes (de banco) 1156
emisión de bonos 392
emisión de capital 549
emisión de obligaciones 392
emisión de títulos-valores 1639
emisión en serie 385
emisión fiduciaria 1300
emisor 1644
emitir obligaciones 1637
emitir un empréstito 1157
emolumentos 1158
empeñado 952
empeñar 1018
empeñar valores 671
empeño de efectos 1501
empeño de títulos 1501
empeño de valores 1501
empeños 961
empleo de capital 1160
empresa 467
empresa del estado 1448
empresa de servicio(s) público(s) 2009
empresa de utilidad pública 2009
empresa estatal 1448

empresa, libre ~ 1391
empresa nacional 1448
empresa privada 1977
empresa pública 1448
empresario 1171
emprestar 415, 1671
empréstito 1705
empréstito a (la) su(b)scripción, ofrecer un ~ 1634
empréstito amortizable 141
empréstito, amortización de un ~ 142
empréstito a prima 1720
empréstito a sorteo 1720
empréstito comercial 473
empréstito con garantía oro 1438
empréstito con prima 1720
empréstito convertible 784
empréstito de amortización 141
empréstito de consolidación 738
empréstito de conversión 774
empréstito de estabilización 2206
empréstito del estado 1453
empréstito del gobierno 1453
empréstito de lotería 1720
empréstito de obligaciones 941
empréstito de sorteo 1720
empréstito en el extranjero 1282
empréstito en obligaciones 941
empréstito estatal 1453
empréstito exterior 1282
empréstito externo 1282
empréstito forzoso 723
empréstito gubernamental 1453
empréstito interior 1099
empréstito legado a un fin determinado 2281
empréstito nacional 1099
empréstito-obligaciones 941
empréstito para el desarrollo 1036
empréstito por bonos de sorteo 1720
empréstito por obligaciones 941
empréstito público 1453
empréstito, redención de un ~ 142
empréstito redimible 141
empréstito, solicitar un ~ 175
enajenabilidad 116
enajenable 117
enajenación 119
enajenador 121
enajenar 118
encaje 587
encarecimiento 1539
encautación 191
endeudado 952
endeudado, estar excesivamente ~ 953
endeudamiento 462
endeudamiento del Estado 1798
endeudamiento excesivo 1207
endeudamiento exterior 420
endeudarse 1294
endosado 1163
endosante 1165
endosante anterior 1944
endosante subsiguiente 2239
endosar una letra di cambio 1162
endosatario 1163
endose 1164
endoso 1164
enjugar 148
enjugar un déficit 836
enterar 1015
entero 1567
enteros (puntos), acusar una baja (una ganancia; un avance) de X ~ 2045
enteros (puntos), registrar una baja (una ganancia; un avance) de X ~ 2045
entrada 409
entrada al debe 946
entrada, aviso de ~ 47
entrada colectiva 717
entrada, dar ~ 401
entrada de capital(es) 99
entrada de rectificación 71
entrada de rescuentro 281
entrada en contra 281
entrada en el debe 946
entrada intermédiaria 2249
entradas 1532
entradas en caja 585
entradas en efectivo 585
entradas y salidas 1525
entrada transitoria 2249
entrampar 466
entrar en liquidación 1428
entrega 119
entrega a plazo 1380
entrega a término 1380
entrega contra reembolso 589
entrega del cupón, contra ~ 1958
entregar 118
enviar 2080
envilecer 1028
envilecerse 970
envilecimiento 1029
envilecimiento de la moneda 896
envío de dinero 1784
envío de fondos 1784
equilibrar el presupuesto 280
equilibrio 1176
equilibrio del presupuesto 251
equilibrio interior 1098
equilibrio interno 1098
equilibrio presupuestario 251
equipo de producción 1134
equivalencia 822, 1180
equivalente 822
erario (público) 2299
erogaciones 1053
erosión de la moneda 896
erosión monetaria 896
error de cálculo 491
errores y omisiones 1183
error u omisión, salvo ~ 1184
error y omisión, salvo ~ 1184
escala móvil 1348
escalonar los pagos sobre X años 2204
escasez de capital(es) 559
escasez de crédito 878
escasez de dólares 1090
escaso de fondos, andar ~ 2178
escaso de fondos, estar ~ 2178
escritura de arrendamiento 1666
escritura fiduciaria 976
especie 661
especie, aportación en ~ 205
especie, aporte en ~ 205
especie, en ~ 1658
especie, remuneración en ~ 134
especificación 429
especulación 2197
especulación en bolsa 111
especulador 2200
especulador a la baja 332
especulador al alza 455
especulador en bolsa 1647
especular 2196
especular a la baja 1427
especular al alza 456
espiral costos-precios 816
espiral de costos y precios 816
espiral deflacionista 993
espiral de precios y salarios 2363
espiral inflacionista 1559
espiral precios-salarios 2363
estabilidad cambiaria 1239
estabilidad de la moneda 903
estabilidad de los cambios 1239
estabilidad de los precios 1326
estabilidad monetaria 903
estabilización del cambio 1237
estabilización de los precios 1969
establecer el inventario 1124
establecer un balance 279
establecer un saldo 279
establecimiento bancario 294
establecimiento central 607
establecimiento financiero 1315
establecimiento principal 607
estacionario 508
estadística 2220
estadísticas 2219
estadísticas internas 1851
estadísticas operativas 1851
estado 2217
estado de consolidación 739
estado de gastos 2218
estado del mercado 1743
estado de repartición 799
estado detallado 429
estado de una cuenta 1940
estado financiero 1319
estado providencia 2373
estado recapitulativo 2241
estado-resumen 2241
estados consolidados 736
estado social 2373
estagflación 2208
estagnación 1130
estampillado de acciones 2212
estampillar 2210
estancación 1130
estancado 508
estancamiento 1130
estancarse 1663
estar a la par 1884
estar bajo la par 1056
estar en el debe 944
estar por debajo de la par 1056
estar por encima de la par 1883

estar sobre la par 1883
estatificación 1801
estatificar 1802
esterilización 2221
esterilizar 2222
esterlina 2223
estimación 176
estimación aproximada 184
estimación aproximativa 184
estimación del monto imponible 1188
estimación (impositiva) 200
estimar 177, 195
estímulo a la inversión 1625
estipendio 1140
estructura del balance 273
estructura de los costes (costos; gastos) 817
estructura financiera 561
estudio del mercado 1740
estudio de rentabilidad 801
Eurodólar 1193
Euromercado 700
evaluación 176
evaluación de bases imponibles 1188
evaluación (impositiva) 200
evaluar 177, 195
evasión de capitales 527
evasión de impuestos 2266
evasión fiscal 2266
evolución 1200
evolución coyuntural 477
evolución de la coyuntura 477
examen del mercado 1740
excedente 1204, 2244
excedente de beneficios 1213
excedente de (en) caja 599
excedente de explotación 1852
excedente de gastos 1212
excedente de ingresos 2245
excedente de la balanza comercial 266
excedente de la balanza de pagos 263
excedente del presupuesto 452
excedente de pasivo 1207
excedente estructural 2229
excedente monetario 6
excedente presupuestario 452
exceder un crédito 1201
exceso 1204
exceso de ahorro 1872
exceso de beneficios 1213
exceso de cobertura de gastos 1870
exceso de demanda 1206
exceso de deudas 1207
exceso de gastos 1212
exceso de oferta 1210
exceso de poder adquisitivo 1209
exceso de valor 1215
ex cupón 831
ex derechos 1249
ex dividendo 1080
exención de impuesto(s) 1248
exención de una deuda 513
exención fiscal 1248
exención impositiva 1248
exentar de derechos de aduana 1246
exento de derechos (de aduana) 920
exento de interés (intereses) 1590
exento (del pago) de impuesto(s) 1247
exigibilidad 674
exigible 496, 675
exigir demasiado 1866
exigir demasiado poco 2316
eximir de derechos de aduana 1246
existencia 1615
existencias 1496
existencias de divisas 1362
existencias de oro 1430
existencia(s) en caja 587
existencia(s) en efectivo 587
éxodo de capitales 556
expansión crediticia 858
expansión de la masa monetaria 1252
expansión de las inversiones 1623
expansión del comercio mundial 1254
expansión del crédito 858
expansión monetaria 1252
expendedor 2105
expender 2157
expensas de, a ~ 1260
experimentar una pérdida 333
expiración 1262
expirar 1264
exportación 1265
exportación de capital(es) 526
exportaciones invisibles 1632
exportaciones visibles 2351
expropiación 1271
expropiar 1270
extender un cheque 1115
extendido en dólares 1010
extinción 139
extinguir 148
extinguir una hipoteca 511
extorno 281
extracto de cuenta 5
extrapresupuestario 1286

facción del inventario 1616
facilidades de crédito 421
factor de conversión 772
factor deflacionista 996
factor inflacionista 1556
factoring 1293
factorización 1293
factura 17
facturación 366
factura pro-forma 1991
factura proforma 1991
facturar 357
falta 988
falta de beneficio 1718
falta de caja 96
falta de capital(es) 559
falta de dólares 1090
falta de ganancia 1718
falta de liquidez 1504
falta de pago 982
falta de valor 2344
fallido 313, 314
fase coyuntural 1150
favor de, a ~ 34
favor de, abrir un crédito a (en) ~ 1847
fecha de cierre del balance 272
fecha de expiración 1263
fecha (de) valor 2343
fecha de vencimiento 931
fiador 236, 395
fiador, salir ~ 52
fiador, ser ~ 52
fianza 602, 1138
fianza cambiaria 230
fianza, dar ~ 52
fianza de caución 394
fianza de fianza 238
fianza de indemnidad 394
fianza de indemnización 394
fianza, prestar ~ 52
fideicomisario 1298
fideicomiso, en ~ 1185
fiduciario 1298
fijación de las razones de paridad 1343
fijación de los precios 1962
fijación de precios 1515
fijación de un dividendo 964
fijación de un máximo 1342
fijación vertical de los precios 2097
fijar un dividendo 965
fijar un precio 1033
filial 98, 427
financiación 1322
financiación anticipada 1952
financiación con déficit 989
financiación con fondos ajenos 1281
financiación con fondos externos 1281
financiación de compras a plazos 1490
financiación de pagos a plazos 1490
financiación de transición 433
financiación de ventas a plazos 1490
financiación externa 1281
financiación interina 433
financiación interna 1601
financiación mediante la cesión de créditos 956
financiación por fondos propios 1601
financiación provisional 433, 1952
financiación temporal 433
financiación transitorio 433
financiamiento 1322
financiamiento anticipado 1952
financiamiento con fondos ajenos 1281
financiamiento con fondos externos 1281
financiamiento de transición 433
financiamiento externo 1281
financiamiento interino 433
financiamiento interno 1601
financiamiento por fondos propios 1601
financiamiento provisional 433, 1952
financiamiento temporal 433
financiamiento transitorio 433
financiar 1306
financiar anticipadamente 1951

financiar provisionalmente 1951
financiero 1321
finanzas 1304
finanza(s), alta(s) ~ 1486
finanzas del estado 827
finanzas públicas 827
fin lucrativo, asociación con ~ 1986
fin lucrativo, asociación sin ~ 1829
fin, salvo buen ~ 2099
firmar una letra por aval 235
firmeza de los precios 1326
fiscal 1329
fisco 1242
flaqueza 1130
flexibilidad de los tipos de cambio 1154
flojedad 1130
flojo 508
fluctuación cíclica 930
fluctuación coyuntural 930
fluctuación de la coyuntura 930
fluctuación del mercado 930
fluctuación de los cambios 1225
fluctuación de los tipos de cambio 1225
fluctuación económica 930
flujo de capital(es) 528
flujo de crédito 859
FMI 1607
fob 1354
fomento del ahorro 1161
fondo 1404
fondo coyuntural 755
fondo de ahorros 2145
fondo de amortización 132, 140
fondo de comercio 1444
fondo de compensación 710
fondo de contrapartida 823
fondo de crédito 1710
fondo de depreciación 132
fondo de estabilización 2205
fondo de garantía 1472
fondo de igualación 710
fondo de inversión 1624
fondo de inversiones 1624
fondo de pensiones 1918
fondo de perecuación 710
fondo de préstamos 1710
fondo de previsión 755
fondo de reemplazo 2086
fondo de rentas 1455
fondo de reposición 2086
fondo de rescate 140
fondo de reserva 2101
Fondo Europeo de Cooperación Monetaria 1197
fondo fiduciario 2307
fondo fijo de caja 1517
Fondo Monetario Internacional 1607
fondo mutual de inversiones 1624
fondo para contingencias 755
fondo para eventualidades 755
fondo para imprevistos 755
fondos 1406
fondos ajenos 417
fondo(s) de explotación 468
fondos del estado 1244, 2005
fondo(s) de operación 468
fondos disponibles 227
fondos en caja 587
fondos en efectivo 587
fondos prestados 417
fondos presupuestados 444
fondos públicos 1244, 2005
fondos tomados en préstamo 417
formación de ahorros 1374
formación de capital 529
formación del inventario 1616
formación del patrimonio 1373
forma de pago 1375
formar el inventario 1124
formar una reserva 454
formulario de depósito 1022
formulario de ingreso 1022
fraccionamiento de acciones 2175
fracción de acciones 1387
franco (a) bordo 1354
franco de aduana 920
franquear 1389
franquicia (aduanera), con (en) ~ 920
franquicia fiscal 1248
franquicia tributaria 1248
fraude fiscal 2266
fraude tributario 2266
fructifero 1147
fuente, deducir en la ~ 972
fuente de entradas 2193
fuente de financiación 2192
fuente de financiamiento 2192
fuente de ingresos 2193
fuente, retener en la ~ 972
fuga de capitales 527
fundación 1385
fusión 135

ganancia 1409
ganancia de capital 530
ganancia distribuible 1072
ganancia excesiva 1213
ganancia extraordinaria 1213
ganancia fiscal 197
ganancia por acción 1142
ganancias 229
ganancias acumuladas 2108
ganancia(s) bruta(s) 1459
ganancia(s) neta(s) 646
ganancias no distribuidas 2108
ganancias no repartidas 2311
ganancias retenidas 2108
ganga 321
garante 395
garante, salir ~ 52
garante, ser ~ 52
garantía 669, 1138, 1471
garantía, adelanto con ~ 86
garantía adicional 65
garantía cambiaria 230
garantía, constituir una ~ 101
garantía, dar ~ 52
garantía, dar una ~ 101
garantía de buen fin 1474
garantía de crédito 860
garantía de crédito a la exportación 1267
garantía de fianza 238
garantía de indemnización 394
garantía del endoso 1166
garantía del estado 1450
garantía de un empréstito 1473
garantía estatal 1450
garantía gubernamental 1450
garantía gubernamental de un crédito 1447
garantía hipotecaria 2035
garantía, ofrecer una ~ 101
garantía oro 1437, 1437
garantía, prestar ~ 52
garantía, prestar una ~ 101
garantía real 2035, 2258
garantía, sin ~ 835
garantía subsidiaria 65
garantía suplementaria 65
garantizado, no ~ 835
garantizar mediante hipoteca 838
garantizar por hipoteca 838
garantizar una emisión 2320
gastado 2378
gastar 1257
gastar más de lo que se gana 1702
gasto 1258
gastos 1053, 1261
gastos accesorios 61
gastos adicionales 61
gastos ajenos al presupuesto 1823
gastos a pagar 39
gastos bancarios 291
gastos comerciales 472
gastos constantes 1336
gastos corrientes 908
gastos chicos 1764
gastos de administración 79
gastos de adquisición 488, 804
gastos de banco 291
gastos de capital 524
gastos de consumo 748
gastos de crédito 805
gastos de desplazamiento 2298
gastos de emisión 1353
gastos de entretenimiento 810
gastos de expedición 2295
gastos de explotación 1850
gastos de fabricación 811
gastos de inversión 524
gastos de los consumidores 748
gastos de manipulación 1478
gastos de mantenimiento 810
gastos de manutención 810
gastos de operación 1850
gastos de producción 811
gastos de prolongación 569
gastos de reposición 2091
gastos de representación 1169
gastos, descontando los ~ 621
gastos de transferencia 812
gastos de transporte 2295
gastos de viaje 2298
gastos directos 1043
gastos diversos 1764
gastos efectivos 55
gastos efectuados 55
gastos extraordinarios 61
gastos fijos 1336
gastos financieros 1313

gastos fuera del presupuesto 1823
gastos generales 1417
gastos imprevistos 754
gastos incidentales 61
gastos indirectos 1417
gastos, ingresos y ~ 1525
gastos menores 1764
gastos, menos los ~ 621
gastos menudos 1764
gastos no deducibles 1049
gastos, otros ~ 1764
gastos por unidad 813
gastos presupuestarios 446
gastos públicos 2003
gastos sociales 2186
gastos suplementarios 61
gastos unificados 813
gastos variables 2346
GATT 1415
gestión financiera 730
gestión presupuestaria 450
girado 1117, 1163
girador 1118, 1165
girante 1118, 1165
girar 2080
girar contra el Fondo Monetario Internacional 1123
girar en descubierto (sobre una cuenta) 1868
girar una letra de cambio contra alguien 1114
girar un cheque 1115
giro 356
giro a la vista 1003
giro bancario 284, 318
giro contra el Fondo Monetario Internacional 1120
giro de dinero 1784
giro de fondos 1784
giro de negocios 2130
giro en descubierto 1867
giro en metálico 595
giro postal 1781
grado de ingresos 1527
grado de liquidez 45
grado de rentas 1527
gran accionista 633
gran capital 355
gratificación 397
gravable 196
gravamen 460
gravamen hipotecario 1793
gravar con deudas 466
gravar con una hipoteca 465
gravar con una sobretasa 1514
gravar con un impuesto 194
grupo 727
grupo de ingresos 1527
grupo de rentas 1527
grupo fiscal 2267

haber 206, 843, 849
haberes 202
haberes bloqueados 381
haberes del tesoro 2300
haberes en el extranjero 204
hacer economías 924
hacer efectivo un cheque 576
hacer el balance de una cuenta 249
hacer el inventario 1124
hacer el servicio de un empréstito 2165
hacer negocios 1084
hacer negocios de trueque 326
hacer protestar un efecto 1481
hacer recurso a las reservas 1042
hacer una deuda 761
hacer un balance 279
hacer un empréstitio 762
hacienda pública 827
hiperinflación 1500
hipoteca 1790
hipoteca amortizable 137
hipotecar 1791
hipotecariamente, asegurar ~ 838
hipoteca (sobre), tomar una ~ 2019
hoja de cupones 832
hoja de distribución de costes 799
hoja de impuestos 1839
holding 1494
honorarios 1295
honrar un efecto 1054
horas extraordinarias 1875
horas suplementarias 1875
hot money 1498
hueco inflacionista 1557
huída de capitales 527
hundimiento 668
hundimiento de las cotizaciones 431
hundimiento de los precios 431
hurtar 977
hurto 978

igualación 1172
igualación de cargas 1174
igualación de impuestos 1175
igualación tributaria 1175
iliquidez 1504
ilíquido 1503
imponer 1015
imponer una contribución (sobre) 194
imponer un impuesto (sobre) 194
imponer un precio 1033
imponible 196
imponible, no ~ 1247
importación 1509
importación de capital(es) 534
importaciones invisibles 1633
importaciones visibles 2352
importar en total 106
importe 149
importe adeudado 151
importe a tanto alzado 1722
importe bruto 1460
importe debido 151
importe global 107
importe impago 154
importe neto 1808
importe neto de los créditos concedidos 1812
importe neto de los créditos utilizados 1810
importe nominal 1820
importe no pagado 154
importe pendiente 152
importe restante 246
importe su(b)scrito 153
importe total 107
imposición 1135, 1567
imposición de contribuciones 1516
imposición de precios 1515
imposición, doble ~ 1109
improductivo de interés (intereses) 1590
impuesta sobre las donaciones 1422
impuesto 1135
impuesto adicional 66
impuesto a la propiedad 551
impuesto al giro comercial 2014
impuesto al lujo 1723
impuesto a los réditos 1530
impuesto compensatorio 712
impuesto complementario 66
impuesto de compensación 712
impuesto de consumo(s) 752
impuesto deducido en el origen 2268
impuesto (de los impuestos), antes del ~ 1959
impuesto de lujo 1723
impuesto de sellos 2211
impuesto de sociedades 792
impuesto de sucesión 938
impuesto de timbre 2211
impuesto diferido 986
impuesto directo 1046
impuesto en la fuente 2268
impuesto graduado 1456
impuesto indirecto 1552
impuesto inmobiliario 1995
impuesto predial 1662
impuesto progresivo 1456
impuesto real 1995
impuesto regresivo 997
impuestos, después de ~ 1677
impuesto sobre el aumento del capital 532
impuesto sobre el beneficio de capital 532
impuesto sobre el capital 551
impuesto sobre el capital social 560
impuesto sobre el consumo 752
impuesto sobre el excedente de beneficios 1214
impuesto sobre el incremento del capital 532
impuesto sobre el ingreso de capital 565
impuesto sobre el lujo 1723
impuesto sobre el movimiento de capital 564
impuesto sobre el movimiento de ventas 2014
impuesto sobre el patrimonio inmueble 1995
impuesto sobre el patrimonio (mueble) 551
impuesto sobre el rendimiento de capital 565
impuesto sobre el valor agregado 2341
impuesto sobre el valor añadido 2341

impuesto sobre la cifra de negocios 2014
impuesto sobre la herencia 938
impuesto sobre la plusvalía de cesión 532
impuesto sobre la plusvalía del capital 532
impuesto sobre la propiedad 551
impuesto sobre la propiedad territorial 1662
impuesto sobre la renta 1530
impuesto sobre la renta de las personas físicas 1930
impuesto sobre las ganancias de capital 532
impuesto sobre las patentes 476
impuesto sobre la(s) renta(s) del capital 565
impuesto sobre las utilidades 1989
impuesto sobre las utilidades excesivas 1214
impuesto sobre las ventas 2014
impuesto sobre la transferencia de capital 564
impuesto sobre los artículos de lujo 1723
impuesto sobre los beneficios 1989
impuesto sobre los beneficios de sociedades 792
impuesto sobre los bienes raíces 1995
impuesto sobre sociedades 792
impuesto sucesorio 938
impuesto suntuario 1723
impuesto territorial 1662
imputación 123, 613
imputar 615
inactividad 1130
inactivo 508
incautación 191
incautarse (de) 211
incentivo 1519
incentivo a la inversión 1625
incentivo fiscal 2270
incidencia de un impuesto 1521
incluir en el presupuesto 443
incluso dividendo 887
inconvertibilidad 1533
inconvertible 1534
incremento de los precios 1539
incremento del tipo de descuento 1541
incremento del X por ciento 1543
incremento de valor 180
indemnización 708
indemnización de caja 133
indemnización de gastos de viaje 2296
indemnización (de los gastos de representación) 128
indicador 1551
indicar un precio 1728
índice 1546, 1550
índice, ajustamiento por un ~ 1548
índice del coste de vida 809
índice de liquidez 45
índice de los precios al por mayor 2374
índice de los precios al por menor 2106
índice de precios 1964
índice de precios de mercancías 696
índice de ventas 2131
índice económico, variar con un ~ 1547
índice ponderado 2370
inflación 1554
inflación crediticia 861
inflación de costes 803
inflación de costos 803
inflación de demanda 1005
inflación de gastos 803
inflación del crédito 861
inflación desenfrenada 1411
inflación galopante 1411
inflación importada 1511
inflación irrefrenable 1411
inflacionismo 1560
inflacionista 1555, 1561
inflación latente 725
inflación oculta 725
inflación provocada por el aumento de los salarios 2361
inflación reprimida 1919
inflación reptante 882
inflar 1553
informe 2217
informe anual 160
informe de auditoría 217
informe de censura 217
informe de la revisión de cuentas 217
informe del censor de cuentas 217
informe financiero 1319
ingerencia del estado 1452
ingerencia del gobierno 1452
ingresar 1015
ingreso 1567
ingreso de capital 1909
ingreso de transferencia 2292
ingresos 1140, 1522, 1532
ingresos accesorios 64
ingresos adicionales 64
ingresos aduaneros 921
ingresos brutos 1463
ingresos de la sociedad 791
ingresos del capital 535
ingresos del Estado 1451
ingresos de los factores 1292
ingresos del trabajo 1136
ingresos (derivados) de inversiones 1528
ingresos disponibles 1068
ingreso(s) efectivo(s) 2032
ingresos en caja 585
ingresos en efectivo 585
ingresos en especie 1529
ingresos extraordinarios 1287
ingresos fijos 210
ingresos fiscales 1565
ingresos imponibles 2262
ingresos laborales 1136
ingresos netos 1811
ingresos no laborales 2323
ingresos no recurrentes 1287
ingresos, otros ~ 1765
ingresos periódicos 2049
ingresos personales 1929
ingresos presupuestarios 447
ingresos primarios 1970
ingresos privados 1929
ingresos públicos 1451
ingreso(s) real(es) 2032
ingresos recurrentes 2049
ingresos regulares 210
ingreso(s) retenido(s) 1137
ingresos salariales 1136
ingresos secundarios 2146
ingresos seguros 210
ingresos suplementarios 64
ingresos varios 1765
ingresos y egresos 1525
ingresos y gastos 1525
iniciativa privada 1976
inmovilización 1506
inmovilizaciones corporales 518
inmovilizaciones incorporales 1505
inmovilizaciones inmateriales 1505
inmovilizaciones intangibles 1505
inmovilizaciones reales 518
inmovilizaciones tangibles 518
inmovilizar 1507
inmuebles 1508
inmunidad fiscal 1248
inmunidad tributaria 1248
inscribir en el activo 403
inscribir en el activo, a ~ 408
inscribir en el pasivo 402
inscribir en el pasivo, a ~ 407
insolvencia 1569
insolvente 1570
inspección fiscal 1566
institución bancaria 294
institución de crédito 850
institución de descuento 1058
instituto bancario 294
instituto de crédito 850
instituto de crédito inmobiliario 1660
instituto financiero 1315
instrumento crediticio 862
instrumento de crédito 862
instrumento fiscal 1332
integración 135
intensidad de capital 538
intercambio triangular 2280
interconvertibilidad 1584
interdicción de importación 319
interés 1585
interés, a ~ 1586
interés corriente 909
interés del capital 540
interés de X por ciento, arrojar un ~ 334
interés de X por ciento, dar un ~ 334
interés de X por ciento, devengar ~ 334
interés de X por ciento, rendir un ~ 334
interés (en) 1495
intereses 1585
intereses a cobrar 376
intereses acreedores 376

intereses activos 376
intereses acumulados 41
intereses anticipados 165
intereses a pagar 947
intereses a recibir 376
intereses atrasados 190
intereses bancarios 306
intereses calculados 1518
interés(es) compuesto(s) 720
intereses corrientes 909
intereses débitos 1589
interés(es) de demora 983
intereses de próximo vencimiento 42
intereses deudores 947
intereses devengados 1589
interés(es) escalonado(s) 1457
intereses hipotecarios 1794
intereses interinos 1599
interés(es) moratorio(s) 983
intereses pasivos 947
interés(es) usurario(s) 2335
intereses vencidos 1589
interés fijo, a ~ 1338
interés fijo, de ~ 1338
interés (intereses), sin ~ 1590
interés mayoritario 770
interés minoritario 1760
interés, prestar dinero a ~ 1675
interés simple 2179
intermediario de corredores de bolsa 1648
intervención del estado 1452
intervencionismo 1608
interventor (de cuentas) 216
interventor de la quiebra 209
introducir en el mercado 1737
inundar el mercado (con artículos baratos) 1132
inventariar 1124
inventario 1614, 1615, 1616
inversión 1619
inversión de capital 542
inversión del sector público 2006
inversión de rédito variable 2348
inversión desacertada 244
inversión en el extranjero 1368
inversión en títulos (de cartera) 1626
inversión en valores (de cartera) 1626
inversión equivocada 244
inversión errónea 244
inversiones de bolsa 1179
inversiones reales 518
inversión extranjera 1367
inversión fija 1340
inversión horizontal 1253
inversión inmovilizada 1340
inversionista 1631
inversión mal colocada 244
inversión mal orientada 244
inversión nueva 1818
inversión para expansión 1253
inversión para racionalización 1580
inversión privada 1978
inversión pública 2006
inversión vertical 1580
inversor 1631
inversor institucional 793
invertir 1618
investigación del mercado 1740
invitar a la suscripción de un empréstito 1634
inyección de capital 521
inyectar capital 436
IVA 2341

juego en bolsa 111
jugador de bolsa 1647
junta de acreedores 388
justificante 2358
justificante de contabilidad 33
justificante de ingreso 877
justificante de pago 600

keynesiano 1657

lado acreedor 206
lado activo 206
lado del activo 206
lado del crédito 206
lado del debe 943
lado del débito 943
lado del haber 206
lado del pasivo 943
lado deudor 943
lado pasivo 943
laguna de dólares 1089
languidecer 1663
languidez 1130
lánguido 508
lanzamiento 1352
lanzar al mercado 1665
lanzar un empréstito 1157
largo plazo, a ~ 1715
leasing 1668
letra a cobrar 364, 373
letra a la orden 374
letra a la propia orden 1477
letra a la vista 1003
letra al cobro 364, 373
letra al propio cargo 1477
letra a pagar 372
letra bancaria 284
letra comerciable 374
letra comercial 356
letra cruzada 819
letra de acomodación 15
letra de banco 284
letra de cambio 356
letra de cambio, aceptar une ~ 8
letra (de cambio), avalar una ~ 235
letra (de cambio), prestar el aval de (para) una ~ 235
letra de crédito 1678
letra de favor 15
letra de resaca 819
letra de tesorería 2301
letra de vencimiento usual 358
letra endosable 374
letra ficticia 15
letra innegociable 371
letra intransferible 371
letra intransmissible 371
letra negociable 374
letra no a la orden 371
letra no comerciable 371
letra no endosable 371
letra nominativa 371
letra no negociable 371
letra no transferible 371
letra no transmisible 371
letra por aval, firmar una ~ 235
letra proforma 15
letra sobre el extranjero 1357
letra sobre el interior 1091
letra transferible 374
letra transmisible 374
levantamiento del inventario 1616
levantamiento de restricciones 2
levantar el inventario 1124
levantar restricciones 1
leventar un empréstito 762
ley 1325
liberación 950
liberación de los precios 971
liberación total de una acción 1908
liberalización del comercio 1684
liberalizar 1685
liberar 949
liberar una acción completamente 1915
liberar una acción del X % 1899
liberar una acción totalmente 1915
libertad de comercio 1392
libertad de competencia 1390
libertad de empresa 1391
librado 1117
librador 1118
libra esterlina 1943
libranza 356
libranza bancaria 284
libranza de letras de colusión 1659
librar una letra de cambio contra alguien 1114
librar un cheque 1115
libras bloqueadas 382
libras (esterlinas) transferibles 2291
libre cambio 1392
librecambio 1392
librecambista 1399
libre competencia 1390
libre de derechos (de aduana) 920
libre (del pago) de impuesto(s) 1247
libre empresa 1391
libreta bancaria 289
libreta de ahorros 2142
libreta de banco 289
libreta de caja de ahorros 2140
libreta de cuenta 289
libreta de cheques 626
libreta de depósitos 1021
libro auxiliar 225
libro borrador 1754
libro de acciones 1701
libro de balance 250
libro de caja 578
libro de efectos (a cobrar) 360
libro de efectos (a pagar) 359
libro de inventario 250
libro de (los) accionistas 1701
libro diario 932
libro mayor 1418
libro mayor de los accionistas 1701
libros comerciales 28

libros de comercio 28
libros de contabilidad 28
licencia 1686
licencia de exportación 1268
licencia de importación 1512
licitación 212
licitar 213
limitación crediticia 874
limitación de créditos 874
limitación de la liquidez 2104
limitar los gastos 915
límite de crédito 855
límite de endeudamiento 422
límite de los adelantos sobre títulos 604
límite de precio 1965
línea de crédito 855
liquidación 139, 773, 1070
liquidación de una cuenta 254
liquidación, día de ~ 24
liquidador 1694
liquidar 148, 785, 1071
liquidarse 1428
liquidar una cuenta 249
liquidar un déficit 836
liquidar un descubierto 836
liquideces cuasimonetarias 1776
liquideces secundarias 1776
liquidez 1695
liquidez de caja 227
liquidez excesiva 1211
liquidez primaria 1971
líquido 1693
lista de cotización 1228
lista de los accionistas 1701
lista de mercancías exentas de aranceles 1394
locación venta 1487
locador 1676
locatario 1667
logro 2337
lonja 695
lote de acciones 386
lucrativo 1147
lucro 1409
lucro cesante 1718

llamamiento al mercado 506
llamamiento de fondos 494
llamar a licitación 1635
llegar al vencimiento 347
llevar al debe 615
llevar al débito 615
llevar al fondo de reserva 68
llevar al mercado 1737
llevar el inventario 1124
llevar la contabilidad 1656
llevar las cuentas 1656
llevar los libros 1656
llevar una suma al crédito de alguien 566

macroeconómico 1725
mala inversión 244
mal pagador 245
malvender 2158
malversación 978
malversar 977
manco 988
mandante 1973
mandar un efecto al protesto 1481
mandato postal 1781
maniobra bursátil 1730
manipulación bursátil 1730
manipulación de la moneda 898
manipulación de los cambios 1730
manipulación monetaria 898
manos muertas 1795
mantenimiento de los precios 1917
mantenimiento del precio de reventa 2097
marasmo 1130
marcha de los negocios 833
margen 1037, 1732
margen adicional 62
margen comercial 1734
margen de beneficio 1734
margen de beneficio bruto 1465
margen de beneficio neto 1813
margen de crédito 864
margen de fluctuación de los tipos de cambio 1346
margen de ganancia 1734
margen de ganancia bruta 1465
margen de ganancia neta 1813
margen de intereses 1412
margen de precios 1966
margen de utilidad 1734
margen entre los tipos de interés 1412
margenes sobre las operaciones de arbitraje 187
marketing 1742
masa activa 202
masa de la quiebra 317
masa monetaria 1783
masa pasiva 961
masa salarial 2359
materia básica 329
materia de base 329
materia prima 329
matriz 821
mayor auxiliar 225
mayoreo 2376
mayor (general) 1418
mayorista 2375
mayor postor 1485
media 231
media anual 158
médidas de relanzamiento 2011
médidas para estimular la recuperación económica 2011
medio 232
medio circulante 636
medio de circulación 636
medio plazo, a ~ 1752
medios 1406
medios de financiación 558
medios de pago 1751
medios de pago, circulación de ~ 638
medios de producción durables 1134
medios financieros 558
mejor postor 1485
memoria anual 160
menor(es) ingreso(s) 2112
menorista 2105
menor valor 969
menos los gastos 621
mensualidad 1787, 1788
menudeo 2107
mercado 1735
mercado abierto 1395
mercado alcista 458
mercado bajista 345
Mercado Común 700
mercado de acciones 2153
mercado de baja 345
mercado de cambios 1230
mercado de cambios a plazo 1382
mercado de cambios a término 1382
mercado de cambios, doble ~ 2309
mercado de capital(es) 554
mercado de compradores 483
mercado de descuento 370
mercado de dinero 1778
mercado de divisas 1230
mercado de divisas a plazo 1382
mercado de divisas a término 1382
mercado de eurodivisas 1192
mercado de euroemisiones 1191
mercado de letras 370
mercado de rentas 393
mercado (de salida) 1736
mercado de valores de renta fija 393
mercado de valores (mobiliarios) 2153
mercado de vendedores 2160
mercado, Euro~ 700
mercado financiero 554
mercado interior 1100
mercado, introducir en el ~ 1737
mercado libre 891, 1395
mercado libre de cambios 1885
mercado libre de divisas 1885
mercadología 1740
mercado, llevar al ~ 1737
mercado monetario 1778
mercado nacional 1100
mercado negro 377
mercado no oficial 891
mercado paralelo 1885
mercado secundario 2147
mercadotecnia 1742
mercancías de exportación 1266
mercancías de importación 1510
merma 988
mesada 1787
metálico 661
metálico, en ~ 573
microeconómico 1757
mil milliones 368
minorista 2105
minusvalía de cesión 553
minuta de compra 425
minuta de venta 440
mobilización de capital 1405
mobilización de fondos 1405
modalidad de pago 1375
modalidades de pago 2278
modo de pago 1375
moneda 660, 893
Moneda 1761
moneda bancaria 307

moneda barata 623
moneda blanda 2187
moneda circulante 906
moneda controlada 767
moneda corriente 906
moneda débil 2187
moneda de cambio 1780
moneda de cobertura en oro y divisas 1436
moneda de cobre 788
moneda de curso legal 1669
moneda de intercambio 1780
moneda del país 1094
moneda de núcleo aureo (en lingotes) 1431
moneda de núcleo oro 1431
moneda de oro 1433
moneda de reserva 2100
moneda dirigida 767
moneda divisionaria 1083
moneda dura 1479
moneda emitida por el tesoro 2302
moneda en circulación 906
moneda en curso 906
moneda estable 2207
moneda extranjera 1361
moneda fiduciaria 1296, 2283
moneda floja 2187
moneda flotante 1350
moneda fraccionaria 1083
moneda fuerte 1479
moneda giral 307
moneda inestable 1350
moneda legal 1669
moneda manipulada 767
moneda metálica 661
moneda nacional 1094
moneda oro 1402
moneda propia 1094
monedar 662
monedas 665
moneda sana 2191
monedas, billetes y ~ 1834
moneda variable 1350
monedear 662
monedería 1761
monetarista 1768
monetización 663, 1772
monetizar 662, 785, 1773
monometalismo 1785
monopolio 1786
monopolio comercial 2287
monopolio del estado 1454
monto 149
monto bruto 1460
monto neto 1808
mora, en ~ 979
moratoria 1276
moratorio 1789
movilización 1766
movilizar 1767
movimiento bursátil 2225
movimiento de capital 555
movimiento de pagos 1911
movimientos de capital, balance de los ~ 256
movimientos de capital, balanza de los ~ 256
movimientos de tesorería 586
muebles 622
muerto 508
multa 136
mundo de las finanzas 1305
mundo financiero 1305
muro aduanero 918
muro arancelario 918
mutuante 1672
mutuario 418
mutuatario 418

nacionalización 1801
nacionalizar 1802
necesidad de préstamos 424
necesidades de capital 557
necesidades de cobertura 837
necesidades de inversión 1627
necesidades de liquidez 596
necesidades de tesorería 596
necesidades financieras 1316
negativa de pago 2074
negociable 1738
negociación 320
negociaciones bursátiles 1222
negociaciones de títulos 1222
negociaciones de valores 1222
negociante en divisas 509
negociar un empréstito 1807
negocio 320
negocio a la vista 1379
negocio al contado 581
negocio a medias 1653
negocio a plazo 1379
negocio a plazo en moneda extranjera 1381
negocio a plazos 1489
negocio a prima 1855
negocio a término 1379
negocio a término en moneda extranjera 1381
negocio de cambio al contado 2202
negocio de cambio a plazo 1381
negocio de divisas al contado 2202
negocio de divisas a término 1381
negocio en efectivo 581
negocio en participación 1653
negocios bancarios 304
negocios bursátiles 1222
negocios con el extranjero 1358
negocios crediticios 851
negocios de cambio 1241
negocios de trueque, hacer ~ 326
negocios, efectuar ~ 1084
negocios en divisas 1241
negocios en títulos 1222
negocios en valores 1222
negocios, hacer ~ 1084
nivelación de cargas 1174
nivelar el presupuesto 280
nivel de inversiones 1679
nivel de (las) cotizaciones 1680
nivel de (los) precios 1680
nivel de vida 1704
no convertibilidad 1533
no convertible 1534
no distribución de dividendo 1826
no económico 2324
no imponible 1247
no inflacionista 1828
no liquidez 1504
no líquido 1503
no lucrativo 2324
no llegar con su dinero 1702
nómina de sueldos 1912
nominal de una acción 1290
no pago 982
no reconocimiento de una deuda 2093
no rentable 2324
nota 17
nota de abono 847
nota de cargo 948
nota de compra 425
nota de contrato 425, 440
nota de crédito 847
nota de débito 948
nota de venta 440
no valor 242, 2344
no valores 2345
nuestra cuenta 1833
nueva fijación de cuotas 77
numerario 572, 661
numerario, en ~ 573
número índice 1550

objetos de lujo 1001
objetos de valor 1646
obligación 389, 692
obligación ajustable por un índice 1549
obligación al portador 338
obligación al portador con cupón de intereses 830
obligación amortizable 497
obligación a prima 1719
obligación bancaria 288
obligación comunal 1713
obligación con garantía 2149
obligación contributiva 2271
obligación convertible 783
obligación de conversión 704
obligación de garantía 394
obligación del estado 1243
obligación del tesoro 1243
obligación de pagar impuestos 1683
obligación de participación 1526
obligacion en divisas 1223
obligación en dólares 1087
obligación en mora 980
obligaciones 961
obligaciones a corto plazo 910
obligaciones a la vista 1006
obligaciones en cuenta corriente 1023
obligación eventual 758
obligación fiscal 2271
obligación garantizada 2149
obligación hipotecaria 1792
obligación índice 1549
obligación irredimible 1636
obligación irrescatable 1636
obligacionista 390
obligación municipal 1713
obligación no amortizable 1636
obligación no garantizada 2331

obligación no reembolsable 1636
obligación no rescatable 1636
obligación perpetua 1925
obligación redimible 497
obligación reembolsable 497
obligación rescatable 497
obligación sin garantía 2331
obligación tributaria 2271
obligación variable por un índice 1549
obligado por letra de cambio 362
obras públicas 2010
obtención de capital 1405
obtención de fondos 1405
obtener una ganancia 1729
obtener un beneficio 1729
OCDE 1860
OECE 1861
oferta 352
oferta (de concurso-subasta) 2276
oferta de pago 1844
oferta de suscripción 1842
oferta excesiva 1210
oferta y demanda 2242
oferta y domanda 192
oficina central 607
oficina de cambio(s) 1217
oficina de compensación 649
oficina de corredor 439
oficina principal 607
ofrecer a la venta 1841
ofrecer en venta 1841
ofrecer mejor precio 2317
ofrecer una garantía 101
ofrecer un empréstito a (la) su(b)scripción 1634
ofrecer un empréstito en su(b)scripción 1634
ofrecimiento 352
OIT 1606
omisiones, errores y ~ 1183
opción 1854
opción de compra 484
opción de venta 1858
opción, doble ~ 1108
operación 320
operación a la vista 1379
operación al contado 581
operación a plazo 1379
operación a plazo en moneda extranjera 1381
operación a plazos 1489
operación a prima 1855
operación a término 1379
operación a término con divisas 1381
operación de cambio al contado 2202
operación de cambio a plazo 1381
operación de cobertura 839
operación de compensación 327
operación de divisas al contado 2202
operación de divisas a término 1381
operación de doble opción 1108
operación de reporte 753, 2251
operación de reporto 753
operación de swap 2251
operación de trueque 327
operación en efectivo 581
operaciones bancarias 304
operaciones bursátiles 1222
operaciones con el extranjero 1358
operaciones crediticias 851
operaciones de bolsa 1222
operaciones de cambio 1241
operaciones de clearing 643
operaciones de compensación 643
operaciones de crédito 851
operaciones de giro 643
operaciones de pago 1911
operaciones de títulos 1222
operaciones de valores 1222
operaciones en divisas 1241
operaciones por cheque 632
operación switch 2253
operación triangular 2253
operación vinculada 2251
operador 1647
orden, a la ~ 1726
orden bancaria 299
orden de banco 299
orden de pago 221, 590
organismo financiero público 2004
Organización de Cooperación y Desarrollo Económico 1860
Organización Europea de Cooperación Económica 1861
Organización Internacional del Trabajo 1606
organo de compensación 649
orientación 1200
orientación de las inversiones 1044
orientación del capital 1044
oro acuñado 667
oro amonedado 667
oro de ley 1324
oro de título legal 666
oro en barras 323
oro en lingotes 323
oro fino 1324
oro monetario 666
oro monetizado 667
oro y plata en barras 457
oro y plata en lingotes 457
oscilación cíclica 930
oscilación coyuntural 930
oscilación de la coyuntura 930
oscilación del mercado 930
oscilación de los cambios 1225
oscilación de los tipos de cambio 1225
oscilación económica 930
otorgamiento de crédito 220
otorgar un crédito 126
otros gastos 1764
otros ingresos 1765

padecer una pérdida 333
paga 1140
pagable en divisas 1898
pagable en moneda extranjero 1898
pagadero a la entrega 589
pagadero a la presentación 1896
pagadero a la vista 1896
pagadero al contado 1897
pagadero en divisas 1898
pagadero en efectivo 1897
pagadero en moneda extranjera 1898
pagador 1903
pagador, mal ~ 245
pagados los impuestos 1677
pagam(i)ento de, contra ~ 732
pagando interés (intereses) 1586
pagar 148
pagar al contado 1727
pagar anticipadamente 1904
pagar con anticipación 1904
pagar con cheque 1901
pagaré 1477
pagaré de acomodación 15
pagar en dinero 1727
pagar en efectivo 1727
pagar integralmente 1905
pagar íntegramente 1905
pagar los intereses de un empréstito 2165
pagar mediante cheque 1901
pagar por adelanto 1904
pagar por anticipado 1904
pagar por medio de un cheque 1901
pagar una factura, dar orden de ~ 223
pagar un dividendo 1051
pagar un efecto 1054
pago 139, 1567
pago a cuenta 1014
pago adelantado 92
pago a la entrega 589
pago al contado 591
pago anticipado 92
pago a plazos 1571
pago a término 1910
pago completo 715
pago con anticipación 92
pago contra entrega 589
pago de, contra ~ 732
pago de dividendos 1052
pago de intereses 1592
pago de interés (intereses), sujeto al ~ 2231
pago de los atrasos 237
pago en efectivo 591
pago en metálico 591
pago entero 715
pago íntegro 715
pago intracomunitario 1611
pago, no ~ 982
pago parcial 1894
pago por adelantado 92
pago por anticipado 92
pago por cheque o transferencia 588
pago provisional 1999
pagos 1911
pagos externos, balanza de ~ 258
pagos, hacer ~ 1152
pagos parciales, por ~ 987
pago total 715
país acreedor 871
país de moneda débil 2188
país de moneda fuerte 1480
país deudor 959
país excedentario 824
país exportador 825
país exportador de capital 525
país importador 826

pánico bancario 2121
papel a la vista 1007
papel bancable 283
papel comercial 356
papel de comercio 356
papel descontable 283
papeles 2151
papeles bursátiles 1699
papel financiero 1307
papel moneda 1355
papel moneda no convertible 1535
papel monetario 1779
papel negociable 1806
paquete de acciones 386
parado 508
par, a la ~ 1882
paralización 1130
paralizado 508
paralizarse 1663
par, estar a la ~ 1884
par, estar bajo la ~ 1056
par, estar por debajo de la ~ 1056
par, estar por encima de la ~ 1883
par, estar sobre la ~ 1883
paridad 1886, 1889
paridad cambiaria 1182
paridad de cambio 1182, 1890
paridad intrínseca 1762
paridad monetaria 1182
paridad oro 1439
paro 1130
parte de acción 2230
parte de los beneficios 2173
partes de fundador 1386
participación (en) 1495
participación en acciones 2172
participación en comandita 1591
participación en el extranjero 1366
participación en las ganancias 1410
participación en las utilidades 1410
participación en los beneficios 1410
participación extranjera 1365
participación mayoritaria 770
participación minoritaria 1760
participación recíproca 885
partida 409
partida activa 857
partida colectiva 717
partida compensatoria 281
partida compuesta 717
partida de cargo 946
partida de compensación 281
partida de crédito 857
partida de débito 946
partida del debe 946
partida de rectificación 71
partida de rescuentro 281
partida deudora 946
partida doble 1106
partida pasiva 946
partidas presupuestarias 444
partida transitoria 2249
pasar al activo 403
pasar a la reserva 68
pasar al debe 615
pasar al débito 615
pasar al fondo de reserva 68
pasar al pasivo 402
pasar con lo que se gana 1703
pasar una suma al crédito de alguien 566
pase de caja 133
pasivo 943, 961
pasivo a corto plazo 910
pasivo circulante 910
pasivo contingente 758
pasivo corriente 910
pasivo eventual 758
pasivo exigible 910
pasivo no exigible 1825
pasivo no vencido 1825
pasivos, activos y ~ 203
pasivos a la vista 1006
paso por la aduana 645
patente 476
patrimonio inmueble 1508
patrimonio nacional 1804
patrimonio neto 1809
patrimonio social 790
patrón claudicante 1476
patrón cojo 1476
patrón de cambio oro 1436
patrón de (en) divisas-oro 1436
patrón de numerario oro 1402
patrón, doble ~ 375
patrón lingote oro 1431
patrón oro 1441
patrón oro-divisas 1436
patrón único 1785
peaje 2284
peculado 978
pedir demasiado 1866
pedir demasiado poco 2316
pedir prestado 415
penalidad 136
pena pecuniaria 136
penuria de capital(es) 559
penuria de crédito 878
penuria de dólares 1090
percepción de impuestos 683
percibir un impuesto 678
perder (en) valor 970
pérdida 1717
pérdida, absorber una ~ 3
pérdida bruta 1464
pérdida comercial 474
pérdida contable 411
pérdida de beneficios 1718
pérdida de cambio 1229
pérdida de capital 552
pérdida deducible 974
pérdida de explotación 474
pérdida de ganancias 1718
pérdida de lucro 1718
pérdida de operación 474
pérdida de valor 969
pérdida en operaciones de cambio 1229
pérdida neta 651
pérdida total 934
pérdida (una ganancia), acusar una ~ 2046
pérdida (una ganancia), arrojar una ~ 2046
pérdida (una ganancia), registrar una ~ 2046
perecuación 1172
perecuación de cargas 1174
perecuación de gastos 800
perecuación de impuestos 1175
perecuación tributaria 1175
período de validez 894
perito contador 21
perito en leyes fiscales 2264
permiso de exportación 1268
permiso de importación 1512
perturbación del equilibrio 1062
peso 2368
petición de (apertura de la) quiebra 316
PIB 1461
pieza 660
pieza de oro 1433
pignorable 9
pignoración de efectos 1501
pignoración de títulos 1501
pignoración de valores 1501
pignoración, susceptible de ~ 9
pignorar 1018
pignorar valores 671
plafón de crédito 855
plan contable 22
plan de amortización 146
plan de cuentas 22
plan de financiación 1312
plan financiero 1312
plazo 1571
plazo, a breve ~ 2177
plazo, a corto ~ 2177
plazo, a largo ~ 1715
plazo de bloqueo 384
plazo de circulación 895
plazo (de cortesía) 998
plazo de expiración 1263
plazo (de gracia) 998
plazo de pago 1924
plazo de preaviso 1836
plazo de previo aviso 1836
plazo (de respiro) 998
plazo de su(b)scripción 2237
plazo de suspensión 384
plazo (de validez) 894
plazo de vencimiento 931
plazo de vencimiento de X años 1749
plazo largo, a ~ 1715
plazo medio, a ~ 1752
plazo mensual 1788
plazo para un pago, acordar un ~ 1274
plazos, a (en; por) ~ 987
plazo semestral 351
plétora de dinero 6
plétora monetaria 6
plus por carestía (de vida) 808
plusvalía 180
plusvalía contable 412
plusvalía de cambio 1233
plusvalía de cesión 531
plusvalía de cotización 1233
plusvalías de entradas 2246
PNB 1466
poco animado 508
poco lucrativo 2324

poco remunerador 2324
poder adquisitivo 487
poder adquisitivo excesivo 1209
poder de compra 487
política crediticia 872
política de dividendos 1081
política del crédito 872
política financiera 1317
política monetaria 1769
póliza 2209
póliza de seguro 1577
ponderación 2371
ponderar 2369
poner a la venta 1841
poner capital a la disposición 1407
poner embargo (sobre) 211
poner en cuenta 570
poner en venta 1841
pool 1938
porcentaje 1921
porcentaje de participación en los beneficios 1923
por ciento 1922
por ciento, aumento del X ~ 1543
portador 336, 337
portador de valores 341
portazgo 2284
poseedor 336
poseedor de valores 341
posición de divisas 1363
posición de una cuenta 1940
pos(t)fechar 1942
postor, mayor ~ 1485
postor, mejor ~ 1485
postura 353
potencial de crecimiento 1469
preaviso 1835
preaviso, con X días de ~ 1837
preaviso de retirada de depósitos 1840
preaviso, sin ~ 1838
precio 1960
precio al consumidor 749
precio al contado 593
precio al detall(e) 2096
precio al por mayor 2288
precio al por menor 2096
precio a plazo 1384
precio a término 1384
precio baratísimo 322
precio base 330
precio concertado 114
precio contractual 114
precio convenido 114
precio corriente 911
precio de adquisición 488
precio de compensación 650
precio de compra 488
precio de consumo 749
precio de coste 814
precio de coste, a ~ 796
precio de costo 814
precio de costo, a ~ 796
precio de detalle 2096
precio de emisión 1642
precio de fabricación 811
precio de favor 1203
precio del alquiler 2088
precio de las acciones 2174
precio del día 911
precio del dinero 1967
precio de(l) mercado 1744
precio de mayorista 2288
precio de menudeo 2096
precio de oferta 1843
precio de pago al contado 593
precio de paridad 1887
precio de producción 811
precio de prolongación 569
precio de propaganda 1613
precio de reclamo 1613
precio de recompra 2095
precio de redención 2054
precio de reembolso 2054
precio de reemplazo 2091
precio de rescate 2054
precio de reventa 2096
precio de su(b)scripción 2238
precio de venta 2162
precio de venta al por mayor 2288
precio de venta al por menor 2096
precio en plaza 2203
precio especial 1203
precio excepcional 1203
precio excesivo 1208
precio exorbitante 1250
precio fijado 78
precio fijo 78
precio global 114
precio impuesto 78
precio irrisorio 322
precio límite 605, 1965
precio máximo 605
precio mayorista 2288
precio medio 234
precio normal 1832
precio normativo 1832
precio ofrecido 1843
precio para el consumidor 749
precio para el oro, régimen del doble ~ 2310
precio por pieza 2328
precio por unidad 2328
precio preferente 1203
precios constantes, a ~ 742
precio tope 605
precio único 1344
precio unitario 2328
precio usurario 1250
precio, vil ~ 322
preferencia 1328
prefinanciación 1952
prefinanciamiento 1952
prefinanciar 1951
premio 110
prenda 1138
prenda, adelanto sobre ~ 86
prenda hipotecaria 2035
prendas de valor 1646
prescripción 1955
prescripciones sobre (el control de) cambios 900
presentación, a (la) ~ 1956
presentación del balance 1957
presentador 337
presentante 337
presión fiscal 463
presión inflacionista 1558
presión sobre las utilidades 1988
prestación adicional 1285
prestación de capitales 1408
prestación de servicios 2084
prestaciones colectivas 684
prestaciones de servicios 2168
prestación social 2185
prestación suplementaria 1285
prestador 1672
prestador de dinero 1777
prestamista 1672, 1777
préstamo 419, 845
préstamo a la vista 504
préstamo amortizable 141
préstamo a plazo fijo 2277
préstamo, a título de ~ 1706
préstamo bancario 298
préstamo comercial 473
préstamo con (contra) garantía 672
préstamo cubierto 672
préstamo de amortización 141
préstamo de día a día 504
préstamo de los bancos centrales 1708
préstamo diario 504
préstamo fiduciario 1301
préstamo garantizado 672
préstamo hipotecario 1711
préstamo interno 1099
préstamo no cubierto 1301
préstamo no garantizado 1301
préstamo pignoraticio 672
préstamo redimible 141
préstamo revocable de día en día 504
prestamos 1673
préstamo sin garantía 1301
préstamo sobre efectos 1674, 1712
préstamo sobre prenda 672
préstamo sobre títulos 1674, 1712
préstamo sobre valores 1674, 1712
préstamo, solicitar un ~ 175
préstamo usurario 2336
prestar 1671
prestar de nuevo 2079
prestar dinero a interés 1675
prestar el aval de (para) una letra (de cambio) 235
prestar fianza 52
prestar garantía 52
prestar sobre valores 91
prestar una garantía 101
prestatario 418
presupuestar 443
presupuestario 442
presupuesto 441
presupuesto anual 159
presupuesto aproximado 184
presupuesto aproximativo 184
presupuesto coyuntural 929
presupuesto de coste 1190
presupuesto deficitario 95
presupuesto de inversiones 519
presupuesto, del ~ 442
presupuesto de la Comunidad 703
presupuesto del estado 1446

presupuesto (de los gastos) 1187
presupuesto equilibrado 251
presupuesto financiero 1312
presupuesto nacional 1446
presupuesto ordinario 1859
presupuesto público 1446
previo aviso, sin ~ 1838
previsión 129
previsiones presupuestarias 449
previsión por depreciación 132
prima 110, 397, 1856
prima a la baja 1953
prima a la exportación 426
prima al alza 507
prima a la venta 1953
prima a recibir 507
prima de cambio 109
prima de emisión 1641
prima de exportación 426
prima de opción a vender 1953
prima de opción de compra 507
prima de prolongación 569
prima de reembolso 1750
prima de rescate 1750
prima de seguro 1578
prima, tener ~ 1883
primera (de cambio) 1327
principal 1972, 1973
principio de la compensación de saldos 1756
principio del valor mínimo 1721
principio de no compensación 1755
privilegio fiscal 2263
privilegio tributario 2263
procurar capital 1407
procurarse capital 416
producir (un beneficio) 100
producir un interés de X por ciento 334
productivo de interés (intereses) 1586
producto 1982
producto base 329
producto basico 329
producto de base 329
producto de los impuestos 1565
producto de los intereses 1595
producto interior bruto 1461
producto nacional 1803
producto nacional bruto 1466
producto nacional neto 1814
producto(s) 229
productos de lujo 1001
prognósticos presupuestarios 451
programa de financiación 1312
programa financiero 1312
progresividad de un impuesto 1992
prohibición de importación 319
prolongación 567, 1994
prolongación de un crédito 1275
prolongar un crédito 1272
prolongar un término 1273
promedio 231
promedio anual 158
promesa de acciones 1597
promesa de crédito 88
promesa de deuda 1477
promesa de divisas 1223
promoción del ahorro 1161
propiedad fiduciaria 2308
propiedad fundiaria 1661
propiedad inmobiliaria 1508
propiedad inmueble 1508
propiedad mobiliaria 622
propiedad mueble 622
propiedad privada 1979
propiedad territorial 1661
propietario 1878
proporcionar 122
proporcionar capital 1407
proporcionarse capital 416
prorratear 122
prorrateo 123
prórroga 998, 1994
prórroga (del plazo) de pago 1276
prórroga de un crédito 1275
prórroga para un pago, acordar una ~ 1274
prorrogar el plazo de pago 1274
prorrogar un crédito 1272
prorrogar un pago 1274
prorrogar un término 1273
prospección del mercado 1740
prospecto de emisión 1643
prospecto de suscripción 1643
proteccionista 1997
protegido contra la inflación 1562
protestar un efecto 1481
protesto, mandar un efecto al ~ 1481
provecho 1409
provechoso 1147
proveer 181
proveer capital 1407
provisión 129, 182, 1615
provisión de capital 1408
provisión de capital, hacer ~ 1407
provisión para amortizaciones 132
provisión para cuentas dudosas 243
provisión para depreciación 132
provisión para impuestos 2001
provocar una reflación 2069
puesta en pool 1939
punto de apoyo 1609
punto de equilibrio 430
punto de intervención 1609
punto de sostén 1609
punto muerto 430

quebrado 313, 314
quiebra 315
quiebra, declaración (judicial) de ~ 69
quiebra, en ~ 314
quieto 508

rarefacción de capital(es) 559
rarefacción de créditos 874
razón 2029
razón de paridad 1888
reactivación 2048
reactivación de la coyuntura 1251
readquirir 480
readquisición 2094
reajuste de las paridades 2031
reajuste de los precios 76
realizabilidad 2033
realizable 2034
realización 773
realización de beneficios 1990
realización de ganancias 1990
realización de utilidades 1990
realizar 785
realizar una ganancia 1729
realizar un beneficio 1729
rebaja 127
rebaja de comercio 935
rebaja de impuestos 2261
rebaja del precio 927
rebaja de valor 969
rebaja ficticia 1822
rebajar la paridad 2062
rebasar una cuenta 1868
rebasar un crédito 1201
recalentamiento 1871
recargar 1514
recargo 60
recargo impositivo 66
recargo tributario 66
recaudable 675, 676
recaudación 680
recaudación aduanera 921
recaudación de créditos (deudas) 682
recaudación de impuestos 683
recaudación de impuestos en la fuente 681
recaudaciones presupuestarias 447
recaudaciones públicas 1451
recaudador de deudas 955
recaudar una deuda 677
recaudar un crédito 677
recaudar un impuesto 678
recesión 1031
recibí 1879
recibir prestado 415
recibo 47
recibo de depósito 608
recibos 1532
reciclaje de capital 2050
recobrar su dinero 1421
recobro 2048
recoger capital 416
recompensa 2041
recompensar 2042
recompra 2094
reconciliación de cuentas 2043
reconciliar las cuentas 112
reconocimiento de deuda 46
reconstituir la reserva 2039
recortar los gastos 915
rectificación de la balanza de pagos 794
recuperación 2020, 2048
recuperar su dinero 1421
recuperar una pérdida 707
recurrir a las reservas 1042
recurrir a un empréstito 1122
recurrir a un préstamo 1122
recurso 2047
recurso a las reservas, hacer ~ 1042
recurso al mercado 506
recursos 1406
recursos de capital 558
recursos en efectivo 587

recursos financieros 558
recursos pecuniarios 1916
recursos públicos 2007
redención 139, 2053
redención de un empréstito 142
redescontable 2058
redescontar 2057
redescuento 2056
redimibilidad 2051
redimible 2052
redimible por sorteo 498
redimir 148, 502
redimir una hipoteca 511
redistribución 2060
rédito 1522, 1585, 2110
rédito del capital 535
rédito de los intereses 1595
réditos gravados 2262
redituarse 40
redituar (un beneficio) 100
reducción de capital 2063
reducción de impuestos 2261
reducción del capital social 2064
reducción del dividendo 925
reducción de los márgines de fluctuación 2065
reducción del precio 927
reducción del tipo de descuento 926
reducción de valor 969
reducción fiscal 2261
reducir el capital social 2061
reducir los gastos 915
reembolsabilidad 2051
reembolsable 2052, 2073
reembolsable por sorteo 498
reembolsar 148, 502, 1900
reembolsar una hipoteca 511
reembolso 139, 2053, 2072
reembolso, contra ~ 589
reembolso de impuestos 2038
reembolso de los derechos de aduana 1116
reevaluación 2036
reevaluar 2037
reexportación 2066
refinanciación 2068
refinanciamiento 2068
refinanciar 2067
reflación 2070
reflar 2069
reflujo de capitales 2071
reforma fiscal 2274
reforma monetaria 899
reforma tributaria 2274
refrenar la inflación 628
refugio fiscal 2269
régimen de créditos 879
régimen de divisas 900
régimen del doble precio para el oro 2310
régimen fiscal 1334
régimen tributario 1334
registrar 401
registrar una baja (una ganancia; un avance) de X enteros (puntos) 2045
registrar una pérdida (una ganancia) 2046
registro de acciones 1701
registro de efectos (a cobrar) 360
registro de efectos (a pagar) 359
registro de (los) accionistas 1701
registro de (los) socios 1701
registro de vencimientos 359
registro mercantil 687
reglamentación de los cambios 900
reglamentación de los precios 1961
regulación del capital 1044
regulación de los precios 1961
regulador fiscal 1333
rehusamiento de pago 2074
rehuso de pago 2074
reintegrable 2073
reintegrar 1900
reintegro 2072
reintegro de los derechos de aduana 1116
reinversión 2078
reinvertir 1936
relación 2029, 2217
relación capital prestado/capital propio 963
relación de gastos 2218
relación de liquidez 45
relaciones de cambio 1236
relación precio-beneficios 1963
relación real de intercambio 2279
relación sobre las finanzas 1319
relajación del crédito 1145
relajar las restricciones crediticias 1143
relanzamiento 2048
relanzamiento, acciones de ~ 1251
rellenar la reserva 2039
remanente 152, 246
rematar 213
remate 212
remesa 1784
remesa en efectivo 595
remesar 2080
remisión de una deuda 513
remitente 2083
remitir una deuda 510
remuneración 2041
remuneración accesoria 1284
remuneración adicional 1284
remuneración del capital 535
remuneración en especie 134
remuneración especial 1284
remuneración suplementaria 1284
remunerador 1147
remunerar 2042
remunerativo 1147
rendimiento 2110
rendimiento del capital 535
rendimiento de obligaciones 396
rendimiento efectivo 57
rendimiento impositivo 1565
rendimiento real 57
rendimiento sobre el volumen de ventas 1815
rendir (un beneficio) 100
rendir un interés de X por ciento 334
renovación de la hoja de cupones 2087
renovación de un crédito 1275
renovar un crédito 1272
renta 1522, 2088
renta anual 161
rentabilidad 1984
rentabilidad bursátil 57
rentabilidad de las acciones 1082
rentable 1147
renta bruta 1463
renta de la sociedad 791
renta del trabajo 1136
renta efectiva 2032
renta fija 210
renta fija, de ~ 1338
renta imponible 2262
renta media por barba 233
renta media por cabeza 233
renta media pro-capite 233
renta nacional 1799
renta neta 1811
renta perpetua 163
renta personal 1929
renta privada 1929
rentar 100
renta real 2032
rentas 1244
rentas aduaneras 921
renta(s) del capital 535
rentas del Estado 1451
rentas fiscales 1565
rentas públicas 1451
rentas tributarias 1565
renta vitalicia 163
reorganización financiera 1318
reorganizar las finanzas 2044
reparación 708
reparar una pérdida 707
repartición 123
repartición de acciones 125
repartición del capital 1074
repartición del mercado 1745
repartición de mercados 1745
repartición ineficiente de fondos 1763
repartir 122
repartir la diferencia 2201
repartir los pagos sobre X años 2204
repartir un dividendo 1051
reparto 123
reparto de acciones 125
reparto de beneficios 183
reparto de dividendos 1052
reparto de ganancias 183
reparto de utilidades 183
repatriación 2090
repatriar 2089
reportar una posición 568
reporte 567, 569, 753
reporte, operación de ~ 2251
reporto 567, 753
reprimida, inflación ~ 1919
repudiación de una deuda 2093
repudiar una deuda 2092
requerimiento de cobertura adicional 501
requerimiento de liberación 494
requerimiento de margen adicional 501

resaca 819
resarcimiento 708
resarcirse de una pérdida 707
rescatabilidad 2051
rescatable 2052
rescatar 148, 502
rescatar una hipoteca 511
rescate 139, 2053
rescate anticipado 167
rescuentro 281, 512
reserva 129
reserva coyuntural 820
reserva de compensación de dividendos 1079
reserva de depreciación 132
reserva de divisas 901
reserva de los consumidores 750
reserva de oro 1440
reserva de previsión 756
reserva de reajuste coyuntural 820
reserva de reemplazo 2086
reserva de reposición 2086
reserva en caja 597
reserva en efectivo 597
reserva en oro 1440
reserva estatutaria 2102
reserva facultativa 1397
reserva libre 1397
reserva monetaria 1770
reserva para amortizaciones 132
reserva para contingencias 756
reserva para créditos dudosos 243
reserva para depreciación 132
reserva para deudas dudosas 243
reserva para (el pago de los) impuestos 2001
reserva para eventualidades 756
reserva para imprevistos 756
reserva para la igualación de dividendos 1079
reserva(s) 2098
reservas declaradas 966
reservas de (en) oro y divisas 1429
reservas de liquidez 1696
reservas encubiertas 726
reservas invisibles 726
reservas latentes 726
reservas legales 1670
reservas líquidas 1696
reservas mínimas (legales) 1670
reservas no declaradas 726
reservas obligatorias 1670
reservas ocultas 726
reservas tácitas 726
reservas visibles 966
reserva voluntaria 1397
resguardo de almacén 2364
resguardo de depósito 608
resguardo de ingreso 877
resguardo provisional 1597
respiro 998
respiro de pago 1276
respiro para un pago, acordar un ~ 1274
responsabilidad 1681
responsabilidad contractual 763
responsabilidad extracontractual 1824
responsabilidad ilimitada 2329
responsabilidad limitada 1689
responsabilidad solidaria 1652
restitución 2072
restitución de impuestos 2038
restitución de los derechos de aduana 1116
restituible 2073
restituir 1900
resto 246
resto adeudado 252
restricción a la importación 1513
restricción crediticia 874
restricción de créditos 874
restricción de la liquidez 2104
restricción de las importaciones 1513
restricción de los precios 1968
restricciones, abolición de ~ 2
restricciones, abolir ~ 1
restricciones cambiarias 902
restricciones crediticias, relajar las ~ 1143
restricciones de divisas 902
restricciones, levantamiento de ~ 2
restricciones, levantar ~ 1
restricciones, supresión de ~ 2
restricciones, suprimir ~ 1
restringir los gastos 915
retardo, en ~ 189
retención en garantía 2109
retener en la fuente 972
retirable 496
retirada 1119, 2053
retirada en efectivo 601
retirar 502, 1113
retirar (de la circulación) 503
retirarse con pérdida 928
retiro 1008, 1119, 2053
retiro en efectivo 601
retrasar un pago 984
retraso, en ~ 189
retribución 2041
retribuir 2042
retroceso 968
retroceso de las cotizaciones (los precios) 886
retroceso de valor 969
reunir capital 416
revalorar 178
revalorización 2036, 2111
revalorizar 178, 2037
revaluación 2036, 2111
revaluar 178, 2037
revendedor 2105
revisar 215
revisión de cuentas 214
revisión de cuotas 77
revisión interna 1600
revisor de cuentas 216
riesgo de cambio 1238
riesgo en el cambio de divisas 1238
riqueza nacional 1804
ritmo de aumento 1256
ritmo de crecimiento 1256
ritmo de expansión 1256
ritmo de la inflación 1563
rotación de créditos 960
royalty 1686
S.A. 1537
sacar 1113
sacar una ganancia 1729
sacar un beneficio 1729
sacar un empréstito a (la) su(b)scripción 1634
salario 1140
salario a destajo 1907
salario a prima 1520
salario con primas 1520
salario por pieza 1932
salario por unidad 1932
salario según rendimiento 1153
salarios y sueldos 1141
saldar 148
saldarse 248
saldar una cuenta 249
saldo 139, 246, 2128
saldo acreedor 849
saldo activo 849
saldo activo de la balanza comercial 266
saldo activo de la balanza de pagos 263
saldo a cuenta nueva 150
saldo contable 27, 255
saldo debido 252
saldo de compensación 269
saldo de (en) caja 253
saldo deficitario 93
saldo de las transacciones corrientes 268
saldo de las transferencias corrientes 257
saldo del comercio exterior 1277
saldo deudor 93
saldo de una cuenta 254, 255
saldo, día de ~ 24
saldo en banco 286
saldo en cuenta nueva 150
saldo exterior 1277
saldo ganancial 849
saldo global de las transferencias y de los movimientos de capitales 1416
saldo negativo 93
saldo pasivo 93
salida de capitales 556
salidas 1053
salidas, entradas y ~ 1525
salir fiador 52
salir garante 52
sanción (pecuniaria) 136
saneamiento financiero 1318
sanear las finanzas 2044
satisfacción 139
satisfacer 148
sección de costes 461
secreto bancario 305
sector de crecimiento 1470
sector de la distribución 1075
sector privado 1981
sector público 2008
secuestración 191
secuestrar 211
secuestro 191
secuestro (judicial) 2040
sede central 607

sede estatutaria 2075
sede principal 607
sede social 2075
segunda de cambio 2148
seguridad 1138
seguridad adicional 65
seguridad social 2184
seguridad subsidiaria 65
seguridad suplementaria 65
seguro 1576
seguro de crédito(s) 863
seguro sobre el crédito 863
sello 2209
sello de premio 2290
sentar 401
sentar en cuenta 570
sentar en el lado del activo 403
sentar en el lado del pasivo 402
señal 602, 1014
señalar un precio 1728
ser fiador 52
ser garante 52
serpiente (monetaria) 2183
servicio de giro postal 1423
servicio de intereses 1592
servicio de la deuda 962
servicio de un empréstito 2167
servicio de un empréstito, hacer el ~ 2165
servicios 2168
servicios, bienes y ~ 1443
servir de cubierta 2166
S.E. u O. 1184
S.E. y O. 1184
SFI 1605
siguro de vida 1688
siguro sobre la vida 1688
sindicato 2255
sindicato de bancos 303
sindicato de colocación 2322
sindicato de emisión 2322
sindicato de garantía 2322
sindicatura 2040
sindico de la quiebra 209
sistema bancario 301
sistema crediticio 879
sistema de cambios 1240
sistema de contribuciones 1334
sistema de coste integral 4
sistema de coste parcial 1045
sistema de créditos 879
sistema de cuentas 22
sistema de salario inversión 2362
sistema financiero 1304
sistema fiscal 1334
sistema monetario 664
sistema monetario oro 1441
sistema monetario papel 1881
sistema tributario 1334
situación bancaria 312
situación de (la) caja 592
situación del mercado 1743
situación de tesorería 592
situación de una cuenta 1940
S.L. 1690
slumpflación 2182
sobrante 27, 246, 2244
sobrecapitalización 1865
sobrecargar 1866
sobredividendo 398
sobre(e)stimación 1864
sobre(e)stimar 1863
sobre(e)valoración 1864
sobre(e)valorar 1863
sobre(e)valuación 1864
sobre(e)valuar 1863
sobregirar una cuenta 1868
sobregiro 1867
sobreimposición 66
sobreimpuesto 66
sobreoferta 1210
sobrepaga 1288
sobrepasar una cuenta 1868
sobrepasar un crédito 1201
sobrepostura 1484
sobreprecio 60, 1208
sobresaturar el mercado (con artículos baratos) 1132
sobresueldo 1288
sobresuscribir 1873
sobresuscripción 1874
sobretasa 60, 66
sobretasación 1864
sobretasar 1863
sobrevencido 1869
socialización 1801
socializar 1802
sociedad afiliada 98
sociedad anónima 1537
sociedad bancaria 302
sociedad bancaria por acciones 1536
sociedad colectiva 1420
sociedad comanditaria 1692
sociedad comanditaria por acciones 1893
sociedad (comercial) 686
sociedad controlada 98
sociedad controladora 769
sociedad cooperativa 786
sociedad cooperativa de producción 1983
sociedad de capitales 1537
sociedad de cartera 653
sociedad de colocación de capitales 653
sociedad de control 769
sociedad de crédito (mutuo) 787
sociedad de fideicomiso 2306
sociedad de financiación 1308
sociedad de inversión 653
sociedad de inversiones 653
sociedad dependiente 98
sociedad de personas 1892
sociedad de responsabilidad limitada 1690
sociedad dominada 98
sociedad dominante 769
sociedad en comandita (simple) 1692
sociedad fiduciaria 2306
sociedad filial 98
sociedad financiera 1308
Sociedad Financiera Internacional 1605
sociedad holding 1494
sociedad inversionista 653
sociedad madre 769
sociedad matriz 769
sociedad (mercantil) 686
sociedad por acciones 1537
sociedad regular colectiva 1420
socio 2171
socio comanditario 1691
socio general 1419
socio oculto 1105
socio personalmente responsable 1419
sola de cambio 2180
solicitante de (un) crédito 172
solicitante de un empréstito 172
solicitante de un préstamo 172
solicitar un crédito 175
solicitar un empréstito 175
solicitar un préstamo 175
solicitud de (apertura de la) quiebra 316
solicitud de crédito 173
solicitud de empréstito 173
solicitud de préstamo 173
solidaridad pasiva 1652
solidez 873
sólido 846
solvencia 2189
solvente 2190
soportar una pérdida 333
sorteable 498
sortear 1112
sorteo 1111
sostén de los precios 1917
sostenimiento de los precios 1917
split 2175
SRC 1420
S.R.L. 1690
stagflación 2208
standard de vida 1704
stock 1615
subacción 2230
subasta 212
subastar 213
subcapitalización 2315
subcuenta 224
subestimación 2318
subestimar 2319
subida de precio(s) 1539
subir de (en) valor 179
su(b)scribir 2233
su(b)scribir con (en) exceso 1873
su(b)scripción 2236
su(b)scripción de capital 562
su(b)scripción en exceso 1874
su(b)scriptor 2234
subsidiar 2240
subsidiaria 98
subsidio 1458
subsidio a la exportación 1269
subsidio del estado 1449
subvaloración 2318
subvalorar 2319
subvención 1458
subvención a la exportación 1269
subvencionar 2240
subvención de intereses 1594
subvención del estado 1449
subvención del gobierno 1449
subvención estatal 1449

subvención gubernamental 1449
su cuenta 1716
sucursal 427
sueldo 2126
sueldo mensual 1787
sueldos, salarios y ~ 1141
suelto 612
sufrir una pérdida 333
sujeto a aviso con X días de antelación 1837
sujeto a contribución 196
sujeto a (derechos de) aduana 916
sujeto a impuesto 196
sujeto al pago de aranceles 916
sujeto al pago de interés (intereses) 2231
sujeto a tributación 196
sujeto a X días de preaviso 1837
suma 149
suma adeudada 151
suma a tanto alzada 1722
suma compensada 247
suma debida 151
suma de compensación 247
suma excedente 1205
suma final 105
suma restante 246
suma total 105
suma (total) del balance 276
superabundancia de dinero 6
superávit 2244
superávit contable 30
superávit de la balanza comercial 266
superávit de la balanza de pagos 263
superávit de la circulación monetaria 6
superávit monetario 6
superbeneficio 1213
supervaloración 1864
supervalorar 1863
suplemento a una letra 124
suplemento de carestía (de vida) 808
suplemento de copertura 62
suplemento de crédito 63
suplemento de impuesto 66
supresión de restricciones 2
suprimir restricciones 1
surplus 2244
susceptible de pignoración 9
suscripción de un empréstito, abrir la ~ 1634
suspender el pago de un cheque 2227
suspender los pagos 603
suspensión de pago 1276
suspensión de pagos 2250
swap, operación de ~ 2251
swing 864
switch 2253

tabla 2256
tabla de amortización 146
talón 828
talonario de cheques 626
talón claudicante 1476
talón cojo 1476
talón de almacén 2364
talón de compra 425
talón de comprobación 821
talón de control 821
talón de crédito 877
talón de imposición 877
talón de intereses 1588
talón de renovación 2085
talón de transferencia 848
talón de venta 440
talón no vencido 2330
talón oro 1441
tanto por ciento 1921
tardanza de pago 999
tarifa 2260
tarifa aduanera 922
tarifa (aduanera) exterior 1279
tarifa arancelaria 922
tarifa de aduanas 922
tarifa de favor 1947
tarifa de preferencia 1947
tarifa diferencial 1041
tarifa escalonada 1041
tarifa exterior común 699
tarifa graduada 1041
tarifa gradual 1041
tarifa móvil 1041
tarifa preferencial 1947
tarifa preferencial para los miembros del Commonwealth 702
tarifa preferente 1947
tarjeta de crédito 854
tasa 614, 1135, 2021
tasa administrativa 80
tasa bancaria 311
tasación 176, 200, 2265
tasación doble 1109
tasa compensatoria 711, 712
tasa de ahorro 2026
tasa de amortización 144, 145
tasa de aumento 1255
tasa de banco 311
tasa de compensación 711, 712
tasa de conversión 778
tasa de crecimiento 1255
tasa de depreciación 144
tasa de descuento 1061
tasa de expansión 1255
tasa de imposición 2023
tasa de inflación 1563
tasa de interés 1593
tasa de inversión 1629
tasa de las inversiones 1629
tasa del deport(e) 240
tasa de licencia 1686
tasa de(l) impuesto 2023
tasa de monopolio 1245
tasa de perecuación 712
tasa de préstamos con garantía 2022
tasa de préstamos sobre efectos 1714
tasa de préstamos sobre títulos 1714
tasa de préstamos sobre valores 1714
tasa de préstamos su prenda 2022
tasa de progresión 1255
tasa de prolongación 569
tasa de redescuento 2059
tasa de registro 2077
tasa de reporte 569
tasa de transferencia 812, 2081
tasa de transmisión 812
tasa (oficial) de descuento bancario 311
tasar 177, 195
tasa uniforme 1345
tendencia 1200
tendencia a la baja 344
tendencia al alza 459
tendencia alcista 459
tendencia ascendente 459
tendencia bajista 344
tendencia deflacionista 994
tendencia descendente 344
tendencia general, estar contrario a la ~ 2120
tenedor 336
tenedor de acciones 2171
tenedor de libros 410
tenedor de obligaciones 390
tenedor de títulos 2171
tenedor de un efecto por endorso 1902
tenedor de valores 341, 2171
teneduría de libros 20
tener agio 1883
tener los libros 1656
tener prima 1883
tercer deudor 1413
término 894, 1262
término de cortesía 998
término de gracia 998
término de liquidación 18
términos del intercambio 2279
tesorería 227, 2299
tesoro público 2299
timbre 2209
tipo 2021
tipo bancario 311
tipo base 328
tipo comprador 354
tipo de ahorro 2026
tipo de amortización 145
tipo de aumento 1255
tipo de banco 311
tipo de cambio 1216
tipo de cambio, ajuste del ~ 75
tipo de cambio al contado 2024
tipo de cambio a plazo 1383
tipo de cambio a término 1383
tipo de cambio cruzado 884
tipo de cambio de billetes y metálico 1235
tipo de cambio de billetes y monedas 1235
tipo de cambio fijo 1341
tipo de cambio flexible 1347
tipo de cambio flotante 1347
tipo de cambio fluctuante 1347
tipo de cambio forzoso 722
tipo de cambio libre 1347
tipo de cambio obligatorio 722
tipo de cambio oscilante 1347
tipo de cambio preferente 1950
tipo de cambio variable 1347
tipo de comisión 691
tipo de compra 354
tipo de conversión 778

tipo de descuento 1061
tipo de emisión 1642
tipo de interés 1593
tipo de interés del dinero 1782
tipo de intereses de préstamo 423
tipo de interés nominal 1821
tipo de(l) impuesto 2023
tipo del mercado libre 1396
tipo de mercado 1234
tipo de préstamos 423
tipo de préstamos con garantía 2022
tipo de préstamos sobre efectos 1714
tipo de préstamos sobre títulos 1714
tipo de préstamos sobre valores 1714
tipo de préstamos su prenda 2022
tipo de prolongación 569
tipo de redescuento 2059
tipo de rédito 2025
tipo de rendimiento 2025
tipo de reporte 569
tipo de reserva mínima 1759
tipo de venta 193
tipo doble 375
tipo en el mercado libre 1396
tipo forzoso 722
tipo imponible 2023
tipo impositivo 2023
tipo medio 234
tipo monetario 1782
tipo nominal 1821
tipo obligatorio 722
tipo (oficial) de descuento bancario 311
tipo oro 1441
tipo único 1785
tipo vendedor 193
tirantez del crédito 874
titular 336
titular de acciones 2171
titular de obligaciones 390
titular de participaciones de un fondo mutual de inversión 2327
titular de una cuenta 26
titular de valores 2171
título 1011
título a (de) interés fijo 1339
título a la orden 1806
título al portador 340
título de accion(es) 2170
título de crédito 862
título de cuenta 25
título de deuda 609
título de empréstito 389
título de préstamo 1709
título de renta 162
título de renta fija 1339
título hipotecario 1792
título (legal) 1325
título negociable 1806
título pagadero a la vista 1007
título provisional 1597
títulos 2151
títulos admitidos en bolsa 1699
títulos al portador 342
títulos comerciables 1739
títulos cotizados (en bolsa) 1699
títulos de bolsa 1699
títulos de cartera 1630
títulos de especulación 2199
títulos de inversión 1630
títulos de la deuda pública consolidada 734
títulos del estado 1244
títulos de primera categoría 387
títulos de primera clase 387
títulos de primer orden 387
títulos de toda confianza 387
títulos especulativos 2199
títulos inscritos en la bolsa 1699
títulos mobiliarios 1739
títulos negociables 1739
títulos no cotizados (en bolsa) 892
títulos nominativos 1568
títulos públicos 1244
títulos registrados 1568
títulos seguros 387
títulos sin valor 2345
títulos transferibles 1739
títulos-valores 2151
títulos-valores nominativos 1568
tocar las reservas 1042
tomador de(l) crédito 418
tomador de un efecto 1902
tomar a (en) préstamo 415
tomar capital en préstamo 416
tomar inventario 1124
tomar prestado 415
tomar prestado capital 416
tomar una hipoteca (sobre) 2019
tope de crédito 855
total del balance 276
total general 105
totalizar 106
tráfico de compensación 643
tranquilo 508
transacción 320, 718
transacción a la vista 1379
transacción al contado 581
transacción a medias 1653
transacción a plazo 1379
transacción a plazos 1489
transacción a prima 1855
transacción a término 1379
transacción a término en moneda extranjera 1381
transacción de cambio 327
transacción de cambio al contado 2202
transacción de cambio a plazo 1381
transacción de compensación 327
transacción de divisas al contado 2202
transacción de divisas a término 1381
transacción de trueque 327
transacción en efectivo 581
transacción en participación 1653
transacciones bancarias 304
transacciones bursátiles 1222
transacciones con el extranjero 1358
transacciones crediticias 851
transacciones de cambio 1241
transacciones de clearing 643
transacciones de compensación 643
transacciones de crédito 851
transacciones de (en) bolsa 1222
transacciones de (en) títulos 1222
transacciones de (en) valores 1222
transacciones de giro 643
transacciones en divisas 1241
transacciones por cheque 632
transacción facultativa a opción del comprador 485
transacción facultativa a opción del vendedor 1857
transacción switch 2253
transacción triangular 2253
transferencia 119, 2293
transferencia al exterior 1372
transferencia bancaria 318
transferencia de capital 563
transferencia de créditos 208
transferencia de dinero 1784
transferencia de fondos 1784
transferencia monetaria 1784
transferencias corrientes, saldo de las ~ 257
transferibilidad 116
transferible 117
transferidor 1165, 2083
transferir 118, 2080
transferir un crédito 207
transmisibilidad 116
transmisible 117
transmisión 119
transmitir 118
transportar 435
transporte del saldo a nueva cuenta 150
trasladar 435
traspasar 118
traspaso 119
traspaso de créditos 208
trato 320
travellor's cheque 2297
tributación 2265
tributación doble 1109
tributación en el origen 681
tributación en la fuente 681
tributante 2028
tributo 1135
trimestre 2016
trueco 325
trueque 325
trust 2304

UEP 1198
umbral de beneficios 430
umbral de rentabilidad 430
unidad de coste 818
unidad de cuenta 31
unidad monetaria 904
unificación 737
unificar una deuda 733
unión aduanera 923
unión de crédito 787
Unión Económica Belga-Luxemburguesa 348
Unión Europea de Pagos 1198
usado 2378
uso 2333, 2366, 2367
usofructo 2334
usura 2337
utilidad 1409

utilidad bruta 1459
utilidad contable 412
utilidad de capital 530
utilidad distribuible 1072
utilidades 229
utilidades acumuladas 2108
utilidades de explotación 475
utilidades de operación 475
utilidades no distribuidas 2108
utilidades no repartidas 2311
utilidades retenidas 2108
utilidad neta 646
utilización de créditos 228
utilizar las reservas 1042
utilizar un empréstito 1122
utilizar un préstamo 1122

vale 876, 1477
vale de caja 590
vale del tesoro 2301
validez 894
valoración 176
valor actual 912
valor a (de) interés fijo 1339
valor a la orden 1806
valor a la par 1889
valor añadido por la industria 2340
valorar 177
valor bruto 1468
valor bursátil 1234
valor capitalizado 546
valor catastral 199
valor comercial 688
valor contable 32
valor cotizado 1234
valor de adquisición 50
valor de bolsa 1234
valor de cambio 1219, 1234
valor declarado 967
valor de compra 50
valor de coste 50
valor de cotización 1234
valor de (en) balance 277
valor de inventario 1617
valor de la moneda en divisa extranjera 1364
valor del 1° de enero 2342
valor del día 912
valor de liquidación 432
valor de mercado 688
valor de paridad 1889
valor de realización 432
valor de redención 2055
valor de reembolso 2055
valor de reemplazo 2091
valor de rendimiento 546
valor de renta 162
valor de renta fija 1339
valor de reposición 2091
valor de rescate 2055, 2247
valor de sustitución 2091
valor efectivo 56
valor en bolsa 1234
valor en oro 1442
valor en venta 688
valores 1646, 2151
valores admitidos en bolsa 1699
valores al portador 342
valores bursátiles 1699
valores comerciables 1739
valores cotizados (en bolsa) 1699
valores dados en garantía 1895
valores dados en prenda 1895
valores de bolsa 1699
valores de cartera 1630
valores de colocación 1630
valores de especulación 2199
valores de inversión 1630
valores del estado 1244
valores de primera categoría 387
valores de primera clase 387
valores de primer orden 387
valores de tota confianza 387
valores disponibles 227
valores empeñados 1895
valores en efectivo 577
valores especulativos 2199
valores extranjeros 1370
valores inmateriales 1505
valores inmobiliarios 1508
valores inmovilizados 518
valores inmuebles 1508
valores inscritos en la bolsa 1699
valores intangibles 1505
valores mobiliarios 622, 1739
valores muebles 622
valores negociables 1739
valores no cotizados (en bolsa) 892
valores pignorados 1895
valores públicos 1244
valores seguros 387
valores transferibles 1739
valor fiscal 198
valor global 108
valor gravable 198
valor imponible 198
valor intrínseco 1612
valorización 176, 2338
valorizar 2339
valor, menor ~ 969
valor negociable 1806
valor neto 1809, 1817
valor neto de una propiedad 1177
valor nominal 1289, 1889
valor nominal de una acción 1290
valor oro 1442
valor real 56
valor realizable 688
valor residual 2103
valor restante 2103
valor standard 2213
valor total 108
valor unitario 2213
valuación 176
valuar 177
valuta 893
valuta (extranjera) 1361
variar con un índice económico 1547
varios 1764
velocidad de circulación 2027
vence el 15 de agosto, que ~ 1129
vencer 347, 1264
vencer el 15 de agosto 1129
vencido 1126
vencimiento 1748
vencimiento, al ~ 1128
vencimiento, a su ~ 1128
vencimiento de X años 1749
vencimiento, llegar al ~ 347
vendedor 2159
vender 2157
vender a(l) crédito 2163
vender al descubierto 1427
vender al fiado 2163
vender a plazo 2161
vender a término 2161
vender con pérdida 2158
vender en subasta 213
vender más barato 2317
vendible 1738
venta 2127
venta a crédito 875
venta al contado 598
venta al descubierto 346
venta a plazos 1491
venta con derecho de retracto 2132
venta con derecho de retroventa 2132
venta con pérdida 2129
venta en descubierto 346
ventaja fiscal 2263
ventajoso 1147
venta por subasta 212
ventas 2130
ventas brutas 1467
ventas netas 1816
verificación de cuentas 214
verificar 215
viabilidad 2349
viable 2350
vil precio 322
vista, a (la) ~ 1956
vivir dentro de sus recursos 1702
vivir uno de sus ingresos 1703
volumen comercial 2354
volumen de ahorros 2353
volumen de crédito(s) 881
volumen de dinero 1783
volumen de intercambio 2354
volumen de las transacciones en bolsa 2225
volumen del comercio 2354
volumen de negocios 2130
volumen dinerario 1783
volumen monetario 1783
voluntad, buena ~ 1444
volver a comprar 480
vuelta 612
vuelto 612

warrant (de almacén) 2364

zona de comercio libre 1398
zona de la (libra) esterlina 2224
zona del dólar 1086
zona del franco 1388
zona de mercado 1736
zona de venta 1736

FRANÇAIS

F

abaissement des cours (prix) 886
abaissement du prix 927
abaissement du taux d'escompte 926
abaisser la parité 2062
abattement fiscal 2261
abolir des restrictions 1
abolition de restrictions 2
abondance d'argent 6
abonnement, par ~ 987
absorber une perte 3
absorption 2257
accaparement 1493
accaparer 489, 1492
accaparer le marché 789
acceptation 10
acceptation bancaire 284
acceptation commerciale 2286
acceptation, commission d'~ 13
acceptation, crédit d'~ 11
acceptation de banque 284
accepter une lettre de change 8
accepteur 14
accise 752
accommodement 718
accord d'autolimitation 2355
accord de clearing 647
accord de compensation 647
accord de paiement 1906
accord de prix 115
accord de prorogation 2216
accord (de) stand-by 2215
accord de standstill 2216
accorder les comptes, faire ~ 112
accorder un crédit 126
accorder un délai de paiement 1274
accorder une garantie 101
accorder un répit de paiement 1274
accorder un sursis de paiement 1274
Accord général sur les tarifs douaniers et le commerce 1415
Accord monétaire européen 1196
accord moratoire 2216
accord sur les prix 115
accréditer quelqu'un 1847
accréditif 843, 1678
accréditif documentaire 1085
accroissement 38
accroissement de capital 536
accroissement de l'intensité de capital 537
accroissement de valeur 180
accroissement en valeur 180
accroître 40
accroître le capital 1544
accueil à un effet, faire (bon) ~ 1054
accueillir un effet 1054
accumulation 38, 44
accumuler 43
accumuler, s'~ 40
accusé de réception 47
accuser une baisse (un gain) de X points 2045
accuser une perte (un bénéfice) 2046
achat 2012
achat à compte 852
achat à crédit 852
achat à livrer 1376
achat à tempérament 1573
achat à terme 1376
achat au comptant 594
achat comptant 594
achat d'occasion 321
achat spéculatif 2198
achat sur livraison 1376
acheter 479
acheter à tempérament 481
acheter à terme 486
acheteur 482
acompte 1014, 1571
acompte mensuel 1788
acompte semestriel 351
acomptes, par ~ 987
acompte sur le dividende 1598
acquéreur 482
acquérir 48
acquérir, s'~ 40
acquisition 49
acquit 47
acquit de, à l'~ 34
acquit, pour ~ 1879
acquittement 139
acquittement préalable 92
acquitter 148
acquitter de, s'~ 148
acquitter par anticipation 1904
acquitter un effet 1054
acte de caution 394
acte de cautionnement 394
acte fiduciaire 976
actif 202, 206
actif, à inscrire à l'~ 408
actif amortissable 1027
actif circulant 468
actif comptable 2285
actif courant 905
actif de la faillite 317
actif disponible 227
actif et le passif, l'~ 203
actif fictif 1297
actif immobilisé 518
actif libre 227
actif liquide 227
actif net 1809
actif permanent 518
actif réalisable (et disponible) 905
actif social 790
action 2169
action à cessibilité restreinte 2282
action au porteur 343
action à vote plural 1796
action bénéficiaire 400
action de garantie 2015
action de jouissance 400
action de préférence 1946
action de préférence ayant part dans les bénéfices 1891
action de priorité 1946
action différée 985
action gratuite 400
action liée 2282
actionnaire 2171
actionnaire enregistré 2076
actionnaire, gros ~ 633
actionnaire principal 633
actionnaire, principal ~ 633
action privilégiée 1946
action privilégiée participant aux bénéfices 1891
action provisoire 1597
actions à droit de vote 2357
actions d'apport 1386
actions de préférence cumulatives 890
actions de priorité cumulatives 890
actions de relance 1251
actions de travail 1159
actions entièrement (intégralement) libérées 1403
actions nominatives 1568
actions nouvelles 1819
actions ordinaires 701
actions privilégiées cumulatives 890
actions sans droit de vote 1830
actions sans valeur nominale 1831
activité bancaire 301
actuaire 58
adaptation des prix 76
admettre un atermoiement 1274
administrateur de la faillite 209
administrateur de la masse 209
administrateur-séquestre 209
administration de la faillite 2040
administration de la masse 2040
administration des dettes 954
administration fiduciaire, en ~ 1185
administration fiscale 1242
administration-séquestre 2040
admission à la cote (officielle) de la bourse 81
admission en bourse 81
adultération de la monnaie 939
affaiblissement 968
affaiblissement des cours (prix) 886
affaire 320
affaire à prime 1855
affaire à tempérament 1489
affaire à terme 1379
affaire au comptant 581
affaire, bonne ~ 321
affaires avec l'étranger 1358
affaires bancaires 304
affaires, faire des ~ 1084
affaires, traiter des ~ 1084
affaissement des cours 431
affaissement des prix 431
affectation 123, 182
affectation à la réserve 67
affectation de bénéfices 183
affectations budgétaires 444
affecter 122, 181
affecter à la réserve 68
affecter au fonds de réserve 68
affermeur 1676
afflux de capitaux 99
affranchir 1389
affranchir des droits de douane 1246
agence 103
agence de courtage 439
agence de courtier 439
agent 104
agent de bourse 2152
agent de change 361, 509, 1311, 2152
agent de circulation 636

agent de recouvrements 955
agent monétaire 636
agio 109, 110, 438
agiotage 111
agioteur 1647
AID 1604
aide au développement 1034
aide de l'état 1445
aide financière 1310
aide gouvernementale 1445
ajustement 72
ajustement de change 75
ajustement des prix 76
ajustement des quotes-parts 77
ajustement en termes réels 74
ajuster 70
aliénabilité 116
aliénable 117
aliénataire 120
aliénateur 121
aliénation 119
aliéner 118
alignement des prix 76
allégement fiscal 2261
alléger les restrictions du crédit 1143
aller à l'encontre de la tendance générale 2120
allocation 123, 182
allocation de cherté de vie 808
allocation de crédit 220
allocation de renchérissement 808
allocation de vie chère 808
allocation inappropriée de moyens 1763
allonge 124
allouer 122, 181
allouer un crédit 126
altération de la monnaie 939
amassement 44
amasser 43
ambiance de baisse 344
AME 1196
amélioration de gages 1542
amélioration de salaire 1540, 1542
amélioration de traitement 1540
amende 136
amener la déflation 990
amenuisement des cours (prix) 886
amenuisement de valeur 969
amoindrissement de valeur 969
amortir 147, 148, 502
amortir une créance 2379
amortir une hypothèque 511
amortissable 2052
amortissable par tirage (au sort) 498
amortissement 138, 139, 2053
amortissement croissant 1545
amortissement décroissant 7
amortissement dégressif 7
amortissement d'un emprunt 142
amortissement économique 143
amortissement linéaire 2228
amortissement progressif 1545
amortissements fiscalement admis 517
amortissement technique 1030
amortissement variable 2347
analyse du marché 1740
anatocisme 156
année budgétaire 448
année civile 493
année commerciale 478
année comptable 1320
année financière 1320
année fiscale 1335
années d'échéance, X ~ 1749
année sociale 705
annuité 161
annuité à vie 163
annuité d'amortissement 157
annuité viagère 163
annulation 512
anti-conjoncturel 168
anti-cyclique 168
antidater 164
anti-inflationniste 170
appel au marché 506
appel de fonds 494
appel de marge 501
appel de versement 494
appoint 612
appointements 2126
apport 765
apport de capital 521
apport de fonds 521
apport en nature 205
apporter du capital 436
apporteur de capital 1631
appréciation 176, 180
apprécier 177
approprier, s'~ 977
approximation grossière 184
appui de l'état 1445
après-bourse 102
apurement de comptes 2043
apurer 215
apurer les comptes 112
arbitrage de change(s) 186
arbitrage de devises 186
arbitrage sur les changes 186
arbitrage sur les devises 186
arbitrage sur les lettres de change 369
arbitrage sur les matières d'or et d'argent 185
argent (à) bon marché 623
argent à (contre) intérêt(s), prêter de l'~ 1675
argent à echéance (fixe) 1337
argent à terme (fixe) 1337
argent au jour le jour 505
argent à vue 505
argent cher 654
argent circulant 914
argent comptant 572, 573
argent, contre ~ 573
argent courant 914
argent, en ~ 573
argent en caisse 587
argent en circulation 914
argent en espèces 572
argent noir 2314
argent serré 654
arrangement 718
arrérages 188
arrérages (d'intérêt) 190
arrêt 191
arrêté d'un compte 655
arrêter le paiement d'un chèque 2227
arrêter les livres 278
arrêter un compte 652
arrêter un solde 279
arrhes 602
arriéré 152, 189
arrière-caution 238
arrière, en ~ 189
arrière-garantie 238
arriérer un paiement 984
arriérés 188
arriver à échéance 347
article 409
article collectif 717
article composé 717
article d'avoir 857
article de compensation 281
article de contrepassement 281
article de journal 1655
article de régularisation 71
article d'ordre 2249
article inverse 281
article (porté) au crédit 857
article (porté) au débit 946
articles de luxe 1001
articles d'exportation 1266
articles d'importation 1510
article transitoire 2249
articulation du bilan 273
assainir les finances 2044
assainissement des finances 1318
assaut de la banque 2121
asseoir 195
assiette 200
assiette (de l'impôt) 331
assignation d'actions 125
assignation de banque 284
assigner 122
assistance financière 1310
association à but lucratif 1986
association de crédit 787
Association internationale de développement 1604
Association internationale pour le développement 1604
association sans but lucratif 1829
associé commanditaire 1691
associé commandité 1419
associé occulte 1105
assouplir les restrictions du crédit 1143
assouplissement du crédit 1145
assujetti à l'impôt 196
assujetti aux droits de douane 916
assujettissement à l'impôt 1683
assurance 1576
assurance contre les risques de crédit 863
assurance-crédit 863
assurance de crédit(s) 863
assurance sur la vie 1688
assurance vie 1688, 1688
atermoiement 998, 1276
atermoyer un crédit 1272

atermoyer un paiement 984, 1274
atone 508
attestation de versement 877
attribuer 122
attribuer à la réserve 68
attribution 123
augmentation de capital 536
augmentation de gages 1542
augmentation de la liquidité 1538
augmentation de la masse monétaire 1252
augmentation de salaire 1540, 1542
augmentation de(s) prix 1539
augmentation de traitement 1540
augmentation de valeur 180
augmentation de X pour cent 1543
augmentation du taux de (l')escompte 1541
augmenter de (en) valeur 179
augmenter la valeur 178
augmenter le capital 1544
austerité 218
autarcie 219
auto(-)consommation 1497
autofinancement 1601
autorisation de crédit 220
autorisation d'exportation 1268
autorisation d'importation 1512
autoriser un crédit 126
autosuffisance 219
aval 230
avaliser un effet 235
avaliseur 236
avaliste 236
avance, à titre d'~ 84
avance bancaire 298
avance contre garantie 86
avance contre (sur) nantissement 86
avance de (en; sur) compte courant 87
avance (de fonds) 83
avance des banques centrales 1708
avance gagée 86
avance garantie 86
avancer 85
avancer sur titres 91
avance sur titres 90
avantage accessoire 1285
avantage complémentaire 1285
avantage en nature 134
avantage extra-légal 1285
avantage fiscal 2263
avantageux 1147
avant-bourse 937
avertissement d'imposition 1839
avilir 1028
avilir, s'~ 970
avilissement 1029
avilissement de la monnaie 896
avilissement monétaire 896
avis de crédit 847
avis de débit 945
avis d'encaissement 47
avis de paiement 97, 1913
avis de réception 47
avis de retrait de dépôts 1840
avis de versement 97
avis de virement 848
avis d'imposition 1839
avis d'opéré 425, 440
avis préalable, sans ~ 1838
avoir 206, 843, 849
avoir bloqué 381
avoir en banque 286
avoir recours à un emprunt 1122
avoir recours à un prêt 1122
avoir recours aux réserves 1042
avoirs 202, 1496
avoirs à l'étranger 204
avoirs du trésor 2300
avoirs en caisse 587
avoirs en devises 1362
avoirs en numéraire 587
avoirs en or 1430
avoirs immobiliers 1508
avoirs liquides 227
avoir social 790
avoirs sur l'étranger 204
ayant compte 26

bail (à loyer) 1666
bailleur 1676
bailleur de capitaux 1631
bailleur de fonds 1105, 1777
baisse 968, 1031
baisse des cours (prix) 886
baisse de valeur 969
baisser 970
baissier 332
balance à nouveau 150
balance commerciale 264
balance commerciale active 53
balance commerciale défavorable 94
balance commerciale excédentaire 53
balance commerciale favorable 53
balance de caisse 253
balance déficitaire 94
balance des biens et services 259
balance des capitaux 256
balance des comptes extérieurs 258
balance des mouvements de capitaux 256
balance des paiements 260
balance des paiements courants 262
balance des transferts 267
balance du commerce 264
balance économique 1148
balance globale des paiements 1862
balancer les livres 278
balancer, se ~ 248
balancer un compte 249
bancocratie 1486
banque 282, 301
banque centrale 606
banque commerciale 310
banque d'acceptations 12
banque d'affaires 1621
banque d'avances 850
banque de clearing 648
banque de commerce 310
banque de compensation 648
banque de crédit 850
banque de crédit foncier 1660
banque de crédit hypothécaire 1660
banque de dépôt(s) 1020
banque de développement 1035
banque d'émission 309
banque d'épargne 2139
banque de placement 1645
banque de (pour le) commerce extérieur 1371
banque de prêts 850
banque d'escompte 1058
Banque des règlements internationaux 300
banque de valeurs 1645
banque de virement 648
banque d'intérêt privé 1974
banque d'investissements 1621
banque émettrice 1645
Banque européenne d'investissement 1195
banque, haute ~ 1486
banque hypothécaire 1660
Banque interaméricaine de développement 1581
Banque internationale pour la reconstruction et le développement 1602
Banque mondiale 1602
banque par actions 1536
banque privée 1974
banqueroute 315
banqueroute, en ~ 314
banqueroutier 313
barrière douanière 918
barrière économique 1149
base de calcul de l'imposition 331
base de l'imposition 331
base de l'impôt 331
base imposable 331
basse conjoncture 1031
battre 662
bear 332
bénéfice 1409
bénéfice apparent 171
bénéfice au change 1233
bénéfice brut 1459
bénéfice commercial 475
bénéfice comptable 412
bénéfice de cours 1233
bénéfice de monnayage 2154
bénéfice d'entreprise 475
bénéfice d'exploitation 475
bénéfice distribuable 1072
bénéfice, donner un ~ 100
bénéfice en capital 530
bénéfice espéré 166
bénéfice excédentaire 1213
bénéfice exceptionnel 1213
bénéfice fictif 171
bénéfice fiscal 197
bénéfice imaginaire 171
bénéfice imposable 197
bénéfice net 646
bénéfice par action 1142
bénéfice reporté 1985
bénéfices 229
bénéfices accumulés 2108
bénéfices non distribués 2108
bénéfices non prélevés 2108
bénéfices non répartis 2311
bénéfices réservés 2108

bénéfices retenus 2108
bénéfice sur le change 1233
bénéfice sur le cours 1233
bénéficiaire 350
bénéficiaire du crédit 418
bénéficiaire d'un effet 1902
besoin d'emprunts 424
besoins de (en) caisse 596
besoins de financement 1316
besoins d'investissement 1627
besoins en capitaux 557
besoins en couverture 837
besoins en liquidités 596
besoins en trésorerie 596
besoins financiers 1316
bien-fonds 1661
biens 202
biens à l'étranger 204
biens corporels 1747
biens de capital 533
biens de consommation 743
biens de consommation durables 747
biens de production 1134
biens d'équipement 1134
biens d'investissement 533
biens durables 1133
biens en immeubles 1508
biens et services 1443
biens et services, balance des ~ 259
biens immatériels 1505
biens immeubles 1508
biens immobiliers 1508
biens incorporels 1505
biens matériels 1747
biens meubles 622
biens mobiliers 622
biens non durables 1827
bilan 270
bilan actif 275
bilan bénéficiaire 275
bilan consolidé (du groupe) 736
bilan de clôture 1302
bilan déficitaire 274
bilan définitif 1302
bilan d'entrée 1700
bilan de vérification 2303
bilan d'ordre 2303
bilan d'ouverture 1700
bilan excédentaire 275
bilan intérimaire 1596
bilan intermédiaire 1596
bilan passif 274
bilan provisoire 1596
billet à ordre 1477
billet (de banque) 287
billet de complaisance 15
billet de créance simple 1477
billet du trésor 2301
billet promissoire 1477
billets en circulation 308
billets et espèces 1834
billets et espèces en circulation 638
billets et espèces étrangers 1369
billets et pièces 1834
billets et pièces en circulation 638
billet simple 1477
billion 367, 368
bimétallisme 375
BIRD 1602
blocage 383
blocage des importations 319
blocage des prix 1400
bloc d'actions 386
bloc dollar 1086
bloc franc 1388
bloc sterling 2224
bloquer 380
bloquer un chèque 2227
boîte de coffre-fort 2123
bon 389, 876, 1477
bon à lots 1719
bon au porteur 338
bon de caisse 389, 590
bon d'épargne 2141
bon de remboursement 704
bon de revenus 1526
bon du trésor 2301
bon en souffrance 980
boni 127, 397, 398, 2244
bonification 127
bonification de taxe 2038
bonification d'intérêts 1594
bonifier une perte 707
bonifier une somme à quelqu'un 566
bonne affaire 321
bonne fin, garantie de ~ 1474
bonne fin, sauf ~ 2099
bonus 397
boom 413
boomflation 414
bordereau 2217
bordereau d'achat 425
bordereau de compte 5
bordereau de contrat 425, 440
bordereau de paiement 877
bordereau de paie (paye) 1912
bordereau de vente 440
bordereau de versement 877
bourse 1218
bourse à parquet 1845
bourse aux actions 1218
bourse de commerce 695
bourse d'effets 1218
bourse de marchandises 695
bourse de(s) valeurs (mobilières) 1218
bourse officielle 1845
boursicoteur 1647
boursicotier 1647
boursier 1647
branche 427
BRI 300
brouillard 1754
budget 441
budgétaire 442
budget annuel 159
budget communautaire 703
budget conjoncturel 929
budget déficitaire 95
budget de l'état 1446
budget d'investissement 519
budget équilibré 251
budgéter 443
budget financier 1312
budget, hors ~ 1286
budgétiser 443
budget national 1446
budget ordinaire 1859
budget public 1446
bulletin de dépôt 608
bulletin de la bourse 1228
bulletin de la cote (de la bourse) 1228
bulletin de(s) cours 1228
bulletin de versement 1022
bureau central 607
bureau de change 1217
bureau de clearing 649
bureau de compensation 649
bureau de courtier 439
bureau principal 607
but lucratif, association à ~ 1986
but lucratif, association sans ~ 1829

cadrer les comptes, faire ~ 112
c.a.f. 634
caisse 579, 587
caisse, contre ~ 573
caisse de compensation 649, 710
caisse de crédit 850
caisse d'épargne 2139
caisse d'épargne à la construction 453
caisse d'épargne-construction 453
caisse d'épargne postale 1941
caisse de pensions 1918
caisse de péréquation 710
caisse de prêts 850
caisse de retraite(s) 1918
caisse, petite ~ 1931
calcul 492
calculation 492
calcul de coûts 797
calcul de prix coûtants 797
calcul de prix de revient type 2325
calcul du coût prévisionnel 1190
calcul du prix de revient 815
calcul du prix de revient complet, système de ~ 4
calcul du prix de revient intégral, système de ~ 4
calculer 490
calcul erroné 491
call money 505
calme 508, 1130
cambiste 361, 509
capacité compétitive 714
capacité de gain 1139
capacité de rendement 1139
capital 514
capital acceptant les risques 1178
capital-actions 544
capital-actions dilué 2365
capital-actions émis 1638
capital, à fort coefficient de ~ 539
capital, à forte proportion de ~ 539
capital appelé 500
capital-apport 521
capital à risques 1178
capital autorisé 222
capital circulant 468
capital d'actions 544
capital d'apport 1564
capital d'emprunt 1707

capital de numéraire 577
capital d'épargne 2143
capital de roulement 468
capital d'établissement 1564
capital d'exploitation 468
capital dormant 1502
capital émis 1638
capital en actions ordinaires 697
capital engagé 468, 541
capital en numéraire 577
capital-espèces 577
capital exigible 499
capital fixe 518
capital flottant 468
capital, grand ~ 355
capital, gros ~ 355
capital immobilisé 518
capital improductif 1502
capital initial 1564
capital investi 541
capitalisation 523, 543
capitalisation d'intérêts (dus) 156
capitaliser 545
capitaliser les bénéfices 548
capitaliser les intérêts 547
capitaliste 550
capital libéré 1880
capital mobile 468
capital mobilier 468
capital mort 1502
capital nominal 222
capital non (encore) appelé 2313
capital non versé 2313
capital-numéraire 577
capital-obligations 940
capital oisif 1502
capital originaire 1564
capital placé 541
capital privé 1975
capital propre 1996
capital roulant 468
capital social 222, 544
capital souscrit 2232
capital versé 1880
capitaux à l'étranger 515
capitaux d'emprunt 417
capitaux de placement 1622
capitaux d'évasion 1349
capitaux empruntés 417
capitaux errants 1498
capitaux étrangers 1359
capitaux fébriles 1498
capitaux fixes 518
capitaux fugitifs 1349
capitaux propres 1996
capitaux vagabonds 1498
carence de paiement 982
carnet bancaire 289
carnet de banque 289
carnet de caisse d'épargne 2140
carnet d'échéances 359
carnet de chèques 626
carnet de compte 289
carnet de dépôt 1021
carnet d'épargne 2142
carte bleue 854
carte de crédit 854
cartel 571
cartel de prix 115
cash flow 586
cassette 579
catégorie de revenus 1527
catégorie d'imposition 2267
caution 395, 1138
caution, donner ~ 52
cautionnement 394, 602
cautionner 52
caution, se porter ~ 52
caution, se rendre ~ 52
cavalerie 1659
cave des coffres-forts 2125
CCI 1603
cédant 121, 1165
céder 118
céder une créance 207
cédule 1477
cédule d'impôts 2267
cédule hypothécaire 1792
C.E.E. 1194
centimes additionnels 66
centre de coûts 461
certificat d'action(s) 2170
certificat de dépôt 608
certificat d'entrepôt 2364
certificat de prêt 1709
certificat de souscription 2115
certificat du trésor 2301
certificat provisoire 1597
certifier un chèque 610
cessation des paiements 2250
cesser les paiements 603
cessibilité 116
cessible 117
cession 119
cessionaire 120, 1163
cession de créances 208
chambre blindée 2125
chambre de commerce (et industrie) 611
Chambre de commerce internationale 1603
chambre de compensation 649
chambre de liquidation 649
chambre forte 2125
change 1216, 1221
change à terme 1226
change au comptant 1227
change à vue 1003
change commercial 356
change (des monnaies) 1231
changes à terme 1378
changeur (de monnaie) 509
charge 460
charge de, à la ~ 616
charge des dettes 462
charge fiscale 463
charge fiscale latente 759
charge hypothécaire 1793
charger 615
charger de dettes 466
charger un compte de 618
charges 619
charges à payer 39
charges d'amortissement 620
charges de capital 520
charges d'exploitation 1850
charges d'intérêt 1587
charges financières 1313
charges fixes 1336
charges indirectes 1417
charges non déductibles 1049
charges non-incorporables 1202
charges sociales 2186
chèque 624
chèque à barrement 883
chèque à ordre 631
chèque au porteur 339
chèque barré 883
chèque croisé 883
chèque de virement 883
chèque de voyage 2297
chèque en blanc 378
chèque non à ordre 630
chèque non barré 339
chèque ordinaire 339
chèque ouvert 339
chèque, payer par ~ 1901
chèque postal 1425
chèque sans contrepartie 241
chèque sans provision 241
chèque tiré en blanc 378
chéquier 626
cherté de la vie 1483
chiffre d'affaires 2130
chiffre d'affaires brut 1467
chiffre d'affaires net 1816
chiffre indice 1550
chiffrer à, se ~ 106
chiffres ronds, en ~ 2119
chute 1125
chute des cours 431
chute des prix 431
c.i.f. 634
circulant 635
circulation de billets (de banque) 308
circulation de billets et espèces 638
circulation de capital (capitaux) 555
circulation de l'argent 637
circulation de moyens de paiement 638
circulation, en ~ 635
circulation fiduciaire 1299
circulation forcée 1356
circulation monétaire 637
circulation monétaire, excédent de la ~ 6
classe de revenus 1527
classe d'impôt 2267
classification 155
clause dollar 1088
clause d'urgence 1155
clause échappatoire 1155
clause or 1432, 1432
clearing 642, 643
climat des affaires 469
clôture d'un compte 655
clôturer les livres 278
clôturer un compte 652
codébiteur 659
coefficient d'amortissement 144
coefficient de couverture 840
coefficient de liquidité 45
coefficient de pondération 2372

coefficient d'équivalence 1181
coefficient de réserve obligatoire 1759
coemprunteur 658
coffre 2123
coffre-fort 2122
collecte de capitaux 1405
collecte de fonds 1405
combler la réserve 2039
combler un découvert 836
combler un déficit 836
combler une perte 707
commanditaire 1691
commandite 1591, 1692
commandité 1419
commerçable 1738
commerçant de gros 2375
commerçant en gros 2375
commerçant, petit ~ 2105
commerce au détail 2107
commerce de change 1221
commerce d'échange 325
commerce de détail 2107
commerce de devises 1221
commerce de gros 2376
commerce de transit 2294
commerce d'outre-mer 1283
commerce en billets et espèces étrangers 936
commerce en détail 2107
commerce en gros 2376
commerce en transit 2294
commerce extérieur 1283
commerce intérieur 1101
commerce libre 1392
commerce, petit ~ 2107
commerce triangulaire 2280
commercialisation 1742
commettant 1973
commettre un détournement 977
commissaire aux comptes 216
commissaire de société 216
commission 689
commissionaire 690
commission bancaire 293
commission d'acceptation 13
commission d'escompte 1055
commission des créanciers 388
commission de service 80
commission d'ouverture de crédit 693
Communauté économique européenne 1194
compagnie 686
compagnie de financement 1308
compartiment de coffre-fort 2123
compensation 642, 643, 708, 709, 1172
compensation bancaire 292
compensation de chèques 627
compensation de soldes 1199
compensation entre banques 292
compensation interbancaire 292
compenser 706
compenser un chèque 641
compenser un découvert 836
compenser un déficit 836
compenser une perte 707
compétitif 713
compétitivité 714
complément de dividende 1303
composante de la demande 716
comptabiliser 401
comptabilité 20
comptabilité analytique d'exploitation 798
comptabilité autonome 2155
comptabilité de prix coûtants 798
comptabilité du prix de revient 798
comptabilité en partie double 1107
comptabilité en partie simple 2181
comptabilité nationale 1797
comptabilité, plan de ~ 22
comptable 21, 410
comptant 572, 573
comptant, au ~ 573
compte 16, 17
compte, à ~ 19
compte à demi 1654
compte à payer 36
compte à recevoir 37
compte auxiliaire 224
compte à vue 23
compte capital 516
compte capitaux 516
compte chèque postal 1800
compte chèques 625
compte client 617
compte collectif 673, 766, 1649
compte commun 1649
compte conjoint 1649
compte courant 23
compte courant, avance de (en; sur) ~ 87
compte courant, crédit en ~ 87
compte d'actif 201
compte d'attente 2248
compte d'autrui, pour (le) ~ 35
compte de banque 285
compte de bilan 271
compte de caisse 575
compte de capital 516
compte de chèques 625
compte de chèques postaux 1800
compte de clearing 644
compte de compensation 644
compte de consignation 2305
compte de contre-partie 760
compte de dépenses 1259
compte de dépôt(s) 1016
compte d'engagement 2248
compte d'épargne 2138
compte de participation 1654
compte de passage 2248
compte de passif 1682
compte de pertes et profits 1523
compte de, pour (le) ~ 34
compte de prévision 130
compte de profits et pertes 1523
compte de provision 130
compte de recettes 1524
compte de réserve 130
compte de revenus 1524
compte de(s) frais 1259
compte de(s) résultats 1523
compte, détenteur d'un ~ 26
compte de tiers, pour (le) ~ 35
compte de virement 1424
compte d'exploitation 2289
compte d'ordre 2248
compte d'un tiers, pour (le) ~ 35
compte en banque 285
compte en participation 1654
compte giro 1424
compte intermédiaire 2248
compte, intitulé de ~ 25
compte joint 1649, 1649
compte loro 1716
compte non liquidé 1846
compte non réglé 1846
compte non saldé 1846
compte nostro 1833
compte ouvert 23, 1846
compte particulier 1926
compte personnel 1926
compte, pour (son) propre ~ 1877
compte privé 1926
compte propre, pour ~ 1877
compte provisoire 2248
compte recettes 1524
compte rendu annuel 160
compter en trop 1866
compte revenus 1524
compter trop (cher) 1866
compter trop peu 2316
compte rubriqué 2305
comptes de régularisation 73
comptes économiques intégrés 1579
comptes extérieurs, balance des ~ 258
compte specifié 429
comptes réfléchis 802
compte, titulaire d'un ~ 26
compte vostro 1716
comptoir 427
comptoir de liquidation 649
comptoir de règlement 649
comptoir de virement 649
computation 492
computer 490
concentration 135
concession 728
concession de crédit 220
concordance de comptes 2043
concordat 718
concordat préventif à la faillite 719
concurrence, libre ~ 1390
concurrentiel 713
concussion 978
conditions de crédit 856
conditions d'émission d'un emprunt 729
conditions de paiement 2278
conditions de règlement 2278
confection de l'inventaire 1616
confirmation de solde bancaire 290
congé de retrait de dépôts 1840
congélation 383
congélation des prix 1400
congeler 380
conjoncture 477
conjoncture, basse ~ 1031
conjoncture, haute ~ 413
conjoncturel 1146
conseil financier 1309

conseil fiscal 21, 2264
conseiller financier 1309
conseiller fiscal 2264
consentir un crédit 126
consolidation 737
consolider une dette 733
consolidés 734
consommateur 744
consommation 751
consommation des ménages 1499
consommation intérieure 1092
consommation interne 1092
consommation nationale 1092
consommation par habitant 1920
consommation par personne 1920
consommation par tête 1920
consommation privée 1499
consommation propre 1497
consommation publique 2002
consortium 740
consortium de banques 303
consortium d'émission 2322
consortium de placement 2322
constituer en gage 1018
constituer une garantie 101
constituer une réserve 454
consultant financier 1309
contenir l'inflation 628
contingent 2017
contingentement 2018
contingentement des devises 2030
contingenter 122, 1186
contracter une dette 761
contracter un emprunt 762
contrainte 191
contrat d'arrangement 719
contrat de bail 1666
contrat de location 1666
contrat de prise ferme 2321
contrat fiduciaire 976
contravention 136
contre-caution 238
contre-écriture 281
contre-inflationniste 170
contrepartie 281, 822
contrepassation 281, 512
contrepassement 281
contre-prestation 731
contrevaleur 822
contre-valeur 1219
contribuable 2028
contribuer du capital 436
contribution 1135
contribution foncière 1662
contrôle des changes 1224
contrôle des comptes 214
contrôle des crédits 629
contrôle des devises 1224
contrôle des investissements 1044
contrôle des prix 1961
contrôle des salaires 2360
contrôle direct 770
contrôle fiscal 1566
contrôler 215
contrôler l'inflation 628
contrôleur des comptes 216
convenir d'un prix 113
convention sur les prix 115
conversion 771
conversion de dettes 776
conversion d'un emprunt 775
conversion en argent 773
conversion en espèces 773
conversion forcée 721
convertibilité 780
convertibilité extérieure 1278
convertibilité externe 1278
convertibilité intérieure 781
convertibilité interne 781
convertible 782
convertir en argent 785
convertir en espèces 785
convertir un emprunt 779
convertissement 771
coopérative 786
coopérative de crédit 787
coopérative de production 1983
corbeille 1845
costing 797
cotation 1960
cotation (des cours) 1746
cote 200, 1960, 2017
côté actif 206
côté créditeur 206
côté débiteur 943
cote de clôture 657
cote de la bourse 1228
côté de l'avoir 206
cote (des cours) 1746
cote d'ouverture 1849
côté du crédit 206
côté du débit 943
cote du jour 913
cote en bourse 1234
côté passif 943
coter 195, 1698
coter un prix 1728
cotisation 200, 2235
coulisse 891
couper les dépenses 915
coupon 828
coupon attaché 829
coupon, contre remise du ~ 1958
coupon de dividende 1078
coupon détaché 831
coupon d'intérêt(s) 1588
coupon non échu 2330
coupon périmé 1664
coupon prescrit 1664
coupon, sans ~ 831
coupon semestriel 1475
coupure 1011
coupure d'action 2230
courant du marché 911
courir 40
cours 1960
cours acheteur(s) 354
cours actuel 907, 913
cours à l'achat 354
cours à la vente 193
cours argent 354
cours à terme 1383, 1384
cours au comptant 593, 2024
cours au pair 1887
cours coté 1234
cours d'achat 354
cours d'appui 1610
cours de change 1216
cours de change à terme 1383
cours de change au comptant 2024
cours de change des billets et espèces 1235
cours de change fixe 1341
cours de change flexible 1347
cours de change flottant 1347
cours de change fluctuant 1347
cours de change libre 1347
cours de change oscillant 1347
cours de change variable 1347
cours de clearing 650
cours de clôture 657
cours de compensation 650
cours de conversion 778
cours de début 1849
cours de déport 240
cours de la bourse 1234
cours de la demande 354
cours demandé 354
cours d'émission 1642
cours de prolongation 569
cours de rachat 2054
cours de remboursement 2054
cours de report 569
cours, dernier ~ 657
cours des actions 2174
cours des affaires 833
cours de souscription 2238
cours de soutien 1610
cours de vente 193
cours d'intervention 1610
cours d'ouverture 1849
cours du change 1216
cours du comptant 593
cours du disponible 2203
cours du jour 907, 913
cours du marché 1234
cours du marché libre 1396
cours du pair 1887
course aux guichets de la banque 2121
cours forcé 722, 1356
cours libre 1396
cours-limite 1965
cours moyen 234
cours offert 193
cours pratiqué 913
cours, premier ~ 1849
cours sur place 2203
cours unique 2326
cours unitaire 2326
cours vendeur(s) 193
courtage 438
court de fonds, être (à) ~ 2178
courte échéance, à ~ 2177
courtier 437
courtier de bourse 2152
courtier de change 361, 509, 1311, 2152
courtier d'escompte 361
courtier en devises 509
courtier en marchandises 694
courtier en valeurs 2152
courtier intermédiaire de bourse 1648

court terme, à ~ 2177
coût 795
coût alternatif 1853
coût, assurance, (et) fret 634, 634
coût d'acquisition 804
coût de crédit 805
coût de la main d'œuvre 806
coût de l'argent 1967
coût de la vie 807
coût de l'émission 1353
coût de remplacement 2091
coût du capital 522
coût du travail 806
coût effectif 54
coût estimatif 1189
coût marginal 1733
coût par unité 813
coût prévisionnel 1189
coût prévu 1189
coût réel 54
coût(s) de production 811
coûts des facteurs, aux ~ 1291
coûts salariaux 2359
coût unitaire 813
couvert, non ~ 835
couverture 834, 1732
couverture additionnelle 62
couverture à terme 1377
couverture complémentaire 62
couverture en or 1435
couverture or 1435, 1435
couverture requise 837
couverture, sans ~ 835
couverture, servir de ~ 2166
couverture supplémentaire 62
couvrir un déficit 836
couvrir une perte 707
créance 639
créance à recouvrer 37
créance, céder une ~ 207
créance chirographaire 2332
créance comptable 404
créance de péréquation 1173
créance éventuelle 757
créance exigible 37
créance hypothécaire 957
créance irrécouvrable 242
créance, mauvaise ~ 242
créances bancaires 296
créances, cession de ~ 208
créances douteuses 1110
créances, transfert de ~ 208
créances, transport de ~ 208
créances véreuses 1110
créance, transférer une ~ 207
créancier 870
créancier chirographaire 405
créancier étranger 1360
créancier inscrit 405
créancier obligataire 390
création d'argent 842
création de crédit 841
création de monnaie 842
création monétaire 842
crédit 206, 843, 844, 845, 873, 879
crédit, accorder un ~ 126
crédit additionnel 63
crédit à découvert 379
crédit à la consommation 745
crédit à l'économie 470
crédit, allocation de ~ 220
crédit, allouer un ~ 126
crédit à moyen terme 1753
crédit au consommateur 745
crédit automatiquement renouvelable 2114
crédit, autorisation de ~ 220
crédit, autoriser un ~ 126
crédit-bail 1668
crédit bancaire 295
crédit cautionné 670
crédit commercial 470
crédit complémentaire 63
crédit, concession de ~ 220
crédit, consentir un ~ 126
crédit consortial 741
crédit contre garantie 670
crédit contre nantissement 670
crédit d'acceptation 11
crédit d'appoint 63
crédit d'aval 853
crédit de banque 295
crédit de caisse 580
crédit de cautionnement 853
crédit de complément 63
crédit de liquidation automatique 2156
crédit, demander un ~ 175
crédit de notoriété 379
crédit d'escompte 1059
crédit de soudure 434
crédit de transition 434
crédit documentaire 1085
crédit en blanc 379
crédit en compte courant 87
crédit en compte-joint 865
créditer le compte (de) 880
créditer quelqu'un d'une somme 566
créditer une somme à quelqu'un 566
créditeur 870
créditeur à droit de priorité 1948
créditeur garanti 2150
créditeur nanti 2150
créditeur prioritaire 1948
créditeur privilégié 1948
crédit finançant des ventes à tempérament 1488
crédit foncier 868
crédit gagé 670
crédit garanti 670
crédit hypothécaire 866
crédit immobilier 868
crédit interbancaire 1583
crédit intérimaire 434
crédit intermédiaire 434
crédit libre 379
crédit mobilier 867
crédit non couvert 379
crédit, octroi de ~ 220
crédit, octroyer un ~ 126
crédit par acceptation 11
crédit par aval 853
crédit par caisse 580
crédit par cautionnement 853
crédit personnel 1927
crédit privé 1927
crédit provisoire 434
crédit réel 868
crédit révocable 2113
crédit revolving 2114
crédit roll-over 2118
crédit rotatif 2114
crédits budgétaires 444
crédits congelés 1401
crédits d'investissement 1620
crédits gelés 1401
crédits intérieurs 1093
crédit spécial 2194
crédit stand-by 2214
crédit supplémentaire 63
crédit sur hypothèque 866
crédit sur nantissement 670
crédit sur notoriété 379
crédit sur titres 869
crédit swap 2252
crédit syndical 741
crédit temporaire 434
crédit transitoire 434
créer un chèque 1115
créer un emprunt 1157
créer une réserve 454
creux 508
curateur 209
cycle conjoncturel 471
cycle d'affaires 471
cycle économique 471

date d'arrêté du bilan 272
date d'échéance 931
date de l'échéance 931
date de valeur 2343
date d'expiration 1263
débâcle 668
débit 613, 942, 943
débitant 2105
débit de, au ~ 616
débit de, par le ~ 616
débiter 615
débiter à un compte 618
débiter un compte de 618
débit, être au ~ 944
débiteur 958
débiteur de, être ~ 1876
débiteur défaillant 981
débiteur d'une lettre de change 362
débiteur en retard 981
débiteur, être ~ 944
débiteur négligent 981
débiteur retardataire 981
débiteur solidaire 1651
débiteur, tiers ~ 1413
déblocage 950
débloquer 949
débouché 1736
débours 1053
déboursements 1053
débourser 1050
déboursés 1053
décaissement 1119
décaisser 1113
décalage 1037
décalage de prix 1038, 1966
décharge 718
déchéance 1262

déclaration de cautionnement 394
déclaration de douane 919
déclaration de faillite 69
déclaration de faillite, demande en ~ 316
déclaration de garantie 394
déclaration de revenus 1531
déclaration douanière 919
déclaration d'un dividende 964
déclaration en douane 919
déclaration en faillite 69
déclaration fiscale 2275
déclaration provisoire 2000
déclarer un dividende 965
déclin 968
décomposition 155
décompte 246, 429
déconfiture 315, 668
décote 2261
découvert 988
découvert, à ~ 835
découvert (de compte) 1867
découvrir un compte 1868
dédit 136
dédommagement 708
dédouanable 916
dédouanement 645
déductible, perte ~ 974
déduction à la source 975
déduction de l'impôt (des impôts), après ~ 1677
déduction de l'impôt (des impôts), avant ~ 1959
déduction des frais, après ~ 131
déduction des frais, sous ~ 621
déduction d'impôts 2261
déduction d'impôt(s), sous ~ 1677
déduction du report déficitaire 2273
déduction faite des frais 131
déduction faite d'impôt(s) 1677
déduction fiscale 2261
déduction rétroactive d'un déficit 2272
déduire à la source 972
déduire à l'avance 973
défalcation des frais, après ~ 131
défalcation faite des frais 131
défaut de paiement 982
déficit 988
déficit budgétaire 95
déficit budgétaire systematique 989
déficit commercial 474
déficit de caisse 96
déficit de dollars 1089
déficit de la balance des paiements 261
déficit des recouvrements fiscaux 1330
déficit d'exercice 474
déficit d'exploitation 474
déficit du commerce extérieur 265
déficit extérieur 261
déficit fiscal 1330
déficit inflationniste 1557
déflateur 996
déflation 991
déflation, amener la ~ 990
déflationniste 992, 995
dégagement bénéficiaire 1990
dégel 950
dégeler 949
dégradation 2367
degré de liquidité 45
dégrèvement fiscal 2261
dégringolade des cours 431
dégringolade des prix 431
délai de blocage 384
délai de circulation 895
délai (de grâce) 998
délai de paiement 1924
délai de paiement, accorder un ~ 1274
délai de préavis 1836
délai de souscription 2237
délai de validité 894
délégation des créanciers 388
demande 1002
demande de biens de consommation 746
demande de couverture supplémentaire 501
demande de crédit 173
demande d'emprunt 173
demande de prêt 173
demande de remboursement 640
demande de restitution 640
demande des ménages 1097
demande en déclaration de faillite 316
demande intérieure 1096
demande, l'offre et la ~ 192, 2242
demande monétaire 1774
demander trop (cher) 1866
demander trop peu 2316
demander un crédit 175
demander un emprunt 175
demander un prêt 175
demande, sur ~ 495
démarque 927
demeure, en ~ 979
démonétisation 1008
démonétiser 503
dénationalisation 1009
deniers de l'état 2005
deniers, en ~ 573
deniers publics 2005
dénominateur commun 698
dépasser un compte 1868
dépasser un crédit 1201
dépense 1258
dépenser 1257
dépenser plus que son revenu 1702
dépenses 1053, 1261
dépenses accessoires 61
dépenses administratives 79
dépenses budgétaires 446
dépenses courantes 908
dépenses débudgétisées 1823
dépenses de caisse 582
dépenses de capital 524
dépenses de consommation 748
dépenses d'entretien 810
dépenses des consommateurs 748
dépenses d'exploitation 1850
dépenses d'investissement 524
dépenses diverses 1764
dépenses effectives 55
dépenses effectuées 55
dépenses en capital 524
dépenses en consommation 748
dépenses en immobilisation(s) 524
dépenses fixes 1336
dépenses générales 1417
dépenses, menues ~ 1764
dépenses, petites ~ 1764
dépenses publiques 2003
dépenses, recettes et ~ 1525
dépenses spéciales 61
dépenses supplémentaires 61
déplacement 2296
déport 239
déposant 1025, 1026
déposer 1015
déposer des titres en nantissement 671
déposer en nantissement 1018
dépositaire 1017
dépôt 1013
dépôt à échéance (fixe) 1337
dépôt à préavis 1019
dépôt à temps 1337
dépôt à terme (fixe) 1337
dépôt avec préavis 1019
dépôt à vue 1004
dépôt bancaire 297
dépôt collectif 685
dépôt de caution 602
dépôt de garantie (bloqué), en ~ 1185
dépôt d'épargne 2144
dépôt de virement 1024
dépôt en banque 297
dépôt fiduciaire, en ~ 1185
dépôt remboursable avec préavis 1019
dépôt remboursable sur demande 1004
dépôts interbancaires 1582
dépôt sur compte de virement 1024
dépôt sur compte giro 1024
dépouillement 155
dépréciation 138, 969, 1029
dépréciation de change 897
dépréciation de la monnaie 896
dépréciation du change 897
dépréciation monétaire 896
dépréciation technique 1030
déprécier 1028
déprécier, se ~ 970
déprédation 978
dépréder 977
dépression 1031
déprimé 508
dernier cours 657
dernier enchérisseur 1485
descendre en valeur 970
descente (en masse) sur la banque 2121
désépargne 1069
déséqulibre 1062
déshypothéquer 511
désinflation 1064
désinflationniste 1065
désinvestissement 1066

destinataire 2082
détail 429, 2107
détaillant 2105
détaxe 2261
détente au marché monétaire 1144
détente du crédit 1145
détenteur 336
détenteur d'actions 2171
détenteur de titres 2171
détenteur de valeurs 341, 2171
détenteur d'obligations 390
détenteur d'un compte 26
détérioration 2367
détermination de la parité de change 1032
détermination des prix 1962
déterminer un prix 1033
déthésaurisation 1063
détournement 978
détournement, commettre un ~ 977
détourner 977
dette 951
dette active 37
dette amortissable 1574
dette caduque 324
dette civile 1928
dette comptable 406
dette consolidée 735
dette de l'État 1798
dette d'impôt 2271
dette d'obligations 391
dette exigible 37
dette extérieure 1280
dette fiscale 2271
dette flottante 1351
dette hypothécaire 957
dette intérieure 1095
dette nationale 1798
dette non consolidée 1351
dette obligataire 391
dette passive 36
dette personnelle 1928
dette prescrite 324
dette privée 1928
dette publique 1798
dettes 961
dettes à courte échéance 910
dettes arriérées 188
dettes bancaires 296
dettes, être accablé de ~ 953
dettes, être criblé de ~ 953
dette solidaire 1650
dette unifiée 735
deuxième de change 2148
dévalorisation 1029
dévalorisation de la monnaie 897
dévalorisation monétaire 897
dévaloriser 1028
dévaloriser, se ~ 970
dévaluation 1029
dévaluation de la monnaie 897
dévaluation monétaire 897
dévaluer 1028
devis 1187
devis approximatif 184
devise 893
devise dure 1479
devise faible 2187
devise forte 1479
devise légère 2187
devise molle 2187
devise nationale 1094
devises 1361
devises à terme 1378
devise stable 2207
devis estimatif 184
devoir 1876
devoir de l'impôt 1683
devoir fiscal 1683
différence 1037
différence de change 1039
différence de niveau des intérêts 1412
différence de prix 1038
différence entre les prix 1038
différence entre les taux d'intérêt 1412
différer un paiement 984
difficultés d'argent 1314
difficultés de trésorerie 1314
difficultés financières 1314
difficultés pécuniaires 1314
digne de crédit 846
dilution du capital(-actions) 2226
diminuer de valeur 970
diminuer les dépenses 915
diminution 968
diminution des cours (prix) 886
diminution de valeur 969
diminution du dividende 925
direction des capitaux 1044
direction des créanciers 388
direction des investissements 1044
diriger l'inflation 628
dirigisme (économique) 1047
disparité 1067
disparité de(s) prix 1038
disponibilité des capitaux 226
disponibilités 227
disponibilités en banque 286
disponibilités monétaires 1783
disponibilités quasi-monétaires 1776, 2243
disponible 227
dispositions en matière de change 900
dispositions en matière de devises 900
dissolution 1070
dissoudre 1071
distraction 978
distraire 977
distribuer 122
distribuer un dividende 1051
distribution de bénéfices 183
distribution de dividende, non-~ 1826
distribution de dividendes 1052
distribution occulte 1482
divers 1764
divertir 977
divertissement 978
dividende 1076, 1077
dividende, avec ~ 887
dividende, ayant droit au ~ 1170
dividende cumulatif 889
dividende de priorité 1945
dividende en actions 400
dividende en espèces 584
dividende extraordinaire 398
dividende final 1303
dividende inclus 887
dividende intérimaire 1598
dividende prescrit 1954
dividende prioritaire 1945
dividende privilégié 1945
dividende provisoire 1598
dividende, sans ~ 1080
dividende supplémentaire 398
doit 942, 943
dollar de compensation 29
dollar de compte 29
dollar, euro~ 1193
domandeur de (d'un) crédit 172
domandeur d'un emprunt 172
domandeur d'un prêt 172
domicile 1102
domicile fiscal 1331
dommages (et) intérêts 708
don 1103
donateur 1104
donation 1103
données statistiques 2219
donner à titre de garantie 1018
donner aval à (pour) un effet 235
donner caution 52
donner des titres en gage (en garantie) 671
donner en gage 1018
donner en garantie 1018
donner en prêt 1671
donner garantie 52
donner un bénéfice 100
donner une garantie 101
donner un préavis de X jours 1426
donner un prix 1728
donneur d'aval 236
donneur de caution 395
donneur de crédit 1672
donneur d'ordre 1973
dotation 123, 1168
dotation à la réserve 67
dotation en capital 523
doter 122, 1167
douane 917
doublé à la baisse 1857
doublé à la hausse 485
double étalon 375
double imposition 1109
double marché des changes 2309
double option 1108
doubles primes 1108
double taxation 1109
doublure à la baisse 1857
doublure à la hausse 485
drainage de capitaux 556
drawback 1116
dresser l'inventaire 1124
dresser un bilan 279
droit 614, 1135
droit ad valorem 82
droit antidumping 169
droit attaché 888
droit au dividende, ayant ~ 1170

droit, avec ~ 888
droit compensateur 711
droit de commission 689
droit de compensation 711
droit de consommation 752
droit de constitution de dossier 1478
droit de conversion 777
droit de douane 917
droit de douane ad valorem 82
droit (de douane) différentiel 1040
droit (de douane) préférentiel 1949
droit de gage (sur) 1687
droit de garde 2124
droit de licence 1686
droit de mutation 812
droit de nantissement (sur) 1687
droit d'enregistrement 2077
droit de péage 2284
droit de préemption 2013
droit de préférence 1328
droit de priorité 1328
droit de régie 1245
droit de retention (sur) 1687
droit de souscription 174, 2115
droit de succession 938
droit d'établissement de dossier 1478
droit détaché 1249
droit de timbre 2211
droit de transcription 812
droit de transfert 812, 2081
droit de transmission 812
droit de vote des titres en dépôt 2356
droit d'inscription 2077
droit d'option 1854
droit d'usufruit 349
droit préférentiel 1328
droit prohibitif 1993
droit protecteur 1998
droits 1295
droits de tirage speciaux 2195
droits de tirage (sur) 1121
droit supplémentaire 60
droit sur la valeur 82
droit sur les donations 1422
D.T.S. 2195
dû 1127
ducroire 1000
due, somme ~ 151
dû, montant ~ 151
dumping 1131
durée de circulation 895
durée (de validité) 894

écart 1037
écart dans les prix 1038
écart (de prime) 1731
écart des prix 1038
écart entre les taux d'intérêt 1412
écart inflationniste 1557
écarts sur les opérations d'arbitrage 187
écart sur frais indirects 464
échange 325, 1216
échange d'actions 1232
échange de titres 2254
échange libre 1392
échange monétaire 1231
échanger 326
échanges extérieurs 1283
échanges triangulaires 2280
échéable le 15 août 1129
échéance 894, 1748
échéance, à courte ~ 2177
échéance, à l'~ 1128
échéance, à longue ~ 1715
échéance, à moyenne ~ 1752
échéance, arriver à ~ 347
échéance de X années 1749
échéance, venir à ~ 347
échéancier 359
échéant le 15 août 1129
échelle mobile 1348
échelon de revenus 1527
échelonner les paiements sur X années 2204
échoir 347, 1264
échu 1126
économicité 1984
économie déficitaire 989
économie de marché libre 1393
économie dirigée 768
économie du marché 1741
économie financière 1304
économie financière de l'état 827
économie libérale 1393
économie libre (des marchés) 1393
économie monétaire 1775
économie planifiée 768
économie politique 1151
économie privée 1976
économies, faire des ~ 924
économique 1146, 1147
économiser 924
écoulement 1935
écouler 2157
écouler une émission 1934
écouler un emprunt 1933
écriture 409
écriture d'ajustement 71
écriture de clôture 656
écriture de contrepassement 281
écriture de crédit 857
écriture de débit 946
écriture de, passer ~ 401
écriture de redressement 71
écriture d'ordre 2249
écriture inverse 281
écriture passée au débit 946
écriture récapitulative 717
écriture rectificative 71
effectuer des paiements 1152
effectuer des versements 1152
effet à l'encaissement 364
effet à ordre 374
effet à payer 372
effet à recevoir 373
effet à usance 358
effet, avaliser un ~ 235
effet à vue 1003
effet commerçable 374
effet commercial 356
effet de banque 284
effet de commerce 356
effet de complaisance 15
effet de finance 1307
effet de financement 1307
effet déposé en garantie 363
effet déposé en nantissement 363
effet de première banque 1323
effet de (tout) premier ordre 1323
effet, donner aval à (pour) un ~ 235
effet endossable 374
effet en nantissement 363
effet en nourrice 363
effet en pension 363
effet en souffrance 365
effet escompté sur l'intérieur 1060
effet impayé 365
effet innégociable 371
effet intransférable 371
effet intransmissible 371
effet nanti 363
effet négociable 374
effet nominatif 371
effet non à ordre 371
effet non commerçable 371
effet non endossable 371
effet non honoré 365
effet non négociable 371
effet non transférable 371
effet non transmissible 371
effet pour aval, signer un ~ 235
effet renvoyé (impayé) 365
effet retourné (impayé) 365
effets 2151
effets au porteur 342
effets d'état 1244
effets immobiliers 1508
effets mobiliers 622
effets publics 1244
effet sur l'extérieur 1357
effet sur l'intérieur 1091
effet transférable 374
effet transmissible 374
effondrement 668
effondrement des cours 431
effondrement des prix 431
effritement des cours (prix) 886
égalisation 1172
égalisation des charges 1174
égalisation des frais 800
élasticité des cours de change 1154
élévation de(s) prix 1539
élévation du taux de (l')escompte 1541
élever à, s'~ 106
élever la valeur 178
embargo sur les importations 319
embarras d'argent 1314
embarras financier(s) 1314
embarras pécuniaire(s) 1314
émetteur 1644
émettre des obligations 1637
émettre un chèque 1115
émettre un emprunt 1157
émigration de capitaux 556
émission 1352
émission à guichets ouverts 2259
émission au robinet 2259
émission continue 2259
émission d'actions 1640
émission d'actions gratuites 399
émission d'actions nouvelles 2116

émission de billets (de banque) 1156
émission de bons 392
émission de capitaux 549
émission de valeurs 1639
émission d'obligations 392
émission fiduciaire 1300
émission par série 385
émoluments 1158
emploi de capitaux 1160
empocher un bénfice 1937
emprunt 419, 1705
emprunt à charnière 2118
emprunt affecté à un but déterminé 2281
emprunt à lots 1720
emprunt amortissable 141
emprunt, amortissement d'un ~ 142
emprunt à primes 1720
emprunt commercial 473
emprunt convertible 784
emprunt convertissable 784
emprunt d'amortissement 141
emprunt de consolidation 738
emprunt de conversion 774
emprunt, demander un ~ 175
emprunt de stabilisation 2206
emprunt d'état 1453
emprunt de valorisation 2206
emprunt d'obligations 941
emprunt du gouvernement 1453
emprunt en souscription, mettre un ~ 1634
emprunter 415
emprunter du capital 416
emprunteur 418
emprunt extérieur 1282
emprunt forcé 723
emprunt funding 738
emprunt gouvernemental 1453
emprunt hypothécaire 1711
emprunt intérieur 1099
emprunt lié à un but déterminé 2281
emprunt national 1099
emprunt obligataire 941
emprunt-obligations 941
emprunt-or 1438
emprunt par obligations 941
emprunt par tirage au sort 1720
emprunt pour le développement 1036
emprunt public 1453
emprunts 1673
emprunt sur titres 1712
emprunt sur valeurs 1712
encaissable 574
encaisse 587
encaissement 679
encaissement, avis d'~ 47
encaisse-or 1430
encaisser un chèque 576
encan 212
enchère 353
enchère(s) 212
enchérissement 1539
enchérisseur, dernier ~ 1485
encombrer le marché (d'articles bon marché) 1132
encouragement de l'épargne 1161
endetté 952
endettement 462
endettement de l'État 1798
endettement extérieur 420
endetter, s'~ 1294
endos 1164
endossataire 1163
endossé 1163
endossement 1164
endosser un effet 1162
endosseur 1165
endosseur antérieur 1944
endosseur postérieur 2239
endosseur précédent 1944
endosseur subséquent 2239
engagement 692
engagement de change 1223
engagement d'endos 1166
engagement de titres 1501
engagement de valeurs 1501
engagements 961
engagements en compte courant 1023
engager 1018
engager des titres 671
enlever 1113
enquête sur le marché 1740
enregistrement 409
enregistrer 401
enregistrer une baisse (un gain) de X points 2045
enregistrer une perte (un bénéfice) 2046
entamer les réserves 1042
entendre sur un prix, s'~ 113
entente 571
entente sur les prix 115
entrée 409
entrée compensatrice 281
entrée de capitaux 99
entrées 1532
entrées de caisse 585
entrées et sorties 1525
entrepreneur 1171
entreprise 467
entreprise de l'état 1448
entreprise de service public 2009
entreprise d'état 1448
entreprise d'utilité publique 2009
entreprise, libre ~ 1391
entreprise nationale 1448
entreprise privée 1977
entreprise publique 1448
entrer en liquidation 1428
envoi d'argent 1784
envoi de fonds 1784
envoyer 2080
épargnant 2134
épargne 2137
épargne contractuelle 764
épargne (de placement) en valeurs 2135
épargne en compte(s) d'épargne 2136
épargne excessive 1872
épargne forcée 724
épargne intérieure brute 1462
épargne mobilière 2135
épargne obligatoire 724
épargne privée 1980
épargner 2133
éprouver une perte 333
épuisement des réserves 1012
équilibre 1176
équilibre budgétaire 251
équilibre du budget 251
équilibre interne 1098
équilibrer le budget 280
équivalence 1180
équivalent 822
érosion de la monnaie 896
érosion monétaire 896
erreur de calcul 491
erreur et omission, sauf ~ 1184
erreur ou omission, sauf ~ 1184
erreurs et omissions 1183
escompte 127, 1048
escompte au comptant 583
escompte bancaire 311
escompte commercial 935
escompte de banque 311
escompte de caisse 583
escompte de revendeur 935
escompte-intérêt 583
escompte officiel 311
escompter 1057
escompte sur facture 935
escompte sur marchandises 935
espèces 572, 665
espèces, billets et ~ 1834
espèces, en ~ 573
espèces en caisse 587
essor 2117
essuyer une perte 333
estampillage d'actions 2212
estampiller 2210
estimation 176
estimation approximative 184
estimation (fiscale) 200
estimation globale 184
estimer 177, 195
établir l'inventaire 1124
établir un bilan 279
établir un chèque 1115
établir un prix 1033
établir un solde 279
établissement bancaire 294
établissement central 607
établissement de banque 294
établissement de crédit 850
établissement de crédit foncier 1660
établissement de crédit immobilier 1660
établissement de l'inventaire 1616
établissement de prêts 850
établissement du prix de revient 815
établissement financier 1315
établissement principal 607
étalon boiteux 1476
étalon de change-or 1436
étalon de lingots-or 1431
étalon de numéraire-or 1402
étalon d'or 1441
étalon, double ~ 375
étalon imparfait 1476
étalon or 1441, 1441

étalon or de change 1436, 1436
étalon or de lingot 1431, 1431
étalon papier 1881, 1881
étalon unique 1785
état 2217
état de consolidation 739
état de répartition 799
état de(s) dépenses 2218
état des finances 1319
état de(s) frais 2218
état détaillé 429
état du marché 1743
état d'un compte 1940
état financier 1319
étatisation 1801
étatiser 1802
état providence 2373
état récapitulatif 2241
état social 2373
éteindre 148
éteindre une dette 510
éteindre une hypothèque 511
être au débit 944
être au-dessous du pair 1056
être au-dessus du pair 1883
être au pair 1884
être débiteur 944
être en prime 1883
étude du marché 1740
eurodollar 1193
évaluation 176
évaluation approximative 184
évaluation des bases imposables 1188
évaluation en gros 184
évaluation (fiscale) 200
évaluer 177, 195
évasion de capitaux 527
évasion d'impôt(s) 2266
évasion fiscale 2266
évolution 1200
évolution conjoncturelle 477
évolution de la conjoncture 477
excédent 1204, 2244
excédent budgétaire 452
excédent comptable 30
excédent de bénéfice 1213
excédent de couverture des frais 1870
excédent de dépenses 1212
excédent de (en) caisse 599
excédent de la balance commerciale 266
excédent de la balance des paiements 263
excédent de la circulation monétaire 6
excédent de la demande 1206
excédent de passif 1207
excédent de pouvoir d'achat 1209
excédent de recettes 2245
excédent des moyens de paiement 6
excédent d'exploitation 1852
excédent monétaire 6
excéder un crédit 1201
excès 1204
excès de dépenses 1212
excès de la demande 1206
excès d'épargne 1872
excès d'offre 1210
ex coupon 831
ex dividende 1080
ex droit 1249
exempt de droits (de douane) 920
exempt d'impôt(s) 1247
exempt d'intérêt(s) 1590
exemption d'impôt(s) 1248
exemption fiscale 1248
exercice budgétaire 448
exercice (commercial) 478
exercice (comptable) 1320
exercice (financier) 1320
exercice fiscal 1335
exercice social 705
exigibilité 674
exigibilités 910
exigible 496, 675
existence 1615
existence en or 1430
existence (en) titres 1628
exode de capitaux 556
exonération d'impôt(s) 1248
exonération fiscale 1248
ex option 1249
expansion de la masse monétaire 1252
expansion des échanges mondiaux 1254
expansion des investissements 1623
expansion du commerce mondial 1254
expansion du crédit 858
expansion monétaire 1252
expédition en douane 645
expert comptable 21
expert fiscal 2264
expiration 1262
expirer 1264
exportation 1265
exportation de capitaux 526
exportations invisibles 1632
exportations visibles 2351
exposé 2217
exprimé en dollars 1010
expropriation 1271
exproprier 1270
extinction 139
extourne 512
extra-budgétaire 1286
extrait de compte 5

facilités de crédit 421
facteur de conversion 772
facteur déflationniste 996
facteur inflationniste 1556
factoring 1293
facturation 366
facture 17
facture d'avoir 847
facture de débit 948
facture pro-forma 1991
facturer 357
faculté 1854
faculté à la baisse 1857
faculté à la hausse 485
faculté de lever double 485
faculté de livrer double 1857
faible 508
faiblesse 1130
failli 313, 314
faillite 315
faillite, déclaration de ~ 69
faillite, en ~ 314
faire accorder les comptes 112
faire apport du capital 436
faire arrêt (sur) 211
faire (bon) accueil à un effet 1054
faire cadrer les comptes 112
faire des affaires 1084
faire des avances sur titres 91
faire des économies 924
faire entrer en (ligne de) compte 570
faire honneur à un effet 1054
faire la part du feu 928
faire le commerce d'échange 326
faire le protêt d'un effet 1481
faire le service d'un emprunt 2165
faire le troc 326
faire l'inventaire 1124
faire payer trop (cher) 1866
faire payer trop peu 2316
faire perte 1056
faire prime 1883
faire protester un effet 1481
faire remise d'une dette 510
faire rentrer une créance 677
faire rentrer une dette 677
faire ressortir une perte (un bénéfice) 2046
faire traite sur quelqu'un 1114
faire un bénéfice 1729
faire un bilan 279
faire une balance 279
faire une dette 761
faire un emprunt 762
faire une perte 333
faire un prix 1728
faire un profit 1729
faute de calcul 491
faux frais 61
faveur de, ouvrir un crédit en ~ 1847
faveur fiscale 2263
ferme 1666
fermer un compte 652
fermeté des prix 1326
fermeture d'un compte 655
fermier 1667
feuille d'appointements 1912
feuille de contribution(s) 1839
feuille de coupons 832
feuille de paie (paye) 1912
feuille de répartition 799
feuille de versement 877
feuille d'impôt(s) 1839
fiche de versement 877
fidéicommis, par ~ 1185
fiduciaire 1298
fiduciant 1298
filiale 98
finance 1305
finance, haute ~ 1486
financement 1322
financement anticipatif 1952

financement au moyen de la cession de créances 956
financement des achats à tempérament 1490
financement des opérations à tempérament 1490
financement de soudure 433
financement des ventes à tempérament 1490
financement de transition 433
financement extérieur 1281
financement intérimaire 433
financement intermédiaire 433
financement interne 1601
financement par des fonds empruntés 1281
financement par des fonds extérieurs 1281
financement par des fonds propres 1601
financement provisoire 433, 1952
financement transitoire 433
financer 1306
financer provisoirement 1951
finance(s) 1304
finances de l'état 827
finances publiques 827
financier 1321
fin, sauf bonne ~ 2099
fisc 1242
fiscal 1329
fiscalité 1334
fixation des prix 1515, 1962
fixation des rapports de parité 1343
fixation d'un dividende 964
fixation verticale des prix 2097
fixer un dividende 965
fixer un prix 1033
fléchissement 968
fléchissement des cours (prix) 886
flexibilité des cours de change 1154
fluctuation conjoncturelle 930
fluctuation cyclique 930
fluctuation de la conjoncture 930
fluctuation des cours (de change) 1225
fluctuation des taux de change 1225
fluctuation du marché 930
fluctuation économique 930
fluctuation sur le marché 930
flux de capitaux 528
flux de crédit 859
flux de trésorerie 586
flux financier 528
FMI 1607
fob 1354
fondation 1385
fonder une dette 733
fonds 467, 1404, 1406
fonds commun de placement 1624
fonds commun d'investissement 1624
fonds conjoncturel 755
fonds d'amortissement 132, 140
fonds de commerce 468, 1444
fonds de compensation 710
fonds de contrepartie 823
fonds de crédit 1710
fonds de dépréciation 132
fonds d'égalisation 710
fonds de garantie 1472
fonds de l'état 2005
fonds d'épargne 2145
fonds de pensions 1918
fonds de péréquation 710
fonds de placement 1624
fonds de prêts 1710
fonds de prévision 755
fonds de prévoyance 755
fonds de rachat 140
fonds de renouvellement 2086
fonds de réserve 2101
fonds de réserve pour dépenses imprévues 755
fonds de roulement 468
fonds des rentes 1455
fonds de stabilisation 2205
fonds d'état 1244
fonds de terre 1661
fonds d'exploitation 468
fonds d'investissement 1622, 1624
fonds disponibles 227
fonds d'or 1430
fonds empruntés 417
fonds étrangers 417
Fonds européen de coopération monétaire 1197
fonds fiduciaire 2307
fonds fixe de caisse 1517
fonds libres 227
Fonds monétaire international 1607
fonds pour le financement 558
fonds prévisionnel 755
fonds publics 1244, 2005
force inflationniste 1558
formation de capital 529
formation de l'épargne 1374
formation de patrimoine 1373
former une réserve 454
formulaire de versement 1022
formule de versement 1022
fort coefficient de capital, à ~ 539
forte proportion de capital, à ~ 539
fortune nationale 1804
fournir des capitaux 1407
fournir en nantissement 1018
fournir une garantie 101
fourniture de capitaux 1408
fraction d'actions 1387
fractionnement d'actions 2175
fractionner le paiement sur X années 2204
frai 2366
frais 1261
frais accessoires 61
frais à déduire 621
frais à payer 39
frais bancaires 291
frais commerciaux 472
frais courants 908
frais d'achat 488
frais d'administration 79
frais de, aux ~ 1260
frais de banque 291
frais de constitution de dossier 1478
frais de course 2298
frais de courtage 438
frais de crédit 805
frais de déplacement 2298
frais de dossier 1478
frais déduits 131
frais de fabrication 811
frais défalqués 131
frais de gestion 79
frais de manipulation 1478
frais d'émission 1353
frais d'entretien 810
frais de production 811
frais de représentation 1169
frais de route 2298
frais d'établissement de dossier 1478
frais de tournée 2298
frais de transfert 812
frais de transport 2295
frais de virement 2081
frais de voyage 2298
frais d'expédition 2295
frais d'exploitation 1850
frais directs 1043
frais divers 1764
frais financiers 1313
frais fixes 1336
frais généraux 1417
frais indirects 1417
frais, menus ~ 1764
frais, moins les ~ 621
frais, petits ~ 1764
frais semi-variables 2164
frais, sous déduction des ~ 621
frais spéciaux 61
frais supplémentaires 61
frais variables 2346
franc d'impôt(s) 1247
franchise (de droits), en ~ 920
franchise d'impôt(s) 1248
franco (à) bord 1354
franc(o) de (droits de) douane 920
frappe 663
frapper 662
frapper d'une surtaxe 1514
frapper d'un impôt 194
fraude fiscale 2266
freiner l'inflation 628
fruste 2378
fuite de capitaux 527
funding 737
fusion 135
fusionnement 135

gage 1138
gage hypothécaire 2035
gagé, non ~ 835
gager 1018
gager des titres 671
gages 1140
gagé, susceptible d'être ~ 9
gagner en valeur 179
gain 1140, 1409
gain en capital 530
gain manqué 1718
gain net 646
gains 229
garant 395
garantie 669, 1138, 1471
garantie accessoire 65

garantie, accorder une ~ 101
garantie additionnelle 65
garantie, avance contre ~ 86
garantie complémentaire 65
garantie, constituer une ~ 101
garantie de bonne fin 1474
garantie de bonne fin d'un crédit 1447
garantie de crédit 860
garantie de crédit à l'exportation 1267
garantie de l'état 1450
garantie d'indemnité 394
garantie, donner ~ 52
garantie, donner une ~ 101
garantie d'un emprunt 1473
garantie, fournir une ~ 101
garantie hypothécaire 2035
garantie, offrir une ~ 101
garantie-or 1437
garantie réelle 2035, 2258
garantie, sans ~ 835
garantie supplémentaire 65
garanti, non ~ 835
garantir hypothécairement 838
garantir par hypothèque 838
garantir une émission 2320
garantisseur 395
garant, se porter ~ 52
garant, se rendre ~ 52
GATT 1415
gel 383
geler 380
gêne pécuniare 1314
gestion budgétaire 450
gestion des dettes 954
gestion financière 730
gonflement du crédit 861
gonfler 1553
goodwill 1444
grand capital 355
grand(-)livre des actionnaires 1701
grand(-)livre des titres 1701
grand livre (général) 1418, 1418
gratification 397
grever de dettes 466
grever d'une hypothèque 465
grever d'une surtaxe 1514
grever d'un impôt 194
gros actionnaire 633
gros capital 355
grossiste 2375
groupe 727
groupe de revenus 1527
groupement 727

hausse 413, 2117
hausse de(s) prix 1539
hausse de valeur 180
hausser la valeur 178
haussier 455
haute banque 1486
haute conjoncture 413
haute finance 1486
heures supplémentaires 1875
holding 1494
homme de finance 1321
honneur à un effet, faire ~ 1054
honoraires 1295
honorer un effet 1054
hors cote 891
hôtel de la monnaie 1761
hôtel des monnaies 1761
hot money 1498
hyperinflation 1500
hypothécairement, garantir ~ 838
hypothèque 1790
hypothèque amortissable 137
hypothéquer 1791
hypothèque (sur), prendre une ~ 2019

illiquide 1503
immeubles 1508
immobilisation 1506
immobilisations (corporelles) 518
immobilisations immatérielles 1505
immobilisations incorporelles 1505
immobiliser 1507
immunité fiscale 1248
impasse budgétaire 95
importation 1509
importation de capitaux 534
importations invisibles 1633
importations visibles 2352
imposable 196
imposable, non-~ 1247
imposer 194
imposer un prix 1033
imposition 1135
imposition à la source 681
imposition des prix 1515
imposition de taxes 1516
imposition différée 986
imposition, double ~ 1109
impôt 1135
impôt additionnel 66
impôt complémentaire 66
impôt de consommation 752
impôt dégressif 997
impôt de luxe 1723
impôt des patentes 476
impôt des sociétés 792
impôt de timbre 2211
impôt direct 1046
impôt du timbre 2211
impôt foncier 1662
impôt immobilier 1995
impôt indirect 1552
impôt prélevé à la source 2268
impôt progressif 1456
impôt réel 1995
impôt retenu à la source 2268
impôt(s), avant ~ 1959
impôts déduits 1677
impôt somptuaire 1723
impôt successoral 938
impôt sur la consommation 752
impôt sur la fortune 551
impôt sur la succession 938
impôt sur le capital 551
impôt sur le capital social 560
impôt sur le chiffre d'affaires 2014
impôt sur le luxe 1723
impôt sur le patrimoine immobilier 1995
impôt sur le revenu 1530
impôt sur le revenu des biens mobiliers 565
impôt sur le revenu des capitaux (mobiliers) 565
impôt sur le revenu des personnes physiques 1930
impôt sur le revenu des valeurs mobilières 565
impôt sur le revenu du capital 565
impôt sur les articles de luxe 1723
impôt sur les bénéfices 1989
impôt sur les bénéfices des sociétés 792
impôt sur les bénéfices excédentaires 1214
impôt sur les bénéfices exceptionnels 1214
impôt sur les biens immobiliers 1995
impôt sur les capitaux 551
impôt sur les fortunes 551
impôt sur le(s) gain(s) en capital 532
impôt sur les mouvements de capitaux 564
impôt sur les mutations de capitaux 564
impôt sur les plus-values de cession 532
impôt sur les sociétés 792
impôt sur l'excédent de bénéfice 1214
imprévus 754
improductif d'intérêt(s) 1590
improfitable 2324
imputable à (sur) 616
imputation 123, 613
imputer 570, 615
imputer à (sur) un compte 618
inactif 508
inactivité 1130
inanimé 508
incidence d'un impôt 1521
incitation 1519
incitation à l'épargne 1161
incitation à l'investissement 1625
incitation fiscale 2270
inconvertibilité 1533
inconvertible 1534
incorporer aux réserves 68
indemnisation 708
indemnité 708
indemnité de caisse 133
indemnité de cherté de vie 808
indemnité de déplacement 2296
indemnité de renchérissement 808
indemnité de route 2296
indemnité (des frais de représentation) 128
indemnité de vie chère 808
indemnité de voyage 2296
index 1546
indexation 1548
indexer 1547
indicatateur 1551
indice 1546, 1550
indice des chiffres d'affaires 2131
indice des prix 1964
indice des prix au (de) détail 2106

indice des prix de gros 2374
indice des prix des marchandises 696
indice des ventes 2131
indice du coût de la vie 809
indice pondéré 2370
indiquer un prix 1728
inéconomique 2324
inflater 1553
inflation 1554
inflation d'adaptation 59
inflation du crédit 861
inflation galopante 1411
inflation importée 1511
inflation incontrôlable 1411
inflation larvée 725
inflation latente 725
inflationnisme 1560
inflationniste 1555, 1561
inflation par la demande 1005
inflation par les coûts 803
inflation provoquée par (la hausse des) les salaires 2361
inflation rampante 882
inflation refoulée 1919
ingérence de l'état 1452
initiative privée 1976
injecter du capital 436
injection de capital 521
inonder le marché (d'articles bon marché) 1132
inscription 409
inscription au crédit 857
inscription au débit 946
inscrire 401
inscrire à l'actif 403
inscrire à l'actif, à ~ 408
inscrire au budget 443
inscrire au passif 402
inscrire au passif, à ~ 407
insolvabilité 1569
insolvable 1570
institut de banque 294
institut de crédit 850
institut de crédit foncier 1660
institut de crédit immobilier 1660
institut financier 1315
institution de crédit 850
instrument de crédit 862
instrument fiscal 1332
insuffisance de capitaux 559
insuffisance de dollars 1090
intégration 135
intensité de capital 538
interconvertibilité 1584
interdiction d'entrée 319
interdiction d'importation 319
intérêt à X pour cent, porter ~ 334
intérêt à X pour cent, produire ~ 334
intérêt de X pour cent, porter un ~ 334
intérêt de X pour cent, produire un ~ 334
intérêt fictif 1518
intérêt fixe, à ~ 1338
intérêt, rapporter X pour cent d'~ 334
intérêt(s) 1585
intérêt(s), à ~ 1586
intérêts accrus 41
intérêts accumulés 41
intérêts actifs 376
intérêts à échoir 42
intérêts anticipés 165
intérêts à payer 947
intérêts à recevoir 376
intérêts arriérés 190
intérêts bancaires 306
intérêt(s) composé(s) 720
intérêt(s) courant(s) 909
intérêts courus 41
intérêts créditeurs 376
intérêts cumulés 41
intérêt(s) (dans) 1495
intérêts débiteurs 947
intérêt(s) de retard 983
intérêt(s) du capital 540
intérêts dus 1589
intérêt(s) échelonné(s) 1457
intérêts échus 1589
intérêts en retard 190
intérêts hypothécaires 1794
intérêt simple 2179
intérêts intercalaires 1599
intérêts intérimaires 1599
intérêt(s) majoritaire(s) 770
intérêt(s) minoritaire(s) 1760
intérêt(s) moratoire(s) 983
intérêts noirs 376
intérêts passifs 947
intérêt(s), prêter de l'argent à (contre) ~ 1675
intérêts rouges 947
intérêt(s), sans ~ 1590
intérêt(s) usuraire(s) 2335
intérimaires 1599
intervention de l'état 1452
interventionnisme 1608
intitulé de compte 25
introduire sur le marché 1737
inventaire 1614, 1615, 1616
inventorier 1124
investir 1618
investissement 1619
investissement à l'étranger 1368
investissement de capitaux 542
investissement de fonds 542
investissement de productivité 1580
investissement de rationalization 1580
investissement d'expansion 1253
investissement du secteur public 2006
investissement en titres (de portefeuille) 1626
investissement en valeurs (de portefeuille) 1626
investissement erroné 244
investissement étranger 1367
investissement fixe 1340
investissement immobilisé 1340
investissement mal orienté 244
investissement mal placé 244
investissement, nouvel ~ 1818
investissement privé 1978
investissement public 2006
investisseur 1631
investisseur collectif 793
investisseur institutionnel 793
investment-trust 653
inviter à la souscription d'un emprunt 1634

jeter sur le marché 1665
jeu de bourse 111
jobber 1648
joindre les deux bouts 1703
joueur à la bourse 1647
joueur de bourse 1647
jour d'échéance 931
jour de déchéance 1263
jour de liquidation 24
jour de règlement 24
jour d'expiration 1263
journal 932
journal auxiliaire 225
journal de caisse 578
journal d'effects (à payer) 359
journal d'effets (à recevoir) 360
jours de grâce 933
jours de répit 933
jugement déclaratif de faillite 69
justificatif 2358

keynésien 1657
krach 668

lacune de dollars 1089
lancement 1352
lancer sur le marché 1665
lancer un emprunt 1157
langueur 1130
languir 1663
languissant 508
leasing 1668
lettre accréditive 1678
lettre à encaisser 364
lettre à payer 372
lettre de banque 284
lettre de change 356
lettre de change, accepter une ~ 8
lettre de change (à l'extérieur) 1357
lettre de change à usance 358
lettre de change à vue 1003
lettre de change sur l'intérieur 1091
lettre de créance 1678
lettre de crédit 1678
lettre (de gage) hypothécaire 1792
lettre de garantie 394
lettre de rente 162
lettre d'indemnité 394
levée de contributions 1516
levée de restrictions 2
lever des restrictions 1
lever protêt d'un effet 1481
lever un impôt (sur) 194
libellé en dollars 1010
libéralisation des échanges commerciaux 1684
libéralisation du commerce 1684
libéraliser 1685
liberalité 1103
libération 950

libération des échanges commerciaux 1684
libération des prix 971
libération intégrale d'une action 1908
libérer 949
libérer une action de (du) X % 1899
libérer une action entièrement 1915
libérer une action intégralement 1915
liberté de concurrence 1390
liberté d'entreprise 1391
liberté des échanges (commerciaux) 1392
liberté du commerce 1392
libre-commerce 1392
libre concurrence 1390
libre-échange 1392
libre-échangiste 1399
libre entreprise 1391
licence 1686
licence d'exportation 1268
licence d'importation 1512
ligne de crédit 855
limitation des crédits 874
limitation du crédit 874
limite de cours 1965
limite de credit 855
limite d'endettement 422
limite de prix 1965
limite des avances sur titres 604
limiter les dépenses 915
liquidateur 1694
liquidation 24, 139, 773, 1070
liquidation d'un compte 254
liquidation, jour de ~ 24
liquide 1693
liquider 148, 785, 1071, 1428
liquider un compte 249
liquidité 1695
liquidité de caisse 227
liquidité excessive 1211
liquidité primaire 1971
liquidités 227
liquidités quasi-monétaires 1776
liquidités secondaires 1776
liste de marchandises exemptes de droits 1394
liste des actionnaires 1701
livraison à terme 1380
livraison contre remboursement 589
livre auxiliaire 225
livre de caisse 578
livre d'effects (à payer) 359
livre d'effets (à recevoir) 360
livre des actionnaires 1701
livre des actions 1701
livre des balances de vérification 250
livre des titres 1701
livre d'inventaire 250
livre (général), grand ~ 1418
livre-journal 932
livres bloquées 382
livres comptables 28
livres d'affaires 28
livres de commerce 28
livres de comptabilité 28
livres de compte 28
livres des marchands 28
livres (sterling) transférables 2291
livre sterling 1943
livret bancaire 289
livret de banque 289
livret de caisse d'épargne 2140
livret de compte 289
livret de déposant 1021
livret de dépôt(s) 1021
livret d'épargne 2142
locataire 1667
location 2088
location-vente 1487
lombarder des titres 91
long terme, à ~ 1715
longue échéance, à ~ 1715
lot d'actions 386
lourd 508
lourdeur 1130
loyer 2088
loyer (de l'argent) 1585
lucratif 1147
lucre 1409

macro-économique 1725
main courante 1754
mainmise 191
mainmorte 1795
maintien des prix 1917
maison d'acceptations 12
maison de banque 294
maison de change 1220
maison de courtage 439
maison d'émission 1645
maison d'escompte 1058
maison mère 607, 769
maison principale 607
majoration de(s) prix 1539
majoration de X pour cent 1543
majoration du taux de (l')escompte 1541
mali 988
malversation 978
mandant 1973
mandat-carte 1781
mandat de banque 284
mandat de paiement 590
mandat de poste 1781
mandat de virement postal 1781
mandat de voyage 2297
mandat postal 1781
mandat-poste 1781
manipulation de la monnaie 898
manipulation des cours 1730
manipulation monétaire 898
manipulation sur les cours 1730
manœuvre de bourse 1730
manquant 988
manquant de caisse 96
manque 988
manque à gagner 1718
manque de capitaux 559
manque de crédit 878
manque de dollars 1090
manque de liquidité 1504
manque de valeur 2344
manteau 2176
marasme 1130
marchand 1738
marchand de titres 2152
marchandises d'exportation 1266
marchandises d'importation 1510
marché 320, 1735
marché acheteur 483
marché à la baisse 345
marché à la hausse 458
marché à livrer 1379
marché à parquet 1845
marché à prime 1855
marché à tempérament 1489
marché à terme 1379
marché à terme des changes 1382
Marché commun 700
marché d'acheteurs 483
marché de corbeille 1845
marché de couverture 839
marché de l'argent 1778
marché de l'escompte 370
marché des acheteurs 483
marché des actions 2153
marche des affaires 833
marché des capitaux 554
marché des changes 1230
marché des changes à terme 1382
marché des changes, double ~ 2309
marché des devises 1230
marché des devises à terme 1382
marché des euro-devises 1192
marché des euro-émissions 1191
marché des lettres de change 370
marché des obligations 393
marché des rentes 393
marché des titres 2153
marché des valeurs à revenu fixe 393
marché des valeurs (mobilières) 2153
marché de(s) vendeurs 2160
marché (de vente) 1736
marché du change 1230
marché du parquet 1845
marché en baisse 345
Marché européen 700
marché financier 554
marché hors cote 891
marché intérieur 1100
marché, introduire sur le ~ 1737
marché libre 891, 1395
marché libre des changes 1885
marché libre des devises 1885
marché, mettre sur le ~ 1737
marché monétaire 1778
marché national 1100
marché noir 377
marché obligataire 393
marché orienté à la hausse 458
marché ouvert 1395
marché parallèle 1885
marché secondaire 2147
marché vendeur 2160
marge 1037, 1732
marge bénéficiaire 1734
marge commerciale 1734
marge de bénéfice 1734
marge de bénéfice brut 1465
marge de bénéfice net 1813

marge de crédit 864
marge de fluctuation des cours 1346
marge de fluctuation des taux de change 1346
marge de prix 1966
marge d'intérêts 1412
marge entre les taux d'intérêt 1412
marge supplémentaire 62
marketing 1742
masse active 202
masse débitrice 961
masse de la faillite 317
masse monétaire 1783
masse passive 961
masse salariale 2359
matière de base 329
matière première 329
matières d'or et d'argent 457
mauvaise créance 242
mauvais investissement 244
mauvais payeur 245
mauvais placement 244
maximum de crédit 855
mécanographie comptable 1724
mécompte 491
mémoire 17
mémorial 932
mensualité 1787, 1788
menue monnaie 612
menues dépenses 1764
menus frais 1764
mesures de relance 2011
mesures pour stimuler la reprise économique 2011
méthode de la compensation des soldes 1756
méthode de non-compensation 1755
mettre à (la) charge 615
mettre à la vente 1841
mettre arrêt (sur) 211
mettre à (sur) un compte 618
mettre d'accord sur un prix, se ~ 113
mettre de côté 2133
mettre des capitaux à la disposition 1407
mettre en adjudication 1635
mettre en gage 1018
mettre en (ligne de) compte 570
mettre en pension 1018
mettre en (sous) séquestre 211
mettre en vente 1841
mettre les réserves à contribution 1042
mettre sur le marché 1737
mettre un compte à découvert 1868
mettre une créance en recouvrement 677
mettre un emprunt en souscription 1634
mettre un impôt en recouvrement 678
mettre un impôt (sur) 194
meubles 622
mévendre 2158
mévente 2129
micro-économique 1757
milieux financiers 1305
milliard 368
mise 353
mise à (la) charge 613
mise de fonds 521
mise en commun 1939
mise en compte 613
mise en gage de titres 1501
mise en gage de valeurs 1501
mise en pool 1939
mise en recouvrement de créances (dettes) 682
mise en recouvrement d'impôts 683
mise en réserve de bénéfices 1987
mise en (sous) séquestre 191
mises hors 1053
mobilisation 1766
mobilisation de capitaux 1405
mobilisation de fonds 1405
mobiliser 1767
modalité de paiement 1375
modalité de règlement 1375
modalités de paiement 2278
modalités de règlement 2278
mode de paiement 1375
mode de règlement 1375
moins les frais 621
moins-perçu 2112
moins-perçu d'impôts 1330
moins-value 969, 988
moins-value de cession 553
moins-values budgétaires 445
mollesse 1130
monde de la finance 1305
monde financier 1305
monétariste 1768
monétisation 663, 1772
monétiser 662, 1773
monnaie 660, 893
Monnaie 1761
monnaie à couverture or et devises 1436
monnaie ayant cours 906
monnaie bancaire 307
monnaie circulante 906
monnaie contrôlée 767
monnaie conventionnelle 1296
monnaie courante 906
monnaie d'appoint 612
monnaie de banque 307
monnaie de billon 1083
monnaie de change 1780
monnaie d'échange 1780
monnaie de conversion 1780
monnaie de cours légal 1669
monnaie de crédit 307
monnaie de cuivre 788
monnaie (de) papier 1355
monnaie de réserve 2100
monnaie dirigée 767
monnaie divisionnaire 1083
monnaie d'or 1433
monnaie du pays 1094
monnaie émise par le trésor 2302
monnaie en circulation 906
monnaie en cours 906
monnaie étrangère 1361
monnaie faible 2187
monnaie fictive 1296
monnaie fiduciaire 1296
monnaie flottante 1350
monnaie forte 1479
monnaie instable 1350
monnaie légale 1669
monnaie libératoire 1669
monnaie manipulée 767
monnaie, menue ~ 612
monnaie métallique 661
monnaie nationale 1094
monnaie obsidionale 1296
monnaie-or 1402
monnaie-papier 1355
monnaie, petite ~ 612
monnaie propre 1094
monnaie, quasi ~ 1805
monnaie saine 2191
monnaie scripturale 307
monnaie solide 1479
monnaie stable 2207
monnaie variable 1350
monnayage 663
monnayer 662
monométallisme 1785
monopole 1786
monopole commercial 2287
monopole d'état 1454
montant 149
montant au bilan 277
montant brut 1460
montant de la souscription 153
montant dû 151
montant forfaitaire 1722
montant global 107
montant impayé 154
montant net 1808
montant net des crédits accordés 1812
montant net des crédits utilisés 1810
montant nominal 1820, 1889
montant restant 246
montant souscrit 153
montant total 107
monter à, se ~ 106
monter en valeur 179
moratoire 1276, 1789
moratorium 1276
mort 508
mou 508
mouvement boursier 2225
mouvement de capital 555
mouvement des paiements 1911
mouvement de trésorerie 586
mouvement en spirale des prix et des salaires 2363
mouvements de capitaux, balance des ~ 256
moyen 232
moyennant le versement de 732
moyennant paiement de 732
moyennant un préavis de X jours 1837
moyenne 231
moyenne annuelle 158
moyenne échéance, à ~ 1752
moyens 1406
moyens de financement 558
moyens de paiement 1751

moyens de paiement, circulation de ~ 638
moyens de paiement, excédent des ~ 6
moyens de production durables 1134
moyens financiers 558
moyen terme, à ~ 1752
muraille douanière 918
mutation 119

nantissement 669, 1138
nantissement, avance contre (sur) ~ 86
nantissement de titres 1501
nantissement de valeurs 1501
nationalisation 1801
nationaliser 1802
nature, apport en ~ 205
nature, avantage en ~ 134
nature, en ~ 1658
nature, rémunération en ~ 134
négociable 1738
négociations en bourse 1222
négocier un emprunt 1807
ne pas dépasser son revenu 1703
ne portant pas d'intérêt 1590
net de droits (de douane) 920
net d'impôt(s) 1247
nier une dette 2092
niveau des cours 1680
niveau des investissements 1679
niveau des prix 1680
niveau de vie 1704
nombre indice 1550
nominal d'une action 1290
non-convertibilité 1533
non convertible 1534
non-distribution de dividende 1826
non économique 2324
non-imposable 1247
non inflationniste 1828
non liquide 1503
non-liquidité 1504
non lucratif 2324
non-paiement 982
non productif d'intérêt(s) 1590
non rentable 2324
non-valeur 242, 2344
non-valeurs 2345
non-versé 154
note 17
note d'achat 425
note d'avoir 847
note de crédit 847
note de débit 948
note de vente 440
notre compte 1833
nouveau placement 1818
nouvel investissement 1818
nouvelle fixation des quotes-parts 77
numéraire 572, 661
numéraire, en ~ 573

obérer (de dettes) 466
objets de luxe 1001
objets de prix 1646
objets de valeur 1646
obligataire 390
obligation 389
obligation à lots 1719
obligation amortissable 497
obligation à primes 1719
obligation au porteur 338
obligation au porteur avec coupon d'intérêts 830
obligation bancaire 288
obligation communale 1713
obligation contributive 2271
obligation convertible 783
obligation d'annuité 162
obligation de conversion 704
obligation de garantie 394
obligation de rente 162
obligation d'état 1243
obligation d'indemnité 394
obligation du trésor 1243
obligation en dollars 1087
obligation en souffrance 980
obligation éventuelle 758
obligation fiscale 2271
obligation foncière 1792
obligation gagée 2149
obligation garantie 2149
obligation hypothécaire 1792
obligation indexée 1549
obligation irrachetable 1636
obligation irremboursable 1636
obligation municipale 1713
obligationnaire 390
obligation non amortissable 1636
obligation non gagée 2331
obligation non garantie 2331
obligation non remboursable 1636
obligation participant aux bénéfices 1526
obligation perpétuelle 1925
obligation publique 1243
obligation rachetable 497
obligation remboursable 497
obligations 961
obligations à vue 1006
obligations en compte courant 1023
obligé 362
occasion 321
OCDE 1860
octroi de crédit 220
octroyer un crédit 126
OECE 1861
office de clearing 649
office de compensation 649
offrant, le plus ~ 1485
offre 352
offre de paiement 1844
offre de règlement 1844
offre de souscription 1842
offre et la demande, l'~ 192, 2242
offre excédentaire 1210
offre excessive 1210
offrir à la vente 1841
offrir à un prix inférieur 2317
offrir en vente 1841
offrir une garantie 101
offrir un emprunt à la souscription 1634
offrir un emprunt en souscription 1634
OIT 1606
omissions, erreurs et ~ 1183
opérateur 1647
opération 320
opération à prime 1855
opération à tempérament 1489
opération à terme 1379
opération à terme sur les changes 1381
opération à terme sur les devises 1381
opération au comptant 581
opération au comptant sur les changes 2202
opération au comptant sur les devises 2202
opération à vue 1379
opération d'échange 327
opération de change à terme 1381
opération de change au comptant 2202
opération de compensation 327
opération de couverture 839
opération de pension 753
opération de report 753, 2251
opération en compte à demi 1653
opération en participation 1653
opération liée 2251
opérations avec l'étranger 1358
opérations bancaires 304
opérations boursières 1222
opérations de banque 304
opérations de change 1241
opérations de clearing 643
opérations de compensation 643
opérations de crédit 851
opérations de (en) bourse 1222
opérations de paiement 1911
opérations de virement 643
opérations en devises 1241
opérations par cheque(s) 632
opérations sur effets 1222
opérations sur titres 1222
opérations sur valeurs 1222
opération swap 2251
opération switch 2253
opération triangulaire 2253
opérer des paiements 1152
opérer des versements 1152
opposition 1414
option 1854
option d'achat 484
option de vente 1858
option, double ~ 1108
or à monnayer 666
or au titre 666
ordonnancer une facture 223
ordre, à ~ 1726
ordre bancaire 299
ordre de banque 299
ordre de paiement 221, 590
ordre de payer 590
or en barres 323
or en lingots 323
or fin 1324
Organisation de coopération et de développement économique 1860

Organisation européenne de coopération économique 1861
Organisation internationale du travail 1606
organisme public financier 2004
orientation 1200
orientation des capitaux 1044
orientation des investissements 1044
orientation vers la hausse 459
or monétaire 666
or monétisé 667
or monnayé 667
oscillation des cours (de change) 1225
oscillation des taux de change 1225
ouverture de la faillite 1575
ouverture d'un crédit 1848
ouvrir la souscription d'un emprunt 1634
ouvrir un crédit en faveur de 1847
ouvrir un emprunt à la souscription 1634

paie 1140
paiement 139
paiement à compte 1014
paiement à la livraison 589
paiement à l'avance 92
paiement anticipatif 92
paiement anticipé 92
paiement à tempérament 1571
paiement à terme 1910
paiement au comptant 591
paiement comptant 591
paiement contre livraison 589
paiement d'avance 92
paiement de dividendes 1052
paiement de l'impôt (des impôts), après ~ 1677
paiement de l'impôt (des impôts), avant ~ 1959
paiement de, moyennant ~ 732
paiement des arriérés 237
paiement d'intérêts 1592
paiement d'intérêt(s), sujet au ~ 2231
paiement en espèces 591
paiement en numéraire 591
paiement entier 715
paiement intégral 715
paiement intracommunautaire 1611
paiement, non-~ 982
paiement par anticipation 92
paiement par chèque ou par virement 588
paiement, parfait ~ 715
paiement par termes 1571
paiement partiel 1894
paiement provisoire 1999
paiements 1911
paiements, faire des ~ 1152
paiements, recettes et ~ 1525
paiement total 715
pair 1889
pair, au ~ 1882
pair du change 1890
pair (du change) intrinsèque 1762
pair (du change) métallique 1762
pair, être au ~ 1884
pair, être au-dessous du ~ 1056
pair, être au-dessus du ~ 1883
panique bancaire 2121
papier à ordre 1806
papier à vue 1007
papier bancable 283
papier commercial 356
papier de banque 284
papier de commerce 356
papier de complaisance 15
papier de haut commerce 1323
papier en l'air 15
papier escomptable 283
papier financier 1307
papier monétaire 1779
papier-monnaie 1355
papier-monnaie (inconvertible) 1535
papier négociable 1806
papiers au porteur 342
papiers-valeurs 2151
paquet d'actions 386
parfait paiement 715
parité 1886, 1889
parité, à ~ 1882
parité, à la ~ 1882
parité de change 1182
parité monétaire 1182
parité or 1439, 1439
parquet 1845
partage des marchés 1745
partage du marché 1745
partager la différence 2201
part des bénéfices 2173
part du feu, faire la ~ 928
participation (à) 1495
participation à l'étranger 1366
participation aux bénéfices 1410
participation en actions 2172
participation étrangère 1365
participation majoritaire 770
participation minoritaire 1760
participation réciproque 885
partie double 1106
parts de fondateur(s) 1386
passage en douane 645
passation au débit 613
passation (d'écriture) 409
passer à l'actif 403
passer à la réserve 68
passer à (sur) un compte 618
passer au débit 615
passer au débit d'un compte 618
passer au fonds de réserve 68
passer écriture de 401
passer en compte 401, 570
passer une somme au crédit de quelqu'un 566
passible des droits de douane 916
passible d'impôt 196
passif 943, 961
passif à court terme 910
passif courant 910
passif éventuel 758
passif exigible 910
passif exigible à vue 1006
passif inexigible 1825
passif, l'actif et le ~ 203
passif non exigible 1825
patente 476
patrimoine immobilier 1508
patrimoine national 1804
patrimoine net 1809
patrimoine social 790
payable à la livraison 589
payable au comptant 1897
payable à vue 1896
payable comptant 1897
payable contre livraison 589
payable en devises 1898
payable en monnaie étrangère 1898
payant 1147, 1903
paye 1140
payement 139
payer 148
payer à l'avance 1904
payer argent sur table 1727
payer au comptant compté 1727
payer comptant 1727
payer d'avance 1904
payer en argent (comptant) 1727
payer en espèces 1727
payer en numéraire 1727
payer intégralement 1905
payer les intérêts d'un emprunt 2165
payer par avance 1904
payer par chèque 1901
payer préalablement 1904
payer un dividende 1051
payer un effet 1054
payeur 1903
payeur, mauvais ~ 245
pays à monnaie faible 2188
pays à monnaie forte 1480
pays créditeur 871
pays débiteur 959
pays excédentaire 824
pays exportateur 825
pays exportateur de capitaux 525
pays importateur 826
péage 2284
péculat 978
peine pécuniaire 136
pénalité 136
pénurie de capitaux 559
pénurie de crédit 878
pénurie de dollars 1090
perceptible 676
perception d'impôts 683
percevable 676
percevoir un impôt 678
perdre (de) valeur 970
perdre en valeur 970
péréquation 1172
péréquation des charges 1174
péréquation des frais 800
péréquation des impôts 1175
péréquation fiscale 1175
période de grâce 998
période de suspension 384
période de validité 894
permis d'entrée 1512
permis de sortie 1268
permis d'exportation 1268
permis d'exporter 1268
permis d'importation 1512

permis d'importer 1512
perte 1717
perte, absorber une ~ 3
perte au change 1229
perte au cours 1229
perte brute 1464
perte commerciale 474
perte comptable 411
perte de bénéfice(s) 1718
perte de capital 552
perte déductible 974
perte de gain 1718
perte de gestion 474
perte de profit(s) 1718
perte de valeur 969
perte d'exploitation 474
perte en affaires 474
perte en capitaux 552
perte en valeur 969
perte, faire ~ 1056
perte nette 651
perte résultant d'opérations de change 1229
perte sur le change 1229
perte totale 934
perte (un bénéfice), accuser une ~ 2046
perte (un bénéfice), enregistrer une ~ 2046
perte (un bénéfice), faire ressortir une ~ 2046
perte (un bénéfice), se traduire par une ~ 2046
petit commerçant 2105
petit commerce 2107
petite caisse 1931
petite monnaie 612
petites dépenses 1764
petits frais 1764
peu animé 508
peu lucratif 2324
peu rémunérateur 2324
phase conjoncturelle 1150
PIB 1461
pièce 660
pièce à l'appui 2358
pièce certificative 2358
pièce comptable 33
pièce d'argent 660
pièce de comptabilité 33
pièce de cuivre 788
pièce de monnaie 660
pièce de monnaie fiduciaire 2283
pièce d'or 1433
pièce en or 1433
pièce justificative 2358
pièce (justificative) de caisse 600
pièces, billets et ~ 1834
placement 1619, 1935
placement à l'étranger 1368
placement à revenu(s) variable(s) 2348
placement de capitaux 542
placement de fonds 542
placement en titres (de portefeuille) 1626
placement en valeurs (de portefeuille) 1626
placement étranger 1367
placement, nouveau ~ 1818
placements boursiers 1179
placer 1618
placer en (sous) séquestre 211
placer une émission 1934
placer un emprunt 1933
plafond de crédit 855
plafond d'endettement 422
plafonnement 1342
plan comptable 22
plan d'amortissement 146
plan de comptabilité 22
plan de financement 1312
plan financier 1312
planisme 1047
pléthore de capitaux 6
plusieurs versements, en ~ 987
plus offrant, le ~ 1485
plus-value 180
plus-value comptable 412
plus-value de cession 531
plus-value de change 1233
plus-values de recettes 2246
PNB 1466
poids 2368
poids de la fiscalité 463
poids des dettes 462
poids des impôts 463
point d'appui 1609
point d'équilibre 430
point de soutien 1609
point d'intervention 1609
point mort 430
points, accuser une baisse (un gain) de X ~ 2045
points, enregistrer une baisse (un gain) de X ~ 2045
police d'assurance 1577
politique de dividende(s) 1081
politique de la monnaie 1769
politique du crédit 872
politique financière 1317
politique monétaire 1769
pondération 2371
pondérer 2369
pool 1938
pooling 1939
portant intérêt(s) 1586
portefeuille (d')actions 1628
portefeuille (de) titres 1628
portefeuille (de) valeurs 1628
porte-fort 395
porter à la réserve 68
porter à l'avoir du compte 880
porter au débit 615
porter au débit d'un compte 618
porter au fonds de réserve 68
porter au passif 402
porter caution, se ~ 52
porter en compte 570
porter garant, se ~ 52
porter intérêt à X pour cent 334
porter une somme au crédit de quelqu'un 566
porter un intérêt de X pour cent 334
porteur 336, 337
porteur d'actions 2171
porteur de titres 2171
porteur de valeurs 341, 2171
porteur d'intérêt(s) 1586
porteur d'obligations 390
position de place 1743
position devises 1363
position d'un compte 1940
possesseur 336
possesseur d'actions 2171
possesseur de titres 2171
possesseur de valeurs 341, 2171
possesseur d'obligations 390
possibilité d'amortir 2051
possibilité de racheter 2051
possibilité de rembourser 2051
postdater 1942
poste 409
poste au débit 946
poste créditeur 857
poste débiteur 946
poste d'ordre 2249
poste non soldé 2312
poste (porté) au crédit 857
poste porté au débit 946
potentiel de croissance 1469
pour-cent 1921, 1922
pourcentage 1921
pour cent, augmentation de X ~ 1543
poussée inflationniste 1558
pouvoir d'achat 487
pouvoir d'achat en excès 1209
pouvoir d'achat excédentaire 1209
pouvoir des capitaux 1407
pratique des prix imposés 2097
préavis 1835
préavis, à X jours de ~ 1837
préavis de retrait de dépôts 1840
préavis de X jours, avec ~ 1837
préavis de X jours, donner un ~ 1426
préavis, sans ~ 1838
précompte 89
précompte (professionnel) 2268
précompter 973
préférence 1328
préfinancement 1952
préfinancer 1951
prélèvement 89, 1119, 1135
prélèvement à la source 975
prélèvement d'espèces 601
prélèvement en espèces 601
prélèvement sur la fortune 551
prélèvement sur le capital 551
prélèvement sur réserves 2377
prélever 973, 1113
premier cours 1849
première de change 1327
prendre sur les réserves 1042
prendre une hypothèque (sur) 2019
preneur 482
preneur (à bail) 1667
preneur (à ferme) 1667
preneur d'un effet 1902
prescription 1955
prescriptions en matière de change 900

prescriptions en matière de devises 900
présentateur 337
présentation, à ~ 1956
présentation du bilan 273, 1957
pression inflationniste 1558
pression sur les bénéfices 1988
prestation complémentaire 1285
prestation de capitaux 1408
prestation de la sécurité sociale 2185
prestation de services 2084
prestation en retour 731
prestations collectives 684
prestations de services 2168
prestation sociale 2185
prestation supplémentaire 1285
prêt 845
prêt à découvert 1301
prêt à échéance fixe 2277
prêt amortissable 141
prêt à terme fixe 2277
prêt, à titre de ~ 1706
prêt au jour le jour 504
prêt à vue 504
prêt bancaire 298
prêt commercial 473
prêt contre garantie 672
prêt contre (sur) nantissement 672
prêt couvert 672
prêt d'amortissement 141
prêt de banque 298
prêt, demander un ~ 175
prêter 1671
prêter de l'argent à (contre) intérêt(s) 1675
prêter sur titres 91
prêteur 1672
prêteur d'argent 1777
prêt fiduciaire 1301
prêt gagé 672
prêt garanti 672
prêt hypothécaire 1711
prêt non couvert 1301
prêt non gagé 1301
prêt non garanti 1301
prêts 1673
prêt sans garantie 1301
prêt sur hypothèque 1711
prêt sur titres 1674, 1712
prêt sur valeurs 1674, 1712
prêt usuraire 2336
prévenir X jours à l'avance 1426
prévenir X jours d'avance 1426
prévision 129
prévision pour dépréciation 132
prévisions budgétaires 449
prévisions de rentabilité 801
prime 110, 397, 1856
prime acheteur 507
prime à la baisse 1953
prime à la hausse 507
prime à l'émission 1641
prime à l'exportation 426
prime au (de) change 109
prime d'acceptation 13
prime d'assurance 1578
prime d'émission 1641
prime de remboursement 1750
prime de report 569
prime d'exportation 426
prime dont 507
prime, être en ~ 1883
prime, faire ~ 1883
prime pour l'acheteur 507
prime pour le vendeur 1953
prime pour lever 507
prime pour livrer 1953
prime renversée 1953
primes, doubles ~ 1108
prime simple à la baisse 1953
prime simple à la hausse 507
prime vendeur 1953
principal 1972
principal actionnaire 633
principe de la valeur minimale 1721
prise de bénéfices 1990
prise d'espèces 601
priser 177
privatisation 1009
privilège fiscal 2263
prix 1960
prix à forfait 114
prix à la consommation 749
prix à la pièce 2328
prix à parité 1887
prix à terme 1384
prix au comptant 593
prix au consommateur 749
prix au détail 2096
prix comptant 593
prix constants, à ~ 742
prix convenu 114
prix courant (du marché) 911
prix coûtant 814
prix coûtant, au ~ 796
prix d'achat 488
prix d'acquisition 488
prix de base 330
prix de clôture 657
prix de détail 2096
prix de (du) marché 1744
prix de faveur 1203
prix de gros 2288
prix de lancement 1613
prix de l'argent 1967
prix de liquidation 650
prix de location 2088
prix d'émission 1642
prix de plafond 605
prix de production 811
prix de rachat 2054, 2095
prix de réclame 1613
prix de remplacement 2091
prix de revente 2096
prix de revient 814
prix de revient à l'unité 813
prix de revient, au ~ 796
prix de revient unitaire 813
prix dérisoire 322
prix des actions 2174
prix de souscription 2238
prix de vente 2162
prix de vente au détail 2096
prix d'exception 1203
prix d'occasion 322
prix d'offre 1843
prix du jour 911
prix du loyer 2088
prix du pair 1887
prix du report 569
prix exceptionnel 1203
prix excessif 1208
prix exorbitant 1250
prix fait 78
prix fixe 78
prix forfaitaire 114
prix global 114
prix grossiste 2288
prix historique 804
prix immodéré 1250
prix imposé 78
prix le plus haut 605
prix limite 605, 605, 1965, 1965
prix locatif 2088
prix maximum 605
prix normal 1832
prix offert 1843
prix plafond 605
prix pour l'or, régime du double ~ 2310
prix pour paiement au comptant 593
prix préférentiel 1203
prix-réclame 1613
prix sacrifié 322
prix spécial 1203
prix standard 1832
prix sur la place 1744
prix unique 1344
prix unitaire 2328
prix usuraire 1250
prix, vil ~ 322
procurer des capitaux 1407
procurer des capitaux, se ~ 416
productif d'intérêt(s) 1586
produire intérêt à X pour cent 334
produire (un bénéfice) 100
produire un intérêt de X pour cent 334
produit 1982
produit de base 329
produit d'intérêts 1595
produit du capital 535
produit intérieur brut 1461
produit national 1803
produit national brut 1466
produit national net 1814
produit primaire 329
produit(s) 229
produits de luxe 1001
profit 1409
profitable 1147
profit au change 1233
profit espéré 166
profits 229
profits accumulés 2108
profits non distribués 2108
profits non prélevés 2108
profits réservés 2108
profits retenus 2108
programme de financement 1312
programme financier 1312
progressivité d'un impôt 1992
prohibition d'entrée 319
prohibition d'importation 319

projections budgétaires 451
prolongation 567, 1994
prolongation d'un crédit 1275
prolonger un crédit 1272
prolonger un terme 1273
promesse 1477
promesse d'actions 1597
promesse de crédit 88
promesse de devises 1223
promesse du trésor 2301
proportion 2029
propriétaire 1878
propriété fiduciaire 2308
propriété foncière 1661
propriété immobilière 1508
propriété privée 1979
prorogation 1994
prorogation (de la durée) d'un crédit 1275
prorogation du délai de paiement 1276
proroger le terme de paiement 1274
proroger un crédit 1272
proroger un paiement 1274
proroger un terme 1273
prospection du marché 1740
prospectus d'émission 1643
prospectus de souscription 1643
protectionniste 1997
protégé contre l'inflation 1562
protester un effet 1481
protêt d'un effet, faire le ~ 1481
provision 129, 1615
provision de capitaux 1408
provision pour amortissement 132
provision pour créances douteuses 243
provision pour dépréciation 132
provision pour taxes et impôts 2001
provoquer une reflation 2069
purger une hypothèque 511

quasi monnaie 1805
quittance 47, 51
quota 2017
quota d'amortissement 144, 145
quote-part 2017
quote-part d'amortissement 144, 145
quotient 2029
quotient de liquidité 45

rabais 127
rabais fictif 1822
rabais marchand 935
rabaissement du prix 927
rabat 127
rachat 2053, 2094
rachat anticipé 167
rachat de découvert 335
rachetable 2052
racheter 480, 502
racheter une hypothèque 511
radier une dette 510
rafler 489
raison 2029
rajustement monétaire 75
ralentissement 968
rapatriement 2090
rapatrier 2089
rapport 2029
rapport annuel 160
rapportant un intérêt fixe 1338
rapport capitaux empruntés/capitaux propres 963
rapport cours-bénéfice 1963
rapport de liquidité 45
rapport de parité 1888
rapport de vérification 217
rapport d'intérêts 1595
rapport du capital 535
rapport du (des) commissaire(s) aux comptes 217
rapporter (un bénéfice) 100
rapporter X pour cent d'intérêt 334
rapprochement de comptes 2043
rapprocher les comptes 112
raréfaction de capitaux 559
raréfaction des crédits 874
rassembler des capitaux 416
ratio 2029
ratio de liquidité 45
réalignement des parités 2031
réalisabilité 2033
réalisable 2034
réalisation 773
réalisation de bénéfices 1990
réaliser 785
réaliser un bénéfice 1729
réaliser un profit 1729
réaménagement des parités 2031
réappréciation 2036
réapprécier 2037
réapprovisionner la réserve 2039
récépissé 47
récépissé de dépôt 608
récépissé-warrant 2364
réception, accusé de ~ 47
récession 1031
recettes 1532
recettes budgétaires 447
recettes de caisse 585
recettes de l'Etat 1451
recettes des douanes 921
recettes et dépenses 1525
recettes et paiements 1525
recettes extraordinaires 1287
recettes fiscales 1565
recette(s) inférieure(s) 2112
recettes non périodiques 1287
recettes non récurrentes 1287
recettes périodiques 2049
recettes publiques 1451
recettes récurrentes 2049
rechange 819
récompense 2041
récompenser 2042
reconnaissance de dépôt 608
reconnaissance de dette 46
reconstituer la réserve 2039
recouponnement 2087
recourir à un emprunt 1122
recourir à un prêt 1122
recourir aux réserves 1042
recours 2047
recours à un emprunt, avoir ~ 1122
recours aux réserves, avoir ~ 1042
recouvrable 675, 676
recouvrement 680
recouvrement de créances (dettes) 682
recouvrement d'impôts 683
recouvrer son argent 1421
recouvrer une créance 677
recouvrer une dette 677
recouvrer un impôt 678
reçu 47
reçu de dépôt 608
reçu de versement 877
recul 968
recul des cours (prix) 886
récupérable 675
récupération 680, 2048
récupération de créances (dettes) 682
récupérer d'une perte, se ~ 707
récupérer son argent 1421
récupérer une créance 677
récupérer une dette 677
recyclage de capitaux 2050
redevable de, être ~ 1876
redevance 614, 1686
redevance fiscale 2271
redistribution 2060
redressement 2048
redressement des balances de paiements 794
redressement financier 1318
redresser les finances 2044
redû 252
réduction de capital 2063
réduction de l'escompte 926
réduction d'impôts 2261
réduction du capital-actions 2064
réduction du dividende 925
réduction du prix 927
réduction du taux d'escompte 926
réduction en valeur 969
réduction fiscale 2261
réduire le capital-actions 2061
réduire les dépenses 915
réemploi 2078
réemployer 1936
réescomptable 2058
réescompte 2056
réescompter 2057
réévaluation 2036, 2111
réévaluer 178, 2037
réexportation 2066
réfaction fiscale 2261
refinancement 2068
refinancer 2067
reflater 2069
reflation 2070
reflux de capitaux 2071
réforme de la fiscalité 2274
réforme fiscale 2274
réforme monétaire 899
refuge fiscal 2269
refus de paiement 2074
régie 1454
régime des changes 900
régime des crédits 879
régime des devises 900
régime du double prix pour l'or 2310

régime fiscal 1334
registre de commerce 687
registre des actionnaires 1701
registre des actions 1701
registre des sociétaires 1701
registre des titres 1701
règlement 24, 139
réglementation des changes 900
réglementation des prix 1961
réglementation du change 900
réglementation en matière de change 900
règlement des arriérés 237
règlement d'un compte 254
règlement, jour de ~ 24
règlement (judiciaire) 718
régler 148
régler au comptant 1727
régler les livres 278
régler le solde 1914
régler un compte 249
regroupement d'actions 2064
regrouper des actions 2061
régulateur fiscal 1333
régulation des prix 1961
réinvestir 1936
réinvestissement 2078
relâchement 968
relâcher les restrictions du crédit 1143
relance 2048
relance, actions de ~ 1251
relations de change 1236
relevé 2217
relevé de compte 5
relèvement 2048, 2117
relèvement de gages 1542
relèvement de salaire 1540, 1542
relèvement de(s) prix 1539
relèvement de traitement 1540
relèvement du taux de (l')escompte 1541
reliquat 246
remboursabilité 2051
remboursable 2052, 2073
remboursable par tirage (au sort) 498
remboursement 139, 2053, 2072
remboursement, contre ~ 589
remboursement des droits de douane 1116
remboursement d'impôts 2038
remboursement fiscal 2038
remboursement sur banquier 1085
rembourser 148, 502, 1900
rembourser une hypothèque 511
remettant 2083
remetteur 2083
remettre 2080
remettre en nantissement 1018
remettre une dette 510
remettre un paiement 984
remise 127, 689, 1784
remise commerciale 935
remise de revendeur 935
remise d'impôts 2261
remise du coupon, contre ~ 1958
remise d'une dette 513
remise en espèces 595
remise sur facture 935
remise sur marchandises 935
remission d'une dette 513
remploi 2078
remployer 1936
rémunérant 1147
rémunérateur 1147
rémunération 2041
rémunération accessoire 1284
rémunération du capital 535
rémunération en nature 134
rémunération spéciale 1284
rémunération supplémentaire 1284
rémunérer 2042
renchérissement 1539
rendement 2110
rendement boursier 57
rendement des actions 1082
rendement des impôts 1565
rendement des ventes 1815
rendement d'obligations 396
rendement du capital 535
rendement effectif 57
rendement réel 57
rendre 1900
rendre caution, se ~ 52
rendre garant, se ~ 52
rendre (un bénéfice) 100
reniement d'une dette 2093
renier une dette 2092
renouveler un crédit 1272
renouvellement d'un crédit 1275
rentabilité 1984
rente 1522
rente annuelle 161
rente du capital 535
rente perpétuelle 163
rente(s) 2323
rentes d'état 1244
rente viagère 163
rentrées 1532
rentrées de caisse 585
rentrées et sorties 1525
rentrées fiscales 1565
rentrer dans ses fonds 1421
renversement 428
réorganisation financière 1318
réorganiser les finances 2044
réparation 708
réparer une perte 707
répartir 122
répartir les paiements sur X années 2204
répartir un dividende 1051
répartition 123
répartition d'actions 125
répartition de bénéfices 183
répartition de dividendes 1052
répartition des marchés 1745
répartition des patrimoines 1073
répartition du capital 1074
répartition du marché 1745
répit 998
répit de paiement 1276
répit de paiement, accorder un ~ 1274
replacement 2078
replacer 1936
repli des cours (prix) 886
répondant 395
report 567, 569, 753
report à nouveau 150
reporter 435
reporter une position 568
report, opération de ~ 2251
reprêter 2079
reprise 2020, 2048, 2257
reprivatisation 1009
répudiation d'une dette 2093
répudier une dette 2092
requête des créanciers 316
réserve 129
réserve conjoncturelle 820
réserve d'amortissement 132
réserve de caisse 597
réserve de change 901
réserve de devises 901
réserve de prévoyance 756
réserve de renouvellement 2086
réserve des consommateurs 750
réserve d'or 1440
réserve en devises 901
réserve en espèces 597
réserve facultative 1397
réserve fiscale 2001
réserve libre 1397
réserve monétaire 1770
réserve-or 1440
réserve pour créances douteuses 243
réserve pour dépenses imprévues 756
réserve pour les impôts 2001
réserve pour régularisation des dividendes 1079
réserve(s) 2098
réserves cachées 726
réserves déclarées 966
réserves de liquidité 1696
réserves d'(en) or de (en) devises 1429
réserves invisibles 726
réserves latentes 726
réserves légales 1670
réserves liquides 1696
réserves non déclarées 726
réserves obligatoires 1670
réserves occultes 726
réserve statutaire 2102
réserves visibles 966
responsabilité 1681
responsabilité contractuelle 763
responsabilité illimitée 2329
responsabilité limitée 1689
responsabilité non contractuelle 1824
responsabilité solidaire 1652
resserrement des liquidités 1697
resserrement du crédit 874
ressources 1406
ressources en capital 558
ressources en numéraire 587
ressources financières 558
ressources pécuniaires 1916
ressources publiques 2007
restant 246
restant dû 252

reste 246
restituable 2073
restituer 1900
restitution 2072
restitution des droits de douane 1116
restitution d'impôts 2038
restreindre les dépenses 915
restriction à l'importation 1513
restriction de la liquidité 2104
restriction des crédits 874
restriction des importations 1513
restriction des prix 1968
restriction du crédit 874
restrictions, abolir des ~ 1
restrictions, abolition de ~ 2
restrictions de devises 902
restrictions du crédit, alléger les ~ 1143
restrictions du crédit, assouplir les ~ 1143
restrictions du crédit, relâcher les ~ 1143
restrictions (en matière) de change 902
restrictions, levée de ~ 2
restrictions, lever des ~ 1
restrictions, suppression de ~ 2
restrictions, supprimer des ~ 1
rétablir l'équilibre budgétaire 280
retard dans le paiement 999
retard de paiement 999
retard, en ~ 189
retenir à la source 972
retenue à la source 975
retenue de garantie 2109
retenue d'impôts à la source 681
retirable 496
retirer 502, 1113
retirer avec perte, se ~ 928
retirer (de la circulation) 503
retirer un bénéfice 1729
retirer un profit 1729
retournement 428
retraire 502
retrait 1008, 1119, 2053
retrait d'espèces 601
retraite 819
retrait en espèces 601
rétrécissement des marges de fluctuation 2065
rétribuer 2042
rétribution 2041
réunir des capitaux 416
revalorisation 2111
revaloriser 178
revendeur 2105
revenu brut 1463
revenu de la société 791
revenu des facteurs 1292
revenu de sources diverses 1765
revenu de transfert 2292
revenu disponible 1068
revenu du capital 535
revenu du travail 1136
revenu en nature 1529
revenu fiscal 1565
revenu fixe 210
revenu fixe, à ~ 1338
revenu globalisé 2262
revenu imposable 2262
revenu moyen par tête 233
revenu national 1799
revenu net 1811
revenu non gagné 2323
revenu non incorporé 1765
revenu personnel 1929
revenu régulier 210
revenu(s) 1522
revenus accessoires 64
revenu(s) de l'Etat 1451
revenus de placements 1528
revenus d'investissements 1528
revenus divers 1765
revenu(s) effectif(s) 2032
revenus mobiliers 1528
revenus particuliers 1929
revenus primaires 1970
revenus privés 1929
revenus publics 1451
revenu(s) réel(s) 2032
revenu(s) retenu(s) 1137
revenus salariaux 1136
revenus secondaires 2146
revenus supplémentaires 64
revenu taxable 2262
revirement 428
réviseur (comptable) 216
révision des quotes-parts 77
révision interne 1600
richesse nationale 1804
risque de change 1238
ristourne 127, 2072
ristourne d'impôts 2038
ristourner 1900
rogner les dépenses 915
rôle d'appointements 1912
rompu 1387
rotation des créances 960
royalty 1686
ruée sur (les guichets de) la banque 2121
rupture de l'équilibre 1062
rythme d'augmentation 1256
rythme de croissance 1256
rythme de l'inflation 1563
rythme d'expansion 1256

S.A. 1537
safe 2122
saisie 191
saisie-arrêt 1414
saisir 211
salaire 1140, 2126
salaire à forfait 1907
salaire à la pièce 1932
salaire à la prime 1520
salaire à la tâche 1907
salaire au devis-prime 1520
salaire au rendement 1153
salaire aux pièces 1932
salaire de rendement 1153
salaire mensuel 1787
salaires 1141
salle blindée 2125
salle des coffres 2125
S.A.R.L. 1690
sciences économiques 1151
scission d'actions 2175
scrip(t) 1597
seconde de change 2148
secret bancaire 305
secteur de croissance 1470
secteur de la distribution 1075
secteur privé 1981
secteur public 2008
section de coûts 461
sécurité additionnelle 65
sécurité sociale 2184
sécurité subsidiaire 65
sécurité supplémentaire 65
S.E.O. 1184
séquestration 191
séquestre 191, 209
séquestre (judiciaire) 2040
séquestrer 211
serpent (monétaire) 2183
service de la dette 962
service des chèques postaux 1423
service d'intérêts 1592
service d'un emprunt 2167
service d'un emprunt, faire le ~ 2165
services 2168
services, biens et ~ 1443
servir de couverture 2166
servir un emprunt 2165
seuil de rentabilité 430
seule de change 2180
SFI 1605
siège central 607
siège principal 607
siège social 2075
siège statutaire 2075
signer un effet pour aval 235
situation de la banque 312
situation de (la) caisse 592
situation de trésorerie 1319
situation du marché 1743
situation d'un compte 1940
slumpflation 2182
SNC 1420
socialisation 1801
socialiser 1802
sociétaire 2171
société affiliée 98
société anonyme 1537
société à responsabilité limitée 1690
société bancaire 302
société bancaire par actions 1536
société (commerciale) 686
société contrôlée 98
société contrôleuse 769
société coopérative 786
société coopérative de crédit 787
société coopérative de production 1983
société de banque 302
société de capital 1537
société de capitaux 1537
société de contrôle 769
société de crédit 850
société de crédit (mutuel) 787
société de finance 1308

société de financement 1308
société de participation 1494
société de personnes 1892
société de personnes à responsabilité limitée 1690
société de placement 653
société de portefeuille 653
société d'investissement 653
société dominante 769
société dominée 98
société en commandite par actions 1893
société en commandite (simple) 1692
société en nom collectif 1420
société fiduciaire 2306
société filiale 98
société financière 1308
Société financière internationale 1605
société holding 1494
société mère 769
société par actions 1537
solde 246, 1140
solde actif 849
solde après compensation 269
solde bénéficiaire 849
solde comptable 27
solde créditeur 849
solde débiteur 93
solde de compensation 269
solde de dividende 1303
solde de (en) caisse 253
solde déficitaire 93
solde des échanges extérieurs 1277
solde des opérations courantes 268
solde des opérations de biens et services 259
solde des transactions sur biens et services 259
solde des transferts courants 257
solde d'un compte 254, 255
solde en banque 286
solde en bénéfice 849
solde en perte 93
solde excédentaire 849
solde excédentaire de la balance commerciale 266
solde excédentaire de la balance des paiements 263
solde extérieur 1277
solde général des transferts et des mouvements de capitaux 1416
solde migratoire 1758
solde négatif 93
solder 148
solde restant dû 252
solder le redû 1914
solder, se ~ 248
solder un compte 249
soldes 2128
solidarité passive 1652
solide 846
solidité 873
solidité des prix 1326
solvabilité 2189
solvable 2190
somme 149
somme à forfait 1722
somme à recevoir 152
somme à recouvrer 152
somme due 151
somme en excédent 1205
somme finale 105
somme forfaitaire 1722
somme restante 246
somme totale 105
sortie de capitaux 556
sorties 1053
sorties de caisse 582
sorties, entrées et ~ 1525
sorties, rentrées et ~ 1525
sortir au tirage 1112
souche 821
souffrance, en ~ 1869
soulte 247
soumis à l'impôt 196
soumis aux droits de douane 916
soumission 2276
souplesse des cours de change 1154
source, déduire à la ~ 972
source de financement 2192
source de recettes 2193
source de revenus 2193
source, retenir à la ~ 972
souscapitalisation 2315
sous-compte 224
souscripteur 1118, 2234
souscription 2236
souscription de capital 562
souscription d'un emprunt, inviter à la ~ 1634
souscription surpassée 1874
souscrire (à) 2233
sous-estimation 2318
sous-estimer 2319
sous-évaluation 2318
sous-évaluer 2319
soutien des prix 1917
soutien monétaire 1771
spécification 429
spéculateur 2200
spéculateur à la baisse 332
spéculateur à la hausse 455
spéculateur en bourse 1647
spéculation 2197
spéculation en bourse 111
spéculer 2196
spéculer à la baisse 1427
spéculer à la hausse 456
spirale coût(s)-prix 816
spirale déflationniste 993
spirale des salaires et des prix 2363
spirale inflationniste 1559
spirale prix-salaires 2363
split up 2175
S.P.R.L. 1690
stabilisation des cours 1237
stabilisation des prix 1969
stabilité de la monnaie 903
stabilité des changes 1239
stabilité des prix 1326
stabilité monétaire 903
stagflation 2208
stagnant 508
stagnation 1130
stagner 1663
standard de vie 1704
statistique 2220
statistiques 2219
statistiques internes 1851
stellage 1108
stérilisation 2221
stériliser 2222
sterling 2223
stimulant fiscal 2270
stock 1615
stock d'or 1430
stock monétaire 1783
stoppage à la source 681
structure des coûts 817
structure du bilan 273
structure financière 561
subir une dépréciation 970
subir une perte 333
subside 1458
subside de l'état 1449
subvention 1458
subvention à l'exportation 1269
subvention budgétaire 1449
subvention de l'état 1449
subvention d'intérêts 1594
subvention du gouvernement 1449
subvention gouvernementale 1449
subventionner 2240
succursale 427
sujet au paiement d'intérêt(s) 2231
superbénéfice 1213
superdividende 398
superprofit 1213
supplément 60
supplément de couverture 62
supplément de crédit 63
supplément d'impôt 66
support de coût(s) 818
supporter une perte 333
suppression de restrictions 2
supprimer des restrictions 1
supputation 492
supputer 490
surabondance d'argent 6
surcapitalisation 1865
surchauffe 1871
surenchère 1484
surendetté, être ~ 953
surendettement 1207
surestimation 1864
surestimer 1863
sûreté 1138
sûreté réelle 2035
surévaluation 1864
surévaluer 1863
surfaire 1866
suroffre 1210
surpaie 1288
surpasser la souscription 1873
surpaye 1288
surplus 2244
surplus structurel 2229
surprix 1208
sursalaire 1288
sursaturer le marché (d'articles bon marché) 1132
sursis 998
sursis de paiement 1276

sursis de paiement, accorder un ~ 1274
sur-souscrire 1873
surtaxation 1864
surtaxe 60, 66
surtaxer 1514, 1863
survaleur 1215
surveillance des crédits 629
surveillance des prix 1961
susceptible d'être gagé 9
suspendre le paiement d'un chèque 2227
suspendre les paiements 603
suspension de paiement 1276
suspension des paiements 2250
swap, opération ~ 2251
swing 864
switch 2253
syndicat 2255
syndicat de banques 303
syndicat de garantie 2322
syndicat de la faillite 2040
syndicat d'émission 2322
syndicat de placement 2322
syndicat des créanciers 388
syndic de la faillite 209
système bancaire 301
système de calcul du prix de revient complet 4
système de calcul du prix de revient intégral 4
système de prix de revient à coûts partiels 1045
système de salaire-investissement 2362
système des changes 1240
système des crédits 879
système de taxation 1334
système d'impôts 1334
système financier 1304
système fiscal 1334
système monétaire 664

table 2256
tableau 2256
tableau d'amortissement 146
tableau de répartition 799
talon (de contrôle) 821
talon de recouponnement 2085
talon de renouvellement 2085
tantième 1923
tant pour cent 1921
tare de caisse 96, 133
tarif 2260
tarif à échelons 1041
tarif à paliers 1041
tarif de faveur 1947
tarif d'escompte 1061
tarif des douanes 922
tarif différentiel 1041
tarif douanier 922
tarif (douanier) extérieur 1279
tarif échelonné 1041
tarif extérieur commun 699
tarif mobile 1041
tarif préférentiel 1947
tarif préférentiel pour les membres du Commonwealth 702
tassement 968
taux 2021
taux à terme 1383
taux au comptant 2024
taux d'achat 354
taux d'amortissement 144, 145
taux d'augmentation 1255
taux de banque 311
taux de base 328
taux de change 1216
taux de change à terme 1383
taux de change au comptant 2024
taux de change croisé 884
taux de change des billets et espèces 1235
taux de change fixe 1341
taux de change flexible 1347
taux de change flottant 1347
taux de change fluctuant 1347
taux de change forcé 722
taux de change libre 1347
taux de change oscillant 1347
taux de change préférentiel 1950
taux de change variable 1347
taux de commission 691
taux de conversion 778
taux de croissance 1255
taux de dépréciation 144
taux de l'argent 1782
taux de l'épargne 2026
taux de l'escompte 311, 1061
taux de l'impôt 2023
taux de liquidité 45
taux de marque 1734
taux d'émission 1642
taux d'emprunt 423
taux de progression 1255
taux de réescompte 2059
taux de rendement 2025
taux des avances 423
taux des avances contre garantie 2022
taux des avances sur nantissement 2022
taux des avances sur titres 1714
taux des avances sur valeurs 1714
taux d'escompte 1061
taux d'escompte bancaire 311
taux des investissements 1629
taux des prêts contre garantie 2022
taux des prêts contre nantissement 2022
taux de vente 193
taux d'expansion 1255
taux d'imposition 2023
taux d'impôt 2023
taux d'inflation 1563
taux d'intérêt 1593
taux d'intérêt de prêt 423
taux d'intérêt nominal 1821
taux d'investissement 1629
taux du change 1216
taux du déport 240
taux du marché libre 1396
taux du report 569
taux fiscal 2023
taux forcé 722
taux monétaire 1782
taux nominal 1821
taux (officiel) d'escompte 311
taux uniforme 1345
taux usuraire 2335
taxable 196
taxation 176, 200, 1839, 2265
taxation des prix 1962
taxation, double ~ 1109
taxe 614, 1135
taxe additionnelle 66
taxe administrative 80
taxe à la consommation 752
taxe à la valeur ajoutée 2341
taxe antidumping 169
taxe compensatoire 712
taxe d'administration 80
taxe de compensation 712
taxe de consommation 752
taxe de luxe 1723
taxe de monopole 1245
taxe de mutation 812
taxe de péréquation 712
taxe de transcription 812
taxe de transfert 812
taxe de transmission 812, 2014
taxer 177, 194, 195
taxe(s), après ~ 1677
taxe(s), avant ~ 1959
taxe somptuaire 1723
taxe successorale 938
taxe supplémentaire 60, 66
taxe sur la consommation 752
taxe sur la valeur ajoutée 2341
taxe sur la valeur foncière 1662
taxe sur le chiffre d'affaires 2014
technique du marché 1742
tempérament, à ~ 987
tendance 1200
tendance à la baisse 344
tendance à la hausse 459
tendance ascendante 459
tendance ascensionnelle 459
tendance déflationniste 994
tendance générale, aller à l'encontre de la ~ 2120
teneur de livres 410
teneur en or 1434
tenir à parité, se ~ 1884
tenir la comptabilité 1656
tenir les comptes 1656
tenir les écritures 1656
tenir les livres 1656
tenue de livres 20
terme 1262, 1571
terme, à court ~ 2177
terme, à long ~ 1715
terme, à moyen ~ 1752
terme (d'échéance) 894, 931
terme de grâce 998
terme de liquidation 18
terme de paiement 1924
terme de préavis 1836
terme de souscription 2237
termes, à (par) ~ 987
termes de l'échange 2279
terme semestriel 351
terne 508
thésaurisation 1493

thésauriser 1492
tiers débiteur 1413
tiers-saisi 1413
tiers-saisie 1414
timbre 2209, 2211
timbre de rabais 2290
timbre-prime 2290
tirable au sort 498
tirage (au sort) 1111
tirage en l'air 1659
tirage sur le Fonds monétaire international 1120
tiré 1117
tirer à découvert (sur un compte) 1868
tirer au sort 1112
tirer sur le Fonds monétaire international 1123
tirer un chèque 1115
tirer une balance 279
tirer une lettre de change sur quelqu'un 1114
tireur 1118
titre 1325
titre à lots 1719
titre à ordre 1806
titre à revenu(s) fixe(s) 1339
titre au porteur 340
titre d'action(s) 2170
titre de créance 609
titre de crédit 862
titre (d'emprunt) 389
titre de prêt 1709
titre de rente 162
titre (d'obligation) 389, 609
titre hypothécaire 1792
titre négociable 1806
titre payable à vue 1007
titre provisoire 1597
titres 2151
titres admis à la cote 1699
titres au porteur 342
titres commerçables 1739
titres cotés (en bourse) 1699
titres de bon père de famille 387
titres de bourse 1699
titres de la dette publique consolidée 734
titres de père de famille 387
titres de placement 1630
titres de portefeuille 1630
titres déposés en nantissement 1895
titres de premier ordre 387
titres de rentes d'état 1244
titres de spéculation 2199
titres d'état 1244
titres détenus en gage 1895
titres de tout premier ordre 387
titres de tout repos 387
titres d'investissement 1630
titres donnés en gage 1895
titres en pension 1895
titres gagés 1895
titres hors cote 892
titres incotés 892
titres inscrits à la bourse 1699
titres mobiliers 1739
titres nantis 1895
titres négociables 1739
titres nominatifs 1568
titres non admis à la cote 892
titres non cotés 892
titres non inscrits à la cote 892
titres publics 1244
titres remis en nantissement 1895
titres sans valeur 2345
titres spéculatifs 2199
titres transférables 1739
titres vedettes 387
titulaire 336
titulaire d'actions 2171
titulaire de parts d'un fonds commun de placement 2327
titulaire de valeurs 2171
titulaire d'obligations 390
titulaire d'un compte 26
tomber d'accord sur un prix 113
total du bilan 276
total général 105
totaliser 106
toucher un chèque 576
traduire par une perte (un bénéfice), se ~ 2046
trafic des paiements 1911
traite 356
traite à vue 1003
traite bancaire 284
traite de cavalerie 15
traité de clearing 647
traité de compensation 647
traite d'encaissement 364
traite en l'air 15
traitement 2126
traitement mensuel 1787
traiter des affaires 1084
traite sur l'extérieur 1357
traite sur l'intérieur 1091
traite sur quelqu'un, faire ~ 1114
tranche 1572
tranche de revenus 1527
transaction 320
transaction à prime 1855
transaction à tempérament 1489
transaction à terme 1379
transaction à terme sur les changes 1381
transaction à terme sur les devises 1381
transaction au comptant 581
transaction au comptant sur les changes 2202
transaction à vue 1379
transaction compensatoire 327
transaction d'échange 327
transaction de change à terme 1381
transaction de change au comptant 2202
transaction de compensation 327
transaction de report 753
transaction en compte à demi 1653
transaction en disponible 581
transaction en participation 1653
transactions avec l'étranger 1358
transactions bancaires 304
transactions boursières 1222
transactions de banque 304
transactions de change 1241
transactions de clearing 643
transactions de compensation 643
transactions de crédit 851
transactions de (en) bourse 1222
transactions de virement 643
transactions en devises 1241
transactions par cheque(s) 632
transactions sur effets 1222
transactions sur titres 1222
transactions sur valeurs 1222
transaction switch 2253
transaction triangulaire 2253
transférabilité 116
transférable 117
transférer 118, 2080
transférer une créance 207
transfert 119, 2293
transfert à l'étranger 1372
transfert bancaire 318
transfert d'argent 1784
transfert de capitaux 563
transfert de créances 208
transfert de fonds 1784
transfert en capital 563
transferts courants, solde des ~ 257
transmettre 118
transmissibilité 116
transmissible 117
transmission 119
transport de créances 208
travaux publics 2010
traveller's cheque 2297
trésorerie 227, 592, 2299
trésor publique 2299
trillion 367
trimestre 2016
tripotage de bourse 1730
troc 325, 327
troquer 326
trust 2304
TVA 2341

UEP 1198
unification 737
unifier une dette 733
union de crédit 787
union douanière 923
Union économique belgo-luxembourgeoise 348
Union européenne des paiements 1198
uniprix 1344
unité à laquelle sont imputés les coûts 818
unité de compte 31
unité monétaire 904
usager du crédit 418
usance 2333
usé 2378
usufruit 2334
usure 2337, 2366, 2367
utilisation de crédits 228
utiliser les réserves 1042
utiliser un emprunt 1122
utiliser un prêt 1122

valeur actuelle 912

valeur ajoutée par l'industrie 2340
valeur à l'achat 50
valeur à revenu(s) fixe(s) 1339
valeur (au) 1er janvier 2342
valeur au pair 1889
valeur brute 1468
valeur cadastrale 199
valeur capitalisée 546
valeur commerciale 688
valeur comptable 32
valeur courante 912
valeur d'achat 50
valeur d'acquisition 50
valeur de bilan 277
valeur de bourse 1234
valeur d'échange 1219
valeur de change de la monnaie 1364
valeur déclarée 967
valeur de liquidation 432
valeur de rachat 2055, 2247
valeur de réalisation 432
valeur de remboursement 2055
valeur de remplacement 2091
valeur de rendement 546
valeur de rente 162
valeur d'inventaire 1617
valeur du cours 1234
valeur effective 56
valeur en bourse 1234
valeur en or 1442
valeur fiscale 198
valeur globale 108
valeur imposable 198
valeur initiale 50
valeur intrinsèque 1612
valeur liquidative 432
valeur marchande 688
valeur négociable 688, 1806
valeur nette 1809, 1817
valeur nette d'une propriété 1177
valeur nominale 1289, 1889
valeur nominale d'une action 1290
valeur or 1442, 1442
valeur présente 912
valeur réelle 56
valeur résiduelle 2103
valeurs 1646, 2151
valeurs admises à la cote 1699
valeurs à l'étranger 204
valeurs au comptant 577
valeurs au porteur 342
valeurs boursières 1699
valeurs commerçables 1739
valeurs corporelles 1747
valeurs cotées (en bourse) 1699
valeurs de bon père de famille 387
valeurs de bourse 1699
valeurs de père de famille 387
valeurs de placement 1630
valeurs de portefeuille 1630
valeurs de premier ordre 387
valeurs de spéculation 2199
valeurs de tout premier ordre 387
valeurs de tout repos 387
valeurs d'investissement 1630
valeurs disponibles 227
valeurs étrangères 1370
valeurs hors cote 892
valeurs immatérielles 1505
valeurs immobilières 1508
valeurs immobilisées 518
valeurs incorporelles 1505
valeurs incotées 892
valeurs inscrites à la bourse 1699
valeurs intangibles 1505
valeurs matérielles 1747
valeurs mobilières 622, 1739
valeurs négociables 1739
valeurs nominatives 1568
valeurs non admises à la cote 892
valeurs non cotées 892
valeurs non inscrites à la cote 892
valeurs spéculatives 2199
valeur standard 2213
valeurs tangibles 1747
valeurs transférables 1739
valeur sur le marché 688
valeurs vedettes 387
valeur totale 108
valeur unitaire 2213
valeur vénale 688
validité 894
valoir, à ~ 19
valorisation 2338
valoriser 2339
value, moins-~ 988
venant à l'échéance le 15 août 1129
vendable 1738
vendeur 2159
vendre 2157
vendre à crédit 2163
vendre à découvert 1427
vendre à la criée 213
vendre à l'encan 213
vendre à l'enchère 213
vendre à perte 2158
vendre à terme 2161
vendre à un prix inférieur 2317
vendre aux enchères 213
vendre avec perte 2158
venir à échéance 347
venir à expiration 1264
vente 2127
vente à crédit 875
vente à découvert 346
vente à la criée 212
vente à l'encan 212
vente à l'enchère 212
vente à perte 2129
vente à réméré 2132
vente à tempérament 1491
vente au comptant 598
vente aux enchères 212
vente avec perte 2129
ventes 2130
ventes brutes 1467
ventes nettes 1816
ventilation 123
ventiler 122
vérificateur (comptable) 216
vérificateur (des comptes) 216
vérification des comptes 214
vérifier 215
versement 1567
versement à l'avance 92
versement anticipatif 92
versement anticipé 92
versement d'avance 92
versement de capital 1909
versement de dividendes 1052
versement de fonds 1784
versement d'intérêts 1592
versement mensuel 1788
versement par anticipation 92
versement partiel 1894
versement provisoire 1999
versements échelonnés, en (par) ~ 987
versements, faire des ~ 1152
versements fractionnés, en (par) ~ 987
verser 1015, 2080
verser à la réserve 68
verser au fonds de réserve 68
verser du capital 436
verser un dividende 1051
viabilité 2349
viable 2350
viager 163
vignette 2209
vil prix 322
virement (bancaire) 318
virement de fonds 1784
virer 2080
viser un chèque 610
vitesse de circulation 2027
vivre au-delà (au-dessus) de ses moyens 1702
volume d'affaires 2130
volume de crédit 881
volume de l'épargne 2353
volume des échanges (commerciaux) 2354
volume des transactions en bourse 2225
volume du commerce 2354
volume monétaire 1783
votre compte 1716
vue, à ~ 1956

warrant 2364
warrant-cédule 2364

zone de libre-échange 1398
zone de vente 1736
zone dollar 1086
zone franc 1388
zone sterling 2224

ITALIANO

abbassamento del prezzo 927
abbassamento del tasso di sconto 926
abbassare la parità 2062
abbonare una perdita 707
abbondanza di denaro 6
abbuono 127
abbuono d'interessi 1594
abolire restrizioni 1
abolizione di restrizioni 2
accantonamento 123, 129, 182
accantonamento per imposte e tasse 2001
accantonare 122, 181
accantonare nella reserva 68
accaparramento 1493
accaparrare 489, 1492
accaparrare il mercato 789
accertamento (fiscale) 200
accertamento (tributario) 200
accertare 195
accettante 14
accettare una cambiale 8
accettazione 10
accettazione bancaria 284
accettazione commerciale 2286
accettazione, commissione d'~ 13
accettazione, credito di ~ 11
accettazione, provvigione d'~ 13
accisa 752
accomandante 1691
accomandatario 1419
accomandita 1692
accomodamento 718
acconto 1014
acconto dividendo 1598
acconto, in ~ 19
acconto sul dividendo 1598
accordare una dilazione di pagamento 1274
accordare una proroga di pagamento 1274
accordare un credito 126
accordare unrespiro di pagamento 1274
accordo 718
accordo di autolimitazione 2355
accordo di clearing 647
accordo di compensazione 647
accordo d'immobilizzazione 2216
accordo di moratoria 2216
accordo di pagamento 1906
accordo di proroga 2216
accordo (di) stand-by 2215
Accordo generale sulle tariffe (doganali) e sul commercio 1415
Accordo Monetario Europeo 1196
accordo sui prezzi 115
accreditamento 844, 1848
accreditare a qualcuno 1847
accreditare a qualcuno una somma 566
accreditare il conto (di) 880
accredito 844
accumulare 43
accumularsi 40
accumulazione 38, 44
accusare una flessione (un guadagno) di X punti 2045
accusare una perdita (un utile) 2046
acquirente 482
acquisizione 49
acquistare 48
acquisto 49, 2012
acquisto a credito 852
acquisto a (per) contanti 594
acquisto a pronta cassa 594
acquisto a rate 1573
acquisto a respiro 852
acquisto a termine 1376
acquisto di copertura 335
acquisto di rimpiazzo 335
acquisto d'occasione 321
acquisto per consegna futura 1376
acquisto rateale 1573
acquisto speculativo 2198
addebitamento 613
addebitare 615
addebitare un conto per 618
addebito 613, 942
adeguamento 72
adeguamento dei prezzi 76
adeguamento delle quote 77
adeguare 70
adulterazione della moneta 939
affare 320
affare a contanti 581
affare a metà 1653
affare a premio 1855
affare a rate 1489
affare a termine 1379
affare a vista 1379
affare, buon ~ 321
affare in contanti 581
affare in partecipazione 1653
affare per contanti 581
affare rateale 1489
affare sul disponibile 581
affari bancari 304
affari conclusi prima dell'apertura della borsa 937
affari con l'estero 1358
affari di borsa 1222
affari, fare ~ 1084
affari, trattare ~ 1084
affittanza 1666
affitto 1666, 2088
affitto di impianti industriali 1668
affittuario 1667
afflusso di capitali 99
affrancare 1389
agente 104
agente di borsa 2152
agente di cambio 509, 2152
agente di sconto 361
agente per il ricupero di crediti 955
agenzia 103
agenzia di cambio 1217
agenzia di mediazione 439
agevolazione fiscale 2263
agevolazione tributaria 2263
agevolazioni creditizie 421
aggio 109, 110
aggiotaggio 111
aggiotatore 1647
aggiustamento 72
aggiustamento della parità monetaria 75
aggiustamento in termini reali 74
aggiustare 70
aggravio fiscale 463
aggruppamento di azioni 2064
aggruppare azioni 2061
aiuto allo sviluppo 1034
aiuto dello stato 1445
aiuto finanziario 1310
alienabile 117
alienabilità 116
alienante 121
alienare 118
alienatario 120
alienazione 119
aliquota (dell'imposta) 2023
aliquota (d'imposta) 2023
allentare gli restrizioni del credito 1143
allibramento 409
allibrare 401
allineamento dei prezzi 76
allunga 124
allungamento 124
alta congiuntura 413
alta finanza 1486
alterazione della moneta 939
AME 1196
ammanco 988
ammanco di cassa 96
ammanco fiscale 1330
ammassamento 44
ammassare 43
ammenda 136
amministratore giudiziario del fallimento 209
amministrazione dei debiti 954
amministrazione della massa fallimentare 2040
amministrazione fallimentare 2040
amministrazione fiduciaria, in ~ 1185
amministrazione finanziaria 1242
ammissione alla quotazione (ufficiale) della borsa 81
ammissione in borsa 81
ammontare 149
ammontare a 106
ammontare complessivo 107
ammontare globale 107
ammontare lordo 1460
ammontare netto 1808
ammontare netto dei crediti accordati 1812
ammontare netto dei crediti utilizzati 1810
ammontare totale 107
ammortamento 138, 139, 2053
ammortamento d'un prestito 142
ammortamento economico 143
ammortamento fiscale 517
ammortamento fisso 2228
ammortamento per quote crescenti 1545
ammortamento per quote decrescenti 7

ammortamento progressivo 1545
ammortamento tecnico 1030
ammortamento variabile 2347
ammortare 147, 148, 502
ammortare un debito 2379
ammortizzabile 2052
ammortizzamento 138, 139, 2053
ammortizzare 147, 148, 502
ammortizzare un debito 2379
ammortizzare un'ipoteca 511
ammortizzazione 138, 139, 2053
ammucchiamento 44
ammucchiare 43
analisi del mercato 1740
anatocismo 156
ancoramento a un indice 1548
ancorare a un indice 1547
andamento degli affari 833
andare in liquidazione 1428
annacquamento del capitale (azionario) 2226
anno civile 493
anno commerciale 478
anno contabile 1320
anno d'esercizio 1320
anno economico 1320
anno finanziario 448, 1320
anno fiscale 1335
anno sociale 705
anno tributario 1335
annualità 161
annualità d'ammortamento 157
annullamento 512
anticiclico 168
anticipare 85
anticipazione 83
anticipazione, a titolo d'~ 84
anticipazione bancaria 298
anticipazione delle banche centrali 1708
anticipazione garantita 86
anticipazione in conto corrente 87
anticipazione pignoratizia 86
anticipazione su pegno 86
anticipazione su titoli 90
anticipo 83
anticipo, a titolo d'~ 84
anticipo garantito 86
anticipo pignoratizio 86
anticipo su pegno 86
anticongiunturale 168
antidatare 164
antieconomico 2324
antiinflazionistico 170
apatia dei consumatori 750
apertura del fallimento 1575
apertura di un credito 1848
appello al mercato 506
appoggio statale 1445
apportare capitale 436
apportatore di capitale 1631
apporto 765
apporto di capitale 521
apporto in natura 205
apprezzare 177
appropriarsi indebitamente 977
appropriazione indebita 978
approvvigionamento di capitali 1408
appuramento di conti 2043
appurare i conti 112
aprire la sottoscrizione di un prestito 1634
aprire un credito a favore di 1847
arbitraggio di cambio 186
arbitraggio di divise 186
arbitraggio sui cambi 186
arbitraggio sui cambiali 369
arbitraggio sull'oro 185
area del dollaro 1086
area del franco 1388
area della sterlina 2224
arretrati 188
arretrato 152, 189
arretrato, in ~ 189
articoli d'esportazione 1266
articoli di lusso 1001
articoli d'importazione 1510
articolo di giornale 1655
ascendere a 106
ascesa 2117
ascesa dei prezzi 1539
assalto agli sportelli (della banca) 2121
assedio della banca 2121
assegnare 122
assegnare al fondo di riserva 68
assegnare alla riserva 68
assegnazione 123
assegnazione alle riserve 67
assegnazione di azioni 125
assegnazione di utili a riserva 1987
assegno all'ordine 631
assegno al portatore 339
assegno a sbarramento 883
assegno a vuoto 241
assegno bancario 284, 624
assegno, contro ~ 589
assegno di carovita 808
assegno di caroviveri 808
assegno in bianco 378
assegno incrociato 883
assegno non all'ordine 630
assegno non sbarrato 339
assegno non trasferibile 630
assegno ordinario 339
assegno, pagare con ~ 1901
assegno per viaggiatori 2297
assegno postale 1425
assegno sbarrato 883
assegno scoperto 241
assegno senza copertura 241
assegno senza provvista 241
assegno turistico 2297
assicurazione 1576
assicurazione contro i rischi di credito 863
assicurazione (di) crediti 863
assicurazione sul credito 863
assicurazione (sulla) vita 1688
assistenza finanziaria 1310
associazione con scopo di lucro 1986
Associazione Internazionale per lo Sviluppo 1604
associazione senza scopo di lucro 1829
assorbimento 2257
assorbire una perdita 3
assumere garanzia 52
asta 212
attivi 202
attivi e passivi 203
attivi fissi 518
attivi immateriali 1505
attivi immobilizzati 518
attivi intangibili 1505
attivi liquidi 227
attivi materiali 1747
attività 202
attività bancaria 301
attività correnti 905
attività da ammortizzare 1027
attività e passività 203
attività immateriale 1505
attività immobilizzate 518
attività liquide 227
attività materiale 1747
attivi tangibili 1747
attivo 202, 206
attivo ammortizzabile 1027
attivo circolante 468
attivo contabile 2285
attivo corrente 905
attivo, da i(n)scrivere all'~ 408
attivo del fallimento 317
attivo disponibile 227
attivo e passivo 203
attivo fisso 518
attivo fittizio 1297
attivo liquido 227
attivo netto 1809
attivo realizzabile (e disponibile) 905
attivo sociale 790
atto di fideiussione 394
atto di garanzia 394
attribuire 122
attribuzione 123
attribuzione alle riserve 67
attuario 58
aumentare di valore 179
aumentare il capitale 1544
aumentare il valore 178
aumento 2117
aumento dei prezzi 1539
aumento della liquidità 1538
aumento della massa monetaria 1252
aumento dell'intensità del capitale 537
aumento del prezzo 1539
aumento del tasso di sconto 1541
aumento del X per cento 1543
aumento di capitale 536
aumento di paga 1542
aumento di salario 1542
aumento di stipendio 1540
aumento di valore 180
aumento salariale 1542
austerità 218
austerity 218
autarchia 219
autoconsumo 1497
autofinanziamento 1601
autorizzare un credito 126
autorizzazione d'esportazione 1268
autorizzazione di credito 220

autorizzazione d'importazione 1512
autosufficienza 219
avallante 236
avallare una cambiale 235
avallo (cambiario) 230
avanzo 2244
avanzo della bilancia commerciale 266
avanzo della bilancia dei pagamenti 263
avanzo d'esercizio 1852
avere 206, 849
avere bloccato 381
avere in banca 286
avere in divise 1362
averi 202, 1496
averi all'estero 204
avviamento 1444
avviso d'accreditamento 847
avviso d'accredito 847
avviso de bonifico 848
avviso di accertamento 1839
avviso di debito 945
avviso d'incasso 47
avviso di pagamento 97, 1913
avviso di ricevimento 47
avviso di ricevuta 47
avviso di ritiro di depositi 1840
avviso di versamento 97
azienda 467
azienda di credito 850
azienda di stato 1448
azienda nazionale 1448
azienda privata 1977
azienda pubblica 1448
azienda statale 1448
azione 2169
azione a cessione condizionata 2282
azione al portatore 343
azione a voto multiplo 1796
azione a voto plurimo 1796
azione differita 985
azione di garanzia 2015
azione di godimento 400
azione di preferenza con partecipazione al beneficio 1891
azione di priorità 1946
azione gratuita 400
azione preferenziale 1946
azione privilegiata 1946
azione privilegiata nella ripartizione dell'utile 1891
azione provvisoria 1597
azioni comuni 701
azioni con diritto di voto 2357
azioni di fondazione 1386
azioni di lavoro 1159
azioni interamente liberate 1403
azioni nominative 1568
azioni nuove 1819
azioni optate 1819
azioni ordinarie 701
azioni per i fondatori 1386
azioni preferenziali cumulative 890
azioni privilegiate a dividendo cumulativo 890
azioni privilegiate con accumulo di dividendo 890
azioni privilegiate cumulative 890
azioni senza diritto di voto 1830
azioni senza valore nominale 1831
azionista 2171
azionista di un fondo commune d'investimento 2327
azionista, grande ~ 633
azionista, grosso ~ 633
azionista iscritto nel libro dei soci 2076
azionista principale 633
azionista, principale ~ 633

bagarinaggio 1493
banca 282
banca associata alla stanza di compensazione 648
banca centrale 606
banca commerciale 310
banca d'accettazione 12
Banca dei Regolamenti Internazionali 300
banca d'emissione di valori 1645
banca di cambio 1220
banca di clearing 648
banca di commercio 310
banca di compensazione 648
banca di credito 850
banca di credito fondiario 1660
banca di credito immobiliare 1660
banca di depositi 1020
banca di deposito 1020
banca di emissione 309
banca di giro 648
banca d'investimenti 1621
banca di (per il) commercio estero 1371
banca di prestiti 850
banca di risparmio 2139
banca di sconto 1058
banca di sviluppo 1035
banca emittente 1645
Banca Europea per gli Investimenti 1195
Banca Interamericana di Sviluppo 1581
Banca Internazionale per la Ricostruzione e lo Sviluppo 1602
banca ipotecaria 1660
Banca Mondiale 1602
banca per azioni 1536
banca privata 1974
bancarotta 315
bancarotta, in ~ 314
bancarottiere 313
banche 301
bancocrazia 1486
bancogiro 318
banconota 287
bandire una gara di appalto 1635
barattare 326
baratto 325
barriera doganale 918
barriera economica 1149
base aurea 1441
base di calcolo dell'imposta 331
base imponibile 331
bassa congiuntura 1031
battere 662
benefici 229
beneficiario 350
beneficiario del credito 418
beneficiario d'un effetto 1902
beneficio 1409
beneficio da ripartire 1072
beneficio lordo 1459
beneficio netto 646
bene fiduciario 2308
beni 202
beni all'estero 204
beni di consumo 743
beni di consumo durevoli 747
beni d'investimento 533
beni durevoli 1133
beni e servizi 1443
beni e servizi, bilancia dei ~ 259
beni fondiari 1661
beni immateriali 1505
beni immobili 1508
beni immobiliari 1508
beni materiali 1747
beni mobili 622
beni mobiliari 622
beni non durevoli 1827
beni stabili 1508
beni strumentali 533, 1134
biglietti e monete 1834
biglietti e monete esteri 1369
biglietti e monete in circolazione 638
biglietti in circolazione 308
biglietto (di banca) 287
bilancia commerciale 264
bilancia commerciale attiva 53
bilancia commerciale deficitaria 94
bilancia commerciale favorevole 53
bilancia commerciale passiva 94
bilancia commerciale sfavorevole 94
bilancia dei beni e servizi 259
bilancia dei capitali 256
bilancia dei conti esteri 258
bilancia dei movimenti di capitali 256
bilancia dei pagamenti 260
bilancia dei pagamenti correnti 262
bilancia dei trasferimenti 267
bilancia delle partite correnti 262
bilancia economica 1148
bilancia globale dei pagamenti 1862
bilanciare un conto 249
bilanciarsi 248
bilancio 270, 441
bilancio annuale 159
bilancio attivo 275
bilancio congiunturale 929
bilancio consolidato (del gruppo) 736
bilancio deficitario 95, 274
bilancio dei capitali 256
bilancio, del ~ 442
bilancio della Communità 703
bilancio dello stato 1446
bilancio di apertura 1700
bilancio di cassa 253
bilancio di chiusura 1302
bilancio di previsione 441
bilancio di verifica 2303

bilancio di verificazione 2303
bilancio finale 1302
bilancio finanziario 1312
bilancio, fuori ~ 1286
bilancio in equilibrio 251
bilancio in pareggio 251
bilancio interinale 1596
bilancio intermedio 1596
bilancio nazionale 1446
bilancio ordinario 1859
bilancio passivo 274
bilancio preventivo 441
bilancio (preventivo) d'investimenti 519
bilancio provvisorio 1596
bilancio pubblico 1446
bilione 367, 368
bimetallismo 375
bimetallismo claudicante 1476
bimetallismo zoppo 1476
BIRS 1602
bisogni di cassa 596
bisogni di copertura 837
bisogni di liquidità 596
bisogni di tesoreria 596
bloccare 380
bloccare un assegno 2227
blocco 383
blocco dei prezzi 1400
blocco del dollaro 1086
blocco del franco 1388
blocco della sterlina 2224
blocco delle importazioni 319
bollettino di borsa 1228
bollettino di versamento 1022
bollo 2209
bollo premio 2290
bonificare una perdita 707
bonifico 127
bonifico (bancario) 318
bonifico d'interessi 1594
boom 413
boomflazione 414
borsa 1218
borsa delle azioni 1218
borsa di commercio 695
borsa merci 695
borsa ufficiale 1845
borsa valori (mobiliari) 1218
borsista 1647
breve scadenza, a ~ 2177
breve termine, a ~ 2177
BRI 300
brogliaccio 1754
budget 441
budgetario 442
buon affare 321
buona occasione 321
buon fine, garanzia di ~ 1474
buon fine, salvo ~ 2099
buono 389, 876
buono delle entrate 1526
buono del tesoro 2301
buono di cassa 389, 590
buono di deposito 608
buono di magazzino 2364
buono di premio 1719
buono di rimborso 704
buono di risparmio 2141
buono in mora 980

cadere di valore 970
caduta 1125
caduta dei corsi (prezzi) 886
calcolare 177, 490
calcolazione 492
calcolo 492
calcolo consuntivo 815
calcolo dei costi parziali 1045
calcolo del costo complessivo, sistema di ~ 4
calcolo del prezzo di costo 815
calcolo di costi 797
calcolo di spese 797
calcolo errato 491
calcolo preventivo 1190
calcolo sbagliato 491
calma 1130
calmiere 78
calmo 508
calo 1125
calo dei corsi (prezzi) 886
cambiale 356
cambiale, accettare una ~ 8
cambiale all'incasso 364, 373
cambiale attiva 373
cambiale, avallare una ~ 235
cambiale a vista 1003
cambiale bancaria 284
cambiale da incassare 373
cambiale da pagare 372
cambiale, dare il avallo su una ~ 235
cambiale di comodo 15
cambiale di favore 15
cambiale di stato 2301
cambiale fittizia 15
cambiale pagabile secondo l'uso 358
cambiale pagherò 1477
cambiale passiva 372
cambiale per avallo, firmare una ~ 235
cambiale proforma 15
cambiale propria 1477
cambiale simulata 15
cambiale sull'estero 1357
cambiale sull'interno 1091
cambiamento (repentino) 428
cambiamonete 509
cambiare 326
cambi a termine 1378
cambiavalute 509
cambio 325, 771, 1216, 1221
cambio a contanti 1227
cambio alla pari 1887
cambio a termine 1226
cambio d'acquisto 354
cambio del giorno 907
cambio denaro 354
cambio di biglietti e monete 1235
cambio (di denaro) 1231
cambio forzoso 722
cambio incrociato 884
cambio in divise auree 1436
cambio medio 234
cambio (monetario) 1231
cambista 361, 509
camera blindata 2125
camera corazzata 2125
camera di commercio (, industria ed agricoltura) 611
Camera di Commercio Internazionale 1603
camera di compensazione 649
camera di sicurezza 2125
campo di smercio 1736
cancellare un debito 510
cancellare un'ipoteca 511
canone d'affitto 2088
canone di licenza 1686
canone di locazione 2088
capacità concorrenziale 714
capacità di guadagno 1139
capacità di reddito 1139
capacità di rendimento 1139
caparra 602
capitale 514, 1972
capitale all'estero 515
capitale altrui 417
capitale autorizzato 222
capitale azionario 544
capitale azionario annacquato 2365
capitale azionario emesso 1638
capitale circolante 468
capitale d'apporto 1564
capitale d'esercizio 468
capitale d'evasione 1349
capitale di conferimento 1564
capitale di credito 417
capitale di fondazione 1564
capitale d'investimento 1622
capitale di prestito 1707
capitale di rischio 1178
capitale di risparmio 2143
capitale di rotazione 468
capitale emesso 1638
capitale esigibile 499
capitale estero 1359
capitale fisso 518
capitale fuggitivo 1349
capitale, grosso ~ 355
capitale immobile 518
capitale immobilizzato 518
capitale impiegato 541
capitale improduttivo 1502
capitale inattivo 1502
capitale in azioni ordinarie 697
capitale in contanti 577
capitale iniziale 1564
capitale investito 541
capitale liberato 1880
capitale morto 1502
capitale mutuato 417
capitale nominale 222
capitale non richiamato 2313
capitale non versato 2313
capitale obbligazioni 940
capitale prestato 417
capitale privato 1975
capitale proprio 1996
capitale richiamato 500
capitale sociale 222, 544
capitale sottoscritto 2232
capitale versato 1880

capitalista 550
capitali vaganti 1498
capitalizzare 545
capitalizzare gli interessi 547
capitalizzare gli utili 548
capitalizzato, fortemente ~ 539
capitalizzazione 523, 543
capitalizzazione d'interessi (dovuti) 156
caratista 2171
carenza di capitali 559
caricare di debiti 466
carichi sociali 2186
carico 460
carico dei debiti 462
carico di, a ~ 616
carico di debiti 952
carico fiscale 463
carnet d'assegni 626
carovita 1483
caroviveri 1483
carta all'ordine 1806
carta a vista 1007
carta bancabile 283
carta bancaria 284
carta commerciale 356
carta di cavalleria 15
carta di credito 854
carta di prim'ordine 1323
carta finanziaria 1307
carta moneta 1355
cartamoneta 1355
cartamoneta inconvertibile 1535
carta monetaria 1779
carta negoziabile 1806
carta scontabile 283
cartella delle imposte 1839
cartella di cedole 832
cartella di rendita 162
cartella esattoriale 1839
cartella fondiaria 1792
cartella ipotecaria 1792
cartello 571
cartello di prezzi 115
carte-valori 2151
cartolina vaglia 1781
casa d'accettazione 12
casa madre 607, 769
casa principale 607
cash flow 586
cassa 579
cassa di compensazione 649, 710
cassa di conguaglio 710
cassa di credito edilizio 453
cassa di liquidazione 649
cassa (di) pensioni 1918
cassa di perequazione 710
cassa di prestiti 850
cassa di risparmio 2139
cassa di risparmio immobiliare 453
cassa di risparmio postale 1941
cassa di sicurezza 2123
cassaforte (blindata) 2122
cassaforte (corazzata) 2122
cassa, piccola ~ 1931
cassa previdenza aziendale 1918
cassetta dei contanti 579
cassetta di sicurezza 2123
castelletto 855
categoria contribuente 2267
categoria d'imposizione 2267
categoria di redditi 1527
categoria fiscale 2267
cattivo pagatore 245
cauzione 1138
CCI 1603
cedente 121, 1165
cedere 118
cedere un credito 207
cedibile 117
cedibilità 116
cedimento dei (nei) corsi (prezzi) 886
cedola 828
cedola attacata 829
cedola, contro rimessa della ~ 1958
cedola di deposito 608
cedola di dividendo 1078
cedola d'interessi 1588
cedola di riaffogliamento 2085
cedola non scaduta 2330
cedola prescritta 1664
cedolario 832
cedola semestrale 1475
cedola, senza ~ 831
C.E.E. 1194
cenno di ricevuta 47
centro di costi 461
certificato azionario 2170
certificato d'azione (azioni) 2170
certificato del tesoro 2301
certificato di debito 609
certificato di deposito 608
certificato di prestito 1709
certificato di sottoscrizione 2115
certificato di versamento 877
certificato provvisorio 1597
cespite d'entrate 2193
cespite di finanziamento 2192
cespite di redditi 2193
cessare i pagamenti 603
cessazione dei pagamenti 2250
cessionario 120, 1163
cessione 119
cessione di crediti 208
check 624
chèque 624
chiedere troppo 1866
chiudere i libri 278
chiudere un bilancio 279
chiudere un conto 652
chiusura di un conto 655
ciclo congiunturale 471
ciclo economico 471
c.i.f. 634
cifra d'affari 2130
cifra tonda, in ~ 2119
circolante 635
circolazione di biglietti (di banca) 308
circolazione di biglietti e monete 638
circolazione di capitale (capitali) 555
circolazione di denaro 637
circolazione di mezzi di pagamento 638
circolazione fiduciaria 1299
circolazione forzosa 1356
circolazione, in ~ 635
circolazione monetaria 637
circolazione monetaria, eccessiva ~ 6
circoli finanziari 1305
classe di redditi 1527
classificazione 155
clausola di bisogno 1155
clausola di riserva 1155
clausola di salvaguardia 1155
clausola dollaro 1088
clausola oro 1432
clausola-scappatoia 1155
clearing 642, 643
clima degli affari 469
coda 124
coefficiente d'ammortamento 144
coefficiente di copertura 840
coefficiente di equivalenza 1181
coefficiente di liquidità 45
coefficiente di maggiorazione 1734
coefficiente di ponderazione 2372
coefficiente di riserva obbligatoria 1759
collocamento 1619, 1935
collocare 1618
collocare una emissione 1934
collocare un prestito 1933
colmare un deficit 836
colmare un disavanzo 836
colmare un scoperto 836
comitato dei creditori 388
commerciabile 1738
commercializzazione 1742
commerciante all'ingrosso 2375
commerciante al minuto 2105
commerciante, piccolo ~ 2105
commercio al dettaglio 2107
commercio all'ingrosso 2376
commercio al minuto 2107
commercio con l'estero 1283
commercio dei cambi 1221
commercio delle divise 1221
commercio di transito 2294
commercio d'oltremare 1283
commercio estero 1283
commercio in biglietti e monete esteri 936
commercio interno 1101
commercio, libertà di ~ 1392
commercio, piccolo ~ 2107
commercio triangolare 2280
commissionario 690
commissionario di borsa 2152
commissione 689
commissione bancaria 293
commissione d'accettazione 13
commissione di sconto 1055
committente 1973
compagnia 686
compagnia finanziatrice 1308
compartecipazione agli utili 1410
compensare 706
compensare una perdita 707
compensare un assegno 641
compensare un deficit 836
compensare un disavanzo 836
compensare un scoperto 836

compensazione 642, 708, 709, 1172
compensazione bancaria 292
compensazione d'assegni 627
compensazione di saldi 1199
compensazione tra banche 292
compenso 708, 2041
comp(e)rare 479
comp(e)rare a rate 481
comp(e)rare a termine 486
comp(e)rare ratealmente 481
competitività 714
competitivo 713
compilare l'inventario 1124
compilare un bilancio 279
complesso 727
componente della domanda 716
compratore 482
computare 490
computazione 492
computisteria 20
computo 492
comune denominatore 698
Comunità Economica Europea 1194
comutuatario 658
concedere un credito 126
concentrazione 135
concessione 728
concessione di credito 220
concordare i conti 112
concordato 718
concordato fallimentare 719
concordato preventivo 719
concorrenza, libera ~ 1390
concorrenziale 713
concorrenzialità 714
condebitore 659
condizioni di credito 856
condizioni di emissione di un prestito 729
condizioni di pagamento 2278
condizioni di regolamento 2278
conduttore 1667
conferimento (di beni) in natura 205
conferimento di capitale 521
conferire capitale 436
conferma di ricevuta 47
conferma di saldo bancario 290
confirmare un assegno 610
congelamento 383
congelamento dei prezzi 1400
congelare 380
congiuntura 477
congiuntura, alta ~ 413
congiuntura, bassa ~ 1031
congiunturale 1146
conguaglio 247, 1172
conguaglio delle imposte 1175
coniare 662
coniatura 663
coniazione 663
conio 663
consegna a termine 1380
consegna (legale), in ~ 1185
consigliere finanziario 1309
consistenza di cassa 587
consolidamento 737
consolidare un debito 733
consolidati 734
consolidazione 737
consorzio 740
consorzio bancario 303
consorzio d'emissione 2322
consorzio di collocamento 2322
consorzio di garanzia 2322
consulente finanziario 1309
consulente fiscale 2264
consumato 2378
consumatore 744
consumo 751
consumo delle famiglie 1499
consumo interno 1092
consumo nazionale 1092
consumo per abitante 1920
consumo privato 1499
consumo pro capite 1920
consumo proprio 1497
consumo pubblico 2002
contabile 21, 410
contabilità 20
contabilità analitica d'esercizio 798
contabilità autonoma 2155
contabilità dei prezzi di costo 798
contabilità in partita doppia 1107
contabilità in partita semplice 2181
contabilità meccanografica 1724
contabilità nazionale 1797
contabilità, tenuta della ~ 20
contabilizzare 401
contante 572
contanti, a ~ 573
contanti, in ~ 573
contanti, per ~ 573
conteggiare 570
conteggio 613
contenere l'inflazione 628
contenuto in oro 1434
conti di riferimento 802
conti economici integrati 1579
conti esteri, bilancia dei ~ 258
conti, giorno dei ~ 24
contingentamento 2018
contingentamento delle divise 2030
contingentare 122, 1186
contingente 2017
conti, piano dei ~ 22
conto 16, 17
conto a compartecipazione 1654
conto aperto 23, 1846
conto a più firme 1654
conto assegni 625
conto ausiliario 224
conto a vista 23
conto bancario 285
conto capitale 516
conto cheques postali 1800
conto cliente 617
conto collettivo 673, 766, 1649
conto comune 1649
conto congiunto 1649
conto corrente 23
conto corrente, anticipazione in ~ 87
conto corrente, credito in ~ 87
conto corrente di corrispondenza 1424
conto corrente postale 1800
conto da esigere 37
conto da incassare 37
conto d'altri, per ~ 35
conto da pagare 36
conto da riscuotere 37
conto dei ricavi 1523
conto dell'attivo 201
conto (delle) entrate 1524
conto del passivo 1682
conto, denominazione del ~ 25
conto depositi 1016
conto di bilancio 271
conto di capitale 516
conto (di) cassa 575
conto di clearing 644
conto di compensazione 644
conto di contropartita 760
conto di deposito 1016
conto di esercizio 2289
conto di partecipazione 1654
conto di, per ~ 34
conto di riserva 130
conto di risparmio 2138
conto (di) terzi, per ~ 35
conto d'ordine 2248
conto economico 1523
conto fiduciario 2305
conto, in ~ 19
conto in banca 285
conto in comune 1649
conto individuale 1926
conto in partecipazione 1654
conto intermedio 2248
conto, intestatario di un ~ 26
conto loro 1716
conto non liquidato 1846
conto non saldato 1846
conto nostro 1833
conto perdite e profitti 1523
conto personale 1926
conto privato 1926
conto profitti e perdite 1523
conto proprio, per ~ 1877
conto provvisorio 2248
conto riassuntivo 766
conto sospeso 2248
conto spese 1259
conto spese e rendite 1523
conto sussidiario 224
conto, titolare di un ~ 26
conto transitorio 2248
conto vostro 1716
contrario alla tendenza generale, essere ~ 2120
contrarre le spese 915
contrarre un debito 761
contrarre un prestito 762
contrassegno 589
contratti di borsa 1222
contratto a termine 1379
contratto d'affitto 1666
contratto di collocazione vincolata 2321
contratto di locazione 1666
contratto fiduciario 976
contravvenzione 136
contrazione del credito 874
contrazione delle liquidità 1697

contribuente 2028
contribuire capitale 436
contributi sociali 2186
contributo 1135, 1458
contributo erariale 1449
contributo governativo 1449
contributo statale 1449
contribuzione 1135
controciclico 168
controgaranzia 238
controllare 215
controllare l'inflazione 628
controllo degli investimenti 1044
controllo degli scambi 1224
controllo dei cambi 1224
controllo dei conti 214
controllo dei crediti 629
controllo dei prezzi 1961
controllo dei salari 2360
controllo del bilancio 214
controllo delle divise 1224
controllo diretto 770
controllo valutario 1224
contropartita 281, 822
controprestazione 731
controvalore 822, 1219
convenire su un prezzo 113
convenzione sui prezzi 115
conversione 771
conversione di debiti 776
conversione di un prestito 775
conversione forzata 721
conversione in denaro 773
convertibile 782
convertibilità 780
convertibilità esterna 1278
convertibilità interna 781
convertire in denaro (contante) 785
convertire un prestito 779
coobbligato 659
cooperativa 786
cooperativa di credito 787
cooperativa di produzione 1983
coperto, non ~ 835
copertura 834, 1732
copertura a termine 1377
copertura aurea 1435
copertura oro 1435
copertura richiesta 837
copertura, senza ~ 835
copertura, servire da ~ 2166
copertura supplementare 62
coprire una perdita 707
coprire un deficit 836
coprire un disavanzo 836
correntista 26
corresponsione d'interessi 1592
corrispettivo 822
corsa agli sportelli della banca 2121
corso 1960
corso a contanti 593, 2024
corso all'acquisto 354
corso alla pari 1887
corso a termine 1383, 1384
corso azionario 2174
corso d'acquisto 354
corso d'apertura 1849
corso d'appoggio 1610
corso degli affari 833
corso dei cambi 1216
corso dei cambi flessibile 1347
corso dei cambi flottante 1347
corso dei cambi fluttuante 1347
corso dei cambi libero 1347
corso dei cambi oscillante 1347
corso dei cambi variabile 1347
corso del cambio 1216
corso del deporto 240
corso delle azioni 2174
corso delle valute 1216
corso d'emissione 1642
corso denaro 354
corso di borsa 1234
corso di cambio a contanti 2024
corso di cambio a termine 1383
corso di cambio di biglietti e monete 1235
corso di cambio fisso 1341
corso di chiusura 657
corso di compensazione 650
corso di compenso 650
corso di conversione 778
corso di domanda 354
corso d'intervento 1610
corso di offerta 193
corso di rimborso 2054
corso di riporto 569
corso di riscatto 2054
corso di sostegno 1610
corso di sottoscrizione 2238
corso di vendita 193
corso forzoso 722, 1356
corso lettera 193
corso limite 1965
corso medio 234
corso sul mercato libero 1396
corso unico 2326
corso unitario 2326
corto di fondi, essere a ~ 2178
costi addizionali 61
costi aziendali 1850
costi d'acquisto 488
costi da pagare 39
costi di credito 805
costi di emissione 1353
costi diretti 1043
costi generali 1417
costi indiretti 1417
costing 797
costi salariali 2359
costituire in pegno 1018
costituire una riserva 454
costituire une garanzia 101
costituzione di capitale 529
costo 795
costo, a ~ 796
costo alternativo 1853
costo, assicurazione, (e) nolo 634
costo calcolato preventivamente 1189
costo (costi) di fabbricazione 811
costo (costi) di manifattura 811
costo (costi) di produzione 811
costo dei fattori, al ~ 1291
costo del capitale 522
costo della manodopera 806
costo della vita 807
costo del lavoro 806
costo d'esercizio 1850
costo di acquisto 804
costo di credito 805
costo di emissione 1353
costo di gestione 1850
costo di manutenzione 810
costo di rimpiazzo 2091
costo di sostituzione 2091
costo effettivo 54
costo marginale 1733
costo presunto 1189
costo preventivato 1189
costo previsto 1189
costo reale 54
costo unitario 813
cottimo 1907, 1932
coulisse 891
crac 668
creare una riserva 454
creazione di credito 841
creazione di disponibilità monetarie 842
creazione di moneta 842
credenziale 1678
crediti bancari 296
crediti, cessione di ~ 208
crediti congelati 1401
crediti di dubbia esazione 1110
crediti dubbi 1110
crediti incerti 1110
crediti interni 1093
crediti, trasferimento di ~ 208
credito 639, 843, 844, 845, 873
credito, accordare un ~ 126
credito adizionale 63
credito-affitto 1668
credito al commercio 470
credito al consumatore 745
credito al consumo 745
credito all'economia 470
credito allo scoperto 379
credito a medio termine 1753
credito attivo 37
credito, autorizzare un ~ 126
credito, autorizzazione di ~ 220
credito bancario 295
credito cambiario 11
credito, cedere un ~ 207
credito commerciale 470
credito complementare 63
credito, concedere un ~ 126
credito, concessione di ~ 220
credito consorziale 741
credito contabile 404
credito contro documenti 1085
credito da ricuperare 37
credito d'avallo 853
credito di accettazione 11
credito di consumo 745
credito di fideiussione 853
credito di garanzia 853
credito di liquidazione automatica 2156
credito di pareggio 1173
credito di rimborso 1085
credito di sconto 1059
credito di transizione 434

credito documentario 1085
credito, domandare un ~ 175
credito esigibile 37
credito eventuale 757
credito fondiario 868
credito garantito 670
credito immobiliare 868
credito in bianco 379
credito in contanti 580
credito in conto comune 865
credito in conto corrente 87
credito inesigibile 242
credito in essere 37
credito interinale 434
credito ipotecario 866
credito irricuperabile 242
credito libero 379
credito-locazione 1668
credito mobiliare 867
credito non coperto 379
credito pendente 37
credito per la compravendita rateale 1488
credito per scoperto di conto corrente 87
credito personale 1927
credito pignoratizio 670
credito privato 1927
credito provvisorio 434
creditore 870
credito reale 868
creditore chirografario 405
creditore estero 1360
creditore garantito 2150
creditore obbligazionista 390
creditore prioritario 1948
creditore privilegiato 1948
credito revocabile 2113
credito revolving 2114
credito rinnovabile automaticamente 2114
credito roll-over 2118
credito rotativo 2114
credito scoperto 379
credito speciale 2194
credito stand-by 2214
credito su ipoteca 866
credito su pegno 670
credito supplementare 63
credito su titoli 869
credito swap 2252
credito temporaneo 434
credito tra banche 1583
credito transitorio 434
credito, trasferire un ~ 207
crollo 668
crollo dei corsi 431
crollo dei prezzi 431
curatela del (di) fallimento 2040
curatela fallimentare 2040
curatore del fallimento 209
curatore fallimentare 209
custodia fiduciaria, in ~ 1185

dare 942, 943
dare a prestito 1671
dare il avallo su una cambiale 235
dare il X per cento d'interesse 334
dare in garanzia 1018
dare in pegno 1018
dare in pegno di titoli 1501
dare in prestito 1671
dare ordine di pagare una fattura 223
dare titoli in garanzia 671
dare titoli in pegno 671
dare une garanzia 101
dare un interesse del X per cento 334
dare un preavviso di X giorni 1426
dare un utile 100
dare X giorni di preavviso 1426
data di chiusura del bilancio 272
data di scadenza 931, 1263
dati statistici 2219
datore di credito 1672
dazio antidumping 169
dazio compensatore 711
dazio di compensazione 711
dazio di consumo 752
dazio di ritorno 1116
dazio doganale 917
dazio (doganale) ad valorem 82
dazio (doganale) differenziale 1040
dazio (doganale) preferenziale 1949
dazio doganale rimborsato 1116
dazio proibitivo 1993
dazio protettivo 1998
dazio sul valore 82
debiti 961
debiti a breve (scadenza) 910
debiti arretrati 188
debiti di conto corrente 1023
debiti, essere pieno di ~ 953
debiti, essere sovraccarico di ~ 953
debiti verso banche 296
debito 942, 943, 951
debito ammortizzabile 1574
debito attivo 37
debito caduto in prescrizione 324
debito chirografario 2332
debito consolidato 735
debito contabile 406
debito dello Stato 1798
debito d'imposta 2271
debito esigibile 37
debito estero 1280
debito fiscale 2271
debito fluttuante 1351
debito in solido 1650
debito interno 1095
debito ipotecario 957
debito nazionale 1798
debito non consolidato 1351
debito non risc(u)otibile 242
debito obbligazionario 391
debito passivo 36
debito personale 1928
debito prescritto 324
debito pubblico 1798
debitore 958
debitore cambiario 362
debitore di, essere ~ 1876
debitore, essere ~ 944
debitore inadempiente 981
debitore in retardo 981
debitore in solido 1651
debitore moroso 981
debitore negligente 981
debitore solidale 1651
debitore, terzo ~ 1413
debito solidale 1650
debito unificato 735
debole 508
debolezza 1130
declinazione 968
decorrere 1264
decurtare le spese 915
dedotte le imposte 1677
dedotte le spese, dopo ~ 131
dedotte le tasse 1677
dedurre alla fonte 972
dedurre in anticipo 973
deduzione alla fonte 975
deduzione all'origine 975
deduzione della tassa (delle imposte), dopo ~ 1677
deduzione della tassa, prima della ~ 1959
deduzione delle imposte, prima della ~ 1959
deduzione delle spese, sotto ~ 621
deduzione di perdite 2273
deduzione fatta della tassa (delle imposte) 1677
deduzione fatta delle spese 131
deduzione fiscale 2261
deduzione retroattiva di perdite 2272
defalcando le spese 621
defalcate le imposte 1677
defalcate le spese, dopo ~ 131
defalcate le tasse 1677
deficienza di capitali 559
deficit 988
deficit commerciale 474
deficit del bilancio 95
deficit del commercio estero 265
deficit d'esercizio 474
deficit di cassa 96
deficit financing 989
deficit fiscale 1330
deficit in dollari 1089
deficit spending 989
deflatore 996
deflatorio 992
deflazionare 990
deflazione 991
deflazionista 995
deflazionistico 992
deflusso di capitali 556
defraudamento 978
defraudare 977
degno di credito 846
degno di fido 846
del credere 1000
demonetizzare 503
demonetizzazione 1008
denaro a buon mercato 623
denaro a interesse (interessi), prestare ~ 1675
denaro alla giornata 505
denaro a termine (fisso) 1337
denaro a vista 505
denaro caro 654

denaro circolante 914
denaro clandestino 2314
denaro contante 572
denaro contante, in ~ 573
denaro corrente 914
denaro depositato 307
denaro giornaliero 505
denaro in cassa 587
denaro in circolazione 914
denaro in contanti 572
denaro in deposito 307
denaro, lettera e ~ 192
denaro non dichiarato 2314
denaro pubblico 2005
denaro scarso 654
denaro spiccio 612
denominatore, comune ~ 698
denominatore comune 698
denominazione del conto 25
denuncia dei redditi 1531
denunzia dei redditi 1531
deperimento 2367
deporto 239
depositante 1025, 1026
depositare 1015
depositare in garanzia 1018
depositario 1017
depositi interbancari 1582
deposito 1013
deposito a richiesta 1004
deposito a risparmio 2144
deposito a scadenza 1019
deposito a scadenza fissa 1337
deposito a termine (fisso) 1337
deposito a vista 1004
deposito bancario 297
deposito cauzionale 602
deposito collettivo 685
deposito con preavviso 1019
deposito di risparmio 2144
deposito di sicurezza 2125
deposito in banca 297
deposito rimborsabile con preavviso 1019
deposito su conto corrente di corrispondenza 1024
deposito su giroconto 1024
deposito vincolato 1337
depressione 1031
depresso 508
deprezzamento 138, 969, 1029
deprezzamento della moneta 896
deprezzamento monetario 896
deprezzamento tecnico 1030
deprezzare 1028
deprezzarsi 970
destinare 122
destinare al fondo di riserva 68
destinare alla riserva 68
destinatario 2082
destinazione 123
destinazione alle riserve 67
destinazione di utili 183
detentore 336
detentore d'azioni 2171
detentore di obbligazioni 390
detentore di titoli 2171
detentore di valori 341, 2171
deterioramento 2367
determinare un bilancio 279
determinare un prezzo 1033
determinazione dei prezzi 1962
determinazione della parità di cambio 1032
determinazione d'ufficio dell'imponibile 1188
detesaurizzazione 1063
detraibile, perdita ~ 974
detrarre alla fonte 972
detrarre in anticipo 973
detratte le imposte 1677
detratte le spese 131
detratte le tasse 1677
detrazione delle spese, previa ~ 131
detrazione fatta delle spese 131
detrazione fiscale 2261
dettagliante 2105
dettaglio 429
devalutazione 1029
devalutazione della moneta 897
devalutazione monetaria 897
devoluzione 119
devolvere 118
dichiarazione dei redditi 1531
dichiarazione di dogana 919
dichiarazione di fallimento 69
dichiarazione di fallimento, domanda di ~ 316
dichiarazione di garanzia 394
dichiarazione di un dividendo 964
dichiarazione doganale 919
dichiarazione fiscale 2275
dichiarazione provvisoria 2000
dichiare un dividendo 965
differenza 1037
differenza dei prezzi 1038
differenza dei tasse d'interesse 1412
differenza di cambio 1039
differenza di prezzi 1038
differenza di prezzo 1038
differenza sui costi indiretti 464
differimento di pagamento 1276
differire un pagamento 984
difficoltà finanziarie 1314
dilazionare un pagamento 984
dilazione 998
dilazione di pagamento 1276
dilazione di pagamento, accordare una ~ 1274
diminuire di valore 970
diminuire le spese 915
diminuzione 968
diminuzione dei corsi (prezzi) 886
diminuzione di valore 969
direzione degli investimenti 1044
dirigismo 1047
diritti amministrativi 1478
diritti di custodia 2124
diritti di prelievo (su) 1121
diritti fissi 1478
diritti speciali di prelievo 2195
diritto 614, 1135
diritto al dividendo, avente ~ 1170
diritto amministrativo 80
diritto attaccato 888
diritto cauzionale (su) 1687
diritto di conversione 777
diritto di iscrizione 2077
diritto di licenza 1686
diritto di manipolazione 1478
diritto di monopolio 1245
diritto di pedaggio 2284
diritto di pegno (su) 1687
diritto di poziorità 1328
diritto di preferenza 1328
diritto di prelazione 2013
diritto di priorità 1328
diritto di registrazione 2077
diritto di rimessa 2081
diritto di ritenzione (su) 1687
diritto di sottoscrizione 174, 2115
diritto di successione 938
diritto di trascrizione 812
diritto di trasferimento 812, 2081
diritto di trasmissione 812
diritto di voto su titoli in deposito 2356
diritto doganale 917
diritto (doganale) ad valorem 82
diritto (doganale) differenziale 1040
diritto doganale proibitivo 1993
diritto doganale protettivo 1998
diritto d'opzione 1854
diritto d'opzione, con ~ 888
diritto d'usufrutto 349
diritto staccato 1249
disaggio 1048
disavanzo 988
disavanzo con l'estero 261
disavanzo del bilancio 95
disavanzo della bilancia commerciale 265
disavanzo della bilancia dei pagamenti 261
disavanzo di cassa 96
disavanzo, essere in ~ 944
disavanzo inflazionistico 1557
disborsare 1050
disborsi 1053
disciplina dei cambi 1224
disinflatorio 1065
disinflazione 1064
disinflazionistico 1065
disinvestimento 1066
disipotecare 511
disparità 1067
disparità dei prezzi 1038
dispendio 1258
disponibilità 227
disponibilità del tesoro 2300
disponibilità di capitali 226
disponibilità in banca 286
disponibilità in cassa 587
disponibilità in divise 1362
disponibilità in valuta 1362
disponibilità monetarie 1783
disponibilità quasi monetarie 2243
disposizioni valutarie 900
distensione al mercato monetario 1144
distinta delle spese 2218
distinta di deposito 608
distinta di pagamento 877
distinta di versamento 877

distribuire i pagamenti su X anni 2204
distribuire un dividendo 1051
distribuzione di dividendi 1052
distribuzione di dividendo, non ~ 1826
distribuzione di utili 183
distribuzione occulta 1482
ditta bancaria 294
diversi 1764
dividendo 1076
dividendo, avente diritto al ~ 1170
dividendo, con ~ 887
dividendo cumulativo 889
dividendo d'acconto 1598
dividendo extra 398
dividendo finale 1303
dividendo in azioni 400
dividendo in denaro 584
dividendo prescritto 1954
dividendo privilegiato 1945
dividendo provvisorio 1598
dividendo, senza ~ 1080
dividendo straordinario 398
dividendo supplementare 398
dividere la differenza 2201
divieto di entrata 319
divieto d'importazione 319
divisa 893
divisa debole 2187
divisa forte 1479
divisa pregiata 1479
divise 1361
divise a termine 1378
divisionario 1083
divisione di utili 183
documento negoziabile 1806
dogana 917
dollaro di compensazione 29
dollaro, euro~ 1193
domanda 1002
domanda di beni di consumo 746
domanda di credito 173
domanda di dichiarazione di fallimento 316
domanda di mutuo 173
domanda di prestito 173
domanda di restituzione 640
domanda di rimborso 640
domanda ed offerta 2242
domanda interna 1096
domanda monetaria 1774
domandante di (un) credito 172
domandante di un mutuo 172
domandante di un prestito 172
domanda proveniente dalle famiglie 1097
domandare un credito 175
domandare un mutuo 175
domandare un prestito 175
domanda, su ~ 495
domicilio 1102
domicilio fiscale 1331
donatore 1104
donazione 1103
dono 1103
dopoborsa 102
doppia imposizione 1109
doppia tassazione 1109
doppio mercato dei cambi 2309
doppio tallone 375
doppio tipo 375
dotare 1167
dotazione 1168
dotazione di capitale 523
dovere 1876
dovuta, somma ~ 151
dovuto 1127
dovuto, importo ~ 151
drawback 1116
drenaggio di capitali 556
D.S.P. 2195
dumping 1131
duplice imposizione 1109
duplice mercato valutario 2309
durata di circolazione 895
durata (di validità) 894

eccedenza 1204, 2244
eccedenza contabile 30
eccedenza della domanda 1206
eccedenza d'esercizio 1852
eccedenza di bilancio 452
eccedenza di cassa 599
eccedenza di entrate 2245
eccedenza di potere d'acquisto 1209
eccedenza di spese 1212
eccedenza monetaria 6
eccedenza passiva 93
eccedenza strutturale 2229
eccedere un credito 1201
eccessiva circolazione monetaria 6
èccessiva liquidità 1211
eccesso 1204
eccesso di copertura delle spese 1870
eccesso di domanda 1206
eccesso di risparmio 1872
eccesso di spese 1212
eccesso d'offerta 1210
economia deficitaria 989
economia di mercato 1741
economia di mercato libera 1393
economia dirigista 768
economia, fare ~ 924
economia finanziaria 1304
economia finanziaria dello stato 827
economia libera (dei mercati) 1393
economia liberale 1393
economia monetaria 1775
economia pianificata 768
economia politica 1151
economia privata 1976
economia programmata 768
economicità 1984
economico 1146, 1147
economizzare 924
effetti 2151
effetti al portatore 342
effetto all'incasso 364, 373
effetto all'ordine 374
effetto attivo 373
effetto bancario 284
effetto commerciabile 374
effetto commerciale 356
effetto da incassare 373
effetto da pagare 372
effetto dato in garanzia 363
effetto dato in pegno 363
effetto depositato in garanzia 363
effetto di prim'ordine 1323
effetto di ritorno 365
effetto di smobilizzo 363
effetto finanziario 1307
effetto girabile 374
effetto in sofferenza 365
effetto insoluto 365
effetto intrasferibile 371
effetto intrasmissibile 371
effetto negoziabile 374
effetto non all'ordine 371
effetto non commerciabile 371
effetto non negoziabile 371
effetto non onorato 365
effetto non pagato 365
effetto non trasferibile 371
effetto non trasmissibile 371
effetto passivo 372
effetto pignorato 363
effetto restituito 365
effetto scontato sull'interno 1060
effetto sull'estero 1357
effetto sull'interno 1091
effetto tenuto in deposito 363
effetto trasferibile 374
effetto trasmissibile 374
effettuare dei pagamenti 1152
efflusso di capitali 556
elargitore 1104
elargizione 1103
elasticità dei tassi di cambio 1154
elenco degli azionisti 1701
elenco di merci non soggette a dazio 1394
embargo sulle importazioni 319
emettere obbligazioni 1637
emettere un assegno 1115
emettere un prestito 1157
emigrazione di capitali 556
emissione 1352
emissione a rubinetto 2259
emissione azionaria 1640
emissione continua 2259
emissione d'azioni 1640
emissione d'azioni gratuite 399
emissione d'azioni optate 2116
emissione di banconote 1156
emissione di biglietti (di banca) 1156
emissione di buoni 392
emissione di capitali 549
emissione di nuove azioni 2116
emissione di valori 1639
emissione d'obbligazioni 392
emissione fiduciaria 1300
emissione in serie 385
emissione obbligazionaria 392
emittente 1644
emolumenti 1158
entrare in liquidazione 1428
entrata 409
entrata di capitali 99
entrata minore 2112
entrate 1532
entrate del fisco 1565

entrate di bilancio 447
entrate di cassa 585
entrate doganali 921
entrate ed uscite 1525
entrate erariali 1451
entrate fiscali 1565
entrate, minori ~ 2112
entrate non ricorrenti 1287
entrate periodiche 2049
entrate pubbliche 1451
entrate ricorrenti 2049
entrate secondarie 2146
entrate straordinarie 1287
equalizzazione 1172
equilibrare il bilancio 280
equilibrio 1176
equilibrio del bilancio 251
equilibrio interno 1098
equivalente 822
equivalenza 1180
erario 2299
erigere l'inventario 1124
erosione della moneta 896
erosione monetaria 896
errore di calcolo 491
errore od omissione, salvo ~ 1184
errori ed omissioni 1183
errori ed omissioni, salvo ~ 1184
esaurimento delle riserve 1012
esazione 680
esazione di crediti (debiti) 682
esazione d'imposte 683, 1516
esborsare 1050
esborsi 1053
esentare da dogana 1246
esente da dazio 920
esente da diritti doganali 920
esente da dogana 920
esente da interesse (interessi) 1590
esente d'imposta (imposte) 1247
esenzione da imposte 1248
esenzione fiscale 1248
esenzione tributaria 1248
esercizio (commerciale) 478
esercizio finanziario 448, 1320
esercizio fiscale 1335
esercizio sociale 705
esercizio tributario 1335
esigibile 496, 675
esigibilità 674
esistenza 1615
esistenza di cassa 587
esitabile 1738
esodo di capitali 556
esonero da imposte 1248
esonero fiscale 1248
esonero tributario 1248
espansione creditizia 858
espansione degli investimenti 1623
espansione degli scambi mondiali 1254
espansione del commercio mondiale 1254
espansione del credito 858
espansione della massa monetaria 1252
espansione monetaria 1252
esportazione 1265
esportazione di capitali 526
esportazioni invisibili 1632
esportazioni visibili 2351
espresso in dollari 1010
espropriare 1270
espropriazione 1271
esproprio 1271
essere alla pari 1884
essere debitore 944
essere in disavanzo 944
essere sopra la pari 1883
essere sotto la pari 1056
estimare 177, 195
estimazione 176
estimazione (fiscale) 200
estimazione (tributaria) 200
estinguere 148
estinguere un'ipoteca 511
estinzione 139
estrabudgetario 1286
estrarre a sorte 1112
estratto (di) conto 5
estrazione a sorte 1111
eurodollaro 1193
Euromercato 700
evasione di capitali 527
evasione fiscale 2266
evoluzione 1200
evoluzione congiunturale 477
evoluzione della congiuntura 477
ex-cedola 831
ex diritto 1249
ex-dividendo 1080
ex opzione 1249
extra 61
extrabudgetario 1286
extradividendo 398
extra-profitto 1213

fabbisogni di finanziamento 1316
fabbisogni d'investimento 1627
fabbisogni finanziari 1316
fabbisogno di capitali 557
fabbisogno di liquidità 596
fabbisogno di prestiti 424
fabbisogno di tesoreria 596
facilitazione del credito 1145
facilitazioni di credito 421
facoltà al rialzo 485
facoltà a ribasso 1857
facoltà di consegnare il doppio 1857
facoltà di ritirare il doppio 485
factoring 1293
fallimento 315
fallimento, dichiarazione di ~ 69
fallimento, in ~ 314
fallito 313, 314
fare affari 1084
fare economia 924
fare il servizio di un prestito 2165
fare l'inventario 1124
fare onore a un effetto 1054
fare un bilancio 279
fare un guadagno 1729
fare un prezzo 1728
far pagare meno del dovuto 2316
far pagare meno del giusto 2316
far pagare troppo (caro) 1866
far premio 1883
far protestare une cambiale 1481
far quadrare i conti 112
far ricorso alle riserve 1042
far ricorso a un prestito 1122
farsi garante 52
far un debito 761
fase congiunturale 1150
fattore deflazionistico 996
fattore di conversione 772
fattore inflazionistico 1556
fattorizzazione 1293
fattura 17
fattura pro forma 1991
fattura proforma 1991
fatturare 357
fatturato 2130
fatturazione 366
favore di, aprire un credito a ~ 1847
fedecommesso, in ~ 1185
fede di deposito 608
fermezza dei prezzi 1326
fermo su un assegno, mettere il ~ 2227
fiacchezza 1130
fiacco 508
fidecommesso, in ~ 1185
fidecommisso, in ~ 1185
fideiussione 1138
fideiussione di indennità 394
fideiussore 395
fideiussore del fideiussore 238
fido 843
fido bancario 298
fido cambiario 11
fido di sconto 1059
fiduciario 1298
filiale 98, 427
finanza 1304, 1305
finanza, alta ~ 1486
finanze 1304
finanze dello stato 827
finanze pubbliche 827
finanziamento 1322
finanziamento anticipato 1952
finanziamento con capitali altrui 1281
finanziamento con mezzi propri 1601
finanziamento degli acquisti rateali 1490
finanziamento della compravendita rateale 1490
finanziamento di transizione 433
finanziamento esterno 1281
finanziamento interinale 433
finanziamento interno 1601
finanziamento mediante la cessione di crediti 956
finanziamento provvisorio 433, 1952
finanziamento temporaneo 433
finanziamento transitorio 433
finanziare 1306
finanziare in anticipo 1951
finanziare provvisoriamente 1951
finanziatore 1321
finanziere 1321
fine, salvo buon ~ 2099

finezza 1325
fino 1325
firmare una cambiale per avallo 235
fiscale 1329
fiscalità 1334
fisco 1242
fissare un dividendo 965
fissare un prezzo 1033
fissato-bollato 425, 440
fissazione dei prezzi 1515, 1962
fissazione dei rapporti di parità 1343
fissazione di un dividendo 964
fissazione di un massimale 1342
fissazione verticale dei prezzi 2097
fitto 1666, 2088
flessibilità dei tassi di cambio 1154
flessione dei corsi (prezzi) 886
flusso delle disponibilità 586
flusso di capitali 528
flusso di credito 859
fluttuazione ciclica 930
fluttuazione congiunturale 930
fluttuazione dei cambi 1225
fluttuazione dei corsi 1225
fluttuazione dei tassi di cambio 1225
fluttuazione della congiuntura 930
fluttuazione del mercato 930
fluttuazione economica 930
FMI 1607
fob 1354
foglio (di) cedole 832
foglio paga 1912
fondazione 1385
fondi 1406
fondi attinti al credito 417
fondi dello stato 2005
fondi d'esercizio 468
fondi di cassa 587
fondi di finanziamento 558
fondi di gestione 468
fondi disponibili 227
fondi di stato 1244
fondi pubblici 1244, 2005
fondo 1404
fondo cassa in dotazione 1517
fondo comune d'investimento 1624
fondo congiunturale 755
fondo conguaglio dividendi 1079
fondo d'ammortamento 140
fondo dei titoli di stato 1455
fondo d'esercizio 468
fondo di ammortamento 132
fondo di compensazione 710
fondo di contropartita 823
fondo di credito 1710
fondo di equalizzazione 710
fondo di garanzia 1472
fondo d'investimento 1624
fondo di perequazione 710
fondo di prestiti 1710
fondo di previdenza 755
fondo di rinnovamento 2086
fondo di riscatto 140
fondo di riserva 2101
fondo di riserva per spese imprevisite 755
fondo di risparmio 2145
fondo di rotazione 468
fondo di stabilizzazione 2205
fondo di svalutazione 132
Fondo Europeo di Cooperazione Monetaria 1197
fondo fiduciario 2307
fondo fisso di cassa 1517
fondo imposte e tasse 2001
Fondo Monetario Internazionale 1607
fondo pensioni 1918
fondo perduto, a ~ 835
fondo perequazione dividendi 1079
fondo per l'ammodernamento 2086
fonte, dedurre alla ~ 972
fonte d'entrate 2193
fonte, detrarre alla ~ 972
fonte di finanziamento 2192
fonte di redditi 2193
fonte, ritenere alla ~ 972
fonte, trattenere alla ~ 972
formare una riserva 454
formazione dei patrimoni 1373
formazione dell'inventario 1616
formazione di capitale 529
formazione di risparmio 1374
fornare l'inventario 1124
fornire capitale 1407
fornitore di fondi 1777
fortemente capitalizzato 539
franchigia (doganale), in ~ 920
franco (a) bordo 1354
franco di dazio 920
franco dogana 920
frazionamento azionario 2175
frazionamento di azioni 2175
frazione d'azioni 1387
frenare l'inflazione 628
frode fiscale 2266
frode tributaria 2266
fruttante interesse (interessi) 1586
fruttare il X per cento d'interesse 334
fruttare (un utile) 100
fruttifero 1147, 1586
fuga di capitali 527
fusione 135

gap inflazionistico 1557
garante 395
garante, farsi ~ 52
garante, rendersi ~ 52
garantire con ipoteca 838
garantire mediante ipoteca 838
garantire una emissione 2320
garantito, non ~ 835
garanzia 669, 1138, 1471
garanzia accessoria 65
garanzia, assumere ~ 52
garanzia aurea 1437
garanzia collaterale 65
garanzia, costituire une ~ 101
garanzia, dare une ~ 101
garanzia dello stato 1450
garanzia di buon fine 1474
garanzia di buon fine di un credito 1447
garanzia di credito 860
garanzia di credito all'esportazione 1267
garanzia di indennizzo 394
garanzia di un prestito 1473
garanzia ipotecaria 2035
garanzia, offrire une ~ 101
garanzia oro 1437
garanzia, prestare ~ 52
garanzia, prestare une ~ 101
garanzia reale 2035, 2258
garanzia, senza ~ 835
garanzia statale 1450
garanzia supplementare 65
GATT 1415
generi di lusso 1001
gestione di bilancio 450
gestione finanziaria 730
gettare sul mercato 1665
gettito delle imposte 1565
gettito fiscale 1565
giacenza 1615
giacenza di cassa 587
giacenza di numerario 587
giacenza d'oro 1430
giacenza in titoli 1628
giacenza numeraria 587
giocatore di borsa 1647
giocatore in borsa 1647
gioco in borsa 111
giornale 932
giornale ausiliario 225
giorni di grazia 933
giorni di respiro 933
giorni di rispetto 933
giorno dei conti 24
giorno di chiusura del bilancio 272
giorno di liquidazione 24
giorno di scadenza 931, 1263
girante 1165
girante precedente 1944
girante susseguente 2239
girare 2080
girare un effetto 1162
girata 1164
giratario 1163
giro 318
giroconto 1424
giro d'affari 2130
giro d'affari lordo 1467
giro d'affari netto 1816
giro di cambiali a vuoto 1659
giro (di) fondi 1784
giungere a scadenza 347
giustificativo 2358
gold bullion standard 1431
gold exchange standard 1436
gold specie standard 1402
gold standard 1441
gonfiare 1553
grande azionista 633
gratifica 397
gratificazione 397
gravame 460
gravare di debiti 466
gravare di una sovrattassa 1514
gravare di una tassa 194
gravare di un'ipoteco 465
grossista 2375

grosso azionista 633
grosso capitale 355
gruppo 727
guadagni 229, 1140
guadagno 1140, 1409
guadagno di cambio 1233
guadagno di capitale 530
guadagno netto 646

holding 1494
hot money 1498

IDA 1604
illiquidità 1504
illiquido 1503
imbarazzi finanziari 1314
imbarazzo finanziario 1314
immettere capitale 436
immettere nel (sul) mercato 1737
immobili 1508
immobilizzare 1507
immobilizzazione 1506
immobilizzazioni 518
immobilizzazioni immateriali 1505
immobilizzo 1506
immunità fiscale 1248
impegnare 1018
impegnare di titoli 1501
impegnare titoli 671
impegni 961
impegno 692
impegno valutario 1223
impiegare 1618
impieghi di borsa 1179
impiego 1619
impiego di capitali 1160
impiego nuovo 1818
imponibile 196, 331, 2262
imponibile, non ~ 1247
imporre una tassa (su) 194
imporre un prezzo 1033
importazione 1509
importazione di capitali 534
importazioni invisibili 1633
importazioni visibili 2352
importo 149
importo complessivo 107
importo dovuto 151
importo forfettario 1722
importo globale 107
importo lordo 1460
importo netto 1808
importo nominale 1820
importo non pagato 154
importo non versato 154
importo pendente 152
importo restante 246
importo rimanente 246
importo sottoscritto 153
importo totale 107
imposizione 1135
imposizione alla fonte 681
imposizione dei prezzi 1515
imposizione di tasse 1516
imposizione doppia 1109
imposizione, duplice ~ 1109
imposta 1135
imposta addizionale 66
imposta all'origine 2268, 2268
imposta complementare 66
imposta decrescente 997
imposta di bollo 2211
imposta di compensazione 712
imposta di conguaglio 712
imposta di consumo 752
imposta di registro 2077
imposta diretta 1046
imposta di successione 938
imposta fondiaria 1662
imposta generale sull'entrata 2014
imposta immobiliare 1995
imposta indiretta 1552
imposta patrimoniale 551
imposta prediale 1662
imposta progressiva 1456
imposta reale 1995
imposta ritenuta alla fonte 2268
imposta sugli scambi (di merci) 2014
imposta sugli utili 1989
imposta sugli utili delle società 792
imposta sui beni immobiliari 1995
imposta sui consumi 752
imposta sui consumi di lusso 1723
imposta sui dividendi e interessi 565
imposta sui profitti 1989
imposta sui redditi del capitale 565
imposta sui soprapprofitti 1214
imposta sui sovrapprofitti 1214
imposta sui terreni 1662
imposta sul capitale 551
imposta sul capitale azionario 560
imposta sul capitale sociale 560
imposta sul giro d'affari 2014
imposta sulla cifra d'affari 2014
imposta sulla circolazione dei capitali 564
imposta sulla proprietà 551
imposta sull'asse ereditario 938
imposta sulla successione 938
imposta sull'aumento del capitale 532
imposta sulle donazioni 1422
imposta sulle plusvalenze 532
imposta sulle società 792
imposta sul lusso 1723
imposta sul patrimonio 551
imposta sul patrimonio immobiliare 1995
imposta sul reddito 1530
imposta sul reddito del capitale 565
imposta sul reddito delle persone fisiche 1930
imposta sul valore aggiunto 2341
imposta supplementare 66
imposta trattenuta alla fonte 2268
imposte, dedotte le ~ 1677
imposte differite 986
imposte, prima delle ~ 1959
imprenditore 1171
impresa 467
impresa di servizio pubblico 2009
impresa di servizi pubblici 2009
impresa di stato 1448
impresa d'utilità pubblica 2009
impresa, libera ~ 1391
impresa nazionale 1448
impresa privata 1977
impresa pubblica 1448
impresa statale 1448
imprestare 1671
imputabile a 616
imputare 122, 570, 615
imputare al conto 618
imputazione 123, 613
inattività 1130
inattivo 508
incanto 212
incassabile 574
incassare un assegno 576
incassi 1532
incasso 587, 679
incasso, avviso d'~ 47
incentivo 1519
incentivo al investimento 1625
incentivo al risparmio 1161
incentivo fiscale 2270
incettare 489
incidenza di un'imposta 1521
inconvertibile 1534
inconvertibilità 1533
incoraggiamento del risparmio 1161
incremento di valore 180
indagine del mercato 1740
indebitamento 462
indebitamento dello Stato 1798
indebitamento eccessivo 1207
indebitamento esterno 420
indebitarsi 1294
indebitato 952
indebitato, essere eccessivamente ~ 953
indebolimento 968
indebolimento dei corsi (prezzi) 886
indennità 708
indennità di carovita 808
indennità di caroviveri 808
indennità di cassa 133
indennità di contingenza 808
indennità (di trasferta) 128, 2296
indennità di viaggio 2296
indennità (per spese) 128
indennizzo 708
indicare un prezzo 1728
indicatore 1551
indice 1546, 1550
indice dei prezzi 1964
indice dei prezzi all'ingrosso 2374
indice dei prezzi al minuto 2106
indice dei prezzi delle merci 696
indice del costo della vita 809
indice delle vendite 2131
indice di liquidità 45
indice ponderato 2370
indicizzare 1547
indicizzazione 1548
indire una gara per l'appalto 1635
indossamento 1164
indossare un effetto 1162
indossato 1163
indossatore 1165
indosso 1164
inflazionare 1553
inflazione 1554
inflazione creditizia 861

inflazione da costi 803
inflazione d'adattamento 59
inflazione da domanda 1005
inflazione del credito 861
inflazione galoppante 1411
inflazione importata 1511
inflazione larvata 725
inflazione latente 725
inflazione mascherata 725
inflazione provocata da aumenti salariali 2361
inflazione repressa 1919
inflazione serpeggiante 882
inflazione sfrenata 1411
inflazione strisciante 882
inflazionismo 1560
inflazionista 1561
inflazionistico 1555
infruttifero 1590
ingerenza dello stato 1452
iniettare capitale 436
iniezione di capitale 521
iniziativa, libera ~ 1391
iniziativa privata 1976
inondare il mercato (d'articoli a buon mercato) 1132
inscrivere 401
i(n)scrivere all'attivo 403
i(n)scrivere all'attivo, da ~ 408
i(n)scrivere al passivo 402
i(n)scrivere al passivo, da ~ 407
inserire nel bilancio 443
insolvente 1570
insolvenza 1569
insolvibile 1570
insolvibilità 1569
intaccare le riserve 1042
intascare un guadagno 1937
integrazione 135
intensità del capitale 538
interconvertibilità 1584
interesse 1585
interesse composto 720
interesse corrente 909
interesse, dare il X per cento d'~ 334
interesse degli interessi 720
interesse del capitale 540
interesse del X per cento, dare un ~ 334
interesse del X per cento, produrre un ~ 334
interesse del X per cento, rendere un ~ 334
interesse di mora 983
interesse fisso, a ~ 1338
interesse, fruttare il X per cento d'~ 334
interesse (in) 1495
interesse in corso 909
nteresse (interessi), prestare denaro a ~ 1675
interesse (interessi), senza ~ 1590
interesse maggioritario 770
interesse minoritario 1760
interesse moratorio 983
interesse rateizzato 1457
interesse scaglionato 1457
interesse simplice 2179
interesse usurario 2335
interessi 1585
interessi accumulati 41
interessi anticipati 165
interessi arretrati 190
interessi attivi 376
interessi bancari 306
interessi composti 720
interessi correnti 909
interessi creditori 376
interessi da maturare 42
interessi da pagare 947
interessi da ricevere 376
interessi da scadere 42
interessi debitori 947
interessi decorsi 190
interessi di mora 983
interessi fittizi 1518
interessi (in) 1495
interessi in corso 909
interessi intercalari 1599
interessi interinali 1599
interessi ipotecari 1794
interessi maturanti 42
interessi maturati 41, 1589
interessi moratori 983
interessi neri 376
interessi passivi 947
interessi rateizzati 1457
interessi rossi 947
interessi scaduti 1589
interessi scaglionati 1457
interessi usuari 2335
intermediario fra agenti di borsa 1648
interventismo 1608
intervento dello stato 1452
intestatario di un conto 26
introdurre sul mercato 1737
introiti 1532
introiti di cassa 585
introiti e pagamenti 1525
introiti fiscali 1565
inventariare 1124
inventariazione 1616
inventario 1614, 1615, 1616
investimenti immobiliari 518
investimento 1619
investimento all'estero 1368
investimento a reddito variabile 2348
investimento del settore pubblico 2006
investimento di capitale 542
investimento di espansione 1253
investimento di razionalizzazione 1580
investimento errato 244
investimento estero 1367
investimento fisso 1340
investimento immobilizzato 1340
investimento in titoli (di portafoglio) 1626
investimento in valori (di portafoglio) 1626
investimento mal orientato 244
investimento nuovo 1818
investimento privato 1978
investimento pubblico 2006
investimento sbagliato 244
investire 1618
investitore 1631
investitore collettivo 793
investitore istituzionale 793
investment-trust 653
inviare 2080
invio di fondi 1784
invitare a la sottoscrizione di un prestito 1634
iperinflazione 1500
ipoteca 1790
ipoteca ammortizzabile 137
ipotecare 1791
ipoteca (su), prendere un'~ 2019
iscrivere 401
istituto bancario 294
istituto di credito 850
istituto di credito fondiario 1660
istituto di credito immobiliare 1660
istituto di sconto 1058
istituto finanziario 1315
IVA 2341

jobber 1648

keynesiano 1657

lanciamento 1352
lanciare sul mercato 1665
lanciare un prestito 1157
lancio 1352
languente 508
languidezza 1130
languido 508
languire 1663
languore 1130
lato del dare 943
lato dell'attivo 206
lato dell'avere 206
lato del passivo 943
latore 337
lavori pubblici 2010
leasing 1668
lega 1325
lettera credenziale 1678
lettera d'accreditamento 847, 1678
lettera d'accredito 847
lettera di addebitamento 945
lettera di cambio 356
lettera di credito 1678
lettera di garanzia 394
lettera di indennità 394
lettera e denaro 192
levare restrizioni 1
levata di restrizioni 2
libera concorrenza 1390
libera impresa 1391
libera iniziativa 1391
liberalizzare 1685
liberalizzazione degli scambi commerciali 1684
liberalizzazione del commercio 1684
liberare 949
liberare un'azione del X % 1899
liberare un'azione interamente 1915

liberazione 950
liberazione dei prezzi 971
liberazione integrale di un'azione 1908
liberismo 1392
liberista 1399
libero scambio 1392
liberoscambista 1399
libertà di commercio 1392
libertà di concorrenza 1390
libretto bancario 289
libretto (d')assegni 626
libretto di cassa di risparmio 2140
libretto di conto 289
libretto di deposito 1021
libretto di risparmio 2142
libri commerciali 28
libri contabili 28
libri di commercio 28
libro ausiliario 225
libro bilanci 250
libro cassa 578
libro degli azionisti 1701
libro dei bilanci di verifica 250
libro dei soci 1701
libro di cassa 578
libro effetti attivi 360
libro effetti passivi 359
libro giornale 932
libro giornale di cassa 578
libro inventario 250
libro maestro 1418
libro mastro 1418
libro mastro delle azioni 1701
libro scadenze 359
libro sussidiario 225
licenza d'esportazione 1268
licenza d'importazione 1512
lievitazione dei prezzi 1539
limitare le spese 915
limitazione creditizia 874
limitazione dei crediti 874
limitazione della liquidità 2104
limite delle anticipazioni su titoli 604
limite di credito 855
limite di fido 855
limite d'indebitamento 422
limite di prezzo 1965
linea di credito 855
liquidare 148, 785, 1071, 1428
liquidare un conto 249
liquidatore 1694
liquidazione 139, 773, 1070
liquidazione di un conto 254
liquidazione, giorno di ~ 24
liquidità 1695
liquidità (di cassa) 227
liquidità primaria 1971
liquidità quasi-monetarie 1776
liquidità secondarie 1776
liquido 1693
lira sterlina 1943
lire (sterline) trasferibili 2291
listino di borsa 1228
livello dei corsi 1680
livello dei prezzi 1680
livello dell'investimento 1679
locatario 1667
locatore 1676
locazione 2088
locazione-vendita 1487
logoramento 2367
logorio 2367
logoro 2378
lordo delle imposte, al ~ 1677
lotto azionario 386
lotto di azioni 386
lucrativo 1147
lucro 1409
lucro cessante 1718
lucroso 1147
lunga scadenza, a ~ 1715
lungo termine, a ~ 1715

macro-economico 1725
madre 821
maggiorazione dei prezzi 1539
maggiorazione del prezzo 1539
maggiore offerta 1484
maggiori spese 61
maggior offerente 1485
mallevadore 395
malleveria 1138
malversazione 978
mancante 988
mancanza creditizia 878
mancanza di capitali 559
mancanza di dollari 1090
mancanza di liquidità 1504
mancanza di pagamento 982
mancanza di valore 2344
mancata distribuzione di dividendo 1826
mancato guadagno 1718
mancato pagamento 982
mandante 1973
mandare un conto allo scoperto 1868
mandato postale 1781
manipolazione dei corsi 1730
manipolazione della moneta 898
manipolazione monetaria 898
manomorta 1795
mano morta 1795
manovra di borsa 1730
mantello 2176
mantenimento dei prezzi 1917
marasma 1130
marca da bollo 2209
margine 1037, 1732
margine commerciale 1734
margine di credito 864
margine di fluttuazione dei corsi 1346
margine di fluttuazione dei tassi di cambio 1346
margine di guadagno 1734
margine d'interesse 1412
margine di prezzi 1966
margine di profitto 1734
margine di utile 1734
margine di utile lordo 1465
margine di utile netto 1813
margine fra le tasse d'interesse 1412
margine supplementare 62
margini d'arbitraggio 187
marketing 1742
massa attiva 202
massa fallimentare 317
massa monetaria 1783
massa passiva 961
massa salariale 2359
mastro 1418
materia prima 329
matrice 821
maturare 40, 347
maturazione 38, 1748
meccanografia contabile 1724
media 231
media annua 158
mediante il pagamento di 732
media scadenza, a ~ 1752
mediatore 437
mediatore di borsa 2152
mediatore di capitali 1311
mediatore di merci 694
mediazione 438
medio 232
medio circolante 636
mediocredito 1753
medio termine, a ~ 1752
meno le spese 621
mensile 1787
mensilità 1787, 1788
mensualità 1787, 1788
mercatistica 1742
mercato 1735
mercato al rialzo 458
mercato al ribasso 345
mercato aperto 1395
mercato a termine delle divise 1382
mercato azionario 2153
Mercato Comune 700
mercato d'acquirenti 483
mercato degli scambi 1230
mercato dei cambi 1230
mercato dei cambi a termine 1382
mercato dei cambi, doppio ~ 2309
mercato dei capitali 554
mercato dei titoli 2153
mercato dei titoli a reddito fisso 393
mercato dei titoli di rendita 393
mercato dei valori (mobiliari) 2153
mercato del denaro 1778
mercato delle azioni 2153
mercato delle divise 1230
mercato delle divise a termine 1382
mercato delle euro-divise 1192
mercato delle euro-emissioni 1191
mercato dello sconto 370
mercato di cambiali 370
mercato di compratori 483
mercato (di sbocco) 1736
mercato (di vendita) 1736
mercato di venditori 2160
mercato, Euro~ 700
mercato finanziario 554
mercato fuori-borsa 891
mercato, immettere nel (sul) ~ 1737
mercato interno 1100
mercato, introdurre sul ~ 1737
mercato libero 891, 1395
mercato libero dei cambi 1885
mercato libero di divise 1885

mercato mobiliare 2153
mercato monetario 1778
mercato nazionale 1100
mercato nero 377
mercato obbligazionario 393
mercato orientato al rialzo 458
mercato parallelo 1885
mercato secondario 2147
mercato valutario 1230
mercato valutario, duplice ~ 2309
merci d'esportazione 1266
merci d'importazione 1510
meritevole di credito 846
meritevole di fido 846
mesata 1787, 1788
messa en conto 613
messa in pool 1939
metodo dei compensi di partite 1755
metodo del compenso di partite 1756
mettere alla vendita 1841
mettere capitale a disposizione 1407
mettere il fermo su un assegno 2227
mettere in conto 570
mettere in vendita 1841
mettere mano alle riserve 1042
mettere sotto sequestro 211
mettere sul conto 618
mettere una somma a credito di qualcuno 566
mettere una tassa (su) 194
mettere un fermo (su) 211
mettere un'imposta (su) 194
mettere un prestito in sottoscrizione 1634
mezzi 1406
mezzi di finanziamento 558
mezzi di pagamento 1751
mezzi di pagamento, circolazione di ~ 638
mezzi di produzione durevoli 1134
mezzi disponibili 227
mezzi finanziari 558
mezzi liquidi 227
mezzo circolante 636
micro-economico 1757
miglioramento di salario 1542
miglioramento di stipendio 1540
miglior offerente 1485
miliardo 368
minori entrate 2112
minori entrate di bilancio 445
minor valore 969
minusvalenza 969
minusvalenza di cessione 553
misure congiunturali di rilancio 1251
misure di relancio 2011
misure per stimolare la ripresa economica 2011
mobili 622
mobilitare 1767
nobilitazione 1766
nobilitazione di capitali 1405
mobilitazione di fondi 1405
mobilizzare 1767
mobilizzazione 1766
modalità di pagamento 1375, 2278
modalità di regolamento 1375, 2278
modo di pagamento 1375
modo di regolamento 1375
modulo di versamento 1022
mondo della finanza 1305
mondo finanziario 1305
moneta 660, 893
moneta aurea 1402
moneta avente corso 906
moneta bancaria 307
moneta cartacea 1355
moneta circolante 906
moneta contante 572
moneta controllata 767
moneta corrente 906
moneta debole 2187
moneta del paese 1094
moneta di cambio 1780
moneta di conto 307
moneta di corso legale 1669
moneta di giro 307
moneta di nucleo aureo 1431
moneta di rame 788
moneta di riserva 2100
moneta di scambio 1780
moneta divisionale 1083
moneta divisionaria 1083
moneta d'oro 1433
moneta emessa dal tesoro 2302
moneta estera 1361
moneta fiduciaria 1296, 2283
moneta fittizia 1296
moneta flottante 1350
moneta fluttuante 1350
moneta forte 1479
moneta in circolazione 906
moneta in corso 906
moneta instabile 1350
moneta legale 1669
moneta manipolata 767
moneta manovrata 767
moneta metallica 661
moneta metallica, in ~ 573
moneta nazionale 1094
moneta oro 1402
moneta propria 1094
moneta, quasi~ 1805
monetare 662, 1773
moneta regolata 767
monetarista 1768
moneta sana 2191
moneta scritturale 307
moneta sonante, in ~ 573
moneta spicciola 612
moneta stabile 2207
moneta sussidiaria 1083
moneta variabile 1350
monetazione 663, 1772
monete 665
monete, biglietti e ~ 1834
monetizzare 785
monometallismo 1785
monopolio 1786
monopolio commerciale 2287
monopolio di stato 1454
mora, in ~ 979
mora nel pagamento 999
moratoria 1276
moratorio 1789
morosità 999
morto 508
movimenti di capitali, bilancia dei ~ 256
movimento a spirale dei prezzi e dei salari 2363
movimento borsistico 2225
movimento dei pagamenti 1911
movimento di capitale (capitali) 555
multa 136
muraglia doganale 918
mutuamento (repentino) 428
mutuante 1672
mutuare 415
mutuare capitale 416
mutuatario 418
mutuo 845
mutuo ammortizzabile 141
mutuo bancario 298
mutuo d'ammortamento 141
mutuo, domandare un ~ 175
mutuo ipotecario 1711
mutuo redimibile 141
mutuo su titoli 1712
mutuo su valori 1712
mutuo usurario 2336

natura, apporto in ~ 205
natura, conferimento (di beni) in ~ 205
natura, in ~ 1658
natura, retribuzione in ~ 134
natura, rimunerazione in ~ 134
nazionalizzare 1802
nazionalizzazione 1801
necessità d'investimento 1627
necessità di prestiti 424
negoziabile 1738
negoziare un prestito 1807
negoziatore di cambiali 361
negoziazioni di borsa 1222
negozio 320
neto d'imposta, al ~ 1247
non convertibile 1534
non distribuzione di dividendo 1826
non economico 2324
non fruttifero (di interessi) 1590
non imponibile 1247
non inflazionistico 1828
non liquido 1503
non lucroso 2324
non produttivo di interesse (interessi) 1590
non redditizio 2324
non rimunerativo 2324
nota 17
nota d'accreditamento 847
nota d'accredito 847
nota di addebito 948
nota di credito 847
nota di pegno 2364
nota di storno 848
numerario 572, 661
numero indice 1550
nuova fissazione delle quote 77

obbligato cambiario 362
obbligazione 389
obbligazione al portatore 338

obbligazione al portatore con cedola d'interessi 830
obbligazione ammortizzabile 497
obbligazione a premio 1719
obbligazione bancaria 288
obbligazione cambiaria da girata 1166
obbligazione comunale 1713
obbligazione con adeguamento 1549
obbligazione convertibile 783
obbligazione dello stato 1243
obbligazione del tesoro 1243
obbligazione di conversione 704
obbligazione di garanzia 394
obbligazione di indennizzo 394
obbligazione di premio 1719
obbligazione eventuale 758
obbligazione fiscale 2271
obbligazione garantita 2149
obbligazione in dollari 1087
obbligazione in mora 980
obbligazione ipotecaria 1792
obbligazione irredimibile 1636
obbligazione municipale 1713
obbligazione non ammortizzabile 1636
obbligazione non garantita 2331
obbligazione non rimborsabile 1636
obbligazione non riscattabile 1636
obbligazione parametrata 1549
obbligazione partecipante agli utili 1526
obbligazione perpetua 1925
obbligazione redimibile 497
obbligazione rimborsabile 497
obbligazione riscattabile 497
obbligazione tributaria 2271
obbligazione vincolata ad un indice 1549
obbligazioni 961
obbligazioni a vista 1006
obbligazioni di conto corrente 1023
obbligazionista 390
obbligo di pagare le tasse 1683
occasione, buona ~ 321
OCSE 1860
OECE 1861
offerente, maggior ~ 1485
offerta 352, 353
offerta (d'appalto) 2276
offerta di pagamento 1844
offerta di sottoscrizione 1842
offerta, domanda ed ~ 2242
offerta eccessiva 1210
offrire alla vendita 1841
offrire a minor prezzo 2317
offrire in vendita 1841
offrire une garanzia 101
offrire un prestito in sottoscrizione 1634
oggetti di lusso 1001
oggetti di valore 1646
OIL 1606
omissioni, errori ed ~ 1183
onere 460
onere fiscale 463
onere fiscale latente 759
onere ipotecario 1793
oneri 619
oneri di ammortamento 620
oneri di capitale 520
oneri d'interesse 1587
oneri finanziari 1313
oneri sociali 2186
onorare un effetto 1054
onorario 1295
onore a un effetto, fare ~ 1054
operatore di borsa 1647
operazione 320
operazione a contanti 581
operazione a metà 1653
operazione a rate 1489
operazione a riporto 753
operazione a termine 1379
operazione a termine con contropartita 2251
operazione a termine su divise 1381
operazione a vista 1379
operazione di baratto 327
operazione di cambio a (in) (per) contanti 2202
operazione di cambio a riporto 2251
operazione di cambio a termine 1381
operazione di compensazione 327
operazione di copertura 839
operazione di scambio 327
operazione in contanti 581
operazione in partecipazione 1653
operazione per contanti 581
operazione rateale 1489
operazione sul disponibile 581
operazione swap 2251
operazione switch 2253
operazione triangolare 2253
operazioni bancarie 304
operazioni borsistiche 1222
operazioni con assegni 632
operazioni con l'estero 1358
operazioni di banca 304
operazioni di cambio 1241
operazioni di clearing 643
operazioni di compensazione 643
operazioni di credito 851
operazioni di (in) borsa 1222
operazioni di pagamento 1911
operazioni in cambi 1241
operazioni in (su) titoli 1222
operazioni in (su) valori 1222
operazioni in valuta 1241
operazioni su divise 1241
operazioni sui cambi 1241
opere pubbliche 2010
opposizione 1414
opzione 1854
opzione d'acquisto 484
opzione di vendita 1858
orario supplementare 1875
ordinante 2083
ordine, all'~ 1726
ordine di banca 299
ordine di pagamento 221
ore straordinarie 1875
organismo pubblico finanziario 2004
Organizzazione della Cooperazione e dello Sviluppo Economico 1860
Organizzazione Europea della Cooperazione Economica 1861
Organizzazione Internazionale del Lavoro 1606
orientamento 1200
orientamento degli investimenti 1044
orientamento dei capitali 1044
oro al titolo legale 666
oro ed argento in barre 457
oro ed argento in lingotti 457
oro ed argento in verghe 457
oro fino 1324
oro in barre 323
oro in lingotti 323
oro in verghe 323
oro monetario 666
oro monetato 667
oro per monetazione 666
oro per uso monetario 666
oscillazione ciclica 930
oscillazione congiunturale 930
oscillazione dei cambi 1225
oscillazione dei corsi 1225
oscillazione dei tassi di cambio 1225
oscillazione della congiuntura 930
oscillazione del mercato 930
oscillazione economica 930

pacchetto azionario 386
pacchetto di azioni 386
paese a valuta debole 2188
paese a valuta forte 1480
paese con un avanzo della bilancia 824
paese creditore 871
paese debitore 959
paese esportatore 825
paese esportatore di capitali 525
paese importatore 826
paga 1140
pagabile alla consegna 589
pagabile a richiesta 1896
pagabile a vista 1896
pagabile in contanti 1897
pagabile in divisa estera 1898
pagabile in divise 1898
pagamenti 1911
pagamenti, fare dei ~ 1152
pagamenti, introiti e ~ 1525
pagamento 139
pagamento a contanti 591
pagamento alla consegna 589
pagamento a mezzo (di) assegno o accreditamento 588
pagamento anticipato 92
pagamento a pronta cassa 591
pagamento a termine 1910
pagamento completo 715
pagamento contrassegno 589
pagamento contro consegna 589
pagamento degli arretrati 237
pagamento di dividendi 1052
pagamento di interesse (interessi), soggetto al ~ 2231
pagamento di, mediante il ~ 732
pagamento d'interessi 1592
pagamento in acconto 1014
pagamento in contanti 591

pagamento in conto 1014
pagamento integrale 715
pagamento intero 715
pagamento intracomunitario 1611
pagamento, mancato ~ 982
pagamento parziale 1894
pagamento per contanti 591
pagamento provvisorio 1999
pagamento rateale 1571
pagamento totale 715
pagare 148
pagare a contanti 1727
pagare anticipatamente 1904
pagare a pronti contanti 1727
pagare con assegno 1901
pagare gli interessi di un prestito 2165
pagare in anticipo 1904
pagare in contanti 1727
pagare in denaro 1727
pagare in numerario 1727
pagare integralmente 1905
pagare mediante assegno 1901
pagare una fattura, dare ordine di ~ 223
pagare un dividendo 1051
pagare un effetto 1054
pagatore 1903
pagatore, cattivo ~ 245
pagherò (cambiario) 1477
panico bancario 2121
paralisi 1130
paralizzato 508
pareggiamento 1172
pareggiamento di un conto 254
pareggiare il bilancio 280
pareggiare un conto 249
pareggiarsi 248
pareggio 246, 1172
pareggio del bilancio 251
pari 1889
pari, alla ~ 1882
pari, essere alla ~ 1884
pari, essere sopra la ~ 1883
pari, essere sotto la ~ 1056
parità 1886, 1889
parità aurea 1439
parità cambiaria 1182, 1890
parità di cambio 1182
parità intrinseca 1762
parità monetaria 1182
parità monetaria, aggiustamento della ~ 75
parità oro 1439
partecipazione (a) 1495
partecipazione agli utili 1410
partecipazione all'estero 1366
partecipazione azionaria 2172
partecipazione di maggioranza 770
partecipazione di minoranza 1760
partecipazione estera 1365
partecipazione maggioritaria 770
partecipazione minoritaria 1760
partecipazione reciproca 885
parte d'azione 2230
parte del dare 943
parte dell'attivo 206
parte dell'avere 206
parte del passivo 943
partita 409
partita debitoria 946
partita del dare 946
partita di compensazione 281
partita di (in) avere 857
partita di regolarizzazione 71
partita doppia 1106
partita in sospeso 2249
partita non saldata 2312
partitario 225
passare al fondo di riserva 68
passare alla riserva 68
passare una somma a credito di qualcuno 566
passivi 961
passivi esigibili a richiesta 1006
passivi esigibili a vista 1006
passività 961
passività a breve (termine) 910
passività, attività e ~ 203
passività correnti 910
passività esigibili 910
passivo 943, 961
passivo a breve (termine) 910
passivo, attivo e ~ 203
passivo circolante 910
passivo contingente 758
passivo corrente 910
passivo esigibile 910
passivo eventuale 758
passivo inesigibile 1825
passivo non scaduto 1825
patente 476
patrimonio immobiliare 1508
patrimonio nazionale 1804
patrimonio netto 1809
patrimonio sociale 790
pattuire un prezzo 113
peculato 978
pedaggio 2284
pegno 1138
pegno, anticipazione su ~ 86
pegno, anticipo su ~ 86
penale 136
penalità 136
pena pecuniaria 136
penuria creditizia 878
penuria di capitali 559
penuria di dollari 1090
percento 1921
per cento 1922
per cento, aumento del X ~ 1543
percentuale 1921
percentuale d'interesse 1593
percentuale di utile sul giro d'affari 1815
percentuale sugli utili 1923
percepibile 676
percepire una imposta 678
percezione d'imposte 683
perdere (di) valore 970
perdita 1717
perdita, assorbire una ~ 3
perdita commerciale 474
perdita contabile 411
perdita d'esercizio 474
perdita detraibile 974
perdita di cambio 1229
perdita di capitale 552
perdita di gestione 474
perdita di guadagno 1718
perdita di profitto 1718
perdita di proventi 1718
perdita di valore 969
perdita d'utile 1718
perdita d'utilità 1718
perdita lorda 1464
perdita netta 651
perdita sul cambio 1229
perdita totale 934
perdita (un utile), accusare una ~ 2046
perdita (un utile), presentare una ~ 2046
perdita (un utile), registrare una ~ 2046
perequazione 1172
perequazione degli oneri 1174
perequazione dei carichi 1174
perequazione dei costi 800
perequazione delle imposte 1175
perequazione fiscale 1175
perequazione tributaria 1175
periodo di blocco 384
periodo di sospensione 384
periodo di validità 894
perito fiscale 2264
perizia 176
permesso d'esportazione 1268
permesso d'importazione 1512
perturbazione del equilibrio 1062
pesante 508
peso 2368
pezza d'appoggio 2358
pezza di pagamento 600
pezza giustificativa 2358
pezza giustificativa contabile 33
pezza giustificativa di cassa 600
pezzo 660
pezzo d'oro 1433
pianismo 1047
piano contabile 22
piano d'ammortamento 146
piano dei conti 22
piano di finanziamento 1312
piano finanziario 1312
piazzamento 1935
piazzare una emissione 1934
piazzare un prestito 1933
piccola cassa 1931
piccole spese 1764
piccolo commerciante 2105
piccolo commercio 2107
pigione 2088
pignoramento 191
pignoramento presso terzi 1414
pignorare 211, 1018
pignorare titoli 671
plafond di credito 855
pletora di capitali 6
pletora monetaria 6
plusvalenza 180
plusvalenza di cessione 531
plusvalenze di entrate 2246
plusvalore 180

plusvalore contabile 412
PNL 1466
poco animato 508
poco lucrativo 2324
poco rimunerativo 2324
politica creditizia 872
politica dei dividendi 1081
politica del credito 872
politica finanziaria 1317
politica monetaria 1769
politica valutaria 1769
polizza di assicurazione 1577
ponderare 2369
ponderazione 2371
pool 1938
porre sotto sequestro 211
portafoglio (di) azioni 1628
portafoglio (di) titoli 1628
portafoglio (di) valori 1628
portare all'attivo 403
portare al passivo 402
portatore 336, 337
portatore d'azioni 2171
portatore di obbligazioni 390
portatore di titoli 2171
portatore di valori 341, 2171
posizione di un conto 1940
posizione divise 1363
possessore 336
possessore d'azioni 2171
possessore di obbligazioni 390
possessore di titoli 2171
possessore di valori 341, 2171
pos(t)datare 1942
posticipare un pagamento 984
potenziale di crescita 1469
potere d'acquisto 487
potere d'acquisto eccedente 1209
preavviso 1835
preavviso, dare X giorni di ~ 1426
preavviso di ritiro di depositi 1840
preavviso di X giorni, con ~ 1837
preavviso, senza ~ 1838
prediale 1662
prefinanziamento 1952
prefinanziare 1951
prelevamento 1119, 1135
prelevamento alla fonte 975
prelevamento all'origine 975
prelevamento da riserve 2377
prelevamento in contanti 601
prelevamento sul capitale 551
prelevare 973, 1113
prelevare, che si può ~ 496
prelevare sul Fondo Monetario Internazionale 1123
prelievo 1119, 1135
prelievo da riserve 2377
prelievo in contanti 601
prelievo sul capitale 551
prelievo sul Fondo Monetario Internazionale 1120
premio 110, 397, 1856
premio a dare 1953
premio all'esportazione 426
premio al rialza 507
premio al ribasso 1953
premio a ricevere 507
premio d'acquisto 507
premio d'assicurazione 1578
premio d'emissione 1641
premio d'esportazione 426
premio di cambio 109
premio di cui 507
premio di rimborso 1750
premio di riporto 569
premio dont 507
premio, far ~ 1883
premio per non consegnare 1953
premio per non ritirare 507
premio put 1953
premio, transazione a doppio ~ 1108
prendere a prestito 415
prendere capitale in prestito 416
prendere in prestito 415
prendere un'ipoteca (su) 2019
prenditore del credito 418
prenditore d'un effetto 1902
presa di profitti 1990
presa di utili 1990
prescrizione 1955
presentare una perdita (un utile) 2046
presentatore 337
presentazione, a ~ 1956
presentazione, contro ~ 1956
presentazione del bilancio 1957
preso in pegno, suscettibile di essere ~ 9
pressione fiscale 463
pressione inflazionistica 1558
pressione sugli utili 1988
prestare 1671
prestare denaro a interesse (interessi) 1675
prestare di nuovo 2079
prestare garanzia 52
prestare su titoli 91
prestare une garanzia 101
prestatore 1672
prestatore di denaro 1777
prestatore di fondi 1777
prestazione addizionale 1285
prestazione di servizi 2084
prestazione sociale 2185
prestazione supplementare 1285
prestazioni collettive 684
prestazioni di servizi 2168
prestiti 1673
prestito 419, 845, 1705
prestito a cerniera 2118
prestito all'estero 1282
prestito allo scoperto 1301
prestito, ammortamento d'un ~ 142
prestito ammortizzabile 141
prestito a premi 1720
prestito a premio 1720
prestito a scadenza fissa 2277
prestito a termine fisso 2277
prestito, a titolo di ~ 1706
prestito a vista 504
prestito bancario 298
prestito commerciale 473
prestito con garanzia oro 1438
prestito convertibile 784
prestito coperto 672
prestito d'ammortamento 141
prestito dello stato 1453
prestito di consolidamento 738
prestito di consolidazione 738
prestito di conversione 774
prestito di stabilizzazione 2206
prestito di stato 1453
prestito, domandare un ~ 175
prestito estero 1282
prestito fiduciario 1301
prestito forzato 723
prestito forzoso 723
prestito garantito 672
prestito giornaliero 504
prestito giorno per giorno 504
prestito governativo 1453
prestito in sottoscrizione, mettere un ~ 1634
prestito interno 1099
prestito ipotecario 1711
prestito legato ad uno scopo determinato 2281
prestito libero 1301
prestito nazionale 1099
prestito non coperto 1301
prestito non garantito 1301
prestito obbligazionario 941
prestito oro 1438
prestito per lo sviluppo 1036
prestito per obbligazioni 941
prestito pignoratizio 672
prestito pubblico 1453
prestito, redenzione d'un ~ 142
prestito redimibile 141
prestito su pegno 672
prestito su titoli 1674, 1712
prestito su valori 1712
prestito usurario 2336
preventivo 1187
preventivo estimativo 184
previa deduzione 89
previdenza sociale 2184
previo avviso, senza ~ 1838
previsioni di bilancio 449
previsioni sulla redditività 801
preziosi 1646
prezzi constanti, a ~ 742
prezzo 1960
prezzo a contanti 593
prezzo al consumatore 749
prezzo al consumo 749
prezzo al dettaglio 2096
prezzo alla pari 1887
prezzo all'ingrosso 2288
prezzo al minuto 2096
prezzo al pezzo 2328
prezzo a termine 1384
prezzo base 330
prezzo contrattuale 114
prezzo convenuto 114
prezzo corrente 911
prezzo d'acquisto 354, 488
prezzo del contante 593
prezzo del denaro 1967
prezzo del (di) mercado 1744
prezzo del disponibile 2203
prezzo del giorno 911

prezzo delle azioni 2174
prezzo dell'oro, regime del doppio ~ 2310
prezzo del pronto 2203
prezzo d'emissione 1642
prezzo denaro 354
prezzo di compensazione 650
prezzo di compenso 650
prezzo di costo 814
prezzo di costo, al ~ 796
prezzo di domanda 354
prezzo di favore 1203
prezzo di lancio 1613
prezzo di liquidazione 650
prezzo di produzione 811
prezzo di propaganda 1613
prezzo di rimborso 2054
prezzo di riporto 569
prezzo di riscatto 2054, 2095
prezzo di rivendita 2096
prezzo di sottoscrizione 2238
prezzo di vendita 2162
prezzo di vendita al minuto 2096
prezzo d'occasione 322
prezzo d'offerta 1843
prezzo eccessivo 1208
prezzo eccezionale 1203
prezzo esorbitante 1250
prezzo fissato 78
prezzo fisso 78
prezzo forfettario 114
prezzo globale 114
prezzo imposto 78
prezzo irrisorio 322
prezzo limite 605, 1965
prezzo massimo 605
prezzo normativo 1832
prezzo pattuito 114
prezzo per contanti 593
prezzo preferenziale 1203
prezzo réclame 1613
prezzo speciale 1203
prezzo standard 1832
prezzo sul posto 2203
prezzo unico 1344
prezzo unitario 2328
prezzo usurario 1250
prezzo venale 2162
prezzo, vil ~ 322
prima di cambio 1327
principale azionista 633
principio dei compensi di partite 1755
principio del compenso di partite 1756
principio del minimo valore 1721
privatizzazione 1009
procacciare capitale 1407
procacciarsi capitale 416
procurare capitale 1407
procurarsi capitale 416
prodotti di lusso 1001
prodotto (di) base 329
prodotto interno lordo 1461
prodotto nazionale 1803
prodotto nazionale lordo 1466
prodotto nazionale netto 1814
produrre un interesse del X per cento 334
produrre (un utile) 100
produttivo di interesse (interessi) 1586
profittevole 1147
profitti 229
profitto 1409
profitto commerciale 475
profitto d'esercizio 475
profitto eccezionale 1213
profitto lordo 1459
profitto netto 646
profitto sperato 166
profitto sui cambi 1233
programma d'emissione 1643
programma di finanziamento 1312
programma di sottoscrizione 1643
programma finanziario 1312
progressività di un'imposto 1992
proiezioni di bilancio 451
promessa d'azioni 1597
promessa di credito 88
promessa (di debito) 1477
promessa di divise 1223
pronti (contanti), a ~ 573
proporzione 2029
proprietà fondiaria 1661
proprietà immobile 1508
proprietà immobiliare 1508
proprietà privata 1979
proprietario 1878
proprietà terriera 1661
proroga 998, 1994
proroga di pagamento 1276
proroga di pagamento, accordare una ~ 1274
proroga d'un credito 1275
prorogare il termine di pagamento 1274
prorogare un credito 1272
prorogare un pagamento 1274
prorogare un termine 1273
prospetto finanziario 1319
protestare una cambiale 1481
protetto contro l'inflazione 1562
protezionista 1997
prova di debito 609
proventi 229
proventi doganali 921
provento 1982
provocare una reflazione 2069
provvedere capitale 1407
provvigione 689
provvigione bancaria 293
provvigione d'accettazione 13
provvigione d'apertura di credito 693
provvigione di servizio 80
provvista 1615
provvista di capitali 1408
pubbliche risorse 2007
punti, accusare una flessione (un guadagno) di X ~ 2045
punti, registrare una flessione (un guadagno) di X ~ 2045
punto d'appoggio 1609
punto d'intervento 1609
punto di sostegno 1609
punto morto 430
punto-premio 2290

quadrare i conti, far ~ 112
quadro 2256
quadro di ripartizione 799
quantitativo trattato in borsa 2225
quasimoneta 1805
quietanza 47, 51
quietanza, per ~ 1879
quota 2017, 2235
quota d'ammortamento 144, 145
quota dell'accomandante 1591
quota d'incremento 1255
quota di riparto 1077
quota di utile 2173
quotare 1698
quotare un prezzo 1728
quotazione 1960
quotazione d'apertura 1849
quotazione (dei corsi) 1746
quotazione del contante 593
quotazione del giorno 913
quotazione di borsa 1234
quotazione di chiusura 657
quotazione per contanti 593
quoziente 2029
quoziente di liquidità 45

raccogliere capitali 416
raccolta di capitali 1405
raccolta di fondi 1405
rafforzamento 2020
raggruppamento di azioni 2064
raggruppare azioni 2061
ragione 2029
ragione di scambio 2279
ragioneria 20
ragioniere 21, 410
rallentamento 968
rapporti di cambio 1236
rapporto 2029
rapporto annuale 160
rapporto annuo 160
rapporto cambio-utile 1963
rapporto capitale in prestito/capitale proprio 963
rapporto di liquidità 45
rapporto di parità 1888
rarefazione dei crediti 874
rarefazione di capitali 559
rata 1571, 1572
rata mensile 1788
rata mensuale 1788
rata semestrale 351
rate, a ~ 987
ratealmente 987
rateare i pagamenti su X anni 2204
ratei 73
rateizzare i pagamenti su X anni 2204
realizzabile 2034
realizzabilità 2033
realizzare 785
realizzare un profitto 1729
realizzare un utile 1729
realizzazione 773
realizzazione di profitti 1990

realizzazione di utili 1990
realizzo 773
realizzo di profitti 1990
realizzo di utili 1990
recessione 1031
redazione dell'inventario 1616
redditi 1244, 1522
redditi accessori 64
redditi d'investimenti 1528
redditi effettivi 2032
redditi mobiliari 1528
redditi primari 1970
redditi privati 1929
redditi pubblici 1451
redditi secondari 2146
redditi statali 1451
redditi supplementari 64
redditi trattenuti 1137
redditività 1984
redditizio 1147
reddito 1522
reddito da fattori 1292
reddito da trasferimento 2292
reddito del capitale 535
reddito della società 791
reddito di interessi 1595
reddito di lavoro (salariato) 1136
reddito disponibile 1068
reddito d'obbligazioni 396
reddito effettivo 2032
reddito fiscale 1565
reddito fisso 210
reddito fisso, a ~ 1338
reddito imponibile 197, 2262
reddito in natura 1529
reddito lordo 1463
reddito medio pro-capite 233
reddito nazionale 1799
reddito netto 1811
reddito non di lavoro 2323
reddito obbligazionario 396
reddito personale 1929
reddito reale 2032
reddito regolare 210
redenzione 139, 2053
redenzione d'un prestito 142
redigere un bilancio 279
redimere 148, 502
redimere un'ipoteca 511
redimibile 2052
redimibile per estrazione a sorte 498
redimibilità 2051
reflazione 2070
regia 1454
regime creditizio 879
regime dei cambi 900
regime del doppio prezzo dell'oro 2310
regime delle divise 900
regime fiscale 1334
registrare 401
registrare a debito 615
registrare una flessione (un guadagno) di X punti 2045
registrare una perdita (un utile) 2046
registrazione a debito 946
registrazione (contabile) 409
registrazione di accredito 857
registrazione di chiusura 656
registrazione di debito 946
registrazione in contropartita 281
registrazione inversa 281
registrazione per storno 281
registro degli azionisti 1701
registro degli effetti attivi 360
registro degli effetti passivi 359
registro delle azioni 1701
registro delle imprese 687
registro di commercio 687
regolamentazione dei cambi 900
regolamentazione dei prezzi 1961
regolamento 139
regolamento dei prezzi 1961
regolamento di un conto 254
regolare 148
regolare a contanti 1727
regolare il saldo 1914
regolare in contanti 1727
regolare un conto 249
regolatore fiscale 1333
regressione economica 1031
regresso 968, 2047
reimpiegare 1936
reimpiego 2078
reinvestimento 2078
reinvestire 1936
relazione annua 160
relazione annuale 160
relazione dei sindaci 217
relazione di verifica 217
remissione di un debito 513
remunerare 2042
remunerativo 1147
remunerazione 2041
remunerazione accessoria 1284
remunerazione addizionale 1284
remunerazione del capitale 535
remunerazione in natura 134
remunerazione speciale 1284
remunerazione supplementare 1284
rendere 1900
rendere un interesse del X per cento 334
rendere (un utile) 100
rendersi garante 52
rendiconto 2217
rendimento 2110
rendimento azionario 1082
rendimento borsistico 57
rendimento del capitale 535
rendimento effettivo 57
rendimento reale 57
rendita 2110, 2323
rendita annuale 161
rendita borsistica 57
rendita del capitale 535
rendita effettiva 57
rendita perpetua 163
rendita reale 57
rendita vitalizia 163
residuo 246
respiro 998
respiro di pagamento 1276
respiro di pagamento, accordare un~ 1274
responsabilità 1681
responsabilità contrattuale 763
responsabilità extracontrattuale 1824
responsabilità illimitata 2329
responsabilità limitata 1689
responsabilità solidale 1652
restituibile 2073
restituire 1900
restituzione 2072
restituzione di dazio 1116
restituzione d'imposte 2038
resto 246
resto dovuto 252
restringere le spese 915
restrizione all'importazione 1513
restrizione dei prezzi 1968
restrizione del credito 874
restrizione della liquidità 2104
restrizione delle importazioni 1513
restrizioni, abolire ~ 1
restrizioni, abolizione di ~ 2
restrizioni dei cambi 902
restrizioni del credito, allentare gli ~ 1143
restrizioni di cambio 902
restrizioni, levare ~ 1
restrizioni, levata di ~ 2
restrizioni, soppresione di ~ 2
restrizioni, sopprimere ~ 1
restrizioni sulle divise 902
restrizioni valutarie 902
retribuire 2042
retribuzione 2041
retribuzione in natura 134
retrodatare 164
rettifica di cambio 75
revisione contabile 214
revisione interna 1600
revisore (contabile) 216
revisore (dei conti) 216
riacquistare 480
riacquisto 2094
riacquisto di scoperto 335
riaffogliamento 2087
riallineamento delle parità 2031
rialzare il valore 178
rialzista 455
rialzo 2048, 2117
rialzo dei prezzi 1539
rialzo del prezzo 1539
rialzo del tasso di sconto 1541
rialzo del X per cento 1543
ribassare 970
ribassista 332
ribasso 127, 968
ribasso dei corsi (prezzi) 886
ribasso del prezzo 927
ribasso del tasso di sconto 926
ribasso di valore 969
ribasso nel valore 969
ricambio 819
ricavare un profitto 1729
ricavare un utile 1729
ricavato 229, 1982
ricavi diversi 1765
ricavi lordi 1467
ricavi netti 1816
ricavo 229, 1982

ricavo delle imposte 1565
ricchezza nazionale 1804
ricerca del mercato 1740
ricevimento, avviso di ~ 47
ricevuta 47
ricevuta di deposito 608
ricevuta di versamento 877
richiesta 1002
richiesta, a ~ 495
richiesta di copertura supplementare 501
richiesta di fallimento 316
richiesta di fondi 494
richiesta di margine supplementare 501
richiesta di versamento 494
riciclaggio di capitali 2050
riciclo di capitali 2050
ricognizione di debito 46
ricompensa 2041
ricompensare 2042
ricomp(e)ra 2094
ricomp(e)rare 480
riconoscimento di debito 46
ricorrere alle riserve 1042
ricorrere a un prestito 1122
ricorso alle riserve, far ~ 1042
ricorso al mercato 506
ricorso a un prestito, far ~ 1122
ricostituire la riserva 2039
ricuperabile 675
ricuperabilità 674
ricuperare il suo denaro 1421
ricuperare una perdita 707
ricuperare un credito 677
ricuperare un debito 677
ricupero 680, 2020, 2048
ricupero di crediti (debiti) 682
ridistribuzione 2060
ridurre il capitale azionario 2061
ridurre le spese 915
riduzione dei margini di fluttuazione 2065
riduzione del capitale azionario 2064
riduzione del dividendo 925
riduzione del prezzo 927
riduzione del tasso di sconto 926
riduzione di capitale 2063
riduzione di fondi risparmiati 1069
riduzione d'imposta 2261
riduzione di valore 969
riduzione fiscale 2261
riequilibrio della bilancia dei pagamenti 794
riequilibrio delle parità 2031
riesportazione 2066
rifinanziamento 2068
rifinanziare 2067
rifiutare di riconoscere un debito 2092
rifiuto di pagamento 2074
rifiuto di riconoscere un debito 2093
riflazionare 2069
riflazione 2070
riflusso di capitali 2071
rifondere 1900
rifondibile 2073
riforma fiscale 2274
riforma monetaria 899
riforma tributaria 2274
rifornire la riserva 2039
rifugio fiscale 2269
rifusione 708, 2072
rilancio 2048
rilancio, misure congiunturali di ~ 1251
rilevamento 2257
rilevare l'inventario 1124
rimanenza 246
rimborsabile 2052, 2073
rimborsabile per estrazione a sorte 498
rimborsabilità 2051
rimborsare 148, 502, 1900
rimborsare un'ipoteca 511
rimborso 139, 2053, 2072
rimborso di diritti doganali 1116
rimborso d'imposte 2038
rimessa 1784
rimessa della cedola, contro ~ 1958
rimessa in contante 595
rimessa in denaro 595
rimettere 2080
rimettere un debito 510
rimpatriare 2089
rimpatrio 2090
rimpiegare 1936
rimpiego 2078
rimunerare 2042
rimunerativo 1147
rimunerazione 2041
rimunerazione accessoria 1284
rimunerazione addizionale 1284
rimunerazione del capitale 535
rimunerazione in natura 134
rimunerazione speciale 1284
rimunerazione supplementare 1284
rincaro 1539
rinnovare un credito 1272
rinnovo d'un credito 1275
rinvestimento 2078
rinvestire 1936
riorganizzare le finanze 2044
riorganizzazione finanziaria 1318
ripagare 1900
riparare una perdita 707
riparazione 708
ripartire 122
ripartire i pagamenti su X anni 2204
ripartire la differenza 2201
ripartire un dividendo 1051
ripartizione 123
ripartizione dei mercati 1745
ripartizione dei patrimoni 1073
ripartizione del capitale 1074
ripartizione del mercato 1745
ripartizione di azioni 125
ripartizione di dividendi 1052
ripartizione di profitti 183
ripartizione inadeguata di fondi 1763
riportare 435
riportare una posizione 568
riporto 567, 569, 753
riporto a nuovo 150
ripresa 2020, 2048
riprestare 2079
riprivatizzazione 1009
risanamento finanziario 1318
risanare le finanze 2044
risarcimento 708
riscattabile 2052
riscattabilità 2051
riscattare 148, 502
riscattare un'ipoteca 511
riscatto 139, 2053
riscatto anticipato 167
rischio di cambio 1238
riscontabile 2058
riscontare 2057
risconti 73
risconto 2056
riscossione 680
riscossione di crediti (debiti) 682
riscossione d'imposte 683
riscotibile 574, 675, 676
riscuotere il suo denaro 1421
riscuotere una imposta 678
riscuotere un assegno 576
riscuotere un credito 677
riscuotere un debito 677
riscuotibile 574, 675, 676
riserva 129, 2098
riserva aurea 1440
riserva congiunturale 820
riserva di cassa 597
riserva (di) divise 901
riserva di previdenza 756
riserva di valute 901
riserva d'oro 1440
riserva dovuta per legge 1670
riserva facoltativa 1397
riserva fiscale 2001
riserva in contanti 597
riserva in oro 1440
riserva libera 1397
riserva monetaria 1770
riserva ordinaria 1670
riserva per conguaglio dividendi 1079
riserva per crediti dubbi 243
riserva per eventualità 756
riserva per la regolarizzazione dei dividendi 1079
riserva per le imposte 2001
riserva per spese impreviste 756
riserva statutaria 2102
riserva valutaria 901
riserve 2098
riserve auree e valutarie 1429
riserve dichiarate 966
riserve di liquidità 1696
riserve invisibili 726
riserve latenti 726
riserve legali 1670
riserve liquide 1696
riserve nascoste 726
riserve non dichiarate 726
riserve obbligatorie 1670
riserve occulte 726
riserve palesi 966
riserve segrete 726
riserve tacite 726
risorse 1406
risorse di numerario 587

risorse pecuniarie 1916
risparmiare 2133
risparmiatore 2134
risparmio 2137
risparmio coattivo 724
risparmio contrattuale 764
risparmio eccessivo 1872
risparmio forzato 724
risparmio forzoso 724
risparmio in conto di risparmio 2136
risparmio interno lordo 1462
risparmio in titoli 2135
risparmio mobiliare 2135
risparmio privato 1980
ristagnare 1663
ristagno 1130
ristorno di dazio 1116
ritardo di pagamento 999
ritardo, in ~ 189
ritardo nel pagamento 999
ritenere alla fonte 972
ritenuta a garanzia 2109
ritenuta alla fonte 975
ritenuta all'origine 681, 975
ritenuta d'acconto 681
ritenuta d'imposte alla fonte 681
ritenuta per rivalsa 681
ritirare 502, 1113
ritirare (dalla circolazione) 503
ritirarsi con perdita 928
ritiro 1008, 1119, 2053
ritiro in contanti 601
ritmo d'aumento 1256
ritmo dell'inflazione 1563
ritmo d'espansione 1256
rivalorizzare 178
rivalorizzazione 2111
rivalsa (cambiaria) 819
rivalutare 178, 2037
rivalutazione 2036, 2111
rivedere 215
rivenditore 2105
rivolgimento 428
rotazione dei crediti 960
royalty 1686
run ai depositi bancari 2121

safe 2122
saggio 2021
saggio a contanti 2024
saggio del cambio 1216
saggio delle anticipazione su pegno 2022
saggio delle anticipazioni garantite 2022
saggio delle anticipazioni su titoli 1714
saggio delle anticipazioni su valori 1714
saggio di base 328
saggio di cambio a contanti 2024
saggio di cambio a termine 1383
saggio d'imposizione 2023
saggio d'imposta 2023
saggio d'interesse 1593
saggio di riporto 569
saggio di risconto 2059
saggio di sconto 1061
saggio di sconto bancario 311
salari e stipendi 1141
salario 1140
salario a cottimo 1907, 1932
salario a premio 1520
salario a rendimento 1153
saldare 148
saldare un conto 249
saldarsi 248
saldi 2128
saldo 139, 246
saldo a credito 849
saldo a debito 93
saldo a nuovo 150
saldo attivo 849
saldo attivo della bilancia commerciale 266
saldo attivo della bilancia dei pagamenti 263
saldo avere 849
saldo con l'estero 1277
saldo contabile 27
saldo creditore 849
saldo debitore 93
saldo deficitario 93
saldo degli scambi con l'estero 1277
saldo dei trasferimenti correnti 257
saldo delle partite correnti 268
saldo delle transazioni su beni e servizi 259
saldo di compensazione 269
saldo (di) dividendo 1303
saldo di (in) cassa 253
saldo di un conto 254, 255
saldo dovuto 252
saldo generale dei trasferimenti e dei movimenti di capitale 1416
saldo in banca 286
saldo migratore 1758
saldo passivo 93
sbarcare il lunario 1703
sbilancio 1062
sbloccare 949
sblocco 950
sbocco 1736
sborsare 1050
sborsi 1053
scade il 15 di agosto, che ~ 1129
scadenza 1262, 1748
scadenza, a breve ~ 2177
scadenza, alla ~ 1128
scadenza, a lunga ~ 1715
scadenza, a media ~ 1752
scadenza di X anni 1749
scadenza, giungere a ~ 347
scadenza il 15 di agosto, con ~ 1129
scadenzario 359
scadenza, venire a ~ 347
scadere 347, 1264
scaduto 1126
scaglionare i pagamenti su X anni 2204
scaglione di redditi 1527
scala mobile 1348
scambiare 326
scambi con l'estero 1283
scambio 325
scambio d'azioni 1232
scambio di titoli 2254
scambio, libero ~ 1392
scambi triangolari 2280
scarsezza di dollari 1090
scarsità di capitali 559
scarsità di dollari 1090
scarto 1037
scarto dei prezzi 1038
scarto (di prima) 1731
scarto fra le tasse d'interesse 1412
scendere nel valore 970
scienza economica 1151
sciogliere 1071
scioglimento 1070
scomposizione 155
scongelamento 950
scongelare 949
scontare 1057
sconto 127, 1048
sconto al rivenditore 935
sconto bancario 311
sconto cassa 583
sconto commerciale 935
sconto fittizio 1822
sconto per contanti 583
sconto per (pagamento) pronto cassa 583
sconto sulle fatture 935
sconto su merci 935
sconto ufficiale 311
scontrino 821
scontrino di cassa 590
scontrino di magazzino 2364
scoperto 835, 988
scoperto, allo ~ 835
scoperto (di conto) 1867
scopo di lucro, associazione con ~ 1986
scopo di lucro, associazione senza ~ 1829
scoprire un conto 1868
scorta 1615
scorta di divise 901
scorta d'oro e di divise 1429
scorta monetaria 1770, 1783
scorte auree 1430
scorte d'oro 1430
scrittura (contabile) 409
scrittura d'addebitamento 946
scrittura di accreditamento 857
scrittura di debito 946
scrittura di storno 281
scrittura d'ordine 2249
scrittura fiduciaria 976
scrittura in sospeso 2249
scrittura inversa 281
scrittura per storno 281
scrittura registrata a debito 946
scrittura rettificativa 71
scrittura riepilogativa 717
sdaziabile 916
sdaziamento 645
sdoganabile 916
sdoganamento 645
seconda di cambio 2148
sede centrale 607
sede principale 607
sede sociale 2075

sede statutaria 2075
S.E. ed O. 1184
segnare a debito 615
segnare una somma a credito di qualcuno 566
segreto bancario 305
semestralità 351
sensale 437
sensale di borsa 2152
sensale di cambiali 361
sensale di cambio 2152
sensale di merci 694
senseria 438
S.E. od O. 1184
sequestrare 211
sequestratario 209
sequestrazione 191
sequestro 191
sequestro (giudiziario) 2040
sequestro presso terzi 1414
serpente (monetario) 2183
servire da copertura 2166
servizi 2168
servizi, beni e ~ 1443
servizio dei conti correnti postali 1423
servizio del debito 962
servizio d'interessi 1592
servizio di un prestito 2167
servizio di un prestito, fare il ~ 2165
settore della distribuzione 1075
settore in espansione 1470
settore in sviluppo 1470
settore privato 1981
settore pubblico 2008
SFI 1605
sgravio fiscale 2261
sgretolamento dei corsi (prezzi) 886
sicurezza 1138
sicurezza sociale 2184
sindacato 2255
sindacato bancario 303
sindacato (finanziario) d'emissione 2322
sindaco (revisore) 216
sistema bancario 301
sistema contabile 22
sistema creditizio 879
sistema dei cambi 1240
sistema dei prezzi imposti 2097
sistema di calcolo del costo complessivo 4
sistema di costi uniformi 2325
sistema finanziario 1304
sistema fiscale 1334
sistema monetario 664
sistema monetario a (di) cambio aureo 1436
sistema monetario cartaceo 1881
sistema salario investimento 2362
sistema tributario 1334
situazione 2217
situazione analitica 429
situazione consolidata 739
situazione della banca 312
situazione della (di)cassa 592
situazione del mercato 1743
situazione di tesoreria 592
situazione di un conto 1940
situazione finanziaria 1319
situazione sintetica 2241
slittamento dei corsi (prezzi) 886
slump 1031
slumpflazione 2182
smerciabile 1738
smerciare 2157
smobilizzare 949
smobilizzo 950
snazionalizzazione 1009
Snc 1420
socializzare 1802
socializzazione 1801
società affiliata 98
società anonima 1537
società a responsabilità limitata 1690
società bancaria 302
società bancaria per azioni 1536
società (commerciale) 686
società consociata 98
società controllante 769
società controllata 98
società cooperativa 786
società cooperativa di credito 787
società cooperativa di produzione 1983
società di banca 302
società di capitali 1537
società di controllo 769
società di finanziamento 1308
società d'investimento 653
società di persone 1892
società di portafoglio 653
società dominante 769
società dominata 98
società fiduciaria 2306
società filiale 98
società finanziaria 1308
società finanziaria d'investimenti 653
Società Finanziaria Internazionale 1605
società holding 1494
società in accomandita per azioni 1893
società in accomandita (semplice) 1692
società in nome collettivo 1420
società madre 769
società mutua di credito 787
società per azioni 1537
socio 2171
socio accomandante 1691
socio accomandatario 1419
socio occulto 1105
sofferenza, in ~ 1869
soggettamento all'imposta 1683
soggettività all'imposta 1683
soggetto a dazio 916
soggetto a diritti doganali 916
soggetto a dogana 916
soggetto a imposta 196
soggetto al pagamento di interesse (interessi) 2231
soggetto a un preavviso di X giorni 1837
soglia di redditività 430
sola di cambio 2180
soldi spiccioli 612
solidarità passiva 1652
solidità 873
solido 846
sollecitazione ad investire 1625
solvenza 2189
solvibile 2190
solvibilità 2189
somma 149
somma a cauzione 602
somma complessiva 105
somma dovuta 151
somma eccedente 1205
somma finale 105
somma forfettaria 1722
somma restante 246
somma rimanente 246
somma totale 105
sopportare una perdita 333
soppresione di restrizioni 2
sopprimere restrizioni 1
soprappaga 1288
soprappiú 2244
soprapprezzo 60, 1208
soprapprofitto 1213
sopraprezzo 60, 1208
sopraprofitto 1213
soprassaturare il mercato (d'articoli a buon mercato) 1132
soprattassa 60, 66
soprattassare 1514
sopravvalutare 1863
sopravvalutazione 1864
sorteggiabile 498
sorteggiare 1112
sorteggio 1111
sospendere il pagamento di un assegno 2227
sospendere i pagamenti 603
sospensione dei pagamenti 2250
sospensione di pagamento 1276
sostegno dei prezzi 1917
sostegno monetario 1771
sostenere una perdita 333
sottocapitalizzazione 2315
sottoconto 224
sottoscrittore 2234
sottoscrivere 2233
sottoscrivere in eccedenza 1873
sottoscrizione 2236
sottoscrizione di capitale 562
sottoscrizione di un prestito, aprire la ~ 1634
sottoscrizione superata 1874
sottovalutare 2319
sottovalutazione 2318
sottrarre 977
sottrazione 978
sovrabbondanza di denaro 6
sovra(c)capitalizzazione 1865
sovr(a)imposta 66
sovraindebitamento 1207
sovrappiú 2244
sovrapprezzo 60, 1208
sovrapprezzo d'emissione 1641
sovrapprofitto 1213

sovraprezzo 60, 1208
sovraprofitto 1213
sovrattassa 60, 66
sovrattassare 1514
sovvenzionare 2240
sovvenzione 1458
sovvenzione all'esportazione 1269
sovvenzione dello stato 1449
sovvenzione d'interessi 1594
sovvenzione statale 1449
S.p.A. 1537
spartizione dei mercati 1745
spartizione del mercato 1745
specifica 429
specificazione 429
speculare 2196
speculare al rialzo 456
speculare al ribasso 1427
speculare sul ribasso 1427
speculatore 2200
speculatore al rialzo 455
speculatore al ribasso 332
speculatore di borsa 1647
speculazione 2197
speculazione in borsa 111
spedizione in dogana 645
spendere 1257
spendere più di quello che si guadagna 1702
spesa 1258
spese 1053, 1261
spese accessorie 61
spese addizionali 61
spese amministrative 79
spese bancarie 291
spese constanti 1336
spese correnti 908
spese da pagare 39
spese dedotte 131
spese, deduzione fatta delle ~ 131
spese, defalcando le ~ 621
spese d'esercizio 472, 1850
spese, detratte le ~ 131
spese, detrazione fatta delle ~ 131
spese di, a ~ 1260
spese di amministrazione 79
spese di banca 291
spese di bilancio 446
spese di cassa 582
spese di consumo 748
spese di emissione 1353
spese di gestione 79, 1850
spese di manutenzione 810
spese d'immobilizzo 524
spese d'investimento 524
spese di rappresentanza 1169
spese di sostituzione 2091
spese di spedizione 2295
spese di trasferimento 812
spese di trasferta 2298
spese di trasporto 2295
spese diverse 1764
spese di viaggio 2298
spese effettive 55
spese effettuate 55
spese extra 61
spese finanziarie 1313
spese fisse 1336
spese fuori bilancio 1823
spese generali 1417
spese impreviste 754
spese in capitale 524
spese indeducibili 1049
spese indirette 1417
spese, meno le ~ 621
spese minute 1764
spese non incorporabili 1202
spese per consumi 748
spese, piccole ~ 1764
spese pubbliche 2003
spese semi-variabili 2164
spese, sotto deduzione delle ~ 621
spese straordinarie 61
spese supplementari 61
spese variabili 2346
spese varie 1764
spezzatura 1011
spezzatura d'azioni 1387
spiccare un assegno 1115
spiccare una tratta su qualcuno 1114
spicci 612
spiccioli 612
spinta inflazionistica 1558
spirale costi-prezzi 816
spirale deflazionistica 993
spirale dei prezzi e dei salari 2363
spirale inflazionistica 1559
spirale prezzi-salari 2363
spirare 1264
squilibrio 1062
S.R.L. 1690
stabilimento centrale 607
stabilimento principale 607
stabilire un prezzo 1033
stabilità dei cambi 1239
stabilità dei prezzi 1326
stabilità della moneta 903
stabilità monetaria 903
stabilito d'acquisto 425
stabilito di vendita 440
stabilizzazione dei prezzi 1969
stabilizzazione del corso 1237
stagflazione 2208
stagnante 508
stagnare 1663
stampiglia 2209
stampigliare 2210
stampigliatura di azioni 2212
standard di vita 1704
stanza di compensazione 649
stanziamenti destinati agli investimenti 1620
stanziamenti di bilancio 444
stanziamento 123, 182
stanziare 122, 181
stanziare nel bilancio 443
stasi 1130
statalizzare 1802
statalizzazione 1801
statistica 2220
statistica aziendale 1851
statistica interna d'impresa 1851
statistiche 2219
statizzare 1802
statizzazione 1801
stato 2217
stato assistenziale 2373
stato di ripartizione 799
stato finanziario 1319
stato sociale 2373
stellage 1108
stellagio 1108
sterilizzare 2222
sterilizzazione 2221
sterlina 2223
sterline bloccate 382
stima 176
stima approssimativa 184
stima globale 184
stimare 177
stipendio 2126
stipendio mensile 1787
stipendio mensuale 1787
stipendi, salari e ~ 1141
stock 1615
storno 281, 512
stretta creditizia 874
stretta finanziaria 1314
stretta monetaria 1314
strumento di credito 862
strumento fiscale 1332
struttura dei costi 817
struttura del bilancio 273
struttura finanziaria 561
studio del mercato 1740
subire una perdita 333
succursale 427
superare la sottoscrizione 1873
superare un credito 1201
supercongiuntura 413
supervalutare 1863
supervalutazione 1864
supplemento 60
supplemento di copertura 62
supplemento di credito 63
supplemento d'imposta 66
surplus 2244
surriscaldamento 1871
suscettibile di essere preso in pegno 9
sussidiare 2240
sussidiario 225
sussidio 1458
sussidio statale 1449
svalorizzare 1028
svalutare 1028
svalutarsi 970
svalutazione 1029
svalutazione della moneta 897
svalutazione monetaria 897
svendere 2158
svendita 2129
svilimento 1029
svilimento della moneta 896
svilimento monetario 896
svilire 1028
svilirsi 970
svincolo dei prezzi 971
svincolo doganale 645
swap, operazione ~ 2251
swing 864
switch 2253

tabella 2256

tagliando 828
tagliando di controllo 821
tagliando di dividendo 1078
tagliare le spese 915
taglio 1011
talloncino di controllo 821
talloncino di dividendo 1078
tallone aureo 1441
tallone claudicante 1476
tallone, doppio ~ 375
tallone d'oro 1441
tallone unico 1785
tallone zoppo 1476
tantième 1923
tanto per cento 1921
tariffa 2260
tariffa di favore 1947
tariffa differenziale 1041
tariffa doganale 922
tariffa (doganale) esterna 1279
tariffa esterna comune 699
tariffa graduale 1041
tariffa mobile 1041
tariffa preferenziale 1947
tariffa preferenziale per i membri del Commonwealth 702
tariffa scalare 1041
tassa 614, 1135
tassa amministrativa 80
tassabile 196
tassa di bollo 2211
tassa di compensazione 712
tassa di conguaglio 247, 712
tassa di lusso 1723
tassa di monopolio 1245
tassa di perequazione 712
tassa di registro 2077
tassa di riporto 569
tassa di successione 938
tassa di trascrizione 812
tassa di trasferimento 812
tassa di trasmissione 812
tassa, prima della ~ 1959
tassare 177, 194, 195
tassa sugli articoli di lusso 1723
tassa sui soprapprofitti 1214
tassa sui sovrapprofitti 1214
tassazione 176, 2265
tassazione doppia 1109
tasse, dedotte le ~ 1677
tasso 2021
tasso a contanti 2024
tasso d'acquisto 354
tasso d'ammortamento 144, 145
tasso degli investimenti 1629
tasso del cambio 1216
tasso del denaro 1782
tasso dell'imposta 2023
tasso d'emissione 1642
tasso d'espansione 1255
tasso di base 328
tasso di cambio 1216
tasso di cambio a contanti 2024
tasso di cambio a termine 1383
tasso di cambio di biglietti e monete 1235
tasso di cambio fisso 1341
tasso di cambio flessibile 1347
tasso di cambio flottante 1347
tasso di cambio fluttuante 1347
tasso (di cambio) forzoso 722
tasso di cambio incrociato 884
tasso di cambio libero 1347
tasso di cambio oscillante 1347
tasso di cambio preferenziale 1950
tasso di cambio variabile 1347
tasso di conversione 778
tasso di deprezzamento 144
tasso d'imposizione 2023
tasso d'imposta 2023
tasso d'incremento 1255
tasso d'inflazione 1563
tasso d'interesse 1593
tasso d'interesse nominale 1821
tasso d'interesse sul prestito 423
tasso d'investimento 1629
tasso di provvigione 691
tasso di rendimento 2025
tasso di rendita 2025
tasso di riporto 569
tasso di risconto 2059
tasso di risparmio 2026
tasso di sconto 1061
tasso di sconto bancario 311
tasso di sviluppo 1255
tasso di vendita 193
tasso fisso, a ~ 1338
tasso monetario 1782
tasso nominale 1821
tasso sui prestiti garantiti 2022
tasso sui prestiti su pegno 2022
tasso sulle anticipazioni su titoli 1714
tasso sulle anticipazioni su valori 1714
tasso sul mercato libero 1396
tasso ufficiale di banca 311
tasso (ufficiale) di sconto 311
tasso unitario 1345
tavola 2256
tavola d'ammortamento 146
tendenza 1200
tendenza al rialzo 459
tendenza al ribasso 344
tendenza deflazionistica 994
tendenza generale, essere contrario alla ~ 2120
tenere i conti 1656
tenere i libri 1656
tenere la contabilità 1656
tenore di vita 1704
tenore d'oro 1434
tenuta dei libri 20
tenuta della contabilità 20
termine 1262
termine, a breve ~ 2177
termine, a lungo ~ 1715
termine, a medio ~ 1752
termine di grazia 998
termine di liquidazione 18
termine di pagamento 1924
termine di preavviso 1836
termine di rispetto 998
termine di scadenza 931, 1263
termine di sottoscrizione 2237
termine (di validità) 894
terzo debitore 1413
terzo pignorato 1413
terzo sequestrato 1413
tesaurizzare 1492
tesaurizzazione 1493
tesoreria 2299
tesoro pubblico 2299
timbro 2209
tipo, doppio ~ 375
tipo d'oro 1441
tipo unico 1785
tirare a sorte 1112
titolare 336
titolare d'azioni 2171
titolare di obbligazioni 390
titolare di un conto 26
titolare di valori 2171
titoli 2151
titoli al portatore 342
titoli ammessi alla quotazione 1699
titoli commerciabili 1739
titoli dati in garanzia 1895
titoli dati in pegno 1895
titoli del debito pubblico consolidato 734
titoli di borsa 1699
titoli di listino 1699
titoli d'investimento 1630
titoli di prim'ordine 387
titoli di speculazione 2199
titoli di stato 1244
titoli di tutto riposo 387
titoli impegnati 1895
titoli in portafoglio 1630
titoli mobiliari 1739
titoli negoziabili 1739
titoli nominativi 1568
titoli non quotati (in bolsa) 892
titoli pignorati 1895
titoli pubblici 1244
titoli quotati (in bolsa) 1699
titoli senza valore 2345
titoli sicuri(ssimi) 387
titoli speculativi 2199
titoli tenuti in pegno 1895
titoli trasferibili 1739
titolo all'ordine 1806
titolo al portatore 340
titolo a reddito fisso 1339
titolo azionario 2170
titolo d'azione (azioni) 2170
titolo di credito 862
titolo di debito 609
titolo di prestito 1709
titolo di rendita 162
titolo ipotecario 1792
titolo (legale) 1325
titolo negoziabile 1806
titolo (obbligazionario) 389
titolo pagabile a vista 1007
titolo provvisorio 1597
totale complessivo 105
totale del bilancio 276
totale generale 105
totalizzare 106
tracollo 668
tracollo dei corsi 431
tracollo dei prezzi 431

traente 1118
tranche 1572
transazione 320, 718
transazione a contanti 581
transazione a doppio premio 1108
transazione a premio 1855
transazione a rate 1489
transazione a termine 1379
transazione a termine su divise 1381
transazione a vista 1379
transazione di baratto 327
transazione di cambio a (in) (per) contanti 2202
transazione di cambio a termine 1381
transazione di compensazione 327
transazione facoltativa d'acquisto 485
transazione facoltativa di vendita 1857
transazione in contanti 581
transazione per contanti 581
transazione rateale 1489
transazione sul disponibile 581
transazione switch 2253
transazione triangolare 2253
transazioni bancarie 304
transazioni con assegni 632
transazioni con l'estero 1358
transazioni di banca 304
transazioni di cambio 1241
transazioni di clearing 643
transazioni di compensazione 643
transazioni di credito 851
transazioni in cambi 1241
transazioni in valuta 1241
transazioni su divise 1241
transazioni sui cambi 1241
tra(n)sferire 118, 2080
trapasso 119
trarre allo scoperto (su un conto) 1868
trarre una cambiale su qualcuno 1114
trarre un assegno 1115
trasferibile 117
trasferibilità 116
trasferimenti correnti, saldo dei ~ 257
trasferimento 119, 2293
trasferimento all'estero 1372
trasferimento bancario 318
trasferimento di capitali 563
trasferimento di crediti 208
trasferimento di denaro 1784
trasferimento di fondi 1784
trasferire un credito 207
trasmettere 118
trasmissibile 117
trasmissibilità 116
trasmissione 119
trassato 1117
tratta 356
tratta a vista 1003
tratta bancaria 284
trattare affari 1084
trattario 1117
tratta sull'estero 1357
tratta sull'interno 1091
trattato di clearing 647
trattato di compensazione 647
trattenere alla fonte 972
trattenuta alla fonte 975
trattenuta all'origine 681, 975
trattenuta d'acconto 681
trattenuta d'imposte alla fonte 681
trattenuta per rivalsa 681
traveller's cheque 2297
tresoreria 227
tributo 1135
trilione 367
trimestre 2016
trust 2304
trustee 1298

UEP 1198
ufficio cambi 1217
ufficio cambio 1217
ufficio centrale 607
ufficio di mediazione 439
ufficio principale 607
unificare un debito 733
unione di credito 787
unione doganale 923
Unione Economica Belga-Lussemburghese 348
Unione Europea dei Pagamenti 1198
unità di conto 31
unità di costo 818
unità monetaria 904
usanza 2333
uscita di capitali 556
uscite 1053
uscite di cassa 582
uscite, entrate ed ~ 1525
uso 2333
usufrutto 2334
usura 2337, 2366, 2367
utile 1409
utile contabile 412
utile, dare un ~ 100
utile da ripartire 1072
utile d'esercizio 475
utile di capitale 530
utile di coniatura 2154
utile fiscale 197
utile fittizio 171
utile immaginario 171
utile lordo 1459
utile netto 646
utile per azione 1142
utile presunto 166
utile riportato 1985
utile sperato 166
utile sui cambi 1233
utili 229
utili accantonati 2108
utili indivisi 2311
utili non distributi 2108
utili non prelevati 2108
utili non ripartiti 2311
utilità 1409
utilizzare le riserve 1042
utilizzare un prestito 1122
utilizzo di crediti 228
vaglia bancario 284
vaglia cambiario 356, 1477
vaglia di giro postale 1781
vaglia postale 1781
validità 894
valore 1011
valore aggiunto dall'industria 2340
valore alla pari 1889
valore a reddito fisso 1339
valore attuale 912
valore capitalizzato 546
valore catastale 199
valore commerciale 688
valore complessivo 108
valore contabile 32
valore corrente 912, 913
valore d'acquisto 50
valore del cambio 1234
valore del reddito (potenziale) 546
valore di avviamento 1444
valore di bilancio 277
valore di borsa 1234
valore di cambio della moneta 1364
valore dichiarato 967
valore di costo 50
valore di inventario 1617
valore di liquidazione 432
valore di mercato 688
valore di realizzo 432
valore di rendita 162
valore di rimborso 2055
valore di rimpiazzo 2091
valore di riscatto 2055, 2247
valore di scambio 1219
valore di sostituzione 2091
valore di vendita 688
valore eccessivo 1215
valore effettivo 56
valore fiscale 198
valore globale 108
valore imponibile 198
valore in oro 1442
valore intrinseco 1612
valore lordo 1468
valore, minor ~ 969
valore negoziabile 1806
valore netto 1809, 1817
valore netto di una proprietà 1177
valore nominale 1289, 1889
valore nominale di una azione 1290
valore oro 1442
valore reale 56
valore residuo 2103
valore rimanente 2103
valore standard 2213
valore totale 108
valore unitario 2213
valore venale 688
valori 1646, 2151
valori al portatore 342
valori ammessi alla quotazione 1699
valori commerciabili 1739
valori di borsa 1699
valori d'investimento 1630
valori di prim'ordine 387
valori di speculazione 2199
valori disponibili 227
valori di tutto riposo 387

valori esteri 1370
valori immateriali 1505
valori immobiliari 1508
valori in contanti 577
valori in portafoglio 1630
valori intangibili 1505
valori mobiliari 622, 1739
valori negoziabili 1739
valori nominativi 1568
valori non quotati (in bolsa) 892
valori quotati (in bolsa) 1699
valori sicuri(ssimi) 387
valori speculativi 2199
valori trasferibili 1739
valorizzare 2339
valorizzazione 2338
valuta 893, 2343
valuta al 1 gennaio 2342
valuta aurea 1402
valuta debole 2187
valuta del paese 1094
valuta dura 1479
valuta estera 1361
valuta forte 1479
valuta nazionale 1094
valuta oro 1402
valuta pregiata 1479
valutare 177, 195
valutazione 176
valutazione approssimativa 184
valutazione (fiscale) 200
valutazione (tributaria) 200
vantaggio fiscale 2263
vantaggioso 1147
varie 1764
velocità di circolazione 2027
vendere 2157
vendere a credito 2163
vendere a fido 2163
vendere all'asta 213
vendere all'incanto 213
vendere allo scoperto 1427
vendere a minor prezzo 2317
vendere a perdita 2158
vendere a termine 2161
vendere con perdita 2158
vendibile 1738
vendita 2127
vendita a contanti 598
vendita a credito 875
vendita all'asta 212
vendita all'incanto 212
vendita allo scoperto 346
vendita a perdita 2129
vendita a rate 1491
vendita con diritto di riacquisto 2132
vendita con diritto di riscatto 2132
vendita con perdita 2129
vendita per contanti 598
vendite 2130
venditore 2159
venire a scadenza 347
verifica dei conti 214
verifica fiscale 1566
verificare 215
verificatore (dei conti) 216
verificazione dei conti 214
versamento 1567
versamento anticipato 92
versamento di capitale 1909
versamento di fondi 1784
versare 1015, 2080
versare al fondo di riserva 68
versare alla riserva 68
vigilanza sui prezzi 1961
vil prezzo 322
vincolo ipotecario 1793
vista, a ~ 1956
vistare un assegno 610
vitale 2350
vitalità 2349
vitalizio 163
vivere al di sopra dei propri mezzi 1702
vivere alla meglio 1703
voce 409
voce attiva 857
voce de conguaglio 281
voce del dare 946
voce dell'attivo 857
voce d'entrata 857
voce passiva 946
volume d'affari 2130
volume degli affari di borsa 2225
volume degli scambi (commerciali) 2354
volume del comercio 2354
volume di credito 881
volume di risparmio 2353
volume monetario 1783

warrant 2364

zecca 1761
zona del dollaro 1086
zona del franco 1388
zona della sterlina 2224
zona di libero scambio 1398
zona di vendita 1736

NEDERLANDS

aanbesteden 1635
aanbesteding geven, in ~ 1635
aanbetaling 1014
aanbieden, een lening ter inschrijving ~ 1634
aanbieden, te koop ~ 1841
aanbieder 337
aanbieding 352
aanbod 352
aanbod, te groot ~ 1210
aanbod tot betalingsregeling 1844
aanbod, vraag en ~ 2242
aanbreken, de reserves ~ 1042
aandeel 2169
aandeel aan toonder 343
aandeelbewijs 2170
aandeel, bonus~ 400
aandeelcertificaat 2170
aandeel fourneren, X % op een ~ 1899
aandeel, garantie~ 2015
aandeel, gratis~ 400
aandeelhouder 2171
aandeelhouder, belangrijke ~ 633
aandeelhouder, geregistreerde ~ 2076
aandeelhouder, hoofd~ 633
aandeelhoudersboek 1701
aandeelhoudersregister 1701
aandeelhouder van een gemeenschappelijk beleggingsfonds 2327
aandeel in de opbrengst 1686
aandeel, interim~ 1597
aandeel met blokkeringsclausule 2282
aandeel met meervoudig stemrecht 1796
aandeel, onder~ 2230
aandeel, preferent ~ 1946
aandeel, prioriteits~ 1946
aandeel storten, X % op een ~ 1899
aandeel, uitgesteld ~ 985
aandeel van de commanditair 1591
aandeel volfourneren, een ~ 1915
aandeel volstorten, een ~ 1915
aandeel, voorlopig ~ 1597
aandeel, winst~ 2173
aandelen, arbeiders~ 1159
aandelenbewijs 2170
aandelenbezit 1628
aandelenbezitter 2171
aandelencertificaat 2170
aandelenfractie 1387
aandelen, gewone ~ 701
aandelenkapitaal 544
aandelenkapitaal, geëmitteerd ~ 1638
aandelenkapitaal, gewoon ~ 697
aandelenkapitaal, uitgegeven ~ 1638
aandelenkapitaal verkleinen, het ~ 2061
aandelenkapitaal verminderen, het ~ 2061
aandelenkapitaal, verwaterd ~ 2365
aandelenkoers 2174
aandelenmarkt 2153
aandelen met stemrecht 2357
aandelen, nieuwe ~ 1819
aandelen op naam 1568
aandelen, oprichters~ 1386
aandelenpakket 386
aandelenportefeuille 1628
aandelenregister 1701
aandelenrendement 1082
aandelenruil 1232
aandelensplitsing 2175
aandelen, volgefourneerde ~ 1403
aandelen, volgestorte ~ 1403
aandelen voor inbreng in natura 1386
aandelen zonder nominale waarde 1831
aandelen zonder stemrecht 1830
aangaan, een lening ~ 762
aangaan, een schuld ~ 761
aangaan van schulden in het buitenland 420
aangeboden prijs 1843
aangegeven waarde 967
aangifte, belasting~ 2275
aangifte, douane~ 919
aangifte inkomstenbelasting 1531
aangifte, voorlopige ~ 2000
aankondigen, een dividend ~ 965
aankondiging, dividend~ 964
aankoop 2012
aankoop, dekkings~ 839
aankoopkoers 354
aankoop op afbetaling 1573
aankoopprijs 488
aankoop, speculatieve ~ 2198
aankoopwaarde 50
aankopen 479
aanleggen, een reserve ~ 454
aanmoediging, fiscale ~ 2270
aanmunten 662
aanmunting 663
aannemen, een wissel ~ 8
aanpassen 70
aanpassing 72
aanpassing der belastingen 1175
aanpassing, reële ~ 74
aanpassingsinflatie 59
aanpassing van de prijzen 76
aanpassing van de wisselkoers 75
aanrekenen 570, 615
aanrekenen, te weinig ~ 2316
aanrekening 613
aanschaffen 48
aanschaffing 49
aanschaffingskosten 488, 804
aanschaffingsprijs 488
aanschaffingswaarde 50
aanslaan 195
aanslag 200
aanslag, ambtshalve ~ 1188
aanslagbiljet 1839
aanslag op basis van schatting 1188
aansprakelijkheid 1681
aansprakelijkheid, beperkte ~ 1689
aansprakelijkheid, contractuele ~ 763
aansprakelijkheid, hoofdelijke ~ 1652
aansprakelijkheid, niet contractuele ~ 1824
aansprakelijkheid, onbeperkte ~ 2329
aansprakelijkheid, solidaire ~ 1652
aanspreken, de reserves ~ 1042
aantrekken van kapitaal 1405
aantrekken van middelen 1405
aanvangskapitaal 1564
aanvraag, krediet~ 173
aanvraag, lening~ 173
aanvraag, op ~ 495
aanvrage, faillissements~ 316
aanvrage, krediet~ 173
aanvrage, lening~ 173
aanvragen, een krediet ~ 175
aanvragen, een lening ~ 175
aanvrager van (een) krediet 172
aanvrager van een lening 172
aanvullend dividend 398
aanvullende belasting 66
aanvullende dekking 62
aanvullende marge 62
aanvullen, de reserve ~ 2039
aanvullende zekerheid 65
aanvullingskrediet 63
aanwending van kapitaal 1160
aanwijzen 181
aanwijzen, een verlies (een winst) ~ 2046
aanwijzing, bank~ 284
aanwijzing, betalings~ 590
aanzuiveren 148
aanzuivering 139
accept 10
acceptant 14
acceptatie 10
accept, bank~ 284
accept, beleefdheids~ 15
accepteren, een wissel ~ 8
accept, handels~ 2286
accepthuis 12
acceptkrediet 11
acceptprovisie 13
accijns 752
accommodatiewissel 15
accoordloon 1907
accountancy 20
accountant 21
accountantsrapport 217
accountantsverslag 217
accrediteren, iemand ~ 1847
accreditief 1678
accreditief, documentair ~ 1085
accumulatie 38, 44
accumuleren 40, 43
achterborg 238
achterborgtocht 238
achter(en), ten ~ 189
achterman 2239
achterop 189
achterstallig 189, 1869
achterstallige 188
achterstallige int(e)rest 190
achterstallige rente 190
achterstallige schulden 188
achterstand 152, 188
achteruitgang 968

achteruitgang, koers~ 886
achteruitgang, prijs~ 886
actief 202
actief en passief 203
actief, lopend ~ 905
actief, netto~ 1809
actief-rekening 201
actief saldo 849
actief schrijven, op het ~ 403
actiefzijde 206
actieve balans 275
actieve handelsbalans 53
actieve schuld 37
actionair 2171
actionaris 2171
activa 202
activa, af te schrijven ~ 1027
activa en passiva 203
activa, fictieve ~ 1297
activa, immateriële ~ 1505
activa in het buitenland 204
activa, liquide ~ 227
activa, materiële duurzame ~ 518
activa, netto ~ 1809
activa, onaantastbare ~ 1505
activa, realiseerbare ~ 905
activa, reële ~ 1747
activa, stoffelijke ~ 1747
activa, vaste ~ 518
activeren 403
activeren, te ~ 408
actuaris 58
actuele waarde 912
additionele zekerheid 65
administrateur 410
administratiekantoor 2306
administratiekosten 79
administratieve provisie 80
ad valorem recht 82
advies, betalings~ 97
advies, credit~ 847
advies, stortings~ 97
adviseur, belasting~ 2264
adviseur, financiële ~ 1309
adviseur, wiskundig ~ 58
afbetalen 148
afbetalen, een hypot(h)eek ~ 511
afbetaling 1571
afbetaling kopen, op ~ 481
afbetaling, maandelijkse ~ 1788
afbetaling, op ~ 987
afbetalingskrediet 1488
afbetalingstransactie 1489
afbetalingszaak 1489
afboeken, een vordering ~ 2379
afbrokkeling, koers~ 886
afbrokkeling, prijs~ 886
afdoen 148
afdoening 139
affaire 320
affaire, contant~ 581
affaire, dont~ 1855
affaire in deviezen, contant~ 2202
affaire in kopers keuze, noch~ 485
affaire in valuta, contant~ 2202
affaire in verkopers keuze, noch~ 1857
affaire, loco~ 581
affaire, meta-~ 1653
affaire met noch in kopers keuze, premie~ 485
affaire met noch in verkopers keuze, premie~ 1857
affaire met noch te leveren, premie~ 485
affaire met noch te ontvangen, premie~ 1857
affaire, premie~ 1855
affaire, swap~ 2251
affaire, termijn~ 1379
affaire, tijd~ 1379
affaire, valutatermijn~ 1381
afgesleten 2378
afgeven, een cheque ~ 1115
afgeven, een wissel op iemand ~ 1114
afhalen 1113
afhaling 1119
afhaling in contanten 601
afhouden, aan de bron ~ 972
afhouding aan de bron 975
afkoopbaar 2052
afkoopbaarheid 2051
afkoopbare obligatie 497
afkoopgeld 708
afkoopsom 708
afkoopwaarde 2247
afkopen 479
afkoper 482
afloop 1262
aflopen 347, 1264
aflosbaar 2052
aflosbaar door loting 498
aflosbaarheid 2051
aflosbare hypot(h)ecaire lening, in termijnen ~ 137
aflosbare lening 141
aflosbare obligatie 497
aflosbare schuld 1574
aflossen 148, 502
aflossen, een hypot(h)eek ~ 511
aflossing 139, 1571, 2053
aflossing, maandelijkse ~ 1788
aflossingsfonds 140
aflossingskoers 2054
aflossingsplan 146
aflossingspremie 1750
aflossingsprijs 2054
aflossingswaarde 2055
aflossing van een lening 142
afnemen 479
afnemende afschrijving 7
afnemer 482
afrekenen 148
afrekening 139, 254, 429
afremmen, de inflatie ~ 628
afroepkrediet 2214
afschaffing van beperkingen 2
afschrift van een rekening(-courant) 5
afschrijven 147
afschrijving 138
afschrijving, afnemende ~ 7
afschrijving, degressieve ~ 7
afschrijving, fiscale ~ 517
afschrijving, jaarlijkse ~ 157
afschrijving, lineaire ~ 2228
afschrijving op basis van de vervangingswaarde 143
afschrijving op basis van technische slijtage 1030
afschrijving, progressieve ~ 1545
afschrijvingsfonds 132
afschrijvingslasten 620
afschrijvingspercentage 144
afschrijvingsreserve 132
afschrijvingsvoet 144
afschrijving, technische ~ 1030
afschrijving, toenemende ~ 1545
afschrijving, variabele ~ 2347
afschrijving, vaste ~ 2228
afschrijving, wisselende ~ 2347
afslag 127
afslag, prijs~ 927
afsluiten, de boeken ~ 278
afsluiten, een balans ~ 279
afsluiten, een lening ~ 762
afsluiten, een rekening ~ 652
afsluiting van een rekening 655
afsluitnota 425, 440
afspraak inzake zelfbeperking 2355
afspraak, prijs~ 115
afstaan 118
afstand 119
afstemmen, rekeningen ~ 112
afstemming van rekeningen 2043
afstempelen 2210
afstempeling van aandelen 2212
af te schrijven activa 1027
aftrek aan de bron 975
aftrekbaar verlies 974
aftrek, belasting~ 2261
aftrekken, aan de bron ~ 972
aftrekken, vooraf ~ 973
aftrek van de belasting(en), na ~ 1677
aftrek van de belasting(en), voor ~ 1959
aftrek van de kosten, na ~ 131
aftrek van de kosten, onder ~ 621
aftrek van de onkosten, na ~ 131
aftrek van de onkosten, onder ~ 621
afvloeiing van kapitaal 556
afwerpen, een rente van X procent ~ 334
afwerpen, een winst ~ 100
afzetgebied 1736
afzetmarkt 1736
afzetten 2157
agenda, vervaldag~ 359
agent 104
agentschap 103
agentschap, wissel~ 1217
agentuur 103
agent, wissel~ 2152
agio 109, 110
agio doen 1883
agio, emissie~ 1641
agiotage 111
agioteur 1647
akkoord 718
akkoordloon 1907
akkoord, vergelijkings~ 719

akte, trust~ 976
akte van borgtocht 394
algemene kosten 1417
algemene onkosten 1417
Algemene Overeenkomst inzake Tarieven en Handel 1415
alleenhandel 1786
allocatie 123
allocatie van middelen, onjuiste ~ 1763
allonge 124
alternatieve kosten 1853
ambtshalve aanslag 1188
amortisatie 138, 139, 2053
amortisatiefonds 140
amortisatielening 141
amortisatiepercentage 144, 145
amortisatieplan 146
amortisatietabel 146
amortisatietafel 146
amortisatie van een lening 142
amortisatievoet 144, 145
amortiseerbaar 2052
amortiseerbare hypot(h)eek 137
amortiseerbare obligatie 497
amortiseren 147, 148, 502
amortiseren, een hypot(h)eek ~ 511
amortiseren, een vordering ~ 2379
amortizatie 138, 139, 2053
amortizeren 147, 148, 502
analyse, cost benefit ~ 801
analyse, kosten-baten ~ 801
analyse, markt~ 1740
analytische exploitatieboekhouding 798
anatocisme 156
andere inkomsten 1765
annuïteit 161
antedateren 164
anticyclisch 168
antidateren 164
antidumpingrecht 169
anti-inflationistisch 170
anti-inflatoir 170
appreciatie 180
arbeidersaandelen 1159
arbeidsinkomen 1136
arbeidskosten 806
arbeidsloos inkomen 2323
arbitrage, deviezen~ 186
arbitrage, goud~ 185
arbitrage, koers~ 186
arbitrage, valuta-~ 186
arbitrage, wissel~ 186, 369
arrest 191
arrest, derden~ 1414
arresteren 211
artikelen, export~ 1266
artikelen, import~ 1510
artikelen, invoer~ 1510
artikelen, luxe~ 1001
artikelen, uitvoer~ 1266
artikelen, weelde~ 1001
assignatie, bank~ 284
auctie 212
austeriteit 218
autarkie 219
autoconsumptie 1497
autofinanciering 1601
aval 230
avaleren, een wissel ~ 235
aval geven voor een wissel 235
avalgever 236
avalist 236
avalkrediet 853
aval tekenen, een wissel voor ~ 235
avondbeurs 102

baar geld 572
baar geld betalen, in ~ 1727
baar, in ~ 573
baisse 1031
baissemarkt 345
baisseneiging 344
baissepremie 1953
baissespeculant 332
baisse speculeren, à la ~ 1427
baissestemming 344
baissetendens 344
baisseverkoop 346
baissier 332
balanceren 279
balans 246, 270
balans, actieve ~ 275
balans afsluiten, een ~ 279
balans, betalings~ 260
balansblad 270
balansboek 250
balansdatum 272
balans, deficitaire ~ 274
balans, economische ~ 1148
balans, goederen~ 264
balans, goederen- en diensten~ 259
balans, handels~ 264
balans, kas~ 253
balans, nadelige ~ 274
balans, openings~ 1700
balans opmaken, een ~ 279
balans opstellen, een ~ 279
balans, passieve ~ 274
balans, proef~ 2303
balansrekening 271
balans, slot~ 1302
balans, sluitings~ 1302
balanstelling 276
balanstotaal 276
balans, tussentijdse ~ 1596
balans van de overdrachten 267
balans, voordelige ~ 275
balans, voorlopige ~ 1596
balanswaarde 277
bank 282
bankaanwijzing 284
bankabel papier 283
bankaccept 284
bankassignatie 284
bankbedrijf 301
bankbiljet 287
bankbiljettencirculatie 308
bankbiljetten in omloop 308
bankboekje 289
bankbreuk 315
bank, centrale ~ 606
bank, circulatie~ 309
bankclearing 292
bank, clearing~ 648
bankcommissie 293
bankconsortium 303
bankdeposito 297
bank, deposito~ 1020
bankdisconto 311
bank, disconto~ 1058
bank, effecten~ 1645
bank, emissie~ 309, 1645
bank, Europese Investerings~ 1195
bankgeheim 305
bankgeld 307
bankgiro 318
bank, giro~ 648
bank, grondkrediet~ 1660
bank, handels~ 310
bank, hypot(h)eek~ 1660
bankiersfirma 294
bankiershuis 294
bankinstelling 294
bank, Interamerikaanse Ontwikkelings~ 1581
bank, investerings~ 1621
bankkosten 291
bankkrediet 295
bank, krediet~ 850
bank, leen~ 850
banklening 298
bankmaatschappij 302
bankmaatschappij op aandelen 1536
bankmandaat 284
banknoot 287
bankobligatie 288
bankonkosten 291
bank, ontwikkelings~ 1035
bank op aandelen 1536
bankopdracht 299
bankoperaties 304
bankoverboeking 318
bankoverschrijving 318
bank, particuliere ~ 1974
bank, postspaar~ 1941
bank, privé-~ 1974
bankprovisie 293
bankrekening 285
bankrente 306
bankroet 314, 315
bankroetier 313
banksaldo 286
banksaldobevestiging 290
bankschulden 296
bank, spaar~ 2139
bankstaat 312
banksyndicaat 303
banktegoed 286
banktraite 284
banktransacties 304
bankvereniging 302
bankverrichtingen 304
bank voor buitenlandse handel 1371
Bank voor Herstel en Ontwikkeling, Internationale ~ 1602
Bank voor Internationale Betalingen 300
bankvoorschot 298
bank, voorschot~ 850
Bank voor Wederopbouw en Ontwikkeling, Internationale ~ 1602

bankvorderingen 296
bank, Wereld~ 1602
bankwezen 301
bank, wissel~ 12
bankwissel 284
bank, wissel~ 1058, 1220
bankzaken 304
basisrente 328
basisvoet 328
baten 229
baten, bijzondere ~ 1765
batig saldo 849
bedienen, een lening ~ 2165
bedrag 149
bedrag, bruto~ 1460
bedrag crediteren, iemand voor een ~ 566
bedrag, forfaitair ~ 1722
bedrag, gezamenlijk ~ 107
bedrag, globaal ~ 107
bedrag goedschrijven, iemand voor een ~ 566
bedrag in iemands tegoed schrijven, een ~ 566
bedrag in (op) iemands credit boeken, een ~ 566
bedrag, inschrijvings~ 153
bedrag, minder ~ 988
bedrag, netto~ 1808
bedrag, nog verschuldigd ~ 252
bedrag, nominaal ~ 1820
bedrag, onbetaald ~ 154
bedrag, overschietend ~ 1205
bedrag, resterend ~ 246
bedrag, totaal ~ 107
bedrag, uitstaand ~ 152
bedrag van opgenomen kredieten, netto~ 1810
bedrag van toegestane kredieten, netto~ 1812
bedrag, verschuldigd ~ 151
bedrijf 467
bedrijf, bank~ 301
bedrijf, factoors~ 1293
bedrijf, openbaar ~ 1448
bedrijf, overheids~ 1448
bedrijf, particulier ~ 1977
bedrijf, privé-~ 1977
bedrijf, regie~ 1454
bedrijfsbelasting 476
bedrijfsboekhouding 798
bedrijfsjaar 478
bedrijfskapitaal 468
bedrijfskapitaal, vlottend ~ 468
bedrijfsklimaat 469
bedrijfskosten 1850
bedrijfsonkosten 1850
bedrijfsoverschot 1852
bedrijf, staats~ 1448
bedrijfstekort 474
bedrijfsverlies 474
bedrijfswinst 475
bedrijf van openbaar nut 2009
beginkapitaal 1564
beginkoers 1849
begrenzen, de uitgaven ~ 915
begroting 441
begroting brengen, op de ~ 443
begroting, conjuncturele ~ 929
begroting, deficitaire ~ 95
begroting, financierings~ 1312
begroting, gewone ~ 1859
begroting in evenwicht brengen, de ~ 280
begroting, investerings~ 519
begroting, jaarlijkse ~ 159
begroting, nationale ~ 1446
begroting (om), buiten de ~ 1286
begroting, openbare ~ 1446
begroting, overheids~ 1446
begrotings- 442
begrotingsbeheer 450
begrotingsdeficit 95
begrotingsevenwicht 251
begrotingsgelden 444
begrotingsinkomsten 447
begrotingsjaar 448
begrotingskredieten 444
begroting, sluitende ~ 251
begroting sluitend maken, de ~ 280
begrotingsontvangsten 447
begrotingsoverschot 452
begrotingsprognosen 451
begroting, staats~ 1446
begrotingstekort 95
begrotingsuitgaven 446
begroting van de Gemeenschap 703
begunstigde 350
behandelingskosten 1478
beheer, begrotings~ 450
beheer, financieel ~ 730
beheerfonds 2307
beheer, in ~ 1185
beheer, kapitaal~ 1044
beheerloon 80
beheer, schuld~ 954
beheersing, prijs~ 1961
beheerskosten 79
beherend vennoot 1419
behoefte, kapitaal~ 557
behoefte, leen~ 424
behoefte, lenings~ 424
behoeften, dekkings~ 837
behoeften, financierings~ 1316
behoeften, investerings~ 1627
behoeften, kas~ 596
behoeften, liquiditeits~ 596
behoefte, vermogens~ 557
bekentenis, schuld~ 46, 389, 1477
beladen, met schulden ~ 466
belang (in) 1495
belang, meerderheids~ 770
belang, minderheids~ 1760
belangrijke aandeelhouder 633
belastbaar 196
belastbaar inkomen 2262
belastbaar, niet ~ 1247
belastbare grondslag 331
belastbare waarde 198
belastbare winst 197
belasten 194, 613, 615
belasten, met een hypot(h)eek ~ 465
belasten, met schulden ~ 466
belasting 1135, 2265
belasting, aan de bron ingehouden ~ 2268
belastingaangifte 2275
belastingaanslag 200
belasting, aanvullende ~ 66
belastingadviseur 2264
belastingaftrek 2261
belastingaftrek, na ~ 1677
belastingaftrek, voor ~ 1959
belasting, bedrijfs~ 476
belastingbetaler 2028
belastingbiljet 1839
belastingconcessie 2263
belasting, consumptieve ~ 752
belasting, degressieve ~ 997
belastingdienst 1242
belasting, directe ~ 1046
belasting, dividend- en coupon~ 565
belastingdruk 463
belasting, dubbele ~ 1109
belasting, egalisatie~ 712
belastingen, na ~ 1677
belastingen, voor ~ 1959
belasting, extra~ 66
belastingfraude 2266
belastinggroep 2267
belasting, grond~ 1662
belasting heffen (op), een ~ 194
belastingheffing 1516, 2265
belastingheffing, dubbele ~ 1109
belastinghervorming 2274
belasting, indirecte ~ 1552
belasting, inkomsten~ 1530
belastinginkomsten 1565
belasting innen, een ~ 678
belastinginning 683
belasting invorderen, een ~ 678
belastingjaar 1335
belasting, kapitaal~ 551
belasting leggen (op), een ~ 194
belasting, luxe~ 1723
belasting, monopolie~ 1245
belasting, na ~ 1677
belasting, omzet~ 2014
belasting onderhevig, aan ~ 196
belasting onderworpen, aan ~ 196
belastingonderzoek 1566
belastingontduiking 2266
belastingontvangsten 1565
belastingontwijking 2266
belastingopbrengst 1565
belasting op de bedrijfswinst 1989
belasting op de buitengewone winsten 1214
belasting op de gerealiseerde waardestijging 532
belasting op de inkomsten uit kapitaal 565
belasting op de meerwaarde 532
belasting op de toegevoegde waarde 2341
belasting op de vennootschappen 792
belasting op het kapitaalinkomen 565
belasting op het kapitaalverkeer 564
belasting op het maatschappelijk kapitaal 560

belasting op immobiliën 1995
belasting op kapitaalwinst 532
belasting op luxeartikelen 1723
belasting op onroerende goederen 1995
belasting op overwinsten 1214
belasting, overwinst~ 1214
belastingplichtige 2028
belasting, progressieve ~ 1456
belasting, reële ~ 1995
belastingreserve 2001
belastingrestitutie 2038
belastingschijf 2267
belastingschuld 2271
belastingschuldige 2028
belasting(s)consulent 2264
belastingsplichtig 196
belastingstelsel 1334
belasting, successie~ 938
belastingsystem 1334
belastingtekort 1330
belastingterugbetaling 2038
belasting, vennootschaps~ 792
belasting, verbruiks~ 752
belastingverlichting 2261
belastingvermindering 2261
belasting, vermogens~ 551
belasting, vermogensaanwas~ 532
belastingverplichting 1683
belastingverplichting, latente ~ 759, 986
belastingvlucht 2266
belastingvoet 2023
belasting, voor ~ 1959
belastingvoordeel 2263
belastingvrij 1247
belastingvrijdom 1248
belastingvrijheid 1248
belasting, weelde~ 1723
belastingwezen 1242
belasting, winst~ 1989
belast, met schulden ~ 952
beleefdheidsaccept 15
beleenbaar 9
beleende effecten 1895
belegd kapitaal 541
beleggen 1618
belegger 1631
belegger, collectieve ~ 793
belegger, institutionele ~ 793
belegging 1619
belegging, buitenlandse ~ 1367, 1368
beleggingen ter beurze 1179
belegging in effecten 1626
belegging in het buitenland 1368
belegging in waardepapieren 1626
belegging, kapitaal~ 542
belegging met veranderlijk inkomen 2348
belegging, nieuwe ~ 1818
belegging, onjuiste ~ 244
belegging, openbare ~ 2006
belegging, particuliere ~ 1978
beleggingsfonds 1624
beleggingsinkomen 1528
beleggingskapitaal 1622
belegging, slechte ~ 244
beleggingsmaatschappij 653
beleggingspapieren 1630
beleggingstrust 653
beleggingswaarden 1630
belegging, vreemde ~ 1367
beleid, financieel ~ 730
beleid, geld~ 1769
beleid, krediet~ 872
beleid, monetair ~ 1769
belenen, effecten ~ 91, 671
beleningsrente op effecten 1714
beleningsrente op waardepapieren 1714
beleningsrentevoet 2022
belening van effecten 1501, 1674
Belgisch-Luxemburgse Economische Unie 348
belonen 2042
beloning 2041
bemoeiing, overheids~ 1452
benaderen 211
bepalen, een prijs ~ 1033
bepalingen, deviezen~ 900
bepaling, prijs~ 1962
bepaling van de pariteit 1032
bepaling, waarde~ 176
beperken, de uitgaven ~ 915
beperkingen afschaffen 1
beperkingen, afschaffing van ~ 2
beperkingen, deviezen~ 902
beperkingen opheffen 1
beperkingen, opheffing van ~ 2
beperking, invoer~ 1513
beperking, krediet~ 874
beperking, liquiditeits~ 2104
beperking, prijs~ 1968
beperkte aansprakelijkheid 1689
beraamde kosten 1189
berekenen 490, 570
berekenen, teveel ~ 1866
berekenen, te weinig ~ 2316
berekening 492
berekening, kosten~ 797
berekening, kostprijs~ 815
bericht 2217
bericht, beurs~ 1228
bericht, financieel ~ 1319
bericht, jaar~ 160
bericht, koers~ 1228
bericht, ontvangst~ 47
beroep doen, op de reserves ~ 1042
beroep doen, op een lening ~ 1122
beroep op de markt 506
bescheid, boekings~ 33
bescheid, kas~ 600
beschermend recht 1998
beschikbaarheid van kapitaal 226
beschikbaar inkomen 1068
beschikbaar stellen 181
beschikbaar stellen, kapitaal ~ 1407
beschikbaarstelling 182
beschikbaarstelling van kapitaal 1408
beschikbare middelen 227
beschikking stellen, kapitaal ter ~ 1407
beschrijving, boedel~ 1614
beslag 191
beslagene, derde ~ 1413
beslag leggen (op) 211
beslaglegging 191
beslag nemen, in ~ 211
beslag onder derden 1414
besloten vennootschap 1690
besnoeien, de uitgaven ~ 915
besparingen 2137
besparingen, binnenlandse bruto~ 1462
besparingen, contractuele ~ 764
besparingen, particuliere ~ 1980
besteding 182, 1258
besteding, consumenten~ 748
besteding, consumptieve ~ 748
besteding, gezins~ 1499
besteding, over~ 1212
bestedingsoverschot 1557
bestek 1187
bestek, ruw ~ 184
bestemmen 181
bestemming, winst~ 183
bestendigheid van de prijzen 1326
bestorming van de bank 2121
betaalbaar, contant ~ 1897
betaalbaar in buitenlandse valuta 1898
betaalbaar in deviezen 1898
betaalbaar op vertoon 1896
betaalbaar op zicht 1896
betaald 1879
betaaldag 24
betaalkrachtig 2190
betaalmiddelen 1751
betaalmiddelen, circulatie van ~ 638
betaalmiddel in circulatie brengen, als wettig ~ 1773
betaalmiddel, wettig ~ 1669
betaalstaat 1912
betaalstrook 1913
betalen 148
betalen, bij voorbaat ~ 1904
betalen, cash ~ 1727
betalen, contant ~ 1727
betalen, een dividend ~ 1051
betalen, een wissel ~ 1054
betalen, geheel ~ 1905
betalen, in baar geld ~ 1727
betalen kosten, te ~ 39
betalen, per cheque ~ 1901
betalen rekening, te ~ 36
betalen rente, te ~ 947
betalen wissel, te ~ 372
betaler 1903
betaler, belasting~ 2028
betaler, slechte ~ 245
betaling 139
betaling bij ontvangst, tegen ~ 589
betaling binnen de Gemeenschap 1611
betaling, contante ~ 591
betaling, dividend~ 1052
betalingen doen 1152
betalingen opschorten, de ~ 603
betalingen over X jaren echelonneren, de ~ 2204
betalingen over X jaren spreiden, de ~ 2204

betalingen over X jaren verdelen, de ~ 2204
betalingen schorsen, de ~ 603
betalingen staken, de ~ 603
betalingen verrichten 1152
betaling, extra~ 1288
betaling, gedeeltelijke ~ 1894
betaling, gehele ~ 715
betaling, int(e)rest~ 1592
betaling, niet-~ 982
betaling, non-~ 982
betaling op termijn 1910
betaling per cheque of overschrijving 588
betaling, rente~ 1592
betalingsaanwijzing 590
betalingsadvies 97
betalingsbalans 260
betalingsbalans, buitenlandse ~ 258
betalingsbalansdeficit 261
betalingsbalans(en), herstel van de ~ 794
betalingsbalans op lopende rekening 262
betalingsbalansoverschot 263
betalingsbalanstekort 261
betalingsbalans, totale ~ 1862
betalingscondities 2278
betalingsmandaat 590
betalingsopdracht 221
betalingsovereenkomst 1906
betalingsregeling, aanbod tot ~ 1844
betalingstermijn 1924
betalingstermijn verlengen, de ~ 1274
betalingsuitstel 1276
betalingsverkeer 1911
betalingsvoorwaarden 2278
betalingswijze 1375
betaling, termijn~ 1571
betaling, transfer~ 2293
betaling uitstellen, een ~ 984
betaling van een cheque opschorten, de ~ 2227
betaling van een cheque schorsen, de ~ 2227
betaling van het achterstallige 237
betaling van, tegen ~ 732
betaling verdagen, een ~ 984
betaling, vervroegde ~ 92
betaling, volledige ~ 715
betaling, voorlopige ~ 1999
betaling, voortijdige ~ 92
betaling, wan~ 982
betoon, dienst~ 2084
betrokkene 1117
beurs 1218
beurs, avond~ 102
beursbericht 1228
beursfondsen 1699
beurs genoteerde fondsen, aan de ~ 1699
beurs genoteerde waarden, aan de ~ 1699
beurs, goederen~ 695
beurs, handels~ 695
beurskoers 1234
beursmakelaar 2152
beursman 1647
beursmaneuver 1730
beursmanœuvre 1730
beurs, na~ 102
beursnotering 1234
beurs, officiële ~ 1845
beursomzet 2225
beursoperaties 1222
beursspeculant 1647
beursspeculatie 111
beursspel 111
beurstransacties 1222
beursverrichtingen 1222
beurswaarden 1699
beurszaken 1222
beurze genoteerde fondsen, ter ~ 1699
beurze genoteerde waarden, ter ~ 1699
beurze genoteerde waardepapieren, ter ~ 1699
bevestigen, een cheque ~ 610
bevestiging, banksaldo~ 290
bevestiging, ontvangst~ 47
bevoorrechte crediteur 1948
bevoorrechte schuldeiser 1948
bevordering van het sparen 1161
bevriezen 380
bevriezing 383
bevriezing van de prijzen 1400
bevroren kredieten 1401
bewaarkluis 2125
bewaarloon 2124
bewaarnemer 1017
bewaking, krediet~ 629
bewaring, in ~ 1185
beweging, kapitaal~ 555
bewijs, aandeel~ 2170
bewijs, aandelen~ 2170
bewijs, deposito~ 608
bewijs, dividend~ 1078
bewijs, garantie~ 394
bewijs, ontvangst~ 47
bewijs, opslag~ 2364
bewijs, rente~ 162
bewijs, schuld~ 609, 1709
bewijsstuk 2358
bewijsstuk, kas~ 600
bewijs van storting 877
bewijs van voorschot 1709
bewijzen, oprichters~ 1386
bewilliging, export~ 1268
bewilliging, import~ 1512
bewilliging, invoer~ 1512
bewilliging, uitvoer~ 1268
bezit, aandelen~ 1628
bezit, effecten~ 1628
bezit, grond~ 1661
bezit, particulier ~ 1979
bezit, privaat~ 1979
bezit, privé-~ 1979
bezit, roerend ~ 622
bezitter 336, 1878
bezitter, aandelen~ 2171
bezitter, effecten~ 341, 2171
bezitter, obligatie~ 390
bezitvorming 1373
bezoldigen 2042
bezoldiging 2041
bezorgen, kapitaal ~ 1407
bezuinigen 924
bezuinigen, de uitgaven ~ 915
bezwaren, met een hypot(h)eek ~ 465
bezwaren, met schulden ~ 466
bezwaring 460
BIB 300
biedende, meest~ 1485
bieden en laten 192
biedkoers 354
bijboek 225
bijdrage 2235
bijeenbrengen, kapitaal ~ 416
bijkantoor 427
bijkomende dekking 62
bijkomende inkomsten 64
bijkomende kosten 61
bijkomende onkosten 61
bijkomende prestatie 1285
bijkomende uitgaven 61
bijkomende vergoeding 1284
bijkomende zekerheid 65
bijkomend krediet 63
bijkomend voordeel 1285
bijkrediet 63
bijnageld 1805
bijslag 60
bijslag, duurte~ 808
bijstand, financiële ~ 1310
bijstrookje 848
bijzondere baten 1765
biljet, aanslag~ 1839
biljet, bank~ 287
biljet, belasting~ 1839
biljet, order~ 1477
biljet, postgiro~ 1781
biljet, schatkist~ 2301
biljet, stortings~ 1022
biljetten en munten 1834
biljetten en munten, buitenlandse ~ 1369
biljetten en munten in omloop 638
biljetten en munten, vreemde ~ 1369
biljoen 367, 368
bimetallisme 375
binden, aan een index ~ 1547
binding, prijs~ 1515
binding, prijzen~ 1515
binnenhandel 1101
binnenlandse brutobesparingen 1462
binnenlandse handel 1101
binnenlandse kredieten 1093
binnenlandse lening 1099
binnenlandse markt 1100
binnenlandse schuld 1095
binnenlandse traite 1091
binnenlandse vraag 1096
binnenlandse wissel 1091
binnenlands verbruik 1092
binnenstromen van kapitaal 99
blad, coupon~ 832
blad, dividend~ 832
blad, koers~ 1228
blancocheque 378
blancokrediet 379

blancoverkoop 346
blanco verkopen, in ~ 1427
blok, dollar~ 1086
blok, frank~ 1388
blokkade 383
blokkadetermijn 384
blokkeren 380
blokkeren, een cheque ~ 2227
blokkering 383
blok, sterling~ 2224
blue chips 387
BNP 1466
bod 353
bod, hoger ~ 1484
boedelbeschrijving 1614
boedel, failliete ~ 317
boedellijst 1614
boek, aandeelhouders~ 1701
boek, balans~ 250
boek, dag~ 932
boeken 401
boeken afsluiten, de ~ 278
boeken, een bedrag in (op) iemands credit ~ 566
boeken, handels~ 28
boeken houden, de ~ 1656
boeken, koopmans~ 28
boekgeld 307
boek, groot~ 1418
boekhouden 20, 1656
boekhouden, dubbel-~ 1107
boekhouden, enkel-~ 2181
boekhouder 410
boekhouding 20
boekhouding, bedrijfs~ 798
boekhouding, mechanische ~ 1724
boekhouding, nationale ~ 1797
boekhoudkundige meerwaarde 412
boek, hulp~ 225
boeking 409
boeking, credit~ 844, 857
boeking, dubbele ~ 1106
boeking in (op) het debet 946
boekingsbescheid 33
boekingshoofd 25
boeking, slot~ 656
boekingsoverschot 30
boekingspost 409
boekingsstuk 33
boeking, storno~ 512
boeking, tegen~ 281
boeking, terug~ 512
boeking, verzamel~ 717
boek, inventaris~ 250
boekjaar 1320
boekje, bank~ 289
boek(je), cheque~ 626
boekje, deposito~ 1021
boekje, rekening~ 289
boekje, spaar~ 2142
boekje, spaarbank~ 2140
boek, kas~ 578
boek, klad~ 1754
boekschuld 406
boekverlies 411
boek, verval~ 359
boek, vervaldagen~ 359
boekvordering 404
boekwaarde 32
boekwinst 412
boek, wissel~ 359, 360
boete 136
bon 876
bon, kas~ 389, 590
bon, schatkist~ 2301
bonus 397, 398
bonusaandeel 400
bonusuitkering 398
boom 413
boomflatie 414
borderel 425, 440, 2217
borderel, stortings~ 877
borg 395, 1138
borgen 1671
borgsom 602
borg staan 52
borg stellen, zich ~ 52
borgstelling 394, 1138
borgstellingskrediet 853
borgtocht 394, 1138
borgtocht, wissel~ 230
bouwspaarfonds 453
bouwspaarkas 453
brandkast 2122
break-even point 430
breedte-investering 1253
brenger 337
brief, garantie~ 394
brief, hypot(h)eek~ 1792
briefje, koop~ 425
briefje, order~ 1477
briefje, sluit~ 425, 440
briefje, verkoops~ 440
brief, krediet~ 1678
brief, pacht~ 1666
brief, rente~ 162
brief, rentespaar~ 2141
brief, schuld~ 389, 1477
brief, spaar~ 2141
brief, wissel~ 356
bron afhouden, aan de ~ 972
bron aftrekken, aan de ~ 972
bron, financierings~ 2192
bron ingehouden belasting, aan de ~ 2268
bron inhouden, aan de ~ 972
bron van inkomsten 2193
brutobedrag 1460
bruto binnenlands produkt 1461
bruto-inkomen 1463
bruto-inkomsten 1463
bruto-methode 1755
bruto nationaal produkt 1466
bruto-omzet 1467
brutorevenu 1463
brutoverlies 1464
brutowaarde 1468
brutowinst 1459
bruto winstmarge 1465
BTW 2341
budget 441, 442
budget, financieel ~ 1312
budget in evenwicht brengen, het ~ 280
budgetkredieten 444
budget sluitend maken, het ~ 280
budgettair 442
budgettair deficit 95
budgettaire kapitaalverliezen 445
budgettaire ramingen 449
budgettair tekort 95
budgetteren 443
buitengewone inkomsten 1287
buitengewone winst 1213
buitenlandse belegging 1367, 1368
buitenlandse betalingsbalans 258
buitenlandse biljetten en munten 1369
buitenlandse crediteur 1360
buitenlandse deelneming 1365, 1366
buitenlandse handel 1283
buitenlandse handelsbank 1371
buitenlandse investering 1367, 1368
buitenlandse lening 1282
buitenlandse munt 1361
buitenlandse participatie 1365, 1366
buitenlandse schuld 1280
buitenlandse schuldeiser 1360
buitenlandse traite 1357
buitenlandse valuta 1361
buitenlandse waarden 1370
buitenlandse waarde van de valuta 1364
buitenlandse wissel 1357
buitenlands geld 1361
buitenlands kapitaal 515, 1359
buitenlands tegoed 204
buitenlands vermogen 204
buitensporige prijs 1250
buitentarief 1279
buitentarief, gemeenschappelijk ~ 699
bulletijn, stortings~ 1022
bureau, centraal ~ 607
bureau, hoofd~ 607
B.V. 1690

calculatie 492
calculatie, kosten~ 797
calculatie, kostprijs~ 815
calculatieschema voor kostprijsberekening, uniform ~ 2325
calculatie, voor~ 1190
calculeren 490
callgeld 505
call-money 505
cambio 356
cambist 361, 509
carry-back 2272
carry-forward 2273
cash 572
cash betalen 1727
cash flow 586
cautie 1138
cautiesom 602
cedeerbaar 117
cedeerbaarheid 116
cedel 2364
cedel, huur~ 1666
cedel, pacht~ 1666
cedent 121, 1165
cederen 118
cederen, een vordering ~ 207

ceel 2364
ceel, huur~ 1666
ceel, pacht~ 1666
centraal bureau 607
centraal kantoor 607
centrale bank 606
centrale zetel 607
certificaat, aandeel~ 2170
certificaat, aandelen~ 2170
certificaat, deposito~ 608
certificaat, schatkist~ 2301
certificaat van aandeel 2170
certificaat van inschrijving 2115
certificaat, voorlopig ~ 1597
certificeren, een cheque ~ 610
certifiëren, een cheque ~ 610
cessie 119
cessie van vorderingen 208
cessionaris 120, 1163
chartaal geld 572, 914
check 624
check, post~ 1425
cheque 624
cheque aan order 631
cheque aan toonder 339
cheque afgeven, een ~ 1115
cheque betalen, per ~ 1901
cheque bevestigen, een ~ 610
cheque, blanco~ 378
cheque blokkeren, een ~ 2227
chequeboek(je) 626
cheque certificeren, een ~ 610
cheque certifiëren, een ~ 610
cheque emitteren, een ~ 1115
cheque, gekruiste ~ 883
cheque incasseren, een ~ 576
cheque innen, een ~ 576
cheque, ongedekte ~ 241
cheque, open ~ 339
cheque, order~ 631
cheque, post~ 1425
cheque, recta~ 630
cheque, reis~ 2297
chequerekening 625
cheque, traveller's ~ 2297
cheque trekken, een ~ 1115
cheque uitgeven, een ~ 1115
cheque uitschrijven, een ~ 1115
chequeverkeer 632
cheque verrekenen, een ~ 641
chequeverrekening 627
cheque, verrekenings~ 883
cheque waarmerken, een ~ 610
cheque zonder dekking 241
c.i.f. 634
cijfer, equivalentie~ 1181
cijfer, index~ 1550
cijfer, zaken~ 2130
circulatiebank 309
circulatie, bankbiljetten~ 308
circulatie, fiduciaire ~ 1299
circulatie, gedwongen ~ 1356
circulatie, geld~ 637
circulatie, in ~ 635
circulatie onttrekken, aan de ~ 502, 503
circulatie van baar geld 638
circulatie van betaalmiddelen 638
circulerend 635
circulerend medium 636
claimrecht 174
claimrecht, exclusief ~ 1249
claimrecht, met ~ 888
classificatie 155
clausule, dollar~ 1088
clausule, goud~ 1432
clausule, ontsnappings~ 1155
clearing 642
clearing, bank~ 292
clearingbank 648
clearingdollar 29
clearinginstituut 649
clearing, interbancaire ~ 292
clearingkantoor 649
clearingkoers 650
clearingovereenkomst 647
clearingrekening 644
clearingtransacties 643
clearingverrichtingen 643
cliëntenrekening 617
coëfficiënt, dekkings~ 840
coëfficiënt, liquiditeits~ 45
coëfficiënt van de verplichte reserves 1759
coëfficiënt, wegings~ 2372
collectieve belegger 793
collectieve rekening 766
collectieve voorzieningen 684
commanditair 1691
commanditaire vennootschap 1692
commanditaire vennootschap op aandelen 1893
commanditair vennoot 1691
commanditaris 1691
commandite 1692
commerciële lening 473
commerciële wissel 356
commissaris 216
commissie 689
commissie, bank~ 293
commissiekoers 691
commissieloon 689
commissie van de schuldeisers 388
commissionair 690
commissionair, effecten~ 2152
commissionair in effecten 2152
committent 1973
compagnie 686
compagnie, handels~ 686
compensatie 642, 708, 709, 1172
compensatiekas 649, 710
compensatieovereenkomst 647
compensatierecht 711
compensatierekening 644
compensatietaks 712
compensatietransactie 327
compensatietransacties 643
compensatieverrichtingen 643
compenseren 706
comptabiliteit 20
concentratie 135
concern 727
concern jaarrekening 736
concessie 728
concessie, belasting~ 2263
concurrentiekracht 714
concurrentievermogen 714
concurrerend 713
condities, betalings~ 2278
conjunctureel 1146
conjuncturele begroting 929
conjuncturele fase 1150
conjuncturele fluctuatie 930
conjuncturele ontwikkeling 477
conjuncturele schommeling 930
conjunctuur 477, 1146
conjunctuurcyclus 471
conjunctuur, dalende ~ 1031
conjunctuurfase 1150
conjunctuurfluctuatie 930
conjunctuurfonds 755
conjunctuur, hoge ~ 413
conjunctuur, laag~ 1031
conjunctuur, lage ~ 1031
conjunctuurontwikkeling 477
conjunctuurreserve 820
conjunctuurschommeling 930
conjunctuurverloop 477
consent, export~ 1268
consent, import~ 1512
consent, invoer~ 1512
consent, uitvoer~ 1268
consolidatie 737
consolidatielening 738
consolidatiestaat 739
consolideren, een schuld ~ 733
consols 734
consortiaal krediet 741
consortium 740
consortium, bank~ 303
consortium, emissie~ 2322
consortium, overname~ 2322
constante kosten 1336
constante prijzen, in ~ 742
constante prijzen, tegen ~ 742
consulent, belasting(s)~ 2264
consulent, financiële ~ 1309
consulent in belastingzaken 2264
consument 744
consumentenbesteding 748
consumentenkrediet 745
consumentenprijs 749
consumptie 751
consumptief krediet 745
consumptiegoederen 743
consumptiegoederen, duurzame ~ 747
consumptie per hoofd (van de bevolking) 1920
consumptieprijs 749
consumptieve belasting 752
consumptieve besteding 748
consumptieve vraag 746
consumptievraag 746
contango 569
contant 573
contantaffaire 581
contantaffaire in deviezen 2202
contantaffaire in valuta 2202
contant betaalbaar 1897
contant betalen 1727
contante betaling 591
contante inkoop 594
contante koers 593

contanten 572
contanten betalen, in ~ 1727
contanten in kas 587
contante prijs 593
contante reserve 597
contante waarde 912
contante wisselkoers (van deviezen) 2024
contant geld 572
contanthandel in deviezen 1227
contant, tegen ~ 573
contanttransactie in deviezen 2202
contanttransactie in valuta 2202
contant vereffenen 1727
contantzaak 581
contingent 2017
contingenteren 122, 1186
contingentering 2018
contingentering, deviezen~ 2030
continu-emissie 2259
continueren, een positie ~ 568
continu-uitgifte 2259
conto 16
conto a meta 1654
conto corrente 23
conto loro 1716
conto, meta-~ 1654
conto nostro 1833
conto vostro 1716
contra-affaire 839
contract, huur~ 1666
contract, overnemings~ 2321
contract, pacht~ 1666
contractprijs 114
contractuele aansprakelijkheid 763
contractuele besparingen 764
contraminedekking 335
contramineren 1427
contramineur 332
contramine zijn, in de ~ 1427
contrapost 281
contraprestatie 731
controle der boekvoering 214
controle, deviezen~ 1224
controle, fiscale ~ 1566
controle, interne accountants~ 1600
controle, investerings~ 1044
controle, krediet~ 629
controle, loon~ 2360
controle, prijs~ 1961
controle, prijzen~ 1961
controleren 215
controleren, de inflatie ~ 628
controlestrook 821
controleur 216
controle van de administratie 214
controle van de boekhouding 214
controle van de (jaar-)rekening 214
controle, wissel~ 1224
conversie 771
conversiefactor 772
conversie, gedwongen ~ 721
conversiekoers 778
conversielening 774
conversieschuldbrief 704
conversie van een lening 775
conversie van schulden 776
converteerbaar 782
converteerbare lening 784
converteerbare obligatie 783
converteren, een lening ~ 779
convertibiliteit 780
convertibiliteit, externe ~ 1278
convertibiliteit, interne ~ 781
coöperatie 786
coöperatie, krediet~ 787
coöperatie, produktie~ 1983
coöperatieve kredietvereniging 787
coöperatieve produktievereniging 1983
coöperatieve vennootschap 786
corbeille 1845
corbeillemarkt 1845
correctiepost 71
cost benefit analyse 801
costing 797
coulisse 891
coupon 828
couponblad 832
coupon, dividend~ 1078
coupon, exclusief ~ 831
coupon, halfjaarlijkse ~ 1475
coupon, int(e)rest~ 1588
coupon, met ~ 829
coupon, niet vervallen ~ 2330
coupon, rente~ 1588
coupon, tegen inlevering van de ~ 1958
coupon, verjaarde ~ 1664
coupon, zonder ~ 831
coupure 1011
courant 893
courante munt 906
courant geld 914
courtage 438
credit 206, 843
creditadvies 847
creditboeking 844, 857
credit card 854
crediteren, iemand voor een bedrag ~ 566
crediteren (voor, met), de rekening ~ 880
creditering 844
crediteur 870
crediteur, bevoorrechte ~ 1948
crediteur, buitenlandse ~ 1360
crediteuren 36
crediteur, gedekte ~ 2150
crediteurland 871
crediteur, obligatie ~ 390
crediteur, preferente ~ 1948
crediteurstaat 871
creditnota 847
creditopgave 847
creditpost 857
creditrente 376
creditsaldo 849
creditzijde 206
creëren, een reserve ~ 454
cross rate 884
cum claim 888
cum dividend 887
cumulatief dividend 889
cumulatief preferente aandelen 890
cumulatief prioriteitsaandelen 890
curator (in het faillissement) 209
curatorschap 2040
cyclische fluctuatie 930
cyclische schommeling 930
cyclus, conjunctuur~ 471

dadelijk opvraagbaar deposito 1004
dag, betaal~ 24
dagboek 932
dagboekpost 1655
dagen, respijt~ 933
daggeld 505
daggeldlening 504
dagkoers 907, 913
dag, liquidatie~ 24
dagnotering 913
dagprijs 911
dag, rescontre~ 24
dag, verrekenings~ 24
dag, verval~ 931
dagwaarde 912, 913
dalende conjunctuur 1031
daling 968, 1125
daling (een winst) van X punten noteren, een ~ 2045
daling (een winst) van X punten vertonen, een ~ 2045
daling, koers~ 886
daling, prijs~ 886
daling van de munt, waarde~ 896
daling van het geld, waarde~ 896
daling, waarde~ 969
datum, balans~ 272
datum, valuta~ 2343
datum van afloop 1263
datum, verval~ 931
debâcle 668
debet 942, 943
debetboeking 946
debetnota 945, 948
debetpost 946
debetrente 947
debetsaldo 93
debet staan 944
debetzijde 943
debet zijn 944
debiteren 615
debitering 613
debiteur 958
debiteuren 37
debiteurenomslag 960
debiteurland 959
debiteur, nalatige ~ 981
debiteurstaat 959
deblokkeren 949
deblokkering 950
debouché 1736
declaratie, dividend~ 964
declaratie, douane~ 919
declareren, een dividend ~ 965
dedouaneren 645
deelname (in) 1495
deelname, meerderheids~ 770
deelname, minderheids~ 1760
deelneming aan de winst 1410
deelneming, buitenlandse ~ 1365, 1366
deelneming (in) 1495

deelneming in het buitenland 1366
deelneming, kapitaal~ 2172
deelneming, meerderheids~ 770
deelneming, minderheids~ 1760
deelneming, wederzijdse ~ 885
deficit 988
deficitaire balans 274
deficitaire begroting 95
deficitaire handelsbalans 94
deficit, begrotings~ 95
deficit, betalingsbalans~ 261
deficit, budgettair ~ 95
deficit dekken, een ~ 836
deficitfinanciering 989
deficit, handels~ 474
deficit, inflatoir ~ 1557
deficit, kas~ 96
deficit op de (buitenlandse) handelsbalans 265
deficit spending 989
deflateren 990
deflatie 991, 992
deflatiespiraal 993
deflationist 995
deflationistisch 992
deflatoir 992
deflatoire tendens 994
deflator 996
deflatorisch 992
degressieve afschrijving 7
degressieve belasting 997
dekken, door hypot(h)eek ~ 838
dekken, een deficit ~ 836
dekken, een tekort ~ 836
dekken, een verlies ~ 707
dekken, hypot(h)ecair ~ 838
dekking 834, 1732
dekking, aanvullende ~ 62
dekking, bijkomende ~ 62
dekking, contramine~ 335
dekking dienen, als ~ 2166
dekking, goud~ 1435
dekking op termijn 1377
dekkingsaankoop 839
dekkingsbehoeften 837
dekkingscoëfficiënt 840
dekkingsinkoop 335
dekkingsverkoop 839
dekking, vereiste ~ 837
dekking, zonder ~ 835
délai (de grâce) 998
delcredere 1000
delen, het verschil ~ 2201
delgen 148, 502
delgen, een hypot(h)eek ~ 511
delging 139, 2053
delgingsfonds 140
delgingsplan 146
delgingsvoet 145
demonetisatie 1008
demonetiseren 503
denationalisatie 1009
denationalisering 1009
denkbeeldige winst 171
deponent 1025
deponeren 1015
deport 239
deportkoers 240
deposant 1025
depositaris 1017
deposito 1013
deposito, bank~ 297
depositobank 1020
depositobewijs 608
depositoboekje 1021
depositocertificaat 608
deposito, dadelijk opvraagbaar ~ 1004
deposito, direct opvraagbaar ~ 1004
deposito, giro~ 1024
deposito-houder 1026
deposito met (op) (vaste) termijn 1337
deposito met opzegging 1019
deposito met opzeggingstermijn 1019
deposito op girorekening 1024
depositorekening 1016
deposito's, interbancaire ~ 1582
deposito, spaar~ 2144
deposito, termijn~ 1337
deposito, verzamel~ 685
deposito, zicht~ 1004
depotstemrecht 2356
depreciatie 969, 1029
depreciatie, geld~ 896
depreciatie, munt~ 896
depreciatiereserve 132
depreciëren 970, 1028
depressie 1031
derde beslagene 1413
derdenarrest 1414
derdenbeslag 1414
derden, voor rekening van ~ 35
derde, voor rekening van een ~ 35
derving van verdienste(n) 1718
derving, winst~ 1718
desinflatie 1064, 1065
desinflationistisch 1065
desinflatoir 1065
desinflatorisch 1065
desinvestering 1066
detailhandel 2107
detailhandelaar 2105
detailhandelsprijs 2096
détaillant 2105
detaillist 2105
detailprijs 2096
detailverkoopprijs 2096
devaluatie 897, 1029
devaluatie van de munt 897
devaluatie van het geld 897
devalueren 1028
devalvatie 1029
deviezen 1361
deviezenarbitrage 186
deviezenbepalingen 900
deviezenbeperkingen 902
deviezencontingentering 2030
deviezencontrole 1224
deviezenhandel 1221
deviezenhandelaar 509
deviezenkoers, termijn~ 1383
deviezenmakelaar 509
deviezenmarkt 1230
deviezenmarkt, dubbele ~ 2309
deviezenmarkt, termijn~ 1382
deviezenmarkt, vrije ~ 1885
deviezenoperaties 1241
deviezenpositie 1363
deviezenreglementering 900
deviezenreserve 901
deviezenrestricties 902
deviezentegoed 1362
deviezen, termijn~ 1378
deviezentransacties 1241
deviezenverordeningen 900
deviezenverplichting 1223
deviezenvoorraad 901, 1362
deviezenvoorschriften 900
dienen, als dekking ~ 2166
dienst, belasting~ 1242
dienstbetoon 2084
diensten 2168
diensten, goederen en ~ 1443
dienst, giro~ 1423
dienstjaar 478
dienst, postcheque- en giro~ 1423
dienstprestaties 2168
dienst, rente~ 1592
dienst, schulden~ 962
dienst van een lening 2167
dienstverlening 2084
dienstverleningen 2168
dienstverrichtingen 2168
diepte-investering 1580
differentieel douanerecht 1040
differentieel recht 1040
differentieel tarief 1041
differentiële kostenberekening 1045
differentiële kostencalculatie 1045
directe belasting 1046
directe kosten 1043
direct opvorderbare passiva 1006
direct opvraagbaar deposito 1004
dirigisme 1047
disagio 1048
disagio doen 1056
discontabel papier 283
disconteerbaar papier 283
disconteren 1057
disconto 127, 1048
disconto, bank~ 311
discontobank 1058
discontohuis 1058
discontokrediet 1059
discontomakelaar 361
discontomarkt 370
disconto, officieel ~ 311
discontoprovisie 1055
discontotarief 1061
discontoverhoging 1541
discontoverlaging 926
discontovoet 1061
dispariteit 1067
dispariteit, prijs~ 1038
distributie, dividend~ 1052
distributiesector 1075
diverse kosten 1764
diversen 1764
diverse onkosten 1764
diverse uitgaven 1764
dividend 1076, 1077
dividend aankondigen, een ~ 965
dividendaankondiging 964

dividend, aanvullend ~ 398
dividend betalen, een ~ 1051
dividendbetaling 1052
dividendbewijs 1078
dividendblad 832
dividendcoupon 1078
dividend, cumulatief ~ 889
dividenddeclaratie 964
dividend declareren, een ~ 965
dividenddistributie 1052
dividend- en couponbelasting 565
dividend, extra~ 398
dividend in contanten 584
dividend, interim~ 1598
dividend, met ~ 887
dividend, met recht op ~ 1170
dividendpassering 1826
dividendpolitiek 1081
dividend, preferent ~ 1945
dividend, recht gevend op ~ 1170
dividendreserve 1079
dividend, slot~ 1303
dividend, stock~ 400
dividend, super~ 398
dividend, surplus~ 398
dividendtalon 1078
dividend uitbetalen, een ~ 1051
dividenduitbetaling 1052
dividend uitkeren, een ~ 1051
dividenduitkering 1052
dividend vaststellen, een ~ 965
dividendvaststelling 964
dividend verdelen, een ~ 1051
dividendverdeling 1052
dividendverlaging 925
dividend, vervallen ~ 1954
dividend, zonder ~ 1080
dochtermaatschappij 98
documentair accreditief 1085
documentair krediet 1085
dode hand 1795
doeanegelden 917
doeanerecht 917
doen, een lening ~ 762
dollarblok 1086
dollarclausule 1088
dollar, clearing~ 29
dollar, euro~ 1193
dollargebied 1086
dollargebrek 1090
dollarlacune 1089
dollarobligatie 1087
dollarschaarste 1090
dollars luidend, in ~ 1010
dollars uitgedrukt, in ~ 1010
dollartekort 1089
dollar, verrekenings~ 29
dollarzone 1086
domicilie 1102
domicilie, fiscaal ~ 1331
donateur 1104
donatie 1103
dontaffaire 1855
dontpremie 507
dood kapitaal 1502
dood punt 430
doorberekening van een belasting 1521
doorsneekoers 234
doorvoerhandel 2294
dossierkosten 1478
dossierrecht 1478
dotatie 1168
doteren 122, 1167
dotering 123
douaneaangifte 919
douanedeclaratie 919
douanegelden 917
douaneinkomsten 921
douaneontvangsten 921
douanerecht 917
douanerecht, differentieel ~ 1040
douanerechten onderhevig, aan ~ 916
douanerechten onderworpen, aan ~ 916
douanetarief 922
douane-unie 923
douaneverklaring 919
douanevisitatie 645
dragen, een rente van X procent ~ 334
dragen, een verlies ~ 333
drager, kosten~ 818
drawback 1116
driehoekshandel 2280
driehoekstransactie 2253
driehoeksverkeer 2280
druk, belasting~ 463
druk, inflatoire ~ 1558
druk op de winst 1988
dubbel-boekhouden 1107
dubbele belasting 1109
dubbele belastingheffing 1109
dubbele boeking 1106
dubbele deviezenmarkt 2309
dubbele premie 1108
dubbele standaard 375
dubieuze vorderingen 1110
dumpen, op de markt ~ 1132
dumping 1131
duur 894
duurgeld 654
duurtebijslag 808
duurte, levens~ 807, 1483
duurtetoeslag 808
duurzame consumptiegoederen 747
duurzame goederen 1133
duurzame produktiemiddelen 1134

EBU 1198
ecart 1731
echelonneren, de betalingen over X jaren ~ 2204
economie, geleide ~ 768
economie, markt~ 1741
economie, monetaire ~ 1775
economie, plan~ 768
economie, planmatige ~ 768
economie, vrije ~ 1393
economisch 1146, 1147
economische balans 1148
economische fluctuatie 930
Economische Gemeenschap, Europese ~ 1194
economische hindernis 1149
economische schommeling 930
economische wetenschap 1151
economiseren 924
E.E.G. 1194
eenheid, munt~ 904
eenheid, reken~ 31
eenheidskoers 2326
eenheidskosten 813
eenheidsprijs 1344, 2328
eenheidsvoet 1345
eenheidswaarde 2213
eenvoudige int(e)rest 2179
eersteklaswaardepapieren 387
eersteklaswissel 1323
eersterangswaarden 387
eeuwigdurende obligatie 162, 1925
effecten 2151
effecten aan toonder 342
effecten als (in) onderpand deponeren 671
effecten als (in) onderpand geven 671
effecten als (in) pand deponeren 671
effecten als (in) pand geven 671
effecten, als onderpand gedeponeerde ~ 1895
effecten, als pand gedeponeerde ~ 1895
effectenbank 1645
effecten, beleende ~ 1895
effecten belenen 91, 671
effectenbeurs 1218
effectenbezit 1628
effectenbezitter 341, 2171
effectencommissionair 2152
effectenemissie 1639
effectenhandelaar 2152
effectenhouder 341, 2171
effectenkantoor 439
effectenmakelaar 2152
effectenmarkt 2153
effecten op naam 1568
effectenportefeuille 1628
effecten, roerende ~ 1739
effectensparen 2135
effectentransacties 1222
effectenuitgifte 1639
effecten, verhandelbare ~ 1739
effecten, verpande ~ 1895
effecten verpanden 671
effectenverrichtingen 1222
effectenvoorraad 1628
effecten, waardeloze ~ 2345
effectenzaken 1222
effectief rendement 57
effectieve kosten 54
effectieve uitgaven 55
effectieve waarde 56
effekten 2151
egalisatie 1172
egalisatiebelasting 712
egalisatiefonds 710
egalisatievordering 1173
eigenaar 1878
eigendom, grond~ 1661
eigendom, particuliere ~ 1979
eigendom, privé-~ 1979
eigen kapitaal 1996

eigen rekening, voor ~ 1877
eigen valuta 1094
eigen verbruik 1497
eigen vermogen 1996
eindjes aan elkaar knopen, de ~ 1703
eindtotaal 105
eisen, liquiditeits~ 596
eis tot terugbetaling 640
elasticiteit van de wisselkoersen 1154
element, vraag~ 716
emissie 1352
emissieagio 1641
emissiebank 309, 1645
emissieconsortium 2322
emissie, continu-~ 2259
emissie, effecten~ 1639
emissie, fiduciaire ~ 1300
emissie garanderen, een ~ 2320
emissiehuis 1645
emissie, in serie uitgegeven ~ 385
emissiekoers 1642
emissiekosten 1353
emissie per reeks 385
emissiepremie 1641
emissieprijs 1642
emissieprospectus 1643
emissiesyndicaat 2322
emissie van aandelen 1640
emissie van bankbiljetten 1156
emissie van gratis aandelen 399
emissie van nieuwe aandelen 2116
emissie van obligaties 392
emissie van schuldbrieven 392
emissievoorwaarden van een lening 729
emissie waarborgen, een ~ 2320
emittent 1644
emitteren, een cheque ~ 1115
emitteren, een lening ~ 1157
emitteren, obligaties ~ 1637
EMO 1196
emolumenten 1158
endossabele wissel 374
endossant 1165
endossant, volgende ~ 2239
endossant, voorgaande ~ 1944
endosseerbare wissel 374
endossement 1164
endosseren, een wissel ~ 1162
engagement 692
en-gros-handel 2376
en-gros-prijs 2288
enkel-boekhouden 2181
enkele standaard 1785
equivalent 822
equivalentie 1180
equivalentiecijfer 1181
ereloon 1295
erfenisrecht 938
erreur ou omission, sauf ~ 1184
Euro-deviezenmarkt 1192
eurodollar 1193
Euro-emissiemarkt 1191
Euromarkt 700
Europees Fonds voor Monetaire Samenwerking 1197
Europese Betalingsunie 1198
Europese Economische Gemeenschap 1194
Europese Investeringsbank 1195
Europese Monetaire Overeenkomst 1196
evenredige verdeling van kosten 800
evenredige verdeling van lasten 1174
eventuele schuldvordering 757
eventuele verplichting 758
evenwicht 1176
evenwicht, begrotings~ 251
evenwicht brengen, de begroting in ~ 280
evenwicht brengen, het budget in ~ 280
evenwicht, intern ~ 1098
evenwichtsverstoring 1062
evenwicht, verstoord ~ 1062
evolutie 1200
excedent 1204, 2244
excedent van uitgaven 1212
ex claim 1249
exclusief coupon 831
exclusief dividend 1080
ex coupon 831
ex dividend 1080
exorbitante prijs 1250
expansie, krediet~ 858
expansietempo 1256
expeditiekosten 2295
exploitatieboekhouding, analytische ~ 798
exploitatiekosten 1850
exploitatieonkosten 1850
exploitatieoverschot 1852
exploitatierekening 2289
exploitatieverlies 474
exploitatiewinst 475
export 1265
exportartikelen 1266
exportbewilliging 1268
exportconsent 1268
exportgarantie 1267
exportgoederen 1266
export, kapitaal~ 526
exportkredietgarantie 1267
exportland 825
exportlicentie 1268
export, onzichtbare ~ 1632
exportpremie 426
exportsaldo 1277
exportsubsidie 1269
exportvergunning 1268
exportwaren 1266
export, zichtbare ~ 2351
expropriatie 1271
expropriëren 1270
externe convertibiliteit 1278
externe financiering 1281
extrabelasting 66
extrabetaling 1288
extrabudgettair 1286
extradividend 398
extraheffing 60
extrakosten 61
extra-legaal voordeel 1285
extraopbrengsten 2246
extra-reservefonds 755
extrauitgaven 61
extrauitkering 398
extravergoeding 1284

fabricagekosten 811
fabricageprijs 811
faciliteiten, krediet~ 421
factoorinkomen 1292
factoorsbedrijf 1293
factor, conversie~ 772
factor, inflatoire ~ 1556
factoring 1293
factorinkomen 1292
factorkosten, tegen ~ 1291
factor, omrekenings~ 772
factureren 357
facturering 366
factuur 17
factuur, pro forma ~ 1991
facultatieve reserve 1397
failliet 313, 314, 315
failliete boedel 317
failliete massa 317
faillietverklaring 69
faillietverklaring, verzoek tot ~ 316
faillissement 315
faillissementsaanvrage 316
fase, conjuncturele ~ 1150
fictieve activa 1297
fictieve int(e)rest 1518
fictieve korting 1822
fictieve winst 171
fiduciaire bewaring, in ~ 1185
fiduciaire circulatie 1299
fiduciaire emissie 1300
fiduciaire lening 1301
fiduciaire uitgifte 1300
fiduciair geld 1296
fijn goud 1324
filiaal 427
finance, haute-~ 1486
financieel beheer 730
financieel beleid 730
financieel bericht 1319
financieel budget 1312
financieel jaar 1320
financieel overzicht 1319
financiële adviseur 1309
financiële bijstand 1310
financiële consulent 1309
financiële hulp 1310
financiële instelling 1315
financiële kringen 1305
financiële lasten 1313
financiële middelen 558
financiële moeilijkheden 1314
financiële overheidsinstelling 2004
financiële politiek 1317
financiële reorganisatie 1318
financiële staat 1319
financiële steun 1310
financiële structuur 561
financiële wereld 1305
financiële wissel 1307
financiën 1304
financiën, openbare ~ 827
financiën, overheids~ 827

financiën reorganiseren, de ~ 2044
financiën saneren, de ~ 2044
financiën, 's lands ~ 827
financiën, staats~ 827
financier 1321
financieren 1306
financieren, voorlopig ~ 1951
financiering 1322
financiering, deficit~ 989
financiering door middel van de cessie van vorderingen 956
financiering, externe ~ 1281
financiering, huurkoop~ 1490
financiering, interne ~ 1601
financiering met eigen middelen 1601
financiering met vreemd vermogen 1281
financiering, overbruggings~ 433
financieringsbegroting 1312
financieringsbehoeften 1316
financieringsbron 2192
financieringskosten 1313
financieringsmaatschappij 1308
financieringsmiddelen 558
financieringswissel 1307
financiering, tussen~ 433
financiering, voorlopige ~ 1952
financiering, zelf~ 1601
financies 1304
financiewezen 1304
firma, bankiers~ 294
firma, makelaars~ 439
fiscaal 1329
fiscaal domicilie 1331
fiscaal instrument 1332
fiscaal jaar 1335
fiscaal voordeel 2263
fiscale aanmoediging 2270
fiscale afschrijving 517
fiscale controle 1566
fiscale last 463
fiscale regelaar 1333
fiscale regulator 1333
fiscale reserve 2001
fiscale toevlucht 2269
fiscale waarde 198
fiscale winst 197
fiscale zetel 1331
fiscaliteit 1334
fiscus 1242
fixeren van prijzen 1962
flauw 508
flauwheid 1130
flexibele wisselkoers 1347
flexibiliteit van de wisselkoersen 1154
fluctuatie, conjuncturele ~ 930
fluctuatie, conjunctuur~ 930
fluctuatie, cyclische ~ 930
fluctuatie, economische ~ 930
fluctuatie in (van) de wisselkoersen 1225
fluctuatiemarge tussen de wisselkoersen 1346
fluctuerende wisselkoers 1347
fob 1354
fonds 1404
fonds, aflossings~ 140
fonds, afschrijvings~ 132
fonds, amortisatie~ 140
fonds, beheer~ 2307
fonds, conjunctuur~ 755
fonds, delgings~ 140
fonds, egalisatie~ 710
fondsen 1406, 2151
fondsen, aan de beurs genoteerde ~ 1699
fondsenbeurs 1218
fondsen, beurs~ 1699
fondsen, genoteerde ~ 1699
fondsen, incourante ~ 892
fondsenmarkt 2153
fondsen, niet genoteerde ~ 892
fondsen, overheids~ 1244
fondsen, prima ~ 387
fondsen, staats~ 1244
fondsen, ter beurze genoteerde ~ 1699
fondsen, ter beurze niet genoteerde ~ 892
fonds, garantie~ 1472
Fonds, Internationaal Monetair ~ 1607
fonds, krediet~ 1710
fonds, lenings~ 1710
fonds, pensioen~ 1918
fonds, rente~ 1455
fonds, reserve~ 2101
fonds, spaar~ 2145
fonds, stabilisatie~ 2205
fonds, tegenwaarde~ 823
fonds, vernieuwings~ 2086
fonds, vervangings~ 2086
Fonds voor Monetaire Samenwerking, Europees ~ 1197
fonds voor onvoorziene uitgaven 755
fonds, voorzienings~ 755
fonds, waarborg~ 1472
forfaitair bedrag 1722
forfaitaire prijs 114
formulier, stortings~ 1022
fourneren, X % op een aandeel ~ 1899
fouten en weglatingen 1183
fout in de berekening 491
fout, reken~ 491
fractie, aandelen~ 1387
frankblok 1388
frankeren 1389
frankgebied 1388
frankzone 1388
fraude, belasting~ 2266
funderen, een schuld ~ 733
fundering 737
fusie 135

galopperende inflatie 1411
gangbaar geld 914
gangbare munt 906
gang van zaken 833
garanderen, een emissie ~ 2320
garant 395
garantie 1138, 1471
garantieaandeel 2015
garantiebewijs 394
garantiebrief 394
garantie, export~ 1267
garantie, exportkrediet~ 1267
garantiefonds 1472
garantie, goud~ 1437
garantie, krediet~ 860
garantie, leen~ 1473
garantie, overheids~ 1450
garantie, staats~ 1450
garantiesyndicaat 2322
garantie van schadeloosstelling 394
garantie voor een lening, overheids~ 1447
garantie, werkelijke ~ 2258
garantie, wissel~ 230
GATT 1415
geaccumuleerde int(e)rest 41
geaccumuleerde rente 41
geaffilieerde maatschappij 98
geautoriseerd kapitaal 222
gebied, afzet~ 1736
gebied, dollar~ 1086
gebied, frank~ 1388
gebied, sterling~ 2224
geblokkeerde ponden 382
geblokkeerd tegoed 381
geboekte post 409
gebonden lening 2281
gebrek aan liquide middelen 1504
gebrek, dollar~ 1090
gebreke, in ~ 979
gebrek, kapitaal~ 559
gebrek, krediet~ 878
gebruik van kredieten 228
geconsolideerde jaarrekening 736
geconsolideerde schuld 735
geconsolideerde staatspapieren 734
gecontroleerde valuta 767
gedeclareerde waarde 967
gedeelte 1572
gedeeltelijke betaling 1894
gedeelten, bij ~ 987
gedekte crediteur 2150
gedekte lening 672
gedekte schuldeiser 2150
gedekt krediet 670
gedekt voorschot 86
gedisconteerde wissel op het binnenland 1060
gedrukt 508
gedruktheid 1130
gedwongen circulatie 1356
gedwongen conversie 721
gedwongen koers 722, 1356
gedwongen lening 723
gedwongen sparen 724
gedwongen wisselkoers 722
geëmitteerd aandelenkapitaal 1638
geëmitteerd kapitaal 1638
geëndosseerde 1163
gefailleerde 313
gefundeerde schuld 735
gegarandeerde lening 672
gegarandeerde obligatie 2149
gegarandeerd krediet 670
gegarandeerd, niet ~ 835
gegarandeerd voorschot 86
geglobaliseerd inkomen 2262

gehalte (aan edel metaal) 1325
gehalte, goud~ 1434
geheel betalen 1905
geheel verlies 934
geheim, bank~ 305
geheime reserves 726
gehele betaling 715
geïmporteerde inflatie 1511
geïndexeerde obligatie 1549
geïntegreerde economische rekeningen 1579
geïnvesteerd kapitaal 541
gekapitaliseerde waarde 546
gekruiste cheque 883
gekweekte int(e)rest 41
geld, afkoop~ 708
geld, baar ~ 572
geld, bank~ 307
geldbeleid 1769
geld, bijna~ 1805
geld, boek~ 307
geldboete 136
geld, buitenlands ~ 1361
geld, call~ 505
geld, chartaal ~ 572, 914
geldcirculatie 637
geldcirculatie, te grote ~ 6
geld, contant ~ 572
geld, courant ~ 914
geld, dag~ 505
gelddepreciatie 896
geld, door de schatkist in omloop gebracht ~ 2302
geld, duur~ 654
geldelijke moeilijkheden 1314
gelde maken, te ~ 785
gelden, begrotings~ 444
gelden, doeane~ 917
gelden, douane~ 917
gelden, overheids~ 2005
gelden, spaar~ 2137
gelden, staats~ 2005
gelden, tol~ 917
geld, fiduciair ~ 1296
geld, gangbaar ~ 914
geld, gereed ~ 572
geldgever 1777
geld, giraal~ 307
geld, goedkoop ~ 623
geld, hand~ 602
geldhandelaar 1311
geld herkrijgen, zijn ~ 1421
geldhervorming 899
geldhoeveelheid 1783
geldhuishouding 1775
geld, huur~ 2088
geldigheidsduur 894
geldigheidstermijn 894
geld in kas 587
geld in omloop 914
geld, jaar~ 161
geld, kas~ 587
geld, klein~ 612
geldkoers 1782
geld, koper~ 788
geld, maand~ 1787
geldmakelaar 1311
geldman 550
geldmarkt 1778
geldmarktpapier 1779
geld, metaal~ 661
geld, metalliek ~ 661
geldmiddelen 1916
geld, munt~ 661
geldnemer 418
geldnood 1314
geldontwaarding 896, 1554
geldopnemer 418
geld op rente lenen 1675
geld op rente uitlenen 1675
geld op (tegen) int(e)rest lenen 1675
geld op (tegen) int(e)rest uitlenen 1675
geld, optie~ 1856
geldoverdracht 1784
geldovermaking 1784
geldovervloed 6
geld, pacht~ 2088
geld, papier~ 1355
geld, papieren ~ 1355
geld, pas~ 612
geldpolitiek 1769
geldreserve 1770
geld, rouw~ 136
geld, schaars~ 654
geldschepping 842
geldschieter 1777
geld(s)omloop 637
geldstelsel 664
geldstuk(je) 660
geldswaardige papieren 1739
geld, teken~ 1296
geld, termijn~ 1337
geld terugkrijgen, zijn ~ 1421
geld, tol~ 2284
geldverlegenheid 1314
geldverstrekker 1777
geld, vertel~ 133
geldvolume 1783
geldvooraad 587
geldvoorraad 1783
geldvraag 1774
geld, vreemd ~ 1361
geld we(d)erkrijgen, zijn ~ 1421
geldwereld 1305
geldwezen 1304
geld, wissel~ 612
geldwisselaar 509
geld, zegel~ 2211
geldzending 1784
geld, zwart ~ 2314
geleend kapitaal 417
gelegenheidskoopje 321
geleide economie 768
gelijkmatige verdeling van kosten 800
gelijkmatige verdeling van lasten 1174
gelijkwaardigheid 1180
gemanipuleerde valuta 767
gemeenschappelijk beleggingsfonds 1624
gemeenschappelijk buitentarief 699
Gemeenschappelijke Markt 700
gemeenschappelijke noemer 698
gemeenschappelijke rekening 1649
gemeenteobligatie 1713
gemene rekening 1649
gemiddeld 232
gemiddelde 231
gemiddelde, jaar~ 158
gemiddelde koers 234
gemiddeld inkomen per hoofd 233
gemiddeld inkomen per kop 233
gemunt goud 667
genootschapsjaar 705
genoteerde fondsen 1699
genoteerde waarden 1699
genoteerde waardepapieren 1699
geraamde kosten 1189
gereed geld 572
geregistreerde aandeelhouder 2076
gereguleerde valuta 767
geretourneerde wissel 365
gestaffelde int(e)rest 1457
gestaffelde rente 1457
gestaffeld tarief 1041
gestort kapitaal 1880
getallen, in ronde ~ 2119
geünificeerde schuld 735
geven, een rente van X procent ~ 334
geven, een winst ~ 100
gever 1104
gever, geld~ 1777
gever, krediet~ 1672
gewaarborgd inkomen 210
gewaarborgd krediet 670
gewettigd kapitaal 222
gewicht 2368
gewogen index 2370
gewogen indexcijfer 2370
gewone aandelen 701
gewone begroting 1859
gewone schuldeiser 405
gewone schuldvordering 2332
gewoon aandelenkapitaal 697
gewoon voorbehoud, onder ~ 2099
gezamenlijk bedrag 107
gezamenlijke rekening 1649
gezamenlijke waarde 108
gezinsbesteding 1499
gezinsverbruik 1499
gezonde munt 2191
gift 1103
giraalgeld 307
girant 1165
gireren 2080
gireren, een wissel ~ 1162
giro 318, 1164
giro, bank~ 318
girobank 648
girodeposito 1024
girodienst 1423
girokaart 1781
girorekening 1424
giroverkeer 643
glijdende schaal 1348
glijdend tarief 1041
globaal bedrag 107
globaal saldo bij de overdrachten en in het kapitaalverkeer 1416
globale prijs 114
globale schatting 184

globale waarde 108
goederen 202
goederenbalans 264
goederenbeurs 695
goederen, consumptie~ 743
goederen, duurzame ~ 1133
goederen en diensten 1443
goederen- en dienstenbalans 259
goederen- en dienstenverkeer, saldo van het ~ 259
goederen, export~ 1266
goederen, immateriële ~ 1505
goederen, import~ 1510
goederen, investerings~ 533
goederen, invoer~ 1510
goederen, kapitaal~ 533
goederen, lichamelijke ~ 1747
goederen, liggende ~ 1508
goederen, luxe~ 1001
goederenmakelaar 694
goederen, materiële ~ 1747
goederen, niet duurzame ~ 1827
goederen, onlichamelijke ~ 1505
goederen, onroerende ~ 1508
goederenprijsindex 696
goederen, produktie~ 1134
goederen, roerende ~ 622
goederen, uitvoer~ 1266
goederen, vaste ~ 1508
goederen, verbruiks~ 743
goedkoop geld 623
goedmaken, een verlies ~ 707
goedschrijven, iemand voor een bedrag ~ 566
goedschrijven, op de rekening ~ 880
gokker aan de beurs 1647
goodwill 1444
gooien, op de markt ~ 1665
goudarbitrage 185
goudclausule 1432
gouddekking 1435
goud- en deviezenreserves 1429
goud- en deviezenvoorraad 1429
gouden munt 1433
gouden standaard 1441
goud en zilver in baren 457
goud en zilver in staven 457
goud en zilver, ongemunt ~ 457
goud, fijn ~ 1324
goudgarantie 1437
goudgehalte 1434
goud, gemunt ~ 667
goudgerande waarden 387
goud in baren 323
goud in staven 323
goudkernstandaard 1431
goudlening 1438
goud, monetair ~ 666
goud, munt~ 666, 667
goudmunt 1433
goudpariteit 1439
goudprijssysteem, tweevoudig ~ 2310
goudreserve 1440
goudspeciestandaard 1402
goud, staaf~ 323
goudstuk 1433
goudvermogen 1430
goudvoorraad 1430
goudwaarde 1442
goudwisselstandaard 1436
graad, liquiditeits~ 45
gratificatie 397
gratisaandeel 400
grens, krediet~ 855
grensprijs 1965
grens, prijs~ 1965
grens voor leningen tegen onderpandeffecten 604
groeikracht 1469
groeipercentage 1255
groeiritme 1256
groeisector 1470
groeitempo 1256
groeivermogen 1469
groeivoet 1255
groep 727
groep, belasting~ 2267
groepering van de balansposten 273
groep, inkomens~ 1527
grondbelasting 1662
grondbezit 1661
grondeigendom 1661
gronden, liggende ~ 1661
grondkapitaal 544, 1564
grondkrediet 868
grondkredietbank 1660
grondprijs 330
grondslag, belastbare ~ 331
grondslag der belasting(en) 331
grondslagprijs 330
grondstof 329
groot aanbod, te ~ 1210
grootboek 1418
grootboek van de aandeelhouders 1701
groothandel 2376
groothandelaar 2375
groothandelsprijs 2288
groothandelsprijzenindex 2374
grootkapitaal 355
grossier 2375
grossierderij 2376
grossiersprijs 2288
grote geldcirculatie, te ~ 6
grote vraag, te ~ 1206
gunste van iemand een krediet openen, ten ~ 1847
gunstige handelsbalans 53
gunstprijs 1203
gunsttarief 1947

halfjaarlijkse coupon 1475
halfjaarlijkse termijn 351
half lang 1752
halve rekening 1654
hamsteren 1492, 1493
handelaar, detail~ 2105
handelaar, effecten~ 2152
handelaar, geld~ 1311
handelaar, groot~ 2375
handelaar, klein~ 2105
handel, binnen~ 1101
handel, binnenlandse ~ 1101
handel, buitenlandse ~ 1283
handel, detail~ 2107
handel, deviezen~ 1221
handel, doorvoer~ 2294
handel, driehoeks~ 2280
handel, en-gros-~ 2376
handel, groot~ 2376
handel in vreemde biljetten en munten 936
handel, klein~ 2107
handel op het buitenland 1283
handel, overzeese ~ 1283
handelsaccept 2286
handelsbalans 264
handelsbalans, actieve ~ 53
handelsbalans, deficitaire ~ 94
handelsbalans, gunstige ~ 53
handelsbalans, ongunstige ~ 94
handelsbalans, passieve ~ 94
handelsbank 310
handelsbank, buitenlandse ~ 1371
handelsbeurs 695
handelsboeken 28
handelscompagnie 686
handelsdeficit 474
handelskorting 935
handelskrediet 470
handelslening 473
handel(s)maatschappij 686
handelsmarge 1734
handelsmonopolie 2287
handelspapier 356
handelspapier, prima ~ 1323
handelsregister 687
handelstekort 474
handelsvennootschap 686
handelsvolume 2354
handelsvrijheid 1392
handelswinst 475
handelswissel 356
handel, transit~ 2294
handel, valuta~ 1221
handel, wissel~ 1221
handgeld 602
harde valuta 1479
hausse 413, 2117
haussemarkt 458
haussepremie 507
haussespeculant 455
hausse speculeren, à la ~ 456
haussestemming 459
haussier 455
haute-finance 1486
hedging 839
heffen (op), een belasting ~ 194
heffen (op), een toeslag ~ 1514
heffing 1135
heffing aan de bron 681
heffing, belasting~ 1516
heffing, kapitaal~ 551
heffing, voor~ 89
heraanschaffingswaarde 2091
herbeleggen 1936
herbelegging 2078
herdiscontabel 2058
herdisconteerbaar 2058
herdisconteren 2057
herdiscontering 2056
herdisconto 2056

herdiscontovoet 2059
herdistributie 2060
herexport 2066
herfinancieren 2067
herfinanciering 2068
herinvesteren 1936
herinvestering 2078
herkrijgen, zijn geld ~ 1421
herleiding 771
hernieuwd krediet, automatisch ~ 2114
herroepelijk krediet 2113
herschatten 2037
herschatting 2036
herstel 2020, 2048
herstel van de betalingsbalans(en) 794
herverdeling 2060
hervorming, belasting~ 2274
hervorming, geld~ 899
hervorming, munt~ 899
herwaarderen 2037
herwaardering 2036
herwaardering van de pariteiten 2031
herwissel 819
herziening van de contingenten 77
herziening van de quota's 77
hindernis, economische ~ 1149
hinkende standaard 1476
historische kosten 804
hoekman 1648
hoeveelheid, geld~ 1783
hoge conjunctuur 413
hoger bod 1484
holding (company) 1494
holdingmaatschappij 1494
hollende inflatie 1411
honorarium 1295
honoreren, een wissel ~ 1054
honorering, waarborg van ~ 1474
hoofdaandeelhouder 633
hoofdbureau 607
hoofdelijke aansprakelijkheid 1652
hoofdelijke schuld 1650
hoofdelijke schuldenaar 1651
hoofdhuis 607
hoofdkantoor 607
hoofdsom 1972
hoofdvestiging 607
hoofdzetel 607
hoogconjunctuur 413
hoogste prijs, de ~ 605
hot money 1498
houden, de boeken ~ 1656
houder 336
houder, effecten~ 341
houder, obligatie~ 390
houder van een gemeenschappelijk beleggingsfonds, aandeel~ 2327
houder van een rekening 26
houdstermaatschappij 1494
huidige koers 907
huidige prijs 911
huis, bankiers~ 294
huis, disconto~ 1058
huis, emissie~ 1645
huis, hoofd~ 607
huishouding, geld~ 1775
huishoudkunde, staats~ 1151
huis, munt~ 1761
hulpboek 225
hulp, financiële ~ 1310
hulpjournaal 225
hulp, monetaire ~ 1771
hulp, ontwikkelings~ 1034
hulp, overheids~ 1445
hulprekening 224
hulp, staats~ 1445
huur 1666, 2088
huurcedel 1666
huurceel 1666
huurcontract 1666
huurder 1667
huurgeld 2088
huurkoop 1487
huurkoopfinanciering 1490
huurkoop nemen, in ~ 481
huurovereenkomst 1666
huurprijs 2088
hyperinflatie 1500
hypot(h)ecair dekken 838
hypot(h)ecaire lening 1711
hypot(h)ecaire obligatie 1792
hypot(h)ecaire schuld 957
hypot(h)ecair krediet 866
hypot(h)eek 1790
hypot(h)eek afbetalen, een ~ 511
hypot(h)eek aflossen, een ~ 511
hypot(h)eek, amortiseerbare ~ 137
hypot(h)eek amortiseren, een ~ 511
hypot(h)eekbank 1660
hypot(h)eek belasten, met een ~ 465
hypot(h)eek bezwaren, met een ~ 465
hypot(h)eekbrief 1792
hypot(h)eek dekken, door ~ 838
hypot(h)eek delgen, een ~ 511
hypot(h)eekkrediet 866
hypot(h)eeklast 1793
hypot(h)eek nemen (op), een ~ 2019
hypot(h)eekpandbrief 1792
hypot(h)eekrente 1794
hypot(h)eekschuld 957
hypot(h)eek terugbetalen, een ~ 511
hypot(h)ekeren 1791

IAO 1606
IBRD 1602
IDA 1604
IFM 1605
IKK 1603
illiquide 1503
illiquititeit 1504
imaginaire winst 171
IMF 1607
immateriële activa 1505
immateriële goederen 1505
immobiliën 1508
immobilisatie 1506
immobiliseren 1507
import 1509
importartikelen 1510
importbewilliging 1512
importconsent 1512
importgoederen 1510
import, kapitaal~ 534
importland 826
importlicentie 1512
import, onzichtbare ~ 1633
importverbod 319
importvergunning 1512
importwaren 1510
import, zichtbare ~ 2352
inbaar 574, 675, 676
inbaarheid 674
inboeken 401
inbreng 765
inbrengen, kapitaal ~ 436
inbreng in natura 205
inbreng, kapitaal~ 521
incasseerbaar 574
incasseerder, schuld~ 955
incasseren, een cheque ~ 576
incassering 679
incasso 679
incassowissel 364
inclusief claimrecht 888
inclusief coupon 829
inclusief dividend 887
inconvertibiliteit 1533
incourante fondsen 892
incourante fondsen, markt in (voor) ~ 891
incourante waarden 892
indamming van de liquiditeit 1697
index 1546
index binden, aan een ~ 1547
indexcijfer 1550
indexcijfer, gewogen ~ 2370
indexcijfer, omzet~ 2131
indexcijfer van de detailhandelsprijzen 2106
indexcijfer van de groothandelsprijzen 2374
indexcijfer van de kleinhandelsprijzen 2106
indexcijfer van de kosten van levensonderhoud 809
index der prijzen 1964
indexeren 1547
indexering 1548
index, gewogen ~ 2370
index, goederenprijs~ 696
index, groothandelsprijzen~ 2374
index koppelen, aan een ~ 1547
indexobligatie 1549
index, prijzen~ 1964
index van de detailhandelsprijzen 2106
index van de groothandelsprijzen 2374
index van de kleinhandelsprijzen 2106
index van de levensduurte 809
index van het omzetcijfer 2131
indicator 1551
indirecte belasting 1552
indirecte kosten 1417
indossant 1165
indossement 1164
indosseren, een wissel ~ 1162

indruisen, tegen de algemene tendens ~ 2120
industrie toegevoegde waarde, door de ~ 2340
ineenstorting 668
ineenstorting van de koersen 431
ineenstorting van de prijzen 431
inflateren 1553
inflatie 1554, 1555
inflatie, aanpassings~ 59
inflatie afremmen, de ~ 628
inflatiebestand 1562
inflatiebestendig 1562
inflatie controleren, de ~ 628
inflatie, door loonsverhogingen veroorzaakte ~ 2361
inflatie, galopperende ~ 1411
inflatie, geïmporteerde ~ 1511
inflatie, hollende ~ 1411
inflatie, kosten~ 803
inflatie, krediet~ 861
inflatie, kruipende ~ 882
inflatie, latente ~ 725
inflatie, onderdrukte ~ 1919
inflatiepercentage 1563
inflatie remmen, de ~ 628
inflatiespiraal 1559
inflatietempo 1563
inflatie, teruggedrongen ~ 1919
inflatievoet 1563
inflatie, vraag~ 1005
inflationeren 1553
inflationisme 1560
inflationist 1561
inflationistisch 1555
inflatoir 1555
inflatoir aanpassingsproces 59
inflatoir deficit 1557
inflatoire druk 1558
inflatoire factor 1556
inflatoire kracht 1558
inflatoor 1555
ingaand wisselboek 360
ingehouden inkomsten 1137
ingehouden waarborgsom 2109
ingehouden winsten 2108
ingeschreven kapitaal 2232
inhouden, aan de bron ~ 972
inhouding aan de bron 975
inhouding van belastingen aan de bron 681
inhouding, winst~ 1987
initiatief, particulier ~ 1976
initiatief, privé-~ 1976
inklaring 645
inkom 1522
inkomen 1522
inkomen, arbeids~ 1136
inkomen, arbeidsloos ~ 2323
inkomen, belastbaar ~ 2262
inkomen, beschikbaar ~ 1068
inkomen, bruto-~ 1463
inkomen, factoor~ 1292
inkomen, factor~ 1292
inkomen, geglobaliseerd ~ 2262
inkomen, gewaarborgd ~ 210
inkomen in natura 1529
inkomen, loon~ 1136
inkomen, maatschappelijk ~ 791
inkomen, nationaal ~ 1799
inkomen, netto-~ 1811
inkomen, overdrachts~ 2292
inkomen per hoofd, gemiddeld ~ 233
inkomen per kop, gemiddeld ~ 233
inkomen, persoonlijk ~ 1929
inkomen, privé-~ 1929
inkomen, reëel ~ 2032
inkomensgroep 1527
inkomensklasse 1527
inkomens, primaire ~ 1970
inkomensschijf 1527
inkomens, secondaire ~ 2146
inkomens, secundaire ~ 2146
inkomen uit arbeid 1136
inkomen uit beleggingen 1528
inkomen uit investeringen 1528
inkomen uit kapitaal 535
inkomen, vast ~ 210
inkomen, vennootschappelijk ~ 791
inkomen, verdiend ~ 1136
inkomen, volks~ 1799
inkomen, werkelijk ~ 2032
inkomen, zuiver ~ 1811
inkomsten 1522, 1532
inkomsten, andere ~ 1765
inkomsten, begrotings~ 447
inkomstenbelasting 1530
inkomsten, belasting~ 1565
inkomstenbelasting op natuurlijke personen 1930
inkomsten, bijkomende ~ 64
inkomsten, bruto-~ 1463
inkomsten, buitengewone ~ 1287
inkomsten, douane~ 921
inkomsten, ingehouden ~ 1137
inkomsten in natura 1529
inkomsten, netto-~ 1811
inkomsten, niet terugkerende ~ 1287
inkomstenobligatie 1526
inkomsten, periodieke ~ 2049
inkomstenrekening 1524
inkomsten, staats~ 1451
inkomsten, supplementaire ~ 64
inkomsten uit kapitaal 535
inkomstobligatie 1526
inkoop 2012, 2053
inkoop, contante ~ 594
inkoop, dekkings~ 335
inkoopkoers 354
inkoopprijs 488
inkoop, vervroegde ~ 167
inkoopwaarde 50, 2055
inkopen 479, 502
inkoper 482
inkrimpen, de uitgaven ~ 915
inlaag 1013
inlaag, spaar~ 2144
inlage 1013
inlage, spaar~ 2144
inlandsverbruik 1092
inleg 1013
inleggen 1015
inleggen, kapitaal ~ 436
inlegger 1025
inleg, spaar~ 2144
inlevering van de coupon, tegen ~ 1958
inmenging, overheids~ 1452
inmenging, staats~ 1452
innen, een belasting ~ 678
innen, een cheque ~ 576
innen, een schuld ~ 677
innen, een vordering ~ 677
innen wissel, te ~ 373
inning 679, 680
inning, belasting~ 683
inning van schulden (vorderingen) 682
inpandgeving van effecten 1501
inperking, krediet~ 874
inperking, liquiditeits~ 2104
inschrijven 401
inschrijven (op) 2233
inschrijven op een lening uitnodigen, tot het ~ 1634
inschrijver 2234
inschrijving 2236, 2276
inschrijving, kapitaal~ 562
inschrijving op een lening openstellen, de ~ 1634
inschrijvingsbedrag 153
inschrijvingskoers 2238
inschrijvingsprijs 2238
inschrijvingsprospectus 1643
inschrijvingsrecht 174
inschrijvingstermijn 2237
inschuld 37
insolvabel 1570
insolvent 1570
insolventie 1569
insteken, kapitaal ~ 436
instelling, bank~ 294
instelling, financiële ~ 1315
instelling, financiële overheids~ 2004
instelling, krediet~ 850
institutionele belegger 793
instituut, clearing~ 649
instrument, fiscaal ~ 1332
integrale kostenberekening 4
integrale kostencalculatie 4
integratie 135
intekenaar 2234
intekenen (op) 2233
intekening 2236
intekening, kapitaal~ 562
intekenprijs 2238
intekentermijn 2237
intensiteit, kapitaal~ 538
Interamerikaanse Ontwikkelingsbank 1581
interbancaire clearing 292
interbancaire deposito's 1582
interbancair krediet 1583
interbankdeposito's 1582
interconvertibiliteit 1584
int(e)rest 1585
int(e)rest, achterstallige ~ 190
int(e)restbetaling 1592
int(e)restcoupon 1588
int(e)rest, eenvoudige ~ 2179
int(e)resten, moratoire ~ 983

int(e)rest, fictieve ~ 1518
int(e)rest, geaccumuleerde ~ 41
int(e)rest, gekweekte ~ 41
int(e)rest, gestaffelde ~ 1457
int(e)rest lenen, geld op (tegen) ~ 1675
int(e)rest, lopende ~ 909
int(e)rest op int(e)rest 720
int(e)rest, samengestelde ~ 720
int(e)rest, schijn~ 1518
int(e)restsubsidie 1594
int(e)rest uitlenen, geld op (tegen) ~ 1675
int(e)restvergoeding 1594
int(e)rest, verschenen ~ 1589
int(e)rest, verschuldigde ~ 1589
int(e)rest, vervallen ~ 1589
int(e)rest, vervroegde ~ 165
int(e)restvoet 1593
interimaandeel 1597
interimdividend 1598
Internationaal Monetair Fonds 1607
Internationaal Monetair Fonds trekken, op het ~ 1123
Internationale Arbeidsorganisatie 1606
Internationale Bank voor Herstel en Ontwikkeling 1602
Internationale Bank voor Wederopbouw en Ontwikkeling 1602
Internationale Financierings-maatschappij 1605
Internationale Kamer van Koophandel 1603
Internationale Ontwikkelings-organisatie 1604
interne accountantscontrole 1600
interne bedrijfsstatistiek 1851
interne convertibiliteit 781
interne financiering 1601
intern evenwicht 1098
interventiekoers 1610
interventie, overheids~ 1452
interventiepunt 1609
interventie, staats~ 1452
interventionisme 1608
intrinsieke waarde 1612
introductie ter beurze 81
inventaris 1614, 1615
inventarisatie 1616
inventarisboek 250
inventariseren 1124
inventarislijst 1614
inventaris maken, de ~ 1124
inventaris opmaken, de ~ 1124
inventariswaarde 1617
investeerder 1631
investeren 1618
investering 1619
investering, buitenlandse ~ 1367, 1368
investering, diepte-~ 1580
investering in effecten 1626
investering in het buitenland 1368
investering in waardepapieren 1626
investering, kapitaal~ 542
investering, nieuwe ~ 1818
investering, onjuiste ~ 244
investering, openbare ~ 2006
investering, overheids~ 2006
investering, particuliere ~ 1978
investeringsbank 1621
investeringsbegroting 519
investeringsbehoeften 1627
investeringscontrole 1044
investeringsgoederen 533
investeringsinkomen 1528
investeringskapitaal 1622
investeringskredieten 1620
investering, slechte ~ 244
investeringsloonstelsel 2362
investeringsprikkel 1625
investeringsquote 1629
investeringsstimulans 1625
investeringsuitgaven 524
investering, vaste ~ 1340
investering, vreemde ~ 1367
investment-trust 653
invoer 1509
invoerartikelen 1510
invoerbeperking 1513
invoerbewilliging 1512
invoerconsent 1512
invoergoederen 1510
invoer, kapitaal~ 534
invoerland 826
invoerlicentie 1512
invoer, onzichtbare ~ 1633
invoerstop 319
invoerverbod 319
invoervergunning 1512
invoerwaren 1510
invoer, zichtbare ~ 2352
invorderaar, schuld~ 955
invorderbaar 675, 676
invorderbaarheid 674
invorderen, een belasting ~ 678
invorderen, een schuld ~ 677
invorderen, een vordering ~ 677
invordering 37, 680
invordering van schulden (vorderingen) 682
inwisselbaar 782
inwisselbaarheid 780
inzinking 968
inzinking van de koersen 431
inzinking van de prijzen 431

jaar, bedrijfs~ 478
jaar, begrotings~ 448
jaar, belasting~ 1335
jaarbericht 160
jaar, boek~ 1320
jaar, dienst~ 478
jaar, financieel ~ 1320
jaar, fiscaal ~ 1335
jaargeld 161
jaargemiddelde 158
jaar, genootschaps~ 705
jaar, kalender~ 493
jaarlijkse afschrijving 157
jaarlijkse begroting 159
jaarlijkse rente 161
jaarrekening, concern ~ 736
jaarrekening, geconsolideerde ~ 736
jaarverslag 160
jaar, verslag~ 478
jarige looptijd, X-~ 1749
jobber 1648
journaal 932
journaal, hulp~ 225
journaalpost 1655

kaart, giro~ 1781
kaart, krediet~ 854
kadastrale waarde 199
kalenderjaar 493
kalm 508
kamer van koophandel (en nijverheid) 611
Kamer van Koophandel, Internationale ~ 1603
kamer, verreken~ 649
kamer, verrekenings~ 649
kantoor, administratie~ 2306
kantoor, centraal ~ 607
kantoor, clearing~ 649
kantoor, effecten~ 439
kantoor, hoofd~ 607
kantoor, makelaars~ 439
kantoor, verreken~ 649
kantoor, wissel~ 1217
kapitaal 514
kapitaal, aandelen~ 544
kapitaal, aanvangs~ 1564
kapitaalbalans 256
kapitaal, bedrijfs~ 468
kapitaal, begin~ 1564
kapitaalbeheer 1044
kapitaalbehoefte 557
kapitaalbelasting 551
kapitaal, belegd ~ 541
kapitaalbelegging 542
kapitaal, beleggings~ 1622
kapitaal beschikbaar stellen 1407
kapitaalbeweging 555
kapitaalbewegingen, saldo van de ~ 256
kapitaalbezitter 550
kapitaal bezorgen 1407
kapitaal bijeenbrengen 416
kapitaal, buitenlands ~ 515, 1359
kapitaaldeelneming 2172
kapitaal, dood ~ 1502
kapitaal, eigen ~ 1996
kapitaalexport 526
kapitaalexportland 525
kapitaal, geautoriseerd ~ 222
kapitaalgebrek 559
kapitaal, geëmitteerd ~ 1638
kapitaal, geïnvesteerd ~ 541
kapitaal, gestort ~ 1880
kapitaal, gewettigd ~ 222
kapitaalgoederen 533
kapitaal, grond~ 544, 1564
kapitaal, groot~ 355
kapitaalheffing 551
kapitaalimport 534
kapitaal in baar geld 577
kapitaalinbreng 521
kapitaal inbrengen 436
kapitaal in contanten 577
kapitaal, ingeschreven ~ 2232

kapitaal in het buitenland 515
kapitaalinkomen 535
kapitaalinkomsten 535
kapitaal inleggen 436
kapitaalinschrijving 562
kapitaal insteken 436
kapitaalintekening 562
kapitaalintensief 539
kapitaalintensiteit 538
kapitaalinvestering 542
kapitaal, investerings~ 1622
kapitaalinvoer 534
kapitaalkosten 522
kapitaalkrapte 559
kapitaallasten 520
kapitaal, leen~ 1707
kapitaal lenen 416
kapitaal, lening~ 1707
kapitaal, maatschappelijk ~ 222, 544
kapitaalmarkt 554
kapitaal, (nog) niet gestort ~ 2313
kapitaal, (nog) te storten ~ 2313
kapitaal, nominaal ~ 222
kapitaal, obligatie~ 940
kapitaal, onopgevraagd ~ 2313
kapitaal, onproductief ~ 1502
kapitaalopbrengst 535
kapitaal, opgevraagd ~ 500
kapitaal opnemen 416
kapitaal, oprichtings~ 1564
kapitaal, opvraagbaar ~ 499
kapitaaloverdracht 563
kapitaal, privé-~ 1975
kapitaalrekening 516
kapitaalrendement 535
kapitaalrente 535, 540
kapitaal, renteloos ~ 1502
kapitaal, risicodragend ~ 1178
kapitaalschaarste 559
kapitaal, spaar~ 2143
kapitaal, stam~ 544
kapitaal, statutair ~ 222
kapitaal storten 436
kapitaalstorting 1909
kapitaalstroom 528
kapitaalstructuur 561
kapitaal ter beschikking stellen 1407
kapitaaltoevloed 99
kapitaal uitbreiden, het ~ 1544
kapitaaluitbreiding 536
kapitaaluitgaven 524
kapitaal, uitgegeven ~ 1638
kapitaaluitgifte 549
kapitaaluitrusting 523
kapitaaluitvoer 526
kapitaal, vagebonderend ~ 1498
kapitaal, vast ~ 518
kapitaal, vastgelegd ~ 518
kapitaal, vastliggend ~ 518
kapitaalvennootschap 1537
kapitaal, vennootschappelijk ~ 544
kapitaal vergroten, het ~ 1544
kapitaalvergroting 536
kapitaal verhogen, het ~ 1544
kapitaalverhoging 536
kapitaalverkeer 555
kapitaalverlies 552
kapitaalverliezen, budgettaire ~ 445
kapitaalvermindering 2063
kapitaal verschaffen 1407
kapitaalverwatering 2226
kapitaal, vlottend ~ 468
kapitaalvlucht 527
kapitaal, vlucht~ 1349
kapitaal, voltekend ~ 2232
kapitaalvoorziening 1408
kapitaal voorzien, van ~ 1407
kapitaalvorming 529
kapitaal, werk~ 468
kapitaalwinst 530
kapitaalwinstbelasting 532
kapitalisatie 523, 543
kapitalisatie van (verschuldigde) rente 156
kapitaliseren 545
kapitaliseren, de rente ~ 547
kapitaliseren, de winst ~ 548
kapitalist 550
kartel 571
kartel, prijs~ 115
kas 579, 587
kasbalans 253
kasbehoeften 596
kasbescheid 600
kasbewijsstuk 600
kasboek 578
kasbon 389, 590
kas, compensatie~ 649, 710
kasdeficit 96
kasgeld 587
kas, kleine ~ 1931
kaskrediet 580
kas, liquidatie~ 649
kasliquiditeit 227
kasmiddelen 587
kasontvangsten 585
kasoverschot 599
kas, pensioen~ 1918
kas, perekwatie~ 710
kaspositie 592
kasrecettes 585
kasrekening 575
kasreserve 597
kassaldo 253
kas, spaar~ 2139
kas, staats~ 2299
kastekort 96
kastransactie 581
kasuitgaven 582
kasvoorraad 587
kasvoorraad, vaste ~ 1517
kas zijn, niet bij ~ 2178
kelderen van de koersen 431
kelderen van de prijzen 431
kennisgeving van bijschrijving 848
kennisgeving van storting 97
keuzerecht 1854
keynesiaans 1657
kladboek 1754
klasse, inkomens~ 1527
kleine kas 1931
kleine kosten 1764
kleine onkosten 1764
kleine uitgaven 1764
kleingeld 612
kleinhandel 2107
kleinhandelaar 2105
kleinhandelsprijs 2096
kleinhandelsprijzenindex 2106
klimaat, bedrijfs~ 469
klinkende munt, in ~ 573
kluis 2125
kluisloket 2123
koepon 828
koepon, niet vervallen ~ 2330
koers 1960, 2021
koers, aandelen~ 2174
koers, aankoop~ 354
koersachteruitgang 886
koers à contant 593
koersafbrokkeling 886
koers, aflossings~ 2054
koersarbitrage 186
koers, begin~ 1849
koersbericht 1228
koers, beurs~ 1234
koers, bied~ 354
koersblad 1228
koers, clearing~ 650
koers, commissie~ 691
koers, contante ~ 593
koers, conversie~ 778
koers, dag~ 907
koersdaling 886
koers, deport~ 240
koers, doorsnee~ 234
koers, eenheids~ 2326
koers, emissie~ 1642
koersfluctuatie 1225
koers, gedwongen ~ 722, 1356
koers, geld~ 1782
koers, gemiddelde ~ 234
koers, huidige ~ 907
koers, inkoop~ 354
koers, inschrijvings~ 2238
koers, interventie~ 1610
koers, laat~ 193
koerslijst 1228
koerslimiet 1965
koers, limiet~ 1965
koersmanipulatie 1730
koers, midden~ 234
koersniveau 1680
koersnotering 1746, 1960
koers, omrekenings~ 778
koers, openings~ 1849
koers, pari~ 1887
koerspeil 1680
koers, preferentiële omrekenings~ 1950
koers, prolongatie~ 569
koers, rente~ 1593
koers, report~ 569
koersrisico 1238
koersschommeling 1225
koers, slot~ 657
koersstabilisatie 1237
koers, steun~ 1610
koers, termijn~ 1384
koersval 886
koers, valuta~ 1216
koers van terugkoop 2095
koers van uitgifte 1642
koers van wederinkoop 2095

koersverhoudingen 1236
koers, verkoop~ 193
koersverlies 1229
koers, verrekenings~ 650
koersverschil 1039
koers voor contant 593
koers, vrije-markt~ 1396
koerswaarde 1234
koerswinst 1233
koers-winst verhouding 1963
koers, wissel~ 1216
kommissie, kredietopenings~ 693
koop 2012
koop aanbieden, te ~ 1841
koopbriefje 425
koop, huur~ 1487
koopje 321
koopje, gelegenheids~ 321
koopkracht 487
koopkracht, vlottende ~ 1209
koopkracht, zwevende ~ 1209
koopmansboeken 28
koop op krediet 852
koop op levering 1376
koop op rekening 852
koop op termijn 1376
koopoptie 484
koopprijs 488
koop, rouw~ 136
kopen 479
kopen, op afbetaling ~ 481
kopen, op termijn ~ 486
koper 482, 788
koperen munt 788
kopergeld 788
kopersmarkt 483
korf 1845
kort 2177
korte termijn, op ~ 2177
korting 127
korting, fictieve ~ 1822
korting, handels~ 935
korting voor contant 583
korting voor handelaars 935
kortingzegel 2290
kortlopend 2177
kostbaarheden 1646
kosten 795
kosten, aanschaffings~ 488, 804
kosten, administratie~ 79
kosten, algemene ~ 1417
kosten, alternatieve ~ 1853
kosten, arbeids~ 806
kosten, bank~ 291
kosten-baten analyse 801
kosten, bedrijfs~ 1850
kosten, behandelings~ 1478
kosten, beheers~ 79
kosten, beraamde ~ 1189
kostenberekening 797
kostenberekening, differentiële ~ 1045
kostenberekening, integrale ~ 4
kosten, bijkomende ~ 61
kostencalculatie 797
kostencalculatie, differentiële ~ 1045
kostencalculatie, integrale ~ 4
kosten, constante ~ 1336
kostende prijs 814
kostende prijs, tegen de ~ 796
kosten, directe ~ 1043
kosten, diverse ~ 1764
kosten, dossier~ 1478
kostendrager 818
kosten, effectieve ~ 54
kosten, emissie~ 1353
kosten, expeditie~ 2295
kosten, exploitatie~ 1850
kosten, fabricage~ 811
kosten, financierings~ 1313
kosten, geraamde ~ 1189
kosten, historische ~ 804
kosten, indirecte ~ 1417
kosteninflatie 803
kosten, kapitaal~ 522
kosten, kleine ~ 1764
kosten, krediet~ 805
kosten, loon~ 2359
kosten, marginale ~ 1733
kosten, min de ~ 621
kosten, na aftrek van de ~ 131
kosten, niet aftrekbare ~ 1049
kosten, niet in-te-calculeren ~ 1202
kosten, onder aftrek van de ~ 621
kosten, onderhouds~ 810
kosten, overboekings~ 2081
kosten, overdrachts~ 812
kosten, overschrijvings~ 2081
kosten per eenheid 813
kostenplaats 461
kosten, produktie~ 811
kosten, reis~ 2298
kosten, representatie~ 1169
kosten, semi-variabele ~ 2164
kostenstructuur 817
kosten, te betalen ~ 39
kosten, transfer~ 812
kosten, transport~ 2295
kosten, uitgifte~ 1353
kosten van krediet 805
kosten van levensonderhoud 807
kosten van, op ~ 1260
kosten van verkrijging 804
kosten, variabele ~ 2346
kosten, vaste ~ 1336
kostenverdeelstaat 799
kostenvergoeding 128
kosten, verminderd met de ~ 621
kosten, vervangings~ 2091
kosten, vervoer~ 2295
kosten, voorcalculatorische ~ 1189
kosten, voortbrengings~ 811
kosten, werkelijke ~ 54
kostprijs 814
kostprijsberekening 815
kostprijscalculatie 815
kost-prijsspiraal 816
kostprijs, tegen ~ 796
kost(prijs), verzekering, (en) vracht 634
krach 668
kracht, groei~ 1469
kracht, inflatoire ~ 1558
kracht, koop~ 487
krap (bij kas) zitten 2178
krapte, kapitaal~ 559
krediet 843, 845
kredietaanvraag 173
kredietaanvrage 173
krediet aanvragen, een ~ 175
kredietaanvrager 172
krediet, aanvullings~ 63
krediet, accept~ 11
krediet, afbetalings~ 1488
krediet, afroep~ 2214
krediet, automatisch hernieuwd ~ 2114
krediet, aval~ 853
krediet, bank~ 295
kredietbank 850
kredietbeleid 872
kredietbeperking 874
kredietbeperkingen vergemakkelijken, de ~ 1143
kredietbeperkingen versoepelen, de ~ 1143
kredietbewaking 629
krediet, bijkomend ~ 63
krediet, blanco~ 379
krediet, borgstellings~ 853
kredietbrief 1678
krediet, consortiaal ~ 741
krediet, consumenten~ 745
krediet, consumptief ~ 745
kredietcontrole 629
kredietcoöperatie 787
krediet dat automatisch gedekt wordt 2156
krediet, disconto~ 1059
krediet, documentair ~ 1085
kredieten, begrotings~ 444
kredieten, bevroren ~ 1401
kredieten, binnenlandse ~ 1093
kredieten, budget~ 444
kredieten, investerings~ 1620
kredietexpansie 858
kredietfaciliteiten 421
kredietfonds 1710
kredietgarantie 860
kredietgebrek 878
krediet, gedekt ~ 670
krediet, gegarandeerd ~ 670
kredietgever 1672
krediet, gewaarborgd ~ 670
kredietgrens 855
krediet, handels~ 470
krediet, herroepelijk ~ 2113
krediet, hypot(h)ecair ~ 866
krediet, hypot(h)eek~ 866
kredietinflatie 861
krediet in gemeenschappelijke rekening 865
kredietinperking 874
kredietinstelling 850
krediet, interbancair ~ 1583
kredietkaart 854
krediet, kas~ 580
kredietkosten 805
kredietlijn 855
kredietlimiet 855
kredietlinie 855
kredietmarge 864
krediet, meta~ 741

kredietmiddel 862
krediet, middellang ~ 1753
krediet, mobilair ~ 867
kredietnemer 418
krediet, ongedekt ~ 379
krediet, open ~ 379
krediet openen, ten gunste van iemand een ~ 1847
kredietopening 1848
kredietopeningskommissie 693
kredietopeningsprovisie 693
kredietoperaties 851
krediet op hypot(h)eek 866
krediet op onderpand 670
krediet op onroerende goederen 868
krediet op roerende goederen 867
krediet, overbruggings~ 434
krediet overschrijden, een ~ 1201
kredietpapier 862
krediet, persoonlijk ~ 1927
kredietplafon(d) 855
kredietpolitiek 872
krediet prolongeren, een ~ 1272
krediet, rekening-courant~ 87
krediet, rembours~ 1085
krediet, renouvellerend ~ 2114
kredietrestrictie 874
krediet, revolver~ 2114
krediet, revolving ~ 2114
krediet, roll-over ~ 2118
kredietschaarste 878
kredietschepping 841
krediet, speciaal ~ 2194
krediet, stand-by-~ 2214
kredietstelsel 879
kredietstroom 859
krediet, swap~ 2252
krediet tegen effecten 869
krediet tegen onderpand 670
krediet tegen onderpandeffecten 869
krediet toekennen, een ~ 126
krediet toestaan, een ~ 126
kredièttoezegging 88
kredièttransacties 851
krediet, tussentijds ~ 434
kredietuitbreiding 858
krediet van de centrale banken 1708
kredietvereniging 787
kredietvergemakkelijking 1145
krediet verkopen, op ~ 2163
krediet verlenen, een ~ 126
krediet verlengen, een ~ 1272
kredietverlenging 1275
kredietverlening 220
kredietvernauwing 874
kredietverruiming 858
kredietversoepeling 1145
krediet verstrekken, een ~ 126
kredietverstrekking 220
kredietverzekering 863
kredietvolume 881
kredietvoorwaarden 856
kredietwaardig 846
kredietwaardigheid 873
kredietwezen 879
krediet, wissel~ 11
kredietzaken 851
kringen, financiële ~ 1305
kruipende inflatie 882
kruiselingse wisselkoers 884
kwartaal 2016
kwijnen 1663
kwijnend 508
kwijning 1130
kwijtbrief 47
kwijting 47
kwijtschelden, een schuld ~ 510
kwijtschelding van een schuld 513
kwijtschrift 47
kwitantie 47, 51

laagconjunctuur 1031
laatkoers 193
laatprijs 2162
lacune, dollar~ 1089
lage conjunctuur 1031
lagere prijs verkopen, tegen ~ 2317
lage schatting, te ~ 2318
lanceerprijs 1613
lanceren, een lening ~ 1157
lanceren, op de markt ~ 1665
lancering 1352
land, crediteur~ 871
land, debiteur~ 959
land, export~ 825
land, import~ 826
land, invoer~ 826
land, kapitaalexport~ 525
land met harde valuta 1480
land met zachte valuta 2188
land, overschot~ 824
lands financiën, 's ~ 827
landsmunt 1094
landsvaluta 1094
land, uitvoer~ 825
lang 1715
lange termijn, op ~ 1715
langlopend 1715
langzicht- 1715
last 460
lasten 619
lasten, afschrijvings~ 620
lasten, financiële ~ 1313
lasten, kapitaal~ 520
lasten, rente~ 1587
lasten, sociale ~ 2186
laste van, ten ~ 616
last, fiscale ~ 463
lastgever 1973
last, hypot(h)eek~ 1793
last, schulden~ 462
laten, bieden en ~ 192
laten, een winst ~ 100
latente belastingverplichting 759, 986
latente inflatie 725
laten zien, een verlies (een winst) ~ 2046
leasing 1668
leenbank 850
leenbehoefte 424
leengarantie 1473
leenkapitaal 1707
leenwaarborg 1473
leggen (op), een belasting ~ 194
leggen (op), een toeslag ~ 1514
legger 1418
lenen 415, 1671
lenen, geld op (tegen) int(e)rest ~ 1675
lenen, kapitaal ~ 416
lener 418, 1672
lening 419, 845, 1705
lening aangaan, een ~ 762
leningaanvraag 173
leningaanvrage 173
lening aanvragen, een ~ 175
leningaanvrager 172
lening, aflosbare ~ 141
lening, aflossing van een ~ 142
lening afsluiten, een ~ 762
lening, amortisatie~ 141
lening, amortisatie van een ~ 142
lening, bank~ 298
lening bedienen, een ~ 2165
lening beroep doen, op een ~ 1122
lening, bij wijze van ~ 1706
lening, binnenlandse ~ 1099
lening, buitenlandse ~ 1282
lening, commerciële ~ 473
lening, consolidatie~ 738
lening, conversie~ 774
lening, converteerbare ~ 784
lening converteren, een ~ 779
lening, daggeld~ 504
lening doen, een ~ 762
lening emitteren, een ~ 1157
leningen 1673
lening, fiduciaire ~ 1301
lening, gebonden ~ 2281
lening, gedekte ~ 672
lening, gedwongen ~ 723
lening, gegarandeerde ~ 672
lening, goud~ 1438
lening, handels~ 473
lening in het buitenland 1282
lening, in termijnen aflosbare hypot(h)ecaire ~ 137
leningkapitaal 1707
lening lanceren, een ~ 1157
lening, loten~ 1720
lening, nationale ~ 1099
lening negotiëren, een ~ 1807
lening, obligatie~ 941
lening omzetten, een ~ 779
lening onderbrengen, een ~ 1933
lening, ongedekte ~ 1301
lening, ontwikkelings~ 1036
lening, openbare ~ 1453
lening op hypot(h)eek 1711
lening opnemen, een ~ 762, 1122
lening op onderpand 672
lening op vaste termijn 2277
lening, overheids~ 1453
lening plaatsen, een ~ 1933
lening, premie~ 1720
leningrentevoet 423
leningsaflossing 142
leningsbehoefte 424
leningsdienst 2167
leningsfonds 1710
lening sluiten, een ~ 762
lening, staats~ 1453
lening, stabilisatie~ 2206
lening tegen effecten 1712

lening tegen onderpand 672
lening tegen onderpandeffecten 1712
lening tegen woekerrente 2336
lening ter inschrijving aanbieden, een ~ 1634
lening uitgeven, een ~ 1157
lening uitschrijven, een ~ 1157
lening, zicht~ 504
lening zonder dekking 1301
leven, boven zijn middelen ~ 1702
levensduurte 807, 1483
levenspeil 1704
levensstandaard 1704
levensvatbaar 2350
levensvatbaarheid 2349
levensverzekering 1688
levering tegen betaling bij ontvangst 589
levering tegen contante betaling 589
levering, termijn~ 1380
liberalisatie van de handel 1684
liberaliseren 1685
liberalisering van de handel 1684
licentie, export~ 1268
licentie, import~ 1512
licentie, invoer~ 1512
licentierecht 1686
licentie, uitvoer~ 1268
lichamelijke goederen 1747
liggende goederen 1508
liggende gronden 1661
lijden, een verlies ~ 333
lijfrente 163
lijn, krediet~ 855
lijst, boedel~ 1614
lijst, koers~ 1228
lijst, loon~ 1912
lijst van aandeelhouders 1701
lijst van tolvrije goederen 1394
lijst van vennoten 1701
limiet, koers~ 1965
limietkoers 1965
limiet, krediet~ 855
limietprijs 1965
limiet, prijs~ 1965
limiet, schuld~ 422
lineaire afschrijving 2228
linie, krediet~ 855
liquidateur 1694
liquidatie 139, 773, 1070
liquidatiedag 24
liquidatie gaan, in ~ 1428
liquidatiekas 649
liquidatietermijn 18
liquidatie van een rekening 254
liquidatiewaarde 432
liquidator 1694
liquide 1693
liquide activa 227
liquide maken 785
liquide middelen 227
liquideren 148, 1071, 1428
liquideren, een rekening ~ 249
liquide reserves 1696
liquiditeit 1695
liquiditeiten 227
liquiditeitenmassa 1783
liquiditeiten, quasimonetaire ~ 1776
liquiditeiten, secondaire ~ 1776
liquiditeiten, secundaire ~ 1776
liquiditeit, kas~ 227
liquiditeit, overmatige ~ 1211
liquiditeit, primaire ~ 1971
liquiditeitsbehoeften 596
liquiditeitsbeperking 2104
liquiditeitscoëfficiënt 45
liquiditeitseisen 596
liquiditeitsgraad 45
liquiditeitsinperking 2104
liquiditeitsratio 45
liquiditeitsreserves 1696
liquiditeitsverhouding 45
liquiditeitsverhoudingscijfer 45
liquiditeitsvolume 1783
locoaffaire 581
locoprijs 2203
locotransactie 581
locozaak 581
lonend 1147
lonen- en prijzenspiraal 2363
lonen en salarissen 1141
loom 508
loomheid 1130
loon 1140
loon, accoord~ 1907
loon, akkoord~ 1907
loon, beheer~ 80
loon, bewaar~ 2124
loon, commissie~ 689
looncontrole 2360
loon- en prijsspiraal 2363
looninkomen 1136
loonkosten 2359
loonlijst 1912
loon, makelaars~ 438
loon, munt~ 2154
loon naar prestatie 1153
loon, premie~ 1520
loon-prijsspiraal 2363
loonsom 2359
loon, stuk~ 1932
loonsverhoging 1542
loonsverhogingen veroorzaakte inflatie, door ~ 2361
loontoeslag 1288
looptijd 894
looptijd, X-jarige ~ 1749
lopend actief 905
lopende int(e)rest 909
lopende overdrachten, saldo van de ~ 257
lopende prijs 911
lopende rekening 23
lopende rente 909
lopende uitgaven 908
lopende verplichtingen 910
lororekening 1716
losmaken 949
lossen 502
lossing 2053
lotenlening 1720
lotenobligatie 1719
loting 1111
lot, premie~ 1719
lucratief 1147
lui 508
luidend, in dollars ~ 1010
lusteloos 508
lusteloosheid 1130
luxeartikelen 1001
luxebelasting 1723
luxegoederen 1001

maandelijkse afbetaling 1788
maandelijkse aflossing 1788
maandgeld 1787
maandsalaris 1787
maandwedde 1787
maatregelen ter stimulering van de economie 2011
maatschappelijke zekerheid 2184
maatschappelijke zetel 2075
maatschappelijk inkomen 791
maatschappelijk kapitaal 222, 544
maatschappelijk vermogen 790
maatschappij 686
maatschappij, bank~ 302
maatschappij, beleggings~ 653
maatschappij, dochter~ 98
maatschappij, financierings~ 1308
maatschappij, geaffilieerde ~ 98
maatschappij, handel(s)~ 686
maatschappij, houdster~ 1494
maatschappij, Internationale Financierings~ 1605
maatschappij, moeder~ 769
maatschappij, participatie~ 1494
maatschappij, trust~ 2306
maatstaf voor belastingheffing 331
macro-economisch 1725
makelaar 437
makelaar aan de goederenbeurs 694
makelaar, beurs~ 2152
makelaar, deviezen~ 509
makelaar, disconto~ 361
makelaar, effecten~ 2152
makelaar, geld~ 1311
makelaar, goederen~ 694
makelaarsfirma 439
makelaarskantoor 439
makelaarsloon 438
makelaar, tussen~ 1648
makelaar, valuta~ 509
makelaar, wissel~ 361, 509
maken, een schuld ~ 761
maken, een verlies ~ 333
manco 988
mandaat 356
mandaat, bank~ 284
mandaat, betalings~ 590
maneuver, beurs~ 1730
manipulatie, koers~ 1730
manipulatie, valuta~ 898
manœuvre, beurs~ 1730
mantel 2176
marge 1037, 1732
marge, aanvullende ~ 62
marge, bruto winst~ 1465
marge, handels~ 1734
marge, krediet~ 864
marge, prijs~ 1966
marge, rente~ 1412
marges van de arbitrageverrichtingen 187

officiële beurs 1845
omlaagtuimelen van de koersen 431
omlaagtuimelen van de prijzen 431
omloop, bankbiljetten in ~ 308
omloop, geld(s)~ 637
omloop, in ~ 635
omloopsnelheid 2027
omloopsnelheid van de debiteuren 960
omloop stellen, buiten ~ 503
omloop(s)tijd 895
om(me)keer 428
omrekening 771
omrekeningsfactor 772
omrekeningskoers 778
omrekeningsmunt 1780
omslaan 122
omslag 123
omslag, debiteuren~ 960
omvang, zaken~ 2130
omwisseling van effecten 2254
omzet 2130
omzetbelasting 2014
omzet, bruto-~ 1467
omzetindexcijfer 2131
omzet, netto-~ 1816
omzetrendement 1815
omzetten, een lening ~ 779
omzet ter beurze 2225
omzetting van een lening 775
omzetting van schulden 776
onaantastbare activa 1505
onafkoopbare obligatie 1636
onaflosbare obligatie 1636
onbeperkte aansprakelijkheid 2329
onbetaald bedrag 154
onbetaalde wissel 365
onbetaald teruggezonden wissel 365
onderaandeel 2230
onderbrengen 1935
onderbrengen, een lening ~ 1933
onderbrengen, een uitgifte ~ 1934
onderdrukte inflatie 1919
ondergaan, een verlies ~ 333
onderhevig, aan belasting ~ 196
onderhevig, aan douanerechten ~ 916
onderhoudskosten 810
onderkapitalisatie 2315
onderkruipen 2317
onderlinge verdeling der markten 1745
onderlinge verdeling van de markt 1745
ondernemer 1171
onderneming 467
onderneming, particuliere ~ 1977
onderneming, privé-~ 1977
onderneming, staats~ 1448
onderneming, vrijheid van ~ 1391
onderpand 1138
onderpand deponeren, als ~ 1018
onderpand deponeren, effecten als (in) ~ 671
onderpand gedeponeerde effecten, als ~ 1895
onderpand geven, als ~ 1018
onderpand geven, effecten als (in) ~ 671
onderpand geven, in ~ 1018
onderpand, voorschot op ~ 86
onderpand, zakelijk ~ 2035
onderschatten 2319
onderschatting 2318
ondersteuning, prijs~ 1917
onderwaarderen 2319
onderwaardering 2318
onderworpen, aan belasting ~ 196
onderworpen, aan douanerechten ~ 916
onderzetting 1790
onderzoek, belasting~ 1566
onderzoek, markt~ 1740
onderzoek van de boekhouding 214
oneconomisch 2324
onevenwichtigheid 1062
ongedekt 835
ongedekte cheque 241
ongedekte lening 1301
ongedekt krediet 379
ongefundeerde schuld 1351
ongemunt goud en zilver 457
ongesaldeerde rekening 1846
ongunstige handelsbalans 94
oninbare schuld 242
oninbare vordering 242
onjuiste allocatie van middelen 1763
onjuiste belegging 244
onjuiste investering 244
onjuiste toewijzing van middelen 1763
onjuistheden en weglatingen 1183
onkosten 1261
onkosten, algemene ~ 1417
onkosten, bank~ 291
onkosten, bedrijfs~ 1850
onkosten, bijkomende ~ 61
onkosten, diverse ~ 1764
onkosten, exploitatie~ 1850
onkosten, kleine ~ 1764
onkosten, min de ~ 621
onkosten, na aftrek van de ~ 131
onkosten, onder aftrek van de ~ 621
onkostenrekening 1259
onkostenvergoeding 128
onkosten, verminderd met de ~ 621
onkosten, zakelijke ~ 472
onlichamelijke goederen 1505
onopgevraagd kapitaal 2313
onoverdraagbare wissel 371
onproductief kapitaal 1502
onrendabel 2324
onroerende goederen 1508
onstabiele valuta 1350
ontbinden 1071
ontbinding 1070
ontbrekende 988
ontdooien 949
ontdooing 950
ontduiking, belasting~ 2266
onteigenen 1270
onteigening 1271
ontheffing (van belasting) 2261
ontlenen 415
ontlener 418
ontmunten 503
ontmunting 1008
ontpotting 1063
ontsnappingsclausule 1155
ontspanning op de geldmarkt 1144
ontsparing 1069
onttrekken 1113
onttrekking 1008, 1119
onttrekking aan reserves 2377
ontvangen rente, te ~ 376
ontvanger 350, 2082
ontvanger van een wissel 1902
ontvangstbericht 47
ontvangstbevestiging 47
ontvangstbewijs 47
ontvangsten 1532
ontvangsten, begrotings~ 447
ontvangsten, belasting~ 1565
ontvangsten, douane~ 921
ontvangsten en uitbetalingen 1525
ontvangsten en uitgaven 1525
ontvangsten, kas~ 585
ontvangst(en), mindere ~ 2112
ontvangsten, overheids~ 1451
ontwaarden 1028
ontwaarding 1029
ontwaarding, geld~ 896, 1554
ontwaarding, munt~ 896
ontwaarding, valuta~ 896
ontwijking, belasting~ 2266
ontwikkeling 1200
ontwikkeling, conjuncturele ~ 477
ontwikkelingsbank 1035
ontwikkelingshulp 1034
ontwikkelingslening 1036
onverdeelde winsten 2311
onvereffende post 2312
onvereffende rekening 1846
onverhandelbare wissel 371
onvermogen 1569
onvoordelig 2324
onvoorziene uitgaven 754
onzichtbare export 1632
onzichtbare import 1633
onzichtbare invoer 1633
onzichtbare reserves 726
onzichtbare uitvoer 1632
opbod 1484
opbod verkopen, bij ~ 213
opbrengen, een rente van X procent ~ 334
opbrengen, een winst ~ 100
opbrengst 2110
opbrengst, belasting~ 1565
opbrengsten, extra~ 2246
opbrengst, kapitaal~ 535
opbrengst, rente~ 1595
opbrengst van obligaties 396
opcenten 66
opcentiemen 66
opdracht, bank~ 299
opdracht, betalings~ 221
opdracht geven tot uitbetaling van een rekening 223
opdrachtgever 1973
opdracht tot betaling 590
opdrijven 1553

opeenhopen 43
op(een)hopen, zich ~ 40
opeenhoping 44
opeisbaar 496, 675
opeisbaarheid 674
opeisbare schuld 37
openbaar bedrijf 1448
openbaar nutsbedrijf 2009
openbare begroting 1446
openbare belegging 2003
openbare financiën 827
openbare investering 2006
openbare lening 1453
openbare schuld 1798
openbare sector 2008
openbare voorzieningen 684
openbare werken 2010
open cheque 339
openen van een krediet 1848
opening, krediet~ 1848
openingsbalans 1700
openingskoers 1849
openingsnotering 1849
opening van het faillissement 1575
open krediet 379
open markt 1395
open rekening 23, 1846
open reserves 966
openstaande rekening 23
openstellen, de inschrijving op een lening ~ 1634
openstelling van inschrijving 1842
operatie 320
operaties, bank~ 304
operaties, beurs~ 1222
operaties, deviezen~ 1241
operaties, krediet~ 851
operaties met het buitenland 1358
operaties, valuta~ 1241
opgaande tendens 459
opgave, credit~ 847
opgave, stortings~ 877
opgeld 109
opgelegde prijs 78
opgelopen rente 41
opgeven, een prijs ~ 1728
opgevraagd kapitaal 500
opheffen 1071
opheffen, elkaar ~ 248
opheffing 1070
opheffing van beperkingen 2
ophopen 43
ophoping 38, 44
opkopen 489
opkopen, de markt ~ 789
opleggen, een prijs ~ 1033
opleveren, een winst ~ 100
opleving 2048, 2117
oplopen 40
opmaken, de inventaris ~ 1124
opmaken, een balans ~ 279
opmaken, een saldo ~ 279
opmaken van de inventaris 1616
opname 1119
opnemen 1113
opnemen, een lening ~ 762, 1122
opnemen, kapitaal ~ 416
opnemen van krediet 419
opneming 1119
opneming in contanten 601
opnieuw gefundeerde obligatie 704
oppotten 1492
oppotting 1493
oprichtersaandelen 1386
oprichtersbewijzen 1386
oprichtingskapitaal 1564
opschorten, de betalingen ~ 603
opschorten, de betaling van een cheque ~ 2227
opschorting van betaling 1276
opslag 60
opslagbewijs 2364
opstellen, een balans ~ 279
opstrijken, een winst ~ 1937
optie 1854
optiegeld 1856
optie, koop~ 484
optierecht 1854
optie, verkoop~ 1858
opvoeren 1553
opvorderbaar 496, 675
opvorderbare passiva 910
opvraagbaar 675
opvraagbaar kapitaal 499
opvragen 1113
opvraging 1119
opvraging in contanten 601
opvraging, met X dagen ~ 1837
opvragingstermijn 1836
opvragingstermijn van X dagen, met een ~ 1837
opvraging van aanvullende dekking 501
opvraging van bijstorting 494
opvraging van storting 494
opwaarderen 178
opwaardering 2111
opwegen, tegen elkaar ~ 248
opzeggen, met X dagen ~ 1426
opzegging 1835
opzegging, met X dagen ~ 1837
opzeggingstermijn 1836
opzeggingstermijn van X dagen, met een ~ 1837
opzegging van deposito's 1840
opzegging, zonder ~ 1838
order- 1726
orderbiljet 1477
orderbriefje 1477
ordercheque 631
order geven tot uitbetaling van een rekening 223
orderpapier 1806
orderrekening 2248
orderwissel 374
organisatie, Internationale Arbeids~ 1606
organisatie, Internationale Ontwikkelings~ 1604
Organisatie voor Economische Samenwerking en Ontwikkeling 1860
Organisatie voor Europese Economische Samenwerking 1861
overbesparing 1872
overbesteding 1212
overboeken 2080
overboeking 318
overboeking, bank~ 318
overboeking naar nieuwe rekening 150
overboekingskosten 2081
overboekingsrekeningen 802
overboeking van geld 1784
overbrengen 435
overbruggingsfinanciering 433
overbruggingskrediet 434
overdekking van kosten 1870
overdisponeren, op een rekening ~ 1868
overdisponering 1867
overdispositie 1867
overdraagbaar 117
overdraagbaarheid 116
overdraagbare waardepapieren 1739
overdraagbare wissel 374
overdracht 119
overdracht, geld~ 1784
overdracht, kapitaal~ 563
overdracht naar nieuwe rekening 150
overdrachtsinkomen 2292
overdrachtskosten 812
overdrachtsrecht 812
overdrachtstaks 2014
overdrachtstaxe 2014
overdracht van vorderingen 208
overdragen 118, 2080
overdragen, een vordering ~ 207
overdrager 121, 2083
overeengekomen prijs 114
overeenkomen, een prijs ~ 113
overeenkomst 718
overeenkomst, betalings~ 1906
overeenkomst, clearing~ 647
overeenkomst, compensatie~ 647
Overeenkomst, Europese Monetaire ~ 1196
overeenkomst, huur~ 1666
Overeenkomst inzake Tarieven en Handel, Algemene ~ 1415
overeenkomst, pacht~ 1666
overeenkomst, prijs~ 115
overeenkomst, stand-by-krediet~ 2215
overeenkomst, stilhalte-~ 2216
overeenkomst tot opschorting van betaling 2216
overeenkomst, verrekenings~ 647
overeenstemming brengen, rekeningen in ~ 112
overgebrachte winst 1985
overheidsbedrijf 1448
overheidsbegroting 1446
overheidsbemoeiing 1452
overheidsfinanciën 827
overheidsfondsen 1244
overheidsgarantie 1450
overheidsgarantie voor een lening 1447
overheidsgelden 2005
overheidshulp 1445
overheidsinmenging 1452
overheidsinterventie 1452

overheidsinvestering 2006
overheidslening 1453
overheidsmiddelen 2007
overheidsontvangsten 1451
overheidspapieren 1244
overheidssector 2008
overheidssteun 1445
overheidssubsidie 1449
overheidstoelage 1449
overheidsuitgaven 2003
overheidsverbruik 2002
overkapitalisatie 1865
overloon 1288
overmaken 118, 2080
overmaking 119
overmaking in contanten 595
overmaking naar het buitenland 1372
overmaking van geld 1784
overmaking van kapitaal 563
overmatige liquiditeit 1211
overname 2257
overnameconsortium 2322
overnamesyndicaat 2322
overnemen 2233
overnemer 120
overneming 2257
overnemingscontract 2321
overprijs 1208
overschatten 1863
overschatting 1864
overschietend bedrag 1205
overschot 1204, 2244
overschot, bedrijfs~ 1852
overschot, begrotings~ 452
overschot, bestedings~ 1557
overschot, betalingsbalans~ 263
overschot, boekings~ 30
overschot, exploitatie~ 1852
overschot, kas~ 599
overschotland 824
overschot op de handelsbalans 266
overschot, structureel ~ 2229
overschot van ontvangsten 2245
overschrijden, een krediet ~ 1201
overschrijven 2080
overschrijving 318
overschrijving, bank~ 318
overschrijvingskosten 2081
overschrijving van geld 1784
overspoelen, de markt (met goedkope artikelen) ~ 1132
overstelpende schuldenlast 1207
overstromen, de markt (met goedkope artikelen) ~ 1132
overtaxeren 1863
overtekenen 1873
overtekening 1874
overtrekken, een rekening ~ 1868
overtrekking 1867
overtrokken vraag 1206
overuren 1875
oververhitting 1871
oververzadigen, de markt (met goedkope artikelen) ~ 1132
overvloed, geld~ 6
overvoeren, de markt (met goedkope artikelen) ~ 1132
overvragen 1866
overwaarde 1215
overwaarderen 1863
overwaardering 1864
overwinst 1213
overwinstbelasting 1214
overzeese handel 1283
overzicht 2217
overzicht, financieel ~ 1319

pacht 1666, 2088
pachtbrief 1666
pachtcedel 1666
pachtceel 1666
pachtcontract 1666
pachter 1667
pachtgeld 2088
pachtovereenkomst 1666
pachtprijs 2088
pakket, aandelen~ 386
pakket aandelen 386
pand 1138
pandbrief 1792
pandbrief, hypot(h)eek~ 1792
pand deponeren, als ~ 1018
pand deponeren, effecten als (in) ~ 671
panden 1018
pand gedeponeerde effecten, als ~ 1895
pand geven, als ~ 1018
pand geven, effecten als (in) ~ 671
pand geven, in ~ 1018
pandrecht (op) 1687
pandvoorschot 86
papier aan toonder 340
papier, bankabel ~ 283
papier, discontabel ~ 283
papier, disconteerbaar ~ 283
papieren 2151
papieren, beleggings~ 1630
papieren geld 1355
papieren, geldswaardige ~ 1739
papieren, overheids~ 1244
papieren, schatkist~ 1244
papieren, speculatie~ 2199
papieren, staats~ 1244
papieren standaard 1881
papieren, toonder~ 342
papiergeld 1355
papier, geldmarkt~ 1779
papiergeld, niet inwisselbaar ~ 1535
papier, handels~ 356
papier, krediet~ 862
papier op het binnenland 1091
papier op het buitenland 1357
papier op zicht 1007
papier, order~ 1806
papier, verhandelbaar ~ 1806
parallelmarkt 1885
pari 1889
pari, à ~ 1882
parikoers 1887
pari, munt~ 1762
pari staan 1884
pari staan, à ~ 1884
pari staan, beneden ~ 1056
pari staan, boven ~ 1883
pari staan, onder ~ 1056
pari staan, op ~ 1884
pari, tegen ~ 1882
pariteit 1886, 1889
pariteit, goud~ 1439
pariteit, munt~ 1762
pariteitsprijs 1887
pariteitsverhouding 1888
pariteit verlagen, de ~ 2062
pariteit verminderen, de ~ 2062
pariteit, wissel~ 1182
pariwaarde 1889
pari, wissel~ 1890
parquet 1845
parquetmarkt 1845
participatie, buitenlandse ~ 1365, 1366
participatie (in) 1495
participatie in het buitenland 1366
participatiemaatschappij 1494
participatie, meerderheids~ 770
participatie, minderheids~ 1760
participatierekening 1654
particulier bedrijf 1977
particulier bezit 1979
particuliere bank 1974
particuliere belegging 1978
particuliere besparingen 1980
particuliere eigendom 1979
particulier eigendom 1979
particuliere investering 1978
particuliere onderneming 1977
particuliere schuld 1928
particuliere sector 1981
particulier initiatief 1976
pasgeld 612
pasmunt 612, 1083
passering, dividend~ 1826
passief 961
passief, actief en ~ 203
passief-rekening 1682
passief saldo 93
passief schrijven, op het ~ 402
passiefzijde 943
passieve balans 274
passieve handelsbalans 94
passieve schuld 36
passiva 961
passiva, activa en ~ 203
passiva, direct opvorderbare ~ 1006
passiva, opvorderbare ~ 910
passiveren 402
passiveren, te ~ 407
peil, koers~ 1680
peil, levens~ 1704
peil, prijs~ 1680
penningen, spaar~ 2137
pensioenfonds 1918
pensioenkas 1918
pensionwissel 363
percent 1921, 1922
percentage 1921
percentage, afschrijvings~ 144
percentage, amortisatie~ 144, 145
percentage, groei~ 1255
percentage, inflatie~ 1563
percentage, rendements~ 2025
percentage, stijgings~ 1255

percentage, toenemings~ 1255
percent verhoging, X ~ 1543
perekwatie 1172
perekwatie der belastingen 1175
perekwatiekas 710
periodieke inkomsten 2049
personenvennootschap 1892
personenvennootschap met beperkte aansprakelijkheid 1690
persoonlijk aansprakelijk vennoot 1419
persoonlijke rekening 1926
persoonlijk inkomen 1929
persoonlijk krediet 1927
plaatsen 1618, 1935
plaatsen, een lening ~ 1933
plaatsen, een uitgifte ~ 1934
plaatsen, op de reserve ~ 68
plaatsing 1619
plaats, kosten~ 461
plafon(d), krediet~ 855
plafon(d), schuld~ 422
plan, aflossings~ 146
plan, amortisatie~ 146
plan, delgings~ 146
planeconomie 768
planmatige economie 768
polis, verzekerings~ 1577
politiek, dividend~ 1081
politiek, financiële ~ 1317
politiek, geld~ 1769
politiek, krediet~ 872
politiek, monetaire ~ 1769
politiek, munt~ 1769
ponden, geblokkeerde ~ 382
ponden, transferabele ~ 2291
pond sterling 1943
pool 1938
poolen 1939
pooling 1939
portefeuille, aandelen~ 1628
portefeuille, effecten~ 1628
positie continueren, een ~ 568
positie, deviezen~ 1363
positie, kas~ 592
positie, markt~ 1743
positie prolongeren, een ~ 568
positie reporteren, een ~ 568
positie van een rekening 1940
post 409
post aandelen 386
post, boekings~ 409
postcheck 1425
postcheque 1425
postcheque- en girodienst 1423
postchequerekening 1800
post, contra~ 281
post, correctie~ 71
post, credit~ 857
post, dagboek~ 1655
postdateren 1942
post, debet~ 946
posten, transitorische ~ 73
post, geboekte ~ 409
postgirobiljet 1781
postgirorekening 1800
post, journaal~ 1655
post, niet gesaldeerde ~ 2312
post, onvereffende ~ 2312
postrekening 1800
postspaarbank 1941
post, storno~ 281
post, tegen~ 281
post, transitorische ~ 2249
post, tussen~ 2249
postwissel 1781
preferent aandeel 1946
preferent dividend 1945
preferente aandelen, cumulatief ~ 890
preferente crediteur 1948
preferente schuldeiser 1948
preferentieel recht 1949
preferentieel tarief 1947
preferentiële omrekeningskoers 1950
premie 110, 397, 1856
premieaffaire 1855
premieaffaire met noch in kopers keuze 485
premieaffaire met noch in verkopers keuze 1857
premieaffaire met noch te leveren 485
premieaffaire met noch te ontvangen 1857
premie, aflossings~ 1750
premie, baisse~ 1953
premie, dont~ 507
premie, dubbele ~ 1108
premie, emissie~ 1641
premie, export~ 426
premie, hausse~ 507
premielening 1720
premieloon 1520
premielot 1719
premieobligatie 1719
premie, prolongatie~ 569
premie te leveren 507
premie te ontvangen 1953
premie, terugbetalings~ 1750
premietransactie 1855
premie, uitgifte~ 1641
premie, uitvoer~ 426
premie, verzekerings~ 1578
prescriptie 1955
prestatie, bijkomende ~ 1285
prestatieloon 1153
prestatie, sociale ~ 2185
prijs 1960
prijs, aangeboden ~ 1843
prijs, aankoop~ 488
prijsaanpassing 76
prijs, aanschaffings~ 488
prijsachteruitgang 886
prijs à contant 593
prijsafbrokkeling 886
prijs, aflossings~ 2054
prijsafslag 927
prijsafspraak 115
prijsbeheersing 1961
prijs bepalen, een ~ 1033
prijsbepaling 1962
prijsbeperking 1968
prijsbinding 1515
prijsbinding, verticale ~ 2097
prijs, buitensporige ~ 1250
prijs, consumenten~ 749
prijs, consumptie~ 749
prijs, contante ~ 593
prijs, contract~ 114
prijscontrole 1961
prijscourant van de effectenhandel 1228
prijs, dag~ 911
prijsdaling 886
prijs, detail~ 2096
prijs, detailhandels~ 2096
prijs, detailverkoop~ 2096
prijsdispariteit 1038
prijs, eenheids~ 1344, 2328
prijs, emissie~ 1642
prijs, en-gros-~ 2288
prijs, exorbitante ~ 1250
prijs, fabricage~ 811
prijs, forfaitaire ~ 114
prijs, globale ~ 114
prijs, grens~ 1965
prijsgrens 1965
prijs, grond~ 330
prijs, grondslag~ 330
prijs, groothandels~ 2288
prijs, grossiers~ 2288
prijs, gunst~ 1203
prijs, huidige ~ 911
prijs, huur~ 2088
prijsindex 1964
prijsindexcijfer 1964
prijs, inkoop~ 488
prijs, inschrijvings~ 2238
prijs, inteken~ 2238
prijskartel 115
prijs, kleinhandels~ 2096
prijs, koop~ 488
prijs, kost~ 814
prijs, kostende ~ 814
prijs, laat~ 2162
prijs, lanceer~ 1613
prijs, limiet~ 1965
prijslimiet 1965
prijs, loco~ 2203
prijs, lopende ~ 911
prijsmarge 1966
prijs, markt~ 1744
prijs, maximum~ 605
prijsniveau 1680
prijs noemen, een ~ 1728
prijs, normale ~ 1832
prijsondersteuning 1917
prijs, opgelegde ~ 78
prijs opgeven, een ~ 1728
prijs opleggen, een ~ 1033
prijs, overeengekomen ~ 114
prijs overeenkomen, een ~ 113
prijsovereenkomst 115
prijs, pacht~ 2088
prijs, pariteits~ 1887
prijspeil 1680
prijs per eenheid 2328
prijs, produktie~ 811
prijs, reclame~ 1613
prijsreductie 927
prijsregeling 1961
prijs, richt~ 1832
prijs, slot~ 657

prijs, speciale ~ 1203
prijs, spot~ 322
prijsstabilisatie 1969
prijsstabiliteit 1326
prijs, standaard~ 1832
prijsstijging 1539
prijsstop 1400
prijs, stuk~ 2328
prijs, tegen de kostende ~ 796
prijs, tegen kost~ 796
prijs, termijn~ 1384
prijs, uitgifte~ 1642
prijs, uitzonderings~ 1203
prijs van de aandelen 2174
prijs van het geld 1967
prijs, vaste ~ 78
prijs, vastgestelde ~ 78
prijs vastleggen, een ~ 1033
prijs vaststellen, een ~ 1033
prijsverhoging 1539
prijs, verkoop~ 2162
prijsverlaging 927
prijsvermindering 927
prijsverschil 1038
prijs, vervangings~ 2091
prijs, voorgeschreven ~ 78
prijs, voorkeur~ 1203
prijs voorschrijven, een ~ 1033
prijs, wederverkoop~ 2096
prijs, weggeef~ 322
prijs, woeker~ 1250
prijs zeggen, een ~ 1728
prijszetting 1515
prijzenbinding 1515
prijzencontrole 1961
prijzen, in constante ~ 742
prijzenindex 1964
prijzenstijging 1539
prijzen, tegen constante ~ 742
prijzen, vrijgeven van de ~ 971
prijzen, vrijmaking van de ~ 971
prikkel, investerings~ 1625
prima 1327
prima fondsen 387
prima handelspapier 1323
primaire inkomens 1970
primaire liquiditeit 1971
prima waarden 387
primawissel 1327
prime 110
principaal 1973
principe van de laagste waarde 1721
prioriteitsaandeel 1946
prioriteitsaandelen, cumulatief ~ 890
prioriteitsrecht 1328
prioriteitsschuldeiser 1948
privaatbezit 1979
privaat verbruik 1499
private sector 1981
privé-bank 1974
privé-bedrijf 1977
privé-bezit 1979
privé-eigendom 1979
privé-initiatief 1976
privé-inkomen 1929
privé-kapitaal 1975
privé-onderneming 1977
privé-rekening 1926
privé-schuld 1928
privé-sector 1981
privé-verbruik 1499
procent 1921, 1922
produkt 229, 1982
produkt, bruto binnenlands ~ 1461
produkt, bruto nationaal ~ 1466
produktiecoöperatie 1983
produktiegoederen 1134
produktiekosten 811
produktiemiddelen, duurzame ~ 1134
produktieprijs 811
produkt, nationaal ~ 1803
proefbalans 2303
profijt 1409
profijtelijk 1147
profitabel 1147
pro forma factuur 1991, 1991
prognosen, begrotings~ 451
progressief tarief van een belasting 1992
progressieve afschrijving 1545
progressieve belasting 1456
prohibitief recht 1993
prolongatie 567, 753, 1994
prolongatiekoers 569
prolongatiepremie 569
prolongatierente 569
prolongatietarief 569
prolongatie van een krediet 1275
prolongeren, een krediet ~ 1272
prolongeren, een positie ~ 568
prolongeren, een termijn ~ 1273
promesse 1477
promesse, schatkist~ 2301
prompt contant betalen 1727
prospectie, markt~ 1740
prospectus, emissie~ 1643
prospectus, inschrijvings~ 1643
protectionist 1997
protesteren, een wissel ~ 1481
provenu 229, 1982
provisie 689
provisie, accept~ 13
provisie, administratieve ~ 80
provisie, bank~ 293
provisie, disconto~ 1055
provisie, kredietopenings~ 693
publieke schuld 1798
punt, dood ~ 430
punten noteren, een daling (een winst) van X ~ 2045
punten vertonen, een daling (een winst) van X ~ 2045
punt, interventie~ 1609
punt, steun~ 1609
putten, uit de reserves ~ 1042
P.V.B.A. 1690

q.q. rekening 2305
quasimonetaire liquiditeiten 1776
quasimonetaire middelen 2243
quota 2017
quote 2017
quote, investerings~ 1629
quote, spaar~ 2026
quotum 2017

rabat 127
rabatzegel 2290
ramen 177
raming 176
ramingen, budgettaire ~ 449
raming, waarde~ 176
rapport, accountants~ 217
ratio 2029
ratio, liquiditeits~ 45
realisatie 773
realisatiewaarde 432
realiseerbaar 2034
realiseerbaarheid 2033
realiseerbare activa 905
realiseren 785
realiseren, een winst ~ 1729
realisering 773
realizeerbaar 2034
realizeerbaarheid 2033
recapitulatie 2241
recessie 1031
recettes 1532
recettes, kas~ 585
recht 614, 1135
recht, ad valorem ~ 82
recht, antidumping~ 169
recht, beschermend ~ 1998
recht, claim~ 174
recht, compensatie~ 711
recht, differentieel ~ 1040
recht, doeane~ 917
recht, dossier~ 1478
recht, douane~ 917
rechten (op), trekkings~ 1121
rechten, vrijstellen van ~ 1246
recht, erfenis~ 938
recht gevend op dividend 1170
recht, inschrijvings~ 174
recht, keuze~ 1854
recht, licentie~ 1686
recht, monopolie~ 1245
recht op dividend, met ~ 1170
recht (op), pand~ 1687
recht, optie~ 1854
recht, overdrachts~ 812
recht, preferentieel ~ 1949
recht, prioriteits~ 1328
recht, prohibitief ~ 1993
recht, registratie~ 2077
recht, schenkings~ 1422
recht, successie~ 938
recht, tol~ 917
recht, transfer~ 812
recht van conversie 777
recht van inschrijving 174, 2115
recht van retentie (op) 1687
recht van terughouding (op) 1687
recht van voorkeur 1328
recht van vruchtgebruik 349
recht, voorkoop~ 2013
recht, waarde~ 82
recht, zegel~ 2211
recipis 47, 1597
reclameprijs 1613
rectacheque 630
rectawissel 371

reçu 47
reçu, stortings~ 877
recycleren van kapitaal 2050
recycling van kapitaal 2050
reduceren, de uitgaven ~ 915
reductie, prijs~ 927
reëel inkomen 2032
reëel rendement 57
reële aanpassing 74
reële activa 1747
reële belasting 1995
reële waarde 56
reflateren 2069
reflatie 2070
reflatie bewerken, een ~ 2069
reflationeren 2069
regelaar, fiscale ~ 1333
regeling, prijs~ 1961
regie 1454
regiebedrijf 1454
register, aandeelhouders~ 1701
register, aandelen~ 1701
register, handels~ 687
registratierecht 2077
registreren 401
reglementering, deviezen~ 900
reglementering, wissel~ 900
regres 2047
regulator, fiscale ~ 1333
rehabilitatie van de financiën 1318
reischeque 2297
reiskosten 2298
reisvergoeding 2296
rekeneenheid 31
rekenen 490
rekenfout 491
rekening 16, 17, 492
rekening, actief-~ 201
rekening afsluiten, een ~ 652
rekening, balans~ 271
rekening, bank~ 285
rekening belasten met, een ~ 618
rekeningboekje 289
rekening brengen, in ~ 570
rekening brengen, te weinig in ~ 2316
rekening, cheque~ 625
rekening, clearing~ 644
rekening, cliënten~ 617
rekening, collectieve ~ 766
rekening, compensatie~ 644
rekening-courant 23
rekening(-courant)afschrift 5
rekening-courantkrediet 87
rekening(-courant)uittreksel 5
rekening-courantverplichtingen 1023
rekening-courant, voorschot in ~ 87
rekening crediteren (voor, met), de ~ 880
rekening debiteren met, een ~ 618
rekening, deposito~ 1016
rekeningen afstemmen 112
rekeningen, geïntegreerde economische ~ 1579
rekeningen in overeenstemming brengen 112
rekeningen, nationale ~ 1797
rekeningen, overboekings~ 802
rekeningen sluitend maken 112
rekening, exploitatie~ 2289
rekening, gemeenschappelijke ~ 1649
rekening, gemene ~ 1649
rekening, gezamenlijke ~ 1649
rekening, giro~ 1424
rekening goedschrijven, op de ~ 880
rekening, halve ~ 1654
rekeninghouder 26
rekening, hulp~ 224
rekening, inkomsten~ 1524
rekening, kapitaal~ 516
rekening, kas~ 575
rekening liquideren, een ~ 249
rekening, lopende ~ 23
rekening, loro~ 1716
rekening, meta~ 1654
rekening, nostro~ 1833
rekening, ongesaldeerde ~ 1846
rekening, onkosten~ 1259
rekening, onvereffende ~ 1846
rekening, op ~ 19
rekening, open ~ 23, 1846
rekening, openstaande ~ 23
rekening, order~ 2248
rekening overdisponeren, op een ~ 1868
rekening overtrekken, een ~ 1868
rekening, participatie~ 1654
rekening, passief-~ 1682
rekening, persoonlijke ~ 1926
rekening, post~ 1800
rekening, postcheque~ 1800
rekening, postgiro~ 1800
rekening, privé-~ 1926
rekening, q.q. ~ 2305
rekening, reserve~ 130
rekening, resultaten~ 1523
rekening, rubriek-~ 2305
rekening salderen, een ~ 249
rekeningshoofd 25
rekening, spaar~ 2138
rekeningssaldo 255
rekeningstelsel 22
rekeningsysteem 22
rekening, tegen~ 760
rekening te voldoen 36
rekening, tussen~ 2248
rekening, uitstaande ~ 1846
rekening van bezit 201
rekening van derden, voor ~ 35
rekening van een derde, voor ~ 35
rekening van, voor ~ 34
rekening vereffenen, een ~ 249
rekening, verlies-en-winst~ 1523
rekening, verzamel~ 673
rekening, voor eigen ~ 1877
rekening, vostro~ 1716
rekening, wacht~ 2248
rekening, winst-en-verlies~ 1523
rekening, zicht~ 23
rembours 2072
remboursement 2072
rembourseren 1900
rembourskrediet 1085
rembours, onder ~ 589
rembours, tegen ~ 589
remise 1784
remittent 1902, 2083
remitteren 2080
remmen, de inflatie ~ 628
remuneratie 2041
remunereren 2042
rendabel 1147
rendabiliteit 1984
rendement 2110
rendement, aandelen~ 1082
rendement, effectief ~ 57
rendement, kapitaal~ 535
rendement, omzet~ 1815
rendement, reëel ~ 57
rendementspercentage 2025
rendementsvermogen 1139
rendement van obligaties 396
rendement, werkelijk ~ 57
renderen 100
renderend, vast ~ 1338
renouvellerend krediet 2114
rentabiliteit 1984
rentabiliteitswaarde 546
rente 1522, 1585
rente, achterstallige ~ 190
rente, bank~ 306
rente, basis~ 328
rentebetaling 1592
rentebewijs 162
rentebrief 162
rentecoupon 1588
rente, credit~ 376
rente, debet~ 947
rentedienst 1592
rentedragend 1586
rentefonds 1455
rente, geaccumuleerde ~ 41
rente, gestaffelde ~ 1457
rentegevend 1586
rente, hypot(h)eek~ 1794
rente, jaarlijkse ~ 161
rente, kapitaal~ 535, 540
rente kapitaliseren, de ~ 547
rentekoers 1593
rentelasten 1587
rente lenen, geld op ~ 1675
rente, lijf~ 163
renteloos 1590
renteloos kapitaal 1502
rente, lopende ~ 909
rentemarge 1412
rente, met vaste ~ 1338
rente, moratoire ~ 983
rentend, vast ~ 1338
rente, nog te vervallen ~ 42
renteopbrengst 1595
rente op effecten, belenings~ 1714
rente, opgelopen ~ 41
rente op rente 720
rente op waardepapieren, belenings~ 1714
renteplichtig 2231
rente, prolongatie~ 569
rente, rode ~ 947
rentespaarbrief 2141
rentestand 1593
rentestandaard 1593

rentesubsidie 1594
rentetarief 1593
rente, te betalen ~ 947
rente, te ontvangen ~ 376
rente, te vervallen ~ 42
rentetitel 162
rente uitlenen, geld op ~ 1675
rente van X procent afwerpen, een ~ 334
rente van X procent dragen, een ~ 334
rente van X procent geven, een ~ 334
rente van X procent opbrengen, een ~ 334
rentevergoeding 1594
rente, verschenen ~ 1589
renteverschil 1412
rente, verschuldigde ~ 1589
rente, vervallen ~ 1589
rentevoet 1593
rentevoet, belenings~ 2022
rentevoet, lening~ 423
rentevoet, nominale ~ 1821
rentevoet, voorschot~ 423
rente wegens (te) late betaling 983
rente wegens verzuim 983
rente, woeker~ 2335
rente, zwarte ~ 376
reorganisatie van de financiën 1318
reorganiseren, de financiën ~ 2044
reparatie 708
repatriëren 2089
repatriëring 2090
report 567, 569
reporteren, een positie ~ 568
reportkoers 569
reporttransactie 753
representatiekosten 1169
rescontre 139
rescontredag 24
rescontreren 148
rescontretermijn 18
reserve 129
reserve aanleggen, een ~ 454
reserve aanvullen, de ~ 2039
reserve, afschrijvings~ 132
reserve, belasting~ 2001
reserve, conjunctuur~ 820
reserve, contante ~ 597
reserve creëren, een ~ 454
reserve, depreciatie~ 132
reserve, deviezen~ 901
reserve, dividend~ 1079
reserve, facultatieve ~ 1397
reserve, fiscale ~ 2001
reservefonds 2101
reservefonds, extra-~ 755
reservefonds voegen, bij het ~ 68
reserve, geld~ 1770
reserve, goud~ 1440
reserve, kas~ 597
reserve plaatsen, op de ~ 68
reserverekening 130
reserve(s) 2098
reserves aanbreken, de ~ 1042
reserves aanspreken, de ~ 1042
reserves beroep doen, op de ~ 1042
reserves, geheime ~ 726
reserves, goud- en deviezen~ 1429
reserves, liquide ~ 1696
reserves, liquiditeits~ 1696
reserves, minimum~ 1670
reserves, onzichtbare ~ 726
reserves, open ~ 966
reserves putten, uit de ~ 1042
reserves, stille ~ 726
reserve storten, in de ~ 68
reserves, verborgen ~ 726
reserves, verplichte ~ 1670
reserves, wettelijke ~ 1670
reserves, wettelijk voorgeschreven ~ 1670
reserves, zichtbare ~ 966
reservevaluta 2100
reserve, vernieuwings~ 2086
reserve, vervangings~ 2086
reserve voegen, bij de ~ 68
reserve voor dubieuze vorderingen 243
reserve voor onvoorziene uitgaven 756
reserve, voorzienings~ 756
reserve vormen, een ~ 454
reserve, vrije ~ 1397
residu 246
residuwaarde 2103
respijt 998
respijtdagen 933
respijttermijn 998
rest 246
restant 246
resterend bedrag 246
resterende 246
restitueren 1900
restitutie 2072
restitutie, belasting~ 2038
restitutie van douanerechten 1116
restrictie, krediet~ 874
restricties, deviezen~ 902
restwaarde 2103
resultatenrekening 1523
retentierecht (op) 1687
retour 365
retourwissel 365, 819
retraite 819
retributie 614
retroactieve verliescompensatie 2272
revalorisatie 2111
revaloriseren 178
revalorizeren 178
revaluatie 2036, 2111
revalueren 178, 2037
revenu, bruto~ 1463
revenu(en) 1522
revisor 216
revolverkrediet 2114
revolving krediet 2114
richtprijs 1832
rijksschuld 1798
rijkssubsidie 1449
rijkstoelage 1449
risicodragend kapitaal 1178
risico, koers~ 1238
risico, wisselkoers~ 1238
ritme, groei~ 1256
rode cijfers staan, in de ~ 944
rode rente 947
roerend bezit 622
roerende effecten 1739
roerende goederen 622
roerende waarden 1739
roll-over krediet 2118
ronde getallen, in ~ 2119
rondkomen 1703
rouwgeld 136
rouwkoop 136
royalty 1686
rubriek-rekening 2305
rugtekenen, een wissel ~ 1162
rugtekening 1164
ruil 325
ruil, aandelen~ 1232
ruilen 326
ruilhandel 325
ruilhandel drijven 326
ruiltransactie 327
ruilvoet 2279
ruilwaarde 1219
ruiterij, wissel~ 1659
run op de bank 2121
ruw bestek 184
ruwe schatting 184
ruwstof 329

safe 2122
safe-inrichting 2125
safeloket 2123
salaris 2126
salaris, maand~ 1787
salarissen, lonen en ~ 1141
salarisverhoging 1540
salderen 148
salderen, een rekening ~ 249
saldering van een rekening 254
saldo 27, 246
saldo, actief ~ 849
saldo, bank~ 286
saldo, batig ~ 849
saldo bij de overdrachten en in het kapitaalverkeer, globaal ~ 1416
saldo, credit~ 849
saldo, debet~ 93
saldo der lopende transacties 268
saldo, export~ 1277
saldo in kassa 253
saldo, kas~ 253
saldo naar nieuwe rekening 150
saldo, nadelig ~ 93
saldo, negatief ~ 93
saldo opmaken, een ~ 279
saldo, passief ~ 93
saldo, rekenings~ 255
saldo, schuld~ 93
saldo trekken, een ~ 279
saldo, uitvoer~ 1277
saldo van de kapitaalbewegingen 256
saldo van de lopende overdrachten 257
saldo van een rekening 255
saldo van het goederen- en dienstenverkeer 259
saldo vereffenen, het ~ 1914

saldovergelijking 1199
saldo, verlies~ 93
saldo, verrekenings~ 269
saldo, verschuldigd ~ 252
saldo, winst~ 849
samengestelde int(e)rest 720
samensmelting 135
samenwerkende vennootschap 786
saneren, de financiën ~ 2044
sanering van de financiën 1318
schaal, glijdende ~ 1348
schaarsgeld 654
schaarste, dollar~ 1090
schaarste, kapitaal~ 559
schaarste, krediet~ 878
schadeloosstelling 708
schadevergoeding 708
schade verkopen, met ~ 2158
schatkist 2299
schatkistbiljet 2301
schatkistbon 2301
schatkistcertificaat 2301
schatkist in omloop gebracht geld, door de ~ 2302
schatkistobligatie 1243
schatkistpapieren 1244
schatkistpromesse 2301
schatkistwissel 2301
schatten 177
schatting 176
schatting, globale ~ 184
schatting, ruwe ~ 184
schatting, te lage ~ 2318
schatting, waarde~ 176
schenken, een schuld ~ 510
schenker 1104
schenking 1103
schenkingsrecht 1422
schennis, munt~ 939
schepping, geld~ 842
schepping, krediet~ 841
schieter, geld~ 1777
schijf, belasting~ 2267
schijf, inkomens~ 1527
schijnint(e)rest 1518
schijnwinst 171
schommelende wisselkoers 1347
schommeling, conjuncturele ~ 930
schommeling, conjunctuur~ 930
schommeling, cyclische ~ 930
schommeling, economische ~ 930
schommeling in (van) de wisselkoersen 1225
schoorsteenwissel 15
schorsen, de betalingen ~ 603
schorsen, de betaling van een cheque ~ 2227
schrijven, een bedrag in iemands tegoed ~ 566
schrijven, op het actief ~ 403
schrijven, op het passief ~ 402
schuld 951
schuld aangaan, een ~ 761
schuld, actieve ~ 37
schuld, aflosbare ~ 1574
schuldbeheer 954
schuldbekentenis 46, 389, 1477
schuld, belasting~ 2271
schuldbewijs 609, 1709
schuld, binnenlandse ~ 1095
schuld, boek~ 406
schuldbrief 389, 1477
schuldbrief, conversie~ 704
schuld, buitenlandse ~ 1280
schuld consolideren, een ~ 733
schuldeiser 870
schuldeiser, bevoorrechte ~ 1948
schuldeiser, buitenlandse ~ 1360
schuldeiser, gedekte ~ 2150
schuldeiser, gewone ~ 405
schuldeiser, preferente ~ 1948
schuldeiser, prioriteits~ 1948
schulden 961
schuldenaar 958
schuldenaar, hoofdelijke ~ 1651
schuldenaar, nalatige ~ 981
schuldenaar, solidaire ~ 1651
schuldenaar, wissel~ 362
schulden, achterstallige ~ 188
schulden, bank~ 296
schulden bedolven zijn, onder ~ 953
schulden beladen, met ~ 466
schulden belasten, met ~ 466
schulden belast, met ~ 952
schulden bezwaren, met ~ 466
schuldendienst 962
schuldenlast 462
schuldenlast, overstelpende ~ 1207
schulden, nog niet opeisbare ~ 1825
schulden op korte termijn 910
schulden overladen zijn, met ~ 953
schuld(en) steken, zich in de ~ 1294
schuld(en) zitten, in de ~ 1294
schuld(en) zitten, tot over de oren in de ~ 953
schuld funderen, een ~ 733
schuld, geconsolideerde ~ 735
schuld, gefundeerde ~ 735
schuld, geünificeerde ~ 735
schuld, hoofdelijke ~ 1650
schuld, hypot(h)ecaire ~ 957
schuld, hypot(h)eek~ 957
schuldig 952
schuldig zijn 1876
schuldincasseerder 955
schuld innen, een ~ 677
schuldinvorderaar 955
schuld invorderen, een ~ 677
schuld kwijtschelden, een ~ 510
schuldlimiet 422
schuld maken, een ~ 761
schuld, nationale ~ 1798
schuld niet erkennen, een ~ 2092
schuld, obligatie~ 391
schuld, ongefundeerde ~ 1351
schuld, oninbare ~ 242
schuld, opeisbare ~ 37
schuld, openbare ~ 1798
schuld, particuliere ~ 1928
schuld, passieve ~ 36
schuldplafon(d) 422
schuld, privé-~ 1928
schuld, publieke ~ 1798
schuld, rijks~ 1798
schuldsaldo 93
schuld schenken, een ~ 510
schuld, solidaire ~ 1650
schuld, staats~ 1798
schuld unificeren, een ~ 733
schuldvergelijking 709
schuld, verjaarde ~ 324
schuld, vlottende ~ 1351
schuldvordering 639
schuldvordering, eventuele ~ 757
schuldvordering, gewone ~ 2332
scrip 1597
secondaire inkomens 2146
secondaire liquiditeiten 1776
secondaire markt 2147
sector, distributie~ 1075
sector, groei~ 1470
sector, openbare ~ 2008
sector, overheids~ 2008
sector, particuliere ~ 1981
sector, private ~ 1981
sector, privé-~ 1981
secunda 2148
secundaire inkomens 2146
secundaire liquiditeiten 1776
secundaire markt 2147
secundawissel 2148
sekwester 191, 209
sekwestratie 191
sekwestreren 211
semi-variabele kosten 2164
S.E.O.O. 1184
sequester 191, 209
sequestratie 191
sequestreren 211
serie uitgegeven emissie, in ~ 385
sinking fund 140
slaan 662
slang 2183
slap 508
slapende vennoot 1105
slapte 1130
slechte belegging 244
slechte betaler 245
slechte investering 244
slijtage 2366, 2367
slijting 2366, 2367
slotbalans 1302
slotboeking 656
slotdividend 1303
slotkoers 657
slotnotering 657
slotprijs 657
sluitbriefje 425, 440
sluiten 248
sluitende begroting 251
sluitend maken, de begroting ~ 280
sluitend maken, het budget ~ 280
sluitend maken, rekeningen ~ 112
sluiten, een lening ~ 762
sluitingsbalans 1302
slump 1031
slumpflatie 2182
snelheid, omloop~ 2027
sociaal voordeel 2185
sociale lasten 2186
sociale prestatie 2185
sociale verzekering 2184
sociale zekerheid 2184
socialisatie 1801

socialiseren 1802
socialisering 1801
sola 2180
sola-wissel 2180
solde 2128
solidaire aansprakelijkheid 1652
solidaire schuld 1650
solidaire schuldenaar 1651
solide 846
soliditeit 873
solied 846
solvabel 2190
solvabiliteit 2189
solvent 2190
solventie 2189
som 149
som, afkoop~ 708
som, borg~ 602
som, cautie~ 602
som der activa 2285
som, hoofd~ 1972
som, loon~ 2359
som ter gelijkmaking 247
som, totale ~ 105
som, verschuldigde ~ 151
som, waarborg~ 602
souche 821
soulte 247
spaarbank 2139
spaarbankboekje 2140
spaarboekje 2142
spaarbrief 2141
spaardeposito 2144
spaarder 2134
spaarfonds 2145
spaarfonds, bouw~ 453
spaargelden 2137
spaarinlaag 2144
spaarinlage 2144
spaarinleg 2144
spaarkapitaal 2143
spaarkas 2139
spaarkas, bouw~ 453
spaarpenningen 2137
spaarquote 2026
spaarrekening 2138
spaartegoed 2144
spaarvolume 2353
sparen 2133
sparen, gedwongen ~ 724
sparen in effecten 2135
sparen op spaarrekeningen 2136
sparen, verplicht ~ 724
speciaal krediet 2194
speciale prijs 1203
speciale trekkingsrechten 2195
speciale vergoeding 1284
specie 661
speciestandaard, goud~ 1402
specificatie 429
specificatiestaat 429
speculant 2200
speculant à la baisse 332
speculant à la hausse 455
speculant, baisse~ 332
speculant, beurs~ 1647
speculant, hausse~ 455
speculatie 2197
speculatie, beurs~ 111
speculatiepapieren 2199
speculatieve aankoop 2198
speculatieve waarden 2199
speculeren 2196
speculeren, à la baisse ~ 1427
speculeren, à la hausse ~ 456
spel, beurs~ 111
speler aan de beurs 1647
spiraal, deflatie~ 993
spiraal, inflatie~ 1559
spiraal, kost-prijs~ 816
spiraal, lonen- en prijzen~ 2363
spiraal van kosten en prijzen 816
splitsing 2175
split-up 2175
spotprijs 322
spreiden, de betalingen over X jaren ~ 2204
staafgoud 323
staat 2217
staat, bank~ 312
staat, betaal~ 1912
staat, consolidatie~ 739
staat, crediteur~ 871
staat, debiteur~ 959
staat, financiële ~ 1319
staat, kostenverdeel~ 799
staatsbedrijf 1448
staatsbegroting 1446
staatsfinanciën 827
staatsfondsen 1244
staatsgarantie 1450
staatsgelden 2005
staatshuishoudkunde 1151
staatshulp 1445
staatsinkomsten 1451
staatsinmenging 1452
staatsinterventie 1452
staatskas 2299
staatslening 1453
staatsmonopolie 1454
staatsobligatie 1243
staatsonderneming 1448
staatspapieren 1244
staatspapieren, geconsolideerde ~ 734
staat, specificatie~ 429
staatsschuld 1798
staatssteun 1445
staatssubsidie 1449
staatstoelage 1449
staatstussenkomst 1452
staatswaarborg 1450
staat van faillissement, in ~ 314
staat van onkosten 2218
staat van uitgaven 2218
staat, verzamel~ 2241
staat, welvaarts~ 2373
stabiele munt 2207
stabiele valuta 2207
stabilisatiefonds 2205
stabilisatie, koers~ 1237
stabilisatielening 2206
stabilisatie, prijs~ 1969
stabiliteit, monetaire ~ 903
stabiliteit, prijs~ 1326
stabiliteit van de munteenheid 903
stabiliteit van de wisselkoersen 1239
staffeltarief 1041
stagflatie 2208
stagnatie 1130
stagneren 1663
stagnerend 508
staken, de betalingen ~ 603
staking van betaling 2250
stam 821
stamkapitaal 544
standaard, dubbele ~ 375
standaard, enkele ~ 1785
standaard, gouden ~ 1441
standaard, goudkern~ 1431
standaard, goudwissel~ 1436
standaard, hinkende ~ 1476
standaard, levens~ 1704
standaard, papieren ~ 1881
standaardprijs 1832
standaard, rente~ 1593
standaardwaarde 2213
stand-by-krediet 2214
stand-by-kredietovereenkomst 2215
stand der prijzen 1680
stand, rente~ 1593
stand van de markt 1743
stand van een rekening 1940
statistiek 2220
statistieken 2219
statistiek, interne bedrijfs~ 1851
statistische gegevens 2219
statutaire reserve 2102
statutaire zetel 2075
statutair kapitaal 222
stellage 1108
stellen, verkrijgbaar ~ 1841
stelsel, belasting~ 1334
stelsel, geld~ 664
stelsel, investeringsloon~ 2362
stelsel, krediet~ 879
stelsel, monetair ~ 664
stelsel, munt~ 664
stelsel, rekening~ 22
stelsel, wissel~ 1240
stemming, baisse~ 344
stemming, hausse~ 459
stempel 2209
stemrecht, depot~ 2356
steriliseren 2222
sterilisering 2221
sterke valuta 1479
sterling 2223
sterlingblok 2224
sterlinggebied 2224
sterlingzone 2224
steun, financiële ~ 1310
steunkoers 1610
steun, overheids~ 1445
steunpunt 1609
steun, staats~ 1445
stichting 1385
stijgen, in waarde ~ 179
stijging 2117
stijging, prijs~ 1539
stijging, prijzen~ 1539
stijgingspercentage 1255
stijgingstempo 1256
stijging van de geldhoeveelheid 1252

stijging, waarde~ 180
stilhalte-overeenkomst 2216
stille reserves 726
stille vennoot 1105
stilstaan 1663
stilstaand 508
stilstand 1130
stimulans 1519
stimulans, investerings~ 1625
stimuleringsacties 1251
stock 1615
stockdividend 400
stoffelijke activa 1747
stok 821
stokken 1663
stop, invoer~ 319
stop, prijs~ 1400
stormloop op de bank 2121
storno 281, 512
stornoboeking 512
stornopost 281
storten 1015
storten, in de reserve ~ 68
storten, kapitaal ~ 436
storten kapitaal, (nog) te ~ 2313
storten, X % op een aandeel ~ 1899
storting 1567
storting, kapitaal~ 1909
stortingsadvies 97
stortingsbewijs 877
stortingsbiljet 1022
stortingsborderel 877
stortingsbulletijn 1022
stortingsformulier 1022
stortingsopgave 877
stortingsreçu 877
storting van een aandeel, vol~ 1908
S.T.R. 2195
strekking 1200
strook 821
strook, betaal~ 1913 .
strook, controle~ 821
stroom, kapitaal~ 528
stroom, krediet~ 859
stroom van geldontvangsten en -uitgaven 586
structureel overschot 2229
structuur, financiële ~ 561
structuur, kapitaal~ 561
structuur, kosten~ 817
studie, markt~ 1740
stuk, boekings~ 33
stuk, goud~ 1433
stuk(je), geld~ 660
stukken 2151
stukloon 1932
stuk, munt~ 660
stukprijs 2328
sub-grootboek 225
subrekening 224
subsidie 1458
subsidie, export~ 1269
subsidie, int(e)rest~ 1594
subsidie, overheids~ 1449
subsidiëren 2240
subsidie, rente~ 1594
subsidie, rijks~ 1449
subsidie, staats~ 1449
subsidie, uitvoer~ 1269
subventie 1458
successiebelasting 938
successierecht 938
succursaal 427
succursale 427
superdividend 398
superwinst 1213
supplementaire inkomsten 64
surplus 2244
surplusdividend 398
surséance van betaling 1276
surtaxe 60, 66
swap 2251
swapaffaire 2251
swapkrediet 2252
swaptransactie 2251
swing 864
switch 2253
switch-transactie 2253
syndicaat 2255
syndicaat, bank~ 303
syndicaat, emissie~ 2322
syndicaat, garantie~ 2322
syndicaat, overname~ 2322
systeem, rekening~ 22
systeem, wissel~ 1240
system, belasting~ 1334

tabel 2256
tabel, amortisatie~ 146
tafel 2256
tafel, amortisatie~ 146
taks 614, 1135
taks, compensatie~ 712
taks, overdrachts~ 2014
talon 2085
talon, dividend~ 1078
tantième 1923
tarief 2260
tarief, buiten~ 1279
tarief, differentieel ~ 1041
tarief, disconto~ 1061
tarief, douane~ 922
tarief, gestaffeld ~ 1041
tarief, glijdend ~ 1041
tarief, gunst~ 1947
tariefmuur 918
tarief, preferentieel ~ 1947
tarief, prolongatie~ 569
tarief, rente~ 1593
tarief, staffel~ 1041
tarief, tol~ 922
tarief van een belasting, progressief ~ 1992
tarief voor de leden van het Gemenebest, voorkeur~ 702
tarief, voorkeur~ 1947
taxatie 176, 200
taxe 614, 1135
taxe, overdrachts~ 2014
taxeren 177, 195
taxering 176, 200
technische afschrijving 1030
tegeldemaking 773
tegenboeking 281
tegenpost 281
tegenprestatie 731
tegenrekening 760
tegenwaarde 822, 1219
tegenwaardefonds 823
tegoed 843, 849
tegoed, bank~ 286
tegoed, buitenlands ~ 204
tegoed, deviezen~ 1362
tegoed(en) 202, 1496
tegoeden van de schatkist 2300
tegoed, geblokkeerd ~ 381
tegoed in het buitenland 204
tegoed, spaar~ 2144
tekengeld 1296
tekenmunt 2283
tekort 988
tekort, bedrijfs~ 474
tekort, begrotings~ 95
tekort, betalingsbalans~ 261
tekort, budgettair ~ 95
tekort dekken, een ~ 836
tekort, dollar~ 1089
tekort, handels~ 474
tekort, kas~ 96
tekort op de begroting 95
tekort op de (buitenlandse) handelsbalans 265
tekort van de belastingopbrengst 1330
tekort voorzien, in een ~ 836
tempo, expansie~ 1256
tempo, groei~ 1256
tempo, inflatie~ 1563
tempo, stijgings~ 1256
tendens 1200
tendens, baisse~ 344
tendens, deflatoire ~ 994
tendens indruisen, tegen de algemene ~ 2120
tendens, neergaande ~ 344
tendens, opgaande ~ 459
tendens tot dalen 344
tendens tot stijgen 459
tendentie 1200
ten honderd 1922
termijn 894, 1262
termijnaffaire 1379
termijnaffaire in deviezen 1381
termijnaffaire in valuta 1381
termijnbetaling 1571
termijn, betalings~ 1924
termijn, blokkade~ 384
termijndeposito 1337
termijndeviezen 1378
termijndeviezenkoers 1383
termijndeviezenmarkt 1382
termijnen, bij (in) ~ 987
termijngeld 1337
termijn, geldigheids~ 894
termijn, halfjaarlijkse ~ 351
termijnhandel in deviezen 1226
termijn, inschrijvings~ 2237
termijn, inteken~ 2237
termijnkoers 1384
termijn kopen, op ~ 486
termijnlevering 1380
termijn, liquidatie~ 18
termijn, op korte ~ 2177
termijn, op lange ~ 1715

termijn, op middellange ~ 1752
termijn, opvragings~ 1836
termijn, opzeggings~ 1836
termijnprijs 1384
termijn prolongeren, een ~ 1273
termijn, rescontre~ 18
termijn, respijt~ 998
termijntransactie 1379
termijntransactie in deviezen 1381
termijntransactie in valuta 1381
termijn verkopen, op ~ 2161
termijn verlengen, een ~ 1273
termijnzaak 1379
termijnzaak in deviezen 1381
termijnzaak in valuta 1381
terms of trade 2279
terugbetaalbaar 2073
terugbetalen 148, 1900
terugbetalen, een hypot(h)eek ~ 511
terugbetaling 139, 2072
terugbetaling, belasting~ 2038
terugbetalingspremie 1750
terugbetalingswaarde 2055
terugbetaling, tegen ~ 589
terugbetaling van douanerechten 1116
terugboeking 512
teruggang 968
teruggedrongen inflatie 1919
terugkoop 2094
terugkopen 480
terugkrijgen, zijn geld ~ 1421
teruglopen der koersen 886
terugslag van een belasting 1521
terugtrekken, zich met verlies ~ 928
terugvloeiing van kapitaal 2071
terugvoeren 2089
terugvoering 2090
terugvoering van kapitaal 2050
terugvordering 640
teveel berekenen 1866
teveel vragen 1866
thesaurie 2299
tijdaffaire 1379
tijd, loop~ 894
tijd, omloop(s)~ 895
tijdtransactie 1379
tijd, verval~ 1748
titel, rente~ 162
titels 2151
titel van aandeel 2170
titel van aandelen 2170
titel van schuldvordering 609
toedelen 122
toeëigenen, zich wederrechtelijk ~ 977
toeëigening, wederrechtelijke ~ 978
toekennen, een krediet ~ 126
toekenning van krediet 220
toelage 1458
toelage, overheids~ 1449
toelage, rijks~ 1449
toelage, staats~ 1449
toelating tot de beurs 81
toelating tot de oficiële notering op de beurs 81
toenemende afschrijving 1545
toenemingspercentage 1255
toerekenen 122
toerekening 123
toeslag 60
toeslag, duurte~ 808
toeslag heffen (op), een ~ 1514
toeslag leggen (op), een ~ 1514
toeslag, loon~ 1288
toestaan, een krediet ~ 126
toevloed, kapitaal~ 99
toevloeiing van kapitalen 99
toevlucht, fiscale ~ 2269
toevoegen 122
toevoeging 123
toevoeging aan de reserve 67
toewijzen 122
toewijzing 123
toewijzing van aandelen 125
toewijzing van middelen, onjuiste ~ 1763
toezegging, krediet~ 88
toezegging van deviezen 1223
tol 2284
tolgeld 2284
tolgelden 917
tolmuur 918
tolplichtig 916
tolrecht 917
toltarief 922
tolunie 923
tolvrij 920
tolvrij maken 1246
toonder 337
toonderaandeel 343
toondercheque 339
toonderpapier 340
toonderpapieren 342
totaal, balans~ 276
totaal bedrag 107
totaal bedragen, in ~ 106
totaal belopen, in ~ 106
totaal, eind~ 105
totaal generaal 105
totaal oplopen van, tot een ~ 106
totaal uitmaken van, een ~ 106
totaal verlies 934
totale betalingsbalans 1862
totale som 105
totale waarde 108
traag 508
traite 356
traite, bank~ 284
traite, binnenlandse ~ 1091
traite, buitenlandse ~ 1357
tranche 1572
transactie 320
transactie, afbetalings~ 1489
transactie, compensatie~ 327
transactie, driehoeks~ 2253
transactie in deviezen, contant~ 2202
transactie in valuta, contant~ 2202
transactie, kas~ 581
transactie, loco~ 581
transactie, meta-~ 1653
transactie, premie~ 1855
transactie, report~ 753
transactie, ruil~ 327
transacties, bank~ 304
transacties, beurs~ 1222
transacties, clearing~ 643
transacties, compensatie~ 643
transacties, deviezen~ 1241
transacties, effecten~ 1222
transacties, krediet~ 851
transacties met het buitenland 1358
transacties, valuta~ 1241
transacties, verrekenings~ 643
transactie, swap~ 2251
transactie, switch-~ 2253
transactie, termijn~ 1379
transactie, tijd~ 1379
transactie, valutatermijn~ 1381
transactie voor gemeenschappelijke rekening 1653
transferabel 117
transferabele ponden 2291
transferabiliteit 116
transferbetaling 2293
transfereren 2080
transferkosten 812
transfer naar het buitenland 1372
transferrecht 812
transfer van geld 1784
transfer van kapitaal 563
transithandel 2294
transitorische post 2249
transitorische posten 73
transporteren 435
transportkosten 2295
transport naar nieuwe rekening 150
trassaat 1117
trassant 1118
trasseren, op iemand ~ 1114
traveller's cheque 2297
trekken 1112
trekken, een cheque ~ 1115
trekken, een saldo ~ 279
trekken, een wissel op iemand ~ 1114
trekken, op het Internationaal Monetair Fonds ~ 1123
trekker 1118
trekking 1111
trekking op het Internationaal Monetair Fonds 1120
trekkingsrechten (op) 1121
trekkingsrechten, speciale ~ 2195
trend 1200
trimester 2016
trust 2304
trustakte 976
trust, beleggings~ 653
trustee 1298
trustmaatschappij 2306
trustvermogen 2308
tussenbalans 1596
tussenfinanciering 433
tussenkomst, staats~ 1452
tussenmakelaar 1648
tussenpost 2249
tussenrekening 2248
tussenrente 1599
tussentijdse balans 1596
tussentijds krediet 434
tweeledige wisselmarkt 2309
tweevoudig goudprijssysteem 2310

verkoopprijs 2162
verkoopsbriefje 440
verkoop(s)waarde 688
verkopen 2130, 2157
verkopen, bij opbod ~ 213
verkopen, in blanco ~ 1427
verkopen, met schade ~ 2158
verkopen, met verlies ~ 2158
verkopen, op krediet ~ 2163
verkopen, op termijn ~ 2161
verkoper 2159
verkopersmarkt 2160
verkoping bij opbod 212
verkrijgbaar stellen 1841
verkrijgen 48
verkrijger 120, 482
verkrijging 49
verlagen, de pariteit ~ 2062
verlaging, dividend~ 925
verlaging, prijs~ 927
verlaging van de discontovoet 926
verlaging van het disconto 926
verlegenheid, geld~ 1314
verlenen, een krediet ~ 126
verlenen, uitstel van betaling ~ 1274
verlengen, de betalingstermijn ~ 1274
verlengen, een krediet ~ 1272
verlengen, een termijn ~ 1273
verlenging 1994
verlenging, krediet~ 1275
verlengstuk 124
verlening, dienst~ 2084
verlening, krediet~ 220
verlichting, belasting~ 2261
verlies 1717
verlies, aftrekbaar ~ 974
verlies, bedrijfs~ 474
verlies, boek~ 411
verlies, bruto~ 1464
verliescompensatie 2273
verliescompensatie, retroactieve ~ 2272
verlies dekken, een ~ 707
verlies dragen, een ~ 333
verlies (een winst) aanwijzen, een ~ 2046
verlies (een winst) laten zien, een ~ 2046
verlies (een winst) vertonen, een ~ 2046
verlies-en-winstrekening 1523
verlies, exploitatie~ 474
verlies, geheel ~ 934
verlies goedmaken, een ~ 707
verlies, kapitaal~ 552
verlies, koers~ 1229
verlies lijden, een ~ 333
verlies maken, een ~ 333
verlies, netto~ 651
verlies ondergaan, een ~ 333
verlies opvangen, een ~ 3
verliessaldo 93
verlies terugtrekken, zich met ~ 928
verlies, totaal ~ 934
verlies vergoeden, een ~ 707
verlies verkopen, met ~ 2158
verlies, vervreemdings~ 553
verlies we(d)er goedmaken, een ~ 707
verlies, zuiver ~ 651
verloop, conjunctuur~ 477
verlopen 1264
verloten 1112
verloting 1111
vermeerderen, de waarde ~ 178
vermeerderen, in waarde ~ 179
vermeerdering, waarde~ 180
verminderd met de kosten 621
verminderd met de onkosten 621
verminderen, de pariteit ~ 2062
verminderen, de uitgaven ~ 915
verminderen, het aandelenkapitaal ~ 2061
vermindering 968
vermindering, belasting~ 2261
vermindering, kapitaal~ 2063
vermindering, prijs~ 927
vermindering van de fluctuatiemarges 2065
vermindering van de koersen (prijzen) 886
vermindering van de munt, waarde~ 897
vermindering van het aandelenkapitaal 2064
vermindering, waarde~ 969
vermogen, buitenlands ~ 204
vermogen, eigen ~ 1996
vermogen, goud~ 1430
vermogen, groei~ 1469
vermogen in het buitenland 204
vermogen, maatschappelijk ~ 790
vermogen, mobilair ~ 622
vermogen, nationaal ~ 1804
vermogen, rendements~ 1139
vermogensaanwasbelasting 532
vermogensbehoefte 557
vermogensbelasting 551
vermogensverdeling 1073, 1074
vermogen, trust~ 2308
vermogen, vennootschappelijk ~ 790
vermogen, volks~ 1804
vermogen, winst~ 1139
vermogen, zuiver ~ 1809
vernauwing, krediet~ 874
vernieuwingsfonds 2086
vernieuwingsreserve 2086
vernieuwing van het couponblad 2087
verordeningen, deviezen~ 900
verpachter 1676
verpande effecten 1895
verpanden 1018, 1791
verpanden, effecten ~ 671
verpande wissel 363
verpanding van effecten 1501
verplichte reserves 1670
verplichting 692
verplichting, belasting~ 1683
verplichting, deviezen~ 1223
verplichtingen 961
verplichtingen, lopende ~ 910
verplichtingen, rekening-courant~ 1023
verplichting, eventuele ~ 758
verplicht sparen 724
verrekenen 148, 615, 706
verrekenen, een cheque ~ 641
verrekening 139, 613, 642, 709
verrekening, cheque~ 627
verrekeningscheque 883
verrekeningsdag 24
verrekeningsdollar 29
verrekeningskamer 649
verrekeningskoers 650
verrekeningsovereenkomst 647
verrekeningssaldo 269
verrekeningstransacties 643
verrekeningsverrichtingen 643
verrekenkamer 649
verrekenkantoor 649
verrichting 320
verrichtingen, bank~ 304
verrichtingen, beurs~ 1222
verrichtingen, clearing~ 643
verrichtingen, compensatie~ 643
verrichtingen, effecten~ 1222
verrichtingen, verrekenings~ 643
verruiming, krediet~ 858
verschaffing van kapitaal 1408
verschenen int(e)rest 1589
verschenen rente 1589
verschieten 85
verschil 1037
verschil algemene kosten 464
verschil delen, het ~ 2201
verschil in de rentestand 1412
verschil, koers~ 1039
verschil, prijs~ 1038
verschil, rente~ 1412
verschil, wisselkoers~ 1039
verschot 83
verschuldigd 1127
verschuldigd bedrag 151
verschuldigd bedrag, nog ~ 252
verschuldigde 151
verschuldigde int(e)rest 1589
verschuldigde, nog ~ 252
verschuldigde rente 1589
verschuldigde som 151
verschuldigd saldo 252
verschuldigd zijn 1876
verslag, accountants~ 217
verslag, jaar~ 160
verslagjaar 478
verslag van de commissarissen 217
verslapping 968
versobering 218
versoepelen, de kredietbeperkingen ~ 1143
versoepeling, krediet~ 1145
verstaatsen 1802
verstaatsing 1801
versterking van de kapitaalintensiteit 537
verstoord evenwicht 1062
verstoring, evenwichts~ 1062
verstrekken, een krediet ~ 126
verstrekker, geld~ 1777
verstrekking, krediet~ 220
verstrijken 1264
verstrijking 1262

vertegenwoordiger 104
vertelgeld 133
verticale prijsbinding 2097
vertonen, een daling (een winst) van X punten ~ 2045
vertonen, een verlies (een winst) ~ 2046
vertoon, op ~ 1956
vertraging 968
vertraging in de betaling 999
verval 1748
verval, bij ~ 1128
vervalboek 359
vervaldag 931
vervaldagagenda 359
vervaldagenboek 359
vervaldag, op de ~ 1128
vervaldag, per ~ 1128
vervaldatum 931
vervallen 347, 1126
vervallen dividend 1954
vervallen int(e)rest 1589
vervallen op 15 augustus, te ~ 1129
vervallen rente 1589
vervallen rente, te ~ 42
vervalsing, munt~ 939
vervaltijd 1748
vervangingsfonds 2086
vervangingskosten 2091
vervangingsprijs 2091
vervangingsreserve 2086
vervangingswaarde 2091
vervangingswaarde, afschrijving op basis van de ~ 143
vervoerkosten 2295
vervreemdbaar 117
vervreemdbaarheid 116
vervreemden 118
vervreemder 121
vervreemding 119
vervreemdingsverlies 553
vervreemdingswinst 531
vervroegde betaling 92
vervroegde inkoop 167
vervroegde int(e)rest 165
verwachte winst 166
verwaterd aandelenkapitaal 2365
verwatering van het aandelenkapitaal 2226
verwerven 48
verwerver 482
verwerving 49
verwezenlijken, een winst ~ 1729
verzamelboeking 717
verzameldeposito 685
verzamelrekening 673
verzamelstaat 2241
verzekering 1576
verzekering, krediet~ 863
verzekering, levens~ 1688
verzekering, sociale ~ 2184
verzekeringspolis 1577
verzekeringspremie 1578
verzekeringswiskundige 58
verzet van de consumenten 750
verzilveren 785
verzilvering 773
verzoek, op ~ 495
verzoek tot faillietverklaring 316
verzuim, in ~ 979
verzwakking 968
vestiging, hoofd~ 607
vlottend bedrijfskapitaal 468
vlottende koopkracht 1209
vlottende schuld 1351
vlottende valuta 1350
vlottende wisselkoers 1347
vlottend kapitaal 468
vlottend maken 1767
vlucht, belasting~ 2266
vlucht, kapitaal~ 527
vluchtkapitaal 1349
voegen, bij de reserve ~ 68
voet 2021
voet, afschrijvings~ 144
voet, amortisatie~ 144, 145
voet, basis~ 328
voet, belasting~ 2023
voet, delgings~ 145
voet, disconto~ 1061
voet, eenheids~ 1345
voet, groei~ 1255
voet, herdisconto~ 2059
voet, inflatie~ 1563
voet, int(e)rest~ 1593
voet, rente~ 1593
voet, ruil~ 2279
VOF 1420
voldoen 148
voldoening 139
volfourneren, een aandeel ~ 1915
volgefourneerde aandelen 1403
volgende endossant 2239
volgestorte aandelen 1403
volksinkomen 1799
volksvermogen 1804
volledige betaling 715
volstorten, een aandeel ~ 1915
volstorting van een aandeel 1908
voltekend kapitaal 2232
volume, geld~ 1783
volume, handels~ 2354
volume, krediet~ 881
volume, liquiditeits~ 1783
volume, spaar~ 2353
vooraad, geld~ 587
vooraf aftrekken 973
voorafbetalen 1904
voorafbetaling 92
vooraf opzeggen, X dagen ~ 1426
voorbaat betalen, bij ~ 1904
voorbehoud van inkomst, onder ~ 2099
voorbeurs 937
voorcalculatie 1190
voorcalculatorische kosten 1189
voordeel 1409
voordeel, belasting~ 2263
voordeel, bijkomend ~ 1285
voordeel, extra-legaal ~ 1285
voordeel, fiscaal ~ 2263
voordeel in natura 134
voordeel, sociaal ~ 2185
voordelig 1147
voordelige balans 275
voorfinancieren 1951
voorfinanciering 1952
voorgaande endossant 1944
voorgeschreven prijs 78
voorheffing 89, 681
voorkeurprijs 1203
voorkeurrecht 1328
voorkeurtarief 1947
voorkeurtarief voor de leden van het Gemenebest 702
voorkooprecht 2013
voorlegging van de balans 1957
voorlopig aandeel 1597
voorlopig certificaat 1597
voorlopige aangifte 2000
voorlopige balans 1596
voorlopige betaling 1999
voorlopige financiering 1952
voorlopig financieren 1951
voorman 1944
voorraad 1615
voorraad, deviezen~ 901, 1362
voorraad, effecten~ 1628
voorraad, geld~ 1783
voorraad, goud~ 1430
voorraad, goud- en deviezen~ 1429
voorraad, kas~ 587
voorschieten 85
voorschot 83, 1014
voorschot, bank~ 298
voorschotbank 850
voorschot, bij wijze van ~ 84
voorschot, gedekt ~ 86
voorschot, gegarandeerd ~ 86
voorschot in rekening-courant 87
voorschot op onderpand 86
voorschot, pand~ 86
voorschotrentevoet 423
voorschot tegen effecten 90
voorschot tegen onderpand 86
voorschot tegen onderpandeffecten 90
voorschriften, deviezen~ 900
voorschrijven, een prijs ~ 1033
voortbrengingskosten 811
voortijdige betaling 92
vooruitbetalen 1904
vooruitbetaling 92
vooruitfinancieren 1951
vooruitfinanciering 1952
voorwaarden, betalings~ 2278
voorwaarden, krediet~ 856
voorwaarden van betaling 2278
voorwaarden van een lening, emissie~ 729
voorwerpen van waarde 1646
voorzien, in een tekort ~ 836
voorziening 129
voorzieningen, collectieve ~ 684
voorzieningen, openbare ~ 684
voorzieningen voor belastingen 2001
voorzieningen voor dubieuze debiteuren 243
voorziening, kapitaal~ 1408
voorzieningsfonds 755
voorzieningsreserve 756
voorziening voor waardevermindering 132
vordering 639

vordering afboeken, een ~ 2379
vordering amortiseren, een ~ 2379
vordering, boek~ 404
vordering cederen, een ~ 207
vordering, egalisatie~ 1173
vorderingen, bank~ 296
vorderingen, cessie van ~ 208
vorderingen, dubieuze ~ 1110
vorderingen, overdracht van ~ 208
vordering innen, een ~ 677
vordering invorderen, een ~ 677
vordering, oninbare ~ 242
vordering overdragen, een ~ 207
vordering, uitstaande ~ 37
vormen, een reserve ~ 454
vorming, bezit~ 1373
vorming, kapitaal~ 529
vorming van spaarmiddelen 1374
vostrorekening 1716
vraag 1002
vraag, binnenlandse ~ 1096
vraag, consumptie~ 746
vraag, consumptieve ~ 746
vraagelement 716
vraag en aanbod 2242
vraaginflatie 1005
vraag naar geld 1774
vraag, overtrokken ~ 1206
vraag, te grote ~ 1206
vraag van de gezinshuishoudingen 1097
vragen, teveel ~ 1866
vreemde belegging 1367
vreemde biljetten en munten 1369
vreemde biljetten en munten, handel in ~ 936
vreemde investering 1367
vreemde munt 1361
vreemde valuta 1361
vreemd geld 1361
vreemd kapitaal 417
vreemd vermogen 417
vrij aan boord 1354
vrijdom, belasting~ 1248
vrije concurrentie 1390
vrije deviezenmarkt 1885
vrije economie 1393
vrije markt 1395
vrije-markteconomie 1393
vrije-marktkoers 1396
vrije mededinging 1390
vrije reserve 1397
vrije wisselkoers 1347
vrijgave 950
vrijgeven van de prijzen 971
vrijhandel 1392
vrijhandelaar 1399
vrijhandelszone 1398
vrijheid, belasting~ 1248
vrijheid van concurrentie 1390
vrijheid van het handelsverkeer 1392
vrijheid van mededinging 1390
vrijheid van onderneming 1391
vrijmaken 949
vrijmaking 645
vrijmaking van de prijzen 971
vrijmaking van het handelsverkeer 1684
vrijstellen van rechten 1246
vrijstelling van belasting(en) 1248
vrij van belasting(en) 1247
vrij van (douane-)rechten 920
vruchtgebruik 2334

waarborg 1138, 1471
waarborgen, een emissie ~ 2320
waarborgfonds 1472
waarborg gegeven wissel, in ~ 363
waarborg, leen~ 1473
waarborgsom 602
waarborgsom, ingehouden ~ 2109
waarborg, staats~ 1450
waarborg van honorering 1474
waarde, aangegeven ~ 967
waarde, aankoop~ 50
waarde, aanschaffings~ 50
waarde, actuele ~ 912
waarde, afkoop~ 2247
waarde, aflossings~ 2055
waarde, balans~ 277
waarde, belastbare ~ 198
waardebepaling 176
waarde, boek~ 32
waarde, bruto~ 1468
waarde, contante ~ 912
waarde, dag~ 912
waarde dalen, in ~ 970
waardedaling 969
waardedaling van de munt 896
waardedaling van het geld 896
waarde, door de industrie toegevoegde ~ 2340
waarde, eenheids~ 2213
waarde, effectieve ~ 56
waarde, fiscale ~ 198
waarde, gedeclareerde ~ 967
waarde, gekapitaliseerde ~ 546
waarde, gezamenlijke ~ 108
waarde, globale ~ 108
waarde, goud~ 1442
waarde, heraanschaffings~ 2091
waarde, inkoop~ 50, 2055
waarde, intrinsieke ~ 1612
waarde, inventaris~ 1617
waarde, koers~ 1234
waarde, liquidatie~ 432
waardeloosheid 2344
waardeloze effecten 2345
waarde, markt~ 688
waarden 2151
waarden, aan de beurs genoteerde ~ 1699
waarden, beleggings~ 1630
waarden, beurs~ 1699
waarden, buitenlandse ~ 1370
waarden, eersterangs~ 387
waarde, netto~ 1817
waarden, genoteerde ~ 1699
waarden, goudgerande ~ 387
waarden, incourante ~ 892
waarden, niet genoteerde ~ 892
waarde, nominale ~ 1289, 1889
waarden op naam 1568
waarden, op naam gestelde ~ 1568
waarden, prima ~ 387
waarden, roerende ~ 1739
waarden, speculatieve ~ 2199
waarden, ter beurze genoteerde ~ 1699
waarden, ter beurze niet genoteerde ~ 892
waardepapieren 2151
waardepapieren aan toonder 342
waardepapieren, eersteklas~ 387
waardepapieren, genoteerde ~ 1699
waardepapieren op naam 1568
waardepapieren, overdraagbare ~ 1739
waardepapieren, ter beurze genoteerde ~ 1699
waardepapieren, verhandelbare ~ 1739
waardepapier met (een) vaste rente 1339
waardepapier, vast renderend ~ 1339
waardepapier, vast rentend ~ 1339
waarde, pari~ 1889
waarderaming 176
waarde, realisatie~ 432
waarderecht 82
waarde, reële ~ 56
waarderen 177
waarde, rentabiliteits~ 546
waarde, residu~ 2103
waarde, rest~ 2103
waardering 176
waarde, ruil~ 1219
waardeschatting 176
waarde, standaard~ 2213
waarde stijgen, in ~ 179
waardestijging 180
waarde, terugbetalings~ 2055
waarde, totale ~ 108
waarde van de valuta, buitenlandse ~ 1364
waarde van een eigendom, netto ~ 1177
waarde, verkoop(s)~ 688
waarde verliezen, (aan) ~ 970
waarde vermeerderen, de ~ 178
waarde vermeerderen, in ~ 179
waardevermeerdering 180
waarde verminderen, in ~ 970
waardevermindering 969
waardevermindering van de munt 897
waarde, vervangings~ 2091
waarde, werkelijke ~ 56
waarmerken, een cheque ~ 610
wachtrekening 2248
wanbetaler 245
wanbetaling 982
waren, export~ 1266
waren, import~ 1510
waren, invoer~ 1510
waren, uitvoer~ 1266
warrant 2364
warrant-cedel 2364
wedde 2126
wedde, maand~ 1787
wederaankoop 2094

wederaankopen 480
wederbetaalbaar 2073
wederbetalen 1900
wederbetaling 139, 2072
we(d)er goedmaken, een verlies ~ 707
wederinkoop 2094
wederkopen 480
we(d)erkrijgen, zijn geld ~ 1421
we(d)erlenen 2079
wederopleving 2048
wederrechtelijke toeëigening 978
wederrechtelijk toeëigenen, zich ~ 977
we(d)eruitlenen 2079
wederuitvoer 2066
wederverkoopprijs 2096
wederverkoper 2105
wederzijdse deelneming 885
weeldeartikelen 1001
weeldebelasting 1723
wegen 2369
weggeefprijs 322
weging 2371
wegingscoëfficiënt 2372
weglatingen, fouten en ~ 1183
wegvloeiing van kapitaal 556
weigering tot betaling 2074
weigering van betaling 2074
weinig aanrekenen, te ~ 2316
weinig berekenen, te ~ 2316
weinig in rekening brengen, te ~ 2316
welvaartsstaat 2373
wending 428
Wereldbank 1602
wereld, financiële ~ 1305
wereld, geld~ 1305
werkelijke garantie 2258
werkelijke kosten 54
werkelijke uitgaven 55
werkelijke waarde 56
werkelijk inkomen 2032
werkelijk rendement 57
werken, openbare ~ 2010
werkkapitaal 468
wettelijke reserves 1670
wettelijk voorgeschreven reserves 1670
wettig betaalmiddel 1669
wijze, betalings~ 1375
wijziging, wisselkoers~ 75
wind zijn, in de ~ 1427
winst 1409
winstaandeel 2173
winst afwerpen, een ~ 100
winst, bedrijfs~ 475
winstbejag, vereniging met ~ 1986
winstbejag, vereniging zonder ~ 1829
winst, belastbare ~ 197
winstbelasting 1989
winstbestemming 183
winst bij vervreemding 531
winst, boek~ 412
winst, bruto~ 1459
winst, buitengewone ~ 1213
winstcapaciteit 1139
winstdelende obligatie 1526
winstdelend preferent aandeel 1891
winstdeling 1410
winst, denkbeeldige ~ 171
winstderving 1718
winsten 229
winsten, ingehouden ~ 2108
winsten, niet toegewezen ~ 2311
winsten, niet uitgekeerde ~ 2108
winsten, onverdeelde ~ 2311
winst-en-verliesrekening 1523
winst, exploitatie~ 475
winst, fictieve ~ 171
winst, fiscale ~ 197
winstgevend 1147
winst geven, een ~ 100
winst, handels~ 475
winst, imaginaire ~ 171
winstinhouding 1987
winst, kapitaal~ 530
winst kapitaliseren, de ~ 548
winst, koers~ 1233
winst laten, een ~ 100
winst maken, een ~ 1729
winstmarge 1734
winstmarge, netto ~ 1813
winstneming 1990
winst, netto~ 646
winstoogmerk, vereniging met ~ 1986
winstoogmerk, vereniging zonder ~ 1829
winst opbrengen, een ~ 100
winst opleveren, een ~ 100
winst opstrijken, een ~ 1937
winst, overgebrachte ~ 1985
winst per aandeel 1142
winst realiseren, een ~ 1729
winstsaldo 849
winst, schijn~ 171
winstuitdeling 183
winstuitkering 183
winstuitkering, verkapte ~ 1482
winstverdeling 183
winst, verhoopte ~ 166
winstvermogen 1139
winst, vervreemdings~ 531
winst, verwachte ~ 166
winst verwezenlijken, een ~ 1729
winst, voor uitkering beschikbare ~ 1072
winst, zuivere ~ 646
wiskundig adviseur 58
wiskundige, verzekerings~ 58
wissel 356
wissel aannemen, een ~ 8
wissel aan order 374
wisselaar 509
wisselaar, geld~ 509
wissel accepteren, een ~ 8
wissel, accommodatie~ 15
wisselagent 2152
wisselagentschap 1217
wisselarbitrage 186, 369
wissel avaleren, een ~ 235
wissel, aval geven voor een ~ 235
wisselbank 12
wissel, bank~ 284
wisselbank 1058, 1220
wissel betalen, een ~ 1054
wissel, binnenlandse ~ 1091
wisselboek 359, 360
wisselboek, ingaand ~ 360
wisselborgtocht 230
wisselbrief 356
wisselbrief, zicht~ 1003
wissel, buitenlandse ~ 1357
wissel, commerciële ~ 356
wisselcontrole 1224
wissel, eersteklas~ 1323
wisselende afschrijving 2347
wisselende valutakoers 1347
wissel, endossabele ~ 374
wissel, endosseerbare ~ 374
wissel endosseren, een ~ 1162
wissel en pension 363
wisselen van geld 1231
wissel, financiële ~ 1307
wissel, financierings~ 1307
wisselgarantie 230
wisselgeld 612
wissel, geretourneerde ~ 365
wissel gireren, een ~ 1162
wisselhandel 1221
wissel, handels~ 356
wissel honoreren, een ~ 1054
wissel, incasso~ 364
wissel indosseren, een ~ 1162
wissel in pension 363
wissel, in waarborg gegeven ~ 363
wisselkantoor 1217
wisselkoers 1216
wisselkoers, aanpassing van de ~ 75
wisselkoers, flexibele ~ 1347
wisselkoers, fluctuerende ~ 1347
wisselkoers, gedwongen ~ 722
wisselkoers, kruiselingse ~ 884
wisselkoersrisico 1238
wisselkoers, schommelende ~ 1347
wisselkoers (van deviezen), contante ~ 2024
wisselkoers, variabele ~ 1347
wisselkoers, vaste ~ 1341
wisselkoersverschil 1039
wisselkoers, vlottende ~ 1347
wisselkoers voor biljetten en munten 1235
wisselkoers, vrije ~ 1347
wisselkoerswijziging 75
wisselkoers, zwevende ~ 1347
wisselkrediet 11
wissel laten protesteren, een ~ 1481
wisselmakelaar 361, 509
wisselmarkt 370, 1230
wisselmarkt, tweeledige ~ 2309
wisselnemer 1902
wissel, niet betaalde ~ 365
wissel, niet endosseerbare ~ 371
wissel, niet gehonoreerde ~ 365
wissel, niet verhandelbare ~ 371
wissel, noodlijdende ~ 365
wissel, onbetaalde ~ 365
wissel, onbetaald teruggezonden ~ 365
wissel, onoverdraagbare ~ 371

wissel, onverhandelbare ~ 371
wissel op het binnenland, gedisconteerde ~ 1060
wissel op iemand afgeven, een ~ 1114
wissel op iemand trekken, een ~ 1114
wissel op naam 371
wissel, order~ 374
wissel, overdraagbare ~ 374
wisselpari 1890
wisselpariteit 1182
wissel, pension~ 363
wissel, post~ 1781
wissel, prima~ 1327
wissel protesteren, een ~ 1481
wissel, recta~ 371
wisselreglementering 900
wissel, retour~ 819
wissel rugtekenen, een ~ 1162
wisselruiterij 1659
wissel, schatkist~ 2301
wissel, schoorsteen~ 15
wisselschuldenaar 362
wissel, secunda~ 2148
wissel, sola-~ 2180
wisselstelsel 1240
wisselsysteem 1240
wissel, te betalen ~ 372
wissel, te innen ~ 373
wissel, uso~ 358
wissel, verhandelbare ~ 374
wissel, verpande ~ 363
wissel voor aval tekenen, een ~ 235
wissel, zicht~ 1003
woeker 2337
woekerprijs 1250
woekerrente 2335

zaak 320
zaak, afbetalings~ 1489
zaak, contant~ 581
zaak, loco~ 581
zaak, termijn~ 1379
zaak, valutatermijn~ 1381
zachte valuta 2187
zakelijke garantie 2258
zakelijke onkosten 472
zakelijke zekerheid 2035
zakelijk onderpand 2035
zaken, bank~ 304
zaken, beurs~ 1222
zakencijfer 2130
zaken doen 1084
zaken, effecten~ 1222
zaken, krediet~ 851
zaken met het buitenland 1358
zakenomvang 2130
zegel 2209, 2211
zegelgeld 2211
zegel, korting~ 2290
zegel, rabat~ 2290
zegelrecht 2211
zeggen, een prijs ~ 1728
zekerheid 669, 1138
zekerheid, aanvullende ~ 65
zekerheid, additionele ~ 65
zekerheid bieden, een ~ 101
zekerheid, bijkomende ~ 65
zekerheid geven, een ~ 101
zekerheid, maatschappelijke ~ 2184
zekerheid, sociale ~ 2184
zekerheid stellen, een ~ 101
zekerheid, zakelijke ~ 2035
zelffinanciering 1601
zelfgenoegzaamheid 219
zelfstandige boekhouding 2155
zelfvoorziening 219
zending, geld~ 1784
zetel, centrale ~ 607
zetel, fiscale ~ 1331
zetel, hoofd~ 607
zetel, maatschappelijke ~ 2075
zetel, statutaire ~ 2075
zetting, prijs~ 1515
zichtbare export 2351
zichtbare import 2352
zichtbare invoer 2352
zichtbare reserves 966
zichtbare uitvoer 2351
zichtdeposito 1004
zichtlening 504
zicht, op ~ 1956
zichtpapier 1007
zichtrekening 23
zichtwissel 1003
zichtwisselbrief 1003
zijde, actief~ 206
zijde, credit~ 206
zijde, debet~ 943
zijde, passief~ 943
zonder animo 508
zone, dollar~ 1086
zone, frank~ 1388
zone, sterling~ 2224
zone, vrijhandels~ 1398
zuivere winst 646
zuiver inkomen 1811
zuiver verlies 651
zuiver vermogen 1809
zwak 508
zwakke valuta 2187
zwakte 1130
zwarte markt 377
zwarte rente 376
zwart geld 2314
zwevende koopkracht 1209
zwevende valuta 1350
zwevende wisselkoers 1347